1985

The ALA Yearbook of Library and Information Services

A review of
library events 1984
Volume 10 (1985)

American Library Association
Chicago, Illinois

Composed by Precision Typographers, Inc.
Beverly Shores, Indiana, in Melior.
Printed on 50-pound Glatfelter,
a pH-neutral stock, and bound
by Braun-Brumfield, Inc.

Volume   1 (1976)
Volume   2 (1977)
Volume   3 (1978)
Volume   4 (1979)
Volume   5 (1980)
Volume   6 (1981)
Volume   7 (1982)
Volume   8 (1983)
Volume   9 (1984)
Volume 10 (1985)

020.62274 American Library Association-Yearbooks
    Library Associations-Yearbooks. Main entry: title
    (Publisher's cataloging).
LCN 83-8703
ISBN 0-8389-0434-3
ISSN 0740-042X

Copyright © 1985 by the American Library
Association

All rights reserved. No part of this publication may be
reproduced in any form without permission in writing
from the publisher, except by a reviewer who may
quote brief passages in a review.

Printed in the United States of America.

EDITOR
Robert Wedgeworth

MANAGING EDITOR
Richard Dell

COPY EDITOR
Donald E. Stewart

ASSISTANT EDITOR
Linda Bostrom

PICTURE EDITOR
Nora Dell

CONTRIBUTING EDITORS
Ruth Tarbox, *Biographies*
Ruth Warncke, *Biographies; Awards*

INDEXER
Pamela Hori

PROOFREADERS
Mary Huchting
Emily Procissi
Joanne Wilkinson

LAYOUT ARTIST
Joseph Szwarek

THE AMERICAN LIBRARY ASSOCIATION

PRESIDENT
E. J. Josey

VICE-PRESIDENT/PRESIDENT-ELECT
Beverly P. Lynch

TREASURER
Patricia Glass Schuman

EXECUTIVE DIRECTOR
Robert Wedgeworth

DEPUTY EXECUTIVE DIRECTOR
Roger Parent

ASSOCIATE EXECUTIVE DIRECTOR FOR PUBLISHING
Gary Facente

ADVISERS

Warren B. Kuhn,
Dean and Director, Iowa State University Libraries, Iowa State University, Ames
Patricia Battin, *Vice President and Director,*
Columbia University Libraries
Lillian Bradshaw, *Director,*
Public Library System, Dallas, Texas
William DeJohn, *Director,*
MINITEX, University of Washington, Seattle
Mary V. Gaver, *Library Consultant,*
Danville, Virginia
Warren J. Haas, *President, Council on Library Resources, Inc.*
Edward G. Holley, *Dean,*
School of Library Science, University of North Carolina
Clara Stanton Jones, *Director Emeritus,*
Detroit Public Library System
E. J. Josey, *Chief*
Bureau of Specialist Library Services, The State Education Department, The New York State Library
Paul Kitchen, *Executive Director,*
Canadian Library Association
Dan Lacy, *Consultant, McGraw-Hill, Inc.*
John G. Lorenz, *Consultant,*
Library and Information Services,
Bethesda, Maryland
Helen H. Lyman, *Professor Emeritus,*
Library School, University of Wisconsin, Madison
Keyes D. Metcalf (deceased), *Library Consultant,*
Belmont, Massachusetts
R. Kathleen Molz, *Acting Dean,*
School of Library Service, Columbia University
Carol Nemeyer, *Associate Librarian for National Programs,*
Library of Congress
LuOuida Vinson Phillips, *Director of Instructional Resources,*
Dallas Independent School District
Alphonse F. Trezza, *Associate Professor,*
School of Library and Information Studies, Florida State University
Allen B. Veaner, *Library and Information Consultant; Principal,*
Allen B. Veaner Associates

Robert Vosper, *Director,*
Clark Library, University of California, Los Angeles
Leo M. Weins, *President*
H. W. Wilson Company

EDITOR'S INTRODUCTION

The idea for the *ALA Yearbook* emerged in a conversation between the Editor and Donald Stewart, former Director of Publishing Services for the American Library Association, at their first meeting. The need for summaries of the major topics covering the library world produced on a regular basis seemed a perfect match for the yearbook format. From an outline of topics and possible contributors to a group of advisers, the *ALA Yearbook* made its dramatic entrance at the 1976 ALA Annual Conference celebrating the centennial year of the Association.

Over the past ten years the *Yearbook* has involved some 2,100 contributors who have written 3,500,000 words illustrated by more than 2,000 photos, diagrams and drawings on every facet of library and information services. The book has carried 23 major feature articles, 80 special reports and 510 state reports in addition to approximately 1,500 articles on library organizations, issues, people, trends, problems, technology, institutions, management, finances, politics and social change.

The 1985 edition completes the record for a decade. In this volume the editors and contributors survey the events, activities and individuals who have shaped 1984 for the field of library and information services.

"Librarianship Through A Rear View Mirror," a staff-written summary review of the *ALA Yearbook* leads this year's features. Coming on the heels of many responses to "A Nation at Risk," Jim Liesener, University of Kentucky, takes a critical look in "School Media Programs" at the status of this speciality. The newest independent agency in Washington is the National Archives. The Archivist of the United States, Robert Warner, explains the significance of this liberation from the General Services Administration and what can be expected for the nation's archivists and archives. According to Bernard Vavrek, rural libraries are having a revival with some from new funding sources and renewed interest from the profession.

A pictorial feature of the newly renovated Astor Room of The New York Public Library adds visual interest to the 1985 book. These are some of the special features of a book that derives its reputation for its authoritative summaries of topics covered each year.

We continue to learn from Jessie Smith and Bill Katz as they survey "Black Americans" and "Serials" in 1984. Both have written for 10 editions of the *ALA Yearbook*. We welcome new contributor Marcus McCorison, Director of the American Antiquarian Society, who succeeds William Towner as our correspondent on the Independent Research Libraries.

The editors regret that adequate reporting of foundation activity was not possible in this edition but assure our readers of its return next year.

This year as with the previous nine editions we appreciate the efforts of the many contributors and the advisers who provide ideas for many features that appear. It is especially fitting for this 10th edition to recognize the contributions of Ruth Tarbox and Ruth Warncke who write the biographies and obituaries and Pam Hori who has produced a 10-year index cumulating her previous contributions.

The *ALA Yearbook* is also blessed with a husband-wife team. Nora Dell begins each year expressing doubt that she will produce enough illustrations to accent the text, yet manages each year to find bountiful sources. Richard Dell as Managing Editor edits and shapes the copy into the final publication. Each of them has been with the *Yearbook* since its inception.

Physically the *ALA Yearbook* has changed very little in 10 years. Technologically, the changes have been dramatic as we now keyboard and transmit copy for typesetting electronically. This process has not only gained more time for editing but also cleaner galley proofs for contributors to review, resulting in fewer errors.

The *ALA Yearbook of Library and Information Services* is a collective enterprise intended to satisfy you, the reader, and your interests in the highlights of librarianship each year. To the extent we have met that challenge with this and previous volumes we are fulfilled. We remain, however, committed to retain and sharpen your interests by a comprehensive, readable, well-illustrated, authoritative annual volume.

ROBERT WEDGEWORTH
Editor

THE CHALLENGES FACING THE INFORMATION SPECIALIST

The 1985 *ALA Yearbook*, the 10th in this important series, records the vitality and the diversity of the work of library and information specialists. Detailed reports are provided on the state of the profession. Issues of importance to the field are reviewed in the areas of intellectual freedom, access to information, problems of literacy, of rural library services, of scholarly publishing, and international librarianship. Support for library services to children and young adults is discussed, as is financial support for libraries of all types. The *ALA Yearbook*, while recording the events in librarianship in 1984, offers insights into the future of librarianship. That future is one of challenge, opportunity, and great expectations.

We are in the midst of a period of changing societal traditions. What is likely to emerge from the information revolution around us? Information will be an important thrust, yet the role of the information professional is unclear. The book remains the central concern of libraries, yet new information demands and capabilities, with new costs, are being added to the library's program. Much has been accomplished in areas of state, regional and national library cooperation, but the 1980s finds library decentralization growing with libraries returning to local autonomy. The principle of a free public library is guarded and cherished, yet the costs of new technologies seem beyond what many communities are willing or able to pay. The need for information specialists is at an all time high, yet forecasts for employment indicate that the number of library jobs and new library professionals will stay constant or increase only slightly over the next decade.

Each year the American Library Association reaffirms its objectives of promoting and improving library services and librarianship and of providing lifelong learning services to all. Each decade or so the Association takes stock of itself and the profession, assessing who librarians are and where librarianship is going. ALA currently is developing a strategic long-range planning process that will provide a more coordinated approach to association planning. Its Committee on Accreditation is exploring procedures and guidelines for the participation of a variety of associations in the accreditation of programs for library and information science education. Many of its divisions have devised long-range plans and are implementing them. All of these activities attest to the growth and development of librarianship. These activities, many of which are reported in this yearbook, exemplify the creativity and the energy the library community brings to the issues of the day. The fundamental questions raised by new technological developments challenge directly the values and philosophy of librarianship, and test the principle of the free public library. Many of the challenges and the responses to them can be found in the *ALA Yearbook*; it offers unquestionable evidence of the creativity and vitality of librarianship.

BEVERLY P. LYNCH

CONTENTS

Feature

xiii Librarianship Through A Rear View Mirror

Special Reports

52 **Significance and Implications of an Independent National Archive**
ROBERT M. WARNER, Dean of the School of Library Science, University of Michigan, served as Archivist of the United States from 1980 to 1985

84 **After 40 Years, NYPL opens its Restored Exhibition Hall**

111 **Electronic Publishing: Eight Trends of '84**
DAVID GROSSMAN, Data Products Manager, Marquis Who's Who, Inc.

159 **The Impact of U.S. Withdrawal from UNESCO**
THOMAS J. GALVIN, Dean, School of Library and Information Science, University of Pittsburgh; ALA Representative to the United States National Commission for UNESCO

161 **U.S.–China Exchanges of Librarians**
WARREN M. TSUNEISHI, Director Area Studies Research Services, Library of Congress

173 **Building Standards and Public Library Planning**

181 **Books in our Future**
DONALD E. STEWART, Editorial Consultant, former Associate Director for Publishing, ALA

200 **The National Library of Canada: Its History and Function**
F. DOLORES DONNELLY, Professor Emeritus, Faculty of Library and Information Science, University of Toronto

222 **Rural Librarianship in the United States: A Renaissance**
BERNARD VAVREK, Coordinator, Center for the Study of Rural Librarianship, School of Library Science, Clarion University of Pennsylvania

232 **Scholarly Publishing**
MARK CARROLL, former President, Society for Scholarly Publishing

243 **Library Statistics: A Current Review**
MARY JO LYNCH, Director, ALA Office for Research

256 **School Library Media Programs— Struggling into "The Information Age"**
JAMES W. LIESENER, Professor, College of Library and Information Services, University of Maryland

1 Awards
7 Biographies
16 Obituaries
21 Notables

Review of Library Events 1984

25 **Abstracting and Indexing Services**
M. LYNNE NEUFELD, Executive Director, National Federation of Abstracting and Information Services

26 **Academic Libraries**
RICHARD D. JOHNSON, Director of Libraries, State University College, Oneonta, New York

33 **Accreditation**
ELINOR YUNGMEYER, Accreditation Officer, American Library Association

36 **Adults, Library Service to**
KATHLEEN HEIM, Dean, School of Library and Information Science, Louisiana State University

38 **American Association of Law Libraries**
JACQUELYN J. JURKINS, Multnomah Law Library, Portland, Oregon; President AALL

39 **American Association of School Librarians**
BETTIE DAY, Coordinator of Library and Resource Center, Office of the County Superintendent of Schools, Santa Barbara, California; President AASL

40 **American Indians**
VIRGINIA H. MATHEWS, (OSAGE) Vice President, Library Professional Publications, An Imprint of the Shoe String Press

41 **American Library Association**
JOEL LEE, Headquarters Librarian; EMILY MELTON, Assistant Librarian, ALA

49 **American Library Trustee Association**
JOANNA C. WISENER, President, ALTA

49 **American Society for Information Science**
BONNIE COOPER CARROLL, Director, Program Development Office and International Activities, Department of Energy Office of Scientific and Technical Information

51 **American Theological Library Association**
RONALD F. DEERING, President, ALTA

52 **Archives**
ANN MORGAN CAMPBELL, Executive Director, Society of American Archivists, Chicago, Illinois

54 **Armed Forces Libraries**
TONY DAKAN, Air Force Librarian, Randolph AFB

55 **Art Libraries**
MARY ASHE, Art and Music Librarian, San Francisco Public Library

57 **Association for Information and Image Management**
PEGGY LINAUGH, Executive Assistant and Membership Coordinator, AIIM

58 **Association for Library and Information Science Education**
JANE ROBBINS-CARTER, Director, Library School, University of Wisconsin-Madison

59 **Association for Library Service to Children**
MARGARET BUSH, Assistant Professor, Graduate School of Library and Information Science, Simmons College, Boston

61 **Association of College and Research Libraries**
SHARON J. ROGERS, University Librarian, George Washington University, Washington, D.C.

62 **Association of Jewish Libraries**
EDITH LUBETSKI, Hedi Steinberg Library, Stern College for Women, Yeshiva University, New York City

63 **Association of Research Libraries**
NICOLE DAVAL, Information Officer, Association of Research Libraries, Washington, D.C.

68 **Association of Specialized and Cooperative Library Agencies**
JAMES A. NELSON, Commissioner, Kentucky Department of Libraries and Archives; President ASCLA

70 **Beta Phi Mu**
BLANCHE WOOLLS, Executive Secretary, Beta Phi Mu

70 **Bibliographies and Indexes**
SANDRA WHITELEY, Program Officer, Association of College Research Libraries, ALA

72 **Black Americans**
JESSIE CARNEY SMITH, University Librarian and Professor, Fisk University

74 **Blind and Physically Handicapped, Library Services for the**
FRANK KURT CYLKE, Director; ALFRED D. HAGLE, Public Resources Officer, National Library Service for the Blind and Physically Handicapped, Library of Congress

78 **Bookselling**
DONALD E. STEWART, Editorial Consultant, Former Associate Director for Publishing, ALA

79 **Buildings**
RAYMOND M. HOLT, Consultant, Del Mar, California

85 **Canadian Library Association**
PAUL KITCHEN, Executive Director, Canadian Library Association

87 **Cataloging and Classification**
MICHAEL GORMAN, Director of General Services; ARNOLD WAJENBERG, Principal Cataloger, University of Illinois Library, Urbana-Champaign

89 **Catholic Library Association**
MATTHEW R. WILT, Executive Director, CLA

89 **Children's Book Council**
JOHN DONOVAN, Executive Director, Children's Book Council, New York

92 **Children's Library Services**
ELIZABETH HUNTOON, Children's Services Coordinator, Chicago Public Library

95 **Children's Literature**
ZENA SUTHERLAND, Associate Professor, Graduate Library School, University of Chicago

98 **Chinese American Librarians Association**
AMY SETOO WILSON, Executive Director, CALA

ix

99 **Collection Management**
FREDERICK C. LYNDEN, Assistant University Librarian for Technical Services, Brown University

106 **Continuing Professional Education**
ELIZABETH W. STONE, Professor Emeritus and Former Dean, School of Library and Information Science, The Catholic University of America, Washington, D.C.

109 **Copyright**
ROBERT WEDGEWORTH, Executive Director, ALA

110 **Council on Library Media Technical Assistants**
JOANNE WOLFORD, Associate Professor, Ohio University–Lancaster

110 **Databases, Computer-Readable**
MARTHA E. WILLIAMS, Professor of Information Science, Coordinated Science Labs, University of Illinois at Urbana–Champaign

114 **Education, Library**
A. VENABLE LAWSON, Director, Division of Library and Information Management, Emory University, Atlanta

117 **ERIC**
BARBARA MINOR, Publications Coordinator; DONALD P. ELY, ERIC Clearinghouse on Information Resources, Syracuse University

118 **Federal Librarians Round Table**
NINA FRANCIS JACOBS, Librarian, Travis Air Force Base; President FLRT

118 **Films**
WILLIAM J. SLOAN, Librarian, Circulating Film Library, The Museum of Modern Art

121 **Films, Children's**
MARILYN BERG IARUSSO, Assistant Coordinator, Children's Services, New York Public Library

127 **Freedom to Read Foundation**
JUDITH F. KRUG, Executive Director, Freedom to Read Foundation

128 **Friends of Libraries**
FREDERICK RUFFNER, President, FOLUSA, Gale Research Company

130 **Gifts, Bequests, Endowments**
CLYDE C. WALTON, Director of Libraries, University of Colorado, Boulder

134 **Government Documents Round Table**
JAN SWANBECK, Head, Documents Division Texas A&M University, College Station

134 **Government Publications and Depository System**
LEROY C. SCHWARZKOPF, Consultant, Greenbelt, Maryland

136 **Health and Rehabilitative Library Services**
KATHLEEN O. MAYO, Institution Library Consultant, State Library of Florida

139 **IFLA**
MARGREET WIJNSTROOM, Secretary-General, IFLA, The Hague, Netherlands

140 **Independent Research Libraries**
MARCUS MCCORRISON, Director, American Antiquarian Society, Worcester, Massachusetts

143 **Information and Referral Services**
LILLIE J. SEWARD, Specialist, Library Information Services and Programs, Division of Library Development and Services, Maryland State Department of Education

145 **Information Industry**
ELIZABETH C. NANNI, Director, Marketing and Communications, Information Industry Association

147 **Information Technology**
RICHARD W. BOSS, Senior Consultant, Information Systems Consultants, Inc.

149 **Insurance for Libraries**
DONALD L. UNGARELLI, Director of Libraries, Long Island University, C. W. Post Center

151 **Intellectual Freedom**
JUDITH F. KRUG, Director, Office for Intellectual Freedom, ALA

155 **Intellectual Freedom Round Table**
PAMELA BONNELL, Library Manager, Plano Public Library System, Texas; chair, IFRT

156 **International Board on Books for Young People**
JOHN DONOVAN, Executive Director, Children's Book Council, New York

157 **International Relations**
MOHAMMED A. AMAN, Dean, School of Library and Information Science, University of Wisconsin-Milwaukee

164 **International Relations Round Table**
EDWIN S. GLEAVES, Professor and Chairman, Department of Library and Information Science, Peabody College-Vanderbilt University, Nashville, Tennessee

165 **Italian Americans and Libraries**
C. MICHAEL DIODATI, JR., Supervising Librarian, New York Public Library, Wakefield Branch

165 **Junior Members Round Table**
CHARLES E. KRATZ, Associate Director, Rider College Library, Lawrenceville, New Jersey

166 **Labor Groups, Library Service to**
DONNA L. NERBOSO, Reference Librarian, New York University

167 **Law and Legislation**
ALEX LADENSON, Executive Director, Urban Libraries Council

170 **Law Libraries**
JULIUS J. MARKE, Professor of Law and Law Librarian, New York University School of Law

171 **Libraries and Education Improvement, Center for**
MILBREY L. JONES, Policy Coordinator; HAROLDIE K. SPRIGGS, Education Program Specialist, Center for Libraries and Education Improvement, Office of Educational Research and Improvement, U.S. Department of Education

172 **Library Administration and Management Association**
GARY E. STRONG, State Librarian of California

174 **Library and Information Technology Association**
NANCY L. EATON, Director of Libraries, University of Vermont

175 **Library Association**
RON SURRIDGE

176 **Library History**
GEORGE S. BOBINSKI, Dean and Professor, School of Information and Library Studies, State University of New York at Buffalo

177 **Library History Round Table**
LAUREL A. GROTZINGER, Dean and Chief Research Officer, The Graduate College, Western Michigan University, Kalamazoo

178 **Library Instruction Round Table**
LINDA DOUGHERTY, Clearing Branch, Chicago Public Library

179 **Library of Congress**
ROBERT G. ZICH, Director; PAMELA ROPER WAGNER, Staff Assistant, Office of Planning and Development, Library of Congress

182 **Library Press**
PATRICIA TEGLER, Assistant Reference Librarian, University of Illinois at Chicago

184 **Library Research Round Table**
SHIRLEY GRINNELL FITZGIBBONS, Assistant Professor, School of Library and Information Science, Indiana University; Chairperson, LRRT

185 **Literacy Programs, Library**
HELEN HUGUENOR LYMAN, Professor Emeritus, Library School, University of Wisconsin–Madison; Adjunct Professor, School of Information and Library Studies, State University of New York at Buffalo

189 **Medical Libraries**
JAMES F. WILLIAMS, II, Associate Director of University Libraries, Wayne State University, Detroit

191 **Medical Library Association**
RAYMOND PALMER, Executive Director, Medical Library Association, Chicago

192 **Mountain Plains Library Association**
DOROTHY LIEGL, South Dakota State Library

192 **Music Library Association**
MARY WALLACE DAVIDSON, Music Librarian, Wellesley College

194 **National Agricultural Library**
JOSEPH H. HOWARD, Director, National Agricultural Library, U.S. Department of Agriculture

196 **National Commission on Libraries and Information Science**
TONI CARBO BEARMAN, Executive Director, National Commission on Libraries and Information Science, District of Columbia

197 **National Endowment for the Humanities**
THOMAS PHELPS, Program Director, National Endowment for the Humanities

199 **National Library of Canada**
GWYNNETH EVANS, Executive Secretary, National Library of Canada

202 **National Library of Medicine**
KENT A. SMITH, Deputy Director, National Library of Medicine, Bethesda, Maryland

203 **National Technical Information Service**
TED RYERSON, Chief, Office of Policy and Planning, National Technical Information Service

203 **Networks**
ALPHONSE F. TREZZA, Associate Professor, School of Library and Information Studies, Florida State University

209 **New England Library Association**
SHERMAN C. PRIDHAM, Portsmouth Public Library, New Hampshire

210 **Oral History Association**
RONALD E. MARCELLO, Executive Secretary, Oral History Association

210 **Pacific Northwest Library Association**
BARBARA TOLLIVER, University of Washington Graduate School of Library and Information Science

211 **Personnel and Employment: Compensation**
LANCE QUERY, Director of Library Research and Analysis, Northwestern University

213 **Personnel and Employment: Recruitment and Selection**
CAROLYN J. HENDERSON, Library Personnel Officer, Stanford University Libraries

215 **Personnel and Employment: Staff Development**
ROGER PARENT, Deputy Executive Director, ALA

216 **Preservation of Library Materials**
CARLA J. MONTORI, Head, Preservation Department, Indiana University

218 **Public Libraries**
KENNETH D. SHEARER, Professor, School of Library Science, North Carolina Central University, Durham

224 **Public Library Association**
CHARLES W. ROBINSON, Director, Baltimore County Public Library

225 **Public Relations**
JON ELDREDGE, Department of Political Science, University of New Mexico, Albuquerque

228 **Publishing, Book**
DONALD E. STEWART, Editorial Consultant, Former Associate Director for Publishing, ALA

233 **Publishing, Serials**
W. A. (BILL) KATZ, Professor, Library School, State University of New York at Albany

235 **Recordings, Sound**
GORDON STEVENSON, Associate Professor of Library Science, State University of New York at Albany

237 **Reference and Adult Services Division**
GARY R. PURCELL, Professor, Graduate School of Library and Information Science, University of Tennessee, Knoxville

239 **Reference Services**
JAMES RETTIG, Reference Librarian, University of Illinois at Chicago

241 **REFORMA**
SALVADOR GUERENA, Chicano Studies Librarian, University of California-Santa Barbara

242 **Research**
JOHN E. LEIDE, Associate Professor, McGill University Graduate School of Library Science

253 **Resources and Technical Services Division**
WILLIAM J. MYRICK, University Director for Library Planning and Development, Office of Academic Affairs, The City University of New York

254 **School Libraries and Media Programs**
GERALD O. HODGES, Assistant Professor, Department of Library Science and Educational Technology, University of North Carolina, Greensboro

258 **Security Systems**
JOHN F. CAMP, Consultant, Library Technology Reports

259 **Seminar on Acquisition of Latin American Library Materials**
SUZANNE HODGMAN, Bibliographer for Ibero-American Studies, University of Wisconsin-Madison; Executive Secretary, SALALM

260 **Serials**
MARCIA TUTTLE, Head, Serials Department, University of North Carolina, Wilson Library, Chapel Hill

262 **Social Responsibilities**
MARVA L. DELOACH, Head, Cataloging and Records Maintenance Division, Illinois State University, Normal

267 **Social Responsibilities Round Table**
DORIS KIRSCHBAUM, Public Services Librarian, Mary Mount College of Virginia, Arlington

268 **Southeastern Library Association**
REBECCA BINGHAM, Durrett Education Center, Jefferson County Public Schools Louisville

269 **Special Collections**
SAMUEL ALLEN STREIT, Assistant University Librarian for Special Collections, Brown University

276 **Special Libraries**
VIVIAN J. ARTERBERY, Library Director, Rand Corporation

278 **Staff Organizations Round Table**
CHARLES KING, Louisville Free Public Library

278 **Standards**
PATRICIA R. HARRIS, Executive Director, National Information Standards Organization (Z39)

279 **Telecommunications**
MARY DIEBLER CLARK, Director, Information and Research, Public Service Satellite Consortium, Washington, D.C.

283 **Theatre Library Association**
RICHARD M. BUCK, Assistant to the Chief, Performing Arts Research Center, The New York Public Library at Lincoln Center

284 **Trustees**
BARBARA COOPER, Public Affairs Director, Gale Research; Immediate Past President, ALTA

285 **Universal Bibliographic Control**
BARBARA JOVER, UBC Programme Officer, IFLA International Office for UBC, British Library, London

286 **Universal Serials and Book Exchange**
MARY W. GHIKAS, Executive Director, Universal Serials and Book Exchange, Inc.

287 **Urban Libraries Council**
ALEX LADENSON, Executive Director, Urban Libraries Council

289 **Washington Report**
EILEEN D. COOKE, Director, Washington Office, ALA

292 **Women in Librarianship**
KATHARINE PHENIX, Westminster Public Library, Littleton, Colorado

296 **Women's National Book Association**
CATHY RENTSCHLER, Editor, Library Literature, The H. W. Wilson Company

297 **Young Adult Library Services**
EVIE WILSON, Visiting Lecturer, Peabody College-Vanderbilt University, Nashville

300 **Young Adult Literature**
EVELYN SHAEVEL, Executive Director, Young Adult Services Division, ALA

303 **Young Adult Services Division**
PENELOPE S. JEFFREY, Manager, Independence Library, Cuyahoga County Public Library, Independence, Ohio

304 **Canadian Report**
JOHN WILKINSON

312 **United Kingdom Report**
RUSSELL BOWDEN
NICK MOORE

STATE REPORTS
316

Alabama. JAMES D. RAMER, Dean, Graduate School of Library Service, The University of Alabama

Alaska. ISABELLE MUDD, Administrative Librarian, MSA Post Library, Fort Wainwright

Arizona. ARLENE BANSAL, Deputy Director, Department of Library-Archives, State Capital, Phoenix

Arkansas. ROBERT RAZER, Little Rock Public Library

California. GIL MCNAMEE, California Chapter Councilor

Colorado. JOHN CAMPBELL, Director, Pathfinder Library System, Montrose

Connecticut. MIKE SIMONDS, President, Connecticut Library Association; Executive Director, Bibliomation

Delaware. JANE E. HUKILL, Director, Delaware Campus Library, Widener University, Wilmington

District of Columbia. LAWRENCE E. MOLUMBY, Deputy Director, District of Columbia Public Library

Florida. HELEN MOELLER, Library Consultant, State Library of Florida, Tallahassee

Georgia. JULIE V. HUNTER, Acting Director, Robert W. Woodruff Library, Atlanta University

Hawaii. SUSAN F. MAESATO, Public Services Librarian; Kenneth R. Herrick, Director of Libraries, University of Hawaii at Hilo

Idaho. LYNN BAIRD, Head, Serials Department, University of Idaho Library, Moscow; ALA Chapter Councilor

Illinois. ESTELLE BLACK, Assistant Director, Rockford Public Library

Indiana. BETH K. STEELE, Director, Public Relations/Publications, Indiana Library/Library Trustee Associations, Indianapolis

Iowa. CARL F. ORGREN, Director, School of Library and Information Science, University of Iowa, Iowa City

Kansas. TOM MUTH, Assistant Librarian, Topeka Public Library

Kentucky. EDWIN C. STROHECKER, former Dean of Libraries and Chairman, Emeritus, Department of Library Science, Murray State University

Louisiana. BEN BRADY, Associate State Librarian, Louisiana State Library, Baton Rouge

Maine. NANCY E. CROWELL, Head Librarian, Scarborough Public Library

Maryland. J. MAURICE TRAVILLIAN, Network Specialist, Maryland State Department of Education, Columbia

Massachusetts. MARGO CRIST, Worcester Public Library; ALA Chapter Councilor

Michigan. ROBERT RAZ, Director, Grand Rapids Public Library

Minnesota. EDWARD SWANSON, Head, Processing Department, Minnesota Historical Society, St. Paul

Mississippi. JAMES F. PARKS, JR., Head Librarian, Millsaps-Wilson Library, Millsaps College, Jackson

Missouri. MADELINE MATSON, Coordinator of Publications, Missouri State Library, Jefferson City

Montana. GLENDA BELL, District Library Media Specialist, Billings Public Schools

Nebraska. JOHN MAYESKI, Library Director, Calvin T. Ryan Library, Kearney State College

Nevada. ANN BRADY, Library Development Division, Nevada State Library

New Hampshire. LOUISE C. PRICE, Assistant Director, City of Manchester Library

New Jersey. STAFF

New Mexico. PAUL A. AGRIESTI, Deputy State Librarian, New Mexico State Library, Santa Fe

New York. ROBERT E. BARRON, School Library Liaison, New York State Education Department; PATRICA MAUTINO, Director, Institutional Support and Informational Services, Oswego County BOCES.

North Carolina. ROBERT BURGIN, Lecturer, School of Library and Information Science, North Carolina Central University

North Dakota. MARY BRAATEN, Government Services Librarian, State Library, Bismarck

Ohio. BONNIE BETH MITCHELL, Assistant to Executive Director for Administration, OHIONET

Oklahoma. GRETCHEN SHARBAUGH BOOSE, Informational Representative, Oklahoma Department of Libraries, Oklahoma City

Oregon. NADINE PURCELL, Technical Services Library, Jackson County Library System, Medford

Pennsylvania. MARY IVY BAYARD, Librarian, Tyler School of Art, Temple University

Rhode Island. HOWARD BOKSENBAUM, Coordinator, Island Interrelated Library System, Barrington

South Carolina. CARL STONE, Director, Anderson County Library

South Dakota. PHILIP BROWN, Documents Librarian, Hilton M. Briggs Library, South Dakota State University, Brookings

Tennessee. ROBERT B. CRONEBERGER, State Librarian and Archivist, Nashville

Texas. KAY M. STANSBERY, Director, Technical and Printing Services, Tarrant County Junior College

Utah. NATHAN M. SMITH, Director, School of Library and Information Science, Brigham Young University

Vermont. MILTON CROUCH, Assistant Director for Reader Service, University of Vermont, Burlington

Virginia. MARY ALICE SEEMEYER, Virginia State Library, Richmond

Washington. MARGARET E. CHISHOLM, Director, Graduate School of Library and Information Science, University of Washington

West Virginia. SHIRLEY SMITH, Field Consultant, West Virginia Library Commission, Charleston

Wisconsin. SUSAN L. HEATH, Reference and Collection Development Librarian, Nicolet College, Rhinelander

Wyoming, PAUL B. CORS, Head of Collection Development, University of Wyoming Library, Laramie

Librarianship Through a Rear View Mirror

> *The publication of this ALA Yearbook, if continued would provide an excellent historical record in the future....*
> George S. Bobinski in "American Library History," *The ALA Yearbook* (first edition, 1976)

Yearbooks have in common the problem of retrospective myopia. Also, they represent neither news nor history. The events and activities summarized are too old to be news yet too recent to provide an adequate historical view. Therefore, the essential value of a yearbook may lie in its ability to select significant events and activities consistently such that it will provide an accurate basis for a summary over longer periods of time.

As the editors of the *ALA Yearbook* pondered this question of value it emerged that perhaps the major feature of the 1985 edition should be a 10-year review article. Such an article must necessarily be highly selective in coverage as each edition of the *ALA Yearbook* on the average presents summaries of over 40 topics, 12-to-15 special features and articles from the 50 states and the District of Columbia in a volume of about 400 pages.

The editors have selected the following highlights of the *ALA Yearbook*, 1976–1985, as representative of the trends and issues covered in librarianship during the past decade:

FOUR EVENTFUL YEARS: 1975–1978

In the first paragraph of "Academic Libraries" in the First Edition, contributor Richard D. Johnson wrote, "The principal issues have been primarily economic—recession, inflation, prospect of declining enrollments. They will continue into the following years." (Johnson, incidentally, has continued to author his article in all 10 editions of the book.)

C. Lamar Wallis, then Public Library Director in Memphis, lamented, "Some librarians remember the Great Depression budgets and the crowds of patrons pawing over out-of-date volumes, but not since the 30s had most of them seen anything like '75. Here and there a big city came up smelling like roses, and the smaller and medium-sized jurisdictions escaped the jugular cuts for the most part, but everywhere one went at least a few librarians could be heard moaning and groaning about budget slashes either in effect or about to occur."

So began the mid-1970s. "Start with the queen of them all—The New York Public Research Library—down to rock bottom in funds and bailed out temporarily by the Astors with an unprecedented gift," Wallis wrote. When branches started closing in New York City, Mayor Beame felt the heat of public outcry. City Librarian Kevin Starr marched on City Hall in San Francisco to wring budget concessions for student pages.

There were some brighter spots. In "Adult Library Services," Margaret Monroe, of the University of Wisconsin Library School, Madison, noted that Information and Referral (I & R) services were still being sustained by federal money in 1975, though federal funds decreased for other outreach programs. She applauded grants from the National Endowment for the Humanities (NEH) for cultural programs (given to Boston, Chicago, and the District of Columbia Public Libraries). She saw such programs as a way to "carry public libraries to a more significant role in the 1980s."

The story of cutbacks also applied to children's and young adults' services. Peggy Sullivan pointed out, "When metropolitan libraries . . . reported closing of branches or reduction of hours, service to children might not be mentioned, but it was a casualty in the economic cutbacks." Young Adult librarians in 1975, nevertheless, took comfort from one piece of professional news: "The Young Adult Services Division of ALA, under a new dues and budgeting plan, found itself able to support . . . an Executive Secretary of its own . . . ending the 15-year joint employment of an executive secretary with Children's Services Division," Carol Starr recorded. Evelyn Shaevel, formerly of the Lake County Public Library System in Indiana, took that part and continues to hold it in 1985.

Anna Mary Lowrey, of the State University of New York, Buffalo, in "School Libraries and Media Centers" (1975 edition), reviewed the surge in the growth of school libraries in the 1960s, in part due to "generous contributions of federal funds." But she observed that "the professional staffing . . . was inadequate." (Statistics as of Fall 1974 from the Center for Education Statistics, published in the 1976 Yearbook, reported 74,625 schools with libraries—22,315 secondary and 52,310 elementary and combined schools. Staff with certificates numbered 55,281 women and 7,378 men. Pupils totaled 43,929,000.) "The quality and size of the media center staff will continue to make the difference between poor and exemplary programs," she wrote. The eight demonstration school library programs of the Knapp Project, 1962–67, were working examples of the educational value of model media programs.

Of special importance to professionals in school in 1975 was publication of *Media Programs: District and School* (ALA and AECT), which brought new emphasis to qualitative aspects of library services that are user-centered. Proposals for a revision are under discussion.

The mid-1970s saw the rise of databases. Martha E. Williams, of the Information Retrieval Laboratory of the University of Illinois at Urbana, summarized:

> 1975 was a significant year for databases. It was the year in which the fledgling database industry developed into a phenomenon to be reckoned with . . . in the world of library and information science . . . the two largest commercial database search services in the world achieved a status of self-sufficiency solely on the basis of sales of online search services . . . the bibliographic type of database enjoyed unprecedented success, as a class, during 1975. The history of computerized retrieval of information goes back a couple of decades, but it has only been in the past five or six years that computer searching on a large scale, and by significant numbers of users, has become economically feasible and commercially viable . . .

Ten years later for this edition of the *Yearbook* she writes, "Databases continued during 1984 to be used online and, to a much lesser extent, in the batch mode. Online activity increased. More and more information centers and libraries are using databases and end-user searching is increasing. One of the forces beginning to contribute to the expansion of the online market is the introduction of front ends, gateways, and intermediary systems for making online searching easier."

Her article reports that the online database industry has achieved success and is growing at a rate of roughly 20 to 25 percent per year. Both the major vendors and the major databases are firmly established, she writes.

Al Trezza, then Executive Director of the National Commission on Libraries and Information Science (NCLIS), contributed the first article on "Networks." He affirmed a view found increasingly in the professional literature of the time: "No individual library, be it the Library of Congress, Harvard, Yale, or The New York Public Library, can develop the resources and services to meet all of the needs of its users. They, too, must participate in national networking. Libraries serving as state, regional, or national bibliographic and resource center, using the latest in computers, microfilming, and other technological developments, can provide identification, location, and delivery of library materials and information on a timely and effective basis."

Yet many librarians in the field felt that they were losing ground. Gil McNamee, of the San Francisco Public Library's Bay Area Reference Center, wrote that reference librarians, "particularly those in public libraries, found themselves faced with staff shortages and drastic cuts in reference book budgets in 1975. . . . Indeed, it seems that reference librarians in 1975, by and large, had difficulty in even maintaining the past level of service, and reference performance did not change for the better."

McNamee, however, managed to end his article (1976 edition) with a note of collegial pride:

> "Lawrence Kusche, an excellent reference librarian himself, . . . dedicated his best seller, *The Bermuda Triangle Mystery—Solved*, to the Interlibrary Loan Department of Arizona State University. And, in addition, he gave a word of hope and a challenge for all reference librarians: 'There's an answer somewhere!' "

CENTENNIAL CELEBRATIONS

"There probably had never been as much excitement and activity in the area of American library history as during 1975," George Bobinski could say "because of the coming Centennial Celebration of the American Library Association in 1976." He observed the brisk sale of Dewey T-shirts ("Dewey? Sure we do!") and commemorative mugs, bookends, and paperweights. ALA published a special Centennial Calendar. *Library Trends* (July 1976) reviewed "The Last 100 Years of American Library History." Peggy Sullivan's excellent biography of "Mr. ALA" (*Carl H. Milam and the American Library Association*) was published by H. W. Wilson in 1976. In 1977 Dennis Thomison's history of ALA was published by the Association, and Libraries Unlimited published the long-awaited *Dictionary of American Library Biography,* edited by Bobinski, Jesse H. Shera, and Bohdan Wynar (302 biographies by about 200 contributors). Edward Holley and other leading librarian-scholars and historians participated in Library History Seminar V, held in Philadelphia October 3–6, the same site and time of the first ALA Conference 100 years ago.

The historical articles published in *College & Research Libraries* by its editor, Richard Johnson, to honor ALA on its Centennial, were collected and published by ALA in 1977 as *Libraries for Teaching, Libraries for Research.* Looking toward the future was a Festchrift in honor of Jerrold Orne—*Academic Libraries by the Year 2000* (Bowker 1977), Herbert Poole, Editor.

In a Special Report (1978) on the ALA Archives at the University of Illinois at Urbana-Champaign, archivist Maynard Brichford's summary indicated that the shoemaker's children may have shoes after all. ALA, he said, "is one of the few professional organizations" that have archives. ALA's comprised 738 cubic feet (equivalent to about 123 file cabinets) and ALA published a microfiche guide to the collections.

Each edition of the *Yearbook* since 1976 has carried illustrated feature articles and a number of shorter "sidebars," or Special Reports. The titles alone indicate the range, and many still make good reading today. A sampling includes "ALA at 100"; "Micrographics: An Eventful Forty Years—What Next?" "At the Hub: The British Library"; "Women in Canadian Librarianship"; "The Dilemma of Fees for Service"; "Genealogy as it Relates to Library Service"; "Our Fragile Inheritance: The Challenge of Preserving Library Materials;;" "The ALA Archives"; "A Comparison of AACR 1 and 2"; "Trustees: Personnel Policy"; "Proposition 13 Sends California Libraries Reeling"; "ALA's Satellite Seminar on Copyright"; "Libraries and the Information Age"; "The Lister Hill Center"; "Year of the Child: Emphasis on Commitments"; "A Look Back in Defense of Freedom"; "Exchange Mission to U.S.S.R.: Children's Services"; "The Late Great Public Library—R.I.P."; "An Information Agenda for the 1980s"; "Accreditation: A Review of Issues"; "The Eighteenth Century Short Title Catalogue—A Revolutionary Advance to Scholarship"; "Issues for Special Libraries"; "The New Censors"; "Remembrances on the Occasion of LSCA's 25th Anniversary"; "OPM v. ALA: The Controversy over Standards for Federal Librarians"; "Education for Librarianship: The Way It Is"; "Public Lending Right: A Forum Sponsored by the Center for the Book, Library of Congress"; "SLA: A 75th Anniversary Historical Review."

The longest feature of the past 10 editions was Edward H. Holley's "ALA at 100" (32 pages). It was reprinted as a separate booklet and distributed at History Seminar V in Philadelphia. Peggy Sullivan wrote an eight-page feature on "The ALA Centennial Celebration" (1977). Among highlights for her was the presidential inauguration of Clara Jones, Director of the Detroit Public Library, who had served as Acting President after the death of Allie Beth Martin on April 11, 1976 (the Centennial Edition of the *Yearbook* is dedicated to her). President Jones became the first black and the first candidate nominated by members' petition to win that post. Sullivan referred to the series of lectures later published by ALA as *Libraries and the Life of the Mind in America: Essays Delivered at the Centennial Celebration of the American Library Association* (1977). Another highlight was Keyes Metcalf's introduction of Daniel J. Boorstin, Librarian of Congress, from November 12, 1975. "A lesser man than Daniel J. Boorstin might have been nonplussed or upstaged by the introductory remarks at the [Centennial lecture], when Keyes Metcalf shared his memories of the men who have served as Librarian of Congress in his years of professional activity. The period spanned almost half of ALA's own history, and his warmly personal comments brought the era to life again for others. "Boorstin, a historian whose appointment had been opposed by the ALA, spoke chiefly on American public libraries and their tradition. At that meeting he began to win the support of many in the library and publishing community.

Sullivan, then Director of Branches and Regional Libraries for Chicago Public, provided in her feature article an informal list of publications on or related to the Centennial. A first for ALA was a *New York Times* 16-page advertising supplement on "The Great American Library Success Story and Your Information Investment" (October 6, 1976), Arthur Plotnik, Editor.

Another Centennial was recognized in the Sullivan article and elsewhere in he 1977 *Yearbook. Library Journal,* "whose ancestor, *American Library Journal,* made its debut in 1876 with Melvil Dewey as editor, celebrated its first century with a 292-page special issue (January 1, 1976): "The Need to Know." In June 1976, *American Libraries* dedicated its special issue to "Who We Are: A National Profile of the American Librarian" ("Library Press," 1977).

By the end of the Centennial Year, budget cuts were already old news and there was less comment on them. The shock of Proposition 13 (1978) was still ahead.

SOME MAIN CURRENTS

"As the nation began its third century, it appeared that a principal feature in libraries of the nation's second century, the familiar card catalog, was slowly on its way to extinction," wrote Richard Johnson in "Academic Libraries" (1977). By 1976 more than 800 institutions participated in OCLC's system for cooperative cataloging. By 1978, the Ohio College Library Center was formally plain OCLC, Inc., with 4,000,000 records stored and 2,211 terminals in operation. OCLC remained the only tie many libraries had with automation.

Few public libraries in the mid-1970s had any access to computers and the staff to manage them as did their colleagues in academe. Yet, contributor Wallis remarked, "crucial matters of money (aside), the subjects most often heard among public librarians during the year (1976) were networks, computers, and microfilm catalogs . . . the tide was turning." The "public librarian had to embrace computers, ready or not." He noted a rush to COM (Computer Output Microfilm), and public libraries began using small computers "for circulation control and a host of other in-house operations."

In his article on "Social Responsibilities, *Yearbook* adviser and contributor E. J. Josey hailed the new Statement of Mission of the Public Library—"the most auspicious act of (ALA) in support of social responsibility"— at the ALA Annual Conference in June 1977. It "asserts a political and social leadership role for public libraries," he said.

Margaret Monroe continued to see both National Endowment for the Humanities and National Endowment for the Arts grants to public libraries as a "small renaissance" in the mid-1970s. CETA-funded positions and use of volunteers were some of the resources called on by library directors struggling to offset budget reductions. Charges were imposed at some libraries for selective adult services—just as some libraries had done in the 1930s.

Severe cold, ice, and fuel shortages came with the winter of '77. Librarians remember, too, cutbacks, layoffs, and closings, damaged facilities and inoperable equipment. Yet, wrote Edward N. Howard of Vigo County Public Library, Indiana, libraries were still "jammed with kids, teachers, and other adults." He reported, perhaps even more surprising, a record high in public library construction as of June 1977— $130,000,000 was expended (local funding 72 percent, federal 17 percent, gifts 6 percent, and state aid 5 percent). Other public library statistics reported include those from the NCLIS "National Inventory" (1977):

81 percent in professional library staff (36,000 in 1975 v. 19,900 in 1965)

65 percent gain in bookstock (397,000,000 in 1975 v. 241,000,000 in 1965).

But libraries in the United States were, in the NCLIS view, "grossly underfunded . . . to give adequate library service."

Still, in 1977, "a year when the public economy was in trouble, libraries fared better than many had expected," Howard concluded. The typical budget had increased slightly.

The year 1978 will be remembered as "the year of the survey." Writing on public libraries (1979 edition), contributor Ernest A. DiMattia, Jr., of Ferguson Public Library, Stamford, Connecticut, so suggested. An ALA-sponsored Gallup Poll reported that "more than one-half of all Americans 18 and over visited a public library in 1978." Commenting on the poll, ALA Executive Director Robert Wedgeworth pointed up a dilemma: the poll showed high satisfaction with present services at the same time that demands were growing for property tax cuts; he saw it as a problem in years to come. Another important survey was conducted by the Book Industry Study Group. For the 1984 update of that survey in this *Yearbook*, see "Publishing, Book."

DiMattia saw 1978 as "a year of struggle for fiscal survival and stability." He wrote as the winds of Proposition 13 in California chilled the nation.

Commenting on children's services, Peggy Sullivan observed a pattern of use that was the reverse of what it was 20 years earlier. Daytime patrons of the 1970s were younger children. The after-school crowd were the more motivated, individual users rather than those, as in earlier years, seeking group experiences such as storytelling hours. A regrettable result, she wrote, was fewer skilled storytellers in libraries. Another trend included the use of able and willing older people as volunteers. Perhaps the longer years of retirement in good health will lead, she suggested, to the library's becoming "the community agency best able to achieve the link between the old and the young which society has lamented having lost." Special problems she saw include interlibrary loan and resource sharing for children—inquiries "still bring more silence than response"—and is "certainly a major area for future watching (1976)." In 1977 the Children's Services Division changed its name to the Association for Library Service to Children (ALSC).

In subsequent *Yearbook* editions, other contributors continued to return to the need to "find ways to prove that the services and programs that (children's librarians) provide are essential library functions" (Barbara S. Miller, Louisville Free Public Library, 1978 edition).

During the period under review, the editors of the *Yearbook* took appropriate notice of the 75th anniversary of the first publication of Peter Rabbit in 1975 and the 50th birthday of Winnie-the-Pooh in 1976; the latter supplied a piece in autobiographical style under "Biographies" (1977 edition).

Young adult librarians often took note of their need for "survival." They remarked on renewed attention to the use of paperbacks in school and public libraries and *School Library Journal*'s call for more national attention to them.

Other trends in YA service, according to Carol Starr (1977), included drop-in centers for transient teenagers, back-to-school programs (as at Enoch Pratt), catch-up centers for reading help (Denver Public), high/low interest/reading information (Los Angeles Public), and use of video (Richmond, California). Though some saw the YA librarian as an "endangered species," it appeared that YA services held their own—"with enthusiasm and creativity" (Mary K. Chelton, 1978).

DATABASES

By the end of 1978 computer-readable databases were coming "to be *the* way of searching the literature." More than half of the current A & I records were online either in America or Europe (Martha Williams), and the volume of online searching exceeded the 2,000,000 mark.

The "Goals for Action" in *Toward a National Program for Library and Information Services* (NCLIS, 1975) remained a charter as the 1980s approached.

COPYRIGHT

The new copyright law of 1976 (effective in 1978) generated a flood of articles and books. Mildred Vannorsdall, of the Chicago Public Library and ALA Reference and Subscription Books Committee, prepared a special bibliography for the 1978 edition. Various copyright *Guidelines* were also printed in the *Yearbook*. The first major revision of laws governing intellectual property in the U.S. since 1909, the 1976 Act extended copyright protection to the author for life plus 50 years. (It was formerly 28 years from date of publication with one 28-year renewal allowed.) In a prize-winning article in *American Libraries*, September 1977, Richard DeGennaro cautioned librarians not to be unduly timid in working with the new law but "to exercise all the rights and privileges" granted by it.

The *Yearbook* in many articles and reports discussed issues of interest on the topic—CONTU guidelines for Sections 108 (copying) and 107 (educational and non-profit use), revision of interlibrary loan forms and King studies (1977 and 1982). Special libraries copied the most in 1976 (15,000,000 copies), followed by public libraries (12,000,000), and academic libraries (5,000,000). Statutory recognition was given for the first time to the fair-use doctrine, a concept that "does not lend itself to exact definition" (Sara Case, "Washington Report," 1977).

"Enactment of the new law does not end concerns for librarians, libraries, and library users," concluded Frank E. McKenna, Executive Director of the Special Libraries Association and *Yearbook* contributor on "Copyright" before his death in November 1978.

BOOK PUBLISHING

Events reviewed included annual performance of the book business. Prices and revenues kept increasing, 1975–78, as number of units sold dwindled. Publications of the period included *Books for College Libraries* (ALA, 1975) in six paperbound volumes, Patricia Senn Breivik's *Open Admissions and the Academic Library* (ALA, 1978), "the year's most important and discussed statement on interpreting the academic library to students" (Johnson, 1979), and *Anglo-American Cataloguing Rules*, Second Edition (November 1978). The "u" in "cataloguing" was evidence of the decision to prepare one text for use throughout the English-speaking world. Discussion about AACR 2 has filled many lines of type in numerous articles in all 10 editions of the *Yearbook*.

OTHER THAN BOOKS

Some of the liveliest yet informative articles in the Yearbook during the past 10 years have been on library subjects other than books. They include the article "Serials" by Bill Katz of the Library School of the State University of New York at Albany; "Recordings, Sound" by Gordon Stevenson, also on the Albany faculty; "Films, Children" by Marilyn Berg Iarusso, Assistant Coordinator of Children's Services at The New York Public Library; and "Films" by William J. Sloan, Librarian of the Circulating Film Library, The Museum of Modern Art.

The zest and enthusiasm of many of the *Yearbook* contributors for their subjects and profession is reflected in their copy and these four are examples among many others. Their articles represent a 10-year record of what was available in their media to libraries and thus to the public; what was judged good and what was judged indifferent; and, particularly in the case of Katz's articles, a record of spiraling prices.

The four titles represent a slice of social history, 1976–1985, and their authors have one other distinction—they are among 35 specialists who wrote for the first edition of this book and have continued for all 10 editions.

The Katz articles trace the history of CONSER (Conversion of Serials) from its launch in 1975 through its torturous course in following years. Katz recorded the birth in 1975 of the independent *Journal of Academic Librarianship*, edited by Richard M. Dougherty and William H. Webb, and in 1976 of *Serials Librarian* (Peter Gellately, Editor, Haworth Press), "the first quarterly journal devoted exclusively to the subject."

Katz in 1977 reported that circulation revenue had begun to exceed advertising margins for leading consumer magazines for the first time in memory. "Perhaps more reliance on readers than on advertisers will improve commercial magazines," Katz hoped, and he saw the same philosophy seeping down to some of the specialized titles.

In his reports on "Social Responsibilities," E. J. Josey often cited alternative periodicals. Among those he named were *Booklegger Magazine*, edited by "courageous and indomitable Celeste West"; the *Hennepin County Library Cataloging Bulletin* (Minneapolis), edited by Sanford Berman, who was the 1976 H. W. Wilson Periodical Prize Winner; and RAIN, from Portland, Oregon, source on appropriate technology.

LITERACY

Under "Literacy Programs, Library" (1976), Jean E. Coleman of the ALA staff wrote: "Since 1965 numerous Adult Basic Education Programs have been funded by the Office of Education." Its report to Congress (1975) indicated that the programs were "successfully reaching only a small fraction of those needing it—particularly among the more educationally deficient." Robert Wedgeworth in October 1974 had "asked the staff of ALA to look into what the continuing activities of the Association had been toward literacy . . . there was no pointed evidence that the Association had maintained a continuing effort toward encouraging librarians to work with literacy programs in their public libraries." The result was a successful grant proposal to the Office of Education early in 1975. Helen Lyman of the University of Wisconsin at Madison prepared an ALA *Manual* providing guidance for literacy programs in public libraries. ALA continued thereafter to sustain its interest and support, taking a lead in organizing the Coalition on Literacy in 1981.

PRESERVATION AND SECURITY

In the Centennial Edition, George M. Cunha, Director of the New England Document Conservation Center in North Andover, Massachusetts (established 1973), took note of the "marked increase in acceptance by the library profession that something must be done to arrest the alarming deterioration of books." Few could have anticipated then that this once neglected aspect of library care would soon become hot newspaper copy. The "yellow snow" of deteriorating acid paper in books was still to be coined at a Harvard conference (1981) when Pamela W. Darling, Head of the Preservation Department at Columbia University, wrote her timely and influential feature for the 1978 edition. In "Our Fragile Inheritance: The Challenge of Preserving Library Materials," she reported on the further rising awareness of the quiet disasters at work and on what can be done, on deacidification to stop "silent erosion," and on the implications for professionals:

> Does all this add up to an emerging speciality within the profession? Probably yes, but a speciality still in such an infant state that it is impossible to predict the shape it will have taken 5 to 10 years from now.

NEH made a grant in 1979 to Columbia to look into the establishment of a conservation training program in its library school. Columbia now offers such a program.

Reflecting issues and trends in a changing society that affect libraries, Nancy Knight, Library Consultant, for nine years wrote the article "Security Systems." Her first article began, "By the mid-1970s security systems to prevent the unauthorized removal of library materials had become something more than the gimmicks they were once considered. More and more libraries, besieged by a high rate of loss, the high cost of replacement, and restricted budgets, were using security systems."

Two years later she wrote, "By 1978 security systems were no longer considered a luxury item. They were becoming standard equipment for an increasing number of libraries."

Her articles chronicle the techniques and systems and devices that librarians and manufacturers have developed and experimented with in an effort to staunch the flow of pilfered materials. In her final article for the *Yearbook* she covered the Oberlin Conference called by librarians, booksellers, lawyers, and law enforcement officers to probe the problem. The conference was the immediate result of the arrest of James Shinn, the notorious book thief linked to the theft of rare materials valued at more than $750,000 from libraries across the country.

DONATIONS

Under the title "Gifts, Bequests, Endowments" Clyde Walton, Director of Libraries, University of Colorado, Boulder, compiled a fascinating 10-year record of the extraordinary variety of items donated to American libraries of every type. Walton, one of the 35 *Yearbook* contributors who has written for every edition, reports in detail on the manuscripts, journals, rare editions, prints, photographs, special collections, memorabilia, and papers of presidents, politicians, statesmen, musicians, historians, writers that flow into libraries every year. Some *Yearbook* articles, and this is one of them, are interesting to read just for what's happening in a particular area of librarianship.

PROPOSITION 13

"Proposition 13 Sends California Libraries Reeling" by Robert Wedgeworth and Eileen D. Cooke was the lead feature in the 1979 *Yearbook* edition. Proposition 13, or the Jarvis-Gann Tax Limitation Initiative, "brought about, overnight, a dramatic change in local government finance in California." Its effect was to limit property taxes to one percent of market value (four percent of assessed value), and assessment increases were limited to two percent each year as long as the property was not sold. "What may be the most important provision" was one that required a two-thirds majority of each house of the State Legislature for new state taxes and a two-thirds majority of the voters for new local taxes. Proposition 13 passed on June 6, 1978, by a vote of 3-to-1. The *Yearbook* feature details the immediate and severe library services losses by the end of 1978. California libraries "fell victim to the political and administrative mishaps resulting from the reduction under the Jarvis change from 6,300 taxing jurisdictions to the administration of the 58 county boards."

REPORTING ON THE NEW ERA: 1979-1981

Public libraries were the first victims of Proposition 13 in California, but the threat of like measures elsewhere served as an undercurrent to all activities in the following years as writers pointed out in subsequent editions.

In November 1979, the Association of College and Research Libraries observed its 40th anniversary "by holding the first national conference for academic librarians in Boston." More than 2,600 attended, "possibly (the) first major ALA conference without committee or business meetings to interfere with the program." The first Academic/Research Librarian of the Year Award, sponsored by Baker & Taylor and ACRL, went to two giants of the profession, Keyes D. Metcalf and Robert B. Downs.

Much discussion about a national information policy engaged librarians as the 1980s approached. Ambitious plans for a national periodicals center, on the model of the British Library Lending Division at Boston Spa, England, were drawn up, but it remained a dream unfulfilled. Perhaps events and technological achievements and prospects had already made the concept obsolete by the time it was proposed.

Libraries received an extra year of cataloging grace when the Library of Congress decided in late 1978 to wait a year before "closing" its catalog based on AACR 1 and opening a new one in 1980 based on the AACR 2 code of 1978.

The "rise" of the Research Libraries Information Network was "the most striking single event in 1979," Richard Johnson decided. Originally established in 1974 by four major east coast libraries—Harvard, Yale, Columbia, and New York Public—the group later went national. Harvard dropped out, Stanford joined. by 1980 23 members had joined. Its online bibliographic network, RLIN, was an outgrowth of Stanford's BALLOTS.

OCLC, the leading bibliographic utility, by 1979 reported more than 3,000 terminals distributed throughout the United States. Smaller networks included WLN (Washington) and UTLAS (University of Toronto). The father of OCLC, Fred Kilgour, resigned as president in 1980 "to devote his attention to innovative programs for the network."

By 1981, OCLC, then 10 years old, could claim 2,700 members (60 percent academic libraries). The database had grown to 8,000,000 bibliographic records, and it was increasing at the rate of 25,000 a week. As of the end of 1984 the organization reported 5,008 members (56 percent academic) and 11,500,000 bibliographic records.

New approaches to fund raising were seen in the early 1980s. Yale made news in 1981 by selling a rare coin in its collections, the Brasher doubloon (dated 1787), for $650,000 to help pay for its new Seeley G. Mudd Library. The University of Rochester made a comparable sale.

An important event in 1979 for all libraries was the White House Conference on Library and Information Services. Held in November the Conference drew 913 delegates and alternates and 2,650 others. It produced "a group of recommendations which can form the basis of a national information policy for the United States," Shirley Echelman wrote in her feature in the 1980 *Yearbook*. The Conference had been preceded by state and territorial conferences that had addressed the Five Conference Themes: meeting personal needs, lifelong learning, organizations and the profession, governing society, and increasing international understanding. Eileen Cooke said in her "Washington Report" (1980) that the Conference "might well be called a coalition effort in awareness building.... The follow-up implementation stage calls for consensus and commitment to work with old allies as well as newly discovered friends."

1979 was also the International Year of the Child. "Books and Broadcasting for Children: An International Symposium" was conducted in Fall 1979 with the management of the Association for Library Service to Children (ALSC). It provided a 36-day opportunity for sharing ideas with specialists from 30 nations, according to Ruth Tarbox's report in the 1980 Yearbook. Barbara S. Miller, in her review (1980), said that positions dedicated to children's services and once abolished were being reinstated in a number of places. Yet, in subsequent reports she emphasized the vulnerability of such services, essentially because children lack power (1981, 1982). Increases in circulation were often a sign of the unfavorable economic and social conditions of the time, she said, and it was important to be aware of children's responses to those conditions.

The American Association of School Librarians (AASL) held its first national conference for school librarians in Louisville, Kentucky, in September 1980. It drew 1,700 library and media specialists and 2,500 registrants. According to D. Philip Baker (1980), the new AASL series, published by ALA and edited by Jane Ann Hannigan and David R. Bender—"Trends and Issues"— "met with immediate success" after the first title appeared.

In 1980, a presidential election year, Oryx Press brought out E. J. Josey's *Libraries in the Political Process*. Another 1980 publication, *A Planning Process for Public Libraries* "can work ... wonders," Mary Jo Lynch, of the ALA staff and Project Coordinator, said because it takes a very different approach from that taken by the Public Library Association in the past and based on "standards."

Kenneth Shearer, of the School of Library Science, North Carolina Central University, Durham, concluded his public library report (1981) with the observation that "the public library ... is of all institutions, the most conservative agent in preservation of the past, the most liberal in spirit, and the most independent in thought. The work begun in the Governors' and the White House Conferences ... must be pursued ... in the decade ahead."

Shearer summarized recent censuses of the state of the public library in the early 1980s (1982 edition). Eight thousand five hundred systems served 225,000,000 (about one for every 26,500 U.S. citizens) and there were about 71,000 public library service outlets of some description. The costs: about $2,000,000,000 in 1981. State aid provided about nine percent of all operating revenues. The U.S. Office of Education estimated that 8,500,000 persons used a public library each week.

Though Massachusetts in 1981 ushered in Proposition $2^{1}/_{2}$, "and ushered out much library service," Shearer reported that state aid in New York was up 29 percent (1982).

Public Libraries, edited by Shearer, completed its plans to become a quarterly journal in Spring 1982. *Public Library Quarterly* announced that it planned to become more theme-oriented in each issue.

Shearer concluded his 1982 article with the following from former U.S. Senator Jacob Javits of New York: "You must make new friends in Congress to get the message across ... that our libraries are cathedrals of the mind which we can afford to ignore only at the peril of losing our intellectual and creative identity."

PUBLISHING

Book sales totaled more than $7 billion by the beginning of the 1980s. Much of the increase came from inflated prices rather than healthy increases in number of units sold. Bill Katz reported that financial problems still dominated serial acquisitions. The average annual chemistry or physics subscription reached $156.

In 1981, ALA with the Association of American Publishers and others, issued a 40-page report, *Limiting What Students Shall Read*, which found that censorship was increasing.

The Concise AACR 2 (1981), edited by Michael Gorman, found a ready market in the early 1980s. ALA published *An Information Agenda for the 1980s* (1981), proceedings of an ALA-sponsored colloquium in New York in 1980 (edited by Carlton C. Rochell).

YEARS OF CHANGE, SIGNS OF VITALITY: 1982–1984

The Register of Copyright in January, 1983, sent Congress the required five-year review of experience under the Copyright Act of 1976 (1978–83). The report called for a better balance between rights of creators and users. Nancy H. Marshall, of the University of Wisconsin at Madison, in the *Yearbook* article "Copyright," recorded the criticisms of the library world to the report, and librarians once again found themselves in debate with the publishing community. The Act had in fact achieved an appropriate balance, they held, and pointed to the statistical evidence of the 1982 King report for the U.S. Copyright Office.

The first serious discussion began in the United States in 1983 about the "public lending right"—payment of royalties to authors whose books are lent by libraries. The 1984 edition covered that issue in a Special Report by John Y. Cole on PLR, based on a forum sponsored by the Center for the Book of the Library of Congress. The 1985 article "Publishing, Book" summarized the first year's experience with PLR payments in Great Britain. Payments were modest for most authors registered in the plan; money came not from the libraries but from a government fund set up expressly for the purpose of paying PLR royalties.

Many *Yearbook* articles give reactions to *A Nation at Risk: The Imperative for Educational Reform* (1983), issued by the National Commission on Excellence in Education. This *Yearbook* carries a Special Report on "Books in Our Future" (December 1984), a summary of the 56-page report prepared by the Librarian of Congress on "the changing role of the book in the future" with special attention to the implications of technology.

The Higher Education Act of 1965, Title II-A (College Library Resource Programs), ended in 1983. Basic grants had been modest, but a large number of schools had benefited from it over the years (Johnson). Despite Reagan administration disapproval, other grants were continued by Congress. Under Title II-C, the pattern established in the past few years was continued, with support (average grant $122,000) to 49 institutions in 1983 for bibliographic control, preservation, and collection development, according to Johnson's report.

Although the economy was improving, financial restrictions continued to plague academic libraries, and many created their own fundraising campaigns. NEH matching grants, like the large one to the University of Kansas, Lawrence ($1,000,000, 1983), provided an incentive.

An Association of Research Libraries survey (1982) indicated that twice as many libraries charged for interlibrary loan as in a previous survey (1976).

For the bigger picture of the research library holdings, the National Collection Inventory Project, supported by the Research Library Group (RLG) and the Lilly Endowment, was under way in the 1980s. It provides an overview by subject and also surveys RLG members' intentions.

The bibliographic utilities held their central role. OCLC moved to its $25,000,000 facility in Dublin, Ohio, in 1981, and it reached 10,000,000 records in its database (1983). In 1979 it had introduced its interlibrary loan mode, and its four-millionth request was handled only four years later (June 1983), Johnson reported. In 1984 OCLC lost its appeal on an unfavorable court ruling that makes it liable for real estate taxes. There was concern about OCLC's decision to copyright its database; RLG announced that it would not do so. Regional bibliographic utilities—WLN (West); AMIGOS (South); WICHE (Southwest), and MIDNET (Midwest)—suffered setbacks in the early 1980s but still were serving their constituencies in the mid-1980s. One response to higher communications costs and utility charges was the independent approach of Penn State (1983), which developed its own online system.

The past 10 *Yearbooks* reveal that security has remained a problem for all types of libraries, including the elite of academia. The library world applauded when a well-traveled book thief, James Shinn, was arrested at Oberlin in 1981 and again in the same year in Allentown, Pennsylvania, and was later convicted. Librarians gathered in Oberlin in September, 1983, to assay with Lawrence W. Towner of the Newberry Library ways of thwarting those who would steal or mutilate library materials.

Shearer reported that public library use patterns in the early 1980s were very different from those of the early 1970s. Circulation was up—it reached one billion loans a year, an average of more than four items for each U.S. citizen—and continues to rise. Cost of library materials was also rising, and proportionately more of the items circulated were the more expensive adult materials rather than less costly juvenile items. Materials expenditures sunk to only 14 percent of the operating budget in 1981 from 19 percent in 1970.

For the first time after a period of somnolence, the federal government supported substantial new public library construction and renovation in 1983, Shearer wrote, and state aid was increased or reinstated in 21 states. Perhaps the Governor's Conferences and the White House Conference follow-up were showing results. Many new Friends' groups continued to be formed—Friends of Libraries USA had been organized in 1979 at the ALA Dallas Conference with Sandy Dolnick of Milwaukee as President. The White House Conference on Library and Information Services Task Force (WHCLIST) "continues to monitor . . . developments in the state governments," Shearer reported.

Shearer tempered his optimistic reports by reminding readers that library salaries continued in the 1980s to be far below those of other professions requiring a graduate degree.

New York State in 1984, according to reports in the 1985 edition, proved a generous supporter of libraries. At the midpoint of his term as president, 1984–85, ALA President E. J. Josey could point to the leadership shown by his own Empire State in 1984.

As did ACRL and AASL members, members of the Public Library Association in Baltimore, in March, 1983, held their own national conference, the first in ALA history for public librarians only. More than 2,600 attended. Shearer saw growth of "a refreshing collegiality and a more judicious use of information sharing and information technology" as public libraries "continued to improve the quality of American life."

For beleaguered children's librarians, Elizabeth Huntoon of the Chicago Public Library saw "signs . . . that the environment in which children's librarians practice was improving and that children's librarians themselves . . . are contributing to a more optimistic climate." Even before *A Nation at Risk* was published, she noted, the "back to basics" movement was helping to increase both the circulation of children's books and participation in library programs. Increases in summer reading programs were reported, and grants were coming from foundations and corporations in support of storyhours, film series, author talks, and other basic services. Among popular services was microcomputer use by children. Huntoon concluded, "The climate is the best in a decade for librarians to improve and extend their services to children (1984)."

Among young adult librarians in the early 1980s, major concerns included, "Microcomputers, VCRs, youth participation, and paperback originals," according to Barbara Newmark-Kruger, consultant of the Westchester County Library System, New York. "Financial difficulties and lack of administrative support" were still seen as major problems"; for example, the LA Public Library dissolved its YA department (1983 *Yearbook* edition). "On the positive side," she cited an increase in "youth participation in the decision-making process of public libraries."

PUBLISHING

By the early 1980s U.S. book sales topped $8,000,000,000 a year and studies on reading habits provided some cause for optimism. The Book Industry Study Group (BISG), for example, reported that the proportion of heavy readers increased in 1983—35 percent compared with 18 percent in a 1978 survey. Another finding was that women had surpassed men as readers, and specialized reading was increasing.

One statistic in the report on book publishing in the 1985 edition stands out: "For trade paperbacks, the average price was $11.79 (1983), a *decrease* from $12.32 in 1982." Bowker tallies in September, 1984, also showed that the average price of a hardcover book was $31.19 in 1983 compared with $30.14 in 1982. The modest increase may be a sign of future price stability if general inflation continues to subside. The strong dollar contributed to an increase of 16.1 percent in imports in 1983, according to the 1985 *Yearbook*, but book exports were down 5.3 percent in 1983 compared with the previous year.

For serials and libraries, it continued to be clear that "No one has a real solution to the problem of smaller budgets, higher periodical prices, and more titles" (Katz, 1983). "Rapid advancements in union lists and cooperation via OCLC and RLIN, to name only two, have been of great value but have hardly solved the budgetary difficulties."

Matters appear somewhat better for serial publishers, according to Katz, but tracking "the performance of periodical publishing over the next 10 years is likely to be as hazardous as predicting the fate of library periodical budgets. The only certainty seems to be that the intrinsic value of the print media will endure."

What the ALA Yearbook of Library and Information Services has done for the past 10 years is to compile a comprehensive and unique source of information on every facet of librarianship, charting the trends, illuminating the issues, and reporting on the individuals who shaped the library world. It has been and will continue to be unparalleled resource because of the expertise, knowledge, and intelligence of those hundreds of writers who contribute to these pages annually.

Awards Biographies Obituaries Notables

Awards

ALA AWARDS

Through its national awards program, the American Library Association seeks to honor those who have rendered distinguished service to libraries and librarianship. Such recognition is made for individual achievement of a high order in some area of librarianship, for effective participation in library affairs, and for writings and illustrations that enrich collections. In addition, recognition and assistance are given to individuals and groups selected to conduct special studies, and scholarships are awarded to promising candidates seeking to enter the profession or for advanced study. The juries and committees making the selections are charged with the responsibility of maintaining the high standards established by their predecessors in selecting individuals who have furthered to a notable degree the purposes for which libraries were created.

The following are ALA awards and recipients for the period January 1984 through December 1984. [For 1983 recipients, see the ninth edition of this *Yearbook* (1984). For a list of all recipients from the first year offered, see the first edition (1976), pages 456–65.] The following were not awarded in 1984: American Institute of Architects/ALA Library Administration and Management Division Buildings Award Program (biennial); Association of Specialized and Cooperative Library Agencies Exceptional Achievement Award; Samuel Lazarow Fellowship; Eunice Rockwell Oberly Memorial Award (biennial); Laura Ingalls Wilder Medal (triennial).

AWARDS AND CITATIONS

Academic/Research Librarian of the Year

A $2,000 award, established in 1979, recognizing individuals who have made outstanding national or international contributions to academic or research librarianship and library development. Donated by Baker & Taylor Company. Administered by the Association of College and Research Libraries.

RECIPIENT: Richard D. Johnson, State University College Library, Oneonta, New York.

American Association of School Librarians, President's Award

An annual award of $2,000, established in 1977, presented to the individual who has demonstrated excellence and provided an outstanding national or international contribution to school librarianship and school library development. Donated by Baker & Taylor Company. Administered by the American Association of School Librarians.

RECIPIENT: Rheta Clark, New England Educational Media Association, South Glastonbury, Connecticut.

American Association of School Librarians/SIRS Intellectual Freedom Award

An annual award, established in 1976, consisting of $1,000 and an engraved plaque presented to a school library media specialist at any level who has upheld the principles of intellectual freedom as set forth in "Policies and Procedures for Selection of Instructional Materials." Donated by Social Issues Resources Services, Inc. Administered by AASL.

RECIPIENT: Vicki Hardesty, Findlay High School Library, Findlay, Ohio.

American Library Trustee Association Literacy Award

An annual award, established in 1980, given to that individual who has done an outstanding job in making contributions toward the extirpation of illiteracy. Donated and administered by ALTA.

RECIPIENT: Lydia A. Duggins, Bridgeport, (Connecticut) Public Library.

American Library Trustee Association Major Benefactors Honor Award

An annual award, a citation, and a plaque, established in 1976, to recognize benefactors to public libraries. It was previously called the Honors Award. The recipient may be a person, institution, agency, or organization. The significance of the gift will be measured from the point of view of the recipient library. Donated and administered by ALTA.

RECIPIENTS: Bertha Bacot, Pascagoula, Mississippi.
Mr. and Mrs. J. Harwood Cochrane, Rockville, Virginia.
John C. Henley III, Birmingham, Alabama.
John Mosby, St. Louis, Missouri (posthumous).

Armed Forces Librarians Achievement Citation

An annual citation, established in 1964, presented to members of the Armed Forces Librarians Section, Public Library Association, who have made significant contributions to the development of armed forces library service and to organizations encouraging an interest in libraries and reading. Donated and administered by the Armed Forces Librarians Section, Public Library Association.

RECIPIENT: Marjorie Rambo, Langley Air Force Base, Virginia.

Association of Specialized and Cooperative Library Agencies Exceptional Service Award

A citation, established in 1957, presented to a member of ASCLA in recognition of exceptional service to ASCLA or any of its component areas of service—namely, patients; the homebound; medical, nursing, and other professional staff in hospitals; and inmates—and professional leadership, effective interpretation of program, pioneering activity, and significant research or experimental projects. Donated and administered by ASCLA.

RECIPIENT: Eunice Lovejoy, Ohio State Library, Columbus.

(Mildred L.) Batchelder Award

A citation, established in 1966, presented annually to an American publisher for a children's book considered to be the most outstanding of those books originally published in a foreign language in a foreign country, and subsequently published in the United States during the calendar year preceding the appointment of the Mildred L. Batchelder Award Jury. The award will be made annually unless the committee is of the opinion that no book of that particular year is worthy of the award. "Children's book" is to be interpreted as any trade book (including picture books) for children between, and including, the prenursery-age level and the eighth grade. Donated and administered by the Association for Library Service to Children.

RECIPIENT: Viking, for *Ronia, The Robber's Daughter* by Astrid Lindgren.

Beta Phi Mu Award

An annual award, established in 1972, of $500 and a citation of achievement. Presented to a library school faculty member or to an individual for distinguished service to education for librarianship. Donated by Beta Phi Mu, the library science honorary association. Administered by the ALA Awards Committee.

RECIPIENT: Jane Anne Hannigan, School of Library Service, Columbia University, New York City.

(Randolph) Caldecott Medal

A medal, established in 1937, presented annually to the illustrator of the most distinguished American picture book for children published in the United States in the preceding year. The recipient must be a citizen or resident of the United States. Donated by Daniel Melcher. Administered by the Association for Library Service to Children.

RECIPIENTS: Alice and Martin Provensen, authors and illustrators, for *Glorious Flight across the Channel with Louis Bleriot* (Viking).

(Francis Joseph) Campbell Citation

A citation and a medal, established in 1965, presented annually to a person who has made an outstanding contribution to the advancement of library service for the blind. This contribution may take the form of an imaginative and constructive program in a particular library; a recognized contribution to the national library program for blind persons; creative participation in library associations or blind organizations that advance reading for the blind; a significant publication or writing in the field; imaginative contribution to library administration, reference, circulation, selections, acquisitions, or technical services; or any activity of recognized importance. Donated and administered by the Section on Library Service to the Blind and Physically Handicapped of Association of Specialized and Cooperative Library Agencies.

RECIPIENT: Maxine Dorf, National Library Service for the Blind and Handicapped, Library of Congress (retired).

(James Bennett) Childs Award

An engraved plaque established in 1976, presented to a librarian or other individual for distinguished contributions to documents librarianship. Donated and administered by the Government Documents Round Table.

RECIPIENT: The (James Bennett) Childs Award was not given in 1984.

(John Cotton) Dana
Public Relations Awards

An annual citation, established in 1942, made to libraries or library organizations of all types submitting materials representing the year's public relations program or a special project terminated during the year. Donated by the H.W. Wilson Company, the awards program is sponsored jointly with the Public Relations Section of the Library Administration and Management Association.

RECIPIENTS: Dauphin Public Library, Harrisburg, Pennsylvania.
  Houston (Texas) Public Library.
  Lutheran Church Library Association, Minneapolis, Minnesota.
  Nellis (Nevada) Air Force Base Library.
  Plaza Junior High School Library, Virginia Beach, Virginia.
  University of Texas Health Science Center, San Antonio, Texas.
15 additional awards were presented in 1984.

Dartmouth Medal

A medal, established in 1974, presented to honor achievement in creating reference works outstanding in quality and significance. Creating reference works may include, but need not be limited to, writing, compiling, editing, or publishing books or providing information in other forms for reference use, e.g., a data bank. Bestowal of the award shall normally relate to works that have been published or otherwise made available for the first time during the calendar year preceding the presentation of the award. Donated by Dartmouth College, Hanover, New Hampshire. Administered by the Reference and Adult Services Division.

RECIPIENT: *The Times Atlas of the Oceans* (Van Nostrand Reinhold).

(Melvil) Dewey Medal

An engraved medal and a citation, established in 1952, presented annually to an individual or a group for recent creative professional achievement of a high order, particularly in those fields in which Melvil Dewey was actively interested—library management, library training, cataloging and classification, and the tools and techniques of librarianship. Donated by the Forest Press, Inc. Administered by the ALA Awards Committee.

RECIPIENT: Warren J. Haas, Council of Library Resources, Washington, D.C.

Documents to the People Award

A citation of achievement and a cash stipend of $1,000, established in 1976, to be used to promote professional advancement in the field of librarianship. Presented annually to the individual and/or library, organization, or other appropriate noncommercial group that has most effectively encouraged the use of federal documents in support of library services. Donated by the Congressional Information Service, Inc. Administered by the Government Documents Round Table.

RECIPIENT: Jaia Barrett, Perkins Library, Duke University, Durham, North Carolina.

(Miriam) Dudley Award for Bibliographic Instruction

An annual award of $1,000 presented to a librarian who has made an especially significant contribution to the advancement of bibliographic instruction. Nominees should have achieved distinction in such areas as planning and implementation of a bibliographic instruction program that has served as a model for other programs; development of courses on bibliographic instruction in ALA accredited library schools or development of continuing education courses on bibliographic instruction that have served as models for other courses; research and publication that has had a demonstrable impact on the concepts and methods of teaching bibliography; and active participation in organizations devoted to the promotion and enhancement of bibliographic instruction. Nominees need not necessarily meet all the criteria. Funded by Mountainside Press. Administered by the Association of College and Research Libraries.

RECIPIENT: Thomas C. Kirk, Hutchins Library, Berea College, Kentucky.

Equality Award

A certificate and a cash award of $500 given to an individual or group for an outstanding contribution towards promoting equality between women and men in the library profession. The contribution may be either a sustained one or a single outstanding accomplishment. The award may be given for an activist or scholarly contribution in such areas as pay equity, affirmative action, legislative work, and nonsexist education. Donated by the Scarecrow Press, Inc. Administered by the ALA Awards Committee.

RECIPIENT: Margaret Myers, ALA Office for Library Personnel Resources.

Facts on File Award

A $1,000 award, established in 1979, to be presented annually to a librarian who makes current affairs more meaningful to adults. Donated by Facts On File, Inc. Administered by RASD.

RECIPIENT: Catherine Monnin, Maple Heights Regional Library, Cuyahoga County (Ohio) Public Library.

Gale Research Company Financial Development Award

An annual award of $2500 and a certificate, established in 1980, presented to a library organization that exhibited meritorious achievement in carrying out a library financial development project to secure new funding resources for a public or academic library entity. Donated by the Gale Research Company. Administered by the ALA Awards Committee.

RECIPIENT: Harvin-Clarendon County Public Library, Manning, South Carolina.

Grolier Foundation Award

$1,000 and a citation of achievement, established in 1953, presented annually to a librarian in a community or in a school who has made an unusual contribution to the stimulation and guidance of reading by children and young people. The award is usually given for outstanding work with children and young people through high school age, for continuing service, or in recognition of one particular contribution of lasting value. Donated by the Grolier Foundation. Administered by the ALA Awards Committee.

RECIPIENT: Carolyn Sue Peterson, Orlando (Florida) Public Library.

(G. K.) Hall Large Print Community Service Award

A plaque and $1,000, established in 1983. Given to the library or libraries demonstrating the most creative methods and comprehensive efforts in increasing the awareness, availability, and use of Large Print books. Donated by G. K. Hall Company. Administered by ASCLA.

RECIPIENT: Jackson-George Regional Library, Pascagoula, Mississippi.

(John Phillip) Immroth Memorial Award for Intellectual Freedom

An annual award, established in 1976, of $500 and a plaque presented to a fighter of intellectual freedom who has made a notable contribution to intellectual freedom and demonstrated remarkable personal courage. Donated and administered by the Intellectual Freedom Round Table.

RECIPIENT: Gene D. Lanier, East Carolina University, Greenville, South Carolina.

Intellectual Freedom Round Table State Program Award

An annual award consisting of $500 and a citation presented to the state intellectual freedom committee that has implemented the most successful and creative state IFC project during the calendar year. Donated and administered by the Intellectual Freedom Round Table.

RECIPIENT: Intellectual Freedom Committee, South Carolina Library Association.

(Coretta Scott) King Awards

Established in 1969, $250, a plaque, and a set of *Encylopaedia Britannica*, presented annually at the ALA Annual Conference for a book written in the spirit of the life and work of Martin Luther King, Jr. Donated by Coca-Cola, U.S.A., Encyclopaedia Britannica, Gregory's Machine and Tool Service, the John H. Johnson Publishing Company, and World Book-Childcraft International, Inc.

RECIPIENTS: *Everett Anderson's Goodbye* by Lucille Clifton (Holt).

My Mama Needs Me by Mildred P. Walter, Pat Cummings, illustrator (Lothrop).

Kohlstedt Exhibit Awards

A citation and plaque, established in 1972, given each year at the Exhibits Round Table Banquet, recognizing the best single and multiple booth displays at the Annual Conference. The criteria on which judgment is made are as follows: Clear identification of exhibitor and product or service offered, availability of staff, and accessibility of product or service; effective use of design elements such as colors, shapes, and textures, and effectiveness of graphics in communicating about product or service; neat, uncluttered appearance and arrangement of booth(s) for convenient flow of traffic. All booths in each year's Annual Conference exhibits are eligible for the awards even though their companies or organizations are not members of ERT.

RECIPIENTS: Single booth: W. H. Freeman, New York City.

Multiple Linear booths: Oryx Press, Phoenix, Arizona.

Futura: H. W. Wilson, New York City.

Library and Information Technology Association/Gaylord Award

A citation, and $1,000, established in 1979, presented annually to an individual or small group, recognizing distinguished leadership, notable technology development or application, superior accomplishment in research or education, or original contribution to the literature of the field. Administered by LITA.

RECIPIENT: Roger K. Summit, DIALOG Information Services, Inc., Palo Alto, California.

Library Research Round Table Research Award

Established in 1975 to encourage excellence in library research. No more than two awards of $500 each are presented annually to the persons submitting the best completed research reports. Research papers completed in pursuit of an academic degree are not eligible. Donated and administered by LRRT.

RECIPIENTS: George D'Elia, Library School, University of Minnesota, Minneapolis, and Sandra Walsh, Ramsey County Public Library, St. Paul, Minnesota, for "Patron Use and Evaluation of Library Services: A Comparison across Five Public Libraries."

(Joseph W.) Lippincott Award

An award of $1,000, an engraved medal, and a citation of achievement, established in 1937. Presented annually to a librarian for distinguished service in the profession of librarianship, such service to include outstanding participation in the activities of professional library associations, notable published professional writing, or other significant activity on behalf of the profession and its aims. Donated by Joseph W. Lippincott. Administered by the ALA Awards Committee.

RECIPIENT: Nettie Bancroft Taylor, Library Development Division, Maryland Department of Education, Baltimore.

MAGERT Honor Award

A citation, established in 1983, given in recognition of outstanding achievement and a major contribution to map librarianship and to The Map and Geography Round Table. Donated and administered by MAGERT.

RECIPIENT: Jeremiah B. Post, Free Library of Philadelphia.

(Margaret) Mann Citation

An annual citation, established in 1950, made to a cataloger or classifier, not necessarily an American, for outstanding professional achievement in the areas of cataloging or classification either through publication of significant professional literature, participation in professional cataloging associations, introduction of new techniques of recognized importance, or outstanding work in teaching within the past five years. Donated and administered by the Cataloging and Classification Section, Resources and Technical Services Division.

RECIPIENT: Dorothy Anderson, Garrick Club, London, England.

(Allie Beth) Martin Award

A $2,000 award, established in 1979, presented annually to a public librarian who has demonstrated extraordinary range and depth of knowledge about books or other library materials or who has shown distinguished ability to share that knowledge. Donated by Baker & Taylor Company. Administered by Public Library Association.

RECIPIENT: Cecil B. Beach, Broward County Division of Libraries, Fort Lauderdale, Florida.

(Isadore Gilbert) Mudge Citation

A citation, established in 1958, to be given at the Annual Conference of ALA to a person who has made a distinguished contribution to reference librarianship. This contribution may take the form of an imaginative and constructive program in a particular library, the writing of a significant book or articles in the reference field, creative and inspirational teaching of reference service, or other noteworthy activities that stimulate reference librarians to more distinguished performance. Donated and administered by the Reference and Adult Services Division.

RECIPIENT: Sara D. Knapp, Information Retrieval and Computer Search Service, State University of New York at Albany.

(John) Newbery Medal

A medal, established in 1921, presented annually to the author of the most distinguished contribution to American literature for children published in the United States in the preceding year. The recipient must be a citizen or resident of the United States. Donated by Daniel Melcher. Administered by the Association for Library Service to Children.

RECIPIENT: Beverly Cleary for *Dear Mr. Henshaw* (Morrow).

(Esther J.) Piercy Award

An annual citation, established in 1968, presented in recognition of a contribution to librarianship in the field of technical services by younger members of the profession. The recipient is a librarian with not more than ten years of professional experience who has shown outstanding promise for continuing contributions and leadership in any of the fields comprising technical services by means of (a) leadership in professional associations at the local, state, regional, or national level; (b) contributions to the development, application, or utilization of new or improved methods, techniques, and routines; (c) a significant contribution to professional literature; (d) studies or research in technical services. Given each year in which the jury believes that there is a qualified recipient. Donated and administered by the Resources and Technical Services Division.

RECIPIENT: Lizbeth J. Bishoff, ELA Area Public Library District, Lake Zurich, New York.

(Distinguished Library Service Award for) School Administrators

An annual citation, established in 1969, presented to a person, directly responsible for the administration of a school or group of schools, who has made a unique and sustained contribution toward furthering the role of the library and its development in elementary and/or secondary education. Two meritorious school administrators may be cited each year. Sponsored and administered by the American Association of School Librarians.

RECIPIENT: Marilyn Scott, Anchorage (Alaska) School District.

School Library Media Program of the Year Award

A $5,000 cash award, established in 1975, presented annually to the school system that displays outstanding achievement in providing exemplary library media programs in its elementary schools. Up to five school systems can receive national finalist awards and be awarded citations of achievement. Donated by Encyclopaedia Britannica. Administered by the American Association of School Librarians.

RECIPIENTS: Richmond (Virginia) Public School System.

Riverside-Brookfield Township High School, Riverside, Illinois.

(John) Sessions Memorial Award

A plaque, established in 1979, to be presented to a public library or library system in recognition of significant efforts to work with the labor community. Such efforts may include outreach projects to local labor unions; the establishment of, or significant expansion of, special labor collections; initiation of programs of special interest to the labor community; or other library activities that serve the labor community. Donated by the AFL/CIO and administered by the Reference and Adult Services Division.

RECIPIENT: Jackson–George Regional Library System, Pascagoula, Mississippi.

Trustee Citations

A citation, established in 1941, presented to each of two outstanding trustees in actual service during part of the calendar year preceding the presentation, for distinguished service to library development on the local, state, or national level. Equal consideration is to be given to trustees of small and large public libraries. Donated by ALA. Administered by the American Library Trustee Association.

RECIPIENTS: Elmer M. Jackson, Jr., Public Library of Annapolis and Arundel County, Maryland.

Helen Muir, Miami-Dade Public Library System, Florida.

Laura Ingalls Wilder Medal

A medal, established in 1954, presented to an author or illustrator whose books, published in the United States, have, over a period of years, made a substantial and lasting contribution to children's literature. Donated and administered by the Association for Library Service to Children.

RECIPIENT: Maurice Sendak.

(H. W.) Wilson Library Periodical Award

An annual award, established in 1960, consisting of $500 and a certificate presented to a periodical published by a local, state, or regional library, library group, or library association in the United States or Canada that has made an outstanding contribution to librarianship. (This excludes publications of ALA, CLA, and their divisions.) The award is presented only in those years when a periodical merits such recognition. Donated by the H. W. Wilson Company. Administered by the ALA Awards Committee.

RECIPIENT: *Colorado Libraries*, Johannah Sherrer, Editor.

(Justin) Winsor Prize Essay

An essay award (formerly the Library History Round Table Essay Award) of $500 established in 1977 by the Library History Round Table of the American Library Association to encourage excellence in research in library history. The winner will be offered the privilege of having his or her paper published in a future issue of *The Journal of Library History*. Donated and administered by LHRT.

RECIPIENT: Larry Yeatman, Towson (Maryland) High School for "Literary Culture and the Role of Libraries in Democratic America: Baltimore, 1815–1840."

SCHOLARSHIPS

Association of College and Research Libraries Doctoral Dissertation Fellowship

An annual award of $1,000, established in 1982, to a doctoral student working in the area of academic librarianship. Donated by Institute for Scientific Information, Administered by ACRL.

RECIPIENT: Donald B. Gould, University of Southern California Library, Los Angeles.

(David H.) Clift Scholarship

Approved by the ALA Council, January 1969, a scholarship in the amount of $3,000 given annually to a worthy student to begin library education at the graduate level without regard to race, creed, color, national origin, or sex. The recipient must be a U.S. or Canadian citizen and must enter a formal program of graduate study leading to a master's degree at an ALA-accredited school. Funded by an annual contribution from the Xerox Publishing Group and individual contributions, as many scholarships as possible are awarded, depending upon the total amount of contributed funds. The award may be withheld in any year. Administered by the ALA Awards Committee and the Standing Committee on Library Education.

RECIPIENT: Maggie Fernandez, Cambridge, Massachusetts.

(Frederich Winthrop) Faxon Scholarship

An annual scholarship in two interrelated parts, a cash award of $3,000 to be applied to the expenses of a master's level, ALA-accredited program in library or information science, and an expense-paid 10 week internship at F. W. Faxon Company. Established in 1981. Donated by F. W. Faxon Company, administered by the ALA Awards Committee.

RECIPIENT: Charis Bacheller, Newberg, Oregon.

(Louise) Giles Minority Scholarship

Established in 1972 by the ALA Council, and renamed in memory of Louise Giles in 1977, the Minority Scholarship is a $3,000 cash award made to a worthy student who is a U.S. or Canadian citizen and is also a member of a principal minority group (American Indian or Alaskan native, Asian or Pacific Islander, Black, or Hispanic). The recipient must enter a formal program of graduate study leading to a master's degree at an ALA-accredited library school. Funded by an annual contribution from the Xerox Publishing Group and individual contributions, as many scholarships as possible are awarded, depending upon the total amount of contributed funds. Administered by the ALA Awards Committee and the Office for Library Personnel Resources Advisory Committee.

RECIPIENT: F. Nell Thomas, Evanston, Illinois.

(Frederic G.) Melcher Scholarship

An annual $4,000 scholarship established in 1956 to encourage young people to enter the field of library service to children. Donated and administered by the Association for Library Service to Children.

RECIPIENTS: Barbara Gail Freedman, Fayetteville, North Carolina.

Constance N. Kehs, Doylestown, Pennsylvania.

Resources and Technical Services Division Resources Section/ Blackwell North America Scholarship Award

An annual award, established in 1975, consisting of a citation and a $1,000 scholarship grant. The citation is presented to the author or authors of an outstanding monograph, published article, or original paper on acquisitions pertaining to college or university libraries. The scholarship grant is given to the library school of the winner's choice. Donated by Blackwell North America and administered by the RTSD Resources Section.

RECIPIENTS: Nancy E. Gwinn, Research Libraries Group, Stanford, California, and Paul H. Mosher, Stanford (California) University Libraries. Scholarship presented to the School of Library Science, University of Michigan, Ann Arbor.

GRANTS

Carnegie Fund Grants

Grants from the income of an endowment established in 1902 by Andrew Carnegie; they are made to units of the American Library Association to support model, innovative projects and continuing programs in all media. Any membership or administrative unit of ALA may submit a proposal. Administered by the ALA Publishing Committee.

RECIPIENTS: Association for Library Service to Children.

Booklist—Adult, Children's, Nonprint and Young Adult sections.

Reference and Adult Services Division.

Status of Women in Libraries (Committee).

Young Adult Services Division.

Grassroots Grants

A $250 grant to allow a library school, library credential or LTA student to attend his/her state library conference. Recipients must be full time students, members of the state library association, and of its JMRT, if there is one. Established in 1978. Donated by Baker and Taylor. Administered by JMRT in cooperation with state chapters.

RECIPIENTS: 32 students in as many states qualified in 1984.

Grolier National Library Week Grant

An annual $1,000 cash award, established in 1953, presented to the state library association that submits the best plan for a public relations program to increase communications and public awareness of library service. Donated by Grolier Educational Corporation. Administered by the National Library Week Committee.

RECIPIENT: North Carolina Association of School Libraries.

(Bailey K.) Howard—ALA Goal Award

An annual grant of $5,000 established in 1960,

made by World Book-Childcraft International, Inc., to encourage and advance the development of public, academic and/or school library service and librarianship through recognition and support of programs that implement the goals and objectives of ALA.

RECIPIENT: New York Library Association for a membership software base.

(J. Morris) Jones—ALA Goal Award

An annual grant of $5,000, established in 1960, made by World Book-Childcraft International, Inc., to encourage and advance the development of public, academic and/or school library service and librarianship through recognition and support of programs that implement the goals and objectives of ALA.

RECIPIENT: Minnesota Library Association for the project "Building Ad Hoc Coalitions for the Public Good."

(Shirley) Olofson Memorial Award

An annual cash award, established in 1972, made to individuals to attend their second Annual Conference of ALA. The recipients must be members of ALA and be potential or current members of the Junior Members Round Table. Donated and administered by JMRT.

RECIPIENTS: Diane Bronson, Florida State Library, Tallahassee.

Kathleen Moeller-Pfeiffer, Orange County Public Library, Hillsboro, North Carolina.

Heather Smith, student, Graduate School of Library and Information Science, University of California at Los Angeles.

Professional Development Grants

Annual cash awards, established in 1975, are presented to librarians to attend the Annual Conference of ALA. The recipients must be members of ALA and the Junior Members Round Table. Donated by the 3M Company. Administered by JMRT.

RECIPIENTS: Diane Bisom, ORION User Services Library, University of California at Los Angeles.

Dominique Coulombe, Brown University Library, Providence, Rhode Island.

James Mouw, University of Illinois at Chicago.

(Herbert W.) Putnam Honor Award

An award of $500 presented as a grant-in-aid to an American librarian of outstanding ability for travel, writing, or any other use that might improve his or her service to the library profession or to society. The $500 grant is made possible by the income received from the Herbert W. Putnam Honor Fund. Administered by the ALA Awards Committee.

RECIPIENT: Virginia P. Boucher, University Libraries, University of Colorado, Boulder.

Putnam Publishing Group Awards

Four annual $400 cash awards, established in 1983, presented to two school librarians and two public library children's librarians to enable them to attend ALA's Annual Conference. The recipients must also be members of the Association for Library Service to Children, have one to five years of library experience, and never have attended an ALA Annual Conference. Donated by the Putnam Publishing Group. Administered by ALSC.

RECIPIENTS: Jane Belsches, Carrboro (North Carolina) Elementary School.

Ione Cowen, Akron-Summit County Public Library, Akron, Ohio.

Jan Irving, Stewart Public Library, Grinnell, Iowa.

Dean Lyons, Carabec School District, North Anson, Maine.

Whitney Fund Grants

Grants made from the James Lyman Whitney Fund to individuals for bibliographical aids for research. The aids must be aimed at a scholarly audience but have a general applicability. The grants may cover any costs appropriate to the preparation of a useful product and are ordinarily scholarships. As many as possible will be awarded, depending upon the total amount of contributed funds. The award may be withheld in any year when there are no worthy recipients. Administered by the ALA Awards Committee and the Standing Committee on Library Education.

RECIPIENTS: Fay Belcher, Morehead (Kentucky) State University Libraries. Salvador Guereña, University of California at Santa Barbara. Mike Jankowski, Alternative Information Network, Austin, Texas.

(H. W.) Wilson Library Staff Development Grant

A cash grant of $2,500, established in 1980, awarded to a library organization to assist in a current or proposed program designed to further the goals and objectives of the library organization. The criteria for selection of a grant winner includes: clearly defined documentation of need in relation to staff development, a well-defined program to meet the organization's needs, and the commitment and demonstrated ability to implement the program. Donated by the H. W. Wilson Company. Administered by the ALA Awards Committee.

RECIPIENT: Prince Georges County Memorial Library, Hyattsville, Maryland.

YASD/Baker & Taylor Conference Grants

Two annual grants of $500 each awarded to young adult librarians who work directly with young adults in either a public library or a school library, to enable them to attend ALA's Annual Conference. Candidates must be members of YASD, have 1–10 years of library experience, and never have attended an ALA Annual Conference. Donor: Baker & Taylor. Administered by YASD.

RECIPIENT: Michelle Pugh, Cuyahoga County Public Library, Cleveland, Ohio.

YASD/*Voice of Youth Advocates (VOYA)* Research Grant

An annual grant of $500 established in 1983 to provide seed money for small-scale projects to encourage significant research that will have an influence on library service to young adults. Applicants must be a member of YASD, although the research project may be undertaken by an individual, an institution, or a group. Grants will not be given for research leading to a degree. Donor: *Voice of Youth Advocates (VOYA)*. Administered by YASD.

RECIPIENT: The YASD/*Voice of Youth Advocates* Research Grant was not given in 1984.

Other Awards

The following are selected awards, scholarships, and grants given by organizations and agencies other than ALA and its units in 1982 or for years indicated.

American Book Awards

$10,000 awards, established in 1979, to the titles voted best among the year's publications by the member constituency of The American Book Awards (TABA). Sponsored by the Association of American Publishers. In 1984 the categories were reduced to three.

RECIPIENTS: Work of first fiction: *Stones for Ibarra* by Harriet Doerr (Viking).

Overall fiction: *Victory over Japan* by Ellen Gilchrist (Little, Brown).

Nonfiction: *Andrew Jackson and the Course of American Democracy, 1833–1845, Volume III*, by Robert V. Remini (Harper & Row).

Besterman Medal

Given annually (announced in June for previous year) by the (British) Library Association since 1970 for an outstanding bibliography or guide to literature published in the United Kingdom during the preceding year.

RECIPIENT: Jointly awarded to *London Illustrated 1604–1851—A Survey and Index to Topographical Books and Their Plates* by Bernard Adams (published by Library Association) and *Ted Hughes: A Bibliography 1946–1980* (published by Mansell).

Book of the Year for Children Medal Award

Given annually since 1947 by the Canadian Association of Children's Librarians for the best Canadian children's book of the year. Formerly the English Language Book of the Year Award.

RECIPIENT: Jan Hudson for *Sweetgrass* (Tree Frog Press).

Boston Globe—Horn Book Awards

Three $200 prizes given annually since 1967, one for the best work of fiction for children, one for the best illustrated children's book, and one for the best nonfiction work for children.

RECIPIENTS: Fiction: *A Little Fear* by Patricia Wrightson (Atheneum).

Illustration: *Jonah and the Great Fish*, Retold and Illustrated by Warwick Hutton (Atheneum).

Nonfiction: *The Double Life of Pocahontas* by Jean Fritz (Putnam).

Carnegie Medal

Awarded annually since 1937 by the (British) Library Association for the most outstanding children's book published in Great Britain.

RECIPIENT: *Handles* by Jan Mark (published by Kestrel).

(Watson) Davis Awards

Established in 1976 by the American Society for Information Science in recognition of continuous service to the Society's membership. Donated and administered by the American Society for Information Science.

5

RECIPIENT: Robert S. Tannehill, Jr. Library Manager, Chemical Abstracts Services, Columbus, Ohio.

(Robert B.) Downs Award

$500 given annually since 1969 by the Graduate School of Library Science to honor Robert B. Downs for his defense of intellectual freedom and his 25 years of service to the University of Illinois. Recognizes contributions to furthering intellectual freedom in any type of library.

RECIPIENT: Marie Bruce, Huntington Memorial Library, Oneonto, New York.

(Kate) Greenaway Medal

Given annually since 1956 by the (British) Library Association for the best illustrated book for children published in Great Britain.

RECIPIENT: *Gorilla* by Anthony Brown (published by Julia MacRae).

(Amelia Frances) Howard-Gibbon Medal

Given annually by the Canadian Library Association for the best illustrated children's book of the year.

RECIPIENT: *Zoom at Sea* by Tim Wynne-Jones, illustrated by Ken Nutt.

(Association of) Jewish Libraries Award

Given annually for the most outstanding contribution in the field of Jewish literature for children.

RECIPIENT: Barbara Pomerantz for *Bubby, Me, and Memories* (Union of American Hebrew Congregations).

Rose Zar for *In the Mouth of the Wolf* (Jewish Publication Society).

McColvin Medal

An annual award given, since 1970, by the (British) Library Association to the author or compiler of an outstanding reference work published in Great Britain.

RECIPIENT: *Dictionary of the British Book Illustrators: The 20th Century* by Brigid Peppin and Lucy Micelthwaite (published by John Murray).

National Medal for Literature

Established in 1964 by the National Book Committee in memory of Harold K. Guinzburg, $15,000 and a bronze medal given annually to a living author in American literature. Administered in 1975 and 1976 by the American Academy and Institute of Arts and Letters and from 1977 by the Association of American Publishers.

RECIPIENT: Mary McCarthy.

Regina Medal

Given annually since 1959 by the Catholic Library Association to an author, publisher, editor, illustrator, or other person for dedication to children's literature, irrespective of religion or race.

RECIPIENT: Madeleine L'Engle.

Special Libraries Association (John Cotton) Dana Award

Established in 1979 (to replace the SLA Special Citation). Award is granted to an individual or a group of individuals in recognition of exceptional services by members of SLA to special libraries.

RECIPIENTS: Ellis Mount, School of Library Service, Columbia University, New York City.

David Rhydwen, *The Globe and Mail* Library, Toronto, Canada.

Special Libraries Association Hall of Fame

Established in 1959, an engraved medallion and a certificate given to recognize persons who over a period of years have made outstanding contributions to SLA.

RECIPIENTS: Mark Baer, Hewlett Packerd Corporation, Palo Alto, California.

William Budington, John Crerar Library, Chicago, Illinois.

Vivian Hewitt, Shotwell Library, Carnegie Endowment for International Peace.

Robert Krupp, New York Public Library.

Special Libraries Association H. W. Wilson Company Award

An embossed scroll and $500, established in 1979, for the best paper published in *Special Libraries* in the preceding year. Donated by H. W. Wilson Company. Administered by Special Libraries Association.

RECIPIENT: Laura N. Gasaway, Law Library, University of Oklahoma.

Wheatley Medal

Awarded annually (announced in June for previous year) since 1962 by the (British) Library Association for an outstanding index published in the United Kingdom during the preceding three years.

RECIPIENT: Index of *Laws of Trinidad and Tobago* by A. R. Hewitt (published by Government of Trinidad and Tobago).

Biographies

ARTERBERY, VIVIAN J.
Vivan J. Arterbery, Library Director, Rand Corporation, Santa Monica, California, was elected President of the Special Libraries Association for 1984-85.

Born June 21, 1937, in Houston, Texas, she received a B.A. degree from Howard University in 1958 and an M.L.S. from the University of Southern California in 1965. Arterbery joined the Rand Corporation as Library Director in 1979. From 1959 to 1960 she was with Space Technology Laboratories, Los Angeles, as Cataloger, Air Force Library. The group was transferred to the newly formed Aerospace Corporation, El Segundo, California, in 1960. She held various positions there beginning as Cataloger and Reference Librarian, 1960-62, and was Supervisor of User Services, 1967-79.

Active in professional organizations, Arterbery was President of the Southern California Chapter of the Special Libraries Association (SLA), 1973-74, on the Board of Directors, SLA, 1980-83, and on the Board of Councilors, California Library Association, 1973-75. From 1972 to 1973 she was President of the University of Southern California Library School Alumni Association and on the USC Library School Advisory Board, 1970-74 and 1980-83.

Arterbery was appointed to various state boards and committees, including the California State Personnel Board and Qualifications Appraisal Panel for the Librarians Examination, 1977. She was a consultant of the U.S. Office of Education to review library grant applications under Title II-B of the Higher Education Act, 1974-76.

Honors include the USC Outstanding Black Alumni Award, 1983; Community Service Award, Links, Inc., 1982; Santa Monica YWCA recognition award, Woman of the Year, 1981.

ASHEIM, LESTER
Lester Asheim, Professor Emeritus, University of North Carolina, Chapel Hill, was named an Honorary Member of ALA at the 1984 Annual Conference.

In 1979, Asheim was presented with a Festschrift, *As Much to Learn as to Teach: Essays in Honor of Lester Asheim*, edited by Joel Lee and Beth A. Hamilton (Linnet Books).

After his retirement in 1984, he continued to write and to lecture extensively.

The ALA citation with the Honorary Membership reads, in part, "In recognition of his contributions to American Librarianship in library education, intellectual freedom and international relations, the American Library Association hereby cites Lester Eugene Asheim . . . as a Distinguished Librarian . . . " For his biography and portrait, see *The ALA Yearbook* (1977).

BARBER, MARGARET (PEGGY) ELLEN
Margaret Ellen Barber, always known as Peggy, Director of the Public Information Office at ALA since 1974, was appointed Associate Executive Director for Communications in 1984. As head of the new Department of Communications she will oversee the planning and administration of conference arrangements, membership promotion, and public relations and information.

Barber was born in Pasadena, California, on August 26, 1943. She received her B.A. degree from the University of California, Riverside, in 1965, and her M.L.S. degree from Rutgers University, New Brunswick, New Jersey, in 1966. Her professional career began in Orange City, California in 1968, where she served as Special Projects Librarian in the Orange County Public Library. In 1968 she went to the San Francisco Public Library as a Reference Librarian in the Bay Area Reference Center, a federally funded project.

She joined the staff of ALA in 1969 as Director of the Office for Recruitment. Here her concern for interesting able minority people in librarianship, and enlisting community leaders in the search for likely candidates brought a new dimension to the Office. In 1974 she became Director of the Public Information Office, providing striking new materials for National Library Week and around the year, and establishing strong working relationships nationally with people with access to the media.

Barber's abilities have long been recognized. In 1965 she was elected to Phi Beta Kappa and in 1966 to Beta Phi Mu, the library honorary society. The PR Society of America honored her with its Silver Anvil Award in 1975. The Golden Trumpet was presented to her by the Publicity Club of Chicago in 1975 and in 1976.

CARROLL, BONNIE C.
Bonnie C. Carroll, Director of Program Development and International Activities, U.S. Department of Energy, Office of Scientific and Technical Information, Oak Ridge, Tennessee, was elected President of the American Society for Information Science for 1985.

With a B.A. degree from Cornell University, and an M.S.L.S. degree from Columbia University, Carroll became the Assistant Reference Librarian of the Cornell University Undergraduate Library in 1970. In 1972, she moved to Oak Ridge, Tennessee, as a staff member of the Oak Ridge National Library, a government research laboratory of Union Carbide Corporation. In 1977 she was made Technical Information Coordinator. From 1979 to 1981 she was employed as Manager of Oak Ridge Operations, Franklin Research Company, a Philadelphia contract research organization.

Carroll began work for the U.S. Department of Energy in 1981 as Assistant Manager for Program Development at the Technical Information Center (TIC) in Oak Ridge. In 1984, her office was expanded to include international activities under the new Department of Energy Office of Scientific and Technical Information (OSTI), and she assumed her present title.

In the American Society for Information Science, Carroll served on the Board of Directors as the Special Interest Group Director from 1977 to 1981. She has been active on many committees, holding several chairmanships. As a frequent lecturer and author in the field of information science, she is recognized as an authority on energy information and information analysis centers.

CLEARY, BEVERLY
Beverly Cleary won the 1984 Newbery Medal for the most distinguished contribution to American literature for children published in 1983 for *Dear Mr. Henshaw*. It tells the story of Leigh Botts, "the mediumest boy in the class" through journal entries and letters to his favorite author. Warm, subtle, and occasionally funny, *Dear Mr. Henshaw* celebrates an ordinary child's life with extraordinary perception.

Cleary has written more than 25 children's books, published in 10 countries and in various languages. Her two best known series concern Henry Huggins and Ramona. Two Ramona books were Newbery Honor Books: *Ramona and her Father* (1978) and *Ramona Quimby, Age 8* (1982). For a biography and portrait of Cleary, see *The ALA Yearbook* (1976) and *The ALA Yearbook* (1981).

COOPER, KENNETH R.
Kenneth R. Cooper, Director General of the National Federation of

Vivian Arterbery

Lester Asheim

Peggy Barber

Bonnie Carroll

Beverly Cleary

Kenneth Cooper

Fritz Eichenberg

William Ford

Building Trades Employers, was appointed Chief Executive of the British Library, taking office in September, 1984.

Educated at Queen Elizabeth's Grammar School, Barnet, England, and New College Oxford, Cooper entered the English Civil Service in 1954. Until 1962 he served in the Ministry of Labor. It became the Department of Employment, and he was appointed its Under Secretary in 1971. From 1975 to 1979 he served as Chief Executive of the Employment Services Agency and when the Manpower Services Commission was established, Chief Executive of its Training Services Agency. In 1979 he went to the Building Trades Employers Association.

A Fellow of the Institute of Training and Development, he is also a Past President. He is a member of the Confederacy of British Industry Council, and a Fellow of the Institute of Personnel Management.

CUNNINGHAM, GEORGE

George Cunningham, Civil Servant and Member of Parliament, was appointed Chief Executive of the Library Association (Great Britain) in 1984.

Cunningham was born in 1931. After earning B.A. and B.Sc. degrees at Manchester and London Universities, he became a member of the Commonwealth Relations Office in 1956. During his term of duty there, he also served as Second Secretary (Political) for the British High Commission in Ottawa, Canada in 1958–60; was a member of the British delegation to the Vienna, Austria, Conference on Diplomatic Relations in 1961; and a member of the secretariat of the Commonwealth Prime Ministers Conference, 1962.

In 1963, he became the Commonwealth Officer of the Labour Party of Great Britain, and in 1963 joined the Ministry of Overseas Development. He was elected to Parliament as a Labour Party Member in 1970. While serving, he was also a Member of the Parliament of the European Community in 1978–79. From 1981 to 1983, he was a Social Democrat Member of Parliament.

A resident of Hampton, Middlesex, Cunningham is known for his publications. In 1970 he edited *Britain and the World in the Seventies*. *The Management of Aid Agencies* was published in 1974, and his latest book, *Careers in Politics*, in 1984.

DOYLE, ROBERT P.

Robert P. Doyle in April 1984 became the Coordinator of the International Federation of Library Associations and Institutions (IFLA), responsible for organizing, coordinating, and publicizing the IFLA General Conference in Chicago in August 1985. It is IFLA's first meeting in the United States since 1974. Doyle reports to Robert Wedgeworth, Co-Chair of the U.S. Organizing Committee, and has an office at ALA headquarters in Chicago.

From 1984, Doyle was the Assistant to the Director of ALA's Office for Intellectual Freedom (OIF), responsible for writing the monthly *OIF Memorandum*, contributing articles to the *Newsletter on Intellectual Freedom*, the *Freedom to Read Foundation News*, and other magazines. He published *Banned Books Week '85—Celebrating the Freedom to Read: A Resource Book*. During his tenure at OIF, Doyle gave over 40 speeches to national, state and local organizations concerned with intellectual freedom.

He was Reference Supervisor at the Oak Lawn (Illinois) Public Library, 1976-80, and from 1974 to 1975 was Research Assistant, Wisconsin Department of Transportation Division of Highways.

Born July 29, 1951, in Milwaukee, Doyle received his B.A. from the University of Notre Dame in 1973, and an M.L.S. from the University of Wisconsin-Milwaukee in 1975.

EICHENBERG, FRITZ

Fritz Eichenberg, noted graphic artist and book illustrator, delivered the 15th annual May Hill Arbuthnot Honor Lecture April 6 at the Minneapolis Public Library and Information Center.

Born October 24, 1901, in Cologne, Germany, Eichenberg went to the United States in 1933 and became a naturalized citizen in 1941. He attended the School of Applied Arts, Cologne, 1916-20, and in 1923 received the M.F.A. degree from the State Academy of Fine Arts in Leipzig. Honorary degrees include a Dr.F.A. from California College of Arts and Crafts 1978 and a doctorate from Marymount College, Tarrytown (New York) 1984.

Eichenberg began his career as a newspaper artist in Germany (1923). During that time he printed and saw published his first lithographs, which illustrated Dostoevsky's *Crime and Punishment* and Swift's *Gulliver's Travels*, and his first wood engravings for *Tyll Eulenspiegel*, a German folk tale. From 1933, he found work producing prints for the Federal Artists Project, illustrating for the *Nation* and teaching at New York's New School for Social Research.

From 1935 to 1945 he was on the art faculty of the New School for Social Research; 1947-72, a professor of art, Pratt Institute, New York; 1966-71, professor of art, University of Rhode Island, Kingston; and 1972-73, on the faculty of Albertus Magnus College, New Haven, Connecticut.

His work is represented in collections of the National Gallery of Art, Hermitage (Leningrad), Metropolitan Museum of Art, Philadelphia Museum of Art, and other museums.

A member of the National Academy of Design and the Society of American Graphic Artists, Eichenberg is also a Fellow of the Royal Society of Arts, London.

His favorite mediums are lithographs, wood engravings, and woodcuts. He has illustrated dozens of books for children and adults. His best-known children's books include *Ape in a Cape: An Alphabet of Odd Animals* (1952), a Caldecott Honor Book, and *Dancing in the Moon: Counting Rhymes* (1955), an ALA Notable book.

He created widely acclaimed illustrations for numerous adult classics including *Wuthering Heights* by Emily Bronte, *Jane Eyre* by Charlotte Bronte, works by Dostoevsky, Edgar Allan Poe, Tolstoy, Pushkin, Goethe, and Shakespeare.

Throughout his career he has incorporated ideals of social justice, peace, and tolerance in many of his works. In 1984 he was working on illustrations for his 700-page handwritten autobiography.

FORD, WILLIAM D.

William D. Ford, Democratic member of the U.S. House of Representatives from Michigan's 15th Congressional District, was awarded Honorary Membership in ALA in 1984.

Ford was born in Detroit, August 6, 1927. After studying at the Nebraska Teachers College and the Wayne State University, he received his B.S. degree from the University of Denver in 1949, and in 1951, his J.D. degree from the same institution.

Practicing law in Taylor, Michigan, from 1951 to 1964, Ford served as Justice of Peace from 1955 to 1957, Township Attorney, 1957-64; and City Attorney, Melvindale, Michigan, 1957-59. In 1962 he was elected to the Michigan Senate, and in 1964 to the U.S. House of Representatives.

As a member of the Education and Labor Committee and of the Post Office and Civil Service Committee, Ford proved a strong and effective supporter of legislation to establish and improve library service nationwide. Among the acts he helped to write and to pass are the Library Services and Construction Act, the Elementary and Secondary Education Act, the Higher Education Act, the statutes establishing the National Commission on Libraries and Information Science, and the White House Conference on Library and Information Services. He was the House of Representatives' member to the White House Conference.

When the U.S. Office of Personnel Management recommended revision of qualifications and classification standards that would have downgraded federal librarians, Ford, as Chair of the House Post Office and Civil Service Committee, led the Congressional movement that resulted in a Government Accounting Office review and ongoing investigation. Always aware of implications for libraries in proposed legislation, Ford brought to the attention of the House the possible adverse effects of the Federal Communication Commission's proposals regarding access charges and private line tariffs. He cited the problems libraries would have: "discontinue their automated services or choose between paying data communication bills or buying new books."

The ALA Honorary Life Membership citation to Congressman Ford read in part: "In recognition of the staunch leadership and unfailing support he has provided to the nation's libraries and educational institutions . . . the American Library Association hereby cites the Honorable William D. Ford . . . as an endearing friend and supporter of libraries and education, and awards an Honorary Life Membership."

HAAS, WARREN

Warren Haas, Jr., President of the Council on Library Resources, Washington, D.C., received the 1984 Melvil Dewey Medal, presented at the ALA Conference in Dallas.

The citation reads, in part: "Warren J. Haas in his long and distinguished career has made major contributions in those areas of greatest concern to Melvil Dewey—library management, library training, and bibliographic control. He has shown outstanding ability as a library administrator at two of the nation's great research libraries, the University of Pennsylvania and Columbia University, and he has provided leadership to the greater library community. . . ."

For a biography and portrait of Haas, see *ALA Yearbook* (1979).

HANNIGAN, JANE ANNE

Jane Anne Hannigan, Professor, School of Library Service, Columbia University, New York, was given the 1984 Beta Phi Mu Award during the ALA Annual Conference in Dallas, Texas. The award of the library honorary association is presented "for distinguished service to education for librarianship."

Hannigan received her B.A. degree from Manhattanville College, Purchase, New York in 1951. Villanova University conferred an M.S.L.S. degree on her in 1961, and in 1969 she received her Ph.D. degree from Columbia University.

Beginning her career as an elementary school teacher and school librarian in 1951, Hannigan became a Special Collections Librarian at Columbia University Library in 1961, and a Teaching Assistant of the School of Library Service in 1962. At the School of Library Science (now the Graduate School of Library and Information Science), Simmons College, Boston, Massachussetts, she served as an Associate Professor from 1964 to 1973. She joined the faculty of Columbia University in 1973, and was made a full professor in 1977.

A member of the ALA Executive Board from 1980 to 1984, Hannigan has also served for 10 years on Council, and on many Council committees. Particularly active in the American Association of School Librarians, she has served on its Board of Directors as Second Vice-President. She has been the Series Editor for the division's "Focus on Trends and Issues" and "Diversity and Direction in Children's Literature," features in the *School Library Media Quarterly*. Her other publications have been numerous, including the book, with Glenn Estes, *Media Facilities Design*.

Hannigan has been honored with the George Fuller Award from the School of Library Service, Columbia University. Teachers College of the University awarded her a Spencer Foundation Research Grant, and at the 50th anniversary of Villanova University she received a medallion as an outstanding alumna of graduate programs.

The 1984 Beta Phi Mu Award citation reads in part:

"For her persistent commitment to the ideals of excellence in teaching; her distinguished work as author and researcher; and her continuing devotion to the library profession and the future well being of her students, the Association presents its Beta Phi Mu Award to Jane Anne Hannigan."

HERRING, HAROLD F.

Harold F. Herring, an attorney and partner in Lanier Shaver & Herring, Huntsville, Alabama, became President of the Urban Libraries Council in 1984. He was Vice President of that group, 1981–83, and a member of its Board from 1973.

Born in Lanett, Alabama, July 22, 1924, Herring was graduated from the University of Alabama with a B.S. in Industrial Engineering in 1948 and from the Law School in 1951.

He attended the Citadel, Charleston, South Carolina, 1941–43, and was a B-17 pilot in World War II.

He became a member of the Alabama Library Association, the American Library Association, and the National Citizens for Public Libraries and served on the Executive Board of the Alabama Public Library Service from 1982.

Herring is a member of the Board of the Alabama Library Exchange, a cooperative of public, academic, special and school libraries serving eight counties in Northeast Alabama, and also on the Board of the Huntsville–Madison County Friends of the Library.

From 1969 to 1980 he was on the Board of the Huntsville–Madison County Public Library. During that time the first public radio station in Alabama was sponsored by the Library.

JURKINS, JACQUELYN J.

Jacquelyn J. Jurkins, Multnomah Law Library, Portland, Oregon, was elected President of the American Association of Law Libraries in 1984.

Jurkins received her J.D. degree from the University of Wisconsin, Madison, and her M.M.L. degree from the Master of Law program, University of Washington, Seattle. Her first professional position was Assistant Law Librarian, Supreme Court of Washington from 1960 to 1962. She became the International and Comparative Law Librarian, School of Law, University of Washington in 1962, and the Law Librarian, Supreme Court of Colorado in 1963. In 1964 she assumed her present position, and from 1969 to 1971, she also served as Law Librarian and Professor of Law at the Lewis and Clark College in Portland.

Active in a number of professional associations, Jurkins was President of the Western-Pacific Chapter of AALA from 1971 to 73. She was elected to the Executive Board of the parent organization in 1973, and served until 1975. She has chaired a number of committees: Program, for the 1973 Annual Convention; Scholarship, 1971-72; Convention Planning, 1976-77; Job Security, Remuneration, and Employment Practices, 1978-79; and Relations with Publishers and Dealers, 1979-80; Co-chair, 1980-81.

Warren Haas

A frequent contributor of articles and book reviews to the Law Library Journal, Jurkins also writes for the Oregon State Bar Bulletin and the Multnomah Lawyer. Since 1969 she has been the Editor of "Membership News" for the AALA Newsletter.

KIMMEL, MARGARET MARY

Margaret Mary Kimmel became the first President of the U.S. National Section of the International Board on Books for Young People (IBBY), to be known as The United States Board on Books for Young People, Inc. (USBBY), at its organization in June during the ALA Annual Conference in Dallas. The former Friends of IBBY organization was dissolved. Sponsoring members of USBBY are the American Library Association and the Children's Book Council.

Kimmel received a B.A. from Rosary College, River Forest, Illinois in 1960 and an M.L.S. from that institution in 1963. In 1980 she received a Ph.D. from the University of Pittsburgh.

She joined the faculty of the School of Library and Information Science, University of Pittsburgh in 1978, as Associate Professor and later was appointed Professor. In 1980 she became Co-Director, Interdisciplinary Program in Children's Literature.

Kimmel's was Children's Librarian, Enoch Pratt Free Library, Baltimore, 1963–66; assistant to Coordinator of Work with Children, Enoch Pratt, 1966–70, Elementary School Media Specialist, Gary, Indiana, 1972–73.

She was Visiting Lecturer, College of Librarianship, Aberystivyth, Wales, 1970–72. During those years she lectured and participated in workshops at other library schools on the continent and in Britain. From 1973 to 1976 Kimmel was Assistant Professor, Simmons College, Boston.

Active in professional associations, she served on ALSC's Newbery-Caldecott Committee, 1973 and 1976, and was President of the Division, 1982–83. She became a member of the ALA Committee on Accreditation in 1983. In addition to ALA and several of its Divisions, Kimmel is a member of the American Association of Library Schools, Children's Literature Association, and the Educational Film Library Association.

Publications include For Reading Out Loud! A Guide to Sharing Books with Children with Elizabeth Segel (1983); Excellence in School Media Centers: Essays in Honor of Elizabeth T. Fast, Co-editor with Thomas Galvin, Brenda White (1980); and Magic in the Mist, illustrated by Trina Ichart Hyman (1976).

She has had wide experience in radio and television programs for children, and she was named Director of a project funded by the U.S. Office of Education on Fred Roger's Archives.

Kimmel's skill in storytelling and promotion of that art are widely recognized. In November she visited Paris, as a guest of the Ministry of Culture to tour libraries and museums for children.

Honors she has received include Northwest Indiana Woman of the Year 1976; Publisher's Showcase for Magic in the Mist, 1976; Volunteer of the Year, Boston School Committee, Boston, 1975.

L'ENGLE, MADELEINE

Madeleine L'Engle, well-known author, was the 26th recipient of the Regina Medal presented April 24 during the annual meeting of the Catholic Library Association in Boston. It is awarded for excellence, consistent and sustained, in an author's body of work. Engraved on the Regina Medal is the following: "Only the rarest kind of best in anything can be good enough for the young, Walter de la Mare."

L'Engle has written a wide variety of books ranging from poetry to science fiction, from fantasy to prayer, from nonfiction to allegory. She received the John Newbery Medal for A Wrinkle in Time (1962) in 1963; a Hans Christian Andersen Runner-up Award in 1964; and the Sequoyah Award 1965.

Born November 29, 1918, in New York City, L'Engle received a B.A. from Smith College in 1941, and did graduate study at Columbia University.

From 1941 to 1947 she had an active career in the theater. She taught at St. Hilda's and St. Hugh's School, New York City, from 1960 into the 1970s. She has been writer-in-residence and/or lecturer on writing at many universities, including Ohio State, Minnesota, Michigan, Rochester, Indiana University, the University of South Mississippi.

A Wrinkle in Time deals with the "fifth dimension" in the adventures of three young people in space and develops the theme of the eternal struggle between good and evil.

The presenter of the Regina Medal closed her comments with, "As the words pour forth from pen to page and we are caught up in your truth-telling, we learn of life. We watch the struggle between good and evil that is us. Even though the dark forces surround us all and all-ways you show us that there is love, and that too is real, and with that we can win."

Titles written by L'Engle include: Meet the Austins (1960); The Army of the Starfish (1965); The Journey with Jonah (1967); A Wind in the Door (1973); Dragons in the Waters (1976); and The Weather of the Heart (1978).

LERNER, ADELE A.

Adele A. Lerner, Archivist, New York Hospital, Cornell Medical Center, was elected Vice-Chair and Chair-elect of the Council of National Library and Information Associations (CNLIA) in 1984. She is the representative of the Society of American Archivists (SAA) to the Council.

Lerner was born in New York City, November 5, 1938. She received her B.A. degree from the University of Rochester (New York) in 1960, and the M.L.S. degree, with honors, from Columbia University in 1971. She earned certificates in various phases of archival management from the American University/National Archives and Records Service, the American Management Association, the Society of American Archivists, and the Medical Library Association.

From 1960 to 1970, Lerner was employed by various insurance companies as an underwriter. She joined the New York Academy of Medicine, after she received her M.S.L.S. degree in 1971, as the MEDLARS/MEDLINE analyst, and in 1972, was appointed to her present position.

As an archival consultant, Lerner was employed by Brooklyn Rediscovery from 1977 to 1983, the New York Academy of the Sciences, 1977-80, and Johns Hopkins Medical Institutions Archives, 1978-80. Since 1979, she has been a member of the Advisory Board for the Archives, United Negro College Fund. She taught a graduate course in "Management of Archives and Manuscript Collections" at the School of Library Service, Columbia University, in 1980.

In the Society of American Archivists Lerner held a number of committee appointments, including the ALA/SAA Joint Committee on Archives/Library Relations. In 1980 she served as Chair of the Archives of Science Committee. She was Vice-Chair of the Archivists Round Table of Metropolitan New York in 1982-83 and became a member of the Steering Committee. From 1975, she served on the Executive Board of the Medical Archivists of New York, and in 1972 was a member of the Executive Committee of the New York Regional Group of the Medical Library Association. She served on committees of Beta Phi Mu, National Library Honor Society.

Lerner wrote *an Introduction to the Medical Archives of New York Hospital-Cornell Medical Center* (1976). She contributed the chapter on "Archival Services in Hospital Libraries" in *Hospital Library Management,* Jane Bradley, editor (Medical Library Association, 1983).

LINDBERG, DONALD ALLAN BROR

Donald Allan Bror Lindberg, M.D., in June was appointed Director of the National Library of Medicine by Health and Human Services Secretary Margaret M. Heckler. He was sworn in at ceremonies held October 11, becoming the 19th director of the Library.

In remarks during the ceremonies the Director of the National Institutes of Health cited Lindberg's qualifications as a teacher, administrator, pathologist, and computer expert, and reflected on the immensity of the task of directing the varied national and international information programs of the library.

Born September 21, 1933, in Brooklyn, New York, Lindberg received an A.B. from Amherst College 1954, and an M.D. from Columbia University 1958. He received a Sc.D. from Amherst College in 1979. In 1963 he earned the American Board of Pathology diploma.

He began his career as an assistant in pathology, Columbia University College of Physicians and Surgeons, 1958-60. From 1962 to 1984 he was in the Pathology Department, University of Missouri School of Medicine.

Lindberg was Professor and Chairman, Department of Information Science, University of Missouri School of Information Science, 1969-71; Vice President for Academic Affairs, University of Missouri, 1970-71; Consultant for Health Services to Vice President for Academic Affairs, 1972-73; and Director, Health Services Research Center with special emphasis on Health Care Technology, University of Missouri, 1976-84.

Publications include *The Growth of Medical Information Systems in the United States* (1979) and joint editorship of *Computer Applications in Medical Care* (1982). Lindberg has written chapters to many books and has contributed numerous articles and reports appearing in national and international scientific publications.

LYNCH, BEVERLY P.

Beverly P. Lynch, University Librarian and Professor of Library Administration, University of Illinois at Chicago, was elected Vice-President/President-elect of ALA in 1984. In the Association she served as a member of the Editorial Board of *College and Research Libraries* from 1977 to 1984. In 1979 she was elected to Council and has been a member of the Committee on Program Evaluation and Support (COPES) since 1979. She was Chair in 1982-83. In 1983 she was elected to the Executive Board.

Lynch was born in Moorhead, Minnesota, on December 27, 1935. She received her B.S. degree from North Dakota State University, Fargo, in 1957, and her M.A. degree in librarianship from the University of Illinois at Urbana in 1959. Her Ph.D. degree was conferred by the University of Wisconsin-Madison in 1972.

After a year in the Serials Department at the University of Illinois Library at Urbana, Lynch in 1959 became Librarian of the Marquette University Memorial Library, Milwaukee. In 1961 she went to England where she was the Assistant Reference Librarian at the Plymouth Public Library. She returned to Marquette as Assistant Cataloger in 1962. A year later she joined the staff of the Serials Division of the Sterling Memorial Library, Yale University. In 1964, she became Head of the Division.

She was appointed Executive Secretary (now Executive Director) of ALA's Association of College and Research Libraries in 1972. In 1977 she joined the faculty of the University of Illinois at Chicago.

Lynch has served on accreditation teams for the New England Association of Schools and Colleges from 1976, the North Central Association from 1981, and ALA from 1980. She taught as a Visiting Lecturer at the Library School, University of Wisconsin-Madison, 1972; Visiting Lecturer, Graduate Library School, University of Chicago, 1975; Visiting Professor, (now) Graduate School of Library and Information Science, University of Texas, Austin, 1978; and Adjunct Professor, School of Library and Information Science, University of Wisconsin-Milwaukee, 1981.

A frequent speaker on academic library and technology topics, Lynch contributed extensively to library periodicals. In 1982, with Thomas J. Galvin, she edited *Priorities for Academic Libraries* (Jossey-Boss). For publication in 1985, she edited *The Management of Libraries: Basic Readings* (Neal Schuman).

Lynch has been a member of the Executive Committee, National Advisory Board of the Center for the Book in the Library of Congress since 1978. From 1977 to 1983 she was a member of the Board of Directors of the Center for Research Libraries, and was Chair in 1980-81. She has been on the National Board of Consultants to the National Endowment for the Humanities since 1979.

In 1959 she was given the Distinguished Graduate Award of the (now) Graduate School of Library and Information Science of the University of Illinois at Urbana. In 1968 she received a two-year Title II-B Fellowship from the U.S. Government. North Dakota State University conferred an honorary Doctor of Literature on her in 1980, and in 1981 she received the ACRL Academic/Research Librarian of the Year Award. She was made a Senior Fellow of the Graduate School of Library and Information Science of the University of California at Los Angeles in 1982.

McANANAMA, JUDITH ELEANOR

Judith Eleanor McAnanama, Chief Librarian Hamilton Public Library System, Ontario, Canada, from 1980, became President of the Canadian Library Association for 1984-85.

She earned a B.A. from the University of Manitoba, Winnipeg; a B.L.S. from McGill University, Montreal; and an M.B.A. from McMaster University, Hamilton.

McAnanama was Branch Head, Winnipeg Public Library 1964-65. In 1965 she began her career at the Hamilton Public Library, where she was Branch Head and Librarian of Children's Services, 1965-73, Head of Branches, 1971-74, and Head of the central library, 1974-77.

She is active in professional and community organizations, serving as a director of the Hamilton Canadian Club and as a director of the Industry Education Council, and she became Chairman of the Ontario Library Association Fundraising Committee. As a member of the Canadian Library Association statistics study team, she prepared a report to Statistics Canada on improved statistical collection and presentation methods.

MARTELL, CHARLES R.

Charles R. Martell, Associate University Librarian for Public Services, California State University, Sacramento, in 1984 was appointed Editor of *College and Research Libraries*, the quarterly journal of the Association of College and Research Libraries (ACRL), a division of ALA. From 1974 to 1975 he was Guide Editor for the *Journal of Academic Librarianship.* He is Series Editor for that journal, responsible for the "Quality of Work Life" series.

Donald Lindberg

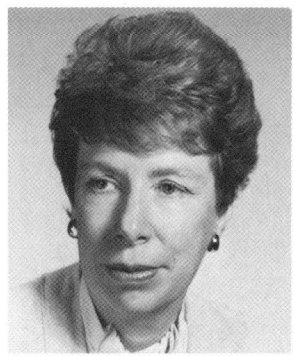
Beverly Lynch

Judith McAnanama

Charles Martell

Phyllis Mirsky

Roger Parent

Carolyn Peterson

Alice and Martin Provensen

Martell was born in Cambridge, Massachusetts, September 18, 1939. He received his B.A. degree from Brown University, Providence, Rhode Island in 1964, and his M.S.L.S. degree from Syracuse (New York) University in 1972. The D.L.S. degree was conferred upon him by the University of California, Berkeley, in 1979.

After four years of business experience, Martell began his professional career in 1968 as a library assistant at the University of Colorado, Boulder. From 1972 to 1974, having acquired his M.S.L.S. degree, he was the Librarian of the California-Canadian Bank of Commerce in San Francisco. For one year, he was Project Leader for the Swedish National Board for Technical Development, studying the information systems of three international corporations to provide models for other Swedish industries.

He went to the University of California in 1979 as Acquisitions Librarian. Until 1981, he served also as Assistant to the University Librarian, and as Reference Librarian in the Education-Psychology Library. It was as Acquisitions Librarian that he joined the staff of the Library of the University of Illinois, Chicago, in 1981. In 1983, he assumed his position at California State University, Sacramento.

Martell has served as a consultant to the California State University, San Jose, the Smithsonian Institute Libraries, the University of California, San Francisco, and the University Librarian, University of California, Berkeley. He wrote *The Client-Centered Academic Library: an Organizational Model* (Greenwood Press, 1983) and many periodical articles. His speeches before professional associations have been almost as numerous as his writings. In addition, he served on many university committees in Illinois and in California. In 1980-81 he was chair of the Librarians Association of the University of California (LAUC), and he was Chair of the Committee for Local Arrangements, ALA/ACRL Annual Conference, San Francisco, 1975.

MIRSKY, PHYLLIS SIMON

Phyllis Simon Mirsky was elected President of the Medical Library Association in 1984. Long an active member of the Association, she served on many of its committees, was Chair of the Study Group on MLA's Role in the Education Process for Health Sciences Librarianship, 1980-81, Chairman, Continuing Education Committee, 1976-77, and member of the Board of Directors, 1977-80.

Mirsky was President of the Medical Library Group of Southern California and Arizona, 1972-73. She was on the NCLIS/SLA Task Force on the Role of the Special Library in Nationwide Network and Cooperative Programs, 1981-83. She is a member of the Library and Technology Association, ALA's Association of College and Research Libraries, and the American Society of Information Science.

Born December 18, 1940, in Israel, she received an A.M.L.S., University of Michigan, 1965, a B.S. in Social Welfare, Ohio State University, 1962, and attended Columbia University School of Social Work, 1962-63, as a Fellow of the National Institute of Mental Health. In 1978 she was certified by the Medical Library Association and recertified in 1983.

Mirsky lectured on various aspects of health science librarianship at the UCLA Graduate School of Library and Information Sciences, 1984; at Catholic University, Graduate School of Library Science 1980; and at the USC and UCLA Library Schools, 1967-78.

She edited *Directory of Health Science Libraries: Arizona, California, Hawaii, Nevada* (University of California, 1979); and, with Lois Ann Colaianni, wrote *Manual for Librarians in Small Hospitals* (University of California, 1978).

MOORE, BESSIE

Bessie Moore, a member of the National Commission on Libraries and Information Science from 1971, was reappointed by President Reagan for a term expiring in 1988.

For a biography and portrait of Moore, a resident of Little Rock, Arkansas, and indefatigable library advocate, see *The ALA Yearbook* (1981).

PARENT, ROGER H.

Roger H. Parent, Executive Director of the Library Administration and Management Division, 1979-84, became Deputy Executive Director of the American Library Association in November 1984.

Parent has been active as a workshop trainer, consultant on library planning, and speaker on personnel management and staff development. For a biography and portrait, see *The ALA Yearbook* (1979).

PETERSON, CAROLYN SUE

Carolyn Sue Peterson, Head of the Children's Department, Orlando, Florida, Public Library from 1970, received the 1984 Grolier Foundation Award.

She was born June 23, 1938 in Carthage, Missouri. She received an A.B. from the University of Missouri in 1959 and an M.A. in Librarianship from the University of Denver in 1960, and she did graduate work at the University of Missouri and Northwest Missouri State College.

Peterson was children's librarian, Town and Country Regional Library, Joplin, Missouri, 1960-62 and Librarian, Elementary and Junior High Laboratory School, Northwest Missouri State College 1962-68. From 1968 to 1970, she was Instructor, Graduate Library-Media Program, University of Colorado.

Active in professional organizations, Peterson served on various committees in the Association for Library Service to Children, was on the Advisory Council, Children's Division, Southeastern Library Association, 1981-82, and held various positions in the Florida Library Association. She is a member of the National League of American Penwomen.

Publications include *Reference Books for Children* (co-author with Ann D. Fenton, 1981); *Index to Children's Songs,* (co-author Ann D. Fenton, 1979); and *Story Programs: A Source Book of Materials* (co-author Benny Hall, 1980). She is a co-owner and Editor of Moonlight Press, a publishing firm dedicated to producing quality storytelling and literature-related materials for librarians, teachers, and early childhood educators.

Peterson frequently lectures at, and is a consultant for, programs related to child development and literature.

Honors she has received include the Florida Library Association Outstanding Library Development Award (1973), and a John Cotton Dana Award (1978).

The Grolier Foundation Award Citation reads, in part: "Carolyn Sue Peterson has made it her life's work to encouarge adults to provide children with unlimited story experiences. Her innovative methods of recruiting thousands of adults to encourage children to enjoy reading are gaining wide use in public libraries and parent education projects around the country."

PROVENSEN, ALICE and MARTIN

Alice and Martin Provensen, illustrators and authors of *The Glorious Flight: Across the Channel with Louis Bleriot,* were awarded the 1984 Caldecott Medal for the most distinguished American picture book published in 1983. *The Glorious Flight* tells the story of pioneer aviator Louis Bleriot, who flew across the English Channel in 1909, eighteen years before Lindbergh crossed the Atlantic. With muted earth tones, dramatic perspectives, and sweeping double spreads, the illustrators convey Bleriot's turn-of-the-century France and vividly record the excitement and triumph of his historic flight.

Alice Twitchell Provensen was born August 14, 1918, in Chicago. She studied at the Art Institute of Chicago, the University of California at Los Angeles, and the Art Students League in New York City. Twitchell worked in animation at the Walter Lantz Studios, Hollywood 1942-43; in graphics at the Office of Strategic Services, Washington, D.C., 1943-45; and has written and illustrated children's books since 1946.

Martin Provensen was born July 10, 1916, in Chicago. He studied at the Art Institute of Chicago and at the University of California in Berkeley. He worked at Walt Disney Studios, Hollywood, 1938-42, and spent 1942-45 in service in the U.S. Navy. Since 1946 he has written and illustrated children's books.

The Provensens were married in 1944. They have illustrated books together for 37 years.

Books written and illustrated by the Provensens include *Our Animal Farm* (1974); *The Year at Maple Farm* (1978); *An Owl and Three Pussycats* (1981).

ROBBINS-CARTER, JANE
Jane Robbins-Carter, Professor and Director, School of Library and Information Studies, University of Wisconsin-Madison from 1981, became President of the Association for Library and Information Science Education (ALISE) in 1984. In 1976 she was the Convenor of the Research Interest Group of the Association. From 1982 to 1983 she was Chair of the Program Committee.

After serving a term on the Board of Directors from 1978 to 1981 she became Chair of the Council of Deans and Directors in 1982-83. Active in other professional associations, she served on ALA committees, and was a Councilor, 1972-73, and 1976-80. She held committee assignments in the Public Library Association (PLA), the Association of State and Cooperative Library Agencies (ASCLA), and the Library Administration and Management Association (LAMA), and was Chair of the Library Research Round Table, 1977-78. A member of the American Society for Information Science (ASIS), and the Continuing Library Education Network and Exchange (CLENE), she was President-elect of the Wisconsin Library Association in 1984.

Robbins-Carter was born in Chicago, September 13, 1939. She earned her B.A. degree at Wells College, Aurora, New York, in 1961, and her M.L.S. degree from Western Michigan University, Kalamazoo, in 1966. In 1972 the University of Maryland, College Park, conferred the Ph.D. degree on her.

Robbins-Carter's first professional positions were with the U.S. Department of the Navy and the Library of Congress, 1966-67. In 1968 she became a reference librarian at the Transportation Center Library of Northwestern University, Evanston, Illinois, and after taking her doctor's degree in 1972, Assistant Professor and Academic Assistant to the Dean, School of Library and Information Science, University of Pittsburgh. In 1973 she moved to the Division of Librarianship (now division of Library and Information Science) at Emory University, Atlanta, Georgia, as Assistant Professor. Following a year, 1974-75, as reference librarian at the University of Northern Colorado, Greeley, she was Board Consultant to the Wyoming State Library, Archives and Historical Department, Cheyenne, from 1975 to 1977. She joined the faculty of the School of Library and Information Science of Louisiana State University, Baton Rouge, as Associate Professor in 1977, and from 1978 to 1981 served as Dean of the School.

As a visiting lecturer and institute director, Robbins-Carter taught in many parts of the country, and has served as a Library Development Plan Consultant in Covington, Louisiana, and Laramie, Wyoming. She was a member of the Board of Editors for the *Journal of Academic Librarianship* from 1977 to 1980, and of *Library Research* (now *Library and Information Science Research*) from 1978 to 1981, when she was appointed Editor.

In addition to contributing frequently to professional journals in the fields of library education, research process and methods, and information agency management, Robbins-Carter published a number of books and papers, including *Public Librarianship: a Reader* (Libraries Unlimited, 1982) and *Public Library Policy and Citizen Participation* (Scarecrow, 1976), based on her doctoral dissertation. She received the LeFevre Outstanding Graduate Award from Western Michigan University, was elected to Beta Phi Mu, the honorary library society, and appointed a Fellow under Title II-B of the Higher Education Act.

RUFFNER, FREDERICK G.
Frederick G. Ruffner, Jr., President of Gale Research Company in Detroit, was elected President of the Friends of Libraries, U.S.A. (FOLUSA) in 1984. He has been a member of the Board of Directors since 1981. In 1967 he became a member of the Board of Directors of the Friends of the Detroit Public Library, and was President, 1975-76. In Fort Lauderdale, Florida, he joined the Board of Directors of the Friends of the Library in 1974, and served as President from 1974 to 1979. He has been President of the Council for Florida Libraries since 1979, in which year he was the Official Observer from the state of Florida to the White House Conference on Libraries.

Ruffner received his B.S. in Business Administration from Ohio State University in 1950. In 1954, when he was working as Research Manager for the General Detroit Corporation, he discovered that no book listing trade associations across the country existed. To fill a need, he and his wife compiled, edited, and published, as the Gale Research Company, the *Encyclopedia of Associations*, still published in updated editions. They sold their products by mail, mostly to libraries and government agencies. Of the many encyclopedias, special dictionaries, guides, and indexes Gale Research Company has published, Ruffner himself has edited the *Code Names Dictionary* and *Acronyms and Initialisms Dictionary*. He is a patent holder in graphic arts.

He is a member of the American Management Association, the Association of American Publishers, and ALA, as well as the American Antiquarian Society.

The Gale Research Company Financial Development Award, administered by ALA, is donated annually by Gale.

SCOTT, MARIANNE FLORENCE
Marianne Florence Scott, formerly Director of Libraries at McGill University, Montreal, became the third director of the National Library of Canada, Ottawa, in April 1984. She is the first professionally educated librarian to hold this position.

For a biography of Scott, see *The ALA Yearbook* (1982).

Jane Robbins-Carter

Frederick Ruffner

Marianne Scott

Ronald Surridge

Richard Talbot

SEGAL, JO AN S.

JoAn Segal, Executive Director of the Bibliographical Center for Research, Denver, Colorado, was appointed Executive Director of the ALA Association of College and Research Libraries in 1984.

Segal was born in Brooklyn, New York, on September 14, 1930. She attended Douglass College and Rutgers University, both in New Brunswick, New Jersey, receiving a BALS degree from Rutgers in 1951. Her MSLS degree was conferred by Columbia University in 1955. She received a Ph.D. degree (communication) from the University of Colorado at Boulder in 1978.

In 1953, Segal assumed her first administrative position, as Librarian of Bergen Junior College, Paramus, New Jersey. She became the Librarian of the Institute of Mathematics and Science, New York University, New York City from 1955 to 1958. In an interesting shift in career, she went to Trident Theatre, Boulder, Colorado, as an actress and instructor, an interlude that lasted from 1963 to 1968. She was appointed Librarian of the Western Interstate Commission for Higher Education, Boulder, Colorado, in 1970, and held the post until 1976. After a period of serving as a consultant to a number of institutions, she joined the Resource Sharing Program, Bibliographical Center for Research as Manager in 1978. In 1980 she became Acting Director and later Director of the Center.

An active member of ALA and the Special Libraries Association, she served the Rocky Mountain Chapter of the latter as President in 1981-82. She is a member of Beta Phi Mu, honorary library association.

Segal's diversity of interests is reflected in her publications. The theater prompted "Mind, Body, and Spirit in the 1976 Colorado Shakespeare Festival" in the *Colorado Shakespeare Annual* and "Group Development in the Casts of the 1977 Colorado Shakespeare Festival" in the subsequent *Annual*. Among her many professional books, papers and articles, three emphasize a special interest in lifelong learning: *A Methodology for Describing Federal Programs That Support Adult Learning Opportunities* (joint author), 1977; *Learning Opportunities for Adults: A Literature Review*, 1977; and *Library Manual in Lifelong Learning*, 1978. Her other special interests are in research, networking, automation, and the field of information science.

SURRIDGE, RONALD GEORGE

Ronald George Surridge, public librarian, editor, writer, publisher, library politician, library activist, and Borough Librarian of the London Borough of Islington, Great Britain, since 1977, was elected President of the Library Association in 1984.

He was born in the East End of London in 1922 and educated at George Green's Secondary School. From 1939 to 1947 he worked for the Poplar Library Service in London with a break of five years for service in the Royal Air Force during World War II. In 1949 he completed the two years toward his Fellowship at the School of Librarianship at Loughborough under the tutelage of Roy Stokes. A succession of posts in London libraries led to his becoming Deputy Borough Librarian in Bromley, returning to his old authority in the East End of London as Chief Librarian and then to Islington.

Long service in the Association of Assistant Librarians (the UK Association for younger librarians), Chair of its Finance Committee, and services as its Assistant Secretary, led to his Presidency of the AAL in 1963. In that year he led a team of 137 members of the AAL touring cities on the Eastern Seaboard of the U.S.

An interest in education for librarianship resulted in membership on many panels and committees of the Library Association including chairmanship of its Education Committee and its Research Development Committee. He was for several years a part-time teacher of bibliography at the Polytechnic of North London. He has been involved with the Council of the Library Association for 25 years, having edited its news periodical *Liaison* for 18 years. As chair of the Grants and Awards Committee of the Library Association since its inception, he initiated and developed the McColvin and Besterman Awards, together with the newly formulated Public Relations Award.

A frequent contributor to journals and seminars, Surridge wrote *Management Information in the Bromley Computerised Library System*, 1973. With Judith Bowen, he wrote *The Independent Learning Project—a Study of Changing Attitudes in American Public Libraries* (1977). With Roy Brown, his colleague in forming the Public Libraries Research Group in 1971, he edited *Output Measurement*, proceedings of a seminar on output measurement for public librarians in 1974, and went on to edit and publish a series of occasional papers on research in public librarianship.

Surridge is known to many American librarians and researchers. He has spoken on occasions at ALA Conferences and in many U.S. library systems and several library schools. His interest is in reciprocal learning and sharing of research methods and findings.

SWERDLOVE, DOROTHY L.

Dorothy L. Swerdlove, Curator, Billy Rose Theatre Collection, New York Public Library at Lincoln Center, was elected President of the Theatre Library Association for 1983-84. She served as Secretary-Treasurer, 1966-70, and as an ex officio Board member 1970-83.

Born January 4, 1928, in New York City, Swerdlove earned her B.A. degree at Swarthmore College 1948, and her M.S. in Library Science at Columbia University, 1961.

In 1948-49 Swerdlove was research assistant, Federal Reserve Bank of New York, and she was social science analyst, Library of Congress, Washington, D.C., 1949-53. She was a research assistant, Princeton University 1953-54; research assistant, Chase Manhattan Bank, New York 1954-55; and an economist, Caltex Oil Corporation, New York 1955-61. In 1961 she went to the Theatre Collection, New York Public Library, becoming first assistant in 1967 and Curator in 1980.

Swerdlove was an assistant editor, *Public Affairs Abstracts* 1950-51, and co-author, *Survey of United States International Affairs* (1954). She contributed to *Oxford Companion to the Theatre* (1976, 1983 eds.); *Performing Arts International Bibliography* (1976); *Notable Names in American Theatre* (1976); *Notable American Women, The Modern Period* (1980); and *Performing Arts Resources* (1980).

TALBOT, RICHARD J.

Richard J. Talbot, Director of Libraries, University of Massachusetts Library, Amherst, became President of the Association of Research Libraries (ARL), in 1984. In addition to serving on committees of the Association, he was Chair of the Task Force (later, Committee) on Statistics from 1980 to 1983 and has been a member of the ARL Board since 1981. Active in a number of professional associations, he was Project Director of the ALA/ACRL (Association of College and Research Libraries) Salary Survey Project, 1975-76, Chair of the Budget and Finance Committee of ACRL, 1980-82, of the Board, 1980-82, and the Executive Committee in those years.

He was a member of the Board of the Center for Research Libraries from 1981, and was a member of the Executive Committee from 1981 to 1983. From 1981 he was also a member of the Board of the New England Library Information Network (NELINET). As an ex-officio member of the Boston Library Consortium, he was elected President for the fiscal year 1981. The Governor of Massachusetts appointed him to the Massachusetts Post-Secondary Education Commission for 1978-79.

He earned an A.B. degree from Manhattan College in 1954 and did graduate work in philosophy at St. John's Seminary, Brighton, Massachusetts, 1957-58, and in theology at the Gregorian University in Rome, Italy, from 1958 to 1960. He received his M.S.L.S. degree from Simmons College, Boston, in 1961. In 1980 Syracuse (New York) University granted him an M.B.A. degree.

After service in the U.S. Air Force from 1954 to 1957, and further study, Talbot began his career in the Circulation Department of the New York Public Library in 1961-62. Then, for eight years he served in various federal libraries as Cataloger, Reference Librarian, Acquisitions Librarian, Library Systems Analyst, and Supervising Librarian. In 1972, he joined the staff of the University of Massachusetts Library in Technical Services and became Acting Director in 1972, Director in 1973.

Talbot is the Author, with Ann von der Lippe, of *Salary Structures of Librarians in Higher Education for the Year 1975-76* (ALA, 1976) and, with the advice of the ARL Task Force on Statistics, *Regression Analysis of the ARL Data* (ARL, 1978). He wrote a number of reports on his research projects, notably on university library standards and periodical usage in research libraries.

Talbot is a member of Phi Alpha Theta, the National History Honor Society. In 1983 he was made a Senior Fellow of the University of California, Los Angeles, by the Council of Library Resources.

TAYLOR, NETTIE BANCROFT
Nettie Bancroft Taylor, who received the 1984 ALA Lippincott Award, is Assistant State Superintendent for Libraries and Chief, Division of Library Development and Services, Maryland State Department of Education, and a leader in the library profession.

She was born in Brownsville, Tennessee, August 6, 1914. She received her A.B. degree from Florida State University, Tallahassee, in 1936. The University of North Carolina, Chapel Hill, awarded her the B.S. degree in library science in 1942. She did further graduate study at the University of Maryland at College Park. In 1967 she received an M.S. degree in Liberal Arts from Johns Hopkins University in Baltimore.

She was Librarian of Taylor County High School in Perry, Florida, from 1936 to 1940. When she went to Leon County High School in Tallahassee, she began work on her library degree. She achieved it in 1942, and became an Army librarian. After service in the United States, she was appointed Command Librarian for the U.S. Army service area in Heidelberg, Germany, where she served from 1945 to 1947. She returned to the United States as Supervisor of Public Libraries, Maryland State Department of Education, a post she held until she was appointed to her present position in 1960.

Always active in professional associations, in ALA, Taylor wa a member of the Editorial (1965-69), Legislation (1965-67), and Planning (1975-79) Committees, and Chairperson of the Nominating Committee (1965). In 1965 she was elected Second Vice-President of the American Library Trustees Association (ALTA), and from 1969 to 1970, President of the Association of State Libraries (ASL), (now incorporated into the Association of Specialized and Cooperative Library Agencies). One of the founders of the Continuing Library Education Network Exchange (CLENE), she was President in 1976. In 1960 she served as President of the Maryland Library Association. She is active in the Chief Officers of State Library Associations (COSLA).

Taylor frequently provided service beyond her immediate position. Florida State University invited her to be a visiting lecturer in the summer of 1959, and she served on the Advisory Committee of the University's State Library Research Project in 1969. She was a member of the Governor's Commission to Revise the Laws of Maryland from 1968 to 1970. She served on two U.S. Office of Education research projects, the Advisory Board for *Public Libraries and Federal Policy* in 1974, and the Advisory Panel for *Evaluation of Title I of the Library Services and Construction Act,* from 1979 to 1981. Nearer home, she was Director of the ALA Library Community Project in Maryland, from 1955 to 1958.

Although there has been steady and remarkable growth in the support and development of Maryland libraries under Taylor, her greatest contribution according to colleagues, was fostering a spirit of cooperation among libraries. She received the Distinguished Service Award of the Maryland Library Association in 1979. In 1983, she was given Honorary Membership in the Maryland Educational Media Association. The citation for the Joseph B. Lippincott Award reads, in part: "Nettie B. Taylor has mastered the art of gentle persuasion and has used it effectively to advance library service in her state, her profession, and her nation."

Nettie Taylor

Linda Wallace

WALLACE, LINDA K.
Linda K. Wallace succeeded Peggy Barber as Director of the Public Information Office of the American Library Association (ALA) in December.

From 1976 Wallace was Community Relations Coordinator for the Mideastern Michigan Library Cooperative, a state-funded service agency for 47 public libraries in three counties with headquarters in Flint. She was a news reporter for *The Flint Journal*, 1971–76.

Active in professional organizations, Wallace was President, Public Relations Association of Greater Flint 1981, and served as Chair of the Public Relations Section of the Library Administration and Management Association (LAMA) of ALA 1983. She participated in library public relations seminars and received two John Cotton Dana Special awards for library programs.

Born in Toledo, Ohio, in 1949, Wallace received a B.S. in Journalism from Ohio University in Athens in 1971.

15

Obituaries

Susan Akers

Bradford Chambers

John Cronin

AKERS, SUSAN GREY

Susan Grey Akers (1889–1984), former Dean of the University of North Carolina Library School, died at the age of 95. Aker's *Simple Library Cataloging*, published by ALA in 1927, with revision in 1944, was the basic text in that field for years.

She went to the Library School in North Carolina in 1931 as an Assistant Professor, becoming Acting Director and Professor, 1932–35, Director and Professor, 1935–42, and Dean and Professor, 1942–54.

Born in Richmond, Kentucky April 3, 1889, Akers received an A.B. from the University of Kentucky 1909, a certificate from the University of Wisconsin Library School 1913, and a Ph.D. from the University of Chicago in 1933.

She began her career as a teacher in public schools in Kentucky and Alabama, 1909–11. In 1911 she went to the Louisville Public Library as a general assistant, and from 1913 to 1920 she was a librarian at Wellesley College (Massachusetts). Akers was in charge of the catalog, North Dakota State Library, 1920–22, and went to the University of Wisconsin Library School as Instructor, then Assistant Professor, 1922–28.

She was Chair of the Professional Training Section of ALA 1937–38, and President of the North Carolina Library Association 1943–46.

BEARD, SARAH ALLEN

Sarah Allen Beard (1902–1984), young adult librarian, died April 1 in Cobleskill, New York.

Born October 16, 1902, in Gloversville, New York, she received an A.B. degree from Cornell University in 1924, a B.S.L.S. from Columbia University in 1943, and an M.A. from N.Y. University in 1944. She was in the 1925 Brooklyn Public Library Training Class.

Beginning her library career as an assistant children's librarian in the Brooklyn Public Library, 1925–27, Beard went to Ridgwood, New Jersey, as children's librarian, 1927–29. In 1930 she returned to the Brooklyn Public Library, where she was a branch young people's librarian, 1930–41, and head of the Young People's Division 1941–43. From 1944–45 she was Supervisor of Work with Young People in the Kansas City (Missouri) Public Library, and was Consultant, School and Public Library Work with Children and Young People, Massachusetts State Department of Education 1945–49.

Beard was Visiting Professor, Department of Library Science, University of Tennessee summers 1949, 1950, and at SUNY (Albany) summers 1951–57. She also was Visiting Professor, Pratt Library School, Brooklyn, 1952–54. She was interim editor of Young Adult Books for *Booklist* (ALA) during the 1950s. From 1959 to 1961 Beard was the organizer and Director of the Hudson Area Library, Hudson, New York.

Active in professional organizations, Beard was a Director of the Division for Library Work with Children and Young People (ALA), 1952–54, and Director of the New York Library Association, 1952–54. She edited *Top of the News*, 1951–52.

Beard contributed many articles to professional periodicals and wrote *Public Library Plans for the Teen Age*, published by ALA in 1948.

CHAMBERS, BRADFORD

Bradford Chambers (1922–1984), both editor and Director of the Council on Interracial Books for Children, an organization devoted to promoting bias-free textbooks and children's literature, died September 22.

He had been director of CIBC for 18 years and previously was a children's book editor. Under his direction the Council developed guidelines to determine whether textbooks and storybooks were racist or sexist. The Council was founded in 1965 by writers, librarians, teachers, and parents to oppose such stereotypes in textbooks and children's books.

Aided by a Carnegie Foundation grant, Chambers established a Racism and Sexism Resource Center at the Council. The Center was awarded the National Education Association's 1982 Human and Civil Rights Award.

He was born in New York City in 1922. Chambers attended Amherst College and was graduated from New York University. While still an undergraduate he undertook a study of New York's Harlem street gangs.

He edited an anthology, *Chronicles of Black Protest*, which documented the Black struggle in the United States for social justice and won the 1969 Brotherhood Award of the National Council of Christians and Jews.

Under his leadership, CIBC campaigned for the hiring of minority personnel in editorial capacities by major publishing houses and promoted the publication of Third World writers.

CRONIN, JOHN WILLIAM

John William Cronin, retired Director of the Library of Congress's Processing Department, had a long career at LC, from which he retired in 1968, marked by numerous national and international achievements in technical processing that were of benefit not only to LC but to libraries everywhere. He died November 24 in Washington, D.C., at the age of 78.

A native of Lewiston, Maine, Cronin received a bachelor of arts degree from Bowdoin College in 1925 and joined the staff of the Library in September of that year. Except for a brief absence in 1926–28 to attend Georgetown University of Law School, from which he received the LL.B. degree in 1929, he served continuously at LC in increasingly responsible positions. He was named Assistant Chief of the Card Division in 1939, Assistant Director of the Processing Department in 1940, and Director in 1952.

His efforts were always pointed toward finding new and practical solutions to the technical problems that beset a large and complex library. His ingenuity in using personnel and facilities led to several major LC programs.

The Library's card distribution service was a major interest of his, and he saw it grow from a modest activity in 1930 to its modern influential status.

Cronin supervised the editing of the original 167-volume *Catalog of Books Represented by Library of Congress Printed Cards* and had major responsibility for the successful publication of the other book catalogs that followed.

His name remains associated with the monumental third edition of the *Union List of Serials* and the retrospective *National Union Catalog*. Library of Congress catalog card numbers in current publications, Library of Congress catalog entries in journals serving libraries and the book trade, and the enclosure by wholesalers and publishers of Library of Congress cards with books supplied to libraries are all programs originated or expanded under his direction.

Cronin combined global acquisitions and shared cataloging to form the National Program for Acquisitions and Cataloging, one of his greatest achievements. His determination that cataloging titles for foreign national bibliographies could be applied in this program was an important forward step in international library cooperation.

In 1961 he received the ALA Margaret Mann Citation for outstanding professional achievement. In 1964 he was awarded the Melvil Dewey Medal.

In 1965 the Library of Congress honored him with its Distinguished Service Award for strengthening "the bibliographic services of the Library of Congress and the extension of these services to other libraries throughout the country and the world to the enduring benefit of scholarship."

DAVID, CHARLES W.

Charles W. David, Director of Libraries and Professor of History at the University of Pennsylvania in the 1940s and 1950s, died April 2 at the age of 99. He was the author of several scholarly works in medieval history, and he played a major role in the development of the Union Library Catalog of Pennsylvania and the revitalization and expansion of the University of Pennsylvania Libraries.

He earned a bachelor's degree from Oxford as a Rhodes Scholar in 1911 and a doctorate from Harvard in 1918. He taught history at the University of Washington for three years and at Bryn Mawr College from 1918 to 1940. In the 1930s he joined historian Conyers Read to become one of the principal architects of the Union Library Catalog of Pennsylvania.

In 1940 David became professor of history and the first full-time Director of Libraries at the University of Pennsylvania. For the next 15 years until he retired in 1955, he worked to achieve a remarkable renaissance of the University's libraries. He also served a five-year term as executive secretary of the Association of Research Libraries, and played a major role in the Farmington Plan and in rebuilding the war-ravaged libraries of Europe.

After his retirement from Penn at the age of 70, David went on to plan and establish the Eleutherian Mills Historical Library, a major research collection for American business and industrial history, at Longwood, Delaware. He also established the Maritime Library at the Mystic Seaport Museum in Connecticut, and served as Chairman of the Board of Trustees at West Chester State Teachers College.

GEER, HELEN

Helen Geer (1903–1984), ALA Headquarters Librarian, 1947–56, and library editor, educator, and active participant in the life of the profession in many roles, died March 10.

Born January 27, 1903, in Newcastle, Pennsylvania, she received an A.B. from Wheaton College (Massachusetts) in 1926, a B.S. in L.S. from the University of Illinois in 1928, and a M.S. in L.S. from Columbia University in 1934.

She began as a circulation assistant, Evanston (Illinois) Public Library, 1928–29, and was Reference Librarian, Flushing Branch, Queens Borough Public Library, 1929–36. From 1936 to 1944 Geer worked in the Queens Borough Public Library, Jamaica, New York. She was a Reference Assistant in Harper Library, University of Chicago, 1944–46, and Editor, *Bibliographic Index*, for the H. W. Wilson Co., New York, 1946–47.

Geer was Headquarters Librarian at ALA from 1947 to 1956. She was Director, The Library Mart (manufacturers' representative), Fairhope, Alabama, 1956–58.

She was Editor, *Library Literature*, H. W. Wilson Co., 1958–62, and Assistant Librarian, Wheaton College, 1962–64. She retired as Associate Professor, Graduate Library School, University of Rhode Island, in 1969, a position she had held since 1964.

She was active in several Divisions of ALA.

HORTON, MARION LOUISE

Marion Louise Horton (1887–1984), California school librarian died in 1984 at the age of 97.

She received an A.B. from Stanford University in 1911 and was graduated from the New York State Library School, Albany, in 1917.

Horton began her library career as a cataloger in the Stanford University Library (1912–13), and from 1913 to 1916 she was Librarian, Fremont High School, Oakland, California. She was Instructor and Principal of the Los Angeles Public Library's Training School 1917–28, and at the Columbia University Library School served as an Instructor, 1928–30.

In 1932 Horton returned to California, where she was Head, Order Department, Library and Textbook Section of the Los Angeles Board of Education until 1952.

After retirement from the Board of Education in Los Angeles, she went to Istanbul, Turkey, where she organized the American Academy for Girls in 1952. The following year she spent as a consultant at the International Youth Library in Munich.

For some years, beginning in 1954 she was an instructor in the Library School at the University of Southern California.

Horton edited the *ALA Catalog* 1926–31, 1932–36, 1937–41. She was compiler and editor of the *Buying List of Books for Small Libraries*, published by ALA, 5th through 7th editions, 1935, 1940, 1945.

She was a member of ALA, NEA, The California Library Association and The School Library Association of California, which she served as Vice-President, 1915–16, and President 1950–51.

JONES, VIRGINIA LACY

Virginia Lacy Jones, library educator, humanitarian, and Dean of Atlanta University School of Library and Information Studies, died December 3. She was often called "the Dean of Library School Deans."

On the occasion of her receiving the honorary Doctor of Letters from the University of Michigan (1979), the commendation read by Russell E. Bidlack expressed the esteem in which she was held by her colleagues and friends:

Virginia Lacy Jones

> Dr. Jones is the personification of wise counselor, inspired teacher, patient mentor, and demanding scholar. In the library profession at large she is acknowledged as a courageous leader who has pointed the way to achievement and success against barriers that most of us would have considered insurmountable.

Born in Cincinnati, Ohio, June 25, 1912, "Dean Jones" as she was called by her students and colleagues, attended public schools in Clarksburg, West Virginia, and St. Louis, Missouri. At Hampton Institute, Viriginia, she received two Bachelor of Science degrees in Library Science and in Education followed by a Master of Library Science from the University of Illinois in 1938. A recipient of two General Education Board fellowships, she received the Ph.D. in librarianship in 1945 from the University of Chicago, becoming the second Black librarian to earn that degree.

From the time she entered the profession, she seemed destined to play an important role in the future development of library science. Her personal commitment, unique abilities, sense of humor, warm personal relationships, and standards of excellence showed the promise that she fulfilled in her long career. She served as Assistant Librarian and Librarian at Louisville Municipal College, Kentucky, for six years. Moving to Atlanta in 1939, she began as the Catalog Librarian at Trevor Arnett Library and became involved in the planning that led to the opening of the Library School at Atlanta University in 1941. After four years as Instructor, she was appointed Dean, a position she held until her retirement in 1981. She was then named the first Director of the new Robert W. Woodruff Library of the Atlanta University Center, a project with which she had been associated since its inception in 1967. On her departure in 1983, she was named Dean Emeritus by the Board of Trustees. The Exhibition Gallery at the Woodruff Library was later named in her honor.

Virginia Jones believed in expanding opportunities for students, librarians, and readers. She had been Supervisor of the Prairie View, Texas, Regional Summer Training Center for li-

Carl Perkins

brarians, one of four sponsored by the General Education Board from 1936 to 1939. She was also instrumental in the establishment of the Library Section of the Kentucky Negro Education Association. She had supported the efforts of Mollie Huston lee of Raleigh, North Carolina, and Charlemae Rollins of Chicago who were working with publishers to improve the images of Black people in children's books. For the Carnegie Corporation of New York, she helped establish a Field Service Program responsible for consultant services to libraries serving Blacks in several southeastern states.

Her knowledge, dedication, and indefatigable efforts extended her impact far beyond the Atlanta University campus. During her long tenure Atlanta University produced over 1,800 trained Black librarians—more than any other school in America. She worked with the National Endowment for the Humanities and the President's Advisory Council on Libraries, to which she was appointed in 1967. Mayor Sam Massell named her to the Atlanta Sister City Program with Montego Bay, Jamaica, in 1973. Governor George Busbee appointed her to the Georgia State Board for the Certification of Librarians, on which she served as Vice-Chair from 1975 to 1980. She was a member of the Committee on Interstate Library Cooperation and the Advisory Committee on the Survey of Southeastern Libraries of the Southeastern Library Association. She served on numerous visitation committees, and in many library and literacy-related organizations. She was in great demand as a consultant and was published widely in professional journals.

In the American Library Association she was four-term member of the Council and a member of the Executive Board from 1970 to 1976. In the Association of American Library Schools (now the Association of Library and Information Science Education), she participated as Secretary-Treasurer from 1948 to 1954, on the Board of Directors from 1960 to 1964, and as President in 1967. She was also active in the Association of College and Research Libraries, the Black Caucus of ALA, the Special Libraries Association, and the Georgia Library Association. At the time of her death, she held memberships in her professional organizations, the NAACP, the Delta Sigma Theta Sorority, and many other organizations.

She received the Alumni Achievement Award from Hampton Institute in 1956 and the Atlanta Bronze Woman of the Year in 1959. She was given Honorary Membership in the West Virginia Library Association in 1971 and the Melvil Dewey Award from ALA in 1973. ALA conferred Honorary Membership on Dr. Jones in 1976. The Black Caucus of ALA presented a citation honoring her 30 years of service to Black librarians in 1977, and the Joseph W. Lippincott Award of ALA was given to her for "distinguished librarianship" the same year. In 1979 she received two honorary doctorates. She was honored with the Mary Rothrock Award from the Southeastern Library Association in 1982 and the same organization elected her to Honorary Membership on October 16, 1984.

She was married in 1941 to Edward Allen Jones (d. 1981), Chairman of the Department of Languages, Morehouse College (Atlanta, Georgia).

The citation of her Beta Phi Mu Award of 1980 read in part: "Virginia Lacy Jones is an excellent model of those who see professional education as encompassing administrative skill, leadership, adherence to principles of human rights, scholarship, and advanced thinking."

A scholarship in her name was established at the Atlanta University School of Library and Information Studies.

KENNEDY, ANNA CLARK

Anna Clark Kennedy (1891–1984), Supervisor of School Libraries, New York State Department of Education from 1929 until her retirement, died in Hudson, New York, in December at 93 years of age.

A nationally recognized leader in school librarianship from the 1930s until retirement, she served as Chair of the School Library Section of ALA 1933–34. She edited a Yearbook on Elementary School Libraries published by the National Elementary School Principals Association in 1942.

Born in Hudson, New York, September 14, 1891, Kennedy received an A.B. from Vassar College in 1915, a B.Lit. from Columbia in 1916, and a certificate from the New York State Library School, Albany, in 1924.

She worked in the news department of the *Hudson Evening Register*, 1916–17, a family-owned firm in which she was interested throughout her life. She was a teacher and librarian in the Hudson Public Schools, 1917–23, and Director of School Libraries for that system, 1924–29.

In 1929 she became Supervisor of School Libraries for the New York State Department of Education, and held that position until her retirement in the late 1950s. Her leadership was a significant factor in the development of school libraries throughout the state.

Active in state and regional, as well as national professional groups, she served as president of the School Library Division of the New York State Library Association, and was on the advisory board of the College of St. Rose, Albany, New York. She was a leader in founding the Hudson Area Library in 1959, serving on its Board of Trustees and as President of that group for a term. Kennedy was also an active member of the Catholic Library Association.

LERNER, LOUIS A.

Louis A. Lerner, community newspaper publisher in Chicago and its suburbs who served on the National Commission on Libraries and Information Science from 1972 to 1977, died on November 14, 1984 in Chicago. See his biography in *The ALA Yearbook* (1978).

MITCHELL, ELEANOR

Eleanor Mitchell (1907–1984), New York Public Library administrator and Project Officer for the ALA International Relations Office, was killed in an automobile accident August 21 near Bedford, Pennsylvania.

Born April 4, 1907, in Orange, New Jersey, she received a B.A. from Douglas College 1928, a B.S.L.S. from Columbia University in 1929, and an M.A. from Smith College in 1936.

Mitchell was chief of the Art division, New York Public Library, 1943–51; Director, Library Services for the United States Information Service (USTS) in Italy, 1951–54; and U.S. Specialist, for the Department of State, Columbia, 1955–57.

She was Executive Director, Fine Arts Commission, People-to-People Program 1957–61, and was a specialist for the Books for the People Fund, Inc., of the Pan American Union, 1961–62. From 1963 to 1968 she was Library Consultant at the University Catolics, Quito, Ecuador. In 1969 she became Project Officer for the ALA International Relations Office, a position she held until 1972.

Mitchell published numerous articles in professional journals. Her contribution to librarianship and international understanding was significant.

PERKINS, CARL DEWEY

Carl Dewey Perkins, United States Representative from Kentucky, and

Honorary Member of ALA died August 6, 1984. The citation presented with his Honorary Membership in 1975 referred to his "remarkable record as a champion of library legislation and as an advocate of excellence in education." For a biography and portrait see *ALA Yearbook, 1975*, p.110.

ROGERS, JOSEPH W.

Joseph W. Rogers (1906–1984) former Chief of the Copyright Office Cataloging Division, died May 15, 1984 in Arlington, Virginia.

Rogers, who was born at Matfield Green, Kansas, was graduated from Baker University with an A.B. degree, received a B.S. in library science from the University of Illinois Library School and an M.S. from the Columbia University School of Library Science.

He began his library career at the Queens Borough Public Library in New York and was later Chief of the Book Selection and Order Department at the Milwaukee Public Library. He was in the Air Force from 1943 to 1946, serving in the China-Burma-India theater with the First Troop Carrier Squadron.

Rogers joined the newly organized Cataloging Division of the Copyright Office in August 1946 as a section head and was chief from 1951 until his retirement in December 1967.

He devoted himself especially to the formulation of rules for cataloging nonbook materials and to the improvement and development of the Catalog of Copyright Entries. He was chairman of the Library of Congress committee which developed the rules for the cataloging of prints and photographs and served on the rules committee for motion pictures and maps.

Rogers was president of the District of Columbia Library Association, 1964–65; chairman of the Special Libraries Association Washington Chapter of the Geography and Map Group, 1955–56; a Council member of the American Library Association (ALA); chairman of the ALA's Subscription Books Committee, 1949–51; and a member of the Decimal Classification Editorial Policy Committee, 1963–65. He was a member of the American Institute of Graphic Arts, the American Documentation Institute, the Bibliographical Society of America, the National Microfilm Association, and the Music Libraries Association.

His special interest was always bookmaking. His extensive knowledge of the graphic arts, printing, and his technical knowledge of the manner in which the diverse materials received as copyright deposits were produced were put to good use in his career at the Library of Congress, and he sought to make bibliographers aware of the unique values of the Copyright Office records in American bibliography.

He was the author of *Industrialization of American Bookbinding* in the Gutenberg Jahrbuch (1938) and *Rise of American Edition Binding* in Lehmann-Haupt's *Bookbinding in America* (1941, rev. ed. 1967). He edited *The Marion Press* by Larremore (1943) and served as editor of the New York Library Association *Newsletter* 1937–39.

A major contribution to the literature of library science and to copyright law was his book entitled *U.S. National Bibliography and the Copyright Law*, published by R. R. Bowker in 1960.

SEALOCK, RICHARD B.

Richard B. Sealock, director of public libraries, editor and publisher, consultant, and association leader, died on November 3, in Wooster, Ohio.

Sealock was born June 15, 1907, in Lexington, Illinois. He attended Eureka College, and received a B.A. degree from the University of Illinois, Urbana, in 1930. The B.S.L.S. degree was conferred upon him by Columbia University, New York, in 1935. His first work in a library was at the University of Illinois. From 1930 to 1939 he was on the staff of the Queens Public Library, New York.

For four years he served at the Enoch Pratt Free Library, Baltimore, Maryland, and in 1943 became Director of the Gary Public Library, a post he held until 1949, when he became the Director of the Kansas City (Missouri) Public Library. In 1968 he resigned to become the Director of the Forest Press, Lake Placid and Albany, New York. He retired in 1977. In his retirement he served as Interim Director of the Andrews Library, College of Wooster (Ohio), the position he held at the time of his death.

In Kansas City, Sealock was responsible for the planning and erection of the 11-story building that now houses the Public Library and the Kansas City Board of Education. He was frequently sought as a consultant. He had been appointed to the Maryland Governor's Commission for the State Library Survey in 1942; from 1964 to 1967 he served as a consultant to Eureka College; he was a member of the Missouri State Library Advisory Committee from 1965 to 1968; and he served as Vice-Chairman, Chairman, and President of the Denver Bibliographic Center.

An active member of professional associations, Sealock was President of the Indiana Library Association, 1946-47, and of the Missouri Library Association, 1955-56. He was elected President of the ALA Library Education Division for 1955-56.

A member of the ALA Board on Accreditation, 1955-56 term, he served as Treasurer of ALA from 1956 to 1960, and was subsequently appointed a Trustee of the Endowment Fund. He was a member of Council from 1961 to 1965, and Second Vice-President, 1963-64.

Sealock was the co-compiler of *Long Island Bibliography* (1940) and the compiler of *Bibliography of Place Name Literature, U.S. and Canada*. Place names were a lifelong interest, and he was a member and Vice-President of the American Name Society.

In 1967, Eureka College conferred an honorary degree on Richard Sealock.

Richard Sealock

SHACTMAN, BELLA EVELYN

Bella Evelyn Shactman (1914–1984), Associate University Librarian at the University of California in Berkeley from 1969, died April 19.

Born in Malden, Massachusetts, May 21, 1914, she received a B.A.L.S. from the University of North Carolina (Greensboro) in 1933. From 1934 to 1936 she worked as a reference and catalog assistant at the Carnegie Public Library in Winston-Salem, North Carolina.

Beginning work in the United States Department of Agriculture National Agricultural Library as a loan desk assistant in 1936, Shactman retired from that Library in 1969 as the Assistant Director of Technical Services.

She was active in ALA, the International Association of Agriculture Librarians and Documentalists, Special Libraries Association (SLA), and others. Shactman was elected to the ALA Council, 1963–67, and served on the ALA Executive Board, 1968–71.

SHEPARD, MARIETTA DANIELS

Marietta Daniels Shepard (1913–84), retired Chief of Library Development with the Organization of American States, was killed in an automobile accident August 21 near Bedford, Pennsylvania.

She was born January 24, 1913, in Mt. Washington, Missouri. Shepard received a B.A. from the University of Kansas in 1933; a B.L.S. from Columbia University in 1943, and an M.A. from Washington University, St. Louis, in 1945.

She was Chief of Circulation, Washington University Library,

Estellene Walker

1938–43; Library Director and Professor of Library Science, Escuela Norma, Panama, 1943–46; Special Assistant to the Librarian of Congress, 1946–48; Associate Librarian, Columbus Memorial Library, 1948–58; and Chief, Library Development Program, Organization of American States, from 1959 until she retired in 1978.

Shepard served on the ALA Council 1956–60 and 1969–74, and as a member of the ALA Executive Board, 1968–72. She was on the RTSD Division Board, 1963–69, and served on various IFLA committees.

She wrote *Bases for Developing an Inter-American Library and Information System* (1981) and contributed to journals and books. An award from the Spanish Book Industry was given to her (1972) in recognition of her contributions to publishing.

WALKER, ESTELLENE PAXTON

Estellene Paxton Walker (1911–84), distinguished South Carolina Librarian, under whose guidance public library service was extended to all citizens of South Carolina, died May 15 in Columbia. Director of the South Carolina State Library Board from 1946 to 1969, Walker was State Librarian, 1969–79, and upon retirement became a consultant to the State Library. From 1945–46 she was a materials-supply librarian for the Army Special Services in ETO.

Born September 11, 1911, in Washington County, Virginia, Walker received a B.A. from the University of Tennessee 1933 and a B.S.L.S. from Emory University, Atlanta, 1935.

She was active in professional organizations, serving as an ALA Councilor 1952–56, as President of the American Association of State Librarians, 1968, and as President of the South Carolina Library Association 1974–76.

Presbyterian College, Clinton, South Carolina, gave her an honorary Doctor of Literature degree in 1975, and Lander College, Greenwood, South Carolina, awarded her an honorary Doctor of Humanities degree in 1979.

Walker's *So Good and Necessary a Work: The Public Library in South Carolina 1698–1980*, was published in 1981.

In 1983 she received the State Library's distingushed Service Award.

Notables

This article covers notable books for general readers, for children, and for young adults; notable children's recordings, notable children's films, and notable children's filmstrips. (See also Young Adult Literature, Children's Literature, and Films, Children's.)

The 1984 Notable Books list was compiled by the Notable Books Council of the Reference and Adult Services Division of the American Library Association. The titles were selected for their significant contribution to the expansion of knowledge or for the pleasure they can provide to adult readers. Criteria include wide general appeal and literary merit.

The Notable Books Council of 1984 included Kenneth L. Ferstl, chair, Denton Public Library, Texas; Jean Adelman, The University Museum, University of Pennsylvania, Philadelphia; Jeri Cole Baker, Dallas Public Library; Lillian H. Barker, Prince George's County Memorial Library System, Laurel, Maryland; Anne K. Halderman, San Francisco Public Library; Jane K. Hirsch, Montgomery County Public Libraries, Rockville, Maryland; Donald Jacobsen, The New City Library, New City, New York; Diane Gordon Kadanoff, Norwell Public Library, Norwell, Massachusetts; Dorothy Nyren, Brooklyn Public Library; Teresa M. Portilla, University of California, Los Angeles; Marcia Lane Purcell, New York Public Library; Dorothy Rasmussen, Skokie Public Library, Skokie, Illinois; and Bill Ott, consultant, *Booklist*.

Notable Books of 1984

John F. Avedon, *In Exile from the Land of Snows* (Knopf)
Mary Catherine Bateson, *With a Daughter's Eye: A Memoir of Margaret Mead and Gregory Bateson* (Morrow)
Robert Bernen, *The Hills: More Tales from the Blue Stacks; Stories of Ireland* (Scribner)
Patricia Bosworth, *Diane Arbus: A Biography* (Knopf)
Rosellen Brown, *Civil Wars: A Novel* (Knopf)
Susan Cheever, *Home Before Dark* (Houghton)
The Chronicle of the Lódź Ghetto, 1941–1944, edited by Lucjan Dobroszycki; translated by Richard Lourie, Joachim Neugroschel, and others (Yale University Press)
J. M. Coetzee, *Life & Times of Michael K.* (Viking)
Evan S. Connell, *Son of the Morning Star* (North Point)
Liza Critchfield Dalby, *Geisha* (University of California Press)
E. L. Doctorow, *Lives of the Poets: Six Stories and a Novella* (Random)
José Donoso, *A House in the County: A Novel* (translated by David Pritchard with Suzanne Jill Levine) (Knopf)
Louise Erdrich, *Love Medicine: A Novel* (Holt)
Ella M. Foshay, *Reflections of Nature: Flowers in American Art* (Knopf)
Ellen Gilchrist, *Victory over Japan: A Book of Stories* (Little)
Germaine Greer, *Sex and Destiny: The Politics of Human Fertility* (Harper)
Kent Haruf, *The Tie That Binds: A Novel* (Holt)
Dolores Hayden, *Redesigning the American Dream: The Future of Housing, Work, and Family Life* (Norton)
Bernd Heinrich, *In a Patch of Fireweed* (Harvard University Press)
Ted Hughes, *River* (Harper)
Jane Jacobs, *Cities and the Wealth of Nations: Principles of Economic Life* (Random)
Susan Kenney, *In Another Country: A Novel* (Viking)
C. C. Lockwood, *The Gulf Coast: Where Land Meets Sea* (Louisiana State University Press)
S. E. Luria, *A Slot Machine, A Broken Test Tube: An Autobiography* (Harper)
Alison Lurie, *Foreign Affairs* (Random)
Ved Mehta, *The Ledge Between the Streams* (Norton)
Jan Morris, *Journeys* (Oxford University Press)
Sharon Olds, *The Dead and the Living: Poems* (Knopf)
Ernst Pawel, *The Nightmare of Reason: A Life of Franz Kafka* (Farrar)
Jayne Anne Phillips, *Machine Dreams* (Dutton/Seymour Lawrence)
Padgett Powell, *Edisto* (Farrar)
Atsushi Sakurai, *Salmon* (Knopf)
William L. Shirer, *The Nightmare Years, 1930–1940* (20th Century Journey: A Memoir of a Life and Times, vol. 2) (Little)
Jonathan D. Spence, *The Memory Palace of Matteo Ricci* (Viking)
Graham Swift, *Waterland* (Poseidon)
Strobe Talbott, *Deadly Gambits: The Reagan Administration and the Stalemate in Nuclear Arms Control* (Knopf)
Studs Terkel, *"The Good War": An Oral History of World War Two* (Pantheon)
Wallace Terry, *Bloods: An Oral History of the Vietnam War by Black Veterans* (Random)
Douglas Unger, *Leaving the Land: A Novel* (Harper)
Eudora Welty, *One Writer's Beginnings* (Harvard University Press)
John Edgar Wideman, *Brothers and Keepers* (Holt)
A. B. Yehoshua, *A Late Divorce* (translated from the Hebrew by Hillel Halkin) (Doubleday)
Paul Zweig, *Walt Whitman: The Making of the Poet* (Basic Books)

Notable Children's Books

Notable Children's Books of 1984 were selected by the Notable Children's Books Committee of the Association for Library Service to Children, a Division of the American Library Association.

Members of the 1984 committee were Dudley Carlson, Princeton Public Library, New Jersey; Sally Dow, Ossining Public Library, New York; Phyllis Kennemer, Jefferson County Schools, Colorado; Phyllis G. Sidorsky, National Cathedral School, Washington, D.C.; Elizabeth Taylor, Chicago Public Library; Caroline Ward, Vermont Department of Libraries, Montpelier; Elizabeth Watson, Fitchburg Public Library, Massachusetts; and Amy Spaulding, Little Red School House, New York, New York, Chair.

The list is composed of children's books published in the United States during 1984 that are of especially commendable quality and that reflect children's interests in exemplary ways. Children and librarians who work with children use these annual lists, which include books of various genres for children of all ages.

Among the criteria used by the Notable Children's Books Committee in its selection are outstanding literary merit and the likelihood of acceptance by children.

Young Readers

Jeanne Baker, *Home in the Sky* (Greenwillow)
Marc Brown and Laurene Krasny Brown, *The Bionic Bunny Show* (Little)
Joanna Cole, *How You Were Born* (Morrow)
Ina Friedman, *How My Parents Learned to Eat* (illustrated by Allen Say) (Houghton)
Paul Goble, *Buffalo Woman* (Bradbury)
Sara Josepha Hale, *Mary Had a Little Lamb* (illustrated by Tomie de Paola) (Holiday)
Lee Bennett Hopkins, *Surprises* (illustrated by Megan Lloyd) (Harper)
Shirley Hughes, *Alfie Gives a Hand* (Lothrop)
Ann Jonas, *Holes and Peeks* (Greenwillow)
Ann Jonas, *The Quilt* (Greenwillow)
Bert Kitchen, *Animal Alphabet* (Dial/Dutton)
Emily Arnold McCully, *Picnic* (Harper)
Barbara Ann Porte, *Harry's Dog* (illustrated by Yossi Abolafia) (Greenwillow)
Maxine Rosenberg, *Being Adopted* (illustrated by George Ancona) (Lothrop)
Alvin Schwartz, *In a Dark, Dark Room: And Other Scary Stories* (illustrated by Dirk Zimmer) (Harper)
Diane Siebert, *Truck Song* (illustrated by Byron Barton) (Crowell)
Seymour Simon, *The Moon* (Four Winds)
John Steptoe, *The Story of Jumping Mouse* (Lothrop)
Nancy Tafuri, *Have You Seen My Duckling?* (Greenwillow)
Vera B. Williams, *Music, Music for Everyone* (Greenwillow)
Ashley Wolff, *A Year of Birds*, (Dodd, Mead)
Audrey Wood, *The Napping House* (illustrated by Don Wood) (HBJ)

Middle Readers

Jim Arnosky, *Drawing Life in Motion* (Lothrop)
Brent Ashabranner, *Gavriel and Jemal: Two Boys of Jerusalem* (Dodd)
Beverly Cleary, *Ramona Forever* (Morrow)
Helen Cresswell, *The Secret World of Polly Flint* (Macmillan)
Camilla Gryski, *Cat's Cradle, Owl's Eyes: A Book of String Games* (Morrow)
Margaret Hodges, *Saint George and the Dragon* (illustrated by Trina Schart Hyman) (Little)
Mavis Jukes, *Like Jake and Me* (illustrated by Lloyd Bloom) (Knopf)
Jill Krementz, *How It Feels When Parents Divorce* (Knopf)
Rika Lesser, *Hansel and Gretel* (illustrated by Paul Zelinsky) (Dodd)
Myra Cohn Livingston, *Christmas Poems* (illustrated by Trina Schart Hyman) (Holiday House)
Bette Bao Lord, *In the Year of the Boar and Jackie Robinson* (Harper)
Jonathan Miller and David Pelham, *The Facts of Life* (Viking)
Philippa Pearce, *The Way to Sattin Shore* (Greenwillow)
Millicent Selsam, *Tree Flowers* (illustrated by Carol Lerner) (Morrow)
Jill Paton Walsh, *Gaffer Samson's Luck* (Farrar)
Terry Tempest Williams, and Ted Major, *The Secret Language of Snow* (Sierra Club/Pantheon)

Older Readers

Avi, *The Fighting Ground* (Lippincott)
Bruce Brooks, *The Moves Make the Man* (Harper)
Paula Fox, *One-Eyed Cat* (Bradbury)
Erik Christian Haugaard, *The Samurai's Tale* (Houghton)
Jamake Highwater, *Legend Days: Part One of the Ghost Horse Cycle* (Harper)
Diana Wynne Jones, *Archer's Goon* (Greenwillow)
Robin McKinley, *The Hero and the Crown* (Greenwillow)
Patricia MacLachlan, *Unclaimed Treasures* (Harper)
Margaret Mahy, *The Changeover: A Supernatural Romance* (Atheneum/McElderry)
Milton Meltzer, *The Black Americans: A History in Their Own Words 1619-1983* (Crowell)
Uri Orlev, *The Island on Bird Street* (Houghton)
Cynthia Rylant, *Waiting to Waltz: A Childhood* (illustrated by Stephen Gammell) (Bradbury)
Isaac Bashevis Singer, *Stories for Children* (Farrar)
William Sleator, *Interstellar Pig* (Dutton)
Susan and Stephen Tchudi, *The Young Writer's Handbook* (Scribner)
David and Charlotte Yue, *The Tipi: A Center of Native American Life* (Knopf)

All Ages

John Bierhorst, *Spirit Child: A Story of the Nativity* (illustrated by Barbara Cooney) (Morrow)
Jack Prelutsky, *The New Kid on the Block* (illustrated by James Stevenson) (Greenwillow)
Chris Van Allsburg, *The Mysteries of Harris Burdick* (Houghton)

Notable Children's Recordings. The 1984 Notable Children's Recordings were selected by the ALSC Recording Evaluation Committee. The list, issued annually, covers children's recordings released in the United States during 1984.

The ALSC Recording Evaluation Committee selecting the recordings were Roslyn Beitler, Washington, D.C.; Eve Wagner, Akron, Ohio; Janet Gilles, Cleveland, Ohio; Jeanette Larson, Mesquite, Texas; and Kathy Woodrell, Woodridge, Virginia, Chair.

Beverly Cleary, *Dear Mr. Henshaw* (read by Gregory Premmer) (Random House Cassette #676-30833-3)
Tomie DePaola, *Strega Nona's Magic Lessons* (read by Tammy Grimes) (Caedmon Phonodisk #TC1714, Cassette CP1714)
Dinosaur Rock (performed by Michelle Valeri and Michael Stein) (Caedmon Phonodisk #TC1739, Cassette #CP1739)
Cathy Fink and Friends: Grandma Slid down the Mountain (Rounder Records/Phonodisk #8010, Cassette #C8010)
Ian Fleming, *Chitty Chitty Bang Bang* (read by Lionel Jeffries) (Listen for Pleasure, two cassettes #7098)
Paul Galdone, *King of the Cats* (Weston Woods Cassette #LTR297C)
Graveyard Tales (NAPPS Phonodisk #NAPPS-4)
Eloise Greenfield, *Honey I Love* (Caedmon/Phonodisk #TC1736, Cassette CP1736)
Howard Hanger Jazz Fantasy, *For Kids Only* (Phonodisk #HHH778, Cassette #HHH778)
Helme Heine, *The Most Wonderful Egg in the World* (Weston Woods Cassette #LTR297C)
John McCutcheon, *HOWJADOO!* (Rounder Records Phonodisk #8009, Cassette #C8009)
Hap and Martha Palmer, *Babysong* (Educational Activities, Inc., Phonodisk #AR713, Cassette #AC713)
Laura Simms Tells Stories Just Right for Kids (Kids Records, distributed by Silo, Inc. Phonodisc #KRL 1008, Cassette #KRC 1008)

Sarah Pirtle, *Two Hands Hold the Earth* (A Gentle Wind, Cassette #GW1028)
Sergei Prokofiev, *Peter and the Wolf*, OP 67 (read by Dudley Moore) Peter Tchaikovsky, *Nutcracker Suite*, OP 71a. (music by The Boston Pops.) (Philips, distributed by Polygram Classics, Phonodisk #412556-1)
Rosenshontz, *It's the Truth* (RS Records/Phonodisk #RS84-03)
Lois Sharon and Bram, *Mainly Mother Goose* (Elephant Records, distributed by Silo, Inc., Phonodisk #LFN8409, Cassette #LFN48409
Shel Silverstein, *Where the Sidewalk Ends* (CBS Records Phonodisk #AL39412, Cassette #FTC39412)
Dodie Smith, *The Hundred and One Dalmations* (read by Joanna Lumley) (Listen for Pleasure, two Cassettes #7132)
The Snowman (words and music by Howard Blake) (CBS Inc. Phonodisk #CBS39216, Cassette #CBS39216)
William Steig, *Dominic* (read by Pat Carroll) (Caedmon Phonodisk #TC1738, Cassette #CP1738)
James Stevenson, *What's under My Bed?* (Weston Woods Cassette #LTR299C)
Tickle Tune Typhoon, Circle Around (Tickle Tune Typhoon Phonodisk #TTTLP001, Cassette #TTTLP001)
Jackie Torrence, *Brer Rabbit Stories* (Weston Woods Phonodisk #WW725, Cassette #WW725C)
Women of Courage: Sally Ride (The Eclectic Company, Inc., Phonodisk #DDR106WOC3)

Notable Children's Films. This list presents 1984 notable 16mm films for children through age 14. It was compiled by the members of the Film Evaluation Committee of the Association for Library Service to Children, a Division of the American Library Association, aided by suggestions from school and public librarians and from media specialists across the United States. Films are in color unless otherwise noted.

The selection committee members were Wendy A. Caldiero, New York, New York, Chair; Elaine P. Goley, Houston, Texas; Grace K. Greene, Arlington, Massachusetts; James Massey, Bel Air, Maryland; Hilda W. Parfrey, Madison, Wisconsin; Linda Rice, Huntington, West Virginia; Jeanette Studley, Washington, D.C.; Gail Terwilliger, Fayetteville, N.C.; and Joyce Wagar, Seattle.

Bamboo Brush (Beacon Films)
Bearskin (Tom Davenport Films)
Burt Dow, Deep Water Man (Weston Woods)
Castle (PBS Video)
Curious George Goes to the Hospital (Churchill Films)
Miracle of Life (Time Life Video)
Pigbird (National Film Board of Canada)
The Plant (National Film Board of Canada)
Please Take Care of Your Teeth (Pyramid Films)
Revenge of the Nerd (Learning Corporation of America)
Sound of Sunshine Sound of Rain (FilmFair)
A Swamp Ecosystem (National Geographic)

Notable Children's Filmstrips. This list presents notable filmstrips (with cassettes) for young people through age 14. Included are filmstrips of especially commendable quality that reflect respect for a child's intelligence and imagination, exhibit venturesome creativity and, in exemplary ways, reflect and encourage a child's interest. In making selections, the committee considered aesthetic and technical aspects, including the effective use of visuals, voices, music, language and sound effects that together create a unified whole. If adaptations, the filmstrips must remain true to, expand, or complement the original work while meeting the general criteria for excellence.

ALSC Filmstrip Evaluation Committee members were: Carol Doll, Chair, Columbia, South Carolina; Donald Adcock, Glen Ellyn, Illinois; Ruth Bacharach, Seattle, Washington; Sheila Carson, Philadelphia, Pennsylvania; Randall Enos, Middletown, New York; Dorothy Evans, Chicago; Gayle Keresey, Wilmington, North Carolina; Elizabeth Ann Long, New York, New York; Donna Rodda, Solon, Ohio; Donna Skvarla, Norman, Oklahoma; Geneva Van Horne, Missoula, Montana.

A Chair for My Mother (Random House/Miller Brody)
Doctor DeSoto (Weston Woods)
The Legend of the Bluebonnet: An Old Tale of Texas (Listening Library)
Shadow (Weston Woods)
Sweet Whispers, Brother Rush (Newbery Award Series) (Random House/Miller Brody)
When I Was Young in the Mountains (Caldecott Series) (Random House/Miller Brody)

Films for Young Adults. The Selected Films for Young Adults Committee of the Young Adult Services Division (YASD) named 11 films to its list of selected films nominated from titles released in the United States in 1983 and 1984. The films were selected on the basis of young adult appeal, technical quality, subject content, and potential utilization with young adult audiences.

Members of the committee included Jeanne P. Leader, Director of Media Services, San Luis Valley BOCS, Chair; Gerald Buchanan, Mississippi Library Commission, Jackson; Steve Crowley, Dunbar Branch Library, Charleston, West Virginia; Lynn Eisenhut, Orange County (California) Public Library; Jennifer Jung Gallant; Cuyahoga County Public Library, Cleveland, Ohio; Jean Thibodeaux Kreamer, University of Southwestern Louisiana, Lafayette; Ryna H. Rothberg, Newport Beach (California) Public Library; Jan Sarratt, East Junior High School, Gaffney, South Carolina; Louise Spain, New York Public Library; Bob Wilson, Jackson County Library System, Ashland, Oregon. Irene Wood, Nonprint Editor of *Booklist*, was a consultant to the committee.

Aliens from Inner Space (Films, Inc.)
Boys and Girls (Beacon Films)
The Car of Your Dreams (Pyramid Films & Video)
How To Be a Perfect Person (Simon & Schuster Communications: Learning Corporation of America)
I Promise to Remember (Cinema Guild)
Just an Overnight Guest (Phoenix/BFA Films, Inc.)
Kiss Me Petruchio (Films, Inc.)
Machine Story (Pyramid Films & Video)
Miraj (Molly Burgess)
Quest (Pyramid Films & Video)
To Bear Witness (Phoenix/BFA Films, Inc.)

Best Books for Young Adults. The books on this list, all published between September 1983 and December 1984, were selected by the Best Books for Young Adults Committee, Young Adult Services Division, ALA, comprising Deborah Kay Ashby, Tucson Public Library, Chair; Elizabeth Acerra, Brooklyn Public Library; Raymond Barber, William Penn Charter School, Pennsylvania; Betty Carter, Landrum Junior High School, Texas; Antoinette Clohessy, Denver Public Library; Beryl Eber, Nathan Straus Young Adult Library, New York; Lucy Marx, Louisville Free Public Library; Margaret Miller, Los Angeles Unified School District (retired); Elizabeth Parker, Enoch Pratt Free Library, Maryland; Mike Printz, Topeka West High School; Hazel Rochman, University of Chicago Laboratory Schools; Claudia Semper, Brookline High School, Massachusetts; Mary Stanton, Tacoma Public Library; Roger Sutton, Chicago Public Library; and Linda Waddle, Cedar Falls High School, Iowa. Sally Estes, *Booklist*, is a consultant to the committee.

FICTION

Barbara Abercrombie, *Run for Your Life* (Morrow)
Lloyd Alexander, *The Beggar Queen* (Dutton)
Piers Anthony, *On a Pale Horse* (Ballantine)
Avi, *The Fighting Ground* (Lippincott)
Nancy Bond, *A Place to Come Back to* (Atheneum)
Eve Bunting, *If I Asked You, Would You Stay?* (Lippincott)
Alden R. Carter, *Growing Season* (Coward)
Barbara Wernecke Durkin, *Oh, You Dundalk Girls, Can't You Dance the Polka?* (Morrow)
Paula Fox, *One-Eyed Cat* (Bradbury)
Donald Gallo, editor, *Sixteen: Short Stories by Outstanding Writers for Young Adults* (Delacorte)
Rumer Godden, *Thursday's Children* (Viking)
Jan Greenberg, *No Dragons to Slay* (Farrar)
Lynn Hall, *Uphill All the Way* (Scribner)
Virginia Hamilton, *A Little Love* (Putnam)
Rosemary Harris, *Zed* (Faber & Faber)
Jamake Highwater, *Legend Days* (Harper/Zolotow)
Diana Wynne Jones, *Archer's Goon* (Greenwillow)
Kathryn Lasky, *Prank* (Macmillan)
Bernie Mackinnon, *The Meantime* (Houghton)
Michelle Magorian, *Back Home* (Harper/Zolotow)
Margaret Mahy, *The Changeover: A Supernatural Romance* (Atheneum)
Norma Fox Mazer, *Downtown* (Morrow; Avon/Flare [paper])
Gary Paulsen, *Tracker* (Bradbury)
Marilyn Sachs, *The Fat Girl* (Dutton)
William Sleator, *Interstellar Pig* (Dutton)
Ivan Southall, *The Long Night Watch* (Farrar)
Joyce Sweeny, *Center Line* (Delacorte)
Joyce Thompson, *Conscience Place* (Doubleday)
John Wain, *The Free Zone Starts Here* (Delacorte)
Jill Paton Walsh, *A Parcel of Patterns* (Farrar)
Robert Westall, *Futuretrack 5* (Greenwillow)
Jane Yolen, *Heart's Blood* (Delacorte)

NONFICTION

Brent Ashabranner, *To Live in Two Worlds: American Indian Youth Today,* (Dodd, Mead)
Jennings Michael Burch, *They Cage the Animals at Night,* (NAL)
Ted Conover, *Rolling Nowhere* (Viking)
Michael Crichton, *Electronic Life: How to Think about Computers* (Knopf)
William Dear, *Dungeon Master: The Disappearance of James Dallas Egbert III* (Houghton)
Gerald Durrell with **Lee Durrell,** *The Amateur Naturalist* (Knopf)
Jay Gale, *A Young Man's Guide to Sex* (Holt)
Gerri Hirshey, *Nowhere to Run: The Story of Soul Music* (Times Books)
Paul Janeczko, editor, *Strings: A Gathering of Family Poems* (Bradbury)
Hanna Kohner and **Walter Kohner,** *Hanna and Walter: A Love Story* (Random)
Bill Kurtis, *Bill Kurtis on Assignment* (Rand McNally)
William Manchester, *One Brief Shining Moment: Remembering Kennedy* (Little, Brown)
Frances McCullough, editor, *Love is like the Lion's Tooth* (Harper)
William D. Montalbano and **Carl Hiaasen,** *A Death in China* (Atheneum)
Eric W. Schirer, editor, *Newton at the Bat: The Science in Sports* (Scribner)
Neil Simon, *Brighton Beach Memoirs* (Random)
Dorothy Sterling, editor, *We Are Your Sisters: Black Women in the Nineteenth Century* (Norton)
Studs Terkel, *"The Good War": An Oral History of World War II* (Pantheon)
Wallace Terry, *Bloods: An Oral History of the Vietnam War by Black Veterans* (Random)
Bonnie Tiburzi, *Takeoff!* (Crown)
Alice Walker, *In Search of Our Mother's Garden: Womanist Prose* (HBJ)

Review of the Library Year

Abstracting and Indexing Services

Abstracting and indexing (A&I) services provide bibliographic aids in the form of references, subject terms, and brief descriptions that are used to identify, locate, and obtain access to published or unpublished documents or nonbibliographic materials. Specific areas of interest in 1984 for A&I (also called secondary) services were international cooperation and marketing, end-user searching, and personal computers. Continuing areas of interest were downloading, pricing, and full-text services.

International Cooperation. In 1984 the U.S. announced that it would drop membership in UNESCO (and with it, the support for UNESCO/PGI), which had been the focus of many international information programs. This pullout provided the impetus to the National Federation of Abstracting and Information Services (NFAIS) to support the founding of an Institute for International Information Programs, designed as a secretariat to arrange for U.S. representation in international organizations, to arrange delegate and study group exchanges with other countries, and to act as a vehicle to communicate interests between the U.S. and international organizations.

International cooperation was also facilitated in 1984 through exchanges and agreements between individual secondary services. The National Technical Information Service (NTIS) signed a new direct exchange protocol with the People's Republic of China (PRC) to promote a greater flow of scientific and technical information between the U.S. and the PRC. The National Agricultural Library (NAL) arranged a tour for a group of Chinese librarians of U.S. libraries and A&I services, including the NAL and the Institute for Scientific Information (ISI). The Centre de Documentation Scientifique and Technique (CDST) in Paris made an agreement with the Japan Information Centre for Science and Technology to set up offices at each other's headquarters with a view to exchanging technical information.

Marketing. Many secondary services further diversified their international marketing. Chemical Abstracts Service (CAS) set up a dedicated communication line from its Columbus headquarters to the Japan Association for International Chemical Information, so that Japanese users could have direct access to CAS online databases. The Derwent patent databases from the U.K., for 10 years exclusive on SDC, were being made available via the U.S.'s Dialog and France's Telesystemes–Questel. The National Library of Medicine's (NLM) MEDLINE was also being tested on Telesystemes–Questel. Mead Data Central, having marketed successfully in Europe and other countries for some time, opened an international headquarters office in London.

Other A&I services concentrated in 1984 on marketing information about foreign technologies to their U.S. customers. The American Institute of Aeronautics and Astronautics announced a monthly current awareness service covering Japanese and Soviet technical publications on several aerospace topics, while NTIS continued to identify reports on foreign technologies through their Office of International Affairs for acquisition into their database.

End User Searching and Personal Computers. In a study of online use patterns conducted in 1984, "personal computers" was the factor mentioned most often by database producers as likely to cause a future increase in database use.[1] New products from A&I services continue to be aimed at the end-user searcher who may have a personal computer.

Information Handling Services and BRS jointly began Tech Data Services, which gives access for engineers and scientists to 15 major technical and engineering databases using a simple interactive language. NLM's Toxicology Information Program began sponsoring an end-user training program for its chemical and toxicological files. NLM has also been testing a "user-friendly" version of MEDLINE. In 1984 two products designed for the end user were made compatible: BioSciences Information Services' (BIOSIS) Information Transfer Service (B-I-T-S), subsets of the BIOSIS database on microcomputer-readable disks, and the ISI's Sci-Mate software for online searching with personal computers. And BRS and W. B. Saunders announced a joint venture aimed at developing online information services, based on Saunders' publica-

25

tions, for medical end users.

NFAIS in July concluded an agreement with Telebase Systems, Inc., to sponsor an end-user-friendly search system called EASYNET. The agreement gives NFAIS member database producers the exclusive right to make their databases available through EASYNET and is designed to open up online access to A&I products and services for entirely new, and untrained, user groups.

Other Trends. Downloading became increasingly accepted as a valid information service, on which can be set a price. Following BIOSIS' lead, NLM provided subsets of its database (on tape or disk) for storage and reuse locally. INSPEC inaugurated a downloading policy for its database, and CAS modified its downloading policy to offer lower fees to low volume users. Pricing continued to be an area of experimentation, with CAS and Mead among the organizations to try out more complex database pricing formulas in 1984, depending less on connect time and more on online retrieval and other factors. Full-text databases continued to grow in quantity, but slowly. New in 1984 were BNA's information services, available through Mead's systems; Information Access Company's ASAP files of business and trade publications available on Dialog; and INVESTEXT, investment banking research reports, available on Dialog.

Among NFAIS member services for which statistics were compiled, coverage of the primary literature in 1984 grew approximately 3.4 percent.[2]

M. LYNNE NEUFELD

REFERENCES
1. M. Lynne Neufeld, "Status of Online Use: A Survey of Database Producers and Vendors" (presented at the International Online Information Meeting, London, December 4-6, 1984).
2. "NFAIS Member Service Statistics," *NFAIS Newsletter*, vol. 27, no. 1 (February 1985).

Academic Libraries

From among the opportunities as well as problems confronting academic libraries in the United States during 1984, this summary presents a brief review of events of the year. At the national level support for academic libraries remained low, and colleges and universities were preparing for further reductions in support as the pool of their principal clientele, college-age students, becomes smaller. Discouraging as these prospects may be, academic libraries sought new solutions to their problems; and here technology presented the most attractive possible solutions.

LEGISLATION

Higher Education Act. For a second year Congress did not appropriate funds for Title II-A, the College Library Resources Program, in the Higher Education Act. It did, however, allocate $6,000,000 for Title II-C, Strengthening Research Library Resources, with 35 grants made to 56 institutions. Three of these grants involved joint activities of several libraries, and 13 grants continued activities begun under earlier grants.

The Higher Education Act was to expire in 1985, and Congress began to consider its revision. The principal criticism of the unfunded Title II-A is that it supplies the same amount of money to all libraries making an application. In recent years the annual grants have been low. Although the act authorizes grants of $10,000, the last grants were for $840 each. The general belief is that such a program must be based on need. Although Congress took no action on reauthorization by year's end, the House Postsecondary Education Subcommittee in its consideration of Title II-A did propose some criteria that would make aid to college libraries based on need. The proposal mandates that the college retain maintenance of effort requirements and assure that it participates in resource sharing. Eligibility for the grants would then depend on two principal factors—the institution's support for the library at less than 2.8 percent of its education and general budget and a low per student expenditure as compared with other similar schools. Once eligibility is settled, the amount of the funding (with a suggested minimum award of $2,000) would be based on four additional criteria: the library's budget for or number of periodicals; low number of hours of opening with professional staff present; deficiencies in basic reference materials; and other factors that may be brought up by the institution.

Copyright. At its January meeting the Board of Directors of the Association of College and Research Libraries (ACRL) recommended that college and university libraries need not conform to the guidelines agreed to earlier by New York University. These guidelines were part of an out-of-court settlement in May 1983 following a suit brought against NYU by nine publishers for copyright violation. Through this action the ACRL Board seconded a similar resolution passed earlier by the Association of Research Libraries (ARL) Board.

The NYU agreement conforms essentially to the "Classroom Guidelines" earlier negotiated by primary and secondary school educators. The ACRL Board, together with other groups in higher education, considers these guidelines too restrictive and unsuitable for postsecondary education. Instead the ACRL Board holds that the 1982 ALA Model Policy Concerning College and University Photocopying for Classroom, Research, and Library Reserve Use is more suitable for academic institutions and that "colleges and universities and their libraries should continue to interpret the Copyright Act in a manner that is in the spirit of the law and consistent with the rights and needs of both copyright proprietors and the academic community."

In March ARL published a survey of its members on "Copyright Policies in ARL Libraries" (SPEC Flyer No. 102) indicating that the responding libraries do not follow uniform practices in interpreting the law; for example, many libraries consider their reserve room an extension of the classroom and thus subject to the same guidelines recommended for classroom copying. In interlibrary loan most libraries do observe the "CONTU Guidelines for the Proviso of Subsection 108(g)(2)" and the related ALA guidelines on record maintenance. Major differences are seen, however, in policies on copying nonprint materials, musical works, and archival items.

Looking at major trends and issues, ARL noted particularly the impact of new technology and the problems in use of optical or video disk storage for preservation purposes as related to copying copyrighted material.

LIBRARY ADMINISTRATION

Strategic Planning. Strategic planning was the subject of ARL's SPEC Flyer No. 108, issued in October. Based on a survey of 30 ARL member libraries, the report shows a number of plans under way, all of which possess certain strategic characteristics. Unlike earlier planning activities, strategic planning "is the deliberate attempt to concentrate resources in those areas which can make a substantial difference in future performance and capabilities." The report concludes that libraries undertaking such efforts become more activist and aggressive in presenting their case for "major new expenditures, shifts in programs, and effective use of available technology."

Library Leadership. Such efforts call for strong library leadership, and another ARL project in 1984 considered "The Assistant/Associate Director Position in ARL Libraries." Summarized in SPEC Flyer No. 103 (April 1984) and later released in a longer publication by Allen B. Veaner, the report observes that while hierarchical structures remain in academic libraries, other factors such as collaboration, collegiality, and personal motivation have become more important. There is the greater use of the associate and assistant director as a member of the senior management team in running the library and in strategic decision making. New technical skills increasingly are required at the top administrative levels.

The report notes that while many such positions are filled from the outside, libraries must also set up programs to allow staffs to advance. Michael E. D. Koenig and Herbert D. Safford in their *Library Journal* article ("Myths, Misconceptions and Management," October 15, 1984) argue that the principal problem in getting managers for academic libraries lies in vertical stratification in the libraries. Increasingly they see good candidates moving into other kinds of libraries and enterprises. Two misconceptions are at the root of this problem—inappropriate specialization and collegial management. They believe some problems can be solved if colleges and universities do not restrict their searches for managers to other academic institutions.

Continuing his own research on library directors (see *ALA Yearbook* 1984, p.41), Ronald Dale Karr in a *College & Research Libraries* article ("The Changing Profile of University Library Directors, 1966–1981," July 1984) compares the university library director of 1966 with the director of 1981. Even though middle-aged male graduates of liberal arts schools predominate, Karr observes changes in regions of origin, library education, other graduate degrees, and career patterns. He concludes that the competition for directorships has become greater because of the larger number of possible candidates.

AUTOMATION

Local Systems. Throughout 1984 individual libraries announced their adoption of various automated systems, possibly a turnkey system

Richard DeGennaro, Director of the University of Pennsylvania Libraries, and Susan Jacobson, Head of Cataloging, examining Harvard University's 1862 card catalog at an exhibit celebrating the University of Pennsylvania's 100th anniversary of its card catalog. The UP libraries are embarking on a five-year plan to convert the catalog to an online machine-readable form christened PennLIN. (Joseph Cigglia)

The Thomas P. O'Neill, Jr., Library at Boston College was dedicated in October and namesake and alumnus Speaker of the House O'Neill was the principal speaker. The library houses 700,000 volumes, nine classrooms, and a computer center. (Lee Pelligrine)

from a commercial vendor, like GEAC or DataPhase, or from a bibliographic network, like OCLC. Possibly it might even be locally developed.

The University of Tulsa entered into an agreement with Pennsylvania State University to use that university's Library Information Access System (LIAS) (*ALA Yearbook* 1984, p.38). Cornell University received a $1,500,000 grant from the J. N. Pew, Jr., Charitable Trust to install a computer-based integrated information system. The two-year project is to link 16 campus libraries into a single information network.

WEBNET, Inc., a network of small academic libraries in Pennsylvania, received a third grant from the Buhl Foundation of $186,570 to make its automated system operational. The four colleges particpating are Carlow, Chatham, Point Park, and Westminster.

The University of California reported its online catalog, MELVYL, up and running in a production version. The University is also building a private telecommunications network, with its campuses to be linked via satellite. Initially, 600 terminals were planned at various sites. One unexpected occurrence in March for MELVYL was a bomb threat communicated through the online catalog via the "comments" command provided for users' feedback. The threat was traced back to the UC San Diego campus, and the library was evacuated so that it could be searched.

Microcomputers. OCLC (Online Computer Library Center) introduced its new terminal early in 1984, a specially modified IBM Personal Computer called the M300 Workstation. When not used as a terminal communicating with OCLC, the M300 Workstation functions as a microcomputer able to handle most software developed for the IBM PC. OCLC also continued development of its Micro Enhancer systems so that libraries can access and use the large online database in Ohio at less cost.

The proliferation of microcomputers in academic libraries is possibly the most dramatic change in academic libraries in 1984. ARL SPEC Flyer No. 104, "Microcomputers in ARL Libraries" (May 1984), reported that in 1982 fewer than one-half of surveyed ARL libraries were using microcomputers. During 1984, 81 percent reported their use; 13 libraries were operating 10 or more microcomputers.

Susan K. Martin, Johns Hopkins University Library Director, writing in *Library Journal* ("New Technologies and Library Networks," June 15, 1984), held that central databases, like OCLC and RLIN, will continue as the source for cataloging and information for interlibrary loan, but she projected that most other functions will be moved to a local system—this fact made possible with the rise of smaller more powerful computers.

As microcomputers spread throughout li-

Top, The Walter Royal Davis Library, University of North Carolina at Chapel Hill, was built to house nearly 2,000,000 volumes. Middle, the Reading Room, and, bottom, the serials section of the Reading Room. (Library Photographic Service UofNC at Chapel Hill)

braries, staff training in their use has been on an ad hoc basis and often limited to those individuals immediately involved in their use. ARL SPEC Flyer No. 109, "Staff Training for Automation in ARL Libraries" (November/December 1984), concluded that such training should be fully integrated into a library's staff development program, with programs reviewed on a regular basis to ensure they will meet the library's changing needs.

NETWORKING

OCLC. OCLC observed its 13th anniversary in August and reported that each day more than 3,800 users catalog approximately 100,000 titles and 500,000 catalog cards are printed. In July OCLC added the 11,000,000th record to its online union catalog. The network also offered its local integrated system (LS/2000) to libraries, introduced the M300 Workstation, and developed Micro Enhancer systems to make OCLC use more cost effective.

The basis for most of the content of the OCLC database consists of cataloging from member libraries. Quality of the data input and ways in which members use the database remain matters for concern. Thus to provide a basic set of guidelines for members, the OCLC Users Council issued a Code of Responsible Use for the Online Union Catalog.

Although a number of member libraries continued to express their concern about OCLC's December 1982 decision to copyright the database, the Copyright Office did register OCLC's claim in 1984.

Telecommunications charges are still not resolved, but a major blow to OCLC was the Ohio Supreme Court decision upholding an earlier court ruling that OCLC is liable for property taxes. OCLC planned to ask for legislative relief from this new burden. Although it did not intend to cancel its $40,000,000 capital expenditure plans, it announced it might relocate its computer installation in another state or distribute its computer network through a restructuring of the organization.

The State University of New York's SUNY/OCLC network continued for a second year its "Solid Service," using Purolator trucks to deliver interlibrary loan materials among member libraries. On an experimental basis the network expanded the service to include libraries in Pennsylvania.

RLIN. The Research Libraries Information Network (RLIN) was to employ in 1984 a small grant received by the Research Libraries Group (RLG) from the Sherman Fairchild Foundation for a one-year test employing telefacsimile equipment for interlibrary loan among six member libraries.

Electronic Mail. Electronic mail continued to emerge as a new method for interlibrary communication. A 1984 survey among ARL libraries reported 43 percent of the responding libraries

The Hawthorne-Longfellow Library, Bowdoin College, Brunswick, Maine, was remodeled and renovated and joined by a skylit link to the underground stacks of Hubbard Hall. (© Nick Wheeler)

use some form of electronic mail. SPEC Flyer No. 106, "Electronic Mail in ARL Libraries" (July/August 1984), pointed out the variety of uses libraries are finding for electronic mail but noted too the increased demands that may be placed on library staffs and facilities as well as the related communication costs. As electronic mail changes into electronic publishing, libraries may also encounter new problems with copyright.

SERVICES

Extended Service. The 1982 ACRL "Guidelines for Extended Campus Library Services" served as a tool for the University of Wyoming in its program to serve off-campus students as well as to set up satellite libraries in other parts of the state. Jean S. Johnson reported on that university library's work in the February 1984 *College & Research Libraries News*.

Academic Reference Librarians. Commenting on academic library reference service, Charles A. Bunge, University of Wisconsin–Madison Library School, reported in the *Journal of Academic Librarianship* ("Potential and Reality at the Reference Desk: Reflections on a 'Return to the Field,'" July 1984) on widespread low morale among academic reference librarians. The condition results, he observed, from the gap between the expectations librarians bring to the job and the realities of what they actually can do, given the various constraints they face. The librarians demonstrate, to Bunge, some of the symptoms of "burnout" noted in other service professions. Responding to Bunge in the same issue of the journal, Nathan M. Smith, Brigham Young University Library School, commented on his own studies of burnout among reference librarians in academic, special, and public libraries. Level of burnout differed in his various surveys, and it seems to vary according to the survey instrument used. Smith concluded, however, that regardless of kind of library "unhappiness and low morale are fairly pervasive among reference librarians."

Database Searching. The *Chronicle of Higher Education* (September 19, 1984) presented a feature on database searching in academic libraries. As is true for electronic mail, libraries experience increased costs with an increase of the use of these services. When the State University of New York at Albany, an early leader in offering this service, instituted database searching in 1972, it had no charges. During 1984 it charged users 30 percent of the cost plus printing charges. Suzanne H. Gallup, University of California, Berkeley, reported the UC Berkeley Library passes on charges for a specialized search, employing the rationale that "it is tailor-made for someone . . . not like a book, which we buy for everyone to use."

SUNY Albany Librarian Sara D. Knapp noted that scholars subsidized by grants spend an average of $27 per search while students with no outside funding spend an average of $5. Knapp expressed her desire for the availability of "pizza-priced" searches—under $5—for students. Shirley Echelman, ARL Executive Director, commented that with information available on the computer we receive a detailed record of who has used the data and for how long. "Because we can count, we can charge. This has serious societal implications. It could result in an information elite."

Some bargain services are now available at off-peak hours, for example, the After Dark program from BRS. Such a service is a do-it-yourself operation, and Knapp said many people are frightened of it. The trained librarian-searcher as an intermediary in a machine search can keep costs down. James C. Andrews, Rensselaer Polytechnic Institute Library Director, stated that it "takes only one attempt to convince a researcher that using someone trained in computer searches will save time and money—and make the results more valid."

One low-priced search service for undergraduate students is the Quicksearch program at Cornell University's Mann Library. Described in the July 1984 *Journal of Academic Librarianship*, the Quicksearch service is performed on a walk-in basis with students charged a $5 fee per search. The library absorbs costs not covered in the charge. Following the first year of the service, Mann Library reported that searches for undergraduates rose from 8.6 percent to 17.59 percent of the total number of searches conducted in that library.

Although most search services concentrate on bibliographic databases, some libraries also have nonbibliographic machine-readable databases, for example, U.S. Census tapes. ARL SPEC Flyer No. 105 (June 1984) surveyed use of such databases. Most of the libraries offering such databases secure them through online vendors. A few libraries have acquired their own. Such databases require trained staff as well as cooperation with the campus computer center. Because the information can be highly specialized, both the user and the librarian may need a training program to use the database properly.

Bibliographic Instruction. Carolyn Kirkendall concluded her service to ACRL as Manager of the Bibliographic Instruction Liaison Project, which was set up to publicize bibliographic instruction to other professional associations. (This work will be continued through the ACRL headquarters office.) As a continuing guide to librarians, the ACRL/BIS Cooperation Committee published a "tip sheet" in the May 1984 *College & Research Libraries News* on techniques to employ to promote libraries and bibliographic instruction through associations representing other subject disciplines.

Although bibliographic instruction has focused primarily on students, a committee in ACRL's Education and Behavioral Sciences Section looked to the needs of college administrators and support staff for library instruction. The committee published its tip sheet on how to reach this campus group in the November 1984 *College & Research Libraries News*.

COLLECTIONS

Collections v. Access. "The emphasis in libraries is shifting from collections to access." These words of University of Pennsylvania Library Director Richard DeGennaro in *Library Journal* ("Shifting Gears: Information Technology and the Academic Library," June 15, 1984) describe the new realities academic

The John Crerar Library moved from Chicago's Illinois Institute of Technology to this new structure on the University of Chicago campus in November. (Jim Wright)

librarians face as they respond to lower funding by sharing resources.

Coupled with this recognition is the fact that many libraries lack space in their present buildings for their growing collections. At the present time, for example, the University of California libraries are adding 650,000 volumes each year—requiring the annual addition of 12 miles of shelving. To handle this situation, the University has decided to rely upon compact shelving in off-campus buildings. There are to be two storage libraries in the state—one in Richmond to serve the northern campuses and a second on the Los Angeles campus for the southern area. Each campus is to deposit a basic number of volumes and then add a given number each year. Once the two regional centers are built, individual campus needs for library facilities will be addressed. The Davis campus, particularly in need of a new library because of grave space problems, is to deposit 400,000 volumes initially in the Richmond storage library and then add 25,000 volumes each year. Reluctant to part with so much of its collection and yet lacking space to house it, the campus faced state objections when it wanted to proceed with planning for a new library building without making the deposits. The resulting dispute made for lively comments in the library press.

In Pennsylvania a much smaller library, at Westminster College in New Wilmington, also faced a similar space problem. With a grant of $151,000 from the Buhl Foundation, the College announced it would develop the concept of a static-capacity library. It proposes to use computer facilities to assist it in managing its library collections in such a way that a new library or an addition will not be needed. Steps included in the Westminster plan are the full use of all remaining library space, conversion of some materials to microform, use of mechanized compact shelving, and increased staff to assist in reviewing use of materials. As a final step during the next decade, the college may transfer some materials to a remote storage area and withdraw others.

Security. ARL's survey of its members on "Collection Security in ARL Libraries" (SPEC Flyer No. 100, January 1984) updated a similar survey from 1977. It reported few changes since that earlier survey. Of the 89 responding libraries, only 13 libraries had written security policies. Academic libraries rely most heavily on electronic security systems (with 78 of the libraries marking their general collections), and some may have separate regulations for their special collections and rare book areas. Most policies emphasize, however, what to do about a theft after it occurs.

Writing in *College & Research Libraries News*, June 1984, University of California Librarian Peter E. Hanff gave a useful account of a major theft from that library and how apprehension of the thief was achieved through cooperation from several San Francisco area book dealers.

The role of the outside thief has received widespread national attention in the library press, particularly following the coast-to-coast activities of James R. Shinn (*ALA Yearbook* 1983, pp. 2-3, 249). But as emphasized at the 1983 Oberlin conference on library security, many library thefts are inside jobs. In October James B. Alsip, former Library Director at George Washington University, Washington, D.C., and earlier a principal library administrator at the University of Oklahoma, pleaded guilty in a federal court to the charge of transporting interstate 175 books stolen from the University of Oklahoma Library. This charge arose following an investigation of what had happened to some $70,000 in George Washington University book orders that were never delivered—the money, it was found, had been deposited in Alsip's bank account.

BUILDINGS

The *Library Journal* survey (December 1984) of libraries built in 1983-84 reported 12 new academic library buildings and 14 additions and renovations. As in 1983, additions and renovations counted for more than 50 percent of new building activity.

Major new buildings of 1984 include:

The Thomas P. O'Neill, Jr., Library at Boston College, a $28,000,000 project with shelving for 1,000,000 volumes and seating for 1,150 readers;

Walter Royal Davis Library, University of North Carolina at Chapel Hill, a $22,396,718 project with shelving for 1,800,000 volumes and seating for 3,013 readers;

Drexel University library, Philadelphia, with a cost of $10,338,188, shelving for 350,000 volumes, and seating for 1,250 readers;

and Southern University library, Baton Rouge, Louisiana, with a cost of $10,000,000, book capacity of 1,500,000 volumes, and seating for 2,100 readers.

Academic Libraries

The John Crerar Library, a private science library, formerly at the Illinois Institute of Technology in Chicago and serving that institution through a special agreement, moved to the University of Chicago and opened in a new structure. It now serves as a central science library for the University.

David Kaser reviewed "Twenty-Five Years of Academic Library Building Planning" (*College & Research Libraries*, July 1984), and the problem areas he named in college and university library architecture are old problems that have simply gotten out of hand: irregular building shapes, interior and exterior courts, monumentality, and too much or too little glass. Kaser concluded that it is understandable why librarians believe they are getting fewer satisfactory buildings than they were a generation ago.

PERSONNEL ISSUES

Placements and Salaries. The 1984 *Library Journal* survey of library placements and salaries for 1983 library school graduates recorded a continuing downward trend, with minor annual variations, for placements in academic libraries—23.8 percent of the total. Increases were recorded for special libraries and other information specialties.

The survey reported an average beginning salary in 1983 of $16,545 for academic librarians ($16,178 for women, $17,327 for men), up from a $15,017 average in 1982. Academic library salaries continued to lag behind the overall 1983 average $17,705. (*See further* Personnel and Employment: Compensation; Women in Librarianship.)

University of California. The University of California concluded a first contract with the University Federation of Librarians for its librarians—a two-year agreement that recognizes librarians as academic employees, not staff, and provides an earmarked professional development fund. In a perhaps unprecedented action, a separate memorandum of understanding between the university and the union recognized the role of the Librarians Association of the University of California (LAUC) in dealing with professional and governance concerns of librarians.

University of Minnesota. As reported in the 1984 *ALA Yearbook* (p. 40), a sex discrimination charge was resolved at the University of Minnesota on behalf of 37 women librarians. The case was filed under provision of the Rajender consent decree, and in 1984 Linda de Beau Melting, a university librarian, benefited from that same decree in a court case that awarded her tenure, previously denied by the university. Even so, the university terminated her employment, pending an appeal to the U.S. District Court.

Faculty Status. A disheartening note to the issue of faculty status for academic librarians was contained in Thomas G. English's survey of academic administrators, reported in *College & Research Libraries* ("Administrators' Views of Faculty Status," May 1984). Conclusions of the survey were that administrators feel there is, at present at least, no substantive advantage to an institution's granting faculty status to its librarians and that the terms and conditions of faculty appointments are largely unsuited to the daily activities and responsibilities of academic librarians.

APPOINTMENTS AND AWARDS

Included among the individuals selected during 1984 to direct U.S. college and university libraries were the following:

In the East: Millicent D. Abell, Yale University, New Haven, Connecticut; Alan Benenfield, Northeastern University, Boston; Stanton F. Biddle, Baruch College, City University of New York; Daniel Davila, Queensborough Community College, City University of New York; David H. Eyman, Skidmore College, Saratoga Springs, New York; David Gillespie, Frostburg State College, Maryland; Mary Ann Griffin, Villanova University, Pennsylvania; B. Donald Grose, University of Massachusetts, Boston; Jean Walstrom Haley, La Salle University, Philadelphia; Nancy L. Herron, McKeesport Campus, Pennsylvania State University; Dorothy M. Kijanka, Sacred Heart University, Bridgeport, Connecticut; P. Robert Paustian, Wilkes College, Wilkes-Barre, Pennsylvania; Sharon J. Rogers, George Washington University, Washington, D.C.; Larry E. Sullivan, Herbert H. Lehman College, City University of New York; Richard T. Sweeney, Polytechnic Institute of New York, Brooklyn; and Sidney Verba, Harvard University.

In the South: Nancy M. Adams, College of Boca Raton, Florida; J. Wayne Baker, Florida Junior College, Jacksonville; Wendell A. Barbour, Christopher Newport College, Newport News, Virginia; Dale B. Canelas, University of Florida, Gainesville; Oakley Herman Coburn, Wofford College, Spartanburg, South Carolina; Miriam A. Drake, Georgia Institute of Technology, Atlanta; Malcolm Getz, Vaderbilt University, Nashville, Tennessee; Sharon A. Hogan, Louisiana State University, Baton Rouge; and Elaine E. Wiltse, University of Southern Mississippi, Gulf Coast Regional Campus, Long Beach.

In the Midwest: Doris R. Brown, DePaul University, Chicago; Bob Carmack, University of Wisconsin–Superior; Mary J. Cronin, Loyola University of Chicago; D. Kaye Gapen, University of Wisconsin–Madison; David Phillip Jensen, Hope College, Holland, Michigan; Janet S. Kenney, College of St. Catherine, St. Paul, Minnesota; John P. Kondelik, Butler University, Indianapolis, Indiana; John M. Meador, Jr., Southwest Missouri State University, Springfield; Imre Meszaros, Wittenberg University, Springfield, Ohio; Thomas M. Peischl, Mankato State University, Minnesota; Henry Stewart, Emporia State University, Kansas; Stuart A. Stiffler, Kentucky Wesleyan College, Owensboro; Don L. Tolliver, Kent State University, Ohio; and Paula N. Warnken, Xavier University, Cincinnati.

In the West: John K. Amrhein, California State College, Stanislaus, Turlock; Melvin R. George, Oregon State University, Corvallis; Rodney M. Hersberger, California State College, Bakersfield; Kathy McGreevy, Mendocino College, Ukiah, California; Larry R. Oberg, Lewis–Clark State College, Lewiston, Idaho; Charles R. Ritcheson, University of Southern California, Los Angeles; Jordan Scepanski, California State University, Long Beach; Alan Edward Schorr, California State University, Fullerton; Judith Sessions, California State University, Chico; and John Sheridan, Colorado College, Colorado Springs. The University of California appointed Michael K. Buckland as Assistant Vice-President for Library Plans and Policies.

There were also major changes at ALA's Association of College and Research Libraries. JoAn S. Segal succeeded Julie A. Carroll Virgo as Executive Director, and Patricia E. Sabosik followed Rebecca D. Dixon as Editor and Publisher of *Choice*. Charles R. Martell was appointed Editor of *College & Research Libraries*, succeeding C. James Schmidt.

ACRL introduced a new award in 1984, the Miriam Dudley Bibliographic Instruction Librarian of the Year Award. Thomas Kirk, Berea College in Kentucky, was named as its first recipient. Richard D. Johnson, State University of New York, College at Oneonta, received the Academic/Research Librarian of the Year award.

CONCLUSION

Patricia Battin's vision of the future, her description of "The Electronic Library," serves as an appropriate conclusion to this year's review of academic libraries. Battin, Columbia University Library Director, shared her vision in an April Columbia University address (subsequently published in the *EDUCOM Bulletin*, Summer 1984). Acknowledging that libraries have been at the center of the research process in universities for the past century, she now looks to the rise of the "university Scholarly Information Center," which will combine the library and the computer center. The cliché of the library as the heart of the university must be abandoned. It is time to select a new image, and she chose DNA. "As the genetic code of the University, the character and quality of the Scholarly Information Center will determine the character and quality of the institution."

RICHARD D. JOHNSON

Accreditation

Accreditation Project. January 1984 saw the addition of a new activity for the ALA Committee on Accreditation (COA). At the ALA Midwinter Meeting the COA approved the final draft of a proposal, developed by Robert Hayes, COA Chair, for an 18-month project to explore ways to involve a variety of associations in the ALA accreditation process. The proposal, forwarded to the U.S. Department of Education, was subsequently funded under Title II–B of the Higher Education Act.

As the body formally recognized by the Council on Postsecondary Accreditation (COPA) and the U.S. Secretary of Education, ALA has the responsibility for the review and accreditation of programs leading to the first professional degree in library and information science. With the many changes occurring in the profession nationally and internationally, the COA believes that this is an opportune time to involve in the accreditation process other societies concerned with the quality of these educational programs.

The purpose of the project is to explore procedures and guidelines for the participation of a variety of associations in the accreditation process for which ALA has the responsibility. The project will also serve to identify the interests of participating societies and will result in specific recommendations to further the involvement of these societies. The project has two main objectives. The first is to develop recommended procedures and guidelines providing a basis for the participation of concerned societies. Such arrangements include financial responsibilities, administration, and policy determination. The second objective is to examine the 1972 ALA *Standards for Accreditation* to determine how they do, or do not, meet the concerns of the several organizations.

Eight major national societies were formally invited to participate in the project, and other relevant societies have been informed of the project and encouraged to participate by identifying observers to working sessions of the project. Each participating society was asked to nominate a person to serve as a member of the project Steering Committee that will coordinate the work of the project and be responsible for submission of a Final Report. Societies were also asked to appoint representatives for a set of six Working Groups, each focused on a specific set of issues: organization of the accreditation process; finance of the accreditation process; guidelines for program goals and objectives; guidelines for faculty; guidelines for curriculum; and guidelines for society-specific objectives. The Steering Committee and the six Working Groups were scheduled to convene and initiate their discussions in January 1985. A plenary session of the COA was planned for the ALA 1985 Midwinter Meeting for the purpose of presenting the results of the first group of meetings.

Ongoing Activities. COA received and accepted 11 self-study reports from library schools in application for site visits to evaluate the master's program for continuing ALA accreditation, and formally scheduled site visits to the applicant schools in the spring and fall of 1984. An additional site visit was conducted to a program that had undergone major changes in 1983. The COA also held four formal conferences with library schools to receive additional information regarding the annual report or to hear reports of progress toward improvement of the library education program. Accreditation actions were taken by COA to continue the accredited status of nine master's programs and to withdraw accredited status from one program.

Fifty-eight annual reports from ALA-accredited programs were reviewed by COA at its 1984 fall meeting. Nine other accredited programs had been released from the annual report since self-study reports from these programs were to be reviewed in January 1985 as applications for spring 1985 site visits, or the programs were visited by COA in fall 1984. Readers on COA review each annual report in terms of the most recent COA report made to the school subsequent to a site visit and in reference to preceding annual reports made by the school. Programs are asked to report on all COA recommendations made in the final report at each annual reporting

Graduate Library Education Programs Accredited by the American Library Association under Standards for Accreditation, 1972

(Accredited programs are revisited periodically for evaluation purposes. The date in parentheses indicates the next scheduled evaluation visit.)
(October 1984)

NORTHEAST

[1]**Catholic University of America,** *Master of Science in Library Science*
School of Library and Information Science, Washington, D.C. 20064 Raymond F. Vondran, Dean (1990)

[1]**Clarion University,** *Master of Science in Library Science*
College of Library Science, Clarion, Pennsylvania 16214 Elizabeth A. Rupert, Dean (1988)

[1,2]**Columbia University,** *Master of Science*
School of Library Service, New York, New York 10027 R. Kathleen Molz, Acting Dean (1991)

[1,2]**Drexel University,** *Master of Science*
College of Information Studies, Philadelphia, Pennsylvania 19104 Guy Garrison, Dean (1990)

[1]**Long Island University,** *Master of Science in Library Science*
Palmer School of Library and Information Science, Greenvale, New York 11548 Lucienne G. Maillet, Dean (1990)

[2]**University of Maryland,** *Master of Library Science*
College of Library and Information Services, College Park, Maryland 20742 Claude E. Walston, Dean (1984)

[1]**State University of New York, Albany,** *Master of Library Science*
School of Library and Information Science, Albany, New York 12222 Richard S. Halsey, Dean (1990)

[1,2]**State University of New York at Buffalo,** *Master of Library Science*
School of Information and Library Studies, Buffalo, New York 14260 George S. Bobinski, Dean (1991)

[1,2]**University of Pittsburgh,** *Master of Library Science*
School of Library and Information Science, Pittsburgh, Pennsylvania 15260 Thomas J. Galvin, Dean (1984)

[1]**Pratt Institute,** *Master of Science*
Graduate School of Library and Information Science, Brooklyn, New York 11205 Nasser Sharify, Dean (1984)

[1,4]**Queens College, City University of New York,** *Master of Library Science*
Graduate School of Library and Information Studies, Flushing, New York 11367 Thomas T. Surprenant, Director

[1]**University of Rhode Island,** *Master of Library and Information Studies*
Graduate School of Library and Information Studies, Kingston, Rhode Island 02881 Lucy V. Salvatore, Acting Dean (1985)

[1,2]**Rutgers University,** *Master of Library Service*
School of Communication, Information and Library Studies, New Brunswick, New Jersey 08903 James D. Anderson, Chairperson (1988)

[1]**St. John's University,** *Master of Library Science*
Division of Library and Information Science, Jamaica, New York 11439 Mildred Lowe, Director (1989)

[2]**Simmons College,** *Master of Science*
Graduate School of Library and Information Science, Boston, Massachusetts 02115 Robert D. Stueart, Dean (1991)

[1]**Southern Connecticut State University,** *Master of Library Science*
School of Library Science and Instructional Technology, New Haven, Connecticut 06515 Rocco Orlando, Acting Dean (1988)

[1,2]**Syracuse University,** *Master of Library Science*
School of Information Studies, Syracuse, New York 13210 Evelyn H. Daniel, Dean (1989)

SOUTHEAST

[1]**University of Alabama,** *Master of Library Service*
Graduate School of Library Service, University, Alabama 35486 James D. Ramer, Dean (1986)

[1]**Atlanta University,** *Master of Science in Library Service*
School of Library and Information Studies, Atlanta, Georgia 30314 Lorene B. Brown, Dean (1987)

Emory University, *Master of Arts; Master of Librarianship*
Division of Library and Information Management, Atlanta, Georgia 30322 A. Venable Lawson, Director (1987)

[1,2]**Florida State University,** *Master of Science; Master of Arts*
School of Library and Information Studies, Tallahassee, Florida 32306 Harold Goldstein, Dean (1988)

University of Kentucky, *Master of Science in Library Science; Master of Arts*
College of Library and Information Science, Lexington, Kentucky 40506-0027 Timothy W. Sineath, Dean (1989)

Louisiana State University, *Master of Library Science*
School of Library and Information Science, Baton Rouge, Louisiana 70803, Kathleen M. Heim, Dean (1986)

[3]**University of Mississippi,** *Master of Library Science*
Graduate School of Library and Information Science, University, Mississippi 38677 Steven B. Schoenly, Acting Director

[2]**University of North Carolina,** *Master of Science in Library Science*
School of Library Science, Chapel Hill, North Carolina 27514 Edward G. Holley, Dean (1985)

University of North Carolina at Greensboro, *Master of Library Science*
Department of Library Science/Educational Technology, Greensboro, North Carolina 27412 Kieth C. Wright, Chair (1988)

North Carolina Central University, *Master of Library Science*
School of Library Science, Durham, North Carolina 27707 Benjamin F. Speller, Acting Dean (1988)

[1]**University of South Carolina,** *Master of Librarianship*
College of Library and Information Science, Columbia, South Carolina 29208 F. William Summers, Dean (1986)

[1]**University of South Florida,** *Master of Arts*
Graduate Department of Library, Media and Information Studies, Tampa, Florida 33620 John A. McCrossan, Chairperson (1987)

University of Southern Mississippi, *Master of Library Science*
School of Library Service, Hattiesburg, Mississippi 39406 Onva K. Boshears, Jr., Dean (1987)

University of Tennessee, Knoxville, *Master of Science in Library Science*
Graduate School of Library and Information Science, Knoxville, Tennessee 37996-4330 Ann E. Prentice, Director (1986)

[1]**Vanderbilt University, George Peabody College for Teachers,** *Master of Library Science*
Department of Library and Information Science, Nashville, Tennessee 37203 Edwin S. Gleaves, Chair (1988)

MIDWEST

Ball State University, *Master of Library Science*
Department of Library and Information Science, Muncie, Indiana 47306 Ray R. Suput, Chair

[2,3]**Case Western Reserve University,** *Master of Science in Library Science*
Matthew A. Baxter School of Information and Library Science, Cleveland, Ohio 44106 Sarah S. Gibson, Executive Officer

[1,2]**University of Chicago,** *Master of Arts*
Graduate Library School, Chicago, Illinois 60637 W. Boyd Rayward, Dean (1991)

[1,2]**University of Illinois,** *Master of Science*
Graduate School of Library and Information Science, 1407 West Gregory, 410 DKH, Urbana, Illinois 61801 Charles H. Davis, Dean (1989)

[1,2]**Indiana University,** *Master of Library Science*
School of Library and Information Science, Bloomington, Indiana 47405 Herbert S. White, Dean (1985)

University of Iowa, *Master of Arts*
School of Library and Information Science, Iowa City, Iowa 52242 Carl F. Orgren, Director (1986)

[1]**Kent State University,** *Master of Library Science*
School of Library Science, Kent, Ohio 44242 A. Robert Rogers, Dean (1990)

[2]**University of Michigan,** *Master of Arts in Library Science*
School of Library Science, Ann Arbor, Michigan 48109-1346 Richard M. Dougherty, Acting Dean (1990)

[1,2,3]**University of Minnesota,** *Master of Arts*
Library School, 117 Pleasant Street, S.E., Minneapolis, Minnesota 55455 George D'Elia, Director

University of Missouri, Columbia, *Master of Arts*
School of Library and Informational Science, Columbia, Missouri 65211, Mary F. Lenox, Dean (1989)

Northern Illinois University, *Master of Arts*
Department of Library Science, DeKalb, Illinois 60115 Cosette N. Kies, Chair (1989)

[1]**Rosary College,** *Master of Arts in Library and Information Science*
Graduate School of Library and Information

Science, River Forest, Illinois 60305 Richard Tze-chung Li, Dean (1989)

[1]**Wayne State University,** *Master of Science in Library Science*
Division of Library Science, Detroit, Michigan 48202 Edith B. Phillips, Director

[1,2]**University of Wisconsin–Madison,** *Master of Arts*
School of Library and Information Studies, Madison, Wisconsin 53706 Jane B. Robbins-Carter, Director (1985)

[1]**University of Wisconsin–Milwaukee,** *Master of Library Science*
School of Library and Information Science, Milwaukee, Wisconsin 53201 Mohammed M. Aman, Dean (1989)

SOUTHWEST

University of Arizona, *Master of Library Science*
Graduate Library School, Tucson, Arizona 85719 Margaret Maxwell, Acting Director (1986)

[1,2]**North Texas State University,** *Master of Science*
School of Library and Information Sciences, Denton, Texas 76203 Dewey E. Carroll, Dean (1991)

[1]**University of Oklahoma,** *Master of Library Science*
School of Library Science, Norman, Oklahoma 73019 Sylvia G. Faibisoff, Director (1985)

[1,2]**University of Texas at Austin,** *Master of Library and Information Science*
Graduate School of Library and Information Science, Austin, Texas 78712-1276 Ronald E. Wyllys, Dean (1985)

[1,2]**Texas Woman's University,** *Master of Arts; Master of Library Science*
School of Library Science, Denton, Texas 76204 Brooke E. Sheldon, Dean (1988)

WEST

Brigham Young University, *Master of Library Science*
School of Library and Information Sciences, Provo, Utah 84602 Nathan M. Smith, Director (1988)

[1,2]**University of California, Berkeley,** *Master of Library and Information Studies*
School of Library and Information Studies, Berkeley, California 94720 Robert D. Harlan, Acting Dean (1988)

[1,2]**University of California, Los Angeles,** *Master of Library Science*
Graduate School of Library and Information Science, Los Angeles, California 90024 Robert M. Hayes, Dean (1989)

[1]**University of Denver,** *Master of Arts in Librarianship; Master of Law Librarianship*
Graduate School of Librarianship and Information Management, Denver, Colorado 80208 Bernard M. Franckowiak, Dean

University of Hawaii, *Master of Library Studies*
Graduate School of Library Studies, Honolulu, Hawaii 96822 Miles M. Jackson, Dean (1986)

San Jose State University, *Master of Library Science*
Division of Library Science, San Jose, California 95192 Robert E. Wagers, Interim Director (1985)

[2,3]**University of Southern California,** *Master of Science in Library Science*
School of Library and Information Management, Los Angeles, California 90089-0031 Roger C. Greer, Dean

University of Washington, *Master of Librarianship*
Graduate School of Library and Information Science, Seattle, Washington 98195 Margaret Chisholm, Director (1991)

CANADA

University of Alberta, *Master of Library Science*
Faculty of Library Science, Edmonton, Alberta T6G 2J4 John G. Wright, Dean (1985)

University of British Columbia, *Master of Library Science*
School of Library, Archival and Information Studies, Vancouver, B.C. V6T 1W5 Basil Stuart-Stubbs, Director (1984)

Dalhousie University, *Master of Library Service*
School of Library Service, Halifax, Nova Scotia B3H 4H8 Norman Horrocks, Director (1990)

McGill University, *Master of Library Science*
Graduate School of Library Science, Montreal, Quebec H3A 1Y1 Helen Howard, Director (1987)

Université de Montréal, *Maîtrise en bibliothéconomie*
Ecole de bibliothéconomie, Montréal, Québec H3C 3J7 Richard K. Gardner, Directeur (1985)

[2]**University of Toronto,** *Master of Library Science*
Faculty of Library and Information Science, Toronto, Ontario M5S 1A1 Ann H. Schabas, Dean (1987)

[2]**University of Western Ontario,** *Master of Library Science*
School of Library and Information Science, London, Ontario N6G 1H1 Jean M. Tague, Dean (1989)

[1]Offers post-Master's specialist or certificate program. (The ALA does not accredit post-Master's specialist or certificate programs.)
[2]Offers program for Doctoral degree. (The ALA does not accredit programs leading to the Doctoral degree.)
[3]Admitting no new students.
[4]Conditionally accredited June 1983 for a period of two years.

---

period until released from so doing by COA.

COA may also have raised concerns about information in previous annual reports, and schools are asked to respond directly to these comments also. Based on the annual report, the COA takes one of three actions: (1) accepts the report, with or without comment, and continues the program's accredited status; (2) defers action on the report until additional information is supplied through documentation or in conference with a COA subcommittee; or (3) declines to accept the report and arranges to schedule a site visit to the program at the earliest possible date. At the 1984 fall meeting, the COA accepted the report and continued the accreditation of the master's program for 53 schools, with comments being returned to all of them; deferred action on four reports pending receipt of additional information; and requested that university and library school representatives of another school confer with COA at the 1985 Midwinter Meeting regarding the current status of the master's program.

The library school at the University of Mississippi closed in December 1984. Four other library schools with ALA-accredited programs (Ball State University, Case Western Reserve University, University of Denver, and the University of Minnesota) announced that they would close in 1985. A sixth ALA-accredited program at the University of Southern California is scheduled for closing in 1986. In circumstances such as these, COA monitors the annual reports of these programs with special care, and with particular reference to the ability of students enrolled in the program prior to the announcement of the closing of the program to complete their planned programs of study with appropriate faculty and resources. Interim reports from these programs are also requested to allow COA to review the continued accreditability of the programs during the phase-out period.

Orientation of Site Visiting Team Members. The librarians and library educators who serve on COA visiting teams to evaluate master's programs are crucial to the accreditation process—they serve as the eyes and ears of COA as they visit library education programs on site. Although the COA *Manual of Procedures* specifies in detail the areas to be covered and the individuals to be interviewed on the site visit, COA annually provides a training session for site visitors who will be making their first site visits in the following academic year. The training sessions focus on such things as how to use the sources of evidence specified in the *Standards for Accreditation*, writing the visiting team report, interviewing techniques, due process, and the like.

Over the past several years, a variety of teach-

Adults, Library Service to

ing tools have been developed by COA: sample team reports, projected materials, a series of hypothetical team recommendations for discussion and analysis, and several role-playing situations. A videotape, developed and produced by Margaret Kimmel at the University of Pittsburgh School of Library and Information Science, was introduced in 1984. Trainee site visitors are asked to view one of three segments presenting a typical interviewing situation during a site visit, and then analyze and discuss the presentation for criticism by the entire group.

Two training sessions were held in 1984: a special session, before Canadian Library Association meetings in Toronto in June, for 14 new Canadian site visitors and the annual session at the ALA Annual Conference in Dallas, which trained ten other new site visitors and four new incoming COA members for 1984–85.

Continuing Recognition by COPA. In late 1982, the COA was notified by the Council on Postsecondary Accreditation (COPA) of the approach of the periodic review by COPA for the purpose of continuing ALA's recognition as a nationally recognized accrediting body for the first professional degree program in librarianship. The petition for recognition materials was prepared in early 1983 and submitted to COPA for review. A hearing on the petition was conducted in October 1983, subsequent to which the COPA Committee on Recognition forwarded its recommendation on the ALA petition to the COPA Executive Board, which in turn took final action on the matter in April 1984. ALA was granted full recognition, without condition, for the maximum five-year period allowable.

COA Members. With the conclusion of the 1984 Annual Conference, Edwin M. Cortez, Philip H. Ennis, Lee Putnam, Bernard S. Schlessinger, and Miriam H. Tees retired from the COA. New appointments to the COA for 1984–85 were Elizabeth Boris, Robert Croneberger, Gwendolyn S. Cruzat, Margot McBurney, and James W. Scheu. Continuing members of the COA for 1984–85 were Dennis D. Goetsch, Alice B. Ihrig, Margaret M. Kimmel, Elizabeth Martinez Smith, Herman L. Totten, and Robert M. Hayes, Chair.

ELINOR YUNGMEYER

Adults, Library Service to

Alliance for Excellence. The centrality of services to adults in the spectrum of library activities was clearly delineated during 1984 in the

A free antique appraisal was sponsored by the Warder Libraries, Springfield, Ohio, during National Library Week. (Warder Libraries)

U.S. Department of Education report *Alliance for Excellence: Librarians Respond to A Nation at Risk*. The report was the product of a series of five seminars, organized as a project titled "Libraries and a Learning Society," developed to examine how public libraries, academic libraries, library and information science training institutions, and school library media centers could best respond to *A Nation at Risk* (1983).

Throughout the *Alliance* document, library services to adults are singled out as critical in the establishment of an enduring Learning Society. Learners advisers are recommended who not only understand community needs but also understand learning resources. Literacy is targeted as a basic library function. Libraries are exhorted to develop resources and services in support of lifelong learning and education.

An overview of adult services in 1984 finds that libraries all over the nation had anticipated and were indeed developing programs that responded to the challenges in the *Alliance* document. This review of adult services summarizes representative services in the light of recommendations identified in *Alliance for Excellence* in the section "Library Leadership in the Learning Society." Such an approach serves as a gauge for the next *Yearbook* article and as a basis for measuring the library profession's response to this new manifesto. (Certain adult services reviewed elsewhere in the *Yearbook* are cited by cross-references.)

Alliance Proposals. *Recommendation I* . . . that libraries accept their central role in the Learning Society as valid learning centers . . . staffed with user-oriented professionals who do not only understand community needs but also know learning resources. These advisers would help patrons to gain the information and skills to function successfully in the Learning Society.

The East Central Network/Illinois Vocational Curriculum Center at Sangamon State University provides technical assistance for vocational education free of charge and functions as a resource

An exhibit at Newark Public Library in the fall explored George Orwell's famous work and its predictions.

Above, Visitors reviewing original art works at the Allied Arts Annual Portfolio Auction sponsored by the Huntington Beach (California) Public Library and Cultural Resources Center.

Above, Olive Gamble, Project Read Coordinator, and John van der Zee, Senior Vice President, McCann Erickson, display public awareness material for San Francisco Public Library's adult literature program, Project Read.

for community college, public, and university libraries that plan to expand their services in job training information. Over 800 task lists have been developed that define skills needed for a particular occupation.

In Newton, Kansas, the public library, a member of the Community Education Clearing House, offers Learning Exchange classes, and provides a "Share a Skill" directory of resource persons for the community. The reference department at Stark County District Library in Ohio is coordinating a language bank that patrons can use to obtain assistance in translating personal documents.

Facilitation of the use of library resources by advisers has been the focus of intensified effort during the last decade. Fulfillment of this aspect of the *Alliance* report is documented in two major publications on bibliographic instruction, *Library Instruction and Reference Services* in the 1984 spring/summer issue of *The Reference Librarian*, and John Lubans' *Educating the Public Library User* (1983).

In all types of libraries linkage of users with community resources is being targeted as an essential service. The learning center concept, an expansion of information and referral, coupled with appointment of learners advisers organizes this approach toward achievement of the learning society. (*See also* Information and Referral, Labor Groups, Library Service to, and Reference Services.)

Recommendation J . . . that libraries become active in adult literacy education programs at local, state, and national levels. Literacy programs are covered in a separate article in the *Yearbook*, yet the importance of literacy aid as a key adult service necessitates its mention here. One state's response to the need for a multi-jurisdictional response is reported in *Libraries: A Discovery for Adult Learners* (Louisiana Department of Education, Bureau of Adult and Community Education, 1984). The Louisiana project was intended to develop a cooperative relationship between local adult education programs and public libraries. Efforts such as this and many others spearheaded by the Coalition for Literacy indicate that libraries are well started in work on this recommendation.

Recommendation K . . . that the nation's . . . public libraries be assessed for their ability to respond to the urgent proposals for excellence in education and lifelong learning . . . in such vital areas as : (1) defining information-seeking skills and behaviors; (2) fostering adult literacy; (3) defining training and retraining; and (4) developing a market strategy.

The assessment of adult services is long overdue. Increased dissemination of techniques outlined in *Output Measures for Public Libraries* (1983) should enable local assessment of some of these services. The RASD Services to Adults Committee Adult Services in the Eighties Project consisting of a 30-year literature review and survey to be conducted in 1985 should provide new baseline descriptive data. The need for impact data persists, however. The publication of the *Alliance* report may spur funding for such studies.

Recommendation L . . . that librarians at local, state, and national levels develop and implement plans to share the resources and services of their institution in support of education and lifelong learning . . . that at the national level, leadership should be exerted to endorse, assist, and support

Roland Richardson, 90, displaying a model of the plane he flew in World War I. He was honored at the annual Veterans Day Memorial Program "Freedom Flyers" at the Cincinnati-Hamilton County Public Library.

Nobel and Pulitzer Prize winning author Saul Bellow appearing at the Chicago Public Library's monthly "Conversations with Chicago Authors." (Gary Degnan)

Topeka (Kansas) Public Library in 1984 presented "Women in the West" film series for patrons.

the states and local communities in their efforts to share resources.

Nationally, the broadest effort in support of lifelong learning through libraries is the "Let's Talk About It" project, reading and discussion group programs funded by the National Endowment for the Humanities and sponsored by the Association of Specialized and Cooperative Library Agencies of the American Library Association. The project was launched with workshop training teams to sponsor programs in their home states. Themes selected include work, ethnicity, family, children's literature from an adult perspective, what America reads, and citizenship.

Adult Services Spectrum. Special focus on types of users and their lifelong learning requirements are treated in the *ALA Yearbook* under specific categories such as American Indians, Black Americans, Blind and Physically Handicapped, and Italian Americans. Each of these categories of users have generic adult services needs but may require modified delivery styles in recognition of unique characteristics of each population group. One example of model service to a special group with generic needs is service to the aging as developed by Brooklyn Public Library's SAGE Program (Service to the Aging). SAGE has developed a realistic and comprehensive plan of library service for older adults with special programs for traditional library users, the homebound, the impaired, readers and nonreaders.

Adult Services have moved to center stage with the publication of *Alliance for Excellence*. New attention to a Learning Society and the call for resources to enable that society to emerge demand a reanalysis of the scope of users targeted, methods and styles of delivery, and evaluative mechanisms. Academic library adult services have become increasingly attentive to user education—a major step in activating the skills of lifelong learning. Many public library adult services have focused on particular modes of service (employment information, services to the aging, parent education) depending on local needs.

It is time for a major reassessment of the scope and breadth of adult services both locally and nationally in order to identify areas for reallocation of funds and reorganization of priorities to meet the recommendations of the *Alliance for Excellence*.

KATHLEEN M. HEIM

American Association of Law Libraries

Activities. The Executive Board in 1984 adopted a recommendation to create an Investment Advisory Committee charged with monitoring the fiscal state of the Association and advising the Treasurer on investment practice. The recommendation was the result of a two-year study of the Association's financial status presented to the Association by the Special Committee on Financial Planning.

The Association funded a number of projects during the year: The Contemporary Social Problems Special Interest Section was granted $5,000 to enable it to distribute, on a gratis basis, the D. E. Manville, *Prisoners Self-Help Litigation Manual*, 2d ed., to state and federal prisons. The Mid-America Law School Library Consortium received a $32,000 grant to sponsor its telefacsimile outreach program, and a minority scholarship for 1984–85 was again funded.

The microfilming of the Roalfe Papers in the Association's archives, at the University of Illinois, was approved.

The National Law Library Committee actively investigated, along with the American Bar Association's Facilities of the Law Library of Congress Committee, the desirability of a National Law Library.

The Special Committee on International Placements (SCIP) was in its second year as a special committee. The Committee acts as a clearinghouse for law librarians, both in the U.S. and abroad, who wish to participate in international employment exchanges or visitations, and for foreign and domestic law libraries who wish to participate in the program.

The Association joined other library associations and bibliographic networks in a telecommunications consortium to monitor federal legislation resulting from the AT&T breakup.

Annual Meeting. "1984: The Future Is Now," was the theme of the AALL's 77th annual meeting in San Diego. The theme was chosen to indicate that Orwellian predictions have not come to pass in the profession. The program and local arrangements committees were headed by Penny Hazelton, U.S. Supreme Court Library, and O. James Werner, San Diego County Law Library.

An Institute on Management Skills for Law Librarians held at the University of Santa Clara campus, under the codirectorship of Robert L. Oakley and Michael Gehringer, preceded the meeting. Two post-convention workshops were conducted: "Program Planning," under the codirection of Donald Dunn and Frank Houdek; and "Editing," under the direction of Carol Boast.

The Conference of Newer Law Librarians, "CONELL-1984," presented a half-day program, "AALL—The Organization: Survival at the Convention," codirected by Mickie A. Voges and Catherine H. Gillette.

The membership addressed several constitutional issues. As the result of a Price-Waterhouse recommendation that non-education based certification was more appropriate to a trade association than to an education association, the members by voice abolished the Certification Board

(*See also* Law Libraries). The members also voted to require payment of dues within three months after dues statements and to change the committee year to allow the committees to begin their year's activities at the annual meeting as the old committee concludes its business.

The 26th chapter was added with the vote to accept the petition of the Colorado Association of Law Libraries.

The 1984 Joseph A. Andrews Bibliographic Award, named in honor of the former Reference Librarian for the Association of the Bar of the City of New York, was awarded jointly to Simone-Marie Kleckner and Blanka Kudej for *International Legal Bibliography* (Dobbs Ferry, New York: Oceana, 1983).

The first Law Library Publication Award, to recognize achievement in creating outstanding in-house user oriented library materials, was awarded to the Reference Staff of Duke University School of Law Library, Michael G. Chiorazzi, Kathryn M. Christee, and Claire Germain. The staff submitted three types of publications: Research Guide Series, DULL NEWS, and Library Guides.

Award. The Association's first Distinguished Service Award was given to Marian G. Gallagher, retired from the University of Washington Law School Library, to recognize her many contributions to law librarianship and to AALL.

Publications. All three AALL publications had new editors in 1984: *Law Library Journal*, Richard Danner; *Index to Foreign Legal Periodicals*, Tom Reynolds; and *AALL Newsletter*, Mary Lu Linnane. The Association continues to sponsor the AALL Publications Series, published by Fred Rothman & Co., Littleton, Colorado, and the *Current Law Index*, published by Information Access, Belmont, California.

Membership. Total membership of the Association was 3,603, representing 1,501 individual members; 57 individual associate members; 1,577 institutional members; 70 institutional associate members; 2 sustaining members; 187 life members; 110 student members; 2 honorary members; and 93 undesignated memberships. Membership in the Association's Special Interest Sections was Academic Law Libraries, 262; Automatic and Scientific Development, 314; Contemporary Social Problems, 98; Government Documents, 323; Micrographics and Audiovisual, 188; On-Line Bibliographic Services, 322; Private Law Libraries, 827; Readers' Services, 219; State, Court and County Law Libraries, 272; and Technical Services, 334.

JACQUELYN J. JURKINS

AMERICAN ASSOCIATION OF LAW LIBRARIES

PRESIDENT (June 1984–July 1985):
Jacquelyn J. Jurkins, Multnomah Law Library, Portland, Oregon

VICE-PRESIDENT/PRESIDENT-ELECT:
Robert C. Berring, Jr., University of California, School of Law Library, Berkeley

EXECUTIVE DIRECTOR:
William H. Jepson

Membership (December 1984): 3,603
Headquarters: 53 W. Jackson Blvd., Chicago, Illinois 60604

American Association of School Librarians

During 1984 the American Association of School Librarians (AASL) placed considerable emphasis on developing a structural plan for the future and assessing members and potential members as to their professional growth needs. These concerns are the basis for reviewing and establishing new directions for AASL.

Future Structure Report. The AASL Board of Directors approved the *Future Structure Report* at the 1984 Midwinter Meeting. The report, begun in 1983, was published in March and sent to all members of AASL, the ALA Executive Board, and ALA Council. It focused on three options for future directions for AASL: (1) Continuing a relationship with ALA providing certain modifications are considered by appropriate ALA bodies. Areas of concern center on program, finance, staff, and governance; (2) Feasibility of federation; and (3) A totally different structure outside ALA. Ad hoc committees were established to study and examine each area in depth.

In 1984 the AASL Board also authorized an opinion survey of AASL members and prospective members. The purpose was to assess how individuals felt about the current structure of AASL and its future direction and to survey the areas and activities respondents would like to have emphasized within the organization. AASL engaged the Lawrence-Leiter Company of Kansas City, Missouri, to conduct the surveys. Twenty percent of the AASL members were surveyed; 43 percent responded. Approximately 2,200 potential members were sent questionnaires; 23 percent were returned.

Four major findings became apparent: (1) AASL is preeminent and effective; (2) present ALA/AASL structure is desirable but not workable; (3) member tolerance for increased dues is low; and (4) the future of AASL is specialist-oriented.

Nine areas were suggested for major emphasis: (1) working to enhance the image of the profession to the public, (2) writing and endorsing professional standards, (3) making a concentrated effort to attract more members, (4) offering continuing education programs for members, (5) lobbying and legislation on behalf of the profession, (6) representing the profession's stand to the news media and public, (7) strengthening ties with state affiliate associations, (8) evaluating print and nonprint materials for the profession, and (9) developing programs and materials that emphasize new technology for the profession. More than half of those concerns and activities were currently being addressed within the committee structure of AASL.

Conference Highlights. The third national conference of AASL, "Challenge '84: Mission Possible," was held in Atlanta, October 31–November 4, 1984. More than 3,200 building level library media specialists, district and regional supervisors, library educators, and school administrators attended. Delegates were from 49 U.S. states, West Germany, Canada, and Panama. Conference participants were challenged to examine their roles as activists, communicators, leaders, managers, motivators, teachers and technologists and to strive toward personal, professional, and program excellence.

Activities. The AASL Professional Development Committee sponsored a preconference in Dallas at the ALA Annual Conference. The theme was "The School Library Media Program and the Curriculum."

During the ALA Midwinter Meeting, the AASL Board adopted "Guidelines for School Library Media Education Programs" developed by the Library Education Committee. The Board and the membership at large approved the establishment of an AASL Library Media Educators Section.

School Library Media Month was established to coincide with National Library Week. To be celebrated for the first time in April 1985, it was to feature the role that library media programs play in the education of elementary and secondary students.

The AASL Board of Directors approved the establishment of a committee on Microcomputers Online for Library Media Centers to increase awareness of microcomputer utilization in schools and school library media centers; to design methods of rapid dissemination of information on microcomputer utilization in the schools; to provide a channel for communication among school library users, potential users, and online agencies; and to share microcomputer experiences in teaching, in management, and in online services.

A 15-member committee of AASL and AECT (the Association for Educational Communication and Technology) was writing new Standards for School Library Media Programs in 1984. Chaired by James Leiesner, University of Maryland, it was working toward a 1986 publication date. A funding proposal was being developed for publication of the Standards.

Awards. The AASL Awards Luncheon in Dallas honored the winners of the first AASL/Encyclopaedia Britannica National School Library Media Program of the Year Award. The Richmond (Virginia) School District, under the direction of Library Media Specialists Beverly Bagan and Delores Pretlow, and the Riverside Brookfield (Illinois) Township High School District, under the leadership of Dawn Heller, Library Coordinator, received $2,500 for each district.

Rheta A. Clark, former school library media consultant, Connecticut State Department of Education, received the seventh annual AASL President's Award, cosponsored by Baker & Taylor. This award, which carries a $2,000 stipend, is given for outstanding contributions in the field of librarianship and school media development.

Marilyn S. Scott, Assistant Superintendent for Communications and Media, Anchorage (Alaska) School District, was awarded the Distinguished Library Service Award for School Administrators in 1984. This award recognizes an administrator for outstanding and sustained contributions toward furthering the role of the library and its development in elementary and/or secondary education.

The 1984 AASL Intellectual Freedom Award, cosponsored by Social Issues Resources Series, Inc. (SIRS), was presented to Vicki Hardesty of Findlay (Ohio) High School. The $1,000 award is given annually to a school library media specialist at the elementary or secondary level who has upheld the Association's principles of intellectual freedom.

The AASL/Follett Library Book Company Microcomputer Award was established in 1984 and will be given annually beginning in 1985. Two awards of $1,000 each were to be provided to two individuals for innovative use of microcomputers in library management and in the integration of computers into the curriculum.

BETTIE DAY

AMERICAN ASSOCIATION OF SCHOOL LIBRARIANS
PRESIDENT (June 1984–July 1985): **Elizabeth B. (Bettie) Day,** Santa Barbara County Schools, California
FIRST VICE-PRESIDENT/PRESIDENT-ELECT: **Shirley L. Aaron,** Florida State University, Tallahassee
EXECUTIVE DIRECTOR: **Alice E. Fite**
Membership (August 31, 1984): 5,324 (4,578 personal; 746 organizational)
Expenditures (August 31, 1984): $130,896

American Indians

Library Service for Indians. When on October 17 President Ronald Reagan signed the amended LSCA legislation, the bill included a new Title IV providing for library service for Indian tribes. The bill is the first title ever to provide for public community library services for Indian people. School libraries under the Bureau of Indian Affairs, administered by the Department of Interior, are not mandated and have no funds provided in the federal budget. The bill's passage began with the formation in 1970 of the first committee within ALA to address the Indian segment of the library's public. When librarians—both Indian and non-Indian—have taken initiatives in asserting the right of Indian people to information access and services, Indian people across the country have responded.

This Title IV of LSCA represents to an unusual degree the grassroots will and desires of Indian reservation and near reservation residents. Its provisions were developed through a process of input and feedback between Indian librarians and tribal leadership over a period of several years which culminated in the 1978 Denver White House Preconference on Indian Library and Information Services On or Near Reservations. From there, the Indian Library Omnibus Bill developed by this all-Indian conference came successfully through the White House Conference on Libraries and Information Services, and most of its elements have been included in all public library legislative proposals amending LSCA since then. Unstinting and dedicated support was provided by the National Commission on Libraries and Information Science through its Deputy Chair, Bessie B. Moore, and its associate director, Mary Alice Hedge Reszetar; and by the ALA through Jean E. Coleman, Director of its Office of Library Outreach Services, and Eileen D. Cooke, Director of its Washington Office. In addition, concerned and sustained support came from the National Advisory Council on Indian Education, the National Indian Education Association, and the National Congress of American Indians and other Indian organizations, as well as through testimony before the House and Senate committees by many tribes. Almost without exception the chief officers of state library agencies were generous in their support of Title IV, and in their understanding of the tribes' desire to have funds disbursed to them directly in order to preserve and reinforce the special relationship between the tribal and the federal governments.

The purpose, as given in the act, is to "assist Indian tribes in planning and developing library services to meet their needs . . . Determination of the best uses of the funds provided under this Act shall be reserved to the Indian tribes." Further, the purpose is to promote the extension of public library services to Indian people living on or near reservations; provide incentives for the establishment and expansion of tribal library programs; and to improve the administration and implementation of library services for Indians by providing funds to establish and support ongoing programs.

Funding. Title IV is authorized through FY 1989, with a set-aside of 1.5 percent of Titles I, II, and III of LSCA for the Indian tribes. At the current level of appropriation this means in the neighborhood of $1,770,000 for the nearly 300 eligible tribes. During the process of coming to an agreement between the House and Senate versions of the legislation, .5 percent of Titles I, II, and III were assigned for the library needs of Hawaiian Natives.

Two types of grant awards are provided. Section 403 of the act provides Basic Grants, awards which are equal in size and available to any eligible tribe applying for them. These grants are noncompetitive and will be made in accordance with the regulations for authorized activities. Section 404 provides funds for Special Project Grants, awarded for the development of a long-range program, implemented by a variety of projects, and planned with the involvement—at least in a consultant capacity—of a librarian. These grants are eligible for up to an 80 percent federal contribution.

The Division of Libraries within the Center for Libraries and Educational Improvement in the U.S. Department of Education was preparing the regulations for Title IV for a "notice of proposed rulemaking" in the *Federal Register* by the end of March 1985. At that time, all tribes, and others, will have a period of time in which to react and respond. The American Indian Library Association and the ALA's Committee on Library Service to American Indian People expect to be able to help to develop a plan for training and technical assistance for the tribes—especially for those that wish to submit long-range plans and apply for special project grants.

Planning. Lincoln White, NACIE, formerly Director of Indian Education Programs in New York State and a special assistant on the secretary's staff at Interior, sent details of the Title IV provisions and of authorized activities relating to library development by the tribes to all Indian Education Act sites and to tribal leadership during 1984. He supported and assisted the staff in the Division of Libraries to provide guidance in what for them is a new set of circumstances—dealing with tribal, rather than state, governments.

Tribal governments were being urged even before regulations were available to plan their priorities and be ready to file applications for their basic grants. It was suggested through *American Indian Library Newsletter* and through other channels that early childhood program specialists, education directors, adult literacy specialists, and those concerned with health, employment, training, youth services, home-school partnership, and family services make known their priorities so that the tribal chairmen may make decisions about what directions the buildup and development of community library services is to take. Tribes were urged to make contact with state library agencies or nearby library systems to discuss the possibilities of seeking technical assistance with such matters as ordering books and other materials, processing and organizing materials, and training staff.

Conference Activities. In other news of American Indian libraries and librarians, the ALA Indian libraries committee and AILA sponsored a daylong workshop preceding the ALA Conference in Dallas. "After the Oral Tradition: Native American Resources" was planned by Lotsee P. Smith and featured such topics as "Native American Literature," "Multi-Disciplinary Approach to Native American Resources," "Resources for Native American Family and Local History," "Making Law Materials Talk," and "Preserving Historical Tribal Records." Speakers included Thomas J. Blumer, a senior editor in the European Law Division of the Library of Congress and a member of the ALA committee. The workshop ended with a pow-wow staged at the Hyatt Regency ballroom by the Dallas-Fort Worth Intertribal Society and the Texas Indian Heritage Society. Highlights included the gourd, shield, and war dances performed by members of the Cheyenne, Kiowa, Apache, and other tribes.

At the end of the 1984 ALA Conference, Janice Beaudin (Winnebago), Historical Archivist at the Winnebago Research Center in Madison, Wisconsin, became Chair of the ALA committee, while Rhonda Harris Taylor (Choctaw), of the Henderson Library at Lon Morris College in Texas, became President of AILA. Janice Beaudin and Jean Coleman worked with the Newberry Library to develop closer relations with Chicago's large Indian community.

Affiliate status with ALA was being sought by AILA.

VIRGINIA H. MATHEWS (OSAGE)

American Library Association

The year 1984 was viewed with general anticipation; the media at large and within the library

American Library Association

Representatives from the Assault on Illiteracy Program and ALA's Coordinated Coalition for Literacy join forces at ALA Headquarters to discuss areas of cooperation. From left, Violet Malone, Benjamin H. Wright, Emille Smith, Calvin Rolark, and Jean E. Coleman. (American Libraries)

field took frequent opportunities to compare the real 1984 with that envisioned in Orwell's novel. The comparisons in both society and librarianship were generally favorable to the present, but such comparisons inevitably identified dangerous trends that give at least some credence to Orwell's picture and that might give both reader and rapporteur some pause. Appropriately, 1984 was a year that might best be characterized as deliberative for the American Library Association.

The chief policymaking and managerial bodies of the Association, the Council and Executive Board, spent a considerable portion of their time deliberating and discussing key issues facing the profession as a whole and ALA in particular. An example is the attention devoted to the lawsuit Merwine v. State of Mississippi, which prompted ALA members to consider not only possible involvement in a particular legal case, but also the very nature of the profession, its educational programs, its status in education and society, and ALA's role in establishing and defending standards for the field. Several hours were devoted to Merwine in Executive Board, Council, and Membership meetings, with discussion remarked by many to be among the most serious, considered, and intense that observers of these groups had seen in some time. Thus the introspection prompted by Orwell and the coming of 1984 had its manifestation within the ALA as well. It can also be observed that programs and deliberations begun in 1983 continued in 1984, and that others begun in 1984 would continue through 1985.

Following the pattern for these "ALA Reports" in the ALA Yearbook, this article summarizes the key issues addressed by the Council and Executive Board, reflecting the way in which ALA's policymaking bodies review profession- and association-wide issues. ALA's primary concerns and accomplishments in the areas of conferences and information services are also addressed, along with the contribution of ALA Publishing in presenting outstanding results of work from across the entire spectrum of librarianship. Other ALA Yearbook articles report on the activities of ALA's many specialist units, including the Divisions, Offices, Committees, and Round Tables, and the topical articles track in detail the year's work in a variety of matters in all areas of the field. The boxes and tables that accompany this text provide some highlights of ALA's organization, officers, membership, and finance; there is also information on many ALA periodicals with a selection of key sources of information about ALA.

Council and Executive Board. Many matters that come before Council are first reviewed by the Executive Board; similarly, actions and concerns of Council may later occupy the Board. In 1984 there were numerous issues of concern common to the agendas of both bodies, including the Merwine case.

A Nation at Risk, a highly critical analysis of education in the U.S. which had entirely omitted the role of libraries in the educational process, had been issued in 1983, and a special task force had been appointed to prepare ALA's response to that report. The result in 1984 was Realities: Education Reform in a Learning Society, a report affirming the role of libraries as a learning resource.

Bronze tablets in the lobby of Huron Plaza, ALA's Headquarters, honor members and friends who helped fund the new facility. (American Libraries)

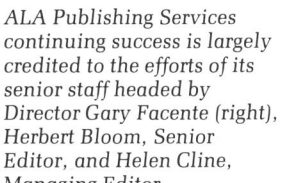
American Library Association

The ALA Commission on Freedom and Equality of Access to Information, appointed during the 1982–83 presidential term of Carol A. Nemeyer, presented the first results of its work at the 1984 Annual Conference. The presentation by Chairperson Dan Lacy at the Membership meeting and the document accompanying that presentation sparked considerable debate and discussion that could clearly be expected to continue into 1985.

Since the Reagan administration first announced its intention to withdraw U.S. financial support for UNESCO, many ALA members, especially in the International Relations Committee and International Relations Round Table, argued the case for UNESCO's substantial contributions to library and information services throughout the world. Among the many lobbying efforts was a Council resolution urging continued support for UNESCO. Secretary-General Amadou M. M'Bow came to the Annual Conference and was among the featured speakers. While ALA's efforts did not prevent the administration from fulfilling its intention at year's end, these efforts do demonstrate the Association's determination and ability to muster forces in support of an important goal.

Administration: Planning to Plan. The need to plan has long been a concern of ALA's management and policymakers, but 1984 saw still more efforts toward systematic planning for ALA. The Committee on Planning and the Committee on Program Evaluation and Support sought to bring to ALA's budget planning more information on the program units' activities on the one hand and more complete financial data on the other. Included in the budget process for fiscal year 1984–85 were a separate capital equipment budget and the first review of the classification/salary matrix that forms a key element in the classification system adopted by the Board in 1983 for ALA Headquarters staff. There were also some preliminary studies concerning the possibility of an office for development at ALA.

Another significant move was the appointment of a "Planning Process Group." Reflecting the members' determination that Association-wide planning should be conducted in a coherent, systematic way, this group, under the leadership of President Brooke E. Sheldon, began the arduous task of formulating a process for "planning to plan," a phrase which perhaps belies the complexity of such an effort in an organization as diverse as ALA. With the participation of numerous members, staff, and a professional consultant, 1984 closed with a program for developing a Strategic Long Range Plan for ALA over the next two years.

Key Headquarters staff positions received attention in 1984. Ruth R. Frame retired as Deputy Executive Director on January 31; in November the position was assumed by Roger H. Parent, previously Executive Director of ALA's Library Administration and Management Association.

Robert Wedgeworth, Executive Director since 1972, announced his intention not to seek renewal of his contract ending July 31, 1985. The Executive Board, which is charged with filling the position, devoted many hours to formulating

ALA Publishing Services continuing success is largely credited to the efforts of its senior staff headed by Director Gary Facente (right), Herbert Bloom, Senior Editor, and Helen Cline, Managing Editor.

the process by which the search for and appointment of a new Executive Director would be conducted in 1984–85. The Board decided early on that among the required credentials of the new Executive Director would be the master's degree in librarianship from an ALA-accredited program.

Conferences. The 1984 Midwinter Meeting was held in Washington, D.C., with a record 5,720 registrants and exhibitors. The Annual Conference was held in Dallas, drawing over 11,400 registrants and exhibitors for more than 3,000 meetings, workshops, and exhibits. Both meetings saw record numbers of exhibitors. Among speakers at the Dallas Conference were former First Lady Rosalyn Carter and civil rights leader Coretta Scott King.

Information Services. Information services continued to be a priority in ALA during 1984. One reflection of this important aspect of the program was a restructuring of public information, conference, and chapter relations activities within a new Department of Communications headed by Peggy Barber. The position of Director of the Public Information Office was filled by Linda Wallace.

Another program announced in 1983 and inaugurated in 1984 was ALANET®, the ALA's electronic information service. Offering subscribers a wide range of services including electronic mail, external databases, and several newsletters of ALA- and library-oriented information, the service grew in only one year of operation to some 800 active "electronic mailboxes" representing all kinds of libraries and information centers, associations, networks and consortia, suppliers, and individual librarians in the U.S. and Canada. ALANET was the service chosen to support the ILLINET (Illinois) interlibrary loan referral network; and a number of ALA units and outside subscribers established communication networks through ALANET among their boards and committees. A special menu of services to library suppliers began to provide for electronic orders and claims for several booksellers and subscription agencies participating in the network. ALANET System Manager is Joel M. Lee, ALA Headquarters librarian.

ALA Report

Far right, Guest Speaker Francis Fitzgerald chats with ALA Councilor Martha Gould at the ALA Conference in Dallas. Right, the ALA store made its debut at the Conference featuring ALA publications, American Libraries tote bags, and a variety of items for sale.

Publishing. ALA Publishing Services continued to improve internal operations with the installation of a turnkey system for order, billing, and warehouse control and for subscription recordkeeping. The move also helped Divisions and other units of ALA that issue their own publications with the management of those functions and began to lead to improved customer service.

Best-sellers of the year covered an extraordinary variety of topics. Among key 1984 publications were revisions of a number of important publications, including Mildred Nickel's *Steps to Service: A Handbook of Procedures for the School Library; Reference Sources for Small and Medium-Sized Libraries;* and *Acquisitions Management and Collection Development in Libraries,* Rose Mary Magrill and Doralyn J. Hickey's update of Stephen Ford's *The Acquisition of Library Materials.*

New and popular bibliographies were YASD's *Outstanding Books for the College Bound;* Richard C. Lynch's *Musicals! A Directory of Musical Properties Available for Production;* and *Exciting, Funny, Scary, Different and Sad Books Kids Like about Animals, Science, Sports, Families, Songs, and Other Things,* compiled by Frances Laverne Carroll. Important treatises published during the year were *The First Freedom Today* by Robert B. Downs; *Security for Libraries* by Marvine Brand; and *Guidelines for Using AACR2 Chapter 9 for Cataloging Microcomputer Software.* Each year's new publications clearly demonstrate the diversity of ALA's interests and activities.

JOEL M. LEE
EMILY MELTON

ALA Report

AMERICAN LIBRARY ASSOCIATION HIGHLIGHTS AND ORGANIZATION

The American Library Association is the oldest and largest library association in the world. ALA was founded in 1876. The first meeting, organized by Melvil Dewey, was held in Philadelphia, October 4–6, and drew 103 librarians. ALA membership was 38,330 in 1982 and 39,124 in 1983, and 39,477 as of August 31, 1984.

THE ALA COUNCIL is the governing body of the Association. It comprises 100 Councilors elected at large and Councilors representing each state, provincial, and territorial chapter. Council convenes at two meetings held each year: Midwinter (early each year) and Annual Conference (summer). The management arm of the Association is the EXECUTIVE BOARD, which comprises the officers of the Association, the immediate Past President, and eight members elected by Council from its membership.

PRESIDENT: E. J. Josey
(June 1984–July 1985)

VICE-PRESIDENT/PRESIDENT-ELECT: Beverly P. Lynch

EXECUTIVE DIRECTOR: Robert Wedgeworth

MEMBERSHIP: 36,544 personal members; 2,923 organization members; total (August 31, 1984) 39,477

ANNUAL EXPENDITURES: (August 31, 1984)
Regular activities	$ 6,521,596
Publishing	5,247,796
Meetings	1,449,104
	$13,218,496

ANNUAL REVENUES: (August 31, 1984)
Membership dues	$ 2,828,303
Publishing	5,953,455
Meetings	2,405,416
Promotional activities	676,382
Other	1,141,552
	$13,005,108

ANNUAL CONFERENCES:
Chicago, July 6–11, 1985; New York, June 26–July 3, 1986; San Francisco, June 27–July 2, 1987

THE GOAL of the Association is the promotion of libraries and librarianship to assure the delivery of user-oriented library information service to all. Much of its work is done through ALA Committees.

ACTIVITIES of the Association include:
  Research on library problems
  Development of standards and guidelines
  Accreditation of library education
    programs

Clarification of legislative issues
Vigorous support for intellectual freedom
Publishing
Awards
Library cooperation
Continuing education

ALA UNITS

DIVISIONS of ALA are membership units that provide resources for special knowledge and for advancing knowledge and service through publications and professional programs. See in this volume:

American Association of School Librarians
American Library Trustee Association
Association for Library Service to Children
Association of College and Research Libraries
Association of Specialized and Cooperative Library Agencies
Library Administration and Management Association
Library and Information Technology Association
Public Library Association
Reference and Adult Services Division
Resources and Technical Services Division
Young Adult Services Division

ROUND TABLES are membership units that deal with aspects of librarianship outside the scope of a Division. See in this volume:

Continuing Library Education Network & Exchange Round Table
Ethnic Materials Information Exchange Round Table
Exhibits Round Table
Federal Librarians Round Table
Government Documents Round Table
Intellectual Freedom Round Table
International Relations Round Table
Junior Members Round Table
Library History Round Table
Library Instruction Round Table
Library Research Round Table
Map and Geography Round Table
Social Responsibilities Round Table
Staff Organization Round Table

ALA OFFICES are headquarters staff units that address issues affecting the entire profession: Accreditation, Intellectual Freedom, Library Outreach Services, Office for Research, Personnel Resources, and the Washington Office (Legislation). See articles in this volume on these subjects.

ALA AFFILIATES are:

American Association of Law Libraries
American Society for Information Science
Asian/Pacific American Librarians Association
Association for Library and Information Science Education
Association of Research Libraries
Canadian Library Association
Chinese-American Librarians Association
Council on Library/Media Technical Assistants
Friends of Libraries USA
Laubach Literacy International (NALA)
Literacy Volunteers of America
Medical Library Association
Music Library Association
National Librarians Association
Oral History Association
Prime Time School Television
REFORMA (National Association of Spanish-Speaking Librarians)
Sociedad de Bibliotecarios de Puerto Rico
Theatre Library Association
Ukrainian Library Association of America
Urban Libraries Council

ALA CHAPTERS are covered under State Reports, the final section of this volume.

HEADQUARTERS

50 E. Huron St., Chicago, IL 60611
Washington Office: 110 Maryland Ave., N.E., Box 54, Washington, DC 20002
CHOICE Magazine: 100 Riverview Center, Middletown, CT 06457

FINDING OUT ABOUT ALA: SELECTED REFERENCES

These key sources provide a wealth of information about ALA, its organization and units, its publications and services, in addition to the many reports in this *ALA Yearbook.*

Exhibit area at the Annual Conference promoted conversation between Christina Carr Young, left, of the American Association of School Librarians, and Claudia Dansby of DataPhase. (American Libraries)

ALA Report

ALA Handbook of Organization and Membership Directory

The annual *Handbook* is a guide to the structure of ALA, with names of current officials, committee members, councilors, and representatives. It includes information about Divisions, Round Tables, and other units. Key documents include the Charter, ALA calendar, Constitution and Bylaws, and Policy Manual.

The *Membership Directory* includes the names and brief addresses of personal and organizational members, as well as historical listings of conferences, presidents, and executive secretaries and executive directors.

The *Handbook* is available separately free to personal members upon request to the Executive Office, and for $10 to others. The combined handbook and directory is sent to organizational members and is $20 to others.

ALA Publications Checklist

An annual comprehensive bibliography of *all* materials currently available from *all* ALA units, compiled by the staff of the ALA Headquarters Library. It describes books, pamphlets, audiovisual materials, and periodicals available from ALA and its units. The *Checklist* contains detailed indexes by subject, issuing unit, and personal author, along with complete ordering instructions and order forms. It is available free upon request from the Sales Manager, ALA Publishing Services.

Announcements of new ALA publications appear regularly in *American Libraries*, as well as in *electroCitations: ALA Publications News* in ALANET.

American Libraries

ALA's official journal reports regularly on ALA activities, policies, publications, and other highlights. It is sent to all ALA members and is also available by subscription to others for $30 from the Subscriptions Dept.

Legislative Report of the Washington Office

Issued twice a year, this report summarizes ALA's many legislation-related activities.

AMERICAN LIBRARY ASSOCIATION COUNCIL

PRESIDENT (June 1984–July 1985):
E. J. Josey, Chief, Bureau of Specialist Library Services, New York State Library, Albany, New York

VICE-PRESIDENT/PRESIDENT-ELECT:
Beverly P. Lynch, University Librarian, University of Illinois at Chicago

SECRETARY:
Robert Wedgeworth, Executive Director, ALA

Council Membership: 100 councilors at large (25 elected by members each year); 1 councilor from each state, provincial, and territorial chapter (52); 1 councilor from each division of ALA (11); 12 members of the **Executive Board** (elected officers—president, vice-president, treasurer, and immediate past-president—plus 5 who are no longer councilors by virtue of election).

Minutes

These are prepared by the Council and Executive Board Secretariat and are indexed annually. For information on current minutes, write to the Executive Office. The Headquarters Library holds complete, indexed minutes of the Executive Board (1906–) and Council (1963–); earlier Council minutes are found in *Library Journal* (1876–1902) and the *ALA Bulletin* (1902–1963).

Treasurer's Report

Submitted at the Midwinter Meeting for the fiscal year (September 1–August 31); for information, contact Fiscal Services Dept., ALA Headquarters.

For other sources and special files, contact the ALA Headquarters Library.

Table 1. ALA Membership (as of August 31, 1984)*

Personal members	36,554
Organizational members	2,923
Total	39,477
Membership in ALA units	
Divisions	
AASL	5,324
ACRL	8,835
ALTA	1,588
ASCLA	1,458
ALSC	3,016
LITA	5,430
LAMA	4,080
PLA	5,571
RASD	4,502
RTSD	5,865
YASD	2,103
Total Divisional membership	47,772
Members selecting no Division 34.1%	
Members selecting one Division 38.2%	
Members selecting two Divisions 19.1%	
Members selecting three or more Divisions 8.6%	
Round Tables	
ERT	271
FLIRT	543
GODORT	1,300
IFRT	1,209
IRRT	574
JMRT	1,047
LHRT	359
LIRT	1,020
LRRT	679
MAGERT	366
SRRT	893
SORT	235
Total Round Table membership	8,496

*Source: Membership statistics, monthly report August 31, 1984 (ALA Administrative Services)

Table 2. ALA Publishing Services, September 1, 1983–August 31, 1984

Publishing Services	Actual Expenditures	Income
Books and Pamphlets	$1,758,070	$1,809,505
Booklist and *RBB*	1,686,540	1,733,012
Library Technology Reports	295,603	335,006
American Libraries (Subscription allowance)[a]	677,723	492,756
		(184,967)
Total	$4,417,936	$4,555,246

Source: ALA Treasurer's Report, August 31, 1984, pp. 18–19.
[a] Transfer from general funds for subscription equivalent for ALA members, who receive *AL* as part of membership benefits.

Table 3. Selected ALA Periodicals (1984)

Periodical	Editor(s)	Publication Frequency	Subscription*	Circulation
ALA Washington Newsletter	Eileen D. Cooke, and Carol C. Henderson, Editors Director, ALA Washington Office	Irregular (minimum of 12 issues)	$15.00 per year.	2,200
ALSC Newsletter	Ann Carlson Weeks, Editor ALA, Chicago	Two issues per year	Free to Division members.*	4,000
ALTA Newsletter	Nancy Stiegemeyer, Editor 215 Camellia Drive Cape Girardeau, Missouri	6 issues a year	Free to Division members.*	1,700
American Indian Libraries Newsletter (OLOS Committee on Library Service for American Indian People)	Cheryl Metoyer-Duran, Editor Graduate School of Library and Information Science, University of California, Los Angeles, California	3 issues a year	$5 to individuals; $7 to institutions; $10 overseas; single issues, $2.	2,000
American Libraries	Arthur Plotnik, Editor ALA, Chicago	11 issues a year; July/August combined	Free to ALA members; available to institutions at $30 per year.	41,290
base line	James M. Walsh, Editor Library University of Wyoming, Laramie, Wyoming	Bi-monthly	Free to Round Table members; subscription $12 per year.	300
Booklist	Paul Brawley, Editor ALA, Chicago	22 issues a year	$47 per year.	36,980
CHOICE (ACRL)	Patricia Sabosik, Editor Middletown, Connecticut	11 issues a year; July/August combined	$95 per year.	5,718
College & Research Libraries (ACRL)	Charles Martell, Editor California State University, Sacramento, California	6 times a year	Free to Division members; subscription $35 per year; single journal issues $7.50.	13,000
C&RL News	George Eberhart, Editor ACRL/ALA ALA Headquarters	11 monthly news issues; July/August combined	Subscription to News $10. Free to Division members; single issues $3.50.	9,600
Documents to the People (GODORT)	Joe Jaros, Editor Texas A&M University College Station, Texas	Bimonthly	Free to Round Table members; subscription $15 per year.	1,700
The Federal Librarian (FLRT)	Doris Beachell, Editor Library of Congress Washington, D.C.	Quarterly	Free to Federal Librarians Round Table Members.*	600
EMIE Bulletin	Vladimir F. Wertsman, Editor Donnell Foreign Language Library Queens College Flushing, New York	Quarterly	Free to Ethnic Materials Information Exchange Round Table members; subscription $4.00 per year; single issues $1.50	200
Financial Assistance for Library Education	Margaret Myers, Editor ALA, Chicago	Annually	$1.00 per copy. Prepaid to OLPR*	8,000
Footnotes (JMRT)	Loretta Turnage, Editor 8750 Georgia Ave. Silver Spring, Maryland	Quarterly	Free to Junior Members Round Table members.*	1,300
Friends of the Library National Notebook (Friends of Libraries USA)	James A. Houck, Editor Youngstown State University Dept. of English Youngstown, Ohio	Quarterly	Free to Friends of Libraries USA members.*	600
IFRT Report (IFRT)	Judith Bradley, Editor P.L. System Plano, Texas	Irregular	Free to Intellectual Freedom Round Table members.*	900
Information Technology and Libraries (LITA)	William Potter, Editor University of Illinois, Urbana, Illinois	Quarterly	Free to Division members; subscription $25 per year; single issues $7.50.	6,800

ALA Report

Title	Editor	Frequency	Availability	Circulation
Interface (ASCLA)	Sue Medina, Editor 663 Hillsboro Rd., Montgomery, Alabama	Quarterly	Free to Division members; subscription $10 per year; single issues $3.00.	2,000
LAMA Newsletter (LAMA)	Edward D. Garten, Editor Tennessee Technological University Cookeville, Tennessee	Quarterly	Free to Division members.*	4,200
LHRT Newsletter	Ronald H. Fritze, Editor Department of History Lamar University Beaumont, Texas	Semiannually	Free to Library History Round Table Members*	400
Leads: A Fact Sheet (IRRT)	William L. Williamson, Editor University of Wisconsin Madison, Wisconsin	Quarterly	Free to International Relations Round Table members; subscription $12 per year.	650
Library Instruction Round Table News (LIRT)	Pamela Engelbrecht, Editor Virginia Tech. Blacksburg, Virginia	Quarterly	Free to LIRT members.	800
Library Resources & Technical Services (RTSD)	Elizabeth Tate, Editor Rockville, Maryland	Quarterly	Free to Division members; subscription $30 per year; single issues $7.50.	9,600
Library Systems Newsletter	Howard S. White, Editor ALA, Chicago	Monthly	$30 per year.	1,375
Library Technology Reports	Howard S. White, Editor ALA, Chicago	6 issues a year	$145 per year; single copies $40.	1,700
LITA Newsletter	Carol A. Parkhurst, Editor University of Nevada Reno, Nevada	Quarterly	Free to Division members.	4,500
Newsletter on Intellectual Freedom (IFC)	Judith F. Krug, Editor ALA, Chicago	6 issues a year	$25 per year; single issues $4.00.	3,000
Openers	Ann Cunniff, Editor ALA, Chicago	Quarterly	Bulk subscriptions only: 100/qtr, $100/yr; 500/qtr, $125/yr; 1000/qtr, $150/yr.	250,000
Public Libraries (PLA)	Kenneth Shearer, Editor 1205 LeClair St. Chapel Hill, North Carolina	Quarterly	Free to Division members; subscription $18 per year; $30 for two years; single issues $4.00	4,500
RASD Update	Steven D. Atkinson, Editor State University of New York at Albany Albany, New York	6 issues a year	Free to Division members; subscription $6 per year; single issues $2.	4,700
RQ (RASD)	Kathleen M. Heim, Editor Louisiana State University School of Library and Information Science Baton Rouge, Louisiana	Quarterly	Free to Division members; subscription $20 per year; single issues $6.	6,800
RTSD Newsletter (RTSD)	Arnold Hirshon, Editor Virginia Commonwealth University Richmond, Virginia	8 times a year	Free to Division members and Library Resources & Technical Services subscribers; available by subscription at $12 per year.	8,200
School Library Media Quarterly (AASL)	Jack Luskay, Editor John Jay Senior High School Katonah, New York	Quarterly	Free to Division members; subscription $20 per year; single issues $5.50.	7,400
SORT Bulletin (SORT)	Sharon K. Adley, Editor Lake County P.L., Merrillville, Indiana	Semiannually	Free to Staff Organizations Round Table members.*	100
SRRT Newsletter (SRRT)	John Hostage, Editor 78 Glenville Ave., Boston, Massachusetts	3 issues a year	Free to Social Responsibilities Round Table members; $20 to institutions.	1,500
Top of the News (ALSC/YASD)	Marilyn Kaye, Editor Division of Library and Information Science St. John's University Jamaica, New York	Quarterly	Free to Division members; subscription $25 per year.	9,500

*Asterisk indicates not available by subscription (December 1983).

American Library Trustee Association

Dallas Conference. A full program for trustees was gathered by Chair Carol Neuhauser for the 1984 Annual Conference. The preconference agenda included two selections, "Access to Information through Literacy" (cosponsored with OLOS and PLA), and "Fund Raising for Libraries" (LAMA, cosponsor). ALTA President Barbara Cooper's reception in the Rare Book Room of the Dallas Public Library was attended by 300 members and guests. A view of changing roles was presented in the ALTA–Public Library Association workshop, "Dynamic Interaction: Professionals and Trustees" featuring panelists from small, medium, and large public libraries. The need for understanding political action was addressed in the ALTA-LAMA workshop "Getting It Passed: How to Use Successful PR Methods with Your State Legislature." A two-part lecture series cosponsored by ALTA and PLA and led by John Alexander of Texas was "Personal Performance Management: The Agony and the Ecstasy." A "first," in that it was an initial gathering of the lay support groups for libraries, was the presentation of "Common Goals—Different Paths: Successful Library Advocacy" cosponsored by ALTA with WHCLIST, ULC, FOLUSA.

A group of 200 enjoyed the representative panelists, including Gloria Glaser, William Asp, A. C. Strip, Laura Chodos, and Joan Hood. Another special guest was Baltimore County Public Library Director, Charles Robinson, speaking at the "People from the States" breakfast on "Risk Taking" and its positive results.

Jonathon Kozol, author, teacher, and writer on literacy, expressed his views and findings to the 300 attendees of the ALTA Literacy Luncheon. The annual ALTA Gala heard Lillian Bradshaw, retired Dallas Public Library Director who was one of the central figures involved in the organization of the Republican Convention in Dallas.

The emphasis on cosponsoring programming was proving economically wise and partially resolved problems of program duplication.

ALTA-WILL. The ALTA Workshop in Library Leadership (ALTA-WILL) has been an effective educational program. Starting with a Minnesota pilot program in 1982, the foundation for future workshops was developed and by 1984 had been replicated in 23 states, Canada and, in a shortened or adapted form, in countless other areas. The main topics are Public Awareness, Planning, Policy, Advocacy, and Law and Funding, which represent the core of the workshop. Many ALTA members have participated in presenting and organizing the programs. During 1983 California produced a series of workshops throughout the state and another series was planned and in progress in 1984.

Organization and Activities. Beyond its Executive Board, ALTA is divided into five Councils including Action, Education, Communications, Conference and Operations, and they preside over 20 committees. Ten Regional Vice Presidents who represent all of the United States are the direct contact for local and state boards.

Publications. The ALTA "Checklist of Materials," available through the ALA Headquarters Office in Chicago, offers 52 publications and media presentations of value to trustees. The titles include current concerns such as "Evaluating the Library Director," "Library Service to Farmers," "Library Trustees and Personnel," "Securing a New Library Director," and "Consultants and Library Boards—A Working Partnership." An advocacy brochure was under preparation for 1985.

Affiliation. In Dallas the ALTA Board approved the concept of affiliation for library boards outlined by Robert Wedgeworth, the ALA Executive Director. It offers, for a single board charge, a quarterly newsletter and is designed to acquaint boards with ALA and ALTA's services and programs for trustees. The structure and concept were being formalized by Peggy Barber of the ALA staff.

Membership. The number of ALTA personal memberships remained stable in 1984, but organizational memberships were reduced by half as a result of the change in the ALA dues structure. That financial setback was partially offset through a raise in Division dues and by members' donations to the ALTA Endowment Fund. Two groups, the PLA/ALTA Task Force on Membership and the PLA/ALTA Common Concerns Committee, were combining Division efforts in areas of common interests, including innovative growth options.

Awards. The 1984 Cited Trustee Awards were presented to Elmer M. Jackson, Jr., Annapolis, Maryland, and Helen Muir, Miami. The Literacy Award went to Lydia Duggins of Bridgeport, Connecticut. Honor Awards to Major Benefactors went to Bertha Bacot of Pascagoula, Mississippi; Mr. and Mrs. J. Harwood Cochrane of Rockville, Virginia; John C. Henley III of Birmingham, Alabama; and, posthumously, to John Mosby of St. Louis for his gifts to the Wolfner Library for the Blind and Physically Handicapped.

JOANNE WISENER

AMERICAN LIBRARY TRUSTEE ASSOCIATION

PRESIDENT (June 1984–July 1985):
Joanne Wisener, Yuma, Arizona

VICE-PRESIDENT/PRESIDENT-ELECT:
Herbert Davis, Brooklandville, Maryland

PROGRAM OFFICER:
Sharon L. Jordan

Membership (August 31, 1984): 1,588 (1,281 personal; 307 organizational)
Expenditures (August 31, 1984): $36,008

American Society for Information Science

Activities. Under President Donald W. King 1984 was a successful year for the American Society for Information Science (ASIS) with an increased membership and a financial surplus used to establish a reserve fund. An Oklahoma ASIS Chapter was chartered during the year, as well as student chapters in Chicago, Taipei, and Atlanta. An all-time high of student members participated in ASIS in 1984. In response to the

American Society for Information Science

growing rate of new professionals entering the field, the society launched an aggressive program to attract newly graduating students.

Continuing efforts to provide information for professionals involved in online searching, ASIS formed a cooperative venture in 1984 with Knowledge Industry Publications to produce the Data Base User Service, the first such service to offer online access to a comprehensive directory of all publicly available online databases. The service also includes personal hotline assistance, a monthly newsletter, and a hardcopy *Data Base Directory*.

The Society's efforts during the past few years to extend information services to rural communities led to the establishment of a Special Interest Group on Rural Information Systems. ASIS has also continued efforts to improve effective education in the problems of rural information exchange by working with Utah State University to develop a certificate undergraduate program in community information services.

ASIS established an annual research award—given for the first time in 1984—as part of its efforts to strengthen research and technology components of the Society. Other actions included the establishment of a National Science Foundation Colloquium at the annual meeting and steps toward improving continuing education programs.

With the assistance of ASIS members Joshua I. Smith, Maxima Corporation, Bethesda, Maryland, and Dale Baker, Chemical Abstracts Service, Columbus, Ohio, Bonnie C. Carroll initiated a development program for ASIS, focusing on major information issues.

Samuel B. Beatty, Executive Director who had served the Society for eight years, resigned in 1984 to return to the private sector. At the close of 1984 a search committee, chaired by Julie A. C. Virgo, was engaged in interviewing candidates for the position.

As ASIS moved toward 1985, the Society finalized plans, the strongest in some years, to enhance the image of the information profession. President Bonnie Carroll said in her presidential address at the annual meeting: "We must make our issues, which are the issues of the information society, better understood . . . . The trends in the technical and professional environments of the information age must be a part of the thinking and planning of ASIS through the many mechanisms we have."

Meetings. The 13th Mid-Year Meeting held at Indiana University, Bloomington, May 20–23, set a record attendance. The conference, "The Micro Revolution," was chaired by Steve Harter, School of Library and Information Science, Indiana University. The 47th annual meeting, "Challenges to an Information Society," was held in Philadelphia, October 21–25. Eugene Garfield, Institute for Scientific Information, Philadelphia, served as Honorary Chairman. Barbara Flood, the Information Doctor, Philadelphia, served as conference Vice-Chairman and Technical Program Chairman.

The 48th annual meeting, to be held in Las Vegas October 20–25, 1985, will mark the 20th year of publication of the *Annual Review of Information Science and Technology* (ARIST).

Publications. Publications issued in 1984 included numbers 1–6, volume 35, of the *Journal of the American Society for Information Science; Bulletin of the American Society for Information Science*, volume 10, numbers 3–6 and volume 11, numbers 1–2; *Annual Review of Information Science and Technology*, volume 19 (1984); *1984: Challenges to an Information Society, Proceedings of the 47th ASIS Annual Meeting* (1984).

Awards. The ASIS 1984 Award of Merit went to Joseph Becker, President of Becker and Hayes of Santa Monica, California, and Martha E. Williams, Professor, University of Illinois, Urbana. The award is presented annually in recognition of "noteworthy contributions to the field of information science." Becker was cited for his leadership as an author, teacher, and adviser in "increasing public and government awareness of the role and impact of information science." He was one of the first commissioners of the National Commission on Library and Information Science, served as president of the Interuniversity Communications Council (EDUCOM), and is Editor-in-Chief of the journal *The Information Society*.

Williams was cited for her extraordinary contributions as a researcher, lecturer, author, editor, and leader. A pioneer in electronic database structures and networks, she edited 10 volumes of the *Annual Review of Information Science and Technology*, served as Chairman of the Gordon Research Conference on Scientific Information Problems in Research, and is Editor of the journal *Online Review*.

The outstanding Information Science Teacher Award, established in 1980 to honor one who has "demonstrated sustained excellence in teaching information science," was presented to Susan Artandi, retired Professor, School of Communication, Information and Library Studies, Rutgers University, New Brunswick, New Jersey. Artandi was cited for 20 years of teaching "that demanded excellence from her students," her leadership in building the information science program at Rutgers, and her contributions through research and authorship of textbooks.

Robert S. Tannehill, Jr., received the Watson Davis Award, established to commemorate the Society's founder, and given "for continuous

---

AMERICAN SOCIETY FOR INFORMATION SCIENCE

PRESIDENT (October 1984–October 1985):
Bonnie Cooper Carroll, Department of Energy, Office of Scientific and Technical Information, Oak Ridge, Tennessee

PRESIDENT-ELECT:
Julie A. C. Virgo, The Carroll Group, Chicago, Illinois

TREASURER:
Frank H. Spaulding, Bell Labs, Holmdel, New Jersey

EXECUTIVE DIRECTOR:
Samuel B. Beatty

Membership (September 30, 1984): 4,458 (4,353 individual; 107 institutional)
Headquarters: 1010 Sixteenth Street, N.W., Washington, D.C. 20036

dedicated service to the membership of ASIS through participation in and support of its programs." Tannehill, in 1984 a Director-at-Large and an ASIS member for 13 years, is Library Manager for Chemical Abstracts Service, Columbus, Ohio. — BONNIE COOPER CARROLL

American Theological Library Association

Annual Conference. The 38th annual conference of ATLA was held at Western Theological Seminary, Holland, Michigan, in June with 190 persons attending. Four preconference continuing education workshops were featured. "Time Management for Librarians" was led by Dwayne Webster of the Association of Research Libraries' Office of Management Studies. "Using Goals and Objectives in the Library" was presented by Margaret Auer of the University of Detroit. Sandra Boyd of the Episcopal Divinity School in Cambridge, Massachussetts, led "Women's Studies in Religion." "Technical Services Management" was presented by Lynn Marko of the University of Michigan Libraries.

Frederick Norwood of Garrett-Evangelical Theological Seminary opened the conference with an address entitled "A Bicentennial Appraisal of Methodist Historical Literature." Theology libraries in relation to networking and OCLC were considered in a paper by Kevin Flaherty of the Michigan Library Consortium. Helen Westra of Hope College presented a paper on the sermons of Jonathan Edwards. A paper on security of library materials was given by William A. Moffett of Oberlin College. Norman J. Kansfield of Colgate Rochester-Bexley Hall-Crozer Theological Seminaries presented a historical paper on New Brunswick Theological Seminary, as did Oscar Burdick of Graduate Theological Union on the origins of Seventh Day Baptists, and Jon Pott of Eerdmans Publishers on current theological publishing.

Conference workshops featured subject headings and anaylsis by Warren Kissinger of the Library of Congress; bibliographic instruction by Carolyn Kirkendall of Eastern Michigan University; retrospective conversion of card catalogs by Robert Kepple of Westminster Theological Seminary; and acquisition of library materials from the Far East by Chester C. I. Wang of the University of Wisconsin.

Important business included the final approval of a revision of the bylaws of the Association. Also a new Preservation Board was established, and the final report of Project 2000 was received and commended.

James A. Overbeck of Columbia Theological Seminary, Decatur, Georgia, and Alice M. Kendrick of the Lutheran Council in the U.S.A., New York, were elected new members of the Board of Directors.

Indexes. One of the most valued contributions of the Association has been the creation and publication of indexes to periodical literature in theology and related subjects. The Index Board, composed of seven members and chaired by Norman Kansfield, publishes two indexes. *Religion Index One* (RIO) indexed 369 periodicals in semiannual and annual editions in 1984; this index assumed its present name in 1977 and continues the former *Index to Religious Periodical Literature* (IRPL), begun in 1949. *Religion Index Two* (RIT) is an annual index to religious and theological essays and articles published in collections, Festschriften, and other sources. RIT has been published annually since 1976, and indexes for 1960–75 have been published retrospectively. The ATLA Religion Database is also available online through Bibliographic Retrieval Services (BRS) for periodicals 1949–59, 1975–84, and for essays 1960–83. In the 1983–84 fiscal year, the Index Board had receipts of $473,581 and expenditures of $363,953.

Other Activities. Microfilming of theological literature was started in 1957 by the Board of Microtext. In 1984 the Board was absorbed into a newly created Preservation Board that in addition to the old program of filming religious periodical literature assumed a new and ambitious second program of filming monographic religious literature. Both programs aim at preservation, wider accessibility of the literature, and potentials of saving library shelf space. The Board is composed of nine members, with John A. Bollier serving as chairperson in 1984.

The periodicals program in 1983–84 had receipts of $94,975 and expenditures of $89,766. The new monographs program has attracted 52 subscribing libraries with a subscription level of $279,000 for 1984–85. Louis Charles Willard of Princeton Theological Seminary has accepted the position of Director of both the monograph and periodicals programs.

An OCLC Theological User Group (TUG) was organized under the leadership of William C. Miller of Nazarene Theological Seminary, Kansas City, and in 1984 served the interests of over 85 theological librarians.

Project 2000. Project 2000, a major study of theological libraries, their current situation, resources, problems and needs for the future, was begun in 1981 by a committee jointly established by ATLA and the Association of Theological Schools funded by a grant from the Lilly Endowment Fund. Stephen L. Peterson was the chief investigator and author of the final report published in fall 1984 as a supplement to volume 20 of *Theological Education* as "Theological Libraries for the Twenty-First Century: Project 2000 Final Report." Both ATLA and ATS accepted the report and committed the Associations to a careful review of its implications and recommendations. — RONALD F. DEERING

AMERICAN THEOLOGICAL LIBRARY ASSOCIATION

PRESIDENT (June 1984–1985):
Ronald F. Deering, Southern Baptist Theological Seminary, Louisville, Kentucky

VICE-PRESIDENT/PRESIDENT-ELECT:
Sara M. Mobley, Pitts Theology Library, Emory University, Atlanta

EXECUTIVE SECRETARY:
Albert E. Hurd, 5600 S. Woodlawn, Chicago, Ill. 60637.

Membership (December 1984): 667 (507 personal; 160 institutional)

Archives

National Archives Independence. After years of lobbying, archivists and researchers succeeded in 1984 in winning independence for the National Archives and Records Service. Congress passed and President Reagan signed legislation creating an independent National Archives and Records Administration, effective April 1, 1985. The National Archives was established as an independent agency in 1934. In 1949 it was incorporated into the General Services Administration (GSA), at the recommendation of the Hoover Commission, as the National Archives and Records Service.

Archivists and researchers had charged that, under GSA, the Archives was subject to political and bureaucratic interference and was unable to properly carry out its mandate to preserve, protect, and make available federal records. Critics charged that GSA officials had failed to seek adequate resources for the Archives. Budget cuts during the Carter and Reagan administrations led to personnel reductions and administrative reorganizations that, in turn, forced the Archives to reduce research assistance and other services for scholars. They also forced the agency to slow down substantially the declassification of sensitive documents.

The National Archives and Records Administration Act of 1984, signed by the President on October 19, transfers all archival authorities from the Administrator of GSA to the Archivist of the United States. It does not, however, expand those authorities. The law provides for the appointment of the Archivist by the President, subject to confirmation by the Senate, for no fixed term. The law provides that the Archivist "shall be appointed without regard to political affiliations and solely on the basis of the professional qualifications to perform the office of Archivist."

It was disclosed just days before the bill was signed that the Archivist of the United States, Robert M. Warner, planned to return to the University of Michigan in spring 1985 to serve as Dean of the School of Library Science. Warner was appointed Archivist in 1980.

Assessment Reports. Published in 1984, *Documenting America: Assessing the Condition of Historical Records in the States*, edited by Lisa B. Weber, summarizes the findings and recommendations of historical records assessment and reporting projects completed in nearly 24 states in 1982–83, with grants from the National Historical Publications and Records Commission (NHPRC). The projects, carried out by State Historical Records Advisory Boards, analyzed the condition of historical records programming in four areas: state government records, local government records, historical records repositories, and statewide functions and needs. They were intended to profile conditions and to provide a basis for establishment of statewide priorities, statewide planning, and the allocation of resources.

Commenting on his analysis of the reports' findings in the area of state records, Alabama State Archivist Edwin C. Bridges states, "The major conclusion about state records that emerges from these assessment project reports is that American state records agencies are in an impoverished condition and are currently unable to provide adequate care for their records." In his analysis of reports on historical records repositories, William L. Joyce, New York Public Library, found, "The prevailing pattern is one in which the majority of historical records repositories are barely capable of providing maintenance of their holdings."

Awards. The winners of Society of American Archivists awards and five new Fellows of the Society were honored at an awards luncheon in Washington, D.C., on September 1.

New Fellows were George M. Cunha, conservation consultant; Max J. Evans, State Historical Society of Wisconsin; Edie Hedlin, National Archives and Records Service; Patrick M. Quinn, Northwestern University; and Charles R. Schultz, Texas A & M University.

The Waldo Gifford Leland Prize, awarded to an outstanding published work in the archival field, was presented to Richard Berner for his book, *Archival Theory and Practice in the United States: A Historical Analysis*. The Philip M. Hamer Award for outstanding work by an editor of a documentary publication went to David Wilson of the U.S. Grant papers.

The first C. F. W. Coker Prize for an outstanding achievement in the area of archival description was presented to Roy Turnbaugh, Illinois State Archives, for *A Guide to County Records in The Illinois Regional Archives*. Frank G. Burke received the Fellows' Posner Prize for his article "Archival Cooperation," which appeared in *The American Archivist* (volume 46).

The Oliver Wendell Holmes Award, given to support travel of a foreign archivist already in the United States, was shared by Alan Ives, Riverina College of Advanced Education, Australia, and Samuel Polkah Toe, National Archival Center of Liberia.

The Distinguished Service Award, presented to an archival repository that has made significant contributions to the archival profession, went to the Public Archives of Canada. The Sister M. Claude Lane Award for outstanding work by a religious archivist was presented to Norbert Brockman, former director of the Marianist Training Network. Colonial Dames Scholarships to the Modern Archives Institute at the National Archives were awarded in 1984 to Gregory Gill, New Jersey State Archives, and to Earl M. Hennen, Jr., Mississippi Department of Archives and History.
— ANN MORGAN CAMPBELL

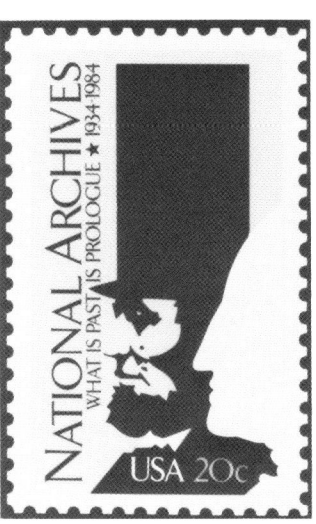

U.S. postage stamp proclaiming 50 years of the National Archives.

Significance and Implications of an Independent National Archives

President Ronald Reagan on October 19 signed into law the bill establishing the National Archives as an independent agency of the federal government effective April 1, 1985.

Thus, in its 50th year of existence, the Archives was returned to the status it enjoyed from 1934 to 1949. Despite the temptation to concentrate on the past during an anniversary year, this legislation turned all thoughts and plans at the Archives to the future.

The new National Archives law creates the National Archives and Records Administration (NARA). The act transfers all archival authorities, functions, and personnel from the General Services Administration (GSA) to the Archivist of the United States. It does not expand these authorities.

Changes in Law. Significant changes in the new law include the following:

The Archivist of the United States will be appointed by the President, subject to confirmation by the Senate, and will serve without a specific term. The appointment is to be made "without regard to political affiliations and solely on the basis of the professional qualifications required to perform the duties and responsibilities of the office."

NARA will be required to report annually to Congress, and the report will cover the National Historical Publications and Records Commission, the National Archives Trust Fund (separate legal entities chaired by the Archivist), as well as the National Archives.

Records management responsibilities that were formerly exercised by the Archives but, in recent years, had been transferred to GSA, are divided between the Archives and GSA. The Archives is charged with "ensuring adequate and proper documentation of the policies and transactions of the Federal government and ensuring proper records disposition." GSA will be concerned with "economical and effective" records management by agencies.

The Archivist of the United States is empowered, as a last resort, to request the Attorney General to initiate action for the recovery of alienated government records and to inform Congress when such a request is made of the Justice Department.

The National Archives Trust Fund Board is empowered to solicit as well as to accept gifts and bequests to be used to benefit the Archives programs.

Any planned disposal of Federal Records by the Archives will be announced in advance in the *Federal Register,* and interested persons may submit their comments on the plans.

These changes, aside from the new elevated status that comes with independence, will make the National Archives more visible to the public. People will be more likely to know who the Archivist is, and, more important, what the Archives is. The annual reports will describe the agency's activities; the ability to solicit funds will mean more and better services and exhibitions for the public; records to be recovered or those slated for disposal will be publicly identified.

Future Direction. But as positive as this legislation is—for the visibility of the agency, for clarification of its functions, for the morale of the staff—it would be a mistake to assume that the problems of the National Archives are now solved. What the legislation provides is a sound basis for the future and an indication of the directions the agency will take in the next few years.

Independence for the National Archives means opportunity. For the first time in 35 years the Archives will be able to set its own priorities, to tell its own story to the Office of Management and Budget and to the Congress, to rise or fall on its own merits, neither protected nor hampered by others.

The significance of these changes cannot be emphasized enough, for the relationship between the National Archives and GSA has deteriorated in the past few years until it produced an intolerable situation that, at times, actually threatened the nation's documentary heritage.

In the early years of GSA, the Archives was treated with benign neglect. But, as the business-oriented conglomerate that is GSA was brought under tighter and more uniform control, policy intrusions began. In time, history (and the archival means to write history) became a bother not a goal. In the process, the National Archives suffered. This undoubtedly is what President Reagan had in mind when, in the statement released by the White House at the time of the signing of the Archives independence legislation, he said: "Many believe [the Archives] has suffered as a result of its placement within the General Services Administration in 1949. I concur in this assessment. . . ."

Past and Future Mission. For half a century it has been the mission of the National Archives to make available to the federal government and to the public those unrestricted records determined to have sufficient historical value to warrant their continued preservation. This will remain the mission of the new independent agency.

But, although the mission of the new NARA is the same as in the past, the means of achieving the goal will be significantly different in the future. The changes will be dramatic, although they may not be immediately apparent in the near future.

First, the new agency will have to reorganize and hire or reassign staff to undertake administrative and other functions that were previously performed for the Archives. These will range from responsibility for the physical state of buildings to financial management, from personnel operations to a congressional liaison staff. The first signs of this change should be apparent when the Archives presents its case for the FY 1986 budget to OMB and the Congress.

Another significant change will occur in the time and effort that the top management of the Archives is able to spend on archival concerns. It has been estimated that more than half of the time of most of the Archives managers has been spent on matters of more concern and importance to GSA than to Archives. It is hoped that independence will mean two extra days in the week for many of the Archives managers. As their talents and energies are redirected to archival matters, the new NARA will inevitably benefit.

New Directions. Areas where change should be apparent in the near future are NARA's involvement with professional archival education and with technology. As the largest archival organization in the country (and one of the largest—if not the largest—in the world), NARA must assume a leadership role in the training of professional archivists. At the same time, the agency must also take the lead in mastering the use of information technology in archives. Both of these are under way; both will require imagination, skill, and funds. But the cost will be small compared to the additional cost of properly preserving current holdings, estimated at over $20,000,000 in the next few years.

During the past decade, as the movement to reestablish the National Archives as an independent, agency grew, historians, archivists, librarians, genealogists, private groups, and other researchers united behind the goal and pressed for change. If the National Archives is to thrive as an independent agency, it is essential that this coalition not disband. Archives are probably the least known of our national treasures; the long-term goals of the National Archives must be both to put its house in order and to change the public awareness of archives and why they are essential.

If those who supported the National Archives in the past continue their interest and involvement in the future, the new independent agency will live up to its unofficial motto, carved on the front of the Archives building in Washington: "What is Past is Prologue."

ROBERT M. WARNER

Armed Forces Libraries

AIR FORCE LIBRARIES

Conference Workshop. A highlight of 1984 for Air Force libraries was the fourth consecutive preconference librarians' workshop in Dallas, which attracted over 100 Air Force librarians from around the world. A feature of the workshop was a one-day miniworkshop on the Zenith Z-100 microcomputer, designated as the standard microcomputer for the Air Force. A 1985 post-ALA Conference workshop will be held in Chicago featuring the theme "Educating Librarians As Managers."

Personnel Changes. Annette Gohlke replaced Nathalie McMahon as Assistant Air Force Librarian in 1984. McMahon was named Air Force Morale, Welfare and Recreation (MWR) Career Program manager, with an office in the Office of Civilian Personnel Operations (OCPO), Randolph AFB, Texas. Gail Knudtson was appointed Command Librarian for the Military Airlift Command (MAC), Scott AFB, Illinois. Mary Lou Sauer took over as Command Librarian for the Strategic Air Command (SAC), Offutt AFB, Nebraska, and Betty Horn was named as Assistant Command Librarian for SAC.

Awards. Marjorie Rambo, Command Librarian, Tactical Air Command (TAC), Langley AFB, Virginia, accepted the Armed Forces Library Section (AFLS) Achievement Award at the joint AFLS/Federal Librarians Round Table (FLRT) banquet during ALA in Dallas. Also during the ALA Conference, Dorothy Hart, Base Librarian, Nellis AFB, Nevada, and Elizabeth Ann De Coux, Base Librarian, Keesler AFB, Mississippi, were honored at H. W. Wilson's John Cotton Dana Library Public Relations Award tea. Hart won the John Cotton Dana Award in the military library division, and De Coux accepted a special award for her library's unique videotape entry system.

Deborah Thompson, Assistant Librarian, Pacific Air Forces (PACAF) Library Service Center, Hickam AFB, Hawaii, was presented with the 1983 MWR Meritorious Award for General Librarian. Eva Haas, Command Librarian, United States Air Forces in Europe (USAFE), received the Meritorious Civilian Service Medal, and Joan Breen, Base Librarian, Lindsey AS, West Germany, was awarded the Wiesbaden (West Germany) Air Force Community's Base Advisory Recognition Award. Sharron Cooper, Base Librarian, Rhein-Main AB, West Germany, won the Air Force Heritage Award for her essay, "Air Force—Only 36 Yet Most Advanced."

Buildings. Both the Air Force Academy and the Air University libraries opened new library wings in 1984, while a new library was constructed at USAFE's newest base, Comiso AS, Italy, and a new academic research library was opened at Einsiedlerhof AS, West Germany, to support the new Warrior Preparation Center. Langley AFB, Virginia, chose an alternative to new construction by purchasing a pre-engineered, 1,600-square-foot PortaStructure library for housing an area branch. PACAF placed an order for four similar libraries.

Career Program. The Air Force librarian career program was expanded to include all 1,410 series positions in grades GS/GM 11 through 15. Centrally funded training was provided for eight librarians who attended Catholic University's "Institute on Federal Library Resources." A librarian intern program was established, with an initial authorization of three positions for 1985. The program provides intern training in general, academic, and technical libraries at three locations. Entry is at the GS-7 level, with promotion to GS-9 at the end of the first year, and a guaranteed GS-11 position upon completion of the program.

ARMY LIBRARIES

Operation and Service Management. During 1984, Army libraries advanced technical and administrative operations to serve the Army library system. The Army Library Management Reporting system (ALMRS) was tested at selected libraries. ALMRS is an Army-wide information system designed to capture data on library services, personnel, and materials collections.

The Army Librarian Intern Program's "Librarian Master Intern Training Plan" was published in 1984. The program provides for the recruitment and training of high-potential librarians to meet the staffing needs of Army libraries.

The automation of Army libraries took a major step forward with the introduction of the Patron-Oriented Automated Library System (PALS) in the USAREUR library community. A contract was awarded to GEAC and the debugging began at test sites in Heidelberg, West Germany. Expansion of the system, to include all 107 of the Army libraries in Europe, was targeted for 1985.

One of the major goals of the project is the development of an online catalog of holdings of all USAREUR libraries, and the eventual networking with other military and U.S. Information Agency libraries in Europe.

An interlibrary loan payment project, sponsored by the Federal Library Committee and tested in 20 Army libraries, proved highly successful and resulted in significant cost savings and faster response times. It simplified the payment of interlibrary loan charges so that Army libraries could borrow from more non-governmental libraries than before. All Army libraries were targeted for coverage in 1985, and all Federal libraries might be covered by the end of 1986.

Training workshops were conducted for librarians in the Training and Doctrine Command (TRADOC) and in USAREUR. As in the civilian library community, Army morale support libraries continued to meet the interests and needs of their communities. The loan of videocassettes and personal computers introduced a whole new group of users to these libraries.

Armed Forces Library Section. The 1984 annual meeting was held in Dallas. Members discussed the status of the Office of Personnel Management's Librarian Register, and voted to take action to get it open for new registrants, and to pressure OPM to keep it open at all times in order to ensure continuing registrations (see also Federal Librarians Round Table). Representatives of each branch of service presented reports on their agency's library programs.

AFLS members joined the Federal Librarians Round Table to hear Fred Goodman, President of

Porta Structures, Washington, D.C., at the annual banquet. The Armed Forces Library Section Achievement Award was presented to Marjorie Rambo, Command Librarian, Tactical Air Command (TAC), Langley AFB, Virginia.

NAVY LIBRARIES

Service and Network Changes. General Navy libraries are administered from the Naval Education and Training Program Development Center, Pensacola, Florida. During 1984 book stocks used to provide libraries for new and reactivated ships and stations were disestablished and made available to all military service libraries.

The General Library Management System (GLMS) was converted from a NASA mainframe computer to an in-house microcomputer. Initial action was taken to extend GLMS to shore general libraries through the development of a standard integrated library operational system based on microcomputers tied to GLMS. The total network was expected to be fully functional in 1988–89.

While many general libraries were in some phase of studying contracting out, none was actually contracted out in 1984.

Peggy Mann, of the Marine Corps Air Station, Cherry Point, North Carolina, was elected Vice-President/President-elect of the Armed Forces Library Section (AFLS). James Aylward, Naval Education and Training Center, Newport, Rhode Island, was elected Secretary.

Technical and research libraries are administered by the organization they serve. The Director of the Navy Department Library, Washington Navy Yard, Washington, D.C., is also coordinator of Navy technical and research libraries. A revised instruction on the function of the coordinator was published.

TONY DAKAN

Art Libraries

Conference Activity. The ARLIS/NA 1984 Annual Conference in Cleveland February 18–22, was hosted by the ARLIS/Ohio Chapter. The Conference Committee, chaired by Jack Perry Brown (at that time Librarian at the Cleveland Museum of Art), organized a wide-ranging series of sessions beginning with the Convocation at the Cleveland Museum of Art, at which Museum Director Evan M. Turner in his address placed the library at the heart of the institution's operations and commented on the problems and prospects of the future. Workshops on management techniques and on career alternatives for art librarians were well-received responses to newer concerns, while more traditional subjects represented were documentation of women artists, oral history, preservation, oriental visual resources, interior design resources, user-related aspects of service to art historians and working artists, slides outside museums and libraries, and picture collections in public libraries.

Sessions on reference tools recently published or in progress and on new serials gave the valuable update these are now counted on to provide each year. The librarian's perspective on architecture for art libraries was presented at a session paralleling one at the 1983 Philadelphia conference on architecture from the architect's point of view.

Intensified interest in computer applications was expressed strongly enough to result in the beginning steps toward establishment of a new Special Interest Group.

The ARLIS/NA Standards Committee was reactivated in 1984 to develop physical facilities standards for art libraries and visual resource collections, in addition to reviewing the previously issued standards for art library staffing and collections. By December 1984 the Committee had completed the final draft of a questionnaire aimed at gathering background statistics. Although 1984 was a year in which ARLIS/NA did not meet in conjunction with the College Art Association, proximity to the CAA conference in Toronto was such that the usual joint session was possible, on the topic "Books as the Artist's Inspiration." Among other meetings during the year were those of the Special Libraries Association's Museums, Arts and Humanities Division, with Guy St. Clair as MAHD Chair and Diane Guzman as MAHD Conference Chair, for the SLA 75th Anniversary Conference in New York, June; ACRL Art Section, chaired by Roland Hansen, jointly with the ACRL Anthropology and Social Sciences Section at the Dallas Museum of Art during the ALA Conference in Dallas; the Visual Resources Curators Group at the Southeastern College Art Conference in Richmond, Virginia, October; and the Association of Architectural Librarians, Washington, D.C., in the fall.

Awards. The ARLIS/NA Gerd Muehsam Award was presented at the ARLIS/NA Cleveland conference to Nancy M. Pike, student of library science at the University of Wisconsin-Madison, for her paper "The Golden Cockerell Press, 1921–1961: A History, Bibliography and Index." The award is given annually to a student in a graduate program of library science for the most outstanding paper on art or visual resources librarianship and is named for the late art librarian of Queens College Brooklyn, author of *Guide to Basic Information in the Visual Arts* (Norton/ABC Clio, 1978). It includes a year's membership in ARLIS/NA and a nominal cash award.

ART LIBRARIES SOCIETY OF NORTH AMERICA

CHAIRPERSON (February 1984–February 1985):
Mary Ashe, San Francisco Public Library

VICE-CHAIRPERSON/CHAIRPERSON-ELECT:
Toni Petersen, Bennington College, Vermont

SECRETARY:
Lynette M. Korenic, University of California, Santa Barbara

TREASURER:
Mary Jane Cuneo, Fogg Art Museum, Harvard University

EXECUTIVE DIRECTOR:
Pamela Jeffcott Parry

Membership (December 1984): 1,197
Headquarters: 3375 Bear Creek Circle, Tucson, Arizona 85749

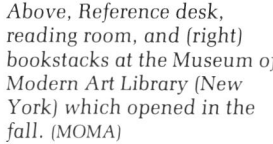
Above, Reference desk, reading room, and (right) bookstacks at the Museum of Modern Art Library (New York) which opened in the fall. (MOMA)

A summary of Pike's paper was published in *Art Libraries Journal*, Summer 1984. For the first time an honorable mention was awarded to Amy Johnsen-Harris, from the school of library science at the University of Rhode Island, for her paper "The Daguerreotype: An Endangered Species."

The 4th Annual George Wittenborn Awards (named for the late New York publisher and art book dealer) for excellence of content and production in art publishing were awarded to the publishers of four 1982 works: the Cooper-Hewitt Museum and Harry N. Abrams for *Scandinavian Modern Design, 1880–1980*, edited by David Revere McFadden; the Macmillan Publishing Company, for the *Macmillan Encyclopedia of Architects*, edited by Adolf Placzek; the Canadian Centre for Architecture, for *Photography and Architecture, 1839–1939*, edited by Richard Pare; the University Press of New England, for *The Work of August Saint-Gaudens*, by John Dryfout. For the first time the paper in all books under consideration was tested for pH in the Paper Conservation Laboratory of the Yale Center for British Arts, with the results entering into the deliberations on the candidates.

Publications. Developments in ARLIS/NA publications included a change in frequency of the Society's bulletin *Art Documentation* from five times yearly to quarterly and the inauguration of a new quarterly newsletter, *ARLIS/NA Update*, to emphasize information and news of a timely nature. Both are edited by Erika Esau and George Boeck, working with the newly established Advisory Board chaired by Caroline Backlund. Among the special features in *Art Documentation* were "American Art Annual: A Guide to Biographical Information, Volume 1 to Volume 30," by Barbara Polowy (Spring 1984); "Viewpoint: What It Takes to Make a Successful Art Periodical," an interview with Milton Esterow, Editor and Publisher of *ARTnews*, by Paula Baxter (Fall 1984); "African Art Periodicals," by Janet Stanley, sixth in a series of annotated bibliographies of art-related journals (Fall 1984); "Art Library Careers: Pivotal Points, Moves and Alternatives: a Bibliography [of post-1977 items]," by Arthur Downing (Fall 1984); "How Art Historians Look for Information," by Deirdre Corcoran Stam (Winter 1984); "Viewpoint: An Inside Look at Art Book Publishing," an interview with Walter Strauss of Abaris Books, by Paula Baxter (Winter 1984). The Summer *Art Documentation* included the customary record of Conference proceedings.

Two new numbers in the ARLIS/NA Occasional Papers series were issued in 1984: "Current Issues in Fine Arts Collection Development," edited by Janet Clarke-Hazlett (OP #3, ARLIS/NA) and "Reference Tools for Fine Arts Visual Resource Collections," edited by Christine Bunting (OP #4, ARLIS/NA). Both are available from ARLIS/NA Headquarters.

Garland Publishing scheduled *Art Books: A Basic Bibliography of Monographs on Artists*, by E. Louise Lucas, revised and expanded by Wolfgang Freitag, for spring 1985. Plans for a second edition of the *Directory of Art Libraries and Visual Resources Collections* (ARLIS/NA and Neal-Schuman, 1978) were cancelled in favor of an agreement with Bowker to enhance art library listings in the *American Art Directory*.

The 600-term *Art Librarian's Glossary*, edited by Ian Sheridan with equivalents of English-language in four other languages, was published by the IFLA Section of Art Libraries.

International Scene Relations. Continuing communication on a worldwide basis is facilitated by the web of sister organizations in other countries: ARLIS/United Kingdom, ARLIS/Australia-New Zealand, CARLIS (Canadian Society of Art Libraries) and ARLIS/Norge, which held its first general meeting in March. The quarterly *Art Libraries Journal* of ARLIS/UK concentrates efforts toward becoming the publication of record for international art librarianship. Serving as an umbrella for these national groups is the Section of Art Libraries of the IFLA Division of Special Libraries, chaired during its development from Round Table to full-fledged Division status by Phillip Pacey of the UK.

The Section of Art Libraries scheduled one session at the August IFLA Conference in Nairobi. Magnus John of the U.K. was present to deliver his paper in person, "The Aesthetics of the Vital Arts: Some Images from Black Africa and the Caribbean," while three others were received: "Developing an Art for Life's Sake" by Gavin Jantjes; "Vision and Design" by Arnold Pacey; "The Designer in a Developing Country and the Information He Needs" by Hl Kuman Vyas. All were summarized in the Section of Art Libraries NEWSLETTER no. 11, October 1984. (The *Newsletter* updates professional affairs and the literature. It is issued about three times yearly.)

Sessions cosponsored by the International Association of Music Libraries (IAML) and the IFLA Audio-Visual Round Table addressed closely related concerns about preserving the musical and performing arts heritage so often threatened like that of the visual arts by development.

Mary Williamson, incoming secretary of the Section, coordinated and completed on the Section's behalf a collection of East African Art slides for presentation to the Kenya Ministry of Culture. Her commitment and dedication were crucial to the project, which included donations of more than 600 slides, three hand-viewers, and a projector, along with a computer-produced catalog. The Visual Resources Association added copies of the *International Bulletin for Photographic Documentation of the Visual Arts* and a membership in the Association. The gift was made in a spirit of recognition of the loss of so much of the African heritage through the removal and dispersal of indigenous art works and as a practical contribution to the study and awareness of East African art in Kenya, where, it was hoped, the materials would be available in the National Archives.

The Second International Conference on Automatic Processing of Art History Data and Documents was held September 24–27 in Pisa, Italy, sponsored by the Scuola Normale Superiore, Pisa, and the J. Paul Getty Trust.

Art History Information Program. A number of projects of great importance and promise in the art information field were operating in the mid-1980s under the aegis of the J. Paul Getty Trust. The program supports a growing number of efforts at improving access and control on a worldwide basis, using the most advanced technology and working toward an international system integrated by a uniform or compatible standard. Included are the Art and Architecture Thesaurus Project, the *Repertoire International de la Litterature de L'Art (RILA)*, the *Avery Index of Architectural Periodicals*, and the *Museum Information Prototype*. Ultimately all will play an important role in the J. Paul Getty Center for the History of Art and the Humanities, as well as in other institutions. The Center as conceived will include a 450,000-volume library with the most sophisticated design and equipment.

The Trust granted $50,000 to the Rutger's Center for the History of Art and the Humanities to support its work as the U.S. body responsible for contributions to the *Lexicon Iconographicum Mythologiae Classicae*, a project of 37 countries to publish a pictorial dictionary of classical mythology. (Two double volumes have been published from 1981 to 1984 by Artemis Verlag of Zurich/Munich; the remaining six were projected at two-year intervals.)

New Library Facilities. Three new art museum libraries were opened in 1984. The Dallas Museum of art designed by Edward Larrabee Jones includes library facilities. The Ingalls Library at the Cleveland Museum of Art is part of a three-story addition to the Museum, with the additional space in the two floors now devoted to the library expected to suffice for at least the next 25 years. The reopening of the remodeled Museum of Modern Art on May 17 saw also the return of the Library from temporary rented space to expanded quarters with 9,000 square feet for its 90,000 cataloged items, 2,250 periodicals titles, and 100,000 vertical files.

ARLIS/NA Founded in 1972, the Art Libraries Society of North America (ARLIS/NA) continued in its second decade as the preeminent subject-oriented professional association for art information specialists. Its membership of 1,197 comprises not only individuals (librarians, library assistants and students) and institutions concerned with all aspects of the visual arts, architecture, slides and photographs, but also a growing component of business affiliates, including specialist dealers, and book and microfilm publishers. A network of 18 regional chapters provides a basis for local activity with direct links to the ARLIS/NA Executive Board through four Regional Representatives who serve as Board members. Four Special Interest Groups (Architecture, cataloging and Indexing System, Serials and Visual Resources) and three Types of Library Groups (Academic, Museum and Public) within the Society give additional focus to the needs and interests of these constituencies, particularly through articles and columns in the Society journals and through sponsorship of programs at the annual conferences.

MARY ASHE

Association for Information and Image Management

Meetings. The Association for Information and Image Management's 1984 executive conference was held in Marco Island, Florida, and included the top leaders in the micrographics and image processing fields. The Service Company Executives Forum, held in New Orleans in October, gave AIIM's service company presidents an opportunity to voice their ideas and needs. A manufacturers meeting was inaugurated in Washington, D.C., in November.

The AIIM Annual Conference and Exposition, held in Chicago, introduced a number of new products, particularly in the engineering micrographics and optical disk areas.

Publications. AIIM's *Journal of Information and Image Management* during 1984 featured a serialized look at "Information Management and Technology—Challenges and Opportunities in a Period of Change." Written by a well-known consultant, lecturer, and author, Klaus W. Otten, the series appeared in all 12 issues of *JIIM* during the year. Other articles covered electronic imag-

Association for Library and Information Science Education

Conferences. The 1984 Annual Conference of the Association for Library and Information Science Education (formerly the Association of American Library Schools) met in January in Washington, D.C. The Conference theme was "Education Information Professionals for the Future: Strategies and Options." Keynote Speaker for the Conference was Anthony Oettinger, Chairman of the Program on Information Resources Policy, Center for Information Policy Research, at Harvard University. The conference included four general sessions focusing on the challenge of the future, library and information science education, professional practice, and strategies for change.

An ALISE-sponsored conference on accreditation in September in Chicago was chaired by F. William Summers, University of South Carolina, and funded by the H. W. Wilson Foundation. Conference sessions examined the national governance of accreditation and the specific accreditation program in librarianship conducted by the American Library Association and models of accreditation in other fields, and it explored issues in library and information science education looking toward the scope, structure and financial support of a new program of accreditation that would represent all relevant groups. Delegates participating in the conference represented the American Association of Law Libraries, American Library Association, American Society for Information Science, American Federation of Information Processing Societies, ALISE, Association of Research Libraries, Association of Records Managers and Administrators, Canadian Association of Library Schools, Canadian Library Association, Council on Library Resources, Federal Library Commission, Medical Library Association, National Commission on Libraries and Information Science, National Federation of Abstracting and Indexing Services, Society of

---

ASSOCIATION FOR INFORMATION AND IMAGE MANAGEMENT

PRESIDENT (April 1984–April 1985):
Roger E. Blue, Total Information Management Corporation, Emeryville, California

VICE-PRESIDENT/PRESIDENT-ELECT:
Edward W. Mackin, MICRO, Cornwells Heights, Pennsylvania

TREASURER:
James E. Weldon, Micro Design Division of Bell & Howell Co., Hartford, Wisconsin

EXECUTIVE DIRECTOR:
O. Gordon Banks

Membership (December 1984): 8,000
Headquarters: 1100 Wayne Avenue, Suite 1100, Silver Spring, Maryland 20910

---

ing, records management, and micrographics applications. A new quarterly newsletter was published in *JIIM* for AIIM's Engineering Special Interest Group (ESIG). It contained engineering news briefs, profiles of industry leaders, new products, and reports from the regional ESIG groups.

Selling Information Systems, a book published in April and aimed at sales and marketing staffs, provided tips and suggestions on how to approach the information management market. A new edition of AIIM's annual *Buying Guide* to the equipment, products, and services offered by AIIM's trade members was published in January.

AIIM's fourth annual *Conference Daily* was published on-site all three days of the Annual Conference and Exposition in Chicago. The tabloid-size, 48-page newspaper featured on-the-spot interviews with conference attendees, product information, and in-depth articles and features on information management written by prominent industry leaders. Fifteen thousand copies were distributed each day.

New standards were published on splices for imaged film; test chart for rotary microfilm cameras; operational procedures/inspection and quality control of first-generation, silver gelatin microfilm of documents, cores, and spools for recording equipment; alphanumeric COM quality test slide; COM input tape formats; and determining illumination uniformity of 35mm planetary cameras.

Activities. AIIM's Engineering Special Interest Group (ESIG) movement moved forward in 1984. Five regional groups were established, with more under consideration. They hold regular meetings and provide special programs and seminars on topics of interest to the active and growing engineering community.

AIIM management during 1984 continued to emphasize the organization's growth. Planning efforts created policies and programs to market the Association's unique position in the information and imaging business environment. More of the Association's resources were to be used to finance growth over a three-year period, with particular emphasis in the membership and annual conference areas. 1984 marked another financially successful year for AIIM.

O. GORDON BANKS

ASSOCIATION FOR LIBRARY AND INFORMATION SCIENCE EDUCATION

PRESIDENT (January 1984–January 1985):
Jane Robbins-Carter, School of Library and Information Studies, University of Wisconsin–Madison

PRESIDENT-ELECT:
Norman Horrocks, School of Library Service, Dalhousie University, Halifax, Nova Scotia

SECRETARY/TREASURER:
Timothy Sineath, College of Library and Information Science, University of Kentucky, Lexington

EXECUTIVE SECRETARY:
Janet Phillips, State College, Pennsylvania

EDITOR: *Journal of Education for Librarianship*
Charles D. Patterson, School of Library and Information Science, Louisiana State University, Baton Rouge

Membership (June, 1984): 651 (558 personal; 93 institutional)
Headquarters: 471 Park Lane, State College, Pennsylvania 16803

American Archivists, Special Library Association, and the United States Department of Education, Division of Library Programs. The proceedings of the Conference were to be available from ALISE headquarters in early 1985.

Awards. Research activities are a top priority within ALISE. Established in 1977, a program of Research Grant Awards for research related to education for library and information science provides support for scholarly activities to personal members of the Association. In 1984 two awards totaling $2,500 were made to John V. Richardson, Jr., UCLA, for "Primary Source Material for a Critical Biography of Pierce Butler," and Alvin M. Schraeder, University of Alberta, for "A Bibliometric Study of the *Journal of Education for Librarianship*."

In addition to the Research Grant Awards, the Association sponsored a Research Paper Competition which recognizes, through $500 awards, outstanding research by members without regard to the topic of the research. The winners of the Research Paper Competition in 1984 were Nancy Van House, University of California–Berkeley, for "The Return on the Investment in Library Education" and Wayne A. Wiegand, University of Kentucky, for "Establishing ALA Headquarters in Chicago: An Analysis of the Forces which Brought the Association to the Midwest in 1909."

A third research-related program of the Association recognizes outstanding doctoral dissertations with $100 cash awards.

Activities. The ALISE Executive Secretary and Past-President Robert D. Stueart, Simmons, served on the Advisory Board for the U.S. Department of Education's project "Libraries and a Learning Society." Through a series of seminars held in early 1984, librarians responded to the 1983 report of the National Commission on Excellence in Education, *A Nation at Risk*. The librarians' response, which is based upon the seminars and a series of papers prepared for the seminars by ALISE members Richard Dougherty, Jane Hannigan, James Liesener, Peggy Sullivan, and Douglas Zweizig, is entitled, *Alliance for Excellence*.

An ad hoc Committee of Association members, chaired by Philip M. Clark, St. John's University, made recommendations to the Board in 1984 on automation of certain operations of the ALISE executive office.

Membership. The full membership category for both institutional and personal members requires that an institution's first professional (master's level) degree in librarianship has been accredited by the American Library Association. All institutional members not so accredited are associate institutional members, and all personal members not associated in a full-time capacity with an accredited program are associate personal members. The ALISE Board recommended that there be only two categories, institutional and personal members, discontinuing the associate designation.

JANE ROBBINS-CARTER

Association for Library Service to Children

Three major concerns emerged as a focus of discussion and activity for the Association for Library Service to Children (ALSC) during 1984: long-range planning, library education for youth services specialists, and interdivisional cooperation in ALA. The ALSC Board of Directors approved a Long Range Planning Proposal submitted by Phyllis Van Orden, 1983–84 Division President. A Task Force on Long Range Planning was subsequently appointed with Van Orden serving as chair. The Task Force will propose new goals and objectives in 1986.

Children's librarians have been attempting dialogue with library schools that have been dropping courses or declining to fill faculty positions in the youth services area of study. Letters supporting the concerns of the local librarians were sent on behalf of ALSC to the deans of such schools. Even in schools offering a strong curriculum in children's, young adult, and school librarianship there seemed to be a declining interest among library school students in youth services careers, and ALSC may join with the Young Adult Services Division and the American Association of School Librarians to develop cooperative efforts with library schools for strengthening professional recruitment and education in this sector of librarianship. ALSC officers and committees have increased their dialogue with other divisions on many fronts in recent years. One result has been a record number of cosponsored programs at the ALA Conference in Dallas and in planning for the Chicago Conference in 1985.

ALSC Activities and Programs. Phyllis Van Orden's President's Program in Dallas had as its

Notable Children's Books Committee of the Association for Library Service to Children session at the ALA Midwinter Meeting in Washington, D.C. (American Libraries)

Association for Library Service to Children

theme "A Retrospective Look at Children's Books, 1976–80" and gave participants the opportunity to participate in the evaluation process used by the Notable Books for Children Committee. Another in-depth program in Dallas was the preconference on Cable Television, "Cable Untangled," cosponsored with YASD. ALSC cosponsored several other conference programs: the ALA Intellectual Freedom Committee's program, "Censors Are People, Too"; the YASD President's Program, "Who Speaks for Youth: Intellectual Freedom, Public Relations and the Library"; the ALSC/YASD Research Forum; the ALSC/PLA cosponsored program, "Toddlers and Their Parents in the Library"; and the ALSC/PLA "Notables Showcase," featuring outstanding children's materials produced during 1983 and 1984.

The Arbuthnot Honor Lecturer for 1984 was Fritz Eichenberg. His speech, "Bell, Book, and Candle: An Artist's Odyssey," was delivered in April in Minneapolis. The event was locally sponsored by the Minnesota Library Association, the Minneapolis Public Library and Information Center, METRONET, the Minnesota Educational Media Organization, and the Kierlan Collection of the University of Minnesota. The lecture is sponsored by ALSC and the Scott, Foresman Publishing Company.

For the second year ALSC supported Library Legislation Day as a cosponsor. ALSC officers and committee members attended and the Division's Legislation Committee distributed buttons reading "Kids Need Libraries."

The Division participated in the ALA exhibit booth at the AASL Conference in Atlanta, and 1984–85 President Margaret Bush attended Conference programs on behalf of the Division. Phyllis Van Orden attended the invitational seminar on Library and Information Science Education held at the University of California–Berkeley in February 1984 and sponsored by the U.S. Department of Education as part of the dialogue stimulated by that agency's publication of *A Nation at Risk*.

Awards and Scholarships. The Caldecott Medal was awarded to illustrators Alice and Martin Provensen for *The Glorious Flight across the Channel with Louis Bleriot*, published by Viking Press. The Newbery Medal was given to author Beverly Cleary for *Dear Mr. Henshaw*, published by William Morrow & Company. The Mildred L. Batchelder Award was presented to Viking Press for *Ronia, the Robber's Daughter*, written by Astrid Lindgren and translated by Patricia Crampton.

The Frederic G. Melcher Scholarships for graduate library school study during 1984–85 were awarded to Barbara Gail Freedman, who is studying at the University of North Carolina at Chapel Hill, and Constance N. Kehs, studying at Drexel University.

The Putnam Publishing Group Award, which provides funds to assist four ALSC members in attending their first ALA Annual Conference, was given to Jan Irving, Iowa; Ione Cowen, Ohio; Jane Belsches, North Carolina; and Dean Lyons, Maine.

In 1984 the ALSC Board of Directors received a proposal from the Bound to Stay Bound Company to establish an annual scholarship of $1,500 to be given to a practicing librarian in the field of children's or school librarianship for academic study beyond the MLS degree. Pending approval by the ALA Council, the award will first be given for study in the 1985–86 academic year.

Available first in 1984, the Helen Knight Memorial Fund provides money for special projects of ALSC members or committees. Grants of $1,000 or less will be made annually for projects that may be long- or short-range and cannot be supported out of the general ALSC funds.

Two ALSC members were honored with prestigious awards during the year. Effie Lee Morris, former Coordinator of Children's Services at the San Francisco Public Library, received the Constance Lindsay Skinner Award given by the National Women's Book Association in recognition of her contributions to children's books and reading. The Grolier Foundation Award, given for outstanding work with children and young people, was awarded to Carolyn Sue Peterson, Head of the Children's Department, in the Orlando, Florida, Public Library.

Publications. *Intellectual Freedom for Children: A Packet of Materials* is available in looseleaf format. A project of the Division's Intellectual Freedom Committee, this collection of forms, bibliographies, policy statements, and guidelines should prove useful for public and school libraries and also for adolescent and adult services. The *Caldecott Calendar*, first published for the year 1984, was also published for 1985. *Coordinators of Children's and Young Adult Services in Public Library Systems Serving at Least 100,000 People*, a directory, became available in a revised edition in 1984.

Several lists of notable materials for children are prepared by ALSC committees each year. The "Notable Films, Filmstrips, and Recordings" lists are now published in the April issue of *School Library Journal*. They are available in folder format through the ALSC office. Three other lists, published in *SLJ*, *Booklist*, and *Top of the News*, are also available as individual folders: "Notable Books for Children," "Caldecott Medal Books," and "Newbery Medal Books." The latter two lists are updated annually to include the current year's medal and honor book awards and all previous winners of the Caldecott or Newbery medals.

Organization Activities. A new committee, the Grants Committee, was established to assist members and committees in the area of funding

---

ASSOCIATION FOR LIBRARY SERVICE TO CHILDREN

PRESIDENT (June 1984–July 1985):
Margaret Bush, Graduate School of Library and Information Science, Simmons College, Boston, Massachusetts

VICE-PRESIDENT/PRESIDENT-ELECT:
Linda R. Silver, Cuyahoga County Public Library, Cleveland, Ohio

EXECUTIVE DIRECTOR:
Ann Carlson Weeks

Membership (August 31, 1984): 3,016 (2,479 personal; 537 organizational)
Expenditures (August 31, 1984): $106,514

sources and grantsmanship. The Division was awarded a $10,000 grant from the Foundation for Children with Learning Disabilities to help with the funding of a preconference to be held prior to the 1985 Annual Conference in Chicago. The focus of this program will be public library services to learning-disabled children and adolescents.

The Membership Committee continued to develop new avenues of attracting new members to the Division. A membership network was established with volunteers identified in local, state, and regional associations.

Cooperative efforts with other national organizations serving the child were expanded by adding liaison relationships with Reading Is Fundamental, Inc., and the Multiple Sclerosis Society. The Division works closely with YASD in developing effective liaison relationships.

As ALSC moved into systematic planning for the future, it appeared in 1984 that the major issues of concern included library education, programming, fiscal matters, the status of children's library services, and the organizational structure of the Association.

MARGARET BUSH

Association of College and Research Libraries

Association Programs. Publications. *College and Research Libraries (C&RL)* published six issues in 1984, the first three under the editorship of C. James Schmidt, and the last three under Charles Martell, whose tenure began in June, for a three-year term. *College and Research Libraries News (C&RL News)* was published monthly (July/August combined) under the direction of George Eberhart. It increased in size to an average of 58 pages per issue in 1984. *Choice*, ACRL's book and nonprint review journal for academic libraries, also appeared monthly (July/August combined). As it passed its 20th anniversary *Choice* changed its policy on the signing of reviews. Beginning with the September 1984 issue, all of the approximately 600 monthly reviews were signed. Rebecca Dixon left *Choice* at the end of July, and Patricia E. Sabosik became the Editor/Publisher.

During 1984 ACRL published *The Bibliographic Instruction Clearinghouse: a Practical Guide; Library Instruction Clearinghouses 1984: a Directory; Curriculum Materials Center Collection Development Policy; Library Statistics of Colleges and Universities, 1982 Institutional Data;* and *Quantitative Criteria for Academic Research Libraries. Academic Libraries: Myths and Realities, The Proceedings of the Third National Conference of ACRL* appeared in a timely fashion, within months of the Conference. In addition, ACRL published course syllabi for six new continuing education courses: *Performance Evaluation; Marketing Fee-Based Services; Interviewing Skills; Job Training; Strategic Planning;* and *How to Teach Science Reference Materials*. A Committee to consider options for publishing a third edition of *Books for College Libraries* (chaired by Richard Johnson) solicited proposals.

Third National Conference. ACRL held its third National Conference in Seattle, April 4–7. Planned and organized by a local committee headed by Gary Menges, the Conference attracted 1,220 participants. The program was based on the theme Academic Libraries: Myths and Realities. Theme speakers (librarians, higher education administrators, and library users) drew on a variety of experiences to address the question. Contributed papers constituted a large part of the program, and 155 exhibitors supported the conference by their participation.

Product Seminars allowed exhibitors to describe briefly the new products and services they were introducing in 1984.

ALA Annual Conference. The ACRL President's Program, Academic Libraries and the Learning Society, featured viewpoints on *A Nation at Risk* and the Libraries and the Learning Society project, by Julie Virgo, Richard Dougherty, and Milton Goldberg, Executive Director of the National Commission on Excellence in Education. Sessions were held by ACRL Sections, including the Anthropology and Sociology Section program on collection management; the Art Section museum tour; the Asian and African Section programs about Third World libraries; the Bibliographic Instruction Section's focus on new technologies; and the College Libraries Section's emphasis on online strategies.

The Community and Junior College Libraries Section featured a program on quality circles; the Education and Behavioral Sciences Section highlighted the involvement of faculty in library services; the Law and Political Science Section examined the political process; the Rare Books and Manuscripts Section discussed rare books from the point of view of the librarian and the patron; the Slavic and East European Section surveyed publishing in the Soviet Union; and the Western European Specialists Section described online services in Europe. Several discussion groups also held programs.

Continuing Education. Fifty participants registered for four courses at the Midwinter Meeting; 184 attended eight courses in Seattle, and seven courses were offered in Dallas. Seven new courses were developed.

Funded Projects. The first two workshops in the joint project of the Public Library Association and ACRL to improve the quality of humanities programming were carried out in October in Madison, Wisconsin, and in December in Santa Barbara, California, with funding from the National Endowment for the Humanities. The ALA Divisional Leadership Enhancement Program, with funding from an ALA Goal Award, conducted its first one-and-a-half-day preconference at the 1984 Midwinter Meeting. About 100 board members from ALA's 11 divisions and the ALA Executive Board attended.

Awards. Richard D. Johnson was honored as the ACRL Academic and Research Librarian of the Year, for (among other contributions) his service as editor of *College and Research Libraries*, his acting editorship of *Choice*, and his work as chair of ACRL's First National Conference. Thomas Kirk was the first person to be awarded the Miriam Dudley Bibliographic Instruction Librarian of the Year Award.

Other. A new edition of the ACRL Speakers Bureau publication was compiled, indicating key officers and staff and the topics about which they are prepared to speak. A program for the overseas exchange of American librarians was carried out at a modest level, hampered by the difficulty of finding comparable placements for European librarians.

Association Units. Chapters. North Dakota became the 34th chapter of ACRL in 1984. Chapters give members the opportunity to work with colleagues locally, to experience quality programming near home, and to exercise leadership skills. *Chapter Topics* appeared quarterly with news of chapter activities and information about chapters and the chapter visits program were carried in *C&RL News*. The chapter visits provided speakers—the Association's top officers and staff—for eight chapters. ACRL also provided funding for special programs at the chapter level and supported a minimum level of chapter activity with its chapter allotments.

Sections. Aside from programming at the ALA Annual Conference, ACRL's 13 sections provided their members with newsletters and other publications, carried out research projects, and sought out continuing education opportunities for their professional development. The Rare Books and Manuscripts Section conducted its 25th preconference in Austin, Texas, on the theme "Collecting the Twentieth Century."

Committees. The Academic and Research Library Personnel Study Group commissioned a paper on the future of the profession; the Continuing Education Committee divided into two parts, the new unit being called the Continuing Education Course Advisory Committee; a new Professional Association Liaison Committee was appointed to enlarge the activities of the Bibliographic Instruction Liaison project; an ad hoc Committee on Research Development was named to help develop the research potential of ACRL members; and a Task Force on Library Statistics explored ways to improve the completeness and timeliness of academic library statistics.

Discussion Groups. The 12 discussion groups met regularly at ALA Conferences; some issued newsletters to keep their members informed about current issues. One new discussion group was formed to discuss microcomputers in academic libraries.

Headquarters Activities. Staff changes in 1984 made it a transitional year: Julie Carroll Virgo left ACRL in July to manage the Carroll Group's Chicago office. JoAn S. Segal became Executive Director on September 1, coming from the Bibliographical Center for Research, Inc., in Denver. Barbara Macikas left her ACRL continuing education position in September to move to the ALA Conference Arrangements Office. Sandra Whiteley was named Associate Executive Director in June. She carried out the fourth statistical study of non-ARL university libraries in the fall. The use of ALANET by ACRL Committees increased during the year.

Planning for the Future. The Association's planning activities continued, with the Planning Committee taking responsibility for reviewing the structure of ACRL, and the new Strategic Planning Task Force building on the work of the earlier Committee on an Activity Model, which had identified ACRL's mission, goals, and objectives. The Task Force activities are designed to help the Association set priorities for action based on member needs and desires, and establish a means for achieving those priorities.

SHARON J. ROGERS

Association of Jewish Libraries

Convention. The opening session of the 19th annual convention in June in Atlanta was devoted to the topic "The History of the Jews in Georgia." It featured an address by Mark Bauman of Atlanta. Perry Brickman of Atlanta gave a slide presentation.

Other major lectures were "Adventures of a Yiddish Book Collector" by Aaron Lansky, Amherst, Massachussetts; "Folk Figures in Jewish Literature" by Jay Jacoby, Charlotte; and "Judaic Studies on the College Campus" by Ellen Umansky, Atlanta. A panel discussing various aspects of the Emory University Holocaust Project was also featured.

One morning was devoted to library concerns according to type of library: Research and Special; Synagogue; School; Community Center. The Council of Archives and Research Libraries (CARLJS) held its annual meeting and the Research and Special Libraries Division of AJL, most of whose members are affiliated with CARLJS, joined this session. Bella Weinberg discussed "Hebraic Computers for Libraries: The State of the Art." Pearl Berger presented a proposal for a cooperative preservation microfilming project.

Topics discussed by the synagogue librarians included "Books as Triggers to Discussion and Thought" by Sylvia Eisen and "There's No Business like Book Business" (i.e., bulletin boards) by Marcia Posner.

Presentations at the school librarian's session were "Assembling and Classifying Books" led

---

ASSOCIATION OF COLLEGE AND RESEARCH LIBRARIES

PRESIDENT: (June 1984–July 1985)
Sharon Rogers, Bowling Green State University, Ohio

VICE-PRESIDENT/PRESIDENT-ELECT:
Sharon A. Hogan, Middleton Library, Louisiana State University, Baton Rouge

EXECUTIVE DIRECTOR:
JoAn S. Segal

DEPUTY EXECUTIVE DIRECTOR:
Cathleen Bourdon

ASSOCIATE EXECUTIVE DIRECTOR:
Sandy Whiteley

EDITOR, *COLLEGE & RESEARCH LIBRARIES*:
Charles Martell

EDITOR, *C & RL NEWS*:
George Eberhart

EDITOR, *CHOICE*:
Patricia Sabosik

Membership (August 31, 1984): 8,835 (7,698 personal; 1,137 organizational)
Expenditures, ACRL and *Choice* (August 31, 1984): $1,651,615

by Gloria Waldenberg; "Integrating Jewish and General History" by Esther Nussbaum; "Teaching Library Skills in the Lower Grades" by Mariessa Anton; "Accreditation" by Nancy Bloom; and "Library Policy" by Margot Berman.

The theme of the Community Center librarians discussion was "Opportunities and Challenges of Jewish Community Center Libraries," and talks were given by Sylvia Firschein, Wayne, N.J.; Anita Wenner, Denver; and Edythe Wolf, Omaha.

A workshop on "Beginning Judaica Librarians" was chaired by Rita Frischer.

Other sessions included Media by Ralph Simon; Old Age in Church and Synagogue Libraries by Barbara Hull; Book Repair, Library Application of Word Processors, Library Use Instructions by Linda Lerman and Charles Cutter; Yiddish Acquisitions and Publishing by Dina Abramowicz and Zachary Baker; and Storytelling by Sue Baranik. "Great Ideas" was chaired by Manne Aronovsky and "Editing a Journal" by Joel Taxel. Cataloging clinics according to various classifications schemes were also held.

Awards. Rose Zar received the Upper Elementary School Children's Book Award for *In the Mouth of the Wolf,* and Barbara Pomerantz received the Primary School Book Award for *Bubby, Me and Memories.*

To encourage excellence in the writing of children's books as well as reference works in the Jewish field, AJL offers a number of awards. The AJL Children's Book Awards consist of a primary school book, an upper elementary school book and a Sydney Taylor Body of Work Award. Judith Greenblatt was named Chairperson of the Children's Book Award Committee for 1984–85. A new award was established for the best reference book.

Three new committees were formed in 1984: a Committee on Library Education chaired by Edith Degani to work toward achieving certification of Judaica librarians; a Cataloging Committee under the direction of Ellen Kovacic to serve as a liaison with the Library of Congress on cataloging policy; and a Job Clearinghouse Edith Lubetski coordinator.

Cooperation. AJL members were actively involved during 1984 with other professional and Jewish organizations, including the Council for Archives and Research Libraries in Jewish Studies, the Jewish Book Council, the Jewish Librarians Caucus, Coalition for Alternatives in Jewish Education, the American Library Association, and the Church and Synagogue Library Association.

AJL continues to be represented at the annual conference of the Coalition for Alternatives in Jewish Education (CAJE). In 1984, in response to AJL Past-President Barbara Leff's proposal, CAJE decided to incorporate library-media centers permanently into its conference structure.

EDITH LUBETSKI

ASSOCIATION OF JEWISH LIBRARIES

PRESIDENT (1983–1985):
Hazel B. Karp, Hebrew Academy of Atlanta, Atlanta

VICE-PRESIDENT-ELECT:
Edith Lubetski, Hedi Steinberg Library, Yeshiva University, New York City

PRESIDENT OF RESEARCH AND SPECIAL LIBRARIES DIVISION:
Pearl Berger, Yeshiva University Libraries, New York City

PRESIDENT OF SYNAGOGUE, SCHOOL, AND CENTER DIVISION:
Sylvia Firschein, Charles Goldman Judaica Library, Wayne, New Jersey

Membership (December 1984): 700
General mailing address: c/o National Foundation for Jewish Culture, 122 E. 42nd Street, New York 10068

Association of Research Libraries

1984 was implementation year for the Association of Research Libraries (ARL) Five-Year Plan, which was developed by the ARL Board of Directors and adopted by the ARL membership during 1983. The plan states the six major objectives for the Association over the next five years and outlines the specific tasks needed to accomplish each objective. The objectives address scholarly communication, access to research materials, preservation, information policy, staffing needs of research libraries, and management. ARL activities and programs during 1984 reflect significant progress toward those objectives.

Collections Inventory. Phase II of the North American Collections Inventory Project (NCIP) was completed during 1984. The goal of NCIP is to build an inventory of significant research collections in North America, using the Online Conspectus developed by the Research Libraries Group. Funded by the Lilly Endowment and conducted in Indiana, Phase II provided a field test of a manual, procedures, and training aids to help librarians complete the conspectus that were developed during Phase I of the project. Three ARL member libraries—Purdue University, the University of Notre Dame, and Indiana University—completed major portions of the conspectus and planned to complete the remaining sections in the near future. The project also tested methods for identifying strong research collections in non-ARL libraries in Indiana, provided information on the costs and time required to complete the conspectus, tested procedures and operating agreements for adding data from non-RLG libraries to the inventory, and developed procedures to verify collection assessment. Phase III, planned to begin in 1985, was expected to bring almost all ARL libraries into the inventory. The ARL Office of Management Studies provided major operational support for the NCIP, and the training resources and manual developed by OMS for NCIP will be available to other libraries early in 1985.

Microform Project. Initial goals of the ARL Microform Project, including development of profile matching, acceptance of standards, development of a clearinghouse database, and establishment of cooperative cataloging projects, were accomplished during 1983 and cataloging for a number of important sets was completed or in progress. The OCLC Major Microforms Proj-

Association of Research Libraries

ect, which makes available tapes of bibliographic records for individual titles for microform sets, is a direct outgrowth of the ARL Project. Efforts in 1984 focused on operation of the Microform Cataloging Clearinghouse to facilitate cataloging of microforms, prevent duplication of cataloging efforts, and assist in development of cooperative projects. A comprehensive update of the database was to be conducted during the summer of 1985. The widespread use of the clearinghouse reflects the need and willingness in the library community to use cooperative action to achieve desired goals. ARL intended to continue to operate the clearinghouse for three years after grant funding ends in 1985. *Microform Sets in U.S. and Canadian Libraries*, published in 1984, is a report of the survey conducted by the Microform Project during 1982.

Preservation. The preservation component of the ARL Microform Project with funding from the National Endowment for the Humanities during 1984 conducted a survey of the state of preservation microfilming and other preservation activities in ARL libraries. A report of the survey, to be completed in 1985, was to be the basis of a plan to expand microfilming and other preservation activities in ARL libraries.

A grant went to ARL from the Mellon Foundation to support preparation of an administrative guide for preservation microfilming in libraries and archives. The project will be carried out jointly with the Northeast Document Conservation Center (NEDCC). NEDCC received a grant from the National Historical Publications and Records Commission in support of the project. The guide is intended as a "practical" tool for administrators of preservation microfilming programs that will "interpret" existing technical sources and standards, describe recommended procedures, and provide advice on both the administrative and production aspects of preservation microfilming.

Reflecting ARL's long-term interest in preservation activities and the renewed interest in such activities reflected in the ARL Plan, the ARL Committee on Preservation of Research Library Materials developed a set of "Guidelines for Minimum Preservation Efforts in ARL Libraries." The Guidelines cover such topics as local program statements, statistics, national participation, environmental conditions, and budgetary efforts. The Guidelines were endorsed in principle by the ARL membership at its October 1984 meeting; the final version was scheduled for distribution during the summer of 1985.

Retrospective Conversion. Late in 1984 the ARL Board of Directors, acting on a recommendation from the ARL Committee on Bibliographic Control, approved plans to seek funding for a study to investigate the feasibility of—and plan of action for—a coordinated North American program for retrospective conversion of bibliographic records for monographs in significant research collections, including those libraries not represented in ARL. Plans for the study reflect widespread interest in the topic within ARL and the library community, including the findings of a meeting on retrospective conversion sponsored by the Council on Library Resources in July 1984 that identified ARL as a logical party to develop and carry out such a program. The three-month study will (1) define the scope of a coordinated retrospective conversion project, including the universe of titles to be converted; (2) identify a process for sharing converted records; (3) establish a consensus on standards for retrospective conversion projects; (4) investigate potential costs and funding strategies; (5) examine efforts required from and benefits accruing to North American research libraries; and (6) develop a plan for implementation. The study, funded by CLR, was to begin in January 1985, and it was anticipated that the final report and possible plan would be considered by the ARL membership in May 1985.

CONSER Abstracting and Indexing Project. The CONSER A&I Project, a joint effort with the National Federation of Abstracting and Information Services, began in November 1983 with the primary goal of providing the needed link between library catalogs and A&I service citations by adding current and reliable information to serials titles in the CONSER database telling where those titles are indexed or abstracted. By the end of 1984, the project had exceeded its original projections, and A&I citations had been added to 62,000 unique CONSER records. Eighty-four A&I services, representing 130 indexes covering almost 120,000 titles, agreed to participate in the project. Funding for the project came from NEH, CLR, the H. W. Wilson Foundation, and the Xerox Foundation; the project was expected to conclude in April 1985.

Library Education. Realizing that in addition to attracting good students to the field, the curricula in library schools must also reflect the complex and changing environment of research libraries, the ARL Committee on Library Education asked OMS Director Duane Webster to work with them in developing and conducting an institute on research library issues for library educators. The institute was funded by CLR and hosted by the University of North Carolina–Chapel Hill Library and School of Library Science. Twelve library educators from 11 library schools were selected for the institute, which included seminars conducted by prominent librarians, educators, and academic administrators, and field visits to nearby research libraries. ARL was also participating in 1984 in ALA's study of accreditation procedures and guidelines for library and information science education.

Legislation. ARL continued in 1984 to monitor legislative and other federal government activities. As usual, major efforts were aimed at support of appropriations for library programs, especially those under Title II of the Higher Education Act and for a number of agencies, including the Library of Congress and the National Endowment for the Humanities. ARL was also a strong supporter of efforts to restore the National Archives and Records Service to independent status (legislation authorizing the change was passed in 1984). Another area of current interest is telecommunications. ARL continued as an active participant in the Telecommunications Coalition of library, education, and information associations, library networks, and bibliographic utilities, set up to monitor telecommunications developments affecting library and education

Table 1. Number and average salaries of ARL university librarians, fiscal year 1985[1]

Position	Number of staff			Average salaries		
	Total	Men	Women	Combined	Men	Women
Director	94	75	19	$63,427	$63,427	$62,183
Associate director	114	55	59	45,219	46,349	44,166
Assistant director	209	108	101	40,166	40,493	39,815
Branch head	527	198	329	30,348	32,004	29,351
Subject specialist	673	311	362	26,870	28,116	25,799
Functional specialist	331	158	173	27,370	28,373	26,455
Department head: Reference	112	48	64	31,515	31,522	31,510
Cataloging	110	30	80	32,899	34,239	32,397
Acquisition	104	44	60	30,990	31,360	30,718
Serials	67	18	49	29,793	29,228	30,000
Documents/Maps	110	42	68	28,462	28,274	28,578
Circulation	91	40	51	27,266	27,054	27,432
Special Collections	100	68	32	33,870	35,417	30,581
Computer	41	29	12	35,598	37,033	32,131
Other	632	250	382	29,453	31,175	28,325
Reference: Over 15 years experience	329	102	227	27,588	28,287	27,274
10–15 years experience	233	67	166	25,370	24,964	25,535
5–10 years experience	277	88	189	21,884	22,242	21,718
Under 5 years experience	231	73	158	18,874	18,785	18,915
Catalog: Over 15 years experience	384	103	281	27,556	28,255	27,300
10–15 years experience	177	53	124	24,559	25,274	24,254
5–10 years experience	206	58	148	21,839	22,059	21,752
Under 5 years experience	221	52	169	18,490	18,851	18,379
Other: Over 15 years experience	307	93	214	29,212	31,447	28,241
10–15 years experience	180	56	124	25,782	27,090	25,191
5–10 years experience	199	61	138	22,199	23,142	21,782
Under 5 years experience	203	50	153	19,154	19,089	19,175
All Positions	6,262	2,330	3,932	$27,935	$30,242	$26,568

[1] Excludes Chicago and staff in law and medical libraries.

Table 2. Number and average salaries of ARL minority university librarians, fiscal year 1985[1]

Position	Number of staff			Average salaries		
	Total	Men	Women	Combined	Men	Women
Director	3	3	0	$ *	$ *	$ -
Associate director	9	2	7	49,287	*	*
Assistant director	9	6	3	37,900	*	*
Branch head	40	12	28	33,302	34,603	32,744
Subject specialist	85	39	46	28,395	29,845	27,166
Functional specialist	23	13	10	29,191	28,301	30,349
Department head: Reference	2	0	2	*	-	*
Cataloging	14	4	10	32,456	34,171	31,769
Acquisition	2	0	2	*	-	*
Serials	3	1	2	*	*	*
Documents/Maps	2	2	0	*	*	-
Circulation	3	0	3	*	-	*
Special Collections	0	0	0	-	-	-
Computer	1	1	0	*	*	-
Other	53	23	30	29,506	31,000	28,360
Reference: Over 15 years experience	36	11	25	27,071	28,271	26,543
10–15 years experience	23	5	18	27,336	23,411	28,426
5–10 years experience	30	8	22	22,488	23,590	22,087
Under 5 years experience	13	2	11	19,278	*	*
Catalog: Over 15 years experience	71	18	53	26,840	27,488	26,620
10–15 years experience	27	8	19	23,723	26,422	22,587
5–10 years experience	22	5	17	21,702	22,495	21,468
Under 5 years experience	22	1	21	19,217	*	*
Other: Over 15 years experience	37	17	20	29,105	30,898	27,580
10–15 years experience	19	6	13	28,407	29,544	27,882
5–10 years experience	8	1	7	21,094	*	*
Under 5 years experience	15	4	11	20,575	18,207	21,463
All Positions	572	192	380	$27,801	$29,958	$26,712

[1] Excludes Chicago and staff in law and medical libraries.
*Salary information is not published when fewer than 4 individuals are involved.

Table 3. Number and average salaries of ARL university librarians by type of institution, fiscal year 1985[1]

Position	All combined (104)[2]		Public (62)		Private (30)	
	Number	Average salary	Number	Average salary	Number	Average salary
Director	94	$63,427	57	$62,049	27	$70,776
Associate director	114	45,219	64	44,845	39	47,080
Assistant director	209	40,166	120	39,869	69	40,641
Branch head	527	30,348	322	29,243	158	32,295
Subject specialist	673	26,870	395	26,528	230	27,236
Functional specialist	331	27,370	182	27,776	119	26,645
Department head: Reference	112	31,515	60	31,340	36	31,050
Cataloging	110	32,899	58	32,322	42	33,423
Acquisition	104	30,990	59	30,971	32	30,275
Serials	67	29,793	39	30,006	22	30,201
Documents/Maps	110	28,462	66	28,323	28	27,850
Circulation	91	27,266	51	27,194	30	26,348
Special Collections	100	33,870	57	34,149	33	33,915
Computer	41	35,598	25	34,509	12	36,692
Other	632	29,453	354	29,065	221	29,873
Reference: Over 15 years experience	329	27,588	227	27,390	68	22,375
10–15 years experience	233	25,370	142	24,978	60	25,764
5–10 years experience	277	21,884	186	21,530	59	22,130
Under 5 years experience	231	18,874	155	18,418	51	19,649
Catalog: Over 15 years experience	384	27,556	205	27,643	135	27,054
10–15 years experience	177	24,559	91	23,587	65	25,509
5–10 years experience	206	21,839	116	21,171	69	22,489
Under 5 years experience	221	18,490	125	17,969	86	19,042
Other: Over 15 years experience	307	29,212	197	29,560	73	27,333
10–15 years experience	180	25,782	105	26,005	54	25,002
5–10 years experience	199	22,199	112	21,959	70	22,094
Under 5 years experience	203	19,154	112	19,049	75	19,240
All Positions	6,262	$27,935	3,682	$27,576	1,963	$28,286

[1]Excludes Chicago and staff in law and medical libraries.
[2]Includes 12 Canadian libraries not included in public/private columns.
( ) Number of ARL libraries included

Table 4. Number and average salaries of ARL university librarians by size of professional staff, fiscal year 1985[1]

Position	Staff over 124 (4)		Staff 75–124 (21)		Staff 50–74 (31)		Staff 1–49 (48)	
	Number	Salary	Number	Salary	Number	Salary	Number	Salary
Director	3	$ *	20	$73,245	26	$62,932	45	$58,516
Associate director	7	55,557	27	47,320	41	44,319	39	42,856
Assistant director	4	47,022	65	43,989	55	40,745	85	36,545
Branch head	46	38,368	230	29,886	108	30,554	143	28,355
Subject specialist	73	32,441	274	27,192	169	26,027	157	24,624
Functional specialist	37	30,188	123	27,775	76	26,961	95	26,077
Department head: Reference	5	33,875	22	33,899	35	31,892	50	29,966
Cataloging	11	38,337	24	35,249	31	33,541	44	29,806
Acquisition	7	38,346	21	31,437	31	31,219	45	29,479
Serials	5	35,506	15	30,796	19	30,183	28	27,970
Documents/Maps	8	36,688	26	28,017	32	28,940	44	26,882
Circulation	7	28,947	19	28,960	29	26,536	36	26,633
Special Collections	8	32,176	25	35,403	31	35,019	36	32,192
Computer	3	*	11	38,352	16	33,616	11	32,056
Other	70	34,730	217	29,812	172	29,027	173	27,290
Reference: Over 15 years experience	26	35,508	95	26,170	119	28,150	89	26,037
10–15 years experience	17	29,649	81	24,986	64	25,537	71	24,634
5–10 years experience	15	25,491	88	21,522	79	21,765	95	21,750
Under 5 years experience	17	22,077	56	18,718	67	19,064	91	18,232
Catalog: Over 15 years experience	65	33,275	114	26,253	92	27,389	113	25,717
10–15 years experience	16	29,982	64	24,731	42	24,278	55	22,997
5–10 years experience	25	23,035	69	21,964	54	22,029	58	20,997
Under 5 years experience	22	19,785	62	18,846	62	18,388	75	17,901
Other: Over 15 years experience	48	36,377	81	27,336	115	28,751	63	27,007
10–15 years experience	21	30,487	46	24,259	74	25,566	39	25,454
5–10 years experience	19	26,682	58	21,654	76	21,739	46	21,795
Under 5 years experience	17	23,558	55	19,213	78	18,667	53	18,398
All Positions	602	$32,485	1,988	$27,900	1,793	$27,667	1,879	$26,768

[1]Excludes Chicago and staff in law and medical libraries.
( ) Number of ARL libraries included
*Salary information is not published when fewer than 4 individuals are involved.

Expenditures, ARL Members, 1983–1984

Library materials	Current serials	Binding	Total materials and bindings	Total salaries and wages	Other operating expenditures	Total library operating expenditures
University libraries						
272,245,325	138,057,103	17,070,379	289,297,704	465,976,354	102,562,591	857,836,649
Nonuniversity libraries						
27,934,211	6,295,250	2,194,884	30,129,095	199,333,112	137,523,820	366,518,027
Grand totals—all ARL libraries						
300,179,536	144,352,353	19,265,263	319,426,799	665,309,466	240,086,411	1,224,354,676

Personnel, ARL Members, 1983–1984

Professional staff FTE	Nonprofessional staff FTE	Student assistant FTE	Total staff FTE
University libraries			
7,919	16,398	7,128	31,446
Nonuniversity libraries			
3,770	4,149	223	8,142
Grand totals—all ARL libraries			
11,689	20,547	7,351	39,588

Collections, ARL Members, 1983–1984

Volumes in library	Volumes added (gross)	Volumes added (net)	Total microform units in library	Current serials
University libraries				
259,451,359	8,251,447	7,348,546	194,306,988	2,855,490
Nonuniversity libraries				
45,728,491	912,360	839,221	21,239,400	393,207
Grand totals—all ARL libraries				
305,179,850	9,163,807	8,187,767	215,546,388	3,248,697

Interlibrary Loans, ARL Members, 1983–1984

	Loaned				Borrowed	
Originals	Photocopies	Total	Originals	Photocopies	Total	
University libraries						
720,164	1,279,050	2,100,659	446,937	332,887	822,479	
Nonuniversity libraries						
194,956	246,822	681,003	2,231	1,323	37,072	
Grand totals—all ARL libraries						
915,120	1,525,872	2,781,662	449,168	334,210	859,551	

data transmission.

New Publications. During 1984 ARL published *Objective Performance Measures for Academic and Research Libraries,* prepared for ARL by Paul B. Kantor of Tantalus, Inc. The manual is the result of efforts of several years by the Committee on ARL Statistics to develop quantitative measures of library service. Kantor was asked to develop several library performance measures for ARL, which were then tested at five ARL libraries. The committee concluded that the measures—including availability of library materials, accessibility of library materials, and delay analysis—would be helpful to libraries, and the resulting manual contains explanatory worksheets and detailed instructions so that libraries can easily adapt the measures to their own needs.

Membership Meetings and Changes. In April ARL membership met in Colorado Springs for a meeting on "Telecommunications and Research Libraries: 1984 and Beyond." The October membership meeting, held in Washington, D.C., addressed "Organizational Futures: Staffing Research Libraries in the 1990s." Proceedings of the meetings are available from the Association.

The University of Waterloo became the 14th Canadian member of ARL during 1984. The John Crerar Library, one of the founding members of the Association, relinquished its membership during 1984 when its collections were merged with the University of Chicago. ARL membership was 117 at year's end; 105 were university libraries.

Staff Changes. In November 1983, Carol A. Mandel left her position as Associate Executive Director. Duane E. Webster, Director of the Office of Management Studies, was appointed ARL's Deputy Director in 1984. Webster continued as Director of OMS. Two program officers, Jaia Barrett and Jeffrey Heynen, joined the ARL staff, and Susan Jurow was appointed OMS Training Specialist.

Center for Chinese Research Materials. The ARL Center for Chinese Research Materials continued its project to make available microfilm copies of local newspapers produced in the People's Republic of China from 1950 to 1966. The project is based primarily on titles held by the School of Oriental and African Studies, University of London, with additional titles from the collections of the Institute of Scientific Information on Social Sciences of the Academy of Sciences of the U.S.S.R., the Hoover Institution, and the Library of Congress. Sixteen titles were available by year's end. The project will cover 38 titles in all. The Center also continued its efforts to reproduce Chinese regional materials on social, economic, and political development of the Republican Period, including newspapers, periodicals, monographs, government publications, and bank reports. The Center was scheduled to publish (1985) a supplement to *The Catalog of the Wason Collection on China and the Chinese, Cornell University Libraries*. The supplement will cover over 11,600 Chinese, Japanese, and Western language monographs and serials cataloged between 1978 and 1980.

Management Studies. In all, 21 self-studies in academic and research libraries were in progress during 1984 as part of the Office of Mangement Studies's Academic Library Program. These include projects as part of the Public Services Program, the Collection Analysis Project, the Preservation Planning Program, and Management Studies.

The National Endowment for the Humanities in 1984 awarded OMS a two-year grant of $65,375 to conduct 10 demonstration Preservation Planning Program studies in ARL member libraries. By the close of 1984 OMS had completed its two-year Public Services Project, funded by the General Electric Foundation. As part of the project, OMS developed and tested a series of aids that academic and research libraries can use to improve their public services programs and help adapt them to changing economic, technological, and user needs. Six libraries were chosen to test a self-study process; reports are available from each of these projects. Also as part of the project, seven ARL libraries were awarded grants under the sponsored research component of the project. The Public Services Self-Study program and manual is available to other libraries.

More than 900 individuals participated in events offered by the Organizational Training and Staff Development Program during 1984. Institutes and workshops included eight Management Skills Institutes—including four advanced institutes—and 15 special focus workshops. Two of the advanced institutes were for senior library managers in Australia. The first Management Skills Institute for Directors was held in 1984. Special focus workshops dealt with planning techniques, time management, cooperative collection development, economic and financial issues, managing small libraries, interpersonal skills, management of change, and performance appraisal.

The Systems and Procedures Exchange Center (SPEC), a publication and information sharing program, issued 10 SPEC kits and flyers. Topics included university archives, branch libraries, collection security, staff training for automation, strategic planning, user studies, copyright policies, the assistant/associate director position, microcomputers, electronic mail, and nonbibliographic machine-readable databases. An Occasional Paper on the assistant/associate director position was published as well. During 1984 SPEC conducted an inventory of automation resources in ARL libraries, and 109 members provided information on the automation status of over 22 library functions. The results were made available in a publication and on a database. Late in the year OMS received a grant from the Council on Library Resources to expand the inventory. (*See also* Academic Libraries)

NICOLA DAVAL

ASSOCIATION OF RESEARCH LIBRARIES

PRESIDENT (October 1984–October 1985):
Richard J. Talbot, Director, University of Massachusetts Libraries

VICE-PRESIDENT/PRESIDENT-ELECT:
Anne Woodsworth, Associate Provost for Libraries, University of Pittsburgh Libraries

EXECUTIVE DIRECTOR:
Shirley Echelman

Membership (December 1984): 117
Headquarters: 1527 New Hampshire Avenue, N.W., Washington, D.C. 20036

Association of Specialized and Cooperative Library Agencies

Highlights. 1984 was a year of significant programs and changes for the Association of Specialized and Cooperative Library Agencies (ASCLA). Achievements included the adoption of two sets of standards, new publications, stimulating programs at Annual Conference, and special projects. ASCLA members carried out through these and other activities the Division's goals of providing access to library service for all citizens and developing and improving library services at all levels.

In June the ASCLA Board of Directors adopted the revised *Standards for Library Functions at the State Level*, and the new edition was to be published in early 1985. The new *Standards* were written following a survey to gather recommendations for the revision and were reviewed by the units of the American Library Association as well as by other national organizations prior to their adoption. Denny Stephens of the Oklahoma Department of Libraries chaired the standards subcommittee.

Revised Standards and Guidelines of Service for the Library of Congress Network of Libraries for the Blind and Physically Handicapped 1984 were adopted in January and published in June. The standards were developed by a subcommittee chaired by Al Trezza, a faculty member at the Florida State University School of Library and Information Studies. Representatives of major national consumer groups acted as consultants in the project, which was funded by the Library of Congress National Library Service for the Blind and Physically Handicapped.

ASCLA continued to carry out its role as the organizational home of library networks and cooperatives by sponsoring the Network Assembly at the Midwinter Meeting and Annual Conference to provide a forum within the American Library Association for discussion of current trends and issues. The January 1984 session featured a panel discussion on online bibliographic databases, telecommunications charges and changes, and network developments. "Networks: New Challenges...New Roles" was a discussion of the future role of state and regional library networks at the Dallas Annual Conference Assembly.

The 1980s have been declared the Decade of the Disabled by the United Nations and by President Reagan. ASCLA formed the Decade of the Disabled Committee (ad hoc) and invited other divisions to appoint representatives to join in planning and presenting activities aimed at improving library services for disabled people. The committee, chaired by Phyllis Dalton, is spearheading an Association-wide action program.

The ASCLA Headquarters Staff, under an agreement with the Chief Officers of State Library Agencies, published a new report on a study of state support for library services. Nancy Bolt, a freelance consultant, carried out the study that resulted in *State Aid 1983: A Report*. This new book updates an earlier ASCLA study, published in 1982 and covering data for fiscal year 1978–79. Both publications are available for purchase from the ASCLA Headquarters Office.

In a major structural change, the ASCLA Board of Directors streamlined the organization by reducing the number of sections from seven to three. The new structure was designed to focus members' energies on providing programs and activities and to enable the division to reduce overhead. ASCLA's three sections are (1) Libraries Serving Special Populations (LSSPS), serving the interests of libraries and librarians working to improve the quality of service for people with special needs including those who are blind, physically handicapped, deaf, developmentally disabled, impaired elderly, in prison or health care facilities, or confined in other types of institutions; (2) Multitype Library Networks and Cooperatives Section (Multi-LINCS); and (3) the State Library Agency Section (SLAS).

Conference Programs. The 1984 Annual Conference in Dallas provided another opportunity to build ASCLA's reputation for quality programs. The State Library Agency Section kicked off the week with a preconference offering assistance in "Dealing with the Media, Political Officials, and Other Often Hostile Audiences." Arch Lustberg, Director of Media Education for the Chamber of Commerce of the U.S., led a dynamic day-long program highlighted by videotaped demonstrations. SLAS joined the Library Administration and Management Association in sponsoring "How to Use Successful Public Relations Methods with Your State Legislature"— another program designed to help librarians increase their visibility and political effectiveness. Yet another program, this one planned by the Multitype Library Cooperatives and Network Section, focused on legislative issues: "Forging Links: State Level Legislation for Multitype Cooperation."

Other ASCLA sections sponsored programs on a variety of topics: "Issues in Public Hospital Library Services to Patients" with segments on bibliotherapy, patient and consumer health information, and programming in hospital libraries; "Your Computer and the Disabled" about using the latest technological developments to improve services for disabled people; "Signs of the Times—Library Programming for Deaf and Hearing Impaired Audiences" featuring Joanne Greenberg, author of *In This Sign*, followed by demonstration story hours and puppet shows and video presentations of sample consumer programs; and "Prison Writing: A Message from the Inside" highlighting the creative efforts of American prisoners.

"Let's Talk about It." ASCLA's special project—"Let's Talk about It: Reading and Discussion Programs in America's Libraries"—celebrated its first anniversary in October. The project is funded with $1,400,000 from the National Endowment for the Humanities for three years (1983–86) and has three major areas of activity:

(1) The project commissioned an Advisory Committee of experts from across the country to develop a program planner's manual, six reading and discussion program themes, and support materials for local and statewide use.

(2) Four member teams from 48 states and three U.S. territories learned about "Let's Talk about It" at three regional workshops.

(3) Cash grants are being awarded on a competitive basis to support "Let's Talk about It" programs in 30 states in 1985 and 1986.

Publications. ASCLA's publications checklist expanded with the addition of two new books in

---

ASSOCIATION OF SPECIALIZED AND COOPERATIVE LIBRARY AGENCIES

PRESIDENT (June 1984–July 1985):
James A. Nelson, State Librarian Department of Libraries & Archives, Frankfort, Kentucky

VICE-PRESIDENT/PRESIDENT-ELECT:
Gail J. McGovern, Funding Sources Consultant, California State Library, Sacramento

EXECUTIVE DIRECTOR:
Sandra M. Cooper

Membership (August 31, 1984): 1,458 (1,093 personal; 365 organizational)
Expenditures (August 31, 1984): $61,955

1984. *The World of Work: A Handicapped Person's Guide to Finding a Job—A Bibliography* is a new bibliographic guide for disabled persons looking for a job, librarians and media specialists selecting materials, and vocational and rehabilitation counselors who work with handicapped people. Along with listing print and nonprint materials on job hunting, the guide also includes information on the availability of materials in large print and braille as well as recorded disk and audiocassette media.

The fifth edition of *The Report on Library Cooperation* was edited by Nancy Wareham and prepared in cooperation with the Chief Officers of State Library Agencies. This biennial compilation on library cooperation and networking has state-by-state entries listing single and multitype cooperatives with name, address, telephone number, administrator, and sources and amounts of support. Each state's entry includes an overview of cooperative and network activities in that state.

Interface, the Division's quarterly publication, continues to expand, offering selection of news, features, and updates on Division activities under Sue Medina's editorship. Phyllis Dalton edited the special Summer 1984 issue on library service for blind and physically handicapped people, and the Winter issue had a mini-feature on library service in jails and prisons. Dottie Hiebing of the State Library of Iowa is Editor of the "Resources" column. The Library Service to the Deaf Forum column reviews materials for and about deaf and hearing impaired people and is edited by Jane Schuerle, a faculty member at the Department of Communicology at the University of South Florida.

Awards. ASCLA's annual Awards Reception at the Dallas Public Library honored two outstanding leaders. Eunice Lovejoy received the ASCLA Exceptional Service Award for the dedication that has made her a national leader in communicating the needs of special populations to those local, state, and national organizations that serve the disabled and elderly. The Francis Joseph Campbell Award went to Maxine B. Dorf for her 32 distinguished years with the Library of Congress and her profound influence on the availability of braille reading materials.

JAMES NELSON

Beta Phi Mu

The 36th annual initiation and reception of Beta Phi Mu was held at the Dallas Public Library on June 23. Hosts for the initiation and reception were members of Beta Lambda Chapter representing North Texas State University, School of Library and Information Sciences, and Texas Woman's University, School of Library Science.

Jane Anne Hannigan, Professor, Columbia University, and member of the American Library Association Executive Board, was presented with the 1984 Beta Phi Mu Award for distinguished contributions to education for librarianship at the inaugural banquet during the American Library Association's 103d Annual Conference in Dallas.

Beta Phi Mu annually awards scholarships to persons who meet designated criteria. The win-

---

BETA PHI MU OFFICERS

PRESIDENT (July 1984–July 1985):
Edward G. Holley, School of Library Science, University of North Carolina, Chapel Hill

EXECUTIVE SECRETARY:
Blanche Woolls, University of Pittsburgh

ADMINISTRATIVE SECRETARY:
Mary Y. Tomaino, School of Library and Information Science, University of Pittsburgh, Pennsylvania 15260

Membership (1984): 44 chapters, 20,000 members

---

ner of the Sarah Rebecca Reed Scholarship for a beginning student was Jean R. Lewis. Lewis, a former Peace Corps volunteer in West Africa and Reference Assistant at the Flagstaff (Arizona) Public Library, was project director for a successful Black Heritage program funded under LSCA. A graduate of St. Lawrence University, Canton, New York, she planned to continue her graduate study at the Graduate Library School, University of Arizona.

The Harold Lancour Scholarship for Foreign Study was awarded to Ann F. Donovan, Curriculum Librarian with the rank of Associate Professor in the Curriculum Laboratory, University Library, Central Washington University, Ellensburg, Washington. She will pursue her research in children's literature among some of the libraries in Europe. Publications resulting from that study will be aimed at those who teach children's literature to prospective children's librarians as well as others who work with children.

Beta Phi Mu continued to receive favorable reviews for *Leaders in American Academic Librarianship: 1925–1975* (1983), edited by Wayne A. Wiegand and distributed through Publishing Services of the American Library Association.

BLANCHE WOOLLS

Bibliographies and Indexes

Compiling bibliographies became easier for the individual bibliographer with the development of microcomputer software specifically for that purpose. The Personal Bibliographic System (from Personal Bibliographic Software of Ann Arbor, Michigan), for example, allows the user to download full MARC records from another system such as OCLC and then edit them into bibliographic citation rather than MARC style.

A helpful guide for the systematic or enumerative bibliographer was published during 1984. D. W. Krummel's *Bibliographies: Their Aims and Methods* (Mansell) covers citation style, annotation, organization, and presentation, and it has extensive bibliographical notes.

While librarians learn to cope with the current *National Union Catalog* on fiche, a British publisher announced the availability of the entire *NUC–Pre-1956 Imprints* on microfiche. *NUC-fiche* is contained on 9,200 fiche. At $11,000 it is probably still too expensive for many libraries that cannot afford the hard copy.

Work continues on the *Eighteenth Century Short-Title Catalog*, aiming for a 1989 completion date. There were 164,000 records in the file by the end of 1984. The British Library joined the Research Libraries Group in 1984 and will be adding ESTC records directly to the RLIN file. Work began on the conversion of the personal names in the ESTC file to AACR2 form.

The H. W. Wilson Company brought up WILSONLINE on schedule, making the following eight indexes available for searching online: *Applied Science & Technology Index, Biological & Agricultural Index, Book Review Digest, Business Periodicals Index, Cumulative Book Index, Education Index, Index to Legal Periodicals*, and the *Readers' Guide to Periodical Literature*. At least one year of indexing coverage is available for each database and all eight files can be searched simultaneously. Each file is updated at least twice a week. Seven more Wilson indexes were to be brought online in 1985. WILSONLINE joined the more than 100 bibliographic databases available online in 1984.

The Council on Library Resources Bibliographic Service Development Program (BSDP) was to have ended in 1984 but it was extended for another two years. The big thrust of BSDP in 1984 was RECON—retrospective conversion of manual cataloging records into machine readable form. Many smaller institutions have already converted all their old manual records, but it is a daunting project for the older research libraries, which have millions of records that are not in the MARC format and do not conform to any cataloging codes. Some represent unique items. The Council issued two reports, *Retrospective Conversion* and *Retrospective Conversion of Music Materials*, which call for developing a coordinated approach to retrospective conversion to avoid duplication of effort. The Association of Research Libraries was studying the feasibility of managing such a program.

The BSDP also issued *The Name Authority Cooperative/Name Authority File Service*, a report of the progress toward a nationwide name authority file service for libraries. NACO is a program of the Library of Congress under which selected libraries transmit authority records to LC, which communicates them to other program participants.

Under another BSDP program, the Linked Systems Project, work continued on efforts to link together the shared cataloging systems. The Council, through BSDP, also made grants to two dozen other organizations to further work in the area of bibliographic control.

The Association of Research Libraries managed the CONSER A&I Coverage Project during 1984. The CONSER database of serials cataloging records was enriched with information on the abstracting and indexing services that included each serial title. Notes were added to the 510 field of the MARC record for up to 65,000 titles. Serials that are indexed or abstracted but are not in the CONSER database will be cataloged and will be issued to MARC subscribers, along with revised records for previously authenticated CONSER records.

ARL's Microform Project was established to improve bibliographic control of microform sets. In 1984 ARL published *Microfilm Sets in U.S. and Canadian Libraries*, which lists the sets held by libraries, the cataloging available for them, and priorities for cataloging microform sets. This should lead to less duplication of effort in the cataloging of microform sets and to their increased representation in library catalogs.

Tables 1 and 2 present data on the number and distribution of bibliographies published 1980–84, taken from category 016 of *American Book Publishing Record* (ABPR). The number of bibliographies published declined for the second consecutive year, though the change from 1983 to 1984 was not as precipitous as in the previous year. While over 80 publishers issued these bibliographies, over one-quarter of them were published by Vance Bibliographies (the successor to the Council of Planning Librarians series). Just three publishers—Vance, Garland, and Greenwood—accounted for half the bibliographies published.

Bibliographic control has moved far beyond the realm of published bibliographies and indexes, with computer files making a far larger contribution.

SANDY WHITELEY

Table 1. Bibliographies and indexes in American Book Publishing Record: 1980–84							
Subject	Category	1980	1981	1982	1983*	1984*	Change from 1983
000	General	40	19	15	10	16	+ 6
100	Philosophy, psychology	10	4	19	10	7	– 3
200	Religion	6	14	16	9	12	+ 3
300	Social sciences, education	257	240	313	203	182	– 21
400	Language	4	2	5	4	4	0
500	Pure science	9	24	21	16	12	– 4
600	Applied science	65	73	99	84	52	– 32
700	Fine arts	131	200	225	142	128	– 14
800	Literature	117	101	75	69	74	+ 5
900	Travel, history, other	73	90	70	68	70	+ 2
	Total	712	767	858	615	557	– 58

*Because December data were unavailable for 1983 and 1984, extrapolation has been done based on the previous 11 months.

Table 2. Comparisons of estimates of bibliography and book publishing: 1980–84					
	1980	1981	1982	1983	1984
Bibliographies	712	767	858	615	557
Total new books	42,377	41,538	38,526	38,053	38,000*
Percentages of bibliographies to new books	1.6	1.7	2.2	1.6	1.5

Source: see text   *Preliminary Estimate

Black Americans

George Orwell's 1984 was of little consequence for Blacks and libraries last year. The year, however, was for those discussed here more than business as usual; it represented a time of continued progress and a host of new ventures. There were promotions and retirements, grants and program development, and full awareness of the need to preserve and promote Black themes as seen in the publication of various new works.

People in the News. E. J. Josey on June 27 became ALA's first Black male president. The position recognizes his leadership ability and many years of service to the profession and to scholarship. New York Public Library's Schomburg Center for Research in Black Culture in 1984 had a new chief—Howard Dodson. A specialist in Afro-American history and consultant for the National Endowment for the Humanities (NEH), Dodson took the helm in September. Also in New York, Stanton F. Biddle became Chief Librarian at City University of New York's Baruch College. The Forsyth County Public Library in Winston-Salem appointed Sylvia Sprinkle-Hamlin Associate Director. Cheney State College Library Director Floyd Hardy was named Director of the Shepard Memorial Library, North Carolina Central University.

Alex Boyd, formerly Associate Professor in the Graduate School of Library Science, University of Alabama, was appointed Assistant Commissioner of the Chicago Public Library. Mary F. Lenox, formerly Associate Professor of Library Science, University of Missouri, Columbia, became its new Dean—the first Black to hold that position. Prairie View (Texas) A&M University named Donald G. Sweet University Librarian of the Banks Library. Walter J. Fraser, library automation specialist, became new Director of Library Services for Advance Library Concepts, Sacramento. The firm produces the ASDLIP Integrated Library System.

Charles D. Churchwell, Dean of library services, Washington University (St. Louis), and since 1976 a member of the Board of the Council on Library Resources, was elected Vice President of the Council's Board of Directors. Dillard University's Chief Librarian, Carole Taylor, was serving in 1984 a four-year term on the Board of the Louisiana Committee for the Humanities. Ulysses Cameron, Head Librarian, College of Education and Human Ecology Library, University of the District of Columbia, received the Doctor of Education degree from Virginia Polytechnic Institute.

Birdie O. Weir, Director of the learning resource center at Alabama A & M University, was elected President of the 1890 Land-Grant and Tuskegee Institute Library Directors Association. She also served as Chairperson of the Symposium Planning Committee of the Association and coordinated the Agricultural Information Symposium held in Atlanta in 1984. The 1890 institutions are the nation's Black counterpart of the original land-grant colleges and universities.

When the U.S. Department of Education invited librarians to respond to *A Nation at Risk*, E. J. Josey, State Library of New York, and Jessie Carney Smith, Fisk University Library, answered. Both attended the Academic Library Seminar held February 6–7 at the University of Chicago, one of five seminars held around the country.

The year 1984 meant the retirement of several of the nation's outstanding Black librarians. Lucy B. Campbell, Head of the Periodicals Department at Hampton University (Virginia), retired after 21 years of service. Penny Perry's retirement from the directorship of North Carolina Central's library in 1984, closed out an illustrious career spanning 20 years at the University. Lucille C. Thomas, noted for her work with Blacks and other ethnic minorities, retired as Assistant Director for Elementary School Libraries at the New York City Board of Education. The former Chief of the Schomburg Center and later NYPL Research Libraries' Assistant Director for Collection Management and Black Culture, Jean Blackwell Hutson, retired in 1984. Hutson had a distinguished career in Black history librarianship.

A Virginia Lacy Jones Legacy. The library profession in many nations, but especially in the United States, has been influenced by the legacy of noted library educator and scholar Virginia Lacy Jones. A graduate of the old Hampton Institute library education program, recipient of a Master's in Library Science from the University of Illinois and a Ph.D. from the University of Chicago in 1945, Dean Jones (as she was called out of respect and admiration) was the second Black to receive the Ph.D. in librarianship.

She is credited with sending out more than 1,800 trained Black librarians; she rightfully earned the title "dean of library school deans"; she directed Atlanta University's library school and raised millions in scholarships and financial aid; she was active in research and publication, and was a dedicated member of ALA and other library and professional associations. She died on December 3. The magnitude of her legacy is yet to be assessed. (*See* Obituaries)

Awards and Honors. Among Black librarians receiving special recognition in 1984 were Mary Biblo and Effie Lee Morris. Mary Biblo received recognition from the University of Chicago as Master Teacher. Head of the University's laboratory school, Biblo, a 1984–85 Joseph Klingenstein Fellow, planned to use the one-year fellowship, awarded by Columbia University's Teachers College, to study at the College.

Morris, noted for pioneering children's library services to the blind and physically handicapped, and a cofounder of the Black Caucus of ALA, received the 1984 Women's National Book Association Award. The honor is awarded annually to "a living American woman who has made an enduring and unique contribution to the world of books, or through books to society."

Oral History. Howard University's Oral History Department recorded interviews with Sarah Williamson Coleman, 87, a pioneer Baptist Missionary to Liberia. Conducting the interview was Pauline E. Myers, 75, a 1931 Howard graduate and an important narrator of the Oral History Project. The project includes photographs of the narrators taken during the recording sessions of the memoirs. Elinor Sinnette, Howard's Oral History Librarian, chaired a session at the 19th

1984–85 ALA President E. J. Josey. (American Libraries)

Library Manager Joyce Sauls, Manager of the Martin Luther King, Jr., Library, poses with photo on the 10th anniversary of the branch opening in Dallas. (Dallas Public Library)

annual meeting of the Oral History Association in Lexington. The session topic was "Black Oral History Sources: A Personal Assessment." Sinnette was elected chairperson of the Oral History Middle Atlantic Region Membership Committee.

Collections. The University of Illinois (Urbana) received a collection of *Little Black Sambo* materials assembled by the late Mimi Kaplan, Children's Literature Professor at Governor's State University. Included in the approximately 100 items covering 75 years of publishing are books, records, games, coloring books, and puzzles.

Dillard University received two small collections that augment the archives. These are the Louisiana Colored Teachers Association journal, and materials related to the Gilbert Academy. Academy alumni are piecing together information on the memoirs of now famous alumni and honoring their early teachers. The Academy, a preparatory school, was connected with Dillard in the 1930s and 1940s. Howard University's Moorland–Spingarn Collection acquired the papers of architect Louis Fry, Sr., and William J. Faulkner, minister and renowned folklorist.

The University of Massachusetts (Amherst) received a significant accretion to the W. E. B. DuBois papers. Included are over 150 letters from DuBois to L. D. Shivery, her daughter Henrietta (Mrs. Herman Long), and family. They were written mostly in the 1930s and 1940s during DuBois' second teaching tenure at Atlanta University. The materials are a gift from Mrs. Shivery's daughter-in-law, Veoria Shivery. The University formed the Chancellor's National Advisory Committee on the DuBois papers. Its purpose is to promote and encourage research on DuBois, whose papers were acquired in 1973 by the Archives at the University. (Other DuBois materials are at Atlanta University and Fisk.)

Exhibitions and Special Programs. The Black Women Oral History Project of Radcliffe College continued its emphasis on a selected group of older Black women who, through professional and voluntary activities, have made substantial contributions to improving the lives of African-Americans and all peoples. Interviews with 72 such women were made from 1976 to 1981, and transcriptions of the oral history tapes have been distributed to selected libraries throughout the nation. The sponsor, Schlesinger Library, prepared an exhibition of photographs by Judith Sedwick based on 55 of the subjects of the oral history project. The exhibition, "Women of Courage," was reproduced in a catalog with the same title and it tours U.S. cities. The New York Public Library's Central Research Library hosted the portraits in December. A smaller group was shown at the Schomburg Center.

The University of Massachusetts (Amherst) prepared the W. E. B. DuBois Traveling Exhibit during 1984. The materials are based on papers in the DuBois Archives at the University.

Other significant exhibitions in 1984 were available at the Schomburg Center, where "Censorship and Black America" was displayed; Moorland–Spingarn, where "Ed Bolden and Colored Baseball" documented the history of the Negro National League; and at the Detroit Public Library, where dance materials from the E. Azalia Hackley Collection were shown.

Celebrities in 1984 were an active part of the library's activities. This was demonstrated in Louisville, where nearly 500 youth and adults crowded into the Free Public Library to see who could best impersonate entertainer Michael Jackson. Conceived by children's librarian Dorothy Seymour, the contest attracted national attention, and represented an innovative means of addressing community interests.

Johnnie Gray, defensive back with the Green Bay Packers professional football team, became storyteller and played the role of a bus driver in "The Elephant on the Bus," which the Brown County (Wisconsin) Library cosponsored with the Visitor and Convention Bureau. The story was a part of a reader's theater, a group of youngsters who perform upon request for community gatherings. Children's Librarian Karan Prevetti trains the library's Treetop Storytellers.

Exploration into folklore and folklife activities in the Black community continued at Fisk University, where in October the library held its second annual "Black Folklife Festival." Supported by a grant from the National Endowment for the Humanities given earlier, the festival represented a part of Fisk's Learning Library Program. Local craftspersons from Tennessee demonstrated their talents in quilts, chair bottoms, marbles, wire sculpture, woodcarvings, needlework, leather crafts, jewelry making, and African batik and crafts. Themes exhibited or demonstrated also included folksinging, children's games, Black American foods, Black American Art, jazz, the cake walk, breakdancing, harmonica playing, folk medicine (including home remedies, voodoo, and hoodoo), and oils and perfumes from Black Africa. A highlight of the festival was the session on storytelling, featuring librarian Jackie Torrence, "The Story Lady." Her scarey tales dramatized the performance of the Odomankoma Kyerema Cultural Troupe, comprised of school youth from Ghana who demonstrated and interpreted African dances and the talking drums of Africa.

Top, Local artistic talent is exhibited as part of the Newark (New Jersey) Public Library's Lorraine Hansberry Lecture Series. Above, The library's Black History Month festivities included a one-woman show by Actress Vinnie Burrows entitled "Walk Together, Children." (Newark Public Library)

73

Blind and Physically Handicapped, Library Services for the

Publications. Of interest to librarians and libraries is the 1984 edition of the New York Public Library's *The Black Experience in Children's Books*. The list of 400 titles demonstrates the decline in publication of such works, and came in response to a panel of authors, publishers, and librarians who discussed the issue at the Countee Cullen Regional Branch. Charlynn Spencer Pyle of Howard University helped to identify Black books for children by compiling "March on Washington: A Guide to Resources," and "Frederick Douglass: A Resource Guide for Young People."

Librarian A. P. Marshall, Ypsilanti, Michigan, in 1984 chronicled the life of Martin Luther King, Jr., in a set of 20 illustrated broadsides designed to introduce him to young people. Text and photographs depict King's youth, the Montgomery boycott, the "Letter from a Birmingham Jail," the March on Washington, the Selma-to-Montgomery walk, and other highlights of his career.

Xavier University (New Orleans) Librarian Leslie R. Morris, and his former staff member Patsy Brautigam, compiled the second edition of *Interlibrary Loan Policies*, published by ALA.

JESSIE CARNEY SMITH

Blind and Physically Handicapped, Library Services for the

In August two major topics were the focus of attention for participants in the 1984 Expert Meeting held in Amsterdam by IFLA's Section of Libraries for the Blind. They were computerized braille production and the role of national libraries in the library services for the handicapped.

Computer-produced braille was discussed by a panel consisting of Peter Hanke, U.S.A.; Theo Van der Graft, Netherlands; Lian Madden, United Kingdom; and Rainer F. V. Witte, Federal Republic of Germany. According to panel members, it is becoming increasingly clear to those engaged in braille production that revolutionary developments are ahead, particularly in the anticipated increase in use of microcomputers. Computers generally have been found to increase the speed of braille production, which in turn shortens the time between a book's publication in print and the book's availability in braille to a blind person. Computers aid publishers of braille and increase the efficiency of transcribers. Complex braille codes can be entered into a system so that less transcriber training is required; the text can be edited before it is committed to hard copy; and master copies can be stored on compact diskettes rather than on bulky paper or metal plates.

transcribers. Complex braille codes can be entered into a system so that less transcriber training is required; the text can be edited before it is committed to hard copy; and master copies can be stored on compact diskettes rather than on bulky paper or metal plates.

Frank Kurt Cylke, of the United States, and Clifford Law, Australia, discussed the topic "Library Service for the Handicapped: Is There a Role for the National Library?" Cylke and Law both advocated a strong coordination role for national libraries if an effective network of service for print handicapped individuals is to be further developed. Cylke stated, ". . . it must be agreed that all activities performed in a national library related to print books must be performed for materials produced for use by blind and physically handicapped individuals."

Sixty-seven participants from 20 countries attended the Expert Meeting under the chairmanship of Winnie Vitzansky, Denmark, and hosted by Henry Fidder, Netherlands. Important directories that were still in preparation in 1983 were published in 1984. The *International Directory of Libraries and Production Facilities for the Blind* lists sources for braille and recorded materials throughout the world and provides pertinent information, such as the languages in which the materials are produced. The directory was under revision in 1984 by Rainer F. V. Witte, Deutsche Blindenstudienstalt in Marburg/Lahn, F.R.G. *The International Directory of Braille Music Collections* is a 41-page directory listing sources for braille music along with detailed information concerning the nature of the material contained in the collections.

Braille music collections received attention in England with the publication by the National Library for the Blind of *Braille Music: An International Survey*, by John Henry. This work consists mainly of two surveys. The first is divided by country and points out the strengths and weaknesses of the collections surveyed. The second part looks at the range of material available instrument by instrument; what material is available to the blind musician on each; and where the

Below, the Washington Army National Guard moves books and equipment to the new location of the Washington Library for the Blind and Physically Handicapped in Seattle. Below, right, Actress/Playwright Leslye Orr in her one-woman play "Hand in Hand" at the School for the Visually Handicapped in Janesville, Wisconsin. Event was co-sponsored by the Madison (Wisconsin) Public Library. (Children's Theatre Company)

blind musician can best obtain needed material.

Regional Librarian's Conference. Using as a theme "Planning Together—Working Together," approximately 250 network, state, public, and special librarians, including participants from Canada, Denmark, and Australia, met in New York City July 9–13. This conference provided National Library Service (NLS) staff from the Library of Congress with an opportunity to exchange information and innovative ideas on a broad range of subjects, including audio-book production, audio-equipment repair techniques, copyright, library policies, computer applications and automation, and library standards.

The revised *Standards and Guidelines for the Library of Congress Network Libraries for the Blind and Physically Handicapped* were accepted at the ALA Midwinter Meeting; the printed revision was distributed at the ALA Conference in Dallas in June. The 1984 standard is a revision of those published in 1979, and was prepared by an ASCLA Advisory Committee headed by Alphonse F. Trezza, Florida State University, who served as project coordinator, together with Donna Dziedzic, New Jersey, formerly regional librarian in Chicago, and Jim DeJarnatt, regional librarian in Georgia.

Internationally, *Approved Recommendations on Working Out National Standards of Library Service for the Blind (August 1983)* has been compiled and edited by the Standards Development Committee of the Section of Libraries for the Blind, IFLA. This committee, chaired by F. K. Cylke, U.S.A., as composed of William C. Byrne, Australia, Henry Fidder, Netherlands, and D. S. Zharkov, U.S.S.R. The standards cover a wide variety of essential topics, including library administration, resource development, lending policies, and response to users.

Regional Libraries. One indicator of progress among libraries serving blind and handicapped persons may be found in the new buildings and moves to new quarters of 1984. The Washington regional library moved to a location nearer to downtown Seattle. The Regional Librarian, Jan Ames, enlisted the cooperation of library personnel, hundreds of volunteers, and numerous agencies to move nearly 200,000 volumes, an 89-hour-a-week radio station, a statewide braille and taping service, plus all of the support equipment and furnishings to a building that provides a great deal of additional space, including space for conference and meeting rooms.

The Broward County, Florida, subregional library moved into the new main library building in Fort Lauderdale, which opened on April 29. Carol Nemeyer, Associate Librarian for National Programs, Library of Congress, spoke at an opening celebration. The subregional library has a collection of disks, cassettes, braille materials, and more than 40 aids and appliances. It is now located in a prominent place in the building visible to all passersby.

Also in Fort Lauderdale, Insight for the Blind opened a one-story, 33-room recording studio. It allows that nonprofit organization to more than double the amount of material it can record and distribute. The building was constructed through the efforts of the Gold Coast Pioneers, Future Pioneers, Pioneer Partners, and phone company employees; together with Insight employees, they contributed more than 175,000 volunteer hours to the project.

The Connecticut regional library occupied its new building in Rocky Hill, a town ten miles

Blind and Physically Handicapped, Library Services for the

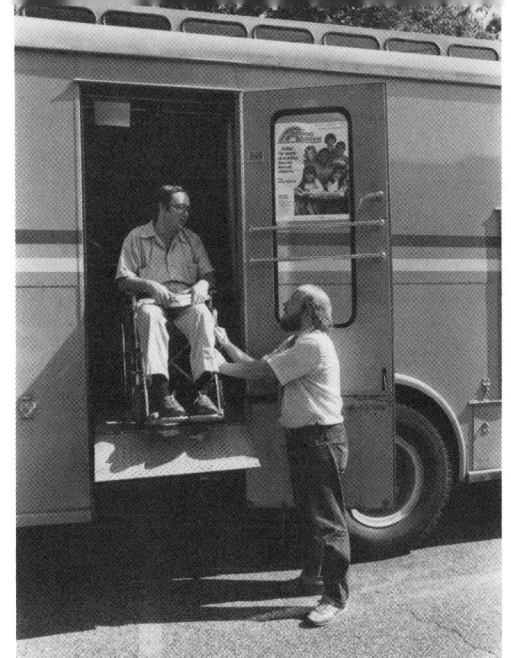

Special Bookmobile with wheelchair lift takes library services to residents of 15 institutions in Memphis and Shelby County. (Memphis Public Library and Information Center)

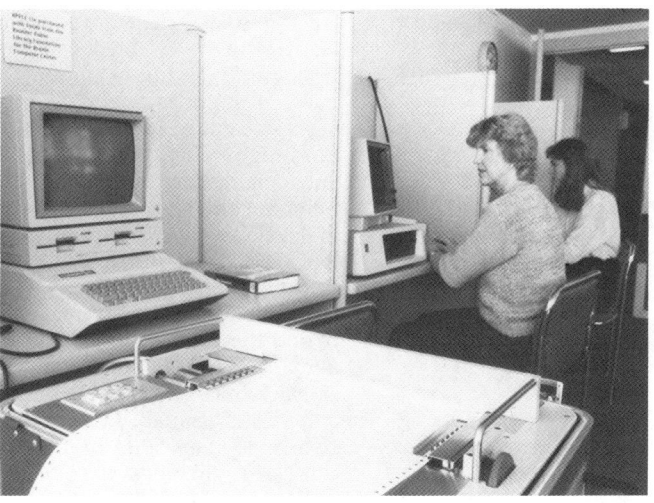

Left, Talking Book Library of the new Broward County, Florida, subregional library in Fort Lauderdale. Below, Denver's Braille Computer Center features minicomputers, a Visual-Tek reading machine, and the only Thiel Braille Embosser in the Rocky Mountain region. (Bob Grzenda)

south of Hartford. Groundbreaking ceremonies took place June 1, 1983, and the completed building was turned over to the state library just 10 months later. The regional library shares the 18,600-foot facility with the state library's Interlibrary Loan Center. As a result of the move, the regional library gained extensive storage, an incoming toll-free line for patrons living outside the Hartford area, and an automated circulation system.

In Milwaukee, three special outreach activities celebrated the opening of the Wisconsin regional library's new reading room area and browsing collection in June. In the Milwaukee Public Library building, the new reading room has tables for using the books, disk and cassette machines, braille maps, games with embossed markings, and reference materials in braille and recorded formats. Braille stacks open for browsing surround the reading area. Coinciding with the opening, the Milwaukee Public Library installed the Smithsonian Institution's exhibit "In Touch: Printing and Writing for the Blind in the Nineteenth Century." This exhibit highlights developments in the history of reading and writing systems for blind persons. Many of the items can be touched, and all are labeled in braille. The regional library also sponsored four performances of the Minneapolis Children's Theatre Company's production of "Hand in Hand" by Leslye Orr. A one-woman play, it was acted by the playwright with audience participation; it is based on the literature of Helen Keller and Anne Sullivan Macy.

Braille Production. The International Conference on English Braille Grade 2, held in September 1982, brought together braille experts from the United States and abroad. It was cosponsored by the Braille Authority of North America (BANA) and the Braille Authority of the United Kingdom (BAUK). *Proceedings* became available in 1984 in print and braille. Also published by BANA is the two-volume *Guidelines for Mathematical Diagrams* primarily intended for the use of sighted transcribers who transcribe mathematics for blind students and professionals. It is designed for those transcribers having a thorough knowledge of Grade 2 English braille as well as the 1972 revision of the Nemeth braille code for mathematics and scientific notation. For transcriptions requiring tactile diagrams, the techniques described are considered the most effective and practicable for the transcriber to execute with a minimum amount of training, practice, and supplies.

As a result of its November 1983 meeting in Washington, the BANA board also voted to consider changes in the literary braille code, music notation, and to establish a technical committee to develop a computer-braille code, based on the ASCII (American Standard Code for International Interchange) code.

Tactile Maps. To further increase knowledge of and the availability and use of tactile maps, and to build a sizable collection of them, the National Library Service for the Blind and Physically Handicapped, Library of Congress (NLS), published *Maps and Graphics for Blind and Visually Handicapped Individuals: A Bibliography.* More than 475 entries deal with broad subjects relating to maps and graphics for visually impaired persons, such as theories of spatial perception, and more specific topics, such as the design of tactile mobility maps.

Interest in tactile maps brought together more than 200 persons representing 40 countries in a four-day international conference in Berlin, German Democratic Republic, in April. The conference was organized into four plenary sessions: (1) the significance of tactile representations; (2) trends in demand in employment, education, and leisure-time activities; (3) technological advances in production; and (4) national cataloging and international cooperation. Conference proceedings were planned for publication in 1985 by the Association for the Blind and Partially Sighted of the German Democratic Republic.

The Library of Congress Program. During fiscal year 1984, readership in the Library of Congress reading program for blind and physically handicapped individuals was in excess of 650,000 and circulation of braille, recorded books, and magazines rose to nearly 19,000,000 items. Given these statistics, the Library of Congress National Library Service for the Blind and Physically Handicapped (NLS) in 1984 continued to seek even more improvements in four areas in timeliness of delivery, quantity, and quality of braille and recorded reading material and equipment: audio equipment, network produced books and magazines, collection building, and automation.

Audio Equipment comprises disk and cassette machines, and forms the "basic unit of service" for the majority of blind and handicapped persons using the NLS service. The first Ad Hoc Audio Equipment Advisory Committee was convened in Washington in 1983 to provide guidance to NLS concerning the design and production of future equipment. Members of the newly formed committee included individuals representing network libraries, user groups, and machine repair personnel.

Network Produced Books and Magazines expand the scope of the NLS collections, and has, since 1981, focused first on magazines produced by network libraries distributed through the four multistate centers (MSCs). The goal of this program is to standardize the quality and format by applying NLS technical and artistic requirements. In the first phase of this program, recorded magazines meeting this requirement were accepted for duplication and circulation via the MSCs through existing interlibrary loan procedures. In the second phase, the quality assurance standards will be applied to network produced books. The NLS microfiche union catalog will indicate the availability of each book and magazine accepted. Both phases are centralized in the Multistate Center for the Midlands (MSCM) in Cincinnati.

In addition, the MSCM has also taken over the production and circulation of masters by reducing them to more compact form. The masters are produced on four-track cassettes for reproduction by the multistate centers, a process that cuts bulk and duplication time by at least half.

Collection Building was the subject of the eighth annual meeting of the Ad Hoc Advisory Group on Collection Building Activities held at the National Library Service for the Blind and Physically Handicapped in Washington in April. Two developments in collection building are worthy of note: the recording of the official history of the war in Vietnam and the added dimension to the collections provided by NLS foreign language program.

Over the next two years, NLS will record 17 official histories of the Vietnam War on cassettes, and circulate them to handicapped persons through the network of regional libraries located around the country. The histories were prepared by the U.S. Departments of the Army, Air Force, Navy, and the U.S. Marine Corps. They deal with not only the events and policies that led to the war but also with troop deployment and tactical strategies.

Foreign Language Program. The Library of Congress foreign language program has grown since 1967 from a few scattered titles to a collection consisting of two distinct elements: (1) the regular collection of 361 titles, predominately Spanish, but including four other western European languages as well (cataloged and circulated through the network libraries in the same ways as other materials); (2) the Special Foreign Language Collection, which consisted in 1984 of 437 foreign language books in 16 foreign languages. The latter are available in limited numbers of copies, and were acquired through exchange, gift, or purchase from agencies in foreign countries and from commercial firms in the United States and abroad. This collection contains titles in both handcopied and press-braille, recorded disks, and cassettes.

The NLS foreign language librarian compiled *Foreign Language Referral Bibliographies and Source Documents*. Copies have been made available to the NLS cooperating network libraries. In addition to listing the mass-produced and Special Foreign Language Collection titles, this loose-leaf bibliography, arranged alphabetically by language, also lists libraries, organizations, and other groups from which braille and recorded materials in foreign languages may be acquired.

In addition to the NLS foreign language collection, the North Carolina Foreign Language Center in Fayetteville provides educational and recreational reading material in 75 non–English languages. The Center also has a bilingual reference service and resources for persons who wish to learn English as a second language. While the collections consist mainly of conventionally printed books and instruction materials, the Center has purchased some commercially available language recordings, many of which are usable by visually impaired persons. The Foreign Language Center has been in operation for more than seven years and was funded by an LSCA grant through the North Carolina State Library.

"A Selection Policy, the Key to Collection Building," is currently being produced by a committee comprising members of the IFLA Section on Libraries for the Blind. Members of the committee are Frank Kurt Cylke, U.S.A.; Clifford Law, Australia; Allan Leach, U.K.; Antun Lastric, Yugoslavia; D. S. Zharkov, U.S.S.R.; and Francis Czajkowski, Poland.

Automation and the use of small computers have been further extended to assist in the registration and circulation functions of the NLS cooperating libraries. The Reader Enrollment and Delivery System (READS) is being developed specifically to address these needs, and to provide them with a system that can operate on as wide a range of devices available in the computer marketplace as possible. In 1983 NLS contracted with Mobius Management Systems to develop READS. The first step involved taking advantage of the local area network LANS, architecture utilizing 2 to 12 small computers as workstations performing a variety of tasks including optical scanning. During 1984, several pilot test sites were selected, and data received from the staff in those test sites will be evaluated; modifications in the system will be made as required; and the system released to requesters, possibly by early 1985. NLS is developing the software for these small computers.

People. Three retirements and an award are worthy of note. Maxine Dorf, a leading authority on the braille code, retired in October 1983 after 32 years with the Library of Congress, the last 16 of which were as head of the Braille Codes (now Braille Development) Section. She received the Francis Joseph Campbell Award in June at the ALA Conference in Dallas. David Scott Thomas retired from NLS after 42 years of providing direct reading service to blind and handicapped readers in the U.S. and abroad. Frances A. Koestler, Editor of the *Matilda Ziegler Magazine for the Blind* and the author of *The Unseen Minority: A Social History of Blindness in the United States*, retired May 31. *The Matilda Ziegler Magazine for the Blind*, begun in 1907, is published in both braille and recording, and has the distinction of being the oldest general interest periodical for people unable to read print.

Newspapers. From a project initiated by the Swedish newspaper *Gotesborgs-Posten*, a research team at Chalmers Technical University in Sweden is developing a daily talking newspaper. The production system under study in 1984 takes the same digital code used for publication of the printed edition and transmits it over regular FM waves to receivers in subscribers' households. A voice terminal translates the coded disks into nonhuman but understandable speech.

The Rome, Georgia, subregional library is recording local papers for 10 of the 11 counties in their service area, and sending them to the patrons in the respective counties. Such papers, for example, include the *Cedar Town Standard* and the *Cherokee Tribune*. The library records 22 newspapers a week. Local newspapers contribute free subscriptions to the project.

Computer and Large Print. The Boston publisher G. K. Hall is using an optical scanner developed by the Kurzweil Computer Products, Inc., of Cambridge, to record the contents of books that it reprints in large-type editions for the visually impaired. This machine is set apart from other such computers by its ability to recognize a great variety of typefaces. Its developers say that this computer marks an advance in artificial intelligence and is gaining acceptance among publishers, linguists, and others who ". . . put it to work 'reading' documents and storing large amounts of information."

Booksetting

Radio Reading. Two new radio reading services were made available in 1984 to patrons in New Jersey. One of the two, Audiovision, is provided by the New Jersey Library located in Trenton. The other is run by the Electronic Information and Education Service in South Orange. EIES started closed-circuit broadcasts in December 1983 on a Sunday-afternoon basis over a regular FM station. Volunteers at both stations read daily and weekly newspapers, magazine articles, and some current books.

Rehabilitation Information. The National Rehabilitation Information Center (NARIC), under a National Institute of Handicapped Research grant of $2,400,000, is developing and enlarging two principal databases, ABLEDATA and REHABDATA. ABLEDATA lists more than 10,000 commercially available products and assistive devices for disabled individuals; REHABDATA provides information about documents and articles on disabilities from the extensive NARIC library. Since its inception in 1977, NARIC has been on the campus of Catholic University of America in Washington, D.C.

FRANK KURT CYLKE
ALFRED D. HAGLE

Bookselling

Trends. The growing interest in the personal computer software market was recognized in February by *Publishers Weekly,* when it introduced a new section on Software Publishing and Selling. By year's end, however, restraint and caution prevailed as booksellers, in a traditionally low-tech business, began to confront the significant differences between selling books and software. The sales of computer books weakened and further tempered booksellers' enthusiasm. Some observers saw the videocassette market as the next big opportunity for bookstores.

Bookstores have been slow to apply computer technology in their own operations. Eighty-nine percent of the stores responding to a survey for the *American Book Trade Directory* [Bowker, 1984] reported no computerized inventory system, and 59 percent had no microfiche readers (useful for keeping abreast of publishers' and wholesalers' stocks).

Marriage of Giants. Hawley Hale Corporation sold Waldenbooks, with almost 900 stores the largest chain in the United States, to the large discount corporation K-Mart. Independent booksellers who like to promote service over price nervously watched for signs of future Waldenbook discount policies.

Richard Fontaine, the Chief Operating officer of another chain, B. Dalton, joined Ingram Book Company, where he was to head new software and video divisions.

As noted in the 1984 edition of this *Yearbook,* price discounting had not been widespread, though Waldenbooks and B. Dalton had started to meet the discounts offered by Crown Books on selected best sellers, and apparently were testing discounts in selected markets. Price laissez faire was rising as an important issue for booksellers in the mid-1980s.

Statistics. The *American Book Trade Directory* (ABTD), in its 30th edition in 1984, reported 23,606 booksellers in the United States and Canada. General bookstores numbered 6,013 in the U.S. and 1,016 in Canada; religious stores, the second highest category, 4,142 in the U.S. and 214 in Canada; and college stores, third, 2,843 U.S. and 148 Canadian. Many stores are small. Defined as "establishments with payrolls," bookstores, according to *Statistical Abstracts of the United States* [1984], numbered only 9,300 [1982] in the United States. For comparison, there were more than 22,000 novelty, gift, and souvenir shops and 19,600 hardware stores.

A survey for *American Book Trade Directory* revealed the scale of bookstore operations: 37 percent reported gross sales under $50,000 annually, 18 percent between $50,000 and $100,000, the same percent between $100,000 and $250,000, 10 between $250,000 and $500,000, 5 between $500,000 and $1,000,000, and only 4 percent over $1,000,000.

General retailers sold books valued at $3,754,000,000, in 1982, the latest year for which figures were available, according to *Book Industry Trends* (Book Industry Study Group, 1984), and college stores' sales totaled $1,792,000,000. (Libraries and other institutional sales for the same period totaled 751,000,000. Sales made directly to the customer totaled $1,939,000,000 and school sales $1,330,000,000).

More than half of the stores bought directly from publishers and 38 percent from one or more wholesalers. There were 825 general book wholesalers in the U.S. (116 in Canada) and 350 paperback wholesalers (37 in Canada), according to the *American Book Trade Directory*. Wholesalers responding to a *Directory* survey reported

The Anderson Library Committee, a group of Friends supporting the Anderson (Ohio) Public Library raised $9,000 in three days at a shopping mall book sale.

that 36 percent used a computerized system for inventory management; 9 percent recorded their stock on microfiche available to stores for ordering information.

Avon Won't Call. Independent booksellers were nettled in 1984 by the decision of Avon Books, the large paperback publisher, to drop 1,700 direct bookseller accounts. The company said a study of its costs showed that it was losing money on the smaller customers. The American Booksellers Association countered by voting $30,000 to conduct its own analysis of the Avon cost study.

American Booksellers Association. On March 1, G. Royce Smith stepped down as Executive Director of the ABA after 12 years of service in that post. He had seen the Association grow from 3,000 to 5,000 members, and he could observe from the sidelines with some satisfaction in May that his organization had drawn a record turnout of 18,000 for its annual conference in Washington, D.C. Royce had seen "Newswire" (book publicity) introduced in 1973, the *American Bookseller* [1977] grow into a full journal, and a new Booksellers Order Service (BOS) begin to operate under full steam by fall 1984. BOS provides centralized services for ordering from publishers, and shipping and billing services. Some 17,000 publishers have books in print, according to 1984 Bowker estimates.

Smith was succeeded by Bernie Rath, formerly with the Canadian Booksellers Association.

At the Cash Register. *Iacocca: An Autobiography* [Bantam], by Lee Iacocca with William Novak, published in November, took only two months in 1984 to soar to a record 1,000,000 copies sold. The American auto executive and public figure made hardcover-book history.

Another two-month wonder was on the fiction side. Records were broken by sales of *The Talisman* [Viking], by writers Stephen King and Peter Straub. Publication was November 8, and by December 31, 1984, 880,000 copies had been sold. The first printing of 600,000 set a record for a hardcover novel. The promotion campaign totaled more than $500,000. No copies were made available to book clubs.

AMERICAN BOOKSELLERS ASSOCIATION

PRESIDENT (May 1984–May 1985):
Gail See, The Bookcase

VICE-PRESIDENT:
J. Rhett Jackson, The Happy Bookseller, Columbia, South Carolina

SECRETARY:
Leroy Soper, University Bookstore, University of Washington, Seattle

TREASURER:
A. David Schwartz, Dickens Books Ltd., Whitefish Bay, Wisconsin

EXECUTIVE DIRECTOR:
Bernie Rath

Membership (December 1984): 3,776 stores, 615 branches
Headquarters: 122 E. 42nd Street, New York, New York 10168

Other names on the best seller lists in fiction were familiar—Robert Ludlum, Mario Puzo, John Jakes, and venerable Dr. Suess—but one was a surprise. On the *Publishers Weekly* list for 1984 sales (published March 15, 1985) is, as sixth in sales, a work by a new novelist, Helen Hooven Santmyer, an octogenarian whose 1,176-page novel— "...*And Ladies of the House*" (Putnam) garnered sales of 368,300 copies by year's end. It was published in June 1984.

For statistics on publishers' sales and other book news, see Publishing, Book. See also Special Reports in this volume on the Librarian of Congress's report, Books in Our Future (1984), and the Book Industry Study Group's report on reading [1984]. For 1984 events in the libel case brought against booksellers, an author, and his publisher by the Governor of South Dakota, William Janklow, see Intellectual Freedom.

DONALD E. STEWART

Buildings

Library construction was on the upswing during 1984, especially in public libraries. Credit must be given to the prodding effect of the Library Services and Construction Act (LSCA) Title II funds and greater success at the ballot box for library revenue measures. Additionally, the earmarking of funds for library buildings as part of state grant programs in an increasing number of states augmented the ground swell of financial support.

LSCA Title II. While LSCA Title II was not funded in 1984, it was restored for 1985 at $25,000,000—just half the $50,000,000 provided in 1983. Even in this reduced amount, however, the prospect of Title II funding was proving to be a further stimulant at year's end.

Observing building activity in their own states, several state librarians made observations about the effect of Title II.

OREGON—This has been a very good year for public library construction in Oregon and much of it is due to the LSCA Title II funds.... The prospect of future funding of Title II has been very important for planning the future of new libraries in Oregon. I know of five cities that are moving ahead with planning of new buildings because there is the possibility of Title II. Other cities are considering expansions, etc. There is no question that Oregon is experiencing the greatest public library construction program since the early 1970s.

MICHIGAN—The $2,600,000 allotted to Michigan has provided funds for 50 libraries varying from small energy conservation projects to new library structures.... As you can imagine, we are very excited with the inclusion of Title II appropriations for fiscal year 1985.

LOUISIANA—We feel that the LSCA Title II funds have sparked an interest in public library building activity in Louisiana which has been very slow for almost a decade.

SOUTH CAROLINA—Title II...has created much interest in public library construction.... It is significant that communities in South Carolina with high levels of unemployment have raised the necessary local funds to construct new buildings.

New checkout counter (left) and new entrance in the remodeled San Francisco Public Library.

INDIANA—The biggest news in construction of libraries in Indiana is the amount of activity occurring.... We feel that LSCA funding has stimulated some of the construction.

MONTANA—The prospect of future Title II funds will certainly mean both new construction and remodeling projects in Montana.

NEW MEXICO—The prospect of future Title II funding has brought direct inquiries...in a recent questionnaire sent to forty-one public libraries in New Mexico, seventeen indicated they have plans for an addition, remodeling or new facility.

MISSISSIPPI—The library building projects that made the news in Mississippi this year were those funded by the welcome allocation of $636,000 of LSCA funds.

WASHINGTON—There is little doubt that the advent of additional LSCA Title II funds in the future has allowed what have been long-range building plans to become more immediate or considered in the light of the near future rather than the far. The severe disappointment felt by those who applied for LSCA monies under the Jobs Bill and were not among the recipients has been replaced by hope that their shelved projects might be funded after all.

FLORIDA—Here in Florida we can honestly say that LSCA Title II funds acted as a catalyst for library construction projects.

Federal funds for 1983 triggered local and state matching funds of almost $100,000,000 and created an estimated 3,600 jobs through September, 1984, according to Nate Cohen of the Division of Library Programs, U.S. Department of Education. He indicated that construction activity still fell far short of that required to meet the public library construction needs for the period 1981–85, which a survey established as $2,300,000,000 for more than 2,800 projects. The Cohen report on LSCA Title II indicated that 1,020 projects were submitted, of about 500 were approved. Funding included federal ($49,146,241), local ($95,500,746), and state ($3,438,680) for a total of $148,085,667.

While many of the smaller projects have already been completed, the full impact will be spread over the next two years.

Building Standards. With so many building projects under consideration, the LAMA Buildings and Equipment Section's Architecture for Public Libraries Committee prepared a special brochure to be available through the LAMA office in lieu of applicable standards. (See Building Standards and Public Library Planning) Geared to parallel the "Planning Process for Public Libraries," the brochure recommends that planners depend on actual needs assessment and programming as a means for establishing space requirements. Reliance on obsolete "standards," "guidelines," and "rules-of-thumb" have been judged to be misleading and fail to adjust building requirements to the local community. New Illinois standards include a section on library facility space planning that provides further guidance.

New Public Library Buildings. Small libraries made big news across the nation, dominating reports of new library construction, additions, and remodeling. The headline announcing the opening of the new Veedersburg Library in Veedersburg, Indiana, may have summed up the meaning of improved library facilities everywhere: a "Flock of Dreams Come True." With community pride running high, typical openings were held in Eldersburg, Maryland; Raton, New Mexico; Vashon, Washington; Rochester, Indiana; and Fisherville, Virginia. News accounts testified to local interest and the unselfish donations of time, labor, and money by volunteers. In Bosque Farms, New Mexico, architectural plans for a new building were donated and shelving supplied for the mere cost of shelving.

Senator Mark Hatfield (R.-Oregon), strong proponent of federal library construction funding, spoke at dedications for several library projects including one in Huntington, Oregon. The new building there replaced the old structure, a picture of which Hatfield had used in his campaign to obtain federal funding for libraries.

In Drain, Oregon, donations included individual sums of $260,000, $100,000 and $45,000.

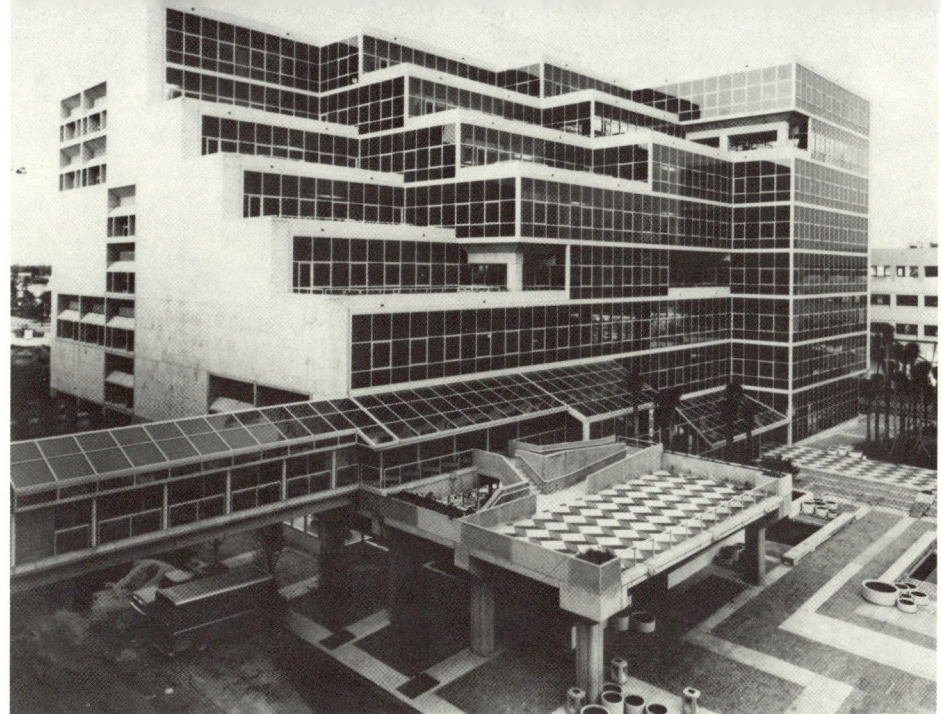

Exterior and first floor interior of the lobby of the Fort Lauderdale (Florida) Main Library. (Stephen Leek)

Contributions by local business to the same project included crushed rock, lumber, landscaping, and maintenance services. In Durham, Connecticut, the $631,000 library project was saved when trustees were able to reduce costs by using work and contributions from town volunteers. The donations of paint and painting labor was one of the major considerations.

Friends of the Clearwater Memorial Library in Idaho underwrote one-third of the $92,000 projected cost for an addition to their library. Actor Paul Newman donated $25,000 toward the Westport, Connecticut, Public Library building fund. This followed a donation of $150,000 from the Stauffer Chemical Co.

Energy conservation and access for the physically handicapped were frequently mentioned project goals. Construction that eliminated stairs, introduced elevators, and enabled physically handicapped persons to use restroom facilities was noted frequently in news reports.

The determination of libraries to accommodate collections and services of special interest to their own communities pervaded many accounts. Meeting rooms and special display areas competed for attention with provision for computers and nonprint materials. It seemed evident that space for programming and nonbook materials, personal computers, and other equipment was as important to the very small library in 1984 as it was to the large libraries.

In many cases, building projects consisted of additions and remodeling rather than new structures. The Clearwater Memorial Library of Orofino, Idaho, for example, acquired gallery space for local artists, a new children's room, and space for enlarged collections.

Smaller libraries for which interesting architectural drawings were seen included the 17,000-square-foot Fulton County Library in Rochester, Indiana, and the 11,950-square-foot Broadneck Branch of the Anne Arundel County Public Library in Annapolis, Maryland. The buildings illustrate creative uses of structures that are essentially square in geometry. Perhaps the most highly publicized library building of the year was the San Juan Capistrano Regional Library in California, designed by Michael Graves.

News of large library buildings was dominated by the opening of the eight-story, 256,000-square-foot Broward County Library in Ft. Lauderdale, Florida. The $39,000,000 building designed by Marcel Breuer received wide attention because of its design and many features that include escalators, a bubble elevator, 300-seat auditorium, and 90-seat restaurant. A six-story atrium provides visual access to the various floors. The library will serve as an academic library for three institutions as well as the headquarters for the Broward County Library system.

The new Lynchburg (Virginia) Public Library opened in October after spending 18 years in a "temporary" location

The San Juan Capistrano Regional Branch of the Orange County (California) Public Library has been called the "Fairy Tale Library" and "The Jewel of California Libraries" because of its open air gazebos, fountains, courtyards, and towers.

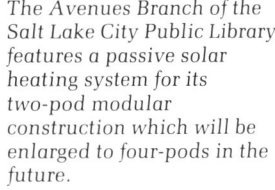

The Avenues Branch of the Salt Lake City Public Library features a passive solar heating system for its two-pod modular construction which will be enlarged to four-pods in the future.

Even larger in scale was the $45,000,000 remodeling and refurbishing of the Central Research Library in New York City. Crown jewel of the facelifting was the restoration of the 6,400-square-foot Gottesman Exhibition Hall, which had been converted to staff space after World War II. New lighting and temperature benefit readers and collections throughout the building.

In Boston a major revamping of branch library buildings was under way. Chicago continued work on the conversion of Goldblatt's Department Store in its central district while Los Angeles Public Library took additional steps toward the restoration and a major addition to its Central Library building to provide a total of 360,000 square feet.

Building Conversions. Those in search of solutions to their library building problems seem to grow ever more inventive. A variety of buildings were being converted in 1984 from other uses to become public libraries. For instance, the city of Farmington, New Mexico, purchased, remodeled, and expanded a former downtown bank building to provide a 25,000-square-foot main library.

The Town of Plains, Montana, converted a former Chevrolet showroom into its new library while the Ventress Memorial library in Marshfield, Massachusetts, moved into a renovated supermarket, as did the Public Library in Beaverton, Oregon. In Oregon, the Oakland Branch of the Douglas County library converted a portion of an old school building while the Reading, Massachusetts, Public Library remodeled the Highland Street School for its new home.

Houses were used in several smaller communities; Columbia, Connecticut, was an example. The Santa Fe (New Mexico) Public Library was busy renovating the City Hall for a new life as a library. The Macon (Mississippi) Public Library renovated and occupied a three-story jail on the National Register of Historic Places. A former Firestone retail store with an ideal location became the branch for the Gloster Public Library in Mississippi.

Academic Libraries. Building activity among academic libraries was fairly limited. Among the larger facilities opened was the Davis Library at the University of South Carolina, Chapel Hill. Designed by Leslie N. Boney with consultants Mitchell/Giurgola, the 438,000-square-foot building has space for 1,500,000 volumes and 3,000 seats. Pace University in Pleasantville, New York, opened a three-story library for 250,000 volumes and 600 readers at a cost of $4,250,000.

The Architects Collaborative of Cambridge was the designer of Boston College's O'Neill Library, providing room for 1,250,000 volumes and 1,350 readers. The new building enables the

New branch libraries of the San Antonio (Texas) Public Library include the Ed Cody Branch (left) and the Collins Garden Branch (above).

College to consolidate several campus libraries while adding new services including a Visions Resources Room for the handicapped. CBN University in Virginia Beach, Virginia, opened a 152,000-square-foot, $13,200,000 library with a capacity for 600,000 volumes and 1,000,000 microforms. The Library is linked to a communications center to launch national and global mass education programs through satellite broadcasts central to the program of the sponsoring agency, the Christian Broadcasting Network. At year's end a $10,800,000 library and computer center was nearing completion on the Lehigh University Campus in Bethlehem, Pennsylvania.

Ursiline College, Cleveland, broke ground for its $3,100,000 library at midyear while a $10,000,000, 107,000-square-foot building was under way for Texas Woman's University in Denton, Texas. Space will be provided for the University's special collections including its extensive Women's Collection.

Money. Financing library construction ran the gamut from bond issues to private donations. Referendums seemed more successsful than in previous years as voters approved issues in such diverse places as Rockland County, New York; Rock Island, Illinois; Anoka County, Minnesota; Tacoma, Washington; Houston, Texas; and Westfield, New Jersey. Nevada voters approved a state bond issue providing matching funds at the ratio of one-to-three for local funding. Illinois joined a steadily growing list of states providing construction grants as part of its state-aid package.

The strategy of challenge grants was repeatedly cited as a strong incentive for acquiring building funds. Depending on the size of the project, challenge grants ran from a few thousands of dollars provided by a local individual, business, or industry to hundreds of thousands of dollars offered by large foundations and the National Endowment for the Humanities, among others.

In Oklahoma, the State Library launched a vigorous campaign to raise private funds, noting that the LSCA Title II is a strong stimulus. The State Library there reminded librarians that:

"80 billion or so a year is given to Americans for charity. Libraries who do not get their share of this money are failing to recognize a resource that has been available for years. The skills are the same if it's $5,000 worth of books or five million dollars worth of building, they must ask or wait for the gifts. For the last two years private funds have been coming to communities in Oklahoma from wills and personal gifts ranging from pocket change to $500,000."

The Oklahoma Department of Libraries spon-

A four-year program to renovate the Boulder, Colorado, 77-year-old Carnegie Branch Library for Local History and restore its "turn of the century" furnishings was completed in 1984.

A gala and glittering evening on May 24, 1984, celebrated the opening of the restored New York Public Library Exhibit Hall, closed since World War II and renamed the Gottesman Exhibition Hall. (Peter Aaron) Distinguished guests dined and danced in a festive tent set up on the Library grounds in a "Celebration of Learning" with living sculptures personifying the arts and sciences. (Anne Day) Library President Vartan Gregorian and Mrs. Vincent Astor, Chairwoman of the Library Trustees and longtime patron, presided over the evening's events. (Bill Cunningham)

After 40 Years, NYPL Opens Its Restored Exhibition Hall

President William Howard Taft presided over the ceremony May 24, 1911, when the great bronze doors of the New York Central Research Library's Exhibition Hall were first opened to the public. The room was designed by architects John Carrere and Thomas Hastings as a major center for public learning and a place to display the Library's most valuable treasures.

Its popular shows of the past included one on Beadle Dime Novels, a Theodore Roosevelt Memorial Exhibition, and an exhibit of ancient Bibles. In 1942 the library packed up its most valuable holdings and shipped them to Saratoga Springs for safekeeping. After the war exhibitions were forgotten and the magnificent hall was unceremoniously subdivided into office space to accommodate a growing library staff.

On May 24, 1984, the restored room—renamed the D. Samuel and Jeane H. Gottesman Exhibition Hall—and its restored doors were again opened to the public at a celebratory ceremony attended by 1,200 distinguished patrons of the Library.

The evening's theme was "In Celebration of Learning" and guests were treated to the first new exhibition in the Hall in four decades.

The evening events were chaired by Mrs. Vincent Astor, Library Trustee for 25 years, and Library President Vartan Gregorian. Astor's family relationship to the Library extends back to the private reference library of John Jacob Astor (1763–1848).

As a part of the Library's $45,000,000 restoration program, the Fifth Avenue facade and the Library's entry Astor Hall were also refurbished and restored.

The Gottesman Exhibition Hall is

entered directly from Astor Hall, and its far doors open to the Library's 88 miles of book stacks. The original architects had commissioned the noted wood carver Maurice Grieve to carve the Renaissance style ceiling, and the ceiling remains one of the rare examples of carved wood ceilings in the United States. The Hall's four arches sit on massive double marble piers. The white marble of the walls is Danby marble from Dorset, Vermont.

The restoration of the Exhibition Hall was filled with unique design challenges. The architects were faced with the task of installing modern electrical and lighting systems as well as temperature and humidity controls, while retaining the original architectural character of the room. Special exhibition furniture was designed to be flexible, portable, and appropriate for the variety of exhibits to be held in the Hall.

Permanent translucent shades for the windows were developed to screen out the damaging effects of natural light on paper and printed works. The architects also designed a set of six bronze and leaded glass inlay chandeliers that are reproductions of the original Carrere and Hastings design. These were installed along with a set of electrical points to allow for mountable track fixtures.

The restoration project was guided by restoration architect Giorgio Cavaglieri. Cavaglieri had previously been responsible for restoring the Library's DeWitt Wallace Periodical Room. The project was made possible through gifts from the D. S. and R. H. Gottesman Foundation, the Rockefeller Brothers Fund, the Uris Brothers Foundation, and Library Trustee Harold W. McGraw, Jr. The restoration of the Exhibition Hall was the keystone project in the Library's restoration program.

---

sored design grants for a year and a half to allow libraries to pay for preplanning. The Department also promoted uniform road signs directing motorists to public library facilities.

Presidential Libraries. Fund-raising for the Carter Presidential Library neared its $25,000,000 goal by midyear. Still unresolved were some of the site problems that have plagued the library since its location at Emory University in Atlanta was announced. Controversy centered on a proposed access road that opponents warned may destroy a historic neighborhood. Meanwhile, architectural planning proceeded on the Library and on Carter Policy Center with which it will be associated.

After much indecision by sponsors, facilities for the Richard M. Nixon Presidential Library were designated: a Spanish-motif building of low profile will stand on a 13-acre bluff overlooking the Pacific in San Clemente, California. Designed by Langdon Wilson, the building was to cost $15,000,000; construction was scheduled to begin in 1985.

Several issues regarding the Ronald Reagan Presidential Library, Museum, and Public Affairs Center, to be built at Stanford University, arose during the year. Partial agreement was reached on the housing of the facilities but governance was still an issue. The Reagan Library Planning Committee identified three potential sites. One near the Center for Advanced Study in the Behavioral Sciences was preferred.

Life Safety Issues and Disasters. Libraries were mercifully spared major disasters during 1984 though some experienced flooding and arson-set fires. Arizona lost two branch libraries to arsonists, one in Phoenix and the other in Tucson. In both cases, the arsonists used the bookdrops for introducing inflammable materials. The fires destroyed several thousand volumes and damaged many more with the total bill running more than $500,000.

There was a rash of reports on problems with asbestos, especially in ceilings and roofs. The Tomkins County Public Library reported that ridding itself of asbestos would cost $400,000. Asbestos removal for the Santa Monica (California) Public Library could cost $1,500,000 and force a shutdown of nine months or more. The Charleston County Library, South Carolina, closed its West Ashley Branch and was replacing asbestos ceilings at a cost of $70,000. The Headquarters Building of a suburban library system in Illinois was expected to be vacated while a $100,000 insulation replacement job was done.

LAMA Buildings and Equipment Section. A capacity crowd attended a two-and-a-half day Building and Equipment Section Committee preconference on library space planning and programming at the ALA Conference in Dallas. Presentations covered needs assessment, programming, architectural selection, and the development of schematic design. Both public and academic libraries were covered. Proceedings were to be published by LAMA. Other conference programs sponsored by the Section reported good attendance—a sign of the revival of interest in library buildings.

RAYMOND M. HOLT

Canadian Library Association

Public Issues. The Canadian Library Association took action on several public issues in 1984. In November, CLA President Judith McAnanama wrote to the Canadian Secretary of State for External Affairs stressing the value of UNESCO, especially in the library context, and urging Canada to take a lead from within the international body in overcoming the problems confronting it in recent years. As an active member of the Canadian Commission for UNESCO, CLA has provided advice and comment on UNESCO's General Information Programme and other endeavors for several years. The Association was concerned in 1984 about the future stability of the organization in view of the announced withdrawals of the United States and the United Kingdom.

On the censorship front, the Association appeared in April before the Special Committee on Pornography and Prostitution appointed by the federal Minister of Justice to speak to the written submission prepared by the then CLA President, Lois Bewley. In response to the Committee's terms of reference on the problems of access to pornography in the context of the fundamental rights of free thought and expression, the Association urged the Committee to propose no further

CLA traveling workshop in the CLA's continuing education program generated enthusiasm throughout the year.

regulations leading to restrictions on certain publications. While deploring the exploitation of children, women, and men in the production of pornographic materials, the Association said that there is sufficient legislation in place that, if judiciously applied, could prohibit the distribution and sale of obscene materials as defined in the Criminal Code of Canada.

The Association endorsed, and member libraries participated in, a national Freedom to Read Week, September 16–23. Sponsored by the Book and Periodical Development Council, of which CLA is a founding member, the Week publicized the dangers of censorship and promoted the concept of freedom of expression through public readings, displays, and media interviews.

CLA's governing Council established a Copyright Task Force in June, following the release in May of the federal government's white paper on copyright, entitled *From Gutenberg to Telidon*. The document refers to the Government's intention to revise and update Canada's 60-year-old *Copyright Act* and outlines proposals for doing so. Of particular concern to libraries are reprography and the fair use principle, exemptions for the benefit of the handicapped, and the creation of copyright collectives. There was a change of government in September, and it remained to be seen when the matter would be reintroduced into the House of Commons; however, in anticipation of that, the CLA Task Force undertook preparation of a detailed response to the published proposals.

Professional Development. In January the Association established a Committee on Canadian Accreditation of Library and Information Science Programs and appointed Beth Miller, CLA First Vice-President, as its convenor. The action followed Council's decision to endorse the concept of Canadian accreditation. Council had concluded that librarianship has matured sufficiently in Canada to warrant this step, and that CLA and possibly other Canadian library bodies should have a greater bearing on professional practice. There are seven schools of library and information science in Canada with master's degree programs accredited by the American Library Association. In embarking on a ways and means study of the Canadian accreditation scheme, the Committee and the Association acknowledged both the longstanding cooperation of ALA in extending its accreditation service north of the border and the excellence of that service.

Council's endorsement of the Canadian accreditation concept has not been without controversy. Several schools and some CLA members have objected to the idea, saying that the present system works well, that Canadian acceptance achieves a desirable North American standard, and that it would be unnecessarily costly for a Canadian system to be set up to serve so few schools. The Committee, which includes a representative from CLA's French-language sister association ASTED, invited briefs from interested parties, and planned to hold hearings in different parts of the country, in preparation for a report for consideration by the membership in June 1986.

CLA accepted in November an invitation from ALA to participate in its project to explore procedures and guidelines for participation of a variety of associations in the accreditation process. Beth Miller was named CLA's appointee to the project's Steering Committee, and appointments were also made to the six Working Groups.

October-November marked the beginning of CLA Seminars, the Association's new professional development program, when a full-day workshop on the dynamics of supervision was presented in six cities across the country. Under the direction of the new Programs Department at CLA headquarters, CLA Seminars will organize three workshops each year that will travel across Canada to help meet the continuing education needs of the library community. At the request of Council, the Programs Department is preparing a proposal for issuing professional development certificates to those attending a prescribed number of seminars. Several provincial associations and CLA chapters are cosponsoring selected presentations.

Meanwhile, the Canadian School Library Association (CSLA), a division of CLA, continued its successful professional development program, commencing its 1984–85 season with an intensive two-day workshop on resource-based learning in Halifax, Nova Scotia. The Canadian Association of Special Libraries and Information Services (CASLIS), also a division of CLA, organized several workshops in 1984 through its five urban chapters.

Other Developments. Following the issuance in 1983 of a consultant's report on the feasibility of CSLA's breaking away from CLA to form an independent association, the CSLA executive and membership considered the pros and cons of such a move for the first six months of 1984. The divisional executive solicited members' views and organized an open meeting on the issue at the annual conference in June. At the annual business meeting of the division immediately subsequent to these deliberations, no motion was moved to form a new body, thus preserving CSLA's status quo.

At the request of the Canadian Association of Public Libraries (CAPL), a division of CLA, CLA

Council, in March, approved the adoption of the library symbol previously recognized by ALA. Also in 1984, CLA promoted, among 700 public libraries, Elderhostel's campus-based educational program for individuals 60 years of age and older.

Conferences and Awards. CLA's 39th annual conference in Toronto in June drew 1,376 delegates and 93 firms and organizations as exhibitors. President Lois Bewley of the University of British Columbia School of Librarianship presided over the 162-event gathering, choosing as her theme "1984 and Beyond—Human Values in the Computer Age." President Judith McAnanama, Chief of Hamilton (Ontario) Public Library, took office at the conclusion of the conference.

With the appointment of an Executive Committee, organizational work began in the winter of 1984 on the joint CLA/ASTED annual conference planned for Quebec City in June 1986. This event will mark the first time that the unilingual English CLA and the unilingual French ASTED will have met together, though the two associations have enjoyed, in addition to their constitutional link, a close working relationship for several years.

CLA awarded the following scholarships in 1984: the Howard V. Phalin–World Book Graduate Scholarship in Library Science ($2,500 Can.) to Kathleen Hogan, Calgary, Alberta; the H. W. Wilson Scholarship ($2,000) to Angela Schmidt of Lethbridge, Alberta; and the CLA–Elizabeth Dafoe Scholarship ($1,750) to Angelica Kurtz of Winnipeg, Manitoba.

The children's librarians section presented two book awards on behalf of CLA. The Canadian Library Association Book of the Year for Children Award went to Jan Hudson for *Sweetgrass* (Tree Frog Press). Ken Nutt received the Amelia Frances Howard–Gibbon Illustrator's Award for illustrations in Tim Wynne-Jones's *Zoom at Sea* (Groundwood Books).

The CASLIS Award for Special Librarianship in Canada went to Melva Dwyer, University of British Columbia Library, Vancouver.

Canadian Library Association President (1983–1984) Lois Bewley (right) passes on words of wisdom to 1984–1985 President Judith McAnanama.

The four CSLA awards for 1984 and their winners were Margaret B. Scott Award of Merit, Pauline Fennell, formerly Education Officer, Ontario Ministry of Education, Toronto; Distinguished Service Award for School Administrators, Rita Spencer, Principal, River Heights Elementary School, Saskatoon, Saskatchewan; Margaret B. Scott Memorial Award (administered jointly with the Ontario Library Association), Anne Galler, Co-ordinator, Library Studies, Concordia University, Montreal, Quebec, Christine Spring-Gifford, Teacher-Librarian, Calgary Board of Education, Alberta, and Patricia Blackburn, Acting Director, Instructional Media Services, Manitoba Department of Education, Winnipeg; Grolier Award for Research in School Librarianship in Canada ($1,000), David Jenkinson, Faculty of Education, University of Manitoba, Winnipeg.

Myrtle Lorimer, Winnipeg Centennial Library Board, received the Canadian Library Trustees Merit Award. The CLA Research and Development Award ($1,000) went to Ruth Jellicoe Sheeran, Bishop's University Library, Lennoxville, Quebec. The CLA Outstanding Service to Librarianship Award was not presented in 1984.

PAUL KITCHEN

CANADIAN LIBRARY ASSOCIATION

PRESIDENT (June 1984–June 1985):
Judith McAnanama, Hamilton Public Library, Ontario

FIRST VICE-PRESIDENT/PRESIDENT-ELECT:
Beth Miller, Special Collections Librarian, D. B. Weldon Library, University of Western Ontario, London

SECOND VICE-PRESIDENT:
Diane MacQuarrie, Chief Librarian, Halifax City Regional Library, Nova Scotia

TREASURER:
Ken Jensen, Regina Public Library, Regina, Saskatchewan

EXECUTIVE DIRECTOR:
Paul Kitchen

Membership (June 30, 1984): 4,765 (3,967 personal; 798 institutional)
Headquarters: 151 Sparks Street, Ottawa, Ontario K1P 5E3

Cataloging and Classification

For bibliographic control, 1984 was a year of consolidation, progress, and steady growth rather than one of spectacular innovation. There were no major new cataloging codes, nor were there complete revisions of major classification schemes, nor were there radical revisions in machine-readable formats. The year, however, was not lacking in interest even though it may have lacked the seismic events of the recent past.

Microcomputer Software. The microcomputer revolution has not been without its consequences for bibliographic control. Libraries of all kinds have acquired games, programs, and data on floppy disks. These are to be used on IBM, Apple, Atari, Commodore, and countless other microcomputers, and present new and, up to now, unanswered problems for technical processing.

Cataloging and Classification

The primary focus of these problems has been on descriptive cataloging as defined by the *Anglo-American Cataloguing Rules, Second Edition* (AACR2). These rules, published in 1978, based their treatment of the description of computer materials upon the previous work of the ALA/Resources and Technical Services Division Subcommittee on Rules for Cataloging Machine-Readable Data Files. That work dated back to the period of 1974–76. It is not surprising, therefore, that the rules as published cover, essentially, the software and machine-readable products of large mainframe computers. This material belongs to the hieratic world of computer experts and large computer systems, and it is almost always unpublished and exists in one copy or a few copies for the use of the initiate and the expert. Small wonder that the rules did not deal adequately with the mass-produced games, programs, and other materials produced for home use on comparatively inexpensive and widely available machines that are, nowadays, not much more complex to use than electric toasters. An extension or revision of the rules in Chapter 9 of AACR2 was clearly needed. It is not too much of an exaggeration to say that, for the last two or so years, standard cataloging of microcomputer software either did not exist or ground to a halt. Cooperative cataloging of these materials was not possible because catalogers were unable to catalog them using national standards, and, even if they essayed a catalog entry, no means were available to add such cataloging to national databases.

The essential first step toward a remedy was taken by a subcommittee of the Committee on Cataloging: Description and Access (CC:DA) of ALA/RTSD. Chaired by Ben Tucker of the Library of Congress, the subcommittee created a set of guidelines (written by Arnold Wajenberg, Vice-Chair of the subcommittee). They were approved by CC:DA in 1983 and were published as *Guidelines for Using AACR2 Chapter 9 for Cataloging Microcomputer Software* (ALA, 1984). The *Guidelines* take advantage of the modular structure of AACR2, Part 1 (Description of library materials), by interpreting the fundamental deep structure of the descriptive rules (based on the ISBD-G), and the working out of that structure in Chapter 9, in light of the peculiar attributes of microcomputer software.

Important features of the Guidelines include: the chief source of information for microcomputer software is the internally encoded data. If such is not available, labels on the carrier (disk, cassette, etc.), the container itself, and accompanying documentation are preferred (in that order); in the physical description area, the carrier is described, resulting, for example, in this description: 1 program file (IBM PC) on 1 computer disk: sd., col.; 5 1/4 in. The instructions for notes include (inter alia) provision for the recording of information on hardware requirements, memory, operating systems, and peripherals.

Beyond the descriptive cataloging problems posed by microcomputer software lies the question of encoding the bibliographic data for use in shared cataloging. Various organizations addressed this in 1984. MARBI (the Committee on Representation in Machine-Readable Form of Bibliographic Information) devised a MARC format for machine-readable data files (MRDF). The proposed format was to be published in early 1985 by the Library of Congress. OCLC, Inc., published its version of the MRDF format in late 1984, and it became available for use in the OCLC system.

Classification of Computer Science. The Decimal Classification Division of the Library of Congress produced a revised draft of a revision of the Dewey DC for computer science and computer engineering. The revised draft is based on work done by a subcommittee of ALA's Subject Access Committee; 004 is being used for Computer science and data processing; 005 for Computer programming, programs, and data; 006 for Special computer methodologies. Revisions of 384 (to include 384.3–Computer communications); and 621.3 (to include 621.39–Computers); and of Table 1 (to include 0285–Data processing) are also proposed. This revision was approved by the Editorial Policy Committee of DDC and was to be published as a separate by Forest Press in 1985.

Minimal-Level Records. Much interest continued to be shown in 1984 in the topic of minimal ("less-than-full") cataloging. The reconciliation of such national "minimal" standards as the National Level Bibliographic Record-Books minimal subset, OCLC "Level K," RLG Minimal Standards, and AACR2 Level 1 continued to be of great interest to libraries faced with backlogs and staff shortages. The Library of Congress continued to produce minimal records but by year's end had not yet decided when, and how, it would disseminate such records. The Technical Service Directors of Large Research Libraries ("Bigheads") Group of RTSD has gathered data and continues to discuss this question.

Revisions to AACR2. The Joint Steering Committee (JSC) published approved amendments to AACR2 agreed by that body in 1983. A number of important, trivial, and typographical matters were corrected or improved. The most important revisions concerned the main entry for sound recordings that were the result of the work of more than one person or body (21.23C and D) and the entry of subordinate corporate bodies that lack distinctive names (24.13, type 3 and 24.18, type 3). It cannot be said that either of these perennially knotty problems has been solved forever. On the other hand, the new revisions are certainly tighter and more easily applied than were their predecessors.

The Library of Congress continued to produce its meticulous and voluminous "rule interpretations" of AACR2. These glosses (to be found in LC's *Cataloging Service Bulletin*) are viewed by all catalogers as a blessing and as a curse, often simultaneously.

The JSC, at its annual meeting in 1984 in Scotland, decided to publish a consolidated edition of AACR2 by the end of the 1980s. The present editors will complete their term of duty by editing the consolidated version, including all approved revisions and contingent amendments and making all corrections known to be necessary.

LC Subject Cataloging Manual. The Library of Congress' Subject Cataloging Division published

Subject Cataloging Manual—Subject Headings in a "preliminary edition." This enormous tome, in a loose-leaf format, contains, in great detail, instructions on the composition and form of LC subject headings. Such information has always been available to LC's own subject catalogers but had not been organized and presented to the wider cataloging community. This Herculean task was under the direction of Eugene T. Frosio and was financed by a grant from the National Commission on Libraries and Information Science (NCLIS). It has been designated "preliminary" because time did not permit the inclusion of every instruction currently available to LC subject catalogers. There should be more than enough, however, for the average toiler in the subject cataloging vineyard to read and digest. The manual will be designated as a "first edition" when all current LC practice is made available. The purpose of the manual is to lead toward great uniformity of subject practice. Its detail and comprehensiveness should guarantee that effect.

Awards. The RTSD Margaret Mann citation for 1984 was awarded to Dorothy Anderson. It was a doubly internationalist award in that Anderson, a native of New Zealand, is also chiefly known for her organizational work on behalf of the International Federation of Library Associations and Institutions (IFLA) and its efforts in the area of universal bibliographic control (UBC).

The Esther J. Piercy Award went to Liz Bishoff, in recognition of her contributions to cataloging, especially from the public library point of view.

MICHAEL GORMAN
ARNOLD WAJENBERG

Catholic Library Association

CLA Concerns. In 1984 the Catholic Library Association focused on developing a cooperative relationship with religious educators. The development of religious education programs in Catholic parishes and schools pointed up a need for supplemental materials, especially bibliographies, to support the educational activities. A new series of bibliographies entitled "Current Concerns in Religious Education" were inaugurated and additional bibliographies, based on recommendations from religious educators, were planned. CLA also participates in diocesan workshops for religious educators to introduce CLA's services and publications.

Through the years, the CLA bylaws have been changed by deletions and additions resulting in some ambiguous and contradictory statements. In 1984 the Executive Board directed the Constitution and ByLaws Committee to make a thorough study to remove sexist language and to resolve the ambiguities. The report of the Committee was due in 1985.

Increases in operating costs at CLA headquarters forced the Finance Committee to recommend a modest increase in membership dues in the Personal and Special Personal categories. At the same time, the Executive Board recommended that the CLA convention registration fee match the National Catholic Educational Association convention registration fee. A financial study of *The Catholic Periodical and Literature Index* revealed that indexing newspapers accounted for a large deficit. The Finance Committee decided to seek subsidies from the newspapers indexed to underwrite the deficit.

CLA responded favorably to the invitation from Elizabeth Stone to be a partner in the promotion of National Library Week. CLA was also represented on the NLW Advisory Council for Pennsylvania.

The September 1984 meeting of the CLA Executive Board was devoted to evaluating CLA's current status and future activities. Those discussions were to be the basis for a mission statement for CLA.

Awards. Elizabeth Stone, in recognition of her commitment and distinguished service to the library profession, was given a life membership in the Association during the Boston Convention. Madeleine L'Engle received the 1984 Regina Medal in acknowledgment of her continued distinguished contribution to children's literature. The Rev. Andrew L. Bouwhuis Scholarship in Library Science was awarded to Melissa C. Flannery of Scranton, Pennsylvania. The World Book Childcraft annual grant of $1,000 was given to Sister Lauretta McCusker and Eileen Noonan, both of Rosary College, to assist in their survey of current periodicals for children in the English language. The John Brubaker Award for the best article published in the *Catholic Library World* in 1983–84 was won by R. Brantley Cagle, Jr.

Other Activities. CLA met jointly with the National Catholic Educational Association in Boston in April. The cooperative venture proved to be a success and resulted in additional cooperative activities with NCEA.

Contributions to CLA's Continuing Education Fund are being reserved until interest from the account is sufficient to offer grants to CLA members for continuing education activities. The videotape series, "On Stage with Children," continued to be popular.

MATTHEW R. WILT

CATHOLIC LIBRARY ASSOCIATION

PRESIDENT (April 1983–April 1985):
Sister Mary Dennis Lynch, SHCJ, Rosemont College, Rosemont, Pennsylvania

VICE-PRESIDENT/PRESIDENT-ELECT:
Mary A. Grant, St. John's University, Jamaica, New York

EXECUTIVE DIRECTOR:
Matthew R. Wilt

Membership (December 1984): 3,100
Headquarters: 461 W. Lancaster Avenue, Haverford, Pennsylvania 19041

Children's Book Council

Children's Book Week was observed for the 65th year in 1984 with a wide variety of display and promotional materials. The theme selected by the Book Week Committee, chaired by Ava Weiss of Greenwillow Books, was "Bring On The Books!" The poster for children was prepared by Caldecott Medalist Gerald McDermott, depicting a parade of children's storybook characters. For

Children's Book Week parade in Springfield, Ohio, featured Miss Piggy personifying the Warder Libraries' theme "Pig Out on Books Day."

Adoptable puppies were made available during Children's Book Week at the Spokane Public Library with volunteers on hand to give advice on pet care.

the second time, a special Book Week poster for young adults was offered: Ken Robbins's photographic depiction of a teenager reading while lounging had great appeal. Other contributors to Book Week were poet Lilian Moore, frieze artist Donald Crews, and streamer artists Felicia Bond, Erick Ingraham and Ann Jonas.

CBC's well-known publication *The Calendar*, after dropping the "Books and Dates" feature that was its sole reason for existing initially, had after nearly 40 years a change of name to *CBC Features*.

Council membership dropped in 1984, in part because of the continuing trend in children's book publishing for houses to purchase, merge with, or otherwise absorb other houses. Perhaps Macmillan Publishing, Inc., proved to be the most notable acquirer in children's books in recent years. By the end of 1984, its children's book publishing program included the following imprints in addition to its own, begun in 1919: Atheneum Publishers, and also Margaret K. McElderry Books; Bradbury Press; Four Winds Press; and Charles Scribner's Sons. Each one of these houses has been a major force in U.S. children's book publishing by any measure. Each sustains its editorial independence, but a great many of the ancillary publishing activities that can distinguish one house from another have been combined. As all of the lists noted are best-known for hardcover publishing, this trend may reflect somewhat that this area of trade book publishing appears to be static. It relies more than in the past on sales of new titles each year. Backlist sales—so long a feature of children's book publishing—continue to be poor as schools and libraries use their limited materials budgets for new works.

The zero-growth characteristic of children's hardcover book publishing in 1984 was not shared by children's paperback publishing, however. According to regularly reported statistics in *Publishers Weekly*, children's paperback publishing has exhibited stronger growth in the past few years than any other area of publishing. The strong showing of this segment of the industry has inspired a substantial number of traditional hardcover children's book publishers to bring out both current and backlist titles in trade paperback format. Meanwhile, mass market children's paperback publishers originated a far greater percentage of their lists in 1984 than was the case only two or three years previously. Much of this publishing is of original series lines

A RIDDLE

What's small,
holds treasure
yet fits in the hand

needs no battery
doesn't chatter
click or clatter

opens with ease
nothing to measure
no locks, no keys?

What takes you to
jungles and castles
and stars?

On day trips to Mars?

Brings you wizards
and witches,
camels and cooks?

Guess.
Yes!
BRING ON THE BOOKS!

© 1984 Lilian Moore

CHILDREN'S BOOK COUNCIL

PRESIDENT (January 1984–January 1985):
Richard W. Jackson, Bradbury Press, Scarsdale, New York

VICE-PRESIDENT/PRESIDENT-ELECT:
Margaret Frith, G. P. Putnam's Sons, New York City

SECRETARY:
Dinah Stevenson, Knopf/Pantheon Books for Young Readers, New York City

TREASURER:
Michael Eisenberg, Farrar, Straus & Giroux, Inc., New York City

EXECUTIVE DIRECTOR:
John Donovan

ASSOCIATE DIRECTOR:
Paula Quint

Membership (December 1984): 66 publishers
Headquarters: 67 Irving Place, New York, New York 10003

Materials made available in 1984 to the Children's Book Council included, far left, a streamer by Felicia Bond; top left and right, posters by Dennis Panek and Gerald McDermott; bottom center, Halley's Comet wall chart by writer Seymour Simon and art by Paul O. Zelinsky; and, above, a bookmark with art by Gerald McDermott and poem by Lilian Moore.

that are popular in both bookstores and libraries.

CBC's committee with the American Booksellers Association sponsored its sixth "Children's Books Mean Business" exhibit and catalog at ABA's 1984 convention in Washington, D.C. The CBC–International Reading Association Joint Committee published "Children's Choices for 1984" in the October issue of *The Reading Teacher*. This annotated listing of about 100 1983 titles voted as favorites by 10,000 children on five teams in the U.S. observed its 10th anniversary in 1984. Other annual lists administered by joint committees are "Outstanding Science Trade Books for Children" (CBC–National Science Teachers Association) that first appears in *Science and Children* and "Notable Children's Trade Books in the Field of Social Studies" (CBC–National Council for the Social Studies) that first appears in *Social Education*. All three lists are reprinted and widely distributed.

Much of the Council's energies in 1984 were devoted to preparations for its second national *Everychild* conference to take place in New York City, August 23–25, 1985.

JOHN DONOVAN

Children's Library Services

Going with the Flow. In 1984 many children's programs focused on crazes that were sweeping the country. The Louisville Public Library attracted a standing room only crowd when they held a Michael Jackson Look-Alike Contest in the children's room of the Central Library. Librarians reported that kids of all ages dressed up like the wildly popular rock star and demonstrated all levels of break dancing.

The West Virginia Library Commission featured a poster with a Michael Jackson look-alike in silhouette carrying the words "Read It," a takeoff on Jackson's chart-topping recording, *Beat It*. Other libraries picked up on the popularity of the copyrighted board game *Trivial Pursuit*. The Morton Grove (Illinois) Public Library sponsored a *Trivial Pursuit* Tournament for children in the 3rd through the 6th grades. The children were divided into teams and played in an eight-week tournament. The Morton Grove staff reported that a waiting list had to be started for players.

Olympic Hassle. Since 1984 was also the year of the Los Angeles Summer Olympics, many children's librarians had enthusiastically planned to use the Olympics as a theme for their summer reading programs. The Los Angeles County Library System was planning a summer program that used the Olympic name when they were informed by attorneys for the U.S. Olympic Committee that this was a violation against the trademark owned by the Committee. The American Library Association quickly got the word out, but many children's librarians could not believe that the Olympic committee was interested in nonprofit children's library programs. Librarians realized this was serious business when they read that the U.S. Committee was suing the March of Dimes Foundation for misusing the Olympic name in the Foundation's annual fundraising program, The Reading Olympics. Children's Librarians dropped "Olympics" from their summer reading themes, but came up with good substitutes. One of the best was from the Los Angeles County librarians—The Bookfest of Champions.

Concern for Children. Children's librarians in 1984 supported the growing national campaign to locate missing children and to prevent child sexual abuse. Some librarians posted fliers describing missing children on their public bulletin boards. Others invited police officers to present "Never Talk to Strangers" programs during story hours. The Chicago Public Library in 30 of its branches hosted a free fingerprint identification service conducted by local police technicians. Children up to the age of 14 were fingerprinted; parents retained the only copy of the prints. The Newark Public Library conducted a series of panel discussions entitled "How to Prevent Sexual Abuse of Children," and the Milwaukee Public Library, working with the Milwaukee County Department of Social Services, distributed a bibliography "It's Okay to Say No: Resources on Child Sexual Abuse."

Reading aloud to children, a cause long endorsed by children's librarians, gained momentum in 1984 because of the national popularity of *The Read Aloud Handbook* (Penguin, 1982) by Jim Trelease. An inspiring speaker, Trelease appeared at professional meetings, schools, and library programs all over the country. He motivated many librarians to reintroduce read-aloud story hours for elementary school children. The Rolling Meadows (Illinois) Public Library started the R*A*P (Read Aloud Please) program to encourage teachers to read aloud to their students.

Classes who visited the library were treated to a tour, film, and a chapter in a book read by the librarian. The teacher was encouraged to check out the book and finish the reading in the classroom. When the Hyattsville Branch of the Prince George's County (Maryland) Memorial Library System opened its new Parent-Child Center,

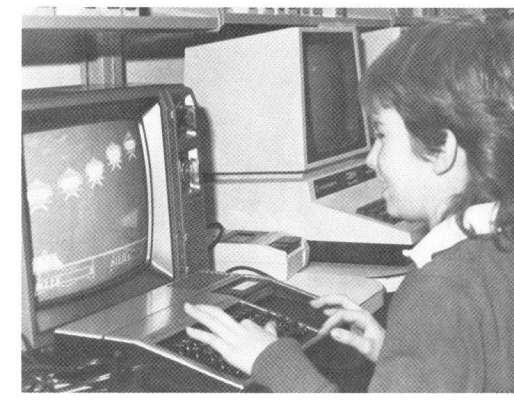

Library computer services for children continued to expand during the year at libraries including the Farmington Community Library, Farmington Hills, Michigan (right); the Kansas City (Missouri) Public Library's Southwest Branch (far right); and the Burbank (California) Public Library (below).

read-aloud materials were cited as a major collection. In Milwaukee at Christmastime, children's librarians visited local bookstores to encourage parents to buy books as presents and to read aloud as a family.

Anti-TV Project. One program begun by a children's librarian gained national media attention. When Nancy DeSalvo, a children's librarian at the Farmington (Connecticut) Village Library, initiated a campaign to encourage residents to turn off their television sets for the entire month of January, representatives from the national and international press corps turned their attention on the Village Library. As Farmington schoolchildren were signing pledge cards to go cold turkey, DeSalvo was spending most of her time giving interviews to reporters. David Letterman, the host of NBC's *Late Night Show*, told his audience that he was going to phone DeSalvo and talk "some sense into this woman." While on the air, Letterman offered DeSalvo a variety of prizes including cash if she would cease and desist the "Farmington Turns Off" campaign. DeSalvo politely refused to give up the campaign.

After the reporters had forgotten the Farmington Village Library, DeSalvo evaluated the program. She reported that of the 4,000 people who signed pledge cards, 1,045 went cold turkey, watching no television during January. Parents reported that their children's school grades improved, school librarians saw book circulation increase, and teachers, especially those who taught kindergartners and first-graders, felt pupils were generally more attentive. Children wrote essays on "What I did when I turned the TV off" with 1,000 winners receiving books as prizes. The project's national visibility encouraged at least 34 towns to call DeSalvo for information on how to start their own campaigns. DeSalvo rated the project a success and planned another "Farmington Turns Off" for 1985.

Computers for Children. Microcomputers continued to be added to children's rooms in public libraries across the country during 1984 although an in-house study, conducted by the R. R. Bowker Company and reported in a *School Library Journal* editorial (November 1984), found that public libraries lag far behind school libraries in the number of computers available for children. Children's librarians often must raise outside grants to purchase basic equipment such as terminals and keyboards, but many persevere, feeling a strong sense of mission to promote computer literacy with their young patrons.

Some libraries experimented with alternatives to purchasing computers for in-house use. The Portsmouth (New Hampshire) Public Library provided computers on a rental basis, but the equipment was available only to patrons, 21 years or older. The Downers Grove (Illinois) Public Library circulated Timex Sinclair 100 models without cost to their patrons (borrowers under the age of 14 had to present a parent's signature on a permission slip).

Other libraries charged rental fees and deposits that virtually excluded children from using the service. While such alternative programs often provided revenue for the purchase of additional equipment or software, children's services professionals viewed the programs as a trend that would limit access by children.

After noting that more boys than girls were using the library's microcomputer, the Rye (New York) Free Reading Room offered a special girls-only club on computer literacy. The club, advised by a teacher who specialized in addressing problems of math anxiety, produced five new tutors for the volunteer corps, which had previously been exclusively male.

The Louisville Public Library chose "Computer Power" as the 1984 summer reading theme, starring a microcomputer named MEM O'REE. By reading books, children earned time on the library's computers. And it should be

Children's Library Services

Summer reading programs featured (far left) a sidewalk coloring contest at Chicago's Public Library; a musical drama for children (center) at the Dallas Public Library; free tickets to a Cincinnati Reds baseball game (bottom) for 10 books read; and (below) a jazz theme for Louisiana summer reading clubs.

Mr. Rogers meets members of his television program audience at the Central Library, Harrisburg, Pennsylvania.

A Read-Aloud Program at the Cleveland Heights-University Heights (Ohio) libraries brought together dedicated volunteers and children for weekly story sessions.

Cabbages and Kings, a children's theatre group, performed "Alice in Wonderland" at branches of the Dallas Public Library during the fall.

The Avenues Branch of the Salt Lake City Public Library opened in December complete with friendly beasts in the children's area.

Branch Librarian Bill Stockey giving karate demonstration in the Hilliard Branch of the Chesapeake (Virginia) Public Library. (Richard L. Dunston)

A 17-foot soft sculpture was donated by Marion Helminiak to the Racine (Wisconsin) Public Library's Children's Department. (Journal Times photo by Charles S. Vallone)

noted that *School Library Journal* in its September 1984 issue began a regular review section featuring recommended software. For children's librarians everywhere this was a sign that microcomputers were no longer an innovative service but a basic part of the children's library program.

Shortage of Children's Librarians. The shortage of librarians to fill positions in children's services, a national trend discussed by children's librarians at local and national meetings for the last few years, finally gained some long overdue visibility in the library press. The Children's Services Section of the New Jersey Library Section reported in its newsletter *Reflections* that at least 30 vacancies existed for children's librarians in the state.

Richard Ashford surveyed a six-state area in New England for the availability of entry-level professional library positions. Writing in *School Library Journal* (November 1984), Ashford reported that positions in cataloging and children's services were more widely available than any other type of entry-level position. Meanwhile library schools continued to cut back or drop courses in children's services, storytelling, and literature largely due to inadequate enrollments. The announcement that library schools at Case Western Reserve, Denver, and the University of Southern California would be closing in the next few years heightened the problem, especially for those regions of the country served by these universities.

Children's librarians applauded the three columns by Will Manley that appeared in *Wilson Library Bulletin* in September, October, and November. Writing in his regular "Facing the Public" column, Manley stated that like the blue whale and the snail darter, children's librarians are on the endangered species list. Manley reported he had trouble filling a $21,000 entry-level children's librarian position. Children's librarians, Manley discovered, are often discouraged by low salaries, inadequate opportunities for advancement within children's services, underfunding for collections and programs, and low esteem given to professions serving children. Manley warned his fellow administrators to make a financial commitment to children's services for, he concluded in his final column, "our futures [i.e., public libraries] are in the hands of our children's librarians."

ELIZABETH HUNTOON

Children's Literature

Statistics, Prices, Changes. While the audience surveyed in Leonard Wood's article "Book Reading, 1955–84: The Trend Is Up" (*Publishers Weekly*, May 25, 1984) was 18 or older, the cheering news that in almost every category of age or schooling people were reading more has significance for children's reading. Reading experts agree that one of the major stimuli for a child's reading (practice and proficiency) is observing adults reading in the home. The available statistics on U.S. sales of juvenile books (*Publishers Weekly*, September 7, 1984) are also

Cover and illustration from the Nutcracker *illustrated by Maurice Sendak and published by Crown Publishers, Inc. (left © Thomas Victor)*

encouraging; the final figures for all trade books, hardbound and paperbound, were 2,967 new titles issued in 1983 as compared with 2,827 in 1982. For all juvenile books, the figures were 3,197 in 1983 and 3,049 in 1982. Not a big jump, but an indication that the market is holding steady.

Prices of hardbound juvenile books rose also. The average price of a hardcover book rose from $8.74 in 1982 to $9.15 in 1983, and for paperbound juveniles the price in those succeeding years rose from $4.04 to $4.76. Also cited were net sales for the first quarter of 1984, as compared to the preceding year: for children's hardbound books the figure rose from $45,600,000 to $48,200,000 and for children's paperback books, from $12,600,000 to $17,300,000.

Within the publishing industry, there continued to be shifts of whole companies or children's books sections. The Macmillan Children's Books Division was celebrating its 65th anniversary, and the General Books Division gave itself some very nice presents in 1984. It acquired Scribner Books, including the children's book divisions of Scribner and Atheneum. It also acquired Four Winds Press from Scholastic, in October. All imprints will be retained, the first two with their established editors and Four Winds Press with Meredith Charpentier, of the Macmillan staff, as editor. Bradbury Press, already acquired by Macmillan and operating as an affiliate, moved from its Scarsdale, New York, offices to Macmillan headquarters in Manhattan in January 1985.

Other changes in the publishing community include the acquisition by Simon & Schuster of the Stratemeyer Syndicate, the establishment of a co-publishing program between Peter Bedrick Books and Blackie & Son Ltd., under which books will be published in the United States that were originally published by Blackie under the

Children's Literature

Blackie and Abelard imprints in the United Kingdom. Under the editorship of Beverly Horowitz, a new mass market paperback line for teenagers, Pacer Books, joined the Putnam Publishing Group.

Seabury Press, subsequent to selling its children's book list, Clarion Books, to Houghton Mifflin, announced its dissolution, while Atlantic Monthly Press announced that it was dissolving its ties with Little, Brown to become wholly independent.

The New American Library took over as sole distributors of Scholastic paperback books. A cautious note in Publishers Weekly (November 2, 1984) announced that Macmillan was considering taking over the assets of the school text division from Harper & Row, which, in this game of "musical publishing," had just announced that it had acquired the rights to the children's book list of Addison–Wesley.

New Ventures, Trends. Among the new ventures in a highly competitive market are a book club for teenagers, the Starlight Romances Book Club, founded by E. P. Dutton, and, announced by Imported Publications of Chicago, the Misha Book Club, specializing in Soviet and other East European children's books. In April Farrar, Straus & Giroux joined the ranks of children's book publishers who have established paperback lines.

A new line of adventure games based on children's classics, Windham Classics, was established by Spinnaker Software. Random House recalled over 70,000 copies of "Button Books" because the attached buttons were deemed a hazard to young children. Coleco Industries announced the signing of a licensing agreement that granted them exclusive rights to manufacture and market home video games and home computer software based on the characters and stories of Richard Scarry. Few of these developments brought joy to the hearts of children's books specialists.

A trend noted under Children's Literature for 1983, the proliferation of books with game elements, toy books, and paper engineering books has continued; indeed, it seems to have burgeoned. Bantam spawned a series of choose-your-own-adventure read-aloud picture books under the series title of "Your First Adventure." The other avalanche, paperback romances, continues unabated, with such series as "Seniors Series," "Electric High" series, and others calculated to draw reader attention by their series titles: "Magic Moments," "Sun Fire," "Sweet Dreams," "Sweet Valley High," or "Wildfire"—a cornucopia of treacle.

Reflecting, as children's books always do, the views and interests of the society from which they emanate, there was a marked increase in 1984 in books about child abuse for all ages, both fiction and nonfiction. Nonfiction in particular emphasized sexual abuse and how to prevent it at best and cope with it at worst. Also noticeable was the large number of picture books as compared with other kinds of children's books, a phenomenon that is probably related both to the continuing interest in all language arts activities of young children and to the fact that there is less competition for audience attention and more parental control of the preschool group.

Distinctive New Books. As is true every year, 1984 had a number of books of special distinction; several of these are notable for their visual appeal. Perhaps the coffee-table book of the year was published by Crown, a version of E. T. Hoffmann's Nutcracker, translated by Ralph Manheim from the original rather than the well-known ballet version, and illustrated profusely and splendidly by Maurice Sendak. Another classic was Oscar Wilde's The Selfish Giant, with delicate paintings by Lisbeth Zwerger (Neugebauer Press).

Using but not abusing techniques of paper engineering, Alice and Martin Provensen concocted a handsome and ingenious book, Leonardo da Vinci (Viking) and another stunning art book came from Piero Ventura, Great Painters (Putnam), which is both an excellent art history and a visual tour de force in combining Ventura's own paintings with small-size reproductions of famous paintings. Dial published Bert Kitchen's Animal Alphabet, its dramatic, highly textured paintings set off by ample space.

Newbery Medal Honor book The Sign of the Beaver and author Elizabeth George Speare who also won the Scott O'Dell Award for historical fiction. (Houghton Mifflin Company)

Sugaring Time by Kathryn Lasky was a Newbery Medal Honor book published by Macmillan. (Christopher Knight)

The artist Leonard Baskin produced *Imps, Demons, Hobgoblins, Witches, Fairies and Elves* (Pantheon), a versatile and imaginative compendium of intriguing creatures. Already popular in England, published here by Random House, *Trouble for Trumpets* is a very large book with cleverly detailed and jewel-toned pictures by Peter Cross and an entertaining fanciful story by Peter Dallas-Smith. From Tundra Books in Canada came *Who Goes to the Park*, by Warabe Aska (Takeshi Masuda), whose paintings of Toronto's High Park are, although not imitative, filled with touches that recall Rousseau and Chagall.

Of the many well-written stories of the year, several stand out as particularly fine examples of writing or their genre or both. *Canadian Fairy Tales* (Groundwood/Douglas & McIntyre) has handsome illustrations by Laszlo Gal (a former winner of the Canada Council's Illustrator Award) to accompany a dozen tales deftly retold by an experienced storyteller, Eva Martin. *The Hero and the Crown* (Greenwillow) by Robin McKinley is another potent tale of magic and adventure.

Adventure at its most picaresque is a feature of Lloyd Alexander's *The Beggar Queen* (Dutton), last of the dazzling Westmark trilogy. Two distinctive realistic stories are Paula Fox's *One-Eyed Cat* (Bradbury), a touching and trenchant story of a child's feelings of guilt and compassion, and for younger children *Thaddeus*, by Alison Herzig and Jane Mali (Little, Brown), a story of a marvelous relationship between a small boy and his great-great-uncle, with soft pictures by Stephen Gammell and an appeal that transcends age demarcations. A third realistic tale came from England; *Gaffer Samson's Luck* by Gillian Paton Walsh (Farrar, Straus & Giroux) is both a tender story of friendship across generations and a perceptive view of the problem a new boy has in being accepted into the rigid juvenile caste system of a village in the English Fens.

Very different in scope and setting, two novels of historical interest were distinctive. Avi's *The Fighting Ground* (Lippincott) takes place in one day of 1778, when a boy of 13 joins a band of soldiers and learns what the war he has glorified is really like. Last, *Bonnie Dundee* (Dutton) by that superstar of historical fiction, Rosemary Sutcliff. She is at her best in this colorful story of the Scottish Royalist who was called "Bonnie Dundee" by his followers and unkind names by his foes.

Organization Activities. Many national organizations showed, in their annual conference programs, an interest in children's books. The International Reading Association held a special session for parents at its convention. Children's authors participated in a program presented by the Children's Book Council at the 1984 conference of the National Association for the Education of Young Children. At the pre-show seminar arranged by the CBC and members of the American Bookseller's Association, so many people arrived to hear discussions of children's books that the meeting hall had to be changed in order to accommodate the 700 people who filled the room. Other news from the indefatigable CBC included its plans for a second "Everychild" Conference, to take place in August of 1985 in New York City. It produced the usual impressive variety of materials for Children's Book Week, which in 1984

Alison Cragin Herzig and Jane Lawrence Mali, authors of Thaddeus *published by Little, Brown and Company. (Adam Reich)*

Ronia, The Robber's Daughter *by Astrid Lindgren, published by Viking Penguin, Inc., won the 1984 Batchelder Award.*

Above, Caldecott Medal winning book Across the Channel with Louis Bleriot *by Alice and Martin Provensen published by Viking Junior Books.*

Newberry Medal winning book Dear Mr. Henshaw *by Beverly Cleary was published by William Morrow and Company.*

was November 12–18 and for which the slogan was "Bring on the Books!" The useful CBC newsletter changed title from *Calendar* to *CBC Features.*

Deaths. The children's book world suffered many sad losses in its ranks in 1984. Authors who died include Helen Boylston, Borghild Margarethe Dahl, Norma Farber, Elizabeth Johnson, Nora Kramer, Ellen Raskin, Mary Renault, and Leonard Wibberley. Jannie Daane, a translator and storyteller, also died. Deaths within the publishing community included Bradford Chambers, for many years the Director of the Council on Interracial Books for Children; Dorothy Bryan, founder of the children's book division of Dodd, Mead; Ellen Knowles Harcourt, first children's book editor for Harcourt Brace; and three former presidents of the Children's Book Council: Doris Patee, Robert Verrone, and Louise Bonino Williams.

Awards. The winners of the Newbery and Caldecott Medals were *Dear Mr. Henshaw* (Morrow) by Beverly Cleary and *The Glorious Flight Across the Channnel with Louis Bleriot* (Viking) by Alice and Martin Provensen. Recipients are chosen by committees of the American Library Association, the first for literary distinction and the second for preeminence in illustration. Honor books for the Newbery Medal were Bill Brittain's *The Wish Giver* (Harper & Row), Kathryn Lasky's *Sugaring Time* (Macmillan), Elizabeth Speare's *The Sign of the Beaver* (Houghton Mifflin), and Cynthia Voigt's *A Solitary Blue* (Atheneum). Caldecott Medal honor books were *Ten, Nine, Eight* (Greenwillow), written and illustrated by Molly Bangs, and *Little Red Riding Hood* (Holiday), a tale by the Brothers Grimm retold and illustrated by Trina Schart Hyman.

Also conferred by the American Library Association, the Mildred L. Batchelder Award for translation was won in 1984 by Viking Press for *Ronia, the Robber's Daughter,* translated by Patricia Crampton from the original Swedish book by Astrid Lindgren. No poetry prize was awarded by the National Council of Teachers of English.

The American Book Awards Program eliminated the children's books category in 1984, an action vigorously protested by many in the children's book world.

The Catholic Library Association conferred its Regina Medal on Madeleine L'Engle for the excellence of her writing for children. The International Reading Association Award for a new author went to Clare Bell for *Ratha's Creature* (Atheneum), and the Scott O'Dell Award for Historical Fiction to Elizabeth Speare for *The Sign of the Beaver* (Houghton Mifflin). The award given by the Jane Addams Peace Association went to Marian Dane Bauer for *Rain of Fire* (Houghton/Clarion).

The Canadian Library Association's Book of the Year for Children was Jan Hudson's *Sweetgrass* (Tree Frog Press) and the runners-up were Dennis Lee's *Jelly Belly* (Macmillan of Canada) and Monica Hughes's *Space Trap* (Groundwood Books/Douglas & McIntyre). The latter was also the publisher of the book that won the Amelia Frances Howard-Gibbon Illustrator's Award for *Zoom at Sea,* illustrated by Ken Nutt and written by Tim Wynne-Jones. The runner-up was Laszlo Gal, illustrator of *The Little Mermaid* by Hans Christian Andersen (Methuen).

Given by the Library Association of Great Britain, the Carnegie Medal for literary merit went to Jan Mark for *Handles* (Kestrel) and the illustrator's award, the Greenaway Medal, was won by Anthony Brown for *Gorilla* (Julia McRae Books/Watts). International prizes chosen by the International Board of Books for Young People are given for the body of an author's and an illustrator's work. For literature the award went to Christine Nöstlinger of Austria; for book art, to Mitsumasa Anno of Japan. Most of their books are available in the United States.

ZENA SUTHERLAND

Chinese-American Librarians Association

Annual Conference. The Chinese-American Librarians Association Annual Program at the ALA Annual Conference in Dallas represented the culmination of the Association's growth since its inception in 1973. It was listed twice in "Pick of the ALA Program: LJ's Choices" (*Library Journal* vol. 109), once for its program "Technologies for Libraries" and again for its Chinese buffet dinner. Keynote speaker William J. Welsh of the Library of Congress presented "China Revisited and the Library of Congress Experimentations in New Technologies." Kenyon Rosenberg of the National Technical Information Service spoke on "Personnel and Technical Information Exchange." Andrew H. Wang of OCLC discussed OCLC and Chinese, Japanese, and Korean language materials. A panel on "Information Technology and Services in Taiwan, ROC" concluded the 1984 program.

The Association's 1984 Distinguished Services Award recipient was Sally C. Tseng, Principal Serials Cataloger at the University of California, Irvine, and author of books and articles on serial cataloging and AACR2.

Awards. As part of its efforts to increase membership, the Association planned to present five certificates to those who recruit the greatest number of new members for 1984–85. To promote and encourage Chinese-American librarianship,

---

CHINESE-AMERICAN LIBRARIANS ASSOCIATION

PRESIDENT (July 1985–July 1985):
Sally C. Tseng, University of California, Irvine

VICE-PRESIDENT/PRESIDENT-ELECT:
William W. Wan, Texas Woman's University, Denton

TREASURER:
Cecilia Chen, California State University, Dominguez Hills, Carson

EXECUTIVE DIRECTOR:
Amy Seetoo Wilson, University Microfilms International, Ann Arbor, Michigan

JOURNAL EDITOR:
John Yung-Hsiang Lai, Harvard University

Membership (December 1984): 300

the Association planned to award a total of $3,000 in scholarship and research grants in 1985.

Goals and Objectives. The Chinese-American Librarians Association continued in 1984 to seek to enhance communication among Chinese-American librarians as well as between Chinese-American librarians and other librarians. Sino-American librarianship and library services were promoted and served as a vehicle whereby Chinese-American librarians cooperated with other organizations that have similar or allied interests.

Organization. In 1983 the Association merged with the Chinese Librarians Association, whose members resided mainly in California. Five regional chapters were active in 1984—Northeast, Midwest, Mid-Atlantic, Southwest, and California. Themes in chapter annual meetings during 1984 ranged from libraries in China to future library services, library automation, and the CJK system. The Association's 1984–85 Committees included: Awards, Constitution and Bylaws, Membership, Program, Local Arrangements, Books to China, Foundation, Public Relations, Finance, Nominating, Publications, and Scholarship and Research Grants Task Force.

Publications. The Association, in cooperation with the National Taiwan Normal University, in 1984 continued to publish the *Journal of Library and Information Science*, a semiannual publication in both English and Chinese. The *Journal* is indexed or abstracted in *Index to Chinese Periodicals*, *Library Literature*, *PAIS*, and *Information Science Abstracts*.

AMY SEETOO WILSON

Collection Management

From beginning to end, 1984 was a bright year for collection managers. There were major accomplishments in resource sharing; collection funding; collection budgeting; collection analysis and use studies; preservation; and continuing education.

Highlights. Some of the highlights of the year included:

In February the National Endowment for the Humanities announced the awarding of $22,000,000 in challenge grants to libraries, including some major acquisition endowments for universities, colleges, and public libraries.

The second phase of the three-phase National Collections Inventory Project (NCIP) was launched in January by the Association of Research Libraries, and was near completion by October after three libraries—Indiana University, the University of Notre Dame, and Purdue—finished major portions of the RLG Conspectus Online.

In August the Fred Meyer Charitable Trust Library Program reported a commitment of an estimated $3,500,000 to a program to enhance access to resources in the Pacific Northwest through the building of a resource sharing network.

In June the U.S. Department of Education announced 35 grants awarded to 56 institutions under the Higher Education Act, Title II-C program. Approximately $6,000,000 was awarded, including $428,255 of funds going directly to collection development.

The October *Library Journal* carried news of the lowest increase in the price of American periodicals since 1977. The American periodical prices increased by 9.4 percent from 1983 to 1984.

The price increases for books were also at a very low level. In September *Publishers Weekly* reported that hardcover average prices had moved up only 2.8 percent from 1982 to 1983.

In September RTSD gave a three-day Institute on Collection Management and Development scheduled to be repeated three more times in 1985–86. The Institute focused on an overview of trends and issues in collection management and development.

A two-day preconference on collection management in public libraries, held by RTSD at the Dallas ALA Conference, looked at topics on public library resource sharing, automation in collection management, and management of internal resources.

The Association of Research Libraries (ARL) published a Systems and Procedures Exchange (SPEC) Kit on Collection Security in January. In June *College and Research Libraries News* published the results of a survey on collection security in combination with an article on a theft at UC Berkeley.

The Association of Research Libraries released a report on the Duke University Library Collection Analysis project (CAP) in October. Nine other CAP studies were in progress. The CAP studies offer a format for studying collection activities and provide data on collection strategies at other institutions with recommendations for changes.

ARL also announced in August that 10 libraries would participate in Preservation Planning Program demonstration studies. Ten libraries were chosen in September and will be directed by the Office of Management Studies in the conduct of their studies on preservation planning. ARL received $65,375 from NEH to direct the program, which will involve a self-study by the 10 institutions.

A major monograph on acquisitions and collection management was published by the American Library Association in September. It updates Stephen Ford's 1973 text, the *Acquisition of Library Materials*.

SOLINET was awarded a grant of $168,401 from NEH to establish a cooperative preservation program in 10 southern states. The two-year project began in October and is expected to help libraries, archives, historical societies, and museums coordinate their preservation activities.

In September the Council on Library Resources released a report on a July meeting in Wayzata, Minnesota, on Retrospective Conversion. The report recommends a coordinated national effort by research libraries for retrospective conversion of their collections based upon the LC classification scheme, or very strong special collections. The special strengths would be identified through the National Collection Inventory Project or by the National Shelf List Count.

During 1984, two major bibliographic utilities—RLIN and OCLC—experimented with electronic transmission of orders to vendors.

Above, physical inventory is done by microcomputer in Pike's Peak Library District, Colorado Springs, Colorado. Right, status of books are checked in Farmington Community Library, Farmington Hills, Michigan, using a GEAC Circulation System.

RESOURCE SHARING

A prerequisite for successful resource sharing has been proximity. With automated interlibrary loan and electronic mail, proximity appears to be less important. In 1984 a number of significant developments improved, or will improve, the resource sharing capabilities of libraries. Changes in the program of the Center for Research Libraries, major grants for resource sharing, and governmental appropriations all contributed to advances in resource sharing. In every case automation was a factor in increasing the potential for sharing. A study on document delivery sponsored by the Council on Library Resources (CLR) published in late October 1983 concluded that over the next five years document delivery will be increasingly initiated by electronic requests and commercial services will increase their share of the market.

CRL Services. The Center for Research Libraries offered some new services in 1984, announced a new pricing schedule, and continued to examine its role as a library of libraries. In February the Center announced that its collections could be accessed through the ILL subsystem of RLIN, the network of the Research Libraries Group. The interaction will be improved through use of electronic mail between the Center and the 26 member libraries of RLG. In July the Center reported that it had reduced its interloan fee for nonmember libraries from $25 to $12 per transaction. There has been much debate over the direction CRL should take. In 1983 the management of CRL proposed using more technology, e.g., transmission of documents via telefacsimile, storage and transmission of documents using optical digital disks. Unfortunately a hefty price was attached to expanded use of such technology—about $10,000,000. In a rethinking of priorities, the Center shifted back to more collection-centered activities. For example, in 1984 35 member libraries contributed $120,000 for the purchase of the complete microfilm edition of the Sanborn Fire Insurance maps. Included in the collection are 623,000 maps of 10,000 American towns and cities for the period 1867–1950. The set will be available for loan to members of the Center.

Cooperative Projects. In December the first task force for the $3,500,000 Fred Meyer Charitable Trust cooperative program among Pacific Northwest libraries was appointed to develop a profile of collections throughout Alaska, Idaho, Montana, Oregon, and Washington. This first step will be followed by cooperative acquisition plans and electronically based document delivery. The W. K. Kellogg Foundation awarded a grant of $836,200 to the Upper Peninsula of Library Cooperation (Michigan) to implement over the next four years an Upper Peninsula automated library system. This network will connect all types of libraries and deliver job-related information to the population of this sparsely inhabited area.

The National Library of Medicine awarded $280,000 to the Cornell University Medical College Library to establish the Cornell Health Sciences Computerized Library Network. The libraries of Sloan–Kettering Cancer Center, Payne Whitney Psychiatric Clinic, the Hospital for Special Surgery, and the Cornell/N.Y. Hospital will be linked by the network. The University of California at Los Angeles received funds amounting to $170,000 (including matching funds from NEH) to support the expansion of an online bibliographic database for resource sharing of U.S.–Mexican borderlands materials.

Government Funded Projects. Governmental funds have been important in promoting resource sharing in a number of states. In March *American Libraries* reported that New Jersey had passed landmark legislation for regional library cooperatives with an appropriation of $125,000 for fiscal year 1984. The new law permits creation of regional multitype library networks and resource sharing among all types of libraries.

New York signed into law the biggest increase in state history, which included funds for resource sharing among school libraries ($3,900,000). The Oregon State Library indicated that LSCA funds would go into local assistance grants, 50 percent of which would support resource sharing among libraries of all types. New legislation in Illinois also permits voluntary conversion into multitype library systems including public, school, academic, and special libraries. The new system is expected to encourage increased cooperative acquisition programs, greater resource sharing, broader planning among libraries, and other cooperative ventures.

In November it was reported that Title III of the Library Services and Construction Act (LSCA) was increased from $15,000,000 to $18,000,000.

NCIP. The National Collection Inventory Project (NCIP) went ahead in 1984 with Phase II, which tested project materials and resources in three Indiana ARL libraries—Indiana University, Notre Dame, and Purdue University. The project identified means of verifying the Collection Conspectus. The training resources and manual were to be available to libraries in 1985. Nine University of California libraries participate in NCIP, a group of 13 Southeastern ARL Libraries agreed to participate shortly, and the Canadian Association of Research Libraries discussed participation in NCIP in November. Phase III will be an implementation of the Inventory in research libraries throughout North America, and the Association of Research Libraries was seeking funding.

Building, Preservation. At a conference on the future of research libraries at the Wye Plantation in Maryland in fall 1983, and reported in Library Issues (March 1984), librarians, faculty, administrators, publishers, and foundation representatives discussed successful cooperation in building and preserving library collections. This gathering concluded that cooperation in building collections and preserving them required (1) basic funding, (2) a management structure for national action, and (3) checks and balances permitting cost effectiveness and responsiveness to institutional priorities. The conferees agreed that the NCIP program and the Center for Research Libraries are making important contributions to a national collection and preservation program. A Committee on Compensation was recommended to address the issues of "balance of trade" in interlending and the problems of copyright. The group also felt that the new Office of Scholarly Communication established by the American Council of Learned Societies will be able to deal with the need for data on publishing, scholarship, and libraries. This Office will study how well scholarly communication is working and will attempt to create closer relationships among the major parties in scholarly communication—research libraries, publishers, and learned journals.

1984 Articles. A number of significant articles were published in 1984 on resource sharing. Maurice Glicksman, retiring Chair of the Center for Research Libraries, indicated in an assessment of the Center in the Journal of Academic Librarianship (July 1984) that commitment to "workable cooperative ventures" is the key to the need for more resources. Judith Feller, East Stroudsburg University, Pennsylvania, reported in Collection Building (Spring 1984) on means for measuring the need for resource sharing as well as the effectiveness of sharing arrangements. Her article defines objective data that can be used in identifying problems, allocating funds, and convincing administrators of the need for resource sharing. Bernard Holicky, Purdue University at Calumet, Indiana, argued in the Journal of Academic Librarianship (July 1984) that small academic libraries must engage in resource sharing to survive the economic situation. Scott Bennett, Northwestern University, made a case in the Journal of Academic Librarianship (November 1984) for pursuing cooperative collection management to improve services, not to reduce costs, but he contends that resource sharing can mean cost containment. He believes that resource sharing would be more successful if collection managers were able to develop a model for cost containment through such sharing.

COLLECTION ANALYSIS, TECHNOLOGY

A number of advances in collection analysis, technology, and use studies appeared in 1984. In the area of collection analysis, ARL continued its CAP program, and as of October nine libraries were participating and Duke University Library had just made its final report. Many libraries had begun to analyze their collections in depth for NCIP and will ultimately make this information available in a database. Libraries were also using vendor-supplied technology from book vendors and bibliographic utilities for acquiring materials, resource sharing, and transmission of orders to vendors. Use studies continued to be an important measure for collection librarians of patron needs, but the debate over how much to rely on use studies continued.

CAP. Libraries participating on the Collection Analysis Project (CAP) in 1984 using ARL assistance were Alberta, Case Western Reserve, Catholic, District of Columbia, Georgetown Law, Howard, Houston, Vanderbilt Management, and Wyoming. The Duke final report was accompanied by task force reports for the following areas: collection policies; organization and staffing; allocation of funds; and collection assessment. The collection assessment task force was particularly significant for Duke, because Duke participates with North Carolina and North Carolina State in cooperative ventures. The Annual Report of the University Library of University of North Carolina noted that those libraries are carefully evaluating collections for narrower resource sharing assignments. For example, Duke and North Carolina divided regional French history by geographic areas in 1984 with Duke covering northern France and North Carolina southern France. Duke, Virginia, and North Carolina share collections in Slavic area studies.

Systems Activities. At the end of October the Online Computer Library Center (OCLC) finished three months of field tests and began direct transmission of orders to vendors using the OCLC system. Three vendors were in production with OCLC—Coutts, Midwest, and Yankee. The Research Libraries Group also began production in 1984 transmitting orders directly to Faxon. These technological developments were reinforced by the increasing use of microcomputer- or minicomputer-based turn-key acquisition systems. Two stand-alone systems were frequently in the news: Innovacq and Bookline (& Perline). The former, available from Innovative Interfaces, is a microcomputer-based system that can be used with large libraries. The latter two systems, available from Blackwell Systems, Inc., are minicomputer-based systems that can handle books and periodicals (including check-in). BA-TAB (Baker & Taylor), Ebsconet (Ebsco), and Datalinx (F.W. Faxon, Inc.) are systems that also received attention in the library press during 1984. These systems connect with a vendor's mainframe computer, but they do not require ordering from that vendor. The two periodical systems also allow check-in. Two advantages of system linkage with a vendor are access to the data in the vendor's files plus prompt delivery of orders. Disadvantages are communications costs and reliance on one vendor.

In 1984 Bowker offered its Bowker Acquisition System (BAS), which can be used by any standard terminal. It can be accessed through BRS, which is a vendor of online databases such as Bowker's *Books in Print*. The BAS system allows libraries to use the International Standard Book Number (ISBN) and SAN (Standard Address Number) for ordering.

The collection manager or acquisition librarian in 1984 had a bewildering variety of options for automated ordering, some of which became available during the year and many of which had begun to flourish. The *RTSD Newsletter* began to cover such systems in 1984 in its "The Marketplace" column.

Standards. Standards were facilitating greater use of technology in 1984. The National Information Standards Organization (formerly ANSI Z39) began circulating the draft of a standard for a machine-readable format for ordering monographs. A standard was developed for the quality of paper in publications. Publications meeting the standard for permanence of paper will carry a symbol in the book to indicate compliance. A draft standard was also prepared for a standard number for computer software. Another standard was under way for criteria for creating romanization systems. At year's end a standard was being proposed for standard numbers for information organizations. All of those standards will aid in ordering library materials.

Use Studies, Weeding. Two topics persisted in the literature of collection management during 1984: use studies and weeding. Nancy Fjällbrant reported in the *Journal of Academic Librarianship* (May 1984) on a use study at the Chalmers University of Technology in Gothenburg, Sweden. Her study supported previous conclusions that 10 percent of the titles met 72 percent of the demand. She concluded that substantial savings could be achieved through cancellation of unused titles after consultation with users. A study of French literature use in Nigeria by Adebayo Olaosun, University of Ife, Nigeria, in *College & Research Libraries* (September 1984) assessed the strength of the French collection at the University of Ife through questionnaires, interviews, and observations of lectures. The study concluded that cooperation should be improved between the Library and the Department of Modern European Languages; the audiovisual section of the Library should be developed more fully; and students should be encouraged to use the library's instructional programs. A citation analysis of library journals by Mary K. Sellen, Pennsylvania State University, Erie, in *College & Research Libraries* (March 1984) indicated, among other results, that librarians use periodicals more than monographic literature (although monographic use is high) and that the majority of references were post-1975.

An article by J. Wesley Miller, in *American Libraries* (June 1984), complained that librarians were weeding classics based upon "circulation" figures. Rejoinders from librarians included points that not everyone is weeding indiscriminately and that libraries have a duty to provide readers with what they want to read and space must be gained for that material. Books remain classics because they continue to be read; therefore, circulation is a good measurement. Proper weeding, it was further argued, results in the books being kept at some library, i.e., there are established practices of weeding that, if followed, will result in retention of classics at a research library from which they can be loaned.

COLLECTION FUNDING

Although the U.S. Department of Education did not request book funds for colleges and universities under the Higher Education Act, Title II-A in 1984, this setback was atypical in a year which was otherwise bountiful for collection funding.

NEH Funding. The National Endowment for the Humanities announced numerous major challenge grants early in the year. Large acquisition grants went to Hoover Institution, Stanford ($900,000 for acquisitions, preservation, and processing); Indiana University ($750,000 for library acquisitions and preservation); the American Academy in Rome, based in New York City ($200,000 for library acquisitions and processing); Hampton–Sydney College ($400,000 for library special collections and equipping of a communications center); Tulsa City–County Library ($250,000 for humanities collections, programs, and services); and Chicago Public ($1,000,000, only part of which goes to an endowment for acquisitions and preservation). These were three-for-one grants designed to bring in three times the award from NEH.

Under the Research Resources program, NEH awarded the American Philological Society $159,528 plus $60,000 in matching funds to support a cooperative microfilming project to select and preserve brittle books and serials in Classics published from 1850 to 1918. Other NEH awards went to the Research Libraries Group ($162,666 in matching funds) to support entry into RLIN (the Research Libraries Information Network), of 21,000 records of manuscript and archival collections at 12 RLG institutions; University of Michigan ($57,715) to support cataloging of a major collection on Thai Studies; Columbia University ($450,000 in matching funds) to support cataloging and preservation of the Avery Library's architectural drawings and development of a database/videodisc interface; and grants to the University of Hawaii, Indiana University, University of Kentucky, and Rutgers for cataloging and entry of newspaper holdings into the CONSER database (part of the U.S. Newspaper Project).

Title II-C Programs. The Higher Education Act Title II-C program resulted in 35 awards to 53 institutions which totaled approximately $6,000,000. The major collection grants went to the University of California at Berkeley ($142,848) for enriching their holdings of Russian émigré imprints; the University of California, San Diego ($169,065) for acquiring published and unpublished research materials in Melanesian Studies; and the American Museum of Natural History ($41,571) for strengthening its film collection. The greatest proportion of the grants ($4,526,772) went to bibliographic control projects which make resources available to libraries through the major utilities.

Each of the above collection projects also requested and received additional monies for cataloging. Two major cooperative grants were received by the University of Florida ($700,000) and Indiana University ($608,522) for bibliographic control projects involving other institutions. The Florida grant was for adding serials records from the Southeastern Area Research Libraries to the OCLC database, adding holdings and locations for 42,000 titles using the new MARC format, ensuring the ability to load the new database, and implementing a consortium coordinated collection development resource sharing program. The second grant to Indiana University went for the purpose of cataloging 25,200 titles on 995 reels of the *Early English Books, 1641-1700* collection of University Microfilms. These records will go into the OCLC database. Harvard University received another grant ($214,133) for preservation microfilming to continue its conservation work in the areas of official gazettes of Latin American nations, European publications of the World War II period, Slavic materials, and other research materials in urgent need of preservation. A total of $1,044,973 went for preservation projects.

Funding and Grants. In addition to federal grants, a number of noteworthy city and private grants for collections were made to institutions in 1984. In Tacoma, Washington, a library bond issue resulted in the purchase of $700,000 worth of books; in Brooklyn increased funding ($1,300,000) from the City of New York allowed Brooklyn Public to increase its book collections; in San Diego the book budget grew by $158,000; and in Winnipeg, Canada, the City Council increased the book budget by $520,000 after being asked to cut the budget.

The University of Cincinnati Library received an endowment of $125,000 from the Miriam P. Urban estate for the purchase of books and journals on the history of Modern Europe. Colgate University Library received $100,000 from the Gladys Brooks Foundation for library materials for the study of non-Western cultures. Westminster College, New Wilmington, Pennsylvania, was awarded a grant of $151,000 from the Buhl Foundation of Pittsburgh for the exploration of the concept of a static-capacity library.

In Tulsa, the City-County Council Library received $600,000 in response to the NEH challenge grant from Donna and Roger Hardesty, owners of a Tulsa real estate firm. The Tulsa City-County Library believes that book buying, which increased from 11.5 percent to 14.5 percent over four years, led to significant circulation increases. Late in the year Exxon Education Foundation awarded $1,500,000 to the Council on Library Resources for a preservation program for the nation's research libraries. The Council intends to fund a Mid-Atlantic Preservation Center.

The University of Illinois annual public library survey showed a leveling off of the median expenditures per capita for library materials. In 1982 the median expenditure per capita was $1.27 and it remained at the same level in 1983. However, this amount was an increase of $.10 from the 1980 figure of $1.17. The percentage of expenditures for materials in public libraries in 1983 went down 2 percent from 1980 expenditures. Fourteen percent of public library expenditures now go for materials.

Academic administrators also recognize the importance of funding for collections for academic libraries. Paul Olum, President of the University of Oregon, said, "We have held the library acquisitions budget, and essentially that budget alone, protected from all reductions . . . . The reason is, I suppose, partly symbolic. It is a declaration to our students, our faculty, the public, and the state government of the crucial importance we attach to the library holdings in the functioning of the university."[1]

CONTINUING EDUCATION

Great strides were taken in 1984 toward further education of collection librarians. Some significant new publications contribute to a better understanding of collection issues. There were several major institutes and conferences related directly or indirectly to collection work. As usual, acquisitions librarians were made aware of shady publishing practices or ventures. New collection guidelines were begun by ALA units. Finally, the Resources Section of ALA made its annual award, the Blackwell North America/Resources Section Award, for the best publication of 1983.

Publications, Meetings. A major new monograph, *Acquisition Management and Collection Development*, by Rose Mary Magrill and Doralyn J. Hickey appeared in 1984. It updates *The Acquisition of Library Materials* by Stephen Ford, published in 1973, and discusses the relationships between collection development and acquisition processes. The Office of Management Studies of the Association of Research Libraries published a SPEC Kit on *Collection Security* (January 1984). The Association of College and Research Libraries also published a collection development guide entitled *Curriculum Materials Center Collection Development Policy*, which contains model statements on the scope and objectives of the collection, personnel roles and responsibilities, selection criteria, weeding, gifts, and interlibrary loan.

Collection Management

The journal *Library Acquisitions Practice and Theory* continued to report the ALA meetings in detail. Issue number 2 covered reports from committees of the Resources Section. The same issue also covered a national conference on "Issues in Acquisitions: Programs and Evaluations," a conference at the University of Oklahoma in March 1984.

The RTSD Collection Management and Development Committee again sponsored a Collection Management and Development Institute at the University of California–Irvine in September. Special issues covered at Irvine were the impact of automation, evaluation of collections, institutional organizational patterns for collection development, and new directions in collection development. Two preconferences prior to ALA's Annual Conference were of interest to collection managers. One, a conference on "Collection Management in Public Libraries," was a first of its kind, and the second, "Who's Afraid of Serials," provided a number of topics of interest to collection librarians, among them serials prices, serials publishers, the LC optical disk program, and the role of the journal in scholarly communication. RTSD also sponsored an institute in October for acquisition (and catalog) librarians on nonbook materials.

Two organizations which have helped collection managers significantly in the past were active in 1984. The annual meeting of SALALM (Seminar on the Acquisition of Latin American Library Materials) was held at Chapel Hill, North Carolina. Although it does not focus on acquisitions alone, the Western European Specialists Section (WESS) of ACRL has also provided acquisition and collection librarians with excellent bibliographies and sources through its *Newsletter*. In 1984 *Collection Management* devoted an issue to the 1983 conference on European Collecting held in Minnesota. The issue includes information on publishing and scholarship in Western Europe, on collection development for Western European studies, and on bibliographic control of Western European materials.

Guidelines to assist collection managers were in preparation in 1984. A subcommittee of the Resources Section Collection Management and Development Committee put out a call in 1984 for collection developer's manuals since the subcommittee is in the process of preparing guidelines for collection development manuals. The same Committee is also revising the 1979 "Guidelines for Collection Development."

RTSD committees have long made librarians aware of shady practices by publishers and vendors. *Library Journal* (February 1, 1984) warned acquisition librarians about a vendor called "Micropublishers International," who had cheated the University of Idaho Libraries of $5,160 by offering microfilm copies of journals and then disappearing without supplying the copies. *Library Journal* (March 1, 1984) also carried reports about a publisher in Albuquerque, New Mexico, operating under nine different names and publishing "junky" materials (handpasted assemblages of photocopies and pages inscribed with magic marker passages), and selling them at a high cost.

Award. The Resources Section of RTSD awarded the 1984 Blackwell North America Scholarship Award, a $1,000 scholarship to the library school of the winner's choice, to Nancy E. Gwinn (Research Libraries Group) and Paul H. Mosher (Stanford) for "Coordinating Collection Development: The RLG Conspectus" in *College & Research Libraries* (March 1983). This article is a detailed explanation of how the RLG conspectus operates. It is the conspectus used in the NCIP program.

COLLECTION BUDGETING

Costs. According to *Publishers Weekly* the price of American hardcover books rose only 2.8 percent from 1982 to 1983 (from an average price of $30.34 to $31.19). The increase was slightly higher when volumes priced at $81 or more were eliminated, with the price increase for 1982 to 1983 occurring at a rate of 3.8 percent. The 2.8 percent rise compares with a double digit increase (13.9 percent) in the previous year. The rate of the price increase for the American periodicals also slowed down. Norman Brown reported in *Library Journal* (August 1984) that the American periodical price increase of 9.4 percent had not been so low since 1977 when the increase was 9.2 percent. The overall average price moved from $50.93 (1983) to $54.97 (1984). It appeared at the end of 1984 that the overall downturn in U.S. consumer prices is having an effect on the prices of materials.

F. W. Faxon, Inc., annually reports on average prices paid for serials by college and university, hospital, public, and school libraries. The Faxon price for colleges and universities, which includes foreign titles, increased by 5.7 percent—from $78.04 in 1982–83 to $82.47 in 1983–84. Foreign price declines due to dollar strength clearly influenced this trend. Rebecca Lenzini, who reports Faxon prices, indicated that whereas domestic prices increased by 9.5 percent, moving from an average of $79.91 in 1983 to $87.47 in 1984, the foreign prices continued to show a decline as the average price dropped 3 percent from $79.50 in 1983 to $77.09 in 1984. Research Associates of Washington, which produces the Higher Education Index, also measured foreign prices. Using the annual study of prices of overseas books purchased by the Library of Congress, Research Associates reported that the overall average price of foreign books increased only slightly from $11.91 to $12.09, or a rise of 1.5 percent. Clearly, the dollar's strength remains a dominant factor in the slowing of increases for library materials.

Efforts were under way in 1984 to produce an international standard for price indexes for library materials. The International Standards Organization, TC46, Working Group 8, chaired by Morten Hein (Denmark), met twice in Loughborough, England, and Providence, Rhode Island. The group was preparing international guidelines for national and local indexes based upon the experience of the *American National Standard for Library and Information Sciences and Related Publishing Practices—Library Materials—Criteria for Price*

Indexes (Z39.20,1983). Greater interest existed in Europe in such data since the dollar had strengthened against European currencies.

The College Book Index, developed from the entries in *Choice* by Richard Werking, Librarian at Trinity University (Texas), was endorsed by the Library Materials Price Index Committee, Resources Section, RTSD. The tables will be published annually in *Choice*. Price data for books reviewed in *Choice* (1983) were published in *Choice* (July/August 1984).

The strength of the dollar accounts in part for another trend, i.e., British publishers charging a differential rate to American libraries for British journals. Ostensibly, this differential rate is to recoup some losses from the dwindling pound, but it has been a practice for a long time. An article by Charles Hammaker and Deana Astle of the University of Missouri in *Library Acquisitions Practice and Theory* showed that subscription prices of British journals increased over the ordinary overseas rates in the dollar price by as much as $169.69 for one title in 1984.

The dollar-to-pound rate for those exorbitant prices was as high as $3.20 per pound for a 1984 subscription when the actual dollar/pound rate in June 1984 was $1.30. According to Hammaker and Astle, "American libraries paid on the average 66.7 percent more for the 548 titles examined than did their counterparts in the U.K. and paid 34 percent more than did other overseas libraries."[2] One American subscription agent sent out a letter with renewals for one British publisher's titles warning about the price gouging.

Budgeting Topics. Two articles in *Library Resources and Technical Services* (April/June 1984) discussed library materials prices. Sally Williams described Harvard's budget justification process for materials and the principles underlying the Harvard budget presentation. Dennis Smith (University of California) explained how the UC system administration uses the price indexes reported in the *Bowker Annual* for its annual prognostications of materials prices. Using a three-year geometric mean price increase, subject by subject, the budget is derived by multiplying the average price increase (over three years) against the expenditures for monographs, serials, and serial services. This formula has proved successful in obtaining requisite funds for materials expenditures at the University of California.

In addition to the "how-to" articles on budgeting, there were some other informative pieces on materials costs in 1984. At the ACRL national meeting in Seattle two talks concerned library materials budgeting: "A Survey of Library Acquisitions Fiscal Problems, 1980–1982," by a group of librarians from Georgia State, and "College Librarians and Professors: Partners in Collection Building and Fund Allocation," by John Allen Wilmert of Manchester College, North Manchester, Indiana.

A resolution by ALA Council at the 1984 Midwinter Meeting may help collection librarians get lower discounts from publishers. An ad-hoc group headed by Annalee Bundy (Providence Public) revised a proposal by Marvin Scilken to favor public libraries with higher discounts on trade books. The group advocated "equal discounts on equal volume orders for all buyers," and asked trade publishers to review their discounts to libraries.

CONCLUSION

Technology increasingly affected the work of collection librarians. The National Collection Inventory Project, which progressed in 1984, used a machine-readable format. NCIP will ultimately be a national database of information about collections and will make resource sharing more dependent on the computer. Electronic transmission of orders was becoming more commonplace, and in 1984 two major bibliographic utilities, RLIN and OCLC, committed to the use of this process. Bowker also began offering its electronic ordering system, the Bowker Acquisitions System, in 1984. BATAB, Bookline (Perline), Datalinx, and Ebsconet were in the news as more libraries were using those systems for ordering books and periodicals, and doing periodical check-ins. The American Library Association made an effort to increase librarians' awareness of technology. A large part of the first issue (January/March 1984) of *Library Resources and Technical Services,* for example, was devoted to electronic publishing and its impact on libraries.

There was also a growing debate among libraries about the degree to which the information revolution will affect collecting. Some would favor access completely over collection building. One English expert has gone so far as to recommend that librarians "reject collection building and focus on building linkages for information users."[3] In 1984 a university librarian, a collection manager, and a library school professor all responded to this issue. The university librarian, Hendrik Edelman, Rutgers University, noted: "We cannot ignore present needs by dreaming of some cheap fix for the future. Change will certainly occur, but in the meantime, we must confront pressing needs for traditional materials . . . . Increased funds are essential."[4] The collection manager, Scott Bennett, Assistant University Librarian for Collection Development at Northwestern University, contended that "collection managers must not become merely middlemen of convenience in the transfer of information . . . if the result is that funds entrusted to us are used to purchase expendable services whose value to the library is lost the moment those services are delivered to the user, then in that measure we have aborted our responsibility in the use of collection funds: to build the capital stock of information available to every user who comes to the library."[5]

Ed Holley, Dean of the School of Library Science, University of North Carolina, perhaps addressed this dilemma best: "In the competition of universities to advance the 'Commonwealth of Learning,' to use Elizabeth Eisenstein's happy phrase, I believe that ways will be found to support both the traditional and added functions of their libraries. Institutional pride and prestige will doubtless assure the needed resources."[6]

FREDERICK C. LYNDEN

REFERENCES

1. Paul Olum, "Myths and Realities: The Academic Viewpoint I," *College & Research Libraries* (September 1984).
2. Charles Hamaker and Deana Astle, "Recent Pricing Patterns in British Journal Publishing," *Library Acquisitions Practice and Theory*, Vol. 8, No. 4 (1984).
3. Meredith Butler, "Electronic Publishing and Its Impact on Libraries: A Literature Review," *Library Resources and Technical Services* (January/March 1984).
4. "Research Library Collections in a Changing University: Four Points of View; Pauline Atherton Cochrane, Oscar Handlin, Hendrik Edelman, and William Herbster," compiled and edited by Dan C. Hazen and J. Gormly Miller, *College & Research Libraries* (May 1984).
5. Scott Bennett, "Current Initiatives and Issues in Collection Management," *The Journal of Academic Librarianship* (November 1984).
6. Edward G. Holley, "North American Efforts at Worldwide Acquisitions since 1945," speech given at the Research Libraries Group, Inc., International Conference on Library Cooperation, October 2, 1984.

Continuing Professional Education

Increasing awareness of the rapid and profound changes in technology, industry, and society that are altering the direction and scope of the library/information profession led to initiatives in the realm of continuing professional education during 1984. The changes reflected the recognition of the need for new skills, methods, and approaches, new understanding of the environment in which professional and end-users operate, and the need for new patterns of collaboration with other groups both inside and outside the library/information science profession. The radical and continuing changes are forcing the development of new patterns and structures toward improving the system of continuing education. Even a cursory review of the literature reveals that it is now universally recognized that no members of the profession can hope to continue working with the same knowledge and understanding they had when starting their professional careers.

International Activity. At the international level, the first World Conference on Continuing Education for Library and Information Science Professions was planned and funded during 1984 with the implementation scheduled for August 1985, in Palos Hills, Illinois. This conference will be held under the auspices of the International Federation of Library Associations and Institutions (IFLA), Section on Library Schools and Other Training Aspects, Josephine Fang, Chair, and the American Library Association (ALA).

This conference will provide a forum for the exchange of ideas, raise issues of mutual concern, and stimulate and foster the exchange of ideas on a continuing basis worldwide. Initiative for the World Conference came from ALA, and the conference is chaired by two former presidents of that association—Brooke E. Sheldon and Elizabeth W. Stone. Funding for the conference has been supplied by the National Endowment for the Humanities, The Council on Library Resources, the H. W. Wilson Foundation, K. G. Saur Verlag (official publishers for IFLA), the Association of College and Research Libraries (ACRL), the Continuing Library Education Network and Exchange (CLENE), the General Bookbinding Company, the Catholic University of America and Texas Woman's University. Registration and copies of the *Proceedings* will be available to participants at no cost.

CEU. Growing out of a concern for a lack of quality and consistency in CE and training activities in the United States, the Council on the Continuing Education Unit (CEU) published *Principles of Good Practice in Continuing Education* (CCEU, 1984), a product of a three-year project to promote stronger standards in continuing education. ALA, represented by the Chair of the Council's Standing Committee on Library Education (SCOLE), Peggy O'Donnell, was one of 21 professional organizations brought in to review and aid in drafting the final report, which consists of 18 principles and 70 additional statements of amplification and interpretation, and a discussion of each principle. *The Principles of Good Practice* consists of five parts: Learning in Continuing Education; Learning Outcomes in Continuing Education; Learning Experiences in Continuing Education; Assessment of Learning Outcomes; and Continuing Education Administration. The ALA Executive Board adopted in principle the tenets set forth by this document during the ALA Board meeting in Dallas in June 1984. Commenting on the importance of this document in a brochure on the *Principles*, Malcolm S. Knowles stated: "For the first time in history we have a single statement of the best knowledge and understanding of how adults can learn most effectively. This is a major breakthrough in this field. The *Principles* focuses attention right where it should be: on the learner and on getting results. Our challenge now is to get this into the bloodstream of every educator or trainer of adults."

CLENERT. After nine years of existence as an independent national organization, the Continuing Library Education Network and Exchange (CLENE), founded in June 1975, was transformed on petition by vote of the ALA Council at its 1984 Midwinter Meeting in Washington, D.C., to the Continuing Library Education Network and Exchange Round Table (CLENERT) of ALA. CLENE was originally created to serve as a coordinating and stimulating body within the profession with two basic missions: (1) to provide equal access to CE opportunities, available in sufficient quantity and quality over a substantial period of time to ensure library and information science personnel and organizations the competency to deliver quality library and information service to all; and (2) to create an awareness and a sense of need for continuing education of library personnel on the part of employers and individuals as a means of responding to societal and technological change.

Its stated objectives as CLENERT are: (1) To provide a forum for the exchange of ideas and concerns among library and information personnel responsible for continuing library education, training, and staff development; (2) to provide learning activities and material to maintain the competencies of those who provide continuing library education; (3) to provide a force for initiating and supporting programs to increase the availability of quality continuing library education; (4) to create an awareness of, and sense of need for, continuing library education on the part of employees and employers.

CLENERT members offered one-to-one tutorials with CE providers and staff development personnel at both the 1984 ALA Midwinter Meeting in January 1984 and the ALA Annual Conference in Dallas. The tutorials provided participants with an opportunity to review projects, discuss proposed plans, and try out new ideas or receive advice and guidance from experienced practitioners. CLENERT proposes to continue this practice at ALA Midwinter and Annual conferences, and, based on a survey of needs of state library agencies in the field of CE, feature preconference workshops on the planning and implementation workshops.

With CLENE's inception as an ALA Round Table, the National Council on Quality Continuing Library and Information Science Education (formerly a CLENE affiliate) was left as an independent agency. During 1984 its Board of Directors carried out investigations to determine whether it should align itself with another organization in the profession or maintain its current independent status. As an interim measure the National Commission on Libraries and Information Science (NCLIS), citing the importance of a monitoring body for quality CE, agreed in April 1984 to distribute information about the Council and encourage CE providers to apply for approval for their CE offerings. NCLIS also agreed to supply some basic support services during this interim period.

Replies received from 10 professional associations surveyed for this article indicate that CE programming during 1984 appeared to be concentrated in two areas: (1) developing managerial ability (in a variety of areas including systems, human relations, finance and funding, marketing, and decision making); and (2) technological innovation, based on the urgent need of existing professionals (as opposed to the new generation of professionals) to be updated not only in technical knowledge, but also in the implications of new technology for organizational structures, job design, staffing, and evaluation of alternative methods of information retrieval.

CE Initiatives. The following paragraphs highlight some of the initiatives taken in the management area by CE providers.

Brooke Sheldon, 1983–84 ALA President, developed a fund-raising training kit based on the design of her 1984 ALA Annual Conference President's Program. The packet includes complete instructions for trainers in conducting half-day or day-long workshops and media presentations and print resources to be presented to workshop participants who promote them in their respective states following the conference program.

Meetings, Institutes. Of the 25 CE offerings at the 1984 ALA Midwinter Meeting and the preconferences held prior to the 1984 ALA Annual Conference, 48 percent were in the area of managerial development. Two traveling institutes produced by the Library Administration Division (LAMA) were "Getting on the Air," designed to teach the practical skills needed to communicate effectively in the broadcast media, and "Management of the Online Catalog," on choices in planning and operating them.

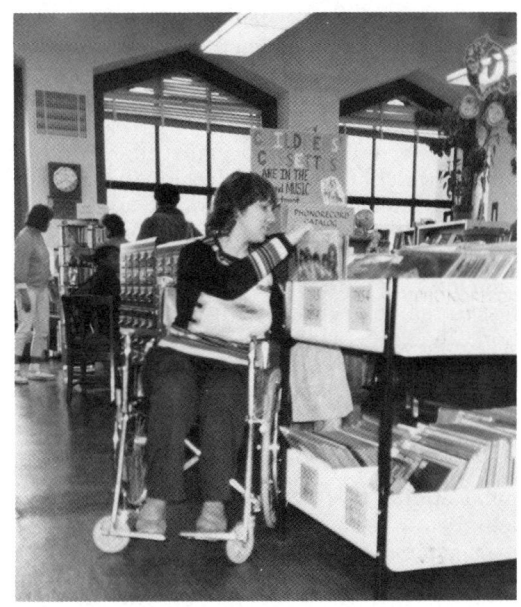

A library technician in Berkeley (California) Public Library participates in a Disability Awareness Training Workshop to familiarize the library staff with problems of the disabled.

Since 1973 the Association of Research Libraries' (ARL) Office of Management Studies has provided more than 1,200 persons with training designed to improve the performance of academic librarians through Library Management Skills institutes. During 1984 such institutes were held in Washington, D.C., Miami, Chicago, San Diego, and Annapolis. Two institutes were held in Australia. A new institute developed in 1984 was designed to aid library science faculty members in exploring the changes taking place in research libraries and assessing the implications of these changes for library education. In addition, special focus workshops were offered on time management, long-range planning methods, performance appraisal, management of change, supervisory and interpersonal skills. Special presentations were made on the economics and financial management concerns of research libraries.

SLA. More than 1,300 registered for the 27 CE courses offered at the Special Library Association's (SLA) Annual Conference in June 1984, a record enrollment for professional development opportunities in SLA.

SLA continued its Middle Management Institute (MMI) series—a formal management training program for special librarians and information specialists moving into supervisory and management positions. The first graduates received their certificates of completion at the 1984 SLA Annual Conference. MMI programming consists of 75 hours of instruction divided into five segments, with each program segment including 15 hours of classwork. The five areas covered are management skills, analytical tools, human resources, marketing and public relations, materials, and machines. Programs may be completed in any sequence. Recognition includes a Certificate of Completion if the series of five is completed within a 24-month period. Participants earn 1.5 continuing education units

Continuing Professional Education

(CEUs) for each completed program; 7.5 CEUs are awarded for completing the entire sequence.

SLA completed plans to offer a winter education conference each year, beginning in February 1985.

A new feature of the *Specialist* (the monthly SLA newsletter) is a "Professional Development" column designed to inform readers about CE and professional development opportunities both within SLA and the field at large. At the June meeting of the SLA Board, CE was identified as the number one priority of the Association. The Professional Development Committee began preparing a policy statement in 1984. Among the many planned committee activities are an executive development program for managers and directors of major information services. Another new feature of the *Specialist* is the publication of the "Management Document Bulletin Board"—members wishing to share useful management documents such as organization charts, user survey questionnaires, and position titles and budgets may communicate and exchange documents.

MLA. The Medical Library Association (MLA) is clarifying concepts of the role of libraries in the management of information science and describing alternatives for the development of professional competency through its current Strategic Planning effort. The ad hoc Committee on Professional Development prepared guidelines for professional development and recognition. New materials designed for use in the development and approval of non-MLA-sponsored CE activities were introduced at the MLA annual meeting in Denver during 1984. Topics include "Criteria for Quality" and "Guide to Quality," and copies are available from the MLA Education Department.

During 1984 MLA announced plans for a winter institute on continuing professional education, combining seminars with evening plenary sessions in an intensive three-day program including sessions on marketing strategies, executive communications, decision analysis, library planning, and human resource management.

MLA sought closer interaction with a variety of professional schools and departments to ensure an adequate supply of entry-level and retrained personnel with appropriate skills and competencies.

IFLA Activities. The need for improved CE opportunities in management was also demonstrated in Miriam Tees's presentation at the IFLA Section on Library Schools and Other Training Aspects during the IFLA Conference in Nairobi, Kenya, in August 1984. The management course outlined for action was developed in response to UNESCO's desire to harmonize education for information professions and is designed to be useful to schools teaching librarians, archivists, and information scientists in all parts of the world. The goal of the course is to teach beginning information professionals the principles of good management. When complete, modules will cover planning, organization, staffing, leading, controlling, marketing, and operations.

UW Extension Program. The Certificate of Professional Development in Library Management is offered by the University of Wisconsin–Extension Communications Programs Unit. This noncredit Certificate Program is structured with required and elective courses designed to provide a more comprehensive examination of administrative problems than is possible during the more generalized education offered in library schools. Open to all library education personnel with supervisory and management responsibilities or aspirations, certification is granted upon successful completion of three core courses and four or five electives (for a minimum of 12 CEUs). Courses are offered at locations throughout the state, and during 1984 the core courses offered were Organizational Management and Personnnel Management. Certificate Eligible Electives offered at various locations across the state included Unionization and Libraries, Planning: A Future Oriented Activity, Grantsmanship and Proposal Writing for Librarians, Problem Solving and Decision Making for Library Managers, Marketing for Librarians, and Output Measures. The program is approved by the National Council on Quality Continuing Library and Information Science Education.

Illinois State Library. The Illinois State Library developed the Online Network of Continuing Education (ONCE). This effective use of technology for furthering CE participation serves as a CE calendar and data bank of human and material resources. Available in Illinois with compatible microcomputers and telephone modems, the library community may access ONCE via a toll-free line. At the Illinois State Library, the system includes three options for users: (1) querying the ONCE database to see available options; (2) displaying the full record of any listed item; and (3) entering CE activities.

Nation at Risk. Two major replies to the challenges presented by the U.S. Department of Education's 1983 report *A Nation at Risk* were published in the summer of 1984. The first, issued in June and prepared by ALA's Task Force on Excellence in Education, is *Realities: Educational Reform in a Learning Society*. The second, issued by the U.S. Department of Education, is *Alliance for Excellence*.

Both contain statements and recommendations concerning the overall goal stated in *A Nation at Risk*—namely, that educational reform should focus on the goal of creating a learning society.

In the ALA publication, four realities were identified for effective educational reform within a learning society: (1) Learning begins before schooling; (2) good schools require good libraries; (3) people in a learning society need libraries throughout their lives; and (4) public support of libraries is an investment in people and communities.

The *Alliance for Excellence* response recommended that libraries accept their central role in the learning society as valid learning centers staffed with user-oriented professionals who provide support for lifelong learning of all people. Both reports accentuate the important role libraries should play in the campaign for literacy as symbolized by the goal of the 1984–85 National Library Week theme, "A Nation of Readers."

ELIZABETH W. STONE

Copyright

Copyright Issues. The long awaited U.S. Supreme Court decision on SONY v. Universal City Studios came on January 17, 1984, when in a 5-to-4 vote, the Court held that the private, noncommercial video taping of television programs does not constitute copyright infringement. The case had been held over from the 1982–83 term and re-argued in the fall of 1983, prior to the decision. The Court found that the principal purpose of home video taping of television programs was for "time-shifting" and is legitimate "fair use." Since the action had been brought against SONY and by implication, other companies involved in the manufacture and sale of video taping equipment, the Court also found that the making and selling of video tape recorders to the general public do not constitute a contributory infringement.

The continuing conflict between the demand for broader access to copyrighted properties via the electronic media and the concerns of copyright proprietors for retaining control over intellectual properties characterized copyright activities in 1984.

Negotiations continued between OCLC, its regional networks and member users regarding the copyright/contract problems initiated when OCLC sought copyright protection for its database while at the same time proposing new terms and conditions for licensing the use of the database. The discussions appear to be long term in that it will require the separate resolution of the copyright limitations and user responsibilities that are attendant to online database use, as well as the contractual issues and the question of to whom they apply. There has been a change in the tenor of the negotiations brought about by the representatives of all parties trying their best to accommodate the several positions on the issues.

Efforts to Influence Copyright Restrictions. Few saw library implications in the resolutions in the New York University (NYU) infringement case settled out of court in 1983. Although the Association of American Publishers sought general adherence by universities to the settlement terms agreed to by NYU, most universities were being advised to consult with legal counsel in order to avoid eroding any of their fair use rights.

In another instance of copyright enforcement, a major publisher of scientific journals announced that it was issuing licenses that would allow reserve librarians in colleges and universities to make no more than six copies of portions of their publications for reserve room use. Springer-Verlag indicated that in the absence of such a license or an arrangement for payment through the Copyright Clearance Center, no copying of their publications would be permitted. ALA and other institutions responded to this effort as a misstatement of the copyright statute that ignores many fair uses of copyrighted materials such as inter-library loans for which permission to photocopy is not required.

Record Rental Problem. Resolution of the record problem occurred in early September when the House of Representatives passed H.R. 5938, the Record Rental Agreement of 1984, prohibiting the commercial lending of phono records without the permission of the copyright owner. Libraries and schools are exempt from the provisions of this bill. The Senate agreed to the House amendments to the Senate Bill #S.32 on September 21 and the President signed the Record Rental Amendment of 1984 into law (PL 98-450) on October 4. The new law would modify the "first sale" doctrine embodied in paragraph 109(a) of the Copyright Act of 1976. Before phono records could be rented, leased or lent for commercial purposes, it would require authorization of the copyright owner.

Semi-Conductor Chips Legislation. New legislation from the 98th Congress in the copyright areas also extended to semi-conductor chips. However, in this case, Congress decided to create the first truly new form of intellectual property protection in nearly 100 years by becoming the first country to explicitly protect the designs of semi-conductor chips against unauthorized copying. The Semi-Conductor Chip Protection Act of 1984 bypasses copyright protection in prohibiting chip piracy by granting 10-year proprietary protection to mask works for semi-conductor chip products through a new Chapter 9 section of Title 17 of the U.S. code. Congressional sponsors of the bills leading up to the passage of the Semi-Conductor Protection Act pointed out that the measure has no implications for protection of computer programs.

Other Issues. Downloading from databases had substantial statistics brought to bear on the question with the completion of a study by Cuadra Associates. The Santa Monica consulting firm headed by Carlos Cuadra focused on downloading and its effect on the online database market. The study, according to *Online Review* notes that downloading is an established aspect of online information retrieval and characterizes the different types of downloading that occurs. The extent to which database proprietors will tolerate downloading that will not be considered an infringement of copyright has not yet been determined.

Another end of year development in connection with the U.S. withdrawal from UNESCO saw the U.S. State Department appoint an ad hoc committee to investigate the basis for U.S. consideration of joining the Berne International Copyright Convention. Major implications of this move that might establish stronger protection for U.S. intellectual properties in many countries around the world involve the assessment of the effect of the removal of all formalities, which is a requirement of Berne, including copyright notice, copyright registration, and legal deposit as a requirement for copyright protection.

People. The end of 1984 saw the resignation of David Ladd, as the Register of Copyright and efforts by the Library of Congress to seek a successor. Ladd's tenure as Register was marked by periodic controversies prompted by his public comments that appeared to be more sympathetic to copyright proprietories than users.

The education and copyright communities were saddened in July by the death of Alan Latman, leading attorney in *William and Wilkins*, v. *U.S.*, New York University Law School professor and a vital force in the Copyright Society of America. In recent years, Latman's influence has been felt in a number of negotiated settlements of copyright issues.   STAFF

Council on Library/Media Technicians

Countless library and information technicians worked during 1984 as support staff in businesses, hospitals, and government agencies. Many technicians were also employed in universities, schools, and public libraries. The Council on Library/Media Technicians (COLT) provides a gathering place for those employees and a means of communicating with each other.

Formed in the mid-1960s, COLT grew out of the need for recognition of support staff and for a forum in which to discuss common concerns. Laboring under the difficulty of being an international organization for workers who found it difficult to receive release time to attend annual meetings, the group in its initial phase relied on directors of college and university technician training programs. In 1984 librarians composed roughly 15 percent of the Board and the membership, thus technicians comprised a majority of its membership and guided the organization. Two professionals who served on the Board in 1984 began as technicians and so bring valuable insight and empathy to technicians' concerns.

College and university programs continued to provide a first introduction to COLT for many technicians. These programs are listed in the *1984 COLT Directory; Institutions Offering or Planning Programs for the Training of Library/Media Technical Assistants*. The directory, in its sixth edition, is only one of COLT's publications. *COLT Newsletter* is published monthly (except in July).

Margaret Myers, Director of ALA's Office for Library Personnel Resources, was keynote speaker at COLT's 1984 Annual Conference meeting. Technicians were featured on the Conference program.

Halfway through the 1980s library and information support staff positions in societies, businesses, and nonprofit organizations continue to expand. For personnel who will fill those jobs and media support staff already employed, COLT provides a home and a voice.

JOANNE WOLFORD

COUNCIL ON LIBRARY/MEDIA TECHNICIANS

PRESIDENT (December 1984–December 1985): **Raymond Roney,** El Camino College, California

VICE-PRESIDENT/PRESIDENT-ELECT: **Joanne Wolford,** Ohio University–Lancaster Library Technology Program

EXECUTIVE SECRETARY: **Margaret R. Barron**

Membership (1984): 800
Headquarters: Cuyahoga Community College Library, Cleveland, Ohio 44115

Databases, Computer-Readable

Databases continued during 1984 to be used online and, to a much lesser extent, in the batch mode. Online activity increased. More and more information centers and libraries were using databases and end-user searching was increasing. One of the forces beginning to contribute to the expansion of the online market is the introduction of front ends, gateways, and intermediary systems for making online searching easier.

The Online Database Industry. The online database industry is dependent on a number of elements; users (both intermediary searchers and end users), databases, online systems, the performance and pricing of the databases and systems and, user receptivity. All of these factors together contribute to the success, or lack thereof, of databases, systems, and the industry as a whole.

The online database industry achieved a success. It has grown continuously at a rate of roughly 20-25 percent per year. The major vendors are also succeeding, and many of the smaller vendors are succeeding in the sense that they are increasing usage rapidly. That does not, however, mean they are yet recovering their costs. The same is true for the databases. The principal databases are profitable but many of the smaller ones do not recover costs.

Based on the continuing Information Market Indicators survey of the online database industry, the number of databases online increases from quarter to quarter, but during 1983 and 1984 much of the growth in hours of use, and growth in revenues was offset by the fact that there were more databases available; thus the pie was cut into smaller pieces. The major systems and databases are few in number and there are many minor ones.

The vendors of word-oriented databases in the U.S. (based on data collected in 1984 for 1983 usage) were: Bibliographic Retrieval System (BRS), CAS Online (CAS), DIALOG, Dow Jones, INFORM, ISI, LegiSlate, Mead Data Central (MDC), National Library of Medicine (NLM), New York Times (now handled by MDC), Pergamon Infoline, QUESTEL, System Development Corporation (SDC), Source, and Westlaw.

U.S. usage within that group of vendors was concentrated within MDC and DIALOG. MDC and DIALOG together accounted for 71 percent of the usage and 85 percent of the expenditures for online databases from the information center/library market. Average expenditures per hour of online usage for all services (connect time, prints, displays, SDIs, training, and anything else that appears on a user bill) across all vendors was $117 ranging from $33 to $272. An average hour on MDC generated $160 and an average hour on DIALOG generated $113. An average hour on NLM generated considerably less ($33) as might be expected of a government service.

The users of databases used a wide variety of databases within the 15 vendors listed. They used more than 300 databases (actually more than 600 vendor database listings as many of the large databases are broken into multiple segments by time or subject), but only five of the 300+ were used more than 50,000 hours in the year. Those five were LEXIS, MEDLARS, CA SEARCH, ERIC, and NEXIS. Approximately half the databases were used fewer than 400 hours in the year and the balance were in the middle. When databases go online, few generate more than 200 hours of use in their first quarter. Among the databases with successful start-ups

Electronic Publishing: Eight Trends of '84

A review of developments in online databases and electronic publishing during 1984 indicates that eight major trends affect libraries. The most significant trend is the reorientation of the entire industry from a "product-driven" environment to "market-driven" operations. This single shift greatly influences all the other trends and developments in the field. The movement is the result of a self-assessment that has been brewing in the industry for several years.

Trend #1: Toward a Market-Driven Industry. Librarians have long been the benefactors of a rapidly proliferating online industry, but 1984 presented strong evidence of changing times. No longer obsessed with unbounded growth, the major players of the industry have realigned themselves over the past several years to expand and grow only in a highly controlled and calculated manner. As a result, most development is occurring primarily in several specific areas.

Since its inception, the industry has been "product driven," using the new technology to make information available via new products. During the decade 1975–84, traditional publishers, for example, scrambled to convert their long-standing print products to machine-readable format—but often without significant market evidence that anyone would use the new database version of the material. The effect was a historical accident that furnished the library community with offerings rich in product.

Although many libraries are still not online, the information producers and vendors are beginning to view the intermediary searcher (libraries) as a saturated market with limited potential for additional revenue. The founding companies in this rapidly maturing industry are now seeking fresh audiences. Furthermore, newcomers to the trade are reshaping the precepts of the entire industry. Unlike the pioneers who first made databases available, recent entrants are experimenting with a variety of products and services with an overriding goal to identify and serve new markets.

The entire industry has moved from the "product-driven" philosophy to one that is "market driven." Companies like Mead and BRS are carefully targeting their new product development to serve only those markets that promise high revenue. Even DIALOG, the "supermarket" vendor of hundreds of databases, began to embrace a more constrained approach to file acquisition.

Trend #2: End-User Services. Purveyors of hardware, software, and databases are plotting their growth cautiously to achieve their ends. While individual segments have been identified in almost every professional and consumer category, the overwhelming push has been in the direction of end users. No longer will libraries be the focus of product development efforts. The end-user market is now center stage. In many cases libraries will be served only by the fallout from the end-user emphasis. As such, the intermediary community—established libraries and technical information centers—will continue to benefit from the creation and improvement of new products, but many of the major developments in the industry will transpire outside the purview of the library world.

Examples of new services designed to reach the end user are the lower priced, menu-driven systems aimed at the microcomputer owner at home and in a small business. The Source and Compuserve have served the market for a number of years, but BRS (After Dark) and DIALOG (Knowledge Index) have also entered the market. The entrance of the established bibliographic majors into this business may be seen as a defensive measure aimed at eliminating the chance that the well-known major online systems could be pushed out of the new markets. Many of the end-user services offer the same files that have been popular with intermediaries for years. To attract new business, the software is usually simpler, menu-driven (offering convenient and wide-ranging options), and priced significantly below the cost of the traditional bibliographic services.

End-user services are becoming specialized as well. Over a half dozen companies compete for physicians' business as well as other segments of the end-user medical market. Fisher Stevens' Phycom, BRS's Colleague, and the American Medical Association's Minet System comprise the three major players, but General Electric (GEISCO), Delphi, Information General Corporation, and IntelliGenetics, in conjunction with the National Institutes of Health, also sell medical databases.

The health care field is not the only specialized market affected by end-user services. ITT–Dialcom's ABA–Net is an example of a system devoted to the legal profession. ALANET (see American Library Association) was formed to serve the same purpose for the library community. These and other specialized online networks strive to support their specific constituency with a variety of products including databases, bulletin boards, online newsletters, and electronic mail services. Most of these services are still new, and their success is yet unproven. It appears that at least one network in each professional area may be viable, however. In addition, systems for communication and access to shared databases are becoming prominent within corporations. As companies adopt these networks internally, the acceptance of other telecommunicated services by the end user will also intensify.

Trend #3: Software Interfaces. The proliferation of these services has established interface and equipment compatibility as major obstacles to conquer in reaching the end-user market. The difficulties encountered by the Viewtron videotex system characterize the compatibility problem. Although the demand for videotex is increasing, Viewtron witnessed a tremendous disappointment during its first year of introduction as the $600 Sceptre terminal was not widely accepted by the intended purchasers. In contrast, the successful services have been those that utilize existing ASCII terminals or microcomputers already in place at the customer site.

Of particular note is Menlo Corporation's IN-SEARCH package, which originally began as the end user's link to the DIALOG retrieval service. The software product utilizes the IBM PC or other similar hardware and has been expanded to include a new version called PRO-SEARCH, which also accesses BRS. Easynet permits users to "gateway" to a wide array of retrieval systems without having to establish contact with or learn each host's command language. A similar service is BCN. Aimed primarily at end users in the business community, BCN offers packaged access to many vendors and databases.

Users of such services do not have to sign agreements or learn each specific protocol to access databases. All of these "value added" wholesale resellers of information feature user-friendly software that allows the inexperienced end user to walk through the sign-on and search using a simple menu-driven language.

The software explosion has also affected database producers significantly. Many individual packages—such as Microdisclosure, BIOSIS-BITS, ISI-Scimate, and IAC Search Helper—have been developed to allow these producers to increase usage of their files by reaching beyond the library clientele. Once again, the proliferation of the personal computer has been instrumental in the development of these products. In

Databases

particular, the establishment of the IBM PC as the industry standard has been a major factor. A notable new story in 1984 was Mead Data Central's acceptance of the IBM hardware. Now that Lexis and Nexis are available to users without dedicated equipment, many nonlegal libraries will be able to take advantage of what formerly was for many a prohibitively expensive information bank.

Trend #4: Standalone and Distributed Products. A new era of standalone products is emerging. Software products like STAR and FINDER allow users to build their own files either through local data entry or conversion of "downloaded" telecommunicated files. These programs are particularly adaptable for library applications, but their eventual market potential is a much broader base of customers. Packages like Knowledge Access were being developed in the mid-1980s to encourage database producers to vend their files directly as standalone, distributed products already loaded on diskettes and ready to be used on microcomputer equipment. These services may grow more rapidly in the later 1980s than any other segment of the industry.

Another standalone product on the verge of major public introduction is the optical or video laser disk. Joint ventures for building and testing the technology have been plentiful throughout the industry over the last several years. Of particular interest to libraries is the Reference Technology venture; BRS took an active part in this project and planned to make many databases available through this medium. The major telecommunicated services are beginning to recognize the potential of this evolving technology as a competitor to their already existing services and therefore worth serious exploration.

Trend #5: Cooperative and Traditional Marketing. Librarians will witness new methods being used to sell familiar products. Traditionally databases have been promoted through direct mail, newsletters, space advertisements, journals, training sessions, and exhibits at the major library and online meetings. Evidence of the market driven philosophy can be seen in the recent efforts at cooperative marketing and training sessions like those being offered mutually by Data Courier, Predicasts, and Disclosure. The emphasis on microcomputers and end users will make these joint campaigns even more cost effective and efficient for database producers.

A related trend of interest to librarians involves the movement of online and database companies toward more traditional marketing methods—among them direct sales forces and distribution through retail outlets such as computer stores. These techniques will be employed increasingly as producers and vendors compete to reach end users in larger numbers.

Trend #6: New Systems. While most of the established industry was concentrating its 1984 efforts to reach new markets, several other developments occurred that will have a positive influence on librarians. Four new major online services appeared on the scene in 1984. Wilsonline, STN, VuText, and Newsnet bring access to a tremendous amount of information not previously available online. Wilsonline consists of all the familiar abstracts and indexes accessible through a software similar to the National Library of Medicine or SDC system. STN is a joint venture of Chemical Abstracts and other scientific database producers to create an international network of technical information. At least two of these services, Wilsonline and STN, characterize a growing desire among information providers for independence.

While the variety vendors were a good way for electronic databases to become established and initially develop a following, the market-driven movement is appealing to many information providers. Producers want more control of their customer base and the ability to reach markets neglected by the established multiple-file vendors. Systems like Wilsonline and STN are expected to abound in future years.

While this trend may currently frustrate librarians because of the necessity of learning an additional command language, the trend toward "front ends" and "gateways," which reduce or obviate the need for such knowledge, will probably begin to offset that predicament soon. Many libraries already operate equipment and systems that have the capability of mitigating many disadvantages of separate systems.

Trend #7: Full Text. Another trend important to librarians is the growing availability of full text online. VuText, for example, offers a core of newspapers and other standard references in the full-text format. Newsnet strives to be a one-stop shopping source for the full text of many industry newsletters. In 1984 Mead Data Central (the original full-text service) continued to grow at a phenomenal rate. A major addition to the system's offerings were the Time, Inc., databases, which comprise the text of many popular magazines.

Information Access Corporation, a well-known library service company, also incorporated full text in many of their bibliographic files. Other major participants include Wiley and Chemical Abstracts, which have introduced numerous full-text files through BRS and other services.

Full text is already popular in online services today. It is likely that the trend toward standalone products will cause rapid expansion.

Trend #8: Source and Reference Databases. Most of the world's abstracts and indexes had become available online by the mid-1980s. The current growth area continues to be reference information. In particular, online catalogs and directories lead the pack of newly available databases. The Electronic Yellow Pages and *Thomas Register* are evidence of this trend and now the online industry has a directory of its own participants available from Marquis's *Who's Who* as the Online PRO-files database on DIALOG.

Conclusion. In all 1984 was a year of controlled and well-planned expansion. The number of new products and usage levels continued to climb. The self-assessment of the industry was nearly complete and future directions highly targeted. Although the online fever is spreading far beyond the arena of the library, intermediaries will continue to benefit from increased awareness and the umbrella effect of new products, technologies, and services that are made available to end users.

DAVID GROSSMAN

---

were the Library of Congress' MARC database on DIALOG, Harvard Business Review on DIALOG, InfoBank on MDC, and LEXPAT on MDC.

Four of the five databases that are responsible for the lion's share of usage are the ones that produced the most revenues—LEXIS, NEXIS, CA SEARCH, and MEDLARS. In addition, Predicasts was a high revenue generator. In this context the revenues are those generated by the databases and paid to the vendors. Those dollars are then split between the vendor and producer according to the agreements between them.

Institutional database users are made up of eight classes—academe, government, industry information brokers, legal, medical, not-for-profits, and public libraries. Each of these classes uses a large number of databases. In fact every class uses at least 64 percent of all online databases. Industry uses all of them and the legal profession uses 64 percent of them. Within specific classes there are only a few databases that account for most of the use.

In academe, eight databases (ERIC, LEXIS, MEDLARS, PSYCINFO, WESTLAW, BIOSIS, CA SEARCH, and SHEPARDS) accounted for 75 percent of all database use and 291 other databases collectively made up the other 25 percent of the use.

In government, 20 databases (ERIC, MEDLARS, NTIS, AGRICOLA, BIOSIS, CA SEARCH, LEXIS, LEXPAT, NEXIS, GEOREF, BOOKS IN PRINT, INSPEC, COMPENDEX, DOE ENERGY, PSYCINFO, EXCERPTA MEDICA, SCIENCE CITATION INDEX, MAGAZINE INDEX, SELECTED WATER RESOURCES, and WESTLAW), made up 70 percent of the usage and 246 other databases made up the remaining 30 percent. It is interesting to note that the four highest use databases in government were government-produced databases.

In industry, 21 databases (CA SEARCH, MEDLARS, ABI/INFORM, CAS ONLINE REGISTRY, CLASS CODE, COMPENDEX, INFO BANK, INSPEC, LEXIS, NEXIS, NTIS, PREDICASTS, WORLD PATENTS, BIOSIS, DISCLOSURE, ERIC, DOW JONES, EXCERPTA MEDICA, NATIONAL NEWS, CAS REGISTRY NOMENCLATURE, and SCIENCE CITATION INDEX) account for 69 percent of the use.

In the legal class only five databases (LEXIS, AUTO-CITE, NEXIS, SHEPARDS and WESTLAW) made up 94 percent of the use. In the medical class the usage is also more restrictive as would be expected in a subject-oriented class. Eleven databases (MEDLARS, CA SEARCH, EXCERPTA MEDICA, CATLINE, HEALTH PLANNING CANCERLIT, BIOSIS, CAS ONLINE REGISTRY, PSYCINFO, ABI/INFORM, and TOXLINE) accounted for 85 percent of database usage in medicine and within the 11 all but ABI/INFORM are databases of obvious use in medicine.

In the not-for-profit class the usage varies considerably from quarter to quarter so it makes little sense to list the 25 databases in the high use group. Two databases—ERIC and NTIS—remained on top consistently. Usage within public libraries is predictable in that the high use databases deal with education, business, health, computers and news. The 16 databases that make up 61 percent of the use in public libraries are ERIC, PREDICASTS, ABI/INFORM, MAGAZINE INDEX, BOOKS IN PRINT, MEDLARS, NATIONAL NEWS, NEWSEARCH, PHILADELPHIA ENQUIRER, PSYCINFO, CLASS CODE, DUN'S MARKET, NTIS, TRADE and INDUSTRY, MANAGEMENT CONTENTS, and MICROCOMPUTER INDEX.

Gateways, Front-Ends and Intermediary Systems. As the number of databases has grown the number of databases used in each class has grown but the increase of number used is likely to plateau unless we can tap the end user market to a significant extent. Producers and vendors are anxious to increase their markets, and consequently, some of them, as well as individual entrepreneurial firms, have developed and are marketing aids in the form of gateways, front ends, and intermediary systems.

These aids are software packages or programs—some for use on personal computers and some for use on host computers—to help users in a variety of ways. They aim to make the complexities of online searching transparent to the user. They generally produce automatic logon. Some let the user use a variety of systems without having to know the commands for specific systems. They may provide automatic database selection, reformatting of output, offline negotiation of searches, assistance in query development, storage of search strategies, downloading and uploading of data, report generation, and other services.

Among the commercial products each providing a subset of the above features are MicroDisclosure, SciMate, Search Helper, MicroCambridge, InSearch, Naturlink, FRED, PC Net Link, iNet, EasyNet, and Business Computer Network. Such systems whether they are database-specific, system-specific, subject-specific, or generalized, help to make the process of searching easier for end users. They increase the speed of becoming acquainted with systems and databases, decrease the need for intermediaries, decrease keying, decrease the need for database and system documentation, and often decrease connect time.

MARTHA E. WILLIAMS

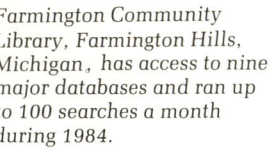

Farmington Community Library, Farmington Hills, Michigan, has access to nine major databases and ran up to 100 searches a month during 1984.

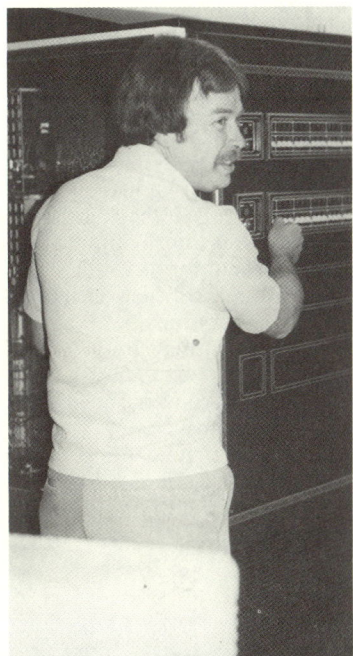

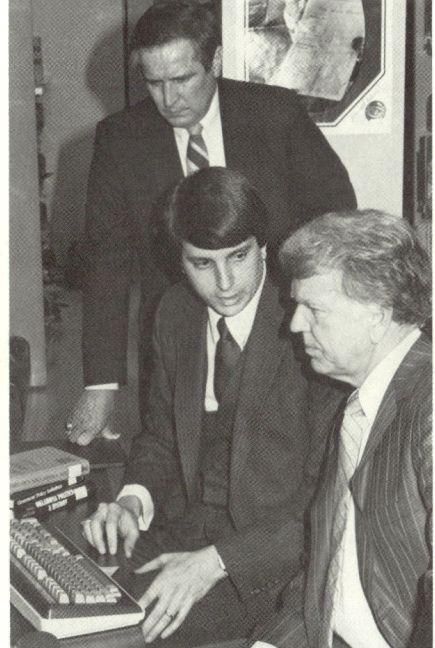

Left, a mainframe computer was installed in 1984 for the Metropolitan Library System, Oklahoma County, Oklahoma, as the first phase in a five-year automation plan. Below, Oklahoma Governor George Nigh (right) at the University of Oklahoma Libraries listens while Bob Seal, Assistant Director of Public Service for the OU libraries, demonstrates the automated circulation system that links OU with the Oklahoma Department of Libraries. Also observing was Joe Leone, Chancellor for the State Regents for Higher Education.

Education, Library

Decreasing Programs. Twice a year the American Library Association publishes a list of the ALA accredited library education programs. A casual comparison of the October listings for 1983 and 1984 suggests only minor changes occurred in the accredited programs during the year. There continued to be 67 programs, 60 of these in the United States. Clarion introduced a post-master's specialists or certificate program, increasing the number of these programs to 39. Doctoral programs continued to be offered by 25 of the schools, 23 of them in the U.S. Rhode Island, Iowa, and Wisconsin-Madison added the word "information" to the title of their programs, bringing the total to 43 schools with "information" now included in their titles. During the year Drexel took this trend a step further by dropping the word "library" from its title and identifying itself as the College of Information Studies.

When these two lists are more closely examined, however, a marked difference is noted. On the 1983 list two programs, Minnesota and Mississippi, had footnote references indicating that no new students were being admitted. On the 1984 list those two schools were joined by Ball State, Case Western, Denver, and Southern California as admitting no new students, bringing a total of six of the accredited programs being phased out. (See Accreditation.)

With the increasing cost of higher education and the decreasing enrollments in many graduate programs, some attrition in accredited programs might be expected. However, the programs being phased out include schools that offer the only accredited program within their state, and in Denver's case, within the region. Four of the schools have been established for 50 or more years, Case Western's program originating in 1904. These are programs that would not have been expected to close. Case Western, Minnesota, and Southern California are three of the 25 accredited programs also offering the doctorate. Library education and the profession generally will be weakened with the absence of these programs that have in many cases made unique contributions to the profession and to education for librarianship.

With the recognition of the importance of information in modern society, it is difficult to understand how schools preparing individuals to effectively collect, organize, and disseminate this valuable resource can become expendable in the academic market place. Have library schools too closely allied themselves with the stereotype of the library as a storehouse of knowledge with the librarian as custodian? Are they failing to present the library as a vital information source and the librarian as the agent for its use?

Kenneth Dowlin in his introduction to *The Electronic Library* urges librarians to recognize the importance of their traditional competencies and with the extension of these competencies through technology "to seek roles in society that increase their value." He notes:

"There is much evidence that people entering the field of library and information science recognize the declining job market in traditional libraries. Many library schools have found that increasing numbers of their students are seeking careers in organizations that do not fit the definitions of a traditional library. The numerous schools of librarianship that have added information science to their name attest to the shift in focus. The change in focus for library schools is accepted as a natural extension of their traditional program. Library schools may be leading the profession into the uncharted waters . . . . Perhaps the educators will lead the rest of the profession during this crucial phase of societal change."[1]

If this is the case the library schools will need the understanding and support of both the profession as a whole and the individual librarians.

Conference on Accreditation. The Association of Library and Information Science Educators (ALISE) with the cooperation of ALA sponsored a September conference in Chicago to discuss the scope, structure, and costs of accreditation as it currently exists and as it might be projected for the future. The three-day conference was promoted by William Summers, South Carolina, as President of ALISE and was funded by the H. W. Wilson Foundation. Participants represented 17 different library and information science organizations and agencies including the U.S. Department of Education. Though a variety of interests and concerns were expressed, there was general agreement that the accreditation process should be broadened to involve other organizations than ALA and that these organizations should share the financial cost of accreditation.

As an outgrowth of the conference, the U.S. Department of Education provided a $46,000 Title II-B Higher Education Act grant to determine procedures and guidelines for involving a variety of professional associations in the accreditation process for library and information science education. Robert Hayes, California at Los Angeles, Chair of the Committee on Accreditation, was named principal investigator for the project and Elinor Yungmeyer, ALA Accreditation Officer, was designated Project Manager. A steering committee and six task forces, composed of representatives of the various organizations participating in the conference, were established to proceed with the project.

STATISTICAL REPORT

Students. In the 1984 *Library and Information Science Education Statistical Report* published by the Association for Library and Information Science Education (ALISE), Agnes Reagan, Texas, reported on data collected on students.[2] Data were provided by 64 of the 67 programs accredited by ALA. The full-time equivalent (FTE) enrollment in the master's programs at these schools totaled 5,515 fall term 1983, an increase of 261 over the 5,254 FTE reported by 65 schools for the previous year. It was the first year in the five the report had been issued that FTE enrollment had not decreased from the previous year (Table 1).

An increase also was reported in FTE enrollments in sixth-year and doctoral programs. An FTE enrollment of 122 was reported by 30 schools in sixth-year programs, an increase of 13 over that reported by 33 schools the previous year. FTE enrollment in doctoral programs totaled 290 in 23 reporting schools, 13 more than the same number of schools reported for the prior year.

Reagan found that the 64 schools awarded 3,784 master's degrees in 1982–83, including 748 males and 3,036 females, 221 minority persons, and 120 foreign nationals. The average number of master's degrees awarded by the accredited programs was 59, continuing the approximately 5 percent reduction in the average that occurred annually for over 10 years. Sixth-year programs in 23 schools had 51 graduates, and 61 doctorates were granted by 21 schools. Table 2 summarizes degrees granted by schools with ALA accredited programs as reported in the five years of the ALISE report.[2]

Placement and Salaries. For the *Library Journal*'s 33rd annual report on placement and salaries of graduates of accredited programs, Carol Learmont, Columbia, received responses from 60 of the 67 eligible schools. The 60 schools reported 3,494 fifth-year graduates for 1983. Of these graduates, 1,845 (53 percent) were reported in permanent professional positions, 401 (22 percent) of them returned to previously held positions, 561 (27 percent) found jobs prior to graduation, and 490 (27 percent) were employed within three months of receiving the degree. Of the 60 reporting schools, 36 identified 30 or fewer graduate placements in permanent professional positions and only 4 reported over 50 such placements for the year, reflecting more the continued limited enrollments in the accredited programs than a limited job market. Information was not available on 737, or 21 percent, of the graduates; 242 (7 percent) were reported in temporary professional positions; 134 (4 percent) were in nonprofessional library assignments, and 536 (15 percent) were not in library positions.

Salary information was available on 1,410 of the 1983 graduates. This represented 76 percent of the known placements and 40 percent of all graduates reported. The average for the reported salaries was $17,705, a 7 percent increase over the 1982 average. The average salary for men continued to exceed that for women, and Learmont found this inequity present in the average salary in each of the different types of libraries and in other information agencies. For the 386 graduates who did not have previous experience, the average beginning salary was $16,328, an increase of $1,080 over the average reported for this group for 1982. Learmont noted that the outstanding need for the year was "for graduates skilled in children's services for both school and public libraries," and that "library and other information related work for which there may be an increasing demand and short supply continue to include cataloging, science and technology, information science, and systems."[3]

Faculty. The ALISE report on faculty, prepared by Gary Purcell, Tennessee, indicates that 66 schools offering accredited programs employed 660 full-time faculty as of January 1984, 20 fewer than reported by 68 schools in the previous year. The number of full-time faculty ranged from a low of 3 to a high of 28; the average faculty size was 10, and the median 9 members.

A total of 47 new faculty appointments excluding deans and directors was reported for 1983–84 in 27 of the reporting schools. These included 26 men and 21 women. Appointments at the rank of Assistant Professor totaled 25 (11 men and 14 women). Completed doctorates were held by 7 of the men and 10 of the women. Of the 20 Assistant Professors appointed in U.S. schools, one was a minority person. The average salary for new Assistant Professors on academic year appointments was $23,722. Purcell noted the increasing disparity between the average salary for males ($24,170) and for females ($21,355) at that rank. When the salary comparison of new Assistant Professors was restricted to those holding the doctorate the disparity proved to be even more extreme, the seven men receiving an average salary of $26,778 and the 10 women $23,870.

Purcell noted the increase in promotions within professorial ranks from 23 in the 1982-83 report to 42 in 1983-84. Earned doctorates are held by 77.1 percent of the faculty in the reporting schools, 82.3 percent of the men, and 70.1 percent of the women. In 1977 only 69.3 percent of the men and 50.9 percent of the women full-time faculty held the doctorate, an overall increase of over 15 percent during the eight-year period. Reporting schools indicated that 67.8 percent of the 1983-84 full-time faculty were in tenured positions. (*See also* Association of Research Libraries; Women in Librarianship, Status of.)

Financial Support. For the income and expenditure section of the ALISE report 61 of the 67 schools with accredited programs provided usable data to Fred Roper, North Carolina at Chapel Hill. Funding for the 61 reporting schools for 1982-83 ranged from a high of $2,596,913 to a low of $212,030, with a mean of $666,334. This was a 9 percent increase over the 1981-82 average. However, Roper noted that 18 of the schools reported some decrease in income over the prior year. Eleven schools, nine in the U.S., reported incomes over $1,000,000, but the incomes of 38 of the schools were still under $600,000. The average income of the 22 schools supporting doctoral programs was reported to be $990,824, over twice the $483,288 average income of the 39 programs not offering the doctorate.

ACTIVITIES OF ORGANIZATIONS

CLR. The Council on Library Resources received a grant from the Andrew Mellon Foundation for the development of research library internships. CLR will offer support to research libraries on a competitive basis to develop internships for recent library school graduates.

The Michigan two-year specialization program for academic research librarianship, instituted in 1981 with a grant from CLR, received additional funding from the H. W. Wilson Foundation in 1984.

ARL. The Association of Research Libraries

Education, Library

Table 1. FTE Enrollments by Degree Programs as Reported by Schools with ALA Accredited Programs

Year (Fall Term)	Master's Programs		Sixth-Year Programs		Doctoral Programs	
	Schools Reporting	FTE	Schools Reporting	FTE	Schools Reporting	FTE
1979–80	63	6,234	35	145	25	312
1980–81	67	5,972	32	140	25	290
1981–82	69	5,820	37	149	24	304
1982–83	65	5,254	33	109	23	277
1983–84	64	5,515	30	122	23	290

Table 2. Degrees Awarded by Schools with ALA Accredited Programs

Year	Master's		Sixth-Year		Doctorate	
	Schools Reporting	Degrees Granted	Schools Reporting	Degrees Granted	Schools Reporting	Degrees Granted
1978–79	58	4,804	20	158	22	77
1979–80	64	4,670	20	60	26	66
1980–81	69	4,717	26	105	13	67
1981–82	64	4,023	20	50	23	74
1982–83	64	3,784	23	51	21	61

sponsored an Institute on Research Libraries for Library Educators. The three-week institute was funded by the Council on Library Resources and hosted by the University of North Carolina Libraries and School of Library Science at Chapel Hill. The 11 leaders in library education participating in the institute explored changes taking place in research libraries and the implication of these changes for library education.

OLPR. Beginning in 1980 the ALA Office for Library Personnel Resources, with the support of participating library schools, has sponsored a reception for prospective librarians at ALA Conferences and Midwinter meetings. During the year OLPR sought to evaluate the impact of the receptions through a questionnaire sent to guests who had attended. Since guests are recruited from paraprofessionals employed in libraries convenient to the conference or meeting site, it could be assumed that many would be geographically limited in their choice of library schools. The majority of the respondents who indicated that they were attending library school identified geographically accessible schools. Even so, the receptions have served to increase the awareness of the guests of the national characteristics of the profession and have provided visibility for the participating schools.

SCOLE. The ALA Standing Committee on Library Education appointed a Library Education Centennial task force to plan for the centennial of the opening of the first library school in January 1887 at Columbia University.

COA. The ALA Committee on Accreditation in 1984 approved continuing the accreditation of the master's degree programs at the following institutions: Catholic, Chicago, Columbia, Drexel, North Texas, Simmons, SUNY at Buffalo, Southern California, and Washington.

ALISE. The Association of Library and Information Science Education, under the leadership of Robert Stueart, Simmons, President, focused its January conference on educating information professionals for the future.

CLENE. Created as an independent organization in 1975, the Continuing Library Education Network and Exchange officially affiliated with the American Library Association as a Round Table.

Changes in Deans and Directors. New appointments to head accredited programs were Raymond Vondran, who moved from Acting Dean to Dean at Catholic, Lucienne Maillet at Long Island, Claude Walston at Maryland, Thomas Surprenant at Queens, Sarah Gibson at Case Western, Mary Lenox at Missouri, Ronald Wyllys from Acting Dean to Dean at Texas, John Wright at Alberta, Helen Howard at McGill, Ann Schabas at Toronto, and Jean Tague at Western Ontario. Of nine acting or interim deans or directors, four had held their acting or interim status for over a year. These changes meant that the leadership of approximately 25 percent of the accredited programs had changed during the year.

Awards and Honors. Library educators honored during the year included Lester Asheim, North Carolina at Chapel Hill, who was awarded ALA Honorary Life Membership. Jane Hannigan, Columbia, received the Beta Phi Mu Award for excellence in teaching. Ellis Mount, Columbia, received the Special Libraries Association John Cotton Dana Award in recognition of exceptional services to special librarianship. George D'Elia, Minnesota, received the ALA Library Research Round Table Development Award. Susan Artandi, Rutgers, received the American Society for Information Science Outstanding Information Science Teacher's Award.

Shirley Aaron, Florida State, was elected Vice President/President-elect of the American Association of School Librarians. Joan Atkinson, Alabama, was elected Vice President/President-elect of the ALA Young Adult Services Division. Brooke Sheldon, Texas Woman's, served as President of the American Library Association, and Gary Purcell, Tennessee, as President of the ALA Reference and Adult Services Division. Lois Bewley, British Columbia, was President of the Canadian Library Association.

Retirements. Lester Asheim, formerly on the faculty and Dean at Chicago and Director of the

ALA Office for Library Education and the International Relations Office, retired as Kenan Professor at North Carolina at Chapel Hill. Bernard Fry, who served as Dean at Indiana from 1968 to 1980, and Margaret Goggin, who was Dean at Denver from 1968 to 1979, retired. Agnes Reagan, who served on faculties at Emory, Syracuse, Illinois, and Texas, and as ALA Accreditation Officer, retired from the Texas faculty.

Deaths. Three former library school deans died during the year: Susan Grey Akers, North Carolina at Chapel Hill; Edgar Behymer, Long Island; and Virginia Lacy Jones, Atlanta. (See Obituaries.)

A. VENABLE LAWSON

REFERENCES

1. Kenneth E.Dowlin, *The Electronic Library: The Promise and the Process* (Neal-Schuman, 1984).
2. Association for Library and Information Science Education, *Library and Information Science Education Statistical Report, 1984* (ALISE, 1984).
3. Carol L. Learmont and Stephen Van Houten, "Placements & Salaries 1983: Catching Up," *Library Journal* (October 1, 1984).

ERIC

Documents. Almost 1,200 documents were announced in each issue of *Resources in Education* (RIE) during 1984. With the 14,247 documents processed during the year, the number of documents entered the database since its inception in 1966 totaled 240,323 at the end of 1984. The Educational Resources Information Center (ERIC) microfiche collection contains the full text of 95 percent of these documents, and individual copies are available on demand from the ERIC Document Reproduction Service in either microfiche or paper copy for 86 percent of these documents, or in microfiche only for the remaining 14 percent. EDRS distributed 14,441,068 microfiche on a subscription basis in 1984, and filled orders for individual ERIC documents totaling 1,748,882 pages of paper copy and 32,585 microfiche (each microfiche contains up to 96 pages).

The microfiche collection is also available for use in some 779 libraries and information centers that had complete or substantial collections of the ERIC microfiche in 1984. Access to the collection is provided by RIE, which has about 2,000 subscribers.

Journal articles indexed for CIJE totaled 18,836 in 1984 (an average of 1,570 per month), bringing the total number of articles announced in the database to 305,036 since the implementation of this service in 1969. Journals covered by CIJE are available through many libraries, and reprints of individual indexed articles are available from University Microfilms International for about 75 percent of the journals. There are about 1,800 subscribers to CIJE.

Database Activities. The final phase of the two-year Education Practice File project was completed September 30. The file developed by the project was tested in nine test sites across the country to determine its strengths and weaknesses in meeting the information needs of teachers and school administrators. Of the 563 searches conducted, over half were requested by K–12 teachers or school administrators. The top 10 types of materials requested (in rank order) were research summaries, research syntheses, curriculum guides, resources materials, learning activities, annotated bibliographies, promising practices, units of study, lesson plans, and handbooks. The project resulted in the development of the new Target Audience data element which is now being assigned on a regular basis to both selected documents and journal articles.

Two additional publication type codes were also added to both documents and articles in 1984, one for the actual listing of a computer program, the other to designate multi-lingual materials in which the full text appears in more than one language.

The ERIC Clearinghouse on Elementary and Childhood Education coordinates the ERIC Digests Online Project, a file of short reports prepared by the clearinghouses for online access via Edline on the The Source. Designed to provide educators, particularly policy makers, with current information on education, the file was expected to be available online in 1985. Access through other vendors in the future was to be explored.

Online Usage. The most recent data on online usage of the ERIC system available in 1984 from Infometrics, Inc. (fourth quarter of 1982), indicate that ERIC is the second most used database offered by both BRS and DIALOG; among all databases and all online vendors, ERIC ranks fourth in total connect time and twelfth in total revenues (partially because no royalty is paid for using ERIC). ERIC is the most used among the social science databases, with usage amounting to over three times that of the second most used: within academia, ERIC is the third most used; within public libraries, ERIC is the second most used; and within the not-for-profit community as a whole, ERIC is the fifth most used database.

Spin-offs of the system designed to make access to ERIC more convenient for the user without prior searching experience include two after-hours online services, DIALOG Information Services's "Knowledge Index" and Bibliographic Retrieval Service's "BRS After Dark." Other spin-offs are MICROsearch, a self-contained microcomputer system developed by the ERIC Clearinghouse on Information Resources for searching selected portions of the database (library/information science, educational technology, and several special topic database disks); EASYsearch from Renaissance Learning Systems, also a self-contained microcomputer system, which provides database disks of resources from the ERIC database for administrators and for teachers of science, foreign language, math, language arts, and social studies; and *Titles 1984—The Classroom Teacher's Guide to ERIC*, a catalog to the 869 books, teaching guides, learning guides, and other instructional publications added to ERIC in 1984.

Current Status. An information system funded through the U.S. Department of Education's National Institute of Education, ERIC is designed to provide access to the ephemeral literature of education, e.g., research reports, project descriptions, conference papers, curriculum guides, and program descriptions. Each of the 16 clearinghouses in the decentralized network collects and processes information on particular areas and aspects of education for inclusion in the ERIC database and announcement in the monthly index, *Resources in Education*. The information base provided by the ERIC documents is broadened by the indexing and announcement of articles selected from the more than 700 professional journals regularly monitored by the clearinghouses for another monthly index, *Current Index to Journals in Education*. The contents of these two indexes make up the ERIC database, which is available for online searching.

Although ERIC is being maintained at a reduced level of publication and service programs because of overall reductions in federal government spending, the clearinghouses in 1984 continued to be active in soliciting documents and processing them for the system. Emphasis on materials useful to practitioners and policy makers continues to be system policy.

BARBARA B. MINOR
DONALD P. ELY

FEDERAL LIBRARIANS ROUND TABLE

PRESIDENT (June 1984–July 1985):
Nina Jacobs, Travis Air Force Base, California

VICE-PRESIDENT/PRESIDENT-ELECT:
Elwynda K. Chapman, Bureau of Census Library, Washington, D.C.

SECRETARY:
Alice Roy, Base Library, Kirtland Air Force Base, New Mexico

Membership (August 31, 1984): 543 (441 personal; 102 organizational)
Expenditures (August 31, 1984): $2,985

Federal Librarians Round Table

Throughout 1984 members of the Federal Librarians Round Table (FLRT) continued their work on a variety of issues, including OMB's Circular A-76 which calls for the wholesale contracting-out of federal libraries; OPM's proposed classification and qualification standards for federal librarians; and federal information access/management policies. FLRT members developed Resolutions on A-76 and on the Department of Labor's pay schedules for certain classes of librarians. Both Resolutions were passed by ALA's Council. At its annual meeting in Dallas, Texas, in June the FLRT membership passed resolutions of thanks to NCLIS Commissioner Margaret S. Warden and to Representative Donald J. Albosta (D-MI) for their hard work on issues of concern to federal librarians everywhere.

FLIPI Committee. During the Dallas meeting, the Final Report of FLRT's Federal Library and Information Policy Issues (FLIPI) Task Force was presented to ALA's Executive Board for action. The Report contains specific recommendations for strengthening and clarifying the roles of library/information science associations when federal library and information policy issues are under debate, subject to change, or newly proposed. Two of FLIPI's recommendations were referred to ALA's Committee on Organization (COO) for implementation. The first calls for the development of formal coordination and action mechanisms so that reaction and debate on federal information matters will be more cohesive, structured and timely. FLIPI recommended that representatives from the Federal Library and Information Center Committee (FLICC), ALA, the Special Libraries Association (SLA) and NCLIS work together to develop such mechanisms. The second recommendation reinforces the first: it requires that a single agency or organization coordinate the community's responses on any one issue. During its Annual Meeting in Dallas, the FLRT Executive Board voted to replace the Task Force with a FLIPI Standing Committee. Patricia W. Berger, FLRT's Immediate Past President, chairs the Committee.

A-76 Task Force. FLRT's efforts on A-76 matters were many and varied. Chief among these was the preparation of an ALA statement on the contracting out of federal libraries which appears in the September, 1984, Hearings on contracting-out which were chaired by Representative Albosta. In addition, the Task Force wrote and contacted FLICC on several occasions to recommend the development of A-76 courses and seminars for federal librarians and the development of a detailed A-76 policy for the federal library community. Adelaide del Frate, FLRT's Director for 1984–87, chairs the Task Force.

Federal Standards Issue. Ellen Cook, Past-President of FLRT, chaired the ALA Task Force studying the controversial development of federal standards for librarians by the Office of Personnel Management (OPM). During ALA's Midwinter Meeting, FLRT's Board voted to pay the first 20 percent of a required fee ($925) to release the data that OPM used to develop the proposal standards. In February OPM announced that all standards development work would be suspended pending OPM's own internal review of its standards development process.

A motion passed at the annual FLRT meeting instructed its Executive Board to take action to persuade OPM to open the Librarian Register as soon as possible. The Board did act, as did other groups, and OPM's Librarian Register opened September 19–October 12, 1984.

NINA JACOBS

Films

The disruptions and problems in the noncommercial film field that characterized 1983 continued and were, if anything, exacerbated in 1984. It was the consensus of those working in the field that the underlying cause of change has been the videocassette revolution. Libraries were allocating more and more of their nonprint budgets to the purchase of videocassettes marketed at low prices to the home-consumer market. These cassettes cost a fraction of a 16mm film, and while they are not effective in programming, and, indeed, are illegal to show in branch programs, significant amounts of library budgets were going toward their purchase. A sizable 16mm market existed but for many distributors the drop in income put their operations in the red.

New Formulations and Mergers. The most

surprising merger of 1984 was the folding of Learning Corporation of America (LCA) into Coronet-Perspective Films. (LCA's production division remained independent.) LCA was the glamour distributor in the education field with its production standards considered to be the highest. It was usually the first choice among filmmakers when they were looking for a distributor and was also the hardest collection to get into. Coronet-Perspective, which had previously subsumed MTI (Motorola) Teleprograms and Centron Films, itself went through corporate change and has become part of the new Simon and Schuster Communications, owned by the Gulf and Western conglomerate. These mergers made Simon and Schuster the largest educational distributor in the U.S. For marketing purposes each of the companies retains its identity.

This type of merging has implications for libraries since it means that there will be fewer titles coming on to the market through normal distribution channels. It has led to more and more independent filmmakers going into self-distribution. It is almost impossible for the acquisition librarian to keep up with the output of these extremely small companies. One result has been that it has made the American Film Festival more important than ever since many little-known independent films turn up at that event.

Group Merges with EFLA. Reflecting the changes in the commercial film sector, the nonprofit organizational sector also went through changes. The Film Library Information Council (FLIC), which was formed in 1967 by film librarians from public libraries, decided to merge with the Education Film Library Association. FLIC's magazine *Film Library Quarterly* will merge with EFLA's *Sightlines*. In recent years FLIC found it increasingly difficult to fulfill its mandate to effectively promote film and video in libraries. FLIC was, for instance, finding that the seminars it once held regularly were becoming too costly to maintain. At the same time it was losing members as public libraries abolished or neglected to fill film librarian positions. New subscribers to the *Quarterly* came more and more from colleges and universities so that it became increasingly difficult for the magazine to hold on to its public library image. FLIC members decided at their annual meeting in New York in May that the most prudent course was to join with EFLA, which shares many of FLIC's goals.

Project to Update *Films on Art*. In a year marked by dislocation and upset, a project sponsored by two major institutions to achieve bibliographic control over an important subject area of film was a major event. The institutions were the Metropolitan Museum of Art and the J. Paul Getty Trust and the goal of their project, called the Program for Art on Film and Video, was to create a computerized catalog to inventory, describe, and index existing films and videotapes on the arts. In effect, it will update and vastly expand the basic reference book on art films, *Films on Art*, compiled in 1977 by the Canadian Centre for Films on Art for the American Federation of Arts and published by Watson-Guptill. Because of the development of database technology, the new compilation will be much more complex

Still from "Godzilla Meets Mona Lisa" directed by Ralph Arlyck. (Ralph Arlyck Films)

Left, Red Ribbon winning film "The Unorganized Manager, Part 1: Damnation" featured actor John Cleese as St. Peter and was shown at the Dallas Public Library as part of its annual program of American Film Festival Winners. Below, scene from "Strangers and Kin," directed by Herb Smith for Appalshop, examined stereotyping of hillbillies. (© Herb E. Smith)

Films

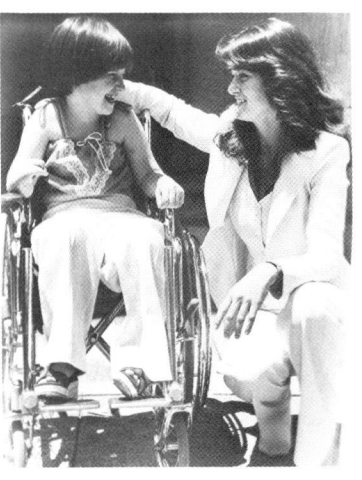 

Scenes from "The Secret Agent" directed by Jacki Ochs portray deforestation of Vietnam by American herbicides (top); toxicologists in Times Beach, Missouri, in 1983 (far right); and birth-defect victims of Vietnam veterans' families exposed to Agent Orange. (First Run Features)

and far broader in scope than the earlier project.

New MOMA Film Catalog. With the commercial sector of film hard pressed, it may be that the nonprofit sector may become more involved in needed projects. During 1984 the Museum of Modern Art in New York published a major source book on the history of film in its *Circulating Film Library Catalog*. The Film Library was established in 1935 and contains over 1,000 titles of films produced from 1894 to the present. The catalog includes full descriptions of the films with credits and interpretive essays on the silent film, the documentary, the European and American avant-garde, the National Film Board of Canada's documentaries and animation films and the British independents. (Inquiries about the availability of the catlaog should be directed to Publications Sales and Service, The Museum of Modern Art, 11 W. 53rd St., New York, NY 10019.)

American Film Festival. Perhaps the major film event of the year is the annual American Film Festival sponsored by the Educational Film Library Association and held each spring in New York. In May 1,700 librarians, distributors, and film and videomakers gathered together to view films and tapes at this largest educational film festival in the world. In spite of the competition from video, film still dominated the event with 724 films entered compared to 310 video entries. Nevertheless, video was up 10 percent over the preceding year and film entries were down by about the same amount.

Outstanding Films of the Year. The winner of the Festival's prestigious John Grierson Award given to the most talented new filmmaker went to a woman documentarian, Jacki Ochs for *The Secret Agent*, color, 56 minutes, a comprehensive report on the effects of the defoliant Agent Orange on the health of Vietnam War veterans. It is distributed by First Run Features, 153 Waverly Place, New York, 10014.

Other outstanding productions released in 1984 were:

Masculine Mystique, color, 86 minutes. Directed by John N. Smith and Giles Walker for the National Film Board of Canada. Distributor: National Film Board of Canada, 1251 Avenue of the Americas, New York, 10020.

This fictional work, which is crafted to look like a Film Board documentary, tells the absorbing story of a number of men taking group therapy together because they are having serious problems relating to the women in their lives. Includes some amusing role reversals in which the women are the dominant figure in the relationship.

Los Sures, color, 58 minutes. Directed by Diego Echeverria. Distributor: Terra Productions, 140 West End Ave., New York, 10023.

A hard-hitting look by an insider at one of the poorest Puerto Rican neighborhoods in Brooklyn.

Godzilla Meets Mona Lisa, color, 58 minutes. Directed by Ralph Arlyck. Distributor: Arlyck Films, 79 Raymond Ave., Poughkeepsie, 12601.

A witty, occasionally profound reflection upon the nature of museums and the processes of appreciating works of art. The film was shot at Pompidou Center and at the Louvre in Paris.

The Great Weirton Steel, color, 58 minutes. Directed by Catherine Pozzo di Borgo. Distributor: First Run Features, 153 Waverly Place, New York, 10014.

Presents the complex story of the takeover of the Weirton Steel company by the workers when the parent company decides to close down the plant.

Strangers and Kin, color, 58 minutes. Directed by Herb Smith for Appalshop. Distributor: Appalshop, P.O. Box 743, Whiteburg, Kentucky 41858.

The director, himself of Appalachian mountain stock, examines the stereotyping of the hillbilly image by the mass media.

Nisei Soldier: Standard Bearer for an Exiled People, color, 28 minutes. Directed by Loni Ding. Distributor: Vox Productions, 2335 Jones St., San Francisco, California 94115.

The story of the Japanese American troops in World War II who served the U.S. while their families were detained in internment camps. Makes extensive use of archival newsreel footage.

Hell's Kitchen Chronicle, color, 60 minutes. Directed by Reed and Maren Erskine. Distributor: Hell's Kitchen Chronicle Project, 361 West 36th St., New York, 10018.

An examination of "Hell's Kitchen," once one of New York's toughest neighborhoods but now in the process of transition as the affluent middle class move into reconditioned buildings, forcing the old residents to find housing elsewhere.

Joint Custody: A New Kind of Family, color, 85 minutes. Directed by Josephine Hayes Dean.

A valuable film on "co-parenting" in which divorced parents work out amicable ways to share in the care of their children after the divorce.

The House That Giacomo Built, color, 47 minutes. Directed by D. S. Pitkin. Distributor: D. S. Pitkin, 27 South Prospect St., Amherst, Massachusetts 01002.

This close examination by an American anthropologist of a rural Italian family reveals the changes that have come about in their life-style from 1951 to 1978 and how a higher standard of living has enhanced family relationships.

Great Branches, New Roots: The Hmong Family, color, 43 minutes. Directed by Rita LaDoux, Kathleen Laughlin, and Nancy Haley. Distributor: Hmong Film Project, 2258 Commonwealth Ave., Saint Paul, Minnesota 55108.

St. Paul and Minneapolis are host to one of the largest groups of Hmong refugees from Southeast Asia. The film follows their remarkably successful adjustment to their new homeland.

WILLIAM SLOAN

Films, Children's

Notable Children's Films. Twelve 16mm films suitable for children through age 14 were cited as Notable Children's Films by the Film Evaluation Committee of the Association for Library Service to Children, American Library Association. Titles selected were *Ballet Robotique* (Pyramid), *Clown of God* (Weston Woods), *Crac* (Pyramid), *Dudh Kosi: Relentless River of Everest* (Indiana University Audio Visual Center), *Itzhak Perlman: In My Case Music* (DeNonno Pix), *Katura and the Cat* (Perspective Films), *Morris's Disappearing Bag* (Weston Woods), *The Snowman* (Weston Woods), *The Sound Collector* (National Film Board of Canada), *Split Cherry Tree* (Learning Corporation of America), *What Energy Means* (National Geographic), and *Zea* (National Film Board of Canada). The Notables film list saturated the library press in 1984, appearing in *School Library Journal* in April, *Booklist* (May 1), and *Top of the News* (Spring). It is available as a separate list, which includes filmstrips and recordings from ALSC.

American Film Festival. At the 26th annual American Film Festival in New York City children's films won awards in the following categories:

Children's Entertainment:

Blue Ribbon—*Bearskin (or the Man Who Didn't Wash for Seven Years)*. Director: Tom Davenport. Distributor: Davenport Films.

Red Ribbon—*Sound of Sunshine, Sound of Rain*. Director: Caroline Heyward. Distributor: FilmFair Communications.

Elementary/Jr. High Instructional:

Blue Ribbon—*Library Report*. Director: Ron Underwood. Distributor: Barr Films.

Red Ribbon (Tie between)—*Henderson Avenue Bug Patrol*. Director: Allen and Cynthia Mondell. Distributor: Media Projects, Inc. *Strange Occurrence at Elm View Library*. Director: Thom Eberhardt. Distributor: FilmFair Communications.

Films appropriate for children were winners in other categories of competition as well, including the following titles:

Film as Art/Animation:

Blue Ribbon—*Monkeys Fishing the Moon*.

Stills from the 1984 Notable Children's Films list include (left) "Ballet Robotique" from Pyramid Films, and (bottom left) "The Clown of God" and "The Snowman" from Weston Woods.

Films, Children's

"Sound of Sunshine, Sound of Rain" distributed by FilmFair Communications won a Red Ribbon at the American Film Festival.

Animation and live action are combined in "The Henderson Avenue Bug Patrol" which tied for a Red Ribbon in the elementary/junior high instructional category at the American Film Festival. (Media Projects)

Producer: Shanghai Animation. Distributor: Distribution 16.

Literature:
Blue Ribbon—*Boys and Girls*. Director: D. McBrearty. Distributor: Beacon Films.

Social Studies:
Blue Ribbon—*Bread*. Director: Albert Kish. Distributor: Chbib Productions.

Sports and Leisure:
Blue Ribbon—*Dudh Kosi—Relentless River of Everest*. Producer: Aled Vaughn. Distributor: Audio Visual Center, Indiana University.

The Disabled:
Red Ribbon—*The Same Inside*. Director: Frank Vitale. Distributor: The March of Dimes.

Family Relations/Parenting:
Red Ribbon—*Oh, Boy! Babies!* Director: Gail Frank. Distributor: Learning Corporation of America.

In the video category productions suitable for children included the following titles:

Instructional-Elementary/High School:
Blue Ribbon—*My Mother the Witch*. Director: Sam Ellis. Distributor: Multimedia Entertainment.

Red Ribbon (Tie between)—*Out & About: Maintaining Friends*. Director: Ed Jakober. Distributor: Agency for Instructional TV. *Tight Times* (Reading Rainbow Series). Director: Larry Lancit. Distributor: Great Plains National.

Mental Health/Guidance:
Red Ribbon—*Rosie*. Director: Tom Robertson. Distributor: Multimedia.

Council on International Nontheatrical Events (Cine):
Among the films for children selected as Cine Golden Eagle titles for submission as American entries in international film events were a number of films suitable for children. They include the following titles: *Adventures of Bunny Rabbit*, *American Storytelling: Michael Parent*, *Animal Babies*, *Boy to Man* (2nd Revision), *The Boy Who Cried Wolf*, *Curious George*, *Doctor De Soto*, *Girl to Woman* (2nd Revision), *Hardlucky*, *I'm Not Oscar's Friend Anymore*, *Oh, Boy! Babies!*, *The Pied Piper of Hamelin*, *A Single Light*, *Then One Year* (Revised), *Three Fox Fables*, *The Thrill of It All*, *Why Mosquitoes Buzz in People's Ears*, and *Winnie the Pooh and a Day for Eeyore*. International honors were received by Cine submissions in many film festivals around the world. *Ballet Robotique* was named in over 12 festivals. Other films of interest to children which were cited frequently were *Bearskin*, *Ben's Dream*, *Clown of God*, *Curious George Goes to the Hospital*, and *Morris's Disappearing Bag*. American children's films made particularly strong showings at the second International Youth Festival in Brussels, Seventh MIFED "The Child in Our Times" International Film Competition in Milan, and the Seventh Kinderkino (Festival of Children's Films) in Oberhausen, Germany, and the Fifth International Festival of Cinema for Children and Youth in Tomar, Portugal. *Ben's Dream* was an award film in Zagreb's Sixth World Festival of Animated Films.

Other Awards. A film about childhood remembered, Ingmar Bergman's *Fanny and Alexander*, was nominated for best director awards for 1983 by both the Directors Guild and the Academy of Motion Picture Arts and Sciences. It won Academy Oscars for best foreign language film, best cinematography, costume design, and art direction.

Other Academy Award nominations went to *Never Cry Wolf* and *Return of the Jedi*. The latter won a special achievement award for visual effects.

A film featuring children, *In the Nuclear Shadow: What Can the Children Tell Us?*, was nominated in the documentary short subject category.

In other Academy Award categories, films for children were cited. Disney's *Mickey's Christmas Carol* and *Sound of Sunshine, Sound of Rain* were nominated for best animated short film.

A film about a girl coping with woman's role stereotyping, *Boys and Girls*, won the Academy Award for best live action short film.

Jacque d'Amboise's *He Makes Me Feel Like*

Dancin', about the National Dance Institute for children, won the Oscar for best feature length documentary.

The 36th annual Emmy awards for network television programming presented several films for or concerning children with major awards.

Outstanding Drama Special went to *Something About Amelia*, a film on incest which also received an Emmy for writing and for supporting actress in a limited series or special.

The Outstanding Children's Program award went to *He Makes Me Feel Like Dancin'*. The Outstanding Animated Program Emmy went to *Garfield on the Town*.

George Foster Peaboy awards for distinguished broadcast programming were presented to the CBS program *What Have We Learned, Charlie Brown* and NBC's showing of *He Makes Me Feel Like Dancin'*.

The Human Family Institute, which presents the Humanitas Prize annually for television programs that affirm human dignity or communicate human values, announced two new $10,000 prizes to be given next year, one for animated programs for children and the other for live-action children's programs.

American Center of Films for Children. The 13th International Children's Film Festival in Los Angeles sponsored by The American Center of Films for Children awarded Ruby Slipper Awards to children's films in two categories. The children's jury selected the following films:

Best Animated Short: *Doctor DeSoto*
Best Live Action Short: *Oh, Boy! Babies!*
Best Feature: *A Minor Miracle*

The Adults' jury selected the following films:
Best Animated Short (Tie between): *Doctor DeSoto; Sound of Sunshine, Sound of Rain*.
Best Live-Action Short: *Oh, Boy! Babies!*
Special Award for Outstanding Documentary Feature for Children: *He Makes Me Feel Like Dancin'*.

In addition to presenting the Film Festival, the Center conducts regular screenings of children's features and short films for its members and children's groups. A screening program in cooperation with the Los Angeles County Public Library System was established, and a brief course on the Creative Use of Media for teachers and other adults was presented at UCLA's Education Extension Division.

The Center acted as the selector for American entries to the Tenth Muse Contest, a competition for films made by young people between the ages of 6 and 25, to be held in Vienna in 1985. The competition is organized by the International Centre of Films for Children and Young People and in 1985 celebrates the "International Year of the Young" with a contest theme of "Development, Participation, and Peace."

Media Center for Children. The New York City based Media Center for Children (MCC) conducted a telephone survey, funded by the New York State Council on the Arts, among 75 New York State museums to determine how museums use media. An information director was hired to expand services at MCC, including the operation of a telephone reference service, The *Children's Media Information Hotline* (212-689-0300), which started operation on Tuesdays and Thurs-

Scene from "Strange Occurrence at Elm View Library," a FilmFair Communications film, tied for an American Film Festival Red Ribbon in 1984. *(FilmFair Communications)*

Megan Follows as Margaret in the film drama "Boys and Girls" from the Rainbow Series that won an Academy Award for best live action short film. *(Atlantis Television International, Inc.)*

Blue Ribbon winner at the American Film Festival, "Monkeys Fishing on the Moon," was produced by the Shanghai Animation Studio, People's Republic of China. *(Distribution Sixteen)*

"Dudh Kosh—Relentess River of Everest" won a Blue Ribbon at the American Film Festival in the sports and leisure category.
(Audio-Visual Center, Indiana University)

days. The information director also assists in the computerization of MCC's collection of film annotations and referral listings of consultants, distributors, filmmakers and organizations and assumed responsibility for MCC's film evaluation program and for its quarterly publication, Young Viewers.

Theatrical Films. The year was not distinguished for feature films for children. Disney re-released The Jungle Book early in the year and Pinocchio for the first time in six years in December. The Neverending Story, based on Michael Ende's internationally best-selling novel, particularly admired by German peace activists and environmentalists, was turned into a fairy tale with themes of positive thinking and imagination. The visual effects enchant children, even though film critics were disdainful and the plot is full of holes. Librarians will appreciate the film's celebration of the book. The film was the most expensive production in the history of German cinema. The Muppets Take Manhattan brought the furry troupe to Broadway and Miss Piggy married universally beloved Kermit the frog.

The Karate Kid, a kind of "Rocky" for adolescents, features a teenager who prevails over the bullies at his high school with the help of his karate teacher, Mr. Miyagi. The chemistry between the Italian American boy from New Jersey and his Japanese American mentor was repeatedly cited for contributing to the success of the film with its audience.

Parents' Choice film reviewer Charles Champlin cited these and the following additional films as of interest to younger viewers in 1984: The Right Stuff, Testament, Star Trek III: The Search for Spock, Cloak and Dagger (starring Henry Thomas of E.T.), Heart Like a Wheel, Splash, Careful He Might Hear You, The Ballad of Gregorio Cortez, Educating Rita, Les Compreres, This Is Spinal Tap, Repo Man, The Last Starfighter, and Ghostbusters.

Science fiction and fantasy films for teenage viewers and others looking for light entertainment dominated the market in 1984. In addition to the films already mentioned, titles included Greystoke, The Legend of Tarzan, Lord of the Apes, Runaway, Starman, 2010, Supergirl, and Dune.

PG-13 Rating. Indiana Jones and the Temple of Doom and Gremlins, both films directed or produced by Steven Spielberg, also part of the science fiction/fantasy trend, were attacked for their gratuitous violence and sadism and led to the new PG-13 rating category for feature films.

Criticism of the rating system of the Motion Picture Association of America, a trade association of large movie companies, had been mounting in recent years. The rating code had not been changed in the 16 years since its initiation and PG and R had become the only functional categories by 1983. Of 342 films rated that year, 123 received PG ratings and 207 were rated R.

Scenes of violence in Indiana Jones, which received a PG rating, caused an outcry for an intermediate category that would fall between PG (parental guidance) and R (restricted to those under age 17 without a parent or adult guardian). In response to criticism of Indiana Jones, Spielberg joined Barry Diller, then Chairman of Paramount Pictures, in recommending a restricted category for children under the age of 13. Despite the objections of Jack Valenti, President of the Motion Picture Association of America, a consensus was reached: a new category, PG-13, came into existence in late June. The new category advises rather than restricts. "Parents are strongly cautioned to give special guidance for attendance of children under 13. Some material may be inappropriate for young children." Religious and other groups worried that the new rating would only weaken the system and lead to unsuitable materials finding their way into the PG-13 category. Many had hoped that the new rating system would be restrictive rather than advisory. Parents have unsuccessfully sued for rigorous enforcement of the age level restrictions by theater owners, but exhibitors have continued to insist that ratings are only an advisory service for parents.

Walt Disney Productions. By the end of the year a domino effect had occurred in Hollywood's executive suites as chairmen and presidents changed companies. According to the *New York Times* more changes had taken place in a six–week period than during any similar time period in the last 40 years. The most interesting development for consumers of children's films was the changes in management at Walt Disney Productions and their implications for increased production and increased availability of old children's productions.

After suffering disastrous movie failures in 1983 with *Tron* and *Something Wicked This Way Comes*, Disney in 1984 fought off two divisive takeover attempts, experienced flagging attendance at its theme parks, suffered from the expense of establishing the promising new Disney pay cable station, and experienced a strike by employees at Disneyland.

Some success was realized under former chief Ron Miller, Walt Disney's son-in-law. The 1983 rerelease of *Snow White* caused it to become the 50th most successful picture of all time in American theaters. In 1984 *The Jungle Book* and *Pinocchio* were rereleased and Donald Duck celebrated his 50th birthday. Seven sets of short cartoon classics sold well in the home video market and "marginal" animated features were being considered for similar release.

Production of animated films was being stepped up with a goal of releasing a new feature every 18 months. A new label, Touchstone, was developed to overcome the resistance of teenagers to the Disney name. It was expected that perhaps half of Disney's projected six to eight movies a year would be released under the new label with PG ratings. The first Touchstone film, *Splash*, the love story of a man and a beautiful mermaid, released in the spring, became Disney's first real hit in years. It also received favorable reviews.

Despite the promising new directions he had taken, Ron Miller was forced by Disney Productions to resign. In September Michael Eisner, the second in command from Paramount Pictures, Hollywood's most financially successful movie studio, was hired as Chairman. A new President, Frank Wells, from Warner Brothers, joined the company, and Jeffrey Katzenberg, former head of production at Paramount, became head of Disney's movie and television division. Arthur Rockwell, Vice-President at MGM/UA and a former movie industry analyst, said, "Three high-powered executives going to Disney clearly signifies Disney's intention of being a major studio."

The new management announced plans to syndicate old Disney television shows, develop new cartoon characters for licensing and put the old characters into contemporary situations in new films, create a children's television show, and increase movie productions from the present 3 a year to 12 to 15. The old management had warehoused the most successful children's films for release every seven years to a new generation of children. The new management seems willing to consider releasing classics like *Pinocchio* on television or in home video format. An additional note of encouragement for Disney watchers who value imagination and originality in children's films comes from the report that film innovators, George Lucas, Steven Spielberg, and Jim Henson actively lobbied for Eisner to get the job at Disney.

There is always a time lag before new management can begin production on new properties. In the meantime several promising projects were under way. The film *Baby* was being filmed in Africa. Described as a mixture of *Raiders of the Lost Ark* and *Dumbo*, it involves a couple who try to save a still extant family of dinosaurs.

Another film in production is a live action sequel to *The Wizard of Oz*—Dorothy returns to the Emerald City to save her friends from the Nome King and wicked witch Mombi and meets the appealing mechanical man Tik Tok. A long awaited animated feature, *The Black Cauldron* based on Lloyd Alexander's award winning books and described as the most complex and expensive animated feature ever produced by Disney, was scheduled for release in summer 1985. According to comments by Ron Miller, the sinister villain in the movie might cause it to be the first Disney cartoon to get a PG rating.

A report by the National Coalition on Television Violence observed that cartoons on the year-old Disney pay television network were almost as violent as the Saturday morning cartoon shows on the commercial television networks. Only 27 percent of the cartoons and 68 percent of the other shows on Disney family cable television were rated "appropriate for children" after studies of 50 hours of programming during a two-month period. The group found an average of 19.3 violent acts per hour in the cartoons and 9.1 violent acts an hour in Disney's non-cartoon programming.

Box Office. *E.T. The Extra-Terrestrial* became Japan's all-time box office success in late 1983. *Ghostbusters* was the runaway hit in the U.S. in 1984. The only big hit that was generally appropriate for children was *The Karate Kid*, but older

Scene from "My Mother the Witch," a Blue Ribbon winner at the American Film Festival in the video category. (Multimedia Entertainment)

Films, Children's

children were no doubt interested in such top grossing titles as *Splash, Star Trek: The Search for Spock, Romancing the Stone, Police Academy, Purple Rain,* the violent *Indiana Jones and the Temple of Doom, Gremlins,* and *Beverly Hills Cop,* with Eddie Murphy.

New Film Formats and Implications. In an article in *Top of the News* (Spring 1984), "Recent Trends in Children's Films," Robert Grover made a timely observation. Because nearly all major film distributors market their products in 16mm as well as 3/4-inch and 1/2-inch videocassette formats, "it is quite apparent . . . that the term film must be expanded to include video as well as the 16mm format; we must think of the generic film as motion pictures available in numerous formats, including videocassettes, videotapes, and videodiscs."

It has long been recognized that productions made for theatrical release or for network television and cable television would someday be available for library markets. This process seems to be accelerating because of the popularity of home video formats, and material from educational producers is also being issued on video. Weston Woods, one of the most important distributors to educational markets, has begun to make many of its films based on children's books available in 1/2-inch home video formats. The increase in popularity of home video has raised several interesting issues.

One of the immediate concerns was about restrictions against use of commercial or theatrical productions of home video for public showings in libraries. Although many videos from educational producers can be used in libraries for scheduled group showings, commercial producers allow only impromptu small group showings and require special contractual arrangements before an institution has the right to use home video for public programs. The legal situation will remain unclear until a test case is brought.

Another issue that concerned libraries in 1984 was the circulation of R rated films in home video formats to borrowers under age 17. Philip Levering, head of Audiovisual Services, Suffolk Cooperative Library System, New York, strongly recommended in *The Bookmark* (Fall 1983) that librarians restrict the loan of R-rated video to borrowers with adult cards.

The ALA Council passed a new "Interpretation of the Library Bill of Rights" at the Annual Conference in regard to circulation of motion pictures and video productions to minors to become part of the *ALA Intellectual Freedom Manual.* It points out that libraries must be very cautious about using MPAA rating codes as a basis for deciding whether to circulate films and video disks or cassettes to minors. ALA Counsel advised that the MPAA codes have no standing in law and cannot be used legally as a standard for permitting or prohibiting viewing or use. Librarians are advised that state statutes vary widely on denying minors access to materials constitutionally available to adults. It is the state statutes—not the ratings—which must be consulted in setting circulation policy. *Voice of Youth Advocates* in the October issue further pointed out that affixing MPAA ratings codes to motion pictures or video productions is "labeling" and is considered "an attempt to prejudice attitudes." (See "Statement on Labeling," *Intellectual Freedom Manual,* ALA, 1983.)

The other side of this issue is that removing MPAA ratings from containers can be considered expurgating them similar to removing publishers' age-level recommendations from books. After four states introduced bills to require video store owners to label cassettes with the MPAA ratings, store owners began work on a voluntary system of self-policing with the help of the MPAA to prevent a patchwork confusion of local laws. Soon most cassettes and disks will probably be manufactured with MPAA ratings premarked on packages.

Another concern of librarians was that the economy and convenience of video formats would lead to the demise of 16mm films. Film experts presently refer to the loss of visual quality and aesthetics in transferring from film to video because of the different proportions of film and video, and in depth of field. (See Levering's article.) In addition a *Media and Methods* editorial (October 1984) described a decline in student performance when the Glenview (Illinois) School District converted from 16mm to video and an improvement when the District returned to 16mm. The consensus in 1984 seemed to be that both 16mm and videocassettes were important.

Amid the questions one thing is certain, more and more film will be available on video cassettes. By 1983 a typical movie earned 13 percent of its revenues from cassettes and disks, according to Wertheim & Company, a New York investment banking house. The video cassette recorder is not only triumphing over the videodisk player but is challenging pay-cable movie channels as a way of seeing movies. By the end of 1984, estimates placed the number of video cassette recorders in U.S. homes at 17,000,000 or 18,000,000, three times more than the highest estimate made two years previously. A survey by the A.C. Neilsen Company showed that 70 percent of video cassette recorder owners rent films on cassettes and 24 percent buy them. The January decision by the Supreme Court that home taping for later viewing did not violate existing copyright laws was seen by Arthur Morowitz, President of New York's Video Shack chain, as encouraging home purchase of video cassette recorders. Furthermore, theater owners seem no longer to be anxious about video cassettes' negative impact on theater going. Some theaters are even selling cassettes.

Films Based on Literature. In addition to titles mentioned earlier, children's literature turned into film or in production in 1984 included Barbara Robinson's *The Best Christmas Pageant Ever* and Robert Tallon's *Latouse My Moose* for ABC television; Alexander Key's *Escape to Witch Mountain* and *Return to Witch Mountain* for Disney's cable channel; Stephanie Tolan's *The Great Skinner Strike* as *Mom's on Strike* for an ABC Afterschool Special; John Masefield's fantasy *The Box of Delights,* Katherine Paterson's *Bridge to Terabithia,* and Virginia Hamilton's *The House of Dies Drear,* for PBS "Wonderworks"; Marlene Shyer's *Welcome Home,*

Jellybean, and Barbara Dana's *Zucchini* for CBS television; S.E. Hinton's *That Was Then, This Is Now* for theatrical release.

Other intriguing productions include the reports that Steven Spielberg is contemplating a remake of *Peter Pan* and that Francis Ford Coppola is directing an hour long video production of *Rip Van Winkle* for Shelley Duvall's Faerie Tale Theatre for Showtime Cable.

Tom Davenport's "From the Brothers Grimm: American Versions of Folktale Classics," including *The Frog King, Bearskin, Hansel and Gretel, Rapunzel, Rapunzel, Bristlelip, The Goose Girl* and the two-part *Jack and the Dentist's Daughter*, were broadcast on educational television stations in spring 1984 through the Public Broadcasting Service.

Publications of Interest. George W. Woolery, *Children's Television: The First Thirty Years, 1946-1981, Part I. Animated Cartoon Series.* (Scarecrow Press, 1983, $27.50).

"Films, Young People and Libraries," a reprint of the *Top of the News*, Spring 1984, special theme issue, which includes 11 articles, filmographies, and bibliographies, available from the Association for Library Service to Children, ALA Headquarters, $6.50.

Stuart Fischer, *Kid's TV: The First 25 Years* (Facts On File, $12.95 paper), looks at classic and popular children's programs from 1947 through 1972.

Lynn Minton of McCall's Magazine, *Movie Guide for Puzzled Parents* (Delacorte Press, $19.95).

Pre-School Films, a special issue of *Young Viewers* annotating 124 short 16mm films that have been successfully tested with preschool children; suggestions for related follow-up activities. Available from Media Center for Children, 3 West 29th Street, New York, N.Y. 10001. $7.50 prepaid.

Philip J. Sleeman, Bernard Queenan, and Francilia Butler, *200 Selected Film Classics for Children of All Ages: Where to Obtain Them and How to Use Them*, includes suggestions for programming and classroom use (Springfield, Ill. Charles C. Thomas Co., $19.75 paper).

MARILYN BERG IARUSSO

Freedom to Read Foundation

Libel Case. Contrary to predictions and Orwellian premonitions, 1984 was a good year for the Freedom to Read Foundation. First, librarians, booksellers and publishers were victorious in the case of *Janklow* v. *The Viking Press, et al.* in their effort to limit the chilling effect of libel litigation on the distribution of books and information materials. The case, a $24,000,000 libel suit filed by South Dakota governor William J. Janklow against the publisher and author of *In the Spirit of Crazy Horse* and three South Dakota booksellers, was dismissed by the trial court in the spring.

In its *amicus curiae* brief, the Foundation challenged the use of libel actions as a means of enforcing prepublication censorship. The Foundation's argument that booksellers should not be held liable for the mere republication of an allegedly defamatory statement of a public figure focused on the potential effect on librarians and other distributors of information and ideas, and the potential stress to the First Amendment rights of the public.

South Dakota Circuit Court Judge Gene Paul Kean dismissed not only the booksellers' but the entire action on the basis that the statements Governor Janklow contended were libelous were not, in fact, defamatory. Under the concept of "neutral reportage," a party is not liable if the statement of another party is accurately reported.

In August, learning that Governor Janklow was planning to appeal the trial court decision, the Foundation Board of Trustees agreed to continued support of the booksellers. A second *amicus curiae* brief was filed in November in the South Dakota Supreme Court.

School Litigation. In the school arena, 1984 saw the successful conclusion of two related students' rights suits in Minnesota. Partially funded by the Foundation and litigated by the Minnesota Civil Liberties Union, both cases concerned the right of students to hear outside speakers in Minnesota elementary and secondary schools. *Stark v. School District No. 1* involved speakers on "alternative life styles"; this case was voluntarily dismissed. *Stark v. Osseo School District* challenged a school board decision that prevented Matthew Stark, Minnesota Civil Liberties Union Executive Director, from speaking at the Osseo High School. The case was settled with a directive to the school district to adopt a new policy consistent with First Amendment guarantees of free speech.

In another school related action, the Foundation supported a lawsuit against the Evergreen (Washington) School District. The suit, *Marian English, et al.* v. *Evergreen School District, et al.*, involved the removal of over 30 books from district school libraries, without notice to parents and students, without opportunity for a hearing, and in direct violation of the school district's policies. By the time the Foundation Board of Trustees met at its annual meeting in June, all but one book had been returned to the shelves of the Evergreen schools. Plaintiffs and attorneys were working with the school board to ensure that similar violations would not occur in the future.

NSA Challenge. On February 15 the long awaited suit challenging the security classification practices and policies of the National Security Agency (NSA) was filed on behalf of the American Library Association, the District of Columbia Library Association, the Virginia Library Association, and other historical and research organizations, in cooperation with the American Civil Liberties Union Foundation National Security Project. The suit challenges the constitutionality of NSA's removal of classified and unclassified documents from public access. The documents consist of letters of William F. Friedman, a pioneer in cryptology and one of the agency's top code breakers. Several of the letters were mentioned by James Bamford in *The Puzzle Palace*, a highly critical account of NSA. While this case was far from settled in 1984, the very act of filing it impelled the NSA to remove classification designations from most of the materials challenged and to return them to open access.

Pornography as Civil Rights Violation. The fi-

Friends of Libraries

nal major issue that the Foundation dealt with in 1984 involved an Indianapolis ordinance that characterizes pornography as a type of civil rights violation that denies women equal opportunities in society. This ordinance, similar to one vetoed twice in late 1983 by Minneapolis mayor Don Frazer, was litigated in the case of *American Booksellers Association et al. v. William Hudnut, et al.* The case was filed in early May; hearings on the constitutionality of the ordinance were held in Indianapolis on July 30 before U.S. District Court Judge Sarah Evans Barker.

The complaint filed by the plaintiffs, of which the Foundation is one, argued that the ordinance was unconstitutional, void, and of no effect in that it goes beyond the standard for obscenity established by the United States Supreme Court; imposes an unconstitutional prior restraint; is unconstitutionally vague; and unconstitutionally restrains access to First Amendment-protected materials. Because library collections in all Indianapolis libraries and, by implication, in all libraries throughout the state of Indiana, would be affected if this ordinance were to become effective, the Indiana Library Association and the Indiana Library Trustee Association filed an *amicus curiae* brief on behalf of the plaintiffs.

On November 19 Judge Barker held that the Indianapolis ordinance was an unconstitutional attempt to regulate speech protected by the First Amendment. In December the defendants made known their intention to appeal Judge Barker's decision. The notice of appeal was filed on December 19. It was anticipated at year's close that the case would be argued in 1985 in the U.S. Court of Appeals for the Seventh Circuit in Chicago.

A Look Back. In his final report to the ALA Council outgoing Foundation President William D. North took a few moments of personal privilege to look back over the years of his association with the foundation. He said:

"Today, the Freedom to Read Foundation has become what it was intended to be when it was created a decade and a half ago—the action arena of libraries and librarians in support of intellectual freedom. It is credible, it is experienced, it is influential, and it is unafraid to attack censorship and suppression in any form or forum.

"The Foundation exists because of one inescapable reality—the only legal rights we have under the First Amendment or any other law are those we are able and willing to assert or defend. Without resources to defend our rights, they cannot exist; without the will to assert our rights, they will be usurped . . . .

"There is no final victory in the war against censorship. There is only continuing vigilance and commitment to the predicate of a free society. In the end, the Freedom to Read Foundation is your best—and possibly, your only—insurance policy."

JUDITH F. KRUG

Friends of Libraries

Friends of Libraries U.S.A. (FOLUSA) celebrated its 5th birthday during the 1984 ALA Conference in Dallas—a full-circle anniversary since the organization was initiated there at the 1979 Conference.

Sandy Dolnick, FOLUSA's founding President, Robert Wedgeworth, Executive Director of the America Library Association, and Joan Hood of the University of Illinois Library, Urbana, were incorporators of the organization that began with a five-member interim Board: Dolnick, Hood, Cecil Young, James Houck, and Richard Cruce. After adopting bylaws and a constitution the Board increased its size to 12 directors and then 20 to ensure representation of various types of libraries—public, academic, and special—as well as geographic areas of the country.

During its five years membership increased to nearly 1,000, most of whom represent Friends organizations.

Meetings and Activities. FOLUSA participated in the 1984 Tournament of Roses parade in Pasadena, California, where the Baskin Robbins Company float saluted Friends of Libraries U.S.A. and Library Friends volunteers throughout the country. Sandy Dolnick rode the float honoring Friends.

At the Midwinter Meeting, FOLUSA cosponsored a forum with the Center for the Book at the Library of Congress on "Winning Ideas for Friends Groups." Speakers included: Frederick G. Ruffner, who discussed his citizens advocacy group, which has as its goal enlisting increased support for libraries from decision makers at state and local levels. The Council also sponsors a statewide Book and Author Festival and a literary seminar in Key West each January.

Pamela Darling, of the Columbia University School of Library Service, described preservation needs for library collections and ways in which Friends could help. Don Fadden, Past-President of Pennsylvania Citizens for Better Libraries, discussed a successful essay contest conducted by PCBL in 1982 and explained how the essay contest demonstrates the value of libraries to legislators and other citizens.

John Cole, Executive Director of the Center for the Book of the Library of Congress described the oral history projects sponsored by the Center and pointed out that the idea can be applied easily at the community level.

Joan Hood discussed the purpose of the national Friends organization and observed that one of its goals is to help form local Friends groups by sharing useful information and ideas and to strengthen useful information and ideas and to strengthen existing groups through FOLUSA's publications another projects. Its quarterly newsletter *National Notebook*, published by Brodart, Inc., at no cost to FOLUSA, provides a wealth of information for Friends groups throughout the country.

The June 1984 Dallas Friends meeting included a celebration on the steps of the Dallas Public Library celebrating FOLUSA's 5th birthday. Wally Amos, entrepreneur and supporter of libraries, organized the event, attended by Mayor Starke Taylor of Dallas, FOLUSA's President, directors, and representatives of Friends groups throughout the United States. The Dallas Public Library's staff aided in the organization. Rosalyn Carter was guest speaker at the annual luncheon. She discussed her book *First Lady from Plains*.

A Friends program meeting on "Paths to Power: Friends, a Valuable Asset" involved participants in several discussion groups; they emphasized starting and sustaining successful Friends groups, fund-raising projects, legislation and advocacy, publicity and public relations, volunteers, and relationships among directors, trustees, and Friends.

Awards. The 1984 FOLUSA awards to outstanding Friends groups were presented to: the Friends of the Thomas Branigan Memorial Library, Las Cruces, New Mexico; Friends of the Salt Lake City Public Library; State University of New York at Albany Library Friends; and Friends of the North Carolina Public Libraries.

FREDERICK G. RUFFNER, JR.

President Barbara Kerney (right) of Friends of the Huntington Beach (California) Library and Chair of the Allied Arts Board Marilynn Tom at an artists' reception at the library.

Display rack holds newsletter OPENERS provided by the Friends of the Topeka Public Library.

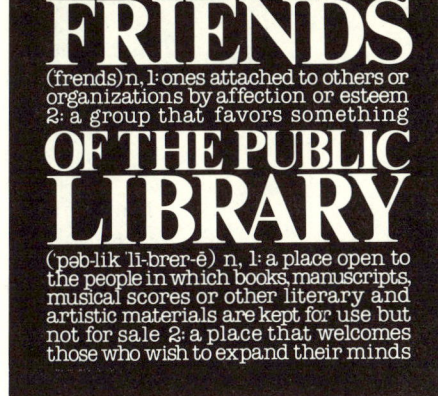

This design can be customized to include the name of any library and can be obtained from the Griendling Line, 144 Barbara Circle, Elizabeth, Kentucky, 42701.

Janet Leigh discusses her book There Really Was a Hollywood at a book and author dinner sponsored by the Memphis Friends of the Library. (Janet McClure)

The "What My Library Means to Me" essay contest sponsored by the Friends of the Newton Free Library elicited hundreds of entries. Many of the children attended this Awards Announcement Party.

Rosalyn Carter talked about books and politics at the Friends of Libraries U.S.A. luncheon at the ALA Annual Conference in Dallas. (American Libraries)

Gifts, Bequests, Endowments

A wide variety of gifts were placed in libraries during 1984. They ranged from a $1,000,000 gift to single volumes, rare and not so rare. There were some early manuscripts, several large collections of papers and substantial additions to the field of music.

Music. In memory of his late wife Blanche, Irving Laurie gave $200,000 to the Rutgers University Music Library. General improvements, including additional acquisitions, will be made to the Music Library and it will be renamed the Blanche and Irving Laurie Music Library. Paul E. Bierley gave the Music Library of the University of Kansas, Lawrence, a collection of over 500 78rpm recordings of military and concert bands. The records are from the first three decades of the 20th century and include a "unique 1902 test pressing of a Sousa Band recording" manufactured in Montreal.

The music library at UCLA, using funds provided by the Henry J. Bruman Educational Foundation, acquired the *Dictionary of American Hymnology: First Line Index*. This reference work, in microform, indexes first line citations to more than 120,000 separate hymns "from denominations as various as the Defenseless Mennonites, the General Six-Principle Baptists, and the Shakers, as well as the more established Protestant, Catholic and Jewish sects."

Friends of the University of Tennessee Library made it possible for that Library to acquire a third collection of Grace Moore materials. This new collection is "rich in correspondence, scripts, scores, photographs and scrapbooks" and amounts to more than 3,000 pieces. The late Ellen Winston established the Sanford Richard Winston Music Collection at the North Carolina State University Library as a memorial to her husband. In addition, "she also bequeathed her personal library as well as a beautiful piano that will be used by the Student Center."

The manuscripts of Bernard Herrmann (1911–1975) were received by the University of California, Santa Barbara. He composed music for such films as *Journey to the Center of the Earth*, *Fahrenheit 451*, *Taxi Driver*, *Vertigo*, *North by Northwest*, *The Trouble with Harry*, *Psycho*, and *Citizen Kane*.

The Trustee of the Cole Porter Estate, Robert Kimball, presented to Yale's American Musical Theatre Collection the manuscript of Porter's song "Let's Fall in Love" (later known as "Let's Do It, Let's Fall in Love") and the set of parts and conductor's score used in the original production of the musical *Gay Divorcée*.

The Music Library at the University of Colorado, Boulder, received a collection of sheet music which includes a copy of every piece of music published by the Tolbert R. Ingram Publishing Company of Denver. The company was active early in the 20th century and published popular music, much of which dealt with Denver and Colorado.

Laurence Witten gave Yale University a fine copy of Giambattista Marino's *Diciere Sacra* (Venice, 1626), Part Two of which is devoted to music. It is one of two known copies, the other being in the British Library. Cecilia Drinker Saltonstall, Stratham, New Hampshire, gave the Music Library at the University of Pennsylvania a large wooden cabinet once owned by Ludwig van Beethoven. The wardrobe "was a part of the furnishings in his Vienna home until his death in 1828."

Grant. The Pew Memorial Trust, Philadelphia, "earmarked $1,000,000 of a $2,000,000 grant to Columbia University for the automation of the catalog." Columbia has chosen the BLIS system and has been testing it; this grant will allow them to proceed with implementation.

Ruth Case, widow of the late United States senator from New Jersey, gave $50,000 to the Rutgers University Libraries. The money will be used by the Department of Special Collections and Archives "to develop a guide to their political papers and to implement an automated archives/manuscript management system."

George W. and Mildred K. White donated $10,000 to the University of Illinois Library Friends to pay for the publication costs of *Geology Emerging: A Collection of Rare and Early Books Held in the Library of the University of Illinois at Urbana-Champaign*.

Theater. T. Edward Hambleton has given to the Yale Collection of American Literature, New York's Phoenix Theatre Archive, 1953–83, comprising 200 linear feet of papers. In the collection are correspondence, business and production

James Warwick, Director of the Rock Island (Illinois) Public Library, at the terminal of the library's IBM-XT computer, while board member Jack Leiby looks on. The computer was purchased with a $13,000 grant from the Melvin McKay Trust and provides a telecommunications hook-up to databases nationwide. Right, youngsters operate a keyboard of an Apple computer in a Chicago Microcomputer Learning Center. Four Centers were established under an Apple Corporation grant.

files, financial records, play scripts, tapes, films, sheet music, publicity materials, reviews, playbills, books, newspaper clippings and other printed ephemera, framed photographs, posters, and awards.

Theater critic Elliot Norton donated to Emerson College, Boston, a collection of theater clippings and reviews of plays that opened in Boston "from the late 1890s thru the 1970s." There are also "files pertaining to opera and dance performances and biographical information on noted individuals in the performing arts." Ira Wolff, of Larchmont, New York, gave a collection of some 2,400 film scripts, ranging in date from the 1920s to the 1980s, to the Lilly Library at Indiana University. About 650 are originals and the remainder are copies made from scripts in other collections. Original scripts include *The African Queen, The Big Sleep, Casablanca, High Noon, Psycho, The Lost Weekend, Rear Window, White Heat,* and *The Wizard of Oz.*

Shane O'Neil, President of RKO General, Inc. presented to the Library of Congress "disks containing news, music, and drama, as well as scripts, musical arrangements and information about the operation of WOR-AM in New York." The collection contains news stories from 1922–80, including the attack on Pearl Harbor, the opening of the UN, and the plane crash into the Empire State Building in 1945.

Children's Literature. The family of the late Mimi Kaplan enriched the Library of the University of Illinois, Urbana, with a fascinating collection of the children's story *Little Black Sambo.* Mrs. Kaplan had become interested in the story while doing research on racism in children's literature. First published in 1899, *Little Black Sambo* "was released in at least 30 versions between 1905 and 1953." In the collection are not only printed versions, but allied materials, including films, dolls, puzzles, games, and records.

Richard Scarry, "one of the world's most popular and prolific authors and illustrators of bestselling children's books," put the original artwork for 27 of his books on deposit in the Homer Babbidge Library of the University of Connecticut. The collection includes 774 drawings. Each illustration includes both the pen and ink drawing on an acetate overlay covering a full-color painting. The University reports that Scarry decided to give his artwork to the library when he read an article that described Mrs. Billie Levy's deposit of some 5,000 illustrated children's books in the Babbidge Library.

Rose Diaz Pinan, owner of a local bookstore, bequeathed $64,000 each to the Los Angeles Public Library and the Los Angeles County Public Library. The funds are to be used for the purchase of children's books. The Los Angeles Public Library said it will earmark the money for "books which encourage and motivate young people to read."

The SLIS Library of the University of Pittsburgh received 1,893 volumes from Clifton Fadiman. "The collection contained his handwritten annotations in a library international in scope and included extensive files of notes and articles on children's literature."

George Mendoza, author of the *Sesame Street Book of Opposites* as well as some 100 other books, placed his papers in the Boston University Library. Antiquarian book dealer E. R. Meyer presented a first edition of the *Wizard of Oz* in an unusually fine state of preservation to the Library of Congress.

Manuscripts. In preparation for its 20th anniversary, Yale's Beinecke Library acquired a major 15th-century English manuscript, Nicolas de Lyra's *Postilla,* on the Psalms and Proverbs. "The exuberant decoration and drawings of this manuscript are carried out on a grand scale unheard of in English manuscripts of the period. The illustrations concentrate on the ritual and regalia of Judaism, including the plan of the temple at Jerusalem, Tables of the Law, High Priest's dress and a fortress. Many margins are filled in with remarkable large panels of floral decoration."

Yale University was given a gift of more than 100 rare Tibetan manuscripts. They are 13th-century copies of the religious teachings of an 8th-century teacher, Padma Sambhave.

The manuscripts and literary correspondence of Rupert Hughes (1872–1956) have been donated to the University of Southern California, Los Angeles, by the widow of the author's brother.

Mr. and Mrs. Richard Koella provided funds for the purchase of a three-page letter written by Davy Crockett on February 11, 1828. Crockett letters are quite rare and this one constitutes a sig-

Clinton T. Peoples (left), U.S. Marshal for the Northern District of Texas, donated his personal papers and photographs to the Dallas Public Library in 1984. With him to accept the gift is Patrick M. O'Brien, Library Director.

McCann Erickson contributed concept, art work, and production costs for a 30-second TV message to attract volunteer tutors and adult students to San Francisco Public Library's Project Read. From left are John van der Zee of McCann Erickson, Olive Gamble, Project Head Coordinator, and John Tormey of McCann Erickson.

Gifts, Bequests, and Endowments

nificant addition to the Library of the University of Tennessee.

Plantation Papers. The papers of the Johnston and Wood families of Hayes Plantation, near Edenton, North Carolina, were presented to the Library at the University of North Carolina, Chapel Hill, by John Gilliam Wood and his children. This is a large and valuable collection of material from the 18th and 19th centuries, dealing with the political history of the late Colonial, Revolutionary, and early national periods, and with social and economic history from the mid-18th through the early-20th centuries.

The Library of Congress received the papers of John Osborn, *New Republic;* Norman Podhoretz, editor of *Commentary;* and Associated Press correspondent Roland Shackford. The records of the Gridiron Club of Washington also went to the Library of Congress.

Mr. and Mrs. Lee Ragsdale, Jr., gave, in honor of their daughter Margaret Welles Ragsdale, an important group of documents relating to the Insurance Company of North America, Philadelphia. Consisting of 140 pieces dated between 1792–1843, these papers "are primary sources of information that provide valuable insights into many facets of American history."

The papers of the late Rabbi Jacob M. Rothschild, Atlanta, have been received by the Emory University Library. Rabbi Rothschild was "an active supporter of the Civil Rights movement in the south during his controversial career at the Benevolent Hebrew congregation, better known as the Temple." This collection augments Emory's other collections dealing with race relations.

The Royal Library of Denmark received the papers of Christine Jorgensen, who pioneered sex change operations in 1952. Included in the collection are letters, documents, films, and photographs.

The Department of Special Collections of Boston University's Mugar Memorial Library received the personal and professional papers of the French actress Annabella, actors Ralph Bellamy, Rex Harrison, and Cliff Robertson, and actress Lee Patrick.

The archives of the late Ladislas Farago, an authority on international espionage and intrigue, on escaped war criminals, and the author of *Patton* and of *Game of Foxes,* were presented to the Department of Special Collections, Mugar Memorial Library, Boston University. The Farago archives "are huge and are a rich source for the history of the 1930s and the 1940s."

The papers of a former governor of Massachusetts, John A. Volpe, arrived at Northeastern University, Boston. In the collection are correspondence files, documents, photographs and memorabilia from 1953 to 1977.

The Billy Graham Center at Wheaton College, Illinois, acquired the papers of the Women's Union Missionary Society. Founded in 1861, the evangelical group documented by the papers did missionary work in India, China, Japan, Burma, Pakistan, Greece, and Cyprus.

The University of Michigan, Ann Arbor, received the papers of Vernon Dale Tate, pioneer in micrographics. The collection "takes up approximately 230 linear feet, covers the history of micrographics and related subjects such as photoduplication, photography and information storage and retrieval." Tate's career included service at the Library of Congress, the National Archives, MIT, and the U.S. Naval Academy.

Literature. The Friends of the Texas Christian University Library gave "an important collection of 160 first and early editions, along with biographical and critical works, of British novelist Anthony Trollope." There are 160 editions in the collection, among them an almost complete set of *Barsetshire* and *Palliser* novels, many in original cloth.

Paulette Goddard Remarque has given the Fales Library, New York University, her husband's (Erich Marie Remarque) diaries. They consist of "22 composition books (well over 1,000 pages), are written in German, and cover the years 1918, 1936–1954, and 1964–1965." They will be located in the Remarque Room, where are kept many of his manuscripts, works, and personal library donated by his wife.

The papers of John Malcolm Brinnin, Director of the Poetry Center in New York City, 1949–56, are now at the University of Delaware, Newark. There are over 17,500 pages of primary-source materials, including correspondence with T. S. Eliot, Dylan Thomas, Katharine Porter, Robert Lowell, Richard Eberhart, and Elizabeth Bishop. Manuscripts of all of Brinnin's works are in the collection.

The University of California, Santa Cruz, received from Robert and Genevieve Hahn, Aptos, California, a collection of books by and about Upton Sinclair. In the collection are "118 of Sinclair's titles, as well as reprints and variant editions, issues of *Upton Sinclair's Epic News . . .*" and the files of the *Upton Sinclair Quarterly.*

The University of Illinois Library Friends have made it possible for the Library to acquire one of the rarest of all of the first editions of John Milton, *Declaration; or, Letters Patents of the Election of This Present King of Poland John the Third. . . .* Only seven copies are known to exist worldwide.

The Houghton Library, Harvard University, acquired Samuel Taylor Coleridge's *The Poetical Works,* London: Pickering, 1828. This is one of 12 large-paper copies "of an edition replaced in the following year by its dissatisfied author with a new edition."

Cookbooks. Louis Szathmary, Chef and owner of The Bakery Restaurant in Chicago, presented to the University of Iowa Libraries "one of the finest collection of books on the culinary arts and sciences in existence today." The collection consists of more than 10,000 rare and exotic volumes on cookery and gastronomy, including "a number of incunables collected during the past 25 years as well as 15,000 pamphlets, menus," and "letters from Presidents and cookbooks owned and used by them."

The Szathmary Collection is unusually strong in American cookbooks beginning about 1650. The Chef used the collection for reference while preparing his 15-volume history on American cooking and living, *Cookery Americana.*

Natural History. Ostrom Enders gave Trinity

College, Hartford, Connecticut, a major natural history library of about 6,000 volumes. Valued at $1,200,000, the library is primarily of ornithological interest. Highlights include *The Birds of America, from the Original Drawings of John James Audubon,* 1860; François Le Vaillant, *Histoire Nouvelle des Oiseaux d'Afrique,* 6 volumes, 1802–8; and Buffon's *Histoire Naturelle des Oiseaux,* 1770–85.

The Hanes Foundation gave to the Library of the University of North Carolina, Chapel Hill, a collection of 300 titles produced by the Estienne family, distinguished printers-publishers-scholars of Paris, active in the 16th and 17th centuries. This collection, put together over a period of a quarter of century by book dealer Fred Schreiber, is believed to be the largest single collection of Estienne publications in the United States.

The Henry J. Bruman Educational Foundation made it possible for UCLA to acquire the microfiche edition of *Börsenblatt für den deutschen Buchhandel, 1834–1945.* This journal "documents the history of German publishing" for a period of 110 years.

The Connecticut Audubon Society gave to the Homer Babbidge Library of the University of Connecticut an almost complete set of *Forest and Stream* (1870–1930). This journal was started by George Bird Grinnell and was the most important of the late-19th-century popular magazines dealing with environment.

An alumnus of Case Western Reserve University gave that institution's Library a collection of 250 autographs, consisting of letters and documents designed by members of the "British Royalty, politicians, statesmen, writers and composers." There are also autographs of all the first Lords of the Treasury from Sidney Godolphin on, and examples from every Prime Minister from Robert Walpole on.

Nathaniel C. Browder, a retired professional cryptanalyst, gave the D. H. Hill Library of the North Carolina State University a full transcription of *The William Thomas Prestwood Enciphered Diary, 1808–1859.* These coded diaries are a record of the day-to-day life of one man living in rural North Carolina.

Early Manuscripts. Philip Hofer donated eight early manuscripts to the Houghton Library, Harvard University. Among them was a three-volume manuscript of a French translation of Augustine's *De Civitate Dei,* written and illuminated for Jean, duc du Berri, around 1380. Mr. and Mrs. H. P. Kraus presented to the Houghton Library, Harvard University, a 15th-century manuscript of Euclid's *Elements* from the library of Luca Paccioli, who was later to edit this text.

Collections. Thirty-five members of the Center for Research Libraries contributed a total of $120,000 to purchase the complete microfilm edition of the Sanborn Fire Insurance Maps. On the film are "623,000 maps of 10,000 American towns and cities for the period 1867–1950."

The Cultural Division of the Republic of China gave 594 books and 212 other items to the Ohio University Libraries, Athens, Ohio. The collection provides reference resources and "general works on philosophy, political science, medicine, history and other topics." In turn, the libraries are "providing training and practical experience in modern library systems and management for librarians from the National Central Library."

Ambassador Mircea Malitza delivered a collection of more than 300 volumes on Romanian civilization and history to the Library of Congress. The gift "represents a broad range of subjects and imprint dates and contains many retrospective works on Romanian history not previously held by the Library."

A major collection of "portraits of international political, theatrical, and other personalities," taken by the late Bern Schwartz, was presented to the Library of Congress.

Berta Bascon presented a collection of 800 Yoruba items, including Akinola Lakesan's *Nigeria in Cartoons,* Lagos: Igaiye Press, 1944, to the Bancroft Library. Ada Tucker Green, of Birmingham, Michigan, has given Michigan State University a collection of 83 boxes of clippings and ephemera concerning clothing, fashion and related subjects from Detroit and the vicinity.

Virginia Scharfman, co-owner with her late husband of the East-West Bookshop, gave the University of Oregon Library, Eugene, a collection of more than 1,500 volumes of "Eastern religions, mysticism, and philosophy"; included are works by Alice Barley, P. D. Ouspensky, and G. I. Gurdjieff.

John P. Vander Mass presented the Library at the University of Iowa, Iowa City, with "40 document boxes of employee and public timetables from railroads throughout the world." Also in the collection are a variety of railroad miscellany, such as train orders, menus, and streetcar transfers.

Gifts. The Hardesty Company gave $600,000 to the Tulsa City–County Library endowment fund drive, bringing the drive over its target of $2,000,000 by $195,000. It is likely the money will be used to "refine and enhance existing collections and services and to develop new services that could not otherwise be funded by the Library budget."

The public library at Virginia Beach, Virginia, received the entire estate, worth $540,000, of a civic-minded couple. The pair were heavy library users and wanted "to give the city something for everyone." The money probably will be put into an endowment that will be used for the purchase of books.

Elizabeth and Paul Selley pledged $300,000 to the Tulane University Library "to provide a Social Sciences Periodicals Reading Area and a compact, mobile storage system." The Periodicals room will allow the display of 500 current social sciences journals, while the compact storage area will provide shelving space needed for social science materials.

The Mardag Foundation gave $60,000 to the Minnesota Library Foundation, the first gift to the recently established Foundation.

Individual Items. Robert B. Honeyman gave a copy of Jean François Champollion's *Precis du Systeme Hieroglyphique des Anciens Egyptiens . . .* Paris: Treutt et Wurtz, 1824–27, to the Bancroft Library.

Mr. and Mrs. Max Alvarez made it possible for the University of Tennessee Library to acquire the third edition of Jonathan Carver's *Travels Through the Interior Parts of North America in the Years 1766, 1767 and 1768* (London, 1871).

The Library Associates of the University of California–Davis, have made it possible for the library to acquire Jacques Besson's *Theatre des Instruments Mathematiques et Mechaniques* (Lyons, 1579). This first French book on machinery contains 60 copper plate engravings and is one of four copies recorded in U.S. libraries.

From the Dorothy K. Thomas bequest, the Bancroft Library acquired *Rubaiyat of Omer Khayyam, the Astronomer-Poet of Persia, Translated into English Verse* (London: B. Quaritch, 1859).

Former Representative James Symington gave "a copy of Henry Adams's rare, privately printed book, *The Memoirs of Arii Taimai* (Paris, 1901)," to the Library of Congress. The book had once belonged to John Jay. Bernard M. Rosenthall presented a copy of *Biblia Latina* (Lyon: Jacob Saccon, 1522) to the Bancroft Library. (See also Special Collections.)

CLYDE C. WALTON

Government Documents Round Table

Task Force Activity. The Federal Documents Task Force (FDTF) initiated several resolutions during 1984 that were passed by the GODORT membership. These involved the distribution of audiovisual material to depository libraries, input by GODORT into the development of GPO's new automated system, the cataloging of Department of Energy publications by GPO, and the publication of the *Numerical List and Schedule of Volumes to the Serial Set.*

The Education Task Force continued to discuss procedures for preparation of the *Notable Documents List.* The first annual list (1983) was published in the Spring 1984 issue of *RQ.* In a joint meeting with the Machine Readable Government Information Task Force, a committee was formed to discuss appropriate actions GODORT might undertake for the improvement of the education of government information professionals, particularly in response to issues raised by speakers at the program presented by the two Task Forces at the Dallas conference.

Topics covered by the International Documents Task Force included USDA's distribution of FAO documents to land grant institutions; UNBIS II, an online database from the United Nations; ALA's efforts to oppose U.S. withdrawal from UNESCO; and the *Foreign Documents Directory.*

The Statistics Task Force continued to discuss minimal statistics to be collected by depository libraries. The State and Local Task Force reviewed the situation with state documents at the Center for Research Libraries and shared information on current events in their state on state documents and state GODORT organizations.

Conference Programs. GODORT's Cataloging Committee presented a program at the ALA Annual Conference entitled, "Documents Cataloging Issues in an Online Environment." The Education Task Force and the Machine Readable Government Information Task Force cosponsored a program designed to create a dialogue with educators to identify and articulate issues within the area of the education of government information specialists. GODORT also cosponsored two other programs: a mapping information update with MAGERT and a program on the use of U.S. federal documents in historical research with the History Section of RASD.

Publications. The Congressional Information Service published two GODORT-sponsored works in 1984: the fourth edition of the *Directory of Government Documents Collections and Librarians* and *The Complete Guide to Citing Government Documents: A Manual for Writers and Librarians.*

Awards. The eighth CIS/GODORT/ALA Documents to the People Award was presented to Jaia Barrett in 1984. Barrett indicated that she would use the $2,000 award to establish the GODORT Friends of Documents Fund. The fund will make money available to members or affiliates of GODORT to support activities that simultaneously promote government documents and establish alliance with key individuals or organizations outside the library profession.

JAN SWANBECK

Government Publications and Depository System

Joint Committee on Printing Regulations. On November 11, 1983, the Chairman of the Joint Committee on Printing, Rep. Augustus F. Hawkins (D.–Cal.), had inserted for comment in the *Congressional Record* revised "Government Printing, Binding, and Distribution Regulations, no. 25." Hawkins remarked that "principal revisions include a redefinition of printing that eliminates the distinction between copying, duplicating and printing, and which includes new processes and procedures for electronically capturing, reproducing, and distributing information." Another significant revision is a new procedure for monitoring federal printing. Instead of seeking JCP approval for each piece of printing equipment on an ad hoc basis, agencies would submit "an annual printing and publishing plan enumerating equipment, printing environments, planned purchases of equipment, and titles and types of publications to be issued, and the means of their distribution."

GOVERNMENT DOCUMENTS ROUND TABLE

PRESIDENT (June 1984–July 1985):
Carol A. Turner, Jonsson Library of Government Documents, Stanford University Libraries, California

ASSISTANT CHAIRPERSON/CHAIRPERSON-ELECT:
Diane H. Smith, Pennsylvania State University, University Park

SECRETARY:
Sharon McClure Anderson, Central University Library, University of California-San Diego, LaJolla

Membership (August 31, 1984): 1,300 (1,060 personal; 240 organizational)
Expenditures (August 31, 1984): $16,968

Above, examples of the promotional materials being distributed by the Federal Depository Library's public awareness campaign in 1984. Left, production of a television public service announcement on the program. (U.S. Government Printing Office)

The proposal met a hostile reception by executive agencies. On April 11, 1984, the Department of Justice at the request of the Office of Management and Budget (OMB) issued an opinion that the regulations "are statutorily unsupported and constitutionally impermissible" in accordance with Supreme Court decisions in Buckley v. Valeo (1976) and Immigration and Naturalization Service v. Chadha (1983). The opinion concluded that a Congressional committee can issue "regulations" only for the legislative branch; that under the regulations Congress seeks to perform executive branch functions in violation of the "separation of powers" principle; and that such a major redefinition of "printing" is a legislative function that cannot be done unilaterally by a committee but must "undergo bicameral passage and presentment to the President."

On June 26 Rep. Hawkins inserted in the Congressional Record for comment revised "Government Printing, Binding, and Distribution Policies and Guidelines No. 25." On August 8 the JCP staff held an open meeting to explain the revision and to invite public comment. The JCP Staff Director, Thomas J. Kleis, explained that the "regulations" were changed to "policies and guidelines," and all executive branch actions that required JCP approval were deleted due to the Chadha decision, which made the legislative veto unconstitutional. However, the expanded definition of "printing" to encompass the broad range of information activities and publishing was not significantly changed despite the Justice Department opinion.

On August 21 the Justice Department issued an opinion on the revised guidelines at the request of OMB and again concluded the guidelines "are without statutory authority [and] even if authorized by statute would represent a constitutionally impermissible trespass upon the rights . . . of the Executive Branch." The JCP staff suspended action on the guidelines until the 99th Congress. On September 6 Rep. Hawkins "moved up" to chair the Committee on Education and Labor following the death of Rep. Carl D. Perkins (D.-Ky.) and was replaced as chair of the JCP and Committee on House Administration by Rep. Frank Annunzio (D.-Ill.). Chairmanship of the JCP reverts to the Senate in the 99th Congress, and there was expected to be a significant turnover in membership.

Public Printer Changes. On January 25 the controversial Public Printer, Danford L. Sawyer, Jr., announced his resignation effective January 27. On May 9 Reagan submitted to the Senate the nomination of Ralph E. Kennickell, Jr., to be Public Printer. After joining the Reagan administration in 1981, Kennickell had served as assistant secretary of the Treasury for administration and as an aide to three officials at the Small Business Administration. He was formerly Vice-President and Manager of the Kennickell Printing Company of Savannah, Georgia. When the Senate Committee on Rules and Administration failed to conduct hearings on the nomination during the 98th Congress, Reagan gave Kennickell a recess appointment on December 11, which expires at the end of the first session, 99th Congress. During the interim period, the Deputy Public Printer, William J. Barrett, served as Acting Public Printer.

GPO Sales Publications Program. At the 1984 fall meeting of the Depository Library Council to the Public Printer, the Superintendent of Documents, Michael F. DiMario, announced plans by GPO to start a program of on-demand printing of titles not stocked for sale in paper copy. GPO plans to sell either microfiche, or a "blowback" (photocopy or equivalent) copy produced from a microfiche master. Three categories will be available: all titles that were distributed in microfiche through the depository library program and the international exchange program; all titles stocked in paper for the sales program after

Uncle Sam display at the Memphis Public Library introduces young readers to government publications.

they go out of print, at which time a microfiche master will be produced if not already available; and documents originally published in microfiche by issuing agencies. While this will greatly expand the number of sales titles, the program will not include all titles listed in the Monthly Catalog of U.S. Government Publications. The pricing structure will be similar to that of the National Technical Information Service (NTIS) since GPO is required by Congress to recover all costs.

With the departure of Sawyer, the plan to close some of the 25 bookstores became a dead issue. However, GPO did not plan at year's end to open additional bookstores, although plans called for existing facilities in federal buildings to be upgraded. More stores will be relocated to commercial buildings. The fifth store to be relocated by the end of 1984 was the Kansas City bookstore.

Depository Library Program. At the close of fiscal year 1984, 1,391 depository libraries were functioning, a net gain of 9 from 1983. There was no change in the status of regional libraries. Six states remained unserved by a regional depository: Alaska, Delaware, Missouri, South Carolina, South Dakota, and Tennessee.

The number of titles distributed in paper copy increased from 18,292 in FY 1983 to 23,100 in FY 1984, and the number of pieces increased from 8,663,839 to 10,066,583. The number of titles distributed in microfiche decreased from 43,850 in FY 1983 to 35,540 in FY 1984, and the number of pieces from 21,748,730 to 16,680,651. The 1983 figure had been inflated by a one-time distribution of U.S. census block statistics maps. Average number of libraries selecting an item distributed in paper was 428, and in microfiche was 440, representing a decrease from FY 1983 figures of 473 and 494, respectively.

The Library Programs Service (LPS) was scheduled to move from leased office/warehouse facilities in Alexandria, Virginia, back to the main GPO building in downtown Washington, D.C., on expiration of its lease in February 1985. In 1974 LPS had moved from crowded quarters in Washington to Alexandria. During the decade excess space had been generated on the sixth floor of the main GPO building as hot metal printing operations were phased out and replaced by automated photocomposition equipment. The move is expected to result in annual savings of $500,000 as well as improved operational efficiency.

The JCP Ad Hoc Committee on Depository Library Access to Federal Automated Data Bases concluded its two-day monthly sessions in early 1984. The Committee "unanimously supported the principle that the Federal Government should provide as defined in section 1901, Title 44, United States Code access to federal information in electronic format through the depository library system," and it recommended that the economic feasibility of providing such information be investigated through pilot projects. The JCP and GPO FY 1985 budget did not contain funds for such pilot projects, however.

LEROY C. SCHWARZKOPF

Health and Rehabilitative Library Services

Although no single event marked 1984, the field of health and rehabilitative library services experienced steady growth and development in many areas. Publications flourished. Individual libraries continued traditional services and experimented with some new approaches. Computer applications for disabled persons became a key concern for individuals as well as for many libraries. Institution libraries felt the tight budgets of their parent agencies and coped with the problems of filling librarian positions.

Publications. A concern for all librarians working in health and rehabilitative library services was keeping up with the flood of current information in the many related fields. It was not enough to read library publications, for librarians needed to know about events in fields such as corrections, mental health, rehabilitation research, and disabliity related legislation.

Some of the key titles that appeared in 1984 included More Notes from a Different Drummer (Baskin and Harris), a selective guide to titles on disabilities for children and young adults that described and evaluated 450 works of fiction. New bibliographic titles were Health, Illness, and Disability: A Guide to Books for Children and Young Adults, by Pat Azarnoff, and ASCLA's World of Work: The Handicapped Person's Guide to Finding a Job, compiled by Dorothy Minor.

Computer applications for disabled persons was a topic that continued to grow in importance during the year. "Computer-Disability News: The Computer Resource Quarterly for People with Disabilities" was a free publication developed by the National Easter Seal Society, Chicago. Peter McWilliams's Personal Computers and the Disabled was a thorough examination of what is available for five specific disabilities. Frank Bowe's 1984 book, Personal Computers and Special Needs, showed how computers can assist daily living needs and overcome difficulties with vision, hearing, mobility, and learning. Two additional periodicals in the field were "Closing the Gap," a bimonthly newspaper, and "Link and Go," a newsletter from the Committee on Personal Computers and the Handicapped, Chicago.

Several key library publications had limited circulations but were noteworthy for their continued contributions to the field of health and rehabilitative library services. They included "LSPI News," produced by Samuel Huang at the library of Northern Illinois University; the "Bibliotherapy Forum Newsletter," from the ASCLA Bibliotherapy Forum; *Keystone Technical Bulletin*, from the State Library of Florida; "Patients' Libraries Newsletter," from the Patients' Libraries Committee of the New York Library Association; and "FOCUS: Library Services to Older Adults and People with Disabilities," produced by Eunice Lovejoy.

Periodicals published special issues devoted to health and rehabilitative library services in 1984. *Bookmark* (New York State Library) dedicated its winter issue to library services to the aging; the summer issue of *Interface* (Association of Specialized and Cooperative Library Agencies) featured library services to the blind and physically handicapped and the winter issue was devoted to service to prisons and jails; and *Keystone Technical Bulletin* featured information on hearing aids and sound amplification for meeting rooms in its January/April issue.

In one of its final activities, the Pomona (California) Public Library's Program for Libraries in Service to Developmentally Disabled Adults produced two sound filmstrips on library use by the developmentally disabled. The kit, "The Library Is for You; The Library Is for Everyone," was available commercially from Stanfield House, Santa Monica.

Hearing Impaired. The number of libraries actively serving deaf and hard-of-hearing persons was on the increase and there were more reports of traditional activities such as sign language story hours, sign language classes, and information desks with telecommunciation devices for the deaf (TDD's).

Closed-captioned television programs continued to grow in number and importance for the hearing impaired community. Some libraries with video collections purchased the many new closed-captioned movies that were released and publicized them to the hearing-impaired community for viewing with their closed-captioned decoders. Public libraries, among them those in Volusia County (Daytona Beach) Florida, continued the practice of loaning out decoders for helping patrons determine whether or not they wanted to own similar devices.

ALA was involved in promoting Deaf Heritage Week (December 2–9) through a resolution passed at its Midwinter Meeting urging President Reagan to issue a Presidential Proclamation observing the week. A free Deaf Heritage Week materials packet was developed by Alice Hagemeyer at the District of Columbia Public Library and distributed to interested libraries. Miami-Dade Public Library System presented signed entertainment, discussions, and films at four libraries.

Self-Help-for-Hard-of-Hearing-People emerged as an important new consumer group offering valuable information and contacts through its bimonthly journal, *SHHH*. At its first

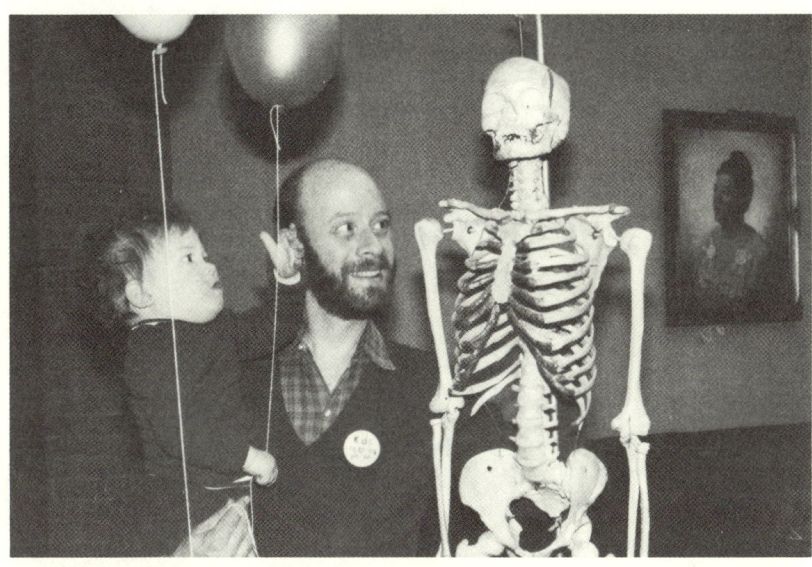

national conference in May, members learned about the use and design of assistive listening devices—devices that can help individuals and groups to improve conversational listening, TV viewing, and group listening. Librarians who had difficulty locating useful information in this area found *SHHH* to be an important tool for serving the 14,000,000 hard-of-hearing Americans. Many librarians also saw the need to install sound amplification devices in their meeting rooms. A chart produced by SHHH, Bethesda, describes the four types that are available and gives a comprehensive assessment of their use.

ASCLA Activities. During the year the Association of Specialized and Cooperative Library Agencies (ASCLA) finalized its internal reorganization to create the Libraries Serving Special Populations Section. It incorporates the activities of the former sections and discussion groups concerned with health and rehabilitative library services and created six Forums: Bibliotherapy, Health Care Libraries, Library Services to the Blind and Physically Handicapped, Library Services to the Deaf, and Library Services to Prisoners.

At the Annual Conference in Dallas the Health Care Libraries Program covered services to pa-

Arlington Heights (Illinois) Memorial Library sponsored a health fair in February featuring displays on health, food, and fitness.

The visually handicapped may use this electronic reading machine free of charge at the Daniel Boone Branch of the St. Louis County (Missouri) Library. The machine, a gift from the Lions Club, can enlarge standard type to eight inches in height. Librarian June Sommer is demonstrating it.

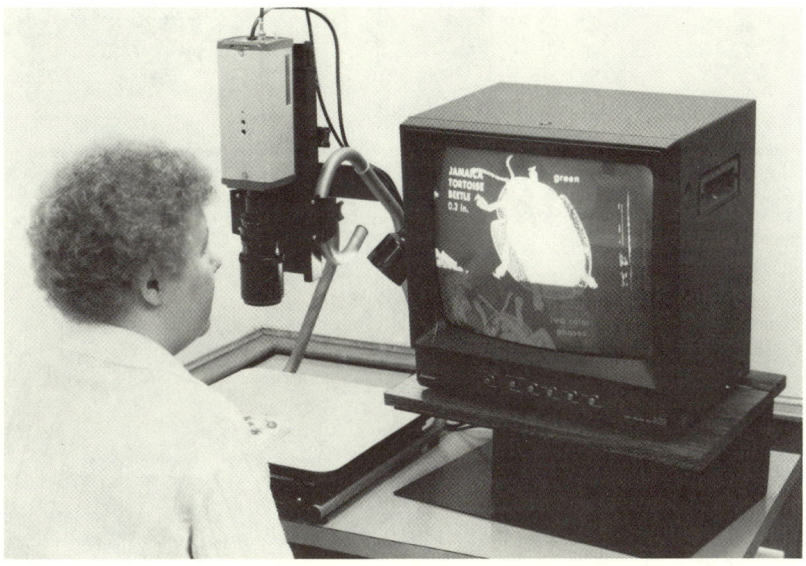

137

Health and Rehabilitative Library Services

Demonstrating a new Visual-Tek machine at the Library for the Blind and Physically Handicapped in Farmington Hills, Michigan, are Carol Hund and Karen White. The machine was a gift of the local Lions Club.

tients and focused on Houston Public Library's program for cancer patients at M. D. Anderson Hospital; Florida State Hospital's extensive programming activities for its forensic, geriatric, and retarded patients; and a California hospice that provides for the individualized information needs of its patients and family members. "Prisoners Writing: A Message from Inside" was the topic of the Library Services to Prisoners Program that featured Joseph Bruchac, Editor of *Prison Writing Review*, and Michael Hogan, a well-known poet and former prisoner who spoke of the role of poetry in developing self-expression for confined inmates. Author Joanne Greenberg, the keynote speaker for the Library Services to the Deaf program, shared her family's experiences with the deaf community that led

Helen Wang (left), Reference Coordinator for the Burbank (California) Public Library, accepts the gift of a tape rack from the Burbank Noon Lions Club represented by Richard Sowby, Bill Vitolo, and Linda Hackett. Rack is used to display tapes and cassettes for the library's Talking Book program.

her to write *In This Sign*. There were also demonstrations of storytelling using sign language and discussions of other programming activities for deaf audiences. "Your Computer and the Disabled" was the Library Service to the Blind and Physically Handicapped Program that presented current and possible adaptations of the library computer for disabled patrons. All of the programs were audiotaped, copies are available for purchase from ALA Publishing Services in Chicago.

At the Annual Conference, ASCLA presented its Exceptional Service Award to Eunice Lovejoy, retired consultant for services to the elderly and disabled with the Ohio State Library. She publishes "FOCUS: Library Service to Older Adults and People with Disabilities."

In June a new ASCLA Committee began work on writing standards for library service for the residents of mental health facilities. These standards represent the first attempt to write national library standards for this population; they have been requested by administrators and librarians for many years.

The Decade of Disabled Persons Committee was established in 1984 to support the National and International Decade of Disabled Persons and to promote cooperation at the local, state, and national levels among libraries and other agencies serving disabled persons. The committee's membership is drawn from all ALA divisions.

Programs of Note. Leon County Public Library, Tallahassee, Florida, completed a two-year LSCA-funded project to serve developmentally disabled persons who live in community-based cluster and group homes. Staff set up bookmobile stops and programs to six agencies serving the handicapped; eight other agencies were also provided with in-service training of staff, library tours, reference assistance, and bibliographies of materials for the staff and clients of programs. Handicap awareness training was available for all public service library staff, including tours of one of the residential centers.

Emphasis was placed on adding and promoting AV and print materials for parents and staff who work with the mentally handicapped in the areas of mental retardation, physical disabilities, and behavior modification.

Elderly, disabled, and others unable to attend book talks at the DeKalb Library System, Decatur, Georgia, could call a 24-hour "Dial Book" service in 1984 and hear capsule book reviews.

The Library Committee of the President's Committee on Employment of the Handicapped (PCEH) sponsored a reception at the Annual PCEH Meeting to honor 12 authors who wrote books in the disability field. This will become an annual activity for the Committee.

G. K. Hall awarded its first Large Print Community Service Award to the Jackson-George Regional Library in Pascagoula, Mississippi, for its efforts to promote and use its large print collection. Activities included "Large Print Month" (February) promoted with buttons, bookmarks, posters, and handouts to libraries and community agencies; rotating collections of large print books placed in senior centers, nursing homes, and hospitals; publicity materials displayed in doctors' offices and senior centers; and a workshop on serving the visually impaired attended by librarians and staff from community agencies.

The School of Library and Information Science of the Catholic University of America, with the National Rehabilitation Information Center (NARIC), formed D:ATA Institute (Disability: Appropriate Technology Applications) in 1984. D:ATA Institute combined the expertise and skills of each sponsoring organization to foster broad-based research, educational programs, and other services related to the impact and applications of technology on the fields of rehabilitation and special education.

Consumer health information continued to be a growing interest for many libraries. With resources like the Medical Library Association's excellent continuing education course, "Consumer Health Information Services," and Alan Rees and Jodith Janes's new edition of *The Consumer Health Information Source Book*, librarians had good advice on setting up even a limited service program. Library schools also offered continuing education courses like the one on general health information presented in September by Palmer Graduate Library School of Library and Information Sciences, Long Island University.

Under a $19,000 grant from the New York State Office of Mental Retardation and Developmental Disabilities Planning Council, the Onondaga County (New York) Public Library established Project Adapt. It set up a resource center with toys that were adapted with special electromechanical devices that persons with physical impairments could operate. Parents and community agencies borrowed the adapted toys, special switches, and leisure equipment to see what works for their children.

Institution Services. Few changes were evident in the library services provided to the residents of prisons, mental hospitals, retardation centers, and youth training schools. The states with active institution library programs maintained or strengthened those services and those states with weak programs continued to ignore this area. Most of the large-scale institution phase outs occurred in the 70s, but a few states reported mental health and retardation facilities closing in 1984. Correctional institutions were the only institutions that appeared to be increasing in numbers. Florida and New York continued their annual continuing education programs for institution librarians, and the California Department of Corrections continued a major study of its library programs.

A continuing concern for all states was keeping institution librarian positions filled. This was ironic since state library agencies worked for years to have the jobs established as professional level positions and then had difficulties attracting qualified persons to fill them. Although the salaries were generally comparable with those of entry-level positions in public libraries, they did not compensate for the special working conditions and long evening and weekend hours required for many jobs.

KATHLEEN MAYO

IFLA

IFLA activities during 1984 were diverse and widespread. They included the 50th annual General Conference of IFLA, held for the first time on African soil (Nairobi, August 1984), the launching of a number of core programs (preservation and conservation, transborder data flow), and the continuation and intensification of the existing core programs of UAP (Universal Availability of Publications), UBC (Universal Bibliographic Control), International MARC, and the advancement of Third World librarianship.

Periodical Publications. *IFLA Journal*, issued quarterly, reported on the activities and projects of IFLA's 41 Sections and Round Tables, and gave highlights of the meetings of IFLA's steering bodies—the Executive Board, the Professional Board, and the Programme Management Committee. In 1984 the *IFLA Journal* published issues on Libraries in a Technological World, the theme of the 1983 Conference, covering such diverse aspects as the economics and politics of information, technology for schoolchildren, and technology and rare book cataloging. It is traditional each year to feature an article on libraries and librarianship in the host country of the annual Conference. The library situation in Kenya was presented in detail, and other articles that reflected the theme of the 1984 Conference, The Basis of Library and Information Services for National Development, also appeared in the *Journal*.

IFLA Annual 1983 contained the annual reports of the Treasurer, the Secretary General, and IFLA's professional groups. It recorded in full the speeches delivered at the opening session, and gave an overview of the more than 200 meetings held. IFLA officers provided abstracts of the papers given during the professional sessions, and the local organizers provided copies of all papers to IFLA's 18 Clearinghouses, located worldwide, including the new Clearinghouse established in Spain in 1984, and also the Clearinghouse at ALA Headquarters.

International Cataloguing, the quarterly bulletin of the UBC program, in 1984 reported specifically on the projects and activities of the Division of Bibliographic Control. Several articles highlighted bibliographic control and cataloging in Kenya. Progress reports were also given on the ISBD (International Standard Bibliographic Description) Five-Year Review.

The UAP program and the International MARC program issued newsletters during 1984. Both newsletters were sent free to all IFLA members, and both included information on new developments, activities, and projects undertaken or coordinated by the responsible bodies associated with the programs. The *UAP Newsletter* was issued in a Spanish version in 1984, and covered national initiatives in promoting the UAP concept and the progress made in involving IFLA's Sections in the program. The *IMP Newsletter* was directed to those involved with or interested in the development of MARC (Machine-Readable Cataloging) formats, especially UNIMARC, at the national and international levels and of an international network for the exchange of MARC records.

The first IFLA Conference held in Africa at Nairobi, Kenya, attracted an international gathering of library and information officials. This group included, from left, Elinor Hashim, NCLIS chair; Guy Brown of USIA; Gerald Thomas, U.S. Ambassador to Kenya; William Lukasavich, Director of the American Cultural Center in Nairobi; Anne Mathews, University of Denver Library School; and Robert Wedgeworth, ALA Executive Director.

Series. In the IFLA Publications series, published by K. G. Saur Verlag, four new monographs were issued in 1984: *Library Work for Children and Young Adults in the Developing Countries*, edited by Geneviève Patte and Sigrun Klara Hannesdóttir; *Supplement to the Guide to the Availability of Theses*, compiled by G. G. Allen and K. Deubert; *A Guide to Developing Braille and Talking Book Services*, edited by L. Clark; and *World Directory of Map Collections*, edited by J. Wolter.

During 1984 the Professional Board initiated a new series, IFLA Professional Reports, published by IFLA Headquarters. The intention of the new series is to ensure that successful IFLA projects receive due recognition. Titles issued in 1984 include *Books for the Mentally Handicapped: A Guide to Selection*, compiled by M. Marshall, S. Simonis-Rupert and S. Holst; *Guidelines for Libraries Serving Hospital Patients and Disabled People in the Community*, compiled by a working group chaired by J. Clarke; and *Poster Sessions in Library Science: Guidelines*, by D. Schmidmaier.

Other Monographs. Other titles issued during 1984 included *Guidelines for Authority and Reference Entries* (UBC program); *Proceedings of the International Cataloguing-in-Publication Meeting, Ottawa, 16–19 August 1982* (UBC program); *A Brief Guide to Centres of International Lending and Photocopying* (UAP program); *Improving the Availability of Publications—A Comparative Assessment of Model National Systems* (UAP program); and *International Guide to MARC Databases and Services* (International MARC program).

IFLA hopes to make itself more visible in the U.S.A. through the 51st IFLA Council and General Conference to be held in Chicago, August 18–24, 1985. — MARGREET WIJNSTROOM

Independent Research Libraries

Changes at the Top. L. W. Towner, the preceding author in this space, suggested a year ago that the leadership of the libraries making up the Independent Research Libraries Association was undergoing substantial change after a full decade of relative stability. At the beginning of 1984, Robert Middlekauff was already installed as the director of the Huntington Library, but successors to the chairs of O. B. Hardison at the Folger Shakespeare Library, James E. Mooney at the Historical Society of Pennsylvania, and Edwin Wolf, II, at the Library Company of Philadelphia had not yet been filled. Successors are now in place at each of those institutions.

Werner L. Gundersheimer, an Italian Renaissance scholar from the University of Pennsylvania took up the directorship of The Folger Shakespeare Library in July. Peter J. Parker and John C. Van Horne are the new neighbors in Locust Street in Philadelphia. Parker had served for several years as Curator of Manuscripts at the Historical Society of Pennsylvania before moving to the directorship. Van Horne moved uptown from the American Philosophical Society, where he was assistant editor of the *Papers of Benjamin Latrobe*, to the librarianship of the Library Company.

Filling the bibliographical shoes of Edwin Wolf there will be no easy task for Van Horne. Wolf's career at the Library Company was marked not only by its duration (more than three decades), but more importantly by Wolf's success in leading an all-but-moribund social institution into new life as a research library with formerly neglected resources for the exploration of Philadelphia's (and by extension the nation's) cultural and intellectual history. If the Library Company's operations are accurately likened to a "mom and pop grocery store," as denominated by Wolf himself, then its collections must be compared to the stock of a "supermarket."

There has been some considerable hullabaloo over the fate of the Folger's theatrical enterprise which was inaugurated some years ago by Hardison in an effort to insert the institution more vigorously into the intellectual and artistic life of the Washington community. In that it was highly successful. Financially, it proved to be less so, which resulted in the long run in a diminution of resources that were available for library operations. The newspaper account of the separation of the theater company from the library and the resulting hue and cry came shortly after Gundersheimer assumed the directorship, thereby plunging that former academic squarely into the difficulties of truly making his tub stand upon its own bottom!

INTERNATIONAL FEDERATION OF LIBRARY ASSOCIATIONS

PRESIDENT (1979–85):
Else Granheim, Director, Statens Bibliotektilsyn, Oslo, Norway

FIRST VICE-PRESIDENT (1983–1985):
Hans-Peter Geh, Director, Württembergische, Landesbibliothek, Stuttgart, FRG

SECRETARY GENERAL:
Margreet Wijnstroom

Membership (1984): 170 association members; 868 institutional members and affiliates; 162 personal affiliates
Headquarters: IFLA Secretariat, P.O. Box 95312, 2509 CH The Hague, Netherlands

IRLA statistics for fiscal 1984

	Total volumes	Net volumes added	Total current periodicals & journals	Total microform units
American Antiquarian Society	621,690	6,122	550	139,934
American Philosophical Society	—	—	—	—
The Folger Shakespeare Library	224,170	1,638	205	(reels) 1,320
Linda Hall Library	567,950	18,555	16,822	919,560
The Historical Society of Pennsylvania	203,260	1,090	562	24,050
The Huntington Library	600,000	5,715	600	N/A
The Library Company of Philadelphia	458,000	3,436	125	84,000
Massachusetts Historical Society	386,250	1,245	281	1,681
The Pierpont Morgan Library	100,115	1,169	212	1,464
The Newberry Library	1,380,586	8,677	—	—
The New York Academy of Medicine	666,376	7,417	4,076	7,036
The New-York Historical Society	634,620	620	490	54,000
The New York Public Library	5,940,652	166,504	29,905	2,120,418
The Virginia Historical Society	259,093	3,692	292	2,172

	Total manuscripts (running feet)	Total reader days	Total circulation	Total interlibrary loans
American Antiquarian Society	2,270	4,289	21,383	310
American Philosophical Society	—	—	—	—
The Folger Shakespeare Library	40,000[a]	7,753	30,389	0
Linda Hall Library	N/A	39,422	60,972	80,587
The Historical Society of Pennsylvania	17,935	15,890	21,840	65
The Huntington Library	2,200,000	16,813	403,693	—
The Library Company of Pennsylvania	301	1,837	3,546	106
Massachusetts Historical Society	9,268	2,361	N/A	N/A
The Pierpont Morgan Library	118,191[a]	2,350	1,778	N/A
The Newberry Library	—	28,296	90,932	0
The New York Academy of Medicine	288	12,722	68,249	21,511
The New-York Historical Society	6,600	7,640	19,800	N/A
The New York Public Library	5,355	1,401,771	2,084,284	6,307
The Virginia Historical Society	6,600	2,892	23,300	0

[a] Items

	Cost of material acquisitions	Cost of binding & conservation	Binding & conservation salaries	Total cost of acquisitions	Cost of physical maintenance
American Antiquarian Society	$ 245,513[c]	$ 12,852	$ 49,692	$ 344,657	$ 85,855
American Philosophical Society	—	—	—	—	—
The Folger Shakespeare Library	129,725[a]	8,552	42,986[b]	181,263	246,005
Linda Hall Library	1,029,372	46,896	—	1,076,268	228,655[d]
The Historical Society of Pennsylvania	28,926	4,650	5,600	39,176	123,837
The Huntington Library	548,877	16,078	74,001	638,956	176,869
The Library Company of Philadelphia	117,352	3,523	28,799	149,676	52,927
Massachusetts Historical Society	21,500	4,500	25,000	51,000	95,000
The Pierpont Morgan Library	49,367	17,986	51,516	118,869	170,870
The Newberry Library	248,874	27,023	147,389	423,286	325,612
The New York Academy of Medicine	429,486	34,846	0	464,332	181,477
The New-York Historical Society	63,600	2,500	2,500	68,350	67,000
The New York Public Library	2,735,448	671,088	642,330	4,048,866	1,472,522
The Virginia Historical Society	48,872[e]	1,904	0	50,782	12,169

[a] does not include gifts in kind of books and manuscripts
[b] does include conservation salaries funding by grants
[c] $36,600 additional gifts in kind
[d] includes security service contract
[e] does not include gifts appraised at $339,838

	Maintenance salaries	Total other salaries	Total fringe benefits	Total fringe as % of total salaries	Other operating expenditures
American Antiquarian Society	$ 38,673	$ 402,309	$ 100,668	21	$ 225,876
American Philosophical Society	—	—	—	—	—
The Folger Shakespeare Library	373,043	1,070,645	243,449	17	3,123,592
Linda Hall Library	85,287	891,878	158,857	16	186,836
The Historical Society of Pennsylvania	78,690	328,690	61,640	15	46,280
The Huntington Library	39,229	778,855	228,172	26	70,822
The Library Company of Philadelphia	26,491	172,282	32,805	14	149,267
Massachusetts Historical Society	37,000	273,400	95,000	19	175,000
The Pierpont Morgan Society	238,138	514,860	152,857	19	340,989
The Newberry Library	156,711	1,535,880	367,253	20	905,148
The New York Academy of Medicine	135,161	850,924	251,340	26	175,936
The New-York Historical Society	70,000	326,200	79,000	20	16,000
The New York Public Library	1,571,544	13,147,969	4,608,533	30	4,972,488
The Virginia Historical Society	14,589	203,406	66,428	33	55,257

	Total library expenditures	Fellowships	Other R & E expenditures	Total R & E expenditures	Grand total expenditures
American Antiquarian Society	$ 1,198,038	$ 60,360	$458,127	$518,487	$1,716,525
American Philosophical Society	—	—	—	—	—
The Folger Shakespeare Library	5,237,997	—	—	—	5,237,997
Linda Hall Library	2,627,781	—	10,298	10,298	2,638,079
The Historical Society of Pennsylvania	678,313	0	0	0	678,313
The Huntington Library	1,932,903	127,832	602,076	729,908	2,662,811
The Library Company of Philadelphia	583,450	N/A	N/A	N/A	583,450
Massachusetts Historical Society	726,400[a]	2,500	5,000	7,500	733,900[b]
The Pierpont Morgan Library	1,536,583	0	0	0	1,536,583
The Newberry Library	3,713,890	183,199	399,377	582,576	4,296,466
The New York Academy of Medicine	2,059,170	0	0	0	2,059,170
The New-York Historical Society	626,550	—	—	—	626,550
The New York Public Library	29,821,922	—	—	—	—
The Virginia Historical Society	402,631	0	0	0	402,631

[a]excluding Adams Papers Program $170,000 [b]including Adams Papers $903,900

	Total endowment	Gifts & grants for endowment	Endowment income	Operations income	Gifts for current use
American Antiquarian Society	$ 9,781,524	$ 482,787	$ 950,011	$ 60,137	$ 129,545
American Philosophical Society	—	—	—	—	—
The Folger Shakespeare Library	27,329,840	—	1,675,348	1,691,344	998,829
Linda Hall Library	49,861,781	—	2,787,019	308,427	—
The Historical Society of Pennsylvania	5,939,569[c]	204,790[d]	412,323[e]	178,625	79,425
The Huntington Library	37,057,434[a]	2,487,726	3,483,960	602,369	837,359
The Library Company of Philadelphia	6,144,244	75,000	406,254	27,929	16,594
Massachusetts Historical Society	11,000,000	85,000	700,000	50,000	55,000
The Pierpont Morgan Library	23,246,081	2,260,094	770,679	272,128	237,392
The Newberry Library	22,538,188	1,409,343	2,484,474	165,005	1,484,135
The New York Academy of Medicine	38,259,945[a]	107,372	281,756	225,844	1,749
The New-York Historical Society	13,350,000[a]	—	58,100	6,200	49,200
The New York Public Library	127,810,052	582,506	9,101,250	2,559,956	6,345,661
The Virginia Historical Society	6,886,835[c]	191,282	245,183	34,307	0

[a]income figures for the institution as a whole
[b]serves other purposes
[c]includes $410,000 endowed publications fund (as of 1/31/84)
[d]includes $100,000 funds acting as endowment awaiting 1:1 match
[e]includes all endowment income for general operating support

	Cash received from grants for current use	Cash from government contracts for current use	Other income	Total income	Surplus or (deficit)
American Antiquarian Society	$ 349,233	0	$ 104,689	$ 1,593,615	$ (122,910)
American Philosophical Society	—	—	—	—	—
The Folger Shakespeare Library	658,931	—	88,162	5,094,614	(143,383)
Linda Hall Library	—	—	—	3,095,446	457,367
The Historical Society of Pennsylvania	0	$17,905	18,345	706,623	28,310
The Huntington Library	154,154	—	25,467	5,103,309	N/A
The Library Company of Philadelphia	10,313	—	9,050	584,108	1,436
Massachusetts Historical Society	26,000	0	25,000	856,000	(18,722)
The Pierpont Morgan Library	385,476	0	0	1,665,675	129,092
The Newberry Library	362,653	0	3,969	5,909,579	1,613,113
The New York Academy of Medicine	8,000	113,249	1,428,572[a]	0	0
The New-York Historical Society	204,600	—	31,200	349,300	(277,250)
The New York Public Library	11,062,570	—	1,572,761	30,642,198	820,276
The Virginia Historical Society	15,000	0	25,987	320,470	(82,159)

[a]income from general endowment

So, changes in leadership have occurred and will, of course, continue. Larry X. Besant of the Linda Hall Library in Kansas City has announced his resignation in mid-July 1985 from the librarianship there. One of the factors which helped IRLA become a vigorous and effective proponent of the value of independent research libraries to the nation was the coherence of its leadership. Now, the group looks forward to an infusion of new energies from these and other new colleagues.

Fund Raising and Balance Sheets. Despite the cheering and thoroughly salutary effects of a round of special Incentive Grants made to IRLA institutions in December 1982 by the National Endowment for the Humanities (most of the 13 independent research libraries have successfully met the $3 to $1 matching requirement imposed by the grants), financial worries of the most profound kind still dog several of these libraries.

The John Crerar Library is no longer a member of IRLA because its trustees failed to meet the challenges of adequate funding. It has been absorbed into the library system of the University of Chicago. Although the newly completed science library building on the campus still carries the Crerar name, the collections have been broken up and are merged with those of the university.

The New York Public Library is renovating its beautiful building at the corner of Fifth Avenue and 42d Street but many professional positions on its table of organizations are unfilled. Deficits appeared on the balance sheets of others, also. In an effort to maintain an active (some think overactive) acquisitions program, the American Antiquarian Society overspent its annual income in 1984 and the Newberry, still in the throes of an extensive rehabilitation project for its building, shows red at the edges. So, it goes for many of these institutions.

But, if the financial picture remains cloudy (it was *ever* thus), a half dozen of these libraries are improving climate control systems and at least three others are renovating their conservation laboratories. The Pierpont Morgan Library is in the midst of a $12,000,000 endowment fund drive, while the American Antiquarian Society is well over half way toward its goal to add $8,000,000 to its endowment funds.

Collections. The independent research libraries also make substantial additions to their collections. For example, the Virginia Historical Society acquired the earliest known example of a painting by John Hesselius, the 18th-century Maryland portraitist. The Berg Collection at the New York Public Library obtained 1,630 letters exchanged between William Butler Yeats and Lady Gregory, 1897–1931. The American Antiquarian Society purchased on its Henry F. DePuy Fund the earliest known American edition of DeFoe's *Life of Robinson Crusoe, of York, Mariner* (Boston: Fowle & Draper, *ca.* 1757–1762). The Massachusetts Historical Society was given an important collection of manuscripts pertaining to the American trade with China in the 18th and 19th centuries and the Pierpont Morgan acquired a great, illuminated manuscript of *Livre de la Chasse* by Gaston Phebus made in the Paris workshops of the Bedford Master, *ca.* 1410. The American Philosophical Society received 54 linear feet of the papers resulting from the work of the editors of *The Papers of Charles Darwin,* including copies of all known Darwin letters.

Research Availability. The difficult task of making research materials available to scholars confronts independent research libraries just as it does our academic or public library brethren. Some independents are associated with national computer networks. The New York Public Library is a founding member of the Research Libraries Group (RLG) and its cataloging utility, the Research Libraries Information Network (RLIN). David Stam, chairman of the Independent Research Libraries Association, is also chairman of the RLG Committee on Collection Management and Development. The American Antiquarian Society (AAS) joined RLG as a full member in 1980 after several years in the OCLC network. Marcus McCorison and Georgia Bumgardner of the AAS staff have just completed terms as the chairs of the RLG committees on Preservation and on Art and Architecture. The New-York Historical Society also is a full member of RLG, while the Folger Shakespeare is an associate member. The Pierpont Morgan Library and the American Philosophical Society are special members of RLG. The Newberry Library, the Massachusetts Historical Society, and the Linda Hall Library are participants in OCLC.

Readers who wish more factual data on independent research libraries are referred to the statistics appended hereto and to the leaflet *Independent Research Libraries Association,* available from the chairman of IRLA at the New York Public Library, or to the article on IRLA in J. C. Kiger's *Research Institutions and Learned Societies* (Westport, Connecticut, 1982).

Thus, one way or another, and for yet one more year, independent research libraries still fulfill their goals of collecting, preserving, and disseminating the very stuff of our mutually held civilization for the benefit of all who are curious about it.
M. A. MCCORISON

Information and Referral Service

New Standards. "Because of the increasing importance of Information and Referral as a vital human service utilized by increasing numbers of people seeking help with their problems, the need for a uniform set of standards by which to judge the efficacy of such services seems essential if Information and Referral is to achieve its highest potential," said United Way of America, in its *National Standards for Information and Referral Services*. It thus joined AIRS (Alliance of Information and Referral Systems, Inc.) and other human service agencies in 1984 to undertake the gigantic task of drafting new standards for Information and Referral (I & R) Service. *National Standards for Information and Referral Services* was intended to provide a framework within which Information and Referral Services should operate. Standards have been developed because I & R is becoming an increasingly specialized social service of significant value. Further, these standards have been "designed to be flexible enough to apply to a wide range of Information and Referral Services," including public libraries, "yet stringent enough to meet professional levels of acceptance . . . the major concerns of human service orgainzations have been incorporated in the standards and criteria in order that the final document would reflect the needs of the voluntary and public organizations that have interest in Information and Referral Services"(*National Standards,* p.ii). *National Standards* supports and strengthens the public library's efforts in legitimizing Community Information and Referral Services.

Computerization. Automation of manual files continues as a key element to the provision of public library community Information and Referral. Two public libraries developed similar ser-

Information and Referral Service

The Southern California Answering Network (SCAN) is centered at the Los Angeles Public Library and provides reference referral services to six public library cooperating systems encompassing 173 libraries in southern California. The service performed 1,500 searches in 1984. Shown at the terminal is Evelyn Greenwald, SCAN Director.

vices without ever talking to each other: the Memorial Hall Library in Andover, Massachusetts, and the Enoch Pratt Free Library in Baltimore. Using the CLSI System, Memorial Hall converted its records into a bibliographic database. As the conversion reached completion, the library decided to add its Information and Referral Service file—that is, its own "answers"—to the database. Writing in American Libraries (May 1984), Nancy C. Jacobson observed that "CLSI does offer a software package of its own for Information and Referral, but Andover's I & R file did not require the large amount of storage provided by the CLSI program." She further notes that patrons "can use the public access terminals to search the I & R file themselves." Ten other libraries in a consortium gained online access to the Andover records.

Established in the early 1970s, the Pratt Library's INFER (Information for Every Resident) database grew to an unwieldly card file of over 2,800 organizations. Improved computer facilities prompted the decision to automate the file and integrate it into the automated book catalog. Assistant Director John Blegan developed the format for the INFER entry to their CLSI System database and the INFER staff loaded the data. A TRS-80 word-processing program is used to update the file. INFER is available in the library's bibliographic database, and entries automatically show up when users are searching for book information. A Pratt library user calling up print materials will now also find community information and resources under an INFER call number.

During the year, many other public libraries have joined these two in automating their files, both in online systems and on popular microcomputers.

A special issue of Information and Referral: The Journal of the Alliance of Information and Referral Systems in 1983 was devoted to computerization of I & R services. The major intent of the issue is to serve as a resource for those I & R agencies and services involved in computerization. The issue is arranged in two parts: Part I covers general I & R issues including step-by-step help on the decision process to automate and on design of a system to meet identified needs; Part II gives five case studies.

Conferences. I & R for Special Population was the focus of discussion at the annual conference program of the Community Information (CIS) Section (PLA/ALA). Over 200 people were attracted to the CIS program at the ALA Annual Conference in Dallas to hear a panel of I & R providers discuss their experiences and services developed to meet the information needs of populations they serve. I & R service to the elderly, the deaf, and handicapped children were spotlighted.

The theme "Looking Inward, Moving Outward" attracted 272 conferees to the Asilomar Conference Center near Monterey, California, for the 1984 AIRS Conference. Conference keynoters set the tone for the "Looking Inward" series of workshops that followed. These workshops provided time for role examination as it relates to techniques and methods of quality I & R delivery. Topics included "Image Building," "Training Trainers," and "Planning Techniques." The conference's "Moving Outward" workshop provided time to discuss ways I & R programs are affected by socioeconomic and technological changes, and strategies librarians can use to initiate as well as to respond to those changes. Workshops included "Emergency Times," "Lobbying and I & R," and "The Electronic Connection."

Cooperation Continues. During the American Library Association Midwinter Meeting, the Public Library Association Board voted to become an organizational member of AIRS and to appoint a PLA–CIS (Community Information Section) representative to AIRS in consultation with each CIS President. In turn, to assure consistent communication, the CIS Executive Committee drew up a set of Guidelines for the PLA representative to AIRS.

The PLA Board formally endorsed the Community Information and Referral Services final report to the National Commission on Libraries and Information Science from the CI & R Task Force. The Board further agreed to request key ALA units (CIS, ALA Executive Board, ALA Washington Office) to work with NCLIS in carrying out the 13 recommendations.

Risha Levinson of the Adelphi University School of Social Work, Garden City, New York, was named to direct a grant to fund a cooperative project involving the Adelphi University School of Social Work and the Palmer School of Library and Information Science at C. W. Post Center, Long Island University. The project is to combine the information/retrieval skills of the librarian with the human relations skills of the social worker in a service that helps the elderly link with services in their communities through a library-based Information and Referral Service. Library School and Social Work students will receive training under interdisciplinary auspices. Concurrent training will be offered to elderly volunteers. Teams of students and volunteers will be assigned to eight selected libraries in the Nassau Library System. New instructional materials, including a course syllabus and an I & R Training Manual, were to be developed.

LILLIE J. SEWARD

Information Industry

Divisions. The Information Industry Association's growth in 1984 kept pace with the rapid development in the information industry, both in numbers and diversity of interest and function represented by the membership. IIA began to mirror the activities of the marketplace, as specific interest areas evolved to form Divisions in the Association's organizational structure.

In fall 1984, the Board of Directors approved the creation of the Videotex and Database Publishing Divisions. Divisions provide interested companies opportunities for concentrated and specialized attention on marketing, operating, legislative, and technology issues relevant to the specific means for handling or distributing information. Divisions carry their own mandate and objectives, and maintain representation on the IIA Board of Directors. Association members can join as many Divisions as they find necessary.

The Database Publishing Division, chaired by Lois Granick, PsycINFO, consists of producers, distributors, and retailers of machine-readable databases. Proposed Committees for 1985 included product development, marketing, legal and regulatory policy, and operational interests.

The Videotex Division, chaired by James Holly, Times Mirror Videotex Services, consists of information providers, transaction service providers, hardware producers, and systems operators. Committees include content, government/regulatory affairs, information/service providers, international, marketing, and technology.

Over 50 financial information services firms chose to align with the IIA as a Division rather than their own Association, thus creating the Financial Information Services Division.

Councils. Core Association services are provided through IIA's Councils. Issues and opportunities that broadly affect the information industries and cut across product and service lines are addressed. The Technology and Innovation Council focuses attention on the new technical developments expanding business frontiers. The Council, through programs and publications, keeps members abreast of the latest innovations and the implications for industry strategy and development. The Task Forces include Artificial Intelligence, Steve Sieck, LINK Resources Corporation, and Marvin Weinberger, MIW Associates; Marketing, James Dillon, Media General; Product Development, John Jenkins, BNA; Policy Liaison, James McGinty, The Dun & Bradstreet Corporation; Standards, L. John Rankine, IBM Corporation; and Technology, Peter Genereaux, consultant.

The Business Operations Council, chaired by Haines Gaffner, LINK Resources Corporation, in 1984 dealt with the profitability of information companies. The Council went electronic in 1984 with the development of an electronic communications system for the membership—IIANET. Through the cooperation of ITT Dialcom, Texas Instruments, and Participation Systems, Inc., the IIA membership and staff can communicate via this new channel.

The committees include Doing Business With Government, Marina Young, IDC; Human Resources, Jim Cornehlsen, Handy Associates; Industry Survey, Andy Clapp, Equifax; International, Larry Day, Business International Corporation; Production, Larry Berul, Berul Associates; Salary Survey, Robert Krammer, Business International Corporation; IIANET, Haines Gaffner, LINK Resources Corporation.

Public Policy & Government Relations Council, chaired by Charles Tower, Dun & Bradstreet Corporation, for the second year, spearheaded efforts to monitor, identify, and analyze legislation and regulation impacting the information business, and to communicate these findings to the membership.

Committees include Proprietary Rights, Marsha Carow, Harcourt Brace Jovanovich, Inc.; Electronic Filing, Mel Day, Research Publications; Freedom of Information Act, Cindy Braddon, McGraw-Hill, Inc.; Government Printing Office, Peyton Neal (PRN Associates); Patent and Trademark, James Terragno (Pergamon Infoline, Inc.; Trade Information, Ronald Plesser, Blum, Nash & Railsback; INFOPAC, William Giglio, McGraw-Hill, Inc.

Government Relations. Perhaps in no other point in its history was IIA more effective in representing the concerns of the information industry to public policy makers and in reporting the effect of public policy decisions to members of the industry than in 1984. Acting through the Public Policy and Government Relations Council and with a highly experienced professional staff, IIA made its presence felt in Washington.

IIA monitored hundreds of legislative proposals dealing with information, and concentrates significant efforts on some of the most im-

---

INFORMATION INDUSTRY ASSOCIATION

CHAIRMAN OF THE BOARD OF DIRECTORS
(November 1984–December 1985):
Robert S. November, LINK Resources Corp., New York City

CHAIR-ELECT:
Carl Valenti, Dow Jones Information Services

PRESIDENT:
Paul G. Zurkowski

VICE-PRESIDENT, GOVERNMENT RELATIONS:
Robert Willard

TREASURER:
Paul P. Massa, Congressional Information Service, Bethesda, Md.

SECRETARY:
Daniel M. Sullivan, Frost & Sullivan, Inc., New York City

Membership (December 1984): 365 corporate members
Headquarters: 316 Pennsylvania Avenue Southeast, Suite 400, Washington D.C. 20003

Information Industry

portant to member company operations. The organization supported legislation dealing with computer crime and with copyright-like protection for microcircuit chips, and both of those bills passed in 1984. IIA opposed amendments to the existing Copyright Act (dealing with work-for-hire) and the Freedom of Information Act (concerning special fees); neither bill became law. A great deal of effort was devoted to a quasi-legislative proposal put forth by the Congress' Joint Committee on Printing that would have extended the GPO printing monopoly into all areas of government information. A coalition spearheaded by IIA successfully beat back the proposal.

In summer 1984 IIA filed with the U.S. Supreme Court an *amicus* brief in the case of *Dun & Bradstreet* v. *Greenmoss*. This case, which deals with libel damage awards, is a landmark case for information companies that do not fall within the libel guidelines earlier established by the Court for traditional media publishers. This decision, expected in spring 1985, will have far-reaching effects on companies in the information business.

A two-day meeting, "Public Policy and the Information Industry: Issues, Impact, Strategy," featured many of the key policy makers in the information world. It provided a significant opportunity to discuss private sector information concerns with a host of policy makers in both the Congress and Executive Branch.

Publications. The IIA's publication program channels information about the Association's activities and services to its membership. The widely distributed weekly newsletter, *Friday Memo*, during 1984 reported member company happenings for an audience of over 2,800 information executives. The year witnessed ever increasing efforts to bring to members the message about the importance of public policy for their businesses. *Information on Washington*, a new supplement to the *Friday Memo*, was introduced in March and published on a monthly basis.

In 1984 *Information Times* emerged as an important source on the business of information. Published semiannually in conjunction with IIA's two major meetings, this magazine provides a platform for discussion of technological, economical, and societal developments important to information companies. It promotes an understanding of the industry and of the role of the Association in fostering its growth. It goes free to more than 30,000 executives in business, government, academia, the library community, the media, and the information industry.

The annual membership directory, *Information Sources*, in its 10th edition in 1984, provided "yellow pages" of all the players in the information industry.

In 1984 IIA released the *Outlook for the Information Industry*, the companion volume to the A. C. Nielsen study, *The Business of Information 1983*, a biannual survey. The *Outlook* highlights the survey data as a new portrait of the competitive positions being taken by both large and small information companies in the U.S.

For the first time, IIA released in 1984 a one-of-its kind industry-wide survey of compensation practices. Prepared by the Business International Corporation, it highlighted salary and benefit data of key management positions in information companies.

A series of "on-demand" publications are created each year, based on key presentations delivered at IIA Conferences.

Communications. During 1984, the IIA created a communications and marketing department. Heavy emphasis was placed on increasing the visibility of the Association to the membership, to the industry, to the government, and to selected business audiences.

The public relations efforts focus on positioning the IIA as the trade group representing the umbrella interests of firms in the private sector that provide information creation, storage, management, or distribution.

Conferences. IIA's most outstanding fete was focusing the attention and participation of over 2,000 industry executives for the 16th Annual Conference and Exhibition in San Francisco in November. The intensive three-day gathering brought together the industry's entrepreneurs, inventors, and champions from the Silicon Valley to Boston's Route 128 corridor.

The Annual "Hall of Fame" Awards, created in 1975 to honor individuals who have made landmark contributions to the growth and development of the information industry, were presented at this forum. The pioneering efforts of three leaders were recognized: Andrew S. Grove, founder and chief operating officer, Intel Corporation; Warren H. Phillips, chairman of the board, Dow Jones & Company; and Otto Eckstein, founder and chairman, DRI.

The launching of the Information Industry Management Institute (IIMI) at this Conference provided over 60 mid-level management "students" with intensive courses focusing on information industry marketing, technology, management and government policy issues—all taught by recognized leaders from leading companies.

In 1984, over 200 information company executives gathered in Boston for an interactive Conference exploring the revolution in information markets created by the personal computer. Three seminar programs were implemented, focusing on specific subject areas under scrutiny by IIA's Councils.

"Exporting Information Products: The Markets, National Policy and Delivery Channels" was jointly sponsored by the Business Operations Council and Technology & Innovation Council. "Artificial Intelligence in the Information Industry: Ideas into Action" was hosted by the Technology & Innovation Council. "Public Policy and the Information Industry: Issues, Impact, Strategy" was produced in Washington, D.C., by the Public Policy & Government Relations Council.

Membership. For two successive years more than 100 new members joined IIA in 1984. The need to provide a systematic method for assimilating executives from these organizations into the activities of the Association has become the top priority for the staff for 1985.

ELIZABETH C. NENNI

Information Technology

While more than 5,000 libraries were using bibliographic utilities for online cataloging support and twice that many were doing remote database searching by the end of 1984, local library automation continued to be leading information technology in expenditures—over $65,000,000 of the $125,000,000 expended.

Circulation Automation. Circulation automation continued to be the keystone of local library automation. It was the most mature module of the "off-the-shelf" options available, and it has become a relatively low-risk undertaking. Circulation systems control the movement of items in a library collection and facilitate the recovery of materials from borrowers. In 1984, as in most of this century, the large majority of libraries relied on book-card, mechanical, and photographic circulation systems. While these systems can reliably record what is currently charged out from a library, they are deficient when it comes to responding to queries about the status of materials, handling holds or reservations, and processing a large number of overdues. They also cannot normally account for items on order or still in processing.

By the end of 1984, more than 850 libraries had automated circulation control, most of them using turnkey systems (those for which a single vendor provides hardware, software, installation, training, and ongoing support). More than a dozen options were available, including turnkey minicomputer-based systems from CL Systems, Inc., Data Phase Corporation, Data Research Associates, Dynix Inc., Geac Computers International, OCLC Local Systems, and Universal Library Systems Ltd.—all firms with sales over $1,000,000 for the year. Two firms—CLSI and Geac—achieved sales of more than $20,000,000 for the year. Supported software packages for medium and large-size libraries were available from the Northwestern and Virginia Tech University Libraries, although the circulation module of the former was being extensively rewritten and improved. Each organization sold several packages during 1984.

Children caught on quickly to the CLSI touch terminals installed in the new Avenues Branch of the Salt Lake City Public Library.

Major Developments. Major developments in local automation during the year were: (1) The continuing and growing interest on the part of most libraries in integrated library systems in which a number of functions—including circulation–share the same bibliographic file.

(2) A tendency for large academic libraries to purchase separate systems for different functions.

(3) Increasing emphasis on circulation control as inventory control.

(4) The availability of a broader range of central processing units from supermicros to superminis.

The first trend—interest in integrated systems—was the most significant. While the auotmation of circulation continued to be the first in-house automation effort of most libraries, a large majority of the libraries issuing requests for proposals in 1984 stipulated that the system include software for several additional functions, among them acquisitions, serials control, and patron-access catalog modules. Most of the RFPs, even those which did not call for the delivery of other than circulation software, called for

C.L. Systems, Inc., moved to this new facility in West Newton, Massachusetts, following a quadrupling of sales of library automation systems since 1978.

Information Technology

the provision of a system that could be expanded to include additional functions at a later time.

Patron Access/Circulation Control. By the end of the year, at least 10 percent of the libraries with online circulation systems also had online patron-access catalog software operational—albeit on a limited basis. This development not only increased interest in integrated multifunction systems, but also appeared to be leading to the emergence of a broader perspective of circulation automation.

Rather than thinking of circulation control solely as the charging and discharging of materials and overdue control, librarians and their patrons began to think of programs for controlling the inventory of the library. Using a system with both patron-access catalog and circulation software, a patron or staff member can determine both holdings and the current availability of materials through a single look-up. Some special libraries—with low circulation levels—installed patron-access catalog software and subsequently added the circulation control function to provide availability information to terminal users.

Inventorying/Acquisitions. There was also evidence of growing interest in electronic inventorying. By scanning items on the shelf and subsequently comparing the label numbers against the holdings in the system and the items checked out, inventorying can be accomplished in a fraction of the time required for manual checking. The turnkey vendors who did not have that capability in 1984 generally committed to provide it before the end of 1985. A number of libraries were also scanning all materials being reshelved to determine patterns of in-library collection use.

Some 10 percent of the libraries with multi-function local library systems were using an acquisitions module. In addition to providing support for ordering, claiming, receiving, and funds accounting, the software made it possible to respond to queries of the patron-access catalog with information about materials on order. Very few libraries were using the serials-control module of their local library systems because most vendors had delivered little if any of the software by the end of 1984. It was generally promised for mid- to late 1985.

The trend toward integrated systems was not universal. Several large academic libraries purchased turnkey patron-access catalog systems—primarily from Biblio-Techniques and Carlyle, both relatively new entrants in the market. Most of those libraries already had automated circulation systems from turnkey vendors and planned future interfaces or electronic linkages between the separate patron-access catalog and circulation-control systems. None appears to have commitments from vendors to develop those interfaces. Several other academic libraries purchased stand-alone acquisitions and serials-control systems—primarily from Innovative Interfaces and Blackwell—rather than waiting for the completion of software for these functions by their circulation system vendor. There appeared to be no provision for interfaces among those systems. Interfacing is, therefore, likely to emerge as a major issue in 1985 and 1986.

Hardware. There was a wider range of hardware available in 1984 than ever before. Some vendors offered options ranging from supermicros to superminis. Several offered multiprocessor systems. For the first time there were several complete system options for under $85,000. A number of small, but sophisticated special libraries were thus able to purchase systems. At least 80 supermicro-based systems were sold during the year. Some 75 supermini and multi-processor-based systems were sold. Only 60 mid-size minicomputer-based systems were sold—the lowest number in three years—suggesting that the availability of a broader range of hardware was very much needed. Mainframe-based systems were popular—with nearly 20 turnkey systems and software packages sold–reflecting greater activity on the part of academic libraries.

Several dozen software packages were available for personal micros such as the Apple II from several vendors, primarily well established general suppliers to the library market. Acquisitions and serials control were both popular. Surprising was the popularity of circulation packages. While they are suitable for charging and discharging library materials and processing overdues, these packages represent a dead-end. They usually require the creation of a database of the library's holdings that is not suitable for patron-access catalog and other functions. Such databases—which represent a considerable investment—will subsequently have to be replaced.

Personal micros continued to enjoy great success as back-up devices for circulation control. Almost all vendors offered software for a micro to permit the collection of charges and discharges when the central site is down. The concept of the micro as a work station had also become established. The micro began to function as an access tool to various databases with the capability to download and manipulate data; and to support word processing, accounting, and electronic mail. So competitive had the local system market become that most libraries seeking bids found themselves with three or more attractive options. Factors influencing libraries' choices appeared to be compliance with the functional requirements for a multi-function system, true integration of the functions, hardware expandability, the vendor's past performance, and, of increasing importance, the perceived viability of the vendor: an assessment of its chances of being in business five years hence.

Vendor viability became an important issue because, despite the growing size of the market, it probably could not support more than a dozen vendors. Total sales of local library systems apparently exceeded $65,000,000 for the year, with CL Systems, Inc., and Geac Computers International accounting for over half of the revenue. Both companies increased their total sales only by achieving dramatic increases in European installations. Data Phase—one of the top three in revenue for the past four years, but suffering from poor sales in 1983—bounced back as the result of the acceptance by Chicago Public Library of its system and major upgrades by a number of existing customers.

Dynix, a new Utah-based firm, experienced the greatest percentage growth in sales, selling

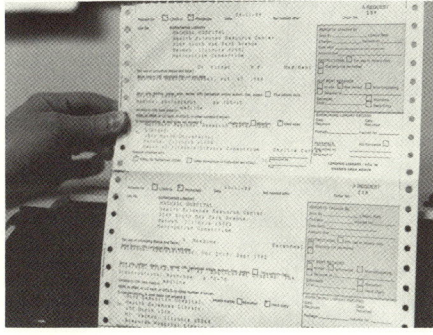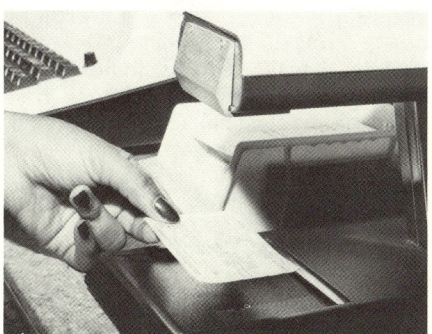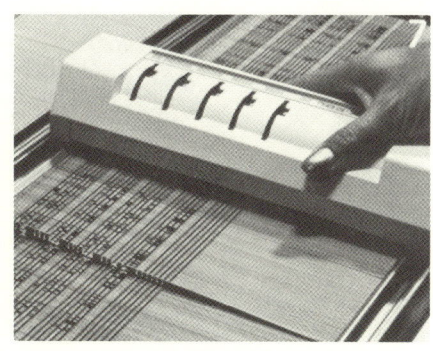

20 systems as against two in the previous year. Northwestern—a supplier of software only—sold more than a dozen systems, thus nearly doubling its installed user base. Data Research Associates also nearly doubled its sales. OCLC Local Systems experienced only modest growth—apparently because it was still adjusting to its acquisition of Avatar late in 1983.

Only three of more than a dozen firms in the market achieved sales of more than $5,000,000 for the year and four others achieved sales of $1,500,000–$5,000,000. While those with sales of more than $5,000,000 a year were each putting $1,000,000 or more into new product development, those with sales of $1,500,000–$5,000,000 were each spending as little as $300,000. Firms with sales under $1,500,000—the majority of the vendors—were generally funding product development from venture capital and may have expended as little as $150,000. Deliverable product, particularly software, determines the attractiveness of a vendor even more than price. The long-term prospects of a number of firms, therefore, appeared uncertain.

The bibliographic utilities achieved only modest growth during the year. OCLC realized most of its new revenue from retrospective conversion services, its local library system, and the sale of micro-based terminals and software products. UTLAS, the Canadian-based utility, established itself in the United States by attracting two major accounts in New York. It also signed marketing agreements with several vendors of local systems. RLIN and WLN saw only minor increases in use.

Brodart was recognized as a commercial bibliographic utility by California, thus permitting state funds to be used for services supplied by it. A Virginia-based firm, The Computer Company, also began to offer online cataloging support. The effect of these ventures on the established utilities was negligible in 1984, but was cited frequently as justification for copyrighting bibliographic databases.

Remote database searching continued to grow, but by the end of the year there was evidence that databases mounted on compact disks or videodisks might eventually displace reliance on database services and value-added networks such as Tymnet and Telenet. Two bibliographic databases were available on disk by December and at least one full-text database was scheduled to be distributed in early 1985. At least two turnkey vendors were making provision to integrate the new mass-storage media into their local library systems so that commercially marketed databases could be accessed from the same terminals used for the local database.

While there were a number of applications of other technologies, such as digital telefacsimile, satellite transmission, and local area networks, none appeared to have gained broad acceptance by the end of 1984.   RICHARD W. BOSS

Insurance for Libraries

NFPA Reported Fires. A fire caused a $4,000,000 loss on the campus of the College of William amd Mary, Williamsburg, Virginia, in January 1983. All 184 students were evacuated from the three-story structure without injuries. The fire spread to concealed spaces throughout the building that were not protected by sprinklers and firefighters were unsuccessful in their efforts to combat the blaze. Firefighters had to be withdrawn from the building when the first floor corridor collapsed. The entire West Wing was destroyed, and there was extensive damage to the East Wing.

According to James R. Bell, NFPA Legislative Technical Specialist, the following factors contributed to the property loss: (1) fire developed within combustible concealed spaces beyond the reach of automatic sprinklers, (2) lack of sprinklers in combustible concealed spaces above suspended ceilings, (3) lack of firestopping in horizontal and vertical concealed spaces, and (4) openings in walls and partitions above suspended ceilings, allowing fire to spread above the ceilings through those openings. The successful evacuation of the students was attributed to: (1) immediate sounding of the general evacuation alarm upon discovery of smoke conditions in the building, (2) prior practice of evacuation procedures by occupants during required fire drills, (3) the training of resident assistants on each floor in evacuation procedures, and (4) resident assistants' exercising their responsibilities in ensuring evacuation of occupants.

A college in Michigan sustained only a $600 property loss in a four-story science building from a basement fire in February 1983. The building was equipped with a partial wet-pipe sprinkler system, waterflow alarm, and a complete standpipe system. A single sprinkler head controlled the spread of the fire.

Officials determined that a short circuit started the fire by igniting insulation on the wiring of a circulating tank pump and motor. The sprinkler did not extinguish the fire because the motor and pump were under a table, shielding the fire. It was extinguished by firefighters.

In April 1983 a fire that was deliberately set

Far left, an interlibrary loan form generated by Fast Inter-Library Loans and Statistics (F.I.L.L.S.), a microcomputer program designed by a librarian and systems analyst which may be used by clerical staff as well as professionals. Center, computerization of the San Antonio Public Library system includes bar-coded "credit cards" for 120,000 library patrons to speed up check-out procedures. Above, the Bassett Retrix system can produce a desired fiche from a random file of up to 12,000 with one sweep of the hand.

Insurance for Libraries

Three months after a fire of "suspicious origin" gutted the library of the James Monroe High School, Bronx, New York, librarians are trying to service 2,100 students with approximately 20 percent of the collection salvaged from the fire. School officials estimate that rebuilding and restocking the library will cost $500,000. Meanwhile the school must use lockers for shelving and the woodworking shop for storage.

during a school session in an Alabama grade school auditorium caused approximately $1,500,000 in property damage. Three students sustained minor injuries. Two teachers who re-entered their classrooms for personal items were trapped in the blazing building and had to jump from the second-floor windows. They suffered serious injuries.

The three-story structure was built in 1943, and several additions had been constructed around the original building. The fire was started by arsonists on the auditorium stage and spread through the attic space to the original building site. All 546 students were evacuated after the building's fire alarms sounded. An automated sprinkler protection system was not provided in the structure.

In June 1983 an incendiary fire in a junior high school in Maine caused $1,550,000 in property damage. The two-story structure was concrete and metal with the walls between the classrooms and corridors constructed with one-hour, fire-rated materials. A detection or suppression system was not installed for the classrooms, but a wet-pipe sprinkler system provided protection for the corridors.

According to officials, a gasoline fire bomb was thrown through a first-floor window. Apparently, the fire went undetected for approximtely 45 minutes because of the fire-rated walls separating the classroom and the corridor and the lack of a detection system.

The fire eventually spread to the second floor as well as throughout the first. A sprinkler in the corridor opened signaling the police department.

A university in Missouri in August 1983 sustained a $1,500,000 loss in a two-story warehouse and physical plant. Mattresses and box springs and 55-gallon drums of flammable liquids had been stored on the second floor over first-floor shops and offices. The fire burned undetected for two hours because the building did not have a detection or suppression system.

The cause of the fire was not immediately determined; however, it was unofficially determined that the fire could have been caused by a carelessly discarded cigarette in the mattress area or by a malfunctioning exhaust fan.

According to the information reported to the National Fire Protection Association, several factors greatly contributed to this large-loss fire: (1) lack of a detection or suppression system to contain the spread of the fire, (2) improper storage of flammable liquids, (3) stockpiling of mattresses and box springs eight feet high near stockpiled bulk paper, (4) combustibles stored in one location, (5) missing fire doors, and (6) loss of water pressure.

In September 1983 an incendiary fire caused $4,000,000 in property damage to a one-story elementary school in Colorado. The fire department received an alarm at approximately 2:35 p.m. and responded within two minutes after the alarm was received. The blaze destroyed most of the classroom areas. The music room and the cafeteria had a wet-pipe automatic sprinkler system that controlled the spread of the fire into these areas.

A $100,000 property loss was sustained in a language laboratory at a community college in Ohio in October 1983. The language laboratory was on the third floor of the Humanities Building. The building was not equipped with a sprinkler system, but it did have a smoke detection system connected directly to a control panel in the maintenance and operations building.

On a Saturday evening the control panel indicated an activated smoke detector signal on the third floor of the Humanities Building. The security office was notified by the man on duty. Guards attempted to enter the floor but the fire flashed when oxygen was let into the room through a broken window. The fire department was called and arrived on the scene two to three minutes later.

Because of the 30-minute delay in notifying the fire department, damage was heavy to equipment. An electrical fault in one of the tape units or wiring in a carrel may have occurred if one of the tape units had been left operating after the class left the room, firemen concluded.

In December 1983 a carelessly disposed cigarette caused a fire in a student lounge in a Humanities Building at a university in Pennsylvania. The 13-story building was constructed with fire-resistant materials. A dry stand-pipe system was located on each floor, but there was no automatic sprinkler or smoke detection system.

Fire officials indicated that the student lounge was equipped with a hydraulic automatic closure on the door that would normally keep the door closed, but it had probably been propped open by students. The propped door contributed to the increased damage. Smoke and fire damage was contained to the seventh floor because of the fast actions of university personnel, but the total property damage was estimated at $110,000.

National Statistics. According to data reported to the National Fire Protection Association, an 8.3 percent decrease was reported in the number of fires in 1983. An estimated 2,326,500 fires caused property damage of $6,598 billion, a 2.6 percent increase over the 1982 figure. Some 122,000 incendiary or suspicious fires, a drop of 5.4 percent from the previous year, were reported. There were, however, 970 fatalities due to suspicious fires, an increase of 6.6 percent. The NFPA also reported that the South continued to lead the nation in civilian fatalities and loss of property while the Northeast leads the country in fire incidents and civilian fire injuries.

Protection and Prevention. A lack of recognition of the importance of protective and preventive systems apparently continues in educational structures. The literature indicates that this trend has continued for years. Protection (insurance coverage) and prevention (smoke detectors and sprinklers) can significantly lower the risk of large financial losses and bodily injury. Protection against financial loss should be a high priority on every administrator's list.

DONALD L. UNGARELLI

Intellectual Freedom

1984 **and 1984.** In *1984*, George Orwell created a haunting vision of the future. It was a fictional account, but prior to actually living through the year of the title, there was a suspicion that Orwell may have been more than a novelist with a story to tell; he may have been a seer.

The year 1984 has now come and gone, and while the Orwellian specter hovered throughout the 12 months, it did not fulfill its prophecy. This is not say that 1984 was a year in which intellectual freedom made great strides, for it was not. And yet, the dire predictions imagined from Orwell's *1984* and seen—by some—in the events of 1983, did not lead to a substantially worsening environment. In fact, in retrospect, it can be said that 1984 was a year of coalescing and consolidating, of strengthening positions and building new alliances—in short, of preparing for the post-1984 years.

At least one aspect of the intellectual freedom picture did not change at all in 1984, namely, the three sources of censorship pressures. These continued to emanate from individuals and groups on the local level who took umbrage at individual titles in local libraries and classrooms; from technological advances; and from the government.

In regard to attacks on local institutions, the number did not dramatically increase; but neither did it decrease. In general, the number of incidents remained relatively stable. As in the past few years, these attacks came from all parts of the country, and touched widely disparate topics. Indeed, the focal points of such attacks constituted yet another list of who's who and what's what of 20th-century American literature.

Technology, another potential source of pressure on intellectual freedom principles, did not create new and seemingly unsolvable mysteries in 1984. Intellectual freedom problems associated with technological advances grew, to a large extent, only because such problems became visible. Solution begins with identification, and in this regard 1984 showed positive results. The profession concerned itself with the effect on intellectual freedom principles of automating library circulation records. In other areas as well, the issues were formulated. For instance, electronic publishing raised a host of questions about the integrity of materials produced in this manner. Such issues will be the focal points of inquiry and review by the Intellectual Freedom Committee during the next few years.

If there was only a slight change in quality and quantity resulting from the first two sources of censorship pressures, the same cannot be said for the third source, the U.S. government. More pronounced than ever was the adage that *no* government, including ours, "loves" a free press. At best, governments "tolerate" a free press.

During 1984, the administration continued its attempts to restrict or keep secret from the public vast amounts of information. Such attempts encompassed broadening the definition of what could be classified as secret, limiting the use of the Freedom of Information Act, censoring former government employees, licensing foreign publications, barring travel by Americans to

The New York Public Library opened its newly renovated exhibition hall in June with a collection illustrating the theme, "Censorship: 500 Years of Conflict." Above, Collier's 1906 cover relating to a controversy over Augustus Saint-Gaudens' nude Diana atop Madison Square Garden; a French lithograph protesting press restrictions from 1834; a special edition of Mother Goose Rhymes published in 1926 as a satirical comment on censors; and Mark Twain's classic Huckleberry Finn, banned from the Concord Public Library in 1886 because of its language. Far right, the exhibit on display in Gottesman Hall.

some foreign countries, refusing entry visas to foreign scholars, and controlling scientific research publications. As in the past, these actions seriously affected librarians' ability to acquire information for their collections.

National Security Directive. In February, however, it appeared that the administration was taking a new tack. Indeed, as far-fetched as it appeared, it seemed as if the administration had reconsidered its previous actions and had decided that a nation of self-governing citizens was not only entitled to, but could be trusted with, a wide variety of information. On Valentine's Day, President Reagan announced that he was suspending the censorship provisions of the National Security Decision Directive 84 (NSDD84).

Initially issued by the President on March 11, 1983, the directive's purpose was to prevent unauthorized disclosure of classified information. Its effects, however, went far beyond that purpose, for among other provisions, NSDD84 attempted to subject all government officials to lifetime prepublication review. The directive provided for an agreement to be signed by all government officials with access to high-level classified information and required those officials, for the rest of their lives, to submit for prepublication review by the government anything they wrote for the general reading public, including newspaper and magazine articles, books, lectures, and even fiction. It was estimated that if the directive had been implemented when issued, it would have affected as many as 128,000 people, including senior officials and senior military and foreign service officers. How many the directive would affect in the future was anybody's guess; many people contended that it could reach the millions.

Among former government officials who would have had to participate in prepublication review were former Presidents Nixon, Ford, and Carter; Vice-Presidents Humphrey and Agnew; and Secretaries of State, including Kissinger. Public information through newspapers would also be affected. For instance, William F. Buckley, Jr., Cord Meyer, Lewis Lapham, and Tom Braden, all syndicated newspaper columnists, are also former CIA employees who had access to classified information. As a result, each column these men write would be subject to prepublication review.

In the fall of 1983, the United States Senate voted to block the implementation of NSDD84 until April 15, 1984. The Senate believed that prepublication review would unconstitutionally violate First Amendment rights of current and former federal employees. But on Valentine's Day, President Reagan announced that he was suspending the censorship provision of the security directive. He stated that there was a lack of understanding by Congress about the National Security Decision Directive 84, and promised to seek a compromise with that legislative body. One official said the White House was hoping "to remove it as a sore spot, a source of controversy" in an election year. It was also suggested that if the White House did not reach a compromise with the Congress, the president would reissue the order if reelected.

Prepublication Censorship Continued. Pleasure over the President's Valentine's Day actions, however, was short-lived. On June 11, 1984, the General Accounting Office (GAO) reported that, notwithstanding the White House

The New York Public Library censorship exhibit displayed these seed packets, pudding packets, and joke book covers containing anti-Nazi material circulated within Germany during the Hitler years.

152

statement of February 14, prepublication review requirements had already been systematically imposed upon thousands and thousands of government employees.

The GAO report made starkly clear that the March 1983 National Security Decision Directive was merely one tentacle of an octopus-like censorship program spreading throughout the administration. According to the GAO, hundreds of thousands of federal employees had already signed lifetime prepublication agreements; more than 3,000,000 employees were potentially covered by such procedures; through their review procedures, numerous agencies of the federal government had become self-appointed "publishers" (more than 15,000 books and articles reviewed during 1983 alone); and that all of the foregoing measures were implemented in the virtual absence of evidence that there had been any injury to the national security arising out of unauthorized disclosures of classified information.

The GAO report also made public the fact that prepublication review had been in operation since 1981. That was the year when form 4193, the prepublication agreement that each federal employee must sign, was issued. Since that time, approximately 156,000 military and civilian employees have been required to sign such agreements at the Department of Defense alone. In addition, as reported by GAO, employees in 22 other federal agencies have also signed these agreements.

GAO's disclosures made apparent that the administration accomplished indirectly what it could not accomplish directly. The disclosures also reaffirmed that the Reagan administration had not made any radical changes in its outlook. (*See also* Publishing, Book.)

Freedom of Information Act. On another front, the administration continued its attempts in 1984 to limit the scope of the Freedom of Information Act (FOIA). Responding to the administration's request for substantial revisions in the act, the Senate passed S. 774 on January 27, by voice vote. The bill amended the FOIA, by providing for increased confidentiality for certain law enforcement, private business, and sensitive personal records. In addition, it promoted uniform fee schedules among agencies, which would lead to the recovery of reasonable processing costs in addition to the current search and copying costs; the agency could keep half of the fees to offset the costs. S. 774 also clarified public interest fee waivers.

Nevertheless, many of the substantive and procedural changes proposed in S. 774 were controversial. Representative Glen English (D.-Okla.), Chair of the House Government Operations Subcommittee on Government Information, Justice and Agriculture, indicated that his subcommittee, which would hold hearings on the senate-passed version of S. 774, "must proceed very carefully and thoughtfully in considering amendments."

Congressman English did indeed proceed as he had indicated he would—in a thorough and deliberative, but not dilatory, fashion. The result was that only one amendment was made to the Freedom of Information Act, specifically, the operative files of the Central Intelligence Agency are now exempt from disclosure. This action, in theory, merely confirmed standard operating procedures.

It was believed at year's end that new attempts would be made to revise the Freedom of Information Act in the 99th Congress.

Strategies for Future. 1984, then, did have its setbacks. The number and intensity of such setbacks, however, were substantially below anticipation. As a result, 1984 became a year of opportunity—opportunity to prepare for the future by strengthening existing alliances and forging new working relationships.

One of the most important alliances of the ALA Intellectual Freedom program is that with the Association of American Publishers' Freedom to Read Committee. Continuing their long tradition, the ALA Intellectual Freedom Committee and the AAP Freedom to Read Committee held joint sessions at both the 1984 Midwinter Meeting and Annual Conference. Taking advantage of Midwinter's Washington, D.C., location, the committees invited to meet with them several individuals who had first-hand information about government attempts to keep information secret. The discussion, involving Mark Lynch and Larry Adler of the American Civil Liberties Union, Richard Schmidt, counselor to the American

Intellectual Freedom

Newspaper Publishers Association (ANPA), and Bruce Rich, counsel to the Freedom to Read Committee led to a decision to focus the committees' joint program at the 1984 Annual Conference in Dallas on the issue of government secrecy.

In Dallas, speaking in favor of making information freely and widely available was Richard Schmidt. Schmidt is ANPA counsel, AAP Washington counsel, and a partner in the Washington law firm of Cohn and Marks. Joining Schmidt on the podium was Cecile Shure, former special assistant in the Office of the Deputy Assistant Secretary of Defense of International Economic Trade and Security Policy. Shure spoke on what she called the alarming results of this country's "too easy access to information," expressing great concern over the ability of the Soviet Union and the Eastern bloc countries to gain access to American technology and to convert what they learned into sophisticated defense weaponry. The texts of Shure's and Schmidt's speeches were published in the *Newsletter on Intellectual Freedom* (September 1984).

Banned Books Week. The ALA in September joined with the Association of American Publishers (AAP), the American Booksellers Association (ABA), the National Association of College Stores (NACS), and the American Society of Journalists and Authors (ASJA) in celebration of the Third Annual Banned Books Week. The week provided an opportunity for bookstores and libraries to bring to the attention of their publics the importance of the right to read and freedom of expression.

As in past years, Banned Books Week 1984 had a subtheme, namely, "1984"—not only in the Orwellian sense, but also in regard to National Security Decision Directive 84. Sponsors of the successful week committed themselves to making the event an annual celebration.

Conference on Free Exchange. A few days after the end of Banned Books Week a major national conference in Washington, D.C., September 18, focused on the importance of the free exchange of information and ideas across the American border. While the conference idea was developed by the American Civil Liberties Union Foundation Center for National Security Studies, the conference itself was sponsored by a broad range of civic, educational, legal, and community groups, including ALA. Among the speakers were playwright Arthur Miller; constitutional lawyer Floyd Abrams; Mexican author and scholar Carlos Fuentes; and South African author and scholar Dennis Brutus. Panel discussion topics included the right of travel, the right to import and export information, and the ideological exclusion of visitors.

The conference brought to the public's attention the many problems engendered by government secrecy. The coalition which sponsored the conference is developing further activities concerning public information and legislation.

Bicentennial of the Constitution. At its 1984 spring meeting the ALA Executive Board voted unanimously to accept the American Bar Association's (ABA) invitation to ALA to become a co-sponsor of "We The People . . . ," a national project celebrating, in 1987, the bicentennial of the United States Constitution. Other major co-sponsors include the American Newspaper Publishers Association Foundation, the National Community Education Association, the Smithsonian Insitution, and KQED-TV in San Francisco. Plans for the celebration include eight one-hour television programs to be broadcast over PBS; 13 half-hour radio programs to be broadcast over National Public Radio; a series of newspaper articles that will support the television programs, to be prepared in cooperation with the American Newspaper Publishers Association; and a series of community forums to be held throughout the United States. ALA's primary responsibility is for development and conduct of the forums.

A related project, scheduled for 1985, marks the 250th anniversary of the trial of John Peter Zenger. Zenger, a Colonial printer charged with seditious libel, was defended by Andrew Hamilton of Philadelphia; from this trial grew the famous "truth as a defense to libel" doctrine and the U.S. tradition of free press and free speech.

In order to involve as many librarians as possible, the 250th anniversary of John Peter Zenger's trial was also selected as the subtheme of the 1985 Banned Books Week.

Public Library Study. *Limiting What Students Shall Read,* a report on a survey of how learning materials are selected for and removed from public schools, was sponsored by ALA, AAP, and the Association for Supervision and Curriculum Development in 1981. The report kindled an interest among the members of the Intellectual Freedom Committee and the AAP Freedom to Read Committee on surveying public library collections. The purpose of the project would be to elicit basic information on diversity of library collections and how it is achieved. The instrument was tested in the fall of 1984; it was anticipated that the questionnaire would be mailed to a full sample in the spring of 1985.

Censorship and Libraries. The Office for Intellectual Freedom early in 1984 joined with the New York Public Library to develop "Censorship and Libraries," which became a part of the New York Public Library's highly acclaimed 1984 censorship exhibition. At the end of November, the OIF received a $123,000 grant from the National Endowment for the Humanities, which will underwrite a national tour of "Censorship and Libraries." The display will have traveled to 16 public libraries throughout the United States by its conclusion in late 1987. The tour was conceived as a means to build popular understanding of the nature and importance of intellectual freedom. Through the use of graphic panels, books and audiovisual materials, the exhibition focuses on key censorship problems in American libraries during the last few decades. The show features information and images concerning censorship in school, university and public libraries, and examines both internal and external restrictions on access to books and materials.

In conjunction with the exhibition, local host libraries will develop special programs that encourage community members to participate in discussions, examine issues, and learn more about the realities and threats of censorship. The exhibition highlights the library's unique role as the only public institution where information and materials covering all points of view and all questions and issues are made freely available to anyone who desires or requires them.

IF Glossary. In addition to building alliances and cementing friendships, the ALA Intellectual Freedom Committee took some action during 1984 that will strengthen its future position. There has long been confusion over the precise definitions of terms used to describe the various levels of incidents which may or may not lead to censorship. Such confusion, as well as repeated questions, prompted the IFC to develop an intellectual freedom glossary. The definitions that will be used to report censorship controversies include:

(1) INQUIRY An informational request, usually informal, which seeks to determine the rationale behind the presence of a particular item in a collection.

(2) EXPRESSION OF CONCERN An inquiry that has judgmental overtones. The inquirer has already made a value judgment on the materials in question.

(3) COMPLAINT An oral charge against the presence and/or appropriateness of the material in question.

(4) CHALLENGE A formal written complaint filed with the library questioning the presence and/or appropriateness of specific material.

(5) ATTACK A publicly worded statement questioning the value of the material, presented to the media and/or others outside the library organization, in order to gain public support for further action.

(6) CENSORSHIP The removal of material from open access by any governing authority.

Access for Minors. In another area the IFC recognized that libraries are adding motion pictures and video productions to their collections. In fact videocassettes and disks are now as common in many libraries as best-selling novels. Questions arise concerning circulation of such items to minors. There is no doubt as to where ALA stands: it stands strongly in favor of free access for minors to all library materials. However, some states prohibit libraries from lending to minors certain types of motion pictures or video productions (usually those deemed to be of a sexually explicit, harmful, or obscene nature). The Motion Picture Association of America (MPAA) ratings—namely, the letters: G, PG, R, and X—are usually assigned to films distributed in the United States. A new interpretation of the *Library Bill of Rights, Circulation of Motion Pictures and Video Productions*, gives practical and timely guidance to librarians about this issue. The new interpretation stated that the MPAA ratings have no standing in law and were devised solely to inform parents and theater owners of the contents of motion pictures and video productions. Furthermore, the interpretation recommended that librarians apply the same standards to circulation of motion picture and video productions as they do to the circulation of books.

Repeal of Fairness Doctrine and Equal Time Provision. Since the mid-1970s attempts have been made from time to time to repeal the equal time and Fairness Doctrine provisions. The issue again became a focal point of IFC concern in 1984 when Senator Robert Packwood (R.-Ore.) proposed a "Freedom of Expression Bill," and sought ALA's support for this legislation. The bill, S. 1917, focused on TV and radio and sought to remove the equal time and Fairness Doctrine provisions. Packwood's position was that the provisions created a double standard that unfairly limited the electronic media in ways that did not affect the print media.

The issue, which generated lively debate among IFC members, appeared to offer a choice of being for "fairness," a moral imperative, or being for freedom of the press, a constitutional imperative. The debate continued throughout the year, and it was not until the 1985 Midwinter Meeting that the committee reached closure. At that time, a resolution was presented to the ALA Council, supporting the retention of the Fairness Doctrine and equal time provisions. The resolution was unanimously passed by the Council.

ALA Leadership. 1984 may well become known as the year of opportunity. The alliances that were strengthened, the bonds that were forged, will undoubtedly stand librarians in good stead during 1985 and beyond. It must be remembered that every battle won in the fight for intellectual freedom, for free speech and a free press, is significant. In the end, however, it is merely a temporary victory. Librarians especially understand the importance of the mind, the power of books, and the implications of censorship. On behalf of librarians, and in support of intellectual freedom, ALA has taken and will continue to take the lead in educating not only the profession but also the public that librarians serve to the dangers of censorship of all kinds and the importance of intellectual freedom.

JUDITH F. KRUG

REFERENCE

Congressional Record, page S1794-1822, February 27, 1984, and "Statement of Rep. Glen English on the passage by the Senate of Freedom of Information Act Amendments," news release from the House Committee on Government Operations February 28, 1984.

Intellectual Freedom Round Table

1984 marked the beginning of a new award established by the Intellectual Freedom Round Table and funded by Social Issues Resources Series (SIRS). This first IFRT State Program Award was presented at the 1984 ALA Annual Conference to the South Carolina Library Association Intellectual Freedom Committee. The award of $1,000 will be presented annually to a state intellectual freedom committee project.

John Swan, IFRT Vice-Chair/Chair-elect, was developing in 1984 a third IFRT award in memory of Eli M. Oboler, a past chairman of IFRT and longtime intellectual freedom activist and writer. The proposed award would be in recognition for a significant body of published writing of a high literary quality on intellectual freedom topics.

At the Midwinter Meeting in Washington, the IFRT assumed responsibility for the Task Force on Coalitions from the ALA Intellectual Freedom Committee.

Top, Gene D. Lanier (center) receives the Intellectual Freedom Round Table Immroth Award, from David Cohen, Award Committee Chair, while James Nelson, IFRT chair, looks on. Above, Daniel Barron (center) accepting award for the South Carolina Intellectual Freedom Committee from Elliot Goldstein while Laurence A. Miller, Chair of the Award Committee, observes.

Under the leadership of 1983–84 Chairman Jim Nelson, the annual membership meeting featured the Roll Call of the States, which gives state IFCs the opportunity to share their activities with other IFC chairs. Gene D. Lanier was the recipient of the John Phillip Immroth Memorial Award. Lanier was selected as a prime example of a fighter for intellectual freedom on the grassroots level.

The IFRT cosponsored with the IFC and the Division IFCs the program "Censors Are People, Too." Beginning in 1984, the IFRT took responsibility for organizing and implementing the annual intellectual freedom program in conjunction with the IFC and the Division IFCs.

PAMELA BONNELL

INTELLECTUAL FREEDOM ROUND TABLE

CHAIR (July 1984–July 1985):
Pamela G. Bonnell, Plano Public Library System, Plano, Texas

VICE-CHAIR/CHAIR-ELECT:
John C. Swan, Lilly Library, Wabash College, Crawfordsville, Indiana

SECRETARY:
Judith Sessions, Meriam Library, California State University, Chico

TREASURER:
Amanda R. Bible, Columbus County Public Library, Whiteville, North Carolina

Membership (August 31, 1984): 1,209 (1,040 personal; 169 organizational)
Expenditures (August 31, 1984): $5,927

International Board on Books for Young People

Biennial Congress. The International Board on Books for Young People attempts to assure that its National Sections exchange information through its biennial Congresses. The 1984 IBBY Congress was in Nicosia, Cyprus, October 9–14. Theme of the congress was Children's Book Production and Distribution in Developing Countries and programming covered Africa, Asia, and Latin America on successive days. The presentations were varied, thoughtful, and provocative. It would be hard to imagine a more successful exchange among such a diverse number of experts concerned with literature and reading development coming together so briefly. Credit for the Congress's success goes to IBBY's Executive Committee (EC) and its worldwide network of contacts with children's book specialists and to Doros Theodoulou of Cyprus, that republic's IBBY representative for the past several years. IBBY's 19th Congress stands as one of its most successful.

Of the nearly 250 advance registrants, 12 were from the U.S. and three from Canada. For the first time at IBBY, an official representative, Yan Wenjng, attended from the People's Republic of China. He is an author of children's books, as well as Vice-Chairman of the Chinese Center of P.E.N. He participated in discussions during the day of programming on Asia. In addition to regular registrants, about 70 students—most studying to be teachers—attended from the Pedagogical Academy of Cyprus.

On the day devoted to Africa, major presentations were made by Francis Nyarko, with a continent-wide survey of children's book publishing and distribution. Irina Tokmakova, the Soviet writer and translator, spoke of her workshops for African writers. Briefer remarks were made by representatives of several African countries, including Molly Melching, an American who has been engaged in literacy and literature work in Senegal for a decade, and also by Helme Heine, German artist whose books are popular in the U.S. and who lived in Africa for a dozen years.

The major presentations on Asia were by Kuldip K. Roy of India and Akemi Asano of Japan. Latin American presentations were led by Lucila Martinez, who was Secretary General for CERLAL in Columbia. Her remarks included a description of the program begun in 1979 in 14 Latin American countries in which one publishing house in each country agrees to cooperate with houses in other countries to co-produce children's books that no one of them could afford to produce alone and publish at a price the public can afford. Seven titles were to be published under that program in 1985.

Anne Pellowski of the U.S. gave the second major presentation on the Latin America day. Departing from her prepared text, she expressed her strong conviction that *story* will indeed endure. While her optimism was not shared by some of the delegates, she made a persuasive and appealing case through a story.

Awards. The high point of every IBBY Congress is the presentation of the Hans Christian

Andersen Medals. Both medalists were in Nicosia for this opening ceremony of this Congress, at which a message from President Spyros Kyprianou was read. Illustrator Mitsumasa Anno's comments were, mainly, a touching tribute to Hans Christian Andersen. Accepting the medal for writing, Christine Nostlinger was thought by some to be overly pessimistic; her remarks are likely to be controversial.

General Assembly Activities. IBBY's General Assembly convened on the final day of the Congress. Without opposition, Miguel Azaola of Spain was elected IBBY President and Patricia Crampton of Great Britain Hans Christian Andersen Jury President. The eight members elected to the EC for 1984-86 were Sergei Alexeyez, U.S.S.R.; Hisako Aoki, Japan, Vice-President; Peter Cervonka, West Germany; Ana Maria Machado, Brazil, Vice-President; Ena Noel, Australia; Dusan Roll, Czechoslovakia; Veronica Uribe, Venezuela; and Minna Vuorinen, Finland. There was no U.S. candidate.

IBBY's other major work in 1984 was to assemble an international exhibit and catalog on the theme "Literature for Language Retarded Children." To be unveiled at the 1985 Bologna Book Fair, the exhibit will subsequently tour the world. Brazil was the sponsor of International Children's Book Day in 1984. IBBY, in cooperation with the International Reading Association, published its second leporello (11-panel foldout) on the theme of "Cats."

Reorganization. In the U.S., the IBBY National Section was reorganized as the U.S. Board on Books for Young People, Inc., a nonprofit educational/charitable organization with a broad-based membership. The first two Patron Members are the American Library Association and the Children's Book Council. The U.S. Board's first President was Margaret Mary Kimmel of the Graduate School of Library and Information Science, University of Pittsburgh.

JOHN DONOVAN

International Relations

Concerns about the inability of library associations to mount expanding programs in international library activities and the curtailment of government support for library expansion in many countries continued in 1984. The year marked the United States State Department giving notice of its intent to withdraw the U.S. membership from UNESCO citing three areas of concern: politicization, hostility toward the basic institutions of a free society, and unrestrained budgetary expansion.

The UNESCO Issue. With respect to politicization, UNESCO is most often criticized for its actions against Israel in 1974, its support for a New World Economic Order and a New World Information and Communication Order (NWICO), and, more recently, for attempts at UNESCO to redefine human rights.

The International Relations Committee invited three speakers who are familiar with UNESCO and its programs to address the ALA conferees in Dallas in June. They were Amadou-Mahtar M'Bow, Director General of UNESCO; Leonard R. Sussman, Executive Director of Freedom House, a nonpartisan, national organization devoted to strengthening free societies; and Else Granheim, President of IFLA. M'Bow spoke of UNESCO's long history of close cooperation with ALA as well as his gratitude and sensitivity to ALA's position on the U.S. withdrawal. He responded to the State Department's complaints against the organization. He believed that whatever the merits of the U.S. grievances, it would be tragic for the U.S. to leave UNESCO. He urged the U.S. to stay and negotiate with the rest of the world on such crucial issues as the free flow of information.

The IRC drafted a resolution that was approved by the ALA Council expressing ALA's regrets over the U.S. decision to withdraw from UNESCO. Another resolution was passed expressing the Association's support for the concepts embodied in H.R. 5686, extending United States membership in UNESCO to December 31, 1985, and requiring consultation with Congress prior to any decision concerning termination of U.S. participation.

The sponsor of H.R. 5686, Rep. James Albert Smith Leach, acknowledged problems with UNESCO, but pointed out that the U.S. decision to leave UNESCO has enormous philosophical as well as practical implications for American foreign policy. He said Congress should review the administration's decision carefully and present alternative perspectives, if warranted.

The full text of the two resolutions on continued United States membership in UNESCO follows:

CONTINUED UNITED STATES MEMBERSHIP IN UNESCO

WHEREAS, The United States was a founding member of the United Nations Educational, Scientific and Cultural Organization; and

WHEREAS, UNESCO's programs are vital to the international flow of publications and information, to Universal Bibliographic Control, to international copyright, to the worldwide promotion of books, libraries, publishing and literacy; and

WHEREAS, The American Library Association has been a longstanding member of the United States National Commission for UNESCO; and

WHEREAS, ALA has a strong and continuing concern for the issues of press freedoms which are addressed in the UNESCO forum; and

WHEREAS, The United States National Commission for UNESCO, on the basis of an extensive study of the views of the American Library Association and other U.S. non-governmental organizations qualified to evaluate the UNESCO program, affirmed on December 16, 1983, that continued United States membership in UNESCO is in the national interest; now, therefore, be it

RESOLVED, That the American Library Association deeply regrets the decision of the President of the United States, on recommendation of the Secretary of State, to issue notice of the intention of the United States to withdraw from membership in UNESCO effective December 31, 1984; and, be it

FURTHER RESOLVED, That the American Library Association calls upon the Secretary of State and the Director-General of UNESCO to initiate prompt, se-

International Relations

rious and productive negotiations leading to timely and satisfactory resolution of differences in order to preserve the many positive benefits of continuing U.S. participation in UNESCO; and, be it

FURTHER RESOLVED, That copies of this resolution be transmitted to the President of the United States, the Secretary of State and the Director-General of UNESCO and other appropriate bodies.

RESOLUTION ON UNITED STATES MEMBERSHIP IN UNESCO

WHEREAS, The United States has given notice of its intention to withdraw from the membership in the United Nations Educational, Scientific and Cultural Organization effective December 31, 1984; and

WHEREAS, The Council of the American Library Association, on January 11, 1984, called upon the U.S. Secretary of State and the Director-General of UNESCO to initiate negotiations leading to timely and satisfactory resolution of differences in order to preserve the many positive benefits of continuing U.S. participation in UNESCO; and

WHEREAS, These negotiations have not yet been initiated; now, therefore, be it

RESOLVED, That the American Library Association expresses its support for the concepts embodied in H.R. 5686 extending United States membership in UNESCO to December 31, 1985, and requiring consultation with the Congress prior to any decision concerning termination; and, be it

FURTHER RESOLVED, That copies of this resolution be transmitted to the President of the United States, the Secretary of State, appropriate members of Congress, the Director-General of UNESCO, The United States National Commission for UNESCO and other appropriate bodies.

In addition to the IRC sponsored president's program, the International Relations Roundtable (IRRT) sponsored two program meetings at the ALA Dallas Conference: one on European databases with ACRL's Western European Specialist Section; and one on technological developments in libraries in the Third World, cosponsored with ACRL's Asian and African section.

IFLA. For the first time in its history, the 1984 IFLA General Conference was held on African soil in Nairobi. The conference in August was sponsored by the Kenya Library Association on behalf of the government of Kenya. Guest of honor was the Vice-President of the Republic of Kenya, Mwai Kibaki. In his opening remarks at the first Plenary Session, he urged librarians in developing countries to promote children's reading habits and adult education, while being aware of the important role of oral tradition. The conference theme was "The Basis of Library and Information Services for National Development," a theme that underlined the indispensability of library and information services in national development.

The theme was covered in plenary sessions as well as professional meetings emphasizing the following aspects: promotion of the reading habit and adult education, personal resources for library and information services, and library and information systems and services.

A preconference seminar focused on aspects of grassroots training, resulting in the "Nairobi Manifesto, 1984," which reaffirmed the need for effective library services, stressed the importance of oral tradition, and called on governments for support. The seminar also urged all governments to adhere to both the spirit and the letter of the Florence Agreement and the Nairobi Protocol. It urged UNESCO to undertake a survey to determine the extent to which those agreements are being observed and to take all possible steps to ensure that any existing obstacles are removed and that the agreements are implemented in an effective manner. A resolution to repeat such an event every five years led to the recommendation to have IFLA's auspices and assistance for a Seminar on Library Education Programs in Developing Countries with special reference to Asia to be held in 1986 in Manila as an IFLA preconference event and as a follow-up to the 1980 Manila Seminar.

The Black Caucus of the ALA joined the Kenya Library Association (KLA) in organizing the first Seminar of African and African-American Librarians. The Pre-IFLA Conference Seminar brought together African librarians and American Black Librarians who presented papers and exchanged ideas on a variety of issues such as literacy programs, services to children, ethnic collections, library and bibliographic instruction, public library services, and transfer of information technology. The seminar was organized by E. J. Josey, President of the American Library Association (1984–85) and J. S. Musisi, President of the Kenya Library Association.

IFLA Conferees interested in African book publishing joined publishers and authors in Zimbabwe for the Second Zimbabwe International Book Fair in Harare.

IFLA Programs. The IFLA Executive Board approved a Medium Term Program (MTP) for 1986–89 patterned on the 1981–85 MTP with one section devoted to the work coordinated by the Professional Board (Divisions, Sections, Round Tables) and a second section on the new core program monitored by the Program Management Committee (PMC) with a special emphasis on the new core programs: advancement of librarianship in the Third World, preservation and conservation, and transborder data flow and related problems of data exchange. These core programs will be incorporated in IFLA activities.

During 1984 IFLA signed the following contracts with UNESCO:

(1) A study on transborder data flow of bibliographic information. The objectives of the study are to: (a) describe appropriate data and bibliographic references; (b) examine the impediments, the economic, financial, and legal barriers to the international circulation of bibliographic data; (c) ascertain the consequences of the impediments and barriers for the services to users of library and documentation institutions; (d) make proposals for solutions to problems identified and for actions that might be taken at the national and/or international levels.

The Impact of U.S. Withdrawal from UNESCO

The United States withdrew from membership in the United Nations Educational, Scientific and Cultural Organization (UNESCO) December 31. This decision was based upon persistent and long-standing complaints by the United States (and other Western bloc members) of excessive politicization resulting in diversion of resources from UNESCO's original goals; hostility toward Western values, notably in the areas of human rights and press freedom; and unrestrained budgetary and program growth. The special significance of this last concern is that the United States has been obliged, under UNESCO's funding formula, to contribute 25 percent of whatever total budget is approved by a majority of the 161 member states.

Professional Response. As reported elsewhere in this volume (see International Relations) the American Library Association urged negotiation of differences between the United States and UNESCO, while consistently expressing opposition to U.S. withdrawal. ALA was joined in this effort in 1984 by the Special Libraries Association, the Society of American Archivists, and other national scholarly and civic organizations. The United States National Commission for UNESCO, a 100-member citizen body created by Congress to advise on UNESCO matters, and including representatives from the library, information, and communications fields, concluded after careful study that despite UNESCO's shortcomings, the national interests of the United States were best served by continued membership. Similarly, the American Library Association has affirmed the importance of UNESCO's library and information-related programs to the North American and the world library communities.

U.S. Position. In announcing the intention of the United States to withdraw from UNESCO, the Department of State expressed a commitment to redirect the approximately $47,000,000 annual U.S. contribution to the support of alternative bilateral and multilateral activities in international education, science, culture, and communications, including selected UNESCO programs that are judged to be meritorious and/or of high priority interest to the U.S. The United States National Committee for the UNESCO General Information Program (PGI), representing a broad range of organizations and institutions concerned with international programs in the library, information and archival fields, has developed a proposal for alternative mechanisms to channel U.S. support to key international programs in the Committee's areas of competence and to maintain linkages with the world professional community during the period of American absence from UNESCO.[1]

The United States government has frequently expressed its intention to rejoin UNESCO at some future time when that organization has accomplished what are considered essential reforms. In the interim, three concerns become paramount: (1) to find ways to continue participation in and support for those UNESCO programs that are of special importance to the U.S. library and information communities; (2) to maintain essential contacts between American library and information professionals and institutions and their overseas counterparts; and (3) to protect vital U.S. interests in the free and unrestricted flow of information in all forms across national boundaries.

PGI Activities. Historically, UNESCO has given a high priority to the charge under its original charter to "promote the free flow of ideas by word and image" among all the peoples of the world. It has developed and implemented a broad range of effective programs to strengthen library and information infrastructures both nationally and internationally and to enhance access to information worldwide. Since 1976, many of the major UNESCO programs relating to books, libraries, information, and archives have been administered through the General Information Program (PGI).

Among PGI's most notable accomplishments have been publication of many useful books, reports, and pamphlets as well as the influential *UNESCO Journal of Information Science, Librarianship and Archives Administration* (recently suspended for budgetary reasons); active support of IFLA's Universal Bibliographic Control (UBC) and Universal Access to Publications (UAP) programs; the highly regarded Records and Archives Management (RAMP) training program to preserve the documentary and cultural heritage of the developing nations; formulation of international policies, norms, standards, and agreements in the information field in conjunction with the International Organization for Standardization (ISO); support for training of professional personnel and establishment of library demonstration projects in the less-developed countries. As the successor to UNESCO's UNISIST program, PGI has emphasized creation of regional networks to facilitate the sharing of scientific and technical information, accompanied by the provision of support and technical assistance to the developing countries in acquiring modern electronic information storage and transfer capabilities. By virtue of its status as an intersectoral program, operating under the guidance of a 30-nation Intergovernmental Council on which the United States has been represented, the PGI has been able to distance itself from the highly controversial proposals for restrictions on the press that have been debated (although not implemented) in other UNESCO forums under the rubric of a "New World Information and Communications Order" (NWICO).[2]

Other UNESCO Activities. Other areas of the UNESCO program that are of major importance to the U.S. library and information communities include international copyright. UNESCO acts as the Secretariat for the Universal Copyright Convention, in which the United States holds both membership and a seat on the Intergovernmental Copyright Committee. It is widely speculated that the latter could be lost as a consequence of withdrawal.

Closely related are the UNESCO-sponsored Beirut, Florence, and Nairobi Agreements, which provide for reciprocal lowering of tariff barriers to facilitate the import of print and audiovisual materials of an educa-

Amadou-Mahtar M'Bow, Director General of UNESCO, addressed the ALA Conference in Dallas. At right is ALA Executive Director Robert Wedgeworth.

International Relations

International Relations

tional nature, as well as scientific instruments. The Department of State has acknowledged, in a recent report to the Congress, the significance of these agreements to American libraries in obtaining materials published overseas, as well as their importance for the economic well-being of the U.S. publishing and media industries. Access to publications from other countries is essential to meeting the informational needs of U.S. scholars, scientists and other researchers in a time when, as the Director of the U.S. Department of Commerce National Technical Information Service points out, between 75 and 80 percent of all scientific research and development is now being carried on outside the United States. Noting that withdrawal from UNESCO could result in a reduction or even loss of access by the U.S. scientific community to information in both print and electronic form, the National Academy of Sciences concluded that "in the area of the sciences at least, there is no real alternative to UNESCO at the present time."[3]

Among other UNESCO activities of special significance to librarians are its worldwide literacy programs, especially in the training of literacy personnel. Its Action to Promote Books and Reading, under the leadership of the International Book Committee, has been an important force in supporting the development of indigenous publishing and bookselling capabilities in the Third World through such activities as sponsorship of the International Year of the Book (1972) and the World Congress on Books (1982). Literacy Training and Books and Reading are both currently ranked among the "15 best UNESCO programs" by the Western nations.

Consequences and Concerns. American librarians are also concerned about the future of UNESCO depository collections in U.S. libraries and the continuation of UNESCO's important role as the major source of reliable international statistical data relating to books, media, and libraries. Special note should also be taken of the International Program for the Development of Communications (IPDC), established in 1978 at the initiative of the Western nations as a positive response to the expressed desire of the developing countries to achieve parity in the critical area of information and communications. This relatively new and modest UNESCO program, in which the United States has played a major role, has already served as an effective counterforce to the more objectionable proposals to restrict journalistic freedom originally advanced by Third World advocates of the New World Information and Communications Order, with active support from the Eastern bloc.[4]

ALA Past President Thomas Galvin (right) with Representative Douglas Walgren of Pennsylvania. Galvin testified before two subcommittees of the House Committee on Science and Technology, urging the U.S. to stay in UNESCO. (American Libraries)

During the period of U.S. absence from UNESCO, it is likely that library and information professionals from the United States will experience a significant reduction in opportunities both to influence and to participate in a range of significant international activities and programs. It is important that the several national professional organizations take effective action, both individually and collectively, to minimize this potential isolation from the emerging world information community. Every effort should be made to encourage reinstatement of U.S. membership in UNESCO at the earliest practicable date, and, in the interim, to assure that book, library, and information programs receive a priority of support from any funds that become available as a consequence of the U.S. withdrawal.

Declining Participation. The last decade has witnessed a significant decline in the level and quality of U.S. involvement in several of the important international nongovernmental organizations in the library and information field. The U.S. National Committee for the UNESCO/PGI reports, for example, that United States' membership has lapsed in the International Council of Scientific Unions Abstracting Board (ICSU/AB), that there is at present no U.S. national member of the International Federation for Documentation (FID), and that the United States is currently represented on only two of the six active subcommittees of Technical Committee 46 of the ISO, which addresses international information standards. By contrast, the Soviet Union is actively represented on all six subcommittees, as are West Germany and Japan.

Implications. The decision of the United States to withdraw from UNESCO has immediate and potentially profound implications for the American library community. A major individual and organizational effort will be needed to identify, find, and implement alternatives to some UNESCO-sponsored activities. In other instances, there indeed appears to be no viable alternative to UNESCO. In such cases, every effort needs to be made to maintain a U.S. presence in international forums that are essential to U.S. libraries or that will shape future policies governing the flow of information and data in all formats across international boundaries.

THOMAS J. GALVIN

REFERENCES

1. United States National Committee for the UNESCO/PGI, "Proposal for Alternative Mechanisms to Accomplish U.S. Objectives in the International Library/Information Area" (July 23, 1984).
2. "ALA, UNESCO and NWICO," *ALA Newsletter on Intellectual Freedom* (May 1984).
3. National Research Council, Office of International Affairs, *UNESCO Science Programs: Impacts of U.S. Withdrawal and Suggestions for Alternative Interim Arrangements* (Washington: National Academy Press, 1984).
4. UNESCO International Commission for the Study of Communication Problems, *Many Voices, One World* (London: Kogan Page, 1980).
   Anthony Smith. *The Geopolitics of Information* (New York: Oxford University Press, 1980).
   U.S. National Commission for UNESCO. *Toward An American Agenda for a New World Order of Communications* (Washington, 1981).

U.S.-China Exchanges of Librarians

Beginning with the visit of a single American librarian in 1972 after the U.S. opening to the People's Republic of China engineered by Secretary of State Henry Kissinger and President Richard Nixon, the flow of librarians between the two countries has swelled to a significant stream, especially in the five years since the establishment of diplomatic relations in 1979. Some 72 Chinese librarians have been reported in North American library schools and institutions primarily for the 1983–84 and 1984–85 academic years, with at least a dozen American librarians traveling to China during the same period for professional purposes. Among the estimated 10,000 students from China (out of about 338,400 foreign students enrolled in American college and universities), the number of librarians is still quite low, but the trend in recent years has been upward.

Official interchange has been encouraged by the implementing accords governing the U.S.–People's Republic of China Cultural Agreement signed in 1979 and the U.S.–China Science and Technology Protocol originally signed in 1982 providing, inter alia, for the promotion of exchanges of information science specialists. In the private sector, the interchange has increased with institutional support, especially by the Simmons College Graduate School of Library and Information Science, the Columbia University School of Library Service, the UCLA Graduate School of Library and Information Science, and the University of Pittsburgh library system, with substantial funding provided by the United Board for Christian Higher Education in Asia and other private and federal government sources.

Chinese Students and Faculty in North American Institutions. Some 58 students or visiting scholars were reported in residence during the 1983–84 and 1984–85 academic years by 28 library schools in the United States and Canada responding to a questionnaire in which names, home institutions, and sources of funding were requested. (The questionnaire, mailed in September 1984, was sent to 69 library schools in North America, as well as to selected East Asian collections in university libraries, known funding sources, and other organizations. Of the 69 library schools, 28 reported students from China, 7 reported none, and 34 did not respond. The numbers of librarians given in this article, therefore, are probably well under the actual numbers involved in international interchange.)

Most of the Chinese librarians were found to be enrolled in MSLS programs, but four were seeking the doctorate, and 14 were listed as visiting scholars. The library schools were those at Brigham Young, California–Berkeley, California–Los Angeles, Chicago, Clarion, Columbia, Denver, Drexel, Emory, Hawaii, Illinois, Indiana, Kent State, Maryland, McGill, Michigan, North Carolina, Pittsburgh, Rosary, Rutgers, Simmons, Southern Mississippi, SUNY–Albany, Syracuse, Toronto, Washington, Western Ontario, and Wisconsin. In addition to the 58 students and visiting scholars, 14 librarians or information scientists were reported in residence as interns or as participants in extended work/study programs during 1982–84 at the university libraries of Ohio, Seton Hall, Washington, and Yale, as well as at the Library of Congress, the National Agricultural Library, and the National Technical Information Service of the Department of Commerce.

Most of the library schools reported single students but several had 2–3 librarians in residence. Topping the list were Illinois and West Ontario (4 librarians each), Columbia and UCLA (5 librarians each), and Simmons (6). Some 28 Chinese institutions have sent students, with by far the largest contingent coming from Wuhan University (11 students), the university with the first and still the largest library school in China. Wuhan was followed by the Institute of Scientific and Technical Information of China (ISTIC, in Beijing, with branches in Shanghai and Chengdu, sent 7 staff members), Beijing [Peking] University and the Chinese Academy of Sciences (5 each), Sichuan University and the Ministry of Machine Building Industry (4 each), and Shanghai Jiaotong University (3). Other universities or government bodies represented were Beijing Foreign Languages Institute, Beijing Normal University, Chinese Academy of Agriculture and Forestry, Chinese Academy of Social Sciences, Dalian Institute, East China Normal University (Shanghai), Fujian Normal University, Guangdong Foreign Languages Institute (Canton), Huazhong University, Institute of International Studies (Beijing), Ministry of Agriculture, Nanjing [Nanking] University, National Library of China, Shenyang Agricultural University, Tianjin [Tientsin] College of Economics, Tianjin Foreign Languages Institute, Tianjin Municipal Library, Tianjin University, Wuhan Medical College, Xian Normal University, and Zhongshan University (Canton). While institutions throughout China are represented, clearly students from North China (Beijing, Tianjin) and Central China (Wuhan, Shanghai) are the most numerous.

Most of the students/scholars are supported in full or in part by their home institutions. The single most important U.S. source of scholarship support is the United Board for Christian Higher Education in Asia, which provides partial funding for 15 students and faculty, mostly at Columbia and Simmons. Other sources of funding include the Asia Foundation, the Ford Foundation, the World Bank, and UNESCO. Tuition or other support are also provided by the host universities, through such mechanisms as the BYU Chinese Students Scholarship Program, the Rosary College Visiting Scholars Program, the Wisconsin graduate assistantship program, and the University of Michigan Barbour scholarship for Asian women.

Individual and Group Exchanges. In 1972 Chi Wang, who was on leave from the Chinese and Korean Section of the Library of Congress and serving as the University Librarian of the Chinese University of Hong Kong, was the first American librarian to visit China in recent decades when he called on libraries in four cities during a two-week trip. In the following year an official delegation of 12 Chinese librarians headed by Liu Jiping, director of the then National Library of Beijing, toured libraries in the U.S. under the sponsorship of the Committee on Scholarly Communication with the People's Republic of China headquartered at the National Academy of Sciences. It was not until 1979 that an official U.S. delegation of 12 headed by William J. Welsh, Deputy Librarian of Congress, was able to accept the invitation tendered by the National Library for a reciprocal visit. That delegation included representatives of the American Library Association, the Association of Research Libraries, and the Association for Asian Studies as well as the Library of Congress.

Agreement was reached on official exchanges of publications and personnel between the Library of Congress and the National Library of China, in keeping with the implementing accord to the cultural exchange signed earlier that year. In the following year, ALA organized a China study tour that included 26 librarians representing university and public libraries and library schools in the U.S. and Canada. In 1982 the second official delegation of Chinese librarians, a group of four from the National Library of China, visited American libraries under USIA auspices following the delegation's attendance at the IFLA conference in Montreal. It was followed in spring 1984 by the second official American delegation to China, once again headed by Welsh but this time con-

International Relations

sisting of five members of the Library of Congress staff. During the two-week visit to Beijing, Wuhan, Shanghai, Hangzhou, and Guilin, the delegation met with some 800 librarians eager for news of developments in American librarianship. Prepared lectures were presented, on managing change in libraries faced with technological developments, on the national and international role of the Library of Congress in automation and networking, and on collections and services for research. Motion picture films on LC and on high technology preservation advances were also screened.

In recent years, moreover, individual librarians have lectured extensively in their areas of specialization. They include Warren J. Haas, President, Council on Library Resources; Rutherford D. Rogers, University Librarian, Yale University; Henriette Avram, Assistant Librarian for Processing Services, Library of Congress; Frederick G. Kilgour, founder of OCLC; and Josephine R. Fang, Simmons College. Fang, who is responsible for selecting library and information science materials for the Wuhan library school library, has received the honorary title of "Professor" from that institution for this and other activities in support of librarianship in China.

Register of Copyrights David Ladd spent two weeks in Shanghai in July 1984 on a training program on copyright for 120 trainees from publishing houses in China. It was supported by UNESCO and involved consultants from Algeria, Sweden, the Soviet Union, India, Italy, and the U.S. In 1981 LC's Copyright Office had dispatched a small delegation for consultation and to conduct training sessions in copyright in Beijing and Shanghai. It had received a Chinese copyright delegation in Washington in 1983 and planned to bring a Chinese delegation to the Copyright Office for two to three weeks in spring 1985. Unusual experiences have been gained by Michael Nilan and Walter Zahaki, faculty members at the Rutgers University School of Communication, Information, and Library Studies, who are engaged in a research project with Professor Cheng Peiwei of Fudan University, Shanghai, to investigate mutual images in communications exchanges involving businessmen. Perhaps the first American library school student in China was Cheryl M. Boettcher, who is enrolled in the Certificate of Advanced Study degree program at the University of Illinois at Urbana–Champaign Library School and who was an exchange student at Beijing University during the 1983–84 academic year.

Of special interest have been the activities of Chinese-speaking specialists invited to China under various auspices. Thus Hwa-Wei Lee, Director of Libraries, Ohio University Libraries, taught a short course in the management of scientific and technical information centers in China, in Kunming in December 1982. Hwa-Wei Lee was sponsored by ISTIC and the International Development Research Center. Eugene W. Wu, Librarian, Harvard-Yenching Library, Harvard University, and Karl K. Lo, Head of the East Asian Library, University of Washington, conducted library training workshops in southwest and northwest China, in programs sponsored by the United Board for Christian Higher Education in Asia.

Nelson Chou, Librarian, East Asian Library, Rutgers, lectured on library science during summer 1983 at Jilin University in northeast China. Ching-chih Chen, Simmons College, has lectured extensively in China, most recently conducting workshops for UNESCO and the World Health Organization during fall 1984. Hsiao-chiang Chen, Principal Catalog Librarian, East Asian Collection, Yale, spent a month in fall 1984 as a guest of the Chinese Academy of Sciences library. She lectured on library automation not only in Beijing but also at the academy's branches in Chengdu, Wuhan, and Canton.

Special Institutional Programs. In addition to the substantial movement of individuals and groups, a variety of projects have been conceived both in the private and government sectors to bring librarians from the U.S. and China into cooperative relationships. Perhaps the most interesting in the private sector are the initiatives of the United Board for Christian Higher Education in Asia, working with library schools in the United States and with universities in China.

In addition to providing partial funding for students and faculty at American library schools, the United Board by 1984 had provided major grants totaling $430,000 over a five-year period toward the establishment of regional library resource centers at universities in the hinterlands, the first at Sichuan University in Chengdu in the southwest, and the second at Shanxi Teachers University in Xian in the northwest. The funds were used for acquisitions programs primarily in the humanities and the social sciences and for the purchase of library equipment by the two libraries, as well as for library training workshops in the two cities and elsewhere conducted by Wu of Harvard and Lo of the University of Washington.

The United Board has also provided smaller grants for book and equipment purchases to a limited number of institutions—such as the Beijing Foreign Languages Institute and Xiamen University in Amoy—as well as small book grants to returning scholars to enrich departmental libraries, particularly in the humanities and social sciences. Assistance was also provided to the Foundation for Books to China to ship microfilmed dissertations to the National Library.

In an entirely different area, Simmons College has been awarded a $219,000 grant from the National Endowment for the Humanities to conduct an innovative videodisk project covering the archeological site in Xian discovered in 1974. This is the enormous burial vault for a life-size army of imperial guards and horses in terra cotta protecting the tomb of Qin Shi Huang, the first emperor of the Qin (Ch'in) dynasty, who unified China in 221 BC. The experimental use of videodisk technology to bring the extraordinary finds being unearthed to the American library public is being conducted by Ching-chih Chen of Simmons College as project director with the assistance of Robert D. Stueart, Dean of the Simmons graduate library school, and Charles Goldstein, Chief, Information Technology branch, National Library of Medicine, and with the advice of anthropologist K. C. Chang, Harvard University, and the art historian Wu Tung, Boston Museum of Fine Art.

Another innovative program and one with great potential in a country accustomed to the closed-stack philosophy of librarianship is a venture involving the University of Pittsburgh library system and Shanghai Jiaotong University, a major polytechnic university with which Pittsburgh has had a cooperative relationship for five years. Jiaotong had received a $10,000,000 grant from Y. K. Pao, a Hong Kong shipping magnate, to construct China's most modern university library facility featuring an open-stack, open-access system integrated into the university's instructional program.

Under a $53,070 grant from the Office of Academic Programs, Bureau of Educational and Cultural Affairs, U.S. Information Agency, Pittsburgh is administering an exchange-of-personnel program to provide training for Chinese librarians and to support consultants. Three Jiaotong students were in residence at Pittsburgh in 1984–85, two of whom, as full-time students in the School of Library and Information Science, were specializing in the organization and automation of libraries. They were expected to complete requirements for their master's degrees in 1986. The third, working as an intern in the university library learning about computerized cata-

International Relations

loging and technical processes, was also auditing courses at the library school.

Anne Woodworth, Associate Provost and Director of University Libraries, spent one week in October–November 1984 in Shanghai to study the library and to make arrangements for a Pittsburgh specialist to be sent to Jiaotong for a three-month consultancy in spring 1985.

The Seton Hall University Library has developed a unique ongoing staff exchange program with the library of the Chinese Academy of Sciences. The University had earlier entered into a "sister" relationship with Wuhan University and the Foreign Trade Institute in 1979. In 1982 James C. Sharp, University Librarian, and Charles Yen, Chief Reference Librarian, began an exchange of librarians program by accepting an invitation extended by the Chinese Academy of Sciences. Each year since then the Academy has sent a librarian to Seton Hall for a six-month internship of practical training, and Seton Hall has sent a librarian to China in return.

The Asia Foundation has concentrated on its well-known Books for Asia Program. During fiscal 1984 it shipped a total of 38,722 books and 17,364 journals to 36 libraries and research institutes in China. The Foundation is also brokering proposed sister law library relationships entered into throughout Asia, including China, and will provide shipping for exchanges of legal materials. The Foundation has provided a fellowship in the past for a Chinese librarian, but it will continue to give books priority for its program in China.

In the field of technical information interchange, the U.S. National Technical Information Service (NTIS) and the Institute of Scientific and Technical Information of China have cooperated from 1982 in the exchange of technical information specialists. A report by American technical information specialists conducting workshops in 1983 was issued as a technical report by the Mitre Corporation. Meanwhile, a new U.S.–China protocol has been adopted calling for technical information exchange activities, including further work study programs such as those conducted during 1983–84 by NTIS for Chinese information specialists from ISTIC. Two were in residence at NTIS in 1984, one a specialist in computers, the other in micrographics. At the same time, the Office of International Affairs of NTIS was seeking qualified U.S. information specialists to lecture in China. International transportation must be paid by the selectee, but costs in China will be borne by ISTIC, the host organization.

The National Agricultural Library reported the extended visit of a five-man study team from the Chinese Academy of Agricultural Sciences and its Institute of Information on Agricultural Science and Technology. NAL planned the tour, which began in San Francisco on September 4, 1983, and concluded in New York on November 10. The team visited libraries and information and computer centers in California, Colorado, Wisconsin, Michigan, Ohio, and Maryland, spending about three weeks studying the organization, services and resources of NAL.

As 1984 drew to a close another project, led by Dean Robert D. Stueart of Simmons, was reaching fruition under the auspices of the Citizen Ambassador Program of People to People International in the U.S. and of the Society of Library Science in China. A team of library and information science specialists was to be organized for a three-week lecture tour of Chinese libraries in spring 1985 to share information on all aspects of librarianship and information exchange with counterparts in China. By December the delegation was already oversubscribed. The Special Libraries Association was also working, at the invitation of the Council on Foreign Relations, on plans with the Council's committee on International Relations Exchanges for cultural exchange with the People's Republic of China. Discussions were in the preliminary planning stage at year's end.

Stueart also assumed the chairmanship of the Advisory Committee on Liaison with Chinese Libraries, an ad hoc group appointed by the ALA International Relations Committee. According to Stueart, the advisory committee will continue to function as a sounding board for various exchange proposals and as an information resource for American librarians interested in cooperative programs with China.

The two-way flow of librarians between China and the U.S. has developed significantly in the past five years. During the visits of the two official U.S. delegations to Beijing in 1979 and in 1984, virtually identical observations on the importance of the interchange were made by Chinese officials. Thus, during the first trip, Vice Premier Fang Yi, in a meeting with the American delegation, expressed his desire to have Chinese librarians learn library modernization techniques from the U.S. Five years later Zhu Muzhi, Minister of Culture, expressed the same sentiments to the second delegation, noting that China's libraries had fallen behind their Western counterparts despite a long history of libraries covering 2,000 years and expressing appreciation to American librarians for reaching out to their Chinese colleagues. Such sentiments augur well for increased interchange in coming years.

WARREN TSUNEISHI

---

(2) A study on the tools to improve the availability of materials for the blind. The study will include a survey of lists and directories of institutions and libraries holding materials for the blind; an investigation of the various means and mechanisms that might improve the availability of materials for the blind at the national and international levels, and suggestions for action.

Exchanges and Aid to Overseas Libraries. The ALA International Relations Committee explored forms of assistance to libraries and librarians in developing countries. These include paying a national association's IFLA subscription; financing particular projects and needs; training by means of personnel exchange; and exchange of professional literature.

The IRC in cooperation with the International Relations Round Table established a joint committee on Librarians' Exchange. The joint committee includes representatives from the Seminar on the Acquisitions of Latin American Library Materials (SALALM), the Association for Library and Information Science Education (ALISE), and interested divisions within ALA.

The ALA received a grant from the USIA and the International Institute of Education under the short-term enrichment program to encourage foreign students to attend the ALA Annual Conference in Dallas. Eleven students were selected; each received $250.

The Special Libraries Association was invited by the Council on Foreign Relations to participate in the planning for a cultural ex-

International Relations Round Table

change with the People's Republic of China. The Council's Committee on International Relations Exchanges with the People's Republic of China coordinates this effort.

To enrich collections of library schools in developing countries that could not pay membership dues, the Association for Library and Information Science Education, through its International Education Committee, decided to ship surplus issues of its *Journal of Education for Library and Information Science* to select library schools in Latin America, Asia, and Africa. Cost of shipping issues of the journal will be born by such organizations as the Asia Foundation and the Organization of American States.

The Carl Milam lecturer for 1984 was Graham Corr, Head of the Department of Librarianship at Melbourne College of Advanced Education. His lecture on models of Library Education in Australia was presented during spring 1984 at 10 library schools.

MOHAMMED M. AMAN

International Relations Round Table

The major event of 1984 for IRRT was the foreign visitors' reception at the Annual Conference in Dallas. Largely through the efforts of Ana Cleveland of Texas Woman's University, the reception was successful, attracting what may have been a record number of foreign visitors and a large number of paying guests. The receiving line included, in addition to IRRT officers, Brooke Sheldon, ALA President; William Welch, Deputy Librarian of Congress; and Else Granheim of Norway, President of the International Federation of Library Associations (IFLA). Among the nations represented at the affair were Australia, China, Germany, Hungary, Jordan, Mexico, Nigeria, Pakistan, Taiwan, and Yugoslavia.

The Hospitality Booth, another regular service of IRRT, operated during the Dallas Conference, providing assistance to foreign visitors. IRRT also cosponsored a program at the Conference in cooperation with the Asian and African section of ACRL.

Among the actions taken at the 1984 Midwinter Meeting in Washington, chaired by Warren Tsuneishi, was a vote to support the resolution proposed by the ALA International Relations Committee opposing U.S. withdrawal from UNESCO. At the ALA Annual Conference in Dallas the Executive Committee approved the appointment of a joint committee with the International Relations Committee and other groups to study possible programs for international exchanges of librarians, educators, and students.

IRRT in 1984 continued to publish *Leads* quarterly, under the editorship of William L. Williamson of the University of Wisconsin at Madison. *Leads,* published continuously under its present title since 1957, features articles, news, and notes on international activities, including reports from the area chairpersons.

Though a small organization, IRRT involves a significant number of members in its activities through its officers, area chairpersons, and representatives to other organizations. Area chairpersons for 1984–85 were *Africa*, David Easterbrook, University of Illinois at Chicago; *East Asia,* Hideo Kaneko, Yale University; *Latin America,* Louella Wetherbee, AMIGOS Bibliographic Council, Inc., Dallas, Texas; *Middle East and North Africa,* E. Christian Filstrup, New York Public Library; *South Asia,* Ravinda Sharma, Freedom, Pennsylvania; and *Southeast Asia,* Kent Mulliner and Lian Mulliner, Ohio University, Athens, Ohio. IRRT representatives to other organizations were Boris Raymond, Freedom to Read Foundation; Ana D. Cleveland, SCOLE Library Education Assembly; and Elizabeth A. Widenmann, Columbia University, Committee on Cataloging: Description and Access, Cataloging and Classification Section, Resources and Technical Services Division.

IRRT's visibility within ALA has been blurred somewhat in recent years by the lack of a full-time international relations officer, although the parent organization provides a liaison staff person to facilitate communication with IRRT.

Deaths. IRRT and international librarianship lost two important members upon the deaths of Eleanor Mitchell and Marietta Daniels Shepard in 1984. Both of these dynamic people had devoted much of their lives to promoting librarianship and library education in Latin America. At the time of her retirement in 1972, Eleanor Mitchell was project officer in the International Relations Office of ALA. Prior to her retirement, Marietta Shepard had served as chief of the Li-

> **INTERNATIONAL RELATIONS ROUND TABLE**
>
> CHAIRPERSON (July 1984–July 1985):
> **Edwin S. Gleaves,** Chair, Department of Library Science, Vanderbilt University, Nashville.
>
> VICE-CHAIRPERSON:
> **Esther J. Walls,** State University of New York at Stony Brook
>
> SECRETARY-TREASURER:
> **Joan Collett,** Public Library, St. Louis, Missouri
>
> Membership (August 31, 1984): 574 (487 personal; 87 organizational)
> Expenditures (August 31, 1984): $4,265

Three generations of International Relations Round Table officers gathered at the ALA Annual Conference. They are, from left, Edwin S. Gleaves, Vanderbilt University, 1984–85; Ester J. Walls, SUNY–Stony Brook, 1985–86; and Warren Tsuneishi, Library of Congress, 1983–94.

brary and Archives Development Program of the Organization of American States. *Leads* dedicated portions of the fall 1984 and winter 1985 issues to Mitchell and Shepard.

EDWIN S. GLEAVES

Italian Americans and Libraries

Immigrants and Libraries. According to the *International Handbook of Contemporary Development in Librarianship*, Italian immigrants in the United States today have a more sophisticated appreciation of libraries and librarianship than the earlier immigrants of the 1900s. Because of the Italian government's attempt to eradicate illiteracy and to move the Italian library system from an elitist service to one of mass appeal, use of Italian public or community libraries increased more than 700 percent in the last 30 years.

Furthermore, there has been an increase in Italian publishing. There are 1,000 publishers in Italy with 350 publishers accounting for more than 90 percent of materials printed. The largest publishing centers are Milan, Rome, and Turin.

Some immigrants coming into the United States are not familiar with the open access of American Libraries. To bridge the gap in this functional knowledge, library systems with identified foreign language populations have offered film and referral services in the Italian language while at the same time offering programs in English as a second language. At the Chesterfield County Public Library, volunteers speaking foreign languages are made available through the library. At the Queensborough Public Library, Italian films with English subtitles are shown through the New Americans Project under Adrianna Tandler.

Continued interest in library service to language groups is shown by the number of articles on this subject during 1983 in *Library Journal*, *Wilson Library Bulletin*, *Catholic Library World*, *Library Trends*, and *Public Library Quarterly*. The importance of this subject may also be inferred from the spirit of the National Commission on Library and Information Science Report of 1981–82 on meeting the special needs of cultural minorities and seen in the direction of the work of the North Carolina Foreign Language Center.

The American Library Association's SRRT Ethnic Materials Round Table provides a vehicle for Association members to work to provide specific data to librarians in the field who work with foreign language groups. The American Library Association's Minority Concerns Committee presents policy recommendations to the Council of the Association relevant to minority concerns.

The Italian American Librarians Caucus. The Italian American Librarians Caucus has tried to anticipate and promote Italian American use of libraries and encourage participation of Italian American librarians within the ALA. Though it did not produce any major studies during 1984, it supported the formation of the Ethnic Materials Information Round Table and presented its position on the question of the professional library degree. Aware that some librarians would use foreign language specialists with or without a library degree to work with foreign language populations, the Caucus is also aware that the federal government's need for a balanced budget will place on the states a greater burden for the services now funded wholly or in part by the federal government.

Future Projects. The Caucus plans to provide a study of the information field relevant to the Italian American population in the United States as well as a specific guide for local library referral agencies.

1984 marks the 200th anniversary of the Constitutional Society of 1784. It was organized by Philip Mazzei when he returned from Europe, where he had been Virginia's agent from 1779 to 1783.

Sister Margherita Marchione edited a three-volume set of *Selected Writings and Correspondence* of Mazzei and deposited original manuscripts at the American Philosophical Society Library in Philadelphia. Sister Marchione is at Fairleigh Dickinson University, Florham-Madison Campus, Madison, New Jersey.

C. MICHAEL DIODATI

Junior Members Round Table

JMRT Activities. During its 53d year the Junior Members Round Table in 1984 served the diverse needs and interests of its members from all types and sizes of libraries and information centers in three significant ways: "as a gateway to the profession, a pathfinder through the maze of ALA, and a stepping-stone to higher places."

Awards. Through professional and career development programs, professional development grants and scholarships, and contacts with more experienced librarians, JMRT serves as a gateway for new members entering the library profession. The 3M/JMRT Professional Development Grant, established in 1975, encourages professional development and participation by beginning professionals in ALA and JMRT. Funding in 1984 from the 3M Company provided the opportunity for four librarians to attend the 103d ALA Annual Conference in Dallas. For the first time in the Program's history, the award was given to an applicant from the Canadian Library Association. The 1984 recipients included Diane Bisom, Orion User Services Librarian at UCLA; Dominique Coulombe, Copy Catalog Librarian at Brown University; James Mouw, Acquisitions Librarian at the University of Illinois at Chicago; and Terri Tomchyshyn, Legal Services Librarian at the Saskatoon Public Library in Saskatchewan.

The Shirley Olofson Memorial Awards provide three grants of $100 to JMRT members who have demonstrated a commitment to professional development and involvement in national, state, and local activities, to attend their second Annual Conference. Recipients were Diane Bronson, Public Library Consultant for Federal Programs at the State Library of Florida; Kathleen Moeller-Peiffer, Librarian at the Orange County Public Library in Hillsborough, North Carolina; and Heather Smith, a student at the UCLA Graduate School of Library and Information Science.

During the 1983–84 year, Baker & Taylor

Members of Junior Members Round Table gathered at a social reception during the 1984 ALA Annual Conference in Dallas. (American Libraries)

Grassroots Grants were presented to students in 34 states. Established in 1978, the grants provide $250 to one library school student from each state and the District of Columbia to attend a state or regional conference.

The 1984 Friendly Booth Award was presented during the JMRT Membership Meeting to Ebsco Subscription Services.

Committees. Several new committees and positions were formed this year, bringing the total organization to 30 committees and 11 liaison positions. The new ones were the Awards Breakfast Committee, formed to plan an awards breakfast to recognize all JMRT national and state award winners; the Fund Raising Committee, to help in obtaining additional finances to support the Round Table's many efforts; the President's Program Committee, to plan a second Annual Conference program; the Scholarship Committee, to establish a JMRT scholarship to be given annually to a worthy student to enroll in a program of library education at the graduate level; and a Liaison Coordinator, to define the roles of liaisons and establish guidelines for this important part of the organization.

Committees, established in 1983, accomplished much in their first year. The Brochure Committee updated the newly printed listing of JMRT committees and their functions and distributed the brochures through the Membership and Minorities Recruitment committees. The Clearinghouse Committee provided JMRT members with the service of assisting those who wish to be considered for an ALA committee appointment in Divisions, Sections, or Round Tables.

Annual Conference. The JMRT Orientation Program at the Annual Conference featured Texas folklorist and humorist John Henry Faulk, who spoke about the hysteria that existed during the McCarthy era and his experience of being blacklisted. Establishing career goals, interviewing, skills marketing, position development, and promotability were among the topics addressed at the JMRT Membership Committee program, "Pounding the Pavement." Ginnie Cooper, Head Librarian at Alameda County Library, and Charles McClure, Associate Professor at the University of Oklahoma School of Library Sciences, were speakers. The topic of "ALA's Hidden Agenda" was addressed by Dorothy Anderson of UCLA's Graduate School of Library and Information Science at the JMRT President's Program. Thomas Galvin, Past ALA President, Richard Dougherty, ACRL 1982 Academic/Research Librarian of the Year, June Breland, Past President of JMRT, and Beverly Lynch, ALA President-elect, discussed their involvement and strategies for success in ALA.

JMRT cosponsored two programs at the Annual Conference: "Training Issues in Changing Technology" with the LAMA/PAS/Staff Development Committee and LITA and "Who's Afraid of Serials" with the RTSD/Resources Section/Acquisitions Committee.

Other Conference activities included the annual Students to ALA Reception at the Dallas Public Library; the first annual JMRT Awards Breakfast with featured speaker Hugh Atkinson of the University of Illinois; and the Annual All-Conference Social.

CHARLES E. KRATZ

Labor Groups, Library Service To

Organization Activities. The AFL/CIO–ALA Joint Committee on Library Service to Labor Groups, Reference and Adult Services Division, presented the program "Recession/Recovery: Libraries Serve the Unemployed" at the 1984 ALA Annual Conference in Dallas. Keynote speaker was Robert Glover, Director of the Center for the Study of Human Resources, University of Texas, who addressed the impact of current economic conditions on the labor force. A reactor panel followed, featuring Jane Bryan, Director of the Jackson–George Regional Library System, Pascagoula, Mississippi, and Isaac Jackson, Special Assistant to Texas U.S. Senator Lloyd Bentsen and a laid-off steel worker.

Those attending indicated a special interest in working with unions, locating materials useful to blue-collar workers, and sharing literature. To help meet the latter need, the Joint Committee developed a table-top display of library and union brochures for the unemployed, available for loan to state associations and other interested groups through Arthur S. Meyers, Muncie (Indiana) Public Library. The exhibit was displayed at

---

JUNIOR MEMBERS ROUND TABLE

PRESIDENT (June 1984–July 1985):
Charles E. Kratz, Jr., Rider College Library, Lawrenceville, New Jersey

PRESIDENT-ELECT:
Anders C. Dahlgren, Hoffman Estates, Illinois

SECRETARY:
Diane J. Cimbala, Reese Library, Augusta College, Georgia

Membership (August 31, 1984): 1,047 (968 personal; 79 organizational)
Expenditures (August 31, 1984): $8,096

the ALA Conference and at the October Nevada Library Association Conference.

In preparation for the Conference program, the Joint Committee conducted a survey of library services for the unemployed under the direction of Joint Committee Co-chair Arthur Meyers. A summary of survey results was published in *RQ* (Fall 1984). The special services being offered are varied, ranging from workshops on job-search strategies to educational counseling to special resource centers in the library and the community.

Many services utilize new technologies, thus expanding the range of information delivery and the scope of problem-solving services. The Columbus and Franklin County Public Library, for example, offers free searches on the Ohio Career Information Service Data Bank. The Arrowhead Library System (Janesville, Wisconsin) uses a microcomputer to help displaced workers evaluate work skills. The Hammond (Indiana) Public Library offers a computer-generated résumé service.

A Michigan library network (Upper Peninsula Region of Library Cooperation, Inc.) received a large grant from the W. K. Kellogg Foundation to develop a centralized database of job-related information to be available to all types of libraries in the region. The planning group will include representatives of public, academic, school, and special libraries.

The AFL–CIO was invited to participate in ALA's National Library Week as part of its National Partnership program. The newsletter *Partnership Exchange* featured the Joint Committee's program on libraries serving the unemployed and also described the AFL–CIO's long history of library support. Joint Committee Co-chair Jim Auerbach, of the AFL–CIO Department of Education, was particularly active in fostering this partnership.

Award. The John Sessions Memorial Award was won by the Jackson–George Regional Library System of Pascagoula, Mississippi, whose staff efforts to involve all relevant public and private agencies in analyzing and addressing the area's severe unemployment problem were felt to serve as a model for all public libraries. As a result of community meetings initiated by the library, agencies were better able to coordinate services to the unemployed. The library also developed kits of agency brochures that were distributed to laid-off workers and job seekers through libraries, union halls, and city offices.

Library History. In addition to these special services, libraries have also been involved in preserving labor history. The Robert Wagner Labor Archives of New York University, in collaboration with the AFL–CIO George Meany Archives and the Cornell University Labor-Management Documentation Center, was conducting in 1984 a two-year survey of labor records in the metropolitan New York City area. Supported by a grant from the National Historical Publications and Records Commission, the survey will lay the groundwork necessary for a comprehensive cooperative collecting strategy for the three institutions.

The Birmingham (Alabama) Public Library organized an extensive archival program in conjunction with the Alabama Labor Council and the Center for Labor Education and Research at the University of Alabama. The Archives of Alabama Labor collects and preserves records of local unions, particularly those related to the basic steel industry, child labor, and convict labor, and has microfilmed complete runs of local union newspapers.

Materials. There are varied materials on American labor available from labor organizations. One example is "Organizing: The Road to Dignity," a videotape developed by the United Food and Commercial Workers Union to introduce unionism in the United States to high school students. The tape was shown at the Dallas Conference as an example of curriculum material available on labor (an often neglected subject). The AFL–CIO Labor Institute of Public Affairs has continued its "America Works" series with six new episodes that were broadcast on public television. The series presents "real life" people involved in labor programs and activities that address current economic and social problems. Episodes are available for rental from the AFL–CIO Film Library.

DONNA L. NERBOSO

Law and Legislation

Federal Level. The most significant library legislation approved at the federal level in 1984 was the extension of the Library Services and Construction Act for the years 1985 through 1989. The amended act retains the following existing Titles: Title I—Library Services; Title II—Public Construction; Title III—Interlibrary Cooperation and Resource Sharing. It also includes three new Titles: Title IV—Library Services for Indian Tribes; Title V—Foreign Language Material Acquisition; and Title VI—Library Literacy Programs.

Authorized appropriations included: Title I—$75,000,000 for fiscal year 1985, $80,000,000 for fiscal year 1986, $85,000,000 for fiscal year 1987, $90,000,000 for fiscal year 1988, and $95,000,000 for fiscal year 1989;

Title II—$50,000,000 for each of the fiscal years 1985 through 1989;

Title III—$20,000,000 for fiscal year 1985, $25,000,000 for fiscal year 1986, $30,000,000 for fiscal year 1987, $35,000,000 for fiscal year 1988, and $30,000,000 for fiscal year 1989;

Title IV—1.5 percent of the amount appropriated for Titles I, II and III for each of the fiscal years 1985 through 1988;

Title V—$1,000,000 for each of the fiscal years 1985 through 1988;

Title VI—$5,000,000 for each of the fiscal years 1985 through 1988. The amended act also contains provisions spelling out in great detail the purposes for which the funds are to be used.

The FY 1985 appropriations for library programs signed into law included: Library Services and Construction Act, Title I—$75,000,000; Title II—$25,000,000; Title III—$18,000,000; Higher Education Act, Title II-B, Training and Research—$1,000,000; Title II-C, Research Libraries—$5,000,000; and National Commis-

Against a political backdrop at the Third Annual Conference of AASL in Atlanta, Mary Margaret Rogers offered tips on lobbying legislators for school librarians as Thomas Hart, chair of the Legislation Committee of the Florida Association for Media in Education, smiles over her remarks.

Joan Rohan of the Friends of the Racine (Wisconsin) Public Library pleads for greater library funding from the city council for the 1985 budget. (Journal Times Photo, Mark Hertzberg)

sion on Libraries and Information Science—$720,000.

The Education for Economic Security Act (PL 98-377) includes libraries as potential recipients of federal grants under this act. Section 206 provides that local educational agencies may conduct teacher training programs through agreements with libraries. Section 207 provides that state higher education agencies may engage in cooperative programs with libraries. Section 212 authorized the Secretary of Education to make grants to libraries "for programs of national significance in mathematics, science instruction, computer learning, and foreign language instruction in critical languages."

An act to authorize the Library of Congress to construct a mass deacidification facility was approved by Congress in 1984. This facility is to be constructed near Frederick, Maryland, and will have the capacity to treat 500,000 books annually. The plant would also serve as a prototype for smaller facilities to be erected in other areas of the country. It is expected that the deacidification process will extend the life of the books treated between 400 to 600 years.

The FY 1985 appropriation for the National Endowment for the Humanities included $3,000,000 for library projects.

The U.S. Copyright Office in September presented to the Subcommittee on Patents, Copyright and Trademarks of the Senate a report entitled "To Secure Intellectual Property Rights in Foreign Markets." The report outlined what government actions are possible to procure protection of U.S. copyrighted works including computer software, books, recordings, and motion pictures in world markets. The 169-page report relates to piracy of American works in various regions of the world and the problems of fostering adaptation of copyright laws throughout the world to accommodate new technologies for use of copyrighted works.

In response to a request from the Senate Subcommittee on Education, the National Commission on Libraries and Information Science appointed a committee to solicit information from academic libraries on a revised Higher Education Act as it affects libraries.

The U.S. Supreme Court ruled in the case of *Sony Corporation of America* v. *Universal City Studios* that individuals may tape TV shows for home use. This decision was hailed as a victory for fair use and ranks as a landmark decision in the protection of library and user rights. In 1983 ALA had joined 29 other educational associations in filing an amicus brief in the case. The brief contended that the fair use provisions of the Copyright Act would be eroded if the Supreme Court outlawed home videotaping.

In a ruling issued by the Federal Communications Commission on June 24, the AT&T private line service tariff scheduled to take effect July 1 was declared to be unlawful. AT&T proposed major increases on the tariff under which libraries are connected to bibliographic databanks. The existing rates continue to remain in effect.

State Activities. Governor Cuomo of New York in July signed into law an omnibus state aid library bill totaling $57,200,000. This landmark

act increased state aid to public library systems from $38,500,000 to $45,200,000. It also provided $3,900,000 for school libraries and $3,000,000 for public library construction, the latter being a first-time effort. Other innovations included $1,300,000 for automation programs, $1,100,000 for preservation of research materials, and $280,000 for public libraries designed to serve state correctional facilities. The law also provides six cents per capita for public library outreach totaling $1,900,000. New groups specifically targeted are persons educationally disadvantaged and those in need of job placement.

The state of California increased state aid to public libraries $10,000,000 to $37,000,000. Included was an appropriation of $2,700,000 for literacy programs, a program which Gary Strong, State Librarian, had inaugurated the previous year with LSCA funds. The new budget also contains $12,000,000 for the Public Library Foundation Program, which represents a 100 percent increase over 1983. Another vital appropriation was $3,900,000 for transaction-based reimbursement for interlibrary loan services.

California voters rejected Proposition 36, which sought to reduce public library financial support drastically.

In Georgia a new formula of state aid for the construction of public libraries was approved by the state library agency. Designed to assist smaller communities, the formula provides that for all library building projects, the state will fund 90 percent of the first $500,000 of the total project, and two-thirds of any additional project cost above $500,000. Library planners expected to obtain funding in 1985 for 15 projects totaling over $6,000,000.

The New Jersey legislature enacted a law that provides for the establishment of regional multitype library networks to include academic, public, institutional, school, and special libraries. An initial appropriation of $125,000 was included for planning grants for six regional networks and provides start-up funds for two of the networks. Illinois also adopted legislation that permits voluntary conversion of a public library system into a multitype library system. No conversion can take place unless approved by 51 percent of a system's public libraries, serving at least 51 percent of the population served by the public libraries.

The Nebraska legislature overrode the Governor's veto of $270,000 in funds voted for public library systems. The supporters of the system concept convinced the legislators of the need of communities with inadequate library services to be linked with the bibliographic resources of the larger libraries across the state.

In Pennsylvania the Governor released a plan for improving public library service developed by a group of leading citizens representing business, education, industry, labor, government and libraries under the leadership of Elliot Shelkrot, State Librarian. The plan calls for a statewide library card that will permit a citizen to use every publicly supported library in the state. The Governor planned to ask the legislature to provide funds that will reimburse libraries for interlibrary lending. He also requested the Education Department to develop a course teaching schoolchildren to use library computer catalogs. His budget for 1985 calls for $3,000,000 in additional state funds and $1,500,000 in federal funds to launch this program.

Local Level. The number one referendum of the year was Proposition L, staged by the Detroit Public Library requesting voter approval of a one mill increase in the property tax to be used solely for library purposes. The proposal was passed 3 to 1. The new money will be used to restore hours of service at branches and the main library. It will also make it possible to restore funds for the purchase of books and to reopen the Rare Book Room.

Tucson voters approved a bond issue of $15,900,000 for the construction of a new central library building of some 80,000 square feet. The library is to be housed in a downtown building to be jointly developed with a private firm.

When home rule was discontinued in Rockford, Illinois, in 1983, the library tax rate dropped from 24.5 to 15 cents per $100 of assessed valuation. In a referendum held on March 20, citizens voted to double the tax rate to 30 cents 20,701 to 17,141.

Long-time library user Sylvester Jerry urged the Racine, Wisconsin, city council to increase its funding of the library.

Indiana State Representative Ralph Ayres was honored as legislator of the year and was a featured speaker at a regional meeting of the Indiana Library Trustee Association.

Law and Legislation

The Brooklyn Public Library said its increased funding of $1,341,000 would largely pay for the purchase of new books. The library hoped to increase its book collection by 80,000 volumes. It also planned to use part of the money to open a branch in each section of the borough on Sunday afternoon, a benefit especially for its working population.

The San Diego Public Library received an increase of $1,300,000 in its annual budget, bringing the library's total budget to $9,300,000. The additional funds will be used to increase staff and will allow branch libraries to remain open six days a week (48 hours). Additional funds will also be available for the automated circulation system, the book budget will be increased, and improvements in the branch system will be made possible.

The Cleveland Public Library secured copyright registration for the "Cleveland Public Library Database," which currently contains 1,200,000 items. Additions are made to the database continuously, and the library plans to update the copyright quarterly.

Under a Board of Tax Appeals ruling, upheld by the Ohio Supreme Court, OCLC lost its tax exempt status as an educational and charitable institution. Moreover, it must pay $1,027,316 in real estate taxes reaching back to 1980. Originally OCLC had been exempt from real estate taxes since its founding. After the utility moved from Columbus to Dublin, an adjoining suburb, however, the local board of education challenged OCLC's exempt status. The Supreme Court ruled that OCLC, which offers a product to educational and charitable institutions for a fee exceeding cost, is not a charitable institution.

The University of California System and the University Federation of Libraries concluded a tentative agreement on a first contract in Berkeley. The contract and an accompanying compact codify the administration's recognition of its librarians as academic employees. The two-year contract dating from July 1 preserves for its members a 9 percent increase in academic employees' salaries voted by the state legislature and an additional 3.8 percent hike scheduled for January 1985. The contract also provides that the university earmark professional development funds for unit members to attend conferences and workshops. The union also won a grievance procedure culminating in a final and binding arbitration.

In a significant case dealing with the value of a library science degree, Glenda Merwine, who held a master's degree in education, applied for a position in the Mississippi State University Library for which the M.L.S. degree was required. When she failed to be appointed, she filed suit against the University Library claiming discrimination. A jury ordered the MSU Library to pay Merwine $10,000 in damages for discrimination agaist her sex by hiring a male librarian. A U.S. magistrate, however, overruled the jury decision. In his memorandum decision he stated: "The evidence clearly establishes that the (MLS) degree is a standard widely recognized by academic and professional employers, including the United States Supreme Court." The Court concluded that Merwine had failed to establish a prima facie case of discrimination in hiring on the basis of sex.

A contract concluded between the Minneapolis Public Library and the MPL Classified Employees Local 99 provides—among other salary and benefit matters—for a comparable worth study to be made by a consultant.

ALEX LADENSON

Law Libraries

The membership of the American Association of Law Libraries in 1984 addressed the problem of Certification of Law Libraries. The AALL had a program of Certification allowing for a formal recognition that a person had attained a standard of competence in Law Librarianship of significant value to the profession. A Certification Board evaluated the qualifications of applicants for certification and recommended the issuance of certificates to those applicants found to be qualified. Standards of experience and education were applied.

Upon the recommendation of Price Waterhouse that noneducation-based certification was more appropriate to a trade association than to an educational association, the membership at the San Diego meeting voted to abolish the Certification Board.

Of the approximately 3,600 members of AALL in 1984, 55 percent are in the private sector, 30 percent in the academic field, and 15 percent in government and related areas. Of the 1,297 attending the annual convention, 357 were men and 954 were women, a ratio of approximately 38 percent men to 62 percent women; reflecting almost precisely the ratio of men and women in the total membership.

The membership in 1984 also resolved that inasmuch as sexual harassment is a form of discrimination in employment prohibited by Title VII of the Civil Rights Act of 1964, as amended, the AALL and its members deplore any occurrence of sexual harassment and call upon all employers and its members to develop a written policy prohibiting sexual harassment, utilize training programs for employees and administrators to prevent it, and institute a grievance procedure providing for the prompt, impartial handling of complaints and for the discipline of anyone found to have engaged in such activity.

The cost of legal publications increased in 1983–84. Monographs went up in price 2.66 percent and all categories of serials increased 6.59 percent.

Category of material	Mean cost per title	Percentage increase over 1982–83
Monographs	$ 35.16	2.66
All serials	143.47	6.59
Legal periodicals	23.82	5.73
Looseleafs	538.27	9.29
Commercially published court reports	441.55	.30
Legal continuations	178.80	11.77

For a more complete listing for 1983–84 prices, see *Law Library Journal*, volume 77, no. 1.

JULIUS J. MARKE

Libraries and Education Improvement, Center for

Under the U.S. Office of Education the Center for Libraries and Education Improvement (CLEI) contains three units—the Division of Library Programs, the Division of Technology, Resource Assessment and Development, and the Division of National Dissemination Programs. The three Divisions administer nine legislatively mandated programs with a total appropriation in FY 1984 of $121,886,038.

Division of Library Programs. DLP makes grant and contract awards to state library administrative agencies, state educational agencies, institutions of higher education, and other public or private agencies, institutions, and organizations for (1) improvement of public library services; (2) construction of public libraries; (3) interlibrary cooperation; (4) training and education in librarianship; (5) support of research and demonstrations in library and information science; and (6) strengthening of major research library collections and services.

Public Library Construction. In FY 1984, $21,015,075 was awarded to 33 states for approximately 200 library construction projects. Under the Emergency Jobs Act, $50,000,000 is available for public library construction. The Jobs Act is intended to provide jobs for long-term unemployed Americans and create federal projects of lasting value to the nation and its citizens.

Interlibrary Cooperative Services. Under LSCA, Title III, for 1984 $15,000,000 was available. A major trend seems to be the increased use of computers and communications technologies. States reported support of activities such as (1) development of statewide and multi-state databases for monographs, serials and audiovisual materials, both for current materials and for retrospective conversion of older records; (2) centralized technical services including ordering, processing, and cataloging, both statewide and within regions within a state; (3) automated circulation systems; (4) machine-assisted reference and information services; (5) library automation consultant services for assistance in planning and designing systems; and (6) training for planning and implementing technology-based activities and services.

College Library Resources. Under the Higher Education Act, Title II-A, for fiscal year 1984, no funds were appropriated for the program and no awards were made. Since the beginning of the program in 1966, an average of 2,300 institutions of higher education participated annually in the receipt of nearly 44,000 grant awards exceeding $195,000,000.

Library Career Training. Under HEA, Title II-B, for fiscal year 1984 $638,800 was available. In fiscal year 1984, funds were awarded to 41 universities in support of 76 fellowships primarily for minorities or economically disadvantaged groups or both and for the upward mobility of minorities and women. The stipends ranged from $1,750 to $6,000 per student depending on the degree level pursued in the field of library and information science.

Library Research and Demonstration. Under HEA, Title II-B, for 1984 $240,000 was available. Awards were made to (1) E. H. White Company, to identify the role of the nation's libraries in responding to the findings and recommendations of the National Commission on Excellence in Education. Activities in FY 1984 included a series of five seminars and production and publication of the report entitled *Alliance for Excellence: Librarians Respond to A Nation at Risk;* (2) Center for the Book, Library of Congress, to study the changing role of the book in the future. This project is jointly sponsored by the Library of Congress, the National Center for Education Statistics, and the Higher Education Act, Title II-B, program office; and (3) American Library Association, to explore procedures and guidelines for participation of a variety of associations in the accreditation of programs for library and information science. Eight organizations with primary interest in library and information science programs of study are to be involved in developing procedures and guidelines for evaluating such programs of study for accreditation.

Strengthening Research Libraries. Under HEA, Title II-C, for 1984 $6,000,000 was available. In its seventh year in 1984, an average grant of $171,429 was made in support of 35 proposals benefiting 53 institutions for strengthening research library resources. Funding provided approximately $4,500,000 for program activities related to bibliographic control, $1,000,000 in support of preservation activities, and over $400,000 for collection development.

Division of Technology, Resource Assessment and Development. DTRAD is responsible for administering a number of programs of national significance with discretionary funds made available to the Secretary of Education. DTRAD's primary focus is the administration of programs designed to stimulate and support the systematic application of television programming and other advanced technologies to improve teaching and learning. The Division also administers programs of high priority to the Secretary in areas such as teacher incentives, school board training, mathematics and science instruction, and the education of gifted and talented students.

Educational Television and Technology. During 1984 and 1983, a number of television series were completed and aired on the Public Broadcasting System for use in homes and school settings. The focus of several was on science and mathematics for children:

3-2-1 CONTACT! Twenty new half-hour programs, focusing on weekly themes of space, measurement, earth, and electricity, constitute the third season of this television series produced by Children's Television Workshop under joint funding by the U.S. Department of Education, National Science Foundation, and the Corporation for Public Broadcasting.

SPACES. The purpose of this series of six 30-minute television programs produced by WETA-TV, Washington, D.C., is to introduce students to careers in science and technology. SPACES is targeted at students, especially minority children, in grades 4–8.

VOYAGE OF THE MIMI. A science and mathematics series produced by Bank Street College of Education for students in grades 4–6. The series contains 26 programs—thirteen 15-minute adventure episodes aboard a seagoing whale research sailing vessel and thirteen 15-minute documentary "expeditions" in which a variety of scientific and mathematical concepts in real-world settings are used. Holt, Rinehart, and Winston market four modules consisting of software and teachers' and students' guides.

A number of other television programs completed during the same period focused on adolescents and their problems. These programs, —*K-I-D-S, Somebody Else's Place,* and *Yes, Inc.*—are available from Great Plains National Instructional Television Library, Lincoln, Nebraska.

Three major software development projects were completed in FY 1984. Their products are available through commercial vendors: QUILL (writing) from D. C. Heath; IRIS (reading comprehension) from WICAT, Inc.; and TABS (mathematics) from Encyclopaedia Britannica.

In late 1983, 12 geographically dispersed school-based technology projects were funded for two years to demonstrate effective use of microcomputers and other technologies in improving reading, writing, and science and mathematics instruction in elementary and secondary schools.

Division of National Dissemination Programs. Under the Education Consolidation and Improvement Act of 1981, Chapter 2, Subpart D, Section 583, the Secretary's Discretionary Fund, $10,000,000 was made available for fiscal year 1984. The National Diffusion Network (NDN) is a school improvement system that makes exemplary educational programs available for adoption by schools, colleges, or other institutions. It does so by providing dissemination grants to exemplary education programs, known as Developer Demonstrators, for two purposes: (1) to enable programs to make public and nonpublic schools, colleges, or other institutions aware of what they offer and (2) to enable the programs to provide in-service training, follow-up assistance, and in some cases instructional materials. NDN also provides funds to organizations known as State Facilitators, who serve as matchmakers for NDN programs and schools and organizations that could benefit from adopting NDN programs.

During FY 1984, new grants were made to Developer Demonstrators in the following areas: adult literacy, science, pre- and in-service training, reading, math, writing, technology, health, social studies, special education, career and vocational education, early childhood education, and programs for gifted and talented students. Technology Lighthouses were also funded to serve as demonstration centers throughout the U.S. for the range of educational technology applications. NDN has also been experimenting with the use of video teleconferencing for awareness presentations. Grants were made available to facilitators in every state, the District of Columbia, Puerto Rico, and the Virgin Islands.

Data from the 1982-83 school year indicates that nearly 18,000 schools adopted NDN programs, affecting over 60,000 classrooms and benefiting over 1,700,000 students. Over 56,000 teachers and over 7,300 administrators were trained to implement NDN programs. The average cost to the NDN was $545 per school or $160 per classroom. This compares favorably with the average cost of developing a new program with unknown potential, which was estimated to be substantially higher, ranging from $300,000 to $500,000.

Territorial Teacher Training Assistance Program. Under P.L. 95-561, Title XV, Part C, Section 1525 of the Education Amendments of 1978, $1,000,000 was made available for fiscal 1984. This program is designed to provide assistance for the training of teachers in schools in Guam, American Samoa, the Commonwealth of the Northern Marianas Islands, the Trust Territory of the Pacific Islands, and the Virgin Islands.

MILBREY L. JONES
HAROLDIE K. SPRIGGS

Library Administration and Management Association

Organization, Administration. Strengthening the planning process and cementing direction drew much attention during 1984. Building on the planning session held in San Antonio in 1983, the LAMA Board, Division-wide committee chairs, and chairs and vice-chairs of Sections met to examine goals and objectives and to assess progress. The representatives shared information about planned activities and sought to coordinate efforts among various LAMA entities to use maximum resources and efforts in meeting the Association's objectives.

The results of hard work by a variety of task forces created to address short-term activities were reported at the Dallas Annual Conference. A Governmental Affairs Committee was appointed as a result of recommendations from one task force. The state membership network was once again established to promote membership in LAMA. Likewise, a task force to examine alternative funding for LAMA began its work.

Section Executive Boards were asked to review their activities against the goals and objectives to be sure that activities planned were supportive of the overall direction of the Association. The Budget and Finance Committee, Publications Committee, and Program Committee completed extensive reviews of LAMA operations and established procedures for handling the business of the Association. LAMA Executive Director Roger Parent completed a long-awaited manual of *Practices and Procedures* covering all of the operational activities of LAMA for distribution to the Board and all officers and committee chairs.

Parent, Executive Director for six years, re-

LIBRARY ADMINISTRATION AND MANAGEMENT ASSOCIATION

PRESIDENT (June 1984–July 1985):
Gary Strong, Librarian, California State Library, Sacramento

VICE-PRESIDENT/PRESIDENT-ELECT:
Ronald G. Leach, Dean of Libraries, Indiana State University, Terre Haute

EXECUTIVE DIRECTOR:
Roger Parent

Membership (August 31, 1984): 4,080 (3,308 personal; 772 organizational)
Expenditures (August 1984): $137,536

Library Administration and Management Association

The editors of LAMA's "Persuasive PR for Libraries" campaign were feted at a reception at the ALA Dallas Annual Conference.

signed to accept the position of Deputy Executive Director of the American Library Association. His fine work and support assisted the Association's leadership in strengthening its work.

Activities and Projects. LAMA presented a number of preconferences and programs associated with the 1984 ALA Dallas Conference. President Nancy McAdams issued a call for papers, "Accessing the Future: Managing Growth and Change." She selected several papers submitted by LAMA members that were presented during a program and issued as a set.

Conference programs covered the topics of "Training Issues in Changing Technology," "Getting It Passed Passed with an 'A Plus,'" "Microcomputers for Library Managers: Beyond the Basics," "Automated Circulation and Beyond," "Swap 'n' Shop Roundup," "Planning Library Buildings: From Decision to Design," "Problem Employees: Improving Their Performance," "Why Library Buildings Win Awards," "Access to Special Format Statistics: The New ANSI Z39.7 Standard and Problems of Implementation," and "Fund-Raising for Libraries." LAMA also conducted its first regional institutes on "Management of the Online Catalog." Continuation of the regional institute program was planned.

The John Cotton Dana Library Public Relations Awards, cosponsored by the LAMA Public Relations Section and the H. W. Wilson Company, recognized outstanding public relations programs by many libraries. Copies of the submissions are available for interlibrary loan from the American Library Association.

The *LAMA Newsletter*, edited since 1982 by Edward Garten of Tennessee Technological University, continued to improve and expand coverage. Themes were selected, and the "Administrator's Update" series began during the year. The *Newsletter* accepted its first advertising during the year. A major supplement highlighting Conference programs was published in the September 1984 issue in an effort to share informa-

Building Standards and Public Library Planning

The American Library Association and the Library Administration and Management Association (LAMA) endorse no standard for public library facilities or for allocating space within an existing facility. A statement prepared in 1984 by the LAMA Building and Equipment Section (BES) Architecture for Public Libraries Committee comments on past standards and sketches an alternative method of determining space needs:

Previous standards for facilities have usually taken the form of a recommended overall space allocation per capita. Such measures, though based on empirical observation and study, become arbitrary in application. The space needs of a library serving a community of 15,000 in a rural setting are likely to be different from those of a library serving a community of 15,000 in a metropolitan area, yet the application of a per-capita measure would result in the same overall space requirement for each library. Because a per-capita measure may not account for differences in service patterns from community to community, the use of such measures is discouraged.

Instead, the Architecture for Public Libraries Committee recommends that planners *program* for space needs. It is most effective to identify as specifically as possible the types of space that an individual library may seek to provide and then estimate the square footage the library will need to meet its service goals for the activities planned to occur in the respective areas. Some of those types of space include: material storage (for book and nonbook material, for adult and juvenile material), user seating, staff space, meeting facilities, special service space (for public-access microcomputers, or in-house listening stations, for example), and nonassignable space (for mechanical equipment, elevators, etc.).

One short example: Upon the determination that a library will need to make available 125,000 volumes to meet the future demands of its community, one can calculate the amount of space required to house those materials. Depending on the type of material (adult trade, children's books, reference) and the type of shelving to be used (standard height, 60-inch, 42-inch), one can house between 10 to 15 volumes per square foot. With that information, one can project the space needs for materials housing for that library in that community.

By programming for these different types of space within a building—with the assistance of a consultant or a staff member familiar with the planning of library facilities—a library will define a preliminary projection of space needs specifically tailored to the needs of that library and community.

A more detailed exploration of this space needs process can be found in Raymond M. Holt, *Wisconsin Library Building Project Handbook* (Madison: Wisconsin Department of Public Instruction, 1978).

LAMA BES APLC

tion with a broader audience of LAMA membership.

Publications. LAMA continued its practice of developing brief, inexpensive publications addressed to the particular interests of library administrators. They included *Getting It Passed: Lobbying Libraries*, by Dean Burges, Patricia Groseck, and Diana Young, edited by Patricia H. Latshaw; *Staff Development in Libraries: Bibliography*, prepared by the Staff Development Committee of the Personnel Administration Section, and *State Publications on School Library Media Facilities*.

GARY E. STRONG

Library and Information Technology Association

Organizational Focus. Technology is now so pervasive in library operations that automation programs are becoming common in other ALA divisions as well as in LITA. The 1982 report of the LITA Goals and Long-Range Planning Committee recommended that LITA concentrate its programs on cutting-edge technology and reorganize to make the creation of interest groups around new developments easy to create and easy to phase out as those developments become common practice within the library and information field. Based on those recommendations, the follow-up Implementation Committee drafted a new function statement and a new organizational structure (approved by membership in fall 1984) that replaces Sections with Interest Groups. Interest Groups can be started by petition of 10 members, can accommodate small memberships of 10 to large memberships of hundreds, can sponsor programs, publications, and discussion groups, and can be phased out easily when a topic is no longer of interest to members.

Function Statement. LITA's current focus is summarized in its new function statement: "LITA is concerned with the planning, development, design, application, and integration of new technologies within the library and information environment, with the impact of emerging technologies on library service, and with the effect of automated technologies on people. Its major focus is on interdisciplinary issues and emerging technologies. Within these areas, LITA encourages and fosters research, promotes development of appropriate technical standards, monitors new technologies with potential applications in information science, develops models of library systems and networks, examines the effect of automation on people, disseminates information, and provides a focus for the discussion of common concerns."

As part of its efforts to reorient LITA and to infuse new energy into membership programming, the LITA Board in 1984 approved the creation of a new position in the LITA office to give additional support to the publications and programming efforts of members.

DataPhase Systems of Kansas City will present LITA with a $10,000 special grant to be used in strengthening LITA's programming and publications program.

LITA/CLSI Scholarship. C.L. Systems, Inc., agreed to sponsor a LITA scholarship for five years, to be awarded to a student specializing in information science. The scholarship program will be the responsibility of the LITA Education Committee, which has prepared guidelines and procedures for the jury. The first scholarship will be awarded at the 1985 Annual Conference in Chicago.

LITA/Gaylord Award. The 1984 LITA/Gaylord Award for Achievement in Information Technology, and the $1,000 cash award which accompanies it, was presented to Roger Summit for his contributions to online bibliographic database systems.

Publications. A new LITA monograph series was initiated by the Publications Committee. The proceedings of the LITA National Conference, *Information and Technology: At the Crossroads*, edited by Michael Gorman, was published in 1984 as the first volume in the series. The second volume of the series, *Online Catalogs/Online Reference*, edited by Brian Aveney, also was published in 1984. The *LITA Newsletter* continued under the editorship of Carol Parkhurst. LITA's journal, *Information Technology and Libraries*, continued under the editorship of William Potter. The LITA Publications Committee sought authors and manuscripts for future monographs in its series.

The Publications Committee appointed a subcommittee to review issues involved in electronic publications, including such matters as need, editorial policy, revenue generation, and formats.

Section Activities. The Video and Cable Communications Section (VCCS) continued to host the Video Showcase of library-produced videotapes at the annual conference. In the planning stages by VCCS in 1984 was a new video magazine to be called the *LITA Video Quarterly*. Its first issue was scheduled for summer 1985.

The Information Science and Automation Section (ISAS) sponsored the 1984 Dallas preconference on "The Art and Politics of Contract Negotiation," which was suggested by the Vendor/User Discussion Group. ISAS discussion groups continue to be popular. The new Application of Computers to Serials Control Discussion Group focused on automated serials check-in systems. The Programmer/Analyst's Discussion Group covered the topic of "Matching Bibliographic and Authority Control Files." All of the

---

LIBRARY AND INFORMATION TECHNOLOGY ASSOCIATION

PRESIDENT (June 1984–July 1985):
Nancy L. Eaton, University of Vermont Libraries

VICE-PRESIDENT/PRESIDENT-ELECT:
Lois Kershner, Peninsula Libraries Automation Network

EXECUTIVE DIRECTOR:
Donald P. Hammer

Membership (August 31, 1984): 5,430 (4,433 personal; 977 organizational)
Expenditures (August 31, 1984): $281,905

current discussion groups will be restructured as Interest Groups under the new organizational structure, which allows them to present programs and produce publications, in addition to discussing topics of current interest.

Committees. The Education Committee assumed the charge of preparing procedures and selecting each year's jury for the awarding of the new LITA Scholarship. In addition, in conjunction with TESLA, it prepared a kit on technical standards (distributed to library schools).

The Legislation and Regulation Committee continued to work closely with the ALA Washington office and the Telecommunications Coalition in monitoring the impact of deregulation of AT&T. In process at year's end was a kit on the pertinent regulatory agencies in each state, an explanation of utilities commission procedures, a list of consumer groups that monitor these issues, and suggestions for representing library concerns to these agencies.

The Program Planning Committee assumed the task of organizing several LITA institutes during 1984–85. The first institute, on telecommunications, was to be repeated three times in various geographic regions.

A special review committee, chaired by Sue Martin, was appointed jointly by LITA, RTSD, and RASD to review the present composition and effectiveness of MARBI (Machine-Readable Form of Bibliographic Information). Hearings were held at ALA Midwinter in Washington, D.C. The final report was due at the 1985 Annual Conference.

Members of the Technical Standards for Library Automation Committee (TESLA) continue to be active on the national standards committees "NISO Z39" and "ANSI X3." Paul Peters was preparing a matrix of standards applicable to library automation. TESLA planned to sponsor a 1985 program on "Standards in Action," focusing on why standards exist, how they are used, what happens when standards are not available, and how standards are promulgated.

The Emerging Technologies Committee, established to identify new information technologies, met for the first time in 1984. As the committee identifies new technological trends or products, it will work with Interest Groups and the Program Planning Committee to ensure that these new interests are reflected in programs and publications as early as possible, in keeping with LITA's new function statement and focus.

NANCY EATON

Library Association

Reshaping Headquarters and Association. An American librarian visiting the Library Association headquarters in London in most of 1984 would have seen a building encrusted in scaffolding as builders strove to preserve its exterior and to remedy many defects. It epitomized an Association fighting its way out of a major financial crisis and beginning to redefine its role in librarianship and society.

All Council and Committee meetings had to be held elsewhere in London as the Association wrestled with a restructuring of its management and faced mounting problems in its relations with a government bent on reducing public expenditure and local authorities, other public bodies, and many a private institution embarking on the further cutting of library services.

At the beginning of the year, the LA Secretary-General, Keith Lawrey, had announced his intention to return to higher education. In his place as Chief Executive Officer and after much interviewing and evaluation came George Cunningham, former Member of Parliament and previously a civil servant, writer, and broadcaster. He was soon to make his mark with a clarity of thinking and decision making and no-nonsense style of management. Any committee, subcommittee, or working party that was not effective within his sphere of influence had its existence seriously questioned.

Relations with the media became more effective as did contact with other collateral organizations in the field of librarianship and information science. Disaster struck in midyear with the sudden and unexpected death of the Editor of the Association's main and monthly journal, *The Library Association Record*. Roger Walter was its first professional editor and his perceptive contributions and imaginative editing were a considerable contribution to the Association's worth. (See *Obituaries*.) Jane Jenkins, formerly editor of the *Museums Journal*, succeeded him. To cope with increasing demands for services some modest replacement and increase of staffing saw the Association toward the latter part of the year in much better shape and coming more to grips with the issues of the day.

Reduced Budgets and Services. What follows may well have a familiar ring to it to American readers. The continual cuts in services in libraries of all kinds—libraries fully closing; opening hours reduced by full or half-day closures; severe cutbacks on book and media funds; entire school library services for large regions were either in dire risk of nonfunding or very sparse resourcing; mobiles were taken off the road and many a development halted. The President opened only one library in the whole year and capital library building seemed virtually to be abandoned. One library system stopped the purchase of all fiction and another (the Western Isles of Scotland) had its book fund reduced to the joke amount of £5,000.

With reenforced staffing level in its membership section, the Association was able to advise MPs more effectively and in quantitative terms affect governmental statements on library resources both in current terms and in its projected spending levels. It began to cooperate in a university-based research project to further sophisticate this as it further maintained its liaison with other and separate groupings of activists such as the Sheffield-based "Libraries against the Cuts" and "LOAF" (Libraries open and free). At best people are now better informed about the position and on occasion authorities take the advice offered and ameliorate the position. It is, however, one of a most serious nature in Britain—a great and indeed noble tradition of service is at risk.

Charge for Services. A Cabinet Office report, "Making a Business of Information," developed the thrust toward charging for information and either by design or neglect did not involve libraries. Much of the comment was discounted, essentially by the Association, and the result to date has been the creation of a Confederation of Information Communication Industries (CICI). This, with LA involvement, will concern itself with the information side of Information and Technology (I.T.) and bring together commercial and noncommercial interests that operate in the field of information. Linked with the fee-or-free concept is the increasing concentration on the privatization of services. The LA is firmly against those moves and has been particularly concerned at the increasing cost of government publications and ordnance survey maps.

Evaluation and Qualification. Education and qualification for librarianship is a continual item on the agenda and the institution of a longer period toward full qualification and an initial stage of being licensed, i.e., as a *licentiate*, one, two or three years prior to becoming fully chartered had led the Council of the Association to reexamine the complexities of the newly instituted scheme. This new evaluation will form part of a major development in policy as the LA comes to grips with the question "What business are we in?" As much as anything, the question had been brought to the fore by the efforts of the Deputy Chief Executive, Russell Bowden, who over a number of years advocated the movement away from books and for the profession to take a wider view.

The publication of the report of the Futures Working Party initiated a national debate. The report's main recommendations were toward widening membership to take in disciplines that are of a collateral kind: in information technology, marketing, automation, and the rest. It would also in a sense be deepened by more advanced studies in specific areas of librarianship leading to higher levels of qualifications. As in many areas of library work, the diagnosis of the issues is really excellent—the prognosis is the problem.

Annual Conference. The Annual Conference was held in Brighton in September. At around 1,000 delegates that included authority delegates, the event had certain characteristics of note. A preconference seminar was held for librarians on business, industrial, and government concerns. Cooperation with the British Council, celebrating its 50 years of existence, enabled some 200 librarians from overseas to participate. This was truly an international library event of importance, further reinforced by a postconference two-day seminar on libraries and race.

1984 Activities. There were success stories during 1984—a Bill before Parliament on Data Protection was amended on the floor of the House on specific intervention by the LA. Concerns over freedom of information developed into a major campaign with the LA playing a prominent role. Though not as political, the long and continuing saga of copyright has occupied hundreds of hours of committee work.

Politically the LA has taken the leading role in attempting to keep the Chancellor of the Exchequer's hand off the imposition of value added tax on books. The campaign was a big one; librarians everywhere displayed leaflets, posters and petitions—the world of book people worked well together. It had the desired effect. No tax was imposed and for that much credit went to the LA Executive.

RON SURRIDGE

Library History

Library History Seminar VII. Planning was finalized in 1984 for Library History Seminar VII entitled "Libraries, Books and Culture" scheduled for March 1985 at Chapel Hill, North Carolina. This national library history seminar was to explore the historical role and significance of graphic records in society, particularly as they are gathered into collections and provide insight into cultural history. Cosponsorship was provided by the School of Library and Information Science at the University of Texas and the School of Library Science at the University of North Carolina at Chapel Hill.

Speakers scheduled to address general sessions included John P. Feather of Loughborough University, England; David D. Hall of the American Antiquarian Society; David Kaser of Indiana University; and Margaret W. Rossiter of Harvard University. In addition, 24 selected papers were to be presented and discussed.

Donald G. Davis, Jr., Associate Professor at the University of Texas School of Library and Information Science was named the Seminar Coordinator. The National Endowment for the Humanities has awarded a $30,000 grant to help fund the Seminar.

Library Education Centennial. Planning continued during 1984 for the celebration of the centennial of library education during 1986–87. Melvil Dewey established the first library school at Columbia University in January 1887. ALA and the Association for Library and Information Science Education (ALISE) are actively engaged in celebration plans.

The ALA Standing Committee on Library Education (SCOLE) named a Library Education Centennial Task Force (Fay Ann Golden, Chair) to plan various events for ALA and to assist libraries and library schools in planning their own observations.

The Association for Library and Information Science Education organized a Library Education Centennial Committee (George S. Bobinski, Chair) to cooperate with the ALA–SCOLE Library Education Centennial Task Force and to plan a library education centennial symposium for New York City in June 1986.

The ALA Archives. The American Library Association Archives, at the University of Illinois Archives, continued to provide source material for researchers in the history of librarianship. Reference uses totaled 403 for 1984. Scholars from 18 states, Australia, England, and Japan used the records. Topics included biographical studies of Tommie Dora Barker, John Billings, and Thomas Blue, and studies of library services to Appalachia and libraries in Evansville, Indi-

Library History Round Table

Photo from the ALA archives shows an ALA camp library during World War I. The archives at the University of Illinois reported 402 users during 1984.

ana, and Kansas City, Missouri. Other ALA users included staff at the Chicago Headquarters and seven dissertation writers. Research topics included the distribution of federal government publications to libraries, the feminization of French libraries, Nigerian and Ghanian library services, library development and support in the Philippines, Carnegie fellowships for librarians, intellectual freedom in the 1950s, research grants for library students, and the role of ALA in promoting financial support for libraries.

Among the major acquisitions processed in 1984 were files from the Washington Office, 1939–81 (29.3 cubic feet), the CLENE Archives, 1975–83 (9.3 cubic feet) and the Office of Accreditation, 1949–70 (15 cubic feet). The archives staff planned to issue a revised version of the 1979 *Guide to the ALA Archives* in 1985. The new *Guide* contains administrative histories of ALA offices.

Charles Babbage Institute. The Charles Babbage Institute for the History of Information Processing needs to be brought to the attention of those interested in American library history. At the Walter Library of the University of Minnesota in Minneapolis, it is named after a 19th-century English mathematician credited with designing the first calculating machine that contained all the functional components of the modern computer. The Institute promotes the study of the history of information processing, bringing historical perspective to the study of its impact on society and fostering the development of a network of historical archives and repositories.

Publications. Wayne A. Wiegand, Associate Professor at the College of Library and Information Science of the University of Kentucky, in 1984 was awarded a grant-in-aid from Forest Press (Albany, N.Y.) to cover all research and travel costs for a comprehensive biography of Melvil Dewey (1851–1931). Wiegand hoped to complete the project in two volumes by 1989.

Among important monographs published in late 1983 and during 1984 were Margaret Beckman, Stephen Langmead, and John Black, *The Best Gift: A Record of Carnegie Libraries in Ontario* (Dundurn Press, 1984); Michael H. Harris, *History of Libraries in the Western World* (Scarecrow Press, 1984); Evelyn Geller, *Forbidden Books in American Public Libraries, 1876–1939* (Greenwood Press, 1984); Kathleen Heim and Katharine Phenix, *On Account of Sex: An Annotated Bibliography on the Status of Women in Librarianship, 1977–1981* (ALA, 1984); Kathleen L. Maciuszko, *OCLC, A Decade of Development, 1967–1977* (Libraries Unlimited, 1984); R. Kathleen Molz, *National Planning for Library Service, 1935–1975* (ALA, 1984); Neil A. Radford, *The Carnegie Corporation and the Development of American College Libraries, 1928–1941* (ALA, 1984); and Gordon Stevenson and Judith Kramer-Greene, *Melvil Dewey: The Man and the Classification* (Forest Press/Lake Placid Education Foundation, 1983).

GEORGE S. BOBINSKI

Library History Round Table

Annual Conference. The 1984 annual conference sessions of the Library History Round Table in Dallas illustrated, in six presentations, the depth and breadth of contemporary library history research. Beginning with Frederick Stielow, University of Maryland, the June 25 program session heard an interpretation of censorship in the late 19th century in his paper "Censorship and the Dilemma of a Moral Culture." Lee Shiflett,

Louisiana State University, followed with an examination of early library training and personal characteristics of the students in "Early Library Education as Gatekeeping." The session closed with a description by Mark Tucker, Purdue University, of the difficulties encountered in the preparation of Josiah Root's biography in an essay on the "Nature and Problems of Library Biography."

On the second day three papers focused on the historical evolution of library science vis-a-vis information science. In setting the stage, Boyd Rayward, University of Chicago, analyzed the history of library science, documentation, and information science in a paper entitled "Library and Information Science: The Integration of Complementary Fields." He argued that library science incorporated documentation and automated information systems; computers serve as a catalyst in the merger of libraries and information science. "Machlup's Categories of Knowledge as a Way of Viewing the 20th-Century Library," by Francis Miksa, Louisiana State University, theorized that knowledge cannot be classified by type, but only by how it is used. Libraries serve to organize and disseminate information; they must play a key role in information (and knowledge) transfer, he maintained. Finally, Curtis Wright, Brigham Young University, used the writings of Jesse Shera to epitomize the evolution of the relationship between machine and man. In "Jesse Shera as an Interface between Library and Information Science Fields," Wright outlined the changing perceptions of Shera on the use of machines in an humanistic environment.

Justin Winsor Prize. In addition to the annual conference program, LHRT continued a number of activities related to the advocacy of library history. Its $500 Justin Winsor Prize winner, selected by the Committee chaired by Haynes McMullen, was a non-library historian from Maryland. Joseph Lawrence Yeatman, a high school English teacher from Towson High School, Baltimore, received the award for his research on early 19th century Baltimore libraries. The paper was developed from Yeatman's Ph.D. dissertation, "Baltimore Literary Culture, 1815-1840." The Winsor Award Committee also recommended and received Executive Committee approval to place a one-year ineligibility limitation on submissions, i.e., the person who received the prize in one year will be ineligible to receive the prize the subsequent year.

Other Activities. In other actions, the Executive Committee approved the format and content modifications initiated by Editor Ronald H. Fritze for the LHRT Newsletter. The Newsletter now serves as a forum for information related to library history and history in general. This expanding interaction is also evident in the continuing appointment of liaison persons with the Association for the Bibliography of History, Donald G. Davis, Jr.; the Journal of Library History, Philip A. Metzger; the National Coordinating Committee for the Promotion of History, Ronald H. Fritze; other history-related organizations, and several ALA Divisions, Sections, and Round Tables.

A bylaws revision was approved by the membership present at the Annual Business/Program meeting in Dallas. Because of financial commitments of the Round Table to support the Seventh Library History Seminar (Chapel Hill, March 1985), the Justin Winsor Prize, and an increased assessment of ALA for expenses associated with LHRT, the annual membership dues were increased from $5 to $8. The increase will also be used to support activities such as the Oral History Survey. Investigator Doris Dale reported in Dallas that the database, now on microcomputer, included 162 data sheets identifying the directory entries. The preliminary draft is being checked for accuracy, and a table of contents, arranged by repository, along with a detailed index will be included in the final manuscript scheduled for the 1985 Annual Conference.

LAUREL GROTZINGER

Library Instruction Round Table

One hundred fifty 1984 Dallas Conference attendees heard presentations on the use of audiovisual materials in library instruction and viewed examples of them. The program "Getting the Most for the Least" emphasized the production of professional-looking audiovisuals as economically as possible. The presentation reminded the audience that while people tend to retain only 11 percent of what they are told, they can retain up to 60 percent of what they see. This is of special importance to adult learners who may be ill suited to the lecture format of instruction.

Chuck Haskins, Manager of Visual Products for 3M Company in Grand Prairie, Texas, and Larry Hardesty, Director of Eckerd College Library, were the two major speakers. The Media in Instruction Exchange followed. Program Planning Committee Chair J. Randolph Call created a poster session atmosphere with 10 libraries presenting library instructional audiovisual items designed by staff members.

Other LIRT committees were equally active throughout the year. The Long Range Planning Committee, chaired by Mary Pagliero Popp, began planning a retreat for Steering Committee members at Midwinter 1985 to establish a strategic planning mechanism for LIRT.

Tobeylynn Birch, Chair of the Public Relations/Membership Committee, worked to sponsor a successful Conference booth and mealtime discussion program at the Annual Conference.

LIBRARY HISTORY ROUND TABLE

CHAIRPERSON (July 1984–July 1985):
Laurel Grotzinger, Graduate College, Western Michigan University

VICE-CHAIRPERSON/CHAIRPERSON-ELECT:
Arthur P. Young, University of Rhode Island, Kingston

SECRETARY-TREASURER:
Robert V. Williams, College of Librarianship, University of South Carolina, Columbia

Membership (August 31, 1984): 359 (294 personal; 65 organizational)

Expenditures (August 31, 1984): $1,224

> **LIBRARY INSTRUCTION ROUND TABLE**
>
> PRESIDENT (June 1984–July 1985):
> **Mary Pagliero Popp,** Undergraduate Library, Indiana University, Bloomington
>
> VICE-PRESIDENT/PRESIDENT-ELECT:
> **Marilyn Berry Segal,** St. Mark's School, Dallas, Texas
>
> SECRETARY:
> **John C. Tyson,** Northern Illinois University Libraries, DeKalb
>
> Membership (August 31, 1984): 1,020 (817 personal; 203 organizational)
> Expenditures (August 31, 1984): $6,882

Eileen Dubin chaired the Research Committee, which completed a questionnaire on the use of computers for library instruction and will publish its findings in *RESIN* (Resource Sharing and Networking).

"It Really Works," a publication of the Continuing Education Committee, chaired by Thelma Tate, describes successful bibliographic instruction programs, workshops, courses, and leaders.

Phyllis Rearden, Chair of the Liaison Committee, coordinated LIRT's effort to maintain contact with instruction-related groups within ALA with the goal of avoiding duplication.

The *LIRT News* was produced by the Publications Committee, chaired by Eddy Hogan. May Brottman chaired the Elections Committee.

LIRT is extending its national base by developing an affiliates council. Christina Woo, President of the LIRT affiliates council, is working with the LIRT board to establish this structure. A network of local, state, and regional chapters of LIRT would enhance the LIRT national mission.

With special cooperation from the Instruction in the Use of Libraries Committee, LIRT sought to provide continued leadership in promoting instruction in the use of libraries as an essential library service. The LIRT officers also worked to maintain a strong liaison with the other Round Tables.

LINDA ANNE DOUGHERTY

Library of Congress

In 1984 the Library of Congress continued exploring new applications of technology, especially in the areas of preservation, compact book storage, online bibliographic access, and information networking. The Library looked forward to the development of its collection of materials published in machine-readable formats, while at the same time concerning itself with preserving and developing its retrospective holdings and with the promotion of reading and the printed word. Preparations began for the retirement of the Library's immense public catalog, to be replaced by computerized and microform catalogs, and for the renovation and restoration of the beautiful, 19th-century Thomas Jefferson Building.

Preservation and Compact Storage. A major step toward the implementation of an effective preservation program was achieved in 1984. Congress authorized and funded the design, construction, and operation of a mass book deacidification facility at Ft. Detrick, Maryland. When completed, this facility will provide chemical treatment with diethyl zinc of books from the Library's collections, extending their useful life for hundreds of years. Construction of the 40,000-square-foot plant was to begin in early 1985, with completion projected for 1987. Both incoming materials and some books in the retrospective collection will be treated. The facility is expected to handle some 500,000 items each year.

The Optical Disk Pilot Program, begun in 1982, received extensive press coverage during 1984, drawing much attention to the Library's leadership in testing this new technology for compact storage and preservation. Representatives of large and small firms, governments, libraries, and archives the world over contacted the Library for information on the three-year experiment in the use of laser disk technology. Several hundred visitors toured the Library and saw demonstrations of the equipment, and Library staff members gave presentations to a variety of audiences across the country.

As the year began, the design and planning phase of the Optical Disk Pilot Program came to an end, and the project implementation phase began. Throughout 1984 attention was focused on the installation and testing of the optical disk and analog videodisk systems. For the digital optical disk project, LC installed a high-resolution scanner, which digitally records a full page in .7 seconds, as well as a microfiche scanner for conversion of film micro-images to digitized images. An Optical Disk operations center was constructed in the Automated Systems Office and a document preparation area in the Preservation Microfilming Office. At year's end, several thousand pages of periodical articles and government documents selected for inclusion in phase one of the project had been scanned and put on disk.

The Library also installed eight high-resolution terminals, two to be used in inputting documents and six in public reader stations. From these terminals, a patron will be able to recall digitized documents in a few minutes at most. A Xerox 2700 and Xerox 5700 make it possible to copy images from the disk. During 1984 the Library secured copyright clearances for the more than 70 periodical titles to be included in phases one and two of the project. All pages of the 1983, 1984, and 1985 issues of those titles will go on disk during phase two, followed by a selection of maps, music, manuscripts, and legal publications, in phase three.

Analog videodisk system equipment was installed, including two Sony videodisk players and monitors, a Sony microcomputer, and five of the six videodisks of pictorial materials Sony is to create for the Library. On June 15 in the Prints and Photographs Reading Room, the Library of Congress opened its first public videodisk reader station. There the public has access to a disk containing excellent electronic reproductions of color slides, political posters, photo albums, lantern slides, and architectural renderings. These materials are accessible through a menu system created by LC staff. Staff is working on a level of access that will provide full bibliographic descriptions of the disk images.

Library of Congress

Postmaster General William F. Bolger with U.S. Postal Service Librarian Jane F. Kennedy took part in ceremonies dedicating the Nation of Readers postage stamp at Library of Congress ceremonies.

The Library's Optical Disk Advisory Group, co-chaired by Robert Wedgeworth (ALA) and Kurt Steele (McGraw-Hill) and comprised of representatives of the library and publishing communities, met three times during the year to consider such matters as the relationship between the private and public sectors in the use of the optical disk, and the need, if any, for securing licenses from and paying royalties to copyright holders of materials put on disk.

Early in 1984 the Library signed a contract with K. G. Saur, Inc., of New York to have the Library's Main Card Catalog reproduced in microform. The filming operation began in March and is being conducted on site at the Library, with a projected four years to completion. The microform edition of the Main Card Catalog will have a reduction of 48:1 and will be made available by K. G. Saur on both 105-millimeter roll film and standard 105-millimeter by 148-millimeter cut fiche (approximately 10,000 fiche).

Collection Development. Some major rarities were acquired by the Library in 1984. Leading the list are two globes constructed about 1688–93 by Vincenzo Coronelli and the 1501 edition of Virgil's *opera* printed by the great scholar-printer Aldus Manutius. Another important acquisition was Serge Lifar's collection of books, manuscripts, and graphic works documenting the career of Serge Diaghilev, the art critic and organizer of the Ballet Russe.

After extensive investigation of its acquisition policies, the Library issued a new policy statement providing that materials in machine-readable form will be acquired according to the same criteria applied for printed materials.

Outreach. The first George and Ira Gershwin concert was held on September 29 in the Library's Coolidge Auditorium, featuring the American premiere of George Gershwin's two-piano arrangement of "An American in Paris" by the Labecque sisters. At the concert, the Librarian of Congress announced plans for a Gershwin Room in the Library's Jefferson Building to be completed as part of the renovation of that building.

The Center for the Book sponsored symposia on topics as diverse as books in the future, biography as a genre, U.S. books abroad, the role of textbooks, and "calligraphy and the Japanese word." By request of Congress, the Center sponsored a report delivered in 1984 on the impact of new technology on the book and the printed word. (See also *Publishing, Book.*) The Center continued to collaborate with several organizations on projects using reading promotion themes developed in previous years, for example, CBS Television and Network Radio ("Read More about It"), ABC Children's Television ("Cap'n O. G. Readmore"), Xerox Education Publications and Book-of-the-Month Club ("Books Make a Difference"), and the U.S. Postal Service and the American Library Association ("A Nation of Readers").

The Publishing Office brought out a number of major reference works this year, including *Historic America; Buildings, Structures, and Sites Recorded by the Historic American Buildings Survey and the Historic American Engineering Record*; the tenth volume of *Letters of Delegates to Congress, 1774-1789*; *Revolutionary America, 1763-1789*, a definitive, 14,810-entry bibliography; and *Railroad Maps of North America: The First Hundred Years*, an oversize volume that displays a sampling of the Library's cartographic and photographic treasures.

Federal Library Committee. During 1984 the Federal Library Committee underwent a reorganization that included changes in its purpose statement and the expansion of its membership, as well as the change of the Committee's name to the Federal Library and Information Center Committee (FLICC). FEDLINK opened a microcomputer demonstration center, which offers federal libraries a consulting service on microcomputer applications.

Copyright. New information technologies were a major concern of the Copyright Office during 1984. In February the Office hosted a Symposium on New Technologies at which nine members of Congress and more than 70 representatives from the judiciary, high-technology industries, libraries, publishing industry, and education community discussed the interaction of law and information technology.

After legal analysis and a great amount of correspondence, the Copyright Office, in March, registered the 628 copyright compilation claims of OCLC in its bibliographic database. In making the registration, the Register of Copyrights noted that, although there may be conflicting claims as to portions of the database, the Office registered claims to copyright after determining that the work on its face constitutes copyrightable subject matter and that legal requirements had been met. Claims of other libraries to their databases were registered as well.

In September 1984, Congress enacted the Record Rental Amendment of 1984, an amendment to the copyright law that would provide for a royalty for copyright owners whenever phonograph records are leased or rented. During hearings, the impact of the amendment on nonprofit libraries and educational institutions was discussed; in response, the final version included language confirming that the legislation would not apply

Books In Our Future

> There could be no more appropriate effort to fulfill the hopes of our nation's founders, nor any more appropriate celebration of the bicentennial of our Constitution, than to aim to abolish illiteracy in the United States by 1989.
>
> Daniel J. Boorstin
> Librarian of Congress

Books in Our Future (December 1984) is a 56-page report from the Librarian of Congress prepared in response to a Congressional Resolution of November 18, 1983, calling on the Librarian to provide "a timely study of the changing role of the book in the future."

Assessment. The report assesses the state of book publishing and bookselling and finds it healthy:

U.S. expenditures on books rose by 47.8 percent from 1979 ($7,304,500,000) to 1983 ($10,798,300,000).

Bookstores increased from 11,786 in 1973 to 19,580 in 1983.

New U.S. book titles increased from 38,053 published in 1972 to 53,380 in 1983.

Book publishers increased from 1,250 in 1972 to 2,128 in 1982.

Even though the "general bookstore with a large stock of older as well as current books has become harder to find," books have become "visible in drugstores, supermarkets, and airports. Discount book chains find locations in shopping malls and at traffic centers downtown," the report observes.

The report takes note of the Book Industry Study Group finding that about half of the American public may be called "book readers" (one who has read at least one book in the past six months). Active people, it turns out, are also book readers. Book reading, Boorstin emphasizes, is *not* a passive condition but "an engaging activity."

"*Elastic Time.*" Time given to TV viewing and other leisure activities is not necessarily taken from that devoted to reading, according to the report. "In our technological society, time seems to have become uncannily elastic. People do more these days."

"*Twin Menaces.*" The Culture of the Book is threatened, Boorstin argues, not by new technologies but by "the twin menaces of illiteracy and aliteracy—the inability to read and the lack of will to read." He cites *A Nation at Risk* (1984):

23,000,000 adults are functionally illiterate.

The pool of adult illiterates is growing by about 2,300,000 each year.

40 percent of U.S. 17-year-olds cannot draw inferences from written material.

"Most disturbing is the . . . decline in emphasis on reading and writing in our elementary and secondary schools," Boorstin says. "Many school libraries have been neglected or abolished. . . . In the very neighborhoods where people most need constructive leisure and self-improvement activities, libraries often cease to be accessible."

Computer "literacy." Mastering a machine "is no substitute for the ability to read, and computer competence itself depends on the ability to read," Boorstin holds.

On Technology. All technologies are our allies: "Our task is to recognize and promote their alliance." TV, for example, whets "appetites for reading," according to the report, "and a few projects, such as the Library of Congress-CBS "Read More about It" trailers to notable TV programs "have begun to use television to invigorate the Culture of the Book."

Recommendations. Proposed ways to promote reading offered in the report include reading aloud to children, educational reform, computer-based writing and reading instruction, improved textbooks, adopt-a-school partnerships between public schools and local businesses, and library literacy and readers' advisory programs.

Recommendations for Congress include providing a literacy impact statement, to assess the effect of new programs on "literacy environment"; giving special attention to early childhood and children's services in public libraries and elementary school libraries; continuing federal assistance for library services and construction, adult education, and reading and library training programs for students; and balancing the interests of creators of intellectual materials and the general public through copyright law.

The Executive Branch should intensify the adult literacy initiative of 1983; strengthen the National Center for Education Statistics; expand Adult Basic Education and related programs; take into account the importance of literacy to community development when making funding decisions; develop plans to increase U.S. book exports; continue NEH support of scholarly publishing and public library humanities programs; continue NEA assistance to writers, literary magazines, and small presses; and establish a private telecommunications line service for libraries.

The Library of Congress and the Center for the Book will "continue to promote books and reading and support the Culture of the Book." LC, further, "is expanding the scope of its National Referral Service to include current information about organizations throughout the country that are concerned with literacy and reading development."

In December 1984 the Coalition for Literacy launched a three-year campaign in cooperation with the Advertising Council.

Evaluation. This report is a welcome contribution. It arrives as a worthy companion piece to *Alliance for Excellence: Librarians Respond to a Nation at Risk* (1984). Though Boorstin breaks no new ground in his assessment of technology, his generally optimistic account helps to clarify issues facing a learning society. Its summaries of projects under way and its prescriptions of what citizens and government can do—combined in a well designed booklet enhanced by apt quotations—could be important in advancing public dialog.

"Some advisers do not agree with some of the conclusions," Boorstin reports, and a "supplementary volume containing the views of project advisers and consultants will be published in 1985."

DONALD E. STEWART

Books in Our Future: A Report from the Librarian of Congress to the Congress (Joint Committee on the Library, Congress of the United States. Washington, D.C.: 1984). For sale by the Superintendent of Documents, U.S. Government Printing Office, Washington, D.C. 20402.

---

to the lending of phonorecords for nonprofit purposes by nonprofit organizations, thereby not interfering with the usual lending activities of nonprofit libraries.

Cataloging. Major progress was made on the Linked Systems Project (LSP) in 1984, as the Library of Congress completed its telecommunications software, called the Standard Network Interconnection (SNI), and its Record Transfer Software. The SNI will enable the different computer systems of the participating utilities, the Washington Library Network (WLN) and the Research Libraries Group (RLG), to communicate. The Record Transfer Software will support the first application using SNI—the online distribution of authority records from LC and the online contribution of authority records to LC's NACO authority file. Online authority record distribution to RLG was expected to be under way in early 1985.

Library Press

Copies of this Library of Congress engagement calendar could be purchased during 1984 for fund-raising activities of library and Friends groups.

In order to increase the consistency of the Library's bibliographic database, a contract was let in late 1983 to upgrade name headings on bibliographic records to the AACR2 form. The project, which was nearly 40 percent complete in 1984, resulted in the revision and redistribution of well over 100,000 book records and the identification of around 30,000 map and serial records that require change. Late in 1984, upgrading began on the series headings in the Library's database for books.

Management. On August 22 the President signed into law an act that authorized an appropriation of $81,500,000 to the Architect of the Capitol for restoration and renovation work to restore and preserve the architectural and artistic features of both the Thomas Jefferson and John Adams buildings. In addition, major mechanical, electrical, fire, and safety improvements will ready the Library to serve in the 21st century.

At the request of Congress, the Library in 1984 conducted the first comprehensive survey of its patrons to be undertaken since 1976. All of the Library's services to Congress and to the public were included in the survey, except those provided by the Congressional Research Service. The Legislative Liaison Office and the Associate Librarian for Management were assigned responsibility for the congressional survey, while the Office of Planning and Development was assigned the responsibility of surveying noncongressional users of the Library's services. The Library planned to submit a final report to Congress in early 1985.

The restoration of the Jefferson Building, the construction of the deacidification facility, the Optical Disk experiment, and the microfilming of the catalog were all under way at year's end. For the Library of Congress, 1984 was a year in which these and other major projects, long planned for, began to be realized.

ROBERT ZICH
PAMELA ROPER WAGNER

Library Press

In 1984, as in the previous year, the major theme in the literature was the role of computers in the library and the role of the library in the information society. The influx of microcomputers into libraries, and into the homes of the general public, forced the library world to examine both how it could use these machines to improve, enhance, and streamline services and processes and to question what effect the decentralization of electronic information would have on the library profession. Despite the increasing emphasis on new technology and its impact, the library press managed not to turn its back on the issues that have always concerned libraries. Debates on library education, collection development, catalog use, and user education raged on the pages of the general library publications, and seemed to coexist comfortably with the new problems of computer system selection, compatibility, and utilization.

New Publications. The major general library periodicals made relatively few changes in direction. The shifting emphasis of the profession was exhibited less in established journals and more in the pages of the new publications introduced during 1984. New journals focusing on computer technology and online information include Meckler's *M300 and PC Report*, a library-oriented source of information for developments, trends, forecasting, and use of the IBM PC; *Database Alert*, a monthly news and reference service notifying readers of online database changes; *Information Today*, a newspaper covering the electronic delivery of information with special emphasis on online database retrieval services; and *Microcomputers for Information Management*, devoted to the innovative application of microcomputer and information management by librarians and information specialists. With the acquisition of *Small Computers in Libraries*, previously published by the Graduate Library School of the University of Arizona, Meckler Publishing became a major publisher of computer-oriented library journals, including *Library Software Review*.

Other journals with a less high tech focus were introduced during the year. JAI Press announced the publication of *Government Information Quarterly: An International Journal of Resources, Services, Policies and Practices*. Edited by Peter Hernon and Charles R. McClure, it provides a forum for research, theory, and practice related to government information in society. Additional new titles include *Book Research Quarterly*, a new periodical exploring the past, present, and future role of the book in our society, and *Judaica Librarianship*, devoted to the management and organization of Judaica and Hebraica collections.

Wilson Library Bulletin. The September issue of *Wilson Library Bulletin*, with its blazing photograph of a neon sculpture, introduced *WLB*'s new larger-size, larger-type format. The familiar 6½ x 10 size was replaced by an 8¼ x 11 size and three-column layout. Throughout the year despite a few changes in the Editorial Board, most conspicuously the loss of Associate Editor Renee Gold, *WLB* maintained the high quality that readers have come to expect. The magazine's writers are refreshingly opinionated and controversial and are as likely to be from fields outside the library profession as within it. The 1984 issues introduced articles on "Censorship and Junk Food Journalism" by Carl Jensen, a professor of communication studies, alternatives to the current copyright law by copyright attorney Daniel Toohey, and biographical profiles by New York Times journalist Joseph Dietch. The 1984 volume contained WLB's familiar mix of historical articles, analysis of contemporary issues, and library profiles.

There was relatively little change in the editorship of the magazine's regular columns. A new column edited by Patricia Berglund on school library technology was introduced in the February issue. The column addresses the "how, what, where, and why" concerns of those school librarians who are just beginning to make use of microcomputers. Of continuing interest is Norman Thomas's monthly column, "Our Profession," which offers a rare focused analysis of current professional publications. Complementing his reviews of library literature are a series of review columns on reference books, young adult and children's literature, records, magazines, crime fiction, and films. The most stimulating and controversial of WLB's regular columnists is Will Manley with his "Facing the Public" column. His ruminations on public library service provide food for thought for librarians in all settings. During the year he addressed the issue of quality in public library programming and collections. He came down firmly on the side of offering cultural/educational and informational opportunities rather than "giving them what they want."

American Libraries. *American Libraries* continued to offer a highly popularized overview of the issues and events in the library world. A few new columns and features were introduced but the general tone of the publication remained essentially unchanged. The January issue introduced a microcomputer "Software Showcase" (later to become part of the Source) and "Quick-Bibs," current bibliographies on timely topics including love, the movies, travel, rock music, and baseball. The magazine also experimented with its first in-magazine continuing education series, a six-part series on modern subject access in the online age taught by Pauline A. Cochrane. Physically *AL* was unchanged except for the introduction of color photographs in the Library Life photo essay.

The April issue of *American Libraries* introduced the second annual special section on new reading for librarians. The reviews of significant new offerings from library publishers were introduced by Norman D. Stevens. In his essay he had some encouraging words to say about the state of the professional literature. "There is much now being published that truly deserves our attention. The literature . . . has grown and matured with me." For *AL* the topic of the year seemed to be the Merwine case and ALA's role in it. Articles on the case appeared in at least three issues of the magazine and letters of response appeared in each issue. Other controversial articles were Bill Miller's "What's Wrong with Reference" and J. Wesley Miller's on library weeding, "Throwing out the Belles Lettres with the Bathwater."

School Library Journal. School librarians and others involved with children's and young adults' services continued to be well served by the lively and informative *School Library Journal*. Editor Lillian Gerhardt has continued the journal's traditionally strong emphasis on collecting materials and developing programs to serve youth. This in itself has been a rather courageous move, since so many other professional journals seem to be giving up many of their pages to the impact of the computer on library services. *SLJ* has not been reactionary in its approach to new technology; according to the Editor, the journal changes its focus or format based on the interests and needs of its readers. The September issue, for example, introduced a new monthly column of software reviews and a quarterly column of reviews of Spanish-language books for children and young adults. Both columns were instituted in response to reader requests.

One of the most interesting items of the year was Gerhardt's October editorial entitled "Back Sassing the President." She takes Reagan to task for stating that he had "attended six elementary schools . . . and one high school. And in none of them was there a library. I think the facilities aren't nearly as important as the humanity in the facilities." Her editorial is a celebration of freedom of the press.

Library Journal. After having made changes during 1983 in format, regular features, and frequency, *Library Journal* settled into a year of stability in 1984. The regular features which readers have come to expect in *LJ* remained unchanged. The Annual Buyer's Guide, conference reports, Outstanding Sci-Tech books, Religion and Business books, Periodical Price Indexes, and Placement and Salaries were all found in the pages of the 1984 volume. New was *LJ*'s own "Reference Sources of 1983." The RASD list of "Outstanding Reference Sources of 1983" that formerly appeared in *LJ* was published in ALA's *American Libraries*.

Perhaps because of the addition of several new columns in 1983, fewer feature articles were published in *LJ* during 1984 and 1983. Features that did appear in the pages dealt most frequently with the effects of technological developments. The June 15 issue focused on "Information Technology" and featured articles on online catalogs, technical processing, library networks, and the effect of technology on library management. Other issues included articles on topics such as the privacy of circulation records, romance novels in the public library collection, rural library service, and preparing libraries for change. One of the most popular columns is A. J. Anderson's regular selection of case studies, "How Do You Manage?". During the year readers faced the problems of recalcitrant and dishonest staff members, absentee directors, and demanding patrons.

Milestones and Miscellanea. The growing number of journals in the field of librarianship, and the increasingly fast moving developments in the field, point to the importance of a library professional's finding some way to keep up with this mass of literature without drowning in it. The recently announced *Library Currents* addresses the problem of current awareness by

Library Research Round Table

summarizing articles in over 100 publications, including many from outside the library field. According to its publicity, the busy librarian could read the newsletter in about 20 minutes and review summaries of articles from such different publications as *Harvard Business Review, Aslib Proceedings, Library Journal, College and Research Libraries,* and *American Way,* the American Airlines publication. Earlier efforts to develop a current awareness newsletter, by Sam Goldstein (*CALL: Current Awareness Library Literature*), K. G. Saur, and the Southwestern Library Association proved short lived.

Two other publications mark the increasing maturity of professional literature. Gary R. Purcell and Gail A. Schlacter produced a long overdue reference guide to the literature of librarianship: *Reference Sources in Library and Information Services: A Guide to the Literature* (ABC-Clio). What promises to become a lively biennial anthology of alternative library literature also appeared. Sanford Berman and James P. Danky published *Alternative Library Literature, 1984/1985* (Oryx Press), which they describe as a deliberately unbalanced collection of material dealing with library and information issues from a critical, nontraditional, socially responsible perspective. The items included are often written with exceptional flair and vitality and address topics usually overlooked or minimized in standard library media.

The *Journal of Academic Librarianship,* for so many years the new kid on the block, celebrated its 10th anniversary with its first 1984 issue. In the editorial marking the event, Editor Richard M. Dougherty commented on journal literature by stating that "the fact that the output of articles can support so many additional journals reflects well on the vitality of librarianship and information science." The year brought changes for the other major academic library journal, *College & Research Libraries.* The July issue introduced a new Editor, Charles Martell, who indicated that he will move the journal away from its almost exclusive emphasis on quantitative research and include the "best that our profession's minds can offer, whether through critical analysis, essay, or other forms of thinking that glorify the wonders of the creative mind."

An intriguing question was posed by Jerry W. Mansfield in the *Journal of Academic Librarianship* in his article "Why Not a Uniform Citation System." Mansfield asks why the field of librarianship, which is so concerned with bibliographic accuracy and control, contributes to "biblioconfusion" by permitting each journal to establish a different citation format. He suggests that the profession establish a uniform citation system that is acceptable to editors, librarians, and researchers, and which is compatible for machine readability.

Colorado Libraries, published by the Colorado Library Association and edited by Johannah Sherrer, won the 1984 H. W. Wilson Library Periodical Award. At the ALA Annual Conference, the Council voted to change the name of the Ralph R. Shaw Award for Library Literature to the Knowledge Industry Publications, Inc., Award for Library Literature.

PATRICIA TEGLER

Library Research Round Table

1984 Activities. In 1984 the Research Forums Committee was chaired by Charles Curran of the School of Library and Information Science at the University of South Carolina. Three research forums were part of the 1984 ALA Dallas Conference. Research Forum I, "Important Findings for Practicing Librarians," featured several reports. "Competence in Library Administration in Large Public Libraries" was presented by Darlene E. Weingand, University of Wisconsin Library School; "Attitudes of Librarians toward Disabled Persons" was presented by Henry C. Dequin, of the Department of Library Science at Northern Illinois University; "Structured Observation as a Methodology for Information Transfer Research" was presented by Robert Grover and Jack Glazier of the School of Library and Information Management at Emporia State University at Kansas; and "CLSI Service and Software; the Users' Perspective" was presented by Richard Van Orden and Renee Crabtree, Marriott Library, University of Utah, Salt Lake City.

Research Forum II featured research "Of Special Interest to Academic Librarians" and included three presentations: "Academic Needs Assessment; A Syllabus Study," by Herbert Achleitner of SLIM at Emporia State University and Edward Neroda of Eastern Montana College at Billings; "Cognitive Style of Online Search Analysts," by Julia M. Rholes and Judith B. Droessler of Texas A & M University Library; and "Functions Performed by Beginning Academic Librarians and Their Perception of Their Preparation for These Responsibilities," by Adeline Wilkes of the Library Science Library at Florida State University.

Three different topics were the subjects of research reports at Research Forum III: "Collection Division in a Large Academic Library and How the Consultants Helped," presented by Maurine Pastine and Jo Whitlach, of San Jose State University Library (California); "A Historic Review of HEA Title II-B Fellowships," presented by Mildred Lowe, Abdul Huq, and Philip Clark of St. John's University; and "Library and Information Science Literature—A Map of Its Place in Abstracting and Indexing Services," presented by Tim LaBorie, of the Drexel University Library.

A special Research Forum, cosponsored by the Library Education Committee, on the topic of "A Foundation for a Theory of Information Science," featured Roger Greer of the School of Li-

---

LIBRARY RESEARCH ROUND TABLE

CHAIRPERSON (July 1984–July 1985):
Shirley Fitzgibbons, SLIS, Indiana University

VICE-CHAIRPERSON/CHAIRPERSON-ELECT:
Maurice P. Marchant, Brigham Young University, Provo, Utah

SECRETARY-TREASURER:
Irene Hoadley, Library Director, Texas A&M University, College Station

Membership (August 31, 1984): 679 (573 personal; 106 organizational)
Expenditures (August 31, 1984): $3,310

brary and Information Management at USC, followed by reactions of Evelyn Daniel of the School of Information Studies at Syracuse and Paul Deane, of the Allen County Public Library at Fort Wayne (Indiana).

Award. The 1984 Research Development Prize Paper competition, chaired by Robert Williams of the University of South Carolina, was awarded to George D'Elia of the Library School at the University of Minnesota and Sandra Walsh of Ramsey County (Minnesota) Public Library. The paper, presented by George D'Elia at Research Forum I, was entitled "Patron Use and Evaluation of Library Service: A Comparison across Five Public Libraries."

Maurice Marchant, of Brigham Young University, was the 1984 membership chairperson with recruitment of doctoral students as a target group for membership in LRRT.

SHIRLEY GRINNELL FITZGIBBONS

Literacy Programs, Library

The year 1984 was noteworthy for fast-breaking developments in the area of illiteracy and literacy education. Awareness and action occurred at national, state, regional, and local levels in government, in the public and private sectors, and among organizations and agencies as well as the citizenry in general. Libraries, particularly public libraries, were involved closely in the events and the new and immediate demands. Library trustees and commissioners, librarians, and adult educators who have been in the vanguard of the literacy education effort for many years saw their efforts realized. The role of the public library and community college resource centers became more visible and acceptable both within and outside the library profession.

Existing library literacy programs have been expanded, new programs initiated, coalitions and working partnerships strengthened or begun, services and resources developed through training programs, technical assistance, collection development, evaluation, and a few research projects. Librarians and library trustees, and Friends groups were engaged actively in working with organizations and agencies. The American Library Association and its Divisions continued to give priority to the literacy effort. Leadership and concrete assistance continued with its support and active involvement in the 11-member Coalition for Literacy.

This increased awareness and consequent demands that were seen as immediate or in the near future aroused delight, alarm, and optimism: delight in seeing attention and cooperative support to a significant educational and social issue; alarm that the newly intensified demands for services and resources exceed abilities to meet them; optimism that opportunities created would stimulate the resources, the knowledge, and ways to make possible a truly literate population.

Developments during 1984 ensured plans and support for improving existing programs and for new ones—more collaborative arrangements in coalitions, a national awareness media campaign, more literacy resource collections, more learning resource centers, more money, more tutors and learners in learning situations across the nation. During the last quarter of the year months of effort culminated in a variety of actions.

National Events. The reauthorization for extension and expansion of the Library Services and Construction Act, Public Law 98-480, was approved by the Congress October 17. It includes three new titles providing services for Indian tribes, foreign language materials, and library literacy programs that have a direct relationship to the development of literacy resources and services. Literacy, by inclusion as a separate title, Title VI, has a designated priority. Although $5,000,000 was authorized between 1984 and 1988, no funds were appropriated. The Higher Education Act, Title II-B for training and research, also suggest funding for personnel, research, and demonstrations that relate to librarianship in specific areas of literacy.

The White House Conference on Library and Information Services (WHCLIS) Taskforce in its five-year review of progress made toward the implementation of resolutions adopted at the 1979 WHCLIS emphasized "the serious illiteracy problem in the United States" and that "libraries and information centers can be increasingly important to the solution of this problem." In multiple resolutions it was proposed that States identify, coordinate, and encourage library literacy programs and cooperation among education agencies.

At the spring meeting of the National Advisory Board of the Center for the Book in the Library of Congress, members discussed the role of the book in the future as well as illiteracy and literacy education. On December 7, the Librarian of Congress, Daniel J. Boorstin, delivered a report, *Books in Our Future*, to Senator Charles McC. Mathias, Jr., Chairman of the Joint Committee on the Library. The report called for a national goal of abolishing illiteracy in the United States by 1989, the bicentennial of the Constitution. A program for combating "the twin menaces: illiteracy and aliteracy" is outlined with examples of what is being done and recommendations for action by private organizations, the Congress, the Executive Branch, and the Library of Congress. (*See* Library of Congress—Books in Our Future.)

Chief Officers of State Library Agencies (COSLA) at an October meeting in Vermont adopted a two-point resolution that COSLA "endorse efforts by State library agencies and public libraries to take an active role in literacy programs" and "encourage each state to support efforts to develop and provide library coordinated community based literacy programs for adult Americans."

The Coalition for Literacy—initiated in 1981 by the American Library Association and with Jean E. Coleman (Director of ALA's Office for Library Outreach Services) as Coordinator—brings together 11 national agencies or volunteer organizations with the purpose of conducting a three-year campaign to inform the nation of the illiteracy problem and solutions. ALA representatives to the Coalition were Jane C. Hiser, Library Resource Librarian, Enoch Pratt Free Library, and Virginia H. Mathews, Vice President, Shoestring Press.

Wally Amos of "Famous Amos" cookie fame and Pat Kuhns of the Drake University Reading/Learning Center. Amos, who has actively supported literacy programs, helped promote a Literacy Awareness Day at the Des Moines Public Library.

The Coalition for Literacy and the National Advertising Council, Inc., on December 12 at the New York Public Library, announced a three-year awareness campaign—Volunteer Against Illiteracy ("The only degree you need is a degree of caring"). For the media campaign designed by Benton & Bowles and administered by the Ad Council, professional materials for television, radio, press, billboard, and brochures were designed to recruit leaders and tutors, to encourage individual and corporate involvement and support for the effort to eradicate illiteracy, and to provide on-site technical assistance and training to those who are developing literacy programs or coalitions. The Ad Council materials are aired, printed, and disseminated on a no-charge basis, with an estimated donated broadcast and print value exceeding $20,000,000 per year. The Coalition has sought funding to cover out-of-pocket production and printing costs and for support of the clearinghouse responses. Grants received totaled $657,275, including $400,000 matching grant from the Business Council for Effective Literacy, $132,275 from the U.S. Department of Education, $50,000 from B. Dalton and $75,000 over a three-year period from the General Electric Foundation.

Throughout 1984 the Coalition for Literacy worked not only in planning with the Ad Council but also in fostering meetings throughout the United States toward the development of statewide coalitions. The Contact Literacy Center at Lincoln, Nebraska, serves as the national information and referral agency by means of a free access telephone number (1-800-228-8813). The Center links literacy resources and providers services. Its computer data bank of resources and service agencies makes possible responses to inquiries and service requests. Library sponsored literacy programs are registered for referrals along with 7,000 literacy resources nationwide and 6,000 human service agencies.

Libraries across the nation also act as centers for volunteer assistance and information referral. Although the campaign is not designed to recruit students, many prospective clients or their families and friends will call to seek help. During a test period in the first six months of the year, a total of 12,227 calls were received—59.6 percent from potential volunteers, 31.5 percent from potential students, and 9 percent from individuals and groups.

The Coalition has other linkages to recently organized groups. It is cooperating with a private foundation, The Business Council for Effective Literacy, which seeks to stimulate private sector corporations to fund literacy activities (1221 Avenue of the Americas, New York, N.Y. 10020). In the spring representatives from the Coalition and the Assault on Illiteracy Program (AOIP) met at ALA headquarters to plan areas of cooperation. AOIP concentrates on the problem of illiteracy in the Black community. Furthermore, the theme for National Library Week 1985, "A Nation of Readers," supports the national awareness campaign.

Urban libraries with long established literacy programs continue to move ahead with collaborative, innovative efforts. At Philadelphia, the Mayor's Commission on Literacy sponsored a national Urban Literacy Conference, September 9-10, on the introduction of literacy programs in urban areas. Adult educators, city representatives of volunteeer programs, and librarians from 40 cities participated. Representatives from literacy programs in cities that were affiliated with public libraries included Cleveland, Newark, New York, Philadelphia, Pittsburgh, and San Francisco. In Philadelphia, Keith Doms, Director of the Free Library of Philadelphia, served as liaison between the Mayor's Commission and the library staff as well as being an active proponent of literacy education.

Activities and Events. State and local activities and events indicate a strengthening of existing programs and development of new projects.

The 1983-84 Annual Report of Literacy Volunteers of America, Inc., listed several libraries as affiliate or organization members including Bergenfield and Trenton Area Public Libraries (New Jersey), Wilmington Library (Delaware), Bay County (Florida), Enoch Pratt (Maryland), Tulsa City/County, Brooklyn, Spokane, and the American Library Association. In November the Detroit Public Library and Adult Basic Education helped initiate the establishment of a Citizens of Detroit LVA affiliate.

The Beaver County Federated Library System (Pennsylvania) and Mary H. Weir Library, Weirton, West Virginia, celebrated International Literacy Day September 8 along with the 100th anniversary birthday of Frank C. Laubach. A special anniversary birthday celebration was held at the Frank and Effa Laubach Memorial Library Association in Benton, Pennsylvania, where Laubach was born September 2, 1884. The U.S. honored this world literacy advocate and educator with a 30-cent "great Americans" stamp featuring a sketch of Laubach.

The Buffalo and Erie County (New York) Public Library purchased 600 new volumes for learners in English as a second language program. An LSCA grant of $46,000 makes it possible to add other materials and resources, two part-time librarians as staff, and staff for the Buffalo educational TV Channel 17, which is developing a statewide program.

Many state libraries provide technical assist-

ance, encouragement, and financial grants for developing literacy projects. The Connecticut State Library granted $1,000 to 18 public libraries.

In Wisconsin attention was focused on libraries' roles in achieving a literate population by the state's long-range plan for library services for 1982 to 1987, by a mission statement for public libraries, and through LSCA grants for special users. The Wisconsin Division of Library Services awarded LSCA funds totaling $86,541 to six library literacy projects. They included the Arrowhead Library System, Janesville; Oakhill Correctional Institution, Oregon; the Dane County Library; Manitowoc–Calumet Library System; Fond du Lac City–County Federated System, and Kenosha Public Library–Southwest Project.

The California Literacy Campaign, authorized by the California State Library, initiated 27 community-based adult literacy programs through the leadership and coordination of California's public libraries. The purpose was to "lay the groundwork for a state and statewide long-term structure that will reach and help adults in California attain an English-language ability they want and need." In 1984 the programs were funded by LSCA awards totaling $2,515,000. This demonstration was to move into a transition period in 1985. For 1984–85 the state budget provided $2,635,000 in local assistance to public libraries to maintain and expand the program along with $212,000 in state operations.

The Bay Area Literacy Coalition brings together separate area projects of Alameda County, Oakland, San Francisco, Richmond, and Contra Costa County. Contra Costa County Library's adult literacy program, PROJECT: SECOND CHANCE, reaches out to 65,000 functionally illiterate adults and is designed to serve 20 percent of the county adult population. The project was initiated by Doris Headley, Coordinator of Adult Services and has a full-time Project Coordinator, Carole Talan. It has $62,000 in funding from LSCA. The Project serves as a support group to other organizations and schools and the needs of English-speaking adults who are not being served by existing programs.

In the Roots and Wings: Reading Program for Adults at the Ventura County Library Services Agency (California), conducted by reading specialist Patricia Gannon, the non-reader was helped to move from zero or beginning level to a high-school reading level through a 40-hour instructional program.

Project READ at the Elyria (Ohio) Public Library and Project LITE at the Lorain (Ohio) Public Library joined the city schools and other service programs in the Lorain County Literacy Coalition.

The library literacy program in New York State has many facets. *The New York State Library: 1984*, a report, devoted more than one-fourth of its coverage to information on Library Development Division support of public library literacy programs. Both the LSCA program documents and objective 1.B.2 in *The Regents Long Range Plan for the Office of Cultural Education* commit the State Library to assisting public libraries to develop appropriate programs for service to persons needing help to develop literacy. The Library Development Division encouraged and LSCA grants supported library-based literacy programs through the years. Some of the $1,000,000 in new state aid for outreach programs was to be used in 1985 for literacy services in libraries. A study by Kevin Smith, Director of

California's Literacy Campaign of 1984 included many tutoring sessions for adult learners including these at the State Library (left) and the Contra Costa County Library, Pleasant Hill.

Dallas Public Library Director Patrick M. O'Brien, surrounded by staff and volunteer tutors, accepts a $6,000 donation from B. Dalton Booksellers to support the Library's "Literacy for Dallas" program. Volunteers are being trained to tutor Dallas citizens who cannot read above the 5th grade level.

187

Literacy Programs, Library

Literacy Volunteers of New York State, found that over 50 libraries provided resources, services, and staff in cooperative literacy programs. Established literacy programs were continued at public libraries in Brooklyn, Onondaga County, Queens Borough and at the Library Systems of Chemung-Southern Tier, Mid-York, and Westchester.

In November, anticipating increased citizen interest as a result of the nationwide campaign initiated by the Coalition for Literacy and the National Advertising Council, Joseph F. Shubert, State Librarian and Assistant Commissioner for Libraries, sent a Literacy Information packet of 14 items to the Directors of the 22 Public Library Systems. He outlined steps to ensure that accurate information is provided to prospective tutors and students.

At the end of December, Shubert invited Directors and the staff of Library Systems in New York State, of Central and Co-Central Libraries, and of School Library Systems to attend an adult literacy closed circuit TV meeting at nine local Public Television Stations for the purpose of increasing providers awareness in an up-to-date national campaign and state activities, promoting a dialog among existing regional and local service agencies, and developing partnership among local resources. TV stations involved included Plattsburg, Liverpool, Plainsview, Schnectady, Buffalo, Watertown, Binghamton, Rochester, and New York.

Awards. Recognition for distinguished and significant work over the years was given during 1984 in award honoring events. ALA's American Library Trustee Association Literacy award went to Lydia A. Dwiggins of Bridgeport, Connecticut.

For her efforts and activities on behalf of literacy Jane Cathcart, head of Extension Services, Onondaga County Public Library (Syracuse, New York), was designated the 1984 recipient by the Central New York Coalition for International Literacy Day.

Among the awards to six Exemplary Outreach Programs sponsored by ALA's Office for Library Outreach Services and presented by Art Kirschenbaum, Program Analyst, U.S. Department of Education Program Service at the ALA Annual Conference in Dallas, were two recognitions of exemplary literacy services: the Adult Program at the Free Library of Philadelphia with its strong component Center for Literacy and multidimensional Reader Development Program and the Fresno County Public Library (California) adult Literacy Project to help the many Hmong refugees. The program provides cultural awareness as well as literacy skills for Hmong refugee families.

At the 1984 Baltimore Conference of Literacy Volunteers of America, Inc., Jean E. Coleman, Director of ALA's Office of Library Outreach Services, received the LVA President's award, which recognizes distinguished and exceptional service. The award recognized her "long standing commitment to literacy," her activity as "catalyst in the cooperative match between literacy and ALA," and her "dedicated, successful work in the Coalition for Literacy."

Resource Aids. At the beginning of the year Capitol Cities Television Production aired the documentary "Can't Read, Can't Write" to television viewers across the nation. The hour-long film helped to create awareness of the illiteracy problem and referred viewers to Contact Literacy Center. In the fall "Wall of Words," another television documentary on the problem of adult illiteracy produced by WBZ-TV Westinghouse in Boston, aired in five major cities.

An 11-minute videotape was produced explaining Coalition for Literacy and the national literacy awareness campaign. It can be copied on 1/2- or 3/4-inch VHS tape. State library agencies and ABE directors acquired copies. In New York State, it was made available upon request to Carol Ann Desch, Assistant in Library Services, Division of Library Development, New York State Library, Albany.

The Coalition for Literacy distributes several information brochures, such as *Illiteracy in America, How to Form a Community Volunteer Literacy Campaign,* and *27 Million Americans Can't Read.* They may be obtained upon request from the Coalition office, ALA Headquarters, 50 East Huron St., Chicago, Illinois 60611.

Lions Clubs International joined the U.S. literacy effort. In *The Lion Magazine* (October 1984) attention was called to the decline of functional literacy. "Can We Improve Our Grades," by Catherine Lazers Bauer, reviews the current situation in schooling and looks at suggested causes and remedies. ALA President E. J. Josey discusses "Working Together to Solve the Problem" and Milton Goldberg, Executive Director, National Commission on Excellence in Education, points out ways to reform "Improving Our Schools."

"Libraries and Adult Literacy Education in Wisconsin 1965-1984" by Helen H. Lyman (*Wisconsin Library Bulletin,* Summer 1984) traces the development of literacy education programs and services and research for the 20-year period.

Of special interest and value to public librarians and trustees is "The Public Library in the Coalition Against Illiteracy," a special section of *Public Libraries* (Winter 1984) with Jane C. Heiser as guest editor. The issue provides an up-to-date review of past, present, and future roles of libraries in the literacy education movement. Special focus is on coalitions and organizational activities.

Books for Adult New Readers, a second revised edition of the bibliography developed by Project: LEARN (2238 Euclid Avenue, Cleveland, Ohio 44115) was compiled and annotated by Roberta Luther O'Brien. There are about 100 new titles in this edition and 60 titles from earlier editions were removed. It is an annotated, indexed bibliography of nearly 400 titles selected from an examination of over 3,000. The materials cover reading, mathematics, coping skills, leisure reading for English-speaking adults (18 years of age and over) and reading at the seventh-grade level or below.

A computer program for measuring readability levels was developed by Michael Schuyler, Assistant to the Director of the Kitsap Regional Library in Bremerton, Washington. The computer program analyzes passages for difficulty in text materials and calculates the reading grade level according to nine different readability formulas.

The formulas include: ARI, Coleman, Dale-Chall, Flesch, Flesch-Kincaid, Fog, Fry, Holmquist, and Powers. The analyses make possible comparisons of the formulas in a composite graph of results. Two versions of the program are available for Apple II and for IBM PC computers.

Research. In 1984 the Enoch Pratt Free Library in Baltimore and the Mary Weir Library in Weirton, West Virginia, were conducting two pilot projects for testing the adaptability for civilian use of an adult learning program developed by the Armed Forces. After nearly a year of study, a Steering Group representing the National Commission on Libraries and Information Science (NCLIS), the United States Army Human Engineering Laboratory (USAHEL), Jane Heiser, Literacy Resources Librarian at the Pratt Library, Helen Crouch, Director, Literacy Volunteers of America, Inc., and David Promisel, Army Research Institute for Behavioral and Social Sciences (ARI), chose the pilot projects. The six-month demonstration project was to test a computer-assisted instructional program developed initially by Robert Wisher and Thomas Duffy, formerly of the Naval Research Development Center. Duffy supervised and assisted in training aspects. Federal funds for the Project are channeled through USAHEL under guidelines laid down in 1980 by the Stevenson-Wydler Technology Innovation Act (PL 96-480) in the Army's Technology Transfer program. The pilot project in Baltimore began October 15 at the Pimlico Branch's Reading Resource Center. The Pratt staff supervises and administers the project. The Mary Weir Library project functions similarly under the direction of the Library Director, Jane Eiselstein.

Continuing Education. Continuing Education programs for librarians and literacy volunteer staff provided training and learning experiences in workshops, conferences, lectures, and discussions. Conspicuous among LSCA grant programs was the inclusion of plans for developing library staff competencies. Workshops have been organized around relevant topics with a group of resource persons from the literacy field and the exchange of experiences among participants as resources. A major part of tutorial programs for adult learners has been the training of tutors and community leaders in cosponsored workshops with volunteer organizations, such as Laubach Literacy Action and Literacy Volunteers of America, Inc.

"Libraries & Literacy '84 Conference, May 9-11, at Janesville, Wisconsin, was sponsored by The Arrowhead Library System and the Wisconsin Library Association Outreach Services Round Table. Coordinators were Debra W. Johnson and Coral S. Swanson. A majority of the 115 conferees were librarians from Wisconsin representing at least 34 libraries or library systems. Collaborative members included technical institutes, literacy councils, university extension, library school students, and out-of-state librarians.

The ALA preconference "Access to Information Through Literacy," cosponsored by ALA's Office for Library Outreach Services, American Library Trustee Association, and Public Library Association/Alternative Education Programs Section, was held June 20-22, at Texas Woman's University, Denton, Texas. It brought together experienced librarians, literacy programmers, and state library personnel who in turn would provide similar training of a statewide scope. The conference focused on the role of libraries in adult literacy.

During the ALA Conference in Dallas Jonathan Kozol, author and authority on literacy, spoke at a meeting of the American Library Trustees Association about the meaning of illiteracy to Americans who cannot read and of his own experiences. Alfred B. Bennett, Jr., consultant, California State Library, at a PLA's Alternative Education Program Section, Basic Education and Literacy Services Committee meeting, discussed "Future Trends in Basic Education and Literacy Services" with a panel of authorities.

A panel of specialists at the New York Library Association Annual Conference in October, discussed "What Does the Adult New Reader Read? Effective Collection Development." The panel included Melissa F. Buckingham, Free Library of Philadelphia, Brian Martin, New York Public Library Learner Advisory Service, and Beverly Provost, Mohawk Valley Library Association.

At the Maryland Regional Library Association, David Harman, researcher in literacy, and George Eyster, Morehead State University (Kentucky), presented their views on the meaning of illiteracy and solutions.

The Ohio State Library sponsored a workshop September 18-22, at Columbus, on "New Readers and Small Libraries" with specialists Sandra Scott, George Eyster, and Roberta O'Brien.

At the mid-November Conference of the American Association for Adult and Continuing Education in Louisville, a session was devoted to the subject of change, the training needs of the practitioner—the librarian who may need new competencies to administer literacy education services.

In California a special Technical Assistance Program was developed to meet the needs of Public libraries participating in the California Literacy Campaign.

The year's accomplishments and realization of some primary objectives prepared a foundation for libraries of all types—and for librarians as well as community volunteers—to meet the many opportunities and demands of the future.

HELEN HUGUENOR LYMAN

Medical Libraries

Automation. Medical Libraries operated under the mantle of a future-oriented agenda during 1984, with the present and future impact of electronic information delivery systems as the first order of business. The topics of discussion throughout the year included (1) full-text access, (2) information analysis (synthesized information) vs. bibliographic compilations (undigested information), (3) new computing power via high density storage, (4) the impact of electronic manuscript preparations, (5) the proliferation of online databases, public vendors, database publishers, communications networks, and information-conscious database users, (6) archival and preservation functions as related to an online environment, (7) the shifting economics of information services, and (8) the viability of librarians vis-a-vis new systems.

The excitement of 1983's discussions on integrated library systems carried forward into 1984 as the National Library of Medicine announced four contracts to conduct strategic planning for the development of integrated Academic Information Management Systems (IAIMS). The conceptual model for these IAIMS projects is one in which a library's own information service system is viewed as one in a series of information systems that must be integrated. The totally integrated system might include, for example, bibliographic databases, knowledge bases, patient records, laboratory test data, statistical databases, and electronic mail systems. The four IAIMS contractors are Columbia University, Georgetown University, the University of Maryland at Baltimore, and the University of Utah. IAIMS projects will take a variety of forms, depending on the computing environment at the respective institutions, but they all share a common objective: to explore the development of new ways for institutions to manage and relate a proliferation of information for operational efficiency. A resource grant program is also available through the National Library of Medicine to support strategic planning for IAIMS development. Two grants were awarded during 1984 (University of Cincinnati and the Baylor College of Medicine), and those institutions are to begin planning the development of integrated information system models. These efforts assume a partnership role for medical libraries with other groups, libraries, databases, and users in the academic health science center. They portend an extension of the library's traditional role, for 1984 and beyond.

The use of personal computers had dramatic effects on medical libraries as they responded (with other libraries) to increasing numbers of information-conscious users. In the U.S. today, it is estimated that there is one computer terminal for every 48 job holders, with expectations that by 1986 the ratio will be one for every ten job holders. For medical libraries, inquiries from health professionals about personal online access have grown over the past few years and their attendance at training sessions has more than doubled. This new group of health professionals intend to perform their own database searches at times and places convenient to them. In response to this new independence among some library users, the National Library of Medicine announced its plans to offer subsets of its MEDLINE database for storage and reuse in a local processing mode. Managed through a licensing agreement, these subsets (floppy disks) are available on an annual subscription basis.

National Library of Medicine. As the National Library of Medicine celebrated the 20th anniversary of its MEDLARS (Medical Literature Analysis and Retrieval System) during 1984, the medical library community welcomed the news that a contract had been awarded to a commercial software and development consulting firm to develop and implement the third generation of the system, MEDLARS III. The MEDLARS III project will introduce a higher degree of automation into NLM's internal processing operations and external services. Its first phase (scheduled to be completed during 1985) will include software development for selection and acquisitions, cataloging, and information retrieval.

U.S. medical libraries also welcomed NLM's implementation of a new online indexing and management system. This system supports journal receipt and checkin and automated subject indexing. For medical libraries it has meant a two-fold decrease in the amount of time between receipt of journals at NLM and the appearance of citations in the MEDLINE database. The primary reason for this reduction in turn-around time is online indexing, whereby keywords in the title and abstract of each journal article are matched by indexers (online) against a stored dictionary of subject terms.

In the Regional Medical Library Program during 1984, two developments in automated networking were of particular interest to medical libraries. The first was a pilot project to determine the feasibility of establishing a national cooperative reference network, using electronic mail. The second was the design and development of completely new system software for automated document request and referral. Both of these pilot programs were to be fully implemented during the latter part of 1984.

Legislation. The most significant legislation directly affecting medical libraries during 1984 was the two-year extension of the Medical Library Assistance Act (MLAA). It is through the MLAA that the Resource Projects, Research, Training, and Regional Medical Library Network of the National Library of Medicine are funded.

On other legislative fronts it was a busy year as the Medical library community maintained a keen self-interest in the following:

Telecommunications. Of particular interest to medical libraries were the divestiture of AT&T; the levying of access charges for local connection to long distance circuits; and the proposed AT&T tariff for telecommunications charges. At year's end, the FCC had ordered AT&T to reduce long distance rates by 6.1 percent, but allowing access charges to go into effect. The concern of libraries over telecommunications charges was acknowledged by the FCC during the summer of 1984, but specific action on library private line service was judged premature and the private-line tariff investigation was still in process at year's end.

Federal Information Policies. During fall 1984 the Office of Management and Budget (OMB) and the Joint Committee on Printing (JCP) issued notices which could have significant impact on the management and distribution of federal information. With their heavy reliance on the publications of the National Library of Medicine, the notices of the OMB and JCP were alarming to medical libraries as they proposed changes in pricing policy, the relationship between public and private sector publishers, the inclusion of electronic format publications in federal depository programs, and the role of the private sector in the publication of government information. In each of these, the OMB and JCP were to take on an additional measure of authority than presently exists. At year's end, there was no resolution to these controversial policy issues.

National Library of Medicine Pricing Policy. In

response to questions surrounding the issue of cost recovery for information produced with federal funds (see above), the National Library of Medicine issued its conclusions on NLM's pricing policy during summer 1984. This pricing policy was welcomed by medical libraries as it rejects differential pricing by type of user, and reiterates the principle to recover the full cost of access (not production costs) for its online services.

Quality of Hospital Library Service. At the end of 1984 there was no resolution to the proposed revisions of the Health Care Financing Administration (HCFA) regarding hospital libraries. The HCFA revision in the regulatory requirements for Medicare/Medicard programs calls for the elimination of the requirement that hospitals have a library. There was also no resolution to the effort of the Office of Personnel Management (OPM) to develop new classification standards for federal libraries. For those librarians working in Veteran's Administration Hospitals, for example, the OPM effort would lower the entry-grade level and levels of qualifications for such libraries.

Meetings. The Medical Library Association (MLA) held its 84th annual meeting in Denver during June. The Association of Academic Health Science Library Directors (AAHSLD) held its annual meeting during the 95th annual meeting of the Association of American Medical Colleges in November. At the 50th general conference of the International Federation of Library Associations (IFLA) in Nairobi, Kenya, during August, the Section on Biological and Medical Sciences of IFLA held sessions on the basis of library and information services for national development.

JAMES F. WILLIAMS II

Medical Library Association

Annual Meeting. The 84th Annual Meeting of the Medical Library Association was in Denver in May. Preconference continuing education courses drew 740 registrants. Courses stressed the adoption of new technology and explored new roles for librarians. The meeting attracted 1,538 participants, including 21 international visitors from 14 countries and 91 exhibitors.

The theme of the meeting, "Linkages to the Future: Stages and Strategies," was the focus of general sessions that enabled participants to explore topics such as the impact of technology on the workplace, electronic publishing, and the social and political ramifications of scientific information delivery. The emphasis was on coping with the future or preparing oneself for it and on actively planning and shaping the future. A subtheme of the meeting deriving from the Association's newly stated mission was "Excellence in Health through Access to Information."

President Phyllis Mirsky tied together the themes planning, imagination, and exellence characterizing the Annual Meeting in her inaugural speech.

1984 Honors and Awards. The Association's highest honor, the Marcia C. Noyes Award, was conferred upon Frederick Kilgour for his role in the development of online library systems. The Frank Bradway Rogers Information Advancement Award, sponsored by the Institute for Scientific Information, was awarded to Louise Darling for her contributions to the application of technology in health sciences information management. Alice D. Ball, James W. Barry, Frederick Kilgour, Miriam H. Libbey, and Priscilla M. Mayden were made lifetime fellows of MLA in recognition of their advancement of the purposes of the Association. Marjorie P. Wilson's contributions were recognized with lifetime honorary membership.

Other awards conferred were the Ida and George Eliot Prize to Jana Bradley for her editorship of *Hospital Library Management*, the Murray Gottlieb Prize to Christopher Hoolihan for the best unpublished paper in the history of medicine by a librarian, and the Rittenhouse Award to Linda Boettcher for the best student paper. Two scholarships were awarded, the MLA Minority Scholarship to Eric Brasley and the Cunningham International Fellowship to Lise Norregaard Christensen of Aalborg, Denmark.

Lectureships. The Janet Doe Lecturer for 1984 was Irwin Pizer. His address, presented at the Annual Meeting, gave a different perspective to strategic planning by looking at the past. In his paper, "Looking Backward—1984–1959: Twenty-five Years of Library Automation—A Personal View," Pizer presented a history of the early efforts at using computer technology in medical libraries. Frank Bradway Rogers, the 1984 John P. McGovern Award Lecturer, delivered the Annual Meeting's keynote speech, an Orwellian allegory entitled "Down on the Farm."

In conjunction with the National Library of Medicine (NLM), the Association established the Joseph Leiter NLM/MLA Lectureship. It provides for an intellectual dialog on subjects related to biomedical communications. Presentations will be held alternately at the NLM and at the MLA Annual Meeting. The lectureship was established by a donation from Joseph Leiter, former Deputy Director for Library Operations, NLM. Monies donated by colleagues and friends of Leiter, in honor of his retirement in 1983, were also added to the fund. The first Joseph Leiter NLM/MLA Lecture, delivered May 13 by Martin Cummings, recently retired Director of the National Library of Medicine, was titled "The Effect of U.S. Policies on the Economics of Libraries."

The Medical Library Association was to receive the Edward R. Loveland Memorial Award in March 1985. The award is presented by the Board of Regents of the American College of Physicians to organizations or to persons other than physicians who have made significant contributions to the health field.

Publications. During 1984 the Association published the second edition of *Introduction to Reference Services in the Health Sciences* by Fred Roper and Jo Anne Boorkman. MLA announced that in 1985 it would introduce a series of short, softcover books to provide practical treatment of timely topics. Entitled the MLA Information Series, the books will cover basics of MEDLINE searching for the end user, management of personal information files with microcomputers, drug information resources, and consumer-health/patient-care information.

MEDICAL LIBRARY ASSOCIATION

PRESIDENT (June 1984–June 1985):
Phyllis S. Mirsky, University of California at San Diego

PRESIDENT-ELECT:
Jean Miller, Health Science Center, University of Texas, Dallas

EXECUTIVE DIRECTOR:
Raymond A. Palmer

Membership (December 1985): 3,726 individual; 1,349 institutional
Headquarters: Suite 3208, 919 N. Michigan Avenue, Chicago, Illinois 60611

MOUNTAIN PLAINS LIBRARY ASSOCIATION

PRESIDENT (April 1984–May 1985):
Dorothy Liegl, South Dakota State Library, Pierre, South Dakota

VICE-PRESIDENT/PRESIDENT-ELECT:
Tom Jones, Veterans Memorial Public Library, Bismarck, North Dakota

EXECUTIVE SECRETARY:
Joseph R. Edelen, Jr., University of South Dakota Library, Vermillion, South Dakota

Membership (December 1984): 760

Legislative Activities. The Governmental Relations Committee in 1984 successfully supported the reauthorization of the Medical Library Assistance Act at more favorable funding levels and urged additional funding for Integrated Academic Information Management Systems (IAIMS). The Association opposed the Health Care Financing Administration proposal to eliminate any reference to hospital library service in the conditions for participation by hospitals in Medicare/Medicaid reimbursement programs. MLA, through its Governmental Relations Committee and its Executive Director, also opposed telecommunications rate increases. In response to the Office of Information and Regulatory Affairs' request for comments on developing a Circular on Federal Information Management, the Association emphasized the concept of information as a vital free good in a democratic society, not to be confused with commodities such as food and clothing for which price is established by the marketplace.

The Association continued to monitor contracting out federal library services; the potential impact on the support hospital libraries might receive, following publication of the interim final rule for Medicare payments to hospitals for inpatient services; postal rates; and proposed restrictions on the use of federal funds for lobbying by nonprofit professional associations.

RAYMOND A. PALMER

Mountain Plains Library Association

During 1984 the Mountain Plains Library Association continued to offer members an information exchange on library science techniques and activities common to members of this far-flung organization. Emphasis during the year was on development of knowledgeable librarians, trustees, and employees in rural, small, and remote library service in the states that make up the organization—Colorado, Kansas, Montana, Nebraska, Nevada, North Dakota, South Dakota, Utah, and Wyoming. The nine member states comprise 25 percent of the area of the continental United States.

Educational programs on technological development were sponsored throughout the year for MPLA libraries. Professional development grants were made available to members for course work, institutes, and workshops. A variety of continuing education opportunities, including preconference and conference workshops, were provided. The organization newsletter emphasized continuing education opportunities.

Annual Conference. The 1984 MPLA Conference was held in Cheyenne in conjunction with the Wyoming Library Association and the Wyoming Association for Educational Communication and Technology. Theme of the Conference was Humanities and the Western Horizon.

Preconference programs included "Getting Started: TV Production for Beginners," "Discrimination and Sexual Harassment in the Workplace and on Campus," "This Way to Books," "Humanities Programs and Grants Available to Public Libraries," "The Faculty Handbook and the Library Professional—Legal, Contractual, and Professional Issues," and "Teleconferencing for Educators."

The Conference program included many programs cosponsored by the Wyoming Council for the Humanities. Featured were "Trends Affecting State Libraries Now and During the Next Five to 10 years," "Laughter on the Frontier, a Study of Frontier Humor," "Nonfiction Books for Children, Books that Make a Difference," "Microcomputers and School Library Management," and "Everything you Wanted to Know about Intellectual Freedom but were too Confused to Ask," and "Once Upon a Mind."

Awards. Peggy Simpson Curry, Casper, Wyoming, was presented the 1984 Library Contribution Award in recognition of published writings deemed highly significant for furthering appreciation and understanding of professional standards.

The News Media Support Award went to the *Howells Journal*, Howells, Nebraska, and the Legislative Leadership Award was presented to L. M. (Bud) Cornich, Topeka, in recognition of his leadership in forwarding the cause of libraries in Kansas.

DOROTHY M. LIEGL

Music Library Association

In 1984 the Music Library Association began to enjoy the benefits of attention paid by recent Boards of Directors to administrative and financial matters. A new business manager was named, membership was up, and the Association's books were ready for the transition to a new accounting system.

Annual Meetings. The 1984 annual meeting in February took place in Austin. The week included an intensive two-day preconference workshop, "Computers and the New Technology in the Music Library." Networks, online systems, retrospective conversion, hardware, and optical and videodisk technologies were the topics of 10 impressively presented sessions. The conference proper, encompassing board and committee meetings, included sessions on space design in music libraries, grants and fundraising, a workshop on preparing for NASM (National Association of Schools of Music) accreditation visits, music research and resources at the University of Texas, resources and collection development, and historical bibliography. Although the Music OCLC Users Group did not meet in conjunction with MLA as it often does, there were the customary meetings of the RLG Music Program Group and IAML-U.S. (the U.S. branch of the International Association of Music Libraries, Archives and Documentation Centers).

Projects and Committees. Among MLA's cooperative projects, new departures in two international activities were notable. First was the establishment, with support also from the International Association of Music Libraries and the American Musicological Society (AMS), of a U.S. RILM office at Cornell University. The office will collect and convey to the International RILM Center at CUNY Graduate Center all U.S. material for *RILM Abstracts of Music Literature*. Previously, the International Center had taken responsibility for U.S. citations and abstracts. Second was the revitalization, also with AMS, of the joint committee on RISM (International Inventory of Musical Sources) for the U.S. RISM, which has published over 30 volumes and has compiled a database of 30,000 additional entries, will receive as the focus of present U.S. efforts information for the supplement to series A I, pre-1801 imprints of individual compositions, and for series A II, manuscripts from 1600 to 1800.

MLA in 1984 participated in two conferences sponsored by the Council on Library Resources on a National Program for Music Retrospective Conversion Projects. Cooperative cataloging received further attention as MLA's Committee on Contributing Libraries to *Music, Books on Music and Sound Recordings* was invited by the Library of Congress to formulate recommendations for the music registers that will be published as part of the *National Union Catalog*. The July issue of MLA's *Music Cataloging Bulletin* conveyed a Library of Congress questionnaire about subject headings for jazz and popular music. Responses were promptly reported and will assist LC in future revisions.

The Audiovisual Committee began a national equipment inventory, a referral service similar to one the Committee offers for new audio installations. Using information contributed by libraries in North America, the Committee will compile a database of model numbers and locations. Libraries contemplating purchase of audio equipment will be able to submit consumer inquiries, first to the database at Greer Music Library, Connecticut College, and, using those responses, then to the libraries that already have in use the equipment specified.

Also among new committee activities was the establishment of a GEAC Music Users Group. Its objectives are to share information and concerns about the coding and display of citations to musical scores and sound recordings and to intitiate dialogue with the firm on such matters.

Publications. MLA's quarterly journal, *Notes*, reached its 41st year. Nancy Bren of SUNY/Buffalo took over the editorship of the quarterly *Newsletter* in 1984. New publications were *The Acquisition and Cataloging of Music and Sound Recordings: A Glossary*, compiled by Suzanne E. Thorin and Carole Franklin Vidali, a volume in the series "Technical Reports," and in the Index and Bibliography Series the second edition of *Analyses of 20th-Century Music* and *Analyses of Nineteenth-Century Music, 1940–1980*, both by Arthur Wenk.

Awards. Citations presented at the annual meeting honored two distinguished senior members of the Association, Richard S. Angell and Carleton Sprague Smith. The annual publications prizes (1982 imprints) went to Carol J. Oja for her *American Music Recordings: A Discography of 20th Century U.S. Composers* (Institute for Studies in American Music at Brooklyn College), to James Bradford Young for his article in *Fontes artis musicae*, "An Account of Printed Music ca. 1724," and to Andrew Frank for his reviews in *Notes* of musical scores by contemporary composers.

The Future. Reflecting on long-range goals, the Association in 1984 began a review of its publications program that is intended to examine premises as well as products. And upon investigation of financial development prospects, MLA committed itself to increasing its fund-raising in order to provide more substantial support for activities in progress and also to increase the scope of its program of awards.

GERALDINE OSTROVE

MUSIC LIBRARY ASSOCIATION

PRESIDENT (March 1985–March 1987):
Geraldine Ostrove, New England Conservatory of Music

PAST PRESIDENT:
Mary Wallace Davidson, Eastman School of Music

RECORDING SECRETARY:
Ruth Tucker, University of California, Berkeley

EXECUTIVE SECRETARY:
Suzanne E. Thorin, Library of Congress

TREASURER:
Karen K. Griffith, The Cleveland Institute of Music

Membership (1984): 2,200
Headquarters: P.O. Box 487, Canton, Massachusetts 02021

National Agricultural Library

Reorganization Structure. The National Agricultural Library (NAL) was extensively restructured in 1984. The primary objective was to revitalize and modernize Library operations and service, expand user access to a greater variety of agricultural information, and coordinate and strengthen a national network of agricultural libraries. Emphasis was placed on development and adoption of standardized formats and procedures and on establishment of cooperative working arrangements with other libraries and concerned private and public institutions.

Structural changes include strengthening library services by organizing the reference function into agricultural subject areas such as economics/marketing and farming/forestry, incorporating the former Food and Nutrition Information Center as part of a Food, Nutrition, and Human Ecology Staff, and expanding the information systems function to recognize the greater significance of computers, telecommunications, and other new technologies in the operation of a modern library. The D.C. Branch Library was under renovation to serve primarily as a reference information center. A new special collection program was established to handle a growing collection of manuscripts, archival materials, rare books, early periodicals, maps, photographs, audiovisual materials, and a variety of other items.

The reorganization will provide the basis for expansion of and emphasis on NAL's role as one of three national libraries (the Library of Congress and the National Library of Medicine are the others) and its international responsibility as the largest agricultural library in the free world.

The Library is expanding its work with the Library of Congress to acquire both foreign and domestic materials in the agricultural field with significant assistance from LC field libraries abroad. The two libraries also cooperated in the NACO and CONSER cataloging projects. The NAL and the National Library of Medicine engaged in mutually beneficial interlibrary loan activities and are sharing responsibility for the collection, processing, and dissemination of information in veterinary science.

Internationally, the Library worked with the Commonwealth Agricultural Bureaux (CAB) in 1984 to implement its controlled vocabulary in the AGRICOLA database beginning in 1985. In a cooperative arrangement, CAB and the Food and Agriculture Organization (FAO) agreed with NAL to work for as much compatibility as possible regarding controlled vocabuláries.

In the rapidly growing area of aquaculture, the NAL initiated a venture with the National Oceanic and Atmospheric Administration (NOAA) and the Aquatic Sciences and Fisheries Information Systems (ASFIS) coordinated by the FAO. The Library will provide backup document delivery service for aquaculture materials collected worldwide and processed by ASFIS.

In 1984 the Library was conducting four separate evaluation studies involving electronic storage and dissemination of information in cooperation with the Science and Education agencies of the United States Department of Agriculture (USDA). Three of the studies are directly related to full-text database transmission, representing a significant step forward from the citations contained in the AGRICOLA bibliographic database currently available online. Pilot studies include laser disks, full-text online storage and retrieval, and photocomposition tapes for a full-text database. A fourth study concerns potential online availability of agricultural source directories.

Automated Systems. In response to the high priority placed by the NAL Blue Ribbon Panel on improving the Library's automated database, a comprehensive review and evaluation of the AGRICOLA system, the Library's master bibliographic database, was completed by MITRE Corporation. The final report issued in March, "Long Term Automation Guidelines—The National Agricultural Library," made several recommendations. The most important was that the present system for bibliographic support be replaced. NAL has followed up by letting a second contract to MITRE for the completion of a detailed requirements document that will be used as the basis for the competitive procurement of an integrated library system. It was expected that procurement would be complete in fall 1985.

An automated system was under development to support the decision to use the CAB thesaurus. It will support the capabilities to load and update the CAB thesaurus file and the subsequent validation of thesaurus terms will be used in NAL indexing records. As of January 1985, validated thesaurus terms were to be used on all indexing records distributed as part of the AGRICOLA subscription service.

AGRICOLA. Preparations were made for some important changes to the AGRICOLA database in 1985. Foremost was to be the addition of Commonwealth Agricultural Bureaux (CAB) thesaurus terms to indexing records. Since AGRICOLA's inception, the sole controlled subject access to its indexing records has been through broadly structured subject category codes. Over the years, the codes have become somewhat more detailed, but many online users have expressed a

An American folk artifacts exhibit was part of the National Agricultural Library's 1984 exhibition on the German housebarn in America.

need for even greater controlled subject access.

Another change to AGRICOLA effective in January 1985 was to be the official U.S. MARC Component Parts approach to recording "host item" information for indexing records. When NAL first adopted the MARC Communication Format in 1979, there was no appropriate mechanism available for describing the "host" or "containing item" (i.e., the containing journal when a journal article was being described or the containing monograph when a book chapter was being described). The Library adopted a provisional mechanism for filling that void, but the eventual official MARBI/MARC approach turned out to be different from that used by the U.S. This change brings NAL back into line with the mainstream of the library community.

Cooperative Cataloging/Indexing. The NAL proposed establishing a network of libraries to participate in a cooperative cataloging project of agriculture monographs. Although the proposed project is initially addressing coordination only with OCLC and participation of OCLC member libraries, future plans include expansion to interested member libraries of other bibliographic utilities. The records prepared as a result of this project will be accessible in AGRICOLA and for the Library of Congress Cataloging Distribution Service.

Cooperative arrangements were established for the indexing of agricultural journals and state publications by two institutions: the University of Georgia and the Arid Lands Information Center at the University of Arizona. Indexing is currently performed by these two institutions according to standard formats established by NAL. The indexing records supplied by the two cooperating institutions are incorporated into the NAL national bibliographic database. Inclusion of these records in the NAL database makes these agricultural materials available both nationally and internationally. Negotiations continue with other institutions that may wish to participate in a similar agreement in order that indexing data can be incorporated into the NAL database.

CONSER, NACO Participation. The Library has been an active member of CONSER, assuming national responsibility for the coordination and quality control of information on current agricultural journals and periodicals input into the CONSER file. As a member of the NACO project at LC, NAL is creating and maintaining name authority records for agricultural serials publications. The NAL also cooperated with the CONSER Abstracting and Indexing Coverage Project in the National Serials Data Program at the Library of Congress, submitting surrogates of agricultural journals and verifying accuracy of information in the agricultural related records of the CONSER file.

Expanded Translations Program. Translation of foreign-language publications on agricultural science and technology will be more broadly available to U.S. Department of Agriculture personnel and other agricultural researchers and extension workers nationwide under a new agreement between the National Agricultural Library and the Office of International Cooperation and Development. Special Foreign Currencies, as authorized under Public Law 480, will be used to pay for overseas translation of journal articles, monographs, reports, and other materials. The memorandum of understanding between the two agencies continued a program previously under way, extending the scope of translations and shifting additional responsibility to the library.

Stack Retrieval. In a major effort to improve document delivery service to the Department, libraries, and the general public, NAL stack retrieval operations were put under contract for the first time in 1984. The Macro Corporation agreed to sort, shelve, and retrieve up to 30,000 document requests per year with a 24-hour turnaround time. The same firm had been previously awarded the photolab contract.

Microfilming of State Documents. In cooperation with NAL, the University of Georgia will coordinate the microfilming of 416,051 pages of state experiment station and extension service publications on land-grant university campuses

The National Agricultural Library will distribute floriculture information to growers, wholesalers, and retailers under an agreement signed by Secretary of Agriculture John R. Block (seated, left) and Mabel Simmons of the American Florists Endowment. Observing the agreement are NAL Director Joseph H. Howard (right) and Orville G. Bentley, Assistant Secretary for Science and Education.

in 12 southeastern states—Alabama, Florida, Georgia, Kentucky, Louisiana, Mississippi, New Mexico, North Carolina, Oklahoma, South Carolina, Tennessee, and Texas. All of the material to be filmed dates from 1970 to 1982; all prior literature has already been filmed. Pennsylvania State University completed its project to coordinate the microfilming of agricultural publications of six states (Pennsylvania, Delaware, Michigan, New Jersey, New York, and Maryland). The material filmed in many cases dated back to the 19th century with the latest issue published in 1980. Approximately 3,000,000 pages had been microfilmed in 42 states by 1984.

Current Awareness. The Library continues to provide a current awareness service to members of USDA on a monthly service embracing 12 databases: Chemical Abstracts; Telegen; Water Resources Abstracts; AGRICOLA; Biological Abstracts; BioResearch Index; Commonwealth Agricultural Bureaus (CAB); Engineering Index;

National Commission on Libraries and Information Science

Primary NAL activities	1984 estimated productivity
Serial issues added	157,481
Number of titles cataloged	19,434
Articles indexed	157,509
Volumes bound	12,432
Document requests filled	229,269
Reference inquiries answered	22,208
Automated searches conducted	8,145
Current awareness searches	212,190
Current awareness profiles by all databases	2,987

Food Science Technology Abstracts; Government Reports Announcements (NTIS); World Textile Abstracts; Zoo Record. A project was under way in 1984 to include AGRIS in the CALS service. Procurement of a text array processor was also under way. Installation at the USDA Washington Computer Center was expected in spring 1985.

Extension Collections. NAL completed processing two special Extension collections donated by the USDA Extension Service and the State Cooperative Extension Service of the Northeastern Region. The USDA Extension Service repository collection consists of dissertations and theses written by USDA Extension personnel and selected Federal and State extension publications related to the Extension Service.

Floriculture Gift. Secretary of Agriculture John R. Block signed an agreement under which the American Florists Endowment made a $30,000 gift to the NAL to be used for distribution information on floriculture to growers, wholesalers, and retailers in the floriculture industry. The agreement was prompted in part by the recent donation to the Library of a major collection of bibliographic and related materials in floriculture economics from the Fossum Foundation Library of North Dakota State University. These materials will be added to the extensive literature on floriculture now in the National Agricultural Library.

Cost Recovery. The Library reviewed and updated its fee schedules for FY 1985. Under the thrust for user fee services, procedures were implemented to charge user fees for computer and reference services beyond a threshold level. Other fees for photoduplicating copies and for AGRICOLA tape uses and sales were also updated. Fees were to be reviewed annually.

JOSEPH H. HOWARD

National Commission on Libraries and Information Science

In 1984 the work of the Commission fell into four major program areas: (1) policy, planning, and advice, (2) improving library and information services to meet changing needs, (3) access to information, and (4) information technology, innovation, and productivity.

Policy, Planning, and Advice. NCLIS in 1984 released the published report of its Blue Ribbon Panel on the Information Policy Applications of Archiving Satellite Data. This panel was established at the request of the Department of Commerce after the President directed the Secretary of Commerce to transfer the nation's remote sensing satellite systems to the private sector. The 47-page study examines the issues related to archiving the nation's weather and land-sensing satellites, provides an overview of the needs of users of satellite data in both the public and private sectors, and summarizes the findings and recommendations of the panel. In her introduction, Elinor Hashim, NCLIS Chairman, stated, "Perhaps the most important policy consideration addressed in the Panel's report is the importance of protecting the needs of the public and insuring continued access to satellite data."

NCLIS served as secretariat for the U.S. National Committee for the UNESCO General Information Program (PGI) and advised the State Department on matters relating to this program. In light of the U.S. decision to withdraw from UNESCO at the end of 1984, NCLIS and the U.S. National Committee were charged with identifying alternative mechanisms to accomplish the objectives of the PGI. A proposal for alternative mechanisms was officially transmitted to the State Department in July 1984. The NCLIS Executive Director headed the U.S. delegation to the PGI Intergovernmental Meeting in Paris in November.

Improving Library/Information Services. NCLIS expressed deep concern that special populations such as the aged, cultural minorities, the geographically isolated, and the illiterate have access to accurate and timely information to meet their personal needs and that barriers to access to such services be eliminated. During 1984 the Commission focused on the special needs of rural populations, the elderly, and the illiterate. NCLIS and the U.S. Department of Agriculture (USDA) worked together for five years to develop and implement programs and projects that would improve the delivery of library and information services to America's rural population. In 1984 the two agencies copublished the proceedings of a Joint Congressional Hearing on "The Changing Information Needs of Rural America—The Role of Libraries and Information Technologies." The hearing explored rural information needs in the context of public policy, modern communications technologies, education, quality of life, productivity, and other major concerns. At its April meeting the Commission adopted a resolution that a study and planning committee be convened by NCLIS to examine and evaluate the concept of a National Advisory Board on Rural Information Needs (NABRIN).

The steady increase in the U.S. population of persons 65 years and older requires that adequate library and information services be available to meet the special needs of this important group. NCLIS signed a memorandum of understanding with the Administration on Aging; its purpose is, through cooperative work at the federal level, to promote the improvement and better use of library and information services for the aging.

According to the U.S. Department of Education, approximately 27,000,000 American adults are functionally illiterate. In an attempt to alleviate this problem, NCLIS and the U.S. Department of Defense through its Army Human Engineering Laboratory have jointly undertaken an innovative technology transfer project. The purpose of the project is to measure whether a computer-assisted instruction program designed to teach military recruits without basic reading skills can be used with adults and out-of-school teenagers in community volunteer literacy programs based in public libraries. The libraries chosen as initial test sites, one urban and one nonmetropolitan, have existing volunteer literacy programs. The demonstration sites are the Enoch Pratt Free Library, Baltimore, and the Mary Weir Library, Weirton, West Virginia. Evaluation of the pilot project was under way at year's end. The possibility of a third test site in Pittsburgh was being explored.

During 1984 the U.S. Department of Education held a series of small regional seminars to bring together librarians, educators, patrons, and other interested groups to identify the most effective role for libraries in a learning society. The purpose of the seminars was to identify the role of libraries in responding to the National Commission on Excellence in Education's report, *A Nation at Risk*. NCLIS was represented at each seminar.

At its January meeting, NCLIS issued a statement on library and information skills in elementary and secondary education. It urged that (1) decision makers recognize the importance of the ability to find and use information effectively; (2) elementary and secondary schools have school library media services of strong quality; and (3) each student be provided with effective library and information services by elementary and secondary school personnel well qualified in library and information science and able to teach information skills and manage library resources.

Access to Information. A primary goal of the Commission is to promote and support efforts at all levels to provide equal opportunity of access to library and information services for all the people in the United States. During 1984 NCLIS began an investigation into the role of fees in supporting library and information services in public and academic libraries. A brief overview study was in progress in 1984 to determine the extent to which fees are charged, the percentage of libraries charging for any services, and the services for which fees are charged.

Technology, Innovation, and Productivity. A small group of experts on information and productivity and other key decision makers met in July at the Cranfield Conference Center in Bedford, England, to discuss information and productivity and their implications for education. The meeting was the first in a proposed series of bilateral meetings between individuals in the library/information field in the U.S. and the U.K. The meeting was sponsored by The British Library, the Library and Information Services Council (U.K.), and NCLIS.

Nominations. During 1984 President Reagan nominated four new members to the Commission for five-year terms: Margaret Phelan, of Phelan Business Research, Shawnee Mission, Kansas; Wanda Forbes, Advisory Council member, Museum of Education, University of South Carolina, Clover, South Carolina; Patricia Barbour, National Advisory Council on Community Education member, Dearborn Heights, Michigan; and Daniel Casey, former NCLIS Commissioner, Syracuse, New York. The new nominees would replace Commissioners Philip A. Sprague and Francis Keppel, whose terms expired in 1983, and Margaret S. Warden and Helmut A. Alpers, whose terms expired in 1984.

Future Plans. NCLIS is the federal agency responsible for providing policy and planning advice to the executive and legislative branches on library/information matters. At the request of Congress, NCLIS will conduct a brief study to provide an overview of the extent of censorship in American libraries and how U.S. society is responding to it. Congress also requested that an overview of the censorship trends over the past 10 years in public and school libraries be presented.

1984 NCLIS Publications. Publications in 1984 included: *Joint Congressional Hearing on the Changing Information Needs of Rural America: The Role of Libraries and Information Technologies*, with the U.S. Department of Agriculture.

National Commission on Libraries and Information Science/Special Libraries Association Task Force, *The Role of the Special Library in Networks and Cooperatives: Executive Summary* (Special Libraries Association, New York). *Annual Report*.

Panel on the Information Policy Implications of Archiving Satellite Data, *To Preserve the Sense of Earth from Space*.

Single copies are available from NCLIS on request; *The Role of the Special Library* is available from the Special Libraries Association in New York.

DIANE YASSENOFF RAFFERTY

National Endowment for the Humanities

The National Endowment for the Humanities (NEH), an independent federal grant-making agency created by Congress in 1965, supports research, education, and public understanding in the humanities through grants to organizations, institutions, and individuals. According to the legislation that established the Endowment, the term *humanities* includes, but is not limited to, the study of archaeology, ethics, history, the history and criticism of the arts, the theory of the arts, jurisprudence, language (both modern and classical), linguistics, literature, philosophy, comparative religion, and those aspects of the social services that have humanistic content and employ humanistic methods.

The Endowment's grant-making operations are conducted through five major divisions and one office. (1) The Division of General Programs endeavors to fulfill the Endowment's mandate to foster public understanding and appreciation of the humanities. The division includes programs that assist institutions and organizations (including libraries and library organizations through the Humanities Projects in Libraries Program) in developing humanities projects for presentation

National Endowment for the Humanities

Graphics for the "Writers of the Purple Sage" regional project on Southwest culture funded during 1984 by the National Endowment for the Humanities and the Tucson Public Library.

to general audiences. (2) The Division of Research Programs provides support for basic research projects in the humanities, for research resources (especially library collections), for the preparation of research tools, and for the publication of these tools and other scholarship in the humanities. (3) The Division of Education Programs supports projects through which institutions endeavor to renew and strengthen the impact of teaching at all levels. (4) The Division of Fellowships and Seminars provides stipends for scholars and teachers and support for centers of advanced study and independent research libraries. (5) The Division of State Programs makes grants to citizen's committees in each state and several territories for local humanities projects, many of them in libraries. Finally, in addition to support through each of the five divisions, support is also available to libraries through the Office of Challenge Grants, which aims at helping institutions to develop new and increased nongovernmental, long-range sources of support in order to improve the quality of their humanities resources and activities. Grants from the Office are made on a matching basis—one federal dollar for every three private dollars.

1984 Grants. In FY 1984, the National Endowment for the Humanities made 29 grants to libraries for a total of $4,685,338. It made more grants to parent institutions and organizations that directly benefit libraries. In addition, in FY 1984, the Endowment re-created the Humanities Projects in Libraries as a separate program within the Division of General Programs and issued guidelines specifically for the program. It encourages public, academic, or special libraries to plan and present humanities programs. The development of cooperative projects between public, academic, or special libraries, and between libraries, museums, historical societies, and other cultural institutions are also encouraged. The primary objective for projects is to foster public understanding and appreciation of the humanities through the use of library resources.

Several examples of grants illustrative of those awarded by the various divisions of the Endowment include:

The Office of Challenge Grants. (1) An award of $250,000 was made to the Tulsa City/County Library System to establish an endowment fund for humanities collections, programs, and services.

(2) Georgia Southern College received a $100,000 award to establish separate endowment funds for library acquisitions in the humanities.

(3) $71,000 was awarded to the Ventress Memorial Library in Massachusetts to support the renovation of a portion of the library for the Daniel Webster Historical Center.

The Division of Research Programs. (1) The American Antiquarian Society in Worcester, Massachusetts, was awarded $282,373 to support the completion of cataloging and database entry of records of the society's U.S. newspapers (some 14,000 titles from 50 states).

(2) An award of $194,573 was made to the Los Angeles Public Library to support the cataloging and conservation of selected images from an extensive collection of nitrate and glass plate negatives illustrating places, events, and people in the Los Angeles area from the 1880s to the 1930s.

Division of Fellowships. (1) In 1984 funds were provided to support stipends for resident scholars at centers for advanced study. Among those receiving support were the Huntington Library, the Newberry Library, and the American Antiquarian Society.

Division of General Programs. (1) An award of $195,806 was made to the Fauquier County Public Library in Warrenton, Virginia, to support literature discussion groups in more than 40 libraries in the state of Virginia. Reading and discussion programs of six to eight sessions each provide programs about "Literary Reflections of the New South" using works by William Faulkner, Robert Penn Warren, James Agee, Eudora Welty, Carson McCullers, Frederick Douglass, Ellen Glasgow, and Russell Baker.

(2) The Rutland Free Library, Rutland, Vermont, received an award to organize a series of reading and discussion programs in rural sections of Vermont and New York State devoted to important books on American history from 1780

to 1900. Works to be studied include *The Federalist Papers, Uncle Tom's Cabin, The Significance of the Frontier in American History,* and *The Uprooted.*

(3) The Tucson Public Library was awarded $92,000 to continue a project designed to examine the literature and history of southwestern United States. The project, entitled "Writers of the Purple Sage," will examine works by popular writers, their scholarly critics, and historians of the Southwest for the period between 1875 to 1925. Programs will present the critical analysis of southwestern literature, the history, and the imagery that combines to make up the "myth" of the Southwest.

(4) An award of $219,245 was made to Simmons College in Boston to support public programs about the literary, historical, cultural and artistic dimensions of the relatively short reign of the Ch'in Dynasty's first Emperor. Particular emphasis will be given to the excavation at Xien. The programs will be produced for use on videodisk hardware for public programming.

The Public Affairs Office at NEH supplies guidelines, deadlines, and other information about any Division, Program, or Office at the National Endowment. For further information, contact that office at 1100 Pennsylvania Avenue, NW, Washington, DC 20506, or call (202) 786-0446. Guidelines and application deadlines for the individual state humanities councils should be obtained from the appropriate councils.

THOMAS PHELPS

National Library of Canada

In 1979, following an extensive review of its programs and services, a report entitled *The Future of the National Library of Canada* identified four areas of concern which had been endorsed as priorities by the Canadian library community. They were the development of a voluntary, decentralized Canadian library/information network; resource sharing; increased support for Canadian studies; and preservation. Adherence to those priorities has guided the planning and management of National Library services since 1979, and the achievements of 1984 are grouped under the first two headings.

Networks. The successful completion of the Bibliographic and Communications Network Pilot Project in 1983 demonstrated the feasibility of basing the Canadian bibliographic network on the Open Systems Interconnection (OSI) reference model, which allows independent systems to intercommunicate. The National Library has developed and is testing and evaluating protocols or standard specifications to permit file and record transfer in support of the exchange of bibliographic records; to support messaging between users of varied telecommunications services (e.g., electronic mail and Telex) for interlibrary loan; to accommodate book-ordering and attendant accounting functions for the acquisition of library materials; and to develop directories to provide access to multiple databases. The development of the technical specifications and their testing and assessment are done in cooperation with a number of libraries across Canada. Following successful application of the protocols, they will be made available to information providers in the private and public sectors. While such technical network developments in a country of small population and great distances are important, equally significant has been the degree of consensus on network issues and principles among libraries of many types and jurisdictions.

Resource Sharing. The decentralized network has been developed with a view to achieving the most effective sharing of library resources in Canada. Significant progress was made in 1984 in resolving some of the issues related to interlibrary loan and document delivery through the promulgation of "Interlending in Canada: Issues and Recommendations" and "Location and Lending Services." The *Canadian Union Catalogue of Library Materials for the Handicapped* and the *Registry of Canadian Works in Progress* (for special format materials) were mounted on DOBIS, the federal government's bilingual bibliographic database and system which functions as the automated national union catalog for serials and monographs. The DOBIS Search Service, whereby libraries across Canada may search the DOBIS database, was first offered in January 1984 and at year's end had 84 subscribers; this service has made an important contribution to immediate and decentralized access to a database of over 3,334,000 records, including 1,735,641 LCMARC, 194,554 CANMARC, 160,766 CONSER and 844,000 catalog records added online by the 16 federal libraries that share the DOBIS system.

To encourage resource sharing, the National Library's reference policy and guidelines on the way libraries may refer reference queries to the National Library to make the best use of its reference resources were developed and disseminated. The policy defines the reference service as a backup to other Canadian libraries and as a direct service to individuals who have been formally referred by their local library, those who do not have access to a library or whose research requires the use of the collections and expertise of the National Library. The Library held workshops and open houses to publicize the interlending and reference services. In May 1984, the Library invited librarians from different types of libraries across Canada to explore options for developing a referral network among Canadian libraries. One option examined was the model presented by the Library of Congress agreements with some of the State libraries.

Implemented in 1984, the Decentralized Program for Canadian Newspapers, provides a flexible and pragmatic model which establishes federal and provincial responsibilities for collecting, preserving, and accessing Canadian newspapers. The National Library assumed responsibility for the coordination, liaison, and overall planning of the program, and provided support to each province to compile checklists of all newspapers published within the province, to plan for the comprehensive collection of the newspapers in the jurisdiction and to microfilm holdings for the purposes of preservation and interlibrary loan. This program as designed con-

National Library of Canada

The National Library of Canada: Its History and Function

Editor's note: With this edition of the *ALA Yearbook of Library and Information Services,* the National Library of Canada will receive annual coverage. This special article provides an historical insight into the library, the principles upon which it was founded, and the principals responsible for its founding and guidance.

History. In comparison with the Library of Congress, the National Library of Canada is a newcomer. Canada's National Library came into existence on January 1, 1953, 70 years after the question of a national library was first raised in Parliament by Sir John A. Macdonald, the Father of Canadian Confederation. Though aware of the need, he was perhaps less clear about the role that a national library should play and his prototype of "the library of the nation" was the British Museum Library. He made an explicit if not too complimentary distinction between it and the Library of Congress, which he considered, despite its number of volumes, to be "commonly and technically merely a Parliamentary Library."

Ironically, it was Canada's Library of Parliament which MacDonald's 1885 compromise eventually cast into the role of parliamentary and national library, under two heads instead of one. Macdonald's decision may have served to postpone the realization of a true national library for 70 years.

There were, of course, other contributing factors in the delay. A powerful one was the absence of any organized effort on the part of librarians that would pressure and propagandize as Canadian scholars and writers had done so successfully for the establishment of a national archives. In 1872 the archival function was taken away from the Library of Parliament and established in a separate government-supported institution called the Public Archives of Canada—years before its counterpart in the United States was realized.

Until almost midway in the 20th century, librarians in Canada depended on the American Library Association for a professional outlook and on the Library of Congress for support and services. True, the province of Ontario had a provincial organization established in 1901 and at least two outstanding Canadian librarians served as President of the ALA. It was the highly visible and prestigious librarians of Ontario who spearheaded the movement for a national library association and brought into existence in June 1946 the Canadian Library Association. It in turn unanimously adopted as its first crusade the establishment of a National Library for Canada.

This was the period of the successfully implemented bibliographical centers in the United States—in Philadelphia, Denver, the Pacific Northwest, and elsewhere. The function of these centers in providing access to scarce library resources was skillfully exploited in the campaign of political pressure and popular persuasion organized by members of the Canadian Library Association. The government responded with the establishment of the Canadian Bibliographic Centre in 1950, housed in cramped, borrowed quarters in the Public Archives building in Ottawa.

In 1948 William Kaye Lamb, writer, historian, editor, former Provincial Librarian and Archivist of British Columbia and at the time Librarian of the University of British Columbia, was named by Prime Minister Mackenzie King as Dominion Archivist "with the special assignment of preparing the way for the establishment of a National Library in Ottawa." The unexpected decision of Mackenzie King to link the administrative function of the Dominion Archives with that of a future national library, affirming "a natural relationship between the two," decided a dual role for the National Librarian of Canada until the end of his tenure. In May 1952, King's successor, Prime Minister Louis St. Laurent, introduced legislation for the establishment of a National Library. The Act came into effect on January 1, 1953, when W. Kaye Lamb officially assumed his duties as National Librarian of Canada.

National Library: First Phase (1953–1967). The National Library Act made mandatory the compilation of a national union catalog in which the contents of the principal library collections throughout Canada would be listed and of a national bibliography in which books produced in Canada, written or prepared by Canadians, or of special significance to Canada, would be listed and described. These functions were under way in the Canadian Bibliographic Centre established in 1950. The act also directed the National Librarian to "undertake the collection, by purchase or otherwise, of books for the Library." As an aid to the Library's book collecting responsibility, the act provided for the legal deposit in the National Library of two copies of every book published in Canada. (The term *book* was to be understood in its generic sense and provided for the later deposit of other types of material published in Canada and included in the national bibliography, *Canadiana*.)

The limited overview permitted in this article cannot adequately convey the achievements of the first 15 years of the National Library's existence, nor the enormous difficulties under which the small, dedicated, knowledgeable staff worked as they sought to meet the expectations of the public and of their mandate. In the phenomenal growth of the union catalog, there was the almost impossible task of keeping abreast with the daily input of thousands of cards into its manual files, the restrictions of space as the prospect of the new library building continued to be a promise rather than a priority, the inadequacy of staff at a time when libraries everywhere were expanding and library schools in Canada had not yet begun to keep pace with the national need.

It was during these years, nevertheless, that the foundation of the National Library's goals of service was established. A head start was made on the collection building that would include an unparalleled collection of Canadian newspapers resulting from the merging of the comprehensive newspaper collections acquired from the Public Archives and the Library of Parliament; on the beginnings of a prestigious music collection that would later become a division of the National Library; and on the nuclei of several special collections from which would emerge a Rare Books and Manuscripts Division.

Canada's centennial year 1967 brought an appreciable enhancement to the collections as gifts poured in from national and international well-wishers. The most highly valued gift of the Centennial Year came from the government of Canada—the new and imposing National Library and Public Archives building officially opened on June 20, 1967. At the time it looked as if space accommodations would be ample for years to come even with the provision of one floor allocated to house the Public Archives. What was not anticipated was that within 10 years, with the spiraling increase of staff and services, the National Library would once again be redistributing its operational units in and around other Ottawa locations in an attempt to cope with a recurring and vexing space problem.

Phase Two (1968–1983). In 1968 W. Kaye Lamb retired from his joint position as National Librarian and Dominion Archivist. The latter post was separated from the National Library appointment and Guy Sylvestre, writer, scholar, and at the time Associate Parliamentary Librarian, was named Canada's second National Librarian.

The first significant event for the

new administration was the revision of the National Library Act in June 1969, bestowing enlarged powers upon the National Librarian in the planning and coordination of federal library resources and the power to enter into new voluntary agreements with other libraries inside and outside Canada.

In the same year, Sylvestre was called upon to present a brief on behalf of the National Library to the Senate Committee on Science Policy. In it he concentrated on NLC's past achievements, its current problems, and future commitments with recommendations for increasing support for its services, improving library coordination on a national basis, and preparing for cooperative commitments on an international level. This document, considered as a sort of manifesto, served as a guideline for NLC research and development policy in the decade ahead.

In the first year of his appointment, Sylvestre had identified a leadership role for the National Library in the development of a national information network, in planning and developing library systems, and in contributing to the rationalization of research collections. To promote those ends, he established a number of task groups including one to recommend standards for bibliographic records and another to provide specifications for the development of a Canadian MARC. An Office of Library Standards was set up at the National Library and worked closely with the Library of Congress as well as with other international agencies developing modes of bibliographical control.

A third task group was set up in 1972 to study the feasibility of converting the Canadian union catalog to machine-readable form, with its long-term goal the creation of a computerized national bibliographic database that would contain records from many sources. It did not report until 1976. The Task Group became a research-oriented project supported by a variety of studies on the history and development of interlibrary cooperation, the use and availability of union lists and catalogs, and the patterns of interlibrary lending. One of the studies found that the National Library of Canada was the second largest net lender of library materials in Canada—the Canada Institute for Scientific and Technical Information being the largest—with almost 80 percent of the titles requested coming from NLC's own collections.

In 1977 the Canadian Library Association endorsed a recommendation emanating from the Task Group study that the concept of a national union catalog, as set out in the National Library Act, be replaced by that of a "national bibliographic network"—a decentralized network of existing bibliographic centers and location tools. Since then, the actual strategy for achieving such a network has been sought after through renewed studies and experimental projects. The realities involved in its attainment constituted the main thrust of an epoch-making document—*The Future of the National Library of Canada*—submitted by the National Librarian in 1979, as the final report of an intensive review of the National Library's roles, services, and objectives carried out over a period of three years to mark the 25th anniversary of the Library.

Although the concentration of effort on the part of NLC's Research and Planning Branch in this second phase of the National Library's development pertained to its bibliographic functions, annual reports of the National Librarian provide convincing evidence of the many-faceted programs that were in progress in public services and elsewhere.

In 1974–75 the name of the Reference Branch was changed to Public Services Branch to reflect the increasing diversity of its operations. Online current awareness and retrospective search services became part of the reference functions; a multicultural/multilingual biblioservice, unique among national libraries, made available to provincial and regional library centers cataloged books on a long-term loan basis in a variety of languages common to the ethnic populations across Canada.

Library service to the visually and physically handicapped was initiated and a full-time consultant on children's literature appointed. During the same period, the Music Division, Rare Books Division, and Library Documentation Center were inaugurated, each with its own chief of staff, while Collections Development was given Branch status incorporating the former Office of Library Resources and initiating a series of significant national resources surveys. The National Library of Canada in 1984 ranked fourth in Canada in holdings—approximately 5,400,000 books and other documents—after the Universities of Toronto, British Columbia, and Alberta. It ranked second in staff with a complement of 545. NLC started in 1953 with a staff of 14.

On an advisory level, it is assisted by a National Library Advisory Board of 16 members and three working committees: the Bibliographic and Communications Network Committee; the Resources Network Committee; and the Committee on Bibliographic and Information Services for the Social Sciences and Humanities, appointed to advance the implementation of the National Library's *Five-Year Plan* in which numerous other task groups and minor committees are also involved.

Although the National Library of Canada does not yet offer the range and depth of services that give the Library of Congress and the British Library their prestige in the national and international library community, NLC takes seriously and has already demonstrated its leadership in such areas as national information and lending networks, library standards, and, more recently, in book conservation and preservation.

In November 1983 Guy Sylvestre retired as National Librarian and was succeeded by Marianne Scott, former Director of Libraries at McGill University, Montreal, marking an end of the second phase of NLC's comparatively short history.

F. DOLORES DONNELLY

---

tributes to the four identified priorities: availability of bibliographic records, promotion of resource sharing, support of Canadian studies, and preservation of the national written heritage.

Outreach. Marianne Scott, former Director of Libraries, McGill University, assumed her duties as third National Librarian, in April 1984. She spent her first nine months becoming acquainted with the staff and programs of the library and in an effort to learn firsthand of the major concerns of the Canadian library community, Scott embarked on a program of visits to every part of Canada and attended the meetings of many library associations.

In addition to exhibits and musical events which make known Canada's cultural heritage, the National Library during 1984 hosted a series of readings by eminent Canadian writers: Gilles

Henault, Michael Ondaatje, Mavis Gallant, Roger Lemelin and Robertson Davies. Exhibits of each author's works, often complemented by examples of manuscripts when the author's papers are held by the Library, were featured at the readings.

GWYNNETH EVANS

National Library of Medicine

New Director. Donald A. B. Lindberg, M.D., was appointed Director of the National Library of Medicine in May 1984. He succeeded Martin M. Cummings, M.D., who retired in 1983 after two decades as director. Lindberg, a prominent pathologist and information scientist, was Director of the Information Science Group and Professor of Pathology at the University of Missouri School of Medicine in Columbia.

Pricing Policy. NLM's Board of Regents took the unprecedented step of sponsoring an open meeting on March 26 at which representatives of various interest groups were invited to comment on the issue of differential pricing for the Library's computerized MEDLARS bibliographic services. The Board was responding to a suggestion in a recent study by the Department of Health and Human Services. The study had approved the present method for establishing and reviewing pricing policies and levels, and it found that the current method of basing charges on the actual cost of providing access is reasonable. The study also concluded that the present policy of differential pricing by type of database and time of day is reasonable, but that the possibility should be explored of expanding that policy to include charging different prices to different types of users (commercial and noncommercial, for example).

The Board of Regents, in May, approved a report that concurred with the findings of the Department's study. While the Board rejected the notion of differential pricing by type of domestic MEDLARS user, it recommended a modest increase in the cost of foreign access (based on the premise that since foreign users do not support the generation of MEDLARS databases through taxes, it is reasonable to impose a higher rate on them). In its report, the Board expressed concern that the American public have rapid and easy access to biomedical information, regardless of the source. In keeping with that philosophy, the NLM was encouraged to work cooperatively with database producers in the private sector to create linkages between databases, reduce production costs, and to otherwise facilitate access to all relevant health information.

Databases. MEDLARS continues to grow—both in number of using institutions and in use made of the databases. By the end of 1984 more than 2,500 U.S. institutions were on the Library's online network. More than 2,800,000 searches were done during 1984 on all MEDLARS databases, about 70 percent of them on MEDLINE and its backfiles. It is apparent from the spiraling usage statistics that these databases, which in the aggregate contain some 8,500,000 references to journal articles, monograph and serial records, and chemical/toxicological data entries, are immensely useful to the health science community.

To improve the currency and accuracy of NLM's databases, an online indexing system was installed in 1984. The system tracks each journal as it moves from step to step in the workflow: check-in, input typing of descriptive information, subject indexing, correction and validation, and management statistics are all supported by the new online indexing system. The system will be an important part of MEDLARS III, the enhanced bibliographic system being developed for the Library under contract. MEDLARS III will be implemented in three phases, the first of which is scheduled for completion in 1985.

Developing Technologies. The Library's research and development component, the Lister Hill National Center for Biomedical Communications, continued to develop prototype information systems utilizing videodisk technology. One, the Electronic Document Storage and Retrieval System, is intended to assist in the Library's archival efforts to capture on disk those parts of the NLM collection that are deteriorating because of the poor quality of paper and because of age. Several other prototype videodisk-based systems for health science education are being developed by NLM staff. One of these, the TIME (Technological Innovations in Medical Education) Project, uses an approach that incorporates microcomputer, videodisk, and voice recognition technologies.

The application of computer and communications technologies to information processing in the health sciences is a field that has come to be known as "medical informatics." The Library has supported this field of research for more than a decade through a variety of grant-supported computers-in-medicine training initiatives. Much of the research training fostered by NLM has focused on developing computerized systems with which human users may consult interactively, much in the way that physicians now consult with their colleagues.

IAIMS. One such area of high visibility in 1984 was the emphasis on developing what are called Integrated Academic Information Management Systems (IAIMS). A study sponsored by the Library and conducted by the Association of American Medical Colleges pointed out the need for academic health sciences centers and hospitals to find new and better ways to cope with the myriad information sources and systems available in such institutions. A typical scenario envisions the health professional, with a small desk top terminal, having rapid and easy access to a variety of computerized files—calling up patient records, ordering laboratory tests and reviewing their results, examining the professional literature, consulting clinical decision-making systems, monitoring the progress of students, and communicating with colleagues. NLM is supporting with contracts the development of several prototype integrated systems that will serve these purposes.

Information about the Library's document delivery, bibliographic, and technical services is included in the article Networking in this *Yearbook*.

KENT A. SMITH

National Technical Information Service

With the addition of 75,000 new research reports in 1984, the National Technical Information Service information collection approached 2,000,000 titles, several hundred thousand of which contain foreign technology or foreign marketing information. All are permanently available for sale, either directly from 80,000 titles in shelf stock or from microform master copies of documents that are less in demand. During 1984 NTIS supplied its customers with more than 6,000,000 documents and microforms, shipping about 24,000 information items daily. Total revenues exceeded $21,000,000.

Among notable developments during 1984 was NTIS's new capability to provide more than 1,000 different data files on floppy diskettes, compatible with IBM Personal Computers. NTIS also signed a direct protocol between it and the State Scientific and Technical Commission (SSTC) of the People's Republic of China that provides for work-study and lecture exchanges and facilitates technical information exchange.

NTIS's Center for the Utilization of Federal Technology (CUFT) produced the following publications on opportunities for American businesses: *1984 Directory of Federal Technology Resources*—a detailed guide to more than 800 federal government sources of specialized R&D expertise and facilities; *Catalog of Government Patents*—describes nearly 1,000 government inventions available for licensing, often on an exclusive basis (entrepreneurs have committed over $140,000,000 to market inventions licensed through this program); and *Federal Technology Catalog*—describes some 1,000 practical technology applications processes and equipment.

1985 Objectives. During 1985 NTIS will continue its efforts to stimulate innovation and productivity through the U.S. economy by channeling U.S. and foreign government-sponsored research, development, and other specialized information to industry, small U.S. businesses, educational institutions, government at all levels, and the general public. Fiscal 1985 objectives include:

(1) Development of new and improvement of current information products for U.S. business and industrial clients.

(2) Continuation of the development of a program to improve access and to expedite transfer of technology from government laboratories to private sector and state and local governments.

(3) Enter into agreements with additional foreign industrial, technical, and government information organizations to acquire, process, and issue foreign technical information.

(4) Increase the accessibility of machine-processable data produced by or for the federal government.

Mission. The National Technical Information Service (NTIS) is a key participant in the development of advanced information products and services for the achievement of U.S. productivity and industrial innovation goals in the 1980s.

NTIS is the central source for the public sale of U.S. government-sponsored research, development and engineering reports and for sales of foreign technical reports and other analyses prepared by national and local government agencies and their contractors or grantees. And it is the central source for federally generated machine processible data files and software and for the licensing of U.S. government-owned patents.

NTIS plays a key role in the international exchange of technical information. It has become the leading federal agency responsible for participation in bilateral, regional, and worldwide activities involving technology transfer and information. More than 300,000 research reports based on foreign technology are in the NTIS collection.

NTIS sells its technical information products and services under the provisions of Title 15 of the U.S. Code. The law established a clearinghouse for scientific, technical and engineering information within the Department of Commerce and directed that it be self-supporting.

TED RYERSON

Networks

Continued technological advances, the wide use of microcomputers by libraries of all types and sizes, advances in the development of telecommunications protocols and distributed processing—all contributed to the continued growth and expansion of networks during 1984.

The year saw growing interest and development of integrated library systems (ILS) by a variety of vendors. ILS can be defined as a computer-based set of library functions using a common or shared database, to achieve institutional goals. To be successful it must offer a high degree of reliability and efficiency supporting principal bibliographic functions such as public access catalog, cataloging, catalog maintenance, authority control, acquisitions, serials check-in, and circulation control. No ILS currently available on the market today can meet all of those requirements. The gap between promise and reality is considerable—the effect of ILS on networking is still speculative. Meanwhile national, regional, and statewide networking continues to grow and improve. The Library of Congress (LC) and the Council on Library Resources (CLR) are still providing leadership, resources, funds and opportunities for discussion, debate, and resolution of many networking problems.

CLR. The Council on Library Resources Bibliographic Service Development Program seeks to develop and employ a nationally acceptable strategy for acquiring and sharing bibliographic control over resources available to users of the nation's libraries. Since 1979 many areas such as linking computer systems, computer-assisted interlibrary loan services, and online catalogs were supported by evaluation studies, working with producers of bibliographic records and encouraging cooperative activities.

A change in focus occurred in 1984—the program has become a means for encouraging communications among many who share similar interests. However, one of its most important efforts—to assure the development and implementation of linkages between shared cataloging services—was continued. Testing and imple-

Networks

mentation of telecommunication links between the computers of LC, the Research Libraries Group, and the Washington Library Network by the exchange of authorities records was planned in 1985.

Another BSDP report, of long-range importance to national resource sharing, recommends that retrospective conversion of bibliographic records activities be coordinated on a national basis and involve the creation of a national database with research libraries taking the lead and LC establishing priorities for converting special subject collections. Consensus of standards for conversion and a long-range fundraising plan involving universities, the federal government, and foundations must be developed as a first priority.

LC. The Library of Congress Network Advisory Committee consisting of the directors of state, regional, and national network organizations met in April and November to discuss the issues of electronic information delivery systems and the information economy in the U.S. and its effect on libraries and library networks. Proceedings of these meetings are available from LC.

LC's processing services staff continued its work on the Linked Systems Project. Major progress was made as LC completed its telecommunications software, called the Standard Network Interconnection and its Record Transfer software. The SNI will enable the different computer systems of the participating institutions to communicate. The Records Transfer software will support the online distribution of authority records from LC and the online contribution of authority records to LC's authority file.

In 1984 the MARC books database passed the 2,000,000 mark while the authorities file grew to over 1,250,000.

FLICC. The major achievement of the Federal Library Committee during FY 1984 was the reorganization of the Committee, effective October 3. The name changed to the Federal Library and Information Center Committee (FLICC) and the expanded membership includes: Administrative Offices of the U.S. Courts, Defense Technical Information Center, Government Printing Office, National Technical Information Center, and Office of Scientific and Technical Information (DOE). The Library of Congress, the National Agricultural Library, and the National Library of Medicine remain as members, as do each of the executive departments and the National Archives and Records Service, National Aeronautics and Space Administration, National Science Foundation, Smithsonian Institution, Supreme Court of the United States, U.S. Information Agency, and the Veterans Administration.

Rotating members were increased from six to ten, and selections are made from the three branches of government, agencies, boards, committees, and commissions. In addition to OMB, observers' status include: General Accounting Office, General Services Administration, Joint Committee on Printing, and National Commission on Libraries and Information Science.

The Committee makes recommendations on federal library and information policies, programs, and procedures to federal agencies and to others concerned with libraries and information centers.

The Committee sponsored a major forum on "Federal Information Policies; Emerging Issues on Managing Information Resources" on February 15 at the Library of Congress.

A number of FLC seminars on the application of OMB Circular A-76, contracting for commercial services, were held at the Library of Congress: Three seminars on the management effectiveness study, the first phase in implementing A-76, and two seminars on performance-oriented work statements. Preparation for a seminar on cost comparison study was under way.

The Federal Library and Information Network (FEDLINK) is a network organization of cooperating libraries and information centers that derives its authority from FLICC. The FEDLINK program offers any federal agency through its library or information center the opportunity to enhance the information resources available to meet the requirements of its personnel. Through FLICC/FEDLINK federal agencies have cost effective access to a number of automated services for online research database searching, as well as online cataloging, interlibrary loan, acquisitions, and serials control.

During FY 1984, FEDLINK participation grew nationwide to approximately 600 agency libraries, information centers and offices, cooperating in the use of 30 contractual services that resulted in 1,246 interagency agreements for approximately $20,000,000 of service.

Access to OCLC's database of over 12,000,000 records and 150,000,000 holding symbols input by 3,600 members is available to FEDLINK members via the OCLC telecommunications network and also through Tymnet and Telenet via dial access. The federal records added to the OCLC database consist of over 5,000,000 logical records, which are growing at a rate of 65,000 records a month.

NAL. The National Agricultural Library was restructured in 1984 to reflect its expanded national and international responsibilities. A primary objective was to coordinate and strengthen a national network of agricultural libraries with emphasis on development and adoption of standardized formats and procedures and on the establishment of cooperative working arrangements with other libraries and concerned private and public institutions.

In the context of its redefined mission, the NAL initiated new efforts to strengthen its networking activities consistent with the 1982 recommendations of the interagency panel on the NAL. Progress has been made in such areas as cooperative cataloging and indexing, coordination and standards, OCLC-interlibrary loans, and microfilming. Specific steps taken include: (1) The NAL proposed establishing a network of libraries to participate in a cooperative cataloging project of agriculture monographs. (2) Cooperative arrangements were established by the National Agricultural Library for the indexing of agricultural journals and state publications by two institutions: The University of Georgia and the Arid Lands Information Center at the University of Arizona. (3) The Library has been an active member of the CONSER project assuming national responsibility for the coordination and quality control of information on current agricultural journals and periodicals input into the CONSER file. The NAL has been a member of the NACO project at the Library of Congress, creating and maintaining name authority records for agricultural serials publications. (4) In cooperation with NAL, the University of Georgia will coordinate the microfilming of 416,051 pages of state experiment station and extension service publications on land-grant university campuses in 12 southeastern states.

NLM. During 1984 the seven Regional Medical Libraries focused on outreach to health professionals, document delivery, resource sharing, online services, and training and consultation—all aimed at improving access to biomedical information for the health professional. Each RML has identified underserved areas within its regional boundaries and is implementing programs to meet the information needs of the health professional in those targeted areas.

The RML contracts continued to emphasize document delivery and resource sharing. Approximately 2,000,000 journal articles, book and audiovisual loans are provided annually to health professionals through the network. NLM, as backup, satisfies more than 140,000 requests annually. Six RMLs earmarked funds for strengthening regional collection resources to improve resource sharing.

Significant progress was made in providing automated support to document delivery activities. SERHOLD currently contains over 600,000 automated holdings statements for 1,233 biomedical libraries. The Regional Medical Libraries coordinate the gathering of holdings data for the database and provide it to NLM in machine-readable form.

SERHOLD was built primarily to support automated routing of requests for journal articles in DOCLINE, NLM's automated document request and referral system. During 1984, progress was made in developing an improved DOCLINE system suitable for use by all RML network libraries during the transition to MEDLARS III. As components of the system were completed and tested, they were made available for testing and use by the RMLs, which constitute the current DOCLINE user group.

Significant progress was made toward the goal of achieving compatibility in descriptive cataloging produced by the three national libraries. This will reduce the effort required by health sciences libraries to merge NLM records with records produced by other cataloging sources. Since 1972, NLM has been cooperating with the Library of Congress (LC) to provide MeSH headings and NLM classification data for inclusion in the Cataloging in Publication copy for biomedical books. Until very recently, however, NLM and LC have each produced descriptive cataloging independently for these items. In March 1984, NLM and LC began a pilot project in which NLM provided LC with descriptive cataloging for a portion of the biomedical books receiving CIP treatment. Due to the success of this test, NLM provided LC with descriptive cataloging, MeSH headings, and NLM class numbers for all biomedical CIPs beginning in October 1984. LC will use NLM descriptive records and add LC subject headings and classification numbers for publication in the CIP records.

In conjunction with the CIP pilot project, NLM also expanded its contributions to the national Name Authority Cooperation (NACO) file, which is maintained at LC. NLM has been contributing all name headings associated with its serial cataloging and some pre-1871 books since July 1981. After the initiation of the CIP pilot, most names associated with CIP cataloging also were checked against the NACO file and contributed if necessary. Beginning with calendar year 1985, all names associated with full cataloging records were to be reconciled with the NACO file and added to that file as appropriate. NLM's role as a participant in the CONSER (Consolidation of Serials) project was expanded to include responsibility for authentication of all name headings and final editing of all records which it contributes. LC previously performed final review for other CONSER participants. To reduce the duplicate keying now required by these cooperative efforts, NLM is investigating how to implement the Linked System Protocol (being tested by LC, the Research Libraries Information Network, and the Washington Library Network) in the MEDLARS III system.

In 1984 NLM introduced an important new service for domestic users—the availability of subsets of the MEDLINE database. Two options were available: "individualized subsets," specified by the subset requester and provided on a onetime basis with no updates. Subsets are currently distributed on magnetic tape only; some subsets will be available on diskette in the future.

Network libraries were to begin to use DOCLINE in early 1985; first, the Resource Libraries will be brought on to the system region by region; in the second phase all network libraries will become participants, a region at a time. The phase-in period is expected to last 12 to 18 months.

An early test of the ability to link DOCLINE to other automated interlibrary loan systems was completed successfully in January 1984, when procedures were established for automatic transfer of unfilled requests from OCTANET to NLM's system.

In order to provide an improved interim document request capability while DOCLINE availability is gradually extended throughout the network, NLM is accepting interlibrary loan requests via electronic mail.

RLG/RLIN. The Research Libraries Group has four principal programs—shared resources, collection management and development, preservation, and technical systems and bibliographic control. By the end of 1984, RLG had 29 owners and 25 associate and special members. The Research Libraries Information Network, the automated information system supporting RLG's programs, has a database in excess of 12,000,000 records. Services provided include searching, acquisitions, cataloging, and interlibrary loan.

The first machine-readable record in the RLIN database for a manuscript collection (Yale University) was entered in 1984. Records now in the Archival and Manuscript Control are part of the same database that contains records in six MARC formats: books, films, maps, music, and serials. Online access to information on manuscripts and archives represents an important resource for scholars.

By the end of 1984 RLIN had completed its work of adding to the central database the GPO *Monthly Catalog*, cataloging from April 1976 to December 1984.

OCLC. 1984 was another year of problems and issues as well as one of accomplishments and expansion of services. In June the Ohio Supreme Court reaffirmed a Board of Tax appeal decision denying tax-exempt status for real property owned by OCLC in Dublin. OCLC made its first installment payment on back taxes of over $1,000,000, but continues to pursue legislative relief from taxes based on its broad public purpose of furthering ease of access to information. Approximately $375,000 in annual taxes will be assessed.

Contract negotiations between OCLC and the regional networks continue. Unresolved issues include contract terms and termination record use, and roles and responsibilities of the various parties. A core contract was still the goal of the regional networks. OCLC and the networks have continued to work together successfully, and service by OCLC to its members has continued unaffected and at a high level despite the protracted negotiations.

The applicability of copyright is still a matter of concern to members of OCLC. Rowland Brown, President of OCLC, stated that copyright is not intended as a method of enforcement relating to use of data by those institutions with whom OCLC has contracts. For those institutions OCLC will forgo rights under the copyright of the database. Approximately 300 libraries signed contracts that include standard use-of-record provisions. OCLC will rely on contracts rather than copyright where members are concerned.

OCLC announced participation in the Linked Systems Project and was in the process of acquiring hardware for the computer link in the name-authorities phase of LSP. This will make possible computer-to-computer links between LC, RLIN, WLN, and OCLC.

After successful testing for four months, the OCLC M300 workstation was made available for member libraries. The M300, a IBM personal computer to which OCLC has added special hardware and software, serves libraries as an online terminal for access to the OCLC central computer system and performs a wide range of stand alone functions as a multipurpose microcomputer.

WLN. As of October, the Washington Library Network had 158 libraries using its services and products. The database size was 3,138,253 titles.

WLN's accomplishments for the year include the acquisition and initial installation of the participant's new WLN PC terminals, the addition of the MARC music format, the loading of Carrollton Press bibliographic records via tape, implementation of the IMAIL interim ILL subsystem, and completion of major preliminary work for design of a full ILL subsystem. WLN continued participation with LC and RLIN on the Linked Systems Project.

CRL. The Center for Research Libraries Board of Directors appointed a Consultation Panel on Center Operations. The panel reviewed internal operations of the Center, focusing on staff and system utilization, and procedures in acquisitions, cataloging, circulation, and their related functions. Based on the panel's report, changes in the Center's internal organizational structure were implemented.

Regional Library Organizations. The AMIGOS Shared Resources System (SHARES) database of 1,300,000 bibliographic records became operational online, and was utilized by the AMIGOS Bibliographic Resource Center for retrospective conversions. AMIGOS completed a study of the potential of electronic mail for communication by its member libraries, using ALANET. A decision was expected in early 1985. Another service introduced in 1984 was the AMIGOS Collection Analysis Service. This process analyzes library bibliographic tapes to determine holdings in predefined subject areas. AMIGOS and SOLINET met to explore possible cooperative programs and strategies and to discuss the issues surrounding the OCLC Network contract negotiation and the copyright claim by OCLC.

BCR. In October 1984 David Brunnell, formerly Assistant Network Coordinator for FLICC/FEDLINE, was appointed Executive Director of the Bibliographic Center for Research. JoAn Segal, former Executive Director, resigned as of the end of August to accept a position as Executive Director of ACRL.

In the spring, of 1984, BCR opened a branch office in Ames, Iowa. The office operates out of Iowa State University and serves to improve communications, visit libraries in the area, conduct workshops, and generally be in more frequent contact with BCR members.

BCR's Reference Systems and Services (RS&S) added two new online services, Pergamon's INFOLONE and SDC Orbit. RS&S continues to expand its services to areas outside of nearby states. Services were initiated to libraries in California, Indiana, Maryland, Massachusetts, Michigan, New Hampshire, Ohio, Oregon, Pennsylvania, and Washington, D.C.

CAPCON. The CAPCON Library Network continued to flourish, adding five new members, inaugurating a new document delivery service and union list of serials service. CAPCON merged and consolidated its database, converted its computer system to IBM compatibility, and implemented a micro services and training program.

SOLINET. The Southeastern Library Network entered into a cooperative project with 13 of the ARL libraries in the Southeast to develop an online system that can support serials holdings records in the new MARC format for holdings and locations. Starting in October, the participants entered a new phase involving the use of the SOLINET system to record and maintain information in the serials database, and the establishment of coordinated collection development strategies. SOLINET's retrospective conversion service converted the 1,000,000th record. ReCon projects for 11 libraries were completed and 37 others were in progress.

The SOLINET and AMIGOS boards met in October to explore cooperative programs and strategies. The issues surrounding the OCLC/Networks contract negotiations and the copyright claim by OCLC resulted in a resolution affirming (1) their "commitment to proceed expeditiously with network group negotiations with OCLC, (2) that appropriate uses of the database be governed by a cooperatively developed and approved code of responsible use, and (3) their continued opposition to any exclusive claim by OCLC of ownership of the database."

State Networking Activity. Alabama. The network of Alabama Academic Libraries Advisory Council convened as a permanent Advisory Council in September 1984. Approval of a $500,000 budget, a search committee for a network director, a schedule of allocations for retrospective conversion funds to member institutions, and an agreement to cosponsor with the Alabama Public Library Service (State Library Agency) a statewide automation study were the initial actions of permanent Advisory Council. The State Department of Education and the Department of Post-Secondary Education (junior colleges) also agreed to be cosponsors of the automation center. The study will examine systems installed in Alabama and examine possibilities of linking the systems, and at will prepare a detailed plan to expand the application of automation to libraries of all types in a state network.

California. The California State Library selected OCLC as the database system vendor to house, mantain, and provide access for the CLSA Database for California public libraries, both OCLC participants and non-OCLC participants. Peat, Marwick and Mitchell conducted a study of the California Union List of Periodicals—its database and current operation. The State Library is sponsoring a project to test the possibilities of using the programming of a microcomputer communications software package to provide an intelligent front end to library staff to access a variety of circulation systems for ILL purposes without knowing the particular search protocols of the different systems.

Colorado. The final report of the Colorado State Library's Library Network Development calls for the formation of the Colorado Library Network—a statewide communications network and the formation of a Network Implementation Council to investigate the feasibility and cost of a statewide communications system for the network and to define the duties and structure of a network office under the State Library, to monitor, administer, and operate the network.

Connecticut. The Connecticut State Library formed an Automation/Resource Sharing Task Force that was to present a proposal for a "full-service" statewide library and information network. An LSCA grant was approved to establish dial access between LEAP (five public libraries sharing a CLSI system in Connecticut) and NOBLE (a cluster of Massachusetts libraries also using a CLSI system). The purpose of the project is to provide the interconnection for searching each system's circulation control databases by author, title, and subject for ILL purposes.

Delaware. Of Delaware's 150 libraries 125 were members by 1984 of the three networks established in 1982 to serve Delaware's three counties. The networks provide ILL statewide, manage a delivery system, and provide an effective means of communication. The 1984 edition of the Delaware Union COM catalog included 500,000 records representing 30 libraries.

Florida. Networking in Florida continued to be guided by the principles that (1) state-funded activities should be compatible on a statewide basis; (2) the principal database will continue to be SOLINET/OCLC; and (3) where possible, efforts will be directed toward retrospective conversions to include additional holdings in the major database.

The State Legislature took a strong interest in networking for the State University System providing $3,154,454 in the 1984–85 budget for the extension of automated networks for the SUS.

This action in effect took the position of extending the state's interest in networking to all types of libraries, although the funds provided were specifically for the State University System.

Projects were funded for the Southeast Florida Library Information Network (SEFLIN) and the Tampa Bay Library Consortium (TBLC). The activities projected for the first year range from initial planning and retrospective conversion in TBLC to mutual access to other databases and telefacsimile service in SEFLIN.

Illinois. ILLINET, the Illinois Library and Information Network, set up its network for ILL, photocopy requests, and reference questions on ALANET—the American Library Association's electronic mail and information service. Illinois is one of the first states using ALANET for its entire statewide ILL and reference system. Fiscal 1984 figures for ILLINET show 597,761 author-title requests—88 percent of the requests were filled. There were 63,028 information inquiries and 97.4 percent were satisfied. Seven of Illinois' library systems and the State Library make up the FAX system—an electronic facsimile transmission of documents service.

Funding for the 18 regional library systems in Illinois reached $15,000,000—$1.145 per capita. The reference and research centers appropriation was $918,750, although public library-based the regional systems include affiliate members representing academic, school, and special libraries. Four systems were in the process of converting from a public library system to a multitype library system—two of the four had full status and two provisional status.

Effective in mid-year the Illinois State Library's continuing education database—Online Network of Continuing Education (ONCE)—became operational.

Indiana. The Indiana State Library continued development of three shared microcomputer circulation "clusters" of three or more public libraries each. In addition installation of microcomputer-based telecommunications systems in four area Library Services Authorities continued. Software was being developed to manage electronic mail, continuing education opportunities, and an integrated ILL record-keeping system.

INCOLSA, the Indiana Cooperative Library Services Authority, completed planning work for two shared minicomputer cluster sites that will include 101 terminals.

Kansas. The Kansas State Library prepared a model Interlibrary Resource Sharing Network proposal for consideration of the State Legisla-

Networks

ture in 1985. It recommends funding for a telecommunications network demonstration project. In 1984 the Kansas Library Network worked on the implementation of an ILL development plan, retroactive conversion of unique holdings in the statewide Kansas Union Catalog, and extension of reciprocal borrowing privileges through a statewide Kansas Library card.

Maine. The Maine State Library contracted in 1984 for a study on the potential for statewide library automation. The final study was due in early 1985 and will have major impact on networking in Maine.

Maryland. The Maryland Division of Library Development and Services made continued progress in the development of the State Network. The eighth edition of MICROCAT, the statewide union catalog, was produced containing approximately 1,500,000 unique titles and 2,500,000 holders from 60 public, academic, school, and special libraries. The fourth edition of the Maryland Union List of Periodicals was also produced containing approximately 27,000 titles and approximately 75,000 holders from 60 libraries.

Negotiations were completed with Autographics to implement "MILINET: Phase One" based upon major system upgrades to the AGILE system. Groundwork was laid for 13 public, regional, and academic libraries to be tied together via leased lines to the AGILE online interlibrary loan system via Sperry PCs. Selection of sites was based upon referral volume and effective fill rates for the major network libraries in Maryland.

Mississippi. The Mississippi Library Commission reported that plans were under way to install a micro-based ILL system in 28 Mississippi public libraries. The system will allow participating libraries to initiate and respond to author/title, subject, periodical, and audiovisual ILL requests on a scheduled polling basis.

Nebraska. Nebraska funded an LSCA title III study on library automation and resource sharing. The study recommendations and implementation plan were to be available in 1985.

Nevada. Nevada introduced a statewide library card. Nearly all of Nevada's public and academic libraries and the State Library agency are tied into one of four CLSI circulation system databases. A telecommunications network designed to communicate with each of the four CLSI computers as well as other computers or networks in the state regardless of protocol differences was operative in the Clark County and Carson City area and will be available to the rest of the state by mid-1985.

New Jersey. A comprehensive law authorizing the New Jersey State Library to establish and fund a statewide multitype library network was signed by the Governor January 17. The law carried an initial appropriation of $125,000; an additional appropriation of $685,000 for FY 1985 was passed in June. Six regional library cooperatives composed of all types of libraries will be organized over a five-year period. Membership is voluntary, open to all types of libraries. The funding formula will include three elements—a uniform factor, population served, and geographic area.

New Mexico. Two regional consortia feasibility studies were funded under LSCA Title III by the New Mexico State Library. The first is in the northern New Mexico area. Twenty-nine libraries representing public, academic, and special participated in the study proposal. Issues of legal establishment, governance, funding, and staffing will be studied. The second study involves school, public, and university libraries and will concentrate on the development of an integrated automation database that would include the consideration of circulation, online catalog, periodicals, and ILL.

New York. Increased support for public library systems from $38,500,000 to $45,200,000, plus $1,300,000 in annual grants to assist in machine-readable database development, kept New York State as first in the nation in funds for state-aid programs. There were 1,600,000 bibliographic and 30,000,000 holdings for monographic records in machine-readable form, an additional 83,000,000 bibliographic and 158,000,000 holding records were yet to be converted. The bibliographic records are included in the OCLC, RLIN and New York Public Library MILCS database and the State Library online catalog.

Pennsylvania. *Access Pennsylvania, an Agenda for Knowledge and Information Through Libraries,* containing the 19 recommendations made by a Library Planning Council of 95 leading citizens, was endorsed by the Governor, who promptly added $3,000,000 in his state budget request to start implementation. Plans call for developing a statewide library card, the expanded use of technology for more effectively sharing resources, and the improvement of state assistance for support of libraries in low-income communities. Three requests for applications were issued to begin implementation of major components of the recommendations: a plan for ILL compensation for all types of libraries, including a formula; a compensation plan for libraries for direct borrowing by users other than the library's regular clientele; and a plan for converting catalogs of high school libraries to machine-readable form.

Twenty-nine Pennsylvania public libraries were participating in the use of facsimile as a means of resource sharing. ILL transactions using facsimile are expected to take few hours delivery time as compared to mail or truck delivery. Facsimile costs are minimal but a photocopy of the material to be sent, capable of being fed into the machine, must first be made.

South Carolina. Plans call for the development of a South Carolina Library Network to be developed in three phases over a period of three years. The first phase calls for the development of a host system—the South Carolina State Library online catalog and a circulation/ILL module. The second plan is the communications access with state agencies, institutions and academic libraries. It will include catalog access, electronic mail, ILL, and a state document depository system. The third phase will include linking local systems, developing a statewide union list of serials, federal documents online, and communications access for school libraries.

South Dakota. South Dakota was developing an integrated online automated system with a projection of phase one in the fall of 1985. The State Library withdrew, after 14 years, its mem-

projection of phase one in the fall of 1985. The State Library withdrew, after 14 years, its membership from BCR as well as from the Minnesota–North Dakota–South Dakota Online Catalog Inc., a non-profit corporation whose goal was resource sharing between the three states.

Texas. The Texas State Library Communications Network was projected to handle 195,000 unique requests in 1985 with a predicted fill rate of 75 percent. Cost per fill increased from $10.42 in 1984 to $10.75 for 1985 for public libraries. Academic libraries will be reimbursed $14 for each net loan. The Texas State Library funded a new project designed to build a union list of serials. Three union lists, using OCLC capability, will serve as the basis for the statewide list.

Utah. The Utah Network of Cooperating Libraries was formally organized in June 1984. The multitype library organization will facilitate and support bibliographic access and resource-sharing among Utah libraries. UNCL has a netlender reimbursement program which reimburses net lenders at $16 per hour net loan.

Virgin Islands. The Virgin Islands established, by law, VILNET. The immediate focus was the adoption of an interlibrary loan code. In addition the feasibility of accessing the computerized database of the Division of Libraries was under consideration. Within three to five years, online access to a common database of all VILNET members is expected.

Virginia. The Virginia General Assembly approved, in 1983, legislation authorizing a multitype statewide library network, but in 1984 it failed to appropriate any funds. Lack of unanimity by Virginia libraries on a plan of action resulted in the issuance, late in 1984, of an RFP for a consultant.

West Virginia. The West Virginia union catalog database was expected to be fully online by early 1985. Eight regional computer networks linking all public libraries is the goal.

Wisconsin. The Wisconsin State Superintendent's Task Force on Library Legislation, in its final report in July, recommended the development of multitype library systems. As a first step, a request for $750,000 will be included in the 1985–87 budget request. Grants will be made to public library systems for the purpose of pilot projects providing for demonstrations of cooperative library service among all types of libraries. Participation by academic, school and special libraries will be voluntary.

ALPHONSE F. TREZZA

New England Library Association

Activities. The New England Library Association (NELA) began 1984 by seeking ways to improve its newsletter while cutting printing and mailing costs. For improved production, speedy delivery, and current news, a lightweight but attractive tabloid-style publication was produced, and it received favorable comments. Software and a modem were purchased to aid the newsletter editor in preparing and delivering articles for the print shop. At the first conference cosponsored with another organization—the New England Educational Media Association (the NELA/NEEMA Conference)—both attendance and exhibitor participation increased.

Librarians found much at the conference to interest them no matter what their specialty. Issues such as pay equity, library education, censorship, copyright, and several others found librarians forgetting to ask whether the meeting was sponsored by public, academic, or school librarians. The joint Conference was so successful that there were preliminary plans to repeat it in 1986.

Three sections that had become practically nonexistent and nonsupportive in recent years were eliminated in 1984. They were Institutional, School, and Special Librarians. NELA President, Jan Sieburth, attended all New England State Library Association Conferences on behalf of NELA. A charter flight was arranged for the ALA Conference in Dallas. NELA was instrumental in forming the New England Council on Library Education comprising the President of NELA, deans of three library schools, and at least three NELA members. Some of the matters the Council planned to address are recruitment, work study internships, more involvement between students and practicing librarians, and sponsoring programs on practical matters of concern to the profession.

NELA in 1984 was in a very healthy position with membership up and a budget firmly in the black.

Programs. Special programs sponsored by sections during the year included "Designing Physical Work Spaces for the 80s" by the New England Technical Services Librarians; "Video on View" drew a large attendance for the media section, and "Page Turners: Children and Reading Motivation" was a hit by the New England Round Table of Children's Librarians. The Hospital Librarians featured "Marketing the Health Science Library." Counterparts Day brought together officers, committee chairs, newsletter editors, and others having common interests from the six state library associations.

The need for interstate communications is evident as is the need for new ideas and programs that make this event so successful. The Membership Committee worked to increase membership. The Continuing Education Committee proposed a grant program whereby librarians can receive up to 50 percent of continuing education costs paid from interest generated by the existing scholarship fund. NELA will continue in 1985–86 to address the educational needs of members.

SHERMAN PRIDHAM

NEW ENGLAND LIBRARY ASSOCIATION

PRESIDENT (November 1984–October 1985):
Sherman C. Pridham, Portsmouth Public Library, Portsmouth, New Hampshire

VICE-PRESIDENT/PRESIDENT-ELECT:
Benita Davis, State Library, Augusta, Maine

EXECUTIVE SECRETARY:
Ronald B. Hunte, Acton, Massachusetts

Membership (December 1984): 1,300

Oral History
Association

Oral History Association

The 1984 annual meeting of the Oral History Association was held in Lexington, Kentucky, September 20–23. The OHA Council tried to gain scheduling flexibility by producing a single four-day conference featuring a variety of program formats. As a result, the meeting included workshop sessions tailored to different interests and levels of experience, formal papers on important topics, panel and Round Table sessions on timely issues, and an assortment of media presentations.

Program speakers were Byron Crawford, John Egerton, William Greider, and Joan Hoff-Wilson. Crawford, a columnist for the Louisville *Courier-Journal* who writes humor, history, and folklore of the state, based his talk on those subjects. Egerton's most recent book, *Generations: An American Family*, chronicles the story of a Kentucky family from pioneer days to the present. He spoke on "The Lost Art of Listening."

Greider, presently National Editor for *Rolling Stone*, discussed his interview experiences with a variety of national political figures. Wilson, a specialist in American and diplomatic history and the Executive Secretary of the Organization of American Historians, addressed the audience on "Political Oral History: Interviewing Nixon."

During 1984 the Association continued to publish the annual *Oral History Review* and the quarterly *Oral History Association Newsletter*. The Association also distributed a number of other publications, including the *Evaluation Guidelines*, bibliographies, and proceedings from earlier meetings. A new publication, *The Annual Report and Directory*, was also provided to each member, and it will continue to be published annually. It includes a membership listing with addresses and telephone numbers, minutes, constitution and bylaws, recognition of officers and standing committees, identification of the state and regional oral history organizations, financial reports and budgets, and membership statistics. Work continued on the development of a pamphlet series addressing the issues and methodology of oral history. The first pamphlet, dealing with the legal aspects of oral history, was to be published in 1985.

The Association was in the process of defining its relationship with regional and state oral history organizations that have developed in the past 10 years. Some years ago OHA issued a policy statement concerning mutual interests and reciprocal support. Efforts were under way to revise and update the policy text to reflect more accurately this relationship. In addition a formal liaison between OHA and the regional groups was established.

RONALD E. MARCELLO

ORAL HISTORY ASSOCIATION

PRESIDENT (October 1984–October 1985):
Martha Ross, University of Maryland, College Park

PRESIDENT-ELECT:
Samuel Hand, University of Vermont, Burlington

EXECUTIVE SECRETARY:
Ronald E. Marcello, North Texas State University, Denton, Texas

Membership (December 1984): 1,400
Headquarters: North Texas State University, Denton

Pacific Northwest Library Association

The Pacific Northwest Library Association celebrated its 75th anniversary in 1984 with a year of activity that was distinguished by increased membership, involvement in significant issues, and a superb annual conference.

PNLA is a unique international association comprising five Northwest states and two Canadian provinces: Alaska, Idaho, Montana, Oregon, and Washington and Alberta and British Columbia.

PNLA does not have an executive secretary, so the officers, particularly the President, bear heavy responsibility. The Association prospered during 1984 under the leadership of Vicki R. Kreimeyer. Kreimeyer's goals for her term as President included increased visibility for PNLA in the region, increased membership, increased quality and quantity of communications and response to issues critical to libraries in the region.

The Association got off to a strong start in October 1983, when the Board met in a retreat setting at Menucha Conference Center near Portland. The planning and commitment that took place there, reinforced by the subsequent quarterly 1984 meetings in Seattle and Portland, resulted in substantial accomplishments.

The main focus of the Board was to implement the recommendations of a regional planning team whose report, *Planning for the Development of Cooperative Library Services in the Pacific Northwest*, was adopted by the membership in 1983. The recommendations will be implemented in stages.

The Resource Sharing Committee, chaired by Sherry Taber of Alaska, conducted a survey and analysis of resource sharing activities in the region. The Committee report was presented at the Annual Conference in Billings, Montana, in Au-

A "Women of Courage" photo exhibit at The New York Public Library in December was co-sponsored by the Black Women Oral History Project of Radcliffe College's Schlesinger Library. Subjects included (left) Dorothy West, author, and Deborah Wolfe, Associate Pastor of the First Presbyterian Church, Cranford, New Jersey.

gust and published in the Fall issue of the PNLA Quarterly. Entitled "Current State of Resource Sharing Among Libraries of All Types in the Pacific Northwest," this body of data about interlibrary access to information is a significant contribution.

The Bibliography Committee, chaired by Nancy Pryor of Washington, is comprised of members from each state and province. Its annual bibliography, "A Checklist of Books and Pamphlets of the Pacific Northwest," is published in the PNLA Quarterly.

The Division structure was under examination in 1984. Divisional memberships were decreasing, and it was recommended that the Board consider a structure that will better respond to the needs and interests of the membership. Nevertheless, each of the seven divisions sponsored excellent programs at the annual conference, and some undertook special projects.

The Academic Division, chaired by W. Bede Mitchell of Montana, published *Library Statistics of Colleges and Universities in the Pacific Northwest, 1982–83.*

The Children's and Young Adult Division annually sponsors a major award, the Young Readers' Choice Award. Over 26,000 ballots were cast by the children in the PNLA region, and the 1984 award was won by *Indian in the Cupboard,* by Lynne Reid Banks.

The *PNLA Quarterly*, the award winning voice of the Association continues to be an effective combination of substantive information, current developments, and news from the region.

The Association's annual meeting and conference were held in Billings, Montana, August 22–24. The conference theme, High-Tech, High-Touch, was reflected in every facet of the conference, from speakers and workshops to souvenir T-shirts.

A preconference workshop was sponsored by the Continuing Education Committee. "The Impact of Automation on Library Organization," presented by Richard Boss, was attended by 90 participants.

The keynote speaker was Michael Annison, President of the Westrend Group, formerly with the Naisbitt Group of *Megatrends* fame. Annison's speech on "Global Trends—Information Technology and Changing Social Patterns" was followed the next morning by a unique group process experience in which he led an all-conference workshop in an examination of the impact of these trends on libraries.

The conference concluded with a High-Touch emphasis with the banquet speech of poet Kim Stafford, "The Place of the Humanist in the Technological Age." With the voice of an ancient bard, Stafford somehow bridged the gap between Beowulf and the word processor.

The Local Arrangements Committee was chaired by Jane Howell. Anna Green of Idaho was Exhibits Chair. Barbara Tolliver of Washington organized the program. As the association year ended, membership had increased to 922, and other vital signs were good.

BARBARA J. TOLLIVER

Personnel and Employment: Compensation

"Go west, young man, go west." In 1984 advice for librarians might also have been: "Get some experience, go into special libraries, and, of course, eventually into administration. And being a man, young man, won't hurt, either." This advice would surprise few librarians and, now, more than ever, data supports such assertions and predicts employment trends. Although historically comparisons and trends about librarians' salaries have been tenuous because of the uneven and ad hoc nature of surveying and reporting data, during the last few years new and important surveys have emerged and existing ones improved.

In 1984 the ALA Office for Research and Office for Library Personnel Resources issued a second and refined *ALA Survey of Librarian Salaries;* it was previously published in 1982. Data included positions, geographic regions, and type of library (small public, large public, two-year college, four-year college, and university). Interpretation of salary and placement data and prediction of the library job market are more credible than ever thanks to the publication in 1983 of *Library Human Resources: A Study in Supply and Demand,* a research report by King Research, Inc., and sponsored by the National Center for Education Statistics and the Office of Libraries and Learning Technologies of the Department of Education. (See also Statistics.)

Entry-level Positions. The King Research report's prediction of an upward trend in the job market through 1990 was borne out by the results of *Library Journal's* 33d annual report on placement and salaries of ALA-accredited library schools. For the first time in many years the increase in entry-level salaries exceeded the cost of living. The mean salary for 1983 was $17,705, an improvement of 7 percent from the previous year. Improvements over the previous year for the period 1980 through 1982 were 6, 9.9, and 8 percent, respectively. Means for those with prior experience were $19,400 (up from $17,687) while those without experience earned an average of $16,382 (up from $15,248).

In 1983 the mean beginning salary for women was $17,563, an 8 percent increase over 1982; for men $18,303, a 4 percent increase. Median salaries were $16,994 for all graduates, $16,829 for

---

PACIFIC NORTHWEST LIBRARY ASSOCIATION

PRESIDENT (October 1984–September 1985): **Barbara J. Tolliver,** University of Washington Graduate School of Library and Information Science, Seattle

VICE-PRESIDENT/PRESIDENT-ELECT: **Fr. Joseph P. Browne, C.S.C.,** University of Portland Library, Oregon

SECRETARY: **Betty Galbraith,** Eielson AFB Library, Fairbanks, Alaska

TREASURER: **Audrey Kolb,** Alaska State Library, Fairbanks

Membership (August 1984): 922

Personnel and Employment: Compensation

women and $17,190 for men. While the economic status of women in the profession is dealt with in another part of the Yearbook, it should be noted here that placement results indicate that women's salaries are improving. Fifteen women reported placement at salaries of $30,000 or more, triple the number from 1982. For library school's reporting placement salaries for both men and women, the women's average was higher than the men's in more than half of the schools reporting against one-third in 1982.

School Libraries. Comparing data from the Education Research Service, Inc., annual survey of salaries and wages of personnel in public schools for the 1982–83 and 1983–84 school years, the mean salary of school librarian salaries went from $22,040 to $23,171, a 5.1 percent increase, down from the previous two years' 7.5 and 9.7 percent increases. Highest salaries were in the West, Southwest, and Rocky Mountain regions.

Classroom teachers' mean salaries increased 5.9 percent to $22,039. The survey does not include the mean, a more useful statistic in salary analysis, nor does it separate district-level supervising librarians from other categories. When comparing the salaries of school librarians and when considering the $14,321 mean minimum of scheduled salaries ($14,206 for classroom teachers), it should be noted that many school librarian positions require library science courses rather than a master's degree from an ALA-accredited library school. School librarians with the degree fared relatively well according to the LJ placement survey. Of the 58 lowest salaries in 1983, school librarians accounted for only 14 percent, which is within one percentage of the previous two years' placement record for school librarians. School librarians worked an average of 187 days during 1983–84.

Public Libraries. The 1984 ALA Survey provided low, mean, and high salaries for many positions and geographic areas. Data are for small public libraries (serving populations of from 25,000 to 99,999) and large public libraries (serving populations of 100,000 or more). The lack of comparable ALA data for 1983 precludes comparability with the previous year for small public libraries. The Allen County (Indiana) Public Library biennial survey of 1983 for all libraries serving populations 100,000 or more allows a comparison for the large public libraries. The mean salary for directors of large public libraries for 1984 was $39,861 (range $16,800 to $77,945); this compared to the Allen County figure of $39,314 for 1983 and ALA's average of $35,060 for 1982. As in previous years, the 1984 average varied considerably by region: $37,938 in the North Atlantic, $41,858 in the Great Lakes and Plains, $34,900 in the Southeast, and $44,569 in the West and Southwest. Nationwide Deputy/Associate Directors and Assistant Directors averaged $31,968 and $31,742, respectively.

Directors of small public libraries averaged $27,090 overall in 1984, with a remarkable regional differential between the Southeast ($20,942) and the West and Southwest ($32,307). Similar differentials between these two regions occur for virtually all positions.

The 1984 mean salary for beginning professionals in large public libraries was $16,583, up 8 percent from 1983. Again, however, there were important regional differences: $14,727 in the North Atlantic, $15,588 in the Great Lakes and Plains, $15,334 in the Southeast, and $18,497 in the West and Southwest.

The LJ placement survey found public librarians accounting for 9 percent of the 58 highest salaries and 28 percent of the lowest salaries.

Academic Libraries. Between the ALA Survey and the Association of Research Libraries' (ARL) Annual Salary Survey, salary data for academic libraries for 1984 was excellent. Unfortunately, because of differences in surveying and presentation of the data, the ALA data and ARL data are not comparable. Data for the ARL members in the United States are included in the ALA category "University"; other ALA categories for academic libraries are two-year college and four-year college. Aggregate mean and median salaries for all academic librarians are not available from ALA.

Generally, salaries are higher at university libraries than at four-year colleges while salaries at two-year colleges are higher than at universities. For administrative positions, the university libraries are highest, followed by two-year colleges and four-year colleges, respectively. For beginning professionals, the mean was $20,439 for two-year colleges, $18,373 for four-year colleges, and $15,699 for universities.

The 105 United States and Canadian ARL libraries had a median salary of $26,100 for 1983–84, an increase of 4.65 percent over the previous year. The median beginning professional salary increased by 4.5 percent to $16,500. Both of these measures grew faster than the increase in the Consumer Price Index; so for the third year in a row, ARL librarians regained another small portion of purchasing power lost in the preceding decade. Salaries paid to librarians in private ARL libraries averaged 2.6 percent higher than those paid in their counterparts in publicly supported institutions. Highest average ARL salaries were paid in the Pacific and Middle Atlantic regions, and the lowest were paid in the East and West South Central regions.

The King study predicted little job expansion in academic libraries during the 1980s and this appears to be borne out by recent placement data. According to the LJ survey, academic libraries accounted for 12 percent (down from 16 percent in 1982) of the 58 highest placement salaries and 33 percent (up from 25 percent) of the lowest salaries.

Special Libraries. The Special Library Association polls a 25 percent sample of its membership as an update of its in-depth triennial salary survey, last conducted in 1982. Between 1983 and 1984 the overall median in the United States went from $25,000 to $27,000, an 8 percent increase; the mean rose 7.3 percent from $26,489 to $28,421. The Canadian members' median rose 9.3 percent from $28,500 to $31,146. Over the past three years, the U.S. and Canadian medians have increased 28.4 percent and 32.5 percent, respectively.

For 1984, U.S. and Canadian managers' salaries ranged from $19,080 to $56,561 with a mean of $34,643. Assistant/Section Heads earned from $16,985 to $41,448, the mean being $26,976. Individuals holding the title Librarian/Information Specialist had salaries ranging from $15,567 to $39,624 with a mean of $25,343. Support staff salaries ranged from $12,987 to $35,763, the mean being $20,054.

According to the *LJ* survey, 41 percent of the highest placement salaries in 1983 were in special libraries, up from 27 percent in 1982. Seventeen percent of the lowest salaries were in special libraries, up from 13 percent in 1982.

Employee Benefits. During 1984 legislators looked ever more closely at the tax-exempt status of many fringe benefits. However, the object of such investigation tended to be the kinds of benefits not usually enjoyed by librarians. Given the unsettled status of tax "reform" and the prospects for important changes in the tax structure, benefits will continue to be an increasingly important part of the librarian's compensation package. The *ALA Survey* shows an average of 19 percent of payroll is spent on benefits. This figure varies slightly by geographic region; the Southeast has the lowest average of 16.9 percent. The figure is highest in large public libraries and two-year colleges (20 percent) and lowest in four-year colleges (15.8 percent). By way of comparison, businesses typically spend 37–40 percent of their payroll on benefits.

Pay Parity. The notion that one should receive equal pay for work of equal *value*, which goes well beyond the narrower concept of equal pay for equal work as defined by the Equal Pay Act of 1963, continued to be pressed ever more vigorously by librarians during 1984. A definitive resolution of the "comparable worth" issue appears unlikely in the near future. The conservative Heritage Foundation, which enjoys the ear of the Reagan administration, resisted the concept.

Nevertheless, public library administrators sought and received salary adjustments to bring librarian salaries closer to parity with other municipal employees. Countywide voluntary comparable worth investigations resulted in salary adjustments for librarians.

Of special future interest will be the impact of a Minnesota comparable worth law concerning municipal employees. In an interesting variation on the issue, North Carolina pay parity was being sought for public librarians and school librarians. Adjudication was expected in 1985 concerning a pay grade-level reallocation in the Fairfax County (Virginia) Public Library system for entry-level librarian positions to make them comparable with other county positions.

Clerical and paraprofessional employees at Yale University obtained wage increases while framing their demands, in part, in the context of comparable worth. ALA's position has been in favor of pay equity bills. Margaret Myers, Director of ALA's Office for Library Personnel Resources, has solicited documents relating to specific comparable worth cases.

Trends. While inflation and the devastating effect it wreaked upon librarians' salaries for over a decade has eased, not all librarians have shared equally in that relief. Indeed, both short-term and long-term prospects for librarians' salaries will depend upon the type of library in which one is employed and one's specialized training.

Placement officials were optimistic in 1984 about job vacancies for 1985. There was still a critical and unmet need for graduates with undergraduate majors in chemistry, physics, computer science, business, engineering, and foreign languages. Increasing demand and short supply continues to include cataloging, science and technology, information science, and systems.

Longer-term projections indicate little change is expected in employment overall, with decreases in school and academic library positions and increases in public libraries and non-library settings.

There are important variables. Will the much heralded stress on quality of education mean more school library positions? What will be the impact of the federal government's new policy on contracting out library services and the Office of Personnel Management's lowering of educational requirements for the GS-9 classification?

Concern continues that the low salaries paid to librarians might preclude the profession from attracting the best and brightest. There is increasing concern too that, within the profession, salaries and benefits in public institutions—schools, colleges, universities, and public libraries—are falling ever farther behind special libraries in the private sector.

LANCE QUERY

Personnel and Employment: Recruitment and Selection

Literature. As in 1983 the expertise of librarians and library school graduates continued to be a focus of the library community during 1984. Administrative skills, as well as technical expertise, were viewed by many library directors as critical elements in the education of librarians. The *Journal of Academic Librarianship* and the *Journal of Education for Library and Information Science*, among others, contributed articles on the need for both theoretical and scholarly curricula. The Association of Research Libraries established a task force to study and review the educational needs of librarians working in research libraries. Public library directors also felt the need for increased competencies among library school graduates; however, they give high marks to the traditional library competencies such as general reference, bibliography and cataloging.

It is important that those institutions which offer graduate programs in library and information science evaluate the curricula offered and readjust them where necessary in order to provide sound programs in areas such as computers, programming and telecommunication, as well as management and human relations.

F. W. Lancaster in an article published in the May 1983 issue of the *Wilson Library Bulletin*, "Future Librarianship: Preparing for an Unconventional Career," wrote that the future librarian will become more actively involved in education and training. Librarians will be qualified to teach people how to select, access, and exploit electronic networks in order to retrieve requested information. Library schools will need to provide the resources and skills necessary for librarians of the future to access computers and to be

Personnel and Employment: Recruitment and Selection

knowledgeable of the limitations of electronic networks, understand their characteristics, and become more specialized in the subject matter. With these factors in mind, many librarians have begun to take courses in the information sciences in order to meet the electronic demands now in place in libraries. Typically, these in-depth courses are offered in schools outside the traditional library school. Although some library schools provide moderate educational experiences in electronic media, these are viewed as insufficient in meeting the current and future demands being placed on librarians.

Comparable Worth. Comparable worth, an issue for the 1980s, continues to be at the forefront in the public and private sectors. While varied opinions exist are numerous studies are being conducted throughout the United States, librarians must not lose sight of the need to continue to upgrade salaries and to serve as role models for those in other professions.

The American Library Association continued in 1984 to challenge the federal government in its efforts to deal with the equal pay issue. *American Libraries* reported that Eileen Cooke, ALA Washington Office Director, challenged a House committee, the Post Office, and a Civil Service subcommittee on compensation and employee benefits to review their actions in charging the Office of Personnel Management with the responsibility to identify and study wage discrimination practices and to propose methods for eliminating them. The Office of Personnel Management data is viewed as inadequate and includes standards which are discriminatory. Further, the Office of Personnel Management did not respond to the American Library Association's request that the standards as they were submitted be rewritten and withdrawn. The American Library Association has requested that an independent study be conducted by "experts" reporting to the General Accounting Office with a review by the President and Congress.

Advertising and Recruitment. The Master of Library Science degree has once again been scrutinized through the widely publicized Merwine case. The primary focus of the case was whether or not Mississippi State University could require the MLS degree from an ALA accredited school as a condition of employment. A judge overturned a jury verdict and found that the ALA sanctioned MLS degree was the minimal educational requirement.

Many libraries during 1984 were reviewing their methods of recruitment, including advertising and program development. In the high technology library environment the need for more automation expertise has created a shift in the methods traditionally used to generate applicants. As reported in 1983, online listings of employment opportunities are on the rise. Some libraries have begun to use employment agencies and search firms to find qualified applicants for positions that require expertise in automated systems. Libraries continue to use the traditional advertising sources such as trade publications and newspapers for most other types of positions.

The trend of promotion from within established during the late 1970s continued in 1984. Many library personnel administrators felt that this recruitment technique was a positive approach in retaining staff and that it created flexibility to hire beginning-level librarians, keeping the staff diverse and dynamic. In addition, greater emphasis was being placed on the recruitment of minorities. Some libraries developed community awareness programs geared toward the recruitment of minority professionals and para-professionals. Others enlisted the aid of individual minority colleagues and minority associations for recommendations of potential applicants.

Libraries continued to experience difficulty in recruiting staff with science, mathematics, engineering, and business backgrounds. The profession must become more competitive with the private sector in the range of salaries offered to such individuals.

Overall salary levels continued to improve throughout the United States in all types of libraries. The ARL *Annual Salary Survey* and the ALA *Survey of Librarian Salaries* are useful tools in determining salary placement nationally, regionally, and locally. Academic and public libraries are offering more per capita support toward moving expenses as an employment inducement when salaries need to be offset for some positions. In addition, many academic libraries are reviewing their retirement packages with an eye toward implementing early retirement programs. In some academic libraries where librarians are faculty, and in many research and development libraries, the early retirement option already exists.

The interview process did not change in 1984. Most libraries preferred the search committee approach. The prescreening telephone interview continued to be a popular and practical means for determining finalist candidates for on-site interviews. The ALA Conference Placement Center offered great opportunities for candidates and employers alike during the search process.

Good human resources management is a key factor in the recruitment and retention of staff. As libraries continue to apply automation, the need to implement good staff development programs, cross-training, and continuing education opportunities for staff increases. It is no longer good management to provide these opportunities only to professional librarians; they must also apply to support staff who are taking on more of what used to be termed as routine librarian tasks. It was not unusual to find high-level support staff serving at the reference desk, providing copy and variant edition cataloging, and managing the day-to-day operations of a work unit in libraries during 1984.

Trends toward using support staff in newer areas of service increased the necessity for personnel administrators to look closely at job levels. Job evaluation and analysis are critical factors in an organization's struggle to cope with rapid change. Libraries must determine internal relationships and in effect establish a hierarchy of positions within the organization. While many feel that the evaluation process is subjective, it is nevertheless important that the organization establish a system to determine the "value" of the position in relation to the skills required to perform the job when compared with others in the organization.

Job analysis, then, requires that personnel administrators continuously monitor job content and competitive pay levels relative to the local and national labor market. They must establish salary levels that are equitable internally. The system that establishes the "value" of the position must be flexible enough to accommodate changing circumstances and organizational need.

CAROLYN J. HENDERSON

Personnel and Employment: Staff Development

Continuing Education. The American Library Association's leadership in developing and sponsoring institutes at the regional level has expanded during the past few years, particularly since ALA's Association of College and Research Libraries (ACRL) developed one- and two-day courses. These numbered more than 14 in 1984. They include traditional programs of interest to librarians in all types of libraries, on topics such as time management, conducting effective meetings, and interviewing skills. Other ACRL courses address current concerns of academic librarians, such as marketing fee-based services and establishing the college BI (bibliographic instruction) program. ACRL also produces syllabi that are available for purchase and can form the nucleus of staff development programs in individual libraries or at library association meetings.

Other ALA divisions, notably the Resources and Technical Services Division (RTSD) and the Library Administration and Management Association (LAMA), are also active in developing regional institutes. In 1984 LAMA cosponsored "Management of the Online Catalog" with library schools, state libraries, and library associations in Wisconsin, South Carolina, and Ohio. These two divisions offer the same packaged programs on the online catalog, fund raising, and preservation of library materials in various locations throughout the country, thus making it possible for libraries to send several staff members at once.

Although traditionally staff development integrates learning activities into the operations of an institution, ALA and many libraries and regional systems are now cooperating to develop training opportunities that address staff needs across library boundaries. This allows them to share resources and expensive developmental costs and to learn from each other's experiences. Joan Durrance, Continuing Education Coordinator, University of Michigan School of Library Science, writing in Public Libraries (Fall 1983), described her experience with an "Issues Forum: Creative Staff Development in Times of Economic Stress."

This forum is cooperatively planned and financed by an informal group of sponsors from all types of libraries in Michigan who recognize the need to bring librarians together to discuss and debate issues and challenges. The cost of nine programs held over a two-year time span was estimated at close to $20,000—an expense that neither a single institution nor the participants themselves would be able to bear.

Among the topics the forum addressed are "Productivity in Libraries" and "Libraries in Times of Economic Stress." Michigan invited outstanding and recognized library leaders to each forum. Major Owens, for example, covered "Libraries in the Political Process."

Most cooperative staff development activities continue, however, to emphasize staff knowledge and skills directly related to job responsibilities, for example, human resource management, job design, motivation, and performance appraisal. Within the past few years many libraries have begun to develop training programs in newer areas such as preservation of library materials and library automation, especially use of microcomputers.

Awards. The 1984 Staff Development Award went to the Prince George's County Memorial Library System, Maryland, "Orientation and Training for Hourly Employees." Other recipients of this $2,000 award have included Southern University, Louisiana, "Library Skills Workshop," 1980; Indiana University, Bloomington, "Computer Assisted Training Modules for Student Workers," 1981; Rhode Island Department of State Library Services, "Group Process Techniques," 1982; Jackson–George Regional Library System, Mississippi, "LIFT: Librarians Improve from Training," 1983.

The ALA and the H. W. Wilson Company initiated the annual Library Staff Development Award in 1980. The award recognizes learning activities that further the on-the-job capability of library personnel and that contribute to the overall effectiveness of an individual library, a library system, cooperating libraries, state governmental agencies, and associations. The jury looks for programs of special merit that clearly relate the

Using standard voting machines to familiarize the public with voting procedures, the Miami-Dade Public Library system in 1984 conducted a Library User Survey to improve services.

learning activity to the organization's goals and objectives, address a clear and pressing need in the organization, show evidence that the activity is part of a coordinated program, and include evaluation.

Entries covered a wide range of traditional and innovative staff development activities including orientation using audiovisual materials, workbooks for hourly employees describing and explaining specific tasks and procedures, training in collection development, applications of microcomputers in school library media centers, handling employee performance problems, short supervisory courses for middle managers, working with problem patrons, training the trainer, interagency long-range staff development programs, preservation of library materials, automated information management techniques on personal computers, basic consultation skills in online reference services, leading and participating in effective committee meetings, workshops on grantsmanship and proposal writing, and training for facilities planning.

Resources and Institutes. Librarians with staff development responsibilities continually seek existing programs and resources that can be used to improve their own efforts. Two new sources for locating library staff development materials and programs appeared in 1983–84. *Learning Packages To Go: A Directory and Guide to Staff Development and Training Packages* by Barbara Conroy (Oryx Press, 1983) is a basic reference tool for trainers, personnel managers, and librarians. LAMA published *Staff Development in Libraries* (1984), an annotated bibliography of materials from both library and management literature. This selective guide to recent literature covers affirmative action, career development, counseling and mentoring, stress, and other topics.

In 1984 the Office of Management Studies of the Association of Research Libraries continued to offer their basic and advanced library management skills institutes intended to develop staff supervisory skills. Over 1,000 persons have participated in the institutes and other OMS workshops geared for librarians in academic, public, or special libraries who have managerial, administrative, or supervisory responsibilities. The basic sessions address specific skills including problem solving, motivation, decision making, effective use of groups, supervision, performance appraisal, and communication. The five-and-one-half-day advanced library management skills institutes are designed for more experienced managers.

CLENE Round Table. In January the Continuing Library Education Network and Exchange officially became the ALA CLENE Round Table. This move helped integrate CLENE's major programs and services more closely to the meetings and activities of ALA itself, placed CLENE in closer contact with thousands of librarians, increased its opportunity for visibility to the entire library community, and helped promote continuing library education more effectively. CLENE continues to publish its newsletter, *CLENE Exchange*, which serves as an idea exchange and carries workshop reviews of quality library continuing education programs. The reviews examine workshops' purpose, audience, presenters, duration, content, cost, and evaluation.

CLENE also continues to sponsor free counseling and one-to-one tutorials on continuing education and staff development at ALA conferences. Such services provide librarians with a chance to review projects, discuss proposed plans, try out new ideas, and receive feedback on activities from experienced professionals.

Developing Skills. Lynn Roberts, Training Officer of the Denver Public Library, draws implications for staff development from John Nasbitt's *Megatrends: Ten Directions Transforming Our Lives* (1982) in an article in *Colorado Libraries* (Spring 1983). Although she recognized long-standing staff development needs for supervisory skills, reference interview techniques, and training in new library technology, she stressed that with the increasing importance of high technology staff must learn, understand, and use computer technologies to create, maintain, and access databases. High technology, however, needs to be balanced by an equally strong move to more human forms of interaction, which Nasbitt calls "high touch." This results in the need for increased training in public relations, outreach, communications and other interpersonal and community-centered skills.

As many organizations shift from a centralized structure to a decentralized structure, bringing more involvement of more diverse elements, library staff need increased political skills of negotiation, conflict resolution, assertiveness, and persuasiveness. These skills are increasingly necessary as libraries move toward more cooperative sharing of resources and expertise and move away from centralized and hierarchical forms of administration. The idea of participation is spreading and radically altering the way institutions are governed. Supervisors particularly need skills in group process, problem solving, brainstorming, and meeting management in order to manage libraries effectively.

ROGER PARENT

Preservation of Library Materials

Growth in the field of library preservation and the growing interest in the subject were reflected in many ways in 1984. Conferences, seminars, and workshops focused on preservation issues were held throughout the year, and professional meetings in other fields had preservation components. Publication continued apace; preservation programs were funded by government agencies and private foundations alike; professional training opportunities increased; and major institutions opened preservation departments.

Conference, Seminars, and Workshops. "Library Preservation: Implementing Programs," the second of three conferences sponsored by the Resources and Technical Services Division of ALA, with the cooperation of LC's National Preservation Program, was held in St. Louis, in mid-April. The major presentations, numerous breakaway sessions, and superb exhibits were intended for librarians involved in the planning, development, and implementation of an institution's preservation program. The Preservation of

Library Materials Section (PLMS) of RTSD, in its regular meetings at ALA Conferences, discussed issues of concern to the Section members.

The preservation of library and archive materials was the focus of conferences, seminars, and hands-on workshops held by various groups during the year. Topics at those meetings included the preservation of photographs; disaster preparedness and recovery; the utilization of commercially available binding technology as a conservation measure; and staff and user education on preservation issues. Other meetings saw major presentations on preservation as related to archives management or rare books and manuscripts librarianship.

The Book and Paper Group (BPG) of the American Institute for the Conservation of Historic and Artistic Works (AIC) continued its research into and development of archivally sound repair and restoration procedures for library materials. An important project initiated in 1984 by the BPG was an inventory of treatment methods and materials used in paper conservation. Another professional group important to library preservation, the Guild of Book Workers, held its third annual seminar on excellence in hand bookbinding.

Grants. Preservation activities were generously supported by funds from both government agencies and private foundations. The support not only allowed new preservation projects to begin, but also helped established programs to continue or expand services. The Illinois Cooperative Conservation Program (ICCP) at Morris Library of Southern Illinois University at Carbondale received $77,000 in Library Services and Construction Act funds, through the Illinois State Library, to carry out the third phase of its activities. This phase will continue the established information services and hands-on workshops, and will emphasize the need for and development of treatment services for local history collections.

Morris Library also received a grant from the National Endowment for the Humanities to develop a cooperative conservation program for the research libraries and archives in a five-state region of the Midwest. This NEH grant funds the Midwest Cooperative Conservation Program for its two-year start-up period. MCCP will initially concentrate on stimulating the development of preservation programs in Illinois, Indiana, Kentucky, Missouri, and Tennessee. Information and on-site services are offered, as are workshops and training sessions. Training materials are distributed, and other materials are available for loan.

NEH made other major grants to preservation programs. The Southeastern Library Network, Inc. (SOLINET), received $168,400 to establish a cooperative preservation program for the libraries and archives of the Southeast. The new project is funded for a two-year period, and has two primary objectives: to promote the development and growth of local programs by offering information, training, and assistance; to cooperate with other preservation programs, especially those with regional or national responsibilities.

The Association of Research Libraries received funding from NEH for distribution to 10 of its member libraries for conducting the self-study

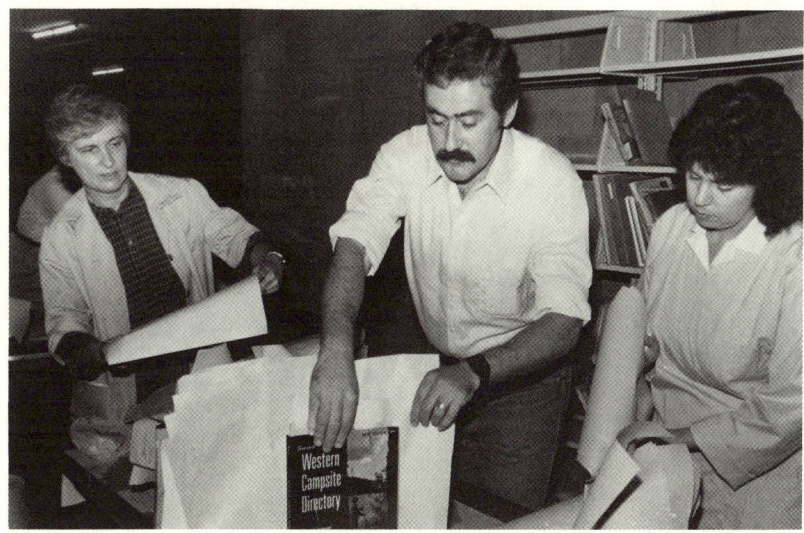

The Damage Limiting Action Team of the Dallas Public Library practices conserving valuable library materials in the event of a disaster.

Preservation Planning Program. With assistance provided by ARL's Office of Management Study, that program allows the staff of participating libraries to conduct a collection condition survey, evaluate the efficacy of existing programs, expand current programs, and develop new ways of dealing with problems.

NEH made $22,000,000 in challenge grants available to 75 educational and cultural institutions, including libraries, with emphasis put on the creation or augmentation of endowments. These endowments support a variety of ends, including preservation.

The Exxon Education Fund granted $1,500,000 to the Council on Library Resources, Inc., to fund a long-term project aimed at preserving the essential holdings of American research libraries. The project's activities are to include: formation of a Mid-Atlantic Preservation Center; development of strategies for preservation within the region; and dissemination of information to the public in support of preservation goals.

Other grants were made during the year to fund other preservation projects. In addition, preservation is becoming an increasingly common component of grants not made specifically for preservation purposes.

State and Regional Programs. The established state and regional preservation programs in 1984 continued to make valuable information and assistance available to their constituents. In addition to performing conservation treatment in its labs, the Northeast Document Conservation Center continued its field survey program, and held seminars and workshops on a variety of topics. The Northwest Conservation Center continued to provide information and treatment services to institutions in the Pacific Northwest.

In addition to the SOLINET preservation program and the MCCP, cited previously, other state and regional programs got under way in 1984. AMIGOS, the bibliographic network serving the Southwest, created a Preservation Committee to review needs and activities in the region, investigate the benefits of further organization for preservation, and recommend action to the AMIGOS board. The Ohio Conservation Committee was formed in response to the need for cooperative

Conservation Administration News (CAN) *quarterly devoted to library and archival preservation added 10 regional/national reporters in 1984 and extended geographical coverage to Australia, Canada, Germany, Britain, and Japan. CAN is published at the University of Tulsa.*

statewide effort to solve conservation problems. It will place strong emphasis on the education of the general public on conservation needs, will serve as a forum for discussing issues, and will work to link existing programs in the state in cooperative effort. The Ohio Cooperative Conservation Information Office completed its first year's efforts to develop statewide conservation resources by conducting workshops and distributing information.

LC and the National Preservation Program. The NPP expanded its staff with the appointments of Merrily A. Smith and Carolyn Clark Morrow as program specialists, an expansion directed toward improving the NPP response to the need for information, educational support, and program coordination among U.S. libraries, and institutions engaged in preservation activities. LC continued development of its Opitcal Disk Pilot Program—a three-year program designed to investigate the use of optical-disk technology in the storage and preservation of high-use and fragile or rare items. The first of six analog videodisks produced during the program's first phase was made available in 1984, giving the user high-speed access to 40,000 images from the Prints and Photographs Reading Room.

Research. Research continued into efficient, effective, economically feasible, and environmentally safe mass deacidification of library materials. The major project at LC's Research and Testing Office was in its diethyl zinc deacidification system. Funds have been allocated to construct a facility capable of treating 500,000 items a year at Fort Detrick, Maryland. Another mass deacidification process, the Wei T'o system, has been developed by Richard D. Smith. The Wei T'o process is used at the National Library of Canada as part of that library's preservation program. A third system was developed by the Koppers Company of Pittsburgh; it has, however, been abandoned since market research indicated there would be insufficient profit to warrant continued development.

Two methods of paper-strengthening were reported by LC's Peter Sparks at ALA's Midwinter Meeting. One was under development by Nova Tran, Inc., of Wisconsin, the other by the British Library.

Professional Education. The Columbia University School of Library Service continued to offer a wide range of professional educational opportunities. It has established degree-granting programs in preservation administration and conservation science, and offers a summer Rare Books School, with some courses directed at professional conservators and preservation officers. Many other graduate M.L.S. programs offered courses in library materials preservation in 1984. Further, the Mellon Foundation funded internships in preservation administration at Yale, Columbia, Stanford, the Library of Congress, and the New York Public Library. These internships provide librarians the opportunity to work in an established preservation program for up to one year in an administrative capacity.

Publications. Many additions were made to preservation literature in 1984. The MCCP began publication of a regular *Newsletter,* edited by Sally Roggia. The newsletter carries current news of the field, reports on regional activities, and contains information on materials and technology. The *RTSD Newsletter* began publishing a regular "Preservation" column, edited by Ann Swartzell, of Yale University Library. *The Abbey Newsletter, Conservation Administration News,* and the *New Library Scene* continue to publish articles on various aspects of preservation, and all remain vital sources of information. The *Journal of the American Institute for Conservation, The Paper Conservator,* and the *American Archivist* are among the many publications written for specific audiences that are likely to carry articles of importance to the library preservation officer. Moreover, as library materials preservation becomes a more widely recognized concern, articles about preservation begin to appear more frequently in the general press.

CARLA MONTORI

Public Libraries

Fostering Literacy and Eliminating Illiteracy. Predictably, the best-selling book in the United States at the beginning of 1984 was George Orwell's *1984.* Unpredictably, Eudora Welty's *One Writer's Beginnings* and Daniel J. Boorstin's *The Discoverers* both enjoyed extended stays on the *New York Times Book Review's* "Best Sellers list" during 1984. The attention to all three books indicates an appreciation of good writing and a life of the mind more widespread than many commentators seem to believe.

The people who accounted for the success of these books tend overwhelmingly to be among the approximately one adult in ten who uses the public library often. Just as there is reason to rejoice that there is a large and irrepressibly curious adult population that is very literate, so there was reason to regret that there is an equally large adult population who are either entirely illiterate or so very nearly illiterate that print media in libraries is virtually useless to them. At least 26,000,000 Americans fall into that category.

A Coalition for Literacy, spearheaded by the American Library Association, in 1984 brought together many of the public and private organizations in America committed to fighting illiteracy today. Volunteers and professionals work with adults eager to acquire the skills of reading and writing. Public libraries are generally seen as natural centers for literacy efforts because they so

Public Libraries

The Memphis Shelby County Public Library and Information Center gets a boost from the restored Orpheum Theatre with a message on the marquee.

clearly symbolize the respect for learning and knowledge of the American people. The Chief Officers of State Library Agencies (COSLA) at their 1984 fall meeting endorsed the idea that public libraries should become the centers and coordinators of those efforts.

The reauthorization of the Library Services and Construction Act (LSCA) passed late in the congressional year includes for the first time a title to fight illiteracy, a position personally championed by Barbara Bush, wife of the Vice-President. Although appropriations were not made in the first attempt for funding of this title of LSCA, the attempt was planned at the end of 1984 to seek supplemental appropriations for this purpose.

COSLA resolved on October 24 to endorse "efforts by State library agencies and public libraries, working in cooperation with existing literacy programs, to promote and encourage libraries to take an active role in national, state, and local literacy programs." This group also encouraged the development of library-coordinated literacy programs that are based in local community efforts in every state.

Another aspect of the public library commitment to the growth of literacy in America in 1984 is the emphasis on "computer literacy." "Computer illiteracy" in the adult population is, of course, common since three-fourths of adults completed formal education before the invention of the microcomputer. But, as with efforts to promote universal print literacy, public libraries can be only a modest partner in attempting to bring about universal computer literacy. The money, the staff, the expertise for computer literacy universally simply are not there. Given funding levels for all public library collection, staff services, and programs at little more than $10 per person nationwide, on average, it is clear that funding levels are insufficient for public libraries to do much more than cooperate with those committed to computer literacy and, increasingly, to take a role in coordination of these efforts. Recent success in both print and computer literacy efforts in some public libraries assures them a meaningful role in both undertakings.

The need for dedicating effort to both of them was made clear in the Department of Education's widely studied report, *A Nation at Risk*. A large number of public libraries welcomed this challenge during the year.

Funding, Use, and Facilities. According to the most recent data from the National Center for Education Statistics, combined state and local government spending for public libraries during fiscal year 1981–82 was $8.61, which was supplemented by federal expenditures of a little under a

The new Orange County (California) Public Library logo is a zebra whose midsection is the computer code bar of the Library's automated circulation control system.

Above, Warder Libraries' float in the Memorial Day parade in Springfield, Ohio. Right, Cincinnati Public Library Bookfest '84 featured a banner contest with 140 entries hung in the library's atrium for two weeks.

A Computer Fair at the Boulder (Colorado) Public Library promoted the use of the Library's seven computers. (Paul Lavelle)

$1 per person that fiscal year. Just under 0.5 percent of all state and local expenditures were expended on public libraries.

The state of Connecticut spent proportionately most of its state and local government monies (0.74%) for public libraries, closely followed by Washington (0.73%) and Utah (0.70%). The 1983 Index of American Public Library Expenditures estimated per capita support from all sources at $9.78, which in view of the official figures for fiscal 1981 given above, is probably a bit low. According to the latter source, 1983 was the second year in succession that an increase in purchasing power for public libraries was experienced (data from Herbert Goldhor, "University of Illinois Annual Survey," *American Libraries*, July/August 1984).

Yet another survey, this one of state sources only, revealed a spread in support ranging from zero funding in some states to more than $2 per capita annually from state sources in West Virginia, Maryland, New York, and Georgia. Since that survey, Virginia has greatly increased its support. Although the improvement in public library funding in 1984 was uneven, the evidence of modest increases overall was convincing.

For a second record-setting year more than one billion items were borrowed for use in homes and businesses by Americans in 1983 (latest year for which figures are available). The median figure for average per capita circulation from public libraries was 5.4 circulations during that same year. Adults continue to account for most of that circulation (just over two-thirds of the total). That figure should continue to rise as the age of the population and the availability of school library materials continue to rise.

During recent years, studies of indicators of public library use other than the traditional one of circulation have been developed and are being applied. They indicate very high levels of satisfaction with the public library as a place to browse with the hope of finding books and other material of interest. Although people are less often able to find the specific title or subject matter they want available at the moment they want it, the studies also indicate a high degree of satisfaction in this regard.

Marked upward movement has been seen in the Sunbelt toward equity in public library service levels. For the large public library in the South "per capita expenditures exceeded the CPI [growth in the Consumer Price Index from 1972 to 1982] by 40 percent." On a per capita basis circulation grew 16 percent "during the decade studied" (Ray L. Carpenter, "The Sunbelt's Public Libraries: 1972–1982," *Public Library Quarterly*, Winter 1983). This study also notes, unfortunately, that the earning power of public librarians in the South, as elsewhere, declined during the decade and that "imbalances in gender distribution among directors continued" there as elsewhere. Progress was made during 1984 in some places which have experienced real economic hardship, including Detroit, where a special library bond to reinstate branch services and staffing levels passed handily. In New York City private gifts have contributed substantially to a $45,000,000 renovation of the great 42nd Street New York Public Library with leadership coming from Brooke Astor, great-great-granddaughter of an earlier cofounder of the library, John Jacob Astor.

The effort to get unemployed Americans back to work in the form of a jobs bill to underwrite necessary public building projects brought some funding for the first time in over a decade to the con-

Left, Tex Schram, General Manager of the Dallas Cowboys, presents Dallas Mayor Starke Taylor with a Cowboy jersey at the opening of the Dallas Public Library's exhibit of the Cowboys' Silver Anniversary. Above, the Texas Stadium scoreboard promotes the exhibit at a game in the fall.

struction title of the Library Services and Construction Act (LSCA). In 1984 the funding led to many projects, including a 1,600-square-foot portable library in the Capitol to replace an outgrown kiosk on a busy site there. The State of Illinois ventured into public library construction beginning with a major addition to the Niles Public Library, which features a computer lab for the public. Welcome as these relatively piecemeal efforts are, a reincarnation of the spirit of Andrew Carnegie and his massive commitment to public library construction is much needed in the land.

Should Library Funding Be Changed? Certain policies are widely held to be at the heart of the public library's success since the implementation in Boston in the mid-19th century of the free library. The cost for library service was to be borne by all taxpayers, the nonusers with the users, the absentee landlords with the business people who benefit from the traffic generated by the nearby library. These policies have stood the test of time and were readily transplanted from the soil of Massachusetts to the other U.S. states and throughout much of the rest of the world. Why, then, bring these time-honored principles under scrutiny as they are increasingly in the 1980s? Perhaps the increasing claims for the future role of computers and telecommunications systems in information-related behavior and the growing fraction of the national economy devoted to information processing have generated thinking about the public library in a fundamental manner. Perhaps the conservative think tanks' questioning of all government spending is partly responsible. In any case, the number of policy studies concentrating on the public library is growing. (Dan Bergen, "Thinking about Librarianship: The Policy Approach," *Rhode Island Library Association Bulletin*, July/Aug./Sept. 1984).

Perhaps even more important as explanations for this trend are the recent developments of library services offered commercially by contract, rulings by the Office of Personnel Management concerning federal grading of librarians, and marketing possibilities for libraries to provide sophisticated information services by contract to businesses. All these developments together raise questions which librarians must monitor and carefully assess.

The first three items in the November 12 issue of *Library Hotline* indicate that uncertainties and opportunities of relevance abound. First, there is an item on the National Agricultural Library, which has a contract with a private firm, Macro Corporation, "to sort, shelve, and retrieve up to 300,000 documents per year . . . within 24 hours of receipt." The second item reveals that the National Music Publishers Association has gotten the University of Texas at Austin to agree to stop unauthorized photocopying of scores in the Music Department. The third item is potentially most revolutionary for public libraries: Denver Public Library has contracted with the United Bank of Denver to provide the Bank with computer-based information services, and the package includes 65 hours per month of a subject specialist's time. Denver Public Library officials view this as the prototype for similar arrangements with other private organizations. Since the U.S. Postal Service has become a self-supporting operation, and tax-

The Detroit Public Library staff and supporters gather in front of the Library attended by the media to thank voters for the passage of Proposition L, which increased library funding from property taxes. In the center of the photo is Paul Scupholm, Executive Director of the Friends of the Detroit PL, who was Co-Chair of the drive for the funding. He is flanked by (at right) Jane Hale Morgan, Library Director, and Jessie Kennedy, Co-Chair.

Rural Librarianship in the United States: A Renaissance

Because of the cultural and economic differences in the United States, access to information is disproportionately available to its citizenry. Unfortunately the cliche "the rich get richer and the poor get poorer" has a validity in relation to information access. Technology has the potential to mitigate real or imagined economic boundaries. At the present, however, information dissemination augments already-established resource centers, and these tend to be located in the metropolitan areas of the United States. As a consequence of this natural tendency, rural America shares unfavorably in the information pie.

Rural Growth. Ironically, the need to consider the infrastructure of information in nonmetropolitan America has never been greater. For the first time in the history of the United States, more people are moving to rural areas than metropolitan places. "Rural" is defined by the Census Bureau as a place of 2,500 or fewer individuals. During the period of 1970–80, the rural population of the United States grew by 16 percent, while metropolitan growth was charted at 10 percent.

In reality, the nonmetropolitan growth was even larger but hidden by the effect of the Standard Metropolitan Statistical Area (SMSA), which classifies the population of an entire county as urban regardless of the characteristics of the individual towns or townships it comprises. In 1980 the SMSA was changed to a Metropolitan Statistical Area (MSA), which adds the tests of population growth, density, travel to work, and other factors for defining urban places. Under the 1980 definition, 49 previously named metropolitan counties have been reclassified as rural. In addition 38 new areas have been listed as MSA's that contain a large number of rural people. In 1984, 85,000,000 people lived in 45,000 rural communities, 35 percent of which were incorporated cities. In absolute numbers, Pennsylvania's rural population, of over 3,000,000, leads all other states. While there is some suggestion that the rural migration has slowed, there is no indication of permanent population decline.

A complex number of reasons account for the rebirth of rural America. Interstate highway systems, population mobility, an expanding service economy, the availability and growth of institutions of higher education, and the movement of job opportunities into the countryside are among causal considerations. While rural America has become decidedly less agrarian since its founding, renewed interest in farming is also a mitigating factor in augmenting rural population growth. Over the last several years, for instance, there has been a 17 percent increase in the number of small farms in the United States.

Another factor must be considered in accounting for the urban exodus. Simply put, but difficult to analyze completely, Americans are looking for a "better way of life." The real and imagined values of small-town living have created an appealing social environment in which the new rural people hope to participate. Satisfying interpersonal relationships, safe places, clean air and water, the backyard garden, close proximity to recreational areas, and so on, are all part of this new rural outlook. Small-town America has also encouraged older Americans to remain in their community rather than seeking health-related services traditionally characteristic of metropolitan areas. Consequently, the countryside is presently "older" than urban places. In a real sense, we are witnessing a new melting pot at work in rural America.

In spite of decided gains, most rural areas lack the services taken for granted in cities. And no greater disparity exists between rural and urban America than in access to information services. In many ways the information needs of rural Americans are similar to those of their urban counterparts. The differences are created by the distances separating both human and physical resources in the rural countryside. Most urbanites have entree to a plethora of information resources—libraries, museums, data centers, specialized agencies of various types, all within the mass transportation radius of a city. Rural Americans must travel an average of over 50 miles to reach a city of 25,000 people to gain access to some of those information services.

Renaissance of Rural Services. This report considers the dynamics of the rural public library. They have always existed, but American librarianship finally has become more aware of them. In fact, it is quite accurate to state that the backbone of public librarianship in the United States can be discovered in nonmetropolitan areas. Beyond numerical superiority—the majority of libraries are found in small towns—other factors have helped to create a renewed interest in rural librarianship. While not an exhaustive list, the following events have been important to a renaissance of the rural library movement:

First, the publication of the Spring 1980 issue of *Library Trends* was a singularly important matter. This particular document gave a national presence to the issues facing rural librarians through a needed identification of problem areas. Previously, one could discover more currently being written about rural librarianship by librarians overseas than by individuals in the United States.

Second, the continuing effort of the U.S. National Commission on Libraries and Information Science to provide for the information needs of rural Americans is also of special significance. The Joint Congressional Hearing sponsored by NCLIS at the meeting of the World Future Society in 1982, and more recently the formation of the National Advisory Board on Rural Information Needs (NABRIN), have helped to focus national attention on information access in rural America.

Third, the efforts of individuals associated with state library associations, particularly those involved in services for small and medium-sized libraries, have created a flurry of meetings aimed at identifying both local and national commonalities. State programs have also attempted to overcome the librarian's sense of geographical isolation, which is a major concern. Among the states recently holding such conferences are Indiana, Kentucky, North Dakota, Michigan, and Texas.

Fourth, added to the above must be the mediations of the consultants at state library agencies who have consistently and quietly provided support to rural staff people at the local level.

Fifth, local librarians, themselves, have also contributed greatly to the renaissance of the rural library movement because they have endured at the delivery end of the rural information chain, frequently out of the limelight and perspective of the national library press.

Sixth, while the organizational structure of ALA has been somewhat slow in recognizing the uniqueness of rural libraries, the Public Library Association has contributed to the rural library movement through the formation of the Committee on Rural Library Services. This group provides another needed forum through which individuals may present their views.

Finally, at least for this tabulation, the author, in modesty, would like to add the establishment at Clarion State College (Pennsylvania) of the Center for the Study of Rural Librarianship in 1978 as another element in this rural kaleidoscope. Others will have to comment on whether or not the CSRL has realized its goals and objectives. But one would like to believe that the publication of *Rural Libraries* has had some measured impact on the ability of librarians to communicate with each other.

Though events augur well for the future of rural library services, the problems that exist temper optimism. On paper they appear insurmountable.

Challenges. Only 25 percent of the full-time rural staff members are certified as professional librarians at the Master's level. An additional 25 percent are degreed through undergraduate programs with specialization in Library Science. "Full-time" is emphasized, because with limited personnel available each person is expected to perform a little of everything. The national average for the number of staff members in communities of 2,500 or fewer people is three. The one-person library manager is more than just an idea in the rural library.

The issue of upgrading educational skills in rural America has not gone unnoticed by state agencies or schools of Library and Information Science. They offer a wide variety of programming in an effort to meet training needs. The problem, however, is to coordinate the disparate needs of staff members within any geographical area. For example, research has shown that rural personnel who have completed their certification are interested in continuing education activities because of the topics offered.

Noncertified librarians, who are also interested in the subjects being conducted, additionally seek academic credit. There is also another concern that is symptomatic of the rural environment in relation to training activities. Those wishing to participate in any type of conference or workshop are often precluded not only because of the geographical distances, but also because no one is available to keep the library open while the librarian is away.

In spite of the adversities and disadvantages—the national average salary for rural librarians is $14,500—the number of individuals choosing rural service as a professional area is apparently increasing. This influence is based not only on the number of students who have been graduated from Clarion and opt for rural positions but also on discussions with colleagues. At the same time, a curious aspect is developing. Some "new" recruits who have had no previous experience with small town life find rural living not genial and ultimately leave their jobs. This does not appear to be a major problem, but something that should be watched. Perhaps it should have been stressed earlier that not all rural communities are as idyllic as their perceived images sometimes suggest—ask my teenage son.

Proposals to Improve Service. American librarianship, including the educational community, must act decisively to mitigate the certification shortcomings presently inherent in the countryside. Because of the locations of schools of Library and Information Science across the United States, commuting to centers of learning is not feasible for most rural staff people. Where it is impossible for an institution to bring its program to an area, other schemes must be considered such as a combination of interactive video, cable television, and correspondence activities. While the description of a "mail-order librarian" may be anathema to the sensibilities of the academically trained professional, the realities must be faced.

Geographical remoteness is a major concern not only for staff. It is also a problem for library patrons, some of whom must travel an average of 14 miles for information services. And, as previously mentioned, 50 miles separate the average library community from a city of 25,000 or more people. Isolation, of course, is a relative matter. But in an information providing sense, it means that there are virtually no other libraries, except those in public schools, to support the local rural librarian. While the concept and reality of interlibrary cooperation provide a lifeline of resources, immediacy is sometimes lacking. Further, though state library agencies deserve praise for their outreach services, there are simply not enough consultants to provide the regular support needed for so many. Microprocessing would appear to be a likely vehicle for alleviating the numbing effects of geographical remoteness. And, interestingly, the number of rural libraries having microcomputers has doubled to 20 percent over the last two years.

ALA can help to reduce the psychological and geographical barriers inherent in the countryside by continuing to identify rural librarians as a constituency that has gotten less than its fair share of attention. In addition, perhaps the membership's dues structure could be made more sympathetic for the librarian who receives an annual salary of only $9,000.

The final issue for consideration here is the lack of informational resources. Consistently, librarians indicate that the most difficult problem in providing reference services is the unavailability of special resources. Interpreting "special" takes on more meaning when one is aware that the average rural library holds only 25,000 books, and only 10 percent of U.S. rural libraries provide online services.

Are there corrective measures for the resource problem? Yes, improve the reference skills of those currently in need so that existing resources may be used to the fullest extent; provide computer training so that online information access will be a viable option; and, send more money. The annual budget for the typical rural library is $42,000.

A fitting end to this report was recently offered by a colleague from Massachusetts who in a letter said, "Providing library services to rural towns should be a national priority." Agreed. It should also be a major goal for American librarianship.

BERNARD VAVREK

---

payer revolts have led to diminished library staffs and collections, at least temporarily, directors seeing a potential and a need are tempted by new mixes of public and private revenues, including fees for entry to the library building, annual charges for library cards, special recreational library service to condominium residents, and other services.

Countability and Accountability. As a result of a study directed by Mary Jo Lynch, Director of the ALA Office for Research, for the National Center for Education Statistics, the state and federal public library census efforts in the U.S. may be very substantially altered in the future. If the study recommendations are accepted, the new directions will include standardized definitions based on those of the American National Standards Institute (ANSI), coordinated procedures at the state and federal levels, and a core of categories collected for public, academic, and, to a lesser degree, school libraries. Also recommended by Lynch and an Advisory Committee for the "Analysis of Library Data Collection" project is the inclusion periodically of ad hoc surveys in order to monitor important trends in the way automation is influencing library service, the speed in growth of videocassette circulation, and fee-based services, for instance. COSLA adopted a resolution at its fall meeting to endorse the Lynch recommendation to gather core data in each state and forward them to the NCES. After they are processed at NCES it is recommended that the results be forwarded to the library press for prompt reporting of current statistics.

The need for accountability is a major reason for cost analysis studies in public libraries. In 1982 the Public Library Association established a Cost Analysis Task Force to review public library costs.

Public Library Association

This task force is overseeing development of a simple cost-finding manual by Phillip Rosenberg, author of *Costing and Pricing Municipal Services.* Accountability was also a reason for the development of output measures, and the 1984 ALA Annual Conference was the scene of the first attempt to analyze output measurement nationally.

Both of these attempts at greater accountability are seen to be leading toward the possibility of new standards for public library service in the U.S. A New Standards Task Force created in 1983 focused on four components of public library development: planning, role setting, output measurement, and national data collection ("Report from the New Standards Task Force," *Public Libraries,* Spring 1984). Eighteen public library systems representing 14 states formed a Coalition for Public Library Research and contracted with the Library Research Center at the University of Illinois Graduate School of Library and Information Science to study how library materials are used in six systems in the coalition.

Awards. Cecil P. Beach, Director of the Broward County Division of Libraries of Fort Lauderdale, Florida, was the 1984 recipient of the Allie Beth Martin Award. The award is given annually to a public librarian who has demonstrated an extraordinary range and depth of knowledge about books and other library materials and exhibits a distinct ability to share it. The award carries with it a $2,000 stipend provided by Baker & Taylor Company.

The outstanding military librarian in 1984 was Marjorie Rambo, TAC Command Library at Langley Air Force Base, Virginia.

Two awards were to be offered for the first time in 1985: the Advancement of Literacy Award and the Leonard Wertheimer Multilingual Award. The literacy award will go to an American publisher or bookseller who makes a significant contribution to the advancement of literacy. The multilingual award will be given to a person, group, or organization.

Kieth C. Wright, Department of Library Science/Educational Technology, University of North Carolina at Greensboro, was awarded the 1984 Frederick A. Thorpe Traveling Fellowship worth £2000. Wright will use the fellowship to develop a course of instruction on "serving the unserved" (the disabled, the institutionalized, the newly literate, and the poor) in the West Indies. The biennial award fosters research and development in library service.

Conclusion. 1984 was a generally good year for public libraries: more use, more support, reauthorization of LSCA, the chief federal legislation for public libraries, and solid gains for the improved evaluation of public library performance at the local, state, and federal levels. It was a year of dedication to reducing illiteracy in the adult population, It was a time of cooperation with other constructive organizations with compatible goals. Coalitions were advanced and solid achievements of public librarians were noted to a high degree. Major gifts to public libraries and fees for extraordinary levels of information service by public libraries seemed more prominent than in the past. Best of all, America was reading *1984,* not living it.

KENNETH D. SHEARER

Public Library Association

Strengthening the Association. As a result of the 1983 national conference of PLA and the increase in interest of many librarians in various PLA activities, it became obvious that staff additions would be necessary to meet the demands of the members. In addition, the work of the Task Forces appointed by the two previous Presidents, Donald Sager and Nancy Bolt, was placing increasing pressure on PLA staff. As a result, the Board of Directors authorized the creation of additional positions, the most important of which was a Program Officer. The appointment of Vee Friesner to fill that post allowed the consolidation of many of the educational facets of PLA into one office and more efficient and effective planning and organization of such activities as national conferences and programs at ALA Conference.

One of the most significant actions of 1984 was the appointment of a new Planning Committee with the specific charge from the Board of Directors to undertake a long- and short-range planning process for PLA. One of the most important products foreseen is a list of PLA priorities, both for action and for funding, that will guide the association and the PLA staff on a yearly basis.

Planning was initiated for the second national conference with the appointment of a National Conference Committee headed by Pat Woodrum of the Tulsa City–County Library. St. Louis was selected as the site for the April 1986 event.

Task Forces. The New Standards Task Force held a number of special working sessions and public hearings in 1984 leading to the completion of a proposal for a Public Library Development Program, designed to assist library boards and directors to identify appropriate service roles and engage in planning and measurement. Also envisaged in their proposal was a customized public library database to be housed at PLA headquarters to aid public library planning efforts with statistics and other information. At year's end, the NSTF proposal had not yet been funded, although a principal investigation had been chosen and detailed plans for the development of manuals on roles, planning and measurement had been made. President Charles Robinson had made a presentation to the State Librarians of the various states regarding the Public Library Development Program, inviting their participation. Their role in the process was seen as vital.

Grants, Publications, Awards. PLA and the Association of College and Research Libraries in 1984 held the first two of six two-day workshops on the development of techniques of successful programming for the humanities. Emphasized in these workshops, the final four to be held in 1985, were the opportunities inherent in cooperative programming between public and academic libraries. The workshops are being conducted under a grant from the National Endowment for the Humanities.

PLA publications distributed both by ALA Publishing and by PLA during 1984 included *Mobile Ideas,* on bookmobile services, and *Traditional and Non-Traditional Delivery Systems for Remote Areas.*

> **PUBLIC LIBRARY ASSOCIATION**
>
> PRESIDENT (June 1984–July 1985):
> **Charles Robinson,** Baltimore County Public Library, Towson, Maryland
>
> VICE-PRESIDENT/PRESIDENT-ELECT:
> **Patrick O'Brien,** Dallas Public Library, Texas
>
> EXECUTIVE DIRECTOR:
> **Shirley Mills-Fischer**
>
> Membership (August 31, 1984): 5,571 (4,825 personal; and 746 organizational)
> Expenditures (August 31, 1984): $156,793

During 1984 the United States Department of Education published its companion piece to the school-related *Nation at Risk* entitled *Alliance for Excellence.* This publication on the importance of libraries in the education process was developed partially with the cooperation of PLA in the seminars and papers leading to the publication.

The 1984 Allie Beth Martin Award was presented by PLA to Cecil P. Beach, Director of the Broward County Division of Libraries in Fort Lauderdale, Florida. The Award Committee said, "Cecil P. Beach's entire career has been aimed at bringing books to people. Ever since his first job as extension/outreach librarian, he has been firmly committed to the strong belief that books and other information sources are extremely important to all."

The Armed Forces Library Section gave its Achievement Citation Award to Marjorie Rambo, Librarian at Langley (Virginia) Air Force Base, for her significant contributions to Armed Forces library services.

CHARLES W. ROBINSON

Public Relations

The past decade has witnessed a remarkable transformation of library public relations. The evolution and maturation of this area of interest, once believed by most to be on the periphery of librarianship, can be attributed to two key factors. First, in a competitive environment where library budgets have proven to be surprisingly vulnerable, library administrators have become more responsive to the notion of promoting their services. Second, public relations practitioners in the library world have concretely demonstrated the value of their skills to their professional colleagues. Currently, public relations techniques are becoming more widely recognized as essential ingredients in successful library management.

Librarianship clearly reflected this long-term trend of increased acceptance for public relations during 1984. The events of the year also revealed a profession mastering greater sophistication in promoting its valuable services. The Annual Conference in Dallas featuring the third annual series of poster sessions, a President's Program on fund-raising, and several major conference programs devoted to developing public relations skills confirmed the existence of a high level of interest for this subject. Throughout 1984 ALA's Public Information Office continued to produce outstanding promotional products and to seize every opportunity to generate national visibility for libraries. The Public Relations Section of LAMA, chaired by Sally Brickman, also maintained its role as a vital center of activity and growth during 1984.

Academic librarianship provided the most dramatic public relations developments in 1984. Only recently has a large segment of academic librarians arrived at a significant level of appreciation and understanding of the importance of public relations. Although they have previously lagged behind other types of librarians in PR awareness, in 1984 academic librarians proved to be good students of the techniques pioneered by their public, special, and school librarian colleagues. Effort by academic librarians in adapting public relations to their particular environments appears to be one of the noteworthy trends of 1984.

At the ACRL's third national conference, for example, Barbara Pinzelik presented a paper on the contrasting image of libraries held by users and librarians. The ACRL Discussion Group on Public Relations in Academic Libraries (PRIAL) enjoyed a busy and productive year under the leadership of its Chairperson Patricia Kelley. At the Midwinter Meeting PRIAL held a discussion on the appropriate image for academic libraries. PRIAL next tackled the public relations aspects of introducing an online card catalog during the Annual Conference in Dallas. During 1984 the journal literature in academic librarianship reflected a heightened awareness of the need to promote libraries. The *Journal of Academic Librarianship* (vol. 10, no. 2) ran a major article by David W. Lewis on the adaptation of marketing techniques to academic libraries. *College and Research Libraries News* (vol. 45, nos. 3, 5, 7) published two cover story articles and two other major articles concerning library promotion. It was clear to observers by the end of 1984 that, generally speaking, academic librarians were rapidly catching up to their colleagues from other types of libraries in developing their own public relations techniques.

ALA Public Information Office. The ALA PIO pursues two fundamental goals: first, to present an accurate, positive image of librarianship to the American public; second, to assist libraries in the successful promotion of their services. To achieve these ends the PIO has engaged in a variety of activities including the placement of advertisements in the mass media, publishing two weekly syndicated newspaper columns, and the production of posters and other library paraphernalia for use in local public relations efforts.

In 1984 the PIO engaged in a number of special projects to further promote librarianship including the production of a ten-minute slide-tape program, *Always in Season,* that celebrates the services of public libraries. The program was developed to assist public librarians with their speaking engagements by providing their audiences with an inspirational view of libraries. The program is designed so it can be easily adapted to specific public libraries and is available in videotape.

With help from a grant made by Public Broadcasting Station WNET, PIO produced and distributed library promotional materials for the

Strange headgear replaced football helmets for members of the Green Bay Packers who dramatized bedtime stories for children at the Packer Hall of Fame. More than 400 children and parents attended the event sponsored by the Brown County (Wisconsin) Library. (Green Bay News Chronicle/Photo by H. Marc Larson.)

The New York Public Library's 1984 Censorship Exhibition included nearly 300 items examining historical and contemporary censorship issues.

PBS series Heritage: Civilization and the Jews. In anticipation of what was termed "the most ambitious documentary series in public broadcasting history," PIO used grant monies to develop bibliographies and program suggestions (discussion groups, displays, etc.) for inclusion in promotional packages to be sent to over 6,000 libraries. The PIO continued during 1984 to assist public libraries in anticipating patron requests generated by the second season of the immensely popular PBS series "Reading Rainbow."

Other PIO activities included the introduction of promotional materials for libraries, the joint sponsorship of Banned Books Week in September, plus coordination of an international competition for posters that promote libraries, books, and reading to be exhibited at a 1985 International Federation of Library Associations (IFLA) preconference in Illinois.

The most important personnel news in 1984 was the promotion of Director Peggy Barber to the new post of Associate Executive Director. For a decade Barber provided the PIO with energetic, innovative, and enthusiastic leadership. Barber's post as head of PIO was filled by Linda K. Wallace, former Community Relations Coordinator for the Mideastern Michigan Library Cooperative.

Public Relations Section. The Public Relations Section held 49 percent of the total LAMA personal membership during 1984. This active Section furnishes a forum for all types of librarians interested in public relations to share their ideas and develop their skills.

Early in 1984 PRS released news of its latest book Persuasive Public Relations for Libraries (ALA, 1983). The book contained 23 essays on various aspects of library promotion. It represented the culmination of an effort over the course of several years to disseminate current public relations theory and techniques to the profession. Meanwhile, the PRS Publications Committee initiated a regular column in the *LAMA Newsletter* in which guest authors offered advice on solving perennial public relations problems.

PRS sponsored its traditional "Swap 'n' Shop" program in 1984 at the ALA Annual Conference in Dallas. This program gave librarians the opportunity to obtain samples of promotional materials from different libraries. Items judged to be the "Best of the Show" were featured in a central display area. Judges from the John Cotton Dana Award contest were available to discuss with interested visitors the merits of the JCD 1984 Award and Special Award contest entries. Swap 'n' Shop featured a series of miniworkshops on improving PR techniques, an innovative departure from past programs that proved highly successful. The workshops included sessions on formulating a PR plan, communicating the library's message through newsletters, dealing with the mass media, and the evaluation of PR programs.

PRS also cosponsored four other major programs in Dallas. Its timely program "Getting It Passed: How to Use Successful Public Relations Methods with Your State Legislature" featured a panel of speakers that included a professional lobbyist, a state senator from Texas, and three librarians with extensive experience in legislative lobbying. In conjunction with ALA's Young Adult Services Division, PRS cosponsored "Who Speaks Up for Youth: Intellectual Freedom, Public Relations and the Library," a program that explained the use of public relations methods in educating the public about intellectual freedom.

PRS and LAMA's Fund Raising and Financial Development Section jointly sponsored a program on using special events to increase library revenues. Some of the illustrations cited gourmet dinners, fashion shows, and library gift shops as means to raise funds for libraries. PRS also cosponsored a program in Dallas with the Library Instruction Round Table on producing inexpensive, but effective, audiovisual materials for library instruction.

JCD Contest. The John Cotton Dana Library Public Relations Award contest recognizes libraries that have exhibited excellence in their promotional activities during the past year. The H. W. Wilson Company and PRS have jointly sponsored the contest since 1946. In 1984 a panel of 10 contest judges reviewed 144 entries to select six JCD Award Winners and 16 recipients of Special Awards. A statistical breakdown by type of library of the awards granted is shown in the accompanying table.

JCD Award Winners for 1984 were Dauphin County Library System (Harrisburg, Pennsylvania); Houston Public Library; Lutheran Church Library Association (Minneapolis); Nellis Air Force Base (Nevada); Plaza Junior High School Library (Virginia Beach); and University of Texas Health Science Center (San Antonio).

Special Award recipients were the Bobst Library at New York University; Campbell County Public Library (Gillette, Wyoming); Clark County Library District (Las Vegas, Nevada); Council for Florida Libraries (Tallahassee); D. C. Everest High School Library (Schofield, Wisconsin); Eufaula Memorial Library (Oklahoma); Hurst Public Library (Texas); Kentucky Department for Libraries and Archives; Mann Library at Cornell University; Keesler Air Force Base (Michigan); McIntre Public Library (Zanesville, Ohio); Oklahoma Department of Libraries; Sheridan County Fulmer Library (Wyoming); St. Louis County Library (Missouri); Tucson Public Library; and Ventura County Library (California).

JCD judges have reported experiencing greater difficulty in selecting winners because of the trend of higher levels of sophistication of PR techniques reflected in typical entries. The panel of judges in 1984 noted this same trend and winning entries demonstrated that imagination and resourcefulness alone constitute the essential ingredients of a successful PR program. Although some noteworthy entries described programs

Left, ALA's Public Information Office and the Sociedad de Bibliotecarios de Puerto Rico cooperated to produce the popular Snoopy READ posters in Spanish. Above, ever popular Superman poster produced by the ALA.

Contestant mimicking the moves of rock star Michael Jackson in a Jackson look-alike contest sponsored by the Louisville Free Public Library.

costing thousands of dollars, most winning entries revealed surprisingly small budgets for their outstanding programs. One exemplary entry that received a Special Award cost only $180 to implement.

The judges and their types of libraries were Marg Chartrand, Chair (public); Bev Bagan (school); Dale Carrison (academic); Ann Eastman (academic); Jon Eldredge (academic); Jack Frantz (public); Corrine Frisch (public); Darrel Hildebrant (public); Jan Olsen (PR consultant); and Sam Simon (public).

Following the week-long judging session three JCD judges and LAMA Executive Director Roger Parent remained in New York to compile a book based upon good PR ideas found in various entries. Entitled *Great Library Promotion Ideas 1984* (ALA), this work identifies valuable ideas that librarians will find useful even if the entries from which they were taken did not win awards. In selecting items for inclusion in the book, the editors sought to find examples of programs that seemed "fresh or especially effective, or in which a discrete idea seemed noteworthy."

Public Awareness. Ten years ago ALA assumed sponsorship of National Library Week (NLW) from the National Book Committee. During its 27th annual observance in 1984, NLW celebrated the theme "Knowledge Is *Real* Power." In 1984 former ALA President Elizabeth Stone's NLW committee secured the cooperation of 46 national organizations including the AFL–CIO, the American Association for the Advancement of Science, and the International Association of Lion's Clubs to promote NLW in a new partnership program. Every year the ALA Public Information Office publishes and distributes about 15,000 copies of a publicity book to assist local library promotional efforts. Sandra Lieb of PIO in 1984 coordinated the annual publication of a 115-page work, *Power Tools Publicity Book 1984*, as a service to libraries around the nation participating in NLW.

Libraries captured the attention of national television audiences on several occasions during 1984. At the 1984 Tournament of Roses Parade an ALA affiliate, Friends of Libraries USA (FOLUSA), won a special award for its floral swan float that consisted of 7,000 square feet of blossoms. CBS's *60 Minutes* produced a show on a Falmouth Public Library (Massachusetts) patron who uses its law collection to argue cases successfully in state and federal courts.

Libraries were honored for the third time in two years with the issuance by the U.S. Postal Service of a commemorative stamp "A Nation of Readers." The National Archives also was celebrated during 1984 in a commemorative stamp.

A record-breaking number of library supporters participated in the ALA Washington Office's 10th Annual Legislative Day. More than 350 advocates for libraries devoted the day to reminding Congress of the importance of continued federal funding for libraries. Representative Major Owens (D–NY), a former librarian, plus 26 of his House colleagues gave inspiring floor speeches during a one-hour program celebrating libraries. Later in 1984, Congress extended and expanded the Library Services and Construction Act through fiscal year 1989.

The Government Printing Office embarked on an ambitious promotional campaign in 1984 with materials generated by its own marketing staff. GPO targeted 60,000 libraries for distribution of information (including publicity brochures and bookmarks) about the selective and regional depository programs. At the same time, the GPO heightened public awareness about government documents through messages carried by the mass media.

JON ELDREDGE

Publishing, Book

U.S. book publishers enjoyed continued growth in dollar and unit sales in most categories reported in 1984. They went on the attack against pirates outside the country and censors within. Three new studies—on reading, on the future of the book, and on electronics in manuscript preparation and processing—sparked wide interest during the year.

Statistics. In the first nine months of 1984, U.S. book publishers' net sales ($6,876,600,000) showed an increase of 6.5 percent over the comparable period in 1983 but only a half percent improvement in unit sales. "General retail sales, while displaying a respectable increase over 1983, did not maintain the vigorous pace" of the first half of 1983, John P. Dessauer reported in *Publishers Weekly*. Library and institutional purchases at $647,700,000 for the nine-month period held firm with an 8.8 percent increase in dollars and 2.7 percent increase in units bought. Schools accounted for a healthy 12 percent increase in dollars spent and a 7 percent unit increase.

For the full year 1983, U.S. book sales totaled almost $8,600,000,000, an increase of 9.5 percent over 1982, according to the Association of American Publishers (AAP) in 1984. Trade book sales were up 17 percent, and religious, professional, reference, and other categories showed good gains. Only losing categories were mail order publications (down 8.3 percent) and AV and other media (down 3.4 percent). Generally speaking, the favorable publishing picture reflected growth and real economic gains in the U.S. economy.

U.S. book publishers issued more than 53,000 new titles and editions in 1983, an increase of 13.7 percent over 1982, according to tallies made from various sources by R. R. Bowker in September 1984. The average price of a hardcover book was $31.19 compared with $30.14 in 1982. For

JCD Contest Awards 1984*		
Type of Library	JCD Awards	Special Awards
Academic	–	2
Consortia**	1	1
Military	1	1
Public	2	9
School	1	1
Special	1	–
State	–	2
Total	6	16

*Contest entries involved PR activities for calendar year 1983, or the 1982–1983 academic year.
**Includes library associations.

trade paperbacks, the average price was $11.79, a *decrease* from $12.32 in 1982.

Exports of U.S. books ($607,122,207) in 1983, according to the U.S. Department of Commerce, dropped by 5.3 percent compared with 1982 sales; imports ($365,828,034) increased by 16.1 percent.

Book Industry Trends 1984 of the Book Industry Study Group (BISG) estimated that "publishers' sales, which showed an average growth rate from 1979 to 1983 of 9.7% in dollars and 3.7% in units," would "post an average increase from 1983 to 1988 of 12.2.% in dollars and 6.4% in units." Trade books were expected to be strongest, subscription reference books weakest. Acquisitions by U.S. libraries (2.9 percent annual increase, 1979–83), according to *Trends*, "will post a growth rate of 9% between 1983 and 1988." Special libraries were expected to show fastest growth (10.5 percent), school libraries the slowest (2.3 percent).

BISG Reading Study. Commissioned by the Book Industry Study Group, the *1983 Consumer Research Study on Reading and Book Purchasing* updated a similar survey done in 1978. Findings were in large part reassuring to book lovers: The percentage of adult book readers in 1983 held at 56 percent (55 percent in 1978). The proportion of "heavy" readers increased (35 percent compared with 18 percent in 1978). The report also found that 8,000,000 new readers were in the 21–60 age group. Twenty-one percent of all books read were borrowed. Some less optimistic findings were: Book reading declines as people age—only 39% or those surveyed over age 60 are book readers. Book readers in the group under age 21 dropped from 75 percent in 1978 to 63 percent in 1983. The average American may read books, newspapers, or magazines 11.7 hours a week but he or she spends 16.3 hours watching television. The study was generally optimistic—"books are thriving."

Boorstin Report. In a report to Congress on the future of the book, Daniel J. Boorstin, Librarian of Congress, demolishes the American "habit of writing premature obituaries." He presents a lively account of the activity of reading and makes recommendations to the Congress, Executive Branch, and Library of Congress on ways to keep books thriving. His aim? No less than abolishing illiteracy in the United States by 1989 (See Special Report: Books in Our Future).

Book Biz. The big grew bigger in 1984. Gulf & Western (parent company of Simon and Schuster) acquired Esquire, Inc., in early 1984 and at year's end completed purchase of Prentice-Hall (annual sales of $448,200,000). The acquisition made the G&W giant the biggest in U.S. publishing. McGraw-Hill became number two.

Random House bought New York Times Books (about 50 titles a year). The Scribner Book Companies came under the corporate aegis of Macmillan in April 1984, and Macmillan also acquired Harper & Row's School Division for a reported $25,000,000. Harper & Row in turn bought Gower Medical Publications from Addison-Wesley.

Waldenbooks, the largest bookstore chain, became part of K-Mart. Encyclopaedia Britannica, Inc., renewed an agreement with Waldenbooks to use its stores for sales promotions. (Most EB sales were still made in home presentations by commission salesmen.) Mattel agreed to sell Western Publishing, which includes Golden Books, to a management group of the firm, and Funk and Wagnalls was sold to a group of its executives by Dun and Bradstreet.

Seabury Press was dissolved. Harper & Row discontinued its electronic publishing division. Time-Life Books, reflecting a trend toward leaner permanent staffs, said it would rely more frequently on book packagers (editorial and production freelancers who deliver completed projects to publishers).

McGraw-Hill reorganized itself into 11 "market-oriented" units—financial services, economic information, education, energy, and others—moving away from "media" as its principle of organization. *Telling Right from Wrong* is a book Random House had accepted but later decided not to publish after learning that its author had faked a letter of endorsement from a Harvard professor of philosophy. The author agreed to return his $10,000 advance.

The U.S. Postal Service revised its rule about the minimum length to qualify a book for the fourth-class "book rate." Formerly 24 pages, it is now only 8, which makes many more children's books eligible. Paul Carlin, a career employee, was named the new Postmaster General in November. (For postage rate changes and legislation affecting books and library acquisitions, see Washington Report.)

A commemorative stamp issued on October 16 pays tribute to "A Nation of Readers." It is based on a daguerreotype of Abraham Lincoln and his son Tad.

AAP. 1984 was a stormy year for the Association of American Publishers (AAP). A survey early in 1984 revealed that about a third of the larger member companies (who pay the most dues) were not satisfied with the benefits they received; more than 80 percent of the smaller companies were. Debate was heavy at Board and membership meetings over reorganization, programs, and budgets. Finally, at a special meeting in December, AAP voted to reduce the Board from 29 to 16 members, eliminating seats for division chairmen among others. Across-the-board budget cuts were approved instead of radical surgery on its divisions, which conduct many programs of special interest to smaller publishers. Dropped were the in-house reference library (moved to CUNY Graduate Center) and the Education for Publishing program.

Electronic Publishing. Though many publishers still counted only small returns from electronic ventures, few wished to be left behind a "quantum leap that will drastically alter the creation, organization, and transfer of knowledge" (*Publishers Weekly*).

Aspen Systems delivered a report for the AAP Electronic Manuscript Project's study (AAP, Washington, $75). One finding was the need for industry-wide standards. Another showed a lag between author and publisher readiness to embrace the new technology. Whereas 80 percent of the authors surveyed fully expected to prepare manuscripts electronically by 1985, only half of the publishers had answered that they expected

Posters prepared by the ALA Public Information Office for National Library Week 1985 feature prominent Americans promoting libraries.

authors to do so—and even fewer were prepared to handle the electronic input. In June AAP began an electronic bulletin board that grew out of an informal communications system devised for participants in the Electronic Manuscript Project.

Baker & Taylor conducted a survey (1983) that indicated that more than 20 percent of public and academic libraries had collections of computer software for use by patrons (1,500 academic libraries and 2,900 public libraries were surveyed; annual acquisitions budgets totaled $10,000 or more).

The *Oxford English Dictionary* reported that it was being computerized at the cost of some $10,000,000. Merriam-Webster announced an electronic thesaurus of the English language; the company had previously marketed an electronic dictionary of American English and online dictionaries in law and medicine. Computer use is a topic in *Dictionaries: The Art and Craft of Lexicography* (1984) by Sidney I. Landau. In a burst of enthusiasm unusual in the staid pages of *Reference Books Bulletin*, the journal lauds Landau's superior style and recommends the treatise to "all would-be and practicing reference librarians, English teachers, writers, editors, and reviewers."

Doubleday formed a new computer books imprint—Quantum Press, featuring books by Peter McWilliams, popular computer and word-processing maven. McGraw-Hill said early in 1984 that it planned to issue more than a 100 software titles during the year.

Copyright. *Pirates.* In January 1984 AAP organized the International Copyright Protection Group to zap "international book pirates." Among targets were operators in Taiwan and in Singapore. The AAP Group and the British Publishers Association cooperated in an effort that led to customs officials' raids on 27 shops and copying mills in Hong Kong.

CCC. Publishers hailed the General Electric Company's agreement with the Copyright Clearance Center. A blanket license to photocopy under the Center's "Annual Authorization Service," it was considered the first significant agreement of its kind. Warner-Lambert Company also signed a similar agreement for a year. "Annual use" is projected based on samples. Previous agreements proved awkward to administer, and the Center had struggled from its inception in the late 1970s to develop a workable system.

David P. Waite, President of the Center from its beginning, died August 10, at the age of 58.

First Amendment. The Second Judicial Circuit Court of South Dakota ruled against the Governor of the State, who had argued that he had been libeled by a *report* of accusations made against him by an opponent and published in a Viking book, *In the Spirit of Crazy Horse*, by Peter Matthiesen.

The third Banned Books Week was September 8–15. ALA prepared kits that included lists of challenged books, posters, and other materials. They were distributed by AAP's Washington Office. Other sponsors included the American Booksellers Association and the American Society of Journalists and Authors.

At the New York Public Library, an exhibit on "Censorship: 500 Years of Conflict" opened June 1 as part of the ceremonies celebrating the reopening of the 6,400-square-foot Gottesman Exhibition Hall.

"Four more years of Ronald Reagan is indeed a withering prospect for those of us interested in freedom of information issues," said Nancy Manaham, National Editor of *USA Today,* speaking to Sigma Delta Chi, the Society of Professional Journalists, on November 15, 1984. The Reagan administration announced, only a few days before congressional hearings were to begin, that its controversial Presidential Directive of 1983 on lifetime prepublication review for federal employees would be shelved at least until January 1985. But disquieting news soon followed. The General Accounting Office (GAO) disclosed that in fact federal agencies were increasing prepublication censorship. Reviews are done under agreements signed by employees using a 1981 form that binds them to lifetime review as a condition of access to "sensitive compartmented information" (*Federal Times*). In 1983 over 200 government employees worked full-time doing such reviews. About 28,000 items were subjected to clearance in 1983. Representative Jack Brooks (D.-Texas) sponsored a bill to restrict polygraph testing and censorship in the federal government. GAO concluded that over 3,000,000 employees and federal contractors could be subjected to polygraph tests, censorship, or both, under administration policies.

Best-Sellers. On the *New York Times* hardcover nonfiction list *Iacocca* was first at year's end. Leo Buscaglia (*Loving Each Other*), Erma Bombeck (*Motherhood: The Second Oldest Profession*), and Andy Rooney (*Pieces of My Mind*) continued to attract large audiences. An autobiographical work that won both critical acclaim and a place on the best-seller list was *One Writer's Beginnings* by Eudora Welty. Also represented in nonfiction were Edward I. Koch (*Mayor*), Barbara W. Tuchman (*The March of Folly*), and Studs Terkel (*"The Good War"*).

Hardcover fiction was led by Robert Ludlum (*The Aquitaine Progression*) followed by *The Talisman* by Stephen King and Peter Straub. Helen Hooven Santmyer's "*. . . And Ladies of the Club*" attracted wide attention. Interest in fictionalized biography was served by Gore Vidal's *Lincoln*. A fiction paperback, *The Name of the Rose*, an elaborate tale that revolved around the mysteries of a monastery library, held its own, appearing near *Nineteen Eighty-Four* on the *New York Times* list.

Megatrends by John Naisbitt headed the nonfiction paperback list. *Webster's Ninth New Collegiate Dictionary*, which introduces dated citations and astute usage notes, shared honors with *Eat to Win* by Robert Haas and *Nothing Down*, among others, on the *New York Times*'s catch-all "miscellaneous" list. (See also Bookselling.)

People. Does publishing need to join baseball, football, and other sports and activities with its own "Hall of Fame"? *Folio* magazine's idea may or may not catch on, but it established a Publishing Hall of Fame in New York in November 1984. Initial inductees from book publishing (the new Hall also recognizes magazine stars) were: Ian and Betty Ballantine of Ballantine and Bantam Books, Cass Canfield, Sr., of Harper & Row, Harold McGraw, August Frugé, Director Emeritus of the University of California Press, and Daniel Melcher.

Bonnie Ammer, former Director of Subsidiary Rights, was named Publisher and General Manager of Bobbs-Merrill Co. (a unit of ITT Publishing).

Frances Gendlin, Editor of *Sierra* magazine and Director of Public Affairs for the Sierra Club, became Executive Director of the Association of University Presses in February.

David Ladd, Register of Copyrights from June 1980, resigned effective January 1, 1985, to enter private law practice. On January 25 Public Printer Danford L. Sawyer announced his resignation. He was a controversial administrator whose proposals to close a number of government bookstores were widely criticized.

Lisa Bayard became President of the College Unit of CBS Educational and Professional Publishing.

Howard Kaminsky, President and Chief Operations Officer at Warner Books, became Publisher and CEO of Random House's trade department in August. At Warner, Laurence Kirshbaum was appointed President (formerly Publisher and CEO).

Deaths. Alfred A. Knopf died August 11. In 1915 he founded the firm that still carries his name. It was independent until 1966, when it was sold to Random House.

Ellen Knowles Harcourt, first children's book editor for Harcourt-Brace & Co., died in New Milford, Connecticut, at 94. Married to Alfred Harcourt, she created the awards named after her and her husband and given annually for biography and memoirs by Columbia University.

Sir Basil Blackwell, British publisher and bookseller, died April 9 in Oxford, England. He headed a publishing conglomerate that included, in the U.S., Blackwell North America and Basil Blackwell, Inc., founded in New York in 1984.

Meetings. The Frankfurt Book Fair, October 3–8, drew more than 6,000 publishers and 70,000 trade visitors and displayed some 300,000 titles. The German Book Trade Peace Prize went to Octavio Paz of Mexico.

The tenth annual New York Book Fair on Labor Day weekend put on view hundreds of small

Publishing, Book

Racine (Wisconsin) Public Library's Adult Services Head Nancy Elsmo posing with books banned at various times during the library's Banned Books Week. (Journal Times Photo by Mark Hertzberg)

Scholarly Publishing

State of the Art. Amid the proliferation of satellite communications dishes and swelling streams of electrons used for the creation, storage, and retrieval of information, traditional bookish ways persisted during 1984.

Example: With justifiable pride, the Museum at the University of Pennsylvania published the first of some 17 volumes of the only dictionary of Sumerian, the world's first written language. The 750-copy edition is expected to be published over the next few decades.

Example: Congress voted to spend $11,500,000 to build a book preservation facility to help the Library of Congress to deacidify and preserve millions of decaying books in its collections.

Example: At several splendid ceremonies, Cambridge University Press, now publishing nearly 1,000 books annually, celebrated the 400th anniversary of its existence and entered its fifth century—the oldest press in the world.

Example: The American Council of Learned Societies opened an Office of Communication and Technology to monitor the application of communications technology to the transmission of scholarly knowledge.

Example: A committee of the National Endowment for the Humanities, in a report on the decline of the humanities in higher education, found that it is easy to get a B.A. knowing FORTRAN, but requirements seldom call for mastery of elements of world history or French or music. The Committee recommended that a core curriculum teach the basic humanistic values and texts.

These examples are only a few of the events and stirrings and observations that indicate that scholarly endeavors and the publishing that proclaims and preserves them are persisting in a time of accelerating cultural change and technological innovation.

True, there are shifts in markets, and eroding buying power as a result of inflation, but the climate for modest success with, say, a Sumerian dictionary, is as good as ever. The consumer, whether as an individual, or as a librarian, or academic, has an increasing number of worthy products from which to choose.

This increasing array means selectivity in acquisitions, both for the publisher and for the publisher's customers. As a rule, clones and lookalikes don't do as well in the marketplace of ideas unless they are better or faster or truly new and improved.

In addition to fighting against the chilly inertia of the marketplace, scholarly publishers are facing an increasing need to be as wily as possible in establishing and enhancing their niches in it. There is a continuing trend toward bigness and concentration in general publishing as exemplified by Simon & Schuster's spectacular purchase of Prentice-Hall (a company with sales of $285 million a year buying a company whose 1983 revenue was $448 million). This trend toward agglomeration does not drive out competition, but makes it harder to compete in the marketplace. But there are many many marketplaces (Simon & Schuster, before acquiring Prentice-Hall, already consisted of 25 companies in publishing and related fields.) The nichemakers, of whatever size, are the successful ones.

Publishers vs. Librarians. We are all engaged in constant redefinition of our roles and reponsibilities (and our niches), and one of the results is the continuing display of the results of our cogitations, be they attempts to assay the present or, with varying degrees of confidence, estimate the future. For example, there seems to be no end to the arguments that persist between publishers and librarians, but at least the discussions, however shrill, are continuing.

In May 1983 the Graduate Library School at the University of Chicago sponsored a conference of publishers and librarians to foster dialog on the possible improvement of their common lot. As is customary on such occasions, sparks flew (*The Chronicle of Higher Education* headlined its account, "Publishers vs. Librarians: Economic Woes Pit Former Allies Against One Another").

The published results of this conference do not replicate the ardent tenor of some of the discussions, but frequently allude to it. In his conclusion to the volume, Lester Asheim of the University of North Carolina reminded the audience of its shared goals with the statesmanlike observation that "A certain responsibility rests with those of us who represent the tradition—the culture—of communication: to discover before it is lost that which is still needed, over and beyond what the machine is capable of providing. To retain the best of both the old and the new is part of the gatekeeper/guardian function that publishers and librarians share, and, as always in the cultural aspect of our occupations, the responsibility that is entailed is not just to our own self-preservation but to the preservation of societal values. In the face of some recent, immediate pressures, publishers and librarians have frequently found themselves in confrontation, voicing recriminations that have harmed us both. But the real point is that they have harmed not only us; they could harm values and needs that far transcend our problems of turf and title."

The problems of turf and title were recently addressed by the Society of Scholarly Publishing, as part of its continuing endeavors to link all sectors of scholarly communication. At a September seminar in Providence on Libraries, Publishing, and Scholarship: Strategic Issues, the participating publishers and librarians considered how the changing nature of scholarly dissemination, using the computer and its mutations, was altering the role of the author and his relationship both to the publisher and the library.

There was no single consensus resulting from the discussion, save for the realization that all those who were occupying stations along the spectrum should hang together, lest they hang separately: a reaffirmed respect for turf and title, but no foreseen cession of traditionally perceived values. That the dialog will continue is deemed fundamental to the continued application of the precepts of scholarly publishing.

MARK CARROLL

---

publishers' books at Madison Square Garden.

At the 22d Congress of the International Publishers Association (a quadrennial meeting), March 11–17, about 600 publishers met. Principal themes concerned high tech and copyright.

The London Book Fair in April drew 9,700 attendees and 500 exhibitors. Spain's Second Annual Book Fair was in Barcelona, September 26–30.

Awards. The American Book Awards Advisory Committee concluded that less is more. Twenty-seven categories were cut to three. Winners for 1984 were: fiction, Ellen Gilchrist, *Victory Over Japan* (Little, Brown), a collection of short stories; nonfiction, Robert V. Remini, *Andrew Jackson and the Course of American Democracy, 1833–1845,* Volume III (Harper & Row); and first work of fiction, Harriet Doerr, age 70, author of *Stones for Ibarra* (Viking). Awards were presented in a short ceremony to a standing audience in Astor Hall of the New York Public Library. Each winner receives $10,000.

Kenneth D. McCormick, consulting editor for Doubleday, received the ninth Curtis Benjamin Award.

William Kennedy received the National Book Critics Circle Award and the 1984 Pulitzer Prize for *Ironweed* (Viking), a compassionate novel about Depression-era derelicts in Albany, New York. The Pulitzer in biography went to Louis R. Harlan for *Booker T. Washington*, Volume II (Oxford University Press). The Prize for Poetry was awarded to *American Primitive*, by Mary Oliver (Atlantic-Little, Brown), and for general nonfiction to *The Social Transformation of American Medicine*, by Paul Starr (Basic Books).

Mary McCarthy received the National Medal for Literature ($15,000 and a bronze medal) at the New York Public Library on May 3.

A Czech poet, Jaroslav Seifert, 83 received the Nobel Prize for Literature. England's Booker Prize for 1984 went to Anita Brookner for *Hotel du Lac* (Pantheon Books). For the Newbery and Caldecott Medals for children's books, see Children's Literature.

The Special Libraries Association presented the Fannie Simon Award to Sandra K. Paul, publishing consultant, at its June conference.

New Publications. *U.S. Books Abroad* (Center for the Book of the Library of Congress), by Curtis G. Benjamin, who died in 1983, covers the faltering state of exports and recommends ways to promote what is "far more than an ordinary commercial commodity." The book's subtitle is *Neglected Ambassadors*.

Book Research Quarterly, edited by John P. Dessauer, is a new journal sponsored by the Center for Book Research at Scranton University and the Transaction Periodicals Consortium at Rutgers University, New Brunswick, New Jersey ($50 for institutions, $30 for individuals).

PLR Royalties. British authors began receiving royalties under Britain's Public Lending Right—intended to give authors a royalty for each library loan of registered authors' books. In 1984 some 6,000 authors received payments, though 3,878 received less than £100. Forty-five received the maximum payment of £5,000. The plan was funded by the government with £2,000,000. Calculations were based on samples at 16 libraries. (See also Intellectual Freedom, Awards, and UK Report.)

DONALD E. STEWART

Publishing, Serials

Online Serials. During 1984 the biggest news in magazine publishing was the behind-the-scenes activities of online vendors. At long last the full text of a periodical may be read at a computer terminal. While this is hardly new, in 1984 Mead Data Central carried it toward the time when not a few, but almost all, serials will be available in this form.

Through its NEXIS, Mead expanded its coverage of online newspapers and periodicals to more than 120 titles. While many of these are business oriented, an increasing number of popular magazines became available. By 1984, for example, the company had added the Luce entries from *Time* and *Sports Illustrated* to *Money* and *People*. Newspapers include *The New York Times* and *The Financial Times of London*.

At the same time, the publishers of *Magazine Index*, *National Newspaper Index*, *Newsreach*, and other publications announced that the complete text of 130 newsletters and magazines is now available online. At least 50 of the titles may be considered popular. The publisher, Information Access Company (IAC), promises to expand the number. At the same time IAC made available what they call *Abstrax*, which offers abstracts of over 225 periodicals online.

Other vendors—from Dow Jones News/Retrieval to NewsNet—offer online material, but most of this is highly specialized, closely associated with business. BRS has some, and promises more periodicals online, as does Dialog.

The H. W. Wilson Company announced it was at long last making its major indexes available online. It appears that unless Wilson and other indexing firms move faster, they will be bypassed by others who not only have indexes, but full text available.

Of course there are numerous catch-22s involved with the marvels of the electronic age. Not the least of these is cost, and the online version of a magazine can run from $20 to much more for a search and printout. Indexing is not up to the quality established by the Wilson Company, and, in fact, some vendors offer only free text searching and key-word-in-context entry. Still, despite the problems, the day of the online magazine is here and the frustration of trying to find a missing periodical may soon be over. The magazine always will be right there at the terminal.

Top Sellers. Turning to the old-fashioned printed magazine, college and university librarians anxious to attract readers for the periodical room might pay attention to a 1984 survey. According to the College Store Executive's study, the top 10 bestsellers in college stores are: *Cosmopolitan*; *Playboy*; *People*; *Penthouse*; *Time*; *Glamour*; *Newsweek*; *TV Guide*; *Vogue*; and *Mademoiselle*. For those interested, the 1984 study shows that *Cosmopolitan* edged out *Playboy* for the number one spot. Women's magazines are becoming more popular, although computer titles are at least making a dent. While not in the top 10, *Personal Computing* and *Popular Computing* are extremely popular.

Computer Magazines. Although there are now well over 600 computer titles available to librarians, even more were published in 1984. Among the new entries: *Software Author* for the writer who needs information on word processing and may think an even better program will appear in the next issue of the magazine. *Personal Software Magazine* is concerned with the quality of the product, and each number reviews about 25 to 30 new programs. *Online Data Access* is a tabloid that deals with the commercial aspects of online information service. Then there are *MacWorld* and *TI Professional Computing*, two of a number of magazines tied to individual types of computers.

For the librarian trying to pick the best of the computer magazines, the 4th edition of *Magazines for Libraries* (R. R. Bowker, 1982) and the recently published *Magazines for Children*

Publishing, Serials

Mini-sized microcomputer index published by Syncon indexes more than 800 articles from 40 computer magazines.

(American Library Association, 1983) are among the leaders.

The Audit Bureau of Circulation (ABC) in 1984 reported that the top personal computer magazines are *Computer and Electronics* (550,000 circulation); *Personal Computing* (460,000); *Byte* (420,000); *Popular Computing* (310,000), and *Compute* (270,000). *Creative Computing* is another highly regarded title, although it lacks a large circulation.

Court Cases. Leaving the computer for the courts, 1984 saw several decisions that strongly affect magazines and publishers. A libel suit cannot be filed against a magazine because of an evaluation of a product made by that magazine. That was the finding in the case involving *Consumer Reports* and Bose Corporation. Bose manufactures loudspeakers that *Reports* found less than satisfactory. The company sued the magazine for its criticism and lost.

The U.S. Supreme Court reaffirmed the decision that a magazine may be taken to court in any state or community, not simply in the state or city in which it is published. That decision was directed against *Hustler* and the *National Enquirer*. The result is that the two magazines, plus others, may be fighting brush fires in all 50 states when someone take exception to what is printed.

After a court decision upheld the right of *The Nation* magazine to publish material from former President Gerald Ford's then unpublished book, syndication of memoirs appears more difficult. Usually such material is sold exclusively to a single magazine or newspaper. Under the ruling, memoirs by public officials may be termed news and not subject to copyright, hence difficult to sell to a single firm.

Claiming a February 1983 issue of *Time* "grievously" harmed then Israeli Defense Minister Ariel Sharon, the attorney for Sharon brought a $50,000,000 libel suit against the news magazine. The story concerned Sharon's involvement in the September 1982 massacre of Palestinians in Lebanon refugee camps. Efforts to dismiss the case failed, and it was clear at year's end it would go to the jury for decision early in 1985.

Magazines and TV. The cooperation between magazines and television continued in 1984, particularly in cable, for which titles from *Tennis* to *Good Housekeeping* are a major source of programming. Joining the ranks in 1984 was *Family Computing* and *Business Week*. During the programs the viewers see a compendium of much of the magazine, usually because the editorial staff of the magazine help to plan the television presentation. The bond between print and cable TV offers the latter medium a convenient source of news and public affairs. The magazines see the opportunity to recruit new subscribers. Viewers who are now watching magazines on television are doing so literally. The number of magazines in both media is likely to increase in the years to come.

Other Magazine Issues. There is still no answer to the *Columbia Journalism Review*'s (July/August, 1984) query: "Reader's Digest: Who's in Charge?" With the death of the founder's widow and the forced retirement of its editor, one of the country's largest privately held corporations seemed without definite direction. There is nothing to indicate how, if at all, the magazine's conservative editorial policy will change.

The most spectacular magazine story of 1984 concerned the abdication of Miss America. The first Black to win the crown, Vanessa Williams, had to give it up when it was reported that she had posed in the nude for a photographer. In itself this was not bad enough, but *Penthouse* added the final blow by publishing some of the photographs. The furor brought an abrupt end to a reign that includes a $25,000 scholarship and usually over $125,000 in appearance fees. *Penthouse*'s circulation, needless to say, increased dramatically when the pictures appeared.

Experts in the matter of twins are the authors of articles in the newest magazines for parents. Yes, it is called *Twins*, for "the parents of multiples." Appearing bimonthly, it covers everything from whether to have separate birthday parties to how to select playmates for the youngsters. Other notable contributions to the periodical scene in 1984 included the usual wide assortment of Little Magazines. *Slow Mountain* is an "ugly little magazine of poems and art in unpolished manuscript form." The editor goes on to explain his little magazine, out of Binghamton, New York, is "somewhat different from the mainstream." Different, yet typical of the ever growing number of Littles. There are now, by estimate, about 3,500 such titles published in the United States alone.

At a more conventional pace, the new titles in 1984 included such as: *ProEducation*, devoted to funding and support programs for schools; *World Policy Journal*, concerned with what political science professors think of international politics; *Tribal Arts Review*, an ongoing bibliography of literature dealing with African, native American, and Oceanic art; *Bop* for the teenager with a fascination for rock; *Walking World*, aimed at promoting walking (not jogging or running); and *Video Movies*, which reviews videotapes and disks available for rent. These are only representative of more than 300 new commercial or education-oriented magazines published over the year 1984.

Among the several new indexes *PMR: Popular Magazine Review* shows the most promise. It offers librarians an annotated guide to about 250 to 300 different articles that have appeared in about 75 popular magazines over the previous month. Unlike *Readers' Guide*, *Access*, or *Popular Periodical Index*, PMR offers abstracts that are unique and provide a much needed service. The online, but not in print, service *Abstrax* has abstracts from more than 225 periodicals.

Costs. In the "play the song again" department, the price of periodicals went up over 9 percent in 1984. Using 1977 as the base year, the 1984 index was 223.5. In their annual report in *Library Journal* (August, 1984) Norman Brown and Jane Phillips observed the increase "has not been this low since the middle 1970's."

Awards. During 1984 there were the usual lists of best and better. The National Magazine Awards went to 11 national magazines. Among those celebrated for above average editorial excellence, as well as superior design: *The New Yorker, Seventeen, Vanity Fair, The New Republic, New York Magazine, Esquire, House and Garden* (two awards), *Outside, National Geographic,* and *The American Lawyer.*

Freelancers' List. *Writer's Digest* listed the top 10 market for freelance writers. *McCall's* was first with $1.75 maximum price per word submitted. Next comes *Travel & Leisure* with only 80 cents maximum, but with other benefits (such as a high kill fee—if the article is not used) to give it second place. Other winners, in order: *Reader's Digest, Mademoiselle, New York, Parents, Woman's World, Signature, Science Digest, Sport.*

The New Yorker did not figure in the freelance writer's top 10, but neither did its hard-earned standard for accuracy—at least in 1984. Veteran writer Alistair Reid admitted he had concocted anecdotes and quotes in several of his *New Yorker* articles. He claims he no longer uses such questionable practices, but does admit to having doctored up a story on the Spanish dictator Franco. He made up dialog between two people who were supposed to be real, but were figments of his imagination. Commenting on the situation, the Editor of the *New Yorker* had only this to say: "He made a journalistic mistake. . . . It was meaningless, it was done for literary reasons."

Censorship Opposition. Both for literary reasons and for freedom, a party was held in the Metropolitan Museum of Art last year. The occasion was to raise funds for the magazine *Index on Censorship.* Each monthly issue reports on censorship and particularly on authors being held in jails throughout the world. Since 1972 the articles have championed what seems to be lost causes, yet often the jailed dissidents have been set free because of them. Published in Great Britain, the journal has had the support of numerous individuals, as well as the Ford Foundation.

BILL KATZ

Recordings, Sound

As has been the case for several years, the most enduring contributions to progress in the area of recorded sound during 1984, related to the functions of libraries and archives, were in three areas: (1) the continued strengthening of archival collections, (2) improved discographical control, and (3) improved technology for preservation and restoration. What may be thought of as the information or cultural environment within which these developments took place was one

More than 300 compact disks were available for lending from the Boulder (Colorado) Public Library, which began its recording collection in 1984.

characterized by a changing technology, a shifting of musical tastes, and the emergence of new styles.

Music Tastes. The audience for rock music—which once consisted only of the young and the restless—now includes a substantial number of adults. In 1984 each of the two male presidential candidates invoked the name of Bruce Springsteen to show their commitment to mainstream American values. Apparently, Springsteen did not suffer from the presidential endorsements, and rock remains a vital force in our musical culture. Country chic (e.g., western clothes and other artifacts) has been declining for several years, but there are still many all-country and western radio stations catering to a half dozen or so sub-species of the genre. Its traditional, middle-class rural orientation is such that country and western music fills a need for a vast audience, a need that cannot be filled by rock or the classics. All things considered, it seems that the days when the main thrust of the record industry was oriented to the needs of teeny boppers and adolescents has past.

An interesting trend in 1984 was the sale of sound-track albums of film music. Ten such albums sold more than 1,000,000 copies in 1984, and all but one were rock music. What cultural chemistry accounts for such a trend? For one thing, a considerable number of media producers (in TV and the movies) are recent graduates of the rock generation. For these people, "music" is virtually synonymous with "rock music." Another factor is the nature of the audience that supports movies. It has been estimated that 75 percent of this audience is under the age of 30. As Norbert Weiner once said of mathematics: "It's a young man's game"—in the case of music, it's also a young woman's game," for there were an unprecedented number of women high on the rock charts last year.

The development of audiences for classical music has never been as spectacular as, say, the development of audiences for prime-time television. Yet, the classical audience found some new members, judged by the increased sale of classical records in 1984. This audience remains substantial enough to make it economically feasible to provide materials that satisfy the most esoteric tastes, with representative material covering the whole range of Western music from the Middle Ages to the current productions of our minimal-ist composers. Some of these audiences simply would not exist if they had to depend on live concerts and radio broadcasts. As the old R.C.A. Victor advertisement put it, sound recordings give you "the music you want when you want it."

The repertory of available material continues to grow, and each year new material is released, much of it from past eras. Several manifestations of this in 1984 were the rebirth of the Blue Note label (of legendary importance in the history of recorded jazz), and from quite a different cultural milieu the entry of the Book-of-the Month Club into the business of producing new recordings—the Club has been selling records for 10 years, but these have been repackaged material that had been produced and available through other commercial channels.

The Association for Recorded Sound Collections (ARSC). The focal point for the serious study of recorded sound, particularly those studies subsumed under the term "discography," is ARSC. Although those interested exclusively in classical music represent a strong faction in the Association, the considerable efforts to broaden the base of the membership has indeed pulled in scholars and collectors (but relatively few librarians) interested in many "non-music" areas and genres other than the classics, including folk and popular music.

Despite its considerable progress, the Association still had to solve the problem of getting its *Journal* out on time. Numbers 2 and 3 of volume 15 (issued as a "double" number and dated 1983) reached the membership in August 1984. On the other hand, the quality of material published in the *Journal* remains high. Of particular interest to librarians is an instructive article by J. F. Weber, "Clues to Composer Discography" (*ARSC Journal*, vol. 15, nos. 2-3, 1983, pp. 46-65), which is an excellent introduction to the problems of constructing a "composer discography"—it is customary to divide discographies into three broad areas: (1) composer discographies, (2) artist discographies, and (3) "label" (i.e., manufacturers) discographies. Some ideas of the problems facing the serious discographer is evident in Weber's list of 129 recordings of Berlioz' "Symphonie Fantastique." In the same issue of the *Journal* (pp. 6-18), James Smart writes about the rise of the Library of Congress's collection of sound recordings during the era when Carl Engel was Chief of the Library's Music Division.

Compact Discs (CDs). The introduction of the CD recording with its laser and digital technologies did not have the immediate revolutionary impact experienced when the long-playing disk and, a decade later, the stereophonic disk were introduced. But by the end of 1984, these wonder disks had become a commercial success. Perhaps their relatively slow adoption on a mass scale reflected high costs of the disks and the very expensive play-back equipment needed (both of these factors, but to a lesser extent, have had an impact on the adoption of other innovative technologies). It appears that the "early adopters" of CDs were found in the burgeoning Yuppie market. But beginning in mid-1984, a concentrated effort was begun by manufacturers to deliver CDs to what some industry people believe will soon be a mass market.

The complete standard repertory, during the next decade or so, will probably be rerecorded on CDs. The role of the United States in this enormous enterprise is not at all clear. In 1984 there were only ten manufacturing plants in the world geared to the production of CDs, and only one was in the United States. The first purchasers of CDs were those interested in classical music, but in 1984 around half of those available were popular music (the CD edition of Michael Jackson's "Thriller" is said to have sold 50,000 copies).

The systematic collecting of CDs as archival material is, then, a new problem to archivists. For the Library of Congress, the collecting of CDs was expedited by a gift of around 1,000 disks from the Compact Disc Group, an association of record companies and equipment manufacturers involved in the production of CDs. Furthermore, because of the use of a laser beam rather than a stylus, a CD is not damaged when it is played, its life expectancy is independent of its use, and it will remain in mint condition forever—this is indeed revolutionary. It is obvious that the CD is an ideal storage media for archival collections (rare and fragile material can be rerecorded on CDs). Work along this line is now being done at the Library of Congress.

Despite the many advantages of the CD, it does not seem likely that it will quickly replace LP and tape recordings. For one thing, there are many millions of traditional turntables in use, and the enormous repertory available on LPs will take a long time to be rerecorded, and much of it will be neither rerecorded nor reformatted. In 1984 there were fewer than 3,000 CDs on the market compared to around 50,000 in-print LPs.

Restoration. The restoration of early cylinders and disks has been of concern to sound archivists for several decades. Despite the considerable progress made in restoration techniques, little information is generally available. The issue is examined in considerable detail by William D. Stone, in his "Proposal for the Establishment of International Re-recording Standards" (*ARSC Journal*, vol. 15, nos. 2-3, 1983, pp.26-37) and by Tom Owen, in his "Fifty Questions on Audio Restoration and Transfer Technology" (*ibid.*, pp.38-45a). Some of the most interesting and innovative work is being done at the Belfer Audio Laboratory and Archive at Syracuse University. There, in a project to rerecord 1,500 early cylinder recordings, laser beams and fiber optics are used to extract sound from the cylinders for permanent storage and replaying. The cylinders are so old and fragile that if they were to be played with a stylus they would be destroyed.

Discography. A little known and little used source of basic research materials on American culture is being made accessible in the series *The Federal Cylinder Project: A Guide to Field Cylinder Recordings in Federal Agencies*. The series, which eventually will run to 20 volumes, is published by the American Folklife Center at the Library of Congress. Recordings on wax cylinders made by musicians and anthropologists, and dating back to the 1890s, are described in detail. Volumes 1 and 8 in the series were published in 1984 and are available from the Superintendent of Documents.

The Greenwood Press (Westport, Connecticut) continues to be one of the most prolific publishers of substantial discographical works. Six titles were issued in 1984. Particularly interesting were Aaron J. Cohen's *International Discography of Women Composers* and *The Essential Jazz Records: Vol. 1, Ragtime to Swing*, by Harrison, Fox, and Thacker.

The Institute of Jazz Studies at Rutgers University (on the Newark campus) continues to develop as a leading center for the documentation of jazz. A continuing project is the cataloging and indexing of the Institute's record collection. As part of this effort, the Institute is currently preparing a *IJS Jazz Register*, to be made available to individuals and institutions. Dan Morgenstern, Director of the Institute, is responsible for the analysis of the sound content of the recordings. The cataloging follows international standards. The indexing, once completed, will result in one of the most detailed jazz indexes ever published and will be a model of jazz discography.

Access to Speech Recordings. For obvious reasons, the technology of recorded sound plays a basic role in the study of human speech, especially in the comparative study of dialects. Most such recorded data is in the hands of individual collectors and scholars. In a project designed to make such resources accessible, and as a by-product to provide "bibliographical" control, the Center for Applied Linguistics undertook a comprehensive survey of tape-recorded speech samples of American English. When the project is completed, the Center will issue a reference guide describing and locating the collections. As a service to the advancement of research, the Center plans to assemble a representative sample of recorded materials.

A Professional Specialty. On several occasions, the ARSC membership discussed and attempted to define the qualifications of a "sound archivist." The issue was never resolved to everyone's satisfaction. But still today this is an important issue. The question is whether there are clearly defined bodies of knowledge and skills that are requisite to function as a professional. Clearly, one cannot speak of "sound librarianship" or "record librarianship" in the same sense as, say, one speaks of "music librarianship." ARSC is in close contact with many users of sound recordings from quite different disciplines and professions. In this lies its strength. On the other hand, most of the practitioners are pragmatists. Theory, philosophy, and a broader view of the role of archives and record collections within the larger context of the cultural functions of public and academic libraries have been slow to develop.

GORDON STEVENSON

Reference and Adult Services Division

The Reference and Adult Services Division carried on an active program during 1984, ranging from the publication of the 4th edition of the widely accepted *Reference Sources for Small and Medium-sized Libraries* to the implementation of a far-reaching new planning process. The dedicated efforts of the chairpersons and members of the various committees and the two sections resulted in one of the most productive years ever for the Division. A dues increase, passed by the members of the Division, was implemented during 1984, adding more resources to support the expanding program. The strong membership vote for a dues increase signified a vote of confidence for the programs and activities of the Division.

Conference Programs. RASD, its sections, and committees sponsored or cosponsored several programs at the 1984 Annual Conference. The divisional program was entitled "The Future of Fiction in an Information Age," and featured three speakers, each bringing a different perspective to the topic. Bobbie Mason, author of *Shiloh and Other Stories*, described her experiences as a writer. Charles Scribner, Jr., of Charles Scribner's Sons, spoke of the continuing need for good fiction, both in short-story and novel form. Larry Swindell, Arts/Entertainment editor of the Fort Worth *Star-Telegram*, stressed the importance of increased financial support for new, promising, and, as yet, unknown authors.

The Machine-Assisted Reference Section's program, entitled "The Ready Reference Use of Online Resources: Ready or Not," was an all-day activity, with five speakers in the morning session and displays of equipment and publicity, budgeting and financing, staffing and training, statistics and record-keeping, vendors and bibliographic databases, nonbibliographic resources, and bibliographic utilities. It featured a significant amount of individual exchange. In all, more than 1,200 people attended at least one of the sessions.

The History Section's program—"The Uses of U.S. Federal Documents in Historical Research"—featured several speakers. Topics covered access to government publications in history, information needs of historians, with special emphasis on their use of government publications, U.S. documents as history, and government publications and the decision making process in a public library setting.

The AFL-CIO/ALA Library Service to Labor Groups Joint Committee sponsored a program on "Recession-Recovery: Libraries Serve the Unemployed." The speaker was Robert Glover, Director of the Center for the Study of Human Resources at the University of Texas in Austin.

The Business Reference Services Committee program, cosponsored by the Machine-Assisted Reference Section, was titled "Getting Down to Business-Online!" It dealt with the nature and effectiveness of online searching in dispensing business information and the difficulties in keeping up with new techniques and options in the face of the proliferation of business databases.

The Catalog Use Committee's program was titled "Communicating Effective Use of Online Catalogs" and featured speakers who discussed how to maximize instruction on the use of the online catalog.

Awards. The Isadore Gilbert Mudge Citation, awarded annually to a person who has made a distinguished contribution to reference librarianship, was presented to Sara D. Knapp, Coordi-

Reference and Adult Services Division

nator of Information Retrieval, Computer Search Service, State University of New York, for her roles as a pioneering reference librarian in the introduction of computerized information retrieval services, as a teacher, as an expert searcher, and as a national professional leader.

The Dartmouth Medal, to honor achievement in creating reference works of significance and outstanding quality was presented to *The Times Atlas of the Oceans*, published by Van Nostrand Reinhold Company, Inc., and the award was accepted by Robert Ewing, Chairman of the Board of the publishing company.

The Facts On File Award was presented to Catherine Monnin, Maple Heights Regional Library, Cuyahoga County (Ohio) Public Library. The award of $1,000 is presented to an individual librarian who has made current affairs more meaningful to an adult audience. Monnin received the award for a project she implemented to increase community awareness and understanding of the experiences of local Vietnam veterans. The award was presented by Howard Epstein, president of Facts On File, Inc.

The John Sessions Memorial Award was presented to the two-county Jackson–George Regional Library System (Pascagoula, Mississippi), under the direction of Jane C. Bryan. This award is presented to a public library or library system in recognition of significant efforts to work with the labor community. Under the direction of Bryan, the library set up special collections of materials and provided assistance to job seekers. It also worked with labor unions to determine what should be done to help the unemployed and to publicize the library's services and collections.

Publications. The major publication issued by the Division during 1984 was *Reference Sources for Small and Medium-sized Libraries*, edited by Father Jovian P. Lang and Deborah C. Masters. This is the 4th edition of a work that has come to be a mainstay in reference departments of small and medium-sized libraries.

Interlibrary Loan Practices Handbook by Virginia Boucher, published by ALA in 1984, had its origins in the work of the Division's Interlibrary Loan Committee. The author is the former Chair of that Committee and is a Past-President of the Division.

Several other publications of significance originated in the work of the Division, and were printed in the Division's journal, *RQ* or elsewhere. The fully annotated annual list of "Outstanding Reference Sources for 1983," compiled by the Reference Sources Committee, was published for the first time during 1984 in *American Libraries*. Previously this list had been published in *Library Journal*. The list without the annotations also appeared as a regular feature of *RQ* and *Booklist*. The Fall 1984 issue of *RQ* carries "Notable Books from 1983." The annual list has 44 outstanding books selected by the RASD Notable Books Council. Published for more than 30 years, the list is intended for use by the general reader or for the use of librarians who work with adult readers.

The Winter 1984 issue of the Division's journal *RQ* included an article by Charles Andrews, another Past-President of the Division, on the Committee on Wilson Indexes. The article provided a history of the Committee and details its functions. The Winter 1983 issue of *RQ* was devoted to "The Challenge of Genealogical Reference Services." The issue featured seven articles and serves as a good introduction. The History Section of RASD completed "Guidelines for Reprinting or Republishing Books of Historical Interest," a resource intended to aid publishers considering this type of publishing venture. It was published in *RQ* (Fall 1984).

Other Activities. Two new committees were established by RASD during 1984: the Committee on Fee-Based Reference Services, which is intended to provide the Division with a contact point with this growing area of interest, and the Speakers and Consultants Directory Committee.

An Information Request Form was developed by the Cooperative Reference Service Committee in 1984. The form, intended by the committee to be used by libraries to standardize the form through which information requests are referred to other libraries, was tested in the field. Upon completion of the testing process, it will be submitted for approval by the RASD Board. If approved, it will be available for use by libraries throughout North America.

The Division cosponsored a workshop with the Southeastern Library Association in Atlanta May 10–11. Titled "Improving Reference Management," it is the first of several projected regional workshops designed to bring RASD program activities to the members of the division.

A project funded by a World Book-ALA Goal Award that gained momentum during 1984 is the Adult Services in the Eighties Project. This project, which will replicate the 1952–54 landmark survey of Helen Lyman Smith, will result in a document that can be used in planning new directions for adult library services. The first phase, a comprehensive review of the literature of adult services from 1953 to 1983, will organize and categorize major articles, theses, reports, and monographs written about adult services during the period. The next phase entails the mailing of approximately 1,500 survey questionnaires to obtain information on current adult services practice.

During 1984, RASD cooperated with the American Association of Retired Persons (AARP) in their "Book Purchase Project." Through this project, AARP asked its 3,200 local chapters and the 2,500 local units of the Retired Teachers Association (RTA) to form planning committees

---

REFERENCE AND ADULT SERVICES DIVISION

PRESIDENT (June 1984–July 1985):
Gary R. Purcell, Graduate School of Library and Information Science, University of Tennessee, Knoxville

VICE-PRESIDENT/PRESIDENT-ELECT:
Rebecca Kellogg, College of Arts and Sciences, University of Arizona, Tucson

EXECUTIVE DIRECTOR:
Andrew M. Hansen

Membership (August 31, 1984): 4,502 (3,501 personal; 1,001 organizational)
Expenditures (August 31, 1984): $142,972

with librarians and other community members to compile lists of books that convey a positive, realistic view of aging, and to donate selected books to local public and high school libraries.

An action that will ultimately have major importance for the planning of RASD activities was the adoption and initiation of a new RASD planning process, developed by the Division's Planning Committee. The adoption and the implementation of the process occurred in 1984, with the first results of the process expected in 1985.

An activity undertaken by the RASD Board during the final six months of 1984 was an experimental effort to determine the value of ALANET to the conduct of business within the division. The project was proposed by the Machine-Assisted Reference Service Section, and included provision for an evaluation at the conclusion of the project.

GARY R. PURCELL

Reference Services

Reference Deep Winter. "Winter came early that year." An elusive novel opens with that line. The search for it begun in 1983 in the pages of *RQ*'s "The Exchange" column continued there in 1984. If the answer is found, it will probably be through serendipity rather than through a systematic search, thus making no difference in the climate of reference librarianship, a field whose deep winter set in during 1983 when results of several unobtrusive studies were published reporting that reference librarians give correct answers to simple factual questions no more than half the time. That winter persisted through 1984, but there was a "January thaw" of sorts through the agency of three articles.

William Miller's "What's Wrong with Reference," published in the May *American Libraries*, preceded the others and generated the most discussion. The other two, Charles Bunge's "Potential and Reality at the Reference Desk," and James Rettig's "The Crisis in Academic Reference Work," sounded similar themes. All three discussed reference librarians' declining job satisfaction and focused on the increasing number of activities reference departments, especially in academic libraries, are expected to provide. These activities—providing bibliographic instruction, conducting online searches, maintenance of extensive lists of in-house publications, and keeping knowledgeable about an incredible number of reference tools in various formats—deplete the departments' finite (and usually constant) resources and divert attention from reference departments' traditional concern of providing service on demand at the reference desk. In labor-intensive reference, those finite resources are reference librarians. And, the articles note, reference librarians are also dissatisfied in their traditional desk role. The mind-numbing repetitiveness of explaining the simplest reference tools to patron after patron combined with the difficulties inherent in dealing with an increasingly diverse clientele have increased the risk of burnout. Some librarians even go a step beyond and drop out of the profession.

Bunge wrote his article after working part-time at the reference desks of a university library and a public library during a sabbatical from his position as a professor at the University of Wisconsin Library School. Of the trio of articles, only his attempts to offer solutions to the complex problems facing reference departments today. Perhaps it is telling that the other two were written by full-time reference practitioners, both heads of large reference departments in large universities.

It remains to be seen whether or not Bunge's suggested solutions will thaw reference librarianship's winter of discontent. It is clear, however, that reference librarians will not allow themselves to be snowed in permanently by their problems. Miller's article became the main topic at meetings of formal discussion groups and informal groups of reference librarians gathered in Dallas in June for the ALA Conference. Another sign of the profession's determination to make its sun shine again was a two-day workshop on reference management held in May in Atlanta under the joint sponsorship of the Southeastern Library Association and ALA's Reference and Adult Services Division (RASD).

Lively discussions throughout the year considered topics beyond Miller's article. Reference librarians, many of whom consider themselves the sole guardians of public service spirit in their libraries, also followed the progress of the Public Services in Research Libraries Project conducted by the Association of Research Libraries' Office of Management Studies. The project encompasses all public services, but reference librarians eagerly attended discussion group presentations about it at the ALA Midwinter Meeting in Washington and a formal program in April at the ACRL conference in Seattle. Project Director Patricia Swanson from the University of Chicago and participants from Michigan State, Columbia, the University of California–Riverside, and the University of North Carolina described the project's purpose and scope and the procedures of the project's assisted self-study methodology.

Online Services. Beleaguered reference librarians, already overwhelmed by the number of services they must provide, added one more to their bag of tricks when the long wait for online access to the H. W. Wilson Company's indexes ended. November 1 WILSONLINE went online, offering access to recent items in the *Business Periodicals Index, Education Index, Readers' Guide to Periodical Literature, Book Review Digest*, and five other databases with the promise of more databases to come. WILSONLINE's innovative feature is the ability to search multiple files simultaneously.

Cuadra Associates reported that at least 72 databases were dropped during one three-month period during which more than 180 were brought up. Cuadra was able to identify more than 2,400 databases offered worldwide by approximately 350 vendors. The major vendors used by libraries continued their intense competition. BRS announced its intention to offer online document ordering, and DIALOG announced plans to emphasize full-text files. Such competition may someday be cause for renaming the two vendors Tweedledum and Tweedledee.

Reference Services

New software packages designed to simplify end-user searching through microcomputers came on the market. *In-Search,* from the Menlo Corporation of Santa Clara, received the most attention. Useful only for searching the DIALOG system and compatible with IBM and Texas Instruments hardware, *In-Search* screens ape the appearance of a library card catalog while helping the user select a database.

Although hard to believe, it is true that some libraries do not yet offer online searching. These who want to join the ratrace described by Miller could choose between two guides to the basics of managing an online search service, Joann H. Lee's *Online Searching* (Libraries Unlimited, 1984) and Christine Borgman, Dineg Moghdam, and Patti Corbett's *Effective Online Searching* (Dekker, 1984). Librarians more interested in nuts-and-bolts, how-to information about system commands could turn to Patricia Klingersmith and Elizabeth Duncan's *Easy Access to DIALOG, ORBIT, and BRS* (Dekker, 1984). The usefulness of this last title will diminish, however, as DIALOG phases in its DIALOG II software changes.

Sara D. Knapp of the State University of New York at Albany received the Mudge Citation for her work as a pioneer in bringing online search services into libraries. This selection showed that a search service is not some Orwellian machination but an integral part of reference service.

Bibliographic Instruction. Bibliographic instruction, a service questioned in Rettig's article but endorsed in Miller's, received its share of reference librarians' attention. A workshop on BI in May at Kingston, Ontario, addressed the year's themes of stress and burnout. An issue of *The Reference Librarian* (Spring/Summer 1984) devoted to BI took a mostly sanguine view of the task as it is carried on in various types of libraries and with various constituencies. In years past, it would have been heresy to question the value of library instruction. In the chill climate of 1984, this theme issue carried a condemnation of BI by Donald Davinson and a reassessment by C. Paul Vincent.

After a one-year hiatus, the annual pilgrimage of BI believers to Ypsilanti for the conference sponsored by LOEX (Library Orientation-Instruction Exchange) resumed. Participants heard a series of papers on marketing and its practical applications to bibliographic instruction in colleges and universities. Those who were not able to attend the previous LOEX conference, the 12th annual conference held in May 1982, could at long last read its proceedings in *Bibliographic Instruction and the Learning Process* (Pierian Press, 1984).

Reference Sources. The traditional, of course, held on amidst uncertainties about the future. But even in as presumably traditional an area as reference tools, portents of change could be detected. In the continuum of tradition, *The Times Atlas of the Oceans* (Van Nostrand Reinhold, 1983) received RASD's Dartmouth Medal as the year's outstanding new reference work. A reversal, if not of a tradition, then at least of a trend, was the debut of the *Business Publications Index and Abstracts* (Gale), the hardcopy counterpart of "Management Contents," a business database previously available only online.

With regard to reference publishing options, Gale Research company was able to have its cake and eat it too. Even as it was acquiring distribution rights for the hardcopy version of the "Management Contents" database, Gale announced the availability of "custom selections [by computer] of information appearing in many of its major directories." Since most of these directories are not available online through vendors, users interested in convenient, made-to-order lists from the Gale directories have little choice but to have them prepared by Gale. The impact on libraries, however, has been minimal since the presumed principal consumers of this customized service are direct-mail advertisers, a market Gale should know well as a result of its own extensive direct-mail advertising to libraries.

An unexpected manifestation of computerization coming to reference tools was the conversion into a machine-readable file of the venerable *Oxford English Dictionary,* a tool conceived and planned in the 19th century. This loading will permit the creation of specialized dictionaries and will simplify updating of the whole. The University of Waterloo was investigating the online dictionary's potential.

Another monumental reference work began publication in the traditional codex format. *The Nineteenth Century Short Title Catalogue* was announced in Washington during the ALA Midwinter Meeting and the first volumes were published by Chadwyck-Healey in the course of the year.

Facts on File, Inc., received the hoped-for blizzard of suggestions for needed new reference tools in traditional printed form. At year's end, the future of its program of awards for reference publishing ideas was assured by the acceptance of one of the approximately one hundred ideas submitted. The winning suggestion from Susan C. Jamisen, librarian at the Corbit-Calloway Memorial Library in Odessa, Delaware, led to the creation of *State Maps on File.* Three of the set's seven volumes were published in November.

Caution Advised. From firms called American Biography Service, Inc., and Somerset Publishers, librarians received advertisements for *Contemporary Biography—Women* (from the former) and for a one-volume encyclopedia tailored to their specific state (from the latter). Experienced reference librarians immediately noted the similarities of style, surefire popularity of the topics, and company names of these brochures and similar brochures, topics, and company names of several years earlier. In fact, sharp-eyed librarians spotted that Somerset, at 200 Park Avenue, suite 303, New York, NY 10017, is one of the names and addresses used several years ago on brochures for reference works advertised by Frank and Michael Gille. Libraries ordered Gille books and prepaid those orders to take advantage of prepublication discounts, but the books never arrived. The Gilles pleaded guilty to two counts of mail fraud in federal court in 1980 in the face of evidence gathered by United States postal inspectors and Robert Montavon of the University of Dayton.

Two similar, competing guides to reference works were published. RASD's *Reference Sources for Small and Medium-Sized Libraries*

(4th ed., American Library Association, 1984), by virtue of its greater historical depth, enjoyed a slight superiority over G. Kim Dority's *Guide to Reference Books for Small and Medium-sized Libraries, 1972–1982* (Libraries Unlimited, 1984).

The Reference Press. *RQ* solicited proposals for articles for its 25th anniversary issue and its Editorial Board selected those for publication in 1985. The annual annotated list of the year's best reference books compiled by the ALA RASD Reference Sources Committee, for 25 years a fixture in the April 15 issue of *Library Journal,* moved to the May reference theme issue of *American Libraries*. Undaunted by the RASD Board's decision to move an ALA product to an ALA journal, *LJ* kept its April 15 number a reference issue, publishing a list of 1983's best reference books compiled by *LJ's* book review editors from reviews published in *LJ* and other review media.

The *Reference Books Bulletin* annnounced a series of special issues, including its first annual encyclopedia roundup in its December 1 issue. It also unveiled a new occasional feature, bibliographic essays on topics such as science and technology reference sources for high school and college libraries.

Conclusion. Reference librarianship in 1984 found itself beset not by Big Brother imposing upon it a bogus version of reality. Rather it suffered from a crisis of faith; the accepted verities were questioned from within, but no answers were found. Tradition continued, of course. A reader of new editions of two guides to reference tools and services, Agnes A. Hede's *Reference Readiness* (3d ed., Shoe String, 1984) and Bill Katz's *Your Library: A Reference Guide* (2d ed., Holt, Rinehart, and Winston, 1984), would form the impression that reference service has been stable and unchanged since the days of Isadore Mudge. Both books, within their limited purposes, simply ignore online services. A perusal of Marjorie Murfin and Lubomyr Wynar's *Reference Service: An Annotated Bibliographic Guide, Supplement 1976–1982* (Libraries Unlimited, 1984) would correct that impression.

JAMES RETTIG

REFERENCES

Bunge, Charles. "Potential and Reality at the Reference Desk: Reflections on a 'Return to the Field,'" *Journal of Academic Librarianship* (1984), pp. 128–133.

Miller, William. "What's Wrong with Reference: Coping with Success and Failure at the Reference Desk," *American Libraries* (May 1984), pp. 303–306, 321–322.

Rettig, James. "The Crisis in Academic Reference Work," *Reference Services Review* (Fall 1984), pp. 12–13.

REFORMA

An affiliate of ALA, REFORMA, the National Association to Promote Library Services to the Spanish-speaking, in 1984 reached its 13th year as an advocate for improved library services to the nation's 19,000,000 Latinos.

The 1984 REFORMA annual program at the ALA Conference in Dallas was on "Library School Recruitment and Education of Hispanics." A panel of library school deans addressed this issue from the perspective of their particular schools. The REFORMA Scholarship Fund drive was kicked off through major contributions from members of the panel. Other ALA programs involving REFORMA collaboration included those that focused on the report of the National Commission on Library and Information Service's Task Force on Library Services to Cultural Minorities.

The REFORMA Executive Board in 1984 reaffirmed its desire to see REFORMA increase its involvement and visibility within ALA while continuing to collaborate with other library groups concerned with services to minorities. The Board decided that the next REFORMA annual program would support the ALA theme "Forging Coalitions for the Public Good."

At the state level REFORMA was active in California. Programs at the California Library Association Conference included "Literacy and the Spanish-Speaking" and a "Reference Update" on Spanish reference materials. REFORMA members were also involved in planning the first Binational Conference on Libraries in the Californias, held in Tijuana, Baja California, in January, sponsored by the Serra Latino Services Project in cooperation with the California State Library. REFORMA members helped to host a follow-up visit to UCLA by a delegation of Mexican librarians following the conference. REFORMA cooperated with the California State Library by participating on the California Library Services Task Force and defined its role in relation to the implementation of *California Libraries in the Eighties: Strategies for Service*, a comprehensive planning document developed by the State Library.

A variety of successful activities were held at the local level during 1984, including fund raisers such as "A Night at Los Alamitos Race Track" (Orange County Chapter) and a production of Garcia Lorca's "Bodas de Sangre" starring the actress Carmen Zapata and involving the Bilingual Foundation of the Arts (Los Angeles Chapter). Other activities included a workshop for the Black Gold Cooperative Library System,

---

REFORMA

PRESIDENT (June 1984–July 1985):
Salvador Guerena, University of California at Santa Barbara

VICE-PRESIDENT/PRESIDENT-ELECT:
(Vacant, December 1984)

SECRETARY:
Anita Peterson, Inglewood Public Library, California

TREASURER:
Rene Amaya, Braille Institute Library, Los Angeles

NEWSLETTER EDITOR:
Doug McLaughlin, Oxnard Public Library, California

Membership (December 1984): 250; 7 local chapters
Headquarters: P.O. Box 832, Anaheim, California 92805-0832

"Information Sources for the Spanish-Speaking" (Santa Barbara/Ventura Chapter). Tucson, Arizona, was the site of a REFORMA cosponsored banquet paying tribute to Arnulfo D. Trejo, who is retiring as a professor in the Graduate Library School at the University of Arizona and is a founder of REFORMA. Trejo also directed the Graduate Library Institute for Spanish-speaking Americans (GLISA) at Tucson.

SALVADOR GUERENA

Research

Library research had a good year during 1984; progress continued to be made in a number of areas.

ALA Office for Research. At the 1984 Midwinter Meeting ALA's Executive Board endorsed the recommendation of the Committee on Research that there are three research functions essential to ALA and that the Office for Research (OFR) should be charged with carrying them out:

(1) To collect, analyze, and interpret data about the membership of ALA and users of ALA products and services on an ongoing basis for organizational decision making.

(2) To collect and/or promote the collection of statistics about libraries and librarians so that ALA and other organizations will have pertinent and consistent data available to them.

(3) To monitor ongoing research related to libraries and disseminate information about such studies to the profession.

OFR pursued the second goal in two major ways during 1984. Working with the Office for Library Personnel Resources (OLPR), OFR collected statistics that were published in the *ALA Survey of Librarian Salaries, 1984*. OFR was also involved in the promotion of statistics collection by others through a contract with the National Center for Education Statistics (NCES) for the "Analysis of Library Data Collection and Development of Plans for the Future."

Academic Libraries. The Association of College and Research Libraries (ACRL) appointed an Ad Hoc Committee on Performance Measures for Academic Libraries to "plan and advise the ACRL Board of Directors on a contract for the publication of an initial set of performance measures for academic libraries; to monitor the contract work; to recommend program, policy, and projects related to performance measures for academic libraries."

Paul Kantor's *Objective Performance Measures for Academic and Research Libraries* describes three measures—"Measurement of Effort by Simulation," "Measurement of Availability Using Patron Requests and Branching Analysis," and "Measurement of Delay by Flow Analysis"—and includes introductory and explanatory text describing how the principles used in the construction of those measures could be applied elsewhere. It will provide a useful start.

ACRL inaugurated a new column in *College and Research Libraries News*. The "Research Forum" gives ACRL members the opportunity "to describe the conceptualization and development of their research projects, to explain the sources of research ideas, to suggest ways of locating methodological and financial support on local campuses and within ALA." This column will be a useful supplement to the "Research Notes," which have appeared for some time in *College and Research Libraries*.

Another ACRL initiative was the appointment of an ad hoc committee on Research Development charged "to stimulate the extension and improvement of research by academic librarians; to inform academic librarians about the value and application of a variety of research techniques; to provide opportunities for development and critiquing research ideas and projects; to recommend general program and policy related to research by academic librarians."

Preliminary Reports from the Public Service Projects, initial findings of research on current public service concerns conducted in seven Association of Research Library (ARL) member libraries, sponsored by the General Electric Foundation as part of a two-year, $250,000 grant to ARL, were published by ARL's Office of Management Studies (OMS) in September. Small grants of up to $4,000 were made for studies of potential usefulness to other research libraries. These studies were presented at the Dallas Conference in a program sponsored by the ACRL Science Technology section. Two other studies sponsored by the General Electric Foundation examined online catalogs.

ACRL awarded its $1,000 doctoral dissertation fellowship to Donald Gould, University of Southern California, for "An Examination of Levels of Work in Academic Library's Technical Service Departments for the Purpose of Determining Levels of Work Performed According to Time Stratified Systems Theory." The $1,000 Samuel Lazerow Fellowship for Research in Acquisitions or Technical Services in an Academic or Research Library, sponsored by the Institute for Scientific Information, was not awarded because no proposals were submitted.

Public Libraries Interest. The Public Library Association's "President's Program" at the ALA Dallas conference focused on *Output Measures for Public Libraries*. Douglas Zweizig used tables prepared by OFR plus commentary provided by participating libraries to produce a first national report on the use of output measures, to be published in *Public Libraries* (Spring 1985).

The newly formed Coalition for Public Library Research, a group of 18 public libraries organized by Herbert Goldhor, Director of the Library Research Center at the University of Illinois' Graduate School of Library and Information Science, funded a study to develop methodology for measurement of in-house use of materials. The four main aspects of the study are (1) collection and dissemination of hard data from nine agencies on in-house use of materials by children and adults one day a month for at least six months, (2) testing alternative methods for measuring in-house use, (3) correlating in-house use with other more readily measured variables, and (4) testing the applicability of the 80/20 rule to materials used in-house.

PLA is seeking funding for the Public Library Development Program, a four-part project to update and improve *A Planning Process for Public*

Library Statistics: A Current Review

This report—the second in a series in the *ALA Yearbook*—updates *Sources of Library Statistics, 1972–1982* published by ALA in December 1983. Like that pamphlet the updates describe published statistics about public, academic, school, and special libraries as well as statistics on related topics such as library buildings, costs, salaries, and library education. The focus is on national statistics published periodically and expected to continue.

1984 was not a good year for the appearance of such statistics although it was a very important year for developments that should lead to more and better statistics in the future. In the *1984 ALA Yearbook of Library and Information Services* this article described work under way in the ALA Office for Research under contract to the National Center for Education Statistics (NCES) on a project entitled "Analysis of Library Data Collection and Development of Plans for the Future." The report of that contract was delivered to NCES on November 15. The report made specific suggestions for data collection procedures related to each of the three publicly supported types of library (academic, public, school), as well as 12 general recommendations. The report also included recommended survey forms for each of the three types. Findings and recommendations for each type of library were noted in the Executive Summary of the report as follows:

(1) Public Libraries. All 50 state library agencies collect statistics from public libraries annually but the amount of data collected varies widely as do the topics covered. In general, topics covered by NCES in recent surveys are also covered by states though the exact language use on survey forms often differs. It would seem useful for NCES to work with state library agencies to develop an integrated data collection system.

(2) College and University Libraries. In 23 states there is annual data collection from college and university libraries in addition to the data collection done every two or three years as part of HEGIS (Higher Education General Information Survey). Topics covered are very close to those covered by HEGIS. NCES should continue the survey of college and university libraries as part of HEGIS but make it an annual part.

(3) School Library Media Centers. School library media center statistics are collected by state government in only 13 states. Evidently NCES will need to function alone for this type of library.

The Executive Summary also summarized the 12 general recommendations by suggesting: (1) An expanded system of communication with the library community. (2) Annual collection of data from each type of library noted above and occasional surveys of other types of libraries and surveys on special topics. (3) Rapid publication of results (i.e., within one year of data collection) in print form and in a machine-readable form that is easy to use and well documented. (4) Use of microcomputer technology whenever possible to collect and disseminate statistics.

Just before the report was submitted to NCES, OFR Director Mary Jo Lynch presented the recommendation on public library statistics to the October meeting of the Chief Officers of State Library Agencies (COSLA). Their support of the idea was expressed in the following resolution: "Moved that the COSLA endorse the concept of a national collection of core public library data by the NCES and that the Chief Officers individually and collectively resolve to ensure to the extent possible state cooperation with the national efforts."

As of year's end, the Department of Education had been asked to support a pilot project that would develop an integrated system in five or six states in order to solve problems likely to occur in implementing a national system.

College and university library statistics from NCES were released in two forms during 1984. In February, ALA's ACRL published *Library Statistics of Colleges and Universities, 1982 Institutional Data* using camera-ready copy from NCES. An NCES Bulletin of highlights from a summary report on the 1981–82 survey was published in February. The 1984 *Bowker Annual* carried an edited version of this Bulletin as did the July 1984 issue of *C&RL News*. The summary report was released by NCES very late in 1984 as *Library Statistics of Colleges and Universities*.

NCES gathered statistics from a sample of public libraries about microcomputers for public use in a "Fast Response Survey" taken late in 1984. Results are expected in spring 1985. In October 1984, NCES signed a contract with Westat for a survey of public and private school library media centers. This survey will build on a similar survey done in 1978 and on work done by ALA in the contract described above.

The *School Library Journal* survey of expenditures in school library media centers was again conducted by Marilyn Miller and Barbara Moran in fall 1984. Results were to be published in *School Library Journal* in 1985.

The *ALA Survey of Librarian Salaries, 1984* was published in July. This is a repeat of the 1982 survey, which covered salaries in academic libraries and in public libraries serving more than 25,000 persons.

MARY JO LYNCH

Libraries and *Output Measures for Public Libraries*.

Grants, Awards. The American Association of School Librarians (AASL) Research Committee sponsored its 11th Annual Research Forum at ALA Dallas. The Association for Library Service to Children (ALSC) Research and Development Committee and the Young Adult Services Division (YASD) Research Committee jointly sponsored another forum session. The $500 YASD/VOYA (*Voice of Youth Advocates*) Research Grant was not made in 1984 because none of the proposals submitted was judged to be worthy of support by YASD's Research Committee; $1,000 was made available for 1985.

ALA's Library Research Round Table presented its Research Development Award of $500 to George D'Elia and Sandra Walsh for "Patron Use and Evaluation of Library Service: A Comparison across Five Public Libraries." Their paper was to appear in *Library and Information Science Research*, a cornerstone in library research.

The Association for Library and Information Science Education (ALISE) awarded research grants to Alvin Schrader, University of Alberta, for a bibliometric study of the *Journal of Education for Librarianship*, and to John Richardson, UCLA, for a study of Pierce Butler. Nancy Van House's "The Return on Investment in Library Education" and Wayne A. Wiegand's "Establishing ALA Headquarters in Chicago: An Analysis of the Forces Which Brought the Association to the Midwest in 1909" were each awarded a $500 prize. The "Research Record" in the *Jour-

Research

Table 1. National Science Foundation, Division of Information Science and Technology Awards, FY 1984

Institution/ Principal Investigator	Award Number/ Title of Project	Award Date Duration	Expiration Date	Amount
Bolt Beranek & Newman Ralph Weischedel	IST-8419162 User Goals as a Basis for an Intelligent System's Ability to Understand Ill-Formed Input (Information Science)	12		$ 63,864–ISP 50,000–IIP 113,864
Brandeis University Ray Jackendoff	IST-8442592 Information Structure of a Natural Language Lexicon (Information Science)	04/05/84[a] 12[b]	10/31/85[a]	27,915
Brown University James Anderson	BNS-8440635 Cognitive Applications of Matrix Memory Models	03/29/84 12	09/30/85	26,133–ISP 52,265–BNS 78,398
Brown University James A. Anderson	BNS-8415236 Cognitive Applications of Matrix Memory Models	—	—	6,660–ISP 13,320–BNS 19,980
University of California–Berkeley Robert Wilensky	IST-8342714 Evaluating a Knowledge Representation for Planning and Natural Language Understanding (Information Science)	10/21/83 —	05/31/85	66,860
University of California–Berkeley Robert Wilensky	IST-8443810 Evaluating a Knowledge Representation for Planning and Natural Language Understanding (Information Science)	07/26/84 12	05/31/86	93,000
University of California–Berkeley Lotfi Zadeh	IST-8320416 Management of Uncertainty in Expert Systems (Information Science)	03/21/84 12	09/30/85	87,254
University of California–Los Angeles Judea Pearl and Norman Dalkey	IST-8405161 Studies in the Organization of Information Structures (Information Science)	06/15/84 12	11/30/85	46,379
Carnegie–Mellon University John Anderson	IST-8318629 (T&L AWD) Structures for Plan-based Tutoring: Applications to Geometry (Information Science)	08/15/84 36	02/15/88	0–ISP 328,361–BBS
Carnegie–Mellon University Marc Kellner	IST-8409622 (RI AWD) Optimal Query Processing in a Distributed Data Base Management System with Data Fragmentation (Information Science)	07/17/84 12	01/31/86	31,284
Colgate University Allen B. Tucker	DCR-8407114 Knowledge-Based Multilingual Machine Translation	07/20/84 12	01/31/86	15,000–ISP 32,100–DCR 47,100
Columbia University Zellig S. Harris	IST-8442537 Conjunction–Hierarchies in Structures of Arguments (Information Science)	04/10/84 12	10/31/85	141,998
Columbia University Charles Parsons and Isaac Levi	IST-8313989 The Structure of Information in Science: Fact Formulas and Discussion Structures in Related Subsciences (Information Science)	10/20/83 12	04/30/85	175,057
Columbia University Joseph F. Traub	DCR-8441590 Information and Complexity (Computer Research and Information Science)	03/05/84 12	08/32/85	15,000–ISP 56,103 71,013
Cornell University Gerard Salton	IST-8316166 Advanced Models for Information Retrieval (Information Science)	01/12/84 18	01/31/86	118,223

Institution / PI	Award / Title	Start / Months	End	Amount
University of Denver Anselm Blumer David Haussler	IST-8317918 (RI AWD) A New Data Structure for Text Processing and Pattern Recognition (Information Science)	02/08/84 24	07/31/86	99,796
Duke University Bruce W. Ballard	MCS-8402803 Workshop on Transportable Natural Language Processing, Durham, N.C.–October, 1984 (Computer Research)	03/21/84 12	05/31/85	6,496–ISP 6,496–MCS 13,992
Florida State University Abraham Kandel	IST-8405953 Analysis and Modeling of Imprecise Information in Uncertain Environments (Information Science)	06/13/84 36	03/31/86	30,713
Georgia Institute of Technology Janet L. Kolodner	IST-8317711 (T&L AWD) Extracting Information From Experience: Experience-Driven Incremental Learning (Information Science)	06/29/84 36	11/30/87	0–ISP 210,000–BBS
Georgia State University Thomas H. Whalen	IST-8317870 (RI AWD) An Intelligent Index of Problem-Solving Tools (Information Science)	02/14/84 12	02/28/86	45,380
Harvard University Richard J. Herrnstein	IST-8441763 Studies on Natural and Artificial Visual Categories (Information Science)	02/14/84 06	06/30/84	24,877
Harvard University Richard J. Herrnstein	IST-8409824 A Comparative Approach to Natural and Artificial Visual Information Processing (Information Science)	08/06/84 12	01/31/86	100,000
Harvard University R. Duncan Luce	IST-8442589 Fundamental Information Issues in the Theory of Measurement (Information Science)	06/20/84 12	12/31/85	95,505
University of Illinois–Urbana Gerald DeJong	IST-8317889 Explanatory Schema Acquisition (Information Science)	07/18/84 12	01/31/86	44,546
Indiana University Foundation Marshall C. Yovits	IST-8312728 Value and Effectiveness of Information as Related to Decision-Making (Information Science)	12/22/83 24	06/30/86	104,713
Iona College Maria Nowakowska	IST-8411304 Dynamic Theory of Expertise: Multimodel Approach (Information Science)	07/17/84 12	12/31/85	30,245
University of Kansas Glenn Shafer	IST-8405210 Belief Functions and Fuzzy Sets (Information Science)	05/16/84 24	01/31/86	82,375
Lehigh University John J. O'Connor	IST-8441723 Computer Selection of Search Words for Text Searching Retrieval (Information Science)	04/03/84 12	09/30/85	67,320
Louisiana State University Donald H. Kraft	IST-8402152 Travel to the International Conference on Research and Development in Information Retrieval: Cambridge, England, on July 2–6, 1984 (Information Science)	04/20/84 03	11/30/84	10,000
University of Maryland Panos A. Ligomenides	IST-8408063 Knowledge Representation and Measures for Relational Experiential Data Base (Information Science)	07/20/84 12	01/31/86	29,839

Research

Institution / PI	Grant / Title	Start	End	Amount
University of Maryland Jack Minker	DCR-8443100 Artificial Intelligence, Parallel Logic Programming, and Deductive Databases (Computer Research and Information Science)	06/28/84 12	02/28/86	47,142–ISP 49,922–DCR 97,064
University of Maryland Azriel Rosenfeld	MCS-8405503 Workshop on Human and Machine Vision, Montreal, Canada, August 1–3, 1984	04/02/84 12	10/31/84	7,251–ISP 7,251–MCS 14,502
MIT Edward Fredkin	IST-8441700 Information-Preserving Dynamics (Information Science)	03/07/84 12	07/31/85	122,604
MIT Whitman A. Richards	IST-8312240 Natural Computation: A Computational Approach to Visual Information Processing (Information Science)	04/13/84 12	10/31/85	115,953–ISP 57,976–MCS 173,929
University of MA.–Amherst Paul Cohen	IST-8409623 (RI AWD) Heuristic Reasoning About Uncertainty: An Artificial Intelligence Approach (Information Science)	07/12/84 12	12/31/85	55,285
University of MA.–Amherst Wendy G. Lehnert	IST-8351863 (PYI AWD) Presidential Young Investigator Award (Information Science)	06/28/84 12	12/31/85	35,000
University of MA.–Amherst Wendy G. Lehnert	IST-8442538 Information Representations for Text Summarization (Information Science)	04/04/84 12	08/31/85	97,883
University of Miami David B. Hertz	IST-8415398 Workshop on the Application of Supercomputers to Information Science, December 5, 6, 7, 1984 (Information Science)	07/18/84 06	05/31/85	24,133
NLM/SRI Jerry Hobbs	IST-8443682 Natural Language Access to Text (Information Science)	08/15/84 12	02/28/84	73,303
U.S. Naval Academy Bao-Ting Lerner	IST-8409621 (RI AWD) Joint Applications of the Theory of Semi-groups and the Theory of Fuzzy Sets to Problems in Computerized Pattern Recognition (Information Science)	00/00/84 24	00/00/86	17,540
Office of Naval Research Gerald S. Maleck	BNS-8401047 Committee on Human Factors	03/09/84	00/00/85	23,000–ISP 23,000–BNS 46,000
University of Nebraska, Lincoln John H. Flowers	IST-8319016 The Processing of Visual Information From Displays Containing Multiple Elements (Information Science)	12/06/83 24	07/31/86	65,600
New Mexico State U. Hung T. Nguyen	IST-8320433 Analysis of Uncertainty in Knowledge Representation (Information Science)	12/06/83 24	11/30/86	30,642
New York University Naomi Sager	IST-8314499 Language as a Database Structure (Information Science)	03/05/84 12	08/31/85	135,000
Ohio State University Don W. Miller	CPE-8400840 Application of the Knowledge Based System Approach to Operational Problems of Engineering	06		10,000–ISP 0–CHE 10,000

Institution / PI	Grant / Title	Start Date / Months	End Date	Amount
Oregon Graduate Center David Maier	IST-8351730 (PYI AWD) Presidential Young Investigator Award (Information Science)	06/25/84 12	12/31/85	54,000
Oregon Graduate Center David Maier	IST-8444028 (PYI AWD) Presidential Young Investigator Award (Information Science)	08/14/84 0	12/31/85	8,500
Penn. State Univ. Joseph Jordan	CHE-8443086 Computer Assisted Studies of Structure-Property Relationships (Chemistry and Information Science)	07/11/84 12	11/30/85	12,051–ISP 36,151–CHE 48,202
University of Pennsylvania Bonnie L. Webber	DCR-8443391 Extended Natural Language Interaction with Database Systems (Computer Research)	07/03/84 12	12/31/85	37,171–ISP 37,171–DCR 74,342
Purdue University King Sun Fu	IST-8405052 Research on Inference Procedures with Uncertainty (Information Science)	05/04/84 12	10/31/85	55,570
Rutgers University David Rozenshtein	IST-8408970 (RI AWD) Toward a Flexible User Interface to Relational Database Systems (Information Science)	06/29/84 12	12/31/85	38,071
Rutgers University Charles Schmidt	IST-8442542 Information Processing Analysis of Human Understanding of Action Sequences and Computational Traces (Information Science)	04/05/84 12	11/30/85	67,189
San Francisco State U. Serge V. Ovchinnikov	IST-8403431 A Normative Approach to Some Issues in the Theory of Computational Linguistics (Information Science)	05/30/84 24	11/30/86	28,913
University of South Carolina James C. Bezdek	IST-8407860 Information Retrieval from Normal Mixtures (Information Science)	06/15/84 12	12/31/85	53,961
University of Southern California Richard B. Hull	IST-8306517 Theoretical Investigation of Semantic Database Concepts (Information Science)	10/17/84 24	03/31/86	78,849
University of Southern California William C. Mann	IST-8408726 Research on Constructive Characterization of Text (Information Science and Computer Research)	07/20/84 24	01/31/87	59,996–ISP 59,996–DCR 119,992
SRI International Jane Robinson	IST-8307893 Research Toward Computer Implemented Natural Language Systems—Configurational Variation (Information Science)	10/24/83 12	03/31/85	99,947
Stanford University Robert L. Blum	IST-8317858 (RI AWD) Representation and Use of Causal Relationships for Inference from Databases (Information Science)	03/05/84 24	02/28/86	89,597
Stanford University Bruce G. Buchanan	IST-8312148 Information Structure and Use in Knowledge-Based Expert Systems (Information Science)	03/05/84 12	08/31/85	99,410
Stanford University Stanley Peters	IST-8443681 Toward Automated Natural Language Processing: Phrase Linking Grammars for Syntax and Semantics (Information Science)	07/18/84 12	12/31/85	111,744–ISP 17,000–DCR 13,000–DCR 141,744

Research	SUNY at Binghamton George J. Klir	IST-8401220 Possibilistic Information: Theory and Applicability (Information Science)	07/16/84 12	12/31/85	53,153
	Syracuse University Jeffrey Katzer	IST-8313716 Impact of Anaphoric Resolution in Information Retrieval (Information Science)	11/03/83 12	07/31/85	69,403
	Syracuse University Jeffrey Katzer	IST-8341810 Research on Information Retrieval: Document Representation Information Systems (Information Science)	10/26/83 12	03/31/85	79,231
	Tantalus, Inc. Paul B. Kantor	IST-8318630 Application of the Maximum Entropy Principle to Optimal Retrieval from Very Large Databases (Information Science)	04/24/84 18	04/30/86	56,461
	University of Texas–Arlington Billy P. Buckles	IST-8318559 Collaborative Research: Development of Retrieval Principles and Languages for Fuzzy Databases (Information Science)	04/03/84 15	02/28/86	53,283
	University of Texas–Arlington Billy P. Buckles	IST-8408345 Travel to Sino-American Conference on Fuzzy Sets July 14–21, 1984; Peking, P.R.C. (Information Science)	04/02/84 06	12/31/84	20,500
	University of Texas–Austin Robert F. Simmons	IST-8403028 (T&L AWD) Representation and Query Logic for a Text Knowledge System (Information Science)	05/17/84 24	11/30/86	0–ISP 124,231–BBS
	Thinking Machines Corp. Stephen Wolfram	IST-8410691 Workshop on Theories of Complexity: Common Frontiers of Physics, Biology, and Computation (Information Science)	07/20/84 08	02/28/85	32,900–ISP 5,000–DCR 5,000–SES <u>2,000–DMS</u> 44,900
	Tulane University Frederick E. Petry	IST-8318025 Collaborative Research: Development of Retrieval Principles and Languages for Fuzzy Databases (Information Science)	04/03/84 15	02/28/86	53,224
	Tulane University Larry H. Reeker	IST-8410510 Methodology and Evaluation of Specialized Information Extraction from Scientific Texts (Information Science and Computer Research)	08/15/84 24	01/31/87	48,010–ISP <u>30,000–DCR</u> 78,010
	Yale University Beth Adelson	IST-8409618 (RI & T&L AWD) Problem Solving Strategies in Computer Program Generation and Comprehension (Information Science)	07/06/84 24	02/28/87	0–ISP 99,406–BBS
	Yale University Elliot M. Soloway	DCR-84429120 Mapping Between Programmer's Conceptualizations and Programming Language Constructs	07/19/84 0	00/00/00	6,000–ISP 12,048–DCR 18,048

[a]Month, day, year
[b]Months

Information Technology Program Awards, FY 1984

Institution/ Principal Investigator	Award Number/ Title of Report	Award Date Duration	Expiration Date	Amount
Aerodyne Research, Inc. H. John Caulfield	IST-8313824 (SBIR AWD) Holographic Display—Phase II (Information Science)	05/29/84[a] 06	04/30/85[a]	$ 0–ITP 49,307–ISTI
UCLA–LA Judea Pearl	IST-8316957 Computer-Based Systems for Problem Structuring (Information Science)	10/14/83 12	04/30/85	95,647
University of California–Santa Barbara Terence R. Smith, & Donna A. Peuquent	SES-8400799 Constructing a Self-Modifying Knowledge-Based Geographical Information System (SES and Information Science)	03/09/84 18	02/28/86	25,000–ITP 49,955–SES* 74,955
Carnegie-Mellon University M. Granger Morgan	IST-8316890 Experiments on Interactive Exploration and Modification of Data and Model Structures (Information Science)	10/20/83 12	04/30/85	180,410
Dartmouth College Carole R. Beal	IST-8413621 (T&L AWD) Acquisition of Expertise in the Revision of Written Texts (Information Science)	07/06/84 12	03/31/86	0–ITP 19,319–BBS
University of Florida Julius T. Tou	IST-8442284 Advanced Information Technology for Document Processing (Information Science)	04/19/84 12	09/30/85	113,415
Lehigh University Donald J. Hillman	SES-8311990 Novel-Purpose Retrieval from Administrative Archives (SES and Information Science)	12/07/83 18	10/31/85	75,000–ITP 78,045–SES 153,045
MIT Edwin Kuh	IST-8443603 Guided Computing and Graphics for Modeling in the Social Sciences (Information Science)	07/18/84 12	09/30/85	10,030
National Academy of Sciences Gesina C. Carter	IST-8440671 Partial Support of the Numerical Data Advisory Board and the U.S. National Committee for the Committee on Data for Science and Technology USSC/CODATA (Information Science)	02/01/84 12	05/31/85	41,000
Perceptronics, Inc. Baruch Fischoff	IST-8312482 Decision Making in Information Retrieval (Information Science)	11/02/83 12	04/30/85	87,237
Relational Tech., Inc. Robert Kooi	IST-8313829 (SBIR AWD) Managing Text as Data (Information Science)			0–ITP 39,953–ISTI
Resources Planning Assoc. Peter N. French	IST-8361006 (SBIR AWD) Low-Cost Digitizing of Color Imagery for Cartographic Analysis Systems	02/08/84 06	06/31/84	0–ITP 28,610–ISTI
Rutgers University Natesa S. Sridharan	MCS-8318075 Exploration of Problem Reformulation and Strategy Acquisition (Computer Research and Information Science)	04/16/84 12	09/30/85	24,178–ITP 72,532–MCS 96,710

Research

Institution/Principal Investigator	Award Number/Title of Report	Award Date Duration	Expiration Date	Amount
Southern Methodist University Robert R. Korfhage	IST-8442174 Interaction of Queries with User Profiles (Information Science)	03/16/84 12	11/30/85	55,684
Stanford University Gordon H. Bower	IST-8403273 (T&L AWD) Information Processing of Graphic Displays (Information Science)	08/13/84 36	01/31/88	0–ITP 185,756–BBS
Stanford University Donald E. Knuth	IST-8442010 Theoretical Basis for the Development of Document Preparation Systems (Information Science)	03/12/84 12	11/30/85	180,157
SUNY–Buffalo Deborah K. Walters	IST-8409827 (RI AWD) Selection of Image Features for Machine Vision (Information Science)	07/06/84 12	12/31/85	50,733
Virginia Polytechnic Institute H. Rex Hartson	IST-8310414 Structure of Human-Computer Interaction (Information Science and Computer Science)	10/18/83 12	04/30/85	87,607–ITP 29,202–DCR 116,809

[a] Month, day, year
[b] Months

Information Impact Program Awards, FY 1984

Institution/Principal Investigator	Award Number/Title of Report	Award Date Duration	Expiration Date	Amount
University of Arizona Gregory B. Northcraft	IST-8408717 (RI AWD) The Role of Expertise in Human Information Processing and Decision Behavior (Information Science)	07/06/84[a,b] 12	12/31/85[a]	$ 23,465–IIP 23,500–SES 46,965
California Institute of Technology Charles R. Plott	SES-8440572 A Laboratory Experimental of Investigation of Institutional Influence on Political Economic Processes	07/06/84 12	12/31/85	50,000–IIP 54,222–SES 20,000–SES 124,222
University of California–Berkeley Thomas A. Marschak	IST-8313704 Information and Incentive Issues in the Theory of Iterative Resource Allocation Mechanisms (Information Science)	10/18/83 12	04/30/85	52,270
University of California–Berkeley Nancy Van House	IST-8409625 (RI AWD) Occupational Segregation Among Information Professionals (Information Science)	07/17/84 12	12/31/85	16,487
University of California–Irvine Nicholas P. Vitalari	IST-8313470 A Longitudinal Analysis of the Social Impact of Computing in the Home (Information Science)	10/18/83 24	03/31/85	152,657
Carnegie-Mellon University Thomas Palfrey	IST-8406296 Oligopoly with Private Information (Information Science)	06/26/84 24	12/31/86	24,678–IIP 24,677–SES 49,355
Cornell University Maureen O'Hara	IST-8408770 (RI AWD) Transactions, Intermediaries, and the Transmission of Information (Information Science)	07/20/84 12	12/31/85	9,726–IIP 9,726–BBS 19,452
CUNY Charles Kadushin	SES-8411914 Micro-Computers and Social Networks	08/17/84 24	01/31/87	8,500–IIP 48,693–SES 57,193
Georgetown Universiy Wilhelmina R. Cooke	IST-8405614 (RUI AWD) Support of Twelfth Annual Telecommunications Research Conference,	03/23/84 07	09/30/84	11,322–IIP 7,000–PRA 18,322

					Research
University of Hawaii–Manoa William Remus	IST-8403844 Tracking and Optimality in Managerial Decision Making (Information Science)	07/06/84 12	12/31/85	0–IIP 15,000–ISP*	
University of Hawaii Marcellus S. Snow	IST-8320473 Research Workshop on Economics of Telecommunications, Information and Media Activities in Industrial Countries April 30 thru May 2, 1984 (Information Science)	01/18/84 07	10/31/84	17,138–IIP 5,000–PRA 22,138	
Hofstra University Harvey J. Levin	IST-8406092 (*RUI AWD*) Studies in Orbit Spectrum Economics (Information Science)	07/06/84 12	12/31/85	49,993	
University of Houston J. H. Kagel	IST-8408396 Information Impact and Information Processing in Common Value Auctions: Experimental and Theoretical Investigations (Information Science)	07/18/84 12	12/31/85	25,146–IIP 25,146–SES 50,292	
King Research, Inc. Donald W. King	IST-8400619 Statistical Indicators of Scientific and Technical Communication in the U.S. (Information Science)	12/02/83 0	12/31/84	0–IIP 59,136–DOE	
King Research, Inc. Donald W. King	IST-8443193 Statistical Indicators of Scientific and Technical Communication in the U.S. (Information Science)	06/26/84 12	12/31/85	76,327	
MIT Marvin A. Sirbu	IST-8318199 The Determinants of Information Technology Standards (Information Science)	01/23/84 24	07/31/85	92,665	
University of Michigan–Ann Arbor Lawrence E. Blume	IST-8406457 The Demand for Information by Rational Agents and the Information Market (Information Science)	06/29/84 24	12/31/86	34,204–IIP 32,915–SES 67,119	
University of Minnesota Leonid Hurwicz	SES-8441288 Comparison and Analysis of Systems and Techniques of Economic Organizations	00/00/84 12	—	10,086–ISP 9,914–SES 38,255 58,255	
University of Minnesota James S. Jordan	IST-8319164 Information Flows Intrinsic to the Stability of Economic Equilibria (Information Science)	02/14/84 12	12/31/85	21,732–IIP 17,000–SES 38,732	
New York University William J. Baumol	IST-8315159 A Study of Productivity Performance and Scientific and Technical Information (Information Science)	12/21/83 12	07/31/85	65,964	
Northwestern University Stanley Reiter	IST-8314504 Computational Complexity of Resource Allocation Mechanisms (Information Science)	01/23/84 12	09/30/85	69,493	
University of Pennsylvania Beth E. Allen	IST-8314096 Alternative Representations of Information in Microeconomic Systems (Information Science)	01/12/84 21	06/30/85	42,325–IIP 13,000–SES 55,325	

Research

Institution / PI	Grant # / Title	Start	End	Funding
University of Pennsylvania Richard E. Kihlstrom	IST-8442693 Studies in the Economics of Asymmetric Information in Financial Markets (Information Science)	07/18/84 12	12/31/85	0–IIP 72,668–SES
University of Pennsylvania Edwin Mansfield	IST-8410689 Industrial Robots in Japan and the United States (Information Science)	08/23/84 36	02/29/88	0–IIP 53,583–ISP
University of Pennsylvania Michael H. Riordan	IST-8317249 (RI AWD) Optimal Contracting with Asymmetric Information (Information Science)	11/30/83 12	06/30/85	38,622
University of Pennsylvania David Sappington	IST-8315690 Collaborative Research (Information Science)	04/16/84 12	09/30/85	9,000–IIP 8,340–SES 17,340
Princeton University Joseph E. Stiglitz	SES-8440607 Information, Innovation, and Market Structure	07/26/84 12	08/31/86	31,506–IIP 39,124–SES 70,630–SES

Table 2. National Library of Medicine Research Grant Awards, FY 1984

Institution	Principal investigator	Title	Funding
Mt. Sinai School of Medicine	Thomas C. Chalmers	Technical Evaluation of the Clinical Literature	$ 225,784
Massachusetts Institute of Technology	Richard S. Marcus	A Computer Assistant for Information Retrieval	123,120
SRI International	Jerry R. Hobbs	Natural Language Access to Medical Text	139,926
Johns Hopkins University School of Medicine	Grover M. Hutchins	Formal Analysis of Patient Data Index by Computer	156,348
Latter Day Saints Hospital–Deseret Foundation	Paul D. Clayton	Computer Based Clinical Decision Analysis	73,534
University of Pittsburgh	Harry E. Pople	Caduceus: A Computer-Based Diagnostic Consultant	209,622
University of Wisconsin	John H. Greist	Computer-Based Interactive Medical Knowledge	124,012
University of Maryland School of Pharmacy	Winifred Sewell	End User Requirements for Optimal Online Searching	85,977
University of California–San Francisco	John A. Starkweather	Support of Individual and Group Information Needs	73,857
New York University	Naomi Sager	Applications of Medical Language Processing	169,213
New England Medical Center Hospital	Stephen G. Pauker	Clinical Decision Analysis and the Individual Patient	107,376
Case Western Reserve University	Peter E. Politser	Patterns, Partial Knowledge and Test Interpretation	26,896
Stanford University School of Medicine	Edward Shortliffe	Therapy-Planning Strategies for Consultation by Computer	118,089
University of Washington School of Medicine	Ira Joseph Kalet	A Cancer Radiotherapy Expert System Using Simulation	85,277
Case Western Reserve University	Miranda L. Pao	Information Retrieval by Semantic and Pragmatic Relevance	30,645
Georgetown University	Leroy B. Walters	Enhancing the Information System for Bioethics	201,888
Stanford University	Gio C. Wiederhold	Deriving Knowledge from Clinical Databases	103,371
Massachusetts Institute of Technology	Benjamin J. Kuipers	Expert Causal Models in the Medical Knowledge Base	74,441

nal of Education for Library and Information Science is an excellent source of research in progress. A database of dissertations in progress can be accessed through Larry Osborne, Graduate School of Library Studies, University of Hawaii, 2550 the Mall, Honolulu, 96822; "results of a computer search on specific topics or a book catalog of the entire data base (about 220–225 records) are available on request."

The American Society for Information Science (ASIS) established an ASIS Award for Research in Information Science to be given annually "for outstanding research contributions in the field of information science." The honorary first award was given posthumously to Fritz Machlup, Derek de Sola Price, and Ithiel deSola Pool.

The Council on Library Resources (CLR) continued to fund faculty-librarian research through the Professional Education and Training for Research Librarianship (PETRL) program. Other CLR grants included $24,300 to Stanford University to investigate end user searching of publicly available databases, $15,000 to New York University to assess users' actual success in using NYU's online catalog in relation to their reported satisfaction level, and $5,000 to Malcolm Getz, Vanderbilt, for research and development for a data collection protocol for library economics data. A planning grant was given to the University of Wisconsin at Madison to design a program that would increase the ability of research librarians to undertake library-related research in cooperation with scholars from other disciplines.

Federal Projects. Projects funded during fiscal 1984 by the National Science Foundation, Division of Information Science and Technology, and by the National Library of Medicine (NLM) are listed in Tables 1–4. Funding for the National Science Foundation (NSF) Division of Information Science and Technology (DST) increased from $6,589,453 in fiscal 1983 to $8,331,681. This represented 117 awards as compared to 88 the previous year. The National Library of Medicine awarded grants totaling $2,129,376 in fiscal 1984. The 18 grants were one-third fewer than in 1983 and only five were new awards.

Research Publications. The July 1984 issue of *Library Trends* was devoted to "Research in Librarianship." Editor Mary Jo Lynch developed the theme of the increasing popularity of team research and suggested that researchers in several social science fields had much to contribute to research in librarianship.

The volume begins with her essay on "Research and Librarianship: An Uneasy Connection." Articles are by Nancy Van House on Economics, Lee Shiflett on History, Ed O'Neill on Operations Research, Jane Robbins-Carter on Political Science, Sara Fine on Psychology, Ann Prentice on Public Administration, Helen Howard on Organizational Theory, Leigh Estabrook on Sociology, Rose Mary Magrill on Publications of and about Research, Thomas Childers on Research and Schools of Library and Information Science, and Shirley Fitzgibbons on Funding for Research.

"Alliance for Excellence: Librarians Respond to *A Nation At Risk,*" a Department of Education publication based on a series of invitational seminars discussing how the library might respond to the challenge of educational excellence, issued a call for research. Recommendation K identifies five areas for investigation: (1) defining information-seeking skills and behaviors, (2) fostering adult literacy, (3) promoting adult learning, (4) defining training and retraining, and (5) developing a marketing strategy. It also recommended the assessment of school library media centers and public libraries for their ability to respond to urgent proposals for excellence in education and life-long learning. Clearly there is much research to be done.

JOHN E. LEIDE

Resources and Technical Services Division

The 28th year of the Resources and Technical Services Division (RTSD)—the largest type-of-activity Division and the second largest in membership of the 11 Divisions of the American Library Association—was dynamic and productive.

Awards. Divisional and Sectional awards were presented at the Division's annual membership meeting in June. The Esther J. Piercy Award, given to a librarian with fewer than 10 years professional experience who has made a substantial contribution in the areas of technical services, was presented to Lizbeth J. Bishoff.

Dorothy Anderson received the Margaret Mann Citation for her outstanding accomplishments in the field of cataloging and classification.

The RS/Blackwell North America Scholarship Award, given for the best publication during the past year in the field of acquisitions, collection development, and related areas of resource development, was presented to Nancy E. Gwinn and Paul H. Mosher for their article, "Coordinating Collection Development: The RLG Conspectus," published in *College & Research Libraries* (March 1983).

Planning and Research. The RTSD Planning and Research Committee, chaired by Judith N. Kharbas, was charged with developing a long-range plan for RTSD. An open hearing in Dallas as a part of a major effort to determine the effectiveness and future directions of the Division provided an opportunity for RTSD members to express their views on the goals, mission, organization, and effectiveness of RTSD. To solicit evaluations of how well the Division is presently meeting the expectations and needs of RTSD members, the Committee mailed a membership survey to a random sample of RTSD members. A preliminary analysis of the data collected was presented to the Board of Directors in Dallas. The final analysis was to be given at the Midwinter Meeting in 1985.

Publishing. The Division's journal, *Library Resources & Technical Services* (*LRTS*), under the editorship of Elizabeth Tate, continued to publish high-quality articles during the year. The action taken the previous year of discontinuing services of an outside sales representative for *LRTS* and of establishing a staff position for advertising promotion and sales for *LRTS*, *RQ*, and *Top of the News*, with costs and benefits to be shared with the Divisions as appropriate, proved profitable and successful.

The *RTSD Newsletter*, which began publication as an information exchange among members, continued to evolve into a substantial periodical containing articles as well as information on forthcoming RTSD events. During 1984 its frequency was increased from six to eight issues per year. The term of its editor, Arnold Hirshon, was scheduled to end in July 1985, and the Board confirmed at the Annual Conference the appointment of Thomas W. Leonhardt of the University of Oregon as the next Editor (for the period July 1985 through the 1988 Annual Conference).

Programs. During 1984 the Division continued to present programs in all regions of the country in the form of institutes on topics of great current interest. A Collection Management and Development Institute was cosponsored with the University of Cincinnati and the Greater Cincinnati Library Consortium. Additional Collection Management and Development Institutes were scheduled at the University of California at Irvine, Trinity University in San Antonio, Texas, and the University of Washington, Seattle. A Library of Congress Subject Heading Institute was held in both Seattle and Boston; an additional LCSH Institute was scheduled for Chicago, given in cooperation with the Resources and Technical Services Section of the Illinois Library Association. The first Nonbook Materials Institute was held in San Diego; additional nonbook institutes were scheduled for Washington, Chicago, Boston, and Orlando, Florida, given in cooperation with the Technical Services Caucus of the Florida Library Association.

Authorities institutes were held in Albuquerque, New Mexico, and Fort Lauderdale, Florida, and were to close with a final one in Boston. Two preconferences prior to the Dallas Annual Conference were given, one on collection management in public libraries and another on serials. Other programs planned for the future include a classification preconference and an acquisitions preconference prior to the Annual Conference in Chicago. In addition, an RTSD program was planned for the IFLA General Conference in Chicago, and preservation regional institutes were scheduled for Chicago and Palo Alto, California. Planning also continued for a series of serials cataloging regional institutes, with the first probably to be held in 1986.

Other Activities. The Board voted at the 1984 Midwinter Meeting to change the name of the Division to the Association for Library Resources and Technical Services (ALRTS). The rationale for the proposed change was provided in the *RTSD Newsletter*. To provide a wider perspective on the issue, the Board conducted a nonbinding mail ballot to solicit membership opinion about the proposed change. Although this nonbinding vote was passed by the membership, the proposed change in name was defeated at the annual membership meeting in Dallas.

New guidelines for the election and appointment of RTSD members to represent RTSD at international meetings were adopted by the Board. The Board also revised its procedures for adopting its annual budget, and established an intern policy for service on RTSD Divisional and Sectional committees.

A loss of membership occurred in the Division during 1984, particularly from organizational members, presumed to be a result of the dues increase from $15 to $25, but a loss felt to be recoverable over a period of time. In 1983 the total membership was 6,071. In 1984 the total membership was 5,506, a loss of 565 personal and organizational memberships. Total revenue, however, increased, leaving the Division in sound fiscal health.

In January an American Library Association Divisional Leadership Enhancement Program, organized by the Association of College and Research Libraries, was held and attended by over 100 ALA Division leaders. RTSD was represented at the program, which included attendance of three Past-Presidents and the Executive Director of the Division.

Within the Association, RTSD is charged with addressing and monitoring activities in the areas of acquisition, identification, cataloging, classification, the preservation of library materials, and the development and coordination of the country's library resources. To carry out its charge in 1984, RTSD utilized its 18 division-level committees, its 21 discussion groups, its Council of Regional Groups, and its five sections.

William I. Bunnell completed six years as Executive Director of the Division in 1984. William Drewett, Deputy Executive Director, left that position in November.

WILLIAM J. MYRICK

School Libraries and Media Programs

Many groups focused attention upon school library media programs in 1984. Most noteworthy were the concerted response of librarians and others to *A Nation at Risk*; the moderate expansion of federal and state funding for educational programs; the intense scrutiny by members of the American Association of School Librarians (AASL) and others regarding the appropriate structure of a school librarians' association; the re-examination in many states of certification standards for professional school library media personnel; and the continued pattern of conferences and publications geared specifically to the diverse and changing needs of school library media specialists.

Alliance for Excellence. One of the most exciting developments in librarianship, in recent years, was the concerted response of all sectors of the profession to the recommendations made in *A Nation at Risk*. The various position papers and the seminars on "Libraries and the Learning Society" resulted in a challenging document published in July 1984. It is *Alliance for Excellence; Librarians Respond to A Nation at Risk* (U.S. Department of Education, 1984). Thirteen major recommendations stress the need for all types of libraries to participate in planned endeavors for implementing a Learning Society in the United States. The base library for most school-age children and young adults is the school library media center, and many of the rec-

---

RESOURCES AND TECHNICAL SERVICES DIVISION

PRESIDENT (June 1984–July 1985):
William J. Myrick, Jr., City University of New York

VICE-PRESIDENT/PRESIDENT-ELECT:
Marcia Tuttle, Davis Library, University of North Carolina, Chapel Hill

EXECUTIVE DIRECTOR:
William I. Bunnell

DEPUTY EXECUTIVE DIRECTOR:
Bill Drewett

Membership (August 31, 1984): 5,865 (4,772 personal; 1,093 organizational)
Expenditures (August 31, 1984): $393,129

ommendations in this document are directed to improvement of the quality of media programs.

The professional staff—well-trained and in sufficient numbers—is emphasized as critical for improvement of education in the schools. Particularly important are skill in critical thinking and competence in dealing with information. Professionals need to assume a leadership role in the school and in the development of curricula that will provide students with opportunities to gain those skills. Furthermore, the document stresses, there is the need for all professional school personnel to work together in developing and implementing such a curriculum.

It is important that teachers and administrators understand the pivotal role of the media specialist in a school's instructional program. A number of the recommendations in the document stress the need for the improvement of the recruitment, training, and certification of prospective media specialists. Library education programs have a particular obligation to assist in the upgrading of the profession. A series of the recommendations in *Alliance for Excellence* make the point that the school library media program cannot be expected to shoulder the responsibility alone. All types of information agencies within a community should systematically plan the most appropriate partnerships to achieve the objectives of a Learning Society for the boys and girls in that community.

The major authors of the issues papers, which formed the basis for 1984 seminars, were Richard M. Dougherty, Peggy Sullivan, Douglas L. Zweizig, James W. Liesener, and Jane A. Hanningan.

Funding for Library Media Programs. The Department of Education identified the Education Consolidation and Improvement Act (ECIA), Chapter 2, as the major Department program that could assist state and local activities in the areas covered by the recommendations of *A Nation at Risk*. An initial fiscal year 1985 request of $728,879,000 for Chapter 2 represented a significant increase over the FY 1984 appropriation of $479,420,000. End-of-the-year reductions resulted in an appropriation of $531,909,000. $500,000,000 of this was included in the state block grant program, which includes libraries. The amount of federal funds actually allocated to library resources at the local level has been difficult to determine precisely. Chapter 2 funds can be used for basic skills development, special projects, and library resources and textbooks. There is a clear need for distinctions and clarity, in record keeping at the school system level so that appropriate data can be gathered in the evaluation of the effects of Chapter 2 on library media programs.

In 1984 the majority of states also responded to the spirit of *A Nation at Risk*. State commissions made recommendations for the improvement of education, and many state legislatures responded with increased funding for schools. Appropriations related to the "new basic" of computer literacy and to vocational education will result in substantially increased expenditures for educational hardware, software, and other materials. Each school should take care to evaluate new acquisitions according to accepted criteria, using selection procedures already in place within the school and the school system.

Hundreds of Dade County schoolteachers and librarians attended the Miami-Dade County Public Library Systems semiannual exhibit of books recommended for home and school libraries.

Professional Association Activities. The American Association of School Librarians (AASL) undertook a survey of members and nonmembers in 1984 to identify the most appropriate structure of a professional association serving school library media personnel. The results, "The Future Structure Report," were presented at the ALA Annual Conference in Dallas and provided the basis for discussion of the relationship of units of ALA to the parent association. The majority of respondents felt that the most appropriate location for a school library media association was within ALA, but they also indicated that there were numerous problems with that relationship. Representatives from AASL met with representatives of ALA's Executive Board in fall 1984 to discuss concerns related to dues structure, autonomy of Divisions, regional conferences, services of ALA to divisions, and other matters. Although some respondents to the survey concluded that AASL should withdraw from ALA, the prevailing sentiment at year's end was that AASL, in conjunction with other ALA Divisions, it was hoped, would work to ameliorate conditions by helping define the terms of the 1982 Operating Agreement.

The regional approach to delivery of continuing education appeared in 1984 to be a significant way of reaching school library media personnel who do not attend ALA Annual Conferences. Attendees of the AASL Regional Conference in Atlanta in November 1984 were able to choose from workshops, programs, and tours related to the conference theme of "Challenge '84: Mission Possible." Programs and workshops on topics such as computer and video technology, the use of literature with children and young adults, managing the school library media program, correlating media skills instruction with the curriculum, standards, staff development, and others enriched the five-day conference.

The visibility of school library media programs in each community will likely be enhanced in future years by the passage in ALA Council of a resolution to make April School Library Media Month. Progress was also made in 1984 regard-

School Library Media Programs—Struggling into the Information Age

Libraries and information agencies of all types face challenges in making the transition into the information age. School library media programs are no different in this regard and face some particular challenges that originate from the environment they serve. The Office of Technology Assessment of the U.S. Congress (1982) in its study of the impact of information technology on American education described these challenges as follows:

> Modern society is undergoing profound technological and social changes brought about by what has been called the information revolution. This revolution is characterized by explosive developments in electronic technologies and by their integration into complex information systems that span the globe. The impacts of this revolution affect individuals, institutions and governments—altering what they do, how they do it, and [how] they relate to one another. If individuals are to thrive economically and socially in a world that will be shaped, to a large degree, by these technological developments, they must adapt through education and training.
>
> The so-called *information revolution,* driven by rapid advances in communication and computer technology, is profoundly affecting American education. It is changing the nature of what needs to be learned, who needs to learn it, who will provide it, and how it will be provided and paid for.

This same study also concluded that the impact of the information revolution is affecting all institutions but "particularly those such as public schools and libraries that traditionally have borne the major responsibility for providing education and other public information services."

Significant progress has been made in the last 25 years in terms of the numbers of school library media programs as well as the extent of the collections provided to users. However, it is truly exciting to consider the even greater potential that now exists for significant improvement in the physical and intellectual access to information of all kinds that we can or will be able to provide to users.

Understanding User Behavior. An overly simplistic view of the information world and information use has dictated past approaches to the provision of library and information services and the teaching of information seeking skills. The advent of computerized database and online searching has forced us to evaluate our understanding of information seeking behavior and some of what we have learned challenges our previous perspectives. At this point, a more realistic and knowledgeable approach to the provision of information services to children and youth is required if more clients are to be served effectively and if students and teachers are to develop the necessary higher-level problem solving skills that require more sophisticated information skills and knowledge.

Users evidently have a considerably different perception of how much information is "reasonable" to satisfy a particular need than information professionals. The time and energy required to find and use information is a serious consideration for most people and it appears that less pertinent or less adequate information is frequently preferable to the expenditure of more time and effort to get more and/or better information to satisfy a need. The time for information gathering and use is limited and there are a number of competing factors. Time needs to be considered a valuable commodity and not "free" for children and youth.

Numerous studies indicate that when confronted with an information problem, many individuals' first preference is to consult another person whom they know and perceive to be knowledgeable and who will assist (1) in refining the question, (2) in screening or presifting the information alternatives, and (3) in some cases, in providing the answer. This strong preference for personal assistance at least in the early stages of an information inquiry needs to be taken into account when planning and developing library and information services.

In addition to trying to understand the information behavior of youth, it is also critical to recognize the information needs of teachers. Teachers probably have a greater diversity of information needs than most other categories of users but yet fewer serious and sophisticated efforts are being made to provide them with realistic and effective assistance.

Is it possible that our failure to reach a larger proportion of our potential client population and the apparent ineffectiveness of our public relations and instruction in the past could be largely due to our unrealistic expectations of users or at least due to our lack of understanding of information seeking behavior? We can no longer afford to ignore these possibilities.

Role Confusion. Considerable confusion exists regarding the roles library media specialists do or do not perform and the roles they are capable of performing. Roles cannot be performed and services cannot be used effectively if they are not perceived accurately by potential clients or if there is a lack of acceptance of these roles by either the individuals receiving the benefits of them or the individuals attempting to perform them.

The value and utility of information of all kinds has become more visible and appreciated and it appears that an expectation of a more active and a broader approach to providing information services is developing. It would seem that if we are serious about the learning needs of children in our society, a quantum leap is not only required of what we expect of educational agencies generally but also in what we expect of the sophistication and contribution of such a key ingredient as the information intermediary (library media specialist) and information laboratory (library media program).

The development of higher-level intellectual and problem solving skills can only be developed in an environment where they can be repeatedly applied and tested throughout the learner's school experience. The cumulative effect of many of these kinds of experiences is what leads to the development of a self-directed learner, capable and motivated for lifelong learning. This kind of information learning laboratory requires a level of sophistication and responsiveness far beyond the current service level of "materials availability" combined with the possibility of some limited assistance.

The primary function performed by the school library media specialist or program should be viewed as a mediation function. From this perspective the specialist plays the role of the primary intermediary between the incredibly complex and rapidly expanding information world and the client. In this sense, the library media specialist is no different than a librarian or information specialist in any other environment. It is the particular environment and the particular needs of the clients served that provides the special focus and in this case the intermediary function is performed for the purpose of facilitating the achievement of learning and instructional objectives.

The older view of the role as a relatively passive culture repository or center for developing in children an enjoyment and appreciation for reading good books identifies a very important function. But it is not actively responsive to the entire range of needs identified as crucial for survival and achievement in an extremely complex, information abundant and rapidly changing world. The concept of information intermediary implies that some active assistance is frequently required for users to effectively and efficiently interact with the information world. The term information is used here in its broadest sense to include all representations of ideas, including the arts, and in any media format. Assistance is used to indicate anything from a little help to higher-level services such as formal instruction, assessing and interpreting information needs, initiating current awareness services, consulting with teachers regarding information use and instruction, and actually providing the information in some cases.

Children and teachers are in desperate need of more effective and sophisticated information systems and services. Considering how much research and development activity is currently under way in the information field, it is extremely discouraging to see how little is being done to develop and make available better and more extensive information systems for children and youth. Subject access to information for children which is not only extremely weak but actually getting worse in a number of ways even though it is the most used approach. School library media specialists and information intermediaries of all sorts who are responsible for serving children and youth need to speak out aggressively for those needs that are not being met or even addressed.

Economics. America has historically expected a great deal of its educational institutions. Every new societal problem becomes a new challenge to be partially solved at least by some addition to the educational mission. A national opinion poll suggested that the public views education as the major foundation for the future and that it should be the top priority for additional federal funds; it took first place of the 12 funding categories covered in the survey. In spite of these ever growing expectations, the level of resource allocations and the priority and status given to education do not by any means parallel the expectations.

The reality for school library media programs in the last 10 years is that the expenditures for materials have remained constant in spite of roaring inflation in the cost of materials. In addition, there has been a loss of school library media positions at the district and elementary levels, even though we are far short of the goal of having a professionally staffed program in every school in the United States. In other words, we are currently losing ground.

Manpower and Training. The supply and preparation of highly qualified personnel is becoming a serious problem. It is true that there has been a decline in the number of positions of possibly 5 or 10 percent. However, the supply side of the picture reveals a very serious decline (90 percent in a number of cases) in enrollments of students planning to be school library media specialists. In addition, a number of both the graduate and undergraduate preparation programs have folded. Several parts of the country, which have not been as severely affected economically as others or have shown increases in population, are already faced with serious shortages.

The diminished scale of the school library media components in the programs that remain also creates additional dangers. Many of these programs were never very strong, but we are now losing relevant faculty positions and our future capacity to continue these programs. The danger of relegating these programs for token attention to Colleges of Education or maintaining them at a token level in Schools of Library and Information Science should be a major concern.

At this time we need the highest level of competence by professionals who have been thoroughly trained in their discipline and not some minimal level of performance by individuals who have had only superficial preparation.

It also appears that we are having difficulty attracting the level of talent that we once did. This has been pointed out as a problem in the field of education generally but it also appears to be occurring in the school library media field. This very likely is the inevitable result of comparatively low financial incentives and low status combined with attempts to maintain extremely high performance expectations. An environment that does not respect or treat individuals as professionals and does not provide adequate or appropriate supporting services may very well be the most serious part of this problem.

Confusion regarding the primary field of the school library media specialist continues. One perspective conceives of this person as a teacher who dabbles with media on the side. However, if the information intermediary function is paramount, then the discipline of the school library media specialist is the discipline of any library and information specialist except that the particular application is in the school. Even from the standpoint of instruction, the discipline or instructional specialization of the library media specialist is library and information science.

It is absolutely crucial that the responsibility for the substantive or subject matter content of the programs be with the discipline (library and information science) if the quality of these programs is to be raised and maintained. Faculty who are at the cutting edge of their field should be providing the substantive input here and that inevitably means they are in departments devoted to their discipline. This is not an attempt to diminish the importance of the application environment but simply to clarify the role and, as a result, the educational preparation implications. An understanding of the application environment, in this case education, is obviously required and in the case of the school library media specialist a thorough knowledge and skill in the design of instruction is particularly crucial. Direct instruction as well as a consultative part of instruction are crucial elements of their role.

Conclusions. This society has the resources and the capability to achieve educational excellence but does it have the will? The educational community has been the whipping boy for all kinds of social issues. It is time that the first-class expectations of education be supported with something significantly more than the third-class support of the past. More rhetoric is not the answer. Possibly even more important, an attitude of respect and regard for the fostering of learning and intellectual health must be developed that is comparable to the weight given the fostering of physical health.

A shift in national priorities must be combined with a direct attack on the problem areas identified here. In addition, national information policy discussions cannot continue to ignore children and youth. Teachers must also be information literate if kids are to be information literate, and teachers must be able to capitalize on the information resources and services available to them. We must be able to recruit and keep a high level of talent. The current shuffling pace in our move into the information age must be accelerated not only to achieve excellence but to simply sustain our competitive capacity.

JAMES W. LIESENER

---

ing the revision of the 1975 standards for school library media programs. The need for a national statement of standards on quality becomes more and more acute, and the publication in 1985 or 1986 of such a statement was widely anticipated.

AASL in 1984 formed a Library Educators Discussion Group to provide a forum for identification of solutions to problems in the pre-service preparation of school library media personnel. A concern that must be addressed is the status of youth services in many library education programs. Recommendations in *Alliance for Excel-*

lence underscore the essential need for more specialization and more extensive education if a school library media specialist is to assume a major role as a leader in the curriculum planning, implementing, and evaluating process.

Intellectual Freedom and Censorship. Proponents of freedom of access to information for children and young adults continued to be vigilant in 1984. People for the American Way made many efforts to educate the public regarding First Amendment rights, particularly in the arena of Church and State.

The Freedom to Read Foundation also supported school personnel in the battle against censors. A spokesman for intellectual freedom for youth, Gene D. Lanier, was awarded the Immroth Award at Dallas. The battles were likely to continue after 1984. The content of, and methods of presenting, instructional materials were to come under scrutiny in all areas of the country, according to reports from groups associated with Phyllis Schafley and others who called for such review under certain federal policies. Updating and use of materials selection policies provide a major avenue for protecting the rights of school administrators, teachers, media specialists, and students in the face of such groups.

People and Publications. Shirley L. Aaron and Pat R. Scales published the second volume of *The School Library Media Annual*, an extremely valuable source. Sections on administering the school library media program and on future trends are essential professional reading. Among many significant additions of high quality to the literature of school librarianship, the following titles are representative: *Supporting K-5 Reading Instruction in the School Library Media Center*, by Lea-Ruth C. Wilkens; *Ready for Reference: Media Skills for Intermediate Students*, by Barbara B. Zlotnick; Alice R. Seaver's *Library Media Skills: Strategies for Instructing Primary Students*; *Media Skills for Middle Schools: Strategies for Library Media Specialists and Teachers* by Lucille W. Van Vliet; *Media Center Management with an Apple II*, by Janet Noll Naumer; Selma K. Richardson's *Magazines for Young Adults; Selections for School and Public Libraries*; and the revised edition of Mildred L. Nickel's *Steps to Service: A Handbook of Procedures for the School Library Media Center*.

The 1984 recipient of the AASL/SIRS Intellectual Freedom Award was Vicki Hardesty of the Findlay City Schools, Ohio. Hardesty, a High School Library Media Specialist, was honored for her regular involvement in activities to raise awareness of students, teachers, administrators, and the community to intellectual freedom issues.

The 1984 AASL President's Award, given in recognition of outstanding contributions to the field of librarianship and to school library development, went to Rheta A. Clark of the Connecticut State Department.

The AASL Distinguished Library Service Award for School Administrators was presented in 1984 to Marilynn S. Scott, Assistant Superintendent for Communications and Media of the Anchorage School District, Alaska. AASL and the Follett Library Book Company announced that they will present, beginning in 1985, awards recognizing the creative use of microcomputers in America's school library media centers, particularly in the areas of library management and integration into the curriculum.

GERALD G. HODGES

Security Systems

Assaults. Two deadly attacks on library staff took place in 1984. In August Linda Feldman, Reference Librarian at Chicago Public, was stabbed and seriously wounded by a man she was helping at the reference desk. In December three women were shot in Cleveland Public by a drifter and ex-convict who started shooting without warning. Kathleen Bowman, a library clerk, was killed; Judith Scott, also a library clerk, was wounded in the shoulder and back; a female patron was critically wounded in the head. The assailant told police he was "tired of being rejected by women."

In Chicago Kathleen Prendergast, President of Local 1215, American Federation of State, County, and Municipal Employees, called for 45 new guards in addition to the force of 60 already employed by Chicago Public. The day after the shooting Cleveland Public's trustees asked for a report and considered whether to hire off-duty police officers as guards. Stanley Deka, Director of Security, said that violence was rare in the library and its branches. But in March 1983 a library security guard was shot by her former boyfriend in Cleveland Public's Science and Technology building.

The Literature. ARL's new SPEC Kit (#100) on Collection Security in ARL Libraries compiles policy statements that should be useful to any library faced with security problems. *Security for Libraries: People, Buildings, Collections*, edited by Marvine Brand (ALA, 1984), brings together recommendations published in *Library and Archival Security* and in other library sources for ten years or more. *Security* stresses the growing consensus within the profession that library administrators must provide users and staff with a "safe place for both their persons and their belongings. . . . Of all questions that come to mind," writes Brand, "the most haunting has to do with tolerance: Has our tolerance for crime and negligence increased to the extent that our libraries are in jeopardy?" And the responsibility is perceived to be not only the Director's. Writing in the October issue of *Library Journal*, Andrew Graf said, "The librarian must think of the personal act of intervening in a problem situation as a positive act, very much in line with the job of serving patrons." *Crime in the Library: A Study of Patterns, Impact, and Security* (R. R. Bowker, 1984) is probably the first study of the subject on a national level to use the statistical methods of criminology. The study is by Alan Jay Lincoln, Associate Professor of Law and Justice at the University of Lowell in Massachusetts. Lincoln's conclusions are based on 1,657 replies to a survey of public libraries in 50 states. His findings indicated that only 7.7 percent of public libraries had guards or police in the building, and only 10 percent had book detection systems. High-crime libraries—with total crime index scores in the top 10 percent of the sample—are more likely to have protection: 19.6 percent have guards or police and 36 percent have book detection systems.

Both *Crime in the Library* and *Security for Libraries* offer checklists for security programs, but neither addresses the problem of keeping weapons out of libraries. The shooting of President Reagan, President Ford's two near misses, the assassination of President Kennedy demonstrate rather conclusively that dozens of guards are unable to protect even a President against a sociopath with a gun. Referring to the shooting in Cleveland Public, Police Chief William Hamton is quoted as saying that "you can have 1,000 policemen nearby and still not prevent something like that."

If libraries are to be safer than other public places in high-crime areas the only option seems to be airport-style metal detectors, and guards to monitor them, at building entrances. This measure would give more real security to library staff and patrons than almost any number of guards, armed or unarmed, elsewhere in the building.

Equipment. The University of Wisconsin–Whitewater Library said that its Knogo book detection system caused a "painful, high-pitched noise" in a Walkman or Walkman-type cassette player. Knogo recommended signs warning of the danger. Engineers at 3M were unable to reproduce such a sound on 3M equipment, although Walkmans in the detection aisle will pick up a clicking noise the loudness of which depends on the volume setting of the player.

In response to another published report 3M confirmed that the activate/deactivate unit, but not the detection aisle, of its EM (electromagnetic) systems will erase or degrade magnetic tapes. The November 1976 and the May–June 1979 *Library Technology Reports* point to this problem in all EM systems (Gaylord–Magnavox, Knogo, and 3M). 3M recommends that video and audio tapes, microcomputer software, and 8mm film with magnetic sound tracks be kept at least a foot away from activate/deactivate units. Leon Drolet, AV Director for the Suburban and North Suburban Library Systems in Illinois, found the magnetism of such units can extend up to three feet.

Until 1984 Checkpoint was the only manufacturer to market a book detection system based on radio frequency (RF). In 1984 3M introduced its own RF systems, the Echotag 2100 and 2200. Unlike any other book detection system, Echotag panels do not have to operate as a pair of parallel screens forming the usual detection aisle. An RF transmitter requiring no receiver, each Echotag panel can stand and operate alone. The ET 2100 wall-mounted panel projects a detection field approximately three feet. A pair of facing ET 2100s can cover a doorway or corridor six feet wide. The free-standing ET 2200 projects detection fields three feet on either side. One unit can protect a space six feet wide; two parallel units can protect a space 12 feet wide. In the full-circulating mode Echotag targets are shielded by treated date-due cards or tabs similar to those used in Checkpoint systems. The ET 2200 free-standing panel costs less than $3,000 installed.

Checkpoint introduced a new Checktab gun that prints the due date on mylar-coated tabs used to shield Checkpoint targets in full-circulating systems. Checkpoint estimates that 85 percent of its library systems are full-circulating; only about 15 percent are by-pass.

Conferences. In January the New York Metropolitan Reference and Research Library Agency (METRO) sponsored an all-day workshop, "Facing Up To Library Security," attended by some 60 participants. Emphasis was on what librarians can do to combat security problems. A slide presentation looked at a library from the thief's point of view. Speakers suggested mirrors and rearranging book stacks to improve visibility into nooks and crannies, and called for staff involvement and training in assertiveness and even self-defense. Speakers agreed that security heads should talk directly with administrators. John Erickson, Head of Security at New York Public, reviewed the laws relating to book theft. Frank DeRosa, Chief of Brooklyn Public's security force of 65 peace officers, described that library's electronic surveillance—26 video cameras in main library and book detection systems in main and in 57 branches. But DeRosa emphasized that in the end security depends on an alert and watchful staff.

JOHN F. CAMP

Seminar on the Acquisition of Latin American Library Materials

Annual Conference. Each annual conference is devoted to (1) a specific aspect of the acquisition of Latin American library materials, of Latin American bibliography, or of related matters and (2) consideration of the progress made, and further action necessary, by SALALM and its committees and cooperating organizations in solving problems related to its concerns. Approximately 200 registrants from the United States, Latin America and the Caribbean, and Europe participated in SALALM XXIX, held at the University of North Carolina, Chapel Hill, June 3–7. The theme of the conference was Collection Development: Cooperation at the National and Local Levels.

The José Toribio Medina award for outstanding contributions to scholarship in Latin American Studies was presented to Robin M. Price for his *Medical Americana in the Library of the Wellcome Institute for the History of Medicine.*

SALALM accomplishes most of its work through committees and subcommittees in which more than one-third of the personal members participate. The Executive Board Committees are Constitution and Bylaws; Policy, Research and Investigation; Editorial Board; Membership; Finance; Nominating; Conference Planning. The substantive committees are Acquisitions, Bibliog-

---

SALALM

PRESIDENT (September 1984–August 1985):
Don Hazen, Stanford University

VICE-PRESIDENT/PRESIDENT-ELECT:
Iliana Sonntag, San Diego State University

TREASURER:
David Lee, National Agricultural Library

EXECUTIVE SECRETARY:
Suzanne Hodgman, University of Wisconsin-Madison

Membership: 408 (30 percent outside U.S.) (279 personal; 127 organizational)

raphy, Library Operations and Services, and Inter-Library Cooperation. There is also a Joint Committee on Official Publications.

Publications. Publications issued in 1984 included *Latin American Economic Issues: Information Needs and Sources* (Papers of the 26th Seminar on the Acquisition of Latin American Library Materials); *Public Policy Issues and Latin American Library Resources* (Papers of the 27th Seminar on the Acquisition of Latin American Library Materials); *Directory of Vendors of Latin American Library Materials* by David Block and Howard Karno (Bibliography and Reference Series, 9); *Bibliography of Latin American Bibliographies, 1982-83* by Lionel Lorona (Bibliography and Reference Series, 10); and *Bibliography of Latin American Bibliographies, 1983-84* by Lionel Lorona (Bibliography and Reference Series, 11).

SUZANNE HODGMAN

Serials

Not unexpectedly, the major issues in serials librarianship during 1984 were prices, resource sharing, and online systems. These topics are reviewed in this article, along with concerns such as standards, preservation, and communication through meetings and publications.

Serial Prices. In their annual article published in *Library Journal*, Norman Brown and Jane Phillips found that American periodical prices had increased 9.4 percent, the smallest annual increase since 1974. Still, the average price of a journal in 1984 was $54.97, significantly higher than $50.23 in 1983. Psychology periodicals had the highest percentage increase—17.6 percent—followed by history at 13.1 percent; the lowest percentage increase was in the field of labor and industrial relations (2.2 percent), a subject that had an 18.2 percent rise in the previous year.

For several years serial publishers' practice of dual pricing, one price for individuals and a higher price for institutions, has been widely discussed and decried by librarians. This year, however, the issue of dual pricing has been replaced by that of discrimination in serials pricing against U.S. subscribers by foreign—especially British—publishers. The claim is that these publishers have one price, the lowest, for domestic (United Kingdom) orders; a second, somewhat higher, for "overseas" or "foreign" subscriptions; and a third, dramatically higher, for U.S. subscriptions. No correlation is evident between the American surcharge and either exchange rates or postage charges.

British publishers give several reasons justifying the discriminatory prices: handling charges, use of optimum means of transportation, even subsidy for Third World subscriptions. What is said but seldom printed is that the publishers know that Americans, and especially American libraries, will continue to subscribe to the British journals, whatever the cost, so their price will continue to rise out of proportion to domestic and "foreign" rates. There may well be truth to this charge; it has been used often in the context of dual pricing. Thus it would behoove American serials and collection development librarians to look carefully at the value they are receiving for their money with respect to foreign journals and to discontinue the practice of accepting automatically the price increases appearing on their invoices. The concern about discriminatory pricing is becoming widespread. The topic was being examined by groups within ALA, and a letter from a leading American subscription agent called special attention to what were seen as disproportionately high 1985 prices charged American libraries by one British publisher.

Resource Sharing. The CONSER project experienced steady progress in several programs designed to make the database more useful to both catalogers and public service librarians. Under the leadership of Julia Blixrud, based at the Library of Congress, OCLC staff has been adding abstracting and indexing (A & I) data to the 510 field of serial records at the rate of 10,000–12,000 a month. The project, sponsored jointly by the Association of Research Libraries and the National Federation of Abstracting and Information Services, has as its goal "to provide the needed link between library catalogs and A & I service citation by adding current and reliable information to serial titles in the CONSER data base about where those titles are indexed or abstracted." Other objectives are to ensure through this inventory that all serials covered by the participating A & I services appear in the database; to add records for missing titles; to provide quick access to notice of where a given serial is indexed or abstracted and which serials are covered by more than one service; to provide standardized bibliographic data for the A & I services to use in their products; and to make possible the capability to produce a core list of abstracted and indexed serials that could serve as the nucleus of a nationwide serials location and holdings system. (*ARL Newsletter* 119; the 1984 issues of this publication provide detailed progress reports on the A & I project.)

It is difficult ot locate statistics describing the CONSER database and nearly impossible to determine its current size. The 1984 issue of *CONSER* printed figures updated to December 1984. At that time the total number of records entered by CONSER participants was 319,883. To this may be added 7,265 related records modified or created and 140,440 records to which holdings were appended. The total number of records, then, in the CONSER database was 467,588. Of these, 178,617 had been authenticated by either LC or the National Library of Canada. Just over 60,000 records had been added to the CONSER database since the end of July 1983 (the date of statistics reported in the 1984 *ALA Yearbook*).

There appears to be a growing effort to alleviate the common problems serials catalogers have with CONSER records. For example, in May personnel from the Library of Congress and OCLC met with CONSER Operational Staff liaisons from participating institutions to discuss technical and procedural matters. Two topics of general concern were related to authentication. CONSER member catalogers will now be able to modify LC-authenticated records and authenticate their own records, thus helping to reduce the unreasonable workload at LC. As a result, MARC serials tapes should be available to subscribers more quickly than at present.

OCLC. In fall 1983 the long-awaited Claiming Component of the Serials Control Subsystem was activated. Claiming through OCLC can be Semiautomatic (notification of potential claim), Automatic (claim issued if next expected issue not received), or Manual (user-initiated claim). With better control over serials receipts, more claims are being produced by libraries using the system. OCLC is working with serials vendors (recipients of most of the claims) as well as with users to smooth the component's rough edges.

The Union List Users Group (now renamed SOUL, for Serials Online Union Listers), begun in 1983, meets regularly twice a year at ALA conferences. A second group, the Serials Control Users Group, met for the first time at Midwinter 1984. It plans to gather at each ALA Conference and perhaps at the Special Libraries Association meeting. The Serials Control Users Group began a newsletter as a means of furthering communication about the Check-in and Claiming components of the Serials Control Subsystem.

As with the size of the CONSER database, current statistics describing the size and characteristics of the OCLC serials database are difficult to come by. CONSER for 1984 reports that the online catalog contained 222,525 LC records and 504,984 records entered by other OCLC participants, a total of 727,509 serial records. Fifty-two percent of the records are for current titles, a slight drop from six months earlier (reported in this article last year), but understandable. As libraries continue with retrospective conversion projects they find that a single title cataloged several years ago under latest entry rules becomes several titles in the database cataloged under successive entry. The top frequency among OCLC serials is still annual at 23 percent, and more than 73 percent of the titles are English-language publications. The disturbing fact about these statistics is the large category designated "unknown." For example, 36 percent of the serials in the OCLC database have a stated frequency of "unknown," and a further 8 percent have no frequency listed. This lack of specific information probably can be attributed to catalogers' sacrificing detail for quantity in records entered, not to the oddities of serials.

Standards. Fortunately, the name change of American National Standards Committee Z39 to National Information Standards Organization (Z39) did not require a title change for its useful newsletter, *Voice of Z39*. As reported in that source, Subcommittee E, Serial Holdings Statements, is working on a standard incorporating both summary and detailed levels of serial holdings. The first draft produced three negative votes and extensive comments, which the committee is reviewing. A revised draft is projected for late 1984. A new subcommittee, CC: Serial Item Identifier, has circulated a draft of its standard defining "the requirements for providing in coded form an identifier for each issue of a serial and each item published in a serial." This work resulted directly from a recommendation by SISAC (Serials Industry Systems Advisory Committee). In addition, the newest revision of Periodicals: Format and Arrangement is nearing completion.

Cataloging. During the summer the Library of Congress relaxed somewhat the rules for determining a title change, thereby reducing the number of serial title changes to be acted upon. When a change (1) occurs after the first five words of the title, and (2) does not change the meaning of the title or indicate a change in the scope, and (3) might easily be overlooked, then the title proper is not considered to have changed. Even within the first five words of the title, the following changes may be ignored: "(1) abbreviated word vs. full form of word; (2) initialisms and letters with separating punctuation vs. those without separating punctuation; (3) numbers or dates vs. spelled out form; (4) signs and symbols (e.g., "&") vs. spelled out forms; (5) hyphenated words vs. unhyphenated word(s); (6) one-word compounds vs. two-word compounds" (*Cataloging Service Bulletin* 25). This change frees the cataloger from having to produce new bibliographic records and/or sets of cards and frees other librarians from the need to change all serial records for such inconsistencies as "on-line" vs. "online" and "yearbook" vs. "year-book." These changes require a note, but no new bibliographic record. As one cataloger says, "It's getting easier all the time!"

Serials Vendors. During 1984 subscription agents and the vendor-related Blackwell Library Systems continued to refine their online serials systems, and libraries continued to select one of these systems to use for some or all of their serials functions. EBSCONET, while continuing to market its OSS (Online Subscription Service), had the other component—Serials Control System—on hold during the first part of the year. In May a new function of OSS, ROUTING, was introduced. ROUTING software is also available for use on a personal computer.

The Faxon Company brought up its INFO-SERV component, which makes available information about all new serial titles entered into its database during the immediate past three years, plus additional promotional and information materials from journal publishers. INFOSERV is useful beyond the serials acquisitions unit; collection development and public service personnel can access this data in the selection process and in responding to patrons' queries. Faxon's Union Listing module was also fully operational in 1984.

Blackwell Library Systems' PERLINE is becoming established in U.S. libraries as a stand-alone serials system. In 1984 its binding and report writing functions were introduced, increasing its usefulness. The accompanying BOOKLINE, a monograph acquisitions system, is under continual development. In early 1985 a new version of the Blackwell products, combining PERLINE and BOOKLINE in one system, will be available.

Additional online serials systems are on the horizon; both SAILS (Swets Automated Independent Library System) and Dawson's SMS (Serials Management Services) were being tested in England in 1984. While SMS is limited to the full range of serials processes, SAILS claims that it will provide in addition, monograph acquisitions, cataloging, circulation, interlibrary loan, and other nonserials functions. It should not be long before they reach the United States.

Meetings and Publications. American serials librarians were more aware in 1984 of international activity concerning serials. About 25 persons from the United States attended the annual meeting of the United Kingdom Serials Group in Guildford, Surrey, in March, and several Americans participated as speakers and panelists. The UKSG attracts not only Americans, but also librarians and vendors from the Netherlands, Switzerland, Germany, Ireland, and Canada. This group has no counterpart in the United States; it is a forum for discussion of mutual problems among librarians, vendors, publishers, library school faculty members, and others interested in serials work. During its three-day conference, information and advice are given and received, business relationships are strengthened, friendships are established, problems are shared.

Not wanting to lose control of their own group because of international interest in it, the UKSG leaders are encouraging persons in other countries to start their own serials groups, with an eye toward a federation. Interest exists in the United States, but there is a strong feeling that serials personnel cannot afford another organization with its membership fee and conference expenses. The possibility of a U.S. Serials Group is being discussed, but the costs seem to be the stumbling block.

An ALA/RTSD preconference in Dallas, "Who's Afraid of Serials?", was directed toward librarians who do not work primarily with serials. It attempted to quell their fears by explaining collection development, acquisitions, cataloging, and public service related to serials. Major themes of the conference included the need for clear communication among those who publish, distribute, organize, and use serials, and the urgency of developing and adhering to standards to codify sound practice and to enhance the quality of communication.

The Serials Section of RTSD was in the early stages of planning a series of regional institutes on serials issues, mainly cataloging and CONSER practices. The Serials Section Executive Committee, in presenting the resolution to the RTSD Board, felt that three factors indicated a need for such institutes: CONSER practices and procedures are of vital importance to cooperation and standardization in creating machine-readable records for serials, not only by CONSER participants, but by all serials catalogers; the adoption of AACR2 has caused many changes in serials cataloging and CONSER practices; other instruments for cooperation and standardization, namely, the MARC format for holdings and the NISO standard for holdings, are likely to be available soon. The Library of Congress has a large role in the planning of the institutes, and it is likely to supply a number of the speakers. The interaction between leaders and participants at these institutes will be a big step toward resolving serials librarians' frustration with CONSER records (discussed in the 1984 ALA Yearbook).

Publications. Both Serials Review and Serials Librarian continued in 1984 as established (ten and nine years, respectively) means of formal written communication for persons concerned with serials. They were joined by Technical Services Quarterly, edited by former serials librarian Peter Gellatly. One wonders, however, if traditional journals are the only appropriate format for today's communication needs. Several years ago the newsletter Title Varies was on the right track, but it was not able to provide the rapid dissemination of information to which it aspired—and which serials librarians need. In Great Britain the UKSG Newsletter, in its sixth volume in 1984, is somewhat successful. Is the time right for another American newsletter for those involved with serials? Perhaps an electronic bulletin board is the direction to look. Clearly, there is a need for news and information to be available while it is still relevant. No more evidence is needed than the surprisingly high number of subscriptions Title Varies maintained and the more than 250 registrants at the UKSG Annual Conference.

MARCIA TUTTLE

Social Responsibilities

Socially sensitive programming has long been an important aspect of the services provided to library users. Current social problems propel libraries to make timely responses to user needs. As in previous years, libraries in 1984 parlayed their responses into a myriad of programs on a variety of critical issues such as missing children and the plight of the poor, homeless, elderly, institutionalized, and disabled persons. Library personnel also gained increased understanding of social problems and users' needs by being receptive to social changes.

During 1984 libraries confronted many problems in their communities and developed innovative ways to assist the public in making intelligent, informed decisions about problems. To better serve their clientele, libraries formed coalitions with police departments, governmental units, child care centers, literacy organizations, medical and health groups, businesses, religious organizations, and social agencies. Public, school, special, and college and university librarians joined forces with library educators and with each other to serve as voter registration centers, campaign corners, career and job information centers, and unemployment compensation offices. Lecture series on critical issues, children's fingerprinting clinics, health fairs, and services to ethnocultural groups were among other socially responsible programming.

State Library Agencies. State library agencies aggressively promoted socially responsible programs through grant awards for innovative local projects and by initiating and coordinating statewide activities through the state agencies. Several representative state agency programs in 1984 include:

CALIFORNIA. The State Library launched a California Literacy Campaign on January 1. The program, directed toward developing and coordinating community-based services to an estimated 20 percent of California's adult population, complements existing services of the State Department of Education and the volunteer sector by fostering working partnerships at the local level with volunteer literacy organizations, educational institutions, businesses, churches,

Social Responsibilities

Chicago's Mayor Harold Washington (center) joins winners of the Chicago Public Library's "Sharing It" holiday poster contest. The contest was held in conjunction with the city's annual Christmas food drive. (Phil Moloitis)

social agencies, and individuals. Twenty-seven projects were funded and resulted in the initiation of literacy programs in about 100 communities. A total of $2,635,000 was approved by Governor George Deukmejian for the 1984–85 campaign. State Librarian Gary Strong began the California Literacy Campaign in 1983.

Other activities included a Teenage Outreach Service to Seniors program at the Contra Costa County Library, which established library services to convalescent hospitals serving seniors; the Burbank Media Project, which established an information and job skills center for unemployed craftspersons and technicians in the motion picture industry at the Burbank Public Library; the Ontario–CLIP (Community Library Involvement Project), which established outreach services via bookmobile to Ontario's (San Bernardino County) rapidly increasing Spanish-speaking population and seniors; and the Pre-school Agencies Cooperative Team, also at San Bernardino, which sought to increase preschool literacy through the cooperative efforts of the county library and local preschool agencies in conjunction with parents, library students, and educators. Library Child Care Link established library outreach to child care centers and trained teachers and parents in Santa Clara County. The Latino Services Project established systemwide service programs for the Hispanic populations of San Diego and Imperial Counties. A highlight of this project was a conference on library services for the Spanish-speaking held in Tijuana in conjunction with librarians from Baja California, Mexico. Oakland Public Library continued its California Spanish Language Data Base, a statewide bibliographic database for Hispanics and Spanish-language acquisitions and cataloging services for public libraries; and Project ASIA continued its cooperative selection, acquisition, and cataloging of Chinese, Japanese, Korean, and Vietnamese language materials for 28 libraries throughout the state.

ILLINOIS. Illinois State Library funded a deaf services project through the Chicago Public Library/Chicago Library System to establish and conduct a program of service to the deaf and hearing impaired. The Deaf Services Program sought to incorporate innovative techniques through state-of-the-art equipment; utilize specialized approaches through its program design; and create acceptance, interest, and awareness on a broad scale through topical programming, workshops, and public awareness activities. Other programs for disabled persons included a videocassette collection of materials captioned for the hearing impaired and a community education program aimed at reducing attitudinal barriers on the part of the general public by heightening community awareness of the capabilities of disabled persons. A unique aspect of the latter is its utilization of the award-winning Kids on the Block puppets.

WEST VIRGINIA. The state agency instituted a "Campaign Corner" in libraries statewide. Posters and bookmarkers ("the Candidates, the Issues, the Library") highlighted the areas in which folders of information on national, state, and local candidates were available for voters.

Branch libraries of the Chicago Public Library during 1984 took finger and footprints of young children for family records. Purpose was to help identify missing children.

263

Social Responsibilities

The state agency also worked out arrangements with the Secretary of State's office to enable every librarian or designated library worker to become a notary, thereby enabling each library to become a voter registration site. Many libraries offered career/job centers and job banks; Raleigh, Fayette, and Jackson Counties had notable programs. McDowell Public Library served as the Unemployment Compensation Office.

The Governor's office donated a series of movies dealing with teenage alcoholism to the state film library. Teachers, churches, and community organizations could obtain the films through their public libraries. Statewide, libraries were actively involved in literacy programs with Literacy Volunteers of West Virginia, Laubach and Friends of the Library groups.

Public Libraries. Many public libraries in 1984 provided outstanding programs reflecting their sense of social responsibility.

ARLINGTON HEIGHTS. Marilyn J. Shuman, Public Information Officer at the Arlington Heights (Illinois) Memorial Library, indicated that the Library maintained its strong record of socially responsible activities. In cooperation with the police department, the Library continued programs such as fingerprinting young children for identification.

The Body Shop, a health awareness program for parents and children, included a fitness trail, health screening tests, health foods sampling, and a display of health services equipment. It was sponsored in cooperation with the local hospital, the park district, and village health officials. Women's health, divorce law, child abuse, wife abuse, retirement, and poverty were topics of lectures and bibliographies during the year. The library also sponsored six programs as part of the North Suburban Library System and Lake Forest College series: 20th Century Voices: Six Nobel Prize Writers. Programs were made possible through a National Endowment for the Humanities (NEH) grant.

A Handicapped Arts Fair coincided with National Employ the Handicapped Week in October. The Community Services Department continued its outreach program of bookmobile visits to nursing homes, parks, and schools. Free delivery of books and materials is offered to the homebound. The Talking Books program and the use of the *World Book Encyclopedia* on cassettes, with instructions for use in braille, are two services for the blind. The latter resulted from a $1,500 gift to the library. A grant of $5,000 supported the development of a Job Information service for job seekers and for assisting employers to plan for future needs.

BROOKLYN. The Brooklyn Public Library provided some valuable and successful programs for special populations. The most active was the Literacy Program: adults received free one-to-one tutoring in reading from trained volunteers. Tutoring for the program was expanded from 5 to 22 libraries via community Block Grants from New York City.

SAGE (Service to the Aging) continued to offer free events for older people in 16 libraries. Senior Assistants, older adults who plan recreational and educational events for their peers in their own neighborhoods, were hired by the Library and functioned as valuable role models. Outreach, the other component of SAGE, involved extensive visits to senior centers where programs were held and large-print books loaned. A workshop, Reading Readiness and the Preschooler, scheduled to be offered at all 58 Brooklyn public libraries, provides information about the needs of preschoolers and offers parents practical suggestions for preparing youngsters to read.

The Child's Place, a special area for and about preschoolers, continued to flourish at three branch libraries. In addition, eight mini–Child's Place areas, with special programming, were set up around the borough. The Kids Project, a special free program featuring puppets three and a half feet tall, makes the point that "being disabled never stopped anyone from being a good classmate or a good friend." The puppets, of whom five are disabled and two are not, share their experiences and draw the audience into spirited dialog. Barbara Aiello, a special education teacher, designed the project and coordinated it for the New York State Office of Mental Retardation and Developmental Disabilities. Several branches presented the Kids Project.

The Education and Job Information Center served more adults in 1984 than ever before. Free help included a résumé revision service, high school equivalency classes on videotape, and some special programs for women entering or re-entering the job market. The center also continued its operation of the Special Needs Area, where people with limited or no vision received free training and help with a variety of special tools that made the library and information more accessible to them.

El Centro Hispano de Information provided bilingual information and referral, reading materials in English and Spanish, and a bilingual Education and Job Information Center. The bilingual staff made this a useful tool for Brooklyn's large Spanish-speaking population, and further increased library and information accessibility.

CHICAGO. The Chicago Public Library continued its commitment to providing programs that stressed social responsibility during 1984. Homework Centers were established in each of the System's 88 branch libraries. These centers consisted of a designated area of the branch and special book collection for use by elementary and high school students preparing after school assignments. Reference and other materials to be specifically used in the homework centers were obtained from a grant. The homework centers were especially effective during the Chicago Board of Education Teacher's Strike that took place shortly before the end of the year. Staff of the Chicago Public Library provided dedicated service to the overflow number of children who came to the local libraries as an alternative to school. Many branches established informal classroom instruction with the assistance of teachers, parents and community groups.

The "Sick Kits For Kids" program established in 1984 provided library resources to hospitalized children. All hospitals in the Chicago area who had at least a 30-bed unit for immobile kids and a full-time specialist were eligible to receive materials such as coloring books, crayons, and activity kits for their patients. Participating hospitals also received long term loans of books from the nearest branch library.

A similar program entitled "Special Kids Need Libraries Too" was sponsored by Portage-Cragin Branch. This program addressed the library service needs of approximately 350 handicapped children in the Portage-Cragin community. It consisted of a series of coordinated programs using books, illustration, and puppets to convey verbal language to multi-handicapped children. These story programs were reinforced with specialized books and learning aids for the children and their parents. In addition a browsing collection for the special child was established, and book displays for parents and special education teachers were created.

EVANSVILLE–VANDERBURGH. Margaret J. Kyle, Assistant Director of the Evansville–Vanderburgh County Public Library of Evansville, Indiana, reported an array of activities. The Library was developing a coalition on literacy with several local agencies. NEAR (New Evansville Adult Readers), a literacy project, continued to flourish. A Visualtek Reader, donated by the National Federation of the Blind in Vanderburgh County, magnifies print up to 60 times the size of an original and supplements the Library's Talking Books Service. Another gift, from the local General Foods Community Service Committee, is a Teletypewriter for the deaf that connects the hearing-impaired of the community to the Adult Information and Children's Departments.

The Homebound Library Service, the Senior Citizens' Book Corner, and the AARP (American Association of Retired Persons) tax-aid program continued to thrive. Deposit collections in nursing and retirement homes and a collection at the County Jail also aid persons who are usually unable to visit the library. Story hours were given for hearing-impaired children and other handicapped children. Open invitations were extended to nursery schools, day care centers, and Headstart. Story hours for area Mental Health Center's adult day care people were also sponsored.

Medical needs of the community were being served cooperatively by county and hospital and health industry librarians and coordinated through the Evansville Area Health Sciences Library Consortium. The library also continued to be the Reference and Referral Center for area libraries in counties in Indiana and supported many cultural, educational, and recreational activities in the community.

HOUSTON. The Community Information Service (CIS) expanded its information and referral services to low-income, disabled, minority, and senior citizens. As a result of its comprehensive computerized database of children's services, CIS and the Houston Committee for the Public Sector Initiative (PSI) received a grant to develop Child Care Resource and Referral. The focus of the service is to further enhance child care provider information, to provide information and advice on quality child care to corporations on a fee-for-service basis, and to provide an abridged version of the service to the public.

The Library continued to cooperate with the Houston Community College in providing adult basic education. In addition, Houston Public Library branch personnel worked with the Houston Effective Literacy Project (HELP), a joint venture of public- and private-sector organizations coordinating literacy efforts and raising funds to increase those efforts. The program served as an impetus for the organization in Houston of an affiliate of Literacy Volunteers of America.

MERRICK. In an effort to increase voter participation in elections, the Merrick Library (New York) became a permanent voter registration center. To increase public awareness about the availability of voter registration cards at the library, a major publicity program was undertaken to advertise the center.

MONROE. The Monroe County Library System's central branch in Rochester (New York) reported a variety of socially responsible programs. Training of library personnel is an important part of Monroe County's service to its users. Training during 1984 was provided in such areas as the problem patron, English as a Second Language, and services to the deaf and visually handicapped; orientation programming was offered to agency personnel dealing with the elderly and persons in institutions. Staff members also were enrolled in sign-language classes.

The Library printed the program guide for a newly established Radio Reading Service; provided services to shut-ins, prisons, jails and a detention center; developed and conducted workshops for day-care providers; issued brochures and directories relating to special needs; instituted collections for English as a Second Language students and printed a directory of programs; conducted special programs for children; purchased BiFolkal kits for use in nursing homes and special toys for children with disabilities; assisted community groups in the establishment of a community toy library and a resource center on racism; and published a newsletter, *Clippings*, for library staff and agency personnel (*Clippings* has been taped and Brailled).

Bookmobiles, including one which is accessible to the handicapped, served geographically isolated areas, schools, industry, and a youth correctional facility. Deposit collections were provided to more than 50 community agencies, and the homebound were served by library staff and volunteers. Kay C. Adams coordinated the many outreach and extension services of the Monroe County Library System.

Volunteers staff the Reader's Table for visually impaired patrons at the Boulder (Colorado) Public Library. (Bob Grzenda)

265

Social Responsibilities

NEW YORK PUBLIC LIBRARY. The New York Public Library (NYPL) provided many outstanding programs to its users during 1984. In addition to its services for the handicapped, the library continued the Children's Events and Events for Adults and Young Adults calendars. Covers for the Children's Events calendars featured illustrations that were donated by well-known children's illustrators. John Steptoe, Chris Demarest, Tracey Campbell Pearson, Martha Alexander, Robert Quackenbush, Ann Jonas, James Stevenson, and William Steig were among the donors. NYPL enlarged its rare collection of campaign memorabilia during 1984. The collection includes memorabilia from a broad segment of the country. Some items date back to the 18th century.

QUEENS. The Queens Borough Public Library greatly expanded its English as a Second Language program for adults. Free English courses were offered through the New Americans Project to adults who spoke a limited amount of English. Other features of the New American Project were the Mail-a-Book program, the foreign language film series, coping skills programs, and programs celebrating the art and literature of various ethnic groups.

A National Endowment for the Humanities (NEH) grant to Queens College provided sponsorship for the Meet Your Ethnic Author/Filmmaker Series; 40 performances by authors and filmmakers were presented at branch libraries during the series. The series was directed by David Cohen. A directory of service agencies assisted the diverse ethnocultural populations in Queens. The library in cooperation with the Jamaica Community Employment Office also offered up-to-date job information on microfiche at eight branch libraries in Jamaica.

Education. COLLEGE AND UNIVERSITY LIBRARIES. Outreach and special services are an integral part of college and university programs. Representative programs include subject-centered bibliographic instruction, term-paper clinics, specialized research consultations, lecture series on social issues, open houses for faculty, and other services to special populations.

Anne Commerton, Director of the State University of New York at Oswego Library, reported a week-long Elderhostel course, Library Ventures and Adventures; classes for high school students; and PLUS (Personal Library User Service) tutorials. In addition, the library presented special programs for BOCES (Board of Cooperative Educational Services), Phi Delta Kappa, and alumni Weekend.

LIBRARY AND INFORMATION SCIENCES EDUCATION. Special courses and projects for underserved populations were popular offerings in many library and information science education programs. Atlanta University continued its Annual Black Book Fair. The Library School and the Special Library Association's student chapter donated books to the Fulton County Jail. The School of Library Science at North Carolina Central University (NCCU) continued to assist public libraries in developing and supporting programs that increase the ability of local residents to become involved in public affairs. NCCU sought public library involvement in meeting the civic literary needs of users through teleconferencing and conducting planning sessions to discuss various economic, educational, and social problems.

Queens College (New York) maintained its leadership through the Ethnic Materials Information Exchange Program and special projects with the Queens Borough Public Library. Texas Woman's University reported Projects LEER, a special collection of bilingual and Spanish materials. An annual doctoral assistantship is a feature of the project. The University of Wisconsin–Madison cosponsored a program with the Child Care Book Center that addressed war as a metaphor in children's literature. The purpose of the program was to provide information to teachers and librarians about the depiction of war in children's literature and its impact on the development of children.

Financing and Budgets. Although libraries generally continued to be underfunded, they fared comparatively well during 1984. The California State Library budget grew by more than $4,000,000 for 1984–85. State Operations and Local Assistance programs benefitted. Clarence Walters, Connecticut State Librarian, reported a 7.4 percent increase in state aid to libraries.

Georgia's public libraries won a constitutional amendment in the November elections that promised to have long-term positive impacts on library construction in that state; the amendment enhanced prospects that the state library's annual budget package would get through the legislature.

Threats of a $225,000 deficit in the Rockford (Illinois) Public Library budget were averted when voters passed a referendum that increased the property income tax.

Jane Morgan, Director of the Detroit Public Library (DPL), indicated that passage of Proposition L rescued the library budget. It was expected at year's end that DPL would receive $5,000,000 a year for the next five years from that increase in the property tax. In Minnesota, Hennepin County Library, Minnetonka, received a 7 percent increase in its operating budget. The 1984–85 capital budget was set at $1,950,000, most of which was to help build three new community libraries.

Election day brought Nevada public libraries approval of a $10,000,000 bond issue for library construction and defeat of a tax revolt measure. The bond issue, overwhelmingly approved by the voters, called for state matching funds in a ratio of one to three to local funding for projects approved by the legislature.

Barbara Thiele, Director of the Westfield (New Jersey) Memorial Library, reported the passage of a nonbinding referendum asking for a bond issue of $3,500,000 for a new building. New strength was added to school and local libraries, library systems, networks, and institutional services by passage of the New York Library Omnibus Bill. The bill provided a major increase for public library outreach to the educationally disadvantaged, members of ethnic or minority groups, and persons in need of job placement.

Voters in Norman, Oklahoma, approved a $3,400,000 expansion of their 1966 library building but rejected three other library funding proposals. State aid to public libraries in South Carolina was increased by nearly $1,000,000. A huge bond issue was passed in Houston. Sally Hunt, Director of the Loudon County Public Library (Leesburg, Virginia), reported passage of a $6,595,000 bond issue. A countywide citizens group is given much of the credit for victory. Kevin Hegarty, Director of the Tacoma (Washington) Public Library, reported the largest library bond issue passed in the history of the state, the first in 21 years for Tacoma. The $15,800,000 will rehabilitate the main library, build two new branches, remodel two others, rehabilitate the rest of the branches, purchase a $1,000,000 state-of-the-art automation system, and buy $700,000 worth of books. Passage can be credited largely to direct mail appeals and a "Libraries Please" sign campaign by library promoters.

Publishing. Social responsibilities remained popular in publishing during 1984. Marguerite Weibel's handbook, *The Library Literacy Connection: Using Library Resources with Adult Basic Education Students*, was distributed to public libraries through the Ohio State Library. The ALA Ethnic Materials Information Round Table (EMIERT) updated, revised, and enlarged its *Directory of Ethnic Publishers and Resource Organizations*.

Two of the many publications addressing social responsibilities from the Council on Interracial Books for Children (CIBC) are *Reconstruction: The Promise and Betrayal of Democracy* and *Presenter's Guide for the Audio-visual Program Childcare Shapes the Future: Anti-racist Strategies*.

The CIBC and the profession mourned the loss in 1984 of Brad Chambers, who during his last 18 years challenged various children's book "isms" such as racism, sexism, ageism, and handicapism. Through the CIBC, Chambers left a legacy of socially responsible publishing.

MARVA L. DELOACH

Social Responsibilities Round Table

Annual Conference Activities. Members of the Social Responsibilities Round Table sponsored a Presidential Candidates Forum during the Midwinter Meeting in Washington, D.C., at which the candidates for ALA President and Treasurer discussed issues and responded to questions. The SRRT Action Council voted to support Herb Biblo for Treasurer; Pat Schuman was endorsed by the Feminist Task Force for the same office. No endorsements were made for the office of President.

Action Council recommended to SRRT membership that dues be increased, and ballots were distributed through the *SRRT Newsletter*. Returns were favorable and annual dues were to be raised to $10 effective January 1985.

During the Annual Conference in Dallas, the SRRT Coordinator met with other Round Table representatives to discuss the advisability of formalizing a committee of Round Table chairs and the possibility of Round Table representation on ALA committees and on Council. SRRT Action Council agreed that a formal relationship with other Round Tables would be beneficial.

SRRT members introduced three resolutions at the ALA membership meeting. Only one, however, was passed by council: The resolution that ALA join the Citizens Against Nuclear War (CAN) as a member organization. A resolution that any personal member of ALA may attend membership and Council meetings, whenever and wherever held, by showing either a conference badge for the day of the meeting or a current membership card was referred to the Committee on Program Evaluation and Support (COPES). A resolution that ALA urge the withdrawal of all American military personnel and the cessation of all military aid and covert intervention in Central America failed.

Task Force Activities. Task Forces sponsored a number of programs at the Annual Conference. The Alternatives in Print and International Human Rights Task Forces cosponsored a program entitled, "New World Information Order: A Third World Perspective." The Coretta Scott King Task Force presented its 15th Annual Award to Lucille Clifton, author of *Everett Anderson's Goodbye*, and to Pat Cummings, illustrator of *My Mama Needs Me*. Coretta Scott King accepted a special citation for her book, *The Words of Martin Luther King, Jr*. The Feminist Task Force presented "The Gender Gap: A Colloquium on Women and Power." The Gay Task Force sponsored a program on "Closet Keys: Gay/Lesbian Periodicals for Libraries." The Library Union Task Force presented, "Managing VDTs for Employee Well-Being," and cosponsored, "Libraries, Unions, and Political Action," with the Staff Organizations Round Table.

The *Field Guide to Alternative Media: A Directory to Reference and Selection Tools Useful in Accessing Small and Alternative Press Publications and Independently Produced Media*, edited and compiled by Patricia J. Case, of the Alternatives in Print Task Force, was published by ALA. The Civil Rights Task Force is preparing a social responsibilities handbook for librarians.

Brad Chambers, Chair of the Civil Rights Task Force and a longtime supporter of SRRT, died in 1984.

SRRT Task Forces and their chair/coordinators for 1984–85 are Alternatives in Print, Jim Williams and Dan Tsang: Civil Rights, Donnarae MacCann; Coretta Scott King, David Searcy;

SOCIAL RESPONSIBILITIES ROUND TABLE

ACTION COUNCIL COORDINATOR:
Doris Kirschbaum, Arlington, Virginia

SECRETARY:
John Sheridan, Colorado Springs, Colorado

TREASURER:
Nancy Gruber, San Francisco

Membership (August 31, 1984): 893 (805 personal; 88 organizational)
Expenditures (August 31, 1984): $8,024

Top, from left, ALA President E. J. Josey, Coretta Scott King, Effie Lee Morris, Chair of the Social Responsibilities Round Table Task Force, and Pat Cummings, winner of the 15th annual Coretta Scott King Award. Above, King with ALA Past President Clara Stanton Jones.

Feminist, Gail Warner; Gay, Barbara Gittings; International Human Rights, Lee Regan; Library Union, Peter Kidder and Mary Rosenthal; Men's Issues, Carl Hays; Peace Information Exchange, Elizabeth Morrissett.

Action Council members for 1984 were Kay Cassell, Joan Goddard, Nancy Gruber, Doris Kirschbaum, Jeanne Kocsis, Barbara Levinson, Betty-Carol Sellen, John Sheridan, Susan Vaughn, David Vespa, Linda Pierce, Past Coordinator, and John Hostage, SRRT Newsletter Editor.

DORIS KIRSCHBAUM

Southeastern Library Association

The Association leadership, through close management discipline, restored the financial health of the Association in 1983–84. Maintaining that achievement and increasing the membership continued to be principal concerns throughout 1984.

A workshop on improving reference management and services was held in May in Atlanta, sponsored jointly by SELA and the Reference and Adult Services Division of the American Library Association. It focused on reference managers and those who aspire to administrative positions.

A conference on intellectual freedom was held in Tallahassee July 29–August 1. Sponsored by SELA in cooperation with Florida State University School of Library and Information Studies and the State Library of Florida, it was the major project of the SELA Intellectual Freedom Committee for the biennium. Evaluation by the 70 people who attended showed that most participants felt the conference had achieved its objectives, which were (1) to help participants become more aware of the effects of censorship through examination of prevailing theories of child development; (2) to assist those working with children and young adults to examine library and media program policies that affect access to information and to develop community policies facilitating access for those age groups; (3) to aid professionals working with children and young adults to develop programming techniques designed to promote information access throughout the community.

The biennial conference of the Association was held in Biloxi, Mississippi, in October, as a joint conference with the Mississippi Library Association. The SELA Special Libraries Section conducted a preconference institute, "Productive Supervision." Featured speakers for the joint conference included actor, critic, folklorist, lecturer, broadcaster, and author Studs Terkel, author Jim Trelease (*The Read-Aloud Handbook*), and a NASA astronaut, Col. Donald H. Peterson. Honorary memberships were awarded to Shirley Brother, Ann Page Bugg, Ann Wimbish Cobb, Virginia Lacey Jones, and Edward Graham Roberts.

The Association's leadership met in Atlanta in mid-December 1984 to appoint an executive secretary and to develop plans to strengthen both communications and services to the membership while maintaining the restored sound state of SELA's financial operations.

REBECCA T. BINGHAM

Special Collections

ORGANIZATIONS AND CONFERENCES

RBMS. The 25th annual conference of the Rare Books and Manuscripts Section of the Association of College and Research Libraries met in Austin, June 19–21. The theme was "Collecting the Twentieth Century." The initial speaker, Richard Landon of the Thomas Fisher Rare Book Library of the University of Toronto, set the tone of the conference in his talk entitled "Embracing the Flood." In particular, Landon discussed the administrative risks of attempting to collect too widely in the vast areas of contemporary social, political, scientific, and literary documentation. But, he added, the rewards can be substantial also, and he illustrated the point with the University of Toronto's acquisition of the papers of an important Canadian foreign correspondent, Mark Gaine, which comment extensively on many of the wars and coups d'etat that have occurred since World War II.

Anthony Rota, the noted London rare book dealer, spoke on collecting 20th-century literary manuscripts, both by private collectors and such important institutional collectors as the Lilly Library, the University of Texas, and Washington University in St. Louis. Rota also addressed such issues as the factors that determine the market for

---

SOUTHEASTERN LIBRARY ASSOCIATION

PRESIDENT (November 1984–November 1986):
Rebecca T. Bingham, Jefferson County Public Schools, Louisville, Kentucky

VICE-PRESIDENT/PRESIDENT-ELECT:
Charles E. Beard, West Georgia College, Carrolton

SECRETARY:
Virginia Benjamin, University of Georgia, Athens

TREASURER:
Georgia R. Stewart, Birmingham Public and Jefferson County Free Library, Alabama

ACTING EXECUTIVE SECRETARY:
David Estes, P.O. Box 987, Tucker, Georgia 30084

Membership (December 1984): 2,109

modern literary manuscripts and the effect on research of manuscript dispersal versus centralization.

Collecting resources that trace the development of science and technology was the topic of Arthur Norberg of the Charles Babbage Institute of Information Processing. Using the example of documenting the development of the computer, Norberg emphasized that collecting strategy must move beyond acquiring the papers of scientists to include such areas as product development, marketing, and sales.

Donald Gallup of the Beinecke Rare Book and Manuscript Library provided a detailed account of Yale University's efforts to build the Ezra Pound Archive, including a variety of legal complications and the many difficulties posed by competing interests within the Pound family.

Speaking from the standpoint of a scholar who relies upon 20th-century material, biographer Michael Holroyd urged institutional repositories to increase their endeavors to ease restrictions on manuscript material and liberalize restraints imposed by copyright laws.

Gerald Ham, of the State Historical Society of Wisconsin, presented strategies for managing vast accumulations of archival collections, strategies that included regional cooperation among institutions, appraisal techniques designed to reduce the bulk of massive collections, and the role of microformats in preserving the content of documents when space considerations preclude retention of the original.

In addition to the formal program, the RBMS conference included a half-day workshop on techniques for conserving 20th-century materials, led by Donald Etherington and his staff at the Humanities Research Center. There also were seminars on legal issues related to collecting 20th-century materials; appraising 20th-century collections for gift and bequest; collecting fugitive political and literary printed matter; processing nonbook materials; and author bibliographies.

Program Chairman for the Austin conference was James Green of the Library Company of Philadelphia. Lynda Claasen, University of California, San Diego, was Section Chairwoman.

APHA. The ninth annual conference of the American Printing History Association took place at Columbia University on September 29. Organized by Francis O. Mattson, Rare Book and Manuscript Division, The New York Public Library, the conference theme centered on "Eighteenth-Century Anglo-American Printing and Publishing." Clinton Sisson of the University of Virginia described "The Construction of the Early Eighteenth-Century English Press," illustrating his talk with slides of a Benjamin Franklin press, a James Franklin press, and the American Antiquarian Society's Isaiah Thomas press.

Donald Farren of the University of Maryland, College Park, investigated the relationship of "Anglo-American Subscription Publishing: East to West and West to East." His talk emphasized that the English and colonial American book trades were closely and knowingly linked and that an important factor in the trade was the widespread practice of subscription publishing.

The Early American paper industry was discussed by John Bidwell of the William Andrews Clark Memorial Library, University of California, Los Angeles. In "An Immigrant's Guide to Early American Papermaking," Bidwell investigated the often elusive origins and careers of colonial papermakers and concluded that a majority of those emmigrating from England were inexperienced prisoners or indentured servants while the real American paper industry was established by better trained and educated German immigrants.

The forces that have shaped the book as object and medium of man's expression were discussed by Roger E. Stoddard of the Houghton Library, Harvard University, in "Some Aspects of Eighteenth-Century Bookmaking." Cultural and technological changes and the relationship of text to the physical shape and size of the book were examined in detail.

Henry L. Snyder, Director and Editor of the Eighteenth-Century Short Title Catalogue/North America discussed "Finding and Using Eighteenth-Century Books: A Historian's Perspective." Snyder addressed the problems of the historical profession in locating and interpreting 18th-century books. He also described the progress and value of ESTC, both to scholars and to libraries.

The annual APHA award for distinguished service to printing history was bestowed upon John Dreyfus, who was cited for his services as typographical advisor to the Cambridge University Press and to the Monotype Corporation and as European consultant to the Limited Editions Club; for his efforts in organizing the Gutenberg Quincentenary Exhibition in Cambridge; for his part in founding the International Typographical Association; for his chairmanship of the Printing Historical Society; and for his many publications, the most recent of which is *Aspects of French Eighteenth Century Typography*.

The Manuscript Society. The Manuscript Society held its annual meeting in Tarrytown, New York, May 23–26. Visits were paid to several historic sites in Dutchess County, including the Rockefeller Archive Center at Pocantico Hills where Archivist Joseph Ernst spoke on the Rockefeller family papers. At the Roosevelt Library and Museum in Hyde Park, the Society was addressed by Library Director William Emerson, who spoke on "FDR as a Collector." A day in New York City featured visits to the Library for the Performing Arts at Lincoln Center; the Pierpont Morgan Library, where D. Rigby Turner, Curator of Musical Manuscripts, presented an illustrated lecture entitled "What Is a Music Manuscript?"; and the New-York Historical Society, where a special exhibition had been prepared that included manuscripts of John Winthrop, Robert Fulton, Peter Stuyvesant, and John Jay.

Grolier Club Centennial Convocation. The Grolier Club, the nation's oldest club devoted to "the literary study and promotion of the arts pertaining to the production of books," celebrated its 100th anniversary during the last week of April with a series of receptions, dinners, and seminars held at several locations in New York.

The first series of seminars, on the history of the book, was moderated by Gordon N. Ray, President of the John Simon Guggenheim Memorial

Special Collections

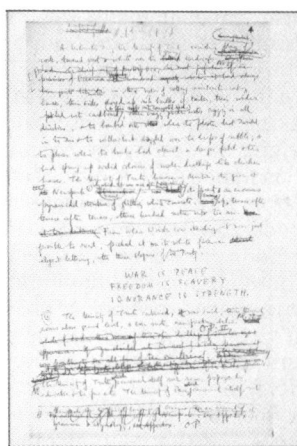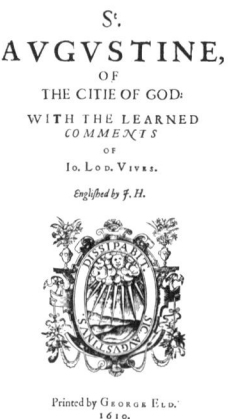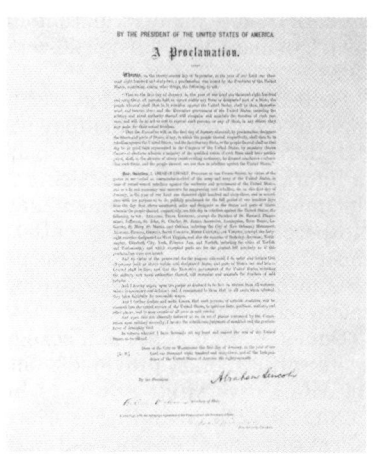

From left, title page from a 16th century Spanish work, part of a 4000-piece collection of Spanish and Portuguese books given to the University of Michigan Libraries in 1984; page from M&S Press 1984 first facsimile of extant manuscript of George Orwell's Nineteen Eighty-Four; *title page of St. Augustine's City of God (1610) acquired by Washington University in St. Louis; one of 48 known copies of the Emancipation Proclamation signed by Abraham Lincoln. Signed in 1864 for the benefit of the Philadelphia Great Central Sanitary Fair, the document sold then for $10 and in 1984 for $297,000.*

Foundation. Collector and author Mary C. Hyde spoke of the days before women were admitted as members of the Club in "Grolier Watching by a Lady, 1943–1966." Her remarks provided insights into the social life of the Club in its all-male days, and sketched the history of American book collecting as reflected in the Club's membership over a 20-year period.

G. Thomas Tanselle, bibliographical scholar and Vice-President of the Guggenheim Foundation, described "The Evolving Role of Bibliography" in a talk that emphasized the inseparability of collecting and scholarship and the need for coordination among the different disciplines that constitute bibliographical scholarship. "History of the Book: Changing Perceptions" was outlined by Robert Darnton, Professor of History at Princeton University. Darnton stressed the need for a closer relationship between the study of the book and such related disciplines as history and literature, particularly as researchers increasingly investigate trends in Western culture through the history of reading.

The second series of seminars—"Prints: Past, Present, Future"—was moderated by Andrew Robison, Curator of Prints at the National Gallery of Art. Frank Stella, representing "The Artist's View," discussed his own work as a printmaker and expressed his opinion that, as art, prints are secondary to painting given the fact that they are produced in multiple copies and are subject not only to the artist's vision but also to the effects of paper size, ink, and machinery.

Eberhard Kornfeld, proprietor of Galerie Kornfeld, Berne, traced the print trade from the 16th to the 20th centuries in "The Dealer's and Auctioneer's View." Both Kornfeld and collector Walter Bereiss, who described his own experience in "The Collector's View," concluded that the supply of old master prints is virtually exhausted and that the only possibilities for new print dealers or collectors are narrow specialization or modern prints. In "The Curator's View," Robison put forth the position that connoisseurship rather than collecting will be the future of print curatorship. He asserted that the aesthetic qualities of prints should take precedence over their "informational value" and that this fact will determine the print curator's future responsibilities.

Robert Graff, Past President of the Grolier Club, moderated the final series of seminars which dealt with "The Future of the Book." Robert Giroux, Chairman of the Board of Farrar, Straus & Giroux, pointed out the inevitability of electronic publishing in "The Publisher's View," and underscored the assumption that it is the author's words that are important rather than the form in which they appear. In contrast to Giroux's thesis, James Thorpe, Director Emeritus of the Huntington Library, expressed his belief in "The Librarian's View" that the change to electronic publishing will be gradual and that books will continue to be produced in traditional ways, though they will be fewer in number and more costly to acquire. Benjamin Compaine, Executive Director of the Harvard University Program on Information Resources Policy, emphasized the coming primacy of electronic publishing. His central theme was that the nature of literacy and its transmission are culturally determined and that there is an increasing relationship between literacy and mechanical skills, which, in combination with the increased cost of traditional publishing, will lead to the ascendancy of electronic publishing.

Daniel Bell, Professor of Sociology at Harvard University, predicted the imminent arrival of a technological revolution based on the codification of theoretical knowledge through electronic, digitalized, and miniaturized mechanical systems. Even so, he added, books will survive as a force for knowledge as opposed to sources of information.

1984. Of the year's many events associated with George Orwell's *Nineteen Eighty-Four*, perhaps the most substantial was the two-day conference April 30 sponsored by the Library of Congress. Held under the auspices of the Gertrude Clarke Whittall Poetry and Literature Fund, Orwell scholars and critics explored the writing, publishing, and impact of one of the most influential novels of the 20th century. Peter Davison of Darwin College, University of Canterbury, and Editor of the recently published facsimile of *Nineteen Eighty-Four,* delivered a lecture on "What Orwell Really Wrote." Jenni Calder, Lecturer in the Education Department of the Royal Scottish Museum, and Peter Stansky, Professor of History at Stanford University, collaborated on a talk entitled "Orwell: The Man." A panel consisting of critic Alfred Kazin, Jeffrey Meyers, Professor of English at the University of Colorado, and Denis Donoghue, Professor of English and American Literature at University College, Dublin, discussed "1984: The Book." Bernard Crick, author of *George Orwell: A Life,* and Nathan Scott, Jr., concluded the seminar with an exploration of "1984: Its Meaning in 1984." The conference papers are to be published by the Library of Congress.

THE TRADE

The Auction Rooms. The antiquarian trade in books, manuscripts, prints, and other rare materials continued to flourish in 1984. Plate books, Judaica, modern first editions, bindings, and presidential manuscripts sold well, continuing a trend of recent years.

Natural history, atlases, and travel books sold extremely well, as evidenced by the February 1 sale at Sotheby's–London which set four records, including those for Audubon's *The Birds of America,* which sold for £1,000,000 ($1,529,000) topping the 1982 record of £890,904, and for Ottens' *Composite Atlas,* which, at £96,800 ($134,500), was the highest price paid to date for a single volume printed atlas. Extraordinarily high prices were paid by a private collector at the Sotheby's-New York sale of the Marcus and Elizabeth Crahan Collection of books on food, drink, and gastronomy. Among the items sold were the first printed edition of the earliest known cookery text, written by the Roman gourmet Apicius; the first printed cookery book, Bartholomaeus Platina's *De Honesta Voloptate et Voletudine,* printed in Venice in 1475; the first edition of Escoffier's *Le Guide Culinaire;* and the first edition of Irma Rombauer's *The Joy of Cooking.*

The record price for a modern illustrated book and an art deco binding was set by the same item, sold from the estate of Florence J. Gould. The binding, a 1920s green leather wrapping by George Cretté, covered the 1899 edition of Jules Renard's *Histoires Naturelles,* illustrated by Toulouse-Lautrec. Christie's-New York conducted a successful sale of bindings in 1984 with art deco bindings again selling especially well, an example being a 1936 binding signed "J. K. Van West," which sold for $19,000, four times the estimate.

Prices for Americana continued to rise during 1984. At the Doyle Galleries sale of Joan Whitney Payson's estate, collector Malcolm Forbes paid $231,000, a record price for any American manuscript or autograph, for the 12-page manuscript of Abraham Lincoln's last public address. In the same sale, a manuscript copy of Whitman's "Oh Captain! My Captain!" was purchased for $82,250 on behalf of the Brown University Library; the last such manuscript copy sold for $15,000 in the 1978 Sang sales. In May Christie's–New York sold an unusually fine set of autographs of the Signers of the Declaration of Independence, again from the Sang estate; 43 of the items were dated 1776 and 33 were autograph letters. The set was purchased for $352,000, 70 percent higher than the price recorded for a set sold by the New Jersey Historical Society the previous year.

Book Fairs. The puzzling fluctuations in attendance and buying patterns at book fairs in recent years continued in 1984, although an improved economy was reflected at several fairs throughout the year. Surveys conducted by *A B Bookman's Weekly* reported general optimism among dealers who participated in the International League of Antiquarian Booksellers in London, the New York and California Antiquarian Book Fairs, and newer, regional fairs such as those held in Tampa, Florida, and Vancouver, British Columbia. At these and other fairs approximately half the dealers agreed that sales met expectations and often, for example, the California fair held in Los Angeles, as many as one-third of the dealers declared that results exceeded their expectations. In contrast, the Boston Antiquarian Book Fair recorded a decline in both attendance and sales after several years of steady growth. The consensus among dealers surveyed by *Bookman's Weekly* at the Boston fair seemed to focus on the proliferation of small one-day fairs that divert attention from more established fairs.

EDUCATIONAL AND RESEARCH PROGRAMS

American Antiquarian Society. Among the first undertakings of the American Antiquarian Society's recently established Program in the History of the Book in American Culture was a "Needs and Opportunities Conference," November 1–3. The purpose of the conference was to bring together scholars from several disciplines including English literature, history, bibliography, religion, and librarianship to explore new interdisciplinary approaches to the history of the book in American culture. Eleven papers were presented on needs and opportunities for research, including: "The Printing Trade and Allied Crafts," by William S. Pretzer, Office of Advanced Studies, Winterthur Museum; "Publishing," by Michael Winship, Editor, *Bibliography of American Literature;* "Networks of Distribution," by James Gilreath, Department of Rare Books and Special Collections, Library of Congress; "Readers and Reading," by William J.

Portrait of the 19th century American composer and pianist, Louis Moreau Gottschalk whose direct descendant Lily B. Glover discovered his diary and more than 130 letters which were added in 1984 to The New York Public Library's collection of Gottschalkiana. The collection is held at the Music Division at Lincoln Center.

Special Collections

Gilmore, Professor of History, Stockton State College; "The Books and Popular Culture," by David A. Grimsted, Associate Professor of History, University of Maryland; "The Morphology of the Book," by Roger E. Stoddard, Houghton Library, Harvard University; and "Social History and the Book," by Robert A. Gross, Associate Professor of History, Amherst College.

The central issue that emerged from the conference was the relationship of analytical and descriptive bibliography to the social and cultural history of the book and the need to pursue the study of that relationship as it applies to the history of the influence the book has had on American culture. This interaction of disciplines relative to the history of the book in America was to continue in the summer of 1985 with a seminar sponsored by the American Antiquarian Society entitled "The Making of Literate America: Diffusion of Culture Based on Printing, 1759–1850." The seminar was intended to introduce recent trends in scholarly interpretation of the history of the book to librarians, bibliographers, and academic researchers.

Columbia University Rare Book School. The Columbia University School of Library Service significantly expanded its summer Rare Book School in 1984. Under the direction of Assistant Dean Terry Belanger, a total of 20 noncredit courses of interest to rare book librarians, booksellers, and to collectors were offered from July 9 to August 17. Subjects ranged from the illustrated book in 16th-century France and Italy to scholarly editing, rare book exhibitions, and microcomputers for rare book libraries. Among the 30 faculty were David B. Gracy II, Director of the Texas State Archives; Elizabeth M. Harris, Curator of Graphic Arts, Smithsonian Institution; Alexandra Mason, Director of the Spencer Research Library, University of Kansas; James Mosley, Librarian of the St. Bride Printing Library; and Michael Winship, Editor of the *Bibliography of American Literature*.

Catholic University Rare Book Program. In 1984 the School of Library and Information Science of the Catholic University of America expanded its program leading to a concentration in rare book librarianship. Already present in the curriculum are courses in archival management, map librarianship, conservation of library materials, the history of the book, and the history of children's literature. New to the program is a course in rare book librarianship and scheduled for fall 1985 are courses in analytical/descriptive bibliography and the automated cataloging of manuscripts and archives. Future plans include a course on historical and documentary editing. Paul S. Koda, Associate Professor in the School of Library and Information Science, coordinates the program.

LIBRARIES

Celebratory Events. In observance of the acquisition of its 5,000,000th volume, the Stanford University library was presented by its Associates with a manuscript of the *Dragmaticon* by the philosopher William of Conches. The manuscript, a 15th-century copy of a 12th-century original that has never been published, is the only copy of the *Dragmaticon* in the United States.

To celebrate the addition of its 2,000,000th volume, Washington University in St. Louis added to its holdings the first English edition of St. Augustine's *The City of God*, printed in London by George Eld in 1610. The volume is heavily annotated by 17th-, 18th-, and 19th-century scholars, including John Ruskin.

On December 6, Columbia University opened to the public its new Rare Book and Manuscript facility on the sixth floor of Butler Library. A climate-controlled structure two floors in height, the Library affords new reading rooms and exhibition and work areas that are intended to make Columbia's special collections properly accessible to scholars and the general public for the first time. An exhibition and an illustrated history of the collections, entitled *The Rare Book and Manuscript Library of Columbia University: Collections and Treasures*, commemorated the event.

The New York Public Library opened its newly restored D. Samuel and Jeane H. Gottesman Exhibition Hall on June 1 with an exhibition entitled "Censorship: 500 Years of Conflict." The opening was marked by a gala reception and dinner held in adjoining Bryant Park. Speakers for the occasion were authors Isaac Bashevis Singer, Toni Morrison, and Stephen Jay Gould, all of whom complemented the theme of the inaugural exhibition in remarks that celebrated the role of libraries as storehouses and guardians of knowledge and culture.

Acquisitions. Notable acquisitions by American libraries in 1984 included:

Arizona State University: A substantial collection of materials by and about American novelist William S. Burroughs including manuscripts and drafts of several of his major works.

Columbia University: Approximately 10,000 items pertaining to the career of Erskine Caldwell added to the manuscript collection of literary agent James Oliver Brown. Covering the period 1951–56, the papers contain over 1,000 letters concerning several of Caldwell's novels including *Claudelle Inglish*, *Close to Home*, and *The Courting of Susie Brown*.

University of Delaware: The papers of Black American poet Paul Laurence Dunbar and his wife, the feminist Alice Moore Dunbar Nelson. Also included in the collection are books from Dunbar's library, photographs, typescripts, and journals.

Library of Congress: A significant collection of notebooks, letters, music scores, photographs, and manuscripts once belonging to Serge Diaghilev and subsequently to Serge Lifar. The collection includes Diaghilev's entire working library of music scores, a diary that details the last three years of his life, and an important collection of drawings by Diaghilev's collaborator, stage, and costume designer Leon Bakst.

University of Michigan: 4,000 Spanish and Portuguese books from the 15th through the 20th centuries, including many rare items from el Siglo de Oro.

Pierpont Morgan Library: The remarkable William S. Glazier Collection of illuminated manuscripts, on deposit at the Morgan since 1962. Included in the 75-item gift was a 5th-century Coptic Acts of the Apostles which contains what may be the earliest extant Christian miniature; the *Chelles Sacramentary*, painted at the French Abbey of Saint-Amand about 860; and the *Hachette Psalter*, a series of large-scale early Gothic miniatures painted in England in the first quarter of the 13th century.

University of Texas: A collection of 89 autograph music manuscripts by Gabriel Fauré, Maurice Ravel, Claude Debussy, Paul Dukas, and Albert Roussel. Some 60 percent of Roussel's repertory is included in the collection as is about half of Ravel's oeuvre.

Trinity College (Hartford, Connecticut): A major natural history collection, particularly strong in ornithology. Included among the 6,000 volumes are *Histoire Nouvelle des Oiseaux d'Afrique* by Francois Le Vaillant, Buffon's *Histoire Nouvelle des Oiseaux*, and numerous color plate books.

University of Wyoming: A significant collection of 350 printed books by the English Romantic poets and essayists, including notable early editions by Coleridge, Byron, Wordsworth, and De Quincy.

Exhibitions. One of the largest exhibitions of 1984, and certainly the most highly touted, was "Censorship: 500 Years of Conflict," which inaugurated the New York Public Library's newly restored Gottesman Exhibition Hall. The exhibition consisted of some 300 books, manuscripts, broadsides, documents, prints, and drawings chosen from the library's collections for their particularly vivid depiction of five centuries of religious, political, scientific, and moral censorship. Among the landmark items displayed were Martin Luther's 1534 translation of the Bible, the scientific writings of Galileo, and *Huckleberry Finn*; essays by John Locke and Thomas Jefferson on freedom of expression; court records from famous censorship trials such as those of John Peter Zenger and Henry Miller; and the satirical graphics of Daumier, Gillray and Rowlandson. The accompanying catalog, with over 100 illustrations, contained eight chronologically arranged essays on various aspects of censorship by, among others, Joel H. Wiener, Paul F. Grendler, Michel Melot, and Margaret C. Jacob.

1984 was a particularly good year for exhibitions of nonbook materials, especially manuscripts. A major exhibition entitled "Illuminated Manuscripts, Masterpiece in Miniature" commemorated the 50th anniversary of the opening of Baltimore's Walters Art Gallery as a public museum. The 185 manuscripts on display provided a capsule history of manuscript production in Western and Near Eastern cultures from the early middle ages through the 16th century. Of particular interest was the selection representing the Walters collection of Armenian illustrated manuscripts, the largest such collection in the U.S. A catalog describing 40 of the items on display was written by the collection's curator, Lillian M. C. Randall.

The Pierpont Morgan Library, to celebrate its 60th anniversary, displayed 30 illuminated manuscripts and 30 autograph manuscripts, several of which were recent acquisitions. Among the earlier manuscripts on display were the Dutch *Hours of Catherine of Cleves*, the *Glastonbury Gospels*, which contain some of the finest English drawings of the 10th century, and the *Histoire Naturelle des Indes*, an illustrated journal made during an early voyage to America, possibly by a seaman who sailed with Sir Francis Drake. The modern manuscripts on view included that for John Steinbeck's *Travels with Charley*, one of Henry David Thoreau's journals, and a summary of the theory of relativity by Albert Einstein.

Drawing exclusively from its own holdings, the Humanities Research Center at the University of Texas mounted a comprehensive exhibition on the work of Samuel Beckett. Printed plays and novels, unpublished manuscripts, and voluminous correspondence were included in the exhibit. Among the featured novels were *Watt, Malone Dies*, and *Murphy*; plays exhibited included "Waiting for Godot," "Krupp's Last Tape," and "Endgame." A catalog with well over 100 illustrations was compiled by curators Carlton Lake, Sally Leach, and Linda Eichhorn.

"Alexander's Feast; or, The Power of Musick" was an exhibit of important 17th- and 18th-century books and manuscripts on music exhibited at the Alderman Library of the University of Virginia. Included in the display were Athanasius Kircher's "Musurgia Universalis," published in Rome in 1650; an opera written by Jean-Jacque Rousseau; a first edition of Beethoven's Fifth Symphony; music copied by Thomas Jefferson; and a series of instrumental instruction manuals.

The Library of Congress displayed a series of rare posters in an exhibition entitled "The Poster as Art in the 1890's." Tracing the fin-de-siècle art poster to its origins in France, the exhibit showed the work of pioneer artists Jules Chéret and Eugène Grasset, who strove to impose artistic integrity upon posters intended for commercial purposes. The exhibit chronicled the brief period during which American businesses, especially publishers such as Lippincott, Harper, and Scribner, commissioned art posters by artists of the caliber of Charles Dana Gibson, Will Bradley, Maxfield Parrish, and Edward Penfield.

One of the most lavish exhibitions of 1984 was "Images of the World: The Atlas through History," mounted in the Madison Gallery of the Library of Congress. Over 200 volumes and plates, drawn primarily from the Geography and Map Division, illustrated the expansion of geographic and scientific knowledge from the Age of Discovery to the rise of the natural and social sciences during the 19th and 20th centuries. Among the rare items on display were a three-color woodcut of the province of Lorraine from Martin Waldsemuller's 1513 edition of Ptolemy's *Geography*; several plates and volumes from atlases produced by Willem Blaeu, including *Le Grand Atlas*, the largest atlas ever produced; and a copper engraving of a world map published in 1478, which is based on a manuscript map by Nicolaus Germanus.

Among the year's more unusual book exhibitions was the Library Company of Philadelphia's "First American Editions," a display of the first American printing of major European books. Included in the exhibition were the Library Company's copy of the first Bible printed in America, John Eliot's Indian Bible of 1663; the first Ameri-

Special Collections

can encyclopedia, published in Philadelphia by Thomas Dobson between 1790 and 1796; and such classics as Cicero's *Cato Major*, printed by Benjamin Franklin, and the *Aeneid*, first printed by Isaiah Thomas in 1796. A second exhibition of note at the Library Company was entitled "China on Our Shelves," and consisted of books and prints that illustrated the Western world's long fascination with China. Featured in the exhibit were early accounts of Jesuit missionaries, descriptions of Italian, Dutch, and English ambassadorial expeditions whose purpose was to open trade with China, and many 18th- and 19th-century accounts written by a wide range of individual travelers. Among the important books exhibited were Athanasius Kircher's encyclopedic *La Chine* and Jean-Baptiste Du Halde's *Description . . . de la Chine*.

During 1984, two of New York's most venerable libraries saluted individuals who were responsible for their early growth. The Pierpont Morgan Library mounted an exhibition that traced the career of its first Director, the legendary Belle da Costa Greene. Comprising correspondence between Miss Greene and many of the leading scholars and book dealers of her era, the exhibition underscored her importance in developing the Morgan Library into one of the world's great research libraries at a time when few women held positions of responsibility in American libraries. The New-York Historical Society honored its founder, John Pintard, with an exhibition of Pintard's gifts to the library. Included in the exhibition were one of two known copies of the first map of New York, engraved and printed by William Bradford, the city's first printer; a first edition of the *Federalist*; and the second edition of the Eliot Indian Bible.

Grants. *American Antiquarian Society:* two grants totaling $125,000 from the National Endowment for the Humanities, the first of which will support the Society's long-term fellowship program. The second grant will underwrite two series of public lectures to be held in 1985 and 1986, one on "Popular Music in Nineteenth-Century America" and one on "Historical Writing in America."

John Carter Brown Library, Brown University: $195,000 from the National Endowment for the Humanities and $81,000 from the Andrew W. Mellon Foundation to continue the projected six-volume bibliographic series entitled *European Americana: A Chronological Guide to Works Printed in Europe Relating to America, 1493–1776.*

Dartmouth College: $183,000 through the Higher Education Act, Title II-C, to preserve, strengthen, and provide improved access to 10,000 pre-1840 New Hampshire imprints.

Harvard College: $188,000 from the National Historical Publications and Records Commission to support a two-year project to survey and improve access to manuscript collections at Harvard and Radcliffe College. The project will improve collection descriptions and expand name and subject access.

Indiana University: $608,000 through the Higher Education Act, Title II-C, to support a joint cataloging project with the University of Arizona, the University of California, Riverside, the University of Delaware, and the University of Utah to create full machine-readable records for 25,000 books selected from the *Wing Short-Title Catalog* of English-language books printed between 1641 and 1700. Records will be created through OCLC.

New York Public Library: $235,000 through the Higher Education Act, Title II-C, to microfilm 3,000 volumes in its World War I collection, to preserve and box 4,000 scarce or unique items, and enter bibliographic records for treated material into the RLIN database.

New York University: $115,000 from the National Historical Publications and Records Commission to the Robert F. Wagner Labor Archives to undertake a two-year survey of labor records in New York City and, in collaboration with Cornell University and the George Meany Archives of the AFL-CIO, to establish a cooperative collecting strategy that will preserve historically important labor collections. A second grant of $185,000 through the Higher Education Act, Title II-C, will catalog and preserve monographs related to labor and radical political movements in the Tamiment Library.

Pierpont Morgan Library: $97,000 through the Higher Education Act, Title II-C, to catalog and preserve autographic materials in the Gilbert and Sullivan Collection.

Research Libraries Group: $163,000 in matching funds provided by the National Endowment for the Humanities for an archives and manuscripts retrospective conversion project. Participating libraries include those of Brigham Young University, Brown University, the University of California–Berkeley, Columbia University, Dartmouth College, Johns Hopkins University, Michigan University, the New-York Historical Society, New York University, Northwestern University, Rutgers University, and the State University of New York–Buffalo.

Stanford University: $350,000 through the Higher Education Act, Title II-C, to create and input into the RLIN database full bibliographic records for 9,500 titles included in the microprint set *Early American Imprints: Second Series*.

University of Texas: $181,000 through the Higher Education Act, Title II-C, to catalog 10,000 monographs in the Benson Latin American Collection, with data to be added to the OCLC database.

Publications. Among the most significant books of 1984 was *Rare Books 1983–84: Trends, Collections, Sources* edited by Alice D. Schreyer (New York, R. R. Bowker). Numerous aspects of the current rare book and special collections scene are surveyed in essays on such topics as recent trends in bibliography, automation, the trade, conservation, periodicals relating to rare books, and institutional collecting in the United States and Canada. Authors include Terry Belanger, G. Thomas Tanselle, William Matheson, Joan Friedman, and Carolyn Harris. Appended to the essays is an extensive Directory of Collections and Sources that includes lists of auctioneers, appraisers, and dealers along with descriptions of U.S. and Canadian special collections repositories.

Revolutionary America 1763–1789: A Bibliography by Ronald M. Gephart (Washington, D.C.:

Superintendent of Documents, Government Printing Office) is a massive two-volume bibliography that lists some 15,000 books and articles pertaining to the American Revolution, many of which are of interest to bibliographic researchers and special collections librarians. Included are citations lists and catalogs of 18th-century imprints that encompass newspapers, periodicals, books, pamphlets, broadsides, almanacs, poetry, and plays; guides to manuscript collections, arranged by state; sections on specific Revolutionary topics such as the newspaper war and the Stamp Act crisis; sections on the printing and papermaking industries and one on book manufacture and the book trade; and a section on public and private libraries of the late 18th century.

The Art of Lettering, The History, Anatomy and Aesthetics of the Roman Letter Form by Albert Kapr (Munich: K. G. Saur, distributed by Gale Research in the U.S.) provides an extensive history of the development of letterforms, both calligraphic and typographic, from cave painting to the 20th century. Kapr also analyzes problems of legibility, the metamorphosis of alphabetic symbols representing sounds, the anatomy of roman letters and examines the characteristics of 600 of the "best" composition fonts of the present day. The book contains some 500 illustrations.

In conjunction with its centennial celebrations, the Grolier Club published two significant books, *The Grolier Club, 1884-1984, Its Library, Exhibitions and Publications* and *Bibliography: Its History and Development* by Bernard H. Breslaur and Roland Folter. Eight of the sixteen essays in *The Grolier Club, 1884-1984* describe various portions of the Club's collections, from incunables to manuscripts, prints, and the Club's own archives. Other essays survey the succession of free exhibitions held in the clubhouses since 1884, the educational use of the library, and the Club publication program—145 major books as well as periodicals, catalogs, and ephemera. Contributors to the volume, all Grolier Club members, included Ruth Mortimer, C. Waller Barrett, G. Thomas Tanselle, Terry Belanger, and P. William Filby. *Bibliography: Its History and Development* was based on a Grolier Club exhibition mounted in 1981 that marked the completion of *The National Union Catalog: Pre-1956 Imprints*. The volume presents an annotated record of key works in the history of bibliography from the 3rd century B.C. to the present, in printed editions from 1472 to 1981.

The Mystique of Vellum (Boston: Bromer Booksellers) is a handsomely designed and printed volume that treats, for the first time, letterpress printing on vellum and parchment. Offering both a history of vellum printed books and a manual for printing on vellum, *The Mystique of Vellum* contains essays by Decherd Turner, Colin Franklin, and Richard Bigus. Two hundred twenty-five copies were printed on handmade Imago paper, each containing a specimen sheet of printed vellum.

It was fitting that one of the most important publications of the year was a facsimile of the extant manuscript of George Orwell's *Nineteen Eighty-Four* (Weston, Mass.: M & S Press; trade edition, Harcourt Brace Jovanovich). The color facsimile reproduces all of the manuscript that is known to have survived, approximately 44 percent of the total. The transcription of the manuscript, prepared by Orwell scholar Peter Davison, is reproduced to a scale that permits line-for-line reference to the facsimile, which is itself reproduced actual size. At the foot of each page of the transcript is a citation for corresponding page numbers of the four current editions, together with an indication of which watermark, if any, is used. Davison also contributed an introduction to the volume which provides a brief history of the writing of *Nineteen Eighty-Four* along with a physical description of the manuscript. In his preface, M & S Press proprietor Daniel G. Siegel writes a fascinating account of how the manuscript of *Nineteen Eighty-Four* came into his possession. In addition to the trade edition, 275 copies of the facsimile were bound in quarter leather and 55 copies in full leather.

Appointments. Noteworthy appointments in 1984 in rare books and special collections libraries and related institutions included: Nancy Burkett, Assistant Librarian, American Antiquarian Society; formerly head of Readers' Services, American Antiquarian Society. David Farmer, Curator of Special Collections, University of Houston; formerly Director of Rare Books and Special Collections, University of Tulsa. Anne Farnam, Director, Essex Institute; formerly Curator, Essex Institute. Sidney Huttner, Director of Rare Books and Special Collections, University of Tulsa; formerly proprietor of The Stege Press and Bindery.

Paul S. Koda, Associate Professor, School of Library and Information Science, The Catholic University of America; formerly Curator for Rare Books, University of North Carolina at Chapel Hill. Gary L. Menges, Head of Special Collections and Preservation, University of Washington; formerly Associate Director for Public Services, University of Washington. Stephen E. Ostrow, Chief, Prints and Photographs Division, Library of Congress; formerly Executive Director, Portland (Oregon) Art Association. John C. Van Horne, Librarian, Library Company of Philadelphia; formerly with the documentary editorial project, which is publishing *The Papers of Benjamin Henry Latrobe*. David Zeidberg, Head, Department of Special Collections, University of California, Los Angeles; formerly Curator of Special Collections, George Washington University.

Deaths. Deaths in 1984 included Sir Basil Blackwell, bookseller and head of the Blackwell Group that included in its holdings Blackwell/North America and over 50 bookshops in England and Europe. Knighted in 1956 for his contributions to bookselling, Sir Basil had been largely responsible for expanding the family firm into the antiquarian trade.

Marguerite Cohn, New York bookseller who with her late husband, Captain Louis Henry Cohn, established the House of Books, for over 50 years a leading firm in the field of modern literature.

Philip Hofer, noted collector, scholar, and former Curator of Printing and Graphic Arts at Harvard University. His major publications included *Baroque Book Illustration: A Short Survey; Edward Lear as a Landscape Draughtsman;*

and *Eighteenth-Century Book Illustration*.

Warren R. Howell, one of the nation's foremost rare book dealers for half a century. Proprietor of John Howell Books in San Francisco, the firm founded by his father in 1912, Howell was instrumental in building many of the nation's most important private and institutional rare book collections. Swann Galleries of New York and Butterfield and Butterfield of San Francisco will sell the firm's inventory and reference library at three auctions in 1985.

J. Ben Lieberman, author, printer, and a founder and the first President of the American Printing History Association. Author of *Type & Typefaces* and *Printing as a Hobby*, Lieberman operated a private press for many years and was president of Myriade Press, which specializes in books on printing and the graphic arts.

Margaret Bingham Stillwell, Professor Emerita of Bibliography and Librarian Emerita of the Annmary Brown Memorial, Brown University, from 1917 to 1953. A prolific scholar, she was best known for *Incunabula in American Libraries: A Second Census of Fifteenth-Century Books Owned in the United States, Mexico, and Canada; Incunabula and Americana, 1450–1800: A Key to Bibliographical Study; The Awakening Interest in Science during the First Century of Printing*; and her autobiography, *Librarians Are Human: Memories in and out of the Rare Book World, 1907–1970*.

Timothy Trace, antiquarian bookseller who at various times in his career specialized in English literature, reference materials and art, and architecture and the decorative arts. He helped strengthen several institutional libraries, including those of the Winterthur Museum and the Avery Architectural and Fine Arts Library at Columbia University.

SAMUEL A. STREIT

Special Libraries

In June, the Special Libraries Association, the second largest library and information-related association in North America and the third largest in the world, commemorated 75 years of accomplishment and achievement. Since the term special library was first applied to libraries in 1909, the Special Libraries Association has grown to just under 12,000 members, in 55 Chapters—throughout the United States, Canada, and Europe—and in 29 subject Divisions.

Conferences. SLA's 1984 75th Anniversary Conference was held in New York City, with record breaking attendance: over 6,000 attendees and 227 company or organization exhibitors. A highlight of the conference was the 75th Anniversary Celebration, which featured a pictorial essay of "SLA Conferences through the Years" and more than a baker's dozen of past SLA presidents.

The conference theme, Information in the Electronic Revolution, was a perfect frame for the Electronic Information Fair, keynote speakers, and Division programs. The Electronic Fair included both informational and amusement components and provided attendees the opportunity to examine a wide range of hardware and software and to have hands-on demonstrations of recent technological developments in information management. Three keynote sessions featured well-known speakers. In a session on Information and Politics, William D. Ford spoke on the federal role in dealing with matters relating to libraries and the dissemination of information. Gail Sheehy in a session on Information and Lifestyles discussed "pathfinders" and the factors in their successful navigation through life. In a session on Information and Productivity, conference attendees heard Donald Marchand admonish that the key to productivity in the information economy is to work smarter, not just harder. Daniel Bell speaking on the Information Era, analyzed the opportunities, limits, and implications for information professionals.

Professional Development. Professional development continued in 1984 as a high priority with special librarians/information specialists. Membership demands for continuing education opportunities led to the expansion of the Association's regional education programs and at the annual conference over 1,200 individuals registered for 25 continuing education courses. Course topics included: Managing in a Changing Environment, Strategic Planning, Marketing Management and Information Services; The Information Professional as a Leader; Microcomputer Basics, Planning for New Technologies, and Planning and Designing Databases.

The Middle Management Institute created in 1982 provides a formal management training program for special librarians/information specialists that focuses on developing decision-making skills, management aptitude, and practical training experiences. In 1984 six special librarians completed the 75-hour program and became the Institute's first graduates.

Public Relations. The Association's Public Relations program began to gain recognition for both special librarians/information specialists and the Special Libraries Association. A major accomplishment included a brochure, Managing Information as a Resource: The Key to Productivity, prepared for the White House Conference on Productivity, which highlighted the importance of special librarians and information resource centers.

Publications. SLA's publications continued to strengthen the image of the Association and provide a means of disseminating news to members and to those outside the profession; to document important professional positions and accomplishments; and to serve as the vehicle for unique presentations by leading authorities. The official journal, *Special Libraries* has gained particular recognition in the profession. During 1984 articles covered such topical areas as: Database Management Systems, Online Database Searching, Education for Librarianship/Information Science, Microcomputers, Private Sector/Public Sector Publishing, Statistical Analysis Systems, Quality Circles, National Information Policy, and Management and Administration.

Books published through the Non-Serial Publications Program provide members with important resources for development of professional and intellectual growth. Six titles were released

Pair of posters promoting library use were made available by the Connecticut Valley Chapter of the Special Libraries Association.

during 1984: (1) *Managing the Electronic Library*, (2) *Position Descriptions in Special Libraries: A Collection of Examples*, (3) *Who's Who in Special Libraries 1983/84*, (4) *Mapping Your Business*, (5) *The Search for Data in Physical and Chemical Sciences* and (6) *Readings in Technology*.

Awards. Recognizing its obligations to the library community, SLA has an awards program, which includes scholarships and stipends, for beginning M.L.S. students and the Plenum and Institute for Scientific Information scholarships for Ph.D. candidates in library and information science. Honors and awards are also given to outstanding special librarians.

Scholarships of $5,000 each were awarded to Adwoa Boateny of Corning, New York, and Susan Borrows, of Washington, D.C. Minority stipends of $3,300 each went to Valerie Ann Railey of Corona, New York, and Frazine Kenneth Taylor of Atlanta, Georgia. Alice Y. Chamis, a Ph.D. candidate, received the Plenum Scholarship.

SLA's highest award, The Hall of Fame was bestowed on four distinguished special librarians upon their retirement from long and productive careers in special librarianship: Mark H. Baer, SLA President 1976/77 and Director of Corporate Libraries, Hewlett-Packard; Vivian D. Hewitt, SLA President 1978–79 and Library Director, Carnegie Endowment for International Peace; William S. Budington, SLA President 1964–65 and Director, John Crerar Library; and Robert G Krupp, who served on the SLA Board of Directors and was Chairman of the 75th Anniversary Celebration. Krupp was also Chief of the Science and Technology Research Center, New York Public Library.

Ellis Mount and David Rhydwen were honored with the John Cotton Dana Awards in recognition of exceptional contributions to special librarianship. William O. Baker was elected an Honorary Member of the Association.

Positions and Issues. The completion of the Association's Long Range Plan was a major achievement. The Board accepted the plan in principle at its fall 1984 Board Meeting. Six priorities were identified for Association focus during 1984–89: (1) Reinforce and expand continuing education programs. (2) Develop a strong public relations program. (3) Review the finances of the Association and its constituent parts and develop a plan for maintaining a strong

This framed tribute to Special Libraries Association's 75th Anniversary Conference in June depicted founder John Cotton Dana with ALA officers and was signed by ALA's Brooke Sheldon and Robert Wedgeworth.

financial base. (4) Reappraise membership services with the specific goal of encouraging greater membership involvement. (5) Develop curriculum objectives for the graduate library and information education accreditation process. (6) Develop a plan and mechanism with full Chapter and Division involvement to improve Chapter and Division programming.

The Association through its Executive Director, with the assistance of the Government Relations Committee, continued in 1984 to monitor legislative activities with significance to the special library community. SLA joined the Coalition to Monitor Telecommunications Development Affecting Library and Educational Transmission in November 1983, and prepared testimony for the Senate Committee reviewing this issue. Among the topics of legislative interests during 1984 were (1) Telecommunications, (2) Pay Equity Act of 1984, (3) Circular A-76. (Contracting Out) (4) Postal Legislation, (5) Federal Information Policy, (6) Computer Technology, (7) Copyright, (8) Government Printing and Binding Regulations, and (9) Author's Compensation.

Future. Special librarians faced many challenges during 1984: the infusion of technological advances, the need for increased productivity, the requirements of a changing business environment, and the desire for increased recognition. The opportunity to create or control the professional future and to respond effectively to what cannot be controlled was even greater.

As David R. Bender, Executive Director of SLA, stated in his address to the Association at the 1984 Annual Business Meeting: "Anniversaries are proper times for summing up and for making new plans. If we are bold. . . we will seek to shape a future that promises not past solutions to perennial problems, but one that embraces a belief that rarely in the history of the Special Libraries Association have we been so much in charge of shaping our own future. . . . Let us be bold.

VIVIAN J. ARTERBERY

SPECIAL LIBRARIES ASSOCIATION

PRESIDENT (June 1984–June 1985):
Vivian J. Arterbery, Rand Corporation, Santa Monica, California

PRESIDENT-ELECT:
H. Robert Malinowsky, Littleton, Colorado

SECRETARY:
Frank H. Spaulding, Bell Telephone Laboratories, Holmdel, New Jersey

EXECUTIVE DIRECTOR:
David R. Bender

Membership (December 1984): 11,612
Headquarters: 235 Park Avenue South
New York, New York 10003

Staff Organizations Round Table

The *Directory of Library Staff Organizations,* published by Oryx Press, is one of the key elements Staff Organizations Round Table members have worked on in the past few years. Frances Jones, one of the authors, is a member of the SORT Executive Board, and SORT helped fund some of the original surveys that form the basis for the book. It gives names and addresses of fellow groups enabling them to seek information and assistance more effectively.

SORT reached out for new members in 1984 with a new brochure produced with assistance from the Louisville (Kentucky) Free Public Library's Community Relations Department. The brochure was distributed at several conferences.

Planning for the 1985 Chicago Annual Conference was one of SORT's primary objectives during 1984. Unions having been one of SORT's prime subjects in the past, the organization is attempting to meet the needs of other groups too. "Show and Tell" sessions from various groups in regard to their programs, activities, fund raising, and especially their constitutions, bylaws, and other documents are planned.

CHARLES D. KING

STAFF ORGANIZATIONS ROUND TABLE

CHAIR (June 1984–July 1985):
Charles King, Louisville Free Public Library, Kentucky

VICE-CHAIR/CHAIR-ELECT:
Doreen M. Lilore, District Council 52, AFSCME, Jersey City, New Jersey

SECRETARY:
Janet Woody, Cabell Library, Virginia Commonwealth University, Richmond

Membership (August 31, 1984): 131 associate members; 104 organizational members
Expenditures (August 31, 1984): $1,764

Standards

Standards under Development. Twenty-four Standards Committees (SC) were engaged in the development of new standards or revising existing standards during 1984. The standards and chairpersons of each SC were: Abbreviation of Titles of Publications (Z39.5–1969), Robert Tannehill, Chemical Abstracts Service, SC A; Language Codes, John Byrum, Library of Congress, SC C; Computer-to-Computer Protocol, Ray Denenberg, Library of Congress, SC D; Serials Holdings Statements, Susan Brynteson, University of Delaware Libraries, SC E; Common Command Language for Use in Interactive Information Retrieval, Charles Hildreth, OCLC, Inc., SC G; Bibliographic Data Source File Identification, Ted Brandhorst, ERIC Processing and Reference Facility, SC J; Romanization, Charles Husbands, Harvard University Library, SC L; Coded Character Sets for Bibliographic Information Interchange, Charles Payne, University of Chicago Library, SC N; Guidelines for Format and Production of Scientific and Technical Reports (Z39.18–1974), Thomas Pinelli, NASA, SC P.

Periodicals: Format and Arrangement (Z39.1–1977), Ed Barnas, John Wiley & Sons, SC Q; Environmental Conditions for Storage of Paper-based Library Materials, Paul Banks, Columbia University School of Library Service, SC R; Permanence of Paper for Printed Library Materials, Gay Walker, Yale University Library, SC S; Standard Order Form for the Purchase of Multiple Titles, Peter Jacobs, Professional Media Service Corporation, SC T; Standard Format for Computerized Book Ordering, Ernest Muro, Baker & Taylor, SC U; Standard Identifier for Information Organizations, Marjorie Bloss, IIT Library, SC V; Non-Serial Holdings Statements at the Summary and Detailed Levels, Stephen Davis, Library of Congress, SC W; Directories of Libraries and Information Centers (Z39.10–1971), Scott Bruntjen, Pittsburgh Regional Library Center, SC X; Eye-Legible Information on Microfilm Leaders, Trailers and Containers of Processed Microfilms, Louis Willard, Princeton Theological Seminary, Speer Library, SC Z; Interlibrary Loan Form, Olive James, Library of Congress, SC AA; Standard Computer Software Number (SCSN), David Cohen, Technique Learning Corporation, SC BB; Serial Item Identifier, Wendy Riedel, Library of Congress, SC CC; Bibliographic References (Z39.29–1977), Robert Tannehill, SC 4; and Romanization of Yiddish, Herbert Zafren, Hebrew Union College, SC 5.

New, Revised Standards. New or revised American National Standards published in 1984 included: Z39.4–1984, Basic Criteria for Indexes; Z39.27–1984, Structure for the Names of Countries, Dependencies, and Areas of Special Sovereignty for Information Interchange; and Z39.48–1984, Permanence of Paper for Printed Library Materials.

The following new draft standards or proposed revised standards were circulated for vote or comment in 1984: Z39.2, Bibliographic Information Interchange; Z39.49 (SC U), Computerized Book Ordering; Z39.50 (SC D), Information Retrieval: Application Service Definition and Protocol Specification for Open Systems Interconnection; Z39.51 (SC L), Romanization; Bibliographic Data Source File Identification (SC J); and Standard Computer Software Number (SC BB).

NISO Officers. The National Information Standards Organization's (NISO) elected officers in 1984 were Chairperson, Sandra K. Paul, President of SKP Associates; Vice-Chairperson, W. Theodore Brandhorst, Director of the ERIC Processing and Reference Facility. Brandhorst was to assume the two-year Chair of NISO on July 1, 1985.

The members of the NISO Board of Directors represent libraries, information services, and publishing. The library community was represented by Joseph Howard, Director of the National Agricultural Library; Mary Ellen Jacob, Director of Library Planning at OCLC, Inc.; and

Linda K. Bartley, CONSER Operations Coordinator at the Library of Congress.

Directors representing information services were James Rush, President of JERA, Inc.; Robert Tannehill, Jr., Library Manager at Chemical Abstracts Service; and M. Lynne Neufeld, Executive Director of the National Federation of Abstracting and Information Services.

Directors representing the publishing community were Ursula Springer, President, Springer Publishing; Seldon Terrant, American Chemical Society; and Jeffrey Heynen, President of Information Interchange Corporation.

Chairpersons of the Executive Council committees were Ted Brandhorst, Program; Sarah G. Bishop (NCLIS), Finance; Joseph Howard, Membership; Linda Bartley, Publicity; Henriette Avram (Library of Congress), International; and Susan Vita (Library of Congress), Future Planning.

During 1984 NISO worked closely with other related groups. Liaisons to such groups were Ray Denenberg (Library of Congress), American National Standards Committee X3 (Information Systems); and Ted Brandhorst, Association of American Publishers' Electronic Manuscript Project. Gary McCone served as NISO's liaison to LITA's TESLA.

International Standardization. NISO is the Technical Advisory Group (TAG) to ANSI on the work of the International Standards Organization's Technical Committee (TC) 46, which is the international counterpart of NISO. NISO is responsible for recommending the U.S. vote on draft international standards prepared by TC 46, suggesting new areas of standardization to TC 46, and representing the U.S. at their meeting.

Sandra Paul, NISO chairperson, served on the TC 46 Advisory Group. TC 46 is organized into six subcommittees and four working groups. The U.S. was actively involved in the work of SC 4, Automation in Documentation, and SC 6, Bibliographic Data Elements in Manual and Machine Processing. A number of important standards were being developed by Subcommittees 4 and 6 in 1984. SC 4 Working Group 5 was defining an international common command language for information retrieval. A draft standard was circulated for a vote in late 1984. The work of NISO's SC G is a parallel to this international activity. SC 4 Working Group 1 Character Sets for Bibliographic Use distributed a draft international standard for the Hebrew character set in 1984. This Working Group has produced extended Latin, African, Greek, and Cyrillic graphic sets and a set of extended control functions.

NISO also represents the U.S. on the TC 46 working groups formed to work on standards for Criteria for Price Indexes for Library Materials, International Library Statistics, Book and Publishing Statistics, and Back of the Book Indexes.

Other Standards Activities. The Book Industry Systems Advisory Committee (BISAC), a committee of the Book Industry Study Group, continued its work to develop computer-to-computer communication protocols for book purchasing, invoicing, and information transfer. A comparable group, established for the serials industry, the Serials Industry Systems Advisory Committee (SISAC) was working with NISO's Standards Committee CC on an identification code for individual issues of serials, as well as a code for individual articles within serials. NISO planned to continue the work begun in SISAC to develop an online ordering and claiming format for serials. The address for BISAC and SISAC is Suite 604, 160 Fifth Avenue, New York, New York 10010.

Sources. American National Standards developed by the National Information Standards Organization (Z39) and international standards produced by the ISO TC 46 are available for sale in the U.S. from the American National Standards Institute, 1430 Broadway, New York, New York 10018. For further information on NISO's program of standards development, a complimentary copy of the NISO newsletter, and an annotated list of published NISO standards, contact the National Information Standards Organization, National Bureau of Standards, Administration Building, Library E-106, Gaithersburg, Maryland 20899, Telephone (301) 921 3241.

NISO offers three categories of membership: voting members, nonvoting information members, and honorary members. Voting members—numbering 55 at the end of 1984—include associations, organizations, and companies who wish to participate and have a substantial concern for and competence in the fields covered by the scope of NISO. Voting members that joined NISO in 1984 included: Academic Press, Information Handling Services, Technique Learning Corporation, Aspen Systems, Reference Technology, Waldenbooks, and CAPCON. Information members—numbering approximately 100 at the close of 1984—include associations, government agencies, and libraries that have an interest in the activities of NISO and wish to maintain liaison with NISO. Information members receive the NISO newsletter and copies of standards in process of development.

PATRICIA HARRIS

Telecommunications

VCRs and TVROs: 1984's Hottest Trends. 1984, the prophetic year of Big Brother, was also the year of 15,000,000 home videocassette recorders (VCR) and 1,000,000 television-receive-only (TVRO) earth stations. Cable TV, now deregulated, penetrated more than 40 percent of U.S. television households. AT&T began to introduce the U.S. public to life with divestiture. USCI completed its first year as America's first commercial Direct Broadcast Satellite (DBS) service. Cellular radio penetrated 24 U.S. cities with mobile phone service. More public and private organizations instituted dedicated telecommunications networks in 1984. Nearly 15 percent of the population owned personal computers, and the public continued to look for new ways to use digital communications. Twenty years from the launch of Early Bird, the growth of U.S. telecommunications was mind-boggling.

Advanced Telephone Systems and Services. For better or for worse, January 1 officially launched the "telephone wars" with the breakup of AT&T and its seven regional operating

Telecommunications

companies. Over 70 percent of companies interviewed in a special survey reported the divestiture had a negative effect on their corporate phone service. With voice communications still accounting for a majority of telecommunications traffic, the race is heated as independent carriers vie with Bell for their share of this lucrative market. Competition is focused on long distance service and telephone equipment.

While more ads appeared in 1984 for alternative long distance services, the fact remained that AT&T Communications still controlled 90 percent of domestic long distance telephone traffic. Carriers, such as MCI, GTE Sprint, and SBS Skyline, were turning toward satellites and fiber optics as ways to eliminate their dependency on leasing AT&T's lines for their services. Yet, AT&T's prices were becoming more competitive, and 1984's general telephone consumer did not stray far from Ma Bell—whether the reason was their satisfaction with the service or their confusion over the other options. While the "equal access" regulation offers an advantage to the independents, the equalization of local access charges is working in Bell's favor. There were 400 long distance service providers in 1984; however, as with computers, the industry expects that only a dozen or so will survive.

The days of the rotary telephone set continue to be numbered, with the creation of advanced telephone equipment, such as the integrated voice-data terminal (IVDT), infrared light-based cordless phones, computer-based audio bridges, and the mobile phone. Some 200 companies are challenging AT&T Information Systems for the telephone equipment market. The rise in use of telephone modems to link computers and phones has inspired the development of computer-based telephone equipment. Telephones appear to be succeeding, where cable is failing, in the provision of interactive narrowband services, such as electronic mail, information utilities, electronic funds transfer, and audio/audiographic teleconferencing.

In 1984, the Electronic Mail Association and the Department of Commerce solved technical message interexchange problems through the adoption of the Message Handling Standard, X.400. The marriage of telephony and computers sparked trends, such as the IVDT, and company mergers, such as IBM and Rolm. More will come as companies vie with each other to provide workstations. IBM and Compaq were the biggest winners in 1984 in personal computer sales. AT&T and ITT were the strongest new PC players in 1984, according to computer consultants.

Audioconferencing remained the most popular, convenient, and affordable form of electronic conferencing, owing in large part to advances in speakerphones and audio bridges. High-quality speakerphones, ranging in price from several hundred to several thousand dollars, enable users to conduct more spontaneous, clear audioconferences, especially when the conference calls are bridged into a special computer controlled device that monitors and adjusts voice levels.

The use of audiographic equipment, in the form of freeze frame systems, electronic blackboards, telewriters, and facsimile machines, increased dramatically in 1984. The use of phone lines to send still graphics and images has become a more acceptable alternative to full-motion videoconferencing and program/course distribution. A nationwide network of slow-scan television facilities, mostly based at educational institutions and called Scan Net, was created to provide an ad hoc audiographic teleconferencing network to the occasional user. 1984 was also the year Federal Express inaugurated Zap-Mail, the product of the merging of facsimile and satellite technologies.

Anyone who has spent hours in a traffic jam can understand the motivation behind cellular radio. While mobile phones are not new, cellular radio has made them more practical. The schematics of cellular radio divide a local area into a number of "cells," each with its own central transmitter and receiver (cell site), which are interconnected by regular phone lines to the Mobile Telephone Switching Office (MTSO). The MTSO, in turn, hands off calls among cells as the mobile user moves from one cell to another. The FCC approved cellular radio in 1982, Ameritech offered the first commercial operational service in Chicago in 1983, but 1984 was the year for mobile phones to come of age with some 55,000 cellular subscribers in over 20 service areas. Cellular franchises are as hot as cable's once were. While this service is targeted at the business user, the individual consumer is expected to be among the 1,500,000 subscribers projected for 1990.

For those who do not want to pay the average monthly cellular service bill of $150, paging is a less expensive (albeit, less convenient) alternative. 1984 trends in paging included pagers with digital display for short messages and phone numbers. Service providers also recognized the value of interconnecting these local services with satellites to produce nationwide cellular and paging services. However, regulatory issues were stalling those efforts in 1984, and industry forecasters predicted such satellite services would not be available until 1986.

Video Communications Distribution Systems. The competition among broadcasters and narrowcasters for the television viewing public was finally experiencing program saturation with fewer than 10 new satellite program services spawned in 1984. The mode of program delivery is finally reaching a plateau as well, although the video consumer is still beset with a number of distribution services from which to choose. It may be easier to understand these services if they are grouped by their delivery medium: broadcast signals, coaxial cable, microwave, or satellite.

Users of video broadcast technology include regular broadcast television, low power television (LPTV), and subscription television (STV). TV broadcasters claim 1984 as their best year yet, in spite of the competitive services. The number of independent television stations doubled between 1978 and 1984. Broadcast television in 1984 was received by 99 percent of the country's households, either off-the-air, or through its competitor, cable.

Television stations, which have been too expensive for the smaller, rural markets, have now been scaled down to mini versions called low power TV stations. Rather than covering 5,000 square miles, an LPTV station signal can reach a range of up to 100 square miles. Start-up costs for a 10-watt VHF or 1-kilowatt UHF LPTV station with a 10-15 mile radius coverage can be as little as $24,000–$82,000. However, LPTV operators were finding programming to be costly, either in the construction of expensive studios for production of local programming or in the purchase of old syndicated network programs. Some LPTV operators were installing earth stations to receive satellite program services. Since the FCC authorized LPTV in 1982, some 260 LPTV stations are currently operational. Once the FCC can process its backlog of 8,000 plus LPTV applications, industry analysts predict around 4,000 stations to be in operation in 1986. Educational institutions are among the applicants.

Subscription TV was born in an effort to capitalize on pay TV public using existing facilities. STV simply uses broadcast TV channels that are idle (usually at night) to distribute its encoded programming to subscribers with special converters. Called wireless cable, sports, movies, and special events are STV's bread and butter. While STV has been around since 1968, the 1980s were witnessing its slow but sure demise. No new STV stations were started in 1984, and several closed their doors.

For years the consumer has heard of the wonders of two-way cable communications. Coaxial cable has been touted as the delivery vehicle for all types of broadcast and interactive communications. Yet, 1984 did not see much innovation in cable-based services. Instead, the economic realities of franchising and upgrading older systems with saturated markets threw the cable industry into a turmoil and stifled the growth of public access programming and services such as videotex/teletext. Many smaller operators sold out to one of several multiple system operators (MSO), and the National Cable Television Association reported the high cost of wiring cities left 65 percent of the homes in the top 10 markets without cable access. However, while the interactive information and communications applications of cable remained largely unrealized, cable TV as an entertainment medium, offering an unparalleled variety of programming, continued to thrive. Cable penetration surpassed 40 percent of U.S. TV households in 1984 and earned $800,000,000 in revenues.

A major cable event in 1984 was the U.S. Congressional passage of the Cable Communications Policy Act, which comprises the first federal cable legislation. Touted as a compromise between the cable industry and local governments, the law favored the interests of the industry.

1984 witnessed the emergence of cable's strongest competitor, not another narrowcast service, but the videocassette recorder. The number of VCRs in homes nearly quadrupled in 1983–84 thanks in large part to 50 percent unit price reductions and the same percentage increase in available video titles since 1980. Consequently, video rental houses sprang up in droves across the nation and were enjoying a healthy business from VCR owners who wanted the convenience and economic benefits of renting particular programs for several dollars to watch at their leisure. The U.S. Supreme Court ruled that time-shifting (the recording of programs for viewing at a later time) did not infringe on copyright laws.

With the price of a television-receive-only (TVRO) earth station dropping to several thousand dollars and the proliferation of satellite programming services available, it is not surprising that a number of video distribution services are satellite based, including satellite master antenna TV (SMATV) and direct broadcast satellites (DBS), or have a satellite component, such as LPTV and CATV.

SMATV, often called private cable, relays satellite programming from the operator's TVRO to the homes of a private subscriber group (usually apartment or condominium complexes) via coaxial cable. Born in 1980, SMATV originally was to provide an alternative to uncabled homes. It capitalized on cable TV's lack of urban penetration and is growing into a noticeable CATV competitor with an estimated 1,000,000 subscribers. SMATV's major advantage is its quick and low-cost system installation.

Three major victories for SMATV occurred in 1984. First, programmers, who had previously remained loyal to CATV, began to negotiate their services with SMATV operators. Secondly, FCC reaffirmed the exemption of SMATV (which operates on private property) from local government regulation. The third major event was the passage of the cable bill without a clause prohibiting SMATV operators from negotiating exclusive agreements with complex owners. With regulatory and programmatic problems now aside, SMATV should be able to grow more rapidly during the rest of the decade.

1984 saw the first shakeout of the direct broadcast satellite (DBS) industry, once proclaimed a sure winner by analysts. The original concept of DBS was to launch higher powered satellites to distribute video programming directly to small three-foot rooftop satellite antennas that would work with converters to process the signal inside the home and onto the TV set. This would bypass the need for the costly local distribution medium, such as CATV. In 1982 eight companies filed DBS applications with the FCC, but half of them dropped their plans during 1984.

The ability to be "first" with the best programming offerings has been a guiding force in the DBS race. Consequently, DBS applicants did not want to wait for their proposed 1986–87 satellite launch dates, and were eager to use existing lower-powered satellites to begin to develop their markets. After some regulatory battles, United Satellite Communications, Inc. (USCI), emerged as the first low-power DBS operator toward the end of 1983. In 1984 USCI and its DBS service were struggling for life. Watching this phenomenon made others shy away from similar activities and made most of the DBS applicants rethink their positions, including those who filed in round two during 1984.

Experts explained this reversal by pointing to the falling prices of currently available backyard TVROs. Consumers could buy and install an earth station and bring receiving 100 channels of their own "DBS-type" programming. While satellite programmers, whose services were meant

Telecommunications

for the paying local operators, fought the "pirating" of their programs by the eavesdropping public, the federal government ruled in favor of the consumer in 1984. A clause added to the cable bill legalized the sale and use of backyard TVROs. If programmers such as HBO choose to scramble their signal, the backyard consumer has the right to try to pay for individual service previously unavailable. The TVRO market has become so lucrative that over 7,000 vendors sell these "dishes." This trend is expected to continue and will greatly affect the evolution of other video services.

The last group of video distribution systems uses microwave technology and includes instructional television fixed service (ITFS) and multipoint distribution systems (MDS). In 1983 an FCC ruling fueled the long-running fire between ITFS and MDS operators. The FCC reallocated 8 of ITFS' 28 channels to MDS so that MDS could become MMDS—multichannel multipoint distribution service—and better able to compete with CATV.

ITFS was created to provide frequency spectrum for private use by nonprofit educational institutions, but until recently was largely ignored or unknown. Because these channels were not being used adequately, MDS operators, whose commercial services also used MHz band frequencies, petitioned the FCC to redistribute some ITFS channel space to MDS, where the channels would be more fully used.

MDS is regulated as a common carrier and used to transmit video, audio, and data programming services. Most MDS channels are leased to pay TV programmers who are eager to use their reallocated ITFS channels to offer their subscribers additional programming. The FCC received 16,000 applications for MMDS licenses.

The FCC finally instituted a lottery that will begin awarding these licenses. Many industry analysts see MMDS as an urban cable alternative, while DBS is the rural alternative. It remains to be seen how successful MMDS will become or what the overall impact will be on ITFS and those who would like to start-up an ITFS system.

One other television advancement was high definition television (HDTV). While still in the planning stages in America, HDTV will ultimately double the number of lines in a TV picture to provide higher resolution, better color, and stereo sound. This technology has already been demonstrated abroad. In 1984 Japan introduced the first HDTV VCR. CBS has been pursuing an interest in HDTV, but no American firm had announced definite operational plans by the end of 1984. Much of the hold-up is attributed to the expense and waste of using two channels to transmit an HDTV signal. What will undoubtedly come sooner to the American home is digital TV. The TV sets of 1984 demonstrated a commitment to an expanded use of the TV receiver. Full-motion video-teleconferencing was moving away from the occasional ad hoc use and more toward the privately owned satellite video-teleconferencing network. The 1984 trend was toward an integrated digital teleconferencing network, which enables an organization to perform a number of communications activities through one closed network.

Fiber Optic Communications. For 15 years, the public has heard about the advantages of fiber optics, a distribution medium consisting of laser beam broadband analog or digital signals traveling through glass fiber tubes. Fiber optic capacity is seemingly endless and boasts lessened signal loss and overall expense. AT&T has installed nearly 1,000 miles of optical fiber cable along the East Coast and plans to build more fiber optic networks throughout the U.S. While fiber was once compared most often with coaxial cable, the subject of many debates in 1984 was fiber versus satellites. Many carriers contend that the cost and capacity of fiber cable rivals that of the distance insensitive satellites. In 1984 South Central Bell inaugurated the first customer telephone fiber optics system. This trend to select fiber cable over coaxial cable, copper wire, satellite, microwave, and submarine cable is destined to continue with the support of the major carriers. Several other companies have begun to build fiber optic networks, particularly for local area networks. Once these networks sufficiently cover the U.S. and pass by major cities, many organizations will begin to use the network for trunking of long distance communications. Now that fiber networks are becoming a reality, the competition between fiber and satellites will intensify. Satellites as we know them today will either disappear, become more advanced, or be relegated to serving specific communications needs, such as remote and rural communications.

Satellite Communications. In 1984 the Space Shuttle launched, both successfully and unsuccessfully, several communications satellites into their geostationary orbit. More than 20 domestic satellites at year's end were operating with more awaiting construction and launch. Even in the wake of competition from fiber optics and an apparent transponder glut, the FCC continues to receive a number of satellite applications. To accommodate these requests, the FCC investigated the feasibility of moving the satellites closer together in their orbital arc. In 1984 the FCC approved the spacing of satellites from four degrees to two degrees apart and ruled this practice would commence in 1987, giving those manufacturers and owners of ground equipment time to modify their earth stations as needed.

Perhaps the biggest activity in the satellite industry in 1984 occurred in the area of international satellite communications. For 20 years, INTELSAT had been the exclusive provider of international satellite communications. This monopoly was being challenged in 1984 by several U.S. firms who planned to build, launch, and operate satellites for the provision of international business communications. To the dismay of INTELSAT and many of its member countries, the federal government gave those firms its blessing. Whether the firms can gain the cooperation of foreign countries in this endeavor remains to be seen. As a result of the challenge, INTELSAT expanded its service offerings and made its earth station requirements more flexible.

Congress voted to maintain U.S. preeminence in the satellite industry when it restored NASA's Advanced Communications Technology Satellite (ACTS) Program budget in 1984. Though the launch slipped in 1989, ACTS will provide the public with the opportunity to experiment on a state-of-the-art satellite. ACTS will be the first satellite to employ on-board switching technology. Used in conjunction with high-powered spot beams some 150-200 feet in diameter, on-board processing will allow for frequency reuse. The ultimate benefits will be conservation of spectrum and orbital arc. ACTS will be the first U.S. satellite to operate in Ka-Band, much higher frequency than the current C and Ku-Bands. NASA in 1984 was searching for public and private sector experiments that could demonstrate and test this digital technology.

Immediate domestic satellite trends are the development of private satellite networks and the move toward Ku-Band or hybrid C/Ku-Band satellites. The satellite industry is working hard to establish a healthy customer base before fiber optic networks are fully operational.

That was the year that was in telecommunications. For some it was the best of times, for others silent disaster. If Big Brother was out there in 1984, he had plenty to see and hear, and 1985 promised to be even more exciting.

MARY DIEBLER CLARK

Theatre Library Association

Awards. The Theatre Library Association's annual book awards were presented May 15 at a reception in the Main Gallery of The New York Public Library at Lincoln Center. The George Freedley Memorial Award, given for an outstanding work in the field of live theatre performance or history, was presented by Jeremy Irons to Martin Meisel for *Realizations: Narrative, Pictorial and Theatrical Arts in Nineteenth Century England.* (Princeton University Press).

The Theatre Library Association Award for an outstanding work in the area of motion pictures or broadcasting was presented by Martin E. Segal, Chairman of the Board of Lincoln Center for the Performing Arts, to Richard Roud for *A Passion for Films: Henri Langlois and the Cinematheque Francaise* (Viking Press). The Theatre Library Association Award Honorable Mention was presented by Vera Zorina to Richard Koszarski for *The Man You Loved to Hate: Erich Von Stroheim and Hollywood* (Oxford University Press). The TLA selection panel of specialists was chaired by Don B. Wilmeth of Brown University.

Activities. TLA's annual summer program and tours, during the ALA Annual Conference in Dallas, were cosponsored by the ACRL Cinema Librarians Discussion Group. The morning panel was devoted to collections in Texas. Barbara Bryant spoke about the historically significant recently rediscovered Black feature films now housed in the Southwest Film Archives at Southern Methodist University, and Raymond Daum discussed the Gloria Swanson collection in the Hoblitzelle Theatre Arts Library at the University of Texas, Austin. The program was chaired by Lee Ash, and arranged by Robert C. Eason, Dallas Public Library.

The afternoon tour arranged by Eason included visits to the Dallas Theater Center, the renovated Plaza, and the experimental New Arts in the warehouse district. Representatives of each theater spoke to the group about the physical plant and the artistic policy of the institution and conducted backstage tours. The day ended with a reception in the Fine Arts Section of the Dallas Public Library.

The annual business and program meeting was held October 19 at the Shubert Archive, Lyceum Theatre building, New York City. Four members were elected to the Executive Board for three-year terms. Board members for 1984–85 were Elizabeth Burdick, Librarian, International Theatre Institute of the U.S. (1983–86); Geraldine Duclow, Librarian in Charge, Theatre Collection, Free Library of Philadelphia (1984–87); Anthony Ibbotson, Archivist, National Arts Centre, Ottawa (1984–87); Gerald Kahan, Department of Drama and Theatre, University of Georgia (1983–86); Martha Mahard, Assistant Curator, Harvard Theatre Collection (1982–85); Julian Mates, Dean, School of the Arts, Long Island University (1982–85); Lois Erickson McDonald, Associate Curator, The Eugene O'Neill Theater Center (1983–86); Louis A. Rachow, Librarian-Curator, Hampden-Booth Library, the Players (1983–86); Elizabeth Ross, Conservation Assistant, Billy Rose Theatre Collection, the New York Public Library at Lincoln Center (1982–85); Anne G. Schlosser, Head Librarian, AFI–Louis B. Mayer Library (1984–87); Wendy Warnken, Associate Curator, Theatre Collection, the Museum of the City of New York (1984–87); and Alan L. Woods, Director, Theatre Research Institute, Ohio State University (1982–85).

The program meeting included a panel discussion on the current practices of photo archives, especially copyright problems, reproduction charges, and permission fees. Among the speakers were representatives from Harvard, The New York Public Library, the Museum of the City of New York, Culver Picture Service, Bettman Archives, and a copyright lawyer. Although many general policies were similar, great diversifica-

Below left and bottom, "The Demille Dynasty" Exhibition at The New York Public Library Lincoln Center in April featured memorabilia of the famous Hollywood family including dancer Agnes deMille and director Cecil B. DeMille. Bottom, the Library's Richard Rodgers exhibit in November included this Hirschfeld 1976 drawing of Rodgers surrounded by stars of his most famous musicals.

> **THEATRE LIBRARY ASSOCIATION**
>
> PRESIDENT (January 1983–December 1984):
> **Dorothy L. Swerdlove,** Curator, The Billy Rose Theatre Collection, The New York Public Library at Lincoln Center
>
> VICE-PRESIDENT:
> **Mary Ann Jensen,** Curator, William Seymour Theatre Collection, Princeton University Libraries
>
> SECRETARY-TREASURER:
> **Richard M. Buck,** Assistant to the Chief, Performing Arts Research Center, The New York Public Library at Lincoln Center
>
> RECORDING SECRETARY:
> **Brigitte Kueppers,** Archivist, The Shubert Archive
>
> Membership (October 1984): 248 personal; 274 institutional
> Headquarters: 111 Amsterdam Avenue, New York, New York 10023

tion in practice and interpretation was evident.

The panel was so basic to research problems that it was recycled as the Theatre Library Association program at the annual TLA/American Society for Theatre Research (ASTR) joint conference, held in 1984 on the campus of Indiana University at Bloomington in November. The subject of the conference was Revisions, Revivals, and Redactions. About 75 ASTR and TLA members heard Mel Gussow, drama critic for the *New York Times*, talk about his unusual experiences as a critic and present his thoughts on the "new" theater in the United States today. They also listened to more than 20 papers on the conference subject ranging from a Plautus revival to the Living Theatre "revival" in New York in 1983.

Publications. The Theatre Library Association publishes *Broadside*, a quarterly newsletter, edited by Alan J. Pally; and *Performing Arts Resources*, an annual publication edited by Ginnine Cocuzza and Barbara Naomi Cohen Stratyner. In 1984 the most recent volume of *Performing Arts Resources* (Vol. 9) was a translation from the Latin by Alfred S. Golding of Franz Lang's *Dissertatio De Actione Scenica* (1727). As *An Essay on Stage Performance*, this first English translation was published by TLA in August.

RICHARD M. BUCK

Trustees

Developing Lay Support. Efforts to establish and maintain statewide lay support groups grew out of state preconferences preceding the 1979 White House Conference on Library and Information Services. While trustees and Friends organizations existed independently or as a part of many state library associations, one goal was to create a high visibility group of citizen leaders to promote the importance of libraries and their needs. Sometimes a conference resolution called for the formation of a state Friends of the Library. In other cases a citizens' council was formed to include lay people who went to the state meeting without prior service as trustees or Friends. Often there was the desire to continue contact with business and civic leaders who had been exposed to the library cause.

Such groups have made progress—some by fits and starts—but the total has risen steadily. Two organizations track them: Friends of Libraries USA (FOLUSA) and WHCLIST, the White House Conference on Library and Information Services Taskforce. FOLUSA began giving awards to statewide Friends/citizens' groups in 1982, along with Friends groups affiliated with libraries. WHCLIST's *Report from the States*, begun in 1980, annually summarizes implementation progress on White House Conference resolutions.

In 1984 30 states and territories reported on statewide Friends/citizens' group activities; however, the number is believed to be as high as 39 states and two territories. Most are concerned with advocacy and creating public awareness, and stimulating vigorous local Friends of the Library is also very important. Some administer grants from federal, state, and private funding sources as high as $100,000.

Leadership has come from many sources. One has been trustees, especially of state library boards or LSCA advisory councils, coupled with support from state library agency heads. Other groups have been started by lay people who emerged from their governors' conferences with a commitment to libraries. Library directors and Friends leaders have frequently taken major roles. In some states the existing statewide trustees or Friends organization has been strengthened to meet the need for increased state funding and legislation dealing with changes in library law. The protracted effort to revise and renew the Library Services and Construction Act also received support from these organizations.

A regional conference sponsored by the Council of State Library Agencies in the Northeast in 1984 underlined the important role of the state library agency and citizens' groups. COSLINE states brought their lay and professional leadership together to participate in a replication of WHCLIST's 1983 Cheyenne meeting on successful strategies for statewide citizens' groups.

ALA's Library Administration and Management Association issued a publication in connection with its 1984 Dallas program on "Getting It Passed: Lobbying for Libraries." In a section reviewing how states get legislation and appropriations passed, many state librarians and library associations gave credit to lay support organizations formed in recent years.

Varied Support Groups. Variety in form and action characterizes lay support groups, as some examples indicate: New York has CLiC, the Citizens' Library Council of New York State, which emerged from the New York Governor's Conference and derived leadership from it. The December 1984 CLiC quarterly focused on citizens' groups around the nation. New York also has a strong independent trustees' organization that in 1984 had 100 percent participation by library boards in the state and conducts educational institutes for new trustees.

Friends of Alabama Libraries was organized for advocacy purposes by a trustee with experience at the national, regional, state and local lev-

els. Principal funding came from a golf tournament that twice raised over $10,000 to finance advocacy efforts.

Friends of Missouri Libraries was started by a young mother "turned on" to libraries by the state preconference. It performs traditional statewide Friends functions: newsletter, state library legislative lay support, and encouraging formation of new Friends groups.

Friends of Virginia Libraries, on the other hand, is a political action committee. Its board is composed of a librarian, a trustee and a vendor, and it has no members or meetings. The PAC was so successful in raising funds and backing political candidates that Virginia leaped from 30th in direct state aid per capita to 4th among the states in one year.

The Coalition of Library Advocates in Rhode Island was an informal liaison of library organizations led by a trustee working with the state library on advocacy initiatives. Its 1984 project was to sponsor a statewide workshop dealing with the role of libraries in education. The organization was being incorporated in order to accept gifts and grants.

ICOLA, the Illinois Coalition of Library Advocates, has been chaired by several citizens who attended the White House Conference. The group received LSCA funds from the Illinois State Library for two years to establish a statewide speakers' bureau. Trustees, Friends, and interested citizens have been nominated by library systems to participate in a training program on library services to enable them to speak before civic groups about what Illinois libraries can offer the public now and in the future.

The Council for Florida Libraries was organized to promote the number one priority of that state's conference—public awareness. It began with a statewide multimedia PR program contributed by the state Advertising Federations. The state library then awarded the Council a series of annual grants for professional PR campaigns promoting services to people and to business.

LIBRA/NJ, Library Advocates of New Jersey during 1984 worked to involve advertising firms headquartered in that state in donating a PR campaign.

Pennsylvania Citizens for Better Libraries established itself through a statewide school essay contest developed by a librarian member. This organization should receive future benefits from a 1984 corporate luncheon sponsored by a Philadelphia bank. Representatives from publishers and other library-oriented businesses heard about PCBL's projects and the need for financial support.

In Arizona the statewide Friends started with trustee and Friend leadership from a metropolitan library system. Their board includes members who are both trustees and Friends, as well as librarians representing large and small libraries.

BARBARA COOPER

Far left, James A. Gary, III, President of the Enoch Pratt Free Library Trustees, Baltimore, joins in the "Tom Sawyer Paint Off" that marked the beginning of the Central Library's $3,000,000 renovation project. Above, Baltimore's Mayor William Donald Schaefer speaking at groundbreaking ceremonies in December.

Universal Bibliographic Control

ISBD Activities. The review of the earliest ISBDs published in 1977–78—*ISBD(M)* for Monographs, *ISBD(S)* for Serials, *ISBD(CM)* for Cartographic Materials and *ISBD(NBM)* for Non-Book Materials—entered a particularly active phase in 1984. Prepared by four specialist subgroups under the supervision of the IFLA ISBD Review Committee, the review drafts were circulated for public comment from September 1983 to March 1984. Comments were received from over 60 organizations, some having polled their own specialized membership to present views from several sources. After the comments were sorted and collated, the four Chairmen had the task of considering them, individually and collectively, to ensure standardization of wording, definitions, and style. The final texts for voting by IFLA sponsoring sections were unlikely to be ready before mid-1985 with publication planned by early 1986.

Meanwhile, the review of *ISBD(PM)* for Printed Music, first published in 1980, has begun with a call for comments and suggestions. This will be a joint project with the International Association of Music Libraries, Archives and Documentation Centres (IAML). Two new ISBD texts under consideration are *ISBD(CP)* for Component Parts (i.e., sections of bibliographic units which are already the subject of a full description: for example, articles in journals, tracks of a record) and an ISBD for machine-readable files and computer software.

CIP. The International Cataloguing-in-Publication Meeting, convened by IFLA in association with UNESCO in Ottawa, 1982, considered the standardization of CIP in several countries. The proceedings and recommendations of that meeting have been published and are available from the IFLA International Programme for UBC, c/o British Library, London. Two working groups are following up the recommendations to design a standard CIP data sheet for publishers to use and to design a standard CIP entry for the verso of the title page of the book. A preliminary report has been circulated to the participants of the meeting. The working groups planned to make their final recommendations in 1985. Their findings will be published as part of the *CIP Guidelines,* an IFLA/UNESCO project to assist CIP agencies in operational procedures and in establishing relationships with publishers.

Authority Entries. The text of *Guidelines for Authority and Reference Entries* was prepared for issue in 1985. The work on standardization of authority entries continues; a new Steering Group will supervise the preparation of UNIMARC format for authority and reference entries.

Further information on UBC activities can be found in the IFLA UBC Programme's journal, *International Cataloguing,* in its 13th year in 1984.

What is UBC? The commitment of the International Federation of Library Associations and Institutions (IFLA) to the quest for Universal Bibliographic Control (UBC) was sustained throughout 1984 by the belief that efficient access to records of the world's imprint is the first step in making that information universally available.

Clearly the knowledge that an article, map, music sheet or report exists does not guarantee that the would-be user will be able to obtain a copy of it. The task of improving access to the material is taken over by the twin IFLA program, Universal Availability of Publications (UAP).

UBC directs its efforts to the rationalization of bibliographic recording. It is accepted that the national bibliographic agency of a country is best equipped in knowledge of local publishing and national terminology to record that country's imprint. It aims to create an authoritative record in a standardized form, as soon as possible after the appearance of the publication and to make those records available nationally to be exchanged internationally in the form of bibliographies—printed, microfiche or machine-readable. Thus, the need for repetitive intellectual analysis of the same items is minimized.

The networks of data thus created should favor the development of union catalogs, interlibrary loan, resource sharing, and national acquisition policies. As more and cheaper information becomes available, individuals and societies will have the opportunity to make informed decisions about their future.

Practical steps to standardize bibliographic recording include: following the International Standard Bibliographic Descriptions (ISBDs) for descriptive cataloging, using internationally recognized subject cataloging and classification schemes and thesauri, agreeing on the structure of headings (corporate and personal and title), employing standard filing rules. Standard records so produced can be integrated into any catalog or listing or checked against an authority file with a minimum of editing.

IFLA also responds to requests to maintain and improve its standards and to extend them to cover all library materials, particularly recent acquisitions, for example, the products of new technology.

BARBARA JOVER

Universal Serials and Book Exchange

Year of Transition. With the retirement of three administrative officers who had directed USBE operations since 1948, the organization's focus in 1984 was on internal change and on the definition of future directions. Incoming Executive Director Mary W. Ghikas was joined by Business Manager Robert Hodges, Director of Membership Services Patricia R. Emerson, Manager of Operations Claude Hooker, Branch Manager Henry Reed, and Administrative Assistant Gerald H. Phillips.

An IBM-PC/XT was acquired at USBE, providing technological resources for expansion of the monthly newsletter, which was combined with the separately issued order lists to form a monthly catalog and newsletter (*USBE/NEWS*); streamlining of mailing list operations; and development of expanded membership files, preparatory to the scheduled 1985 publication of a USBE membership directory.

The trend to online ordering continued, with OCLC, BRS, UTLAS, and DIALOG/DIALORDER orders continuing to grow. Based on member demand, telex service, through MCIMail, was added in 1984. Additional expansion into electronic mail service was scheduled for 1985.

In May the USBE Board of Directors voted to offer USBE subscriptions as well as membership. The subscription program provided an alternative for small libraries as well as for others with highly specialized interests. At the same time, the differential handling charge on orders from outside North America, added in 1980, was dropped.

In addition to expansion of *USBE/NEWS*, USBE began a series of subject catalogs, beginning with *Medicine and Allied Health Sciences* and *Law and Related Subjects.* Scheduled for 1985 was a listing of holdings in science/technology.

Finally, USBE's program of direct contact with members was expanded in 1984 with addition of the Canadian Library Association, the ALA's Association of College and Research Libraries, and the American Society for Information Science conferences to a schedule that already included the American Library Association, Special Library Association, and Medical Library Association conferences. After a long absence, USBE announced it would return to the ALA Midwinter exhibit.

USBE's Mission. From its inception, USBE has been, both in governance and character, a membership cooperative. Libraries and other information centers support each other through contribution to a common pool of useful, *redistributable* information resources. These resources are evaluated, inventoried, organized and made accessible by USBE for *future* acquisition—to replace lost or damaged materials, to extend and develop collections, and to fill specific information demands with appropriate materials, whether or not those materials exist within an individual library's or institution's own collection. This commitment to keeping a broad range of information resources alive has enriched the educational and scientific community for over 35 years.

In 1984 "The Collection Network" includes 1,000 institutions and libraries in 43 countries. In addition to those formally affiliated with USBE, many other libraries and information centers contribute to and draw from the resource pool on a nonmember basis. The continually changing "collection" of information resources includes over 4,000,000 items, primarily serials. Over 3,800,000 issues of some 40,000 serial titles are held, plus a volatile stock of approximately 50,000 monographs, as well as microforms and other formats. Almost 200,000 items are redistributed annually. Almost 1,000,000 items are annually received and evaluated, with retention based on membership demand. USBE also provides its members an effective channel for the direct exchange of material, "brokering" the library-to-library resource redistribution.

Board of Directors. Under the leadership of President Susan K. Martin, Director of the Milton S. Eisenhower Library, Johns Hopkins University, the 1984 USBE Executive Board included Past President Juanita S. Doares, Associate Director for Collection Management and Development, New York Public Library; Vice-President/President-elect Joseph M. Dagnese, Director of Libraries, Purdue University; Treasurer Murray S. Martin, Librarian, Tufts University; and Secretary Joyce D. Gartrell, Head, Serials Cataloging, Columbia University Libraries. Members of the Board of Directors in 1984 were Patricia W. Berger, Chief, Library and Information Services Division, National Bureau of Standards; H. Joanne Harrar, Director of Libraries, University of Maryland; Joseph H. Howard, Director, National Agricultural Library; Nancy H. Marshall, Associate Director of Libraries for Public Services, University of Wisconsin–Madison; Frank H. Spaulding, Head, Library Operations, Bell Laboratories, Holmdel; and Benita M. Weber, Head, Serials Department, University of New Mexico General Library. With the absence of Nancy H. Marshall early in the year, 1982–83 Board Member Richard DeGennaro extended his term through the first half of 1984. Members of the Executive Board and Board of Directors are elected annually, for two-year terms, by USBE member institutions.

MARY W. GHIKAS

Urban Libraries Council

The Urban Libraries Council and the School of Library Science and Information of the University of Pittsburgh sponsored a seminar on "The Urban Electronic Library in the Communications Era" in Washington, D.C., in January during the ALA Midwinter Meeting. Seventy-five librarians from all over the United States as well as a librarian from the Netherlands registered for the program. The papers of the seminar were published by the Council.

The Council's semiannual survey (1984) of state aid to public libraries reported that 43 states provide some form of state aid to public libraries; 36 states provide direct state aid to public libraries; 28 states provide state aid to cooperative public and multitype library systems and networks; 8 states provide state aid for construction of public library buildings.

The 1984 survey indicated an impressive increase in state aid to public libraries. The total amount for 1983 was $252,510,536 as compared with $200,406,433 for the previous year. The 1983 figure represents a nationwide average of $1.11 per capita. The largest per capita amount for state aid to public libraries was $3.32 in Maryland, followed by New York with $2.98, West Virginia with $2.89, Alaska with $2.34, Rhode Island with $2.27, Georgia with $2.04, Illinois with $1.93, Virginia with $1.82, Massachusetts with $1.79, and Michigan with $1.66.

The Council actively promoted federal aid to public libraries during 1984. Several of its members and officers participated in National Library Day in Washington, urging not only the extension of the Library Services and Construction Act, but also increases in the authorization of funds for the various Titles of the Act.

The Urban Libraries Council compiles every other year a comprehensive statistical study of public libraries that are members of the Council. The accompanying tables provide a summary for 1983.

ALEX LADENSON

URBAN LIBRARIES COUNCIL

PRESIDENT (June 1984–June 1985):
Harold F. Herring, Huntsville, Alabama

VICE-PRESIDENT:
Paulette Holahan, New Orleans

SECRETARY:
Marjorie Stern, San Francisco

TREASURER:
David M. Hennington, Houston

EXECUTIVE DIRECTOR:
Alex Ladenson

Membership (December 1984): 171 public libraries
Headquarters: 425 North Michigan Avenue, Room 1102, Chicago, Illinois 60611

Urban Libraries Council — **Annual Statistics (1983)**

ANNUAL EXPENDITURES

Number of libraries	Population served	Low	Median	High
17	50,000–99,999	$ 713,631	$ 1,172,044	$ 2,718,263
41	100,000–199,999	762,495	1,958,160	3,997,567
16	200,000–299,999	1,286,504	2,069,550	7,381,790
18	300,000–499,999	2,438,597	5,416,431	12,170,241
24	500,000 and over	3,948,002	14,148,637	40,334,343

PER CAPITA EXPENDITURES

Number of libraries	Population served	Low	Median	High
17	50,000–99,999	$6.94	$13.72	$40.93
41	100,000–199,999	4.57	13.95	26.45
16	200,000–299,999	4.59	9.50	36.19
18	300,000–499,999	6.66	11.42	24.96
24	500,000 and over	6.67	13.39	29.74

CIRCULATION

Number of libraries	Population served	Low	Median	High
17	50,000–99,999	247,073	615,797	1,065,000
41	100,000–199,999	191,665	828,289	1,596,876
16	200,000–299,999	513,003	1,029,189	2,141,461
18	300,000–499,999	1,170,684	1,796,683	7,150,010
24	500,000 and over	1,168,051	3,950,601	10,061,567

BOOK EXPENDITURES

Number of libraries	Population served	Low	Median	High
17	50,000–99,999	$61,050	$153,800	$462,817
41	100,000–199,999	75,000	238,154	598,420
16	200,000–299,999	171,778	276,299	892,468
18	300,000–499,999	336,867	692,000	1,160,103
24	500,000 and over	434,068	1,527,185	4,260,380

NUMBER OF VOLUMES

Number of libraries	Population served	Low	Median	High
17	50,000–99,999	66,650	170,387	390,480
41	100,000–199,999	160,000	326,389	747,106
16	200,000–299,999	226,065	394,961	1,651,407
18	300,000–499,999	410,041	765,991	1,886,245
24	500,000 and over	802,934	1,900,197	5,388,480

STAFF

Number of libraries	Population served	Low	Median	High
17	50,000–99,999	31	47	132
41	100,000–199,999	19	83	160
16	200,000–299,999	42	80	287
18	300,000–499,999	90	175	353
24	500,000 and over	167	437	2,020

SALARY OF BEGINNING LIBRARIAN

Number of libraries	Population served	Low	Median	High
17	50,000–99,999	$10,500	$16,744	$19,843
41	100,000–199,999	11,000	16,545	22,812
16	200,000–299,999	12,967	16,692	26,600
18	300,000–499,999	12,147	16,644	24,612
24	500,000 and over	13,188	18,221	28,356

SALARY OF LIBRARY DIRECTOR

Number of libraries	Population served	Low	Median	High
17	50,000–99,999	$21,961	$35,970	$49,003
41	100,000–199,999	29,181	39,325	63,076
16	200,000–299,999	35,664	43,440	59,073
18	300,000–499,999	39,306	47,000	63,152
24	500,000 and over	42,375	50,000	86,882

State Aid to Public Libraries (1984 appropriations)

State	Direct aid to public libraries	Public and multitype library systems and networks	Construction of buildings	Total	Per capita	State library agency operations
Alabama	$ 1,946,944	$ a	$ —	$ 1,946,944	$ .50	$1,547,546
Alaska	648,065	293,135	—	941,200	2.34	2,658,800
Arizona	300,000	—	—	300,000	.11	3,286,300
Arkansas	2,144,874	—	—	2,144,874	.94	1,407,404
California	18,624,000	2,458,000	—	21,082,000	.92	7,427,000
Colorado	520,437	1,111,679	—	1,632,116	.56	729,380
Connecticut	989,900	541,800	800,000	2,331,700	.75	6,222,300
Delaware	268,600	—	—	268,600	.41	475,800
Florida	5,623,934	—	687,500	6,311,434	.65	1,549,224
Georgia	11,153,877	—	—	11,153,877	2.04	886,999
Idaho	—	—	—	—	—	1,305,800
Illinois	5,476,167	14,205,597	2,250,000	21,931,764	1.93	3,057,795
Indiana	934,835	843,260	—	1,778,095	.32	1,543,547
Iowa	—	1,099,145	—	1,099,145	.38	910,382
Kansas	413,030	356,515	—	769,545	.33	817,423
Kentucky	1,052,740	907,232	815,600	2,775,572	.76	817,100
Louisiana	1,092,548	—	—	1,092,548	.26	1,097,508
Maine	124,000	221,500	—	345,500	.30	1,122,693
Maryland	10,254,320	3,744,965	—	13,999,285	3.32	1,033,977
Massachusetts	4,369,591	5,817,341	—	10,186,932	1.79	419,544
Michigan	12,558,182	2,831,818	—	15,390,000	1.66	2,371,000
Minnesota	—	4,802,000	—	4,802,000	1.18	776,988
Mississippi	1,711,256	—	—	1,711,256	.68	3,171,604
Missouri	1,605,000	—	—	1,605,000	.33	809,391
Montana	—	495,000	—	495,000	.63	624,080
Nebraska	180,000	394,690	—	574,690	.36	1,328,005
Nevada	143,878	—	—	143,878	.17	1,064,579
New Hampshire	—	—	—	—	—	1,057,473
New Jersey	7,963,000	2,749,000	—	10,712,000	1.45	2,838,000
New Mexico	234,300	—	—	234,300	.18	1,672,900
New York	27,087,932	22,206,125	3,000,000	52,294,057	2.98	6,193,125
North Carolina	4,789,462	—	—	4,789,462	.81	2,468,434
North Dakota	550,000	—	—	550,000	.84	380,000
Ohio	31,540	1,091,730	—	1,123,270	.10	4,584,135
Oklahoma	1,368,086	—	100,000	1,468,086	.48	2,214,332
Oregon	200,000	—	—	200,000	.08	1,746,000
Pennsylvania	16,000,000	a	—	16,000,000	1.35	2,262,000
Rhode Island	453,559	1,015,985	676,825	2,146,369	2.27	709,811
South Carolina	3,121,820	—	—	3,121,820	1.00	1,452,143
South Dakota	—	—	—	—	—	1,300,150
Tennessee	—	6,542,300	—	6,542,300	1.42	1,944,500
Texas	—	4,652,964	—	4,652,964	.33	9,748,438
Utah	—	—	—	—	—	1,863,600
Vermont	—	381,669	—	381,669	.75	1,215,000
Virginia	9,749,300	—	—	9,749,300	1.82	3,356,625
Washington	—	—	—	—	—	3,808,949
West Virginia	5,616,804	a	20,000	5,636,804	2.89	1,682,043
Wisconsin	—	6,095,000	—	6,095,000	1.30	2,318,000
Wyoming	—	—	—	—	—	723,013
Total	$159,301,981	$84,858,450	$8,349,925	$252,510,356	$1.11	$104,000,840

[a] Included with direct aid; [b] average
Source: Alex Ladenson, Executive Director, Urban Libraries Council

Washington Report

1984 was a very good year for libraries and librarians in many legislative areas, despite the ominous overtones of 1984. The election year, with 33 Senate and 435 House seats up for grabs, had something to do with the good news side of the year-end tally. The year started with the Reagan administration's proposing for the third consecutive time zero funding and elimination for categorical library programs. It ended with the President's signature on a five-year authorization bill extending and expanding the Library Services and Construction Act (LSCA) and on a 1985 fiscal year appropriation bill with a 47.5 percent increase in funding for LSCA.

LSCA. Public Law 98-480, the new LSCA, incorporates many of the revisions called for in the resolutions developed at the 1979 White House Conference on Library and Information Services. Changes in the first three titles—I, Library Services; II, Public Library Construction; and III, Interlibrary Cooperation and Resource Sharing—are relatively minor but reflect increased attention to special user needs and information access through technological means. In addition, the law adds three new titles—IV, Library

Washington Report

Services for Indian Tribes; V, Foreign Language Materials Acquisition; and VI, Library Literacy Programs. The authorization levels over the five years are shown in the accompanying table. The new law also authorizes advance funding of LSCA. This would mean winning a double appropriation one year to implement the provision.

Other Funding. Two other programs slated for elimination by the administration were reversed by Congress. The Humanities Projects in Libraries under the National Endowment for the Humanities wound up with $2,940,000 and the National Historical Publications and Records Commission with $4,000,000 to continue their grant programs. Both programs may be of particular interest to those planning activities in looking toward the Bicentennial of the U.S. Constitution in 1987.

Congress also came to the rescue of libraries, educational institutions, and nonprofit organizations in maintaining the $801,000,000 postal subsidy at the current level to avoid the sharp rate increase that would have been necessary if the administration's proposed 44 percent cutback in revenue foregone had prevailed.

Postal Rates. The U.S. Postal Service Board of Governors announced, December 12, that a general postal rate increase for all classes of mail was to take effect February 17, 1985. A first class stamp was to go up to 22 cents, a 10 percent increase, while the library rate first pound cost would go to 40 cents on February 17, about a 15 percent increase for the current step 14 of the phasing cycle. Step 15 was to go to 45 cents and step 16 to 50 cents. Each additional pound through 7 would go up from 12 cents in 1984 to 14 cents, 15 cents, and 17 cents. Altogether, the cost of a two pound book package would increase from 47 cents to 67 cents at step 16, a 42 percent increase over the 1984 cost.

National Archives. A long time in the offing, proposals to separate the National Archives and Records Service from the General Services Administration and create a new independent agency finally came to pass and were signed into law (PL 98-497) October 19. The new agency, effective April 1, 1985, will be called the National Archives and Records Administration, with the U.S. Archivist to be appointed by the President rather than by the GSA Administrator as is now the case.

Copyright. Three significant copyright issues were settled for the time being. Since copyright in the U.S. is a statutory right set forth in the Constitution, it seems to always be in a state of flux and subject to unending debate. On January 17 the Supreme Court, in a 5–4 decision, decided that private noncommercial home videotaping of television programs does not constitute copyright infringement in the Betamax Case (*Sony Corp. of America v. Universal City Studios, Inc.*). The Court found that such home taping is generally done for purposes of "time-shifting" and is a legitimate fair use and that making and selling videotape recorders to the public does not constitute contributory infringement.

On October 4 the Record Rental Amendment of 1984 was signed into law (PL 98-450). Its purpose is to prohibit the 200 commercial record rental operators in the U.S. from renting audio recordings without the copyright owners' permission. It would modify the "first-sale" doctrine embodied in section 109(a) of the Copyright Act to require the authorization of copyright owners before phonorecords could be rented, leased, or lent for commercial advantage. Section 2 of the act, which was instigated by ALA, states that "nothing in the preceding sentence shall apply to the rental, lease, or lending of a phonorecord for nonprofit purposes by a nonprofit library or nonprofit educational institution." The House Judiciary Committee report (H. Rept. 98-987) says:

> By accepting this language, the Committee thereby intends that the legislation not interfere with the usual lending activities of nonprofit libraries or the educational programs of nonprofit educational institutions when the rental, lease or lending of phonorecords is part of their customary activities and not in the nature of a commercial enterprise. These activities must be directly related to the ordinary lending activities of the nonprofit library or the educational mission of the nonprofit educational institution. By requiring the lending activity to be "for nonprofit purposes," the Committee does not intend to bar a small fee to cover administrative costs of the lending program, if that is customary. However, this provision is not intended to allow nonprofit libraries and nonprofit educational institutions to engage in record rentals for the purpose of raising funds to support other activities.

On November 8, the Semiconductor Chip Protection Act of 1984 (PL 98-620) was signed into law as a new form of intellectual property protection to protect the designs of semiconductor chips against unauthorized copying for a ten-year term. The chips, made up of layers of semiconductor material imprinted with traces of other elements in certain patterns through the use of "masks" or stencils, perform electronic functions. Since they are akin to audiovisual or graphic works subject to copyright protection and at the same time like useful articles subject to patent law, Congress compromised on a "sui generis" approach (in a class by itself) with a new Chapter 9 at the end of Title 17 of the *U.S. Code*. The Copyright Act comprises Chapters 1 through 8. Chapter 9 is a form of industrial intellectual property right rather than the usual author's copyright. Penalties are civil rather than criminal. The noncopyright approach limits precedential value for any future copyright legislation. Sponsors made a point of stressing that the semiconductor chip bill has no implications for computer program protection.

Shortly before Congress adjourned, Senator Charles Mathias, Chairman of the Patents, Copyrights and Trademarks Subcommittee, introduced for consideration and hearings in 1985 a bill to protect copyrighted computer programs from illegal copying. S. 3074 would require authorization from the copyright owner before one could engage in the rental, lease, or lending of computer programs for commercial purposes. Of particular concern to librarians and educators is Senator Mathias's introductory statement in the October 5 Congressional Record (pp. S13706f

Eileen Cooke, Director of the ALA Washington Office, welcomes visitors to the organization's new quarters.

Washington Report

Fiscal Year 1985 Budget Appropriations for Library and Related Programs (in thousands)

Library Programs	FY 1984 Appropriation	FY 1985 Budget	FY 1985 House	FY 1985 Senate	Fy 1985 Appropriation
Educational Consolidation and Improvement Chapter 2 (includes school libraries)	$ 479,420	$ 728,879	$ 678,879	$ 531,909	$ 531,909
GPO Superintendent of Documents	25,826	29,747	28,291	28,868	28,868
Higher Education Act Title II	6,880	0	6,880	7,000	7,000
Title II-A, College Libraries	0	0	0	0	0
II-B, Training and Research	880	0	880	1,000	1,000
II-C, Research Libraries	6,000	0	6,000	6,000	6,000
Library of Congress	325,864[1]	239,263	231,290	236,065	236,010
Library Services and Construction Act	80,000	0	80,000	143,000	118,000
Title I, Public Library Services	65,000	0	65,000	75,000	75,000
II, Public Library Construction	0	0	0	50,000	25,000
III, Interlibrary Cooperation	15,000	0	15,000	18,000	18,000
Medical Library Assistance Act	10,000[2]	7,500	deferred	7,500	8,040
National Agricultural Library	9,932	11,661	11,544	11,400	11,400
National Commission Libraries and Information Science	674	690	690	720	720
National Library of Medicine	49,718[3]	43,820	43,820	53,400	47,870
Library Related Programs					
Adult Education Act	100,000	100,000	100,000	100,000	100,000
Bilingual Education	139,183	139,245	143,656	142,245	142,951
Corporation for Public Broadcasting[4]	159,500	100,000	deferred	238,000	200,000
ECIA Ch. 1 (ESEA I Disadvantaged Children)	3,480,000	3,480,000	3,680,000	3,696,620	3,688,163
Educationally Handicapped Children (state grants)	1,068,875	1,068,875	1,125,000	1,135,145	1,135,145
HEA Title III, Developing Institutions	134,416	134,416	134,416	148,000	141,208
IV-C, College Work Study	555,000	850,000	600,000	585,000	592,500
VI, International Education	25,800	0	25,800	27,300	26,550
Indian Education Act	68,780	68,780	68,780	68,780	67,404
National Archives and Records Service	86,805	92,325	94,925	92,325	94,925
National Center for Education Statistics	8,747	8,747	8,747	8,747	8,747
National Endowment for the Arts	162,223	143,875	175,000	162,000	163,660
National Endowment for the Humanities	140,118	125,475	145,000	139,975	139,478
National Historical Publication and Records Commission	4,000	0	4,000	4,000	4,000
National Institute of Education	48,231	54,231	54,231	48,231	51,231
Postal revenue foregone subsidy	879,000	452,000	801,000	801,000	801,000
Postsecondary Education Improvement Fund	11,710	11,710	12,710	12,300	12,710
Public Telecommunications Facilities	11,880	0	24,000	30,000	24,000
Revenue Sharing	4,566,700	4,566,700	4,566,700	4,566,700	4,566,700
Science and Math Education	—	50,000	—	200,000	100,000
Women's Education Equity	5,760	0	5,760	6,000	6,000

[1] Includes supplemental funding of $81,500,000 for renovation and $11,500,000 for mass book deacidification facility.
[2] Includes $2,500,000 in supplemental funding.
[3] Includes $3,400,000 in supplemental funding.
[4] CPB funded two years in advance.

LSCA Authorization Levels

	1985	1986	1987	1988	1989
Title I, Library Services	$75	$80	$85	$90	$95
Title II, Public Library Construction	50	50	50	50	50
Title III, Interlibrary Cooperation & Resource Sharing	20	25	30	35	30
Title IV, Library Services for Indians	1.5% of the amount appropriated for Titles I, II, and III for Indians and 0.5% for Native Hawaiians				
Title V, Foreign Language Materials Acquisition	1	1	1	1	—
Title VI, Library Literacy Programs	5	5	5	5	—

daily edition), in which he says:

> Let me note one area that will certainly deserve careful discussion: Whether the bill should make special provision for the rental of software by nonprofit educational institutions. In the case of record rental, a consensus has developed that nonprofit libraries and schools should be exempt from the new rule prohibiting unauthorized lending of records. While the same accommodation could be made for software, some might argue that organized software rental policies, even on a nonprofit basis, so encourage improper copying that they should be permitted only with the consent of the copyright owner. I am confident that these and related concerns will be fully explored in the coming months, and that we will then know better how to proceed in this regard.

A related measure was signed into law October 30 with the signing of the Tariff and Trade Act (PL 98-573). This includes a sense of Congress declaration that copyright protection is essential for computer software, and if a nation withdraws such protection or provides for compulsory licensing of software, the U.S. should seek appropriate relief. In addition, in renewing the Generalized System of Preferences concerning trade with developing countries, Congress established intellectual property rights as one of the major priorities in U.S. trade negotiations and provided mechanisms for promoting better protection of intellectual property in world trade.

Other Issues. Calls for restoring excellence in education continued throughout the election year of 1984 to be a rallying point, spearheaded by the U.S. Department of Education's *A Nation at Risk* (1983). In June, 1984 ALA's Task Force on Excellence in Education issued its rejoinder, *Realities: Educational Reform in a Learning Society*. And in July, the Department of Education published *Alliance for Excellence: Librarians Respond to A Nation at Risk*. In an introduction, Education Secretary Terrell H. Bell highlighted the need for an alliance of home, school, and library as essential to the attainment of excellence in education and a learning society.

On August 3 Senator Claiborne Pell (D-RI) called attention to the challenges set forth for librarians in the *Alliance for Excellence*. Looking to the future of the learning society, Senator Pell reminded his colleagues that it was time to start thinking about the 1989 White House Conference on Library and Information Services. He planned to introduce such legislation in 1985.

It was also on August 3 that Representative Carl D. Perkins (D-KY) died—a great loss to the library and education community. He was Chairman of the House Education and Labor Committee and a longtime supporter of libraries and Honorary Member of ALA. A number of education programs of interest to librarians were reauthorized during 1984 under the leadership of Carl Perkins. The Education Amendments of 1984 (PL 98-511) included the Adult Education Act, the National Center for Education Statistics, the Bilingual Education Act, Impact Aid, Women's Educational Equity Act, and a new Emergency Immigrant Education Act, which includes special materials and supplies as eligible uses of funds. The Vocational Education Act (PL 98-524) was amended and extended and renamed the Carl D. Perkins Vocational Education Act.

Aside from the various legislative measures tracked during 1984, there still remained the administrative and regulatory issues that had been stewing away, sometimes boiling over during the past few years: reclassification of federal librarian standards, contracting out of federal libraries, and access to government-produced information.

EILEEN D. COOKE

Women in Librarianship

Sources of Information. To take the pulse of women in libraries, and survey the status of 85 percent of the membership of the American Library Association as well as women in other information associations and in other countries, requires a variety of strategies. In 1984 pay equity dominated the status of women in librarianship front. Those important struggles are reported elsewhere in this *Yearbook*.

Annual statistics gathered by the Association for Library and Information Science Education (ALISE) provides clues to the future composition of the profession by its student count (by sex) of ALA-accredited library and information science programs. The faculty portion of the ALISE survey reveals something on the dollar value placed on library science education as offered by women or men and on the composition of library school faculty (by sex) who may be the mentors and role models of future library and information science professionals.

The Association of Research Libraries (ARL) gathers data annually as well. These statistics reveal the number of women who hold directorships in important academic libraries, report their level of compensation as compared to male directors in ARL libraries, and provide male/female salary data in other positions.

Finally, annual "placements and salaries" data reveal sex discrimination at its earliest stage. For example, with the same experience (none), and within the same type of library, women's average salaries lagged behind men's by an average of $1,000–$3,000 directly out of library school in 1983.

A third type of reportage which adds to the general picture of women in libraries is that which emanates from the numerous coalitions, discussion groups, round tables and associations. A number of them publish their own newsletters, which are sometimes the only reliable sources of information about the group.

The year 1984 saw the presentation of the first ALA Equality Award. ALA and the Committee on the Status of Women in Librarianship recognized librarians who had made "an outstanding contribution toward promoting equality between women and men in the profession." The first recipient of the ALA Equality Award was Margaret Myers, Director of the ALA Office for Library Personnel Resources, who has fought for equality for many years and on a number of fronts.

Placements & Salaries. ALA-accredited library school programs in Canada and the United States reported 2,685 women and 694 men graduates in the spring of 1984. Successful placements were reported by 1,122 women and 282 men. Average salary for women was $17,563 (median $16,829) while men averaged a beginning salary of $18,303 (median $17,190). Salary ranges show men with a low of $13,630 as compared to women's $14,634; but a high of $27,333 as compared to women's high of only $24,774. Reportage by schools shows women with a higher average salary in 29 schools; men's were higher in 26 schools. In 1982 men's salaries were higher in 38 schools and women's higher in only 22 schools.

Placement data revealed severe stratification within the profession in 1984. Men were gravitating to institutions that serve high-status clientele, i.e., academic and special libraries, while women continued to move into the low-status and service-oriented institutions, school and public libraries.

The highest percentage of jobs (28 percent) were found in public libraries, followed by special libraries (26.1 percent), academic (23.8 percent), then school (17.3 percent). Analyzing placement by sex, however, finds women and men employed in very different types of libraries. Of the 501 positions filled in public libraries, 413, or 82 percent, were filled by women. Furthermore, while almost 50 percent of the women graduates found positions in school and public libraries (49.3 percent), more than half (63.1 percent) of the men found employment in academic and special libraries. Specifically, 37.1 percent of the men found jobs in academic libraries as compared with 20.4 percent of the women, while only 7.9 percent of the men were employed in school libraries compared to 19.6 percent of the women. In fact, men filled only 9 percent of the school library positions.

Salary data by type of library showed women lagging behind men in every type of library. Reportage from all schools showed average salaries for public libraries: women $16,361, men $17,011; school libraries: women, $18,821, men $22,115; academic libraries: women $18,816, men $19,128; other libraries: women $18,919, men $20,796.

Association for Research Libraries. The 1984 data for the Association of Research Libraries revealed that 75 men and 19 women (20 percent) were directors of ARL libraries in 1984 and that 3,932 women in ARL libraries represented 62 percent of the professional staff. The study revealed that women actually had fewer years of experience (18.3) than men (24.7). Medians were not available.

Salary data showed men making more money than women in all categories except one. In reference departments, the average salary for the 166 women with 10–15 years of experience was $25,535 which topped the average salary ($24,964) for the 67 men with the same number of years of experience. For women and men with one–three years of experience in all libraries, men averaged $19,320, while women received an average salary of $18,838. Male librarians with over 35 years of experience earned $42,213 while women with equal longevity earned an average of $32,761.

Association for Educational and Communications Technology. An AECT poll in 1983 indicated women's participation in instructional media work on the rise during the past 15 years. Membership was still predominately male (64 percent). Intraprofessional stratification was evident here as well as throughout the library and information science professions: women were more likely found in government departments of education and elementary schools. Women and men were equally distributed in individual secondary schools, private/business, industry and other. Men were found to predominate in school districts, regional media centers, academic institutions, nonprofit organizations, and the military. Men's salaries were higher than women's; men $31,104 to women's $27,054 on the average. However, researchers report finding equal pay for equal work: when holding variables such as work setting, job classification, highest degree achieved, or years in present position equal, they found no discrimination by sex.

Association for Library and Information Science Education. Student data which reported number of students enrolled in 64 ALISE member library education programs show that women continued to outnumber men three to one upon entering library school. Fall 1983 enrollment showed 2,495 women to 785 men in master's programs. Those enrolled in post-master's degree programs counted 45 women to 14 men; at the doctoral level, 112 women were enrolled to 71 men. Almost 2.5 times as many women received master's degrees as men; 37 women received post-master's degrees to 14 men; and 39 women to 22 men received their doctorates.

Faculty of 66 ALISE member schools had much the same representation by sex as in previous years. Of 658 full-time faculty positions, 57.9 percent are filled by men and 42.2 percent by women. This ratio was slightly better for women than in 1983, with an increase of female representation of 0.3 percent. Female representation on library school faculties increased only 0.7 percent in eight years since the data were first collected in 1976.

At the lecturer level, six women (66.7 percent) and three men were found. Women comprised 81.2 percent of the instructors, with 13 women and 3 men in this position. Numbers of women

Scene from "Women as an Underserved Population," a slide/tape program produced by the Committee on the Status of Women in Librarianship to help librarians provide more effective service to women.

Women in Librarianship

drop as positions rank higher. There were 105 women (61 percent) at the assistant professor level; 78 (35.6 percent) at the rank of associate professor; 59 (33.7 percent) professors; and 17 (25.8 percent) women reported as deans or directors.

The percentage of women with doctorates lags behind men, 70.1 percent to 82.3 percent, but the rate of increase for females exceeds men's by 6.2 percent. Compared to the 1983 differential of 14 percent more men than women with doctorates, there was a 12.2 percent difference in 1984.

Salary data showed women's salaries still lower than men's. At the dean and director level, for fiscal year appointments, 41 males in 1984 received an average salary of $53,134 (median $52,000). For the 16 female deans and directors, the average salary was $46,460 (median $46,650). While 1983 data showed women received 85.6 percent of what men at the same level earned, the 1984 differential was computed at 87.4 percent. This percentage is still lower than comparative average salaries computed in 1975–76, when women deans and directors earned a full 96.8 percent of what their male counterparts earned.

For both fiscal year and academic year appointments, women's average salaries were lower than men's at all ranks. For fiscal year appointments, men earned $49,786 to women's $49,521 at the professor level. For associate professors, men earned $42,161 to women's $38,151; and men assistant professors earned $33,267 to women's $32,024.

Society of American Archivists. Jacquiline Goggin presented a detailed analysis of the 1982 salary survey in *The American Archivist* (Summer 1984), and compared results with surveys conducted in 1972 and 1979. More than half (54.2 percent) of the 1982 survey respondents were women. Salary disparity has narrowed only slightly in 10 years, and findings showed women archivists earned 25 percent less than their male counterparts, regardless of age, education, or years of experience. Goggin reports that upon closer study of salary data, she found that the gap *widens* with years of experience. Male-held degrees are valued more highly as well: women with Ph.D.s earned $4,000 less than men with equivalent degrees, those with double M.A.s or M.S. $5,000 less, master's were worth $3,600 less, M.L.S. $2,900 less; B.A. $4,800 less than men, and high school $7,800.

Other Research. Terence Mech in 1984 looked at library directors in his "Ohio's Small Private College Library Directors: A Profile" (*Ohio Library Association Bulletin*, April 1984) and studied the 18 men and 9 women who responded to his survey. The men were older by approximately six years on the average, and had more years of experience (22.66 to 12.33), although both men and women entered the profession between the ages of 26 and 27.

In Theresa E. Maggio's study, "Role of Women Directors in Louisiana's Public and Academic Libraries" (*Louisiana Library Association Bulletin*, Summer 1984), the percentage of male directors in Louisiana was found to be on the increase from the 1930s to the 1980s. In public libraries, percentages dropped from 95.5 percent female in 1950 to 74 percent female in 1983. Male academic library directors increased from 38.9 percent in the 1930s to 71.9 percent in 1970 and were 62.8 percent in 1983.

Ronald Dale Karr's "Changing Profile of University Library Directors" (*College & Research Libraries*, July 1984), noted that while the number of female-headed ARL libraries increased from one in 1966, the number of women directors does not in any way approach the two-thirds representation women have in academic libraries. Karr's study found an "old boy" network. Most future directors attended one of three library schools. He also noted that a larger pool of potential library directors will increase the competition for top jobs, and that "women and graduates of less distinguished library schools can no longer be excluded."

Robert Swisher and Rosemary Du Mont continued looking at the status of women in academic libraries (*Library Quarterly*, April 1984). They surveyed members of ACRL in a "search for explanations" for the sex-related occupational stratification of librarianship. They found that 39.1 percent of the men in academic libraries held administrative positions, while only 13.5 percent of the women held similar rank.

Committee on the Status of Women in Librarianship. The Committee received two Carnegie awards in 1984: one, "Equal Pay for Comparable Worth," cosponsored by OLPR will update the 1981 pay equity bibliography. A second, "Library Resources for Women," is cosponsored with RASD Women's Materials and Women Library Users and ACRL Women's Studies Discussion Group. It is designed to develop reading list bibliographies for libraries on women's issues.

COSWL's Legislative Subcommittee chaired by Mary Lou Goodyear produced seven legislative fact sheets on the issues of pay equity, the ERA, pensions, VDTs, childcare, abortion, and insurance. The Subcommittee also developed target groups within ALA with which to network in the future.

On Account of Sex: A Bibliography on the Status of Women in Librarianship, 1977–1981, by Kathleen Heim and Katharine Phenix, was published by ALA and the Committee in 1984. This work represented the Committee's continuing response to its charge "to promote and initiate the collection, analysis, dissemination, and coordination of information on the status of women in librarianship." An essay characterizing the five years documented by the bibliography accompanies over 1,000 citations to the literature on women in libraries.

Poster Sessions. Two poster sessions reported research on women in 1984. Jean M. Ray and Angela B. Rubin presented "Pay Equity in Academic Libraries: Some History and Analysis of the ARL Salary Surveys 1976/77–1982/83." They found that at all levels, female ARL university librarians receive lower salaries than men. Ilene F. Rockman at California Polytechnic State University presented "Job Satisfaction: How Autonomy, Decision-Making Opportunities and Gender Affect Faculty and Librarians." Gender, she determined, is not a factor of job satisfaction.

Pay Equity Commission. ALA President E. J. Josey in 1984 proposed an ALA Commission on

Pay Equity to the Executive Board. The Commission was formed with co-chairs Helen Josephine and Cynthia Johanson presiding over 13 other members. Pay equity was made a presidential priority in 1984.

SLA; Australia, Japan. Outside the American Library Association, library women's groups report much activity in 1984. At the Special Libraries Association Conference in New York City, Pauline Rothstein presented a petition to the Executive Board to establish the Women's Resources and Concerns section of the Social Sciences Division. The group plans to "provide a forum for discussion and analysis of women's resources and materials as well as for the social, economic, and professional concerns of women in libraries." Approved on a provisional basis for its first year, Gurley Turner was named the Chair, with Pauline Rothstein as Vice-Chair.

The Library Association of Australia Status of Women Special Interest Group reported in its newsletter that membership had grown from "a few interested individuals to a national membership of nearly 800." The group organized two public forums, "Towards Democratic Decision-Making? Women in Management" and "Role of Librarians in Public Service."

Japanese women librarians organized a group called FLINT, which is designed to bring together women interested in librarianship and in women's rights.

Specialized and Local Action in 1984. ALISE's Women in Librarianship Special Interest Group, led by Sheila Intner of Columbia, presented its program "Getting to the Top, or How to Succeed in Library Administration" at its annual conference in Washington, D.C. Three university library directors, Patricia Battin of Columbia, Merrily Taylor of Brown University, and Nancy Eaton of the University of Vermont traded advice on success.

At the Library of Congress, the Women's Program Advisory Committee recognized its 10th anniversary in 1984 during an open house on November 8. A report in the *Library of Congress Bulletin* noted "The Women's Program Office works toward the goal of achieving full equality of opportunity for women staff members and applicants for positions at the Library of Congress. The Women's Program Advisory Committee has played an integral role in fulfilling this important mission."

Pay equity was foremost as a topic of concern for many state and regional meetings in 1984. On October 26 the Illinois Library Association Social Responsibilities Round Table presented "Comparable Pay for Comparable Work: An Educational Seminar." Margaret Myers, ALA, Kathleen Prendergast representing Chicago Public Library's employees union, Barbara Flynn Currie, Illinois representative, and Marsh Bates of Hays Associates were speakers.

The ILA SRRT Women's Concerns Task Force took on the monumental chore of compiling an updated national SHARE (Sisters Have Resources Everywhere) Directory of feminist librarians and published it at the end of 1984.

The New York Library Association Round Table on the Concerns of Women discussed "Advancing Legislation for Women in 1984: What Can You Do?" NYLA also offered a "Pay Equity Workshop on Comparable Worth" led by Kate Todd, Labor Relations consultant of AFSCME Council 37. This program offered simulated evaluation problems to demonstrate the feasibility of a pay equity case in a library.

The Round Table on the Status of Women in Librarianship of the North Carolina Library Association was active in pay equity action. The group was one of 14 to sponsor a Gubernatorial Forum on Women's Issues at Meredith College. In May, Wilma Woodard, state legislator, discussed pay equity with the NCLA Executive Board.

Two groups in Louisiana drew attention to pay equity. The ACRL Louisiana Chapter held a program at the University of Southeastern Louisiana, and at the University of New Orleans, the Academic Library Directors meeting presented a panel on pay equity.

At the 1984 Southeast Library Association meeting held in conjunction with the Mississippi Library Association annual conference, Elizabeth Paschall of the White House Office of Public Liaison presented "Women in Management Process in Libraries." In New Jersey, a program featuring Dee Garrison, Patricia Glass Schuman, and Leigh Estabrook was presented by the ACRL chapter called "Myths/Realities of Academic Women Librarians." Indiana's Division on Women in Indiana Libraries sponsored a program on "Treatment of Women in Encyclopedias." Other ILA women's achievements include the publication of the 1984 *Network Directory*, and plans for 1985 programs on censorship and

Table 1. Median Salaries for Entry Level Librarians 1977–1983

	Median salary for women	Median salary for men	Women's salary as % of men's
1977	11,000	11,311	97.3
1978	11,700	12,000	97.5
1979	12,885	13,103	98.3
1980	13,500	14,112	95.7
1981	15,000	15,500	96.8
1982	15,885	16,500	96.3
1983	16,829	17,190	97.9

Source: "Placements and Salaries," *Library Journal* (1978–84).

Table 2. Entry Level Salaries by Sex and Type of Library 1983

Type of library		Women	Men	Women's salary as % of men's
Public				
	mean	$16,361	$17,011	96.2
	median	16,000	17,000	94.1
Academic				
	mean	16,285	17,317	94.0
	median	16,000	16,500	97.0
School				
	mean	17,500	22,115	79.1
	median	17.500	18,500	95.0
Special				
	mean	18,816	19.128	98.4
	median	18,300	18,000	—
Other				
	mean	18,919	20,796	91.0
	median	18,000	20,965	85.9

Source: "Placements and Salaries," *Library Journal* (October 1984).

Women's National Book Association

pornography, and a conference in fall 1985. The Missouri Women in Libraries Committee looked for voting status within the Missouri Library Association.

Other women's associations in information and publishing industries continued work on women's concerns and report their activities to the ALA COSWL chair. The Women's National Book Association continued to recognize significant contributions in the world of the book. Women in Communications, Inc., celebrated a 75th anniversary at the 1984 conference in Seattle. Librarian Laura X of the Women's History Research Center reported on the availability of microfilm copies of the Women's History Library and publications on marital rape. The National Women's Studies Association Librarians Task Force presented "Taking Action: Smoldering Issues in Feminist Librarianship" at their annual meeting.

KATHARINE PHENIX

Women's National Book Association

Activities. WNBA in 1984 participated as a partner in the National Library Week campaign sponsored by the American Library Association. The NLW Partnership Program, launched in the fall of 1983, fosters the development of alliances between ALA and other national organizations. As a partner, WNBA disseminates NLW information to each of its eight local chapters, and encourages each chapter to collaborate with libraries in its area, to promote NLW in chapter mailings, and to present programs on libraries, reading, and literacy.

In December WNBA and Women in Scholarly Publishing cosponsored a program during the Modern Language Association meeting in Washington, D.C., "Publishing Feminist Criticism and Creative Writing in the 1980's: Does Editorial Prejudice Persist?" Panelists were Leslie Mitchner, Rutgers University Press; Marilyn Hacker, Columbia University; W. J. T. Mitchell, University of Chicago; Trudier Harrie, University of North Carolina at Chapel Hill; Emily Toth, Pennsylvania State University; and Loretta Barrett, Doubleday and Company. The session was organized by Ann Heidbreder Eastman of Virginia Tech for WNBA and Carol Orr, Director of the University of Tennessee Press, for WISP.

The role of the WNBA as a nongovernmental organization of the United Nations has been maintained since 1959. Representing WNBA in this activity is Sally Wecksler, Wecksler-Incomco, New York City.

The Bookwoman, edited by Susan B. Trowbridge of Addison-Wesley, is published three times a year.

Awards. The biennial WNBA Award (formerly the Constance Lindsay Skinner Award) is presented to a distinguished bookwoman for her enduring and unique contribution to the world of books and to the larger society through books. The 1984 award was presented in May to Effie Lee Morris, first coordinator of Children's Services at the San Francisco Public Library, at a reception in the Rayburn House Office Building in Washington, D.C. Carol Nemeyer, Associate Librarian of Congress for National Programs, participated in the ceremony. Robert Wedgeworth, Executive Director of ALA, John Frantz, City Librarian of San Francisco, and Virginia Mathews, Vice-President, Library Professional Publications, presented tributes. The citation, presented by WNBA President Sylvia Cross, reads in part: "by honoring Effie Lee Morris, we honor a rare tradition of service to children, a will permanently to engage children with books, and a vision of the intellectual, emotional, and spiritual growth that reading fosters."

The second annual Lucile Micheels Pannell Award was presented at the American Booksellers Association convention in Washington, D.C. to Meg Risser and Jim McLaughlin of the R. M. Mills Bookstore in Nashville, Tennessee. The Pannell Award is given to a living American or Canadian bookseller for a creative effort to bring children and books together. Risser and McLaughlin created and conducted a ten-week program of music classes designed to bring together children and music and books in the store. The award, which honors the late librarian and manager of the Hobby Horse Bookshop for children at Carson Pirie Scott department store in Chicago, consists of $2,500 and a piece of original art by a children's book illustrator. The 1984 artwork was by Tomie de Paola.

Annual Meeting. President Sylvia Cross presided at the annual meeting of the Board of Directors of WNBA in Washington, D.C., in May. Chapter Presidents attending were: Margaret Burns, Nashville; Marie Cantlon, Boston; Lucy Hebard, New York; Lou Keay, Los Angeles; Mary Levering, Washington/Baltimore; and Elizabeth Pomada, San Francisco.

The Women's National Book Association, founded in 1917, is the only organization in the book world open to women and men in all occupations allied to the publishing industry—publishers, authors, librarians, literary agents, editors, illustrators, designers, educators, critics, booksellers, and those engaged in book production, marketing, finance, subsidiary rights, and personnel. Publishers, wholesalers, and other organizations support the work of the WNBA through sustaining memberships.

CATHY RENTSCHLER

WOMEN'S NATIONAL BOOK ASSOCIATION, INC.

PRESIDENT (1984–85):
Sandra K. Paul, SKP Associates, New York City

VICE-PRESIDENT/PRESIDENT-ELECT:
Cathy Rentschler, The H. W. Wilson Company, Bronx, N.Y.

SECRETARY:
Jean K. Crawford, Abingdon Press, Nashville, Tennessee

TREASURER:
Sandra J. Souza, Massachusetts Department of Correction, Norfolk

EDITOR OF THE BOOKWOMAN:
Susan B. Trowbridge, Addison-Wesley Publishing Co., Reading, Massachusetts

Membership (December 1984): 900

Young Adult Library Services

Trends and Issues. In 1984 Michael Jackson, whose favorite books were compiled in a list that became part of a special program at the Chicago Public Library previously, was enjoying a tremendous influence on youth of all ages. Across the United States breakdancing as a performing art form brought together young men and women of all backgrounds who inch and scoot over dance platforms exchanging ideas for movement and rhythm. Many demonstrations were being done in local libraries, and publishers could not produce too many materials on Jackson, his dress, and his music. Rock music videotapes also continued in great demand, and some library programming has been planned around them as well.

Though some past trends continue, slight shifts are apparent. Video game sales and attendance at video game rooms seemed to be declining. "Choose your own adventure" and the many romance paperback series continued to be read in 1984, but one youth librarian reported the beginning of a backlash against the romances. YA patrons have begun to comment that these romances are all the same, a statement that supports the idea that some young people can identify quality as well as some librarians. Interest in science fiction and fantasy continues unabated.

Young adults also are concerned about two issues of a grimmer nature: child abuse and nuclear war. The novels of V. C. Andrews, which tell the frightening stories of children victimized by adults, still enjoy enormous popularity among adolescent readers. Young people are aware that more children die from murder by parents than from childhood diseases. YAs are also concerned about the increase in suicide among their peers. One adolescent suicide frequently triggers a chain reaction resulting in the suicides of other youths within the same community. Parents and youth workers must learn to recognize symptomatic behavior.

One reason given for youth stress and despair is the fear of nuclear war. Several youth librarians from different areas of the United States have testified that this is a growing concern among the young, and an episode of the popular St. Elsewhere television series dealt with a young child who experienced asthmatic-like seizures as a result of fear that any loud or sudden noise was The Bomb.

YA librarians faced some critical professional issues. As automated services increase in libraries, how will librarians be able to continue to provide free access to all library services if young patrons cannot afford to pay for automated reference searches? If American children score lower than Japanese children in both math and reading, how can YA librarians help to improve competency levels? Attempted censorship of library materials (novels by Judy Blume and Mark Twain's *Tom Sawyer*) as well as library programs (Dungeons and Dragons) continues to threaten First Amendment rights of youth.

In a study of the Atlanta and Fulton County Library, Lowell Martin suggests the use of the term "young people" as less ambiguous than "young adult." But YA Services leaders emphasized that adolescents ages 11–18 are assuming more and more adult responsibilities, pregnancy and parenthood being good examples (*Voice of Youth Advocates*, February 1984). Martin also suggests the creation of a Children's and Young People's Coordinator who would have responsibility for services to children as well as adolescents.

Since children and youth lack the financial resources and verbal clout to ensure their own programs, services to them are frequently among the first to be reduced or eliminated in tight budget times. In libraries, cutbacks in YA positions and budgets are especially disturbing in light of the consistent use of libraries by students as a respectable percentage of any given total local population.

YA-serving librarians must begin to take more advantage of automated circulation operations and other methods of documentation to record use and point up increases in YA materials circulation and utilization of other YA services. Diane Tuccillo, YA librarian at the Mesa (Arizona) Public Library, produced an annual report that might serve as a model for documentation of collection utilization and audience served by booktalking in the local schools. Mesa Public also initiated a study to assess the effectiveness of YA outreach services.

Programs. Youth-serving librarians have always exhibited ingenious skills in attracting adolescents to libraries. One of the most creative is Mike Printz, librarian at Topeka West High School in Kansas. Following up on a successful student-conducted oral history program that included interviews with Senators Nancy Kassenbaum and Robert Dole and actress Dee Wallace, Elliott's mother in "E. T.," as well as the discovery by students of a diary kept by one of the Iranian hostages, ex-marine Rocky Sickman, which resulted in its eventual publication, Printz in late 1984 conducted a Win-a-Bear Contest. Students, after careful research in a given list of reliable sources, were asked to submit entries for new names for VIP's along with related library materials about the famous names. Printz also developed a "Culture Vulture" program based on an archaeological dig site and a "Banned Books" bibliography and project for students during Banned Books Week, September 8–15.

Left, a young gymnast studies gymnastics books at the Burbank (California) Public Library. Above, "Homework Centers" created by the Chicago Public Library with a city grant for all its branch libraries put useful reference books together for school children. (Phil Moloitis)

Young Adult Library Services

Other programs stimulated YA use of library materials. For REaders' VIEW, a program of the Arlington Heights Memorial Library in Illinois, junior high students reviewed books choosing those they would enthusiastically recommend to their friends. A discussion of the selected titles was conducted on a local cable television station.

There were 21 different ways for teens to play in the various categories of the popular "Bookjack: Hit the Reading Jackpot!" at the Enoch Pratt Free Library in Baltimore and at the Rochester (New York) Public Library. The Glenarden Branch of the Prince George's County (Maryland) Library offered "B.E.A.T. (Be Encouraged and Think) Books." YAs signed up and were given a list of questions to answer and a crossword puzzle about selected YA books within an announced deadline. Michael Jackson was featured in a program that included a display of his favorite books and the showing of the video "Thriller" as a closing event.

The Grande Prairie Public Library (Hazel Crest, Illinois) offered "Video Stars," during which YAs wrote and performed book "commercials" that were videotaped. "Reading for Gold!" was a summer reading program for YAs offering special prizes as the number of books read increased at the Loutet Library (Grand Haven, Michigan).

The Friends of the Library in Provo, Utah, sponsored an all-night Readathon for YAs that resulted in an increase in interest in library programs. At the Saginaw (Michigan) Public Library's Summer Reading Scavenger Hunt, YAs who participated in all branches requested that the program be repeated next year. Summer reading programs at the Novi (Michigan) Public Library and the Wicomico (Maryland) County Free Library brought YAs and staff together to talk about books, enabling librarians to develop a better feeling for youth needs in relation to future collection development.

Other Ideas. Other library programs for young adults that are not necessarily book related help to establish an appreciation of the goodwill of library staff and to foster a belief among adolescents that the library is an interesting place to visit. Teenagers acted as volunteers to run many of the events for a Medieval Fair at the Greenburgh (New York) Public Library that included jugglers, tumblers, games with prizes, and a pie-eating contest.

Following in the tradition of LEVELS (Great Neck Public Library, New York), the Ashland (Oregon) Public Library's efforts to expand hours in its Ashland Teen Center, housed in the library's basement, were supported in 1984 by the passage of a funding referendum. The Leominster (Massachusetts) Public Library celebrated the founding of its Young Adult Center with a Fifth Anniversary Dance; the Friends of the Library paid for a deejay, prizes, and police chaperones.

Breakdancing contests or demonstrations were held in libraries in Bloomington (Illinois), Rochester (New York), Miami (Florida), Louisville (Kentucky), Streamwood, Illinois (Poplar Creek Library), and Patchogue-Medford (New York). Christine A. Hauke, media specialist at the Manchester (Michigan) High School, uses "Puzzle-of-the-Week," which tests reference skills and visual perception to attract nonusers as well as library regulars. Hauke also involved students in bringing "Ancient Arena: The Roman Colosseum," a traveling exhibit from the Detroit Institute of Arts, to her small-town school library.

A "Paint-a-Shirt" workshop was conducted in Rochester (New York)—participants were furnished with stencils or could do their own imaginative designs. Rochester also offered a Clown Workshop that was enthusiastically received by attending YAs. "Brown Bag Luncheon and Meet the Author" was a program held at the Northport (New York) Public Library. Junior High students read an author's work in advance, than went to the library for lunch provided by the library and to talk with the author.

Linda Waddle, Librarian at the Cedar Falls (Iowa) High School Library, reported an interesting computer-related activity for students called the OnLine Search Project. After reading 1984, English students received instruction on preparation of search strategies, were given a demonstration of online searching, and then researched some aspect of the future to be applied in the composition of a short story about the future.

Lucy Marx of the Louisville Free Public Library organized "Computer Power Summer Reading Program Starring Mem-O-Ree Micro Fighting the Summer Glitches." Under a grant from the Kentucky Department of Libraries and Archives, computers were obtained and rotated throughout the Louisville System with YA volunteers assisting children. YAs also had their own computer program as well. Colorful registration materials, lists, and name tags were given out to each registrant. Despite the cutbacks in library budgets in Massachusetts, Gay Hyson of the Medford Public Library reported a large number of YAs attended a computer orientation program.

Despite some right-wing opposition, Dungeons and Dragons groups, mostly organized by the YAs themselves, continued in Leon County, Florida, Rochester (New York), and Poplar Creek Library (Streamwood, Illinois).

Youth unemployment remains a key issue, and libraries offered useful programs on job opportunities during the year. Babysitting workshops were well received in Mesa (Arizona), Babylon (New York), and Leominster (Massachusetts). Prince George's County, Maryland, provided "You and the Workplace: Practical Job Search Tips for Teens" at four of its branch libraries.

The Bettendorf (Iowa) Public Library presented a forum in which an attorney discussed the legal rights of youth. Kathi Brill at the Lead (South Dakota) High School Library reported a series of programs for National Library Week that included a Baby Photo Contest, Motorcycle Clinic, Punk Day, and Computer Demonstrations. The North Dade (Florida) Regional Library hosted a Hispanic Oral History Event in which local notables of Cuban descent related their experiences as young newcomers in a community with much anti-Cuban feeling. Extensive media coverage reported that the event helped to create a better understanding among ethnic groups concerned. "Cranes for Peace," an origami project at the Scarsdale (New York) Junior High, gave young people a nonpolitical opportunity for expressing their concern for peace through an art form.

Youth-Designed Programs and Publications. Following the leadership of YA Librarians Nancy Rolnick (Croton, New York), Christy Tyson (Spokane, Washington), and Connie Lawson (Cuyahoga County, Ohio), many libraries across the country during 1984 involved youth in various aspects of library operations and planning. Spokane Public Library's Young Adult Advisory Committee selected Beverly Cleary for its 1984 Golden Pen Award, recognizing the author who has given them the most reading pleasure. At the Mesa (Arizona) Public Library, members of the Young Adult Advisory Council were reviewing films for *Voice of Youth Advocates* on a regular basis in 1984. Continuing a school outreach program begun by Jan Ballard in the 1960s, Nancy Bond of the Orlando (Florida) Public Library involved YAs in the production of slide shows that feature various aspects of library services of interest to school students. The Cary (Lexington, Massachusetts) Memorial Library also involves YAs in the review and selection of books and magazines for the library.

Many libraries offered forums for the creative talents of the YAs in their communities. The Provo (Utah) Public Library featured YA poetry on their bulletin board. Each spring the Bloomington (Illinois) Public Library displays student art from the local junior high. A representative from American Youth Hostels presented a slide lecture called "Traveling on Your Own Steam" at the Chappaqua (New York) Library. Writers' workshops were conducted for YAs at the Edgewood School (Highland Park, Illinois) and the Boston (Massachusetts) Public Library. Jointly sponsored with the Watertown Center for the Arts, the Watertown (Massachusetts) Free Public Library held a Science Fiction Short Story and Fantastic Art Contest. At the New Berlin Public Library (Wisconsin), junior-high students worked together for eight weeks during the summer to plan and produce puppet shows for children. Teenage performers of the New York Public Library saluted Black History Month with a talent show that included gospel singers, tap and disco dancers, a dramatic reading and a storyteller. Called "Unique People," the program was funded with a grant from Consolidated Edison Company. The Enoch Pratt Free Library—in cooperation with the Baltimore Council on Adolescent Pregnancy, Parenting, and Pregnancy Prevention, Inc., and the Department of Human Ecology of Morgan State University—presented the Family Circle Theater, Inc., featuring students from Morgan State University portraying real-life experiences that confront teenagers.

YA authors and artists also produced several notable library publications in 1984. Diane Tuccillo of Mesa Public reported that their advisory board's nationally known publication of original science fiction stories, poems, and art, *E. T. 7*, was ready for printing. A poetry workshop funded by the New York State Council on the Arts and held at the New York Public Library resulted in *The Power of Poetry*, a collection by the young poets of the Castle Hill Branch Library. Made possible through a grant from New York's Poets and Writers, *Aim: To Hang Out* was published in spring 1984; it was written by teenagers at the New Dorp Branch of the New York Public Library. YAs who frequent the Young Adult Center at the Leominster (Massachusetts) Public Library have a newsletter called *The Room*, which includes poetry along with announcements of upcoming library events of interest to teens.

R. A. W. Ideas is a newsletter published by YAs of the Mobile (Alabama) Public Library who meet mainly on Saturdays to discuss reading and writing. *Bibliomania* is a literary magazine produced by young people (grades 6–12) from various schools and neighborhoods who meet together to write, illustrate, evaluate, and select the content of each issue at the Lakewood (Ohio) Public Library.

Liaison with Other Agencies. Despite budget cuts and subsequent staff shortages, YA librarians managed to allow time for outreach efforts and contacts with professionals in other community youth-serving agencies. The most notable was the obvious linkage with local public school systems. Enoch Pratt and Prince George's County continued their standard-setting booktalking in the schools. In Hawaii the Honolulu Theater for Youth in cooperation with the state's School Library Services distributed booklists for all YAs who attended a performance of *To Kill a Mockingbird*.

Jose Rodriquez of the Rochester (New York) Public Library planned to work with teenage inmates in the Attica facility as well as with staff of the Monroe County Detention Center in identifying materials on life skills. Brenda Hunter of the Atlanta (Georgia) Public Library reported that contacts with crisis centers and runaway facilities resulted in speakers for library programs on youth in crisis. The Saginaw (Michigan) Public Library began a paperback loan collection in Innerlink, a home for runaways. William Rettig at the South Central Library System in Madison, Wisconsin, received an LSCA grant to serve incarcerated juveniles at the nearby Dane County Juvenile Detention Center.

The Miami-Dade Public Library in joint sponsorship with United Family and Children's Service Bureau provided a reading clinic and tutorial program for teens (12–16) in North Dade County. Working with the local Youth Development Agency, the Northport (New York) Public Library held several programs for parents and YAs on such topics as "My Mother Was Never a Kid" and "Kids, Drugs and Alcohol."

Debbie Taylor, Young Adult Specialist for the Enoch Pratt Free Library, is a member of the Baltimore Council for Children and Youth as well as the Mayor's Advisory Task Force for Schools. Linda Lapides and Jan Baird-Adams, also from Enoch Pratt, are credited with invaluable assistance in the publication of Baltimore's "Service Directory on Adolescent Pregnancy, Parenting, and Pregnancy Prevention."

Prince George's County (Maryland) YA librarians were involved in the planning process and the development of the bibliography used in the exhibit for "Children Raising Children: Overcoming Barriers," a conference cosponsored by Planned Parenthood of Metropolitan Washington and other youth-serving agencies in the county. The New York City area has Community Youth Boards, which are a citywide network of community-based boards, each reviewing proposals and allocating money for youth-serving projects, such as an art contest for teens at the Grand Concourse Branch Library and a Youth Day at Bryant Park at which the library staffed an information booth.

Mary Jane Tacchi, Assistant Coordinator of YA Services for the New York Public Library, reported that YA librarians who attend the meetings of their local boards found the community contacts made there invaluable. For YA librarians in the Brookhaven (New York) area, cooperative projects with the Brookhaven Youth Bureau resulted in a full-page ad for local library branches in Youth, the publication of the Brookhaven Youth Bureau.

Leadership, Professional Publications, Continuing Education. The publication that many rank highest in usefulness for YA professionals, even for those in systems whose budgets have been cut and in which no YA services are formally offered, is Voice of Youth Advocates, referred to by most as VOYA. Other leading journals often cited in the YA literature and useful to YA professionals include The Unabashed Librarian, Booklist, Wilson Library Bulletin, Top of the News, School Library Journal, and English Journal. The editors of Voice of Youth Advocates, Dorothy Broderick and Mary K. Chelton, provided an example of their leadership by addressing the need many colleagues expressed for appropriate fiction and nonfiction titles on YA Christian themes. VOYA, which consistently reviews books from the smaller religious presses, published an article on "Christian Self-Help Books" in June 1984.

Regional YA groups within state library associations continued to provide valuable continuing education programs for YA librarians. For some, it took the form of book reviews, such as those produced by Bay Area (California) Young Adult librarians (BAYA) and the Young Adult Cooperative Book Review Group (Massachusetts). Brigham Young University (Utah) held a conference on YA literature with emphasis on encouraging reading and dealing with censorship. The South Dakota State Library offered a three-part series on booktalking, intellectual freedom, and YA programming. The New England Library Association, the Florida Association for Media in Education (FAME), the South Dakota Library Association, School Media Section, and the Youth Services Section of the New York Library Association all featured programs on various aspects of computers and libraries, as did the Westchester Library System (New York). The California State Library provided a workshop on the early adolescent.

EVIE WILSON

Young Adult Literature

"Should Read" Titles. Attention was focused in 1984 on what young adults (teenagers) "should read" as well as the titles that are popular with the age group.

In August William Bennett, Chair of the National Endowment for the Humanities (NEH), released a survey he had conducted in which he asked over 400 historians, writers, professors, and cultural leaders what writings every high school student should read. Not surprisingly among the works cited most frequently were: Shakespeare (especially Hamlet and Macbeth); Mark Twain, Huckleberry Finn; the Bible; Dickens, A Tale of Two Cities and Great Expectations; Steinbeck, Grapes of Wrath; Sophocles, Oedipus Rex; Orwell, 1984; poems by Emily Dickinson and Robert Frost; Leaves of Grass by Walt Whitman; Marx, Communist Manifesto; Thoreau Walden; J. D. Salinger, Catcher in the Rye; and Jane Austen, Pride and Prejudice.

This list of tried and true "classics" contained no real surprises and also no work published in the last 25 years. Librarians who work with young adults often reacted like Mike Printz, Topeka West High School, Topeka, Kansas, who was quoted in U.S. News & World Report, as saying "Young people are going to have to be led to those books. They won't come to them alone."

A number of titles that young adults do read on their own have remained popular over time, titles that meet their desire to read books that help them to deal with their adolescence and in which they can see their own lives reflected: Among those labeled as "young adult" literature are Judy Blume's Forever and Tiger Eyes; Paul Zindel's Pigman; Are You In the House Alone? and Father Figure by Richard Peck; The Outsiders, Tex and Rumble Fish by S. E. Hinton; Norma Fox Mazer's Someone to Love; Home Before Dark by Sue Ellen Bridgers; The Chocolate War by Robert Cormier; Killing Mr. Griffen by Lois Duncan.

Among the "adult" titles that might be added to a list of books every high school student should read, and which librarians have said are continuing to be popular with teenagers, are: Diary of Anne Frank; To Kill a Mockingbird by Harper Lee; I Never Promised You A Rose Garden by Hannah Green; A Tree Grows in Brooklyn by Betty Smith; Tolkien's The Lord of the Rings trilogy.

Current Publishing Trends. The October 19 Publishers Weekly carried several articles on the current trends in writing, publishing, and marketing of young adult books. In general, the articles reflect the realities that librarians who work with young adults have observed. The mass market paperback format is overwhelmingly popular with young adults, who prefer reading and buying books in this format and often will wait to read a title until it is available in paperback.

Publishers agree that young adults are reading—and buying—books today if they meet their varied interest, including romance, science fiction, and fantasy and the supernatural, the traditional YA or problem novel. As George Nicholson, Editor-in-Chief, books for young readers, Dell/Delacorte, stated: "Any subject is fair game for YA and any publisher who is going to survive has to recognize the overwhelming necessity for diversity." Dell books (as most YA literature) entertain but are always tempered by serious ideas and an awareness of social implications. "Our readers can, and should, worry about the bomb, but they still want a date for Saturday night."

The continued success and growth of the market for young adult paperback books was evident with new paperback imprints such as Putnam's Pacer books and Scholastic's Point, and the emphasis placed by publishers on such well established imprints as Simon & Schuster's Archway, Avon/Flare, Bantam/Starfire, and Dell/Laurel-Leaf.

Whether paperback or hardcover, the basic themes of young adult literature—what is being published and what is being read—was summed up by Charlotte Zolotow of Harper and Row, who said, "YA novels are becoming more honest and realistic, authors writing out of heart, feeling, and genuine motivation. Adolescents experience life with great intensity and any author who can capture that depth is bound to succeed with a YA audience.... Teens want to read about themes that impinge upon their lives... 'transitional novels' concerned with that all important syndrome of adolescence, the movement from one stage of life to the next, always brought with difficulty."

The Young Adult Novel. A number of "YA novels" published in 1984 add to the genre's backlist and appeared on "lists" of best for the year (ALA's Young Adult Services Division's annual "Best Book for Young Adults" list, *Booklist's* "Young Adult Editor's Choices 1984," *School Library Journal's* "Best Books for Young Adults.")

Joyce Sweeney was the first winner of the Delacorte Press Prize for an Outstanding First Young Adult Novel. Her book, *Center Line,* about five teenage brothers who fearing for their safety, steal their abusive, alcoholic father's car and run away from home, was selected to the YASD *Best Books for Young Adults'* list.

In three other "YA novels," young women experience the challenges of adolescence and do indeed move from one stage of life to another. In *A Little Love* by Virginia Hamilton, sensitive Sheema, sustained by the love of her grandparents and her strong tender boyfriend, searches for her father, and discovers that, although she feels fat, insecure, and slow, she is strong and beautiful.

Madeleine L'Engle's *A House Like a Lotus* tells a story of 16-year-old Polly O'Keefe, who, when she learns that terminally ill Max, an older woman who has befriended her, is a lesbian, tries to run away but eventually becomes aware of the special relationship that exists between them.

Back Home by Michelle Magorian is the story of Rusty Dickinson returning to England after five years of being evacuated to America during World War II, who feels lonely and alienated until she and her mother grow toward mutual understanding and acceptance.

Science Fiction, Fantasy and the Supernatural. The speculative genre of science fiction, fantasy and the supernatural, continued their popularity with young adults. Diana Wynn Jones's *Fire and Hemlock* is a fantasy filled with sorcery and intrigue, magic and mystery, all background to an unusual love story between 19-year-old Polly Whittacker and cellist Tom Lynn, who does not exist in her remembered past.

In *The Changeover: A Supernatural Romance,* Laura, with the help of an older boy who loves her, "changes over" into a witch to fight the evil forces that are attacking her little brother.

Another book that combines romance and fantasy is Jane Yolen's *Heart Blood,* in which Jakkin wants only to possess and train his own red dragon—until his love for Akki leads him into the maze of Austarian politics.

Presenting more traditional science fiction is *The Integral Trees* by Larry Niven, the story of intertribal conflict among the descendants of a handful of space mutineers who have created a complex civilization around giant trees in orbit within the ring of breathable air surrounding a neutron star.

In *Futuretrack 5* by Robert Westall, Henry Kitson is one of a small group responsible for keeping the highly computerized manipulative 21st-century British society functioning, and Keri is the London bike-riding champion of *Futuretrack 5.*

Adult Novels for YAs. Novels written for adult audiences continued to find a following among young adults when their subjects or story lines appealed to adolescent interests. Four diverse titles worth noting include Frederick Forsyth's *The Fourth Protocol,* a cold war spy story dealing with a Soviet plan to explode a small nuclear bomb, smuggled into London piece by piece, and blame it on the Americans.

In *Run for Your Life* by Barbara Abercrombie, Sarah, a mystery writer who is also training to run a marathon, finds herself in a race with death as her fiction becomes reality.

Summer of the Barshinskeys by Diane Pearson, begins in an English village in 1902 and tells how the arrival of the Barshinskey family forever changes the lives of the three Willoughby children.

Authors William D. Montalbano and Carl Hiaasen, one of the first American reporters admitted to China and an investigative newsman, pooled their writing skills in *A Death in China,* a novel that blends the spectacular chase through thousands of clay soldiers who guard a Chinese Emperor's tomb at Xian with avarice, political intrigue, romance, and murder.

Nonfiction. Diverse subjects reflecting the myriad interest of adolescents are the topics of nonfiction titles popular with young adults. Topics range from child abuse, sex education, soul and rock music, to sports, history (especially World War II and Vietnam), and biography.

Author Judy Blume (left) was honored by Friends of the Chicago Public Library with the Freedom to Read Award at the Literary Arts Ball. Blume's K.I.D.S. grant paid for special parent and children's workshops at the CPL's Woodson Regional Library.

Above, Jay Gale, author of A Young Man's Guide to Sex *published by Holt, Rinehart and Winston. (Images by Dwayne)*

Brent Ashabranner, author of To Live In Two Worlds: American Indian Youth, Today, *published by Dodd, Mead & Company, Inc.*

Virginia Hamilton, author of A Little Love *published by Philomel Books, a division of The Putnam Publishing Group.*

In *They Cage the Animals at Night* author Jennings Michael Burch recalls the sometimes kind, but often mentally and physically brutal, treatment he received between ages 8 and 11 when he was placed in a series of foster homes by his mother who was ill and could no longer care for him.

Jay Gale's *A Young Man's Guide to Sex* is a comprehensive and explicit guide to the emotional and physiological aspects of sex and sexuality written specifically for young men.

Gerri Hirshey interviewed a number of performers to capture the beat of soul music from Motown to James Brown in *Nowhere to Run: The Story of Soul Music* and Mike Clifford and others produced the 4th edition of *The Harmony Illustrated Encyclopedia of Rock*, which includes many photographs of album covers and musicians.

Newton at the Bat, edited by Erie Schrier and William F. Allman, is a compilation of essays that present the part which physics, physiology and aerodynamics play in baseball, frisbee, skiing, sailing, and other sports.

Personal perspectives on war—both World War II and Vietnam—proved popular with 1984's young adults. Studs Terkel's *"The Good War:" An Oral History of World War II* offers wonderfully readable tales that are alive, spontaneous, and personal as Americans from all walks of life recall their involvement and participation.

Hanna and Walter: A Love Story, by Hanna and Walter Kohner, related how a couple, separated by the Nazi invasion of Czechoslovakia, endure concentration camps and death, but finally are reunited after the war.

In Wallace Terry's *Bloods: An Oral History of the Vietnam War by Black Veterans* 20 Black soldiers give graphically detailed accounts of the Vietnam War and the emotional aftereffects on themselves, their families, and friends.

The stories of other people's lives are real-life adventures that young adults like to read about. In 1973 at 24 Bonnie Tiburzi was the first woman hired as a pilot for a major U.S. airline. In *Takeoff! The Story of America's First Woman Pilot for a Major Airline*. Tiburzi shares her love of flying and tells of her challenging and often frustrating climb to success.

Brent Asabranner's *To Live in Two Worlds: American Indian Youth Today* presents young American Indian men and women, who through words and photographs, tell about their lives, on and off the reservation, as well as their hopes for the future.

We Are Your Sisters: Black Women in the Nineteenth Century, edited by Dorothy Sterling, is a moving documentary history of Black women based on transcripts of interviews with ex-slaves, memoirs, letters, and other primary sources.

EVELYN SHAEVEL

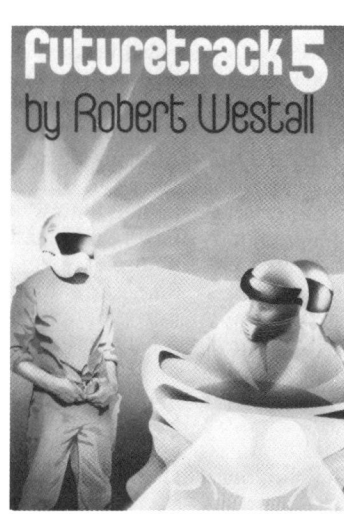

Far right, Joyce Sweeney's Center Line *published by Dell Publishing Company, Inc., won the first Delacorte Press Prize for an outstanding first young adult novel. Right, Robert Westall's* Futuretrack 5 *was published by William Morrow & Company, Inc.*

Young Adult Services Division

In spite of growing budget problems, the Young Adult Services Division continued its commitment during 1984 to producing useful services to members, by members. The Hi-Lo list became an annual publication, accompanying "Best Books" and "Selected Films," and a booklet compiling the "Outstanding List for the College Bound" was published. The "Best of the Best" was compiled at a preconference at Los Angeles to update YASD publications.

Conference Activities. The Annual Conference in Dallas saw several successful YASD programs. The YASD Computer Applications to YA Committee program, "Getting It Together and Getting It Going: Microcomputer Practicalities for Youth Services," featured speakers covering planning considerations, funding sources, choosing software and hardware, youth participation and future trends.

The YASD President's Program was cosponsored by PLA, ALSC, IFC, YASD IFC, and LAMA PRS. Entitled "Who Speaks Up for Youth: Intellectual Freedom and the Library," the program addressed how to effectively mount a public education campaign to explain the library's "mission" of providing access to materials and to build support groups for public libraries. It grew out of a concern to find a positive approach to intellectual freedom, instead of a defensive posture. After the library has adopted a selection policy and complaint mechanism, the public relations effort is aimed at making the public aware of what the library is so that support alliances can be formed before problems arise.

Gene Lenier, winner of the IFRT Immroth Memorial Award, spoke on intellectual freedom as a primary responsibility. Pat Latshaw, PR Director of the Akron–Summit County PL (Ohio) spoke on public relations campaigns as opposed to publicity. Pat Scales, of the Greenville, South Carolina, Middle School described a project run with parents acquainting them with new materials for youth and why the library buys them. Other divisions and committees of ALA cosponsored the program.

Norma Fox Mazer, author of several "Best Books" spoke to a large crowd at the YASD luncheon.

The Selected Films Committee presented some of their latest choices, encouraging use of films with young adults.

The first Baker & Taylor Conference Grant was made to Michelle Pugh of Warrensville, Ohio. Two grants will be available annually for a public library YA specialist and a school library media specialist to attend their first ALA Conference. Applications are available through the YASD Office.

Fiscal Activity. YASD continued to have budgetary problems in 1984. One positive aspect was journal advertising. *Top of the News* (YASD/ALSC), *Library Resources and Technical Services* (RTSD), and *Reference Quarterly* (RASD) joined resources and hired their own advertising sales representative. Advertising quotas were met or surpassed, increasing revenue for the journals.

YASD and Educational Reform. The YASD was asked by ALA in 1984 to respond to *A Nation at Risk*, and passed a resolution that stressed the role school librarians and YA specialists in public libraries have in the personal growth and education of young adults. The Board resolved that because of this involvement " . . . school and public librarians be integral participants in planning for educational reform at all levels." Several YASD members, including President Penny Jeffrey, Director Gerald Hodges, and Susan Madden, participated in a series of seminars sponsored by the U.S. Department of Education on "Libraries and Lifelong Learning." The seminars resulted in *Alliance for Excellence: Librarians Respond to "A Nation at Risk."* This booklet echoed YASD's concerns: "Sustained by alliances among educators, parents, other citizens and librarians, such a Learning Society can be developed and nurtured. Well designed and well maintained, this alliance will assure that the whole will indeed be greater than the sum of its parts."

YASD President Lydia LaFleur and ALSC President Margaret Bush prepared a response to the *AASL Future Structure Report*, which stated in part:

"ALSC and YASD . . . are eager to work with AASL staff and members in positive and cooperative ways to serve the needs of youth in society as well as individuals working with this population. School and public libraries will continue to serve complementary roles in the educational and recreational lives of children and young adults. Likewise the ALA youth divisions should serve complementary roles to fulfill the primary needs of their members and draw upon the specialized expertise of other divisions."

A task force of the Board was formed to draw up an age/grade definition of a "young adult." This is imperative if the work of YA specialists in public and school libraries is to be recognized in statistics gathering. Statistics are important to support or institute service, and most states do not even ask for YA activities. Where they are counted, they are usually included with juvenile or adult statistics, depending on who oversees YA activity in a given library. Acceptance of YASD's definition would give libraries a way to respond to requests for statistics and collect them internally.

PENELOPE S. JEFFREY

YOUNG ADULT SERVICES DIVISION

PRESIDENT (June 1984–July 1985):
Lydia LaFleur, New York Public Library–Manhattan Borough Office, Donnell Library Center, New York City

VICE-PRESIDENT/PRESIDENT-ELECT:
Joan L. Atkinson, Graduate School of Library Science, University of Alabama, University, Alabama

EXECUTIVE DIRECTOR:
Evelyn Shaevel

Membership (August 31, 1984): 2,103 (1,552 personal; 551 organizational)
Expenditures (August 31, 1984): $98,748

Canadian Correspondent's Report

The Canadian correspondent's report for the 1985 *ALA Yearbook of Library and Information Services* differs in several respects from the reports by the same correspondent in the 1983 and the 1984 *Yearbooks*. The Editors of the 1985 *Yearbook* asked R. Brian Land, Director of the Ontario Legislative Library, to prepare an historical overview of the National Library of Canada for the present volume, and they asked Gwynneth Evans, Executive Secretary of the National Library, to prepare an article on the current activities of that Library. Hence the National Library of Canada is covered elsewhere in the 1985 *Yearbook*.

Secondly, the network of subcorrespondents for Canada who report to this correspondent writer has been formalized and given greater recognition than heretofore. The writer and editors wish at the outset to acknowledge with deep gratitude the contributions of Norman Horrocks, Director of the Dalhousie School of Library Service; Diane Mittermeyer, Graduate School of Library Science, McGill University; Alixe Hambleton, Faculty of Education, University of Regina; and Robin Inskip, Faculty of Library Science, University of Alberta. Horrocks covers the Atlantic Provinces, Mittermeyer the Province of Quebec; Hambleton solicited material for Manitoba and Saskatchewan; and Professor Inskip reported for Alberta and British Columbia.

The report also differs from its immediate predecessors in one further respect: no longer does economic recession form the dominant theme. The recession by the end of 1984 had at, least for the moment, abated in Canada as it had in the United States. In Canada, however, continuing high unemployment and a dangerously high national debt remain as barriers to full economic recovery.

Three of Canada's ten provinces drafted public library legislation, and, although this news is not entirely new (reference was made to initiatives in Alberta, Ontario and Saskatchewan in the 1983 report) it *is* noteworthy. As Laurie Bildfell noted in the October 1984 issue of *Quill and Quire*, "Library legislation is normally so far down on the political agenda that it falls somewhere off the bottom of the page." Moreover, because of acts of omission rather than of commission in the three drafts, they do appear in their present form to militate in part against the aspirations of librarians. Alberta proclaimed the Alberta Libraries Act in April 1984 to replace its 1956 Act. Saskatchewan replaced its 20-year old legislation two months later; and, concurrently, Ontario gave first reading to a bill to replace its Public Libraries Act of 1967.

Library Legislation

The new Alberta Act is remarkable for its omission of any standards. It says little about library services as they are or should be. Instead, regulations direct each municipality to assess the needs of the community, decide how those needs can best be fulfilled, and develop its own plan to do so. Paradoxically, although the Alberta Act appears to give local boards more freedom than heretofore, some boards perceived the new regulations as interfering with their autonomy. However, Joseph Forsyth, Director of Library Services for Alberta Culture, assured us that, "Primary responsibility for library service [still] rests with the municipal-government level. The provincial government's role is to facilitate provision of that service." Certainly, however, a modification in the new Alberta Act is that libraries are now prohibited from charging fees for service, although membership fees are still permitted.

In Ontario, the library community, which had expressed general dismay over the plans outlined in the government's Green Paper of March 1983, appeared to be somewhat reassured by the new Bill which received first reading in June of this year. Sections of the Bill that have been widely applauded include those which encourage formation of county libraries; those which attempt to eliminate non-operating library boards; those which mandate open board meetings and the advertising of vacancies on boards; and those which encourage specialized services to francophones, native people, and the disabled. Less popular are those sections which turn over to municipal councils the power to appoint library board members; those which establish three-year terms for board members, concurrent with those of the municipal council; and those which stipulate that henceforth councils will approve library estimates, "subject to any terms or conditions that the council imposes."

The opponents of these latter sections feel, as does Stan Beacock, recently retired Director of the London Public Library, that three years is too short a time for board members to become thoroughly familiar with library needs; that a council veto "virtually obliterates any independence that the board has" (Elizabeth Cummings, President of the Ontario Library Association); and that, as Peter Bassnett, Chairman of the Ontario Public Library Programme Review, has noted, you cannot have "two clauses in the same Act which are mutually exclusive. One clause says that the library board has management and control. The second clause implies that a council can override that management and control. One clause should be amended."

Certainly, the lack of any overall philosophy of public library service in Canada is evidenced by the ways in which the Alberta and Ontario legislation presently differ. The Alberta Act leaves control of policy and expenditures in the hands of the library board; the Ontario Bill gives this control to the local council. The Alberta Act prohibits service fees but not membership fees; the Ontario Bill prohibits membership fees, but leaves open the possibility of charging for certain reference and information services.

Most important, however, and constituting a possible threat to the profession, while the Alberta Act does at least require libraries in communities of over 10,000 to hire a professional librarian, the Ontario Bill omits any mention of library staff qualifications. Nor is this omission accidental, for, according to a senior member of the Ontario Libraries and Community Information Branch, which advised on the provisions of the new Bill, long-term failure clearly to define the meaning of the term "librarian" prevents its use in legislation and may even jeopardize the existence of librarianship as a distinctive specialization. Moreover, according to the Ontario Minister of Citizenship and Culture, a library school degree should specifically *not* be a prerequisite for *any* position in a library.

As 1984 drew to a close, concern with regard to the lack of standards and definition in the Ontario and, to a lesser extent, the Alberta legislation appeared to be increasing. However, reaction to the 1984 Saskatchewan Public Libraries Act appears to have been so muted as to be largely absent. The library community seems to have been more upset by the way the act was hustled through the legislature than by the act itself, possibly because the Saskatchewan Act appears to evidence even less change in underlying philosophy than does the Alberta Act. Thus the new Saskatchewan legislation merely adjusts to meet changes in circumstances. The role of the Provincial Library is modified from one of coordination to one of assisting libraries to develop cooperative services; and the "Provincial Librarian" is renamed the "Saskatchewan Librarian."

The powers of the (renamed) Saskatchewan Library Board are increased; and the autonomy of the seven regional libraries are recognized. If a local council wishes to withdraw from a region it may still do so; but mediation and arbitration procedures are now prescribed prior to the final option. The Minister in Charge of Libraries, rather than the Saskatchewan Librarian, is now responsible for the purchase of books and materials, which will probably mean little change in practice. Yet, according to the Saskatchewan Library Trustees Association's Secretary Treasurer, George Bothwell, "the Minister could [now] be subject to pressure from various groups" on purchase and collection selection decisions. Finally, the Saskatchewan Public Libraries Act recognizes the two municipal libraries in Saskatoon and Regina and the Provincial Library as provincial resource centers, which gives those libraries a legal basis from which to agitate for additional funding but does not in itself provide any such funding.

Again, in the Saskatchewan Act, as in the library acts of the other two provinces, the legal position of qualified librarians remains ill-defined and, in Saskatchewan, at least de jure, a major professional responsibility of the senior Saskatchewan librarians is transferred to a non-librarian. However, with respect to all three acts, it must be recognized that at present, except for the comments of the Ontario Ministry representative noted earlier, few Canadian librarians seem particularly concerned about the impact of the new legislation upon the profession per se.

Political and Economic Background

Presumably political and economic developments in Canada in 1984 did not have such immediate consequences for libraries as did the new library legislation. Nevertheless, no report on Canadian librarianship can omit the federal election of September 4. John Turner, who had replaced Pierre Elliott Trudeau in the early summer as leader of the Liberal Party, called what some would now say was a premature election for the early fall and was soundly defeated. The Conservatives, under their new leader, Brian Mulroney, swept to power with unusually strong representation from every province and from both the French and English segments of the population. Unlike recent Canadian governments, therefore, the newly elected federal Conservatives represent a truly national force, with an overwhelming mandate for change.

Change, carefully measured and skillfully presented, does indeed appear to be the increasingly welcomed initiative of the new Canadian government. The previous protectionist policies of Canada are being reversed and the welcome mat is out to foreign investment. The National Energy Programme, long anathema to much of the business community, was scheduled to be rewritten. There is a new emphasis upon strengthening the nation's ties with the United States: both economically and politically. Inflation has come down, as has the Canadian dollar. Interest rates went up early in the year; but finally dropped to record lows. Growth in Canada continued, though at a slower rate than in the United States.

Many companies, badly threatened by the recession of 1982–83, were again able to get their balance sheets back under control. In particular, Canada's high technology industry made some remarkable advances in 1984 (and met some remarkable defeats). Northern Telecom, for example, which describes itself as the second largest designer and manufacturer of telecommunications equipment in North America, predicted sales of $4,200,000,000, up from $3,300,000,000 in 1983.

Crowntek Incorporated—a new Canadian database, application software, and maintenance service—emerged as a major force in the high tech sector, with several microcomputer outlets: ownership of Toronto's Polaris Computer Systems Ltd.; acquisition of Datacrown Inc., the country's second largest service firm; and the purchase of a small California fiberoptics operation. Spar Aerospace, world famous for its development of the Canadarm used on many space-shuttle flights, continued to prosper and is now developing a remote manipulator for servicing Ontario Hydro's nuclear reactors; but a less well-known firm, Sonotek Ltd. of Mississauga, Ontario, also made a major breakthrough in the high tech field with the development of a sun photometer for Garneau's shuttle mission.

On the other hand, Ottawa-based Nabu Network's bold venture into distributing home computer software proved to be a costly failure; and Montreal-based Comterm Inc. was forced by competition from IBM and Apple to withdraw its much ballyhooed Hyperion from the personal computer market. Moreover, outside the high technology industry, some sectors, such as mining, forest products, merchandising and energy, along with some provinces such as Alberta and British Columbia, still missed out on the general economic recovery in 1984.

There may be a growing (though rarely discussed) schism between a relatively small group of externally-oriented Canadian librarians and the great majority of internally-oriented library practitioners. Clearly, the events selected for mention in this report form but a fraction of the vast array of minutiae that appeared each month in the library literature for 1984. In this year's report, space constraints have precluded, for example, reports on the scores of local, regional, and national conferences and meetings that preoccupy the unflagging efforts of so many librarians. They precluded, too, reports on the achievements of all but a handful of library leaders.

Public Libraries

Despite the weakening recession, city councils

Trivial Pursuit game inventors Chris Haney, left, and Scott Abbot, center, visited the Metropolitan Toronto Library's Arthur Conan Doyle Collection, reputed to be the largest in the world, to ferrett out Sherlock Holmes questions and answers. Money Magazine *photographer Joe McNally photographs the search.*

continued in a few cases to probe, as councils should, at the fiscal support structure of their public libraries; but in most cases proposed cuts were successfully resisted. The most publicized case was that of the Winnipeg, Manitoba, Public Library in which the city council, supported by Chief Librarian Don Mills, proposed the closing of five branch libraries. Opponents, including some councillors, pointed out that Winnipeg's per capita library spending was already lower than that of 26 other Canadian cities and that library use in 1984 was 41 percent above that in 1981.

Eventually, on February 13, 1984, just over two months before the branches were to close and after thousands of protests had been received by the council, the plan was scrapped, leaving the problem of how to provide adequate funding for Winnipeg's 21 branches unsolved but raising the probability of a sharp increase in library book budgets and a more modest increase in the municipal tax level.

On the other hand, despite public protest, the Ottawa Public Library Board did decide to cut summer operating hours after the city council reduced the 1984 increase previously granted to the library—the Board also increased fines on adult overdue books from 10 to 15 cents a day. The Regina Public Library did close its Regina Energy Conservation Information Centre after both the Saskatchewan and federal governments discontinued fiscal support. Finally, the British Columbia Library Network (BCLN) found itself forced to close down with the completion of Phase I of the project, because participating libraries could not commit themselves to maintaining funding levels, even though the Network was deemed in some respects superior to the UTLAS cataloging and acquisitions support currently being used.

As opposed to these few setbacks, however, and especially in contrast to the failure of BCLN, la bibliothéque Nationale du Québec announced early in 1984 its plans to purchase the French and Québécois bank from UTLAS in order to relocate all searching, cataloging, and retrieval facilities in Montreal. The Quebec government is prepared to make initial grants to repatriate the bank; but, once in operation, its services will be made available to users through a commercial firm.

Similarly, the Quebec government announced in May its plans to form a Quebec-based data bank center—IST: Informathèque Inc.—to replace an earlier group (which had been formed in 1966 through a joint Franco-Quebec effort to disseminate scientific and technological information; but which had been terminated because of escalating costs, hardware incompatibility, and poor markets). During the next three years, the Quebec government will thus invest at least $6,700,000 in a wide-scale library automation program for the Province.

Also on the Quebec public library scene, Professor Diane Mittermeyer reported that, in addition to the four province-wide library association now existing in Quebec—The Corporation of Professional Librarians of Quebec; Association pour l'avancement des sciences et des techniques de la documentation (ASTED); the Quebec Library Association; and the Eastern Canada Chapter of the Special Libraries Association—two new associations were formed in 1984. These two new associations, which significantly do not have any official English names, are L'Association des directeurs de bibliothèques publiques de Québec; and Le Regroupement québécois de l'information documentaire.

Each of these two new associations represents a major development. L'Association des directeurs reflects the enormous progress made by public libraries in the province over the past five years, a progress carefully fostered and monitored by the Quebec Ministry of Cultural Affairs. "New and updated buildings, updated collections as well as new services are now a reality," reported Mittermeyer, "Obviously, with all these changes, library directors have felt a need for greater exchange of communication among themselves."

The second new association, Le Regroupement québécois, has a much broader purpose than has L'Association des directeurs. "Its aim is," according to Mittermeyer, "to provide a communication platform for every association having an interest in or dealing with 'document' information (information documentaire).... For now [Le Regroupement] consists largely of archivists, various groups of information specialists, and librarians. Their basic objective is threefold: (a) to share common problems and concerns and to organize a stronger and more unified voice, particularly when lobbying the provincial government; (b) to exchange information and possibly to cooperate in the planning and organization of continuing education activities; and (c) on a longer term basis, to achieve financial savings by sharing such administrative resources as personnel, equipment and office space. [Le Regroupement is important because] it represents an approach to cooperation which until very recently was totally absent in Quebec, even among library associations."

Clearly, the large number of library associations now in the Province of Quebec is indicative of the dramatic surge of library activity taking place in that province. This surge, together with the strong support being offered by the provincial government to both traditional and new information services, is rapidly placing Quebec in the forefront of professional librarianship in Canada.

While the Province of Quebec as a whole made great strides in 1984, a public library in another province made gleeful headlines as the fastest growing library in Canada. The Edmonton (Alberta) Public Library reported that it was now first in the nation in circulation, with 1983 circulation of materials for home use topping 6,600,000 (over 1,000,000 higher than number two Toronto Public Library). In four years circulation at the EPL doubled from the 1979 figure of 3,078,892. The Library also operates Canada's largest automated circulation system with four computers, the fourth of which was purchased in the fall of 1983 for $200,000. "Comparative figures compiled in Eastern Canada show our staff to be the most productive in Canada," says Vincent Richards, EPL Director, "and our costs for the work done [are] the lowest."

Ontario's public libraries, too, should see considerable increases in book stock and, one would hope, in circulation, over and above "traditional" use, as 1984 grant decisions by that province's Ministry of Citizenship and Culture become effective. Through its Library and Community Information Branch, the Ministry announced a grant of over $120,000 for materials needed by francophone, multicultural, and native communities as well as for the print-handicapped, and a $40,000 grant to the Ministry's regional library services in southern Ontario to improve Native people's access to public library service. In addition, approximately $100,000 will be made available to northern Ontario Native staff to help them to develop and maintain library services. In a different context, the Ministry also initiated a $1,200,000 program in 1984 to help Ontario libraries to obtain automation hardware and software from Canadian manufacturers.

Automation, Networking, and Computers. Indeed, automation was very much to the fore in public library developments in Canada during the year. The Brampton (Ontario) Public Library, for example, made headlines with its claim to be, as of May 1, the first library in the Province to provide online terminals for its users to locate library materials. Fourteen terminals at Brampton's two branches were installed at a cost of $400,000 for public access to the new catalog system. The location of a book, whether or not it is available, and the return due date can be obtained using only title, author, or subject.

Where Brampton leads, can others be far behind? Saskatchewan continued to prepare for a provincial automated network with the publication in 1984 of a report by Richard Boss of Information Systems Consultants Inc. on the repatriation of the database currently maintained at UTLAS. Consideration of the Province's public library needs led Boss to conclude that library interests would best be served by taking a separate rather than a combined approach to such repatriation.

It is, incidentally, interesting to note that, as more and more libraries moved to repatriate their UTLAS databases, the University of Toronto continued vigorous efforts to sell UTLAS, most recently to the International Thompson organization. Also in 1984 the Kitchener Public Library signed a $500,000 contract with GEAC: an online catalog was to begin operation there in 1984, with circulation control to follow in spring 1985.

GEAC was also in the news, though less favorably, when Don Miller, Director of the Greater Victoria Public Library (GVPL), reported to his Board that GEAC-Canada was several months behind schedule on its contract. GVPL had signed a contract in December 1982 to supply computer hardware and software worth $465,000. A spokesman for the company was reported as responding that, although some early stages in the computerization had been delayed, compression in later stages could correct the situation.

Automation also had a less than favorable impact on at least two other public libraries in 1984. Further improvements to the circulation and cataloging systems of the Vancouver Public Library were postponed because (unionized) library workers feared the loss of jobs to computers; and, on October 1, more than 380 workers at the Metropolitan Toronto Reference Library walked out, causing the library to close its doors to the public for more than two months.

Susan Genge, President of the Canadian Union of Public Employees local concerned in the Metro Toronto strike, said that money was not an issue; but "we must protect the people whose jobs are being taken over by computers." The Toronto strikers went back to work on November 26, after compromise agreements were reached on such issues as position transfers and the status of part-time employees. Management won the right to transfer employees without their consent; but part-time workers continue to be eligible for sick pay benefits. The new agreement also provided for a five percent wage increase for 1984, and a maximum of five hours a day work on video display terminals (with additional display-work concessions for pregnant employees). In short, the Metropolitan Toronto Reference strike and settlement offered an interesting harbinger of probable personnel developments in the rapidly automating world of librarianship.

In other public libraries the impact of computers was more readily assimilated. The Kingston (Ontario) Public Library enjoyed a second successful summer of computer literacy training programs, using five students hired through a Summer Canada grant and its own computer plus 10 rented TRS-80s and Commodore 64s to instruct 335 registrants for one-week periods over a span of eight weeks at low cost to registrants. On a much larger scale, the Metropolitan Toronto Library Board will purchase a $2,600,000 integrated library system from Biblio-Techniques Library and Information System (BLIS), which will provide a cataloging system and an online public catalog. The online catalog will permit four levels of searching, including an easy access level for novice users, and keyword and Boolean search capabilities for experienced users. The catalog was to be ready by 1985, with 51 terminals operating and 5,000,000 entries on the 2,000,000 items in Metro's collection.

Finally, under news of public library automation, the Public Library Service branch of Manitoba Culture, Heritage and Recreation signed an agreement with the National Library of Canada to directly access DOBIS on behalf of rural Manitoba public libraries; and the Saskatoon (Saskatchewan) Public Library (SPL) Board signed an agreement on November 13, 1984, with Universal Library Systems to purchase an automated circulation system. The SPL schedule called for online circulation to begin in fall 1985.

Other Issues. Although items involving automation have come to dominate library news in recent years, other, more traditional issues do still arise. Among Canadian public libraries in 1984, these issues ranged from celebrations to censorship, and from regional libraries to book selection. One celebration was for the Regina (Saskatchewan) Public Library's 75th birthday. The library put on a week-long program of special events including exhibits, displays, and slide presentations. Another celebration was by the Newfoundland Public Libraries Board, which had its 50th anniversary in October.

The censorship issue involved the Prince George (British Columbia) Public Library and, though somewhat of a storm in a teacup, did serve to show how easily censorship can occur, even within a library dedicated to its prevention. Poet-novelist John Laine had flown in from Montreal to participate in a series of reading when his appearance was abruptly cancelled because of a "naughty word" found in one of his books. The decision, taken apparently unilaterally by a library staff member other than the Chief Librarian, caused considerable embarrassment in view of the library's policy supporting freedom of expression: but Laine was still not heard.

Regional libraries made the news in at least three provinces. In British Columbia the good news was that the Surrey Public Library's 1983 "divorce" from the Fraser Valley Regional System had produced "surprisingly few hard feelings" in 1984. Stan Smith, Surrey's Chief Librarian, reported in March 1984 that his independent system had been able to operate within budget despite 10 to 20 percent increases in circulation, increased book stock, and the decision to install a $500,000 computer system to cover acquisitions, cataloging and circulation. Indeed, the main reason for relaying the Surrey experience is to provide an example of a local system (nurtured by a strong regional system) that now properly and amicably is in a position to stand on its own. The Surrey Public Library thus represents one logical conclusion to regional library development.

A second logical development is presented

Library users with a terminal or personal computer with modem and communications software can dial into the Geac circulation system database of the York (Ontario) University. Beginning in January, the university made the collections in York's five libraries on two campuses available to computer users.

by an Ontario example. In that province, the Library and Community Information branch of the Ministry of Citizenship and Culture, under its new and aggressive Director, Wil Vanderelst, completed the reorganization of the Ontario Regional Library System by consolidating the former 14 systems into eight: Escarpment, James Bay, Nipigon, Rideau, Sauqeen, Thames, Trent, and Voyageur. The new configuration was expected to improve both the efficiency and the coordination of library services in Ontario. In Nova Scotia, the Provincial Library Council proposed a new funding formula for regional libraries in the provinces, details of which were being examined by the Regional Library Boards as the year closed.

Finally, as an isolated but perhaps important news item regarding Canadian public libraries in 1984, the Bathurst Heights Area Branch of the North York (Ontario) Public Library System made headlines with the success of its 20-year-old program of adult education. It had begun when the North York Board of Education decided to give adults over the age of 18 a chance to improve their mathematics and English skills in a non-traditional setting. Hundreds of adults, many of them immigrants or Native people, and most with little more than Grade four or five education, enjoyed the relaxed, informal setting of the library, and the chance to use library resources. The initiative in this case came, properly, from the Board of Education rather than the Library Board; nevertheless, the involvement of the North York Public Library in so direct and high-profile an educational exercise is an excellent example of library involvement in an effective social program.

People. As always, librarianship in Canada focused as much in 1984 upon individuals as upon issues; and appointments, awards, retirements, and occasionally deaths formed an important element of the public library scene. Madeleine Aalto was appointed Chief Librarian, Greater Victoria Public Library. Aalto had served as Chief Librarian of the East York (Ontario) Public Library for the past nine years and was President of the Canadian Association of Public Libraries, 1983-84. She replaces Don Miller, who died September 3. Miller was himself President of CAPL the year before Aalto, and was a Past-President of the British Columbia Library Association.

Karen Adams, Director of Manitoba Public Library Services since 1979, was appointed to the newly named post of Saskatchewan Librarian.

Barbara Baker was appointed Chief Librarian of the Newcastle (Ontario) Public Library. Stanley Beacock retired as Director of the London (Ontario) Public Libraries and Museums after 10 years in that position, and joined the staff at the School of Library and Information Science, University of Western Ontario. Beacock was succeeded by Reed Osborne.

Janice Boudreau was appointed the first full-time bilingual coordinator for the Western Countries Regional Library of Nova Scotia. Janet Clark, formerly with the North West Territories Library Service, was appointed Chief Librarian of the South Shore Regional Library Service, Nova Scotia. Joanne Cournoyer-Farley was appointed Coordinator of French Language Library Services in the Library and Community Information Services Branch of the Ontario Ministry of Citizenship and Culture. The Ministry also appointed Marie Foster Coordinator of Multicultural Library Services; Patty Lawler Coordinator of Children's Services, and Elizabeth Rossnagel Coordinator of Library Services for Disabled Persons.

The Rev. Edmond Desrochers, S.J., retired in 1984 as Library Director, La Maison Bellarimin, Montreal, after 33 years in that position. Desrochers was President of the Canadian Library Association in 1963-64. Pat Fader replaced Juliette Henely as Consultant, Library Services, Alberta Culture.

Gliceria Fimaculangan, Chief Librarian of the Brandon (Manitoba) Public Library until her retirement in November 1982, died July 28. Jill K. Foster became Chief Librarian at the new Kennebecasis Public Library in Quispamis, New Brunswick. Jennifer Gamon was appointed Chief Librarian, Oromocto Public Library, New Brunswick. She succeeded William Molesworth, who became City Librarian, Fredericton Public Library, New Brunswick. Nancy Harsanyi was appointed as Coordinator, Library Services, Seaway Valley Libraries, and Chief Librarian of the Cornwall (Ontario) Public Library. Harsanyi succeeded Ann Nyland, who retired at the end of July. Jocelyne Le Bel, Legislative Librarian, Fredericton (New Brunswick) was named Acting Director, New Brunswick Library Service, replacing Agnez Hall, who left to direct a study of network libraries for the New Brunswick government. Brenda Lennox became the new Chief Librarian of the Collingwood (Ontario) Public Library. Lennox was also President of the Ontario Public Library Association.

Myrtle Lorimer of the Winnipeg Centennial Library Board won the 1984 Canadian Library Trustees' Association Merit Award presented annually for distinguished service as a public library trustee.

Arnold Maizen was appointed Chief Librarian of the Kingston (Ontario) Public Library, succeeding Moira Cartwright, who retired. Maizen was Chief Librarian of the North Bay (Ontario) Public Library. Diana Lockhart Mason, former Assistant Librarian for User Services, Toronto Public Library, died in 1984.

Marion Pape was appointed Executive Director of the Fraser Valley (British Columbia) Regional Library. Andre Paris was appointed Chief Librarian for the new French community center library opened in Saint John, New Brunswick. Les Szollosy was appointed Chief Librarian of the Port Moody (British Columbia) Public Library, succeeding retiring Ian Holter. Aileen Tufts, who had been Acting Director of the Vancouver Public Library since November 1983, was appointed Director of the V.P.L. Leonard Wertheimer, recently retired Languages Coordinator with the Metropolitan Toronto Library Board, was accorded a singular honor by the Public Library Association of the American Library Association: the PLA established the Leonard Wertheimer Multilingual Award to be granted annually to a person, group, or organization in recognition of outstanding contributions to multilingual public library services.

Lynn West became Head of the Corner Brook (Newfoundland) Public Library. Finally, Peter White was appointed in 1984 as the new Curator/Director of the Dunlop Art Gallery of the Regina (Saskatchewan) Public Library.

Academic Libraries

One gets the impression, both from talking to Canadian academic librarians and from the dearth of news about their libraries, that academic libraries were content just to keep going in 1984. They did little that was spectacular. They took few risks. They made virtually no headlines. They survived. One measure of the degree to which fiscal attrition was sapping the energy of Canadian academic librarianship in 1984 is the employment picture. The University of Toronto's Faculty of Library and Information Science reported a dramatic decrease in the number of graduates finding positions with academic libraries: in 1982 15 had found employment; in 1983 the number dropped to four. The University of Alberta's Faculty of Library Science also reported that the largest decrease in positions between 1982 and 1983 came in the college and university library sector, with 29 percent of its graduates reporting positions in that sector in 1983 compared with 35 percent in 1982.

Indeed, one of the few headlines involving academic libraries reflected both the fiscal hardship and the still strong sense of values that pervaded such libraries. A group of about 20 local residents occupied the Library of the David Thompson University Centre (DTUC) in

Nelson, British Columbia, in the late spring of 1984, to protest the provincial government's closure of the Centre on May 1 because it was too expensive to run. The library's occupants, mostly senior citizens whom former university librarian Ron Welwood called his "gray panther division," chose the Library because it was, according to one of the seniors, "the heart of culture in this community." The group refused to leave before they had a written guarantee that books and equipment would not be removed from the Centre until its future had been negotiated.

The number of protestors grew steadily, from half a dozen to six dozen; and on July 18 they had a lawn party to celebrate what they believed to be the guarantees they sought. However, the celebration was premature. The government, having enticed the occupants outside, closed the building and placed security guards. The gray panther division pushed the guards aside and reoccupied the Library; and this time they were joined by the local member of parliament who called the latest development a "total double-cross." Finally, on July 27, the British Columbia government reached agreement with Nelson city officials that no library materials would be removed without the city's agreement, and a representative of the occupiers' group was given observer status during any removal. The Centre and its Library have not necessarily been saved; but community action forced a more participative approach to the DTUC's future, and the Nelson City Council commended the occupying forces for their perseverance and community loyalty concerning the future of the Library.

A different type of group action involving academic libraries occurred also in 1984, this time in Ontario, when, on October 17, the 7,500 full-time faculty of the province's 22 community colleges, including librarians, went on strike. The major issue in the confrontation involved teachers' workloads—according to the teachers, they spent more time in preparation and marking than on the teaching hours covered by their contracts. Thus the librarians were involved largely because of union solidarity; but they were, nevertheless, fully involved, and the strike was a bitter one, ending only with back-to-work legislation by the Ontario government on November 12, just short of the time when it would have begun to cost students their year. The government dictated the formation of a three-person committee to examine the workload issue and report back by the summer of 1985.

If the issues involved in the community college strike did not center on their libraries, another academic institution became involved in a totally library-centered issue in 1984. The University of Calgary and its Library found intellectual freedom itself under attack when the Customs Division of the Royal Canadian Mounted Police seized two copies of *The Hoax of the Twentieth Century*, published in the U.S. Alan MacDonald, Director of Libraries at the University of Calgary, noted that the copies were ordered by the Library in July 1983 and received in January 1984. Canada Customs prohibited importation of the title in June 1984 and confiscated the Library's copies on August 8, 1984. Thus the ban on importation was extended to cover confiscation of a title already imported.

The two copies were subsequently returned to the Library on September 17, 1984, after Revenue Canada's Adjudication Directorate advised the RCMP that it could not justify seizure under the importation clause. Everyone concerned, including the Library Association of Alberta, which had fully supported the position taken by university officials, and Revenue Canada itself, seemed pleased with the decision. However, under current federal hate literature laws, the RCMP can still charge anyone found having possession of the title in question. Thus the CLA's position on intellectual freedom may yet be tested by *The Hoax of the Twentieth Century*.

The remaining news of Canadian academic libraries in 1984 is less issue oriented. Two libraries reported major building developments. The University of Toronto's Planning and Resources Committee approved a $5,700,000 addition to the Faculty of Law Library. Improvements to the heating and lighting systems of the existing Library were also covered in the report approved by the Committee; but no construction schedule was set. The Wilfrid Laurier University Library (Waterloo, Ontario) completed the third and final stage of its building program in 1984, with the official opening of two new floors on October 19. The Library has seven floors in operation, and contains 950,000 items with 53 staff. The total annual budget of the Laurier Library exceeds $2,000,000.

The University of New Brunswick (Fredericton) announced that its library system was beginning a massive catalog conversion project that will see more than 450,000 of its books reclassified on a computer. Initial support is from a $25,000 grant from the University and a similar grant from the city of Fredericton, which accounts for more than 3,000 off-campus library users. The project was scheduled for completion in 1985.

The University of Waterloo (Ontario) Library reported completion of its Materials Acquisition Sub-system (MASS), which now keeps computerized track of approximately $2,600,000 in expenditures annually. MASS, which cost $200,000 to develop (by GEAC to UW design specifications), interrelates nine separate functions, including the names of those ordering, the state of the budget, the 3,500 suppliers of library materials, currencies, searching, requesting, ordering, receiving, and invoicing. The University of Waterloo also announced completion of an agreement with Oxford University Press that will lead to the computerization of the *Oxford English Dictionary* (see also Publishing, Book). The University expects its involvement with the latter project to last more than 100 years and involve costs of approximately $6,000,000.

The University of British Columbia Library passed a milestone in mid-July when the University authorized start-up funding of approximately $250,000 for the acquisition of a library computer. Additional funds will come from diverting funds currently paid to UTLAS. The purchase was approved in an attempt to stabilize cataloging support costs, reduce the burden on the university's central computer, and make possible more efficient and expanded library services.

In a non-automated context, the University of British Columbia Library also made a small headline with its announcement in March 1984 that it had received special funding to strengthen its services to UBC students enrolled in off-campus credit courses. As a first step, the Library appointed a part-time professional to oversee the operation of the extension library; and immediate plans were to expand the extension collection and to offer toll-free telephone service so that all long-distance students can request materials and ask for reference assistance.

In Newfoundland, the Queen Elizabeth II Library of Memorial University acquired its millionth volume: a 17th-century work on Irish history by Roderic O'Flaherty. In New Brunswick, the University de Moncton Library became a full depository for Quebec Provincial documents, the only university library outside Quebec (except for Harvard) to be given this status.

People. Academic librarians in the news in 1984 included Margaret Beckman, former Chief Librarian at the University of Guelph (Ontario), who became Executive Director for Information Technology at the University of Guelph, and John Black, Associate Librarian at the University of Guelph, who was appointed Chief Librarian for a three-year term.

Ellen Hoffman, who had been Acting Director of Libraries at York University (Downsview, Ontario) since 1983, was appointed Director of Libraries at York. Stephen Kees retired from Niagara College of Applied Arts and Technology, where he had been the Chief Librarian from the day the College opened in 1967.

Hans Möller was appointed Acting University Librarian at McGill University (Montreal) after Marianne Scott, Director of McGill Libraries since 1975, was appointed National Librarian of Canada; and E. Ann Rae became the new Chief Law Librarian of the University of Toronto. Prior to her appointment, Rae was assistant and Acting Law Librarian at the University of Alberta. Early in 1984, a one-man Board of Inquiry, appointed under the Nova Scotia Human Rights Act, dismissed the allegation of racial discrimination brought by Acadia University Science Librarian Nirmal K. Jain against Acadia University. Jain's charges stemmed from his failure to secure the position of University Librarian at Acadia in September 1982.

School Libraries

This section of the report perhaps appears to suggest that all that happened in school libraries in 1984 happened west of Ontario. This is obviously an unsupportable view, but this summary is presented with its limitations as the only one this correspondent has, based on news stories and reports received.

From west to east, then, the British Columbia Teacher-Librarians' Association followed up its 1983 initiatives (noted in the 1984 *Yearbook*) by completing a major survey of learning and working conditions in school libraries in the province. All information has been standardized to permit an easy comparison between districts.

In Alberta, the government produced a White Paper on school libraries, based on the 1983 position paper. The new paper, heralded by an 11-point brief by the Library Association of Alberta (LAA), could spell major changes for library service in the province's 1,648 schools. For example, the number of teacher-librarians could double if school libraries are integrated with the school instructional program. Significantly, motivation rather than money is seen by the government as the driving force behind the desired changes.

"If school systems designate libraries as a priority," noted Martin Adamson, Associate Director of Media and Technology for Alberta Education, "the money seems to be there." Some school systems achieved the recommended standards, even though their income per student was below the provincial average. Models and standards, such as those presented in the December 1984 publication *Alberta School Libraries in Action 1984-1985*, are expected to provide the catalyst for change. Individual school boards will be responsible for the local development, implementation, and assessment of the provincial policy.

In Saskatchewan, the Advisory Committee established in 1983 to report to the Minister of Education did so in December 1983. A year later the Minister had not distributed *Directions*, as the report was entitled. Apparently, according to an article in the April 1984 *Saskatchewan Library Forum*, school resource centers received considerable emphasis in *Directions* and a provincial policy was called for; but government reactions to that section of the report were unknown at year's end.

In Manitoba, the government released *Enhancing Equity in Manitoba Schools*, a major review of educational finance chaired by Glenn Nicholls. The most publicized recommendation in the review was the establishment of a new curriculum grant of $60 per pupil, of which $20 was to be spent on libraries. If such a grant were to be approved, it would double the per capita amount presently being spent on library materials.

The Manitoba review did not recommend specific provincial funding for teacher-librarians; but supported instead the general principle of student access to specialists such as guidance counselors and librarians. The Manitoba School Library Audio Visual Association (MSLAVA) cautioned that *Enhancing Equity* is at present no more than a series of recommendations, and has published a supplementary position paper on the roles and competencies of teacher-librarians that emphasizes the leadership role of the professional librarian.

People. Elizabeth Austrom, President-Elect of the British Columbia Teacher-Librarian's Association, won that Association's Award of Merit for 1984 for her outstanding service and leadership to the profession. D. Pauline Fennell, recently retired Education Officer with the Special Projects Branch of the Ontario Ministry of Education, was awarded the CSLA Margaret B. Scott Award of Merit for outstanding contributions to Canadian school librarianship at the national level; and Rita Spencer, Principal of River Heights Elementary School, Saskatoon, Saskatchewan, won the 1984 CSLA Distinguished Service Award for School Administrators.

Special and Government Libraries

By their very nature, special libraries tend to be small, individualistic, and . . . specialized. They rarely make the headlines as a group, or raise issues as a category. Special librarians tend to make news as individuals but there are exceptions. In 1984, the exception was the Library Science (LS) group of the Treasury Board of Canada, which four years ago successfully fought, through its union—the Public Service Alliance of Canada—for parity with the male-dominated Historical Researchers or Archivists (HRA) on the principle of equal pay for work of equal *value* (*not* equal pay for *equal work*).

In the June 1984 issue of *Feliciter* appeared a rather plaintive letter from Christopher Rogers, President of the LS Local, asking if the CLA membership was aware that the Treasury Board was contemplating lumping both LSs and HRs into a single new category: the "Museums, Library and Archival Sciences Group." This move, in Rogers' opinion, would have abolished librarians as an occupational entity, since the minimal qualification for the new group would not have been a library science degree. CLA wrote immediately to the Treasury Board stressing that any dilution of minimum qualifications would result in a lower quality of library service, not only to federal government personnel but also to the public.

The Treasury Board responded by assuring the CLA that the basic requirement of a degree in library science, or post-graduate training in librarianship equivalent to that degree, would be retained; and the amalgamation proposal was subsequently dropped. Score one for the Library Science group and for CLA; but the task of protecting the special identity and status of library science constantly requires such vigilance, and a weakening of the legislated base in provinces can only make that task more difficult.

Manitoba special libraries provided two items of news: one good and one uncertain. The good news was the planned fall opening of a Multicultural Education Resource Centre in Winnipeg as part of the Department of Education Library. The new Centre is intended to provide a physical and information focus for multi-cultural studies from Kindergarten to Grade 12. An operating budget of $13,000 was allocated for 1984–85. The uncertain news, however, tends to overshadow the plans for the Resource Centre. Negotiations continued through most of 1984 over the fate of Manitoba's Legislative Library. On May 3 the provincial government announced that the library would be closed to the public and its staff reduced as a cost-saving measure. On May 10, the announcement was reversed and two full-time staff positions were restored. The final decision may depend upon the results of a study being undertaken for Manitoba's Department of Culture Heritage and Recreation on short-term solutions for the Library.

An earlier Manitoba government decision to close its Alcoholism Foundation Library to the public and cut two of its three half-time positions was reversed after protests from the Manitoba Library Association, from CASLIS, and from users; but several other government and college libraries suffered attrition in staff and hours during 1984. Incidentally, the very active role that CASLIS has been taking in Manitoba was reflected in 1984 by the formation of a Winnipeg Chapter of the Association.

Individual special librarians whose names appeared in the news in 1984 included Maurice Boone, recently retired New Brunswick Legislative Librarian, who died; the Rev. Leonard Boyle, a Canadian Dominican priest and professor at the University of Toronto who was appointed, effective September 15, as Prefect, or Head Librarian, of the Biblioteca Apostolica Vaticana (the Vatican Library); and Melva Dwyer, Head Librarian of the Fine Arts Division of the University of British Columbia Library, who won the 1984 CASLIS Special Award for Special Librarianship in Canada for her publication of seminal works of music library reference materials, music union lists, and finding aids to bio-bibliographic works on Canadian musicians.

In addition, Shirley B. Elliott, former Legislative Librarian for Nova Scotia received an honorary Doctor of Civil Laws degree from Acadia University at its Spring Convocation. Wayne Morgan was appointed Chief Curator of the Winnipeg Art Gallery. Daphne Cross Roloff became the new Chief Librarian, Canadian Centre for Architecture in Montreal (Roloff was formerly Director of the Ryerson and Burnham Libraries, Art Institute of Chicago). Guy Sylvestre, retired National Librarian of Canada, was appointed Executive Director, Canadian Institute for Historical Microreproductions (CIHM). Sylvestre succeeded Ernie Ingles, who became Chief Librarian, University of Regina. Marie Tremaine, founding member of CLA, Project Director for the Arctic Institute of North America, and well-known Editor of *Arctic Bibliography*, died on August 1 in Washington, D.C.

Education for Librarianship

Paradoxically, indeed extraordinarily, the most important development in Canadian library education in 1984 did not initially involve the Canadian library schools themselves. In the January 1984 *Feliciter*, the Canadian Library Association Council reported to the Association on its actions furthering President Lois Bewley's hope that Canada would repatriate the accreditation of its graduate library schools. In November 1983 the Council had endorsed the concept of Canadian accreditation, and the CLA Board had established a Special President's Committee to recommend a course of action by March 1984. Apart from a strong note of nationalism, the major reason for the Council and Board decisions seemed to be a wish to enhance the visibility and viability of the CLA. As Treasurer Ken Jensen, who was one of Bewley's supporters, noted, CLA initiative in the Canadian accreditation of Canadian schools would mean "that you couldn't be a librarian in Canada without acknowledging the CLA. It would help us [the CLA] in many ways."

Whether or not CLA was justified in pushing forward on Canadian accreditation in 1984, the way in which Board and Council acted struck many library school faculty as remarkably insensitive. The Canadian Association of Library Schools (CALS) had in fact recently discussed the issue of Canadian accreditation and had voted against any attempt at repatriation; but the CLA did not consult CALS or the Council [of Deans] of Canadian Library Schools (CCLS) before taking the initiative. Moreover, although Bewley maintained in the March issue of *Feliciter* that "the Board has charged its special committee to investigate thoroughly and objectively, the implications of 'Canadianization,' " the belief remained that Council, by its prior endorsement of just such "Canadianization," had compromised the President's Committee before it had even begun its work.

William Cameron, then Dean of the School of Library and Information Science at the University of Western Ontario and Chairman of CCLS, wrote an open letter to CLA asking that "as CLA has apparently decided to keep

CCLS/CCEB [Conseil Canadien des écoles de bibliothécaires] informed solely through the pages of *Feliciter* . . . I am therefore writing this letter on behalf of the seven Canadian library schools with a request that CLA develop a better consultative mechanism for discussion of the complex issues. . . .''

Samuel Rothstein, of the University of British Columbia's School of Librarianship and President of CALS, wrote in the same issue deploring the way in which the decision had been reached. "Before it goes further in the matter of accreditation," concluded Rothstein, "the CLA Council should give more heed to the importance of due process and professional collegiality."

Bewley then invited her "academic colleagues to contribute their expertise to the consultative process now that this, formally, has begun"; and the President's Special Committee, chaired by Beth Miller, President-elect of the CLA, also solicited opinions. One such opinion was indeed ably expressed by Robert Blackburn, recently retired Chief Librarian of the University of Toronto and a former President of CLA, in the November 1984 *Feliciter:* . . . it would be a serious mistake to move towards a purely Canadian mechanism for accrediting library schools. . . . As I see it, the international nature of the present system is of greater benefit to Canadian librarians than it is to the Americans, who could easily get along without us. I hope the existence and work of the committee on accreditation will not provoke any jingoistic feelings south of the border."

In March 1984 Council agreed to fund an ambitious ($15,000 to $19,000) three-year study of the whole issue. Chairperson Miller indicated that her Committee would hold hearings in at least five cities between September 1984 and June 1985, and present its final report to Council in March 1986. A call for written submissions or briefs from members of the library community was published in the June 1984 issue of *Feliciter*. Meanwhile, CLA Council voted to provide $13,800 to send the requisite seven CLA representatives to the forthcoming ALA study on accreditation.

Less dramatically, the library schools of Canada themselves reported on their own business in 1984. The University of British Columbia's School of Librarianship changed its name to School of Library, Archival and Information Science (SLAIS) to reflect the expanded scope of a program that has included a separate Master of Archival Studies since 1981. In October SLAIS hosted a Committee on Accreditation team as a step in its continuing accreditation process. The COA itself was expected to take action on the UBC report during the 1985 ALA Midwinter Conference.

The SLAIS release of its 1982–83 annual report included the results of a 1982 survey showing that, of the 72.1 percent of graduates who responded, 75 percent had either full-time or part-time positions in libraries and that median salaries offered were in the $21,000 to $27,000 range. The 1983–84 employment picture seemed to be deteriorating, so that fewer 1983 graduates would be likely to find employment. Thus only 43 (out of 133) applicants were admitted to the School in 1983–84, one less than in 1982–83.

The salary range presented by the SLAIS survey found its counterpart in surveys by both the Toronto Faculty of Library and Information Science (FLIS) and the University of Alberta's Faculty of Library Science (FLS). The FLIS survey of 1983 graduates showed a 15 percent annual increase in special libraries starting salaries (to a mean of $22,027 and a median of $20,350). The median starting salary for public libraries was $22,700, with a mean of $22,640; and the median for academic libraries was $20,150, with a mean of $20,300. Seventy-six percent of Toronto's 1983 graduates found jobs in libraries, with the largest number finding jobs in public libraries.

The FLS survey showed that 75 percent of 1983 graduates who responded found jobs in library or information science areas; and the average salary for a professional, permanent, full-time position rose to $29,267 from $24,625 in 1982. Of Alberta's respondents 80 percent indicated that they had remained in Alberta; 10 percent gave Ontario as their place of residence; and Saskatchewan and Manitoba each attracted 5 percent. The Alberta FLS was scheduled to receive its current accreditation visit in September 1985.

The library schools at Alberta, University of British Columbia, Dalhousie, and the University of Western Ontario now communicate by the ENVOY electronic mail system.

The University of Toronto named the building which houses FLIS the "Claude T. Bissell Building," after Professor Emeritus Bissell, whose efforts on behalf of the Faculty when he was President of the University had much to do with FLIS being located in the excellent quarters it now occupies. The Ontario Ministry of Citizenship and Culture made a $125,000 grant to the FLIS Centre for Research in Librarianship of the Faculty for the publication of a new edition of *Canadian Selection: Books and Periodicals for Libraries*; and Professor Ethel Auster and Laurent G. Denis were awarded a $62,000, two-year grant from January 1984 to January 1986 to investigate the management of retrenchment in Canadian academic research libraries.

College programs in library and information science education contributed two important items to the news in 1984. The Ryerson Polytechnical Institute in Toronto, a highly reputable institution somewhere between a college of applied arts and technology and a university, announced that it had established a new certificate program to replace its library technician diploma, which was closed out two years ago. The new program, entitled "Information Studies: How to Manage Information Resources for Optimum Results," offers 10 courses and focuses on the application of communication and computer technologies to information resources.

The second item coming from the college component of library education (as distinct from the graduate library schools) was the 1983 salary survey for library technicians. It noted, as indeed did the graduate library school surveys mentioned earlier, a marked increase in the number of part-time and contract jobs. There are also more technicians actively seeking work. For the first time a significant number of technicians may be finding work in archives and the 1985 survey will thus explore this outlet further. The statistics were incomplete since six colleges had not replied at time of publication; but, from the data published, the lowest salary received by a certified library technician in Canada in 1983 was apparently $8,600 and the highest was $22,000. Government libraries seemed to pay the highest technician's salaries, closely followed by public libraries. The mean salary for all types of library employment from the nine institutions reporting was $14,820.

People. In addition to the more general news arising from the field of library education in 1984, individual library educators as usual made the news. Larry Amey, Dalhousie School of Library Service, became President of the Canadian Association of Library Schools (CALS) in June. Jamshid Beheshti was appointed as an Assistant Professor at the Graduate School of Library Science of McGill University.

Sheila Egoff, recently retired from the UBC faculty, received the British Columbia Library Association's Helen Gordon Stewart Award for her outstanding career in librarianship.

Elizabeth Frick was appointed to the faculty of Dalhousie University's School of Library Service, and was immediately elected Secretary-Treasurer of CALS. Frick was formerly head of user services, University of Colorado. Frances Halpenny was made a Companion of the Order of Canada. Kathleen Hogan was the recipient of the $2,500 Howard V. Phalin World Book Graduate Scholarship in Library Science. Hogan, Coordinator of Public Access Systems, University of Calgary Library, was working toward an MLS at the University of Western Ontario.

Norman Horrocks, Director of the School of Library Service and Dean of the Faculty of Management Studies at Dalhousie University, was appointed Chairman of the Advisory Board on Scientific and Technological Information (ABSTI), which advises the National Research Council on issues and developments related to scientific and technical information resources and services in Canada. Horrocks was also appointed to the National Commission on Libraries and Information Science, and he represented the Canadian Council of Library Schools at the ALISE Conference on Accreditation in Chicago in September.

Helen Howard succeeded Hans Möller as the Director of the McGill Graduate School of Library Science. Robin Inskip was awarded the first Library Association of Alberta's Certificate of Merit for leadership in the area of school libraries. Inskip was also presented with a Meritorious Person's Award by the Alberta Teachers' Association. Marjorie Kennedy became the new head of the Library Technician Programme at the Kelsey Institute of Applied Arts and Science, Saskatoon, Saskatchewan. Kennedy succeeded Alice Hagel, who retired after 13 years with the program.

Angelica Kurtz of Winnipeg, Manitoba, won the $1,750 CLA Elizabeth Dafoe Scholarship. Kurtz was planning a career as a teacher-librarian and was taking her MLS at the University of Toronto.

Fred Matthews retired from the Dalhousie School of Library Service at the close of the 1983–84 academic year. Charles Meadow was appointed to the Faculty of Library and Information Science at Toronto with the rank of full professor. Meadow has been editor of the *Journal of the American Society for Information Science* since 1977 and was made a fellow of the Institute of Information Scientists (U.K.) in 1979. Immediately before joining FLIS, Meadow was Acting Manager, Technology Applications, DIALOG Information Services, Inc.

Sharon Meadows of Cow Bay, Nova Scotia, was named the 1984 winner of the Atlantic Provinces Library Association's award. The award is given each year to the student showing most professional promise among those graduating from the Dalhousie University School of Library Service. Meadows had already won a $1,500 scholarship in 1982 from the Nova Scotia Teachers' Union and holds a $1,200 fellowship from Dalhousie.

Professor Ann H. Schabas was selected to be Dean of the University of Toronto FLIS for a five-year term, succeeding Katherine Packer, who took a one-year research leave before retirement. Angela Schmidt of Lethbridge, Alberta, an employee of the University of Lethbridge Media Distribution Department, won the $2,000 CLA H. W. Wilson Company Scholarship, which she planned to use to pursue her MLS at the UBC School of Library, Archival, and Information Science.

Dean Basil Stuart-Stubbs of UBC's SLAIS, was elected to Fellowship by the Royal Society of Canada; an honor accorded to 49 distinguished Canadian humanists and scientists in 1984, but rarely accorded to librarians. Jean Tague of the University of Western Ontario's School of Library and Information Science became Dean of SLIS July 1, succeeding W. J. Cameron, who had held the post since 1970.

Miriam Tees, McGill Graduate School of Library Science, represented the Canadian Association of Library Schools (CALS) at the ALISE Chicago Conference on Accreditation. Louise White, Provincial Archives of Newfoundland, received the first award given by the newly established Margaret Williams Trust Fund and applied the money toward attending the Dalhousie SLS.

Library Association
Virtually all the news created by library associations in Canada in 1984 came from the Canadian Library Association, which, under the aggressive and sometimes controversial Presidency of Lois Bewley, made an unusually large number of headlines. The CLA initiative on the possible Canadian accreditation of Canadian library schools was the most widely reported. A second initiative was the decision of the CLA Board to change the main Conference hotel for the 1984 Toronto Conference from a downtown to a suburban location in order to save money for both the Association and for individual delegates. Although shuttlebus service was provided to enable delegates to visit downtown Toronto, many attending the conference continued to question the wisdom of a suburban location. However, the difference in a single room price was $27 per night, and the potential saving to CLA on meeting room expenses was $25,000.

A third 1984 CLA initiative was the introduction of continuing education seminars to tour the country coast to coast. Henceforth, CLA expects to use its headquarters facilities to coordinate an annual series of three seminar topics to be presented in each of six Canadian cities. The one-day sessions will be widely accessible in all regions of the country. The three topics announced for 1984–85 were: "The Dynamics of Supervision" by Don Young of Training Strategies Canada, Ltd.; "Statistical Techniques for Libraries," the already highly successful workshop by Gail Schlachter; and the "The Effective Reference Interview: Skills and Strategies," to be given in spring 1985. The inaugural session, given by Young, was cosponsored by the new Manitoba CASLIS chapter on October 20. The arguable aspect of the CLA venture is that librarians in Canada's major urban areas may be already overloaded with continuing education opportunities and that CLA may simply compete with existing provincial and local continuing education programs.

In other decisions, the Canadian Library Association agreed to reverse its 1983 decision to replace the full-time professional editor of fiscally ailing *Canadian Materials* (*CM*) with a part-time non-librarian. Faced with unexpected opposition from the Canadian School Library Association (CSLA) and from *CM* readers, the CLA Board first referred the matter back to its Executive Director (who recommended that the annual saving of $3,800, "begins to look like a poor economy when measured against the probable detrimental effects of the changes involved in producing the saving"), and then finally decided to make no changes in the *CM*'s editorial staff in 1984. However, *CM* Editor Adele Ashby resigned.

The CLA Board addressed in 1984 the allegedly high costs of the *Canadian Periodical Index* (*CPI*), which is managed by CLA. A consultant was hired to look into in-house micro-reproduction of *CPI*, using either a microcomputer or CLA's new IBM computer and, by mid-summer, the CLA Board had voted to bring *CPI* production in-house with the purchase of a $35,000 microcomputer. The Board also voted $30,000 for the purchase of a laser printer if such was deemed desirable to further reduce *CPI* costs (by up to $74,000 a year). *CPI* is, of course, a labor-intensive operation and its costs must, therefore, inevitably increase over the years; but CLA's initiatives on the production end hold promise of reducing operational costs in the immediate future (though at considerable capital expense).

Costs in general continued to be critical to the Canadian Library Association. The Board increased both allocations to CLA Divisions and its proposed budget deficit for 1984–85 in an attempt to make the Association more visible to existing and potential members and to counter a continuing decline in CLA membership—a drop of 93 personal and 128 institutional members since 1983. Of the institutional drop, however, 112 came as a single withdrawal when the Vancouver School Board cancelled the membership of all its schools. By the June conference, membership had picked up slightly; but was still down by 200 to 4,759. One attempt to increase the membership in 1984 was the creation of a new membership category for retired and former trustees; but it remains to be seen how many trustees want CLA services after the expiration of their board term.

In other association news, CLA undertook noteworthy initiatives on issues of copyright and intellectual freedom. The copyright initiative was occasioned by the release of *From Gutenberg to Telidon*, the federal government's White Paper on the revision of Canada's 60-year-old Copyright Act. The government's proposals released on May 2 generally reflected CLA's own position on copyright, including continued adherence to the principle of fair dealing ("fair use"); the extension of protection to unpublished posthumous works; permission for libraries to make limited copies of rare material for reference or preservation; a general exemption for braille, tape, and other special formats for the handicapped; and the decision not to introduce a public lending right in the Copyright Act.

On the other hand, *From Gutenberg to Telidon* did not go nearly as far as CLA had hoped in prescribing reprography collectives (or "societies"). Such societies are encouraged; but are far from compulsory, so that a majority of copyright owners may still choose to negotiate with, or sue, librarians on an individual basis. To discuss these and other issues raised by the White Paper, the CLA Copyright Committee sponsored a workshop on June 7 in Toronto. What effect the change of federal government in Canada in 1984 would have on the time table of the parliamentary committee studying the White Paper remained uncertain at year's end.

The intellectual freedom initiative came when CLA Council asked the Intellectual Freedom Committee, under its Convener Tim Schobert, to prepare a brief on the Association's behalf for the federal Department of Justice Special Committee on Pornography and Prostitution (the Fraser Committee), which held hearings across Canada in 1984. CLA presented its brief April 6. The brief noted the present inconsistency of legal interpretations and practice; stressed the difficulty of distinguishing between erotica and pornography; pointed out the responsibility of the library community to ensure ready access to information; and concluded by urging the Special Judicial Committee "to propose no further regulations which may lead to restrictions on certain publications."

Three other CLA concerns included the relationship of CLA to its major component divisions; the relationship of CLA to external organizations; and the appointment or elected positions which changed within CLA in 1984. Relationships within CLA seemed to have improve in 1984 and the CLA Board placed special emphasis upon divisional satisfaction. Most significantly, the CSLA, which had been engaged in long standing guerrilla warfare with its parent association and which in 1983 thought of withdrawing from CLA, decided at its June 1984 annual general meeting to pass unanimously a recommendation that the division abandon the proposed creation of an independent school library association.

CLA's Council voted to initiate discussions with both the New Zealand and Australian Library Associations on "formal working agreements of cooperation between the associations" and will invite the Commonwealth Library Association to hold its next Council Meeting in Ottawa in 1986.

Winners at CLA's student article contest were Neil A. Campbell, a second-year student at the UBC School of Librarianship, first prize; Susan Chapman, a 1984 graduate of the library techniques program at Seneca College of Applied Arts (Ontario), second prize; and Margaret Ann Wilkinson, a first year student at the Faculty of Library and Information Science, University of Toronto, third prize.

Finally, the CLA made the news with elections and appointments. Judith McAnanama, Chief Librarian of the Hamilton (Ontario) Public Library, became President of the Association for 1984–85. Beth Miller, Special Collections Librarian at the University of Western Ontario, London, Ontario, was elected First Vice-President and President-elect. Diane MacQuarrie, Chief Librarian of the Halifax City (Nova Scotia) Regional Library, was elected Second Vice-President. At CLA Headquarters, a major change occurred when David Porter was appointed Director of Finance and Administration, effective September 5. He succeeds Alister MacLachlan, who left CLA in June 1984 after 11 years with the Association. In a second, less drastic administrative change, Laurie Bowes, who has been CLA Managing Editor for seven years, was named Director of Publishing.

The Atlantic Chapter of the Canadian Association of Information Science received its charter and held its inaugural meeting in Halifax in October. The Prince Edward Island Professional Librarians Association became an official entity, and the Canadian Association of Special Libraries and Information Services (CASLIS) formed a Manitoba Chapter.

Cognate Issues

Quebec's Cultural Affairs Minister, Clement Richard, announced on June 12 that, over the next five years, the Ministry of Education will pay out $6,250,000 to ensure that writers and other creators of copyright material receive compensation for photocopying of their works in the province's CEGEPs (Quebec's version of junior colleges). Initially, since no count of copying has been made, a flat rate of $40 will be paid for every title in the 25,000-title index of the Quebec Writer's Union. From July 1984 to June 30, 1988, when the agreement runs out, the actual number of pages photocopied per author will be calculated and paid for. This compensation for copying is believed to be the first of its type in North America.

The irrepressible firm of McClelland and Stewart, often in financial straights but never yet KOd., survived perhaps its most dangerous crisis when in mid-September the government of Ontario agreed to bail M&S out, provided that the publishing firm could raise more than $1,000,000 in share capital from the private sector. That the firm was able to raise this amount may be attributable in part to the 12 percent annual dividend paid by M&S, and to the government's agreement to rebate 30 percent of the investment in cash to personal investors (30 percent tax credits to corporate investors); but probably the major reason for Jack McClelland's success was the high esteem in which he and his firm are held in Canadian cultural circles. However, unless McClelland and Stewart can move quickly to correct serious management problems—the firm has recently been without either a head of sales and marketing or a production manager—this leading independent Canadian publisher may still be in serious jeopardy.

Finally, as 1984 ended and 1985 began, a second major Canadian publishing firm, this time a branch of a U.S. firm, was very much in the news. Prentice-Hall of Canada, Ltd., one of the largest foreign-owned publishing companies in the country, was acquired by Gulf & Western Industries, Inc., of New York in December 1984 when Gulf & Western bought Prentice-Hall Inc. of Englewood Cliffs, N.J., for $706,000,000.

This indirect acquisition will come under review by the Foreign Investment Review Agency of the new Conservative government, and it will present the government with a difficult test of its new cultural policy. On the one hand, the Conservatives are extremely anxious to encourage foreign investors; on the other hand, the government has made strong commitments to maintaining cultural sovereignty—and several Canadian firms were apparently interested in buying the firm if Gulf & Western are forced by FIRA to sell. The government's decision will be important for all Canadian cultural agencies.

JOHN WILKINSON

United Kingdom Report

LA Membership, Reorganization

The sixth year of severe financial restraint in Britain made itself apparent in every aspect of librarianship. Even the headquarters building of the Library Association showed wear and tear. Early in 1984 large chunks of concrete began to drop off the facade and the building spent most of the year cocooned in scaffolding.

In December, however, the scaffolding came down and a renovated, newly painted building emerged. Unfortunately, work on the facade had only been completed a few weeks when it was discovered that the roof was leaking. Scaffolding once more began to appear.

A similar process of remedial work and renewal took place within the infrastructure of the Association as the leaders attempted to bring about changes that would secure the position of the profession in the years to come.

In the 1960s and 1970s membership of the Library Association had grown rapidly. In the 1980s its growth came to an end, producing, among other things, severe financial problems for the Association.

At the same time, job opportunities were becoming increasingly restricted so that at year's end 15 percent of the LA membership was unemployed.

A group was established to consider remedies. In December the group published its recommendations calling for the LA to broaden its membership to include all those working in the newly emerging information occupations. To accommodate such new members, the report advocated a new qualification structure and revised entry requirements. Not surprisingly, the report provoked discussion and argument that was expected to continue into 1985.

Budgets and Services

Against the background of a second year of a Conservative Government intent on reducing public expenditure, both by central and local governments, library and information services in the public sector continued to suffer reductions in services as a consequence of Government policies. CIPFA surveys indicated that the number of library service points have been reduced. In the period 1974–75 to 1984–85 those open 60 hours or more fell from 229 to 34; those open 30–59 hours increased from 2,087 to 2,148; those open 10–29 hours increased from 945 to 1,239 and those open fewer than 10 hours were reduced from 1,063 to 366. All these reductions took place against increased use, particularly in the many areas of high unemployment, and reduced purchases as a consequence of increased book and journal prices and falling budgets.

In academic libraries a similar picture of reduced services emerges (from an LA census) and is exemplified by 37 full-time posts being abolished in the year ending August 1, 15 being "frozen" and 13 left vacant. A similar picture for a corresponding period was revealed in the polytechnics and higher and further education libraries where 14 full-time posts were abolished, 17 "frozen" and 44 left vacant.

Some growth continued in parts of the private sector particularly in pharmaceuticals and the commercial and service areas.

Some local services were particularly hard hit. Somerset County Council threatened to disband its school library service but in response to pressures from the Library Association and many other organizations decided instead that it would purchase no new fiction in 1985–86. In the far north of Scotland the Western Isles Island Council decided to reduce its book purchasing budget by 82 percent, which, given the time of the year in which the decision was taken, effectively halted the purchase of any further new books for that year.

Unfortunately because of public support for the Government's policies the Minister for Arts and Libraries, who has a statutory responsibility to "improve the efficiency of the public library service" and "promote its development," did not condemn the decisions. His views were made clear in his Annual Report to parliament. "From time to time I am pressed to intervene in the affairs of a library authority, because the advocates of such action . . . believe the level of service to be unsatisfactory. The Act of 1964 is cited to justify intervention in such cases. . . . The power to intervene exists, but I can envisage only extreme circumstances in which it would be my duty to use it. . . . I am reluctant to tell library authorities what they should do."

Ironically while he was extolling the virtues of privatization of previously publicly provided services and encouraging libraries to follow suit, a report commissioned by his own executive, the Office for Arts and Libraries, from LAMSAC (Local Authorities Management Services and Computer Committee) concluded that little could be contributed to funds if libraries adopted such activities: ". . .we do not consider direct income is a realistic way of funding the library service."

Nevertheless, the Government's consultative White Paper, "The Government's Expenditure Plan," and a commentary upon it from the Office suggested that libraries were to do no worse, nor any better, than other local authority services in the Government's future expenditure proposals. Obfuscated data and misinterpretation were the criticisms aimed at the document by the profession.

The Library Association issued its own commentary upon the White Paper figures and the Office's interpretation of them indicating a future of resourcing of services very different to that of the Government. It showed not only reducing staff levels, but also falling total amounts to be spent on books and reducing stocks. "The range of books available, and the physical quality in terms of paper and binding, must have decreased, as non-fiction and hardbacked books become a lesser proportion of the total purchases."

Six years of continual reductions in finances, retraction of services, and reductions in the quality and extent of provision offered inevitably provided further evidence in 1984 of deteriorating standards. Militancy arose not only in those organizations dominated by political parties opposed to the Government's policies but also more generally in the profession and particularly among younger librarians. In February the Library Campaign was inaugurated in Sheffield. It quickly rallied around it professionals who, whatever their political colors, had reached the conclusion that they could no longer stand passively by to see services that had been so painfully established over the past 20 years in the interests of the user community being dismembered without effective protest. In order to help the campaign to more effectively examine the effect of public expenditure cuts on library services, the Library Association contributed a research grant to the University of Bristol's School of Advanced Urban Studies to be undertaken in 1985.

It was hardly surprising when the professionals' energies have to be devoted to finding justifications for services and expenditure upon them that little spare energy remained to innovate or expand services. Despite this, progress was made in particular areas. For instance, in affecting legislation in Parliament that had a bearing upon the quality and extent of library and information services and within the Library and Information Services Council, which is the advisory body to the Minister.

Legislation

Two major pieces of legislation were perceived to have consequences for the practice of librarianship. A Data Protection Bill, to bring the United Kingdom into line with practices overseas and particularly in the countries of the European Community, in its first presentation to Parliament showed little awareness of the effects of the Bill on the operation of libraries.

The Library Association was successful in introducing a new clause into the Bill concerned with the retention of data for archival purposes, and in obtaining clarification from the parent department, the Home Office, on a number of other issues. By the end of the year, and after the Bill had been enacted for only six months, the Library Association produced draft guidelines for its members to assist them in implementing the measures in the Act and was in close consultation with the Registrar responsible for the administration of the law.

The Cable and Broadcasting Bill, which sought to promote franchises to "cable up" 11 local authorities, appeared to many to offer "wall-to-wall 'Dallas.'" Library Association pressures succeeded in amending the Bill to permit local authorities, and particularly their public libraries, to use the cable-supplied services for the promotion of "socially useful" information. The Library Association sought to coordinate the introduction of such services within the authorities involved and issued guidance to its members.

LISC

The Library and Information Services Council (LISC)—under the active and highly successful Chairmanship of Professor Wilfred Saunders (who retired at the end of the year amid plaudits for his energetic and tireless direction of the Council)—continued its examination of the UK's manpower and education and train-

Directions to the Public Library receive the lowest priority on this sign in Cheltenham, U.K., but a new publicity and public relations group organized by the Library Association hopes to enhance the library image and priority.

ing needs. The final three papers in a series of five on the basic professional education for library and information work and on training and on continuing education were published and organizations within the profession submitted their views.

LISC's considered responses were being prepared by the end of the year. The ferment of debate anticipated about the documents showed few signs of happening. Some library and information science schools responded individually but generally the quality of the contributions and the conservatism reflected in many of them were considered to be disappointing responses to the, in many cases, radical proposals in the reports. One exception was the Library Association, which began a fundamental consideration of its role and membership and produced a radical report for its membership's consideration.

By the end of the year this particular initiative of LISC appeared to have moved to the University Grants Committee and the National Advisory Body for Public Sector Higher Education, which had established a Trans-binary Group on Librarianship and Information Studies: "to advise on the current provision of, and likely needs for, library and information courses within the areas of responsibility of" the UGC and NAB and to "review . . . likely future demand (both in terms of numbers and expertise). . . ."

School Libraries

School libraries represent one potential bright spot in an otherwise gloomy sky. In Britain school libraries are not nearly as well developed as they are in the United States. Only a small minority are staffed by a qualified librarian.

1984 saw the publication of a major report on school libraries by the Library and Information Services Council (*School Libraries: the Foundation of the Curriculum*. HMSO 1984).

Although less high powered than the reports of Roberts on public libraries (1957), Parry on university libraries (1967), and Dainton on national libraries (1969), it should be set against these far-sighted and far-reaching reports. It indicated what the profession already knew, but many outside had failed to recognize—school libraries in the United Kingdom are the weakest part of the national library and information system. It made positive recommendations to LISC, to the Government (Department of Education and Science), and to the education and library professions on how they might each contribute to improvement in the future.

The recommendations for the substantial development of school libraries come at a time when many other developments are pointing in the same direction. There has been a major program to install microcomputers in schools at all levels and to use these for, among other things, information retrieval. Furthermore, there is pressure to extend the school curriculum to include a greater appreciation of information technology. Increasingly, teachers and educational administrators are beginning to realize that they have got the technology and now they need someone to handle the information.

Coordinating Library Services

The considerations begun in 1979 with a report on the future development of libraries and information services particularly concentrating on the organizational and policy framework (FDL1), continued in 1981 with considerations "on working together within a national framework" (FDL2). These continued to be investigated in 1984 under a LISC working party examining particularly (in FDL3) cooperation and coordination of the multiplicity of libraries and information services in the UK, the existing and potential role of local authorities, possible new forms of collaborative enterprise, and the desirability and feasibility of promoting an electronic communication network. Finally, it was to define the need for more effective national coordination of library and information services.

Taxation and Licensing

There were other events and initiatives started outside the library and information world to which the profession reacted. In the summer indications became clearer than the Chancellor of the Exchequer was considering the imposition of Value Added Tax (VAT) on books, periodicals, and newspapers. Not since the 1940s, in the worst days for the UK of World War II, had a Parliament been asked to levy a duty on books and printed matter.

Although VAT is imposed on books at varying rates in other countries of the European Community, the UK has no obligation to fall into line with practices in other Community countries. Coordinated by the National Book Committee, the National Book League, author organizations, the Publishers and Booksellers Associations, and librarians united to produce an agreed case that was used to persuade Members of Parliament and the Chancellor of the Exchequer that this would be a tax on reading. By the end of the year there was some hope of success.

Librarians saw a similar threat to the interests of their users in moves made by the Copyright Licensing Agency (representing an indeterminate number of publishers and author organizations) to introduce a license particularly to control the unacceptably high speed of multiple-photocopying from books and journals. The profession rallied to oppose what it saw as an equally unacceptable tilt in the balance that had protected, in the past, the intellectual property rights of the creators and yet provided access for those involved in private study and research as permitted under the 1956 Copyright Act—known as the "fair-dealing" clause.

The license was seen to impose on libraries administrative procedures that, in the current financial climate, they could not afford. Despite opposition the local authority associations signed an agreement for an experimental period for one year with the CLA to monitor how such a licensing scheme would apply.

Aslib (The Association for Information Management—a name adopted in 1984), the Library Association, and SCONUL (Standing Conference of National and University Libraries) had made clear its opposition to the licensing scheme and its support for any other CLA initiatives intended to curb multiple copying, which they believed did not occur in libraries.

Government Actions
In Wales the Government initiated an investigation into the library services and the powers required to provide them from the four district councils granted powers in 1974 and to respond to a request from 10 districts to Government to take over the powers from the counties. Librarians gave careful consideration to the need to retain or move up library powers (from the four districts that currently have them) to the counties, and stated that only the counties have sufficient resources to provide a modern public library service.

The Government continued to press forward with its aim of introducing information technology into all walks of life. Having produced in 1983 the ITAP report "Making a Business of Information," the Library Association had responded to point out that many of the information industries' services provided in the private sector were dependent for success on those in the public sector. Although the report was intended to balance considerations of the technology with those of information provision, it had scarcely succeeded in its intentions. The "I" had taken second place to the "T." Picking up one of the recommendations, the private sector moved to establish a new body to coordinate those involved in information provision and supply. CICI (Confederation of Information Communication Industries) was established in the summer, and Aslib, the Library Association, and the British Library immediately joined. It established a small Executive on which the British Library agreed to keep a watching brief on behalf of the library and information services community. Five panels will be established (on which the profession will hope to obtain membership): copyright, public affairs, export promotion, technology, and education.

Preservation
While the profession continued to give attention to the new technology and the consequences of its adoption for library and information services the majority of its members had tended to ignore the serious deterioration in the documents that provide the backup to the delivery of bibliographical and other information through the IT systems. To survey the need the British Library's Research and Development Department established a research project supervised by Fred Ratcliffe, Librarian of Cambridge University Library which reported during the year. Its recommendations included two of particular significance. The first was concerned with the necessity to establish a National Preservation Office with a National Preservation Advisory Committee (the British Library, to plaudits from the profession, did so during the year). The second was to improve among the profession and in library and information science schools in particular the need for awareness for improved conservation and preservation practices. To encourage the introduction of conservation into the library and information schools' curricula the Library Association organized a Seminar during the year.

International Cooperation
The British Council (originally established as the British Council for Relations with Other Countries) celebrated its 50th anniversary in 1984 and in so doing fully illustrated its close links with the library and information science profession. It helped to turn the Library Association's September Brighton Conference into a mini-IFLA, bringing to the UK librarians from 36 countries and Presidents, Vice-Presidents, or Past Presidents from seven.

Tributes were paid by senior librarians from Africa, Europe, and Asia to the role of the British Council and British librarianship in the international context. During the Conference requests were made to establish bilateral programs of cooperation with the Library Association and library associations in Brazil, Mexico, China and Hungary along the lines of those already in existence with Canada, Poland, Italy, and Spain.

During the year Branches and Groups of the Library Association continued with their financial assistance to library associations and other institutions in the Third World by paying subscriptions to IFLA membership for those in Ghana, Bangladesh, Trinidad and Tobago, Zimbabwe, Zambia, Lesotho, Fiji, Botswana, Belize, and Uganda.

Progress continued in the long-term planning required by the Library Association to host IFLA in the United Kingdom in Brighton in 1987. The British Government gave serious consideration, in the light of the United States federal government's statement of intention to leave UNESCO, to a similar move at the end of 1985. The Library Association stated its support for the work of the General Information Programme of UNESCO.

The Government statement provoked unanimous opposition from all sectors of the library and information community in Britain. The Library Association, in conjunction with Aslib, the Institute of Information Scientists, Society of Archivists, and many others protested in forthright terms to the government. There was, however, little evidence that the protests had any effect.

Information Technology
The pace of technological change accelerated and many libraries, despite their other problems, extended the applications of information technology. In Devon, for example, the public library service set up a system of information centers in small rural communities using a network of microcomputers that were in turn linked to the county mainframe. This will bring computing and some of the latest telecommunication facilities to the sort of small communities that are often overlooked with other technological developments.

On a rather different scale, the British Library Lending Division planned to use a satellite link for the electronic delivery of documents. Using a European Space Agency satellite, full-text documents can be transmitted at high speed from the Lending Division in Yorkshire to users throughout Western Europe.

The number of public libraries introducing microcomputers for such housekeeping activities as circulation control, accessions, and inventory records or to enter and exploit online databases increased considerably from the handful in 1981 to around 40 percent in 1984.

In an attempt to share experience in the application of information technology in libraries, the British Library established a Library Technology Centre at the Polytechnic of Central London.

A considerable increase in competition among the suppliers of library automation systems was seen in 1984. Now that the American market is becoming saturated, the big suppliers are fighting for a stake in the British and European market. OCLC, GEAC, and CLSI, among others, were battling it out to gain a substantial share of the market.

Education for Librarianship
Britain continued to suffer from a surplus of librarians and information workers, and the library schools were becoming vulnerable to the charge of over-production. In response, schools attempted to improve the quality of courses and to demonstrate relevance to the library and information community. There was much talk of curriculum development and the need to increase the technological content of courses.

More significant changes were taking place in the financial arrangements governing the organizations that support library schools. The universities were undergoing financial pressure and departments of librarianships, as small, relatively low status departments, were under threat. In the polytechnic sector a new system of financial control was introduced with the National Advisory Body. This too produced pressures on the library schools. Toward the end of 1984 it was announced that the National Advisory Body and the University Grants Committee were to combine to look at the national provision of library education. This will almost certainly result in recommendations for a major restructuring of the system. Not surprisingly, there was a considerable degree of apprehension.

Meanwhile, library school students still found it difficult to obtain professional employment. Many were forced to take temporary jobs or jobs intended for unqualified staff. Others moved out of librarianship altogether.

British Library
Even the British Library was beginning to feel the pinch after 10 years of steady and sustained growth. In common with many academic libraries, it was greatly affected by the prevailing foreign exchange rates and inflation rate. The arithmetic is simple. The inflation rate at year's end was about 5 percent. Making allowance for the worsening exchange rate for li-

The British Library's display at the 1984 British Library Association Conference.

braries, the British Library departments, if they are to maintain their rate of acquisition, actually need annual increases of between 6.5 percent and 7 percent. But the British Library was to get an increase of only 3 percent in cash terms. In reality, the budget will have been cut by between 3.5 percent and 4 percent. In response, the Library is cutting grants to other libraries, reducing staffing levels, and, according to Chairman Sir Fred Dainton, "examining all sources of revenue we can possibly muster, including the consideration of user charges." In contrast with many other libraries, however, the British Library was well off.

At national level the Government's own advisory body, the Library and Information Services Council, said in its annual report that it "views with concern the effects which the government's financial policies are having on library and information services. Despite the government figures on financial inputs, the reality is that library services are contracting. Furthermore, the government's future financial plans imply further contractions to the point where many library authorities may find it increasingly difficult to provide a fully satisfactory level of service or to meet objectives they regard as fundamental." This is strong criticism indeed when it is remembered that such advisory bodies usually present their views cloaked in the measured phrases of the British Civil Service.

Leadership Changes

In June the untimely death of Roger Walter, the highly regarded Editor of the *Library Association Record*, occurred (*see* Obituaries). His place was filled in October by Jane Jenkins, previously an editor with the Museums Association.

The Library Association, in April, saw the departure of Secretary-General Keith Lawrey and the arrival of George Cunningham, an ex-politician and its first Chief Executive. The change of title was intended by the Association to reflect a change in responsibilities for the initiation of policies and actions by its executive officers.

Tony Anthony (previously and until retirement Deputy Director of Aslib) retired as Secretary to the Joint Consultative Committee of Aslib, Institute of Information Scientists, SCONUL, Library Association and the Society of Archivists. He was replaced by Brian Vickery (until 1983 Head of the School of Library, Archive and Information Studies in University College of London University).

The British Library saw the departure of Sir Harry Hookway from the post of Chief Executive, a position he had held throughout the first 10 years of the Library's reorganized existence. He was elected President of the Library Association for 1985.

His place at the Library was to be taken by Kenneth Cooper of the National Federation of Building Trades Employers. Almost his first initiative was to establish a review of the Library's activities and concerns in order to produce in 1985 an agreed Corporate Plan.

Wilfred Saunders, former Head of the Library School at Sheffield University, who retired as Chairman of the Library and Information Services Council, had steered the Council through a particularly difficult period and had achieved a number of advances in the face of a general lack of interest on the part of Government.

Perhaps the best-known library personality in 1984 was Ron Surridge. As President of the Library Association he made a considerable impact throughout the country, speaking at numerous meetings, attending conferences, and generally making his presence felt wherever he went.

RUSSELL BOWDON
NICK MOORE

State Reports

State correspondents report here on events of general interest during 1983. They provide systematic coverage on state library associations and state agencies. Data are given as of the end of 1983 unless otherwise indicated. ALA membership is given for state associations reporting it.

ALABAMA

**Alabama Library Association
(founded 1905)**

Membership: 2,003; *annual expenditure:* $45,056.

President: Monroe C. Snider, Head Librarian, Livingston University 35470 (April 1984–April 1985).

Vice-President/President-elect: Betty Ruth Goodwyn, Route 1, Box 405-U, Helena 35080.

Executive Secretary: Ruth Waldrop, P.O. Box BY, University 35486.

Annual meeting: April 10–12, 1984, Mobile.

Publications: Alabama Librarian (monthly).

Alabama Public Library Service

Anthony Miele, Director
6030 Monticello Drive
Montgomery 36130

Library Media Consultant

Hallie A. Jordan
Library Media Unit
111 Coliseum Building
Montgomery 36109

Library Funding. After several years of austere funding, including proration, state appropriations improved dramatically, especially those in support of education. Spin-offs from this improvement brought higher salaries for school librarians, substantial increases in the materials budget for college and university libraries, and an increase of 70 percent in state aid to public libraries. In addition to rising revenues from traditional sources, permanently invested money derived from off-shore gas leases establishes a base for continuing income in the future.

State Association. The Alabama Library Association held a highly successful annual conference April 11–13, in Birmingham, with a total registration of 517. Kaye Gapen, at the time Dean of Libraries at the University of Alabama and later Library Director at the University of Wisconsin, was the keynote speaker. The well-organized conference was facilitated by the recently published *Convention Handbook* prepared by the Association. Such a codification of the details involved in planning an annual convention should be of inestimable value to future convention committees.

At the same time a committee neared completion of a revision of the *Association Handbook*.

Beebe McKinley, Reference Librarian at the Tuscaloosa Public Library, assumed the editorship of the *Alabama Librarian* in June.

State Library Activities. The Alabama Public Library Service, which celebrated its 25th anniversary at an open house on May 2, sponsored a number of workshops during the year. Notable was a Trustee Workshop featuring Arch Lustberg, nationally known communications consultant. This workshop was repeated at four locations around the state and resulted in a new *APLS TRUSTEE HANDBOOK*.

In addition to its leadership in continuing education activities, APLS participated in or sponsored a number of surveys and studies during 1984. APLS cooperated with several other organizations in a National Endowment for the Humanities sponsored project that led to the identification and location of Alabama newspapers. APLS also announced the award of a contract to RMG associates to develop an automation/resource sharing plan for all Alabama libraries.

APLS was designated as a partial depository for United States government publications.

Public Libraries. Fifteen public libraries across Alabama sponsored seminars during the summer as a part of the Committee for the Humanities' nationally funded project "Shakespeare: The Theatre in the Mind." Under the direction of humanities scholars, participants studied the historical and cultural contexts of Shakespeare's writings, as well as various interpretations of his plays. At the same time, young readers focused on "Travelin' Alabama," the theme of the 1984 Summer Reading Program, exploring Alabama's rich history and geography through books.

Sharing in the influx of additional revenue for library funding, public libraries enjoyed a building boom during 1984. The Federal Jobs Bill provided a timely assist in the construction of new buildings or the expansion of old ones. In all, 14 libraries received funds from this source, sharing a total of $1,119,784 in federal assistance for construction.

School Libraries. A non-recurring appropriation of $5,000,000 by the State Legislature was designated for the strengthening of school library collections. This amount supplemented local resources at approximately $6.50 per student. Efforts were being marshaled to gain a continuing line item in the State Department of Education's budget for the same purpose and to increase the amount to $15 per student.

A reorganization of the State Department of Education in 1984 placed the Educational Media Unit under Eldon Johnson, Director, Division of Student and Instructional Services. Kenneth Blankenship had responsibility for that unit.

The Children and School Librarians Division of the Alabama Library Association established an Outstanding Library/Media Specialist Award, the first recipient to be announced at the 1985 convention. The Division also continued its sponsorship of the successful Emphasis on Reading Program.

Academic Libraries. The Network of Alabama Academic Libraries (NAAL) received a $500,000 operating budget, of which $410,000 will be used for retroactive conversion of bibliographic records in the libraries supporting graduate programs.

Most state-supported college and universities received substantial increases in their appropriations, several in the neighborhood of 25 percent, and were thereby able to provide much greater support to their libraries.

As the year drew to a close, all three campuses of the University of Alabama System (Tuscaloosa, Birmingham, and Huntsville) were in the process of searching for new library directors.

The Auburn University Library was designated as an official depository of United States patents, joining the Birmingham Public Library as the second such in Alabama.

The Graduate School of Library Service at the University of Alabama announced a new medical/media specialization within its MLS degree program. This specialization is to prepare graduates to work in small hospitals, designing and producing media in support of patient and staff educational programs, as well as administering the library.

Building Programs. The Birmingham Public Library opened its new central library on September 15. Beginning with a parade led by the Mayor, 15,000 patrons entered via a spacious atrium the four-story contemporary structure containing 130,000 square feet. The new building is connected to the old by a suspended walk-across; the limestone facade of the old library is reflected in the glass of the new. The Mountain Brook Public Library saw a doubling of its space with a $700,000 addition and the library of the University of North Alabama underwent extensive remodeling.

One of the most noteworthy contributions to a library's building fund was a $23,000 gift from the famous musical group, "Alabama," that went to the DeKalb County Library in Fort Payne. The gift came from the proceeds of "June Jam," an annual event that aids several organizations in the group's hometown. As an example of determination and dedication, Monroe County, with a total population of 23,000, was able to secure a NEH Challenge Grant of $100,000 and then raise $300,000 matching funds to renovate an existing building.

Networks, Interlibrary Cooperation. Shortly after the two multitype library systems, Alabama Library Exchange (ALEX) and the Pioneer Alabama Library System (PALS), became operational in 1981 as pilot projects, a contract to evaluate the systems was awarded. F. William Summers and Daniel Barron of the University of South Carolina submitted an evaluation in late spring to the Executive Board of the Alabama Public Library Service. Although PALS had ceased to function by the time the report was submitted, the two evaluators saw valuable lessons to be derived from the experience of these demonstration projects. They encouraged the state to continue to develop and test multitype library systems.

In its effort to familiarize librarians with such systems, APLS devoted a public library administrators' meeting to a special program conducted by Robert McClarren of Illinois and

Thomas Alrutz, of New Jersey, directors of multitype library organizations in their states. In the meantime ALEX entered its fourth year of operation and conintued to grow. The total number of member libraries reached 99.

A major project initiated by PALS, the North Alabama Union List of Serials, was being continued by ALEX. Originally a project of ALEX and at present a separate nonprofit corporation, the Library Management Network (LMN) was extending its cooperative automated services to additional libraries in north Alabama. The Muscle Shoals Regional Library and the University of North Alabama were to begin participation in 1985. The Network awarded a contract to CLSI for assistance in developing integrated library systems.

Intellectual Freedom. No dramatic issue or controversy related to intellectual freedom emerged during the year. The Intellectual Freedom Committee of the Alabama Library Association devoted its efforts to revising the *Manual on Intellectual Freedom*, originally published in 1979.

Professional Interests. A Retired Librarians Round Table was formed on April 12 at the annual convention of the Alabama Library Association. Elizabeth Beamguard, former Director of the Alabama Public Library Service, was elected moderator.

Alabamians achieving distinction at the national level included Joan Atkinson, President-elect of the Young Adult Services Division of the American Library Association; Anthony Miele, OCLC Users Council; Harold Herring, President, Urban Libraries Council; George Stewart, Treasurer, Southeastern Library Association; Sue Medina, Editor of *Interface* published by ASCLA; and Virginia McKee, Board member of ALSC.

Awards. The Alabama Library Association presented a Distinguished Service Award to Ruth Holliman, Media Director, Pickens County Board of Education, and the Public Service Award to James F. Vickery, President, University of Montevallo. Alabama Authors Awards were presented in three categories: Fiction (Roy Hoffman, *Almost Family*), Nonfiction (Linda O. McMurray, *George Washington Carver: Scientist and Symbol*), and Juvenile/Young Adult Literature (Emma M. Butterworth, *As the Waltz Was Ending*).

Elected to the Alabama Library Roll of Honor were James Richard Rutland, (1879–1948), Librarian and later Head of the English Department of Auburn University, as well as a charter member of the Alabama Library Association, and Ruby Pickens Tartt (1880–1974), Librarian of the Sumter County Library, whose fascination with the stories, songs, and folklore of rural blacks led to creative collaboration with Carl Carmer and John Lomax.

Mildred Goodrich, Librarian of the public library of Anniston for 37 years, was featured in the July issue of *American Libraries*. "Miss Mildred," as she was known to generations of Annistonians, was also a cofounder of the Alabama Public Library Service.

John C. Henly, III, received an Honor Award from the American Library Trustee Association (ALTA) in recognition of a $250,000 gift to aid in establishing and supporting a major research facility in the Birmingham Public Library.

Recipients of APLS scholarships were Juanita McClain, Director, Tuskegee–Macon County Public Library; Marily Sheehee, Director, Geneva Public Library; and Brian Moore, Circulation Assistant, Huntsville Public Library. The $5,000 scholarships permitted each winner to attend library school on a full-time basis.

Appointments. The year 1984 may be characterized more by retirements and resignations than by appointments. Among those retiring were F. Wilbur Helmbold, Librarian of Samford University for 26 years; Perry Cannon, Assistant Librarian of the Mervyn H. Sterne Library, University of Alabama in Birmingham; and Nina Martin, Professor, Graduate School of Library Service, University of Alabama. The Library School in Tuscaloosa also lost Associate Professor D. Alex Boyd, who joined the Chicago Public Library. Appointed to the faculty were Margaret Stieg and Gordon Coleman. Two prominent librarians, Exir and David Brennan, returned to Alabama, Exir Brennan taking a position with the Alabama Commission on Higher Education and David Brennan with the Jones Law School, Alabama Christian College.

Deaths. Every issue of the *Alabama Librarian* since v. 1, no. 1, December, 1949, carried an advertisement for the Tuscaloosa Library Bindery. The owner, E. W. Rosenfeld, had contributed a scholarship since 1959 for students wishing to attend library school. "Rosie" died on August 29, 1984.

JAMES RAMER

ALASKA

Alaska Library Association (founded 1960)

Membership: 320; annual budget: $17,750.
President: Evelyn Bonner, Box 479, Sitka 99835 (May 1984–June 1985).
Vice-President/President-elect: Mary Jennings, SRA 265, Anchorage 99516.
Annual meeting: March 5–7, 1984, Sitka.
Publications: Sourdough (quarterly); Newspoke (bimonthly).

Division of State Libraries

Richard B. Engen, Director
Pouch G
Juneau 99811

School Library Media Coordinator

Jo Morse
Alaska State Library
650 International Airport Road
Anchorage 99502

Collection development and censorship shared the spotlight in the library news in 1984. Resource sharing/collection development was the theme chosen for the annual Alaska Library Association conference. Censorship became an issue in the Fairbanks North Star Borough School district when a group of citizens endeavored to remove a book from the shelves of the local high school libraries.

State Association. Sitka was the site of the annual AkLA conference in March. Paul Mosher, Director of Collections Development for Stanford University Libraries and consultant for the Alaska Statewide Collection Development Steering Committee, presented the keynote address. Members of the committee presented the program, addressing policy statements, collection surveys, and the Alaska Conspectus.

Kathleen Bowman, Associate Director of the Fred Meyer Trust, provided background on the formation of the trust and insight as to how it has arrived at efforts relating to library services in the Pacific Northwest.

Clark Gruening, Legislative Consultant to the Association, also spoke at the conference and was available to assist individual librarians in their efforts to persuade legislators to provide support for library programs.

State Library Activities. The State Library operating budget included full funding for library grants in 1984 and the capital budget also included $360,000 for the Alaska Library Network, $500,000 for library construction grants, $600,000 for acquisition of the Southeast regional library site, and $30,000 for Alaskana acquisitions for the state library.

Public Libraries. Anchorage Municipal Library's new automated circulation system, Noah, serves as a guinea pig for a new group of generic software programs from Geac. With four local systems in various stages of development in use in Alaska, linking local systems was becoming an essential part of the future planning for automation in the state. The AML Geac system, CLSI at the Fairbanks North Star Borough Public Library, Gnosis at the University of Alaska libraries, and the Alaska State Library's media booking system were all in operation or in development in 1984.

School Libraries, Media Centers. The revised Alaska School Library Media Standards, approved at the AASL/Alaska preconference, were formally endorsed by AkLA at its annual membership meeting.

National Library week was observed by students, teachers, librarians, parents, school administrators, school board members, and the Learn Alaska Audioconferencing Network in 14 school districts throughout the state with the first statewide "Battle of the Books" tournament. Over 1,500 students shared their knowledge of books they had read and in addition many students experienced the value of Alaska's telecommunication system. Meeting other students through the system from around the state to share their knowledge of books made Alaska seem a bit smaller.

Jose Aruego was Artist in Residence in Ketchikan from February 27 thru March 23. His visit was funded by the Alaska State Council on the Arts, the National Endowment of the Arts, the local school district, and the Valley Park Parent Committee.

Academic and Other Libraries. The University of Alaska's online system, dubbed Gnosis by Tom Hassler, the designer of the system, is intended to serve as a circulation system and also for interlibrary loan, statewide collection development conspectus, and the development of and access to a variety of Alaska information indexes, including indexes of oral history collections, film and nonprint media, archival materials, newspapers, and the Bibliography of Alaskana.

Librarians working in special libraries organized to become a Round Table in the Alaska Library Association.

Fort Greely MSA Post Library received an interlibrary cooperation grant to become a Recon only member of the Washington Library Network. This is unique in that a federal library was awarded a state grant to purchase necessary equipment for the project—in this case, an Apple IIe microcomputer to input holdings on floppy disks to be converted to tape and added to the database.

Building Programs. Anchorage Municipal Library headquarters building was in the building process during 1984 and was expected to be completed in 1985. An addition to the Elmer E. Rasmuson Library at UAF was also to be completed in 1985.

Networks, Interlibrary Cooperation. According to a survey reported on at the Sitka Conference, Alaska libraries are overwhelmingly aware of the Alaska Library Network. Of the 93 questionnaires returned, 90 libraries indicated that they know the term and concept and over 70 use the ALN fiche as well as other services.

Proceedings of the Sitka AkLA conference were published through an interlibrary cooperation grant from the Alaska State Library to the University of Alaska, Anchorage. Entitled *Alaska Is a Library: the Alaska Library Network, a Review of Its Components, Status and Dreams for the Future*, the publication was edited by Nancy Lesh, University of Alaska Library staff and B. Jo Morse, Alaska State Library.

Intellectual Freedom. It was an uncomfortable and disquieting year in Fairbanks. The controversy surrounding Hanckel and Cunningham's *A Way of Love, A Way of Life: A Young Person's Introduction to What It Means to Be Gay* divided large segments of the community and raised questions about intellectual freedom within the library community as well. After the school district followed the set procedures for evaluating controversial books and the School Board voted to uphold the superintendent's decision to keep the book on the library shelves, a group called "Parents in Action" was formed and circulated a petition to recall the three School Board members who had voted to retain the book. Working in cooperation with "Citizens for Responsible Government," AkLA's Northern Chapter began an education campaign to alert the community to censorship and to provide historical and political perspectives. School Board election campaigns were based on other issues, but the censorship issue was there. In the end the recall petition was denied by the borough clerk, and two of the three seats up for election were won by candidates opposed to censorship. Although things were relatively quiet at year's end, the library community was continuing to prepare itself for future censorship attacks.

Professional Interests. The Anchorage Chapter of AkLA sponsored seminars for the general public on what library services are available and where to obtain resources in the libraries within the Anchorage area. At each presentation directories of all libraries in the area were distributed. Training workshops for bush librarians were held in Unalakleet and Fairbanks.

Awards. Marilyn S. Scott, Assistant Superintendent, Communications and Media, Anchorage School District, received the Distinguished Library Service Award for School Administrators Award at the AASL convention in Atlanta. She was chosen for her part in effecting change in using technology in education and for interlibrary cooperation and networking. The Anchorage School District was the first school district to become an active member of WLN.

Elizabeth Carroll, Librarian at the A. Holmes Johnson Public Library in Kodiak, was awarded an honorary membership in the Alaska Library Association upon her retirement.

Appointments. Joseph McElroy of New York was appointed librarian of the A. Holmes Johnson Memorial Library in Kodiak. Judith Monroe was named Library Coordinator for the Southcentral Region for the Alaska State Library. Mary Jennings, formerly Librarian for the Alaska Region for Blind and Handicapped Services in Anchorage replaced Monroe as Head of the Anchorage Section of the Alaska Film Library. Nancy Gustavson, formerly with Juneau Memorial Library, became Librarian of the Kettleson Memorial Library, Sitka.

ISABELLE A. MUDD

ARIZONA

Arizona Library Association (founded 1926)

Membership: 800; *annual budget:* $29,422.

President: Don Riggs, ASU Library, Tempe (October 1983–December 1984).

President-elect: June Garcia, Phoenix Public Library.

Annual meeting: December 13–15, 1984, Phoenix.

Publication: ASLA Newsletter (monthly).

Library, Archives, and Public Records Department

Sharon Womack, Director
State Capitol
Phoenix 85007

State Association. The Arizona State Library Association engaged in a vigorous planning endeavor: it established six primary goals and achieved all of them. The first Mid-Year Conference in ASLA's history was held in March; about 400 persons attended the event, which was held in Phoenix. A most successful annual conference was held in December; despite its closeness to Christmas, the Phoenix event attracted many attendees and exhibitors. At the beginning of the conference, 914 members had paid their annual dues as compared with 677 paid members at the beginning of the 1983 annual conference.

State Library. The Department's Library for the Blind and Physically Handicapped moved into new quarters especially designed for it.

One of four Carnegie library buildings built in Arizona has come under the Department to be restored as a museum.

Public library construction projects, made possible by the Emergency Jobs Bill, got into full swing. The majority of the 12 projects that were funded involved enlarging or renovating existing buildings. New library buildings were constructed in the towns of Prescott Valley, Oracle, and San Luis; and after extensive planning, funds will be granted to replace the city-county library in Clifton that was destroyed by floods.

Multi-county planning for public library development, initiated in 1983, was continued with a second areawide planning meeting. Preparations were also made for the development of a Statewide Planning Council to meet early in 1985.

Academic Libraries. Over 1,000,000 persons used Arizona State University's new Daniel E. Nobel Science and Engineering Library during its first ten months of service. The $7 million facility houses all of the University's science, engineering, and nursing materials as well as over 115,000 maps.

Public Libraries. A relatively strong economy during 1984 allowed most public libraries to keep pace with Arizona's continuing growth in population. Local and county support increased, and several communities, notably Mesa, Parker and Prescott, received substantial increases in funding. Fourteen new libraries were opened, two of which serve Indian reservations.

Library service was extended to the largely rural residents of Arizona's newly formed La Paz County with bookmobile service.

School Libraries. Arizona school library/media centers moved into automation more completely in 1984. Many Arizona school districts have provided libraries with computers so that they might function as satellite centers and also advance into automated circulation, periodical, and cataloging services. Arizona librarians have been involved in a new workshop format with other librarians in the state featuring extended cooperation, upgrading of state certification requirements, keeping a close check on censorship, and striving to reestablish a state school library/media consultant in the Arizona State Department of Education.

Building Programs. A successful bond election will provide funds for the construction of a new Main Public Library in Tucson, and a site was selected for a new library to serve the city of Glendale. Planning for new public library buildings was initiated in Apache Junction, Page and Cottonwood.

Networking and Cooperation. The Arizona Interlibrary Loan Center (AILLC), funded by the State and LSCA, operates out of the Phoenix Public Library and provides resource and referral services for book and photocopy requests from multitype libraries throughout the state. At the completion of its second full year of service, at the end of 1984, AILLC staff had processed more than 21,563 requests, of which 16,763, or 77.7%, were filled locally or through OCLC.

The Arizona Research Information Center (ARIC), funded by LSCA, and at the Tucson Public Library, is structured to provide in-depth reference service to public libraries.

The SOLAR (Serials Online in Arizona) project, funded by LSCA, was initiated after more than a year of planning. Utilizing OCLC, the major public and academic libraries will, over a three-year period, input their holdings into the Serials Subsystem. At the completion of the project, fiche or paper copies of the union list will be made available to non-OCLC libraries.

Local and county-wide consortia, involving public, community college, and school libraries were formed in Prescott, Cochise County, Yuma, and Lake Havasu City in response to identified needs for greater cooperation and resource sharing at these levels.

Awards. The Arizona State Library Association awards, presented during the annual conference, went to Alice Scudder, Sierra Vista Public School—Librarian of the Year; Jeanette Daane, Mesa Community College—Distinguished Librarian; Julia Goddard, Libraries Limited—Rosenzweig Award; Phil Hart, Arizona Historical Society—Outreach Services Award; Ann Nolen Clark—Outstanding Arizona Author; Kerin McPherson, Mesa Community College—ALTA Scholarship Award; and Mary Beth Burgoyne, University of Arizona Library School—JMRT/Baker and Taylor.

The Arizona Library Friends (ALF) held the Second Annual Legislator's Reception and Awards Ceremony. Receiving the first ALF Commendations was State Representative Sam A. McConnell, Jr. The first Amigo Award to a non-elected citizen was given to Mrs. Floy May King.

Professional Interests. Programs of continuing education, addressing topics as diverse as "the problem patron" and "book conservation," were held in nearly every county. Public relations and library awareness were also subjects that were thoroughly explored in several county-wide workshops. The major continuing education event of the year was a week-long series of seminars and workshops focusing on all aspects of reference services. This annual event is cosponsored by the State Library and the Maricopa County Library Council.

Transitions. New directors were appointed to sixteen local public libraries. At the county level, Ava Chartz replaced Maggie Nation as Director of the Flagstaff City–Coconino County Library; Sharman Gerdes was named Director of the Prescott City–Yavapai County Library, replacing John Halliday, and Jan Elliott resigned as Head of the Clifton City-Greenlee County Library.

Major changes in academic libraries included Jean Collins, named Director of Libraries at Northern Arizona University; Margaret Maxwell, named Acting Director, University of Arizona Graduate Library School; and the retirement of Arnulfo D. Trejo, founder of the Graduate Library Institute for Spanish Speaking Americans (GLISSA) at the University of Arizona Graduate Library School.

ARLENE BANSAL

ARKANSAS

Fund Raising. The fund raising campaign conducted by the University of Arkansas, Fayetteville, for the University library reached its goal of $2,500,000 in 1984. All money was to go toward materials acquisition; it was hoped that more than 100,000 volumes would be added to the collection as a result of the "Books For Libraries" campaign.

The campaign was directed by Frank Broyles, University of Arkansas Athletic Director, and the initial contribution was $100,000 from the Athletic Department. Donations were received from alumni, students, citizens in the state, and foundations and corporations based in Arkansas, in addition to contributions from national corporations that do business in Arkansas.

The Mullins Library is the state's major research library and a heavy lender of books to other libraries in the state, both academic and public. As a result, many libraries in the state will benefit from the fund drive. In addition,

Arkansas Library Association (founded 1911)

Membership: 850; *annual budget:* $37,000.
President: Bettye Kerns, Sherwood Elementary School, Sherwood (October 1984–October 1985).
Vice-President/President-elect: Nancy Evans, Northeast Arkansas Regional Library, Paragould.
Executive Director: Frank Ivey, Association Mgt. Group, Boyle Building, 103 West Capitol, Little Rock 72201.
Annual meeting: October 7–9, 1984, Little Rock.
Publications: Arkansas Libraries (quarterly); *Newsletter* (six times a year).

Arkansas State Library

John A. Murphy, Librarian/Director
State Capitol Mall
Little Rock 72201

State School Library Media Supervisor

Betty Jean Morgan
State Department of Education
Little Rock 72201

the campaign contributed to increased library public awareness in the state. Arkansas librarians hope to be positively affected for once by a "trickle down" theory since much library goodwill has been generated by the University's library fund drive.

The University has indicated that even though the initial goal has been reached, efforts will continue to improve the library in order to raise Mullins Library to ARL standards.

State Association. The Association's annual conference followed a cultural heritage theme in 1984. Speakers included Bern and Franke Keating, author and photographer for the National Geographic Society's *The Mighty Mississippi;* Hillary Rodham Clinton, who headed the education committee named by Governor Clinton that revamped the state's educational requirements and paved the way for increased state aid to education and libraries; and the authors of a photographic history of Little Rock that featured many previously unpublished mid-19th century photographs.

Other theme-related conference activities included an autograph party featuring authors from two of the state's local publishing houses and a barbeque dinner on the grounds of the Old State House adjacent to the conference hotel. The Old State House served as the state capitol for much of the 19th century and is now a state museum. Musicians playing music familiar to the Ozarks provided entertainment during the casual banquet.

The Association's College and University Division sponsored a workshop conducted by Allan Pratt on microcomputer applications for libraries. Demonstrations of the best-selling microcomputers were also a part of the program. The summer program sponsored by the Association's school librarians/media educators division featured Nancy Polette and a presentation on the library media center's role in curriculum development.

Administratively, the Association formed two new round tables: Library Automation and Children's Services. At year's end, the Association's administrative office was transferred to an association management firm in an effort to maintain membership services while keeping administrative costs contained.

Public Libraries. New standards for public libraries were adopted by the membership of the Association's Public Library Division and by the Association's Executive Board in 1984. The new guidelines, which went through several drafts during a 12-month period, were developed by a committee of public librarians. It was hoped that the higher standards could be incorporated into state aid requirements.

School Libraries. The leadership offered by Arkansas' school librarians in providing continuing education opportunities and in cooperating with other library related groups continued in 1984. In addition to their annual summer workshop, the Association's school librarians conducted a program in conjunction with the Arkansas Audio-Visual Association at the annual conference of the Arkansas Education Association.

The state's school librarians went national with their programming in 1984 as librarians from the Pulaski County School District conducted a two-day preconference for the American Association of School Librarians at the Dallas Conference of the American Library Association. The conference topic was "The School Library Media Program and the Curriculum." The Pulaski County District's efforts in this area have received national recognition in the past including being a finalist for the Encyclopedia Britannica/AASL School Library Program of the Year award.

Academic Libraries. In addition to the University of Arkansas' fund raising efforts, the big news in academic libraries concerned the acquisition and opening of several special collections.

The highly regarded collection of Arkansas materials owned by J. N. Heiskell, owner and editor of the *Arkansas Gazette,* was acquired by the University of Arkansas at Little Rock (UALR) from the Heiskell descendants. The material is considered by historians as the most valuable collection of Arkansiana still in private ownership and is reported to be the most extensive collection of Arkansas materials ever donated to a public institution.

The collection contains pamphlets, manuscripts, and over 3,000 books, including many rare first editions. The collection is particularly strong in accounts of early exploration along the Mississippi and Arkansas Rivers and in diaries and letters of the Civil War period. These materials include accounts written by both federal and confederate military personnel serving in Arkansas during the war in addition to material written by Arkansas civilians describing the war years in Arkansas.

The University of Arkansas, Fayetteville, opened the Francis Irby Gwaltney Papers in 1984. Gwaltney was an Arkansas novelist whose papers include letters and other documents related to his long friendship with Norman Mailer. The University also acquired the papers of D. Y. Thomas, a major Arkansas historian, and a collection of 46 photographs taken in 1939 that depict life on the Wilson Plantation in northeastern Arkansas. Wilson's extensive land holdings have long dominated agricultural activities in eastern Arkansas.

Interlibrary Cooperation. The desire to preserve a valuable collection of books brought about a unique form of library cooperation between a public and an academic library that also involved private and foundation funding.

The Board of Trustees of the Central Arkansas Library System (Little Rock) and the administration of the University of Arkansas at Little Rock agreed to a long-term loan from CALS to UALR of the 4,700-volume book collection of U. M. Rose, an internationally known jurist of the early 20th century. Rose, a Litte Rock resident, collected extensively in foreign language materials dealing with classical studies, economics, history, literature, and western civilization. Books in the collection date from the early 18th century to the early 20th century with the majority of the books being evenly distributed among English, French, and German publications.

A need for proper restoration and a lack of adequate resources to care for such a valuable collection led CALS' Board of Trustees to offer the material to UALR's Special Collections and Archives on permanent loan. UALR secured $10,000 from the local law firm founded by U. M. Rose and a matching sum from the Little Rock based Donaghey Foundation to begin restorative work.

Intellectual Freedom. The major intellectual freedom activities in 1984 dealt with events in the small north Arkansas town of Concord, where the School Board responded to a challenge of three sex education books present in the school library by appointing a citizen review committee that was reportedly dominated by members of a statewide conservative religious and anti-abortion organization known as Family, Life, and God (FLAG). The committee removed the books from the library and later recommended their permanent removal.

The school librarian appealed to the Arkansas Library Association for assistance and petitions were circulated in Concord by local parents in support of the books. ALA President Bettye Kerns of Sherwood Elementary School in Arkansas spoke to the School Board and defended libraries' intellectual freedom principles as supported by the Arkansas Library Association and the American Library Association. Following Kerns' remarks, parents presented their petitions, which indicated overwhelming support for maintaining the books in the library.

The School Board accepted the review committee's report but refused to order the books removed from the school library collection. The books were returned to the library. Though the issue has not been totally resolved by year's end, Arkansas librarians hoped that a victory has been achieved in Concord.

Awards. The Arkansas Library Association established a new award in 1984 to be presented in recognition of "a career of notable service in librarianship in Arkansas." The award was named the Frances P. Neal Award in honor of Neal, who served 30 years as head of the Arkansas Library Commission, the forerunner of the Arkansas State Library.

The first Neal Award was presented to Freddy Schader, formerly Coordinator of Federal Programs at the Library Commission. Schader, too, had served 30 years in her post. Both Neal and Schader retired in 1978. The two librarians were honored during the Association's annual conference.

Other Association awards presented included the Distinguished Service Award to Don Deweese, Administrative Assistant for Information Services for the Fayetteville Public Schools, who has long been active in Association activities. The Asssociation's Compton Award, presented in recognition of the best contribution published in Arkansas Libraries during the last two years, was given to Bob Razer for his continuing book review column, "Arkansas Books & Authors," and other contributions during his four years as editor of Arkansas Libraries. Donald Rader, trustee for the Clay County and the Northeast Arkansas Regional Library, was named winner of the Trustee Award.

The Association's $1,000 scholarship to be used to attend graduate library school was won by Janice Savage, an employee at the Ouachita Baptist University Library. Bill Sheridan, a student at the University of Arkansas, Fayetteville won a Baker & Taylor's Grassrotts Grant to attend the annual conference.

BOB RAZER

CALIFORNIA

California Library Association (founded 1895)

Membership: 2,578; *annual expenditure:* $282,415.

President: Bernard Kreissman, University of California, Davis (January 1984–December 1985).

Vice-President/President-elect: Linda M. Wood, Riverside County Library.

Executive Director: Stefan B. Moses, Suite 300, 717 K Street, Sacramento 95814-3477.

Annual meeting: December 1–5, 1984, Los Angeles.

Publication: CLA Newsletter (monthly).

California State Library

Gary E. Strong, State Librarian
P.O. Box 2037
Sacramento 95809

School Library Media Supervisor

Gerald W. Hamrin
State Department of Education
Sacramento 95814

Major library interest in 1984 centered on several increases in state aid to libraries totaling $37,000,000. The new budget contains a large increase for the Public Library Foundation program. The legislature approved an amount of $27,900,000, but the Governor, though supportive, reduced the amount to $12,000,000.

An appropriation of $3,900,000 was allotted for transaction-based reimbursements for interlibrary loan services.

The California Literacy Campaign started in December 1983, with $2,500,000 in LSCA funds awarded to 28 public libraries. Governor George Deukmejian, who supported library efforts in the literacy campaign awarded an additional $2,600,000.

State Association. One of the most successful activities of the California Library Association was its third Legislative Day held in May. Two hundred and fifty Friends, trustees, commissioners, citizens, and librarians attended. The morning session focused on speakers from the Association's Government Relations Committee, on the State Librarian, on the Legislative Advocate, and on a representative from the Office of the Speaker of the State Assembly. In the afternoon, the group called upon legislative offices encouraging support for California library services. Legislative Day paid off, it was generally believed, in state budget augmentation.

The Association also sponsored some much needed workshops on "Management Change", "How to Deal with Disturbed Patrons", and "Parliamentary Procedures". The latter two have proved popular and are offered at each annual conference.

Members were responsible for placing two important issues on the floor of the Council of the American Library Association: (1) recommendations for changes contemplated by Congress on computer literacy; (2) placing the Merwine case on the agenda for formal discussion by ALA. E. J. Josey, ALA President, and Robert Wedgeworth, ALA Executive Director, participated in CLA's annual conference.

State Library Activities. Gary E. Strong was reappointed State Librarian by Republican Governor Deukmejian. Strong was first appointed by Governor Edmund G. Brown, a Democrat, in September 1980. The State Library staff worked hard on the state's budget in 1984 and was gratified by the outcome. California librarians appreciated the staff's participation in Legislative Day. Included in the many increases was an increase in the budget of the Department of General Services of $525,000 for design plans for a new State Library building.

The State Library Foundation bought an antique Albion handpress for the Library. In his thanks the State Librarian said that it "symbolizes our commitment to the history of the book and the long tradition of fine printing in California."

The Library made a public library survey on fees charged for library services, and continued its sponsorship of workshops for the state's librarians. It presented workshops on "Job Seeking Skills," "Grassroots Fundraising," and "Literacy."

Public Libraries. A survey early in 1984 revealed that California Public Libraries, by and large, were benefiting from the upturn in the general economy. However, they have never fully recovered from the blows received in 1978 after passage of Proposition 13. Open hours were down 22 percent and the number of employees was 8,667, a 10.3 percent decrease. The per capita figures of 4.97 for circulation and 1.31 for reference remained almost static for several years and are significantly below the 5.74 circulation and 1.59 reference per capita marks of 1978.

There were some "up" newsworthy items to note about some individual public libraries. The Hollywood Regional Library received a grant of $300,000 from the National Endowment for the Humanities to help replace the humanities book collection, destroyed by fire in 1982. The matching fund raising effort was spearheaded by Johnny Carson.

Hayward Public Library installed the first public library online integrated catalog on hardware by Hewlett-Packard and software by the Virginia Polytechnic Institute.

Riverside Public received a grant from an estate totaling $90,000 a year. The grant is to be spent on books and materials and may not be used to reduce the existing library budget.

The Los Angeles Public Library and the LA County Library System were bequeathed $54,000 each, to buy children's books. The LA County System celebrated Asian-Pacific American Heritage week with a two-day conference for librarians, educators, and community leaders.

The Los Gatos Library uses off-duty senior citizen vans to take children from preschool centers to visits of the library.

Sixty-four authors participated in the seventh Annual Author Festival at Long Beach. B. Dalton gave the sponsors $2,200.

The San Diego County Library System was awarded a $1,300,000 budget increase, which allows additional personnel, hours of service, and a larger book budget. It installed four token-operated Apple IIe microcomputers. The service eventually would spread to all 34 branches.

The San Diego Public Library opened its first portable structure branch in March. The Terresanter Branch opened in May. In addition, a new expanded facility was opened in San Ysidro, and new construction began at the Otay Mesa Branch.

Academic and Special Libraries. *Academic.* The Academic Business Librarians Exchange (ABLE) was formed in Southern California in 1984 to create a forum for discussion and information exchange. In December, MELVYL, a new satellite network, joined the libraries of all the University of California campuses. The library system contains about 20,000,000 volumes and is surpassed in the U.S. only by the Library of Congress. Under the new system, patrons will be able to request materials from computer terminals in more than 100 libraries.

Special. Special libraries have been making great strides in networking activities. Representatives from both southern and northern California met with the State Librarian regarding the removal of barriers to full participation by special libraries in multitype networks. Some members of the Bay Area Chapter participated in the new Bay Area Library Information Network, composed of libraries of all types.

The San Andreas and the San Francisco Bay Region Chapters sponsored a seminar in February entitled, "Whose Information Is It Anyway?" The purpose was to show the change in the political, social, technological, legal, and economic climates and the impact on information users.

The San Francisco Chapter announced that one of its members had edited and published a much-needed book, *Position Descriptions in Special Libraries.*

Professional Interests. Despite the efforts by the USC Alumni Association and the California Library Association to keep the School open, the Library School at the University of Southern California announced that it would be discontinued in June 1986.

An important milestone was accomplished in collective bargaining. The University of California System entered into an agreement with the University Federation of Librarians: the University's Librarians were recognized as academic employees, not staff. Included in the package were: (1) 9 percent increase in salaries; (2) professional development funds; (3) retention of benefits while on two months' leave without pay; (4) a grievance procedure; (5) an agreement that librarians may rise in rank whether or not they assume administrative duties.

Los Gatos became a leader in recognition of comparable worth when the employees received an adjustment from 4 percent to 20 percent in salaries.

Awards. Clara Breed was named Librarian Emeritus of the San Diego Public Library. Diane Bisom, UCLA, received one of the 3M/JMRT Professional Grant Awards. The Chinese American Librarians Association's distinguished services award went to Sally C. Tseng, UC, Irvine. Paul Mosher, Stanford, received the RTSD Blackwell North American Scholarship award. Roger Summit, President of DIALOG, received the LITA/GAYLORD Award.

The Ventura County Library received one of the John Cotton Dana Public Relations awards. Judith A. Hoffberg, Editor and Publisher of *Umbrella* magazine, Glendale, received a Fulbright grant to organize the records of Len Lye, a New Zealand kinetic sculptor. John Schroeder, Research Libraries Group, Inc., Stanford, received a technology fellowship from Edinburgh University.

Effie Lee Morris, San Francisco, was the 1984 recipient of the Women's National Book Association Award, and was also named the 1984 Bay Area Book Woman of the Year. Nancy Van House, UC, Berkeley, was awarded a NSF grant for a study of "Occupational Segregation Among Information Professionals." Donald P. Gould, USC, received the ACRL Doctoral Dissertation Fellowship award of $1,000 from the Institute for Scientific Information. Heather Smith, UCLA Library School student, received a JMRT Shirley Olofson Memorial Award.

Salvador Guerena, UC, Santa Barbara, received a $600 Publishing Committee Carnegie–Whitney Fund grant for bibliographies. Joyce Ball, CSU, Sacramento, received a special citation from Indiana University for outstanding achievements in library science. Gary Strong, State Librarian, received a special citation from the University of Michigan. Lizbeth Bishoff, Pasadena Public, received RTSD's Esther J. Piercy Award. Karen Howell received CLA's Edna Yelland Memorial Scholarship Fund and planned to study at UCLA.

Appointments. Hal Watson, Pomona Public Library, was appointed President of the California Library Services Board.

Charles Martell, Jr., Associate California State University Library, Sacramento, was named Editor of *College & Research Libraries.*

Effie Lee Morris, California Library Services Board, and Gail Schlacter, ABC-CLIO Press, were elected ALA Councilors-at-Large.

Helen Josephine, Berkeley, Susan Galloway, UC, San Diego, and Joan Goddard, San Jose Public, were appointed by E. J. Josey, ALA President, to serve on the ALA Commission on Pay Equity.

Gary Strong, State Library, was appointed to the Optical Disk Advisory Group by the Library of Congress.

Appointments in the academic field included Paul Birkel, Dean of the Library, University of San Francisco; Joseph Boisse, University Librarian, UC, Santa Barbara; Millicent Abell, UC, San Diego, Chair of the Board of Directors of the Center for Research Libraries; Russell Shank, UCLA Librarian, Chair of the OCLC Board of Directors; John K. Amrhein, Director of Libraries, CSU, Stanislaus; Alan E. Schorr, University Librarian, CSU, Fullerton; Robin Calote, Director of the San Bernardino Valley College Library; Judith Sessions, Director of the Library, CSU, Chico; Michael Buckland, Vice-President, Library Plans and Policies for the University of California Library System; and Rodney M. Hersberger, Director of Libraries, CSU, Bakersfield.

Appointments in California public libraries during 1984 included John J. Sullivan, Daly City Librarian; Linda Glawatz, King City Public Librarian; Victoria Jenkins, Director of Downey City Library; Sharon Hammer, Director, Marin County Free Library; Jane Light, Director, Redwood City Public Library; and Marilyn Cochran, Director, Orland Free Library.

Deaths. Jane Pulis, Librarian for Germanic collections at UC, Berkeley, died November 20, 1983. Esther Mardon, former California State Library Consultant, died September 10, 1983. Blanche Collins, former Library Director, Long Beach Public, died October 2, 1983. Bella Shachtman, Associate University Librarian, UC, Berkeley, died April 19, 1984. She had served on ALA's Council and Executive Board. Ralph Moreno, Mill Valley Library, died July 31.

GIL McNAMEE

COLORADO

Colorado Library Association (founded 1892)

Membership: 700; *annual budget:* $40,000.

President: Bev Moore, University of Southern Colorado, Pueblo (November 1984–November 1985).

Vice-President/President-elect: Brenda Hawley, Pikes Peak Library District, Colorado Springs.

Executive Secretary: Susan Englese, Colorado Library Association, P.O. Box 32113, Aurora 80041.

Annual meeting: October 6–9, 1984, Copper Mountain.

Publication: Colorado Libraries (quarterly).

Colorado Office of Library Services, Colorado Department of Education

Anne Marie Falsone
Assistant Commissioner
Colorado Department of Education
1362 Lincoln Street
Denver 80203

After several interesting years of discussion and debate over what components would constitute an automated Colorado Library Network and what it might look like, 1984 saw continued discussion and some substantial progress toward its attainment. In April, the Colorado State Board of Education accepted the final report of the Network Development Committee. It had worked from 1981–83 to describe and make recommendations concerning the network. The final report recommends a distributed network of linked host computers (automated library systems). They would be linked using the technology developed by the IRVING project (discussed later). In addition, certain basic standards for the network were discussed. While not earthshaking, they do provide some guidelines to avoid any major disasters as libraries purchase automated systems or microcomputers. The committee also recommended the creation of another committee, the Network Implementation Council, to continue their work and discussions on the future of the network. The new committee was operational by year's end and was looking at the costs, strategies, and schedules for the full implementation of a network to improve library service to all of the residents of the State.

Networking. Moving past the important political ramifications of the development of a statewide network, the real success story in automation was the development and use of the CARL public access catalog (CARL is the Colorado Alliance of Research Libraries, composed of the University of Colorado at Boulder, Colorado School of Mines, Auraria Library, University of Denver, University of Northern Colorado, and Denver Public Library.). This system, running on Tandem hardware using locally developed software, has been under development for several years.

During 1984 the database exceeded 1,500,000 records, over 100 terminals were up and running, and dial-up ports were provided for remote users. In addition, circulation control was implemented for the participating libraries. The response from both patrons and librarians was enthusiastic. In October the CARL libraries invited participation by other libraries as associate members of the online system.

The IRVING (not an acronym) group of libraries (Boulder Public Library, Jefferson County Public Library, Denver Public Library, Aurora Public Library, and Littleton Public Library) have been involved for several years in attempting to link different automated circulation systems with automated nodal processors and a common network language. After much work, it was decided to try a pilot project linking the CLSI System at Aurora Public Library with the Sperry Library System (developed at Pueblo Library District in Colorado) at Jefferson County Public Library.

An intriguing microcomputer-based interlibrary loan system, BOOKPATH, was developed by the Pathfinder Library System in Montrose, It runs on IBM PC microcomputers and moves requests from local libraries to the main microcomputer for processing.

Colorado Library Association. The Colorado Library Association held its annual conference in October. The theme of the conference was "People = Libraries = People," and many of the programs focused on the human element in library service. Interestingly, there were few programs on computers and automation—to many this was a welcome change after seeming years of feeling that the computer would finally be the salvation of libraries and librarians.

Among the featured speakers were Will Manley, Director of the Tempe (Arizona) Public Library, who spoke on "Snowballs in the Bookdrop: A Humanistic Approach to Public LIbraries"; and Virginia Baeckler, author of several books on public relations for libraries, who gave a preconference workshop on "People Are the Public in Libraries." Other programs dealt with collection development, young adult services, stress management, and gaining voter support for library bond issues and mill-levy issues—a hot topic in the state.

Awards presented by the Association were: Colorado Librarian of the Year, JoAn S. Segal, formerly of the Bibliographical Center for Research in Denver and Executive Director in 1984 of ALA's Association of College and Research Libraries; Distinguished Service Award, Estes Park Woman's Club; Project of the Year, Colorado Alliance of Research Libraries for their "Online Public Access Catalog"; Media Award, Johannah Sherrer, Editor of *Colorado Libraries*; Library Benefactor Award, Frank I. Lamb Foundation of Pueblo; Special Award for Professional Achievement, University of Denver Graduate School of Librarianship and Information Management.

Colorado Libraries, the quarterly journal of the Colorado Library Association, won the H. W. Wilson Library Periodical Award for 1984. Johannah Sherrer, Editor of the journal received the award at the American Library Association Annual Conference in Dallas.

"1984: Before and Beyond" was the theme of the Colorado Educational Media Association annual conference held in February at the Broadmoor Hotel in Colorado Springs. Author John Neufeld and Illustrator Michael Haugue were among the speakers.

Numerous workshop sessions focused on media production, microcomputers, and book selection in various subject areas. As a result of the microcomputer becoming more of a staple in the school library/media centers, one noticeable change could be seen in the workshop content at this conference. Programs are now focusing more on the types of software available for management of the media center rather than the old standby workshop on "how I do it good with my computer."

Legislation. Only one major piece of library legislation was brought to the Colorado State Legislature. The bill would allow library districts, with voter approval, to increase the maximum mill levy for library service from 2.5 to 4 mills. The bill, along with numerous others relating to special districts such as fire, sewer, or water districts, died in committee. The bill was to be reintroduced in 1985 with the lobbying support of the Colorado Library Association.

State Library. Using LSCA funds, the Colorado State Library awarded three major contracts in the areas of trustee education, training for directors of small public libraries, and telecommunications. The telecommunications study was awarded to the Denver Research Institute. it will identify and report the potential of telecommunications technologies to meet the needs of Colorado libraries.

Nancy Bolt and JNR Creative Enterprises were awarded a contract to assess the educational needs of the trustees of Colorado libraries and to provide education to meet those needs. The University of Denver Graduate School of Library and Information Management was awarded a contract to provide education to directors of small public libraries—those with budgets of $30,000 a year or less. Ed Miller of the Graduate School was named project director.

Library Education. The University of Denver announced its decision to eliminate the ALA-accredited Graduate School of Library and Information Management during the summer of 1985. The Library School had been in operation for 52 years and was a major educational resource throughout the Rocky Mountain West. A large number of concerned Colorado librarians and educators were attempting to relocate the program to another institution of higher education in the state.

After several years of debate over statewide networking and automation, 1984 seemed to be a year when automation was accepted as a reality. Members of the library community began to turn their attention back to the honored profession of librarianship—to working with people and books and media to enrich people's education and lives.

JOHN CAMPBELL

CONNECTICUT

Connecticut Library Association (founded 1891)

Membership: 750; *annual budget:* $51,400.

President: Michael Simonds, Bibliomation, c/o Bridgeport Public Library (June 1984–June 1985).

Vice-President/President-elect: Betsy Wilkins, Windsor Public Library.

Executive Secretary: Jeanne Simpson, State Library, Hartford 06106.

Annual meeting: April 3–4, 1984, Hartford.

Publications: Connecticut Libraries (11 issues per year).

Connecticut State Library

Clarence F. Walters, State Librarian
231 Capitol Avenue
Hartford 06106

Instructional Media Consultants

Brenda White and Betty Billman
Connecticut State Department of Education
Hartford 06106

Library Planning. The major story coming out of the Connecticut Library community in 1984 was that concerning the Year 2000 retreat. Sponsored by the State Library to collect input from the field on creation of a new five-year LSCA master plan, the retreat rapidly turned into a state-wide forum for long-range library planning in Connecticut.

From May 29 to May 31, 53 participants from all sections of the Connecticut Library community gathered at the Mercy Center in Madison. The issues discussed were then referred to three separate task forces that met during the summer, a process that eventually culminated in a second retreat at the Mercy Center in November.

The issues that occupied the participants were (1) Service Measures, (2) Marketing, and (3) Resource Sharing. The Service Measures task force was charged with developing standards by which Connecticut libraries could measure themselves in their efforts to improve service to their communities. The draft developed by this task force was being field tested in 1984 by the State Library and several cooperating libraries around the state. The Marketing task force attempted to develop a program that would help libraries identify the needs of their communities as well as better informing their users and potential users of the services available through their local library.

The Resource Sharing Task Force ended up with a proposal that may help reshape library service in Connecticut. This task force reported that while several local automated networks had been successful in building shared library circulation systems, the day of such independent grassroots efforts was drawing to a close. Most of the libraries in Connecticut that could afford to had either automated through joining such a network or were in the process of doing so. The state was rapidly approaching the point that would find the library community divided into the have and have-not libraries.

Three major issues confronted the task force members: (1) How to aid the networks to expand and take into membership those libraries that could benefit from membership, (2) How to link the existing system (Geac, CLSI, and Dataphase) so that everyone could have access to the whole statewide database, and (3) How to provide access to this emerging unified database to all those libraries that were too small or specialized to participate in it directly.

In order to develop a systematic state-wide approach to these issues, the task force identified two things which were needed: (1) An organization with a state-wide perspective to develop state-wide plans and (2) the hard cash necessary to make those plans a reality. The organization created is known as the CONNILNET COUNCIL, a body created by the State Library Board to advise the Board on networking issues. The Hard Cash is a $4,500,000 bonding issue to be brought to the State Legislature by the Connecticut Library Association. It would provide funding for those libraries that can join the existing networks and linkages of those that cannot.

The issue was before the Connecticut State Legislature, and not resolved by year's end. The hope was that it would be viewed favorably as part of an integrated package of coordinated library development. The State Library, the State Library Association, and the State's four automated networks have come together to work for this common goal.

Professional Education. The other major issue to come before the Connecticut Library Association was the adequacy of professional library education available in the state. The resignation of the Dean of the Southern Connecticut State University Library School early in the year caused an organization of Library Administrators from Fairfield County to ask CLA to investigate the quality of education available to Library students in Connecticut. A special task force was appointed for this task. Library administrators from around the state were surveyed to determine their experiences with Southern Graduates and to identify concerns that they might have about the Library Education program.

The results of the survey were decidedly mixed, although a number of specific concerns were identified. The plan was to use the survey as the basis of discussion when CLA approaches the new Dean of the Library School.

School Media Centers. Library media skills instruction and the use of microcomputers for library management in 1984 became the focus of program efforts by both the Learning Resources and Technology Unit (State Department of Education) and the Connecticut Educational Media Association (CEMA). Several events helped promote a more expanded concept of school library media programs.

The teaching of library media skills received attention when the Learning Resources and Technology Unit and CEMA joined forces to produce and publish *Instruction in Library Media Skills*, a supplement to the state's *Guide to School Library Media Programs*. The supplement presents approaches to teaching information skills through a variety of subject areas. It contains a scope and sequence of library media skills, sample interdisciplinary lessons and a bibliography. *Instruction in Library Media Skills* was formally introduced at a reception in the State Library.

Increasing interest in the role of microcomputers for library media center management was evidenced by continued demand for professional development opportunities, a weeklong CEMA-sponsored Summer Institute, "Managing With Micros," was over subscribed. There was also significant response to a software preview day and programs at the annual conference.

In recognition of the vital role played by school library media programs, the Governor designated May 10 as School Library Media Day in Connecticut.

MIKE SIMONDS

DELAWARE

Delaware Library Association (founded 1934)

Membership: 250; *annual budget:* $5,500.

President: Atlanta T. Brown, Newark High School, Newark (May 1984–May 1985).

Vice-President/President-elect: Jacqueline Paul, Delaware Law School, Wilmington.

Annual meeting: April 26–27, 1984, Rehoboth Beach.

Publication: Delaware Library Association Bulletin (quarterly).

Division of Libraries

Sylvia Short, State Librarian
Edgehill Shopping Center
South DuPont Highway
Dover 19901

State Library Supervisor

(vacant)
Department of Public Instruction
Townsend Building
Dover 19901

State Library Aid. The Delaware General Assembly passed and Governor Pierre S. du Pont IV signed legislation establishing a formula for state aid to public libraries and funds were appropriated for that purpose. This increase in state support of public library services was a goal articulated at the 1978 Governor's Conference for Libraries and Information Services. Governor du Pont invited the members of the State Library Advisory Council Legislative Committee to attend a signing ceremony. This event was covered by a number of media representatives for Delaware and New Castle County.

The Delaware Library Association Legislative Committee and the State Library Advisory Council Legislative Committee worked diligently for passage of the bill. With the passage of HB 436, the public libraries of Delaware were removed from the grant-in-aid process and appropriated public library funds became a line item in the State budget for the first time in Delaware library history. The new formula driven allocations will triple State Aid to public libraries—$50,274 in fiscal year 1984 as against the projected $178,000 for fiscal year 1985.

State Association. The Delaware Library Association held its annual conference in Rehoboth Beach April 27. Dinner speaker for the conference was President-elect E. J. Josey, of the American Library Association. Programs offered at this meeting were "Online Searching—Issues for the Future"; "The Teenage Romance Syndrome"; and "The Librarian's Role in Reducing Illiteracy."

Page Bristow, Assistant Professor of Reading Education at the University of Delaware, was the featured speaker for the literacy program. She is the cofounder of the Literacy Volunteers of Wilmington and was instrumental in the development of Literacy Volunteers of Rhode Island. During 1984 she was active in working with other volunteers to establish Literacy Volunteers of Delaware.

The program sponsored by Children's Services Division on teen romance literature featured author Suzanne Rand. A panel composed of Rand, high school librarian Lois Simon, and Delaware teens discussed this genre.

The Delaware Library Association celebrated its 50th birthday in 1984. The first annual meeting of DLA was held on January 20, 1934. The featured speaker was Josephine Adams Rathbone, Vice-Director of the Pratt Institute School of Library Science, Brooklyn, and President of the American Library Association, 1931–32. It was noted during the meeting that Delaware had 28 public libraries and that with the formation of the Delaware Library Association in 1934 the only state left without a state library association was Nevada.

State Library Activities. In fiscal year 1984 the Delaware Division of Libraries consolidated gains begun in earlier years for improved library services.

The Automation and Resource Sharing for the Libraries of Delaware study prepared by Information Systems Consultants, Inc., affirmed the continuing importance of the Delaware Union Computer Output Catalog and the Delaware Division of Libraries' funding of retrospective conversion projects to increase the number of Delaware libraries' bibliographic records in the COM.

Convinced of the value of the Delaware Division of Libraries' Art Loan Program to both library patrons and Delaware artists, a volunteer committee was established to hold an annual art sale to benefit the Art Loan Program.

The Summer Funmobile visits to the Department of Public Instruction feeding sites throughout the State successfully reached 3,000 minority children not usually involved in public library experience such as storytelling, puppet shows, and related craft activities.

The Delaware Division of Libraries' State Fair Exhibit attracted 3,592 visitors, who participated in a library treasure hunt and learned about the Division's services. Many visitors praised the exhibit's effectiveness in promoting libraries and their use.

The Delaware Library Development Plan, 1984–89, was prepared by the DOL and accepted by the State Library Advisory Council and the U.S. Department of Education, Office of Libraries and Learning Technologies. The State Library Advisory Council established the Standards Revision Committee, which prepared updated *Standards for Public Library Service in Delaware, 1984–89*.

The Special Services Unit for the blind and

323

physically handicapped established county consumer councils to provide user input and opened a new reception area for the use of their patrons and the demonstration of visual aids.

DOL provided three continuing education programs for library directors and staff. The programs included a course on microcomputers, the development of Friends of the Libraries, and the new library technologies. The Large-Print Union List was updated with the Division's new microcomputer. The IBM/XT was utilized extensively in word processing and data management projects. Public use of the Division's facility at Edgehill grew by 1,360 and attendance at programs and exhibits showed a substantial increase. Books-by-Mail provided 36,000 reading materials for patrons without public library access while PDQ Library Line continued to answer 2,000 plus reference inquiries a month.

Public Libraries. The New Castle County Department of Libraries reorganized its Children Services and Reference Committees to become the Library I personnel discussion group to provide a professional forum for exchanging information. Projects of interest were generated from the discussion and were handled by those working in each service. The discussions were reported in writing to the Director and the reports forwarded to the Head Librarian of each library.

A project to explore the feasibility of receiving foundation monies to fund PLATO was undertaken jointly with the Newark Library Friends. This applied to the Claymont, Concord Pike and Kirkwood Highway Libraries for a three-year period. The PLATO Grant awarded to the Newark Library was extended for another year.

All Department libraries served again in 1984 as distribution points for IRS tax forms. VITA provided free tax service for the public within the libraries. The inmates at the Women's Correctional Center contacted the Head Librarian at Claymont Library to discuss ways in which they could make use of the library. An arrangement was worked out that requires the inmates to set aside money from the "Welfare Fund" to cover possible loss or damage of library materials. A list of titles, subjects, or authors is telephoned into the library. Titles are pulled by the staff, and delivered to the Center. The previous shipment is picked up at the time the new shipment is sent.

The NCC Department of Libraries hired the professional services of RMG Consultants to produce a plan for an Integrated Automated Library System. A review group was established to work with the consultant to establish project goals and objectives and to identify critical problems and issues. The consultant's recommendation for automation will be submitted as a project in fiscal year 1986 Capital Budget. LSCA funded the Computer Accessed Job Information project for $5,000. This grant provided for the purchase of a microcomputer to provide online access to DELPHI Employment and Career Information System for public use. It was to run from September 1984 through May of 1985. A major Public Relations packet for the libraries of the system was prepared.

The Wilmington Institute Library established a Council on Library Services to Business and Industry. The initial planning group established a need for a public library collection designed to serve the business community in Wilmington. An operating budget was established for the approval of a Council whose members will include bankers, advertising and communications experts, college presidents, lawyers, governmental officials, and media representatives.

Working on the themes of coalitions, the Wilmington Institute merged with and/or provided space for the Literacy Volunteers of America, and the Volunteer Clearing House. It has actively cooperated with the Urban Coalition, Wilmington Arts Commission, Delaware Humanities Forum, and the Delaware State Arts Council.

In 1984 Wilmington Institute established new fee based services for the circulation of 16mm films and videocassettes, VCR's, 16mm projectors, personal computers, audiocassettes, and charges for reserve books.

Academic Libraries. Construction on the University of Delaware Morris Library continued throughout 1984. This $15,000,000, 137,000-square-foot addition will expand and renovate the existing facilities with an increased capacity of about 80 percent. Built to hold over 2,500,000 volumes and more than double patron seating to 3,000 seats, it was scheduled for completion by July 1985, with major renovations to the existing building to be completed by January 1986.

The Morris Library was completed in 1963, at a time when the electric typewriter represented the latest word in technology for most libraries. The addition, begun in 1983, fully reflects the arrival of the computer age in libraries. The public catalog area will be renovated to support the distribution of computer terminals for public access to an online catalog envisioned for the near future, and terminals will also be located at strategic spots throughout the library stacks. In recognition of the importance of computer-based instructional programs and researchers' need to access the University's main frame computers, separate facilities for those applications will be provided throughout the Library. The Library will also introduce a microcomputer facility with stand-alone personal computers available for patron use.

With the introduction of an extensive nonprint media resource facility, special services to the visually impaired, and vastly expanded individual study and group study facilities, the new University of Delaware Library will be able to provide new and more diverse services as well as house a greater number of resources more effectively.

Funding for the project is being provided on a cooperative basis by the state of Delaware and by private funds raised by the University. $9,000,000 was committed by the state legislature. A University capital campaign begun in October 1982 exceeded its goal of $6,000,000 and met the matching requirement for state support. The architect for the project is Richter, Cornbrooks, Gribble, Inc., of Baltimore.

Ground breaking for the additions to the Delaware Law School Library and the Delaware Campus Undergraduate Library of Widener University occurred in July 1984. During the decade 1975–84, the once modest collection grew to a total of 150,000 volumes, an increase of 300 percent. Although 24 percent of the volumes are on microfilm, only 1,000 feet of the original 16,000 feet of shelf space remain available, and the collection grows at the rate of 4,000 to 5,000 volumes per year. The Law Library occupied in 1984 16,000 square feet on two floors above the Delaware Campus Undergraduate Library. It houses Delaware's finest collection of legal reference materials, including a special collection of Delaware corporate law, subscriptions to more than 500 legal journals, and a rich variety of reports, statutes and treatises. The new addition will give the Library another 12,000 square feet, increasing shelf space by 60 percent and making it possible to accommodate 75 more users at any one time.

The addition to the Delaware Campus Undergraduate Library provides up to 50 percent expanded facilities. The entire collection is to be moved to the new addition, thus allowing the older section to be used for seating, media services, reference center, and the current periodicals collection. An older office will be renovated for a teaching classroom for bibliographic instruction, as well as for special classes requiring specific media presentations. Occupancy was set for September 1985.

An important new addition to the Delaware Campus Undergraduate Library of Widener University is the microcomputer lab. An average of 70 students per day use the computers for classes, assignments, or for word processing to complete papers for course work. Housing 10 IBM-PCs, the lab is available for 91 hours a week.

JANE E. HUKILL

DISTRICT OF COLUMBIA

District of Columbia Library Association
(founded 1894)

Membership: 950; *annual budget:* $25,000.

President: Lawrence E. Molumby, Deputy Director, D.C. Public Library (May 1984–May 1985).

Vice-President/President-elect: Lelia Saunders, Director Arlington County Public Library.

Secretary: Jacque-Lynne Schulman, National Library of Medicine, Bethesda.

Annual Meeting: October 21–24, 1984, Baltimore, Maryland.

Publication: Intercom (monthly).

School Library Media Supervisor

Marie Harris (Acting)
District of Columbia Public Schools
Washington, D.C. 20024

Issues. With the passage of The District of Columbia Confidentiality of Library Records Act of 1984 by the Council, the District of Columbia joined 23 states, including its neighbors Maryland and Virginia, that have provided legal protection for the privacy of library patrons. The law states that any circulation record that can be used to identify a library patron and the specific material that patron has borrowed shall be kept confidential. Such records may not be divulged to a third party without permission of the patron or a court order. The bill was introduced by Council-member H. R. Crawford and supported by the D.C. Board of Library Trustees, the ACLU, Friends of Library groups, the Washington Bar Association, and many more.

Among the issues of greatest concern to federal librarians in D.C. were the continuing threat of downgrading of federal librarians as a result of proposed new standards from the Office of Personnel Management and the contracting out of entire federal libraries to private businesses.

Adelaide del Frate continued to monitor developments on these issues for the Special Libraries Association and the D.C. Library Association. Del Frate, who heads the A-76 Task Force of the Federal Library Round Table of ALA and works closely with the Federal Library Committee and the ALA Washington Office on federal issues, arranged and moderated a symposium on "Library Contracting: Service or Disservice" at the Middle Atlantic Regional Library Federation Conference in Baltimore on October 21.

Peter Durant, an official of the Office of Management and Budget, defended the A-76 procedure and said that the objective was not to replace federal workers with private sector workers, but simply to achieve high productivity. Sal Costabile, a library consultant, said that large-scale contracting out of federal library work could be harmful to small businesses that are now able to compete for federal library contracts. Del Frate quoted a letter from 12 members of Congress opposing the contracting out of those "Library operations which are inherently connected to the government's ability to make sound policy judgements."

State Library Associations. The Middle Atlantic Regional Library Federation (MARLF) Conference was sponsored by five state library associations including DCLA. Lucy Cocke and Bill Gordon represent D.C. on the MARLF Board. Andy Lisowski, David Vespa, Jacque-Lynne Schulman and Melissa Laning also made important contributions to the success of the quadrennial regional conference.

One of the most important annual activities of the D.C. Library Association is its role in bringing librarians from all over the country to Washington during National Library Week to meet with their legislators and discuss the importance of federal support for Library service. National Library Week Legislative Day is a joint effort of the ALA Washington Office and the NLW Committee of the D.C. Library Association. The 1984 Legislative Day set new records for contributed financial support and for the number of state delegations that went to Washington. The reception, attended by members of Congress and their staff as well as librarians, marked the 10th anniversary of this successful lobbying effort by the library community. The DCLA National Library Week Committee was chaired by Molly Raphael.

The D.C. Chapter of the Special Libraries Association voted to place its archives in the Washingtoniana Division of the Martin Luther King Memorial Library.

Rep. Major R. Owens, the only librarian in Congress, was the luncheon speaker at the annual Joint Spring Workshop sponsored jointly by the Law Librarians Society of Washington, D.C.; the D.C. Chapter, Special Libraries Association; the D.C. Library Association; and the Potomac Valley Chapter of ASIS.

Interlibrary Cooperation. Several structures to promote continuing interlibrary cooperation are in the District of Columbia. The Library Council of the Metropolitan Washington Council of Government, a cooperative of all types of libraries, provides information exchange and coordinates library activities in the region. Agnes Griffen served as Chairperson of the organization and provided aggressive and attentive leadership during a difficult year. The COG Library Council has a five-person staff headed by Mollyne Honor-Forte.

A major activity of the Council was "Summer Quest '84," a metropolitan-wide summer reading program for children. More than a hundred branch libraries in nine political jurisdictions participated in the program. Mrs. George Bush opened the "Summer Quest '84" season by reading stories to children at the Parklands-Turner branch of the D.C. Public Library. Library Theater, a local professional theater group that brings book characters to life through dramatizations, also participated in the opening ceremony and later performed at 25 public libraries in the city during July and August.

The Library Council also sponsored the formation of the Association of Liberated Librarians, a group that serves as a communications link for the retired, self-employed, and unemployed.

Hardy R. Franklin, State Librarian, convened regular meetings of directors of city-supported libraries. A major accomplishment of that group during 1984 was the inauguration of the D.C. Public Library's online catalog and Community Information Service on terminals not only in the downtown main library (the Martin Luther King Memorial Library), but also in the library of the University of the District of Columbia and in two public senior high schools. This pilot program, funded by Title III, LSCA, was an instant success. The D.C. Public School system signed a memorandum of agreement to transfer funds to the Public Library for the installation of terminals in all city public high schools in early 1985.

Another interlibrary cooperative effort was the formation of a four-member team representing the D.C. Library Association, the D.C. Public Library, the D.C. Community Humanities Council, and a local humanities scholar to prepare a joint application for a "Let's Talk About It" grant to produce book discussion programs in local libraries. Members of the D.C. team are Larry Molumby, DCLA; Molly Raphael, DCPL; Bea Hackett, DCCHC; and Marcia Greenlee, an independent humanities scholar.

The universities of the Washington area worked together during 1984 through a permanent Consortium under Library Programs Coordinator Darrell Lemke. The two bibliographic networks are FEDLINK and CAPCON, directed by James P. Riley and Joe Ford, respectively.

Public Library. The D.C. Public Library continued to enjoy steady growth in use and in public support in 1984. Circulation figures continued to rise both at the main library (13 percent) and in the branch system (8 percent). The number of people entering the libraries was up 13 percent. During 1984 library visits totaled more than the combined attendance at all the home games of the Redskins, Bullets, and Caps. Visitors to the public libraries would have filled all the theaters of the Kennedy Center 250 times.

As a result of the Jobs Bill (HR 1718) passed by Congress in 1983, the D.C. Public Library was able to replace its Parklands Kiosk with a much larger Porta-Structure in 1984. Although the Parklands Kiosk, built in 1976, has had consistent strong use, it did not appear possible to expand the facility until fiscal year 1989. But the combination of Jobs Bill funding for library construction in 1984 (LSCA Title II) and the permission of the D.C. Board of Education to use an excellent site adjacent to the Turner Elementary School meant that the new Parklands-Turner Community Library could open its doors in early March 1984 across the street from the outgrown kiosk.

The Library's persistence in planning for cable television over the last 14 years began to bear results in 1984. District Cablevision, Inc., which was awarded the franchise for the city cable system, included in its proposal operating and capital grants to the D.C. Public Library to support the Community Information Service and other cable activities by the Library. A one-way Community Information Service will be provided on one channel of the basic service, to be followed later by interactive service on a second channel. The Library will also have ample access to the municipal cable channels.

"Books Plus," a bright new store and gift shop, was opened in the Martin Luther King Memorial Library under new legislation that permits the Library to sell used books and library-related items and use the proceeds to augment the Library's book fund.

A videocassette rental service was also inaugurated at the main Library, making it possible for the Library to offer a popular new service without any budget increase.

Intellectual Freedom. In January the D.C. Library Association joined with the American Library Association, the Virginia Library Association, the American Historical Association, the Organization of American Historians, and the American Civil Liberties Union as co-plaintiffs in a suit against the National Security Agency. The case (*Peterzell v. Faurer*) concerns private papers donated to the George C. Marshall Foundation by William Friedman, a noted American cryptologist. The issue, as stated by the attorney for the plaintiffs, is "whether the National Security Agency (NSA) has the authority to classify privately owned documents that the Agency previously concluded were unclassified and were available to the public in a non-governmental library."

People. Raymond F. Vondran was appointed Dean of the School of Library and Information Science at the Catholic University of America. He had been Associate Dean of the Catholic University library school. Ruth Person, an Assistant Professor at CU since 1979, was appointed Associate Dean of the School of Library and Information Science there. Sharon Rogers was appointed University Librarian at George Washington University. She was formerly the Associate Dean of Libraries and Learning Resources at Bowling Green State University in Ohio. Nancy Gwinn was named Assistant Director for Collections Management at the Smithsonian Institution Libraries. Jacque-Lynne Schulman was appointed Head of Circulation and Control at the National Library of Medicine.

Deaths. Joseph W. Rogers, retired Chief, Copyright Office Cataloging Division, Library of Congress, died on May 15.

LAWRENCE MOLUMBY

FLORIDA

Networking. The State Legislature of Florida provided $3,154,454 in the 1984–85 budget for

Florida Library Association (founded 1920)

Membership: 848; *annual budget:* $92,665.

President: John McCrossan, University of South Florida (May 1984–May 1985).

Vice-President/President-elect: James Wheeler, Volusia County Public Library System.

Association Management: Crow-Segal, Inc., 2020 W. Fairbanks Avenue, Winter Park 32789

Annual meeting: May 16–18, 1984, Orlando.

Publications: FLASH (monthly).

State Library of Florida

Barratt Wilkins, State Librarian
R. A. Gray Building
Tallahassee, Florida 32301

State School Library Media Supervisor

Sandra Ulm
School Library, Media Service
303 Winchester Building
Tallahassee, Florida 32301

---

the extension of automated networks for the State University System. Although the funds provided were specifically for the State University System, this action, by the proviso language included, extends the state's interest in networking to all types of libraries. The State Library of Florida was mandated to oversee the networking plan.

Adult Literacy. The Florida Legislature in 1984 approved passage of the Adult Literacy Act placing special emphasis on the role of public libraries in an adult individualized literacy instruction program. The program will be aimed at adults possessing less than a fourth grade education. The program will be administered by the Commissioner of Education in coordination with the State Division of Community Colleges, local schools, and the State Library.

Florida Center for the Book. The Florida Center for the Book was established by the Broward County Division of Libraries in cooperation with the Center for the Book in the Library of Congress. Its creation was announced on April 29 by Carol A. Nemeyer, Library of Congress Associate Librarian for National Programs, in her speech dedicating Broward County's new $43,000,000 building in Fort Lauderdale. She noted that the two Centers for the Book have the mutual objective of promoting an appreciation of the role of books in society and a closer relationship between those who create books and those who read them. In addition to projects of its own, the Florida Center will use local volunteers and funding to extend to the citizens of Florida several of the reading promotion projects, e.g., Books Make a Difference, Read More About It, and A Nation of Readers, developed by the Center for the Book in the Library of Congress.

State Association. Library Day in Tallahassee drew 620 library supporters to the state's capital to meet with their legislators and discuss library issues. Representative Winston "Bud" Gardner, Brevard County, received the 1984 Outstanding Legislator of the Year award. Leadership awards were presented to Senator Clark Maxwell, Jr., and Representative James Harold Thompson.

Legislative activities were extensive and focused on efforts to obtain full funding of Chapter 257, *Florida Statutes*, which authorizes state aid of 25 cents for each local dollar spent on library services.

The 61st Annual Florida Library Association Conference and Trade Show focused on Management, Legislation, and Service (MLS). This theme highlighted the three primary target areas for professional librarians as they face increasingly demanding professional standards. Automation, executive image, stress management, leadership, and cost effectiveness were major program topics. Kate Rand Lloyd, Editor-at-Large for *Working Woman* magazine, addressed the membership regarding the changing roles and relationships of women and men in our society. Other speaker highlights included Dorothy Broderick, Sol Yurich, and Edward Bernays.

State Library. The State Library of Florida has completed reorganization. Phase one of the recent reorganization by the management team at the State Library was the implementation of a fully operational Information Center for the general public and state government agencies. In the process of establishing the center, a new open physical layout of facilities incorporating three special collection areas was developed. Extended reference services to libraries in Florida will be available through the Information Center. The State Library research staff can search materials in the General Reference, Florida History, and Government Documents Collections beyond what might be found in the local library collection. In phase two, acquisitions, cataloging, mail, and courier operations were transferred to the Bureau of Library Services, headed by Bill Paplinski. The Bureau of Library Support Services was deleted from the agency. Phase two also established the Bureau of Interlibrary Cooperation, headed by Freddie Ann Mellichamp, with Marvin Mounce as Interlibrary Cooperation Consultant.

The new Bureau of Interlibrary Cooperation will fill a need for assistance to libraries in the planning and establishment of cooperative arrangements among libraries of different types. A major focus of statewide coordination and technical consulting support will be automation, communications, and delivery systems. (Grants to support networking and automation projects under state general revenue funds and the Library Services and Construction Act, Title III, will be assisted within the new bureau).

Fifty-nine counties qualified for state aid to libraries. New counties qualifying in 1984 were Hardee and Pinellas. These counties provided free library service to 807,185 persons. 10,561,390 persons in Florida, or 99 percent of the population, had access to free library services.

The State Legislature provided increased funding for the State Library in 1984: $300,000 increase in state aid, $687,500 in public library construction grants, two new positions for the State Library, and a 49 percent increase in the book budget.

The third year of Florida's statewide public awareness program fostered an increase in use by the business community. The 1984 campaign slogan was "Who Gets Over 15,000 Calls a Day and Answers Every One? Your Library." Materials produced and distributed statewide included three television public service announcements, brochures, stickers, buttons, clip art, a full-page advertisement in *Florida Trend*, Florida's business magazine, and a training manual for librarians. The campaign was funded through LSCA.

Florida's statewide Summer Library Program saw an increase of 14 percent in attendance over 1983; 253,250 visits were made to public libraries as part of this LSCA-funded program.

The State Library sponsored eight workshops attended by over 1,200 participants. Topics covered include computer technology, deaf services, multitype library cooperation, public relations, services for rurally isolated, and services for youth.

Public Libraries. Two counties established countywide free public library service. Hardee County established and funded its first library and DeSoto County assumed responsibility for its library. Pinellas County designated the St. Petersburg library as the administrative unit to provide free countywide library service.

Putnam County and Alachua County signed a reciprocal borrowing agreement allowing residents of those counties to use both library systems. Citrus and St. Johns county libraries held successful bond referendum campaigns.

Library Trustee Jean Fletcher of Quincy, Florida, testified before Congress on the importance of Library Services and Construction Act grants to rural residents. The Broward County Division of Libraries moved into its new $43,000,000 building in April.

The Boynton Beach, Delray Beach, and West Palm Beach public libraries formed the Cooperative Authority for Library Automation (CO-ALA) to share the purchase and operation of a computer system which will access collections of the three libraries.

Citizen library supporters Glenda Conley of Seminole County and Barbara Cooper and Roslyn Kurland of Broward County traveled to Washington to encourage Florida's congressmen and senators to support library legislation. While there, the group presented Congressman Larry Smith with a certificate of appreciation from the Florida Library Association for his recent action against the Gingrich Amendment.

School Media. Nearly 20,000 readers in grades 4 through 8 in 201 schools chose their favorite books for the "First Annual Sunshine State Young Readers Award." The winner was *Bunnicula* by James and Deborah Howe and the runner-up was *Ramona Quimby, Age 8* by Beverly Cleary.

Building Programs. An addition to historic (1886) Walton-DeFuniak Library was funded by a State Construction Grant and completed in 1984. The State Grant program awarded funds to Jefferson County, St. Johns County, Volusia County, and Jacksonville Public Library.

Increased interest in public library construction was evidenced by the 46 projects awaiting possible funding during 1984 under the state program. The Clermont Library in Lake County was completed in 1984. The library was built using LSCA funds made available under the 1983 Emergency Jobs Bill and was the first library in Florida to be built using federal money in 10 years.

The North Miami Public Library funded by the Jobs Bill will be completed by the end of 1985.

Networks, Interlibrary Cooperation. The State Library of Florida, which is the headquarters of the Florida Library Information

Network (FLIN), was one of five libraries nationwide selected during 1984 to participate in OCLC's Micro Enhancer Prototype Evaluation. The evaluation, which used an Apple IIe microcomputer and OCLC software to batch process interlibrary loan requests drawing on the OCLC database during non-business hours, proved to be highly successful. The State Library granted funds to 23 FLIN resource libraries to purchase the Micro Enhancer software and hardware. By using the Micro Enhancer, the FLIN network, which serves almost 500 libraries and processes over 70,000 requests annually, reached a fill-rate of over 80 percent for the first time since the network was established in 1968.

In addition, the expansion of FLIN continued as Broward County Division of Libraries reached the minimum standards for becoming a FLIN Resource Center Library. It became the first new Resource Center added to FLIN since 1970, joining the Jacksonville, Orange County Library District, Miami-Dade, and Tampa-Hillsborough public library systems.

The State Library was given the responsibility of coordinating and approving an interlibrary cooperative plan for automated library systems that will include the state university system libraries, private institutions, community colleges, public libraries, and other library resources within the state and those arising out of interstate cooperative agreements.

The newly established State Library Bureau of Interlibrary Cooperation will assist in the planning and establishment of cooperative arrangements among libraries of different types. A major focus will be on automated systems.

Intellectual Freedom. *Playboy* magazine was the target of controversy in Broward County. The Library's subscription caught the attention of a local antipornography group and received much space in the press. Library Director Cecil Beach successfully counterattacked any political pressure to remove *Playboy* from the shelf.

An Intellectual Freedom Conference held in July drew over 60 participants from Florida and the Southeast. The conference was sponsored by the Southeastern Library Association, the Florida State University School of Library and Information Studies, and the State Library of Florida.

Professional. The first Florida statewide Adult Literacy Conference was held in October. The conference included workshops in the areas of tutoring, training, and organization geared to volunteers, adult students, and professionals.

The two ALA-accredited library science master's programs at Florida State University and the University of South Florida cooperated to offer the accredited master's programs in parts of the state not previously reached.

Awards. Carolyn Peterson of the Orange County Library District recieved the 1984 Grolier Foundation Award for outstanding contributions to the stimulation and guidance of reading by children and young people.

Helen Muir of Miami received the 1984 ALA Trustee Citation for her many contributions to Florida libraries, including developing the Miami–Dade Library System and working on Miami–Dade's successful bond campaign. She was inducted into Florida's Women's Hall of Fame by the Governor in 1984.

The Council for Florida Libraries, Inc., received a John Cotton Dana award for its Florida Book and Author Festival. The Festival, in its fifth year, makes available to Friends groups in Florida a how-to kit, publicity posters, and a roster of Florida authors. Twenty-five library systems participated in the Festival in 1984.

Glenda Conley of Oviedo (Seminole County) won the Florida Library Association Trustees and Friends Award for her outstanding service on local, state, and national levels.

Bert Harmon of Pompano Beach (Broward County) received the FLA Outstanding Citizen Library Award in recognition of his activities to advance the stature of libraries.

The Coconut Grove Library Association (Dade County) received the FLA Library Service Enchancement Award.

Frederick Ruffner, Council for Florida Libraries President, was inaugurated as the President of Friends of Libraries, USA.

Barbara Cooper was elected Chair of the White House Conference on Library and Information Services Task Force. The Task Force was making plans for a second White House Conference on Library and Information Services scheduled for 1989.

Santa Fe Regional Library (Alachua County) received awards for Outstanding Outreach Services in two categories from the American Library Trustee Association (ALTA)—for services to the homebound and for institutional services.

Delray Beach Public Library and the Central Florida Regional Library each received honorable mention from the Southeastern Library Association for their public relations materials. Delray Beach received recognition for its creative literary cookbook and Central Florida Regional for its bond referendum campaign materials.

Miami–Dade Library System was a finalist for the 1983–84 G. K. Hall Large Print Community Service Award. The campaign, "Large Print Books—Love at First Sight," received much community recognition and support.

The Northwest Regional Library System received a John Cotton Dana Award for "The Informer: Radio Is the Library Way" program. The Informer produced original public service announcements promoting reference services and offered a toll-free telephone reference line to six counties.

Retirement. Florida Librarian Mary McRory, retired from the State Library after 35 years of service. The Florida Collection became a major research collection under her direction.

HELEN MOELLER

GEORGIA

The Georgia Library Association, in conjunction with the Georgia Council of Public Libraries, in 1984 employed a legislative consultant whose fill-time task was to monitor the legislative activity of the Georgia General Assembly and provide information about library issues to members of the Assembly, to librarians, trustees, Friends of Libraries, local officials, and the general public. The consultant, Lasa Joiner, was to define the role of librarians as professionally trained educators.

In April over 30 Georgia librarians journeyed to Washington, D.C., to join other librarians from across the nation for the ALA's Annual Legislative Day. The Georgia librarians visited their state's senators and ten representatives, discussed issues of concern to them and to the profession, and "presented position papers on independence of the National Archives and Records Service, on LSCA Title II funds for public libraries and on funding for school media centers."

The Coastal Georgia Library Association featured ALA President E. J. Josey as guest speaker at the Association's annual banquet March 9. Formerly Library Director at Savannah State College, Josey is Chief of the Bureau of Specialist Library Services at the State Library in Albany, New York.

State Association. The Georgia Library Association convened a Constitutional Convention in March in Atlanta. The constitution and bylaws were revised to incorporate a newly structured organization that makes provision for specialized library interest groups as functioning parts of the Association. More than 200 members registered for the convention and participated in the debates that preceded the final approval of the changes. A group of 25 librarians entertained members of the Georgia House and Senate Appropriations Committees at a luncheon to convey the needs of libraries.

State Library Activities. One of the more notable state library activities during 1984 involved planning for a materials circulation system at the State Library that was made possible through a special appropriation approved by the Georgia General Assembly. The State Library initiated several continuing education activities for its staff and for public library staff members during 1984. Workshops for public libraries were provided on interviewing skills and collection development policy formation. For the state library staff, performance evaluation techniques were discussed during a one-day workshop.

Public Libraries. Public library funding increased during 1984 as state aid and local sources of financial support increased. Through a grant from the LSCA Act, Title I, the DeKalb Library System produced a trustees' manual (*Georgia Public Library Trustees Handbook, 1984*) and video cassettes of a trustees' workshop, in cooperation with the Georgia Library Trustee and Friends Association and the Division of Public Library Services, Georgia Department of Education. Three staff

---

Georgia Library Association
(founded 1898)

Membership: 823; *annual budget:* $31,168.

President: Jane R. Morgan, Paul W. West Professional Library, Fulton County School System, Atlanta (October 1983–October 1985)

Vice-President/President-elect: Wanda J. Calhoun, Augusta Regional Library, Augusta.

Executive Secretary: Ann W. Morton.

State Department of Education,
Division of Public Libraries Services

Joe Forsee, Director
156 Trinity Avenue, S.W.
Atlanta 30303

Division of Instructional Media Services

Nancy Hove, Director of Media Services Unit
Twin Towers, 20th Floor
Atlanta 30334

members of the DeKalb Public Library System, in cooperation with the Division of Public Library Service, published *Microcomputers in Public Libraries in Georgia—Survey 1983*, which reveals widespread interest in utilizing microcomputers in public libraries.

The Chatham–Effingham–Liberty Regional Library (Savannah, Georgia) received a $10,425 Venture Grant from the Piton Foundation of Denver and the local United Way to establish Homework Assistance Centers in three of its public library branches. Tutors at each branch assist students with homework assignments in person or by phone. Sponsors include the Savannah Area Chamber of Commerce, the Savannah–Chatham Public School System, and Armstrong State College. The Roddenbery Memorial Library (Cairo, Georgia) joined the Social Studies Teachers, the Science Council, and the English Council in its community in enhancing and enriching informational resources for study and learning. With a small LSCA grant, the Dougherty County Public Library developed a small successful traveling play, CHECK IT OUT, on reading and library awareness. It was geared for making children regular library users.

With a second grant from the Georgia Endowment for the Humanities, the Athens Regional Library sponsored a special project entitled "Different Drummers: Women in Literature," featuring lecturers on several authors and issues.

The Friends of the Atlanta–Fulton Public Library held its first library book sale dubbed SMORGASBOOK and raised $20,000 for the library. Friends of the Macon Library System cleared $24,500 during their three-day "Old Book Sale."

In Canton, the fourth annual McDonald's golf tournament for the benefit of the R. T. Jones Memorial Library, headquarters for the Sequoyah Regional Library, netted over $2,800 for equipment. At a Wendy's grand opening in Canton, the Library Director and staff were given the unusual ribbon after the cutting; attached to it were 256 one-hundred dollar bills, representing the number of ways Wendy's prepared hamburgers when the chain first opened.

An exhibit of selected rare titles from Black collectors was displayed at the Atlanta Fulton Public Library during March. The exhibit included 100 rare titles and 2 periodicals covering almost 200 years of publishing.

School Libraries. Georgia hosted the third national conference of the American Association of School Librarians in Atlanta in the fall, attracting more than 3,200 delegates representing 50 states and several foreign countries. The conference featured Mary Cunningham, author of *Powerplay*, Alonzo Crim, Atlanta Public Schools Superintendent, and Maya Angelou, author of *I Know Why the Caged Bird Sings*. Governor Joe Frank Harris proclaimed the week of October 28–November 3, 1984, "School Library Week," noting that "Our Nation's school library media specialists have made invaluable contributions to America's educational system, and their dedication and commitment to maintaining and enhancing our school libraries are to be commended by all."

A self-study of its media program was conducted by the Savannah/Chatham County School System, resulting in the development of a five-year comprehensive plan to address the needs revealed in the study: that of strengthening program, staff, facilities, and resources. Another media program at the Johnson Elementary School in Cherokee County houses an up-to-date media center, staffed by a specialist assisted by student aides and part-time parent volunteers. The facility is equipped with closed circuit television, videotape machines, cameras, computers, and other conventional media equipment. Innovative and creative programs include the production of videotapes by sixth graders to teach reference skills to third and fourth graders and the DIRT (Daily Independent Reading) Program in which everyone in the school reads 17 minutes each day.

Both of these school systems were singled out by the Georgia Board of Education for excellence in school and system media services. Plaques were presented in July as part of the Board's Excellence Recognition Program.

The Georgia Association of Media Assistants (GAMA) held its annual convention in April, drawing some 350 students whose interests lie in library and audiovisual aids for grades six through twelve. The Georgia Library Media Department (GLMD) featured Robert Bohanan, Archivist for the Carter Presidential Materials Project, during its spring meeting. GLMD is an affiliate of the Georgia Association of Educators and of the American Association of School Librarians. One of its highlights is Media Day (first Friday in February), proclaimed by the Governor as a day set aside to mark the importance of library/media centers and programs to the total educational program.

Academic and Special Libraries. David Estes, Librarian for Special Collections for many years at Emory University and active member of the Georgia Library Association, retired and assisted SELA on a part-time basis as Executive Director. In his honor, Emory established the David Estes Book Fund, to be used to purchase materials about Georgia.

Graham E. Roberts retired on June 30 as Director of Libraries at the Georgia Institute of Technology in Atlanta, after 25 years of dedicated service. A strong advocate of cooperation among libraries, he was instrumental in the formation of SOLINET and served on its first Board of Directors. An endowment fund was established in his honor by colleagues at Georgia Tech and a challenge grant of $25,000 was offered by the Price Gilbert, Jr., Charitable Fund. Income from the endowment was to be used initially to purchase materials in technology and science policy, architecture, and applied biology.

Elizabeth Brinson, Acting Director and Head of Technical Services of the H. A. Hunt Memorial Library, Fort Valley State College Library, retired after 23 years of outstanding service. She was an active member of the GLA.

Important acquisitions in academic libraries in 1984 included two valuable and important collections by the Woodruff Library, Emory University. The papers are of Pulitzer Prize winning journalist Claude Sitton, an alumnus and Editor of the *Raleigh News and Observer*, and the papers of the late Rabbi Jacob M. Rothschild of Atlanta. The Sitton papers include materials from his years as Chief Southern Correspondent for the *New York Times* (1958–68), correspondence and writings from his career in North Carolina, and some coverage of Civil Rights activities in the earlier portion of the collection. The Rothschild papers figure prominently on the Civil Rights Movement in the South as he was an active supporter and friend of Martin Luther King, Jr., and Ralph McGill, Pulitzer Prize winning Editor of the *Atlanta Constitution*.

Over 200 cassette tapes, books, and pamphlets by Howard Thurman, noted preacher, mystic, teacher, and author, went to Paine College, Augusta, to form the nucleus of the Library's Howard Thurman Meditation Room. The donation was made by Daniel Collins, President of the Paine College Board of Trustees. An entire set of the publications of the American Institute of Real Estate Appraisers was given to the University of Georgia Libraries by the Southeast Chapter of AIREA.

The first part of the *Southern Recorder Index, 1820–1874*, was completed by Tom Armstrong and Janice C. Fennell. The *Southern Recorder* reflects an important period in Georgia history and its index will be of tremendous help to genealogical users.

The Talking Book Center of the Cherokee Regional Library acquired a Talking Encyclopedia on cassette tape for those visually impaired and handicapped; an anonymous challenge grant was matched by the LaFayette Rotarians.

Building Programs. The General Assembly approved approximately $2,000,000 in state funds for five public library construction projects; the five library systems are Cordele Carnegie Library, the Greene, Baldwin, and Bleckley County Libraries, and the Byron Public Library. In addition, the General Assembly passed a resolution calling for a constitutional amendment that adds library governing bodies, for the purpose of constructing library facilities, to the list of state agencies which allowed use of state general obligation bond funds. The constitutional amendment was approved during the November general election.

A change in the formula for allocation of state construction funds for public libraries by the Georgia State Board of Education allows a more generous use of state monies. Under the new formula, "the State will fund 99% of the first $500,000 of the total library building project cost and 66 2/3% of any additional project cost above $500,000 . . . not to exceed more than $3,000,000 per project in a fiscal year." Fifteen proposals were received, totaling $7,300,000.

The Dougherty County Public Library of Albany formally initiated its final phase of constructing a $1,700,000 new central headquarters. It was to provide 38,000 square feet of space for book stacks, a small auditorium, projection room, and sound system. Every portion of the new building was to be accessible to handicapped citizens.

Two new public libraries were dedicated in 1984. A facility for the Liberty County Public Library, a branch of the Chatham/Effingham Liberty Regional Library, was dedicated March 18. The Bacon County Public Library was officially dedicated Saturday, March 22, as the Sharpe Building, named for the first physician to open a hospital in Alma.

The Oglethorpe County Library, a branch of the Athens Regional Library System, completed renovation of an old building to serve as the county library. Much of the work was done by interested citizens and board members as a community project.

Networks, Interlibrary Cooperation. SOLINET (the Southeastern Library Network) was granted funds for a two-year, NEH-funded cooperative preservation program, serving libraries and archives in 10 states. Its proposal provided for the establishment of an Office of Conservation Studies, which would be the coordinating information site and would provide services for the region; the development of a conservation laboratory for preservation and restoration of materials; and the institution of a security storage facility. There was active participation by the Librarians Council of the University Center in Georgia, which comprises membership of 12 institutions in the Atlanta–Athens region.

The Georgia Library Information Network had a membership increase of five libraries during 1984, bringing the total to 205 libraries or library systems. A pilot project was begun during 1984 that explores the use of IBM PC microcomputers to transfer interlibrary lending requests and related information from small libraries to the State Library and vice versa. The Science Library at the University of Georgia agreed with the Indexing Section of the National Agricultural Library during 1984 to index agricultural experiment station publications and selected horticulture and general agriculture journals for the Agricola database.

Intellectual Freedom. The Georgia General Assembly passed a bill relating to obscenity and related offenses during its session in 1984. The bill prohibited the sale, loan, and exhibition of materials harmful to minors. However, an exclusion for libraries, or at least an interpretation to that effect, came with the language that it would be "unlawful for any person knowingly to exhibit for a monetary consideration to a minor . . . ."

Several activities were sponsored by the Metro Atlanta Coalition Against Censorship (the Intellectual Freedom Committee of the Metro Atlanta Library Association, the American Civil Liberties Union of Georgia, and McGuire's Bookshop). Some worthy of note included displays at the Central Library of the Atlanta–Fulton Public LIbrary and McGuire's Bookshop, an article in *Creative Loafing* and an editorial in the *Atlanta Constitution* (both Atlanta newspapers), radio interviews, feature segments on all three of the local TV network affiliates, a forum on Censorship, "Censorship and Pornography," a panel discussion at the DeKalb Library System, and "An Evening of Forbidden Books," which provided selected readings from banned books.

Professional Interests. Salaries for state-paid public librarians were increased by three percent during the 1984 General Assembly while other state-paid professionals were approved for a 10 percent increment. This action removed state-paid public librarians from the teachers' pay scale, which raised much concern by library leaders throughout the state. As a result, increased activity developed, spearheaded by GLA, GLMD, and other library units. A drive was successful and library media specialists were included in the pay raise.

The Georgia Library Video Association (GLVD) during its fall meeting heard ALA Executive Board member Elizabeth Futas as a workshop leader. Associate Professor in the Emory Division of Library and Information Management, Futas prepared a bibliography on "Video Selection Sources" as part of the workshop materials.

Awards. Elizabeth C. Harris, wife of Georgia Governor Joe Frank Harris, was the 1984 recipient of the Georgia Library Trustee Association Honor Award. Harris was cited for her support of an effort to expand the Governor's Mansion Library through a program that invited Georgia authors to contribute autographed copies of their works to the existing collection.

Wilma S. Cravey, a retired librarian and Past-President of the Georgia Library Media Department, received the 1984 William E. Patterson Service Award, given to honor distinguished service to GLMD and for meritorious service to library/media work in Georgia.

Barbara Loar, Director of the DeKalb Library System, was named Woman of the Year by the *DeKalb News/Sun*. Chosen from among 50 women, Loar was singled out for having initiated programs that have received national recognition from her peers.

The International Reading Association and the Cherokee Council honored the Dalton Regional Library for services in the promotion of literacy. The award was given for its library's Bookmobile program and adult and children's services.

Annual awards in the Atlanta Public School System's Academic Achievement Incentive Program were awarded to Bertha Burnett of Inman Middle School, Joyce Hadley of Venetian Hills Elementary School, and Barbara Mosby of Toomer Elementary School, recognizing distinguished academic achievement in various teaching fields.

Rod Chatham, Media Specialist for Audiovisual Software, Media Services Department of the Fulton County School System, won awards from the Atlanta Chapter of the International Television Association: the Video Communications Award for "Safety Patrols to Washington, D.C.–1983" and the Golden Cassette Award for "Computer Scheduling."

SELA presented the biennial Outstanding Southeastern Library Program Award to the DeKalb Library System's Tobie Grant Homework Library for alternative public library service in a low-income area. The Library is the result of the renovation and conversion of a traditional public library into one designed primarily to provide direct support to the educational achievements of upper elementary and high school students in an economically deprived area. The conversion was funded by an LSCA grant as was the first year of operation.

Appointments. Elizabeth Futas of Emory University was elected to a four-year term on the Executive Board of ALA. Bobi Conti, Children's Literature Consultant for the DeKalb Library System, was appointed to the Nominating Committee for the 1984 Georgia Book Award. Betsy Curry, Staff Training and Library System, was selected to serve as Chair of the Adult Library Materials Committee of the Reference and Adult Services Division of the American Library Association. She is President of the Georgia Library Video Association.

Rosemary K. Evans, Director of the Gordon Junior College Library, and Paula Suddeth were appointed to the State Board for the Certification of Librarians by Governor Joe Frank Harris.

Eugenia Cavender, Director of the Dalton Regional Library System, was chosen to serve on the Public Library Association Network Relations Task Force to review the current status of public library participation in online bibliographic networks and to develop recommendations for the PLA Board.

Deaths. Virginia Lacy Jones, retired Professor and Dean of the Atlanta University School of Library and Information Studies, 1939–81, and the first Director of the Robert W. Woodruff Library of the Atlanta University Center, died December 3 (*see* Obituaries).

JULIE HUNTER

HAWAII

Hawaii Library Association (founded 1922)

Membership: 418; *annual budget:* $27,373.

President: Caroline Spencer, 270 Ilihau St., Kailua 96734 (march 1984–March 1985).

Vice-President/President-elect: Arlene Tibayan, 98-444 Kilinoe Street, Aiea 96701.

Annual meeting: March 9–10, 1984, Waikiki.

Publications: HLA Newsletter (4–6 times a year); *HLA Journal* (annual).

Hawaii State Library, State Librarian

Bartholomew A. Kane
4644 Aukai Avenue
Honolulu, 96816

State School Library Supervisor

Patsy Izumo
Department of Education
641 18th Avenue
Honolulu 96816

The 13th annual conference of the International Association of School Librarians was held on the campus of the Kamehameha Schools in Honolulu, July 30–August 3. The conference theme was "School Libraries/Media Centers: Partners in Education," and it attracted 195 librarians from 11 countries. Speakers included Ken Haycock, Mary Ann Paulin, James Dator, and Rubellite Johnson.

Library automation dominated activites in both the Hawaii State Library and the University of Hawaii's Manoa campus. The University of Hawaii at Manoa Libraries were installing an integrated computerized library system with Advanced Library Concepts (AdLib) of Sacramento, California. The first stage of installation, at a cost of $525,000, includes the conversion of records in the undergraduate library. When complete, the system will support acquisitions, fund accounting, cataloging, and circulation functions as well as an online public catalog.

The State Library's automation project was extended to all public libraries on Oahu and to the largest of the branches on the outer islands in Hilo on the island of Hawaii. The State Library planned to convert all remaining branches during 1985. Automated libraries accounted for 80 percent of all circulation in 1984, and preliminary planning was under way to provide public online catalogs. Indexing of the two major daily newspapers was being performed online through the automation project.

State Associations. The Hawaii Library Association's spring conference was held in Honolulu, March 9–10, with the theme "The Future Is Now." Speakers included the State Librarian, Bart Kane; the Dean of the University of Hawaii Graduate School of Library Studies, Miles Jackson; and Barbara Hennsler,

Frances Enos, and Robert Wedgeworth, ALA Executive Director.

The fall conference was held at the University of Hawaii at Hilo with the theme of "Big Island: Science Showcase." Speakers included Dale Cruikshank, an astronomer with the University of Hawaii's Institute for Astronomy, Jon Erickson of the Hawaii Volcanoes National Park (speaking on the threat to Hilo from Mauna Loa's 1984 eruption), William Mull, a research associate in entomology with the Bernice Pauahi Bishop Museum, and Russ Apple of the National Park Service speaking on the negative aspects of geothermal energy.

The newly formed Hawaii Island Chapter of the Hawaii Association of School Librarians joined in the Hawaii Library Association's fall conference with sessions on "Children as Authors" and the use of puppetry in storytelling.

The Second Hawaii Island Library Conference was held March 26. Boone Morrison spoke on the making of his book "Images of the Hula," Mary Bitterman, Director of the East–West Center's Institute of Culture and Communication on "Journey Towards Excellence," and Professor Gerald Lundeen of the Graduate School of Library Studies at the University of Hawaii on "Using Microcomputers in Libraries."

Public Libraries. The newest addition to the Hawaii State Library System, the Salt Lake-Moanalua Community Library, was opened June 30. The library, in the Salt Lake Shopping Center, is the first in the state that is in a storefront location.

The new Mililani library building was dedicated in October. The Library had been housed in Mililani High School since its opening.

Bartholomew Kane was reappointed State Librarian by the newly elected Board of Education in November. The Board named Francis Hatanaka Acting Superintendent of Education, replacing Donnis Thompson.

Public library staffs benefited from "Library Institute Days" implemented by the State Librarian in 1984. One working day of the year was designated for professional improvement in each of the five library districts and was devoted to workshops and meetings for all library staff. The program parallels "Teachers' Institute Days" for public school staffs in Hawaii.

Public hearings on the reinstitution of a fine system for overdue library material were in process during 1984.

School Libraries. A pilot project for a Computer Review Center and Clearinghouse, funded by ECIA Chapter II, was initiated in August. The Review Center was working toward a centrally coordinated evaluation program that, when fully operational, would systematically review computer resources and act as a clearinghouse to periodically disseminate information at school, district, and state levels.

Computer use in schools was also included in the updated Department of Education State Computer Plan. The two major goals of the Plan are the development of a statewide network of school library resources and the automation of selected library operations at the school level.

Integrating library skills with content areas remained a major in-service training focus in 1984. Workshops included "Children as Authors," "Puppets in the Library," and "Using Secondary Libraries for Learning."

Academic Libraries. The University of Hawaii at Hilo Library was named the Edwin H. Mookini Library in honor of the former Chancellor of that campus. A sculpture by Bumpei Akaji was erected in front of the library as part of a State Foundation on Culture and the Arts program to beautify and enrich public buildings.

Professional Interests. The question of comparable worth was unresolved in 1984 and hearings on the subject continued.

A threatened strike by unions representing four major bargaining units, including all school librarians, teachers, and public and university library staffs, failed to materialize following a dramatic settlement reached 30 minutes before the February 21 deadline. Part of the settlement, effective in January 1985, included changing membership in the State Employees' Retirement System from mandatory to optional. The employer was to continue to contribute to the system on the employee's behalf, but individual employees were given an opportunity to choose between continuing their own contributions to the system or selecting some other retirement plan.

Awards. The 1984 Nene Award winner selected by Hawaii's elementary school children was *Nothing's Fair in Fifth Grade* by Barthe De Clements. The Nene Honor Book was *Jelly Belly* by Robert Kimmel Smith.

Appointments and Retirements. M. Cecil Mackey of Michigan State University was appointed President of the University of Hawaii in December following a year-long search by the Board of Regents.

Oi Yung Chow, who headed the Public Library's main branch in Honolulu, retired in December after 36 years of service.

SUSAN F. MAESATO
KENNETH R. HERRICK

IDAHO

Idaho Library Association
(founded 1915)

Membership: 429; *annual budget:* $18,961.
President: Vera Kenyon, P.O. Box 1, Wilder 83676 (April 1984–April 1985).
Vice-President/President-elect: Jerry Glenn, Madison County Library, 73 North Center, Rexburg 83440
Annual meeting: October 3–5, 1984, Sun Valley.
Publications: The Idaho Librarian (quarterly).

Idaho State Library
Charles Bolles, State Librarian
325 West State Street
Boise 83702

State School Library Media Supervisor
Rudy Leverett, Consultant
State Department of Education
Boise 83720

Idaho Library Association. "Partners in Excellence" described the mood of the first joint conference of the Idaho Library Association and the Idaho Educational Media Association. ILA President Anna Green and IEMA President-elect Ned Stokes presided over the conference at Sun Valley in October.

Two preconferences were held. "Democratization of History" was sponsored by the Institute of the American West. Randy Collver spoke on "You and Your Micro," an entertaining and provocative approach to library applications of microcomputers.

Authors were in abundance; conferees met Terry Davis, Richard Etulain, Bill Hall, Eric Kimmel, and Gloria Skurzynski as they spoke on topics ranging from "I don't want to support my local library" to "Today's kids as western heroes." Richard Etulain, funded by a grant from the Association for the Humanities in Idaho, inspired his audience to further exploration of the area's heritage, western literature. Other aspects of the profession shared the limelight. Online searching, Caldecott award selection criteria, library media programs, and video equipment were among topics covered in workshops.

State Library News. The 1984 legislature appropriated a 24.1 percent increase in general account funds for the Idaho State Library beginning July 1984. A major portion of the increase was to bring funding of the Blind and Handicapped Division under state rather than federal purview. This appropriation also supported a complete reorganization of the Idaho State Library, adding five new positions and streamlining operations. The agency reorganization was to be completed January 1, 1985, and to result in a Library Development Division, an Information Services Division, and an Administrative Support Section under the direction of the State Librarian. Associate Director for the Library Development Division is Ann Joslin. Associate Director of the Information Services Division is Vicki Kreimeyer, and Administrative Support Section Librarian is Rich Wilson.

A casualty of this legislative action was removal of the last elements of state aid to libraries. The state regional library systems were fully funded by LSCA Title I funds effective with fiscal year 1985.

Public Libraries. Public support for libraries increased during 1984. Buhl Public Library received $2,000 from an anonymous donor. Coeur d'Alene Public Library received a check for $1,000 for a movie projector while a local clothing store provided funds for the cart. Boise Cascade Corporation provided Council Public Library with a microcomputer and supporting software. A collection of memorabilia documenting the operatic soprano career of Amelita Galli-Curci was donated to the Ketchum Community Library.

Voters in East Bonner County approved the annexation of the Library into the library district while voters in the Franklin County Library District passed an override levy that will give the Library an additional $15,000 per year for five years. The override levy was approved by a vote of 23 to 17.

Academic Libraries. Academic libraries received public donations during 1984. Two institutions received substantial gifts, enriching Idaho's research collections.

The papers of the late Senator Frank Church of Idaho were donated to Boise State University shortly before Senator Church's death early in 1984. The collection is housed in the BSU Library in an especially constructed suite of two rooms. One room will exhibit the late Senator's memorabilia, and the other houses the manuscripts and includes work space for processing the collection.

The bulk of the collection covers the years 1956–80 and contains files relating to

Church's service on the Senate Foreign Relations Committee, the Special Committee on Aging, his work on wilderness legislation, his campaign for the Democratic nomination for president, issues surrounding the Panama Canal Treaty, and a host of other topics. The collection includes hundreds of motion pictures and video and audio tapes of speeches given by Church and his opponents.

The University of Idaho received the Day Mines collection from Henry Day, past President of Day Mines, Inc. The collection consists of correspondence, records, and files of Day Mines, about nine tons of documents that cover the period 1900–53.

Building Programs. The Pinehurst–Kingston Library, which opened its doors September 21, began in the elementary school cafeteria in June 1976. The school district donated land for a library site adjacent to the school so the library continues to serve as a school–public library. LSCA Title II funds of $76,022, donated land worth $18,562, and local funds of $41,243 went into construction of the library serving 4,753 people. The Library is in the Coeur d'Alene Mining District, which experienced the closure of one of the largest mining companies in the area, Bunker Hill Company. People and businesses, nevertheless, provided enough support to purchase or build all shelving and furnishings.

The Clearwater Memorial Library in Orofino completed an addition. Potlatch Corporation donated $10,000 in time to save a 300-square-foot section of the addition. Friends of the Library were raising funds for stacks and furniture.

An expansion of the Meridian Public Library began in April. Planned were the first phase, to add 800 square feet, and a second phase, a remodeling to open the interior that will result in a new children's library.

Awards. Cheryl Sebold, regional assistant of the Portneuf District–Gateway Regional Library System, was recognized as 1984 Idaho Librarian of the Year by the Idaho Library Association.

Dick Clayborn received the Idaho Library Association's Special Services to Libraries award for his efforts, as Nampa city councilman, to promote Nampa libraries and services.

Stanley Shepard received a life membership to the Idaho Library Association. He retired from the University of Idaho Library after 25 years of service as Documents Librarian, Catalog Librarian, Special Collections Librarian, and head of the Technical Services Department.

Three scholarships were awarded by ILA. The recipients were Janet Wright, Cathy Sitz, and Bette DeBruyne.

The University of Idaho Library Faculty Award was presented to Ron McFarlane, Professor of English. This recognizes the effort McFarlane has made in collection development, library committees, and editing the *Snapdragon*, a literary magazine sponsored jointly by the library and English Department.

Randall Simmons, Reference Librarian at Northwest Nazarene College, received the Northwest Nazarene College Alumni–Faculty grant for 1984. The grant will fund in part efforts to index literature on the history of the Church of the Nazarene.

Appointments. Lynn Melton was named Director of the Boise Public Library in 1984. She went to Idaho from Burlington, Wisconsin, where she was Library Director.

Terry Abraham became the Head of Special Collections at the University of Idaho Library. Abraham was formerly the Assistant Special Collections Librarian at Washington State University Library in Pullman.

Craig Anderson was named Director of the Idaho Falls Public Library when Bill Ptacek left to become the Director of the Louisville Public Library in Kentucky.

The David O. McKay Learning Resources Center had a new director. Thomas Liau assumed the position of Director vacated by Larry Ostler. Ostler became the new Assistant University Librarian at Lee Library, Brigham Young University.

Larry Oberg was named Director of Lewis–Clark State College Learning Resources Center, replacing Danny Wynn.

Deaths. Beulah Brenneman, recipient of Idaho Library Association's Trustee of the Year award in 1981, died July 25. She served 57 years as trustee of the Salmon Public Library, watching the library grow from "a shelf in the local jewelry store to an incorporated body housed in a modern building whose net worth is nearly half a million dollars. . . ." A certified Braillist, Brenneman transcribed over 43 children's books into Braille.

Rex A. White, librarian emeritus of Idaho State University and past president of the Idaho Library Association, died Dec. 21, 1984. White served on many committees for the Idaho Library Association and Pacific Northwest Library Association. He was one of the planners for the new Idaho State University Library, where he served as associate librarian and acting university librarian, retiring in July 1982.

LYNN BAIRD

ILLINOIS

Illinois Library Association (founded 1896)

Membership: 3,700; *annual budget:* $281,290.

President: Valerie Wilford, Assistant Professor, Department of Communication, Illinois State University, Normal (January–December 1984).

Vice-President/President-elect: Harold Hungerford, Department of English, Illinois Wesleyan University.

Executive Director: Willine Mahony, 425 North Michigan, Suite 1304, Chicago 60611.

Annual meeting: May 9–11, 1984, Chicago.

Publications: ILA Reporter (quarterly).

Illinois State Library

Bridget Lamont, Director
Centennial Building
Springfield 62756

School Library Media Supervisor

Marie Sivak
Illinois Office of Education
Springfield 62702

Reflections—Heritage of the Past . . . Promise of the Future was the theme of the 1984 Illinois Library Association Annual Conference in Chicago May 9–11. The Illinois Library Association paused to reflect on its past, present, and future—a reflection of concern for Association members, a commitment to Illinois libraries, and a caring for the interest and activities of those who struggle to bring quality library services to Illinois citizens. Reflecting on the past were achievements and a nostalgic look at the way we were. Reflecting on the present were nearly 75 sessions ranging from the Board and business meetings to special speakers on the practical, how to do it good presentations reflecting quality in what's available for library services in the areas of material, equipment, furnishings, supplies, and customer services from our commercial representatives. Reflecting on the future were programs which challenge us to expand our experiences, increase our service, refine our thinking, ans a special dialog between Peggy Sullivan and Alphonse Trezza who gave their perspective of what will be.

State Library Activities. The Illinois State Library launched the READ ILLINOIS program in 1984. Of great significance to Secretary of State James Edgar and the backbone of READ ILLINIOIS literary programs is community involvement in literature discussion programs at the local level.

The READ ILLINOIS Advisory Committee, using funds appropriated to the Illinois State Library's program by the Illinois Humanities Council, awarded seven communities money to do a program stressing their area or community's literary heritage.

The Suburban Chicago Committee of READ ILLINOIS presented "Illinois Voices: Echoes and Promises" May 31 at Downer's Grove Public Library and June 2 at the Park Ridge Public Library.

The programs included an afternoon discussion session with authors Michael Anania, Robert Bray, Leon Forrest, Kathryn Kerr, and Elizabeth Klein. A book fair was held and the day closed with dramatic-readings presentations by City Lit Theatre Company.

READ ILLINOIS' Galesburg Committee hosted a lecture, "Three Galesburg Writers: Julia Fletcher Carney, Earnest Elmo Calkins, and Mary Allen West," June 9 in Galesburg.

The Peoria Public Library sponsored a READ ILLINOIS week June 18–22 with a word-puzzle contest. A writing/publishing workshop was held June 19; George Chambers, poet and Bradley University professor, spoke on June 20; Jerry Klein, from the Peoria *Journal Star*, discussed Peoria history June 21; and Judith McInerney, children's author, spoke June 22.

Southern Illinois University at Carbondale was the site of a July 20 READ ILLINOIS program. The University Dean of Library Affairs Kenneth Peterson welcomed the public and guest speaker, Herbert Russell. Small group sessions on poetry, journalism, fiction, drama, children's stories, and browsing and autograph sessions were held.

Floyd Olive, Ben Gelman, Henry Dan Piper, Christian Moel, Regina Shelton, and Mary Lamb were group speakers. Special guest speaker was Gwendolyn Brooks talking about her writing in the lecture "Brooks on Brooks."

The READ ILLINOIS' Bloomington Committee developed a literary calendar divided not into seasons but by types of literature—poets, historians, novelists, and dramatists. The committee is also developing an Illinois *Poetry and Place* Chapbook.

On August 5 the Rockford Committee of READ ILLINOIS held an Illinois Heritage Fair at Haskell Park in Rockford. Local authors, folk musicians, and oral traditionalists performed throughout the day. Marita Brake, folksinger and songwriter, and Ron Holm, singer, performed in special presentations. John Cragan, professor of communications at Illinois State University, gave a special presentation on "Folk Stones of Rockford."

In one of the final programs of the year the Champaign-Urbana READ ILLINOIS Committee developed a traveling exhibition of photographs, autographs, biographical information, and anecdotes of area authors. The exhibit was made available to all libraries in the Lincoln Trail Libraries System.

The Champaign-Urbana committee also presented programs, related to the displays, in six to eight libraries. Print materials about the authors and their work were made available to the public.

Public Libraries. The Public Library Section of the Illinois Library Association sponsored several programs during 1984 including a program on the assessment process featuring Thomas Hynes, Cook County Assessor.

The Section also sent a representative to the American Library Association seminar "Marketing for Libraries" in Madison, Wisconsin. One of the on-going activities of this Section will be to sponsor a program on marketing for libraries during 1985.

A revision of the Public Library Section bylaws, working for the improvement of statistical reporting forms, membership campaigns that will attract other librarians were given high priority as activities for the Public Library Section.

The Section was also active in the attempt to override the Governor's veto of $8,000,000 in construction funds. The section printed 100,000 bookmarks and distributed them to library systems and to public libraries for inclusion in interlibrary loan books. The bookmarks featured a concise description of the override case and a list of librarians from the Illinois Library Association Legislative Library Development Committee who could be contacted for further information.

School Libraries and Media Centers. The Illinois Association for Media in Education chose for their annual conference theme "Unlimited Connections." John Ciardi was the featured speaker. School Library Media Day was proclaimed by Governor Thompson during National Library Week. Regional workshops and other sessions were held throughout the year. Topics for these workshops included Public Relations, Professional Image, Censorship, and a video presentation entitled "Pot O' Gold."

Illinois Library Association. The Children's Librarians Section of the Illinois Library Association changed its name to the Youth Services Section to reflect a desire to serve young adult librarians as well as children's librarians. The Section produced a successful statewide library program "Be a Star—Read." They also published four issues of a newsletter entitled "The Children's Crier," cosponsored Storytelling at the Illinois State Fair with the Illinois State Library, and awarded the Davis Cup for Distinguished Service to Ruth Griffith.

The Specialized Library Services Section produced the April issues of *Illinois Libraries*, "*Special Collections in Illinois Libraries.*" The 18 articles included descriptions of library collections and their related activities and services on subjects ranging from the artists' books at the Chicago Art Institute to the library of the Lincoln Park Zoo.

The Government Documents Round Table in 1984 participated in the national action urging the President to nominate and Congress to approve the appointment of Bill Barrett as Public Printer.

The annual fall workshop of the Government Documents Round Table served as an introduction to U.S. government documents and was considered successful in terms of getting "Documents To The People."

The Resources and Technical Services Section sponsored a continuing education conference, "Online in Illinois: Integrating Dreams and Reality." Lucia Rather, Director for Cataloging at the Library of Congress was the featured speaker.

The Illinois Library Trustees Association has approximately 1200 members, making it the largest section of the ILA. Two well-attended workshops on how to be an effective trustee were held during the year, one in Chicago and one in Mt. Vernon.

The Social Responsibilities Round Table sponsored several programs during the year: "Libraries for Peace: A New Emphasis for the '80's," featuring George Lopez, coordinator of the Peace and Global Studies Program, Earlham College; "The Freedom of Information Act: Implications for Librarians," with Susan Bandes, American Civil Liberties Union, and Robert Doyle, American Library Association Office for Intellectual Freedom; and "Illinois Library Resources on Women," a panel of seven librarians representing various Women's Studies collections and libraries in Illinois.

The group also cosponsored with the Illinois Association of Media in Education a program entitled "Censorship or Selection" featuring a discussion between librarians and members of the Moral Majority and Eagle Forum.

Illinois became the second state in the nation to pass a library association nuclear freeze resolution.

The Social Responsibilities Round Table developed a traveling exhibit of controversial titles based on American Library Association's "Banned Books" exhibit. The Illinois traveling exhibit is entitled, "Books Under Fire" and is available to Illinois libraries for a one—month loan period through the Social Responsibilities Round Table.

The group published the 1984 edition of the *SHARE Directory of Feminist Library Workers*. This publication has expanded coverage to include men and women across the nation and in Canada.

A one—day educational seminar entitled, "Comparable Pay for Comparable Worth," featuring Margaret Myers of the American Library Association Office of Library Personnel Resources; Marsh Bates of Hay Associates, Illinois Representative Barbara Flynn Currie; and Kathleen Prendergast, President of AFSCME of Chicago Public Library, was also offered. Video tapes of the session may be borrowed from the Arlington Heights Memorial Library.

The Library Assistants Round Table held two major workshops in 1984. "Solving the Mysteries of AACR2," a self-development workshop for library support staff was offered in two locations. "Library Support Staff and Computer Systems: Let's Learn About That Computer" was repeated on four dates at three locations.

The Library Assistants Round Table Recognition Award was presented to Dorothy Lyles, Past-President and one of the organization's founding members. She currently works at the Carter G. Woodson Regional Library, Chicago Public Library System.

The District Library Round Table developed a slide show showing the benefits of and procedures for becoming a district library. The round table also sponsored several workshops including an insurance workshop covering buildings, public liability, officers and directors insurance, workman's compensation, and medical insurance; a computer workshop, and a financial planning workshop.

Intellectual Freedom. According to Betty J. Simpson, ILA Intellectual Freedom Chair, and Deborah Miller, Director, Governmental Services, three incidents merited attention in 1984:

(1) The action of the Peoria School Board with regard to the removal of three Judy Blume books from its library shelves; (2) public libraries and children's Christmas programming; and, (3) a motion to repeal Cook County's Child Pornography Ordinance.

In the fall the Peoria Board of Education was asked to reconsider a decision by its Faculty Review Committee to remove three Judy Blume books from the library shelves. The books were *Blubber, Then Again, Maybe I Won't*, and *Deenie*. The objection was to their strong language and graphic depictions. Letters of appeal were sent by the American Library Association, the American Civil Liberties Union, and other agencies and by parents in the community. Articulate testimony by residents in Peoria and a strong letter of support from Illinois Library Association's Valerie Wilford resulted in the retention of the books on the shelves with only minor restrictions, but still making them available to all school children.

Lincoln Public Library chose not to use the book *Little Drummer Boy* in its children's programming because of the book's religious connotations. Library board members were contacted regarding this book. The library board met, re-examined its policies, and held firm to the decision not to use the book.

The third incident occurred in December, and concerned a motion before a committee of the Cook County Board of Commissioners to reconsider its child pornography ordinance in light of a new State of Illinois law. The major differences between the two laws were that Illinois law provides for felony penalties while the county ordinance is merely a misdemeanor. The county ordinance does not have an affirmative defense for librarians as does the State law. The motion was defeated, leaving librarians in the same position they were in previously, presuming State law would prevail should an incident occur.

Deaths. Mildred V. Schulz who was the reference librarian for the Illinois State Historical library from 1964 to 1970 and was its head librarian from 1970 to 1976 when she retired died October 13.

ESTELLE M. BLACK

INDIANA

ILA/ILTA. "Your Indiana Library—See What's in it for You" challenged members of the Indiana Library Association (ILA) and Indiana Library Trustee Association (ILTA) in

Indiana Library Association (founded 1891)

Membership: 1,400 (ILA), 1,700 (ILTA); annual budget: $122,000.

President: Harold W. Boyce, 1120 E. 49th Street, Marion 46952 (March 1984-May 1985).

Vice-President/President-elect: Elizabeth Booth-Poor, Bartholomew County Public Library, 5th at Lafayette, Columbus 47201.

Executive Director: Joyce M. Martello, 310 N. Alabama, Suite A, Indianapolis 46204.

Annual meeting: March 8-10, 1984, Indianapolis.

Publications: Focus on Indiana Libraries (monthly); *Indiana Libraries* (quarterly).

Indiana State Library

C. Ray Ewick, Director
140 North Senate Avenue
Indianapolis 46204

School Library Media Supervisor

Phyllis Land Usher
State Department of Public Instruction
Indianapolis 46204

1984. Major events included a joint annual conference with AIME (Association for Indiana Media Educators), an administrative change to an association management firm for the executive offices, participation as *amici* in the Indianapolis anti-pornography ordinance lawsuit, and a number of individual library projects.

Burnison, Martello and Associates, Inc., assumed management of the associations in January, with Joyce M. Martello serving as Executive Director. Membership voted at the March annual conference to increase 1985 dues and approved establishment of discussion groups without division affiliation. November 30 marked the kick-off of the ILA/ILTA Endowment Fund, which will provide additional staff positions, scholarships and awards, and special lectures and seminars.

Former ILA/ILTA Executive Director Ann Moreau was retained by Burnison, Martello and Associates as legislative counsel for the 1985 session, which will see an attempt to secure adequate state funding for the library services authorities.

Legislation. A quiet 1984 "short session" of the Indiana General Assembly saw passage of corrective legislation for library board appointments, which clarified and revised a bill passed in 1983. Mary Elizabeth Pogue served as legislative counsel.

Conferences/District Meetings. A joint conference of the associations and AIME was held in Indianapolis in March and featured authors Peter Spier and Susan Beth Pfeffer, former Minnesota Governor Albert H. Quie, Sara Fine, Ann McGee-Cooper, Sharon K. Rogers, Betty Costa, Nancy Polette, and others. The three-day meeting also featured an organizational meeting for the state Friends of Indiana Libraries and sessions for trustees based on the ALTA WILL.

Seven regional district meetings in the fall included a variety of speakers, workshops, and additional sessions for trustees.

Conferences were held by the Children and Young People's Division, featuring Jack Prelutsky and Lillian Hoban; Small Libraries, with Bernard Vauvek; Medium Size Libraries; and the Reference Division.

The second annual Indiana Library Day held in January brought many librarians and trustees from throughout the state to Indianapolis to talk to legislators.

ILTA continued sessions based on the ALTA WILL topics of public awareness and funding at the annual conference and district meetings.

Networking. Indiana State Library completed a major revision of Indiana's Long Range Plan for Library Services, 1985-90; the biennium budget request for 1985-87 included a major increase for state and regional components of the Indiana Library and Information Services Network, the nine regional Area Library Services Authorities, and the statewide Indiana Cooperative Library Services Authority (INCOLSA). INCOLSA and two ALSAs celebrated completion of a decade of service in 1984.

The State Library provided LSCA support to INCOLSA for implementation in 1984-85 of two automated circulation clusters for 12 participating libraries in the Evansville and Central Indiana regions, and funds to South Bend Public Library for expansion of its system to include two additional libraries.

The Area Library Services Authorities completed the first year of a phased-in project to equip the regional cooperative units with microcomputers to process interlibrary loans and to support administrative tasks, providing a statewide automated link of the nine ALSA areas.

The State Library began conversion to an automated circulation system that includes circulation of materials of the Blind and Physically Handicapped Division, a regional library of the National Service for the Blind.

The Reference and Loan Division and Indiana Divisions provided specialized reference services to state government and the business community. The Indiana Data Center continued its program of training and information referral services in cooperation with regional affiliate data centers.

Continuing Education/CLENE. The Indiana Council for Approval of Providers (ICAP) approved a fundraising workshop, cosponsored by the Indiana State Library and ALA, as a continuing education offering. The CLIME plan was reviewed and updated by the continuing education providers to improve the dissemination of information on continuing education offerings.

Intellectual Freedom. Results of a survey conducted by the Intellectual Freedom Committee working with the Indiana State Library showed a 59 percent response from public libraries. Sixty-five percent formally adopted materials selection policies; 79 percent of those have patron complaint forms; and nearly 28 percent said they treat questionable or challenged materials differently from other materials. Fifty-eight titles were reported challenged.

The ILA/ILTA Joint Executive Board agreed to support a lawsuit in an *amicus curiae* brief against the Indianapolis antipornography ordinance. Challenged by the American Booksellers, Freedom to Read Foundation, and others, the ordinance would have restricted pornography on the basis that it violates women's civil rights. The ILA/ILTA Division of Women in Indiana Libraries joined with the Intellectual Freedom Committee in urging the associations to file the brief. Federal Judge Sarah Evans Barker ruled the measure unconstitutional, but city officials indicated that they would appeal the decision.

Public Relations. "Your Indiana Library—See What's in it for You" was the 1984 public relations campaign theme, and a statewide public relations program continued under an LSCA grant administered jointly by the ILA/ILTA and the Indiana State Library. Under direction of the public relations/publications director, posters, bookmarks, and publicity materials were distributed to all libraries upon request. Workshops featuring hands-on experience with newsletters were presented at annual conference and other meetings throughout the state.

A concentrated statewide publicity effort for Banned Books Week, in cooperation with the Intellectual Freedom Committee, brought excellent media response and focused public attention on the dangers of censorship.

Focus on Indiana Libraries, a joint monthly publication of ILA/ILTA and the State Library, changed from a magazine to newspaper format in January, resulting in a more timely publication with improved service to its readership. Also offered were discount advertising rates to library-affiliated groups and three special four-page inserts to the newspaper were published in 1984.

Public Libraries. Morrisson-Reeves Public Library (Richmond) observed Book Week with a communitywide "Turn Off TV" project that received national attention. Children's Librarian Sue Weller coordinated the cooperative effort between school and public librarians, which received strong community support.

Twelve public libraries in southern Indiana will participate in the ALA-sponsored "Let's Talk About It" reading discussion groups, under direction of coordinator Janna Kosinski.

Public libraries observing anniversaries in 1984 included: Muncie, 80; New Albany-Floyd County, 100; Lake County, 25; Garrett, 70; Batesville, 10; Jasper, 50.

Academic Libraries. Ball State University (Muncie) announced that it would phase out its master of library science degree program by the end of summer 1985. Reasons cited were cost-effectiveness and projected declines in graduate enrollments. Bethel College (Mishawaka) dedicated its new $1,400,000 library on March 23. It is named the Otis R. and Elizabeth A. Bowen Library in honor of the former governor and his late wife.

Awards. In addition to the established awards of outstanding librarian, trustee, and others, the associations, through the legislative committee, honored four Indiana General Assembly legislators as Legislators of the Year for their promotion and support of library legislation.

Muncie Public Library's project, "This Far by Faith: Black Hoosier Heritage," was named the best humanities project in the country by the National Endowment for the Humanities.

Appointments. Included among major library appointments during 1984 were John P. Knodelik, Head of Butler University's Irwin Library system; Martha Gardin Stratton, Coordinator of ALSA II; Bill Laramore, President of state Friends of Indiana Libraries; Ralph Simon, Head of Data Services Division, Indiana State Library; and Ronald G. Leach, Dean of library services at Indiana State University,

Vice-President/President-elect of Library Administration and Management Association.

Deaths. Roger Bryant Francis died May 1. He had been head of South Bend Public Library for 25 years, was a former librarian of the year, and had served as President of ILTA. Maude McMahan, Librarian for 34 years at Brownstown, died January 14. Lois Campbell, former Brownsburg Librarian, died June 6. Rebecca McKelvey, Bloomington, died in November.

BETH K. STEELE

IOWA

Iowa Library Association (founded 1890)

Membership: 1,679; *annual budget:* $67,817.

President: Richard Doyle, Stewart Memorial Library, Coe College, Cedar Rapids (January 1984–December 1984).

Vice-President/President-elect: Lois Siebersan, Sioux Center Public Library.

Executive Secretary: Naomi Stovall, 823 Insurance Exchange Building, Des Moines 50309.

Annual meeting: October 17–19, 1984, Des Moines.

Publication: CATALYST (bimonthly).

State Library Commission of Iowa

Claudya Muller, State Librarian
Historical Building, Des Moines 50319

School Library Media Supervisor

Betty Jo Buckingham
Department of Public Instruction
Des Moines 50319

Confidential library records laws were strengthened considerably in 1984 by a new law designed to prevent law enforcement authorities from "fishing expeditions" into library records. Beginning in 1984, such records can only be accessed by permission of the court when authorities show that a "particular person or organization" is suspected of a known crime and that a "rational connection" exists between the information released and the investigation of the case.

State Associations. The 1984 annual ILA conference produced a record attendance in Des Moines in October under the direction of ILA President Richard Doyle. A preconference on fundraising was conducted by Florence Green, Santa Monica, California. Arch Lustberg, Washington, D.C., conducted a communications workshop, and ALA President E. J. Josey spoke on cooperation among libraries. Other speakers were Maureen Pastine, Director, San Jose State University Library; Karen Harris, Professor of Library Science, University of New Orleans; Karen Van Westering, Vice-President of Doubleday and Company; J. Charles Park, Professor of Education, University of Wisconsin, Whitewater; Zoe Carpenter, Associate Librarian, Johns Hopkins University; Rebecca Whitaker, Information retrieval specialist, Indiana Cooperative Library Service Authority; and Kathleen Balcom, Director of Downer's Grove Public Library.

During the conference, three children's librarians, Robin Currie, Carol Elbert and Rene Lynch, were given a special recognition award for their successful *Rainbows and Ice Cream*, a nationally acclaimed publication sold through the ILA office. Shirley Clark from Jefferson was awarded a $200 check for her work with children in a community under 5,000 population. The Econo-Clad Book Company gave two $100 awards to Ames and Sioux Center for their summer reading programs. John Reinhard gave a $350 award to Dee Ann Miller, a student of library science at the University of Iowa. Baker & Taylor's Grass Roots Grant Award went to Kathryn Nelson, and Jeff Dick received the Iowa Library Trustees scholarship award. Two Iowa trustees, Charlotte Mohr from Scott County Library and Margaret Waechter from the Carnegie–Vierson Public Library in Pella, received outstanding trustees awards.

The ILA Chapter of ACRL Spring Conference was held at Grinnell College. Keynote speaker Sharon Rogers, Director of Public Services, Bowling Green State University Library, spoke on strategic planning in academic libraries.

The Iowa Workshop in Library Leadership (WILL) was held in Des Moines in March. Cosponsored by ILA, the State Library of Iowa, and the Iowa Regional Library System, it covered issues such as public awareness, funding, planning, policymaking, computerization, and advocacy. Speakers included Don Surratt, President of the American Library Trustee Association, Nancy Stiegemeyer, Editor of ALTA *Newsletter*, and Alice Ihrig, Director, Civic and Cultural Programs, Moraine Valley Community College, Palos Hills, Illinois.

Seven District Meetings were again presented around the state with programs on new computer technology, intellectual freedom, and preservation.

The Intellectual Freedom Committee was made aware of two attempts to remove books from shelves in school libraries. The Committee members provided materials and counsel to those who sought guidance, and in one case attended a hearing and spoke to the issue of free access to ideas.

Legislative Activities. The annual legislative day was held in February and featured an ILA display area in the state capitol rotunda and a surprise visit by Governor Terry Branstad. A reception at the Bohemian Club was attended by 87 legislators (about 60 percent of all Iowa legislators) and well over 200 librarians and library supporters from around the state.

Results of the 1984 state legislation program included:

(1) *Confidential records amendment:* limits access to library records by court order to investigations of particular persons committing a known crime and when a need for information is cogent and compelling. *Passed.*

(2) *Regional library formula change:* provides a new formula for allocation of funds among seven regional library systems. Passed by the Senate in 1983, passed by the House in 1984 with "hold harmless" amendment guaranteeing no region would lose funds due to change. *Passed.*

(3) *County library amendment:* provides for financing of county libraries and withdrawal of unincorporated areas from the library district pending a public hearing. *Passed.*

(4) Appropriations for the State Library and Regional Library Systems were approved at the Governor's recommendation for the biennium that resulted in an approximate 2 percent increase for the State Library and 15 percent increase for the Regional Systems.

State Library Activities. The State Library published and distributed *Iowa Libraries: A Time to Grow*. The document was the culmination of a major effort by the Iowa library community to identify the information needs of Iowans and to provide a plan to meet those needs during the next five years.

A major reorganization of the State Library Table of Organization was completed. Three offices with directors that report directly to the State Librarian were established to provide external programs, internal programs, and in-house staff services.

The Medical and Information collections were combined to provide more efficient use of manpower. The first phase of a remodeling project completely revamped the ground floor offices and facilities.

Seven professional positions were filled during 1984. Added to the staff were Dorothea Hiebing, Director of the Office of Library Development; John Montag, Director of the Office of Information Services; William Davis, LSCA Coordinator; Sandra Dixon, Continuing Education Program Planner; Sharon Seide, Medical Librarian; Helen Dagley, AV Librarian, and George Carlson, Reference/Documents Librarian.

The State Library sponsored or cosponsored several statewide workshops of note in 1984. They include the highly successful I-WILL Conference for library trustees; a preconference workshop to the Iowa Library Association Fall Conference titled "Raising Funds for Libraries: Paths to the Private Sector"; "Basic Grant Proposal Writing Workshop" conducted by Brooke Sheldon; and "Managing the Small Library" conducted by Don Sager.

A service added to the AV Department was provided by a telephone answering machine that makes it more convenient for libraries to book films.

Publishing activities of the State Library included the newly completed Union List of Serials, and a revival, after a 10-year hiatus, of the *Iowa Library Quarterly*.

Public Libraries. A bond issue passed in 1984 provides for an integrated automation system for the Public Library of Des Moines. The system will be operational in two years.

Des Moines Public Library sponsored a Literacy Awareness Day, with the highlight being a visit by Wally Amos, of Famous Amos Chocolate Chip Cookie fame. Amos is a strong supporter of libraries and a member of the Board of Directors of Friends of Libraries, USA. The Library received an award from the International Reading Association for its contribution to literacy.

School Libraries, Media Centers. The Iowa Educational Media Association, an affiliate of ALA's American Association of School Librarians, had 500 members and an operating budget of $26,000 during 1984. President for 1984–85 was Pat Meier, Armstrong Elementary School, Bettendorf, Iowa.

In 1983–84 Iowa public schools spent $3,496,526 for library books, about $7 per student. For all materials, supplies, and equipment schools spent $6,763,099 or $13.63 per student.

Approximately $5,444,239 was reported as spent for materials for student and teacher services from Area Education Agency Media Centers in the 1983–84 year, close to $11 per student.

The Iowa Department of Public Instruction published pamphlets on weeding media center collections, media center budgeting, a bill of rights for school library media centers, and a variety of bibliographies to assist media center personnel.

Academic Libraries, Special Libraries. The newly enlarged and remodeled Iowa State University main Library building was formally dedicated in June and renamed the W. Robert Parks and Ellen Sorge Parks Library in honor of the President of Iowa State and Mrs. Parks. President and Mrs. Parks have been long-term supporters of further Library development and growth at Iowa State. Parks was serving his 19th year as President.

Iowa State also inaugurated two new "state-of-the-art" library centers for media and microtext in 1984. Opened in January, the new ISU Parks Library Media Center has seating capacity of 136, providing individual and group listening/viewing. Center equipment includes 72 videocassette VHS phonographs and AM/FM. Listening rooms are equipped with large-screen television, overhead and opaque projectors, and stereo speakers. A computerized central control room provides complete switching capabilities. In October the ISU Library opened its new Microtext Center providing 38 reader stations for all microform formats, reader printers, and portable circulating fiche readers. The Parks Library collections include more than 1,500,000 microtexts and over 25,000 media items.

Iowa State is one of 10 research libraries in the U.S. to be chosen to conduct an assisted self-study and serve as a demonstration site for the Preservation Planning Program supported by the National Endowment for the Humanities and operated by the Association of Research Libraries Office of Management Studies. Preservation of research collections has become a major national priority, and these self-study/demonstration sites will help provide guidelines toward establishing preservation policies usable by all libraries.

The University of Iowa began construction of a new Law Library that will be occupied in the spring of 1986. The building will also house the College of Law.

In preparation for occupancy, the Law Library was completing the retrospective conversion and reclassification of the entire collection with the expectation of having an online catalog operable in 1986. The University of Iowa Library and the Law Library are cooperating in the selection and implementation of a totally integrated computerized library system that will encompass all libraries on campus when completed.

Northwestern College integrated its library, audiovisual, computer, and writing laboratory services into a single administrative unit, directed by Librarian Art Hielkema. The collections of this combined Learning Resource Center are searchable at the various locations of the unit or from home or departmental office microcomputers on a BRS system.

Luther College received a Museum Assistance Program grant to have a consultant examine the college art collection and recommend ways in which it could be better handled and maintained.

The annual meeting of the Midwest Chapter–Medical Library Association was held in Cedar Rapids. The theme was "the User Centered Library."

Building Programs. Renovation of the Burlington Public Library was aided during 1984 by a grant of $110,000 in LSCA Title II funds and matched by city funds generated by a special library tax levy. The 1898 building, which is on the National Register of Historic Places, is undergoing a three-year renovation program.

Des Moines Public Library dedicated the new North Side Library in December. The 10,000-square-foot building houses 30,000 volumes in its print and nonprint collections. Services include a microcomputer for public use.

Greene was the state's largest recipient in 1984 of a federal matching grant for a new library for the community. The library received $202,500 in federal funds, with total cost of the building project to be $405,000. The building was completed by July and dedication took place in August.

The public library in Sibley (population 3,051) passed a $342,000 bond issue for a building addition. Support for the project was generated by activities of Friends of the Library.

Networks, Interlibrary Cooperation. Chiropractic Library Consortium's first comprehensive *Union List of Serials*, edited by Public Services Librarian Alana Ferguson and Serials Librarian Dick Carr, was published by Palmer College in June. Subsequent annual editions were planned.

Chiropractic Library Consortium's first *Annual Statistics of Chiropractic College Libraries in the United States and Canada* is being compiled and edited by Dennis Peterson and Glenda Wiese of Palmer College Library.

The Illinois–Iowa Quad Cities Area Biomedical Consortium's *Union List of Serials*, 2d edition, was edited by Public Services Librarian Alana Ferguson and published by Palmer College in September 1984.

The Iowa State University Library was named coparticipant with the Iowa State Historical Department to direct the Iowa portion of the U.S. Newspaper Project under a grant from the National Endowment for the Humanities. All U.S. and Iowa newspapers will be cataloged and then entered with their locations and holdings into OCLC.

The Kinney-Lindstrom Foundation gave a grant to 73 public libraries in North Central Iowa and to the North Central Regional Library for computers. They will be available both for public and library use and will work together in a library computer network.

The computers will be linked to the North Central Regional Library in Mason City to provide access to the database of book holdings of the libraries in the region. It will be the first regional network on microcomputer within the state of Iowa.

Iowa private colleges entered into a new photocopy agreement with net charges resulting from photocopy activity between each pair of libraries being paid only once yearly.

The Northwest Regional Library completed input for the first edition of its COM Catalog in July. Microfiche will be distributed to all 100 libraries in the region. The first edition contains approximately 22,000 entries, accessible by author, title, and subject and with holdings information (library and call number) for each entry.

Professional Interests. The Workshop in Library Leadership (WILL) for public library trustees originally developed by ALTA and replicated in Des Moines last March by ILTA was made available to trustees of the Northeast Region in November. A series of workshops were held at three sites. The programs included sessions on Trustee Advocacy; Policymaking; Confidentiality and Copyright; and Finances and Budgeting. A total of 148 attended the three programs: 25 librarians; 105 trustees, and 18 others. Forty-six of the 81 libraries in the region were represented.

The University of Northern Iowa's Department of Library Science sponsored its Sixth Annual School Library Media Conference—Evolution or Revolution! A Taxonomy for Change. It included an opening presentation by David Loertscher.

The University of Iowa's School of Library and Information Science offered conferences on conducting library user surveys, renewed dedication to reference service, and sharing books for young people. Forums are provided by the School for library administrators and for children and young adult librarians. The Special Libraries student chapter brought a series of speakers to campus.

Awards. Peg Johnson, Sioux Center Public Library, received the Iowa Library Association's CYP-Econoclad award for an outstanding summer reading program in a small (under 15,000 population) library.

The Iowa Educational Media Association presented the following awards: William J. Rettko, Principal, Muscatine High School, was selected to receive the 1983–84 Outstanding Service Award. Kay Runge, Director, Scott County Library System, was chosen as the winner of the IEMA/SIRS Intellectual Freedom Award for 1983–84. The award carried a $500 grant for the recipient from Social Issues Research Series, Inc. (SIRS), with a $500 grant for the library of the recipient's choice. The Scott County Library System was named to receive the institutional award. Author Berthe De Clements was given the Iowa Children's Choice Award, 1983–84, for her book *Nothing's Fair in Fifth Grade*.

Appointments. John Budrew accepted the position of Director of the David D. Palmer Library, Palmer College of Chiropractic, in June.

Mary Anne Smith, Consultant with the Northeastern Region since January 1983, became Administrator in March.

CARL ORGREN

KANSAS

Legislative work continued during 1984 on funding for the state's resource sharing program, the Interlibrary Loan Development Plan. Annual funding would be $1,200,000 for a five-year period. These funds would be divided among the state's major public and academic libraries, with amounts also going to school, special, or private academic libraries that serve as net lenders within the state. The Plan received much newspaper coverage and support, and was endorsed by groups within the state.

State Association. Kansas Connections was the theme of the tri-conference of the Kansas Library Association, the Kansas Association of School Librarians, and the Kansas Association for Educational Communication and Technology in Topeka.

Major speakers for the tri-conference included James Gunn, Ben Bova, David Loertscher, Barbara Smucker, Joanna Stratton, Peggy

Kansas Library Association (founded 1900)

Membership: 800; *annual expenditures*: $20,000.

President: Louise Snyder, Kelsey Library, Sterling College, Sterling 67579

Vice-President/President-elect: Rachel Senner, Hesston U.S.D. 400, Hesston 67062

Annual meeting: October 10–12, 1984, Kansas City.

Publication: KLA Newsletter (three times a year).

Kansas State Library

Duane F. Johnson, State Librarian
Third Floor, Statehouse
Topeka 66612

School Library Media Supervisor

June Level
State Department of Education
Topeka 66612

Sullivan, and Charlene Joy Talbot. Popular topics included ethical standards and news reporting, adult continuing education, problem employees, time management, and action research.

The College and University Libraries Section of the Kansas Library Association met in Topeka. The keynote speaker was Sharon Rogers, President, KCRL. Contributed papers were presented by several members.

State Library Activities. The State Library in 1984 began publication of the *Kansas Library Automation Newsletter* (a bimonthly) to keep librarians informed on automation trends, new software and hardware developments, training and workshop opportunities, personnel profiles, and research studies.

Through State Library efforts, libraries in Kansas may now take advantage of KANS-A-N authorization cards for making long-distance, business-related phone calls. KANS-A-N is a leased, private-line, long-distance telephone system for making both intra- and interstate calls, 24 hours a day. It can provide up to 45 percent savings in making calls and over 50 libraries were participants.

The Library in 1984 made available the *State Documents of Kansas Catalog*, a comprehensive list of Kansas government publications. It includes all recent documents received by the State Library.

The Library co-hosted a Kansas Automated Library Network Conference in August. More than 60 librarians, library automation experts, and vendors gathered to discuss the future of statewide cooperation in the area of automated networking. The State Library will coordinate efforts by library constituent groups to seek new state funding for this area of library service.

Building Programs. The Morton County Library, Elkhart, was completed in July. Voters in Leavenworth passed a bond issue for a new library building in December. The five construction programs partially funded by LSCA Title II allocations during 1983 were still under construction by year's end.

Networks, Interlibrary Cooperation. The Kansas Library Network Board worked during the year to make civic and educational groups and the Kansas library community aware of the benefits of the Interlibrary Loan Development Plan. Task forces were established to handle interlibrary loan communications, delivery systems and procedures, and to review opportunities to enhance the effectiveness of the Kansas Information Circuit. The report of the Continuing Education Task Force was reviewed and approved. The State Library was assigned the job of implementing the report. The Board promoted use of the Kansas library card. The possible production of a state union list of serials was being evaluated. The Board published *Kansas Newspapers; A Directory of Newspaper Collections in Kansas*. Jasper Schad, Wichita State University, was reelected to chair the Board for 1985. Jane Hatch, Southwest Kansas Library System Director, continued as the Board's Vice-Chair (term ends September 1985).

Professional Interests. The Friends of Kansas Libraries held its second statewide conference in Hutchinson, April 27–28. Five trustees were elected for the period May, 1 1984, to April 30, 1986. State Librarian Duane Johnson discussed the dynamics of legislation affecting libraries. Programs and discussions dealt with the value of talking books, starting Friends groups, funding and budgeting for nonprofits, volunteers, media relations, and Library/Board/Friends relationships. The Friends continued their support of library legislation during the 1984 session.

Awards. *A Light in the Attic* by Shel Silverstein was named the winner of the 32d annual William Allen White Children's Book Award presented by Emporia State University. The Kansas Federation of Women's Clubs (KFWC) presented their first annual library service awards to recognize work done by volunteer groups and individuals on behalf of Kansas libraries. One category of nominations has been designated for those who are not members of KFWC.

Appointments. Bruce Bumbalough was appointed System Director, Northwest Kansas Library System. He went to NWKL from White County Public Library, in Searcy, Arkansas.

Henry R. Stewart was appointed Director of Library Services and University Librarian at Emporia State University. He was Associate Dean for Management and Public Services at the Old Dominion College Library in Norfolk, Virginia.

Sandra Brandt was appointed Interlibrary Loan Librarian at the University of Kansas. She was formerly Reference Librarian and Manager of Interlibrary Loan Services at the University of Missouri–St. Louis.

Livia Perlaky was appointed Head of the Fine Arts Department, Topeka Public Library. She was formerly Head of Acquisitions for the same library.

Deaths. Edna H. Buschow died January 12. Edna Buschow's involvement with libraries spanned many years and at the time of her death she was a member of the State Library Advisory Commission and Board Chairman of the Public Library in Valley Center. The new Public Library was named in her honor.

Mary D. Murphy died in March. She was head of Lawrence Public Library's Reference Department and had long been involved with interlibrary loan activities.

Mary Jane Neff, Head of Serials Division and Associate Professor, William Allen White Library, Emporia State University, died July 21. She was a 20-year employee of E.S.U. and had degrees from the same institution.

Charles Joyce, Jr., Director of the Kansas City Public Library, died October 2. He was a graduate of Tufts University and Simmons College, Boston.

TOM MUTH

KENTUCKY

Kentucky Library Association (founded 1907)

Membership: 1,160; *annual expenditures*: $57,092.

President: Rebekah H. Heath, Associate Librarian, Jefferson Community College, Louisville 40502 (October 1984–October 1985).

Vice-President/President-elect: Jennie Boyarski, Librarian, Paducah Community College, Paducah 42002.

Secretary: Patty Grider, Hart County Public Library, Munfordville 42765.

Executive Secretary: Thomas Sutherland, Paducah Public Library, 555 Washington, Paducah 42001.

Annual meeting: October 10–12, 1984, Louisville.

Publication: Kentucky Libraries (quarterly)

Department of Library and Archives

James A. Nelson, State Librarian and Commissioner of the Department for Libraries and Archives
Box 537
Frankfort 40602

Program Consultant for School Media Services

Judy Cooper
State Department of Education
1830 Capital Plaza Tower
Frankfort 40601

Working within the confines of minimal to no funding, Kentucky librarians continued to strive for better and more effective services and collections throughout 1984. Through the efforts of the school library organization an allotment of $5 per pupil was set by the State Department of Education for library funding.

During the year the Kentucky Library Association Board went on record recommending amendments to the Cable Telecommunications Act of 1983 and urged the Federal Highway Administration to adopt the library symbol as a recognized general information sign. Additional actions by the Board included (1) the establishment of an annual Kentucky Libraries Award for an outstanding article written for the Association's journal, (2) the recognition of the Interlibrary Loan Round Table, and (3) the grant of a year's subscription to the Association's publications to conference exhibitors so that they would be better informed of the Association's activities.

Since the State Department of Education and the State Department of Libraries and Archives are already serving as ex-officio members on the Association's Board, members felt that the Kentucky Library Association could be a more effective agency of promoting library services by adding representation from the Friends of Libraries or Library Trustees membership. Consequently, the President of one of these groups, alternating each year, will attend meetings as an ex-officio member.

State Association. Libraries Offer Lifelong Living was the theme of the Association's annual conference in Louisville in October. Registration totaled 650 as librarians from all areas of the state came together to view 52 exhibits and participate in the varied programs of the meeting. Having declared 1985 as the year of "Read to a Child," the kick-off took place at the meeting's general session. Preconference activities focused on formatting machine readable data files, fitness for librarians, making the library a more human place, and working together in raising funds. At the other sessions the organization's sections sponsored programs on rural librarianship, conducting library research, electronic publishing, and reading programs for children. Emphasis was also given to literature for children and young people with hints on publishing, observations on reading and reviews of picture books, juvenile fiction, and young adult books. Round table discussions covered the activities and publications of the Bureau of Labor Statistics, teaching the use of periodicals, microcomputer program applications, and library service for genealogists. Although the new Children and Young Adult Services Section meets only during the annual convention, the 136 members were as active as those of the other sections—Academic, Public School Media, Special—in contributing to the successful programming of the Association's meeting.

State Library Activities. In order to provide access to another segment of the state, federal funding was made available in 1984 to Bracken County for the establishment of a public library program. A $143,000 grant from the National Endowment for the Humanities for "Reflection of the Past" made possible the initiation of a two-year public library program providing an awareness of archival resources and their educational value. However, lack of funding forced the Kentucky Coalition for Literacy, the state's coordinating agency, to close, resulting in the handling of the coalition's work by the Departments of Libraries and Education. A Steering Committee for a Kentucky Public Library Needs and State Services Study was established in early 1984. This Committee, which includes public library trustees and librarians, will draft the proposal for an independent study to determine the needs for statewide public library services.

Public Libraries. The Public Library Section held its spring meeting in Owensboro on April 4-6 with the theme "Real Libraries for Real People." The program concentrated on practical problems such as hiring, firing, and evaluating staff, innovative approaches to overdues, recruiting, and managing volunteers, bookmobiles and other extension services, problem patrons, and how to sell your library to the entire community.

The Outstanding Public Library Service Award was presented to Veronica Hill of the Marion County Public Library, and the Outstanding Board of Trustees Award was given to the Taylor County Public Library Board of Trustees. Public Library Section Scholarships were awarded to Alice Clay, Kathy Cox, and Sharon Haines.

Concurrently with the Public Library Section meeting, the Kentucky Library Trustees conducted a workshop on the library image, the selection and orientation of trustees, and the responsibilities of library trustees. The Friends of Kentucky Libraries awarded scholarships to Alice Casey, Thelma Creech, Sheryl Cross, and Mary Taylor.

School Libraries, Media Centers. Over 300 members of the Kentucky School Media Association attended their fall workshop at the Drawbridge Inn in Fort Mitchell in August. Concentrating on the theme "Library Skills Are Lifetime Skills," the school librarians explored new methods and activities that promote library usage. In the keynote speech, Jerry Mallett spoke on the avenue of humor being an effective method of motivating a child to read. Jean Ross of Benton was recognized as the Outstanding School Media Librarian. Thomas D. Clarke, Kentucky historian, author, and library supporter, received the Jesse Stuart Media Award.

Academic Libraries. Sixty-four academic librarians registered for their annual spring meeting at Bowling Green in April. The theme of the conference stressed "Personal/Personnel Skills." Topics discussed during the workshop sessions included group dynamics, meeting behavior, interviewing, and intergroup relations.

Special Libraries. With the theme of "Networking: Angles, Avenues, Options," 34 persons registered in March for a two-day spring conference in Berea. Those in attendance heard remarks on such topics as the role of special librarians in providing information, multiple library networks, multi-source budgeting, and library volunteers in medical centers. At the fall meeting the Special Librarian of the Year Award was given to Virginia Neel, Science Librarian at Western Kentucky University.

Building Programs. The Louisville Free Public Library in 1984 received $950,000 for the construction of four new branch libraries.

Networks. The Network Development Committee of the State Advisory Council on Libraries in October reported on its recommendations for the organization structure of a Kentucky Library Network. The resultant action was the presentation of draft articles for the formation of a nonprofit corporation. At the meeting a progress report was made on the merger of Kentucky databases and the Kentucky Union List of Serials.

Intellectual Freedom. The June issue of *Kentucky Libraries* was prepared by the Intellectual Freedom Committee and entitled "Kentucky Library Association—Intellectual Freedom Manual." Divided into two parts—(1) preparation for the censor's pressure and (2) intellectual freedom issues that oppose censorship—the work includes bibliographical sources (available from the Executive Director of the Kentucky Library Association for $3).

Awards. Martha Alexander received the second Annual Bluegrass Award for *Move Over, Twerp* in the reading incentive program for fun.

The 1983 Summer Reading Program, "Dare to Read with Izar from the Planet Daer," of the Louisville Free Public Library received a "Louie" award during the city's annual creative competition event. Presented by the Advertising Club of Louisville, this award recognized the creative professional achievement of the library.

Faye Belcher of Morehead State University was awarded $750 under the American Library Association's 1984 Carnegie-Whitney Fund. She will use the funds to complete a bibliography on coal and coal related subjects. Recipient of the 1984 Miriam Dudley Bibliographic Instruction of the Year Award was Thomas G. Kirk, Library Director at Berea College. Also recognized at the American Library Association's annual conference in June were Pyddney Jones and Sarah Kelly, who received the John Cotton Dana Public Relations Award for outstanding achievement in promoting the use of public libraries. Under the theme of "Reading Time Trek with Wizlet," the summer reading program was promoted in 102 public libraries in Kentucky.

Appointments and Retirements. William Ptacek, former Director of the Idaho Free Public Library System, in 1984 was named Director of the Louisville Free Public Library, replacing Ronald Kozlowski.

Coy Harmon, formerly of the staff of the University of Oklahoma Libraries, became Dean of Libraries at Murray State University. He succeeded Edwin C. Strohecker, former President of the Kentucky Library Association, who retired.

Vera Guthrie, Director of the library science program, retired from the Western Kentucky University faculty. Active in regional and national organizations, she was president of the Kentucky Library Association, 1968-69.

Deaths. Dan M. King, retired Head Librarian of Kentucky Wesleyan College, died in Owensboro. A Past President of the Kentucky Library Association, he was active on the state and national level in promoting academic libraries and library education. After his retirement, a scholarship for Kentucky Wesleyan College students showing promise of becoming a librarian had been established in King's name.

EDWIN C. STROHECKER

LOUISIANA

The taxpayer's "revolt" reported on the national level caught up with Louisiana library tax propositions in 1984. Three library tax propositions in September and in November were defeated. Several common factors were thought to have contributed to the failures including extremely large voter turn-out, numerous unpopular and controversial taxes on the ballot, and a decision by the library boards to try a low-key approach to carry the election. None of the libraries will close since there was adequate lead time to have another election before the library tax expires.

State Association. The 58th Annual Louisiana Library Association Conference held in Baton Rouge in March broke an all-time record for attendance—1,040. Theme was "1984: The Future Is Now."

Some 320 librarians, trustees, and patrons convened in Baton Rouge April 17 for LLA Legislation Day to learn more about the legislative process and to honor the legislators. About 75 lawmakers attended portions of the day's activities. John W. Dean III, former aide to President Nixon and best-selling author, was the featured speaker for the luncheon.

Louisiana Library Association (founded 1909)

Membership: 1,535; *annual budget:* $67,200.

President: Joy Lowe, P.O. Box 3061, Tech Station, Ruston 71272 (July 1984–June 1985).

Vice-President/President-elect: Anthony Benoit, 4265 Hyacinth Avenue, Baton Rouge 70808.

Secretary: Gloria Donatto, 4824 Odin Street, New Orleans 70126.

Executive Director: (Mrs.) Chris Thomas, P.O. Box 131, Baton Rouge 70821.

Annual meeting: March 14–16, 1984, Baton Rouge.

Publication: LLA Bulletin (quarterly).

Louisiana State Library

Thomas F. Jaques, State Librarian
P.O. Box 131
Baton Rouge 70821

State School Library Media Supervisor

James S. Cookston
State Department of Education
Baton Rouge 70804

The organizational meeting for Louisiana's version of the American Library Trustee Association's Workshop in Library Leadership (ALTA WILL) took place in May. Partially funded by the State Library and the Trustee Section of the Louisiana Library Association, the workshop was set for 1985.

The Continuing Education Committee of LLA and the Louisiana State Library teamed up to provide funds and direction to a series of workshops intended for employees of libraries in Louisiana who have no formal library science education. Planning took place during 1984 with the workshops to begin in 1985.

State Library. "Catfiche," the Louisiana State Library's holdings on 377 microfiche, was made available to public, academic, special, and institutional libraries to speed up interlibrary loan processes in the state. The microfiche catalog contains 206,000 titles, which represents the major holdings of films, recordings, Louisiana materials, state and federal documents, and fiction/nonfiction monographs. SOLINET created the COM catalog. Sixteen libraries tested the product before general distribution was made.

The first statewide summer reading program for Louisiana was produced by the State Library in 1984. With permission of the Louisiana World Exposition, Seymore D. Fair, the Fair mascot, was used in connection with the theme "Reading and All That Jazz." Sixty-two of 64 public libraries participated along with the State Library's Section for the Blind and Physically Handicapped, eight state institutions, and the base library at Fort Polk, Louisiana. Some 342,708 pieces of material were distributed over the state. Over 61,000 children registered and 31,400 earned a certificate of completion. Statistics indicate that 147,250 children were involved in some type of library programming during the summer.

The State Library received two grants from the Louisiana Committee for the Humanities. The first grant for $17,000 was used to create a traveling photographic exhibit of the life and times of Huey Long. Designed to travel to all 64 parishes of the state (mostly in public libraries), the exhibit was to be part of a major State Library program planned for 1985 to coincide with the 50th anniversary of Long's assassination. A grant of $29,360 was given to further develop reading/discussion programs for Louisiana public libraries. The "Readings in American Themes" program focused on basic American themes found in literature, especially short stories, with local university professors leading the informal public programs.

Public Libraries. Financial problems within Louisiana government affected the State Aid to Public Libraries grant program. The amount granted was $1,394,553, a reduction of $77,527 from what had been anticipated, for a per-capita amount of $.319.

Lafourche Parish Library completed a five-year plan for library service. The plan includes a capitol improvement project, increase and upgrading of staff positions, an outreach program, studies of service needed, and a public relations program.

Masterpuppet Theatre, a series of 13 puppet shows provided by the Lafayette Public Library Staff for Acadiana Open Channel, won an award for best pre-planning for a series produced in the studio. Including Masterpuppet Theatre, the library has 46 videotaped programs that are broadcast on a rotating basis twice weekly over the cable television channel.

The LaSalle Parish Library and the LaSalle Parish Art Association cosponsored its second annual Hobby and Craft Show. Emphasis in 1984 was on country-style crafts. Several hundred people attended.

Academic and Special Libraries. The College of Education and the Friends of the Earl K. Long Library at the University of New Orleans hosted the opening of an important collection of new books in 1984. Children's and young adult's books solicited from the publishers will reflect the two most recent years of publication. The collection will afford school librarians, reading specialists, or anyone involved in children's services the opportunity to examine firsthand new publications and to select personally those titles which best fit individual programs.

The Louisiana Chapter of the Association of College and Research Libraries sponsored a 1984 regional meeting in Lafayette on the topic "Librarians/Faculty: Working Toward Common Goals in the University Community Together."

School Libraries, Media Centers. An organized effort was made to assist school librarians in every parish to form local library associations. A committee of the Louisiana Association of School Librarians received requests during 1984 from 16 parishes to aid in forming local library organizations or bi-parish library organizations.

A joint appeal from the Louisiana Association of School Libraries and the Louisiana Association for Educational Communications and Technology was made to the state's Board of Elementary and Secondary Education to encourage funding for school library materials.

Building Programs. Four parish libraries received Library Services and Construction Act Title II grants to construct new or enlarge facilities. The Allen Parish Library planned a 5,000-square-foot headquarters facility in Oberlin, while Calcasieu Parish will construct a 10,000-square-foot section of a projected 64,000-square-foot main/headquarters facility in Lake Charles. DeSoto Parish was to construct a 13,676-square-foot facility in Mansfield. St. John the Baptist was to add 7,500 square feet to its LaPlace headquarters library.

Two new branch libraries were dedicated. A 6,000-square-foot Delmont Gardens Branch of East Baton Rouge Parish Library was opened in July. In Rapides Parish, the Carl N. Gunther Branch, a 3,600-square-foot building, was dedicated in August.

One new academic library was contructed and two were expanded. At Southern University–Baton Rouge campus, a 133,000-square-foot multimillion dollar facility named the John B. Cade Library was opened. The Troy H. Middleton Library, Loiusiana State University–Baton Rouge, added a third and fourth floor (125,000 square feet) at a cost of $7,900,000. Likewise, the Earl K. Long Library, University of New Orleans, had a third and fourth floor added to it increasing the library's total square footage to 254,000 at a cost of $11,000,000.

Professional Interest. The School of Library and Information Science, Louisiana State University, revised its curriculum and reduced the total number of hours required for graduation to 37. The number of required courses was reduced from seven to four. The School and the Department of Computer Science in 1984 began a joint degree program to meet the growing demand for information professionals trained in library science and computer science. Students enrolling in the program are able to earn two master's degrees.

Awards. Awards were presented during the 1984 Louisiana Library Association annual conference to individuals and libraries. The Essae M. Culver Distinguished Service Award was presented posthumously to Marcia W. Perkins, public library consultant, Louisiana State Library. The Modisette Awards, given in recognition and encouragement of high standards in library service, were presented to Jackson Parish Library, Jonesboro; Istrouma Middle Magnet School, Baton Rouge; and Captain Shreve High School, Shreveport.

The Educator's Award presented by the Louisiana Association of School Librarians went to Brother Ivy LeBlanc, S.C., Principal of Brother Martin High School, for his dedication and support of the library's activities. The Subject Specialist Section presented the Lucy B. Foote Award to Harriet Callahan, Head of the Louisiana Section of the Louisiana State Library, for her substantial, long-term contributions to the library profession.

State Librarian Thomas F. Jaques was awarded the Mid-Career Award by the New Members Round Table for the dedication, energy, and enthusiasm with which he directs the State Library. Presented by the Louisiana Association of School Librarians, the Sue Hefley Award winner was Tomi dePaola. His book *Big Anthony and the Magic Ring* was selected by a vote of the children of the state as their favorite.

LLA Scholarship winner was Kenneth Paul Neal of Walker, Louisiana. Combining a library degree with a master's degree in art history, Neal planned to pursue a career as an art librarian or art archivist. The Louisiana Literary Award went to Robert Bush for his book *Grace King: A Southern Destiny*, a biography of a noted New Orleans writer.

Charles D. Patterson, Professor of Library Science at Louisiana State University, received the H. M. "Hub" Cotton Foundation

Faculty Excellence Award established to honor and recognize excellence in teaching, research, administration, or public service.

McNeese State University (Lake Charles) Documents Librarian R. Brantly Cagle, Jr., received the Governor's Award at the Governor's Conference for Disabled Persons in Baton Rouge. Cagle was recognized for outstanding personal achievement and service to his community and state.

The Howard–Tilton Library of Tulane University, New Orleans, was recipient of a $300,000 gift from Mr. and Mrs. Paul Selley to be used for a reading/display area for social science journals and shelving.

Appointments. Major personnel changes took place in 1984 in public libraries. Marion K. Bryant was appointed Librarian of the East Carroll Parish Library, while Melissa Crampton, a recent graduate of the University of Southern Mississippi Library School became Librarian in West Carroll Parish. Alloyd P. Lambert, Jr., assumed the position of Director of the St. James Parish Library upon the retirement of Maurin C. Donaldson.

Steven L. Rogge was appointed Rapides Parish Library Director. He had worked in Iowa before going to Alexandria. Elizabeth Rountree was appointed director of the St. Tammany Parish Library. She was formerly Assistant City Librarian of the New Orleans Public Library. Ronald C. Tumey, former Director of the Rapides Parish Library, was named Librarian of the St. Mary Parish Library.

Sharon Anne Hogan became Director of Libraries at the Baton Rouge campus of Louisiana State University. She had served as Acting Director at the Temple University Libraries in Philadelphia. She replaced George J. Guidry, Jr., who retired after 37 years of library service. Kathleen M. Heim was named Dean of the Louisiana State University School of Library and Information Science. She came to LSU from the faculty of the Illinois Graduate School of Library and Information Science in Urbana–Champaign. Elfreda A. Chatman was appointed to the School of Library and Information Science faculty as assistant professor.

Christine Burns Campbell was named Librarian of the Louisiana Training Institute in Bridge City. She had previously taught in several Louisiana parishes.

Deaths. Retired Director of the Trail Blazer Library System, Monroe, Drucilla E. Motley, died February 28. Bess Vaughn, retired Lincoln Parish Librarian, died in Ruston on March 15. Former Arts Librarian and Archivist at Louisiana Tech University, Ruston, Nowlan Nichols, died March 21.

Ruth Elizabeth Baird, retired Librarian with the Webster Parish Library, Minden, died May 17 in Carrolton, Texas. Edith Rogers Abbott died June 8 in Garmisch, West Germany. She had retired as Librarian of Our Lady of the Lake Regional Medical Center. Norris K. McClellan, retired Louisiana State University Professor of Library Science, died September 10 in Baton Rouge.

Margaret W. Walsworth died October 4, in Lafayette. She served as Administrative Librarian for Vermilion Parish Library until her retirement. Clarissa Hall Schindler, Audiovisual Librarian for Jefferson Parish Library, died October 7. Tillie Schenker, retired East Baton Rouge Parish Library Director, died October 9.

BEN BRADY

MAINE

Maine Library Association (founded 1893)

Membership: 692; *annual budget:* $25,335.

President: Glenna Nowell, Gardiner Public Library, Gardiner (May 1984–May 1985).

Vice-President: Edna Mae Bayliss, Maranacook Community School, Readfield.

Executive Secretary: Patricia Smith, Maine Municipal Association, Community Drive, Augusta 04330.

Annual meeting: May 19–21, 1984, Orono.

Publications: Downeast Libraries (quarterly); *Maine Memo* (6-10 times per year).

Maine State Library

J. Gary Nichols, State Librarian
State House Station 64
Augusta, Maine 04333

School Library Media Supervisor

Walter Taranko
Maine State Library
State House Station 64
Augusta 04333

Automation. A statewide automation study began in 1984 with formation of the Maine Statewide Automation Committee. After determining that three tasks were required of a consultant, the committee chose Susan Baerg Epstein, Ltd., to perform the study.

Epstein conducted a two-day workshop intended to acquaint attendees with the state-of-the-art, to solicit information about their automation needs, and to gather their recommendations. A second responsibility was to draft a report on the current status of automation in the state. The final report was to address various scenarios for automated library networking in Maine including an integrated statewide network, regionalization, automation of the Maine State Library, creation of a union catalog, and development of automation on a smaller scale. The final written report was expected by March, 1985.

School Library Service. At their joint annual conference in May, the Maine Library Association and the Maine Educational Media Association drafted coordinated resolutions in response to the Governor's Commission on the Status of Education in Maine. The resolutions affirmed the role of libraries in education and life-long learning. MLA's resolution called for increased per capita support to public libraries. MEMA's resolution recommended a professional library/media specialist for every 400 students within a school district, adoption of guidelines with standards for school library/media centers, incentive and support projects available to rural and isolated areas, and expansion of the cataloging services of the State Library to include schools.

The final report of the Governor's Commission was revised to include some reference to the importance of libraries and adequate educational resources. During a special session devoted to education, the State Legislature passed the "Education Act of 1984." As a result of this act, standards for libraries are included in the review process for school approval. The act also calls for instruction in library skills for all students, although no specifics were provided as to how, when or by whom.

State Association. The Maine Library Association and the Maine Educational Media Association continued the tradition of a joint annual conference at the University of Maine in Orono. The theme for the May meeting was, "Online with the World."

MLA began a new year in June under President Glenna Nowell with the formation of three ad-hoc committees, public relations, ways and means, and library standards. The MLA Executive Council voted to reduce the cost of producing the "Monthly Memo" by publishing it less often. The renamed, "Maine Memo," saw a change of editors as Laura Juraska of Bates College succeeded Aaron Weissman.

State Library Activities. The Maine State Library large print book service received a major boost in support with the passage of legislation providing additional funding for staff and collection. The G. K. Hall Company commended the successful lobbying effort by the State Library during the ALA Annual Conference in Dallas.

State library services which are growing include the Books-by-Mail service which saw a 35 percent increase in 1984. In addition 50,000 card kits were produced for the 85 libraries participating in the catalog card service. The common borrower's card program is now honored by over 80 public, school and postsecondary school libraries.

A library computer newsletter was begun by Karl Beiser, Microcomputer Specialist for the State Library. A directory of small computer users in the state was compiled and flyers are available on various topics of interest to librarians considering purchase of a small computer.

The Information Exchange moved from the Department of Education to the State Library. The Exchange offers free computerized search services to educators and librarians. The Exchange also maintains an electronic file, the Maine Resource Bank, which contains names of human, program, and educational resources in Maine. The program was previously funded by federal monies and is now seeking support from the state legislature.

Public Libraries. The 1984 Maine Storytelling Festival was held in two locations for the first time through support of the Maine Humanities Council. The all-day programs, held in Portland and Bangor, included workshops and lectures with performances by Ashley Bryan and The Folktellers, Barbara Freeman and Connie Regan-Blake.

Portland Public Library expanded its administrative staff to include a Director of Development and Public Affairs. The Trustees sought support from the private sector to supplement funds from state, county and local government sources.

South Portland Public Library has installed a minicomputer integrated library system from Dynix.

School Libraries, Media Centers. The Maine Educational Media Association has developed "Library Skills Curriculum Ideas" under the direction of Julie Tallman. The K-12 curriculum was designed to be flexible and provides local school districts with suggestions for starting or refining their own programs.

Joining 1985 MEMA President Marcia

McGee, Sumner Memorial High School, are newly elected officers, Andrew Abbott, College of Education, University of Maine at Orono, President-elect; and Pat Weeks, Charles Shaw Junior High School, Gorham, Secretary.

Academic Libraries, Special Libraries. Portland hosted the North Atlantic Health Science Librarians' conference in October. The keynote address by Estelle Brodman introduced the conference theme, "Roll Call: defining the role of the Health Sciences librarian in these changing times."

Bates College Library received as a gift the library of the late Rabbi David Berent. The collection numbers over 3,000 English and 500 Hebrew titles. Bates celebrated its centennial as a Government Printing Office Depository, as did Bowdoin College Library and Portland Public Library.

Building Programs. At least 30 libraries in the State have expressed plans to build or renovate. Merrill Memorial Library in Yarmouth and Thomas Memorial Library in Cape Elizabeth had major expansion projects underway.

Networks, Interlibrary Cooperation. In September, the Maine Computer Consortium began helping Maine educators with software decisions, educational computing information and training. The Consortium, housed in Auburn, has an extensive software library and is gathering resource material dealing with planning, developing, implementing, and evaluating computer education programs.

School and public libraries in Biddeford, Saco and Sanford, produced a union list of serials. These same libraries began an interlibrary loan system in which a volunteer picks up a request and searches for the item at subsequent libraries on the route. Two trips to all libraries are made per week with mileage costs reimbursed by the participating libraries.

Intellectual Freedom. In September, the Maine Supreme Court heard oral arguments over the validity of the Portland obscenity ordinance originally enacted by a close referendum vote in November of 1982. In September, 1983, the District Court ruled that the ordinance was invalid due to a procedural technicality although constitutional standards were met. In February, 1984, a Superior Court decision reversed both parts of the decision by the District Court. There is no indication of when the Supreme Court will issue its ruling.

Continuing Education. Maine Library Association's Standing Committee on Continuing Education (SACCE) selected Clarion University's Library School to provide graduate library courses in Maine. SACCE offered library skills courses in book and periodical selection, audiovisual materials and equipment, and computers in libraries, at locations throughout the state.

Awards. Dean Lyons of the Carrabec School District, North Anson, is one of four children's librarians nationally to have won the first Putnam Publishing Group Awards. The grant assisted the winners in attending their first ALA annual conference.

Shirley Helfrich, Southern Maine Library District Consultant, was named School Library Media Specialist of the Year for 1984 by the Maine Educational Media Association. She was recognized for fostering cooperation between school and public libraries.

The Southern Maine Library District presented its first "Certificate of Appreciation" to Mary Hatch who has worked as a volunteer in the District office for more than five years.

Connie Hindman of Bethel was selected as a "1984 Jefferson Award" winner by television station WCSH in Portland. She volunteered over 2,080 hours in 1983 to operate a nonprofit recording library and tape media loan service for the blind.

Appointments. Peggy Stewart has been appointed Central Maine Library District Consultant at the Maine State Library. Benita Davis, Special Services Coordinator, Maine State Library, was elected Vice President/President-elect of the New England Library Association.

Richard C. Holmes was appointed Director of Library, Media and Technology Services at the University of Maine at Farmington. The University of New England named Andrew J. Golub Library Director. Joining the Lewiston Public Library were Richard Speer as Director and Paula Smus as Children's Librarian.

Joan Staats retired after 35 years with the Jackson Laboratory Library. In appreciation of her achievements in the field of mouse genetics, the institution named the library in her honor. Judy Monroe has retired from Waterville High School after more than 25 years of service. Co-author of, *Peoplework*, with Robert LeLieuvre (ALA, 1979), Monroe will continue her writing career. Jan Pierce resigned from Baxter Memorial Library in Gorham to take a marketing position with the L. L. Bean company.

NANCY CROWELL

MARYLAND

Maryland Library Association (founded 1932)

Membership: 900; *annual budget:* $25,000.

President: Kenna Forsyth, Baltimore County Public Library (June 1984–June 1985).

Vice-President/President-elect: Claudia Sumler, Cooperating Libraries of Central Maryland.

Executive Secretary: Robert Greenfield.

Annual Meeting: May 17–18, 1984, Ocean City, Maryland.

Publication: CRAB (bimonthly).

Maryland State Department of Education

Nettie B. Taylor
Assistant State Superintendent
 for Libraries
Baltimore

School Library Media Supervisor

Paula Montgomery
School Library Media Service, Branch Chief
Maryland Department of Education
Baltimore 21201

Reference Information Survey. The State Department of Education conducted an unobtrusive measure survey of the reference and information performance of Maryland Public Libraries. Forty questions were asked by research staff members by telephone and in person in each participating library branch. The results of the survey showed that on a statewide basis only five percent of the questions were answered with inaccurate information. On the other hand, only 38 percent were answered fully and completely including the source of the information. The results of this survey were distributed to each participating system and have been used for an intensive staff training program. The survey will be repeated.

Planning. Maryland Public Libraries continued their extensive efforts in developing long-range plans. By the end of 1984, 15 of the 24 public library systems had long range plans in place or were currently developing them.

Networking. During 1984, plans were developed to operate the Maryland Union Database—MICROCAT—online. This new system, know as MILNET, includes online locations in 12 of the largest public and academic libraries. Plans were being developed to extend the system to other public, academic, and special libraries and to school library media centers.

Statewide Plan. A statewide planning committee was appointed by the Assistant State Superintendent for Libraries, Nettie B. Taylor, to begin the process of developing *The Maryland Plan for Libraries 1986–1991*. The planning committee was divided into four subgroups, each assigned to develop a specific area—public libraries, school library media centers, academic libraries, and statewide networking.

School Libraries. The School Library Media Branch of the Department of Education developed the Maryland Instructional Resource Network, which includes the reviews of instructional materials in an online database. All items included in the database have been used in instruction by the Maryland school system. A task force on school library media programs was appointed by the State Superintendent of Schools, and it developed a report on school library media needs in the state.

Public Library Construction. Three county public library systems opened facilities in fiscal year 1984. Broadneck Branch, an 11,870-gross-square-foot agency of the Annapolis and Anne Arundel County Library, has an automated circulation system, resource security detection system, and passive solar energy features. The South Carroll Multi-Purpose Center in Eldersburg, a branch of the Carroll County Public Library System, has 14,407 gross square feet of library space within a building housing a state police substation and a Health Department outpatient clinic. The third project, the Beltsville Branch of the Prince George's County Memorial Library System, boasts 24,000 gross square feet in an extensively renovated school building. The latter also shares its roof with a county police substation.

New construction costs ran $78 per square foot. Renovated space cost $44 per renovated square foot. Furniture and equipment for new projects ran $8.00 per square foot.

Maryland Library Association. The Annual Conference was held at Ocean City, Maryland, May 17–18, 1984, with the theme "Serving More in '84."

People. Anne Briggs was named as Director of the Kent County Public Library, replacing Carolyn Wiker. Joey Rogers was selected as Chief of Network Services for the State Library Resource Center. Rogers was formerly with the Fairfax County Public Library System in Virginia. William Newman was selected as Director of the University of Baltimore Library, replacing Ellis Hodgins. John Zimmerman retired as Director of Frostburg State College

Library and was replaced by David Gillespie. William Johnston Tubbs was selected as Librarian at Washington College. Lloyd Mayfield was chosen as Director of Libraries at the Community College of Baltimore.

MAURICE TRAVILLIAN

MASSACHUSETTS

Massachusetts Library Association (founded 1890)

Membership: 849; *annual budget:* $44,000.

President: Connie Clancy, South Hadley Public Library (July 1983–June 1985).

Executive Secretary: Ron Hunte, 436 Great Road, Acton 01720.

Annual meeting: May 14–15, 1984, Springfield.

Publications: Bay State Librarian (3 issues per year); Bay State Letter (8 times per year).

Board of Library Commissioners

Roland Piggford, Director
648 Beacon Street
Boston 02215

A two-year campaign to "put libraries in the public eye with an upbeat message" was carried out during 1984 by the Public Relations Committee of the Massachusetts Library Association under the slogan of "Libraries Have MASS Appeal." One series of events calls attention to libraries, using bumper stickers and buttons and TV spots with celebrities like Steven King, Arlo Guthrie, and Wade Boggs of the Red Sox. A second series urges, "Give to the Library of Your Choice," a message carried on radio and TV by local luminaries. A third element provides local libraries with PR materials, including booklists like MASS murder, MASSterpieces, MASSsports and classics old and new set in the Bay State. Milles Cavanaugh, of the South Hadley Library System, chaired the MLA PR Committee that launched the two-year initiative.

Massachusetts Library Association. Membership in the Massachusetts Library Association was stimulated by an active two-year campaign by the Membership Committee, chaired by Christine Kardokas. After bottoming out at 600, membership was back up around 900 in 1984.

Helpful in maintaining member interest were the two yearly conferences of MLA. "Literally Speaking" was the theme of a midwinter conference covering topics related to books, publishing, authors, and collection development. "Back to Basics" was the focus for the spring conference with keynote speaker Beverly Lynch, Vice-President of ALA, on that topic. Other issues covered included legal and business information, library use of micros, networking, and making the political process work for libraries.

A Planning Committee made its report on the future for MLA during 1984 targeting the needs for better legislative networking, a better financial plan, better membership recruitment, and clearer use of Association publications among other issues. The Executive Board adopted the Planning Committee recommendations as their new agenda.

The Massachusetts Library Association resolved that the recommended minimum annual salary for beginning librarians in Massachusetts be $14,964.

Public Libraries. Public libraries joined force in 1984 behind an MLA-sponsored bill to increase funding to the regional library systems. The regional systems in Massachusetts serve only public libraries, and had existed on a static budget for four years. A successful campaign for reaching the legislature and the Governor resulted in an increase of $2,500,000 and restores all three regions to strength and a healthy budget to continue services to public libraries. The restored budgets helped place materials support back at a healthy level, and allowed each region to release funds for automation projects in support of the increasing computer activity across the state.

Academic Libraries. The state college library system received a new boost in the direction of automated networking as the State Board of Regents mandated all state colleges to join OCLC and financed the initial buy-in costs for each college not already a member. The purpose was to have all the state colleges able to share directly on an interlibrary loan network. In addition, eight state colleges were members of local automated networks in various parts of the state.

Building Programs. Massachusetts experienced encouraging building developments in libraries in 1984. The Thomas P. O'Neill, Jr., Library was dedicated at Boston College with the Speaker of the House of Representatives on hand for the ceremony. The overall costs of the building were expected to be $24,000,000.

Innovative building programs included that at Reading, where a school building on the National Register of Historic Places was made an attractive library for under $1,000,000. The new library in Marshfield won an award from the Massachusetts Municipal Association for the year's most innovative municipal project. A $2,000,000 project in Stoneham developed a library building incorporating custom-designed oak millwork, cathedral ceilings, and copper-covered dormer style windows.

Networking. As the state moved forward in implementing the automation plan called Automated Resource Sharing in Massachusetts, one of the groups providing focus for discussion of the plan is the Network Advisory Committee chaired in 1984 by Donald Dunn, Librarian of Western New England College Law Library. The NAC pursued a range of activities including sample network agreements, review of technical development, particularly the area of telecommunications, legislative action related to automation and networking, identification of need for network standards, and funding. The Board of Library Commissioners, which authorized the NAC, continued to allocate substantial LSCA monies to interlibrary cooperation, particularly in an automated environment.

Over 30 librarians served during 1984 on the Network Advisory Committee representing public, academic, school, and special libraries as well as networks and consortia. NAC is developing as a forum for statewide discussion of library automation issues.

MARGO CRIST

MICHIGAN

Michigan Library Association (founded 1891)

Membership: 1,995; *annual budget:* $151,800.

President: Robert Garen, Detroit Public Library, 5201 Woodward, Detroit 48202 (November 1984–November 1985).

President-elect: A. Michael Deller, 2165 Burns Avenue, Detroit 48214.

Executive Director: Marianna Gessner, 415 W. Kalamazoo, Lansing 48933.

Annual meeting: November 2–4, 1984, Detroit.

Publication: Michigan Librarian Newsletter (six a year).

State Library of Michigan

James W. Fry, State Librarian
735 E. Michigan Avenue
Lansing 48909

School Library Media Consultant

Patricia Slocum, Consultant
P.O. Box 30008
Michigan Department of Education
Lansing 48909

State library. The major library news in Michigan centered on the newly formed Library of Michigan, established under the State Legislature. The Legislative Council is responsible for the management, control, and budget of the Library. Governor James Blanchard appointed an advisory Board of Trustees under the public act of 1983, which created the Library. The Board has 14 members, including representatives from all types of libraries, the legislature, and the Michigan Supreme Court.

James W. Fry was appointed State Librarian March 19 and the Board of Trustees approved the Mission Statement, a long-range plan for the Library.

Three major areas covered by the Mission Statement and plan are: (1) Meeting the informational needs of the Legislature and state government; (2) meeting the administrative, developmental, and technical assistance needs of Michigan libraries of all types; and (3) meeting the library service needs of individuals and agencies for which the Library has a statewide resource responsibility. The plan provides detailed action statements that will direct staff in implementing the Mission Statement.

Placing the Library of Michigan under the Legislature resulted in improved budget provisions allowing for the development of a fully integrated automation system and for the hiring of new professional staff members.

Preliminary planning began on the new State Library and Historical Museum complex to be built near the State Capitol. A site was picked and $275,000 allocated for the preliminary design work on the $32,000,000 complex. There was some hope that the facility could be completed in time for the state's 150th anniversary in 1987.

Detroit Public Library. By a nearly two to one margin, Detroit voters increased their property taxes to raise nearly $5,000,000 for

341

the Detroit Public Library. A "Keep the Doors Open" campaign caught the attention of the public. Lack of funds was forcing the reduction of hours at the main library and the Board faced a decision to close nearly one-half of its branches. The successful vote was for a five-year period and the Library began the process of hiring over 100 new staff members for upgrading its services to begin in mid-1985.

Tax Funding. There was a new mood of optimism for libraries around the state as Michgan continues to pull itself out of a recession period. By a three to two margin Michigan voters rejected Proposal C—a major tax cut effort that would have reduced state and local taxes to 1981 levels. If the proposal had passed, many libraries in Michigan would have faced major budget reductions.

Over 20 libraries from all areas of the state waged successful property tax millage campaigns. Libraries in Alpena County, Monroe County, Constantine Township, and Lincoln Township passed .5 mill levies. In Dickinson County, Livonia, and Oxford, voters passed one mill levies and the Oxford and Livonia votes were for perpetuity. Grand Traverse County voters agreed to form a new district library and provided for three years of funding.

Expansions/Renovations. Spurred by Library Services and Construction Act Title II money, over two dozen public libraries were involved in expansions or renovations in 1984. Building expansions costing more than $300,000 included the Shelby Township Library, Sparta Township, and Lapeer County Libraries.

A major success story for a rural library comes from the Pigeon District Library serving a population of just over 8,500 in Michigan's thumb area. Beginning in the early 1970s with a small one-room library with one staff person, the library by 1984 had five staff members and a much enlarged facility. A new $100,000 addition to the library was begun. Funds were raised entirely by private contributions from businesses and individuals.

The City of Troy added 35,000 square feet to its existing facility. The Kresge Foundation provided a challenge grant of $150,000 and $68,000 was raised in community donations. The remainder of the funding came from city appropriations.

The Saginaw State College in University Center, Michigan, was building a new 67,000-square-foot facility that will house 240,000 volumes and seat 826 students. The new library will house the central processing unit for a computerized circulation system to serve the Valley Library Consortium, a multitype library network comprised of Delta College, Saginaw Valley State College, and the Saginaw public libraries. Several other libraries in the Saginaw Valley area were expected to join this consortium.

In Michigan's upper peninsula, voters in Delta County approved a $4,000,000 bonding request to construct a new learning resource center at the Bay de noc Community College in Escanaba.

The upper peninsula region of library cooperation received a grant of $836,200 from the W. K. Kellogg Foundation to be expended over a four-year period to implement an interactive computer based integrated library system serving all types of libraries in the upper peninsula. Meloday Weist was named Automation Specialist and Program Director for the project.

Michigan Library Consortium. The Michigan Library Consortium formed in the 1970s as the OCLC broker for Michigan expanded its membership dramatically. In 1984, 57 percent of its membership was made up of non-OCLC subscribers and its membership base included one-third public and school libraries, one-third academic, and one-third special libraries. *Development News*, a publication on fund raising for libraries, had wide distribution with subscribers in 17 states. The automation program on MLC saved members over $68,000 in 1983-84. Future goals through 1987 were outlined by Executive Director Kevin Flaherty. They include: (1) Maintenance and expansion of OCLC services, (2) expansion of tape management services, (3) continued expansion of timely, professional communications, such as *Development News*, and (4) improved economies in purchase of equipment, supplies, and materials. The Consortium completed a statewide union list of serials in microfiche format distributed throughout the state.

Michigan Library Association. The annual conference of the Michigan Library Association was held in Detroit in November. The annual Legislative Day was held April 4, when librarians, staff members, trustees, and friends came to Lansing to meet and talk with their legislators. The Association followed up its successful campaign to move the State Library from the Department of Education to the Legislature by working on full-funding of the State Aid Act to bring it from its current level of $8,700,000 to $14,500,000.

Library Schools. The Western Michigan University School of Librarianship was closed in December. Michigan was left with two library schools accredited to issue the Master's degree in Librarianship, Wayne State University and the University of Michigan.

Awards. The Michigan Library Association in 1984 granted the following awards: Librarian of the Year, Susan M. Haskin; Trustee of the Year, Hans Fetting; Loleta Fyan Award, Co-winners, Glenda Vandemark and Geri Furi; and Walter Kaiser Award, Alan S. Bobowski.

Appointments. John A. Oliver, Director of the Flint Public Library, retired on March 30, 1984. The new Director of the Flint Public Library is Gloria Coles.

Russell Bidlack, Dean of the School of Librarianship at the University of Michigan, retired; Robert M. Warner, Archivist of the United States, was appointed Dean effective in April 1985.

Susan M. Haskin, Deputy State Librarian, retired on September 30, 1984. She served as an Administrator at the State Library for the past 20 years and was Interim State Librarian before being named as Deputy Director.

ROBERT E. RAZ

MINNESOTA

Minnesota Library Association. The Minnesota Library Association (MLA) received the 1984 J. Morris Jones—World Book Encyclopedia—ALA Goal Award for a project entitled "Building Ad Hoc Coalitions for the Public Good." The MLA project will document and disseminate the process and results of an ad hoc coalition effort. The goal of the coalition is to involve Minnesota libraries in one

Minnesota Library Association (founded 1891)

Membership: 850; *annual budget:* $33,400.

President: W. Joseph Kimbrough, Minneapolis Public Library and Information Center (November 1984–December 1985).

Vice-President/President-elect: Donald Pearce, University of Minnesota, Duluth.

Annual meeting: May 2–3, 1984, Rochester.

Publication: MLA Newsletter (10 times a year).

Department of Education, Office of Library Development and Services

William G. Asp, Director
440 Capitol Square Building
550 Cedar Street
St. Paul 55101

State School Library Media Supervisor

Robert H. Miller
State Department of Education
St. Paul 55101

of the most important problems facing the state—the issue of economic vitality.

The focus of the project will be the development and operation of the Minnesota World Trade Center, itself a symbol for the economic vitality of the state. The project will attempt to teach those involved in Minnesota's economic health to "ask us first" for quality information and to include members of our profession in planning groups. The project will document the processes by which these professional linkages are formed so that the experience can serve as a model for other states.

The MLA project will produce a manual that will provide information about the Minnesota experience to other ALA chapters. In addition, information about the project was to be presented as a part of the President's Program on "Forging Coalitions for the Public Good" during the 1985 ALA Conference.

Degree Program Eliminated. At its meeting in October, the Board of Regents of the University of Minnesota formally voted to discontinue the academic degree programs of the University's Library School effective June 30, 1985. Admissions had been suspended in 1982, pending the report of a task force appointed to explore the possibility of developing a restructured program. The report, which strongly recommended the development of a new information studies program, was still under review by university officials in 1984.

Several library organizations in Minnesota played host to the 15th Annual May Hill Arbuthnot Honor Lecture featuring book illustrator Fritz Eichenberg, which was held April 6.

Associations. "Connections" was the theme of the 89th MLA conference held May 2–3 in Rochester. Featured speakers included Nancy Bolt, President of ALA/PLA; authors William A. Nolen, Nancy Carlson, Joanne Hart, and Patricia Calvert; Congressman Tim Penny; Mary Hutchings Reed, ALA legal counsel; and Eileen Cooke of the ALA Washington Office. Program topics covered output measures for public libraries, dealing with the angry patron, budgeting in a service organization, standards for public libraries, publishing for young readers, public relations, computer literacy for librarians, the correlation between pornography and male violence against women, and current trends in technical services in Minnesota. The annual awards dinner was enlivened with the "First Annual Jo Davies Memorial Musical Revue."

MLA, in cooperation with the Office of Library Development and Services (LDS), inaugurated an online database of library/information science/media positions open in Minnesota and contiguous states.

The Minnesota Educational Media Organization (MEMO) held its annual Upper Mississippi Media Conference in November on the theme "The Life Long Learner in the Information Age." Speakers included Colleen Coghlan, Librarian of Metropolitan State University, and Mary Alice White, Director of the Electronic Learning Laboratory, Teachers College, Columbia University.

The Minnesota Library Foundation began its first full year of operation. The foundation was established in December 1983 to promote the development, and to improve the service capabilities, of school libraries and media centers, public libraries, academic libraries, and nonprofit special libraries and information centers in Minnesota. Its establishment represents the first state-wide effort to build a public and private coalition to help achieve library service goals in Minnesota.

Awards. MLA presented its Trustee of the Year Award to Dorothy Petroskey, trustee of the Arrowhead Library System and immediate Past-President of the Minnesota Library Trustees Association. The President's Award was presented to Bruce Willms, Macalester College, for his outstanding service in helping MLA "identify and meet the challenges of the future."

Certificates of Merit were presented to Mary Birmingham, Director of METRONET, for her work in coalition building and networking, and to the Minnesota Humanities Commission for its strong commitment to libraries, its support of the role libraries play in the study and use of humanities materials, and for its many grants on behalf of library programs in the state.

MEMO honored Don E. Lifto, Superintendent of the Trimont Public Schools, with its Outstanding Service Award for a School Administrator. LaVonne Anderson, also from the Trimont Public Schools, received the Outstanding Service by an Adult Media Aide Award.

Bill Asp, Director of LDS, was honored with a special award from the White House Conference on Library and Information Services Taskforce for his "commitment and special support for the betterment of libraries and the improvement of library services." He chaired the task force in 1982.

George D'Elia, University of Minnesota Library School, and Sandra Walsh, Ramsey County Public Library, received the ALA Library Research Round Table's 1984 Research Development Award.

The Duluth-Superior Area Community Foundation granted the Duluth Public Library $7,000 to expand and improve the Library's collections on world cultures and economic, social, and political systems, to promote these collections, and to provide free public programs at which speakers will discuss world cultures and problems.

The National Endowment for the Humanities awarded an $18,500 grant to the Minnesota Association of Library Friends to fund a series of reading/discussion programs in one public library in each of the regional library systems in Minnesota. The Minnesota project, entitled "Minnesota—Let's Talk About Books," will be patterned on the national NEH/ALA-sponsored "Let's Talk About It" project.

The National Association of Counties presented the Hennepin County Library an Achievement Award for its cooperative program with a local cable television company to provide public access to television production facilities through a jointly operated television production studio.

Buildings. Washington County Library opened its new Park Grove Branch in November. The 80,000-volume building serves as the main information center for the system.

The citizens of Brainerd voted by a margin greater than two to one in September to authorize issuance of $1,700,000 for construction of a new public library building. Voters in Fergus Falls passed a referendum for issuance of $650,00 in bonds for construction of a new library building by an almost three to one margin.

Construction was begun on new library buildings for Aurora and Grand Rapids.

People. William DeJohn, formerly of the Pacific Northwest Bibliographic Center, was named Director of MINITEX in June.

Rheda Epstein, formerly of the Virginia Beach (Virginia) Public Library, was named Technical Services Manager of the Saint Paul Public Library. Jim Godsey, formerly of the Huntington (Indiana) Public Library, was appointed Deputy Director of the Rochester Public Library. Marcia Valance was named Head Librarian of the Grand Rapids Public Library.

Janet Kinney was appointed Director of the St. Catherine Library, College of St. Catherine, and Claire Fleishman McInerney was named to the faculty of the college. Shannon Lang, formerly of the St. Tammany Parish Schools, Slidell, Louisiana, was appointed Children's Consultant for the Arrowhead Library System.

Coordinators were named by two of the multitype library cooperation systems: Lucile Lowry as coordinator of the Southcentral Minnesota Library Exchange (SMILE) and Nancy Alsop as coordinator of the North County Library Cooperative.

Sharon Charles was named to head the Automation and New Technology Specialist Project conducted by LDS and the James J. Hill Reference Library. The project is designed to assist regional public library systems and public libraries in planning and implementing library automation. Roger Sween, formerly of St. Cloud State University, joined the LDS staff as Multi-Type Library Cooperation Specialist.

EDWARD SWANSON

MISSISSIPPI

State Association. "Fair Sailing in Biloxi" was the theme of the joint Mississippi Library Association (MLA)/Southeastern Library Association (SELA) conference in October. The conference drew librarians and exhibitors from over the Southeast and featured a wide selection of presentations, workshops, and entertainment. Writer Studs Terkel spoke, as did NASA astronaut Donald H. Peterson, Lou Williams of Savlin/Williams, and Jim Trelease, author of *The Read-Aloud Handbook*. A number of computer workshops and tours, including one to the World's Fair, were scheduled. John Maxwell presented a one-man show, "Oh, Mr. Faulkner, Do You Write?"

State Library. State funding was again the greatest concern of the Mississippi Library Commission (MLC) in 1984. Lower appropriations by the state legislature caused severe cutbacks in service, materials, and staff. Support services for the state's public libraries were drastically reduced. The purchases of nonfiction books, films, and periodicals were cut as well, but it was hoped a Mississippi Union Catalog project could be salvaged. MLC Director David Woodburn called for resourcefulness and assistance in approaching the next legislative session for relief.

MLC's public relations and printing department won six awards in the annual competition of the Mississippi Chapter of the International Association of Business Communications. The awards were for promotional television spots, photos, newsletters and press kits.

The Commission sponsored a series of workshops throughout the state on film programming.

Public Libraries. Public libraries in the state promoted the New Orleans World Exposition in a unique 1984 tourism effort for Mississippi. The libraries served as information centers for tourists passing through the state to the Fair.

School Libraries, Media Centers. A much-heralded and ambitious Educational Reform Act of 1983 turned sour for Mississippi's school libraries. A Task Force on Accreditation (chaired by Olon Ray, recipient of MLA's 1983 Ed Randsdell Award) failed to follow recommendations of an MLA Ad Hoc Committee on School Libraries and dropped from its proposed standards central elementary libraries and professional librarians and decreased requirements on the secondary level. School and other librarians were alarmed, particularly

---

Mississippi Library Association (founded 1909)

Membership: 1,000; *annual budget:* $66,000.

President: Anice Powell, Sunflower County Library, Indianola 38751 (January 1984–January 1985).

Vice-President/President-elect: Barbara Carroon, 5818 North Dale, Jackson 39211.

Executive Secretary: DeLois Minton, Mississippi College, P.O. Box 470, Clinton, Mississippi 39056.

Annual meeting: October 17–19, 1984.

Publications: MISSISSIPPI LIBRARIES (quarterly).

Mississippi Library Commission

David Woodburn, Director
P.O. Box 10700
Jackson, Mississippi 39209

State Department of Education Educational Media Services

John Barlow, Supervisor
P.O. Box 771
Jackson, Mississippi 39205

since it followed layoffs of professional librarians in some major school systems in the state. The proposed standards were to be tested for two years before full implementation. Librarians were building resistance. Among groups meeting to learn more about the standards and their effects was the Mississippi Association of Media Educators (MAME).

Academic Libraries. Late in December 1983, a federal magistrate ruled in favor of the Mississippi State University Library and its Director in the much publicized Merwine case. Merwine had sued the Library, stating that the ALA accredited degree was not an appropriate criterion for the job she had been denied. The national library press covered the case at length.

The University of Southern Mississippi's 17th annual Children's Book Festival was held in March. Winner of the 1984 USM Medallion was author/artist Peter Spier. Also there as speakers and guests were authors Paul Zindel, Esphyr Slobodkin, and Molly Bang.

Interlibrary Cooperation. In spite of severe budget cutbacks, MLC laid plans for an automated interlibrary loan system for the state's public libraries. Set to begin in 1985 the microcomputer-based system had attracted 22 public library applicants for participation by year's end.

Intellectual Freedom. Much in the news in 1984 were efforts to control selection in libraries, in bookstores, and on television. In Rankin County a group of parents, meeting at a Primitive Baptist Church, sought and got a library book review committee for the public school system after two books were challenged—*Head Man* and *Cujo*.

A Jackson city ordinance aimed at pornography in book shops was passed with little opposition except for bookstore owners. In effect for a few weeks, it was shelved by a judge on the basis of the existence of a previously restrained state law on the subject. Both laws await further action. Librarians and others have expressed concern over a perceived trend toward censorship and, although relieved by the court action, they expected further activity among would-be censors.

Professional Interests. MLA's 10th annual NLW Workshop and Legislative Luncheon was held in February with 500 in attendance. This working meeting provided encounters with state legislators and planning tips for NLW publicity.

MLA's ACRL chapter sponsored a May seminar on "Participatory Management in Academic Libraries" at Jackson State University with William Cooley as principal speaker. The six regional spring meetings of the state association featured a variety of programs, including those on censorship, library instruction, and computer applications, and special workshops on oral history.

Awards. The MLA Peggy May Award was presented to Lelia G. Rhodes, Dean of Libraries, Jackson State University, and the Association awarded its Outstanding Achievement Award to Burl Hunt, Professor of Educational Media, University of Mississippi.

Pamela S. Lambert, Director of the Pine Forest Regional Library, received the Past-Presidents' Award. The two recipients of the Ed Randsdell Award were Ted Alexander, Superintendent of the McComb Public School System, and Ann B. Denison, Media Director of the Biloxi Public Schools.

Baker and Taylor's Grassroots Award went to Liz Abbott, graduate library science student at the University of Southern Mississippi.

Appointments. William D. Majure was appointed Head Librarian of the Moss Point City Library. Dixie Stevens was appointed Director of the Long Beach Public Library. Thomas G. Reid, Jr., became Director of the Reformed Theological Seminary library, and Malone Jackson was appointed to the MLC Board of Commissioners.

Deaths. Iola Magee, former Director of the Lincoln–Lawrence–Franklin Regional Library and 1972 MLA President, died in April. Evelyn West Oswalt, former Librarian of Copiah-Lincoln Junior College, died in late December 1983. Jeannetta Cole Roach, head Librarian of Tougaloo College, died in April. Jeannetta Roach was among the first Blacks to hold major offices in the state library association.

JAMES F. PARKS, JR.

MISSOURI

Missouri Library Association (founded 1900)

Membership: 1,139; *annual budget:* $80,935.

President: Helen Wigersma, Missouri Western State College Library, 4525 Downs Drive, St. Joseph 64507 (October 1984–October 1985).

Vice-President/President-elect: Ray Riddle, Cass County Public Library, 103 Oriole, Harrisonville 64701.

Executive Coordinator: Marilyn McLeod, Missouri Library Association, Parkade Plaza, Suite 9, Columbia 65201.

Annual meeting: October 3–5, 1984, Cape Girardeau.

Publication: Missouri Library Association Newsletter (bimonthly).

Missouri State Library

Charles O'Halloran, State Librarian
2nd Floor, Truman State Office Building
Jefferson City 65102

State School Library Media Supervisor

Carl Sitze
State Department of Elementary and Secondary Education
P.O. Box 480
Jefferson City 65102

The State Library moved to the new Harry S Truman State Office Building in 1984. Library staff spent months planning the move, which took place in late June. Utilizing large postal tubs in which books were packed in Dewey order, 25–30 moving company personnel and 29 State Library staffers completed the move of 300,000 items in five days. The library is on one level and has 32,800 square feet, a 40 percent increase in space.

State Association. MLA's 84th annual conference dealt with the theme "Access to Information: Restricted." The conference offered a variety of programs and workshops. Keynote speaker was John N. Berry III, Editor of *Library Journal*, who spoke on free access to information vs. information as a commodity that is bought and sold in the marketplace. Speakers addressing general sessions included Cecil Beach, Director of the Broward County Library (Florida), who discussed funding, programs, and preparing for change; James Bamford, author of *The Puzzle Palace, A Report on America's Most Secret Agency*, who described his use of the Freedom of Information Act to discover information on the National Security Agency; James Kirkpatrick, Missouri's Secretary of State, who spoke of the need for an open and responsive government; and Penn Kimball, author of *The File*, who told of his problems in obtaining information held on him by the federal government.

Seymour Simon, author of 60 science books, spoke at the annual Thusnelda Schmidt Lecture. Robin Brancato, author of books for young adults, and Jose Aruego, children's book illustrator, were the speakers for the children's and young adults' sessions.

MLA members contributed some $6,000 to be used for the Association's legislative program during 1985.

The MLA Computer and Information Technology Committee conducted a second survey to determine the extent of automation in Missouri's public, academic, and special libraries. Out of 328 surveys mailed, 146 were returned, a response rate of 44 percent. The survey included statistics on hardware, software, and applications of automation.

The MLA and the State Library sponsored a Workshop in Library Leadership in April. The ALTA/Will workshop, which has been replicated throughout the country, offered sessions on finance and planning, policymaking, and awareness and advocacy. Keynote speakers were trustees Virginia Young, Alice Ihrig, and Nancy Stiegemeyer, all nationally known for their work with trustees.

The MLA Jobline, established in 1983, proved a success in 1984 and was to be expanded to a 24-hour service.

Legislation. Three bills affecting libraries were passed in the 1984 Missouri General Assembly. The bills deal with removal of limits on library levies in political subdivisions of a certain population; tax exemptions for creators of musical, scholarly, or artistic work who donate their creations to nonprofit institutions; and authorization of county collectors to deposit funds collected for the library directly to the treasurer of the library rather than routing them first to the county treasurer. The MLA Legislative Committee planned to work on legislation relating to the confidentiality of library records for the 1985 session.

State Library Activities. The State Library formed a staff committee in 1984 to examine ways in which library operations might be more effectively performed with automation. The Committee interviewed library staff members about aspects of their jobs that would benefit from automation. Automation will be applied for interlibrary loan, preparation of mailing lists, library indexes, and statistical manipulation.

The second statewide summer reading program for children had as its theme "Read More '84." A free poster, created for the program by a Missouri artist, went to all public libraries. The State Library provided financial assistance and staff for the program.

The State Library granted 11 staff development fellowships to Missouri librarians for participation in workshops or other educational activities designed to improve job performance.

Public Libraries. A "Printmarket" offering old and rare books, prints, and maps for sale was held in October to benefit the St. Louis Public Library. The proceeds of $3,000 were to be used in support of the library's National Endowment for the Humanities Challenge Grant for the restoration of the Main Library, built in 1912 and designed by the noted architect Cass Gilbert. The grant was made in 1981; by 1984 the Library had raised $131,900 from private donations. It needed to raise $750,000 by July 31, 1986, to qualify for the $250,000 grant.

The University City Public Library held a number of fund-raising activities in 1984 including "Poets Four," a benefit reading by four University City poets—Donald Finkel, Pamela White Hadas, John Morris, and Constance Urdang—which netted $4,600 to be used for the library's book budget. The Library's Friends group developed a series of fund-raising programs described in a booklet entitled "Between the Covers."

Springfield–Greene County Library sponsored a Tennessee Williams Film Festival, made possible by a grant from the Missouri Committee for the Humanities. The project featured seven film showings, each followed by a discussion led by a humanities scholar.

St. Louis County Library expanded its book budget by almost 20 percent ($200,000) in 1984. The expansion resulted from voter approval in 1983 of a library and maintenance tax.

Voters passed tax levies for seven Missouri libraries in 1984: Daniel Boone Regional Library, Montgomery City Public Library, Centralia Public Library, Kansas City Public Library, Brentwood Public Library, Carrollton Public Library, and Trails Regional Library. Voters also approved the establishment of a library district for Adair County.

The Friends of Webster Groves Public Library held their annual fifth-grade visit: all fifth graders in the Webster Groves school system are brought to and from the Library by bus paid for by the Friends. Each group attends classes in four areas: children's card catalog, reader's guide, reference room, and fine arts room. Volunteers from the Friends serve as teachers.

St. Louis Public Library, one of three public libraries in the country chosen to participate in a new one-year program with the U.S. Department of Commerce National Technical Information Service, will offer for sale the latest government-sponsored research, development, and engineering reports and other analyses prepared by government agencies.

School Libraries, Media Centers. The Missouri Association of School Librarians completed a major study of school library media centers in 1984. The survey was undertaken to provide information needed for the formulation of long-range goals and legislative activity, and to define priority needs to improve the state's school libraries. Findings indicated that many students and faculty in Missouri schools have access to less than adequate collections and services.

The MASL spring conference took place in Hannibal. The theme was "A Brave New World?" The 1984 Mark Twain Award was won by Betty Miles for *The Secret Life of the Underwear Champ*.

Academic Libraries, Special Libraries. The Missouri Association of College and Research Libraries held its spring conference, "Coping with Austerity," at the University of Missouri–Columbia. Featured speakers were Shaila Aery, Missouri Commissioner of Higher Education, and Julie Virgo, former Executive Director of ALA's Association of College and Research Libraries. More than 100 librarians attended the conference.

The Japan Foundation, a nonprofit organization dedicated to promoting international cultural exchange, awarded a $3,000 Library Support Grant to the Nelson–Atkins Museum of Art, Kansas City. The grant will be used to fill gaps in the museum's Japanese serial and journal publications holdings.

The University of Missouri–Columbia Libraries and Washington University Libraries were awarded grants from the Higher Education Act, Title II-C ($68,230 and $62,325, respectively).

The University of Missouri–Columbia and the International Graduate School, St. Louis, cosponsored a workshop on "Oral History for Librarians and Archivists" that dealt with basic skills in developing oral history programs.

The Missouri Botanical Garden Library, St. Louis, will share a $300,000 grant with the New York Botanical Garden to continue a joint project of recataloging their collections. The Missouri Botanical Garden Library also was awarded an $85,000 challenge grant by the National Endowment for the Humanities. The money will be used for the remodeling of the library and for the rare book collection. The collection contains volumes dating back to the 15th century and archives of more than 220,000 documents on the history of science.

The University of Missouri–Columbia School of Library and Informational Science organized a Center for Rural Library Development. The Center has tentatively defined "rural library" as one existing outside a Standard Metropolitan Statistical Area (SMSA). It planned to concentrate on continuing education and the publication of *The Center for Rural Libraries Newsletter*. Genevieve Casey, former Michigan State Librarian and faculty member of Wayne State University, consulted with Missouri rural librarians on the development of the Center.

The Concordia Historical Institute, St. Louis, received a major collection of Lutheran catechetical materials from the Reverend Arthur C. Repp, Sr., of St. Louis. Many of the volumes in the collection were printed in Germany in the 1700s and 1800s. After cataloging, the collection will be available for research purposes.

The University of Missouri–Columbia Friends of the Libraries received a $7,500 matching grant from the Kansas City Life Insurance Company. The company helped the Friends to initiate its first fundraising drive so that books and other materials could be acquired for the UMC Libraries and the State Historical Society of Missouri. The UMC Friends also received a gift of $78,000 from the will of Olive Gilbreath-McLorn of LaPlata, Missouri, to be divided between the UMC Libraries and the State Historical Society of Missouri.

The University of Missouri–Kansas City Libraries sponsored a workshop on the preservation and conservation of library materials conducted by staff from the Midwest Cooperative Conservation Program, a multistate project funded by the National Endowment for the Humanities.

Building Programs. St. Louis County Library continued its major building program involving the upgrading of existing facilities and construction of new branches. Tax monies approved in 1973 were used to construct five branches, to renovate and increase the size of one branch, and to remodel two branches. Construction began in 1984 on two new branches, and several more branches were in the planning stages at year's end.

Construction began in October on a 50,000-square-foot addition to the Ellis Library and State Historical Society of Missouri, both on the University of Missouri–Columbia campus. It is expected that the project will take two years to complete.

St. Louis University launched a $75,000,000-dollar development plan, part of which calls for a $4,000,000-dollar library annex.

The Friends of Farmington Public Library commissioned Missouri artist Michael Chomyk to create a mural for the Library's children's room.

Work was completed on nine of the 18 Title II grants made in 1983. Title II funds helped to pay construction costs for an addition to the Rolla Public Library and for new library buildings in McDonald County, St. Charles County, Cass County, Douglas County, and the Ozark Regional Library.

The Archie Library League, a Friends group for the Archie Branch of the Cass County Library, designed and completed a rainbow mural for the library building exterior.

In June the Sarcoxie Public Library moved into new quarters in the former city fire barn. Friends of the Sarcoxie Library raised $6,000 for remodeling.

Networks, Interlibrary Cooperation. The Library Advisory Committee was working in 1984 on the recodification of the state's library laws. The Committee, including librarians from all types of libraries, provides information and makes recommendations to the Missouri Coordinating Board for Higher Education. The Coordinating Board has statutory responsibility for the state's two- and four-year colleges.

The Missouri General Assembly in 1983 gave statutory recognition to multitype library networks. The State Library has since developed a network rule, which was approved by the Missouri Libraries Network Board and the Coordinating Board for Higher Education, to regulate networks and serve as a basis for state funding of networks.

The Kansas City Metropolitan Library Network presented a one-day workshop on "Copyright Law: Current Issues and a Look at the Future." It considered the extent of librarians' responsibility in maintaining copyright compliance. Speakers included law librarians and law faculty from Missouri universities.

Awards. MLA awards went to Mona Van Duyn, St. Louis poet and National Book Award winner, for her literary achievements; to Congressman E. Thomas Coleman of the Kansas City area for his efforts to secure reauthorization of LSCA; and to Daniel Boone Regional Library for its 25th anniversary public relations program. Mid-Continent Public Library was recognized with an honorable mention in public relations for its campaign to raise the library tax.

The Beta Phi Mu Award for Excellence in Librarianship was presented to Esther Gilman, former Director of Trails Regional Library.

Louvan Gearin received the Special Service Award given by the Missouri Association of

School Librarians. Gearin retired from the Hixon Junior High School in 1982 after serving as Librarian for seven years.

Nancy Stoddard, Chief Librarian of the *St. Louis Post-Dispatch*, received a special award from the Newspaper Division of the Special Libraries Association for her editorship of SLA's 60th anniversary commemorative publication.

Appointments, Retirements. Library directors appointed in 1984 include John M. Meador, Jr., Southwest Missouri State University; Marguerite Mitchel, Stephens College; Nancy Hanks, Northwest Missouri State University; Connie Wolf, Missouri Botanical Garden; Evelyn Pypes, Atchison County Library; Ann Sampson, James Memorial Library; and Nina Walsh, Mary Institute.

Fred Raithel was named coordinator of the Mid-Missouri Library Network, and Judy Muck was named coordinator of the Northwest Missouri Library Network.

Mary F. Lenox was appointed Dean of the University of Missouri–Columbia School of Library and Informational Science. She had been a Library School faculty member since 1978. Named to the Library School faculty were Ronald L. Fingerson and Jack D. Glazier.

Susanna Alexander, former Associate State Librarian, was a Visiting Professor at Texas Woman's University.

Mary Ann Mercante was named Executive Director of the Missouri Library Network Corporation. The Corporation provides database services to Missouri libraries and is preparing a microfiche catalog of Missouri library holdings.

Ray Starke, Chief of Library Services at the Harry S Truman Memorial Veterans Hospital, Columbia, was appointed one of five charter members of the OCTANET Advisory Group. OCTANET is a regional online system used primarily in Midwestern medical libraries.

Robert W. Roehr was appointed Manager of the Main Library of St. Louis Public Library.

Dorothy Proper, Director of Atchison County Library, retired after 38 years of service.

Deaths. William C. Mills, Librarian at Parkway North High School in St. Louis for 12 years, died May 6.

Richard B. Sealock, Director of the Kansas City Public Library from 1949 to 1968, died November 3 in Wooster, Ohio.

MADELINE MATSON

MONTANA

The Pacific Northwest Library Association convened its 75th Anniversary Conference, "High-Tech High-Touch," in Billings in August. Long affiliated with PNLA, Montana completed its first year as a member of the Mountain Plains Library Association. PNLA/MPLA/MLA were entertaining the idea of a Tri-Conference in 1989 when the Treasure State celebrates its 100th birthday.

For active professional participation, Montana draws not only from ALA but also from two regional organizations, PNLA to the west and MPLA to the east.

State Association. The Montana Library Association held its 71st annual conference in Helena in April. A snowstorm that made national TV news resulted in light early attendance. "2001: The Future Is Created in the Acts of the Present" was keynoted by Art Plotnik, Editor of *American Libraries*. His talk, "Fu-

Montana Library Association (founded 1914)

Membership: 580; *annual budget:* $30,000.

President: Barbara Rudio, 1119 Lincolnwood, Missoula 59802 (June 1984–June 1985).

Vice-President/President-elect: Karen Fischek, 505 North Valley, Bozeman 59717.

Annual meeting: April 26–28, 1984, Helena.

Publication: President's Newsletter (4–6 issues a year).

Montana State Library

Sara Parker, State Librarian
1515 6th Ave.
Helena 59601

School Library Media Supervisor

Shelia Cates
Office of the Superintendent of Public Instruction
Helena 59601

---

tured to Death," was notable for its humor and insight and won him "favorite son" status by acclamation.

State Library Activities. 1984 saw the reinstituted Montana Library Services Advisory Council launch a long-range plan for Montana libraries. "A Choice of Futures, A Future of Choices" in draft form circulated throughout the state with responses and comment returning to the Council in late September. By year's end the Council was studying the results, anticipating a formal spring report to the State Library Commission.

The newly expanded seven-member State Library Commission formally accepted the Federation Review; acted upon the pilot MONCAT recommendations; and appointed statewide committees to study collection development and automation. The Commission went on retreat to consider the assortment of recommendations coming out of the Program Review (1982), the Federation Review (1983-84), and the draft Long-Range Plan (1984). The distillation and implementation of those recommendations were to occupy the Commission in 1985.

Public Libraries. The 46th session of the State Legislature (1983) provided for an increase in the permissive levies for both cities and counties. This move generated a modest infusion of funds that were quickly absorbed into materials and public library services.

Trustee workshops were held in the six Federations as were Financial Management Training sessions. Well attended and well executed, these continuing education efforts from the State Library had impact on rural libraries in Montana. Indicative of the leadership of State Librarian Sara Parker, the state's public libraries were undergoing revitalization in spite of reduced revenues.

School Libraries, Media Centers. Under the leadership of Sheila Cates, the Office of Public Instruction Library/Media Consultant, representing the State Superintendent on the State Library Commission, school libraries have had an active participant in the political structure that so influences the profession. Recognized as significant members of the Library Community, school libraries were seeing their concerns become the concerns of the entire community. This recognition reassures the Montana school practitioner who often appears to function in virtual isolation in the Big Sky Country.

School librarians of Montana annually attend fall retreats; 1984 saw 121 librarians attend three retreats, one high on the Continental Divide of Glacier Park, one at Big Sky near Yellowstone, and one at the famous Fort Peck Reservoir.

Academic Libraries. Impeded by an April blizzard, MLA Conference attendees nonetheless attended the "Access to Information" Session in good numbers. The attraction was the team of Dick Dougherty and Bernadine Hoduski. Hoduski is a native of Montana and Dougherty is from Michigan.

Montana's academic library community during the conference laid ambitious plans for future conference programming and began preparation for the 47th convening of the state legislature.

Building Programs. Ten projects in Montana received LSCA Title II grants totaling $220,523 during 1984. The rural nature of Montana is evident when these projects are sampled: Big Fork (population 501), Plains (1,046), St. Ignatius (925), Mineral County (county population 2,958).

In addition to the LSCA funds, grass root campaigns achieved success. Havre Public Library and Hill County Library consolidated in 1983 and raised funds during 1984 to remodel the old Havre Clinic, a gift of local physicians.

Citizens of Plains raised nearly $89,000 to purchase an existing building for their new library facility. They applied for and received a $20,000 LSCA grant for remodeling.

Networks, Interlibrary Cooperation. Acronyms that reflect the pervasive cooperation in Montana include KALSHARES in the Kalispell area; HELCAT in Helena; GOLDCAT in Golden Plains Federation; MONCAT; and WLN.

Four MONCAT grants were awarded by the State Library Commission. Additions to the Montana Union Catalog database include four public libraries, two hospital libraries, one film/media library, and five school libraries.

The pilot MONCAT in 1984 included 20 libraries using the WLN Resource Directory in fiche as their base instrument. MONCAT was to be available statewide in fiche format in 1985.

Professional Interests. Three areas emerged in 1984. One was the automation compatibility issue. Many Montana libraries were building files on microcomputers that contained bibliographic records, or they were contemplating developing automated circulation systems. Guidelines for building those files in such a way that the machine-readable records can eventually be added to MONCAT were needed. October saw the appointment of the State Automation Committee.

The second area emerging was collection development. Core collections were developed in outlying areas along with speciality collections. August saw the appointment of the Collection Development Committee.

A third emerging issue was continuing education. The university units, the State Library, and the Montana State Library opened dialog on this issue in October.

Awards. The Montana Library Association annually recognizes a school administrator and a library trustee for outstanding contributions to the advancement of library services. In

1984 those awards went to Peter L. Carparelli, Principal, Helena High School and Jean Koppang, Trustee of the Great Falls Public Library.

Margaret Warden, a member of the National Commission on Libraries and Information Science (NCLIS), was honored by her Great Falls community. The only Commissioner for the vast region that encompasses Montana, North and South Dakota, Wyoming, Idaho, Washington, and Oregon, she made her influence felt nationwide. In an April interview she stated that "without the backing of a public library you don't have the fundamental requisites of a good education."

GLENDA BELL

NEBRASKA

Nebraska Library Association (founded 1895)

Membership: 920; *annual expenditure:* $28,600.

President: Elaine Norton, David City (November 1984–October 1985).

Vice-President/President-elect: Susan Kling, Nebraska Library Commission.

Executive Secretary: Raymond Means, Creighton University, Omaha 68178.

Annual meeting: October 31–November 2, 1984, Kearney.

Publication: NLA Quarterly.

Nebraska Library Commission

John L. Kopischke, Director
1420 P Street
Lincoln 68508

School Library Media Supervisor

Rex Filmer
Department of Education
Lincoln 68509

Legislative Activity. The Nebraska Legislature in March overrode Governor Bob Kerry's veto of $270,000 of state funds to support Nebraska Library Systems. Though the budget amount originally requested was $530,000, the Legislative Appropriations Committee trimmed the request to $270,000 when putting together its total state budget recommendation. The budget bill was passed by the Legislature, and the Appropriations Committee presented a budget amendment that included $240,000 for library system funding and $30,000 for net lending libraries in the state interlibrary loan network. Thirty senators voted for the amendment, 17 against, with two excused. Thirty votes were required for the override.

In April Governor Kerry signed LB 229, an act to change the provisions relating to money recovered in civil actions involving libraries. Money other than any court costs and attorney's fees collected in such actions is to be placed in the treasury of the city, village, township, or county library fund. A provision struck from the bill before passage covered the low priority libraries are given by county and city attorneys when assistance is needed in prosecuting cases dealing with such actions. The Miscellaneous Subjects Committee held hearings in November in regard to lack of prosecution for library theft, mutilation, and damage cases. Efforts will be made to strengthen LB 229 during the 1985 State Legislature.

Two separate developments during the year highlighted the more intense involvement of Nebraska librarians in the political process. The Nebraska Library Association's first Legislative Day was held in February. Librarians met with their legislators to discuss library needs followed by visits to individual legislators in their offices. Concluding the day was a general reception for senators, guests, and other state officials. In June a group of concerned library supporters formed "Nebraskans for Libraries," a political action committee, to offer support to candidates for the Nebraska Legislature and to increase the visibility of libraries in the political process. Fund-raising activities at the annual NLA convention made it possible already in 1984 to make financial contributions. Also at the convention "Nebraskans for Libraries" received the endorsement of the NLA membership.

At the beginning of 1984 the State Board of Education proposed changes to the Nebraska Administrative Code dealing with the operation and accreditation of Nebraska schools. Changes were prompted by the Governor's Task Force on Excellence in Education. Several public hearings were held around the state during the year dealing with the proposed changes that many felt were a watering down of basic standards.

State Library Activities. The Nebraska Library Commission in 1984 approved agreements between the Commission and the Nebraska Union Catalog (NUC) member libraries. Union Catalog participating libraries will be designated state resource libraries and be eligible for financial compensation from the state when their level of lending qualifies them as "net lenders."

Early in the year the Library Commission issued a request for proposals seeking a consultant to examine Nebraska's resource sharing environment and automation needs. The study was intended to assess the components of Nebraska resource sharing (interlibrary loan arrangements, NEUCAT and NEULIST, telecommunications, etc.) and application of computer technology (local applications in shared systems) for presentation of recommendations and options. King Research of Rockville, Maryland, was selected to conduct a five-month study. The study was originally suggested by the NEBASE Advisory Board and was one of the LSCA projects endorsed by the 1983 State Advisory Council on Libraries. The final report was due in 1985.

Implementing LSCA program plans recommended by the 1983 Nebraska State Advisory Council on Libraries, the Library Commission awarded a series of resource sharing enhancement grants to 43 libraries totaling $67,640. In addition, four public libraries received individual grants of $6,000 to acquire equipment and training to utilize services of OCLC. Fifteen Nebraska OCLC libraries received Library Services and Construction Act grants (Title I and Title III) from the Commission to assist in converting previously cataloged material to the OCLC database. Records added to the OCLC database are automatically added to the Nebraska Union Catalog (NEUCAT) by a computer tape including cataloging records of Nebraska OCLC libraries.

In a 1984 reorganization of the Library Commission's Library Development Division, Fern Heim was named Library Services Coordinator–Public Library Specialist. Other appointments were Richard Allen, Library Services Coordinator–Extension Services Specialist; Marla Bouton, Library Services Coordinator–Systems Development Specialist; Mona-Jean Easter, Library Services Coordinator–Resource Sharing Specialist; and James Minges, Library Services Development Director to supervise the Library Services Coordinator staff positions and department activity.

NEMA. The Nebraska Educational Media Association (NEMA) held its annual convention in Kearney in October. Sonya Collison completed her term as President and was succeeded by Rich Urwiler. Tony Schulzetenberg, Supervisor of the Center for Information Media at St. Cloud State University, St. Cloud, Minnesota, presented the keynote address, "Library Media Specialist: Today's Traditions in Tomorrow's World." Mary Calhoun, children's book author from Steam Boat Springs, Colorado, was the luncheon speaker. Robert Stepp received the NEMA Distinguished Service Award. The sectional meetings covered such topics as "Role of the Media Specialist in the School Media Program," "Stress Management," "Documents to the Schools," "Use of Chapter 2 funds in Nebraska," and "Computer Graphics."

Building. A major addition to the Carl M. Reinert Memorial Library at Creighton University was dedicated September 12. The Omaha Public Library received a $116,000 bequest to be used as approved by the Library Board of Trustees but directing that special attention be given to the South Branch Library. The Elkhorn Public Library moved to a new facility in the same location. The lower level of the Elkhorn Community Building was remodeled for library use. The Union College Library in Lincoln moved into its new building during early fall.

The DeWitt and Howells Public Libraries sustained book losses and minor building damage after a June flooding in eastern Nebraska. The Howells Public Library received a matching grant for $5,000 from the Peter Kiewit Foundation of Omaha for new library furnishings. The West Point Library Foundation was awarded a Kiewit Foundation $5,000 matching grant for library furnishings and equipment. The Nelson Public Library doubled its size using an LSCA Title II construction grant to add a 20-by-42-foot addition.

Intellectual Freedom. The Ravenna Public Schools in 1984 asked that the Buffalo County Bookmobile discontinue a stop at the Ravenna schools because a book carried on the bookmobile was held to be inappropriate for a junior high school student. After several school board meetings it was decided that the stop at the Ravenna schools be discontinued. The specific title in question was not identified, but described as an "adult western."

The Nebraska Library Association's Intellectual Freedom Committee worked throughout the year preparing a new Nebraska Intellectual Freedom handbook to give librarians and media specialists guidelines to use in the event of an intellectual freedom challenge.

The Holdrege Public Library was requested to remove the Judy Blume book *Forever* from its collection and the Library Board urged to adopt "a Christian book selection policy." Librarian Paul Holland reported that the book had been moved from the young adult to the adult reading section of the library but that no changes were to be made in the selection policy.

Library Systems. The $240,000 funded by the Legislature for Nebraska libraries was funneled into six multitype library systems across the state which were organized and implemented during fiscal year 1982–83. System Service Plans and budgets were approved for each System for 1984–85. One notable project which involved two of the Systems was the formation of a telecommunications switching center called the Reference/Interloan Center at Kearney (RICK). Sponsored by the Meridian and Republican Valley Library Systems and supported by a grant from the Nebraska Library Commission, the Center provides interloan and reference service for 301 school, public, academic, and institutional libraries in a 35,000-square-mile area of Central Nebraska. The goal of the Center is to generate, gather, and analyze cost data for the provision of interlibrary loan and reference service for the two systems involved in the project.

Professional Interests. With financial support from the Nebraska Library Association, the Library Commission appointed Mary Jackson Continuing Education Coordinator. She will plan and implement a statewide continuing education network and will provide support and assistance to the continuing education efforts of the Library Systems, library-related associations and organizations, and individual libraries. The Annual Fall Children's Conference was held at Kearney State College, where deposits from the Commission have established the Nebraska Archive of Children's Books. Richard Peck was the main speaker.

Awards. The Marie Sandoz Award was presented to Paul A. Johnsgard of the University of Nebraska–Lincoln for his contributions to regional natural history specifically and for his recognized international contributions as an author on the subjects of ornithology, animal behavior, and natural history. The Trustees Citation was presented to the members of the Howells Library Board for their tireless effort to solicit funds, materials, and manpower to construct a 30-by-85-foot one-story library valued at over $80,000. The Nebraska Library Association's Meritorious Service Award was presented to Vern Hazelwood, Professor of Library Science at the University of Nebraska at Omaha, and to Vivian Peterson, Library Director at Concordia Teacher's College in Seward.

Nebraska Library Association. The Nebraska Library Association's annual fall convention was held in Kearney. The convention theme was "Nebraska's Libraries: What's Now? What's Next?" Featured speakers included Fred Kempf, Carol Elbert, Doris S. May and Carol Lechner, Barbara Lutey, Ardys Hansum, Frederick Glazer, and Ivy Ruckman. The opening session and keynote address was given by Brooke Sheldon, immediate Past-President of ALA.

The College and University Section met at Bellevue College in April. The program theme was "Computers—Cure-All or Snake Oil?" Fifteen papers were presented by section members. The Special and Institutional Section met at Southeast Community College in Lincoln. The theme was "Small Library Management." The spring meetings of the Public Library Section were held in Columbus, Valentine, Gering, Holdrege, and Lincoln. The theme of the meetings was "Your Library: A Practical Approach."

People. Several retirements, resignations, and appointments were announced during 1984. Ron Johnson, Director of the Dana College Library for 17 years, resigned to take the position of Director, Library Services, Pacific University. Sylvia Hermone was appointed Assistant Director of the Keene Memorial Public Library in Fremont, replacing Stan Schulz, new Director of the York Public Library. Deb Thomas was named Director of the Kimball Public Library. Ann Birney, Director of the Joslyn Art Reference Library in Omaha, accepted a position with Kansas State University Library.

Gerald Rudolph resigned as Dean of Libraries and joined the Special Collections Division in the Love Library at the University of Nebraska–Lincoln. Irple P. Ruby was named Head of the Learning Resources Center at McCook Community College, Metropolitan Technical Community College's new Director of Instructional Resources Technology was Paul Marsh.

Susan Annette was named Art Librarian at the Joslyn Art Museum. Edna Pfeiffer retired after 20 years as Librarian of the Hooper Public Library. Nancy Chu resigned from the Nebraska Library Commission. Ruth Boettcher returned to Nebraska as Chief of Library Services at the VA Medical Center in Lincoln. Gabrielle Cope, who served on the library staff at Nebraska Wesleyan University for over 16 years, retired on August 31.

Mary Magnusson was appointed the Director of the Hard's Memorial Library in Central City. Carroll Varner was named Assistant Director for Technical Services at Northern Illinois State University. Ella Jane Bailey became Chair of the Technical Services Department at the University of Nebraska at Omaha. Arlene Lindholm retired from the staff of the University of Nebraska at Omaha after 19 years of service. Esther Carrell, Plainview Public Library librarian, retired after 14 years of service, being replaced by Mrs. Lester Swan. Patricia S. Peterson, formerly Coordinator of Branch and Extension Services of the Lincoln City Libraries, was appointed Assistant Library Director. John Dale was named Coordinator of Branch and Extension of the Lincoln City Libraries.

Eleanor Manning, who served as the Library Director of the Thomas County Library in Thedford, died in March. Doris Fritz, Niobrara Public Library Librarian, died July 30 at Creighton.

JOHN K. MAYESKI

NEVADA

Networking in Nevada. The State of Nevada did, during 1984, nearly complete its goal of tying every public library, community college library, university library and the State Library into one of four CLSI circulation system databases. For the most part, the libraries are all on-line circulating agencies with only a few of the smallest and most remote still remaining as dial-up access only. In addition, the Clark County Library District (Las Vegas area) was experimenting with adding secondary and vocational schools. A telecommunications network was being implemented based on the state of Nevada microwave system and networking equipment manufactured by Doelz Corporation. It was designed to maximize use of each channel through multiplexing and allow for communication to each of the four CLSI computers or directly to any other terminal on each of the four systems and to any other computer or network regardless of protocol differences. The telecommunications network was installed in Clark County and Carson City areas in 1984 and was to be completed through the rest of the state by mid-1985.

The State Library produces a Nevada Union Catalog semiannually through General Research Corporation. It represents holdings of almost all public and community college libraries in the state as well as a few public schools. It is used for interlibrary loan and to spin off COM catalogs for many participating libraries. A new development on the Nevada library scene was the elimination of card catalogs in each of the two rural area CLSI systems in favor of a joint COM catalog. In the Carson City area, six counties and the State Library share a common catalog and circulation system. The same is true of five counties in the Elko area. Regional libraries are building toward an online catalog based on MARC records and CLSI expanded title format.

A statewide library card was introduced in Nevada in 1984 and was in use in the southern portion of the state. Other libraries planned to introduce the statewide card as their supplies of existing cards dwindle. Reciprocal borrowing among libraries in the same circulation system and interlibrary loan as well as reciprocal borrowing was expected to climb with the enhancements made for ease of access to all library collections.

At the general election held in November, a construction bond issue was passed by the voters for building and expanding public libraries in the state in the amount of not more than $10,000,000.

State Associations. "Libraries and Learning, the Education Connection" was the theme of the Nevada Library Association's annual conference held in Ely October 11–13. Membership had dropped somewhat from 1983 and attendance at the conference was not as large as usual. Ely is in a remote area and difficult for some residents to reach. Among the guest speakers were Will Manley, *Wilson Library*

Nevada Library Association (founded 1946)

Membership: 216; *annual budget:* $16,000.

President: Gretchen Billow, Western Nevada Community College (January 1984–January 1985).

Vice-President/President-elect: Billie M. Polson, University of Nevada, Las Vegas.

Annual meeting: October 11–13, 1984, Ely.

Publication: Highroller (bimonthly).

Nevada State Library

Joseph J. Anderson, State Librarian
Carson City 89710

School Library Media Supervisor

William F. Arensdorf
Nevada State Department of Education
Carson City 89710

Bulletin; Patricia Holt, *San Francisco Chronicle;* and Arnold Adoff, author and poet.

State Library Activities. Governor Richard Bryan in 1984 appointed a commission to study educational excellence and the legislature appointed a legislative Special Committee to study education. The Nevada State Advisory Council on Libraries and the Nevada Association of School Librarians submitted testimony. The Nevada State Advisory Council on Libraries met in June to review the letters of intent to apply for grant funds. They met again in Ely prior to the Nevada Library Association Conference. During the two meeting days their Council reviewed, discussed, and affirmed its advice on the projects for fiscal year 1985.

School Libraries. Throughout 1984 Nevada State Library cooperated with the State Department of Education and various school district librarians to provide in-service training, particularly in areas of the state that lack professional librarians. The Nevada Association of School Librarians conducted a survey of school libraries to present to the Commission on Excellence. Joseph Anderson, Nevada State Librarian, assisted in providing facts and figures where possible.

More than half of Nevada schools do not meet minimal standards set by Northwest Accreditation for budget levels and staffing. In small, isolated rural communities it is often difficult to hire teachers, let alone librarians. On the other hand, there are some exceptional school librarians in those areas, certified or noncertified. There is also a great deal of cooperation between the schools and the public libraries, sometimes done under contract with school district administration. In Washoe County (Reno) and Clark County (Las Vegas) efforts were being made to bring more schools into the statewide database.

State Division of Archives and Records. The Nevada State Library Division of Archives and Records in 1984 received a $23,993 grant from the National Historical Publications Reporting Project. Project staff assessed the conditions of records programs in state and local government agencies and in historical records repositories. The final report, *Preserving Nevada's Documentary Heritage,* makes short- and long-range recommendations.

In September the American Association for State and Local History conferred a Certificate of Commendation on the State Division for its "contribution to the preservation and conservation of Nevada's historical local government records."

In May the Division hosted the annual meeting of the Conference of Intermountain Archivists, a regional professional organization serving the archivist community in the intermountain states. State Archivist Guy Louis Rocha was elected President of the organization for 1985. The program included training sessions and panel discussions dealing with the preservation of historical records.

ANN BRADY

NEW HAMPSHIRE

The Executive Branch Reorganization Act adopted by the New Hampshire General Court in 1983 (RSA 21-G) mandated the consolidation of over 140 agencies, boards, commissions, authorities and institutions into 12 to 17

New Hampshire Library Association (founded 1889)

Membership: 400; *annual budget:* $8,005.

President: Kathryn Wendelowski, Littleton Public Library (May 1984–May 1985).

Vice-President/President-elect: Barry Hennessey, Dimond Library, University of New Hampshire, Durham.

Secretary: Carol West, Shapiro Library, New Hampshire College, Manchester.

Treasurer: John Courtney, Concord Public Library.

Annual meeting: June 1984, New London; Fall Meeting: November 1984, Manchester.

Publication: NHLA Newsletter (bimonthly).

New Hampshire State Library

Shirley Gray Adamovich, State Librarian
20 Park Street, Concord 03301

departments each of which is to have a commissioner appointed by the governor. The initial indications from the Joint Committee on Executive Branch Reorganization suggested that the New Hampshire State Library become a division of the Department of Education. State Librarian Shirley Gray Adamovich in February alerted the library community to what was considered an unacceptable proposal, stating that the State Library could best perform its statutory requirements as an independent agency.

The library voice was heard by the Joint Committee and as reorganization proceeds inexorably the Subcommittee on Libraries and Education, chaired by Representative Michael V. Hutchings of Plymouth, will recommend to the Joint Committee that an entirely new department be created, a Department of Libraries, Arts and Historic Resources, with its own Commissioner and division status for each of its three entities. To date this will be the only new department to be proposed in the process. Meetings with Representative Hutchings were being held and compromises being made as to the qualifications of Commissioner. It is probable that the present State Librarian will become the first Commissioner if the bill (HB 26) passes both House and Senate. Under the revision the Director of the Division of Libraries will be known as the State Librarian and will be required to have appropriate credentials.

New Hampshire Library Association. The 94th Annual Conference of the New Hampshire Library Association was held at Colby-Sawyer College in New London on June 4 and 5. Katherine VanWeelden, New England College, Henniker, served as chairperson.

Alice Sizer Warner, Information Guild, Lexington, Massachusetts, Barbara Whyte Felicetti, Info/Mation, Pittsfield, Massachusetts, and Patrice A. Rafail, Access, Inc., Goffstown, New Hampshire, formed a panel on the subject of Information Brokering: Lessons Learned (the Hard Way). Discussion focused on business "how-to" tips culled from many years of lecturing, authoring, consulting and practicing in the field.

Jane Perlungher, director of the Keene Public Library, who successfully increased the library's book budget by 67 percent in three years presented her techniques in the budgetary process—strategies for all sizes of public libraries.

The history and tradition of storytelling and folklore surrounding children's literature was addressed by Linda Morley, New Hampshire State Folklorist, formerly Professor of Folklore at New England College for ten years.

Other programs included Automation in New Hampshire Libraries, Personnel, Accountability, and How to Lure the Preschool Parent into the Library following the theme of the conference, "A Chance to Grow." Robert B. Parker, of Spenser fame, was the banquet speaker. He talked on "Books and Scripts"— an inside look at the way things do or do not get done in the movies as well as the absurdities which abound as only Spenser can see and tell it.

The fall meeting at Manchester on November 8, presented programs on educational reform in a learning society and library advocacy. The annual auction, with Frances Wiggin, Bedford, as auctioneer, added funds for Association programs.

Reading/Discussion Series. During 1984 (and continuing into 1985) NHLA sponsored a reading/discussion series "Good Company with Books," funded by the New Hampshire Council for the Humanities and the New Hampshire Charitable Fund. Participating libraries had a choice of one of three themes developed for the project: New England Women and Men; Rural and Small Town America; and Growing Up: Growing Old. Four biweekly programs led by scholars presented discussions based on the four books selected for each theme.

On the state level most of the activity centered around automation. The State Librarian prepared for the 1985 biennial legislative session with the emphasis to be on automation, staffing, book budget and a line item for state aid to libraries. It is expected that the new Public Library Standards will be accepted by the Joint Legislative Committee on Rules early in the new session. January 1, 1988, will be the date approved by the State Library Commission for meeting requirements.

Automation, Cooperation. In April the Concord Public Library began its journey towards full automation. The project is being funded through library trust funds, an LSCA grant and capital improvement funds. The library contracted with Maxwell Library System to convert the collection to machine readable form to be used with the OCLC-ILS Avatar System. The resulting tape will be fed into the State Library's computer, added to the Union Catalog and, together with information from other libraries, will contribute to the creation of a statewide database. Five staff members visited the Allentown, Pennsylvania, Public Library in June to observe their automated circulation system and online catalog which is the one Concord is installing.

In addition Continental Cablevision of Concord is cooperating in the project by installing an institutional loop. Using co-axial cable the loop will link the Concord Public Library with the State Library and allow transmission of data between them. A public access terminal is planned and other peripheral functions anticipated include acquisitions, managerial reports, serial updates, reference and interlibrary loan.

LOUISE C. PRICE

NEW JERSEY

New Jersey Library Association (founded 1890)

Membership: 1,627; *annual budget:* $125,000.

President: Eleanor Brome, Cranford Public Library (May 1984–April 1985).

Vice-President/President-elect: Lynn Miller, Rutgers University.

Executive Director: Abigail Studdiford, 116 West State Street, Trenton 08608.

Annual meeting: April 25–28, 1984, New Brunswick.

Publications: New Jersey Libraries (quarterly); *New Jersey Libraries Newsletter* (monthly).

Division of State Library, Archives and History, State Department of Education

Barbara Weaver, State Librarian
185 West State Street, CN 520
Trenton 08625

State School Library Media Supervisor

Anne Voss
State Library
185 West State St., CN 520
Trenton 08625

New State Network. The big news in New Jersey in 1984 was the initiation of the new statewide network. The Governor signed the Library Network bill into law on January 17. Under that landmark legislation, fiscal year 1984 appropriations provided $125,000 for six planning grants and start-up costs of two Regional Library Cooperatives (RLCs). The RLCs were to be phased in over a five-year period. Two were to be in operation in 1985. Six regions recommended by a Statewide Planning Group were: (1) Hunterdon, Morris, Somerset, Sussex, Warren; (2) Bergen, Passaic; (3) Essex, Hudson; (4) Middlesex, Union; (5) Mercer, Monmouth, Ocean; and (6) Atlantic, Burlington, Camden, Cape May, Cumberland, Gloucester, and Salem.

In 1984 planning committees in each region received $5,000 planning grants and Regional Library Cooperatives $50,000 establishment grants. Basic services provided by each region were to cover supplemental reference, interlibrary loan, delivery, and citation/location.

Six hundred librarians, trustees, commissioners, and citizens representing 283 different libraries attended nine regional meetings on the New Jersey Network. The State Librarian, Barbara F. Weaver, provided overviews at the meetings on the 20-year history of library cooperation in the state and the progress toward a full-service, multitype network. State funding is "new money" in addition to that allocated for per capita aid and other state aid and grants. In his annual budget message on January 30, Governor Thomas Kean requested an increase of $2,000,000, or 30 percent, in aid to local libraries, the largest single increase ever proposed for them. (For the Area Library Program, the state had appropriated $2,300,000 for fiscal year 1984.) The first statewide meeting of network Interim Planning Committees and the Interim Library Network Review Board was convened in Princeton October 11, 1984.

Rutgers. At the School of Communications, Information and Library Studies, Rutgers, plans were well advanced in 1984 for a new master's degree program in communication and information systems.

Children's Services. "The Fine Art of Children's Services" was the theme of the program attended by librarians in Trenton on September 2.

Grants. A grant of $10,000 was awarded to the Trenton Public Library by the state Committee for the Humanities for an index to materials on ethnic groups of Trenton.

The State Library received a $5,400 B. Dalton grant, under the book chain's national literacy program, to support a summer reading program for public libraries.

Somerset County Library, the county College Learning Resources Center, and the county Vo-Tech School Library were jointly awarded an LSCA Title I $5,000 Automation Consultation Assistance grant.

Retirements. After 22 years at the State Library, Henry J. Michniewski, Head of the Library Development Bureau, retired. Robert A. Drescher was named Head of a reorganized Bureau. Selma P. Kessler, on the State Library staff from 1972, retired as Assistant Coordinator of State and Federal Programs.

Appointments. Ocean County Library appointed Elaine McConnell, President of the New Jersey Library Association, its new Director. Donna Benson, formerly I & R Coordinator of Volunteer Services at Ocean County, was named Coordinator of Volunteer Services for the Blind and Handicapped at the State Library.

The retired Assistant State Librarian, David C. Palmer, was elected President of Friends of the Trenton Free Public Library.

STAFF

NEW MEXICO

New Mexico Library Association (founded 1924)

Membership: 600; *annual budget:* $32,000.

President: Cheryl Wilson, Las Cruces (April 1984–April 1985).

Vice-President/President-elect: Marcy Litzenberg, Santa Fe.

Annual meeting: April 25–27, 1984, Albuquerque.

Publication: NMLA Newsletter (five issues per year).

New Mexico State Library

Virginia Downing, State Librarian
325 Don Gaspar
Santa Fe 87503

School Library Media Supervisor

Mary Jane Annand
State Department of Education
300 Don Gaspar
Santa Fe 87503

New Mexico Needs Assessment. Work began in late 1984 on a statewide assessment study of library client needs for the next 15 years. The State Library and the New Mexico Library Association worked together on the study, which will review and revise the Coordinated Library Systems of New Mexico, a planning document developed in 1971 and revised in 1977. A private consulting firm—Cresap, McCormick and Paget of Los Angeles—selected by the study advisory committee was performing the assessment. Results of the needs were to be summarized in a written report to be presented at the New Mexico Library Association annual conference in April 1985. Long-range planning efforts to implement study recommendations were scheduled to begin in the spring of 1985 and to utilize a broad base of librarian input.

Recording Books for Blind and Physically Handicapped. The New Mexico State Library developed a new program of volunteers that includes actors, teachers, clerks, and individuals from all walks of life who are volunteering their time to record books for the blind and physically handicapped. The project greatly expands the materials available to the blind and physically handicapped. The project has a coordinator who works under the supervision of the LBPH director.

State Aid to Public Libraries. In 1984, the Legislature approved a state-aid appropriation of $234,300, or 17 cents per capita. The New Mexico State Library planned to ask an increase of state grant-in-aid funds from the 1985 New Mexico Legislature—$341,750, or 25 cents per capita.

New Buildings, Remodelings. The Tucumcari Public Library during 1984 completed a new program room with a seating capacity of 60. Grand opening celebrations for the $1,800,000 Farmington Public Library were held March 12 through 17. The Santa Fe City Council approved plans for a new $3,900,000 library and ground was broken for a new $3,400,000 library and learning resource center at the New Mexico Military Institute in Roswell. Voters in Belen passed a $500,000 bond issue for a new library building.

Appointments. Jack Carter, Kathryn Gursky and Donna Berg joined the staff of the Library at Los Alamos National Laboratories. Kristine Warmoth was named Reference Librarian at the University of Albuquerque and Bill Richmond was appointed Director of the State Library Media Center. Peter Ives joined the University of New Mexico General Library and Ruth Krug joined the University of New Mexico General Library in the Serials Department. Christine Peterson was appointed Assistant Librarian at the Gallup Public Library, and Karen Hankla was named Librarian at the Cuba Community Library. Glee Wenzel and Ann Penney joined the staff of the State Library's Development Division.

Retirements/Resignations. Artie Mae King, Librarian at the A. W. Thompson Library in Clayton for 15 years, and Barbara Cox, Reference Librarian at the University of Albuquerque retired in 1984. Laura Belle Cole, Head of Technical Services at Mesa Public Library, Los Alamos, retired after 15 years. Sara Beth Galloway resigned as Director of the Roswell Public Library. Jacki Schenck, a Consultant at the New Mexico State Library, resigned, and Frances Sena, Assistant Librarian at Carnegie Public Library, Las Vegas, moved to Nebraska.

PAUL A. AGRIESTI

NEW YORK

New York Library Association (founded 1890)

Membership: 2,825; *annual expenditure:* $265,500.

President: Roy D. Miller, Jr., Executive Assistant to the Director, Brooklyn Public Library (October 1984–December 1985).

Vice-President/President-elect: Ruth A. Fraley, Head, Graduate Library for Public Affairs and Public Policy, SUNY at Albany, Albany.

Executive Director: Nancy Lian, 15 Park Row, Suite 434, New York 10038.

Annual meeting: October 21–24, 1984, Concord Hotel, Lake Kiamesha.

Publication: NYLA Bulletin (10 issues a year).

New York State Library

Joseph F. Shubert, State Librarian and Assistant Commissioner for Libraries
State Education Department
Cultural Education Center
Empire State Plaza
Albany 12230

School Library Media Supervisor

Beatrice Griggs, Chief
Bureau of School Library Media Programs
State Education Department
Albany 12234

On July 10 Governor Mario Cuomo signed legislation increasing state aid to all types of libraries by $13,400,000, bringing state aid to libraries to $55,500,000 annually. The new law increased aid to public libraries, academic, and special libraries, created a $3,000,000 program of library construction and rehabilitation aid, initiated programs for technology and preservation of research materials, and made permanent the 12 pilot-school-library systems as well as providing for the establishment of 36 more school-library systems to complete the statewide network. The bill received unanimous approval in both houses of the legislature.

Throughout New York State in 1984 libraries displayed the slogan "New York—Where Learning Never Ends—The Library" to celebrate the 200 years of educational leadership by the Board of Regents. Carol Nemeyer, Associate Librarian of Congress and former President of the American Library Association, joined Barbara W. Tuchman, historian, former Ambassador George Kennan, James Reston of the *New York Times*, and others in a January 1984 Board of Regents Bicentennial seminar on international exchange of information. The role of librarians in information exchange dominated the discussion and helped set the stage for year-long library participation in the Bicentennial. The Regents Advisory Council on Libraries and the New York Library Association with libraries and library systems cosponsored 14 state events during which Regents met with librarians, trustees, and library users.

Moving toward its goal of establishing student affiliate groups in high schools throughout the state, the Citizens' Library Council of New York State (CLiC) scheduled charter club kickoff celebrations throughout 1984 to coordinate with the Regents' Bicentennial. The charter clubs, selected, in part, after a survey of high schools revealed which districts in the state had well-developed, active student library clubs, will form the basis for development of an organization and activity manual, and will serve as models for the nearly 50 additional schools that either have, or desire to form, library clubs.

State Association. NYLA Council had four goals and many objectives for 1984.

Goal 1: Legislation—to pursue an aggressive legislative program so that libraries are properly funded to sustain and expand existing programs while providing the impetus for exploration and implementation of change. Accomplishments: NYLA joined with NYSALB (New York State Association of Library Boards), CLiC, and the library community of the state to see that goal realized. Throughout the legislative session, NYLA leadership and membership were constant and thorough in attending to the advancement of the Library Omnibus Bill, which became Chapter 348 of the Laws of 1984. A successful Library Day in Albany was held in March and the NYLA Legislative Committee was responsible for organizing the delegation of some 30 people who participated in the April Library Day in Washington.

Goal 2: Awareness—a commitment to raising awareness level of the public to library services presently available, together with immediate and future needs of all libraries. Accomplishments: a major awareness program using the Regents' Bicentennial celebration as its focus. Libraries across the state highlighted their many services while identifying the needs of the future. A Bicentennial Task Force, chaired by Lucille Thomas, was established with representatives from each Section of NYLA. The Task Force developed a booklet "Idea Exchange," which was printed and distributed to all libraries by the State Education Department. In addition a special library logo adopting the official Regents Bicentennial logo was designed. Posters of the logo were printed courtesy of Queens Borough Public Library, decals of the logo were reproduced courtesy of Franklin Watts, and three sizes of the logo were prepared for reproduction courtesy of R. R. Bowker. The Task Force also commissioned Mildred Lowe to write a position paper on the Bicentennial theme to be published in *The Bookmark*, a publication of the New York State Library.

Goal 3: Communication—improve methods of communication with its membership so that members will feel their needs are being met. Accomplishments: The Conference Planning Committee, chaired by Second Vice-President Sam Simon, planned and executed an excellent conference program that provided an opportunity for professional growth and social interaction for the 1,600 librarians, trustees, exhibitors, and Friends attending. There were 140 programs and meetings including speakers Michael Korda and Fran Lebowitz, Intellectual Freedom skits, and Carnival Night, which raised about $3,000 for NYLA's Vitality Fund. The Vitality Fund goal is to develop a reserve fund equal to six months' operating budget. The Personnel Administration Committee coordinated the Job Referral Center; the Continuing Education Committee presented seven in-depth seminars attended by approximately 175 people; and the Exhibits Committee provided an excellent array of exhibitors totaling 141 booths. At the annual meeting the membership passed unanimously the proposed bylaws revision and also approved the new personal membership dues structure at the rate of $2.50 per $1,000 annual gross salary.

The Continuing Education Committee also planned a one-day conference, "Using Books with Children," November 10, 1984, in cooperation with the Buffalo and Erie County Public Library and SUNY at Buffalo.

ALA Chapter Councilor Patricia Mautino worked to improve communication by meeting with the ALA Councilors from New York, served as a member of NYLA Council, and through her column in the *NYLA Bulletin* kept membership informed about ALA activities.

Goal 4: Membership—will increase thus assuring a strong and viable organization. Achievements: The Membership Committee developed promotions that resulted in 90 new institutional members, an increase of 49 percent, and 113 new personal members.

In addition to these Council goals, each Section and RoundTable developed a program that complemented and strengthened NYLA's goals and objectives.

The Academic and Special Libraries Section prepared a Library Day handout and supported a first-class mailing on legislative issues. The Section prepared a publication for sale on "The Impact of Online Databases on the Usage of Printed Equivalents."

The Public Library Section also paid for a first-class mailing to provide all NYLA members with timely information on legislation so that concerted and effective lobbying could be done.

Reference and Adult Services Section used "Organization, Celebration, Legislation, and Publication" as its focus to celebrate 20 years as a NYLA Section. The section held a two-mile "Run with RASS" at the conference, issued three publications, and cosponsored a general NYLA mailing.

The School Library Media Section celebrated its 40th year as a Section of NYLA. The School Library Media Section held its 14th annual two-day spring conference. SLMS members actively sought the inclusion of the role of the school library media center in the *Regents' Action Plan to Improve Elementary and Secondary Education Results*. SLMS gained visibility by participation in the New York State Council of Educational Associations and statewide conferences sponsored by non-library organizations and took an active role with school library systems to secure the passing of the Library Omnibus Bill.

Constance H. Richardson, School Library Media Specialist at Mendon High School, Pittsford, won the SLMS 1984 Elliot Rabner Cultural Media Award. William H. Phillips, Superintendent of the Jordan-Elbridge Central School District, received the 1984 SLMS Administrator's Award for outstanding support of the district's elementary school library media program.

The Youth Services Section sponsored a one-day workshop on "How to Pick 'Em" attended by 100 people. The Section also published revised *Standards for Youth Services in the Public Libraries of New York*, which was the culmination of two years' work. A 1984 calendar noting daily items of interest to youth librarians was sold out as was the *YA program Guidebook* (1984).

The Library Education Section changed its status and name to the RoundTable on Library and Information Science Education. Two new RoundTables were established to serve the needs of members. The first was to serve needs of members interested in library networks, library systems, and library cooperatives. It will be known as STAR (Sharing Through Alliances RoundTable). The second, the Public Relations RoundTable, will provide a forum for the exchange of ideas and public relations expertise and will serve as a clearinghouse for public relations information.

The Association had a severe fiscal problem during the year. It arose from the unauthorized use of NYLA funds by a staff member.

State Library. The State Library served as a research center for government and citizens during 1984. A collection of over 1,900,000 volumes, access to an online state library catalog and over 200 other databases, and special collections of maps, manuscripts, and other special media materials provided the basis for library service to some 84,000 walk-in users, and over 100,000 intelibrary loan requests. Reference inquiries at the library increased 18 percent, rising for the first time to over 100,000 a year. Nearly 5,000 database searches were provided for government clients, a special project provided legal information to 3,400 prisoners, and over 300,000 special media materials were loaned to 25,000 blind and visually handicapped users.

For the Legislature, the Legislative and Governmental Services unit produced announcements on recent library acquisitions, short reading lists, and 25 bibliographies on topics of legislative concern. Among the subjects were acid rain, arts and tourism, computer crime, parental kidnapping, and water quality. The unit also presented four seminars attended by 563 persons. The seminars enabled participants to hear such experts as the Secretary of the Assembly Ways and Means Committee; the State's Chief Budget Examiner; the Assistant Secretary to the Governor; and a professor from the Graduate School of Public Affairs, SUNY at Albany. For the first time the Library had access to the computerized legal database LEXIS. Science, Health Sciences and Technology Reference Service published an extensive report on two consumer health projects completed in 1983.

The Educational Programs and Studies Information Service staff loaned nearly 10,000 reports and books to some 7,400 staff from the Education Department and schools. For users of its genealogical research and services, the staff of Humanities and Manuscripts and Special Collections produced a half-hour introductory videotape.

In addition to state aid for libraries, the Library Development staff administered federal aid programs, which included LSCA I, $4,309,250; LSCA II (appropriated as part of the 1983 Emergency Jobs Act) $2,588,381; and $1,012,170 for Title III. Seventy-four Title I grants, 9 Title III grants, and 13 construction grants were awarded. According to a State Senate report issued in March 1984, more than 2,000,000 New York State residents over the age of 18 or 16 percent of the adult population are functionally illiterate.

Literacy projects are an important part of the 1984 LSCA I program with nearly $200,000 invested in eight literacy projects in library systems. In addition, because of the link between literacy and educational opportunities, nearly a dozen other projects under the adult independent learners program in public libraries have a literacy component. An upgraded automated system replaced the 1973 automated system in the Library for the Blind and Visually Handicapped which served 25,000 readers and loaned 312,000 books in 1984.

Jack B. Spear retired after 33 years with the State Library. Sarah McCain and Carol Desch joined the staff of the Division of Library Development.

School Library Media Programs. The *Regents Action Plan to Improve Elementary and Secondary Education Results in New York*, approved at the March meeting of the Board of Regents, included 17 direct and several indirect implications for libraries. Three of the direct references were (1) "The Department will further study the issue of requiring certified library media specialists for grades K-6. A Department recommendation will be issued by November 1984."

(2) "Students in grades 7 and 8 shall have the equivalent of one period of library and information skills per week. The use of libraries should be taught by a library media specialist in cooperation with classroom teachers. Schools will have flexibility in scheduling this requirement."

(3) "In all subjects, K-12, revisions in the syllabi will include materials and activities related to generic subgoals such as problem solving, reasoning skills, speaking, capacity to search for information, the use of libraries, and increasing student awareness of and information about the disabled." Use of computers and libraries will be encouraged in grades 3-12. Interdisciplinary projects are also encouraged.

The Bureau of School Library Media programs staff began work on the preparation of the grade 7-12 library media skills curriculum to complete the K-12 program. The K-6 portion has been published. Bureau staff were helping the 36 new regional school library systems authorized by the Chapter 348 legislation to become established and develop their first three-year plan of service to member libraries. Staff of the Bureau were active participants in developing Commissioner's Regulations and other activities related to the implementation of the Regents' *Action Plan*. Staff have been part of the Registration Team for New York City High Schools. Their reports helped to get the per pupil allocation for library materials doubled in 1984.

Bureau staff reached over 1,300 participants through programs done for such annual conferences as Towards Humanizing Education, Writing, Reading, Arts in Education, and the School Library Media Section Spring Conference.

Public Libraries. Onondaga County Public Library received a grant of $19,000 under the Developmental Disabilities Assistance and Bill of Rights Act to provide electromechanical services to aid severely disabled persons. Commonly available toys with adaptive switches, able to be controlled by minimal movement, will be available on loan to schools, agencies and individuals. The library will house and distribute the toys and Telephone Pioneers of America will provide training and maintenance.

The New York Public Library held a major exhibit on censorship to open its newly renovated exhibit hall. The $3,000,000 refurbishing of the huge marble room is part of a $44,600,000 restoration program.

Some 26 Nassau County libraries make it possible for residents interested in adopting a child to get information on available children through a set of loose-leaf reference books entitled *New York State's Waiting Children*, published and updated bimonthly by the New York State Department of Social Services Adoption Service. Because their service hours are longer than other agencies and because they offer unhurried browsing close to home, libraries are excellent locations for recruiting prospective adoptive parents.

A seven-week film series on Russian opera and ballet, cosponsored by the Greenburgh Public Library, the Greenburgh Arts and Cultural Committee, and the Westchester Dance Council, set off protests, bomb threats, and three acts of vandalism before the first film was shown on March 13. Robert Trudell, Director of the Greenburgh Public Library, was the recipient of the first annual SIRS/NYLA Intellectual Freedom Award. Marjorie Hasbrouck of the Stone Ridge Public Library received the L. Marion Moshier/Asa Wynkoop award given annually by the Public Library Section for distinguished library service in a rural community serving a population of 7,500 or less.

Alan Kusler retired after 22 years as Public Relations Director of the Rochester Public Library and the Monroe County Library System.

Port Washington Public Library published *It Looks Like Yesterday to Me*, a collection of photographs and reminiscences documenting the community's Afro-American heritage. The 36-page booklet was researched and compiled by Elly Shodell, the Library's oral historian, in cooperation with Gwenderlyn Johnson of the Schomburg Center for Research in Black Culture.

Harrison's Citizen of the Year, Marie Mersky of the Harrison Public Library, retired after 15 years as Director. Gertrude Schwerbish, Directore of the East Islip Public Library, also retired. She had been with the library since 1961.

Academic, Special Libraries. R. Kathleen Molz, Melvil Dewey Professor of Library Science at Columbia University, was named Acting Dean of its library school while Richard Darling, Dean since 1970, was on sabbatical leave. His retirement was to be effective in June 1985.

Awards. Lucille Thomas retired Assistant Director, Office of Library, Media and Telecommunications, New York City Board of Education, and Marie Bruce, Director of the Oneonta Public Library, shared the 1984 NYLA Outstanding Service Award. Bruce also was awarded the 1984 Robert B. Downs Intellectual Freedom Award given annually by the Graduate School of Library and Information Science of the University of Illinois. Thomas also received one of the Regents Bicentennial Medals of Excellence as did Harold S. Hacker, retired Director of the Monroe County Library System and the Rochester Public Library. Richard Johnson, Director of libraries, Milne Library, SUNY at Oneonta, was named Academic Librarian of the Year by the Association of College and Research Libraries.

NYLA Executive Director Nancy Lian was the 1984 recipient of Association Executive of the Year award presented by the New York State Association of Convention Bureaus.

Esther Lopato received the Velma K. Moore award, which is the highest honor given to a library trustee by the New York State Association of Library Boards.

Deaths. Deaths in the New York library world during 1984 included Peggy Overfield, Assistant to the Director of the F. W. Crumb Memorial Library, SUNY at Potsdam; Alice Damon Rider, retired Chair, Department of Library Science, SUNY at Geneseo; Lynda A. Regan, Librarian for the New York State Office of Court Administration; and Robert J. Flores, retired Chief of the Bureau of Regional Library Services, Division of Library Development, New York State Library.

ROBERT BARRON
PATRICIA MAUTINO

NORTH CAROLINA

North Carolina Library Association (founded 1948)

Membership: 1,982; *biennial budget (1984–85):* $88,600.

President: Leland M. Park, Davidson College Library, Davidson 28036 (October 1983–October 1985).

Vice-President/President-elect: Pauline F. Myrick, Moore County Schools, Box 307, Carthage 28327.

Biennial meeting: October, Raleigh.

Publication: North Carolina Libraries (quarterly).

Division of State Library, Department of Cultural Resources

David N. McKay, Director
109 East Jones Street
Raleigh 27611

School Library Media Supervisor

Elsie L. Brumback
Department of Public Instruction
Raleigh 27602

Awards at ALA. Several North Carolina librarians and library organizations were honored at the American Library Association Conference in Dallas. The Friends of North Carolina Public Libraries won the 1984 Friends of Libraries USA Award as the outstanding Friends organization in the country. The North Carolina Friends, in only their third year of existence, were recognized for a broad range of activities that included workshops across the state to assist interested citizens in forming local Friends groups, a speakers bureau, and a newsletter. Friends President Perry White accepted the award at the Dallas Conference.

The North Carolina Association of School Librarians received the 1984 Grolier National Library Week Grant for its proposal to sponsor a statewide School Library Media Day during National Library Week. The award, the first to be presented to a school library media group, was selected by ALA's National Library Week Committee during the 1984 Midwinter Meeting.

Lester Asheim, who retired in 1984 as William Rand Kenan, Jr., Professor of Library Science at the University of North Carolina at Chapel Hill, was given honorary membership in the American Library Association at the Dallas Conference.

The 1984 John Phillip Immroth Memorial Award for Intellectual Freedom was given to Gene Lanier, Chairman of the NCLA Intellectual Freedom Committee and Professor of Library Science at East Carolina University. The award honors the courage and dedication of those who have made notable contributions to intellectual freedom. Lanier has also received the Hugh M. Hefner First Amendment Award in education, presented by the Playboy Foundation, and the Mary Peacock Douglas Award from the North Carolina Association of School Librarians.

Jaia Barrett, head of the Public Documents Department at Duke University, was presented the 1984 "Documents to the People" Award in recognition of her "exemplary record as an active contributor to documents librarianship." The award, donated by the Congressional Information Service, is administered by the ALA Government Documents Round Table and carries with it a citation of achievement and a monetary prize to be assigned to a project of the recipient's choice.

State Library Activities. The State Library-sponsored 1984 statewide summer reading program for children was entitled "North Carolina Celebrates: 1584–1984!" and was designed to coincide with the 400th anniversary of the sailing of the Roanoke voyages, which left England for America in 1584. Deneen Graham, Miss North Carolina, was the program sponsor and starred in a public service announcement publicizing the program.

Building Programs. The Walter R. Davis Library opened at the University of North Carolina at Chapel Hill, following four years of construction and over 11 years of planning. The Davis Library replaces the Louis Round Wilson Library as the central library on the UNC–CH campus and contains over 420,000 square feet. The new library is designed to seat over 3,000 users and to hold 1,800,000 volumes plus a large microform and government documents collection. The building and its furnishings cost $22,400,000.

A library bond worth $9,300,000 to the Public Library of Charlotte and Mecklenburg County was passed with a 70 percent approval rate. The bond includes $8,800,000 for expansion of the main library.

Networks, Interlibrary Cooperation. The North Carolina Library Networking Steering Committee awarded two grants for ZOCs (zones of cooperation) to encourage resources sharing and cooperation. Grants were awarded for a range of services for Cleveland County libraries and for libraries in Wilson County.

The Cleveland County project, known as CLEVE-NET, serves a population of 85,000 and involves seven libraries: Cleveland County Memorial Library, Cleveland Technical College, Cleveland County Schools, Gardner-Webb College, Kings Mountain District Schools, Mauney Memorial Library (Kings Mountain), and Shelby City Schools. CLEVE-NET builds on an existing cooperative effort that provides a common library card and reciprocal borrowing among the public and academic libraries. The project will use electronic mail to transmit messages related to collections, interlibrary loan requests, and reference questions. A merged file of patrons registered at each library, a local resource directory, and community calendar will be developed and maintained online.

In Wilson County, a number of libraries will use microcomputers and an electronic bulletin board system for networking activities, which will include a union catalog of audiovisual materials. Cooperating libraries include the Wilson County Public Library and libraries of Atlantic Christian College, Wilson County Technical Institute, Eastern North Carolina School for the Deaf, Wilson Memorial Hospital, and three high schools.

The two 1984 grants bring to four the total ZOC grants given by the committee. In 1983 grants were received for a union list of periodicals for libraries in western North Carolina and for a union COM catalog for libraries in Nash and Edgecombe Counties.

The Triangle Research Libraries Network made available a gift of 11 sets of their union list on microfiche to the Reference Branch and the IN-WATS Branch of the State Library and to nine large public libraries. The prime value of the union list is the subject access it provides to the large number of resources of the member universities—Duke University, North Carolina State University, and the University of North Carolina at Chapel Hill.

Awards. The Learning Resources Center Library at Guilford Technical Community College was named the Mertys W. Bell Library in honor of Bell, who retired in 1984.

Appointments. Calvin Craft was named Director of the F. D. Bluford Library at North Carolina A & T State University in Greensboro. Janet Freeman became Director of the Meredith College Library in Raleigh. Michael LaCroix was appointed Director of the Wingate College Library in Wingate.

Deaths. Frances Reid, former consultant with the State Library, died in December 1983. Mary E. Morris, acquisitions librarian at Western Carolina University since 1961, died January 20, 1984. Susan Grey Akers, dean of the UNC—Chapel Hill Library School from 1935 to 1954 and the first woman academic dean at the university, died January 30.

ROBERT E. BURGIN

NORTH DAKOTA

North Dakota Library Association (founded 1908)

Membership: 474; *annual budget:* $54,500.

President: Jerry Kaup, Minot Public Library, Minot (October 1983–October 1985).

Vice-President/President-elect: Cheryl Bailey, Mary College Library, Bismarck.

Annual meeting: September 20–22, 1984, Williston.

Publication: GOODSTUFF (quarterly).

North Dakota State Library

Ruth Mahan, State Librarian
Liberty Memorial Building
Capitol Grounds
Bismarck, North Dakota 58505

School Library Media Supervisor

Patricia Herbel
Department of Public Instruction
Capitol Building
Bismarck, North Dakota 58505

On July 1 libraries across North Dakota unplugged their Teletype machines and within a few weeks were all on an electronic mail system called Easy Link. Through this system, interlibrary loan requests and messages could be exchanged between 22 libraries, at year's end. A series of training sessions in four areas of the state were conducted in late June, prior to the electronic link-up. Conducted by State Library staff members, the local libraries' personnel were instructed in start-up procedures and troubleshooting. This link-up was one of the first projects suggested by the NDLAC (North Dakota Library Automation Committee), which was revived in mid-1984 and was continuing to explore automation that will eventually give each library in the state access to the state database.

State Library Activities. In April the State Library formed a Task Force to determine the role and function of the agency. Members of the Task Force, which submitted a Mission Statement to the State Librarian, were Cheryl Bailey, Bismarck; Tom Jones, Bismarck; Elaine Little, Bismarck; Suzanne Mattheis, Bismarck; Cynthia Schaff, Williston; Larry Spears, Bismarck; Shari Stroup, Hazen; Dennis Page, Grand Forks; and Charlotte Whittey, Mandan. A Task Force team comprised of Charlotte Whittey, Cynthia Schaff, Elaine Little, and Kilbourn Janecek, Fargo, were following up the Mission Statement implementation and working with State Library staff.

The Governor's Advisory Council on Libraries with the State Library approved grant awards to the School for the Deaf, Grafton State School, School for the Blind, State Industrial School, Jamestown State Hospital, Soldier's Home, and San Haven to support the library and information needs of the clientele of each institution.

LSCA Title II funds were awarded for building/renovation projects. State aid grants to public libraries were again awarded.

Plans for microfilming the state document collection at the State Library have been developed by the State Librarian and a committee of the Government Documents Round Table, a section of NDLA.

NDLA. The 1984 North Dakota Library Association Convention was held in Williston in September. Keynote speaker for the convention was Bernard Vavrek, School of Library Science, Clarion State College, Pennsylvania, who spoke on rural librarianship. The School Library Media Section sponsored a workshop conducted by Ruth Toor, School Library Media Specialist from Southern Boulevard School in Chatham, New Jersey. Frank A. Stevens, Chief of Library Education, U.S. Dept. of Education, introduced the section to *Alliance for Excellence: Librarians Respond to "A Nation at Risk."* The Media Section awarded the first School Administrator of the Year Award to Ronald M. Stammen, Superintendent of Schools at Divide County School District 1, Crosby. Neil Price, UND, chaired the Media Section.

The Academic Section of NDLA announced new officers at the convention: Marilyn Guttromson, Bismarck, President; Dolores Vyzralek, Bismarck, Secretary; and Jon Boone, Grand Forks, President of the new ACRL chapter. The Governor's Advisory Council on Libraries agreed to use $66,000 of LSCA funds to promote the completion of the state's automated database. These funds will aid public libraries with retrospective conversion projects. Some of the funds will be cost-sharing with the academic libraries, who were given funds last spring to finish their retro projects.

Officers of the Trustee Section of NDLA were Marion Enyeart, Garrison, President; Shari Stroup, Hazen, Vice-President; and Pam Anderson, Ward County, Secretary. Three trustee schools were held in March. The program included Jerry Kaup, Minot Public Library; Diane Caley, Ward County Public Library; and Mary Braaten, State Library, who presented an overview of the newly distributed *North Dakota Public Library Standards.* Jerry Kaup offered suggestions on fund raising. Braaten analyzed intellectual freedom issues in the state.

The Children's Round Table Section of NDLA was chaired by Paulette Nelson, Minot. Plans were under way for a regional summer reading program for the northwest quadrant of the state.

The Junior Members Round Table Section of NDLA, headed by Ann Pederson, Grand Forks, awarded its second annual Baker & Taylor Grassroots Award in North Dakota to Beulah Sears, Minnewaukan Public School Librarian. JMRT also awarded its annual Friendly Booth award at the conference to Timothy Walsh from Ollis Book Corporation.

The Health Science Information Section NDLA was chaired by James Robbins. The National Library of Medicine approved a grant proposal from David Boilard, Director, H. E. French Medical Library, UND, Grand Forks, for regional collection development on Human Nutrition Research. Two underserved/unserved area projects were approved by the Greater Midwest Regional Medical Library Network. In the Northwest and Southwest AHEC Libraries, they included workshops on basic hospital management.

The National Library of Medicine approved two library resource grants from the eastern AHECs to develop essential collections of monographs and journals in the small hospitals.

The Intellectual Freedom Committee, chaired by Mary Braaten, Bismarck, finalized a draft of the *North Dakota Intellectual Freedom Handbook,* which was approved by the convention attendees. The Committee also conducted a survey in spring 1984 on intellectual freedom and confidentiality of records requests.

The Electronic Library Round Table was established as an organizational committee during the convention. Chaired by Dennis Page, Grand Forks, it has three objectives: provide or encourage programming at conference or in continuing education, encourage publication of information dealing with high technology, and convey the importance of technology to the library community.

The Public Library Section of NDLA, chaired by Marlene Ripplinger, helped to sponsor the keynote speaker for the convention. Two Spring Frolics were held in April, with Marlys Ostrem, children's storyteller, Jerry Kaup, on Volunteers and Friends of the Library; and Mary Braaten, on intellectual freedom issues. The Tri-State Automation in Libraries Institute was held in Bismarck in June. The Institute was cosponsored by MINITEX, the North Dakota State Library, and the South Dakota State Library.

Professional Services. Marilyn Guttromson and Mary Braaten, both from Bismarck, conducted the Legislative Documents Workshops in three locations in October, looking toward participation of 46 libraries in the documents program during the next session of the Legislature. These libraries receive bills, journals, resolutions, bill status reports, and miscellaneous documents from the legislature.

The Dakota Radio Information Service (DRIS) became a reality in March. It reaches handicapped persons who cannot read in a 75-mile radius of Bismarck–Mandan. Patrons of the service receive a special closed circuit receiver free of charge that captures the signal for the programs. The organizers of the project were George Saiki, Bismarck, and Sally Oremland, State Library, Bismarck.

Appointments. Val Morehouse began working as the automation consultant for the State Library in April. Darryl Podoll was appointed Director of the Valley City State College Library. Phyllis Bratton became the new Director of the Jamestown College Library. Sue Eisenzimmer was named Media Director at the North Dakota School for the Deaf in Devils Lake.

MARY BRAATEN

OHIO

Ohio Library Association (founded 1895)

Membership: 1,986; *annual budget:* $140,970.

President: Greg Byerly, Kent State University (November 1984–November 1985).

Vice-President/President-elect: Bonnie Beth Mitchell, OHIONET, Columbus.

Executive Director: A. Chapman Parsons, 40 South Third Street, Suite 230, Columbus 43215.

Annual meeting: October 18–20, 1984, Columbus.

Publications: OLA Bulletin (triannually); *Ohio Libraries* (nine issues a year).

State Library of Ohio

Richard Cheski, State Librarian
65 South Front Street
Columbus 43215

School Library Media Supervisor

Theresa Fredericka
Division of Elementary and Secondary Education
65 South Front Street
Columbus 43215

The Public Library Financing and Support Committee worked during the first half of the year in seven open meetings, accepting testimony from the library community and the tax department on the issues of adequacy and distribution. Over the summer the Committee prepared a draft plan that was introduced in open hearings in five locations throughout the state. On December 6 the final recommendations were presented to the Governor.

The first statewide public relations campaign was launched in cooperation with five other associations, supported by a LSCA grant from the State Library of Ohio.

State Association. The Third Concurrent Conference of the Ohio Educational Library Media Association and the Ohio Library Association, held October 18–20, had a record attendance of 2,452 people registered. Charles

Kuralt was the conference banquet speaker.

The Research and Planning Committee conducted an Ohio Census Day March 19. Data were collected on circulation of library materials, library visitors, number of reference transactions, and other subjects.

In light of increased funding for public libraries beginning in 1986, the Board of Directors requested the Library Development Committee to revise the "Standards for Public Libraries of Ohio." The Committee responded and labeled their work "Interim Standards. . .," with the pledge to continue their work and test the standards.

The Ad Hoc Committee appointed to revise the OLA Code of Ethics recommended that the OLA Code be replaced with the endorsement of the ALA Code of Ethics.

Outreach and Special Services planned several publications to aid in serving their special constituencies. A Guideline to Planning Public Library Service to Children was prepared by Children's Services in Libraries and School Media Centers and is available for sale. A *New Members Handbook* produced by the Junior Members Round Table received recognition at the ALA JMRT meeting.

The Reading Promotion Task Force of the Children's Services in Libraries and School Media Centers Division received a Gund Foundation grant for a statewide reading promotion—Get into a Good Book.

The 1984 meetings, coordinated by the Chapter Conference Committee, attracted an attendance of 1,477, a 10 percent increase over the previous year's record. Completion of a *Chapter Conference Handbook*, two years in preparation, promises to facilitate planning.

State Library Activities. The reference staff of the State Library of Ohio responded to more than 1,600 requests for information while the circulation staff loaned nearly 60,000 materials in fiscal year 1984. State employees made over 2,200 requests for interlibrary loan materials. In addition, reference staff performed more than 600 database searches for state employees. During fiscal year 1984 more than 20,000 volumes were added to the Library Control System. The Library's catalog and shelflist were discarded because their functions were absorbed by the online catalog. The addition of two microcomputers helped streamline the reference and information services staffs' work. *State Policy Reports* and the *Council of State Government's Backgrounds* were indexed on a micro; each proved useful and the publishers of the documents asked for copies.

The library's genealogy staff served patrons by responding to almost 14,000 requests for information. More than 80,000 items were cataloged in the Library's Technical and Special Services area for 65 contract libraries.

The Northwest Library Center–Bowling Green doubled its circulation over the fiscal year 1984 as another county was added to the contract list. It also doubled reserve requests and increased interlibrary loan of materials tenfold. Two recreational-style vehicle bookmobiles purchased in fiscal year 1984 increased fuel efficiency without sacrificing space of facilities.

The library's bookmobiles circulated more than 368,000 books and 8,915 16mm films to libraries and residents of 22 rural counties across Ohio. In all, more than 44,000 information requests were answered. The trucks traveled almost 113,000 miles.

Users of the library's Talking Book program borrowed, free of charge, more than 38,000 titles. The nationwide program was faced with a severe shortage of cassette machines, Ohio having a monthly waiting list of up to 700 individuals. In 1984 the Library received 1,939 new and reconditioned cassette players and 1,034 record players through the National Library Service for the Blind and Physically Handicapped. These machines were immediately sent to sublending agencies for issuance to patrons.

Public Libraries. The 250 public libraries reported library circulation of 78,117,285 in 1983, a 6 percent increase over 1982. Total income for public libraries increased 10 percent to $165,879,746. Total intangibles taxes distributed to public libraries increased from $121,766,143 in 1982 to $135,762,297 in 1983, an 11 percent increase. The percentage of intangible collections distributed to libraries stayed constant at 92 percent.

Ohio's public libraries in 1982 contained 30,874,552 volumes, which represented 36 percent of the state's total number of volumes. Total staff increased from 5,398 in 1982 to 5,500 including the number of professionals, which increased from 1,125 to 1,199. The percentage of operating expenditures for salaries decreased from 50.9 to 49.8 while the expenditures for books increased by .6 percent to 16.6.

School Libraries, Media Centers. The total number of volumes held by school libraries increased from 28,274,308 in 1982 to 28,584,857, an increase of only 1 percent; however this total includes a decrease from 3,897 to 3,752 in the number of school buildings reporting and counted in the total. The number of professional staff continued to decline from 2,108 in 1982 to 1,669 in 1983. Total expenditures, including salaries were not available. Expenditures for materials in 1982 comprised 60.3 percent of the total operating expenditures and that percentage stayed the same in 1983.

Academic Libraries, Special Libraries. The 132 academic reporting for 1983 contained 23,404,188 volumes, an increase of 5 percent. Operating expenses increased by 17 percent over 1982, to $76,957,763; professional staff increased from 815 to 834; and total staff increased from 1,948 to 2,063. Total personnel costs increased from $29,424,852 to $33,696,751. The percentage of total operating expenditures for materials stayed constant at 28.2.

Statistics were recorded for special libraries having a minimum of one full-time staff member; the number increased from 151 in 1982 to 162 in 1983. The total number of volumes held in 1983 decreased from 1,552,497 to 1,403,792. Total staff increased from 414 to 452, and the number of professionals increased from 120 to 128. The number of volumes added during 1983 decreased from 46,053 in 1982 to 40,698 in 1983.

Library service in institutions of Ohio is provided by 39 libraries. Volumes reported by those libraries total 160,010 with 6,154 added in 1983.

Building Programs. Eighteen public libraries received LSCA Title II grants ranging from $30,000 to $456,000 for construction, renovation, and handicapped accessibility projects. As a result of these projects, new construction and additions will add 62,425 square feet of space to Ohio libraries. Nine libraries will improve or create public meeting rooms and, in at least two of these cases, will provide the first public meeting facility in the community. Seven buildings will become completely accessible to all their patrons for the first time through the construction of ramps or elevators. Another significant impact of these grants will be the improvement of library services in small communities. All but five projects are in communities with populations of less than 10,000 and four are in communities of less than 2,000 people. With the inclusion of local matching funds, over $6,000,000 will be added to the state's economy.

Networks, Interlibrary Cooperation. Membership in OHIONET reached over 200 by December 1984. In addition to recruitment, training, and accounting for OCLC services, programming toward the implementation of OhioPI, an Ohio public information utility, was the major activity. The OhioPI database will contain the status of Ohio legislation as it is introduced and acted upon by the legislature, directories of calendars of events, and names of organizations and corporations throughout Ohio, newsletters of associations, decisions of the Ohio court system, and Ohio statistical data from the U.S. Census and various state agencies. Access to OhioPI will be available through library members of OHIONET.

Awards. Librarians and trustees honored by the Ohio Library Association and the Ohio Library Trustees Association in 1984 included: Librarian of the Year: Mary Ann Sadlier, Lima Public Library. Trustee of the Year: Dennis Fedor, Lakewood Public Library. Diana Vescelius Memorial Award: Susan Barrick, Grove City Public Library. Supportive Staff Member of the Year: Alice Nodes, Westerville Public Library. OLTA Award of Achievement: Lorain Public Library Board of Trustees.

Deaths. Elnora Portteus, Allen Oakum, and Michael Boylan died in 1984.

BONNIE MITCHELL

OKLAHOMA

Oklahoma Library Association (founded 1907)

Membership: 780; *annual budget:* $36,673.

President: Norman Nelson, Edmon Low Library, Oklahoma State University, Stillwater 74078 (July 1984–July 1985).

Vice-President/President-elect: Lee Brawner, Metropolitan Library System, Oklahoma City 73102.

Executive Secretary: Kay Boies, 300 Hardy Drive, Edmond 73034.

Annual meeting: March 22–23, 1984, Tulsa.

Publications: Oklahoma Librarian (quarterly).

Oklahoma Department of Libraries

Robert L. Clark, Jr., State Librarian
200 North East 18th
Oklahoma City 73105

State School Library Media Supervisor

Clarice Roads
State Department of Education
Oklahoma City 73105

Facing constraints of tight budgets due to revenue shortfalls on a statewide level, Oklahomans anxiously awaited an upswing in the state's economy at the end of 1984. Governor George Nigh at the outset of 1984 emphasized three Rs—reductions, reform, and revenue. Libraries found support through local organizations, businesses, and private donations as they rallied to make the most of tough economic times.

State Association. The Rotunda of the Capitol was filled with library displays during Library Legislative Day in February. Librarians, trustees, and Friends lunched with legislators after an assembly on the floor of the House. Participants presented their legislators with folders of information, buttons promoting school libraries, and laminated copies of the Oklahoma Department of Libraries' "Libraries . . . for All of Us" poster.

The Association's annual conference was in Tulsa in March under the theme "Libraries, Liberty, and Learning." Emphasizing creative learning in libraries and the free flow of information, conference speakers included Melvin Tolson, Jr., Professor of French at the University of Oklahoma; Seymour Hersh, author and journalist; Kaye Gapen, Dean of Libraries, University of Alabama; and Jane Rhoads, Development Specialist for Reading and Study Skills Center, Wichita State University.

State Library Activities. The Oklahoma Department of Libraries launched a campaign against illiteracy with its "Oklahoma . . . Do You READ Me?" project. Ten new literacy councils were established throughout the state in cooperation with public libraries that received grants to fund a coordinator and tutor training.

A statewide archives assessment project got under way with Howard P. Lowell as Administrator and Inez Dillon Prinster as Project Manager. Funded by a grant from the National Historical Publications and Records Commission, the project assessed the needs and conditions of archives and historical records in Oklahoma. A final report was issued in April 1985.

Shared administrators were appointed in two areas of the state—one librarian to work with the staff of the libraries in Bristow and Prague, another with the librarians for Waurika, Frederick, and Walters.

Public Libraries. The Tulsa Library Endowment Fund exceeded its $2,000,000 fundraising goal. A $600,000 donation to the campaign from Roger and Donna Hardesty was the largest single contribution ever given to the library system.

Television cameras were on hand when the Metropolitan Library System, Oklahoma City, celebrated the circulation of the 2,000,000th book for the year. A cascade of balloons and cake and punch for patrons and staff rounded out the celebration. The year 1984 was the first in which the system's circulation figures topped the 2,000,000 mark.

Arts and humanities supporters in Woodward joined forces to explore the history of the Depression era in the Woodward area with a unique program called the "Dirty Thirties." The public library, the Pioneer Museum, Senior Center, Woodward Arts Theatre, and the public schools sponsored a week of events ranging from entertainment films of the 1930s to public lectures about the Dust Bowl. A weekend production of "Annie" by the community theatre concluded the programming.

Shirley Collier, Chairman of the Western Plains Library System Board of Trustees, spoke on behalf of public libraries before the Study Committee on Reform of Oklahoma State Government. Reform committees were organized by the Governor to address the state's funding problems.

School Libraries, Media Centers. The State Reading Section of the State Department of Education initiated a five-year plan to enhance reading achievement with "Read On, Oklahoma!" Schoolchildren throughout the state were checking books out of their school libraries to participate in a special segment of the project, Drop Everything and Read (DEAR).

The Oklahoma Association of School Media Specialists (OASLMS) sponsored "Turn On to Reading" at their fall meeting in Tulsa. Jim Trelease, author of the *Read Aloud Handbook*, was the featured speaker at the day-long workshop.

A total of $2,967,998 was available to fund projects for the Library Media Improvement Program in fiscal year 1983–84. Forty projects were initiated and 130 projects continued, serving 82,265 students. Funds are used according to needs assessments in the areas of personnel, books, and audiovisual materials or equipment.

Academic Libraries. The University of Oklahoma Bizzell Memorial Library added its 2,000,000th volume, a 322-year-old copy of *Instructions Concerning Erecting of a Library*. The University has the largest library collection in the state.

The University of Tulsa Libraries became the first client of the Pennsylvania State University's Library Information Access System, a leased information software package that provides an online catalog and circulation control.

Oklahoma State University's Student Government Association sponsored a "Save Our Library" campaign to garner support for a budget increase for the Library and to raise funds for new books. Governor Nigh donated a signed book to the cause, and declared "Save Our Library Day" in Oklahoma.

Building Programs. Norman voters approved a $3,045,000 expansion project for the public library in a bond election while defeating three other proposals on the same ballot.

The new Reiger Memorial Library, Haskell, was made possible by a memorial contribution from the family of Ted and Neva Reiger, land donated by Mr. and Mrs. Harold French, and a grant from the Oklahoma Department of Libraries.

Eufaula broke ground for a 6,000-square-foot library facility after a successful fund-raising campaign that involved the entire community of 3,000 residents.

Tulsa City–County Library Commission approved plans for three new library buildings, in Broken Arrow, Bixby, and Maxwell Park.

Networks, Interlibrary Cooperation. A successful three-month facsimile transmission project for the interlibrary loan of journal materials was conducted with the Tulsa City–County Library, the University of Oklahoma, Oklahoma State University, Oral Roberts University, and the Oklahoma Department of Libraries. Participants used the microwave network of the Oklahoma Regents for Higher Education.

The University of Oklahoma and the Oklahoma Department of Libraries share a database of their collections through compatible automated circulation systems. Both institutions have access to computerized listings of author, title, and subject records of each library.

The Oklahoma Chapter of the Western Conservation Congress in cooperation with the Oklahoma Department of Libraries formed the Oklahoma Recovery Assistance Team (O–DRAT) to provide access to a network of libraries for advice and assistance when documentary resources are damaged.

Awards. The Oklahoma Library Association presented its highest honor, the Distinguished Service Award, to Alfreda Hanna, formerly Librarian for Bethany Nazarene College.

A Special Meritorious Service Award from the Oklahoma Library Association was presented to Esther Mae Henke to recognize her 30 years of service on behalf of Oklahoma's public libraries during her tenure as Head of the Library Services Branch of the Oklahoma Department of Libraries. She also received a certificate of recognition for her accomplishments as an outstanding woman of Oklahoma at Oklahoma Women's Hall of Fame ceremonies.

The Oklahoma Library Association Certificate of Appreciation was presented to Robert R. Matthews, Ponca City, for his contribution to a comprehensive five-year plan for the city's library.

The Oklahoma Department of Libraries received its sixth John Cotton Dana Award for the publicity surrounding the collection of books for minorities circulating throughout the state. The Eufaula Public Library also received a John Cotton Dana Award for its ambitious fund-raising campaign to build a new library.

The Metropolitan Library System, Oklahoma City, won first place with its annual report in the annual library publicity contest of the Library Public Relations Council.

Appointments. John R. McCracken, formerly at the Fort Worth Public Library and Director of the Yuma City–County Library, Arizona, was appointed Head of the Library Services Branch of the Oklahoma Department of Libraries.

Death. Elsie Lilias Bell, longtime library supporter and Chief Librarian for the Main Library of the Metropolitan Library System, Oklahoma City, died January 10.

GRETCHEN BOOSE

OREGON

Election year 1984 saw many library budgets, special library districts, and library tax levies presented to the voters of Oregon. The one statewide issue uppermost in the minds of Oregon librarians, educators, and public officials was Ballot Measure No. 2, a property tax limitation bill. Measure No. 2 was similar to Proposition 13 in California, and would have had a devastating impact on library service in Oregon. The defeat of the proposal was not official until several days following the election because of a close vote.

State Association. The Oregon Library Association annual conference in April featured a preconference on Intellectual Freedom presented by Edward Jenkinson of Indiana University. Keynote speaker for the conference was Burke M. Raymond, organizational con-

**Oregon Library Association
(founded 1941)**

Membership: 537; *annual budget:* $13,850.

President: Mary Devlin-Willis, Portland General Electric Corp., 121 S.W. Salmon, Portland (April 1984–April 1985).

Vice-President/President-elect: George V. Smith, Oregon State Library, Salem 97310.

Annual meeting: April 11–14, 1984, Welches.

Publication: Oregon Library News (monthly).

Oregon State Library

Wesley A. Doak, State Librarian
State Library Building
Salem 97310

School Library Media Supervisor

George Katagiri
Coordinator of Instructional Technology
Oregon Department of Education
700 Pringle Parkway Southeast
Salem 97310

---

sultant. Ivan Doig, Northwest author, was featured at the banquet.

OLA members adopted a mission statement for the Long Range Plan for Library Development: "All Oregonians shall be guaranteed free access to library services that meet their needs."

A set of four legislative priorities was adopted dealing with funding of the Oregon State Library from state general funds, use of LSCA funds, and per capita state aid to libraries.

Declining conference revenues led the OLA Executive Board to adopt a deficit budget, which was later revised. Priorities established included funding for a year-round lobbyist, legislative/library development committee activities, and representatives to ALA and PNLA.

A special Membership meeting in September considered legislative issues in the coming session. At that meeting the members voted for an increased dues structure as a means to meet rising costs of Association activities.

A public relations firm worked with the OLA Public Relations Committee to develop three television spots designed to encourage library use by the nonuser. The project was partly funded by an LSCA grant.

State Library. The State Library reinstituted its "Letter to Libraries," a monthly newsletter dealing with State Library news, funding news, and other items not generally appearing in OLA's *Oregon Library News.*

LSCA funds totaling slightly over $525,000 were awarded for a number of projects around the state. Projects with statewide impact include funding for ORULS—the Oregon Regional Union List of Serials; funds for the central storage facility for little-used materials; and a statewide Continuing Education Coordinator.

One LSCA grant allows Sherman County to contract for library services with Fort Vancouver (Washington) Regional Library. The two are separated by the Columbia River.

Public Libraries. The year 1984 saw an improvement of the budgets of many public libraries in Oregon and the creation of at least two new library districts in the state.

In Multnomah County, home of the largest public library in the state, voters dealt with two local measures. The first, a charter amendment to establish a new governance structure with an independent library commission appointed by the County Executive, failed by fewer than 100 votes. Discussion of possible changes in the contract between the County and the independent Library Association of Portland was under way. The second measure, a $9,000,000 serial levy for library operations, passed handily. Following the retirement of James Burghardt, Cecile Carpenter was named Acting Director for six months beginning July 1.

A DOBIS automated circulation system became operational in Roseburg at Douglas County Library on March 20. Branch libraries in other locations in the county went online at periodic intervals, culminating a two-year conversion project by library staff.

The theme of the Summer Reading Program in at least 27 public libraries was "Go for the Gold at Your Library." Evaluation reports received indicated that 7,477 participants read 77,800 books during the six-week program.

Friends of the Library groups in Jackson County joined forces to hire a coordinator to raise money to buy books for the 13 libraries of the Jackson County Libary System whose book budget had been decimated by county budget shortfalls. The campaign raised in excess of $40,000, and brought in thousands of gift volumes. The FOL groups were also instrumental in the November approval by the voters of a three-year serial levy for the operation of the Jackson County Library.

Funding levies were also passed in Salem, Washington County, and Crook County. Siuslaw Library District was formed and a budget approved in western Lane County. Tax bases were approved for the Curry Library District in the towns of Brookings, Gold Beach, and Port Orford on the south coast.

School Libraries, Media Centers. "Professional growth in the face of change" was the theme of the Oregon Educational Media Association conference in Corvallis, October 11, 12. Lee Hay, 1983–84 Teacher of the Year, was the keynote speaker.

Other Activities. A joint conference of Oregon and Washington chapters of ACRL was held October 25–26 at Menucha Conference Center with futurist Robert Theobald as speaker.

The search for a new Library Director at Southern Oregon State College was halted early in 1984 because of budgetary constraints. Ruth Monical was appointed Acting Director until the end of the 1984–85 academic year.

The Oregon Health Information Network Coordinator, Steve Teich, was named instructor for Planning Hospital Library Facilities by the Medical Library Association.

Interlibrary Cooperation. Douglas Ferguson, formerly of Stanford University Libraries, was named Director of the Library and Information Resources for the Northwest (LIRN) Program of the Fred Meyer Charitable Trust. Offices of the Program are in Portland. The LIRN Program was announced by the Trust officials in 1983, and was given $3,500,000 to develop a technologically sophisticated resource-sharing network in Alaska, Idaho, Montana, Oregon, and Washington.

Intellectual Freedom. Censorship activities continued to spring up in schools and libraries around the state during 1984. The coastal community of Coos Bay received wide media coverage late in the year when the People Against Pornography group requested that Coos Bay Public Library stop a subscription to *Playboy*. The Library Board refused the request, and also refused to restrict the magazine by age level. People Against Pornography asked the Coos Bay City Council to overrule the Library Board. The City Council could not overrule an autonomous board, but did ask the Library Board to reconsider. On November 28 the Library Board upheld their previous decisions.

Awards. For the second year in a row, a Linfield College Library staff member received the ALA F. W. Faxon Scholarship, which includes a $3,000 stipend and ten-week internship at Faxon corporate offices. The winner in 1984 was Charis Bacheller, Circulation/Interlibrary Loan Manager at Linfield since 1982. She planned to attend the Library School at the University of Illinois in Urbana.

Dixie A. Anderson of Coos Bay Public Library was a winner in the 1984 OCLC Library Literature Contest for her article "Shared Usage: An Experiment that Works." The article was published in the *PNLA Quarterly* (Spring 1984).

The Evelyn Sibley Lampman Award for 1984 was given to Eloise Jarvis McGraw, Oregon author of works for young people.

Douglas County Library received the OLA Outstanding Service Award at the OLA conference in April for its "Read Experience '83" program. The highly successful program brought together library staff and patrons for book review presentations and small group discussion of preselected topics and books.

Appointments. Melvin R. George, formerly Library Director at Northeastern Illinois University, assumed the Director's post at Oregon State University in the spring.

Ronald Johnson became Library Director at Pacific University. He was formerly at Dana College in Nebraska.

Kathleen McHarg of Newport Public Library was named Director of the Oregon State Libary Division for the Blind and Physically Handicapped.

NADINE PURCELL

PENNSYLVANIA

Culminating three years of work by a 95-member planning council, the *Comprehensive Plan for Library Service in Pennsylvania* was presented in 1984 to Governor Dick Thornburgh. At the September annual meeting of Pennsylvania Citizens for Better Libraries, the Governor announced a major proposal, based on recommendations in the plan, to "open the door of information to all Pennsylvanians at every publicly supported library in the Commonwealth." This proposal, called *Access Pennsylvania*, pledges Commonwealth support for three major areas with specific strategies in each area:

(1) Statewide Access to Library Resources: Develop a statewide library card system and strengthen the interlibrary loan program to provide access to resources to all citizens at any publicly supported library.

(2) Sharing Library Resources through Tech-

Pennsylvania Library Association (founded 1901)

Membership: 1,700; *annual expenditure:* $213,000.

President: D. Jean Kindlin, School of Library and Information Science, 3rd floor, LIS Building, Pittsburgh 15260 (October 1984–October 1985).

Vice-President/President-elect: Dwight Huseman, Gettysburg College, Gettysburg 17325.

Executive Director: Margaret D. Bauer, PLA Headquarters, 126 Locust Street, Harrisburg 17101.

Annual meeting: October 14–October 17, 1984, Lancaster.

Publication: PLA Bulletin (eight times per year).

State Library of Pennsylvania

Elliott L. Shelkrot, State Librarian
Box 1601
Harrisburg 17126

nology: Extend the state's automated interlibrary loan network to include school libraries so that materials can be shared within a school district or across the state. Assist all libraries to adopt integrated computerized access systems which can be linked together to form an interactive statewide database. Develop guidelines for the integration of online searching skills into the school library media program.

(3) Revising Financial Support Systems of Libraries: Convene a task force to examine local financial support systems of public libraries and recommend improvements. Revise the state aid program for public libraries to revitalize equalization aid.

In order to finance this program, which will affect all types of libraries, the Governor asked the legislature for $3,000,000 in new state funds to be combined with $1,500,000 of redirected federal LSCA funds.

State Association. Margaret D. Bauer was named Executive Director of PLA following the resignation of Diane Ward for reasons of health.

The Association sponsored, along with Pennsylvania Citizens for Better Libraries, its Fourth Annual Legislative Day, attended by over 350 participants from across the Commonwealth. Partly as a result of this legislative information effort, the state budget included an increase of $1,420,000 for libraries.

Another bill supported by the Association became Act 90 of 1984, removing the 3-mill ceiling on local support for public libraries. It also amends the Library Code to protect the confidentiality of library circulation records.

Directors and officers insurance was offered for the first time to all institutional members of the Association at a competitive rate.

PLA's annual conference was held October 14–17, at the Host Farm in Lancaster. The conference theme, "Exploring the State of the Art," included programs on the future of the book, a PR idea shop, and a Micromagic Computer fair. Dee Alexander Brown was banquet speaker.

State Library Activities. Coordination of the efforts of the Comprehensive Plan that culminated in *Access Pennsylvania* was the focus of State Library activities for the year.

Lois Albrecht, Coordinator of the Advisory Services Section, announced that she would retire after 12 years of State Library service. Albrecht and her husband won $3,250,000 in the Pennsylvania State Lottery in 1984.

The State Library was awarded a grant of $312,418 from the National Endowment for the Humanities for a two-year program to inventory and catalog newspapers published in Pennsylvania and out-of-state papers held in Pennsylvania libraries, historical societies, publishers' files, and other collections.

Public Libraries. The Carnegie Library of Pittsburgh and the Free Library of Philadelphia shared a $60,000 LSCA grant for a large-print catalog.

The Free Library of Philadelphia received a $38,000 LSCA grant to catalog newspapers and atlases.

A party was held at the Free Library of Philadelphia to celebrate the 95th birthday of Philadelphia children's author Marguerite de Angeli.

Academic/Special Libraries. University of Pittsburgh School of Library and Information Science received a 1984 grant of over $71,000 from the Pennsylvania Department of Education to support a study of the library and telecommunications environment in the state. The study is expected to provide a basis for recommendations for a telecommunications network for library service in the state.

Drexel University's School of Library and Information Science became the College of Information Studies with the introduction of a program leading to a B.S. in information systems in addition to their graduate programs. The undergraduate course is a five-year program that includes three co-op work assignments.

Building Programs. Bucknell University in 1984 received a challenge grant of $400,000 from the Kresge Foundation of Troy, Michigan, for the renovation of the university's Ellen Clarke Bertrand Library. The renovation program is part of a comprehensive $2,380,000 library improvement plan that includes construction of a major library addition.

Two grants totaling nearly $800,000 will enable Carnegie Library of Pittsburgh to add 5,000 square feet of public space to its Oakland facility. The three-phase renovation of the building's south wing will affect the Children's Room, the Technical Services Division, the Music and Art Department, the Pennsylvania Division and the Microfilm and Periodical rooms.

Drexel University dedicated its $10,300,000 new library building in 1984. The building has a gross area of 100,000 square feet and the capacity for 350,000 volumes.

Networks, Interlibrary Cooperation. The Council of Pennsylvania Library Networks, once a committee of the State Library, formally organized, adopting by-laws and electing officials. The Council stated its mission: "To promote cooperation among library networks, cooperatives, and consortia when such cooperation will result in improved service to the clientele of constituent libraries and to the Commonwealth generally."

Seventeen libraries from Pennsylvania's community colleges formed a consortium during 1984 to provide Pennsylvania residents in the communities served with expanded learning opportunities through interlibrary resource sharing and to foster use of the libraries for lifelong learning.

Awards. Carolyn Wicker Field was the recipient of the 1984 Drexel Citation, which is awarded to individuals in the Philadelphia area who have made outstanding contributions to literature for children.

Virginia Sternberg was honored as Distinguished Alumnus awardee of 1984 at the annual banquet of the Pitt/Carnegie Library and Information Science Alumni Association.

Pennsylvania Library Association Certificates of Merit were awarded to Dick Cowen, Alice Devers, and Celeste Di Carlo Nolwasky. The New Librarian's Award was presented to Steven Herb.

Governor Dick Thornburgh received the PLA Distinguished Service Award for his support of libraries in the Commonwealth.

Appointments. Elizabeth Smith Aversa joined the Drexel CIS faculty as Assistant Professor. Susan Gale Matusak was named Head Librarian of Wilson College. Marnie Rees, Associate Director of the Scranton Public Library, was named Administrator of the newly created Lackawanna County Library System.

James Myers, Associate Director at Stanford, was appointed Director of Libraries at Temple University. John W. Walter was named Director of the New Castle Public Library. Michael Turbak was named Director of the Monroe County Public Library in Stroudsburg.

Margaret Kimmel, faculty member of the School of Library and Information Science, University of Pittsburgh, assumed office as President of the United States Board on Books for Young People in 1984. Martin P. Wilson from Clarkson University was appointed College Librarian, Juniata College.

Deaths. Howard H. Williams, Reference Librarian Emeritus, Swarthmore College, died July 6 while vacationing in New Jersey. He worked at Swarthmore from 1949 until his retirement in 1975.

MARY IVY BAYARD

RHODE ISLAND

Rhode Island Library Association (founded 1928)

Membership: 698; *annual budget:* $13,500.

President: Frances Farrell-Bergeron, Providence Interrelated Library System, Providence Public Library, 150 Empire St., Providence 02903 (November 1983–December 1984).

Vice-President/President-elect: Constance Lachowicz, South Kingstown Public Library, 603 Kingstown Road, Peace Dale 02883.

Annual meeting: November 18–20, 1984, Newport.

Publication: Bulletin (monthly, except in August).

Rhode Island Department of State Library Services

Fay Zipkowitz, Director
95 Davis Street
Providence, R.I. 02908

Nineteen eighty-four was a special year to the Rhode Island library community as it marked the 20th anniversary of the legislation that established the Department of State Library Services (DSLS) and the Interrelated Library Network (RIILN), the mechanism for multitype library cooperation that has been the keystone of library development throughout the state. Significantly, the major library activities in Rhode Island in 1984 were steps to enhance the effectiveness of that same network. Although transformed by the passage of two decades, Rhode Island's libraries continue to follow the route of improving service through cooperative endeavors.

The biggest news of 1984 was the installation of a statewide electronic mail system that will eventually connect all of the state's libraries. A Digital Equipment Corporation VAX/VMS minicomputer at the DSLS in Providence will accept any off-the-shelf microcomputer as a dial-up terminal, and offer a specially tailored interlibrary loan communication program, electronic mail message service, word processing, calendar, desk and file management, and other services.

In its first implementation phase in 1984, the principal public library and four regional centers were connected by dedicated lines, and the 11 special research centers provided with dial-up terminals, allowing the minicomputer to replace the antiquated Teletype system that previously united them into the Rhode Island Interrelated Library Network. Among the advantages are reduced turnaround time for ILL requests, statistical reporting, and rationalized ILL search strategies.

Rhode Island's automated library networks grew significantly in 1984. The Rhode Island Automated Library Consortium (RIALC), a CLSI LIBS 100-based consortium of the public libraries of Cranston and Barrington and the DSLS, experienced its first year with all members online for circulation control. The network of libraries contracting with the Providence Public Library for the services of their CLSI LIBS 100 system grew to eight during 1984; it was organized into the Cooperating Libraries Automated Network (CLAN).

The Champlin Foundation was instrumental in that growth as it granted start-up funds to the public libraries of Woonsocket, Central Falls, Greeneville, and East Providence, a total of $147,223 and an enhancement grant of $33,064 to Pawtucket Public Library. The public libraries of Westerly, Newport, and North Providence received grants from the Champlin Foundation to join in 1983. The nine libraries of CLAN hammered out agreements for reciprocal borrowing and a network-wide borrower's card. Champlin Foundation support promised to make possible retrospective conversion of the network's 400,000 title entries in 1985.

A third network, also employing CLSI LIBS 100, is planned to connect the libraries of Rhode Island's three institutions of higher learning under agreements worked out in 1984. The University of Rhode Island planned to upgrade its CLSI system to accommodate Rhode Island College and the Community College of Rhode Island in the HELIN network. Representatives of RIALC, CLAN, and HELIN began discussions of cooperative arrangements that would cover most of the state's resources.

Rhode Island Library Association. In 1984 RILA put into effect bylaws revisions of 1983 designed to correct the Association's fiscal problems, increase its accountability to membership, and permit more effective planning. The changes established a standing budget and finance committee and moved the start of the fiscal year to January in accordance with cash-flow patterns and the change of officers at the November annual meeting. The result was a six-month year from the end of June 1984 to the end of December 1984. This meant a lot of overtime for the membership committee, with two membership years in one calendar year, and for the new budget and finance committee, who had two budgets instead of one to prepare.

The focus on Association mechanics did not daunt activity in other vital arenas. An active Government Relations Committee garnered an increase in state grants-in-aid to libraries and the network of $89,000. The Committee, under Chair Anne Parent, then went on to ensure visibility of library support as an issue in statewide election campaigns, eliciting position statements from both major gubernatorial candidates.

The annual conference in November began with a special Sunday session for public library trustees. The following two days were packed with sessions on technical services, public services, and cultural topics. Highlights included a 20th-anniversary panel presentation by instigators of the 1964 legislation that created the DSLS and RIILN and an appearnace by Elizabeth Janeway, who opened the subject of public lending right and author compensation.

John Mills, Professor of Library Science at the Riverina College of Advanced Education in Wagga Wagga, Australia, spoke on Australian and U.S. library development. Mills spent his sabbatical from July through December at the Island Interrelated Library System examining the American style of library networking.

The Association accepted a resolution from Florence Doksansky's Personnel Committee raising the Association's recommended annual starting salary for professional librarians to $17,500. Another resolution called on the governments of the U.S. and the U.S.S.R. to effect a mutual verifiable nuclear freeze.

State Library. LSCA funds provided backing for an ambitious project demonstrating online database searching to the state's public librarians. A $55,000 grant from the Champlin Foundation enabled the DSLS to begin computerization of its statewide library for the blind and physically handicapped.

DSLS was instrumental in the promulgation of a governor's executive order creating an Adult Literacy Council. Representatives of the DSLS and RILA are among those seated on the Council.

A statewide summer reading program organized by consultant Melody Brown, under a grant from the Rhode Island Committee for the Humanities, presented a "storytellers' caravan" that provided 59 programs by three professional storytellers at public libraries across the state. The caravan was part of a "Reading Rainbows" theme adopted by 42 public libraries to capitalize on the public television program of the same name.

The most far-reaching work of the DSLS in 1984 was the establishment of a long-range planning committee responsible for creation of its 1986–91 DSLS five-year plan. Forty representatives of all types of libraries, community groups, and other library users gathered under the chairmanship of Roberta A. E. Cairns, Librarian of East Providence, to follow the general outlines of *A Planning Process for Public Libraries*, issued by ALA's Public Library Association.

School Libraries, Media Centers. School libraries and media centers continued to suffer from the absence of representation at the state level. The last remaining position in the RI Department of Education with any responsibility for library service was abolished in 1983. A joint committee of RILA and the Rhode Island Educational Media Association (RIEMA) continued to press for recognition, however. In 1984 the Joint Committee managed to achieve inclusion of new library/media center standards and standards for library curriculum in the Department of Education's proposed Basic Education Plan. RIEMA also presented testimony regarding the need to upgrade certification of school librarians to include media credentials.

RIEMA convened a Computer Awareness Committee in 1984, chaired by James Kenney of Rhode Island College. The Committee held monthly topical meetings and began a collection of public domain microcomputer software. RIEMA's annual conference in March, chaired by Mike Mello, featured Troy Earhart, new Commissioner of Education in Rhode Island, as guest of honor.

Public Libraries. Many of Rhode Island's public libraries marked 1984 with their entry into the era of microcomputers and cable TV. Half employed microcomputers in 1984 according to surveys by RILA and the newly formed Microcomputer Applications for Children's Services Advisory Council to the DSLS. Uses range from reference indexes and public-use computers to bookkeeping and payroll. Cooperative use of micros also began in RI in 1984—an updated edition of the Island Interrelated Library System Union List of Serials was produced on an Apple.

For cable television, still new in Rhode Island, every one of the nine franchise regions had at least one librarian on its local community advisory board in 1984. Fay Zipkowitz, Director of the DSLS, was appointed to the statewide cable advisory committee.

The East Providence Public Library moved into TV production when Director Roberta A. E. Cairns was appointed PR Director for the city. She produces a weekly half-hour interview called *East Providence Inside*. The children's department at the East Providence library produces a weekly *Storytime*. Coventry Public Library produced 16 cable TV programs in cooperation with Literacy Volunteers of America. Westerly Public Library produced three programs.

Interlibrary cooperation is not only automation in Rhode Island, however. The Northern Interrelated Library System in 1984 received two grants of $14,679 each from the Rhode Island Committee for the Humanities and the Massachusetts Foundation for the Humanities and Public Policy to produce six traveling exhibits, showing the history and architecture of the Blackstone River Valley from Worcester, Massachusetts, to Pawtucket, Rhode Island.

Building Programs. The Providence Public Library took another step toward renovation of its central branch with passage of a $3,000,000 bond issue. Renovation of the old Peck School Building was completed and it became the new home of the Barrington Public Library and Community Center. The Central Falls Public Library rededicated its new wing completed in 1983. South Kingstown Public Library hired building consultant Nolan Lushington to prepare a library needs assessment in preparation for renovation of the three libraries in its system. Remodeling continued at the Apponaug Branch of the Warwick Public Library.

Construction began on a new building for the North Providence Public Library. North Providence was remodeling an old ice skating rink.

Professional Interests. In response to the publication of *A Nation at Risk*, Rhode Island's Coalition of Library Advocates (COLA) held a two-day conference at Rhode Island College on "Libraries in the Future of Education: A Rhode Island Perspective." The 80 conference participants from school, public, and academic libraries in New England focused on finding local applications of ALA's *Realities: Educational Reform in a Learning Society* and the U.S. Department of Education's *Alliance for Excellence: Librarians Respond to a Nation at Risk*.

Academic and Special Libraries. The first Union List of Serials of the Consortium of Rhode Island Academic and Research Libraries (CRIARL) became available in 1984. The list contains over 20,000 titles held by 14 libraries in Rhode Island with academic or research collections.

The Government Documents Committee of CRIARL took a cue from the U.S. GPO early in 1984 and coordinated a statewide publicity campaign with the national GPO campaign.

A new library was established for women inmates of the Adult Correctional Institution (ACI). The collection was begun with books from the ACI library and a $1,000 grant from the DSLS; the Governor's Advisory Commission for Women was spearheading a supporting fund-raising effort.

Awards. One of Rhode Island's greatest friends of libraries, Senator Claiborne Pell, was honored in 1984. The White House Conference on Library and Information Services Taskforce (WHCOLIST) presented its 1984 Award for Outstanding Legislator in Support of the Nation's Libraries to Senator Pell at its fifth annual meeting. Back home, Senator Pell was acclaimed as a RILA Legislator of the Year at the Association's annual meeting.

Also named a RILA Legislator of the Year was state Representative Mary McMahon, whose advice, support, and advocacy were instrumental in passage of RILA-initiated legislation. At the RILA annual meeting, a Trustee of the Year Award was presented to Martha Sherman, longtime trustee of the Providence Public Library. WHCLIST presented Bruce Daniels of the DSLS with an award for special services.

The Providence Public Library received several awards in 1984. A Certificate of Commendation was awarded by the American Association for State and Local History for the 1982–83 program series "A Lively Experiment." The Library was recognized by ALA for Exemplary Public Library Outreach for its Child Learning Centers and project L.I.V.E., which encourage reading among children and young adults of low-income families.

Providence Public Library was also one of three Rhode Island recipients of honors from the Public Relations Committee of the New England Library Association; Newport Public Library and East Providence Public Library were also cited at NELA's annual meeting.

Appointments. The year saw a number of changes in the Rhode Island library community. Beth Perry, formerly Assistant Director of the Adams Library of Rhode Island College, was named State Librarian of Rhode Island, succeeding Eliot Andrews, who had retired in 1983. Richard W. Robbins retired from his post as Director of the Warwick Public Library, and was succeeded by Douglas Pearce.

Debbe Brennan resigned from the directorship of the North Kingstown Public Library. Barbara Mirabelli resigned as Director of the Clark Memorial Library to take the position of Director of the Narragansett Free Library. She was succeeded at Clark by Catherine Hull. Connie Roe became Director of the Foster Public Library. Diana Cardosa assumed the directorship of the Hope Library.

Peter Fuller was appointed Assistant Director at the Lincoln Public Library. Mildred Giusti retired as Head of Reference at the Providence Public Library, and was succeeded by Frances Farrell-Bergeron. Jody Bush left the post of Coordinator of Providence Public Library branches to assume leadership of the central library of Berkeley, California; Shirley Long was appointed Coordinator at Providence.

Sonita Cummings left the Community College of Rhode Island to accept the job of Coordinator of the Western Interrelated Library system, which was vacated by Paul Drake. Drake became the new ILL and Serials librarian at Roger Williams College.

Carol DiPrete was appointed Director of the Library, Computer Center and Learning Center at Roger Williams College. Her predecessor, Rebecca Tildsley, retired in 1983. Jean Sheridan was appointed head of the Library of the URI College of Continuing Education. David Carlson became Systems Librarian at URI. Judith Stokes was appointed Serials Librarian at Rhode Island College. Linda Walton left the State Library to assume the directorship of the Butler Hospital Library.

Deaths. Deaths in 1984 included those of Gladys Segar, Librarian of the Langworthy Library; Alice V. McGrath, Librarian of the Rhode Island School of Design; Catherine E. Hunt, Assistant Director of the Crompton Free Library; Muriel C. Wyman, Librarian Emerita and Trustee Emerita of the William Hall Library; and Marion Lamb, Assistant Librarian at the Coventry Library.

HOWARD BOKSENBAUM

SOUTH CAROLINA

The South Carolina State Legislature in a milestone action increased state aid to public libraries from $.75 per capita to $1 per capita. Public libraries and the State Library had fought for that level of support since 1975, when state aid was $.35 per capita.

Emphasis was on the creation of a South Carolina library network. This program, conceived by State Librarian Betty Callaham, envisions a computerized network linking all libraries in the state for access. It is significant that the State Legislature authorized $50,000 for network planning and development. The project was endorsed by the South Carolina Library Association of the Association of Public Library Administrators.

South Carolina Library Association. The South Carolina Library Association held its annual meeting in Columbia on September 13–15. Stuart Forth, Dean of Libraries, Pennsylvania State University, was the banquet speaker. Kenneth Toombs, Director of Libraries, University of South Carolina, and Elizabeth Ann Lange, Assistant Director for Technical Services, University of South Carolina, presented a program on the "Movietone News Collection." Ron Kozlowski, Director, Charlotte/Mecklenburg Libraries, spoke about methods of service to the public. South Carolina's Lieutenant Governor Mike Daniel, spoke on state support of libraries at the JMRT meeting. The Service to Children and Youth in School and Public Libraries Section presented in the Notables Showcase the author Eleanora Tate, who wrote *Just an Overnight Guest*. This Section also saw a presentation of a children's play by the Charleston Chopstick Theatre.

Forty-nine librarians and trustees attended a breakfast meeting featuring Ann Woodward of Atlanta.

Herbert White, Dean of the School of Library and Information Sciences, Indiana University, presented a program on "Management Communications" to a combined meeting of Special Library Section, College and University Section, Two-Year College Section, and the Archives and Special Collections Section.

The Government Documents RoundTable of SCLA published *Government Documents in South Carolina: A Directory of Collections of Federal, State, Local and Council of Government Publications in South Carolina Libraries*, compiled by Mary R. Bull of USC–Coastal Carolina College. It documents the collections of 136 libraries in the state.

State Library. The South Carolina State Library expanded its film service so that civic organizations could borrow adult and documentary films from county public libraries. A special catalog listing available films was given to each library. Feature films and children's films are available to public libraries for in-house use, but are too heavily booked for general circulation.

The State Reorganization Commission approved the State Library's Certification Program for public librarians in its Sunset Review report for 1984. The certification program sets

South Carolina Library Association (founded 1915)

Membership: 837; *annual budget:* $19,000.

President: Carl Stone, Anderson County Library, Anderson (October 1984–September 1985).

Vice-President/President-elect: Susan Roberts, USC–Aiken Library, Aiken.

Annual meeting: September 13–15, 1984, Columbia.

Publications: South Carolina Librarian (semiannual); *News and Views* (bimonthly).

South Carolina State Library

Betty E. Callahan, State Librarian
P.O. Box 11469
Columbia, S.C. 29211

School Library Media Supervisor

Margaret W. Ehrhardt
Department of Education
Columbia, S.C. 29201

qualification standards for professional librarians based on education and experience. County library systems must employ a certified director to be eligible for state aid.

The State Library issued its latest *Periodical Holdings*. For the first time the list was issued in COM format. The alphabetical listing of the library's 2,229 periodicals was sent to public, academic, and special libraries in the state. The list was compiled by the University of South Carolina School of Medicine Library staff using software developed by the school's Data Center.

The U.S. Government Printing Office approved the South Carolina State Plan for Federal Deposit Libraries. The plan is regional, utilizing the libraries of Clemson University, University of South Carolina, and Winthrop as depository libraries. The South Carolina State Library will provide administrative support and coordinate the discarding of documents. The plan provides two benefits. All citizens of the state will have access to the documents and the depository libraries will be able to discard unneeded documents.

The State Library issued its last Micro Automated Catalog (MAC) in 1984. The catalog, first issued in 1972, consists of 70 reels of microfilm containing the library's card catalog. The issuance of further editions will depend on future networking developments.

Timothy Driggers, Chair, South Carolina State Library Board of Trustees, presented the library's Public Service Awards to State Senator John C. Landis III, State Representative Tom Mangum, and the Chester *News and Reporter*. Senator Landis was honored for his efforts in establishing the Clarendon County Library. Representative Mangum was instrumental in attaining a $.25 per capita increase in state aid. The *News and Reporter* supported efforts to build a new library building in Chester.

Charleston County Library received the State Library's Meritorious Service Award for 1984. The award cited the library's extension of service through community involvement. All awards were presented at the South Carolina Library Association's annual convention.

Public Libraries. The South Carolina Association of Public Library Administrators (APLA) held its third annual Library Legislative Day February 29. The focus of the day was the increase of state aid to $1 per capita. The day drew 150 library supporters representing 41 of the state's 46 counties. An estimated 100 state legislators attended. The South Carolina House of Representatives passed a concurrent resolution in support of libraries sponsored by Representative Irene Rudnick of Aiken. There were 120 cosponsors to the resolution. The meeting was cosponsored by the Trustee Section and the Public Library Section of SCLA.

APLA held its annual meeting at Hilton Head in conjunction with the South Carolina Association of Counties. The program was "Hard Facts about Overdues." Patsy Hansel, Assistant Director, Cumberland County (N.C.) Library, and Robert Burgin, Lecturer at North Carolina Central University, presented the program.

Much of the activity in South Carolina public libraries during 1984 centered around literacy. The South Carolina State Library, the South Carolina Literacy Association, and the Lieutenant Governor's Office cosponsored programs for county libraries using LSCA funds.

York County Library developed a program to reach 10 percent of all first-grade children. The Library, which also supports adult literacy efforts, hoped that the program would prevent future adult illiteracy. The children were identified by local school districts and were enrolled in a program of enrichment to demonstrate the fun of reading. Special programs for parents were also offered. Dillon County Library held a two-day workshop to train Laubach tutors. The programs at Union County Library and the Anderson County Library helped to attract money from agencies such as United Way and other sources. Greenwood County Library and Greenwood Literary Council trained 93 literacy tutors.

York County Library celebrated its 100th anniversary with a dinner featuring Jim Hoagland, Foreign Editor of the *Washington Post*.

The State Library reported that the number of books and other materials circulated by public libraries increased from 110,000 to over 9,500,000. An average of 23,700 reference questions were handled each week. The total number of transactions was 4.84 per person in the state, or 4,200 per library.

School Libraries, Media Centers. The South Carolina Association of School Librarians annual meeting was in Greenville in May. Theme of the meeting was "The Media Connection." Peggy Hanna, Charleston County School District 1, was elected President; Diane Ervin of Greenville County School was elected Vice-President/President-elect; Mary Daniel of Columbia was elected Secretary; and Dottie Hicks of Mauldin was elected Treasurer. Jacqueline Kelly of Olanta was named Regional Network Director. The annual meeting's theme was concerned with communicating the importance of the media center in the curriculum.

The Association is divided into regions with programs based on the desires of the regional members. An example is the Region IV (Richland, Fairfield, Newberry, and Lexington Counties) meeting in October. Two issues were addressed. The main topic was "Communicating with the Principal." Also discussed was *A Nation at Risk*.

Academic Libraries. The Archives Department of the Dacus Library, Winthrop College, published *Women Leaders in South Carolina: An Oral History*, edited by Ron Chepesiuk and Ann Evans, Archives, and Thomas Morgan of the History Department. The South Carolina Committee for Humanities funded project is an edited transcript of 13 video interviews with 13 South Carolina women leaders.

The Furman University Library received half of a $1,000,000 grant by the Duke Endowment. $400,000 was to be used to purchase books for the James Buchanan Duke Library. The remainder was to be used to expand the reference department.

The Allen University Library was damaged by a fire started by lightning. The lightning struck the roof of the building, which was being renovated, and it collapsed, allowing water to pour into the book collections of the Library's top two floors.

Citadel Development Foundation made grants totaling $138,000 to the Daniel Library at the Citadel. The grants were for materials, retrospective conversion of records, and a feasibility project involving free provision of DIALOG searches for faculty.

Converse College Library received a special collection of memorabilia on Helen Keller. The collection belonged to Keller's former Secretary, Nella Braddey Henney. It was presented to the library by Henney's sister, Ann Braddey. An additional gift of $40,000 was presented by Keith Henney for the Nella Braddey Henney Memorial Fund.

A signed and numbered copy of *Finnegans Wake* by James Joyce was presented to the Sandor Teszler Library of Wofford College. It was the 200,000th volume to be added to the library.

Building Program. Spurred by LSCA grants, many construction projects were under way in the state during 1984. Greenwood County Library received $40,000 in state rural improvement funds, a total of $50,000 from the Self Foundation of Greenwood, and $5,000 from Josephine Abney for the construction of the Ninety-Six Branch Library. The Spartanburg County Foundation donated $10,000 toward the construction of the Landrum Branch. The Union County Council voted to underwrite the balance needed by the library to receive a $100,000 LSCA grant. Library supporters had raised $295,000 of the $380,000 needed to qualify. Chester County Council approved an ordinance to issue $1,000,000 in general revenue bonds for construction of a main library building. Bids were let in Colleton County, Richland County, and Dillon County. Astronaut Charles Bolden spoke at the Richland groundbreaking. Bolden is the son of Richland County Board member Ethel Bolden. The Gregg–Graniteville Library of University of South Carolina–Aiken doubled its space to 40,000 square feet in a $1,200,000 expansion project. New facilities include study carrels, seminar rooms, typing, listening, and computer rooms. The West Ashley Branch of Charleston County Library had a $70,000 renovation after asbestos was found in ceiling tiles. The Library received new ceiling tiles, paint, and carpeting.

Networks, Interlibrary Cooperation. The development of a statewide library network became a major priority in South Carolina. Prior to detailed planning for the project, the South Carolina Task Force on Library Automation and Networking held a series of open meetings with experts in the automation of networking areas. The first meeting was held in November 1983, and featured Frank Grisham of SOLINET. The second meeting, held in February 1984, offered Sally Drew, Director, Bureau of Interlibrary Loan and Resource Sharing, Wisconsin Division of Library Services. The March meeting presented Rob McGee, RMG Consultants, Inc. The final meeting in May presented Richard Boss, Senior Consultant, Information Systems Consultants, Inc. Each speaker discussed aspects of statewide networking.

In July the South Carolina State Library outlined a three-year development plan to APLA. Phase I envisioned an integrated system at the State Library, putting the SCSL catalog online, with a circulation/ILL module and communications testing. Phase II calls for network implementation with catalog access, ILL, electronic mail, and communication access for public and academic libraries. Phase III calls for a statewide union list of serials. Various necessary hardware and software requirements were discussed.

At year's end, the project had state funding of $50,000 for network planning and development. Another $150,000 was projected from LSCA. Installation of the host system was expected to begin by September 1985.

Intellectual Freedom. The Intellectual Freedom Committee of the South Carolina Library Association announced that it would present an award to a state resident who made a special contribution to intellectual freedom. The award would be presented jointly by SCLA/SCASL and would include a $500 cash award plus an award of $500 for new material to the Library of the winner's choice. The Committee worked on legislation to ensure the confidentiality of library records. Unfortunately, the bill was caught in legislative delays, and did not come to the floor in time for consideration. The committee was developing a site visit procedure manual in case a team must be appointed to investigate a South Carolina library intellectual freedom case.

Professional Interests. Many workshops were held in South Carolina in 1984. One of the more successful was a puppetry workshop held at the White Oaks Conference Center near Winnsboro in March. A LAMA Institute on Online Catalogs was held in September. It was cosponsored by SCLA, the State Library, and the USC College of Library and Information Science. Joseph R. Matthews of J. Matthews & Associates and Charles Hildreth of OCLC, Inc., were the speakers. JMRT sponsored a grant writing workshop; the Bibliographic Instruction Interest Group sponsored a B.I. Workshop; the Public Library Section held a workshop on supervision; and the Technical Services Section held a meeting on "Coping with the Battered Book."

Awards. Ann Scott Terry, Community Services Librarian, York County Library, was selected as one of the Outstanding Young Women of 1983.

Cherokee County Literacy Association won a National Award for Special Effort for rapid and stable development. The program is part of a pilot project sponsored by the South Carolina State Library, the South Carolina Literacy Association, the South Carolina Office of Adult Education, and the Office of the Lieutenant Governor.

The architectural firm of Craig, Gauldin and Davis was presented with an Award of Merit for Design Excellence by the South Carolina chapter of the American Institute of Architects for its design of the main library building of the York County Library.

Gale Research Company honored the Clarendon County Library with its $2,500 Financial Development Award. The Library also won the $100 award of the Public Relations Section of the Southeastern Library Association.

Appointments. Wanda L. Forbes of Clover, South Carolina, was nominated by President Reagan to the National Commission on Library and Information Service. Forbes, who served as a school librarian in Gastonia, North Carolina, and Clover, is the first South Carolinian to be appointed to NCLIS.

Dennis Bruce, Director, Spartanburg County Library, was elected President of the South Carolina Literacy Association. Bruce was also Vice-President/President-elect of the Association of Public Library Administrators in 1984.

William Summers, Dean, College of Librarianship, University of South Carolina, was appointed to the Executive Search Committee of ALA.

Betty Callaham, State Librarian, was elected to the SOLINET Board of Trustees for a three-year term. Callaham was also appointed Chair of the Planning Committee of the SOLINET board for 1984–85.

Deaths. Estellene P. Walker, 71, retired State Librarian, died on May 15, 1984, in Columbia. Walker joined the State Library in 1946 and served as its administrator until 1979. She created the "unified" county library system in South Carolina that led to the provision of county-wide public library service in every county of the state. She expanded the library agency to provide service to state government, the blind, and physically handicapped, and state institutions. She developed the statewide interlibrary loan network. She was President of the South Carolina Library Association and of the Association of State Libraries, and she wrote *So Good and Necessary a Work: The Public Library in South Carolina.*

Frances Reid died on December 11, 1983. Reid was Director of the Spartanburg County Library and had retired from the North Carolina State Library.

Alice Dodson Callaham died January 21, 1984. Callaham had served as a member of the Anderson County Library Board of Trustees and the Honea Path (S.C.) Board of Trustees. She was engaged in a renovation of the Honea Path Library at the time of her death.

CARL STONE

SOUTH DAKOTA

South Dakota Library Association (founded 1907)

Membership: 520; *annual budget:* $11,600.

President: Joseph Edelen, I.D. Weeks Library, University of South Dakota, Vermillion 57069 (September 1984–October 1985).

Vice-President/President-elect: Judy Johnson, Central High School, Rapid City 57701.

Annual meeting: September 16–18, 1984, Pierre.

Publication: Book Marks (bimonthly).

South Dakota State Library

Clarence L. Coffindaffer, State Librarian
State Library Building
800 N. Illinois Ave.
Pierre 57501

School Library Media Supervisor

Donna Gilliland
South Dakota State Library
State Library Building
800 N. Illinois Ave.
Pierre 57501

During 1984 continuity was more typical than change in South Dakota librarianship. Statistical measures in most libraries showed normal increase, the usual number of modest donations of cash and materials occurred, and microcomputers and security systems continued to spread to more libraries.

The effort to produce a quantum advance in library automation and cooperation in the state accelerated and then received a setback from governing bodies. The Task Force on Automation, advised by RMG Associates, learned that state government has considerable excess capacity in its IBM mainframe computer, and Central Data Processing managers indicated a willingness to mount a major library system on the computer.

Because the opportunity to avoid buying computer space might be transitory, the Task Force on Automation decided to forego the request-for-proposal procedure and to look only at IBM-using, integrated systems featuring online public-access catalogs (OPACs). Northwestern University's NOTIS and Biblio-Techniques' BLIS were selected for demonstration even as the previously appointed specifications committees for machine-readable catalog records, OPAC capabilities, and circulation systems and a newly appointed acquisitions and serials systems specifications committee completed their recommendations. In August the Task Force on Automation selected BLIS as the preferred system and throughout the fall negotiated specifications for the integrated acquisitions, serials, cataloging, OPAC, and circulation components.

Funding was the next hurdle. The Automation Task Force's plan projects service ultimately to the South Dakota State Library and 30 other public and private academic libraries, public libraries, and school systems' libraries. In the initial year of operation the State Library and the libraries in four state colleges and universities would begin utilizing the system. Although the Board of Regents approved the concept of a shared online catalog system in 1982 and has underwritten retrospective conversion of cataloging records, it chose to favor a systemwide online student records system for the funding and the available computer space. As a result, the governor's 1986 fiscal year budget proposal, released in early December 1984, reflected that choice and also omitted funding for the State Library's share of the costs.

Although negotiations with Biblio-Techniques were suspended until preparation for the 1987 budget cycle, the Board of Regents reaffirmed its commitment to shared library automation by ordering that no separate library automation efforts be undertaken in the six state colleges and universities.

Legislation. The library community initiated no new legislation in 1984, although SDLA's Library Issues Committee lobbied against continuance of the law forcing the South Dakota State Library to charge fees to recover postage for lending films. As the year ended the committee failed narrowly to persuade the Joint Appropriations Committee to recommend a bill for repeal. In the 1984 session the Governor issued an executive order to reorganize the agencies in the Department of Education and Cultural Affairs. Subject to a legislative veto, it was withdrawn after librarians lobbied in opposition to a provision that would make the State Librarian report to the State Superintendent of Schools rather than directly to the Secretary of the Department.

State Association. The convention in September in Pierre, with the theme "Cooperation Starts with You," drew more than 180. Featuring Blanche Woolls, Professor at the University of Pittsburgh's School of Library and Information Science, as keynote speaker, the convention also offered two preconferences dealing with computers in libraries and a preconference on children's books. Several sessions enlarged upon the conference theme to detail cooperation between school and public libraries and between local libraries and agricultural information agencies such as the Cooperative Extension Service.

The winner of a contest to design a new SDLA logo was selected by a vote in the business meeting, which also adopted a resolution urging the Legislative Research Council to continue its study of comparative worth. Resolutions supporting a nuclear freeze and directing SDLA to join the South Dakota Advocacy Network for Women were defeated by arguments that such advocacy positions would compromise libraries' position as unbiased dispensers of information.

Bob Carmack, Dean of Library Services at the University of South Dakota for 13 years, was honored by a resolution recognizing his many contributions to SDLA and libraries in South Dakota and awarding him the SDLA Distinguished Service Award.

SDLA received a grant from the National Endowment for the Humanities for over $190,000 to be matched by over $90,000 in local funds and in-kind donations for a project entitled South Dakota: Changing, Changeless 1889–1989. To give libraries a role in celebrating the centennial of South Dakota statehood in 1989, the project will produce three short films, bibliographies of materials on state history, a traveling exhibit, and poster sets, and it will provide programs in public libraries to be led by humanities scholars who teach in South Dakota colleges.

The new Health Sciences Section selected officers, approved a constitution, and was granted recognition as a section in SDLA. The Executive Board directed a mail vote be taken on the merger of the moribund Trustees Section with the Public Libraries Section. In addition, a Paraprofessionals Round Table, the first Round Table in SDLA, was formed.

State Library. The South Dakota State Library's budget advanced almost 10 percent over the previous year after discounting the pass-through of LSCA Title II funds in the previous fiscal year. Additional funds were targeted at collections primarily; staffing remained the same, and the service programs were not enlarged.

After a three-year hiatus the State Library again published *Statistics of South Dakota Libraries*, adding coverage for special and school libraries to that previously provided for public and academic libraries. Directory information was removed to the new *South Dakota Library Directory*, which added school libraries for the first time.

Public Libraries. Harrisburg and Buffalo Gap established new libraries. Buffalo Gap's library was named Bar-O Library in honor of the community's western tradition and the lending tradition of libraries.

The Phoebe Apperson Hearst Library in Lead was extensively damaged in April when a firewall collapsed during a fire that destroyed the adjacent Homestake Opera House. The periodicals collection was destroyed, and most other materials were smoke damaged. The library reopened in a temporary location after one month.

Sturgis Public Library became the first library in South Dakota to have an online circulation system, thanks to a donation from a trustee and her husband. A grant from the community foundation enabled Watertown Regional Library to begin a dial-a-story service. Mitchell Public Library, in cooperation with a local hospital, began a toy library for infants and toddlers under three years of age.

Aberdeen's Alexander Mitchell Public Library received a Telecommunications Device for the Deaf through the local Optimist Club. A collection of 300 original graphic art works and watercolors was given to Deadwood Public Library by three Chicagoans in association with a local retired history professor. The collection is valued at over $100,000.

In the first year of a three-year grant entitled Solo Artists in Libraries, six libraries in communities under 5,000 population were provided with artists-in-residence programs lasting five days. The project is jointly funded by the South Dakota Arts Council and the South Dakota State Library.

The South Dakota Committee on the Humanities began a successful semiannual series of reading and discussion programs on regional authors. Programs on South Dakota Public Television begin each series and are followed by discussion programs in local libraries led by humanities scholars from South Dakota colleges.

Sylvia Minton, Director of Mitchell Public Library, spent seven months in China and Saudi Arabia, where she helped organize technical libraries. Sandra Norlin, Director of Brookings Public Library, was elected South Dakota's ALA Councilor.

School Libraries. Three large school libraries installed what were believed to be the first book detection systems in South Dakota schools: Flandreau and Marty Indian Schools and Sioux Falls Lincoln High School.

South Dakota schools spent more than the national average per pupil for print and audiovisual materials, but collections are smaller than national and regional averages, in large part because of the small enrollments of most schools in the state.

A committee organized in 1983 worked throughout the year toward revising the South Dakota guidelines for school libraries. The wide-ranging document was to be presented to the State Board of Education in 1985 for approval.

Academic Libraries. The University of South Dakota–Springfield closed at the end of the spring semester. A few of the occupational training programs were transferred to other state-supported colleges, and associated library collections were moved with the programs. The college campus was to be converted into a minimum security prison that is to emphasize educational opportunities.

Black Hills State College's Leland D. Case Library for Western Historical Studies received the James Emery, Sr., Lakota language and music tape collection on the culture of the Teton Sioux Indians.

Buildings. Approximately $400,000 in library construction was completed in 1984 utilizing grants from South Dakota's $190,000 share of LSCA Title II funds distributed in 1983. The largest project placed Minnehaha County Rural Library in a new headquarters building in a different community, Crooks, in place of Hartford.

Local funding paid for a moderate remodeling of Potter County Library for energy conservation and upgraded wiring. The Elk Point Library occupied a new building paid for entirely through special fund-raising efforts.

Networks, Interlibrary Cooperation. South Dakota severed membership in Bibliographical Center for Research (BCR) to consolidate all OCLC activity in MINITEX, which also provides effective document delivery. The first South Dakota libraries to join OCLC in 1977 and 1978 did so through BCR, to which South Dakota had belonged since the early days of BCR's union catalog. The initial contract with MINITEX for document delivery brought with it advantages for libraries to obtain OCLC services through MINITEX, and all subsequent OCLC contracts were made through MINITEX. Costs to the South Dakota State Library for BCR membership and the contemplated statewide online catalog made consolidation in one network desirable.

Intellectual Freedom. In 1983 Governor William Janklow filed a libel suit in a state court against Peter Matthiessen and Viking Press, author and publisher of *In the Spirit of Crazy Horse*, and against three bookstores that had refused Janklow's telephoned request to withdraw the book from sale. The inclusion of booksellers as defendants was novel and was seen by critics as a way to ensure trial in a presumably friendly state court. Opposed to what they perceived as an attempt at censorship were the American Booksellers Association, the American Civil Liberties Union, and ALA's Freedom to Read Foundation. Janklow's suit was denied by a state judge in June; he filed an appeal to the South Dakota Supreme Court.

The Freedom to Read Foundation's request for SDLA to join in the suit was rejected by SDLA's Executive Board in February when it reaffirmed its decision to stand aside as long as no attempts were made to prevent libraries from holding and circulating the book. This position brought public criticism from some members who said failure to support the booksellers publicly appeared to condone Janklow's allegations that the booksellers acted maliciously and recklessly.

Awards. Dorothy Liegl, Deputy State Librarian, was named Librarian of the Year by SDLA, and Susan Stow Sandness, Director of Minnehaha County Rural Library, was honored as New Librarian of the Year. Kathryn Giacometto, trustee of Belle Fourche Public Library, was designated Trustee of the Year, and Dorothie Mahoney of Rapid City, Treasurer of the White House Conference on Library and Information Services Task Force, was recognized with the Friend of the Library Award. The South Dakota Reading Council presented its first Literacy Award to Marlys Shaff, Librarian at Winner Elementary School.

Appointments. Bernice C. McKibben was named Director of Devereaux Library at the South Dakota School of Mines and Technology. Connie Holltorf became Director of Yankton Community Library and Naomi Haller Director of Grant County Public Library. Also appointed were Karen Blank, Circulation Librarian, and Bang Kim, Catalog Librarian (both department headships), at Hilton M. Briggs Library of South Dakota State University. Bob Carmack, Dean of Library Services at University of South Dakota for 13 years, resigned to accept a similar position at the University of Wisconsin–Duluth.

PHILIP BROWN

TENNESSEE

Tennessee Library Association. "Information Our Most Valuable Resource" was the theme of the 1984 Tennessee Library Association

Tennessee Library Association (founded 1902)

Membership: 1,113; *annual budget:* $49,550.

President: Evelyn P. Fancher, Director, Tennessee State University Library, Nashville 37703 (April 1984–April 1985).

Vice-President/President-elect: Mary Glenn Hearne, Nashville Public Library, Nashville 37203.

Executive Secretary: Betty Nance, P.O. Box 120085, Nashville 37212.

Annual meeting: April 25–28, 1984, Memphis.

Publication: Tennessee Librarian (quarterly).

Tennessee State Library

Olivia Young, State Librarian, Nashville

Convention held in Memphis. Programs included Charles McClure, School of Library Science, University of Oklahoma, speaking on, "Improving the Quality of Reference Service for Government Publications"; an all-day program on "Microcomputers in Libraries"; a panel of government officials, library directors, and trustees discussing "Perspectives on Lobbying for Libraries"; and a keynote address by ALA President Brooke Sheldon on "Paths to Power for Libraries in 1984."

The College and University Library Section of TLA conducted its annual conference in November at Middle Tennessee State University in Murfreesboro. Theme for the meeting was "Accessing Libraries and Information." A panel discussion on "Public Access to Academic Libraries" was presented by Malcolm Getz, Director of Vanderbilt University Libraries; Dale Manning, Reference Librarian, also of Vanderbilt; Aubrey Mitchell, Acting Head of Public Services, University of Tennessee Libraries; and Robert B. Croneberger, Director, Memphis/Shelby County Public Library and Information Center.

Tennessee State Library. Olivia Young retired as State Librarian in 1984. Robert B. Croneberger was to assume that position effective January 1, 1985. Croneberger was Director of the Memphis/Shelby County Public Library and Information Center, Deputy Director of the Detroit Public Library, and Assistant Chief, Serial Records Division, at the Library of Congress.

Academic Libraries. The University of Tennessee at Knoxville Library was selected by the ARL Office of Management Studies to participate in an assisted self-study as a demonstration site for the Preservation Planning Program supported by the National Endowment for the Humanities. Norman Watkins, Head of Binding and Preservation, was to direct the study in 1985.

The Council on Library Resources PETREL Grant Program has funded a grant to UTK Librarian Angie LeClercq for a high school community access program to allow top high school students use of the library. The UTK Library Day's 36th lecture featured William J. Welsh, Deputy Librarian of Congress.

The University of Tennessee at Chattanooga initiated an online public access catalog in June. The system features hardware from Hewlett-Packard and a software package developed by Virginia Polytechnic and State University. The online catalog initially included 11 public terminals, each with access to 200,000 MARC records representing all of the library's 900,000 volumes.

Memphis State University Libraries installed a CLSI turn-key online catalog automated circulation system. Loading of the database was in process and will ultimately allow for the inclusion of some 600,000 bibliographic records as part of the system's operational database. The BRS/After Dark program was made available, allowing individual library users to conduct their own bibliographic searches.

Reference Librarians Sharon Mader and Betsy Park received a grant from MSU's Information Technology Research Institute Project to study faculty and graduate students' use of the new database. MSU and the Midwest Cooperative Conservation Program presented a Preservation and Conservation Workshop on preservation problems of research institutes.

The Periodicals Department of the Sherrod Library of East Tennessee State University Library became a participant in the Faxon-Linx serials control system, joining the ETSU Quillen-Dishner College of Medicine Library in shared use of that computer-assisted resource. A 3M book theft detection system was also installed in the Sherrod Library after a five-year effort to obtain funding. The Instructional Media Center (IMC), in conjunction with the College of Education, serves as the language arts clearinghouse for the Tennessee State Department of Education. Under the direction of Jean Flanigan, the clearinghouse, one of the six in the state, assists Tennessee school systems in purchasing decisions concerning educational microcomputer software.

Cleveland State Community College Library computerized technical and clerical activities. Circulation is online with a super mini VAX computer. Dialog was accessed through a Radio Shack TRS-80. Bryan College Library in Dayton joined SOLINET in July.

Public Libraries. LSCA funding for Knox County Public Library's retrospective conversion project ended September 30. The two-year grant enabled the library to convert 121,485 bibliographic records into machine-readable form. Local funding will continue the conversion through FY 1985, at which point the entire circulating collection is expected to be in the database.

Chattanooga-Hamilton County Bicentennial Library established a planning committee of board members, staff, and Friends of the Library. A grant of $18,759 was received from the Community Foundation of Greater Chattanooga, Inc., to support the continuation of an oral history project begun in 1982.

Programming for the year included the annual Children's Summer Reading program, coordinated with the city's Riverbend Arts Festival, and a six-week series of informational seminars for senior citizens at the Eastgate Branch. The Library also hosted a special exhibit of black-and-white photographs taken by Eudora Welty on her 1930s tour of Mississippi.

The most significant event of the year at Memphis/Shelby County Public Library and Information Center was the publication of *A Library for Memphis 2000*, a study by consultant Lowell Martin. Following release of the study, Goals and Objectives were developed and committees involving 95 staff members worked on strategies. Nineteen branches were online for circulation. A new service is the Institutional Bookmobile, which visits agencies such as group homes, juvenile reformatories, drug and alcohol recovery centers, and hospitals for the mentally or physically handicapped. Cooperative program efforts for 1984 included work with Memphis State University Gallery on a major exhibit and lecture, "A Divine Tour of Egypt," writers' workshops sponsored in conjunction with the Mid-South Writers Association, and the participation of library storytellers at the Memphis in May International Children's Festival.

Magness Memorial Library, a member of the Caney Fork Regional Library System, received a $5,500 grant from Levi Strauss Foundation to be used for a reader/printer and a photocopy machine.

School Libraries. The Comprehensive Education Reform Act had a significant impact on school librarians across the state during 1984. They are included in the Governor's Career Ladder Program, which provided for three levels of librarians, based on years of experience and other criteria.

An evaluation tool was developed by a statewide committee of school librarians and awaited the approval of the Education Interim Committee. The levels were expected to be implemented during the 1985–86 school year. Evaluations of school librarians for placement on the Career Ladder will be done during three visits by other school librarians over the course of one school year. Questionnaires will be distributed to six faculty members and one class of students for further input. Librarians on the Career Ladders will have the option of selecting 10-, 11-, or 12-month contracts, depending upon level. Responsibilities and salaries will change accordingly.

Through the efforts of Librarians Betty Lumpkin and Linda Robbeloth, Ooltewah High School Library in Hamilton County acquired 50 color monitors to accompany a $50,000 Central Media Distribution System that allows three separate video programs to be channeled to different locations throughout the school.

Special Libraries. Oak Ridge National Laboratory Library System implemented OCLC's LS/2000 System and went to an online catalog in 1984 and the card catalog was closed.

Church Libraries. Dargan-Carver Library announced that it would divide in 1985 to become the E. C. Dargan Research Library of the Baptist Sunday School Board and the Southern Baptist Historical Library and Archives of the Historical Commission, Southern Baptist Convention. The Murfreesboro First Baptist Church Media Library hosted a retreat for the Baptist Library Organization. Principal speaker was Barbara Jenkins.

Building Programs. In the Nolichucky Regional Library System, Blaine Library opened in Grainger County, Marie Ellison Library opened in Cocke County, and the Seymour Branch of Sevier County moved to a larger facility.

The University of Tennessee Center for the Health Sciences Library planned to occupy five floors of a new building early in 1985. Net space is 43,000 square feet. The University of Tennessee at Knoxville Music Library was renovated. In preparation for beginning construction on the new library, the Undergraduate Library collection and services were moved into two locations and the computer and offices into a third. In Franklin County, Sweanee Elementary, Franklin County High, and Cowan Elementary were either being completely renovated or acquiring new buildings.

Awards. The Tennessee Library Association granted the following awards in 1984: the Louise Meredith School Librarian's Award to Helen Simpson Smith, Librarian, Greenville High School, Greenville; the Frances Neel Cheney Award to John David Marshall, Director of Libraries, Middle Tennessee State University, Murfreesboro; the 1984 Honor Award to Jess A. Martin, Director of the Center for Health Sciences Library, University of Tennessee, Memphis; and the Tennessee Children's Choice Book Award to James Howe for *Howliday Inn*. Committee Chair Beverly Youree announced that more than 100 schools and 6,250 students had participated in the selection.

Edward Garten, Director of Libraries, Tennessee Tech University, received the Distinguished Alumnus Award from the Kent State University School of Library and Information Science.

Legislative News. The Tennessee Library Association Legislative Committee during 1984 compiled a "Legislative Handbook," containing practical information necessary for lobbying officials and distributed at the TLA Convention. Three pieces of legislation relating to libraries were passed by the Tennessee General Assembly. One act makes removing library materials from a library without checking them out an offense equal to shoplifting. A second bill adds legislative records to those documents to be sent upon request to the state depository libraries.

The Comprehensive Education Reform Act of 1984 had many implications for professional services by librarians. One of the goals to be achieved within five years is "an improvement in the library holdings of the public technical institutes, community colleges, and universities." A special appropriation of $2,000,000 was included as part of Governor Alexander's Better Schools Program to be distributed to public libraries throughout the state to enhance materials collections.

ROBERT B. CRONEBERGER

TEXAS

Acceleration of change in technology, in the information-providing industry, in the individual's information-seeking habits, and in economics all characterized the year 1984 for Texas libraries. As an effort to keep pace with the accelerated changes affecting their work environment, librarians attended conferences, workshops, and short courses in record numbers.

Texas was host to the 103d Annual Conference of the American Library Association during June in Dallas. Featured speakers were former First Lady Rosalyn Carter; Pulitzer Prize–winning author Frances Fitzgerald; and Ahmadou-Mahtar M'Bow, Director-General of UNESCO.

During the Republican National Convention, Dallas area librarians managed an information center for the press, staff members attached to the Republican National Committee, delegates, and candidates. Reference services were provided from a core collection of materials housed at the center (with back-up resources available at the Dallas Public Library's Central Library) and online database searching.

Texas Library Association (founded 1902)

Membership: 3,888; *annual budget:* $369,203.

President: Margaret I. Nichols, SLIS, North Texas State University, Denton (April 1984–April 1985)

Vice-President/President-elect: Mary Boyvey, Texas Education Agency, Austin.

Executive Director: Ada Howard, 3355 Bee Cave Road, Austin 78746.

Annual meeting: April 2–7, 1984, Corpus Christi.

Publications: Texas Library Journal (quarterly); *TLACast* (newsletter, eight a year).

Texas State Library

Dorman H. Winfrey, Director and Librarian
Box 12927, Capitol Station
Austin 78711

State School Library Media Supervisor

Mary Boyvey
Texas Education Agency
Austin 78711

State Association. Ada Howard became the Association's Executive Director in November succeeding Mrs. Jerre Hetherington, who retired July 1 after 30 years of service to the Association. The Headquarters office moved in October from Houston to Austin to a new 1,240-square-foot office condominium, the first parcel of property acquired by the Association.

At the annual conference in Corpus Christi attendees were able to visit 240 exhibits—a record number at any conference of the Association. During the awards ceremony, James B. Stewart, Director, Victoria Public Library, was selected 1984 Librarian of the Year; John H. Wootters, Library Trustee of Crockett, Texas, was given the Outstanding Services to Libraries and Distinguished Service Awards; Mr. and Mrs. Jess Austin, Jr., Jacksonville, Texas, were given the Philanthropic Award; and the Houston Endowment, Inc., was presented the Benefactor Award.

Texas State Library. The Texas State Library and Archives Commission in February rejected a proposal for direct aid legislation for public libraries until increased funding for libraries is obtained. Although there was general support for direct grants-in-aid, system coordinators and others urged the TLA to continue studying the consequences of direct aid. The primary concerns were that direct grants might increase administrative costs, reduce collection development funding at some levels, and jeopardize cooperative purchasing benefits and discounts available to systems. Both the commission and library professionals agreed in general that a division in the library community on this issue might compromise increased funding attempts for library services in Texas.

The Library Development Division administered establishment grants for library services in five unserved counties (dropping the number of unserved counties from 21 to 17) and distributed more than $2,000,000 in LSCA Title II grants to match local funds for library construction. In September the Division began distributing to systems a total of $335,455 in LSCA funds for literacy programs. The Division sponsored a series of workshops to assist librarians and adult educators in establishing and publicizing local literacy projects. A conference for system advisory council members and lay representatives provided a forum for discussion of statewide library service issues.

The Information Services Division acquired an IBM PC modified as an M300 terminal to handle interlibrary loans through OCLC. The reference unit began a joint project with the Division for the Blind and Physically Handicapped to equip and staff a reading room for the disabled. A Kurzweil reading machine will be supplemented in the future with other state-of-the-art equipment so that visually and physically handicapped patrons can access the entire print collection at the State Library.

The Division for the Blind and Physically Handicapped reorganized to assign reader consultants to specific patrons. Specialists were assigned to serve Spanish-speaking and institutionalized patrons. As a result, circulation per reader increased 20 percent.

Patron usage in the Archives Division increased substantially, possibly in anticipation of Texas' sesquicentennial celebration in 1986. *Guide to the Genealogical Resources at the State Archives* was revised and expanded to include numerous new collections and record series.

Public Libraries. Many Texas public libraries in 1984 expanded cooperative ventures with other types of libraries. Houston Public Library's Carnegie Branch received the TLA Project of the Year Award for its cooperative school/public library project. The project offers library service to a local high school and middle school, as well as the public, and maintains an adult learning center for Houston Community College. A multitype library demonstration project of the North Texas Library System was successful, and other public libraries across the state began serious consideration of cooperative projects. Smaller public libraries, such as the A. H. Meadows Community Library in Midlothian, sought wider utilization and economy by incorporating school libraries and senior citizen centers into their facilities.

Automation continued to be a major thrust in development. Library systems spent approximately $860,000 for automation projects in FY1984. In the South Texas, West Texas, and San Antonio Area systems, computer database searching was studied. The Houston Area Library System continued its implementation of one of the largest shared integrated library systems in the country. Multitype cooperation proved useful in several technological projects. In the Program of Cooperative Utilization of Library Technology, involving four corporate libraries and the Dallas Public Library, new library technology was offered to five historically Black Texas colleges. A united effort by Abilene Public Library and three academic libraries resulted in the first computerized union list of serials available from the Abilene Library Consortium.

Nonprofit corporation status was a growing issue of consideration for Texas libraries. The Attorney General of Texas ruled in 1984 that for purposes of system membership, a public library established as nonprofit should have a contract between its Board of Directors and a local government entity designating the Board as a public agency and responsible for the library's management and operation.

Texas public libraries in 1984 received more response than ever before from children in summer reading programs. Numerous programs and events were organized for National Library Week and Texas Book Month, proclaimed in March by Governor Mark White. Adult literacy projects began developing rapidly as a result of LSCA grants made available for such purposes.

Networks, Interlibrary Cooperation. Beyond the work of Texas' public library member systems, independent organizations, assisted by LSCA Title III grants, extended opportunities for library cooperation in the state. The Library Committee of the Association for Higher Education of North Texas (AHE) attracted new members. Composed exclusively of academic libraries since 1964, the Library Committee became multitype when it was joined in 1984 by the Dallas Public Library. AHE is one of the pioneer users of OCLC's union list component.

The Cooperation Committee of the Texas Library Association's College and University Division focused attention on the benefits of a shared online union list of serials with the result that the Texas State Library won approval and funding to profile a consolidated display of Texas' OCLC union list groups. The Council of Research and Academic Libraries (CORAL) in San Antonio used a second year of Title III funding to complete its union list. LSCA grants in 1984–85 will support new union list groups in West Texas and East Texas.

The Harrington Library Consortium, based in Amarillo, started as a resource-sharing project among four libraries (academic, public, and special) in 1979. After a Title III grant for retrospective conversion and more than $2,000,000 from the Harrington Foundation, HLC is now using Data Research System software and Digital hardware to maintain a public access catalog and circulation and cataloging functions.

School Libraries, Media Centers. As the Texas Legislature convened in special session, school librarians of Texas had originally planned to push for funding for school library resources. The plan was to request the average cost of one book per pupil. This would be the first state funding for school library resources within the state. As the legislative session set its agenda, it became apparent that staffing needs would be more critical than funding for resources.

In a very close vote, librarians were excluded from the career ladder for teachers. The omission shocked librarians, whose certification requirements mandate teacher certification prior to approval of the Learning Resources Specialist (Librarian) endorsement and certification. In additional interpretations of the law, other special teachers were also excluded from the career ladder.

The Texas Library Association Legislative Committee and one of its divisions, the Texas Association of School Librarians, will continue this legislative thrust as the Texas Legislature reconvenes in 1985.

In other school reform, the Texas Education Agency identified the essential elements that must be covered in the basic curriculum. The Texas Education Agency has, on its publication schedule, a suggested course outline for librarians in grades K–12 that will weave library skills into the essential elements.

Academic Libraries. Texas has continued to grow at a dynamic pace since the 1980 census, and that growth is reflected in the new and expanded library buildings throughout the state. Librarians and staff members at the University of Texas, El Paso, moved into a new building in 1984 and those at Texas Woman's University attended ground-breaking ceremonies for a new facility to be completed within the following two years.

The Library of the University of Texas at Austin added important materials to its collections, including unique Yiddish materials and a large music collection, through acquisitions on extensive buying trips in the Middle East, India, and Brazil.

In September North Texas State University and Texas Woman's University were hosts of the first joint meeting of the Texas and Oklahoma chapters of ACRL. The meeting brought library educators and academic librarians together to discuss changes in information technology and how changes impact the preparation of academic librarians for their role in an information society.

At the Library of the University of Houston, an online catalog and integrated library system became operational with 110 terminals at four campuses.

In 1984 the Association for Higher Education of North Texas Library Committee completed a two-year Title III project in preventive and corrective conservation. The Library of Trinity University reported an 11 percent growth rate, and Southern Methodist University received a foundation grant for retrospective conversion of the Library's bibliographic records.

KAY M. STANSBERY

UTAH

Utah Library Association
(founded 1912)

Membership: 600; *annual budget:* $20,000.

President: Brad Maurer, Davis County Library, South Branch, 725 So. Main, Bountiful 84010.

Vice-President/President-elect: Connie Lamb, Brigham Young University, Provo 84502.

Executive Secretary: Gerald A. Buttars, Utah State Library Commission, 2158 South 300 West, Salt Lake City 84115.

Annual meeting: March 22–24, 1984, Ogden.

Publications: HATU (quarterly); *Utah Legislative Newsletter* (irregular).

Utah State Library Commission

Russell L. Davis, Director
2150 South 300 West
Salt Lake City 84115

Coordinator, Media Support Services

Kenneth L. Neal
Office of Education
250 E. South Street
Salt Lake City 84111

Utah Library Association. The Utah Library Association (ULA) held its annual convention in March sponsored by the ULA and the Utah Education Library Media Association (UELMA). The theme for this year's conference was "1984: Then Is Now." George Orwell's projected conception of society in his novel *1984* provided convention planners with an abundance of relevant and exciting program topics.

The keynote speaker, futurist Leon C. Martel, addressed the topic "1984; How Near? How Far?" In his discussion he compared Orwell's fictional world of *1984* with the world that exists today. A former member of the Hudson Institute, he assessed Orwell's fulfilled predictions. Other featured speakers included Gerald R. Shields of the State University of New York (Buffalo), a noted activist in the field of information with a particular interest in issues on intellectual freedom; and Margaret E. Chisolm of the University of Washington, author of books on the media specialist and the media center.

State Library Activities. 1984 saw the publication of *Utah Under Cover*, the first annual edition of a checklist and index of Utah's state agency publications. This was the culmination of improvements in its service programs for state publications. The State Library also automated its circulation system for the Library for the Blind and Physically Handicapped, launched a systematic statewide consulting service for public libraries, and continued its work on Project Upgrade.

The year also saw the completion of a two-year pilot program to test and evaluate the costs and benefits of using OCLC through a host library. A pilot cluster project involving the State Library (the host library), the Utah Technical College of Salt Lake City (representing academic libraries), and the Park City Public Library (representing public libraries) established the feasibility of using the cluster approach to allow smaller libraries to access OCLC's services for cataloging and interlibrary loan. All qualified libraries will be allowed to participate on a cost-sharing basis with the State Library.

A significant advance in audiovisual services occurred when the State Library was granted public performance rights. Twenty new feature-length, family-oriented video titles were leased, and will be available for circulation.

Public Libraries. Several Utah libraries were nominated in 1984 to be placed on the national register of historic places: Brigham City, Ephraim, Garland, Manti, Mount Pleasant, Panguitch, Richfield, Richmond, and Tooele. They were all originally Carnegie Libraries and have made significant contributions to public education in their regions.

The Weber County Library began an Adult Literacy Program that provides individualized tutoring in basic reading and writing skills. The Literacy Program received a $500 grant from the B. Dalton National Literacy Initiative. The Southwest Branch of the Weber County Library System implemented an automated circulation system and an online public access catalog that necessitated remodeling of the interior of the library. Weber County also installed "Dial-A-Story," allowing children to call and hear classic stories around the clock.

In Salt Lake County, public access microcomputers were introduced at Whitmore, Holladay, Peterson, and Kearns Branches. Whitmore also opened a supply-gift-bookshop (the Whitmore Booktique) in the library providing patrons with a convenient source for frequently requested supplies.

Academic, Special Libraries. The Marriner S. Eccles Foundation gave the Southern Utah State College Library an unrestricted gift for the purchase of library materials. It will be used to upgrade the arts and letters and sciences collections. The previous year's gift, used to upgrade the business collection, resulted in the awarding of a fifth-year accounting program for the school. In addition, the register for the William R. Palmer Collection was printed and distributed to all college libraries. This is the largest and most important collection the library has ever received, and contains unique and valuable material on Southern Utah history, particularly on the Paiute Indians.

Following careful evaluation, the NOTIS Integrated Library System developed by Northwestern University was selected by Brigham Young University to provide an integrated library system for the Harold B. Lee Library. It unites all library functions in one centralized system, and also gives patrons online access to the catalog.

The Eccles Health Sciences Library of the University of Utah was awarded a contract from the National Library of Medicine to plan and implement an Integrated Academic Information Management System (IAIMS). It will provide greater availability of a variety of information sources needed by individual users, such as a hospital information system, computer-based education, an integrated library system, other internal databases, and access to external databases. As part of the project an InfoFair was conducted on the operation of microcomputers and some of their applications. In addition, the library began offering public access to microcomputers.

The Marriott Library at the University of Utah received a Title II-C grant to catalog the microform set *Early English Books*, as a joint project with five other libraries under the direction of the University of Indiana. The Library also completed Phase I of the Utah Newspaper Project and received a second NEH grant to begin Phase II, Bibliographic control. The Utah Newspaper Conference, held in November 1983, published its proceedings under the title *Utah's Newspapers—Traces of Her Past* and including a 920-item checklist of Utah newspapers, the most complete in existence. In addition, the Middle East Library was given the books and papers of Fayez Sayegh, former representative from Kuwait to the United Nations.

The LDS Library of the Utah Genealogical Society added a new service, the Family Registry. The Library also developed the Personal Ancestral File, a software program and genealogical management system for home computers. The Genealogical Library obtained rights from Accelerated Indexing Systems (AIS), a private indexing firm for major U.S. records, to duplicate their entire database and distribute it on microfiche to branch libraries.

Building Programs. Both Whitmore and Magna Branches celebrated their 10th anniversary in 1984. The Salt Lake City Avenues Branch opened in October, Granger Branch changed its name to West Valley Branch, and Lehi library was renovated and reopened in September. The Washington County Library began to build their Hurricane Branch with an expected completion date of August 1985.

At the University of Utah Medical Center, the Hope Fox Eccles Clinical Library was dedicated in May. The Clinical Librarian accompanies medical residents on rounds to provide information support for both residents and patients.

During 1984 construction of the LDS Church's new Genealogical Library progressed well past the 50 percent stage. The new 136,00-square-foot facility was to be completed by fall 1985.

Networks, Interlibrary Cooperation. The Washington County Library System is sharing its Dynix Integrated System with Dixie College (St. George) for circulation and public access. Both libraries have direct access to the central PAC, and the local high schools have telephone access. In the future the school district may join the system, resulting in a single listing of all library holdings within the county. Southern Utah State College Library purchased a NEC Telefacsimile machine for use in Interlibrary Loan.

Awards. An endowed award was established in honor of Priscilla M. Mayden, former Director of the Eccles Library. The award will be presented annually to the author of a distinguished paper in the information sciences. At the 103rd ALA Conference in Dallas, the Friends of Libraries USA (FOLUSA) honored the Friends of the Salt Lake City Public Library for their participation in the Reading Is Fundamental (RIF) Program.

H. Wallace Goodard, Media Director at Uinta High School, was selected as Utah Librarian of the Year by the Utah Library Association. The Utah Library Association's Special Service to Libraries Award went to the Park City Library Board. UELMA awarded Florence Tippetts the Outstanding Librarian in Utah award. Marjorie Sower of the Price City Library received the Service Award from the Utah State Historical Society.

Appointments. Glenn N. Rowe was named Director of the Historical Department Library–Archives. Wayne J. Peay became the Director of the Eccles Library. The Phillips Library of Snow College appointed Dorothy Floyd as Head Librarian.

Retirements. Priscilla M. Mayden retired as Director of the Eccles Library after 18 years of service. Donald T. Schmidt, Director of the Historical Library–Archives at the Historical Department of the LDS Church, retired after serving in that position since 1972.

H. Thayne Johnson, first Director of the Brigham Young University Graduate School of Library and Information Science, retired following 19 years of service. Carol T. Smith, Science Librarian at BYU, retired after 36 years of service. At Weber State College Stewart Library, Professor Martie Collett, Director of the Special Collections Department, retired after 20 years there.

NATHAN SMITH

VERMONT

The Department of Libraries (DOL), the University of Vermont, and Middlebury College were ready at year's end to sign a contract with a vendor for a distributed library system. All li-

Vermont Library Association (founded 1892)

Membership: 397; *annual budget:* $3,600.
President: Jean F. Marcy, St. Johnsbury, Athenaeum (January 1984–January 1985).
Vice-President/President-elect: Vivian Bryan, Northfield.
Secretary: Anita Danigelis, Burlington, Fletcher Free.
Annual meeting: May 23–24, 1984, Poultney.
Publication: VLA News (10 issues a year).

Vermont Department of Libraries

Patricia E. Klinck, State Librarian
Montpelier 05602

School Library Media Consultant

Jean D. Battey
State Department of Education
Montpelier 05602

braries within the state may eventually take an active part in this new information and resource sharing system. The process took almost three years, a major portion of the time being devoted to drafting a five-year plan: "A Strategy for Library Development." Both UVM and Middlebury had almost completed retrospective conversion and DOL started in 1984. The four state colleges planned to join OCLC in 1985 and to begin on retrospective conversion of their unique records within the next two years.

State Association. Vermont Library Association had 367 members during FY 1983–84, up nearly 11 percent from 1982. Composition of the membership indicated that 19 percent were also ALA members, 34 percent earn $10,000 or more, 15 percent earn between $5,000 and $10,000, and 47 percent earn less than $5,000. The Public Library Section of the Association is the largest, followed by College/Special Library and the Children and Young Adult sections. Since 1975, average membership in the Association has been 382.

During 1984 a new advertising policy was officially accepted by membership and many changes were made in the bylaws. The Association adopted the "ALA Statement on Professional Ethics." The annual conference, held at Poultney, featured Nat Hentoff and Peter Kurth. Librarians also enjoyed presentations on the use of interactive video and a new film on censorship, "Books under Fire." District meetings were held in 1984 in Chester, Waterbury, and Danville, and discussion centered on conserving energy and ways to make libraries more attractive for users. The College and Special Libraries Section held a fall meeting devoted to new technologies. The Children and Young Adult Section program concerned children's programming with nonfiction. Members of the Public Library Section met in Brandon to attend a program on library volunteers and on what had been called the third fastest growing hobby in the U.S., genealogy.

State Library. Vermont libraries experienced significant changes since state standards were last revised in 1979. The Vermont Board of Libraries in 1984 began a process leading to their revision. A standards revision committee was to prepare a first draft for the reactions of the Vermont library community. Public hearings, one in each of the five regions, were to be held in early 1985. Attention was to be focused on whether or not to retain two levels, Step I and II standards. Under the 1979 standards, only those libraries meeting Step I standards are eligible to use the Vermont Centralized Cataloging Service.

Earlier in 1984, DOL almost exhausted the funds allocated for the card service. Over 60,000 catalog cards were produced and the average cost per card set has been over $1. Libraries were asked to limit requests to titles with current or previous year publication dates. DOL began retrospective conversion during the year. The 190,000 titles in the Department's regional libraries, Law and Documents Unit, Library Science Collection, Reserve Services Unit, and Children's Book Exhibit Center were to be converted to MARC with work to be completed in 18 months.

Statewide van delivery service between regional libraries and local libraries was eliminated in response to a state budget deficit necessitating drastic trimming of all agency budgets in FY 1985.

Public Libraries. Ninety-one libraries met Vermont Board of Libraries Step I standards in 1984. The library receiving the highest per capita tax support ($25.93) was the Vernon Free Library. The Rutland Free Library spent more for books ($55,807), the Brooks Memorial Library in Brattleboro had more books (108,482), and South Burlington Community Library was open longer than any other public library in the state (75 hours a week). Nineteen public libraries sponsored humanities reading/discussion programs during the fall and winter. During National Library Week, libraries made special efforts to spotlight services, concentrating on adult programming. A DOL publication, "Adult Programming: Ideas and Resources for Vermont Public Librarians," was sent to every Vermont public library. The 81-page guide was designed to spark new ideas or provide different perspectives on the old ideas. Brattleboro sponsored a series of talks on neglected books. Children in Brandon scurried around town finding sponsors for a Read-A-Thon fund-raiser. The Library netted over $2,000. Montpelier's Kellogg–Hubbard Library continued its tradition of having adult storytelling at noon. Banned Books Week received considerable attention in Vermont, and libraries helped sharpen community awareness to dangers of censorship. The state had only one incident affecting intellectual freedom in 1984 and that did not involve a book.

Citizens of Bakersfield began making efforts to save their library. The village of 862 people was having problems supporting that attractive library, which opened in 1951 with a $22,000 endowment. A "Save the Library" fund drive raised $2,000. In a month of door-to-door solicitations, the Friends raised a little more than $400 and another $40 at a used book sale. Most residents believe that increasing taxes is the "wrong route."

School and Media Centers. New state standards concerning libraries went into effect, and for the first time in Vermont's history all schoolchildren, K through 12, may eventually look forward to the services of a certified library-media director and access to a collection of cataloged materials housed in one location. Larger school systems were planning to upgrade library-media services and a few librarians have been employed to initiate improvements.

Schools in Chittenden County, Vermont's most populated, were now using Public Access TV during 1984. Much of the responsibility for this programming is the librarian's and programming proved a good way to get students into the library. Burlington High School had a weekly program and Essex Junction planned to start a weekly program as funds permitted. There was a renewed interest in copyright legislation during 1984. Video taping was a major problem for media librarians because many school superintendents were not familiar with new legislation requiring permission for recording. The state's School Library Media Consultant was attempting to address the problem.

Academic Libraries. The four state college libraries completed a plan for improving collections and for providing better reference service. The question becomes: will the state fund it? The first step in the right direction was the decision to join OCLC. St. Michael's College worked to produce a simplified subject authority control file for a microcomputer. The Library was also weeding its collection before embarking on retrospective conversion.

The University of Vermont plans to offer graduate programs in other state locations. Plans were being developed to provide areas with library service, and a distributed library system coordinated by UVM, DOL, and Middlebury College may provide the answer.

Building Programs. New state standards for school libraries will lead to library expansion in the years ahead. In 1984 Enosburg completed a new library building and Richford completed major renovations to its library. The Townshend Public Library celebrated the completion of a new multipurpose room in April. Rockingham Free Library in Bellows Falls opened a new entrance and lift for the handicapped. All projects were funded by Title II matching grant funding. The Winooski Memorial Library opened its new children's room in March. Burlington's public library continued to undergo a renaissance with new programming and a 15 percent increase in circulation. If a proposed branch library in an economically depressed area of the city is built in 1985, it will result in Vermont's second major public library branch.

Networks and Interlibrary Loan. The statewide interlibrary loan system administered by DOL processed over 25,000 requests during 1983–84 and continued to be an efficient service. To expedite this service, the electronic mail system Easy Link was introduced. Networking and interlibrary loan cooperation were about to enter a new phase as the distributed automated network joining the state's largest libraries becomes a reality. A sample of the catalogs of the three participating libraries indicated that only 20 percent of the titles are duplicated among the three collections. A merged database of holdings would maximize access to each other's collections for shared collection development and for statewide sharing of resources through DOL's statewide interlibrary loan network. DOL would take the responsibility for entering the holdings of other Vermont libraries into the database, so that the online system could replace the manual union list.

Intellectual Freedom. The one reported incident during 1984 occurred in the Oxbow Union High School. The principal, acting on the request of two school board members, asked a classroom teacher to remove posters of Marx and Lenin. The superintendent of schools ordered the posters to be put back up again.

Professional Interest. The Vermont Historical Society in 1984 published a catalog of books about Vermont as its *Booklist*. The list offers a wide assortment of titles with a Vermont focus: children's books, cookbooks, country living, humor, poetry. Maps and record albums are also included. The 1984 Olympic Games inspired a piece of animation produced by 25 elementary children, 7 through 13 years of age, and entitled "The Albert Bridge Elementary School Presents the Olympics." This five-minute film is a child's version of the Olympics and had its world premiere at the Olympiad of Animation, July 1, at the Los Angeles Arts Festival.

Seminars and Meetings. The Orange Arts Center, Bradford, exhibited works of over 100 children's book illustrators in February at a seminar, "Words into Pictures." Simmons College and St. Michael's College held a one-week conference on children's literature in July. Entitled "The Book and the Child," the conference drew writers, illustrators, teachers, librarians, and other professionals in children's literature for a series of lectures, presentations, seminars, tours, exhibits, and discussion groups. DOL's two most recent Smith Lecturers were Virginia Hamilton and Jean Fritz. Pat Rhoads Mauser was awarded the 1984 Dorothy Canfield Fisher Award for *A Bundle of Sticks*. Vermont College Archives and the Vermont Historical Society cosponsored a series of miniworkshops on preserving documents, photographs, and family treasures. COSLA held its annual fall meeting in Burlington.

UVM and DOL presented two seminars in 1984. Ellen Hahn, Chief of the General Reading Rooms Division, Library of Congress, discussed the optical disk pilot program. Karen Hunter, Planning Officer, Elsevier Science Publishing, answered questions concerning electronic publishing. The Dana Medical Library (UVM) sponsored a day-long seminar, "InfoFair '84," concerning personal computer access to health science databases.

Grants and Awards. Priscilla K. Fox left $100,000 to the St. Johnsbury Athenaeum to help support a small museum in the library. The bequest provides a sense of security and the opportunity to extend hours of service and new ways of staffing the art museum.

DOL awarded minigrants of $200 each to five public libraries for children's programs: Danville, Stamford, Winooski, Castleton, Middletown Springs. The resulting programs included workshops on puppetry, photography, special programs for toddlers, art projects, and sports programs. Elva Sophronia Smith grants, administered by DOL and amounting to a total of $1,700 in 1984, were awarded to Poultney for a five-part book discussion series for adolescents, St. Johnsbury Athenaeum to develop a preschool toy collection, and Williston for comprehensive services to preschoolers and parents.

Public libraries in Woodstock, Montpelier, Rochester, and Burlington received grants for adult programs from the Vermont Council on the Humanities and Public Issues. In Burlington, a three-week series of panel discussions and a photographic exhibit centered around the issue of the homeless, "From Poor Farm to Shelter: The Fate of the Homeless."

The Special Collections Department, UVM Library, received funding from the Chittenden

County Superior Court to clean and process records damaged several years ago by smoke.

People. Retirements included those of Jane Westover (Bridgewater), Irena Hyde (Bakersfield), Emma Stannard (Dorset), and Ange-Aimee Martin (Middlebury). Ellen Nagle was named the new Dana Medical Librarian, and Gilbert Power became Librarian at DOL's Northeast Regional Library. Appointed Librarian at Newport was Gee Gee Zaveson and at Bennington, Michael Price.

Deaths. Janice J. Byington died April 8 at the age of 83. After teaching for 25 years she became Librarian at Burlington High School in 1948. In 1960 she became the State Library Consultant, working with school libraries throughout the state. For 20 years she was chairman of the Dorothy Canfield Fisher Book Program.

Sister Mary Beatrice Woods, of the Sisters of Mercy, died February 24. She served as School Librarian at Mt. St. Mary's Academy, and for 15 years she had been active in prison ministry.

MILTON H. CROUCH

VIRGINIA

Virginia Library Association (founded 1905)

Membership: 1,110; *annual budget:* $56,500.

President: Christie D. Vernon, Thomas Nelson Community College, Hampton (November 1984–December 1985).

Vice-President/President-elect: Harriet Henderson, Newport News Library, Virginia.

Executive Director: Debbie Trocchi, 80 S. Early St., Alexandria 22304.

Annual meeting: November 1–3, 1984, Norfolk.

Publications: Virginia Librarian Newsletter (bimonthly); *Occasional Papers.*

Virginia State Library

Donald R. Haynes, State Librarian
Richmond 23219

School Library Media Supervisor

Mary Stuart Mason, Libraries and Textbook Adoption
State Department of Education
Richmond 23216

For the first time in 15 years, the state appropriation for state aid to public libraries was sufficiently large in 1984 that libraries were allotted the full amount of aid for which they qualified. The State Library Board approved grants totaling $9,294,699 to 79 public libraries and to institutional libraries and programs for the handicapped. Shenandoah and Lancaster counties met the state-aid eligibility for the first time, in addition to one-time establishment grants. In 10 years, Virginia moved from a position of 30th to 4th in the nation in direct state aid to local libraries.

Changes in the law concerning the licensing of librarians shifted the administration of that program from the office of the state librarian to the Department of Commerce. The Virginia State Board for the Certification of Librarians, one of some 30 boards set up to govern the licensing of members of professional groups, was in the process of rewriting its regulations. Work was expected to continue well into 1985 to redefine requirements for entry level certification, set the time interval for renewal of certification, and discuss the possibility of continuing education requirements for renewal. The master's degree from an accredited library program was expected to remain as the criterion for automatic certification, but other roads to certification were to be discussed. Members of the new certification board are State Librarian Donald Haynes (chair), Benjamin Clymer of Old Dominion University, and Katherine Bland of Virginia State University. The Virginia Library Association created an Ad Hoc Committee on Certification to monitor the Board's activities and to provide input on the issues discussed. The VLA committee is chaired by Caroline Arden of The Catholic University of America.

State Association. Under the leadership of Timothy L. Byrne of Virginia Commonwealth University, the Virginia Library Association in 1984 dealt with legislative issues concerning full funding for public libraries and the certification of librarians.

VLA's 79th annual conference was held on November 1–3 in Norfolk and Portsmouth. The conference theme, "Virginia's Libraries 1984: Freedom, Knowledge, Opportunity, Service, Cooperation," brought to mind the Library's role in safeguarding the public's right to read and providing free access to information. Five hundred librarians, trustees, educators, and other library supporters attended sessions on a variety of topics related to the theme. Among the featured speakers were Morton H. Halperin, Director of the Center for National Security Studies in Washington; Anne Beaubien, Director of the Michigan Information Transfer Service, and Joseph Weizenbaum, Professor of Computer Science at the Massachusetts Institute of Technology. Young adult author Paula Underwood Spencer was the 1984 recipient of VLA's Jefferson Cup Award.

VLA published the *Virginia Library Automation Directory*, a summary of information gathered in a 1983 survey of Virginia libraries conducted by VLA's Technical Services, Automation, and Resources Forum. One hundred twenty-three libraries responded to the survey. Entries include information on a library's collection, population served, automation activities, and vendors used. Addresses for all vendors are included in the directory, as is a vendor/system index.

The VLA Public Relations Committee in 1984 carried out the final stages of producing a 30-second PSA on the dangers of censorship. The project was funded in part by the 1983 National Library Week Grolier Grant. Additional funding from VLA enabled the Committee to distribute copies of ALA's 1984 *Publicity Book* in April. During Banned Books Week, the committee sent public service announcements adapted from the television script to radio stations throughout the state.

VLA became a charter member of the newly formed Virginia Literacy Coalition. Virginia is one of about 20 states in the union to have formed a statewide literacy organization.

State Library Activities. The Virginia State Library Board authorized the establishment of a foundation for the purpose of soliciting and managing endowment for the State Library. The General Assembly at its last session during 1984 amended the law to declare the State Library an educational institution for the purpose of receiving endowment. The change in law permits the Library to turn over to a foundation all gifts and endowments and provides that such endowment shall not be considered by the legislature when appropriating funds for the operation of the Library.

Nine directors—three members of the State Library Board and six public members—will run the affairs of the foundation. At its first organizational meeting, the new foundation board elected the following officers: S. Douglas Fleet, President; Virginius R. Shackelford, Jr., Vice-President; S. Buford Scott, Treasurer and Chairman of the Finance Committee; State Librarian Donald Haynes, Secretary and Executive Director; Leigh B. Middleditch, Counsel and Assistant Secretary. Other members of the board are Robert B. Ball, Sr., Ruth Anne M. Brooks, Alan S. Donnahoe, Mrs. James Lewis Kirby, Jr., M. O. Roache, Jr., and William B. Spong, Jr.

The establishment of a foundation mechanism enabled the library to accept a gift from the estate of Annabelle Cox McAllister, who died in Houston in 1983. The Library will receive more than $1,250,000 from the bequest. Mrs. McAllister and her husband, Edward Nevill McAllister, had used the Library's collections for many years in conducting historical and genealogical research. They published volumes on Braesfield and Estes families that traced their ancestry to Virginia. The copyright of these volumes was included in the bequest to the State Library, along with the McAllisters' library and genealogical notes.

School/public library cooperation is getting stronger, due in part to *The Public/School Librarian's Workout Book*, published jointly by the Virginia State Library and Virginia Department of Education. Capitalizing on the current workout craze, the publication uses an exercise book format to present numerous ideas for cooperative activities between school and public libraries. The project was funded through LSCA Title III and state appropriations. Copies were distributed widely throughout the state and continues to be requested almost daily by libraries around the country.

Public Libraries. The Alexandria Library celebrated its 190th birthday in July 1984. The library is the oldest circulating library in the state and one of two or three oldest libraries in the country.

School Libraries & Media Centers. Richmond Public Schools was one of two libraries in the nation to receive the 1984 National School Library Media Program of the Year Award. Richmond was named the top media program in the country in school districts with 15,000 to 49,999 students. Winners received a $2,500 cash prize and were honored at an awards luncheon during ALA's 103rd Annual Conference in Dallas. Richmond Schools Superintendent Richard Hunter and Media Services Supervisor Beverly Bagan attended the program, during which their school board was commended for its goal to prepare students for a productive role in a technological society. The city's innovative media services program includes in-house television facilities, a Homework Hotline, and a 4000-plus film/video library. Fifty-eight full-time professional library media specialists serve nearly 30,000 students in K-12 schools, in technical, adult-learning, math-science, and humanities centers and in special-education schools.

Virginia Beach Public Schools received a John Cotton Dana Award for producing an outstanding videotape to promote a middle school library in the system.

The State Department of Education's School Libraries and Textbooks Division developed standard learning objectives for library and information skills in grades K-12. These are the first learning objectives of their kind to be produced in the state.

The Division of Instructional Media and Technology of the Department of Education and the Virginia Educational Vendors Association sponsored six regional media congresses around the state in September and October 1984. The theme was "New Horizons for Excellence" and encompassed new resources and approaches to help Virginia's school library media programs achieve excellence. The new standard learning objectives for teaching library/information skills were introduced. In addition, VEMA presented a session on media in the instructional program.

Academic Libraries. Hampden-Sydney College's Eggleston Library received a $400,000 grant from the National Endowment for the Humanities to support humanities collections and develop an international learning center. The challenge grant enables the library to purchase video and computer equipment.

Building Programs. CBN University dedicated its $13,200,000 Library October 13-14. Presidential counselor Edwin Meese III was the main speaker. The new Library has a capacity of 600,000 volumes and space for 650 readers and 68 staff members. The Data Phase automated library system is being installed. Special features of the building include a two-story high central atrium with trees and plants, and small prayer chapel with a stained glass window.

Mr. and Mrs. J. Harwood Cochrane were awarded the ALTA major benefactor's honor award for donating one acre of land and $380,000 to build the Rockville Branch of Pamunkey Regional Library.

Networks, Interlibrary Cooperation. The Virginia State Library in 1984 issued a request for consultant services to review the status of library networking in Virginia and the options open to the state in networking and to recommend future service to all of the state's libraries. Several consulting firms sent representatives to a bidders' conference at the State Library on November 28. A selection team of five persons representing the State Library, the State Network Users Advisory Council, the Council of Higher Education, public libraries, and the Department of Information Technology reviewed the proposals and recommended that a contract be awarded to King Research, Inc., of Rockville, Maryland. It was expected that the contract would be signed in early 1985 and that the final report will be delivered in late 1985 or early 1986.

LSCA Title III funds were used to expand the Virginia State Library-Pamunkey Regional Library shared online system to include the J. Sargeant Reynolds Community College libraries. Terminals placed in the College's centralized technical processing office and three public service branches will be linked via telephone lines to the Hewlett Packard computer at the Virginia State Library. The shared system will provide J. Sargeant Reynolds with VTLS circulation and cataloging services and will make holdings records of all three libraries available to each other online.

CAVALIR, statewide union catalog of holdings in Virginia's libraries, has grown to include 1,800,000 entries. Copies of the microfiche catalog have been distributed to 269 libraries of all types.

The Tidewater Consortium is a cooperative association composed of 15 academic and four public libraries in the southeastern part of Virginia called Tidewater. The consortium is compiling the first edition of the *Tidewater Union List of Serials,* produced through the OCLC union list component in Virginia. It will also be the third OCLC union list group in SOLINET. The project coordinators are Albert C. Liu, Associate Dean for Technical Services, and Gale Nordon, Head of Cataloging and Database Control at Old Dominion University.

Intellectual Freedom. The Virginia Library Association agreed to bring the Association into partnership with the American Civil Liberties Union (ACLU) in a Freedom of Information lawsuit that has attracted national attention. The lawsuit centers on the right of access to certain papers at the George C. Marshall library, a private research library on the campus of Virginia Military Institute. The papers are those of William Friedman, a pioneer figure in United States Intelligence gathering and a former employee of the National Security Agency. The agency reportedly cleared the papers, then began to re-examine and classify some after James Bamford used them in his book, *The Puzzel Palace.* At issue is whether NSA has the legal right to deny access to papers that are not classified and to classify others that have already been available and used by the public. ACLU was to formally request access to the Friedman papers and, if denied by NSA, initiate the suit.

Christie Vernon of VLA played a key role in efforts to obtain statements on Freedom of Information in the Democratic Party platform. Vernon, a member of the National Democratic Platform committee, attended most of the hearings held prior to the drafting of the platform. After consulting with the platform committee Director and with Eileen Cooke, Director of the ALA Washington Office, she prepared testimony from ALA legislative positions, and from an article on the VLA-ACLU lawsuit. The platform committee promised that a strong reference to FOI would be included in the platform as well as criticism of the use of import-export law to diminish the flow of information between the U.S. and other countries.

Professional Interests. VLA's Paraprofessional Forum published *Who Makes What Where How: Library Paraprofessional Salaries in Virginia,* a 68-page report of a survey of paraprofessional job responsibilities and salaries in Virginia libraries. Ninety-five library systems responded to the survey, which may be one of the first of its kind in the country. In addition to other salary data, the survey disclosed that the mean starting salary for paraprofessionals in the state was $10,876. A paraprofessional position was defined as any position not requiring an M.L.S. Positions were grouped by the following categories: circulation, catalog/acquisition, reference, administration, and media. Job types covered by the "administration" category included payroll clerks, budget analysts, secretaries, janitors, computer operators, and administrative assistants. The report also gives information on the number and types of position for paraprofessionals, along with job descriptions.

Festivals celebrating completion of the statewide summer reading program, "Read for the Gold," were held in Abingdon August 7, and in Richmond August 14. A new feature in the celebrations was the First Annual Virginia Storytelling Festival, organized jointly by the Virginia State Library, VLA's Children's/Young Adult Round Table, and School Library Section, and the Virginia Educational Media Association. Approximately 175 children, parents, and librarians representing eight library systems participated in Abingdon and nearly 400 participants from eighteen library systems attended in Richmond. In addition to storytelling, festivities included clowns, balloons, puppets, and costumed cartoon characters, State Librarian Donald Haynes awarded certificates of merit signed by Lynda Robb, a supporter of the program, to representatives of participating libraries.

Governor Charles S. Robb signed a Certificate of Recognition designating December 1984 as Virginia Reading Month. 1984 marked the third year of this observance.

Awards. Robert Grattan, Learning Resource Center Director at the Parham Campus of J. Sargeant Reynolds Community College in Richmond, was awarded a Fulbright Fellowship to teach library automation at the University of Tunis in Tunisia for the spring semester, 1985.

VLA awarded life memberships to H. Gordon Bechanan, former Director of Virginia Polytechnic Institute and State University in Blacksburg and Past-President of VLA; Mary A. Marshall, member of the House of Delegates representing the 48th district; Hannah McLay, retired consultant from the Virginia State Library; Mary-Elizabeth Mather, retired Librarian from the Richmond City Schools; John H. Robertson, former Chair and current member of the Virginia Beach Public Library Board; and Howard M. Smith, retired city librarian of the Richmond Public Library.

1984 recipients of the Professional Development Grant, sponsored by Yankee Book Peddler, were Stephen Marine, College of William and Mary, and Linda Wilson, Virginia Polytechnic Institute and State University. The grant encourages professional activities by librarians who have no more than three years of experience.

Appointments. Augustus C. Johnson, of Syria, Virginia, and Armistead L. Robinson, of Charlottesville, Virginia, were appointed by Governor Charles S. Robb to five-year terms on the Virginia State Library board.

The State Networking Users Advisory Council elected as Chairpersons Patricia U. Thomas, Librarian of the Chesapeake Branch of the Tidewater Community College.

Deaths. Henry Muller Brimm, retired Librarian and Emeritus Professor of Bibliography at Union Theological Seminary in Richmond, Virginia, died on August 1.

James Jackson, Social Science and Documents Librarian at the University of Richmond Boatwright Library, died on December 13, 1983. In his honor, an annual award was to be established to recognize an outstanding research paper completed by a graduate student in the departments with which he worked.

Milton Chamberlain Russell, Head of the Reference and Circulation Department of the Virginia State Library for 36 years, died August 21.

Helen Keeble Scribner, a librarian at the Virginia State Library for 42 years, died on July 25.

MARY SEEMEYER

WASHINGTON

Washington Library Association (founded 1905)

Membership: 1,102; *annual budget:* $54,668.

President: Ann Haley, Walla Walla Public Library (August 1983–July 1985).

First Vice-President/President-elect: Irene Heninger, Kitsap Regional Library.

Corresponding Secretary: Marjorie Burns, 1232-143rd Ave. S.E., Bellevue 98007.

Annual meeting: April 25–28, 1984, Pasco, Washington.

Publications: Highlights (5 times per year); *Washington Library Advocate* (4 times per year).

Washington State Library

Roderick G. Swartz, State Librarian
AJ-11
Olympia 98504

State School Learning Resource Centers

Jean Wieman
Director of Programs and Learning Resources
Office of Superintendent of Public Instruction
FG-11
Olympia 98504

Intellectual Freedom. The intellectual freedom tenets of Washington libraries and librarians were tested in 1984 by individuals, organized groups, and institutions. The most notable incidents were in Vancouver and Seattle. In Clark County, the American Civil Liberties Union of Washington, with support from the Washington Library Association and the Freedom To Read Foundation, filed suit against the Evergreen District for arbitrary removal of over 30 books for which no complaints had been filed and no public review hearings held.

A Seattle group, Eastside Citizens for Decency, launched the Together Against Pornography Campaign. By threatening boycotts and pickets, they were successful in forcing many high-volume, high-visibility retailers to remove *Playboy* and other materials which TAP deemed degrading to women. They carried the complaint to the Boards of the King County and the Seattle Public Library amidst a media blitz. TAP remained active and highly visible at year's end, lobbying for passage of local anti-pornography ordinances, while librarians urged exclusion for public libraries.

With help from the ACLU's school censorship project, the Washington State Coalition Against Censorship has produced a videotape titled "Empty Shelves, Empty Minds." The tape, 13.5 minutes long, has been distributed to many community groups, school districts, and libraries within Washington state. It has also been entered in the American Film Festival sponsored by the Educational Film Library Association in New York.

State Library Activities. The Washington State Library Commission in 1984 awarded $402,000 for Title I competitive grants to public libraries and $72,000 for Title III competitive grants for two or more libraries for different types planning and for implementing cooperative ventures. To assist in the planning and writing of grant proposals for LSCA, the Library Planning and Development Division sponsored Grant Proposal Workshops in three locations of the state.

In cooperation with the Washington Library Friends and Trustees Association, the Library Planning and Development Division sponsored an ALTA designed Workshop in Library Leadership for trustees. Over 105 attended to hear speakers Alice Ihrig, Charles Robinson, Nancy Steigmeyer, and a host of Washington librarians and trustees.

Legislation which would change the governance of the Washington Library Network was drawn up by the WLN Computer Services Counsel for introduction in the 1985 legislative session. The proposal calls for formation of a public non-profit corporation to be known as the Western Library Network.

School Libraries, Media Centers. The Washington Library Media Association held its annual conference at the Yakima Convention Center. Guest speakers included Michael Giammatteo, Brain Research Specialist; Jim Sayles, Futurist; and Bettie Day, AASL President.

Academic Libraries. The Washington State Legislature funded the University of Washington Libraries to organize the papers of Senators Warren G. Magnuson and the late Henry W. Jackson. Also at the University of Washington, in the Health Sciences Library, a three-year National Library of Medicine resource project grant was received to coordinate health science information services in the state of Washington. A major event was the ACRL Third National Conference which was held in Seattle.

Building Programs. A number of library construction projects were either completed or started during 1984. Five were the recipients of LSCA grant monies: Naches completed its energy conservation program involving insulation, and other improvements. Another Yakima Valley Regional Library System library in Granger was dedicated in August. The Goldendale building was scheduled for completion in 1985 as was the renovation of the Bellingham Fairhaven branch and the main library expansion. Also completed was the Newport Public Library. Kitsap Regional library upgraded facilities in Port Orchard and Kingston.

In January the King County Library System dedicated its Vashon Island Branch. The System began construction of its 15,000-square-foot Fairwood Community Library. No LSCA funds are involved in either project. The Fairwood library represents the System's 27th building project since 1967.

The future construction picture is bright in Tacoma since a $15,000,000 library capital construction bond issue was approved in November. The Seattle Library will realize about $2,000,000 from a general capital bond issue approved by the City's electorate. Spokane County successfully lifted a levy limit and will use some of the funds for building projects.

Networks. LSCA Title III funds were used in 1984 to establish a statewide materials delivery system with the goal of improving "library service to the end user by developing a delivery network for resource sharing for libraries in Washington." The project included 24 ground couriers linking present courier networks, selected telefacsimile sites, a telecommunication network and a reference/referral module. The Planning Committee anticipates being able to reduce the average speed of delivery from 14 days to 48 hours, state wide.

The Resource Sharing Program is successfully replacing the Pacific Northwest Bibliographic Center, now defunct, with an LSCA grant from the Washington State Library.

Awards. Marilyn Hawkins of Sharp, Hartwig Advertising, Inc., received the Washington Library Association President's Award for the excellence of her work in public relations as a vocal and visible promoter of public libraries in Washington state.

Raya Fidel, of the University of Washington, received a Best Paper Award—Honorable Mention for her article in the *Journal of the American Society for Information Science* for the year 1983.

Professor Spencer Shaw, of the University of Washington, was a major speaker at the 10th World Congress International Reading Association in Hong Kong in August.

Karen Sy was elected for membership in the Sigma Xi Honorary Research Society in Science in 1984.

Irving Lieberman, Professor and Director Emeritus, Graduate School of Library and Information Science, University of Washington, was honored during the 40th Anniversary of the Armed Services Edition, Library of Congress, for his service in World War II as a librarian promoting the use of "paperbacks" to military personnel.

Barbara Tolliver, Director of Continuing Education in the Graduate School of Library and Information Science at the University of Washington received the College/University Administrator of the Year Award.

Appointments. Margaret Chisholm, Director of the Graduate School of Library and Information Science, University of Washington, was appointed to the ALA Executive Board for the 1984–88 term.

In Washington's academic libraries, Nancy Baker, who was Head of Reference at the University of Utah, was appointed Assistant Director of Libraries, Undergraduate Library Services, University of Washington Libraries. Diane C. Parker, former Director of the Science and Engineering Library, State University of New York at Buffalo, was named Director of Wilson Library at Western Washington University.

Public Library Directors appointed during 1984 include: Jo Davies, North Olympic Library System; John Halladay, Whatcom County Library; Cindy Brennan, Cams Public Library; Diane Kerlin, Milton Public Library; and David Remington, Pend Oreille County Library.

MARGARET CHISHOLM

WEST VIRGINIA

1984 Issues. The annual campaign for libraries brought the state per capita from $2.42 to $2.88, just $.12 shy of the $3 per capita goal. Coming on the heels of two years of budget freezes and cuts, this increase in state funding was sorely needed by public libraries just to maintain basic services.

Public libraries participated fully in the legislative process during the 1984 election year by setting up "Candidates' Corners" with informational material provided by the Library Commission and individual candidates. Red, white, and blue posters, folders, and bookmarks proclaimed "The Issues, The Candidates, The Library." Public libraries participated in a statewide notary public program,

West Virginia Library Association (founded 1914)

Membership: 654; annual budget: $27,582.

President: Charles E. McMorran, Kanawha County Public Library, Charleston (December 1984–November 1985).

Vice-President/President-elect: Susan Vidovich, Raleigh County Public Library, Beckley.

Annual meeting: October 11–13, 1984, Harpers Ferry.

Publication: West Virginia Libraries (quarterly).

West Virginia Library Commission

Frederic J. Glazer, Executive Director
Science and Cultural Center
Charleston, West Virginia 25305

State Library Media Supervisor and Director of ECIA Chapter 2

Carolyn Skidmore
State Department of Education
Building 6, Capitol Complex
Charleston, West Virginia 25305

each library being given a one-time opportunity to register staff members as notaries without paying a fee. This enables each library to become a voter registration site.

The statewide automation plan was running far ahead of its projected schedule, with installations by 1984 in public libraries in Huntington, Fayette, Raleigh, Boone, Mercer, McDowell, Wood, Berkeley, Harrison, Kanawha, Marshall, and Hancock Counties, and at West Virginia State College and Marshall University.

State Association. The 11th annual Library Appreciation Day Dinner February 1 at the Charleston Civic Center saw 690 library trustees, Friends, workers, and librarians letting the 100 legislators in attendance know their needs for libraries. Guest speaker was Bob Greene, author of American Beat.

"Libraries: Lifelines for Lifetimes" was the theme for the 69th annual meeting of the Association October 11–13 at Harpers Ferry. Anne Heanue, Associate Director of ALA's Washington Office, addressed the general session on "Legislation, Libraries, and Lobbying." The Assistant Secretary of Education, Donald J. Senese, spoke on "Alliance for Excellence."

Other sessions featured David Nathanson, Chief, Office of Library and Archival Service, National Park Service, speaking on "Libraries in the National Park System"; Ralph DeVore of Western Maryland Public Library, discussing "Nitty Gritty Graphics"; Peggy O'Brien from the Folger Shakespeare Library, giving an overview of the collection there; Joe McHugh, Storyteller, telling Appalachian tales; Jane Heiser of Enoch Pratt Free Library talking on "Adult Continuing Education and Libraries"; Cynthia Rylant speaking on her writings; and Jean Ambrose, Executive Director of LVA-WV, on "Libraries and Literacy."

Other programs included technology ("VTLS Users Group Meeting," "Librarianship and Technology—Some Reservations about the Future," "The Use and Misuse of Query," and "VTLS and the Academic Library"); Donna Calvert, Consultant with the West Virginia Library Commission (WVLC), presented programs for library trustees; Steven Payne, speech communications instructor at WV University, spoke on "The Nonverbal Librarian," and Karl Hess, author, entertained with his "Confessions and Delusions of a Library Junkie." Also participating were Rebecca Bingham from Jefferson County (Kentucky) Public Schools, Max Gurman from March of Dimes, and Donald Fossedal from GPO.

State Library Activities. The West Virginia Library Commission (WVLC) offered for the 11th time at Marshall University in Huntington the two-week Library Skills Institute. The session was attended by over 100 students from West Virginia, Virginia, Kentucky, Ohio, and Tennessee. In conjunction with the Institute, a two-day continuing education program was offered in cooperation with the University of Kentucky's School of Library and Information Science's CE Department. Over 80 students received credit for participating in "Advanced Reference" or "Public Relations."

The Library Commission continued to coordinate, for the second year, the State Humanities Foundation-funded Great Books program.

WVLC was invited to be a part of a multi-agency Coalition for Literacy in West Virginia, a group dedicated to using any and all resources to combat illiteracy in West Virginia. Many libraries in West Virginia were actively involved during 1984 in holding literacy programs.

A series of posters produced by WVLC's Support Services resulted in thousands being distributed nationally and internationally as well as several appearing as covers on Library Journal.

Public Libraries. The Public Library Section (PLS) of WVLA cosponsored spring workshop with the Junior Members Round Table (JMRT). It included presentations on programming for preschoolers, ideas for reaching the aged with library services, and methods for marketing the library within its community.

The PLS continues to sponsor the West Virginia/Pennsylvania Cooperative Job Hotline.

School Libraries, Media Centers. The School Library Section (SLS) was the initial sponsor of the West Virginia Children's Book Award, which provides an opportunity for children in grades three through six to read from a group of book selections and participate in the voting for their favorite book.

SLS in 1984 became an affiliate of the American Association of School Librarians.

The annual workshop was held in April at Shinnston's Lincoln High School. Key speaker was Kathleen Kawecki, School Services Specialist for WNPB. Other speakers included Jeanne Moellendick, President of WVLA; Elizabeth Howard, WV University; James E. Bennett, Superintendent of Harrison County Schools; and Jerry M. Toth, Principal of Lincoln High School.

Academic Libraries. Academic librarians continued to attempt to resolve the faculty status issue with the Board of Regents. A proposal on classification was in committee at year's end.

The Section's spring working conference was held May 10 at Mountainlair at West Virginia University. The conference, entitled "Preserving Yesterday's News," was concerned with the preservation, accessibility, and research value of newspapers.

Attempts continued in 1984 to revive the Advisory Council to the Board of Regents, a group that would counsel on long-range planning and administrative concerns.

West Virginia University Library received a grant of $88,051 from the National Endowment for the Humanities to support the West Virginia Newspaper Project undertaken by its West Virginia and Regional History Collection. The project, under the direction of Harold M. Forbes, seeks to preserve and establish a bibliographic record of state newspapers published from Colonial times to the present.

Building Programs. Thanks to a windfall from the Emergency Jobs Bill, $642,477 in federal money was matched by $400,000 in state money to enable 21 construction projects to be completed. They included new Instant and Outpost libraries, as well as remodeling and standard construction buildings.

Interlibrary Cooperation. The expansion of the VTLS statewide automation system promises to improve interlibrary cooperation immensely. An invitation was issued to the public school system to participate in the program.

Awards. At its annual conference, WVLA issued resolutions to Jonathan Lowe for his contribution to libraries, Anthony J. Sparacino for his distinguished service as a trustee, to junior high librarian Julia Temple for her exemplary service, and to Hal Shill for his contribution to state and national legislative efforts.

The Dora Ruth Parks Award was presented to Barbara Bonfili for her work at Morgantown High School and 23 years of involvement with library service to the state. The Distinguished Service Award was presented to Ruth Figgatt of Kanawha County Public Library, and Cynthia Rylant received the Literary Award.

JMRT presented the Outstanding New Librarian Award to Kay Boyce Mullins of Taylor County Public Library, and the JMRT/Baker and Taylor Grassroots Award went to Gillian Ellern.

Appointments. Judy K. Rule was appointed Director of Cabell County Public Library. William Muller became Director at McDowell Public Library in Welch, and Dolores Antigo assumed the directorship at Brooke County Public Library in Wellsburg.

David Gillespie resigned as Head of Robert F. Kidd Library at Glenville State College.

Deaths. Perry Emmett O'Brien, past member of the West Virginia Library Commission and trustee of Alpha Regional Library, died in 1984.

SHIRLEY SMITH

WISCONSIN

A 19-member Task Force on Library Legislation was appointed by the State Superintendent of Public Instruction, Herbert J. Grover, in May 1983 to help rewrite and update Chapter 43 of the Wisconsin statutes. During 1984 the Task Force held five meetings and four public hearings around the state during its 14 months of work. The final report was submitted in August 1984 and contained 56 recommendations and eight general policy statements that the members of the Task Force, chaired by Douglas Zweizig, felt would strengthen library services throughout Wisconsin.

Superintendent Grover agreed that public library service was a matter of statewide concern and that adequate provisions of these services was the responsibility of local, county, and state governments. State provision of financial

Wisconsin Library Association (founded 1891)

Membership: 1,760; *annual budget:* $107,202.

President: Dennis Ribbens, Lawrence University, Seeley G. Mudd Library, Appleton (January 1984–January 1985).

Vice-President/President-elect: Milton Mitchell, Indianhead Federated Library System, Eau Claire.

WLA Administrator: Faith B. Miracle, 1922 University Avenue, Madison 53705.

Annual meeting: October 24–26, 1984, LaCrosse Convention Center, LaCrosse.

Publication: WLA Newsletter (bimonthly).

Wisconsin Department of Public Instruction Division for Library Services

Leslyn Shires, Administrator
125 S. Webster, P.O. Box 7841
Madison 53707

Bureau of Instructional Media & Educational Technology

Dianne McAfee Hopkins, Director
Division for Library Services
125 S. Webster
Madison 53707

---

support for state-level library automation was also necessary. While he agreed with recommendations relating to state-level resource libraries, he said he could not propose changes without further study by the Council on Library and Network Development. Certification requirements for public library directors were supported along with increasing the indexing level for public library system aid to 13 percent of local public library expenditures. Grover also supported additional state funding to public library systems for demonstration grants and pilot projects relating to multitype library services. He said he was unable to support prescribed ratios for staffing of school library media centers because of lack of broad support in the educational community.

State Association. 1984 was an important year for Wisconsin Library Association's growing public relations efforts. A bumper sticker contest was sponsored to increase library visibility throughout the state. The winning bumper sticker—"Libraries: A Renewable Resource" (designed by Mary Struckmeyer)—was presented for sale at WLA's annual conference and announced at the annual business meeting. The "WLA Book Bag" was also developed for Wisconsin Public Radio, to promote books about or by Wisconsin authors as an extension of the print media project that provides book reviews to approximately 30 Wisconsin newspapers.

ALA's "Let's Talk About It" program also was promoted in Wisconsin, with the State Library's support and it began September 15 with the hiring of Barbara Morford to oversee its success. Five libraries throughout Wisconsin planned to offer book discussion programs during the first half of 1985, centering on the theme "Making a Living, Making a Life."

The WLA Literary Awards Committee and the Council for Wisconsin Writers cooperated to sponsor "Discover Wisconsin Writers Week" October 7–13 honoring Wisconsin authors living and dead with book fairs, readings, and other activities.

During 1984 a petition was circulated to begin a WLA Automation Round Table for librarians to begin in 1985. A new semi-annual WLA publication, The WLA Journal, was also to be launched in 1985. Jim Gollata, Director at Mt. Senario College Library, was appointed its first editor. The bimonthly WLA Newsletter continued its publication under the new editorship of Patricia Powell.

The Annual WLA Conference with its theme "Books, Bytes, and Bits—A Bridge to the Future" attracted close to 800 Wisconsin librarians, trustees, Friends, and exhibitors. Programs which included Confrontation Techniques, Management for Change, Librarians in a Period of Global Transformation, Planning for Library Technology, Working with Legislators, Access to Information, Automation, and Inservice Education were among many others offered.

WLA's Education Section had an active year. The Committee developed a draft of Guidelines for Library Employment, prepared to assist employers seeking staff members. The Education Section also cosponsored a "Rainbow Coalition" of library/media educators with the Wisconsin Educational Media Association and the Wisconsin School Library Media Association. The Coalition met four times to discuss certification requirements for school/library media specialists.

State Library Activities. The Division for Library Services (DLS) spent much staff time working with the Library Legislation Task Force this year and did an excellent job keeping Wisconsin librarians informed from start to finish.

Wisconsin's MITINET retrospective conversion project had over 244 participating libraries in 1984. With all the new bibliographic records being converted to computer readable format, the second edition of WISCAT, a statewide microfiche union catalog, was published. WISCAT is one of the largest statewide union lists. It is used by over 250 Wisconsin libraries for interlibrary loan, patron use, cataloging, reference, and retrospective conversion.

The Cooperative Children's Book Center (CCBC), which has been in operation for over 20 years, received the third annual Celebrate Literacy Award given by the Madison Reading Council. It was the first institution to be so honored.

Public Libraries. The chief concern of the Wisconsin Association of Public Librarians (WAPL) for 1984 was monitoring the development of the legislative proposals recommended by the State Superintendent's Task Force on Library Legislation. Many have been included in the Department of Public Instruction's Biennial Budget. It was hoped that a legislative declaration would be added to the Wisconsin statutes stating that public library service is a matter of statewide concern, along with clear rationale regarding Wisconsin's role in promoting and funding the development of public library services and interlibrary cooperation.

WAPL cosponsored a representative to the Frontiers Conference on marketing public library services, sponsored by the Education for Public Libraries Committee and the Task Force on Marketing of the Public Library Association. WAPL also assisted in securing the state's participation in the ALA "Let's Talk About It" program.

The Personnel and Professional Concerns Committee of WAPL produced a tabular report on "Salary and Fringe Benefits of Wisconsin Public Libraries," which provides comparable data on 192 public libraries.

Trustees. The Wisconsin Library Trustee Association (WLTA) met for one full day in LaCrosse in conjunction with the WLA and discussed a variety of issues. Trustees working with their own libraries are concerned about funding for libraries and heard from state legislators, staff from the Division for Library Services, and also Task Force members from across the state that have been involved in the State Superintendent of Instruction's Task Force on Library Legislation. The WLTA met several times in 1984 and sponsored two Educational Telephone Network (ETN) broadcasts dealing with projects such as funding, censorship, and legislation. The ETN classes are offered free to all state trustees and others who sign up at an ETN site in their home areas. The Wisconsin Trustee Reference Manual was also revised.

WLTA is led by a Board of Directors composed of 15 Trustees from across Wisconsin, including officers and at-large representatives from the different regions. Each director attempts to keep in contact with Public Library System Directors in the State in order to involve the 'grass roots' level as an integral part of their program. Each public library is governed by a Board of Trustees, but membership in WLTA numbers just over 200. Increasing this number is an ever constant goal.

Academic Libraries. With the support of ALA's Association of College and Research Libraries, the Wisconsin Association of Academic Librarians (WAAL) in 1984 began the quarterly ACRL/WAAL Newsletter, edited by their Publications and Professional Development Committee.

The WAAL Automation Committee produced a Micro Software Directory, Useful for evaluating various microcomputer software packages for purchase in all types of libraries.

To help develop bibliographic instruction programs, WAAL's Education and Library Use Committee published a guide for academic libraries, Minimum Library Use Skills.

A spring conference was held at Green Bay in April. Under the theme "Library Systems," topics ranged from automation to barriers to reference service. Proceeds from the conference made possible publication of conference Proceedings and Papers, the Micro Software Directory, and the Minimum Library Use Skills.

School Libraries/Media Centers. The Wisconsin School Library Media Association (WSLMA) in 1984 made a concerted effort to make the importance of the library/media program and the role of the school library/media specialist better known among other educational organizations through such activities as exhibits and presentations at conferences for the following organizations: Parent-Teacher Association, Wisconsin Association of School Boards, and the Wisconsin School District Administrators. WSLMA presented, and the membership approved, a resolution to support the Department of Public Instruction's Legislative initiatives also, but requested WLA to back the school library/media community's concerns regarding the legislative proposals. WSLMA and the Wisconsin Educational Media Association worked together to publish a job description for district library media directors as well as the annual *Wisconsin Ideas in Media*. At the WLA Fall Conference, WSLMA concentrated on presenting strong programming for its membership through key speakers. They included Betty Costa, Shirley Hughes, and Jane Botham. As part of its awards program for recognizing professional exellence, WSLMA recognized Miriam Erickson, Media Specialist, Gibralter Area Schools, as the Media Specialist of the Year and James F. Krems, Principal, Rosholt Public Schools, as Administrator of the Year.

Building Programs. Twelve Wisconsin public libraries were involved in building and extensive remodeling programs in 1984. They included Barneveld, Beaver Dam, Beloit, Greenfield, Hales Corners, Jefferson, Marshfield, Princeton, Rhinelander, Sauk City, Watertown, and Weyawega.

Networks/Interlibrary Cooperation. Wisconsin Interlibrary Loan Services conducted a federally funded test of telefacsimile equipment for interlibrary loans with 15 participants—seven academic, six public, and one each from the State Library and the network office. Telefax was found to be a cost-effective means of transmitting interlibrary loan materials and requests.

A first fiche product from OCLC-based serials union list project was produced. It included holdings of nearly 300 libraries, many of which are small public, special, and secondary school libraries. Much of this effort was accomplished through support from the network research projects funds.

Wisconsin also participated as a test site for OCLC's Group Access capability, which allows libraries to use the OCLC interlibrary loan subsystems without being full cataloging participants in OCLC. After the test period, more than half of the libraries decided to continue participation.

Intellectual Freedom. Two obscenity bills were introduced by state senators in 1984. The WLA/IFC voted to oppose both bills after they were studied by various WLA committees and the WLA Legislative Advocate. Neither bill survived the legislative session.

The IFC provided excellent programming during WLA's fall conference on "Information Access and Its Ramifications in an Information Age." Frances MacDonald from Mankato State University was the featured speaker. A brochure about the work of the Committee was prepared. The IFC also contributed programming assistance and $500 toward the Wisconsin Intellectual Freedom Coalition's sixth annual conference entitled: "Has the Orwellian World Arrived: Premonitions and Predictions from *1984*"; it was cosponsored by the National Council of Teachers of English.

Awards. The Wisconsin Library Association Awards given at the 1984 annual conference went to Mary Muellenbach, Trustee of the Year, from Manitowoc/Calumet Library System; to Serena Nelson, Librarian of the Year, from Southwest Wisconsin Library System; and to Luther Hospital Library, Eau Claire, Library of the Year. The Special Service Award went to Sally Davis, University of Wisconsin–Madison, Library School Library.

The Banta Literary Award was given to Sara Rath for her book of poetry entitled *Remembering the Wilderness*. Notable Wisconsin authors added to Wisconsin's Notable Authors List included Herbert Kubly, Paul Mackendrick, and Beverly Butler.

Appointments. Several libraries named new directors in 1984. They included D. Kaye Gapen, University of Wisconsin–Madison; Bob D. Carmack, University of Wisconsin–Superior; Donald J. Sager, Milwaukee Public Library; Jane Byers, Waukesha Public Library; William Wilson, McMillan Memorial Library, Wisconsin Rapids; and Joseph J. Accardi, Janesville Public Library. Hsi-Ping Chao is the new Dean of Learning Resources, University of Wisconsin–Whitewater.

Deaths. Val Mae Fenstra, a professor at University of Wisconsin–Madison, Graduate School of Library and Information Studies, died in May.

SUSAN L. HEATH

WYOMING

Wyoming Library Association (founded 1914)

Membership: 475; *annual budget:* $50,000.

President: Henry M. Yaple, University of Wyoming Library, Laramie 82071 (May 1984–September 1985).

Vice-President/President-elect: Lesley D. Boughton, Platte County Library, Wheatland 82201.

Executive Secretary: Lucie Osborn, Laramie County Library, Cheyenne 82001.

Annual meeting: May 2-5, 1984, Cheyenne.

Publication: Wyoming Library Roundup (three times a year).

Wyoming State Library

Wayne H. Johnson, State Librarian
Supreme Court Building
Cheyenne 82002

State School Library Media Supervisor

Jack Prince
State Department of Education
Hathaway Building
Cheyenne 82002

1984 can be described as a year of steady but unspectacular progress for Wyoming libraries, a year in which existing programs grew in size and strength, but a year in which outstanding new developments did not occur. At the same time, it was a year that brought no serious problems or setbacks to most of the state's libraries: in general, budgets held up, and there were no major intellectual freedom battles directly involving libraries. This reflected the overall condition of Wyoming's economy; the rapid economic development and population growth of the late 1970s and early 80s have ended, and most forecasters predict only modest growth for the balance of the decade. The same prediction seems likely to be true for libraries of all types.

Wyoming Library Association. The WLA annual meeting, held in Cheyenne in May with the Mountain Plains Library Association and the Wyoming Educational Media Association, had as its theme "Humanities on the Western Horizon." The pooling of resources resulted in a rich array of continuing education workshops and an outstanding slate of speakers, including folklorist Roger Welsch, authors Aileen Paul and Patricia and Gordon Sabine, and librarians Richard De Gennaro and Jutta Reed-Scott. The membership of WLA amended the Association's bylaws to remove the requirement that the annual meeting be held in the spring and then decided to start a fall meeting cycle in 1985. It was hoped that the change will provide better opportunities for school librarians to attend the annual meeting. WLA's election procedure and committee structure were also revised.

Both the Academic and Special Library Section and the Public Library Section had one-day meetings in the fall, offering their members a selection of workshops on topics of current concern.

Interlibrary Cooperation. A project under way for several years came to fruition when the State Library published the first *Wyoming Union Catalog* at the beginning of the year. Covering the holdings of most public and academic libraries in Wyoming as well as the State Library's own collection, the catalog is in COM format and lists materials acquired by the participating libraries since 1976. Because the catalog is primarily being used as an interlibrary loan tool, its publication led to the need to revise the protocols for in-state interlibrary loans; the final draft of the revised protocols was approved in December.

Partial implementation of the statewide online union catalog/circulation system was accomplished in the fall, but this delay plagued project was still not fully up and running at the year's end.

The Health Sciences Information Network, linking medical libraries throughout Wyoming, saw the publication of its *HSIN Manual for Health Sciences Libraries* in the spring and, unfortunately, the departure of its professional staff in the summer. All the regional consortia are now well established and operating independently, however, and a new state coordinator had been hired by the end of the year.

State Library. The State Library has been increasingly handicapped by lack of space for both personnel and collections in its 50-year-old building, shared with the Wyoming Supreme Court and its Law Library. In September the Library unveiled a bold plan for a new building in central Cheyenne, to be paired with a complementary edifice housing the State Archives and Historical Department and the State Museum. Cost of the complex was estimated at $40,000,000 and the projected completion date is 1990, the centennial of Wyoming statehood. Funding was to be sought from the Legislature in 1985.

At its annual meeting in Saratoga in September the State Library Advisory Council chose Nancy Effinger, Director of the Teton County Library, as its Chair. The Council devoted much of its meeting to revising the criteria and procedures for awarding LSCA grants.

Public Libraries. Especially on issues of copyright, authors sometimes appear to regard public libraries as enemies, but a Wyoming author and library have demonstrated that this need not be the case. Shannon Garst, a popular children's author, not only served as a trustee of the Converse County Library for several years in the 1950s and 60s, but at her death her will named the Library the recipient of all future royalties from her books. The children's room in the Library's headquarters in Douglas was dedicated to Garst's memory.

School Libraries. At its annual meeting in

Cheyenne in May the Wyoming Association for Education Communication and Technology became the Wyoming Educational Media Association. The Association sponsored a workshop on computers for school libraries at Casper in November.

Academic Libraries. The second Articulation Conference, bringing librarians and administrators from the University of Wyoming and the community colleges together for an intensive planning session, was held at Jackson in September. The conference was rated a success by those who were present and promised to become an annual event.

Buildings. Probably reflecting the general slowdown in growth in Wyoming, 1984 saw the opening of only one major new library facility: the Uinta County Library dedicated its new headquarters building in Evanston in September. The building is a creative recycling of a former supermarket.

Other Issues. On the other hand, 1984 was a year of substantial growth in continuing education programs for Wyoming librarians. Besides workshops sponsored by WLA and WEMA, there was a wide range of workshops and short courses offered by the State Library, the University of Wyoming, and the community colleges. Most were designed for Wyoming librarians, but a two-day disaster recovery workshop at Laramie in October, jointly sponsored by the State Library and University Libraries, drew participants from throughout the country; Sally Buchanan of Stanford was the leader.

Cody was the scene of an ongoing intellectual freedom controversy for a good part of the year, when a local group started a campaign to remove "filthy" magazines from local stores. The Chief of Police gave the store owners a deadline, but was overruled when the City Attorney declared the existing municipal obscenity ordinance unconstitutional. The City Council then drafted a new ordinance, but found the issue too hot to handle and decided to submit the proposed legislation to the voters in a referendum. The voters decisively rejected the proposal in November, which seems to have ended the controversy.

1984 was the year for the short budget session of the Legislature, so no major bills affecting library service were considered. 1985 may well be different, since one of the state's more outspoken public librarians, Lisa Kinney, former Director of the Albany County Library and a Past-President of WLA, was elected to the State Senate in November. Kinney, currently a law student at the University of Wyoming, is the first librarian elected to Wyoming's upper house.

Awards. At its annual meeting in May, the Wyoming Library Association presented the following major awards: Outstanding Librarian, Barbara Fraley, Director, Johnson County Library, Buffalo; Milstead Award for exemplary service to children or young adults, Jeannie Ferriss, Natrona County Public Library, Casper; Georgia Shovlain Award, for an outstanding special project, Rose Mary Malone, Special Collections Librarian, Casper College Library; Andy Fisher Award, for continuing distinguished service by a public library, Centennial Branch Library, Centennial, Mary Simpson, Librarian; and Trustee Award, Bette Thompson, Sublette County Library, Pinedale.

PAUL B. CORS

ABBREVIATIONS AND ACRONYMS

Following are selected abbreviations and acronyms used in *The ALA Yearbook*. For page references consult the *Index* under full names in this *Yearbook* and the *Index* in previous volumes (1976-   ).

AAAS American Association for the Advancement of Science
AALL American Association of Law Libraries
AALS Association of American Library Schools
AAP Association of American Publishers
AASL American Association of School Librarians
ABA American Booksellers Association
ACLD Advisory Council on Library Development
ACNO Advisory Committee of National Organizations
ACRL Association of College and Research Libraries
AECT Association for Educational Communications and Technology
AFLS Armed Forces Librarians Section
AIA American Institute of Architects
AIRS Alliance of Information and Referral Services
AJL Association of Jewish Libraries
ALHRT American Library History Round Table
ALSC Association for Library Service to Children
ALTA American Library Trustee Association
AMIGOS Southwestern states network
ANSI American National Standards Institute
APHA American Printing History Association
ARAC Aerospace Research Application Center
ARL Association of Research Libraries
ARSC Association for Recorded Sound Collections
ARLIS/NA Art Libraries Society of North America
ASCLA Association of Specialized and Cooperative Library Agencies (1978); former ASLA and HRLSD
ASIDIC Association of Information and Dissemination Centers
ASIS American Society for Information Science
ASTED L'Association pour l'avancement des sciences et des techniques de la documentation
ATLA American Theological Library Association
BAMBAM Booline Alert: Missing Books and Manuscripts
BARC Bay Area Reference Center
BLLD British Library Division
BNB British National Bibliography
BPDC Book and Periodical Development Council (Canada)
BSO Broad System of Ordering
CACUL Canadian Association of College and University Libraries
CAIN Cataloging and Indexing
CALA Chinese American Librarians Association
CALS Current Awareness Literature Search
CAPL Canadian Association of Public Libraries
CARL Canadian Association of Research Libraries, a section of CACUL
CASLIS Canadian Association of Special Libraries and Information Services
CE Continuing Education
CIA Computer Industry Association
CIP Cataloging in Publication
CISTI Canadian Institute for Scientific and Technical Information

CLASS California Library Authority for Systems and Service
CLENE Continuing Library Education Network and Exchange
CLEP College Level Examination Program
CLIP Coordinated Library Information Program
CLR Council on Library Resources
CLTA Canadian Library Trustees' Association
COA Committee on Accreditation
COLA Cooperation in Library Automation
COLT Council on Library Media Technical Assistants
COM Computer Output Microform
COMCAT Computer Output Microfilm Catalog
CONSER CONversion of SERials
CONTU National Commission on New Technological Uses of Copyrighted Works
COPA Council on Postsecondary Education
COSLA Chief Officers of State Library Agencies
CR Classification Research
CRL Center for Research Libraries
CRS Congressional Research Service
CSAA Council of Specialized Accrediting Agencies
CSLA Canadian School Library Association
CTS Communications Technology Satellite
CUNY City University of New York
DARE International Data Bank for Social Sciences (UNESCO)
DAVI Department of Audiovisual Instruction (of NEA)
DDC Defense Documentation Center
DLC District Library Center
ERIC Educational Resources Information Center
ERT Exhibits Round Table
ESEA Elementary and Secondary Education Act
FID International Federation for Documentation
FIPS International Federation of Information Processing Societies
FLA Federal Librarians Association
FLRT Federal Librarians Round Table
FPT Freight Pass Through
FRACHE Federation of Regional Accrediting Commission of Higher Education
GAC Government Advisory Committee
GODORT Government Documents Round Table
HEA Higher Education Act
I & R Information and Referral Services
IASA International Association of Sound Archives
IASL International Association of School Librarianship
IBBY International Board on Books for Young People
ICBD International Children's Book Day
IDS Interlibrary Delivery System
IFC Intellectual Freedom Committee
IFLA International Federation of Library Associations and Institutions
IIB International Bibliographic Institute
ILLINET Illinois Library and Information Network
ILRA Independent Research Library Association
IRRT Intellectual Freedom Round Table
ISBDS International Standard Bibliographic Description for Serials
ISBN International Standard Book Number
ISDS International Serials Data System
ISO International Organization for Standardization
ISSN International Standard Serial Number
IUC Interuniversity Council
JCET Joint Council on Educational Telecommunications
JMRT Junior Members Round Table
JOLA Journal of Library Automation
JSCAACR Joint Steering Committee for Revision of AACR
LA Library Association (British)
LAMA Library Administration and Management Association
LC Library of Congress
LHRT Library History Round Table
LIRT Library Instruction Round Table
LITA Library and Information Technology Association
LOEX Library Orientation-Instruction Exchange
LRRT Library Research Round Table
LSCA Library Services and Construction Act

MAGERT Map and Geography Round Table
MARBI Representation in Machine-Readable Form of Bibliographic Information
MARC Machine-Readable Cataloging
MARS Machine-Assisted Reference Services
MEDLARS Medical Literature Analysis and Retrieval System
MIDLNET Midwest Region Library Network
MLA Music Library Association
MLSA Metropolitan Library Service Agency
MPLA Mountain Plains Library Association
MRAP Management Review and Analysis Program (ARL)
NACAC National Ad Hoc Committee Against Censorship
NAL National Agricultural Library
NARS National Archives and Records Service
NASIC Northeast Academic Science Information Center
NCA National Commission on Accrediting
NCES National Center for Education Statistics
NCLIS National Commission on Libraries and Information Science
NEA National Education Association
NEDCC New England Document Conservation Center
NEH National Endowment for the Humanities
NELA New England Library Association
NELB New England Library Board
NELINET New England Library Information Network
NFAIS National Federation of Abstracting and Indexing Services
NIAL National Institute of Arts and Letters
NIEA National Indian Education Association
NLM National Library of Medicine
NMA National Microfilm Association
NPR National Public Radio
NSDP National Serials Data Program
NTIS National Technical Information Service
OAS Organization of American States
OCLC, Inc. Online Library Center
OECD Organization for Economic Cooperation and Development
OLLT Office of Libraries and Learning Technologies
OLPR Office for Library Personnel Resources
OMS Office of University Library Management Studies
OSHA Occupational Safety and Health Agency
OSIS Office of Science Information Service
PALINET Pennsylvania Area Library Network
PBS Public Broadcasting Service
PGI UNESCO General Information Programme
PISA Public Interest Satellite Association
PLA Public Library Association
PNBC Pacific Northwest Bibliographic Center
PNLA Pacific Northwest Library Association
PRECIS Preserved Context Index System
PSSC Public Service Satellite Consortium
RASD Reference and Adult Services Division
RICE Regional Information and Community Exchange
RIF Reading Is Fundamental
RLG Research Library Group
RLIN Research Libraries Information Network
RTSD Resources and Technical Services Division
SAA Society of American Archivists
SDI Selective Dissemination of Information
SELA Southeastern Library Association
SHARE Shared Area Resources Exchange
SIE Scientific Information Exchange
SLA Special Libraries Association
SOLINET Southeastern Library Network
SORT Staff Organizations Round Table
SRRT Social Responsibilities Round Table
STAR Serial Titles Automated Records
STC Short Title Catalog
SWLA Southwestern Library Association
TABA The American Book Awards
UAP Universal Availability of Publications
UBC Universal Bibliographic Control
USBE Universal Serials and Book Exchange, Inc.
UTLAS University of Toronto Library Automation System
WLN Washington Library Network
YASD Young Adult Services Division

INDEX

AACR 2: *see* Anglo-American Cataloguing Rules
A & I Services: *see* Abstracting and Indexing Services
Abbot Scott, (photo) 305
abbreviations and acronyms, 378
Abell, Millicent D.: *see* Biographies 82 ed.
ABLEDATA, 78
Abrams, Harry N., 56
Abstracting and Indexing Project (CONSER), 64
Abstracting and Indexing Services, 25–26 (*also* 78–84 eds.) See Indexing and Abstracting Services 76, 77 eds.
  CONSER project, 64
  cooperation with NAL, 195
  microcomputer index, (photo) 234
  online availability, 112
  religious periodicals, 51
Academic Libraries, 26–33 (*also* 76–84 eds.)
  buildings, 82–83
  Canada, 307–308
  performance measures for, 242
  and public relations, 225
  and salaries, 212
  and social responsibilities, 266
  and statistics, 243
Academic/Research Librarian of the Year Award (ACRL), 1, 33, 61
Academy Awards, 123
Accreditation, 33–36 (*also* 76–84 eds.)
  ALA list, (chart) 34–35, 114
  and Canada, 86, 309–310
  new guidelines for, 171
  See also 77 ed., "Patterns of Education and Accreditation for Librarianship: Canada, Great Britain and Australia"
Acquisitions: *see* 76, 77 eds; *see* Collection Development 76–79 eds.; *see* Collection Management 80–84 eds.
acronyms: *see* abbreviations and acronyms
Across the Channel with Louis Bleriot, (photo) 97
Action to Promote Books and Reading, (UNESCO) 160

Adams, Scott: *see* Obituaries 83 ed.
(Jane) Addams Peace Association Award, 98
administration: *see* Management, Library
Adult Services in the Eighties Project, 239
Adults, Library Service to, 36–38 (*also* 76, 78, 80–84 eds.) See Adult Library Services 79 ed.; *See also* Older Adults, Library Services to 76–77 eds.
  special activities, (photos) 36–38
Advanced Communications Technology Satellite (ACTS) Program, 282–283
Advancement of Literacy Award, 224
advertising
  and electronic publishing, 112
  and fraud, 240A
  and job openings, 214
  and library programs, (photos) 135
  library promotion, (photos) 105, 129, 219, 276, 313
  and library volunteers, 131, 186
affirmative action: *see* Personnel and Employment: Affirmative Action 76–81 eds.
aging, library service to: *see* older adults, library service for
AGRICOLA, 194–195
Aiken, George D.: *see* Biographies 83 ed.
Air Force Libraries, 54
AJL Children's Book Awards, 6, 63
Akers, Susan, 16, (photo) 16
Alabama, networking in, 207
Alabama report, 316–317
ALA Honorary Life Membership Award, 116
ALANET, 43, 207
ALA Report, 44–48 (*also* 83 ed.)
  See also American Library Association; Divisions, Offices and Round Tables by name.
ALA Yearbook, retrospective: *see* feature article this ed.
Alaska report, 317–318
Alexander, Mary Louise: *see* Obituaries 77 ed.
Alison, William Andrew Greig: *see* Biographies 80 ed.

Allain, Alex P.: *see* Biographies 76 ed.
Alliance for Excellence: Librarians Respond to A Nation at Risk, 36, 59, 108, 181, 224, 253, 254, 257–258, 292, 303
Alsip, James B., 31
American Antiquarian Society, 143, 271–272
American Association of Law Libraries (AALL), 38–39 (*also* 76–84 eds.)
  and certification of law librarians, 170
American Association of Retired Persons (AARP), 239
American Association of School Librarians (AASL), 39–40 (*also* 76–84 eds.)
  membership survey, 255
American Book Awards, 5, 232–233
American Booksellers Association (ABA), 79
American Booksellers Association et al., v. William Hudnut, et al., 128
American Center of Films for Children, 123
American Film Festival, 119, 120, 121–122, 123, 124, 125
American Indian Library Association (AILA), 41
American Indians, 40–41 (*also* 79–84 eds.) See American Indians and Libraries 76–78 eds.
The American Lawyer, 235
American Libraries, 183
American Library Association, 41–44 (*also* 84 ed.)
  and accreditation, 32–36, (chart) 34–35, 114
  awards, description of, 1–4
  Dallas conference, (photos) 44, 45, 166, 173
  fundraising training kit, 107
  headquarters, (photo) 42
  history of: *see* 76 ed. "ALA at 100"; 77 ed. "The ALA Centennial Celebration"
  kits for Banned Books Week, 230
  librarianship archives, 176–177
  Midwinter Meeting (Washington,

377

D.C.), (photo) 59
organization of: see ALA Report
and pay equity, 214, 294-295
position on UNESCO, 157-158, 159
and problems in education, 292
publishing services, (staff photo) 43
references: see ALA Report
standards for, 242
Washington quarters, (photo) 290
Yearbook, ten-year retrospective: see feature article this ed.
American Library History: see 76-82 eds.; see Library History 83, 84 eds.
American Library History Round Table (ALHRT) : see 76-79 eds.; see Library History Round Table 80-84 eds.
American Library Society: see 76-78 eds.
American Library Trustee Association (ALTA), 49 (also 76-84 eds.)
American National Standards Committee Z39: see National Information Standards Organization
American Primitive, 233
American Printing History Association, 269
American Printing History Association Award, 269
American Society for Information Science (ASIS), 49-51 (also 76-84 eds.)
American Theological Library Association (ATLA), 51 (also 76-84 eds.)
Amey, Larry, 310
AMIGOS and preservation, 217
Shared Resources System (SHARES), 206
Amos, Wally, 128, (photo) 186
(Hans Christian) Andersen Medals, 156-157
Anderson, Dorothy, 3, 89, 253
Anderson, Florence: see Biographies 77 ed.
Andrew Jackson and the Course of American Democracy, 5, 232
(Joseph A.) Andrews Bibliographic Award, 39
Angell, Richard S., 193
Anglo-American Cataloguing Rules, 88-89
Anno, Mitsumasa, 98, 157
ANSI Z39: see National Information Standards Organization
Anthony, Tony, 315
antiquarian trade, 271
Arbuthnot Honor Lecture, 60
architecture: see Buildings
Archival Theory and Practice in the United States: A Historical Analysis, 52
Archives, 52 (also 76-84 eds.)
Canadian history, 200
history of librarianship, 176-177
independence of National Archives, 53
and labor records, 167
new national agency, 290
and satellite data, 196
Archivist of the United States, 52, 53
Arizona report, 318-319
Arkansas report, 319-320
Armed Forces Librarians Achievement Citation, 1, 54, 55, 224, 225
Armed Forces Libraries, 54-55 (also 76-84 eds.)
Army Libraries, 54
arson: see fire, losses due to
Artandi, Susan, 50, 116
Arterbery, Vivian J., 7, (photo) 7

Art Libraries, 55-57 (also 78-84 eds.)
asbestos, in library buildings, 85
A-76 Circular, and federal librarians, 118
Ashabranner, Brent, (photo) 302
Asheim, Lester, 7, (photo) 7, 116-117
Asia Foundation, 163
Asian Americans and Libraries, 263
See also 76 ed.; Ethnic Groups, Library Service to 77, 78 eds.
ASIS Award for Research in Information Science, 252
Assault on Illiteracy Program (AOIP), 186
Association for Educational and Communications Technology, 293
Association for Information and Image Management (AIIM), 57-58 (also 84 ed.)
Association for Information Management (Aslib), 314
Association for Library and Information Science Education (ALSE), 58-59 (also 84 ed.) See Association of American Library Schools 79-83 eds.
and accreditation, 114
faculty statistics, 115
student statistics, 114-115
survey of profession by gender, 292, 293-294
Association for Library Service to Children (ALSC), 59-61 (also 78-84 eds.)
Carnegie Fund Grant recipient, 4
See also Children's Service Division 76-77 eds.
Association for Recorded Sound Collections (ARSC), 236
Association of American Library Schools: see Association for Library and Information Science Education
Association of American Publishers (AAP) Awards, 5, 232-233
decisions and concerns, 229
Association of College and Research Libraries (ACRL), 61-63 (also 76-84 eds.)
continuing education courses, 215
and copyright guidelines, 26
and performance measures, 242
Doctoral Dissertation Fellowship, 4, 242
Association of Jewish Libraries (AJL), 62-63 (also 80-84 eds.)
Association of Jewish Libraries Awards, 6, 63
Association of Research Libraries (ARL), 63-68 (also 76-84 eds.)
Collection Analysis Project, 99, 101
CONSER A & I Coverage Project, 71
and continuing education, 107
management skills institutes, 216
National Collections Inventory Project, 99, 101, 105
Preservation Planning Program, 68, 99, 217
public service research, 242
salary & placement by gender, 292, 293
SPEC Flyers: see SPEC Flyers
survey on copyright policies, 26-27
three-week institute, 115-116
Association of Specialized and Cooperative Library Agencies (ASCLA), 68-70 (also 79-84 eds.)
internal reorganization, 137
"Let's Talk About It" project, 38, 69

See also Association of State Library Agencies; Health and Rehabilitative Library Services Division 77-79 eds.
Association of State Library Agencies: see 77-79 eds.
Astor, Mrs. Vincent, (photo) 84
Atlantic Provinces Library Association's Award, 310-311
audiovisual materials, 178
Austrom, Elizabeth, 309
authors, and lending royalties, 233
Automation
and academic libraries, 27-28
armed forces libraries, 54
in Britain, 314
in Canada, 306
and catalog, 148
and circulation, 146, 148
funding for, 171
and health sciences information, 202
I & R services, 143-144
inventory of ARL resources, 68
and LC, 179
and library education, 213-214
and medical libraries, 189-190
and NAL, 194
uses of, (photos) 100, 113, 130, 147, 149
See also 76-84 eds.
Aveney, Brian Henry: see Biographies 81 ed.
Avenue Branch (Salt Lake City Public Library), (photos) 82, 94
Avram, Henriette, 162. See also Biographies 82 ed.
Award of Merit (ASIS), 50
Award of Merit (British Columbia Teacher-Librarian's Association), 309
Awards, 1-6 (also 79-84 eds.) See Prizes and Awards 76 ed.; Awards and Prizes 77-78 eds.
ABA, 5, 232-233
academic librarianship, 1, 2, 33
ACRL, 1, 33, 61
ALA, description of, 1-4
archival, 52
armed forces, 1, 54, 55, 224, 225
art librarianship, 55
Beta Phi Mu, 1, 70
bibliographic instruction, 2, 33, 61
bibliographies, 5, 39
blind and handicapped services, 2, 70, 138
in Canada, 87, 307, 309, 310-311
cataloging and classification, 3, 89, 253
Catholic Library Association, 6, 89
children's films, 121-123
children's library services, 2, 60
children's literature, 1, 3, 4, 5, 6, 60, 63, 87, 98, 156-157, 211
Chinese-American librarians, 98-99
documents librarianship, 2, 134
equality, 2, 292
exhibits, 3
films, (still photos) 119, 120, (still photos) 121-125
FOLUSA, 129
illustrations, 2, 6, 87, 98
index, 6
information industry, 146
information science, 5, 50-51
information technology, 3, 174
intellectual freedom, 1, 2, 3, 6, 155, 156, 258, 303
labor, library service to, 4, 167, 238
law librarianship, 39
library education, 50, 116
library history, 4, 178
library literature, 184
literacy, 1, 188, 224
literature, 5, 6, 232-233

map librarianship, 3
medical librarianship, 191
music librarianship, 193
periodicals, 4, 184
printing history, 269
professional development, 5, 165
public libraries, 3, 224, 225
public relations, 2, 54, 173, 227–228
reference, 2, 3, 6, 237–238, 240
research, 1, 3, 50, 87, 185, 252
school librarianship, 1, 3, 40, 258
serials, 235
social responsibilities, 267
special librarianship, 1, 2, 6, 70, 87, 138, 277
staff development, 215–216
technical services, 3, 253
theatre librarianship, 283
translation, 1, 60, 97, 98
trustees, 1, 4, 49, 87
WNBA, 296
young adult literature, 301
See also individual awards, eg. Caldecott, Newbery; organizations issuing awards by name; state reports for regional and local awards.
Axford, H. William: see Obituaries 81 ed.
Ayres, Rep. Ralph, (photo) 169

(Charles) Babbage Institute, 177
Bacheller, Charis, 4
Bacot, Bertha, 1, 49
Baer, Mark H., 6, 277, See also Biographies 77 ed.
Baker and Taylor Grassroots Grants, 165–166
Baker, Augusta: see Biographies 76, 82 eds.
Baker, Dale Burdette: see Biographies 76 ed.
Baker, William O., 277
Ballantine, Ian and Betty, 231
Banks, Lynne Reid, 211
Banned Books Week, 154, 230, (photo) 231
Barber, Margaret (Peggy), 7, (photo) 7, 226
Barker, Tommie Dora: see Obituaries 79 ed.
Barrett, Jaia, 2, 134
Barron, Daniel, (photo) 156
BATAB, 102, 105
(Mildred L.) Batchelder Award, 1, 60, 97, 98
Batchelor, Lillian L.: see Obituaries 78 ed.
Battin, Patricia (Meyer): see Biographies 79 ed.
Bauer, Marian Dane, 98
BCR (Bibliographic Center for Research), 206
Beach, Cecil P., 3, 224, 225
Beard, Sarah Allen, 16
Bearman, Toni Carbo: see Biographies 78, 81, eds.
Becker, Joseph, 50
Belcher, Fay, 5
Bell, Clare, 98
Bell, Terrell H., 292
Bellow, Saul, (photo) 38
Belpre-White, Pura: see Obituaries 83 ed.
Belsches, Jane, 5, 60
Bender, David Ray: see Biographies 80 ed.
benefits, employee, 213
(Curtis) Benjamin Award, 233
Bennett, William, 300
Bentley, Orville G., (photo) 195
Benton, Charles: see Biographies 79 ed.
bequests: see Gifts, Bequests, and Endowments

Berger, Mary C.: see Biographies 81 ed.
Berne International Copyright Convention, 109
Berninghausen, David K.: see Biographies 83 ed.
Best Books for Young Adults, 24
Besterman Medal, 5
Betancourt, Virginia: see Biographies 82 ed.
Beta Phi Mu, 70 (also 76–84 eds.)
Beta Phi Mu Award, 1, 9, 70, 116
Bewley, Lois, 8, 87, (photo) 87, 116, 311. See also Biographies 84 ed.
Bibliographic Center for Research: see BCR
bibliographic instruction, 30, 240
Bibliographic Instruction Liaison Project, 30
bibliographic networks: see Networks
Bibliographic Processing Centers: see 78 ed.; see Processing Centers 76, 77 eds.
bibliographic records, conversion of, 64, 71, 204
Bibliographic Services Development Program (BSDP) (CLR), 71, 203–204
Bibliographies and Indexes, 70–74 (also 76–82 eds., 84 ed.)
Biblo, Mary, 72
Bidlack, Russell Eugene: see Biographies 78 ed.
Binding: see 76, 78 eds.
Biographies, 7–15 (also 76–83 eds.)
Bishoff, Lizbeth J., 3, 89, 253
Bisom, Diane, 5, 165
Black Americans, 72–74 (also 79–84 eds.) See Blacks and Libraries 76 ed.
See also Ethnic Groups, Library Services to 77, 78 eds.
Blackburn Patricia, 87
Black Caucus (ALA), 158
Black History month, (photo) 73
Blackwell North America Scholarship Award, 4, 104, 253
Blackwell, Sir Basil, 231, 275
Blind and Physically Handicapped, Library Services for the, 74–78 (also 76–78, 81–84 eds.). See Blind and Handicapped, Library Services for the 79, 80 eds.
bibliographic guide for handicapped, 69
Decade of the Disabled Committee (ASCLA), 69
I & R services, 144
publications about services, 136–137
special activities and programs, (photos) 75, (photo) 107, 138, 139, 264, 265
special equipment, (photos) 75, 137, 138
and volunteers, (photo) 265
See also Association for Specialized and Cooperative Library Services; Health and Rehabilitative Library Services; specific handicaps, eg. deaf.
Block, John R., (photo) 195, 196
Bloom, Herbert, (photo) 43
Blos, Joan W.: see Biographies 81 ed.
Bloss, Meredith: see Obituaries 83 ed.
Blume, Judy, (photo) 301
Boateny, Adwoa, 277
Boettcher, Cheryl M., 162
Boettcher, Linda, 191
Bolden, Connie E.: see Biographies 80 ed.
Bolger, William F., (photo) 180
Bond, Felicia, 91
Bonk, John Wallace: see Obituaries 80 ed.

Booker Prize, 233
Booker T. Washington, 233
book fairs, 231–232, 271
Book Industry Systems Advisory Committee (BISAC), 279
Bookline, 101, 105, 261
Booklist, as grant recipient, 4
bookmarks, (photo) 91
bookmobiles, 264, 265
See also 76 ed.; see Community Delivery Services 77, 78 eds.
Book of the Year for Children Medal Award (CLA), 5, 87, 98
Book Purchase Project (AARP), 239
Booksellers Order Service (BOS), 79
Bookselling, 78–79 (also 78–84 eds.)
Books for Asia Program, 163
Books in Our Future, 181
Boorstin, Daniel J., 181, 229. See also Biographies 76 ed.
Borrows, Susan, 277
Boston Globe—Horn Book Awards, 5
Boucher, Virginia P., 5
(Rev. Andrew L.) Bouwhuis Scholarship, 89
Bowden, Russell, 176
Bowker Acquisition System (BAS), 102, 105
Boyd, Jesse Edna: see Obituaries 79 ed.
Brademas, John: see Biographies 82 ed.
Bradley, Jana, 191
braille
and computers, 74
and foreign language materials, 77
innovations in transcribing, 76
music collections, 74–75
Brasley, Eric, 191
Breland, June, 166
Brink, Carol Ryrie: see Obituaries 82 ed.
British Council, 314
British Library
display, 315
and eighteenth century catalog, 71
present status, 314–315
See also 77 ed. "At the Hub: The British Library"
British Museum Library, 200
Brockman, Norbert, 52
Bronson, Diane, 5, 165
Brookner, Anita, 233
Brother, Shirley, 269
Brown, Anthony, 6, 98
Brown, Guy, (photo) 140
Brown, Marcia: see Biographies 78, 84 eds.
Brown, Rowland, 206
BRS, 240
(John) Brubaker Award, 89
Bruce, Marie, 6
Brunnell, David, 206
Bubby, Me and Memories, 6, 63
Buck, Paul H.: see Obituaries 80 ed.
budgeting
in Britain, 312–313
computerization of (Canada), 308
and library materials, 105–106
See also 76, 77 eds.; costs
Budington, William S., 6, 277
Bugg, Ann Page, 268
Buildings, 79–83, 85 (also 76–84 eds.)
academic libraries, 31–32
armed forces, 54
art museum libraries, 57
Canada, 308
construction of, (photos) 27, 28, 31, 81, 82, 83, 94, 220–221, 285
and energy conservation, (photo) 82
LC renovations, 182
renovations of, (photos) 29, 80, 83, 84, 220, 285
services for blind and

379

handicapped, 75
standards for, 173
See also individual buildings by name; individual state reports by name.
Bunge, Charles A.: *see* Biographies 81 ed.
Bunnell, William I., 254. *See also* Biographies 79 ed.
Burke, Frank G., 52
Burkhardt, Frederick Henry: *see* Biographies 76 ed.
Burns, Robert W., Jr.: *see* Biographies 79 ed.
Burrows, Vinnie, (photo) 73
Bush, Barbara, 219
Business Council for Effective Literacy, 186
Butler, Dorothy: *see* Biographies 83 ed.
Byrnes, Hazel Webster: *see* Obituaries 82 ed.
Byrum, John Donald, Jr.: *see* Biographies 78 ed.

Cabello-Argandoōna, Roberto: *see* Biographies 78 ed.
Cable, Frances, (photo) 238
Cagle, R. Brantley, Jr., 89
(Randolph) Caldecott Medal, 2, 12–13, 60, 97, 98
Caldecott Medal Honor Books, 98
California, networking in, 207
California report, 320–321
(Francis Joseph) Campbell Citation, 2, 70
Campbell, Neil A., 311
Canadian Association of Special Libraries and Information Services (CASLIS), 86
Canadian Bibliographic Centre, 200
Canadian Centre for Architecture, 56
Canadian Correspondent's Report, 304–312 (*also 76–84 eds.*)
Canadian Library Association (CLA), 85–87 (*also 76–84 eds.*)
founding of, 200
overview of, 311–312
travelling workshop, (photo) 86
Canadian Library Trustees Merit Award, 87
Canadian School Library Association (CSLA), 86
Canadiana (Canadian National Bibliography), 200
Canfield, Cass, 231
CAP: *see* Collection Analysis Project
CAPCON, 206
Carlin, Paul, 229
Carnegie Awards, 294
Carnegie Branch Library for Local History (Boulder, Colorado), (photo) 83
Carnegie Medal, 5, 98
Carnovsky, Leon: *see* Obituaries 76 ed.
Carroll, Bonnie C., 7, (photo) 7
Carroll, (Marti) Martha S.: *see* Obituaries 80 ed.
Carson, Johnny: *see* Biographies 84 ed.
Carter, John (Waynflete): *see* Obituaries 76 ed.
Carter, Julia Frances: *see* Obituaries 81 ed.
Carter Presidential Library, 85
Carter, Rosalynn, 43, 128, (photo) 129
Castagna, Edwin: *see* Obituaries 84 ed.
Cataloging and Classification, 87–89 (*also 76–84 eds.*)
catalog for films on art, 119–120
CIP, 205, 286
CONSER project, 71, 102, 195, 205, 260
conversion project in Canada, 308

cooperation with NAL, 195
inventory of research collections, 63
LC and NAL cooperation, 194
national library cooperation, 205
online catalogs and directories, 112
and serials, 261
See also Anglo-American Cataloging Rules.
Cataloging in Publication: *see* CIP
Cathcart, Jane, 188
Catholic Library Association (CLA), 89 (*also 76–84 eds.*)
Catholic University of America School of Library and Information Science, 272
censorship
in Canada, 85–86, 306
and court cases, 127
exhibit on, (photos) 226, 230, 273
and federal employees, 230–231
journal on, 235
NCLIS study, 197
and U.S. government, 152–153
and young adults, 155, 297
See also 82 ed. "The New Censors"
Center for Chinese Research Materials (ARL), 68
Center for Research Libraries (CRL)
internal operations review, 206
services and concerns, 100
Center for the Book, 180
Center for the Study of Rural Librarianship (Clarion State College, Pennsylvania), 222
Center Line, 301, (photo) 302
Certificate of Merit (Library Association of Alberta), 310
Chambers, Bradford, 16, (photo) 16, 267
Chamis, Alice Y., 277
Chanin, Leah F.: *see* Biographies 83 ed.
Chapman, Susan, 311
Cheney, Frances Neel: *see* Biographies 77, 79 eds.
Chief Officers of State Library Agencies (COSLA)
literacy resolution, 185, 219
and public library data, 243
child care resource service, 265
Children's Book Council (CBC), 89–91 (*also 76–84 eds.*)
special materials, (photos) 91
Children's Book Week, 89–90, (photo) 90
Children's Library Services, 92–95 (*also 76–84 eds.*)
and computers (photo) 92
and reading programs, (photos) 93, 94
recommended book exhibit, (photo) 255
special activities, (photos) 94
Children's Literature, 95–98 (*also 76–84 eds.*)
See also Young Adult Literature.
Children's Services Division: *see* 76–77 eds; *see* Association for Library Service to Children 78–84 eds.
(James Bennett) Childs Award, 2
Childs, James Bennett: *see* Obituaries 78 ed.
Chinese American Librarians Association (CALA), 98–99 (*also 78–84 eds.*)
Chiorazzi, Michael G., 39
Chisholm, Margaret Elizabeth Bergman: *see* Biographies 76 ed.
Christee, Kathryn M., 39
Christensen, Lise Norregaard, 191
CIP (Cataloging in Publication) pilot project, 205, 286
Circulation Systems

automation of, (photo) 113
See also 76–84 eds.
Civil Rights Act of 1964, 170
Clark, Rheta, 1, 40, 258
Clausman, Gilbert Joseph: *see* Biographies 78 ed.
Cleary, Beverly, 3, 7 (photo) 8, 60, 97, 98. *See also* Biographies 76, 81 eds.
CLENE (Continuing Library Education Network and Exchange): *see* CLENERT
CLENERT (Continuing Library Education Network and Exchange Round Table), 106–107
as ALA affiliate, 116
new role for, 216
(David H.) Clift Scholarship, 4
Clifton, Lucille, 3, 267
Cline, Helen, (photo) 43
C. L. Systems, Inc., (photo) 147, 148, 174
Coalition for Literacy, 185, 186, 219
Coan, LaVerne Z., (photo) 238
Cobb, Ann Wimbish, 268
Cochrane, Mr. and Mrs. J. Harwood, 1, 49
Coco, Alfred Joseph: *see* Biographies 78 ed.
(Ed) Cody Branch (San Antonio Public Library, Texas), (photo) 83
Cohen, David, (photo) 156
Cohn, Marguerite, 275
(C.F.W.) Coker Prize, 52
Colaianni, Lois Ann: *see* Biographies 80 ed.
Cole, Fred Carrington: *see* Biographies 77, 79 eds.
Cole, John Y.: *see* Biographies 79 ed.
Coleman, Jean E., (photo) 42, 185, 188
Collection Analysis Project (CAP) (ARL), 99, 101
Collection development: *see* Collection Management
Collection Management, 99–106 (*also 80–84 eds.*) *See* collection Development 76–79 eds.
and access, 30–31
LC and rare books, 180
See also Acquisitions 76, 77 eds.
collective bargaining: *see* Mediation, Arbitration and Inquiry 76–81 eds.; Personnel and Employment: Collective Bargaining 81 ed.
Collins Garden Branch (San Antonio Public Library, Texas), (photo) 83
Colonial Dames Scholarships, 52
Colorado Libraries, 4, 184
Colorado, networking in, 207
Colorado report, 321–322
Columbia University School of Library Service, 272
Comaromi, John P.: *see* Biographies 81 ed.
Committee on Accreditation (COA), 116
Committee on the Status of Women in Librarianship, 294
Community Delivery Services, (photo) 75 *See also* 77, 78 eds. *See* Bookmobile 76 ed.
Companion of the Order of Canada, 310
computers
copyright of software, 290–291
and job information, 167
personal: *see* microcomputers
See also Automation: Databases, Computer Readable.
Confederation of Information Communication Industries (CICI) (Britain), 176

conferences, library: *see* individual organizations by name; state reports by name
Connecticut, networking in, 207
Connecticut report, 322-323
CONSER (CONversion of SERials) Project A & I services, 71, 260
　general statistics, 260
　and NAL, 195
　new entries, 102
　NLM's role, 205
construction: *see* Buildings
Contact Literacy Center (Lincoln, Nebraska), 186
Continuing Library Education Network and Exchange (CLENE): *see* CLENERT
Continuing Professional Education, 106-108 (*also* 76-84 eds.)
　ACRL courses, 215
　Canada, 311
　and collection librarians, 103-104
　literacy training, 189
　rare book studies, 272
　special librarianship, 276
　and special programs, (photo) 107
　See also CLENERT; Education, Library; Personnel and Employment: Staff Development; individual state reports by name.
CONTU: *see* 77,78 eds.; *see* Copyrighted Materials, Commission on New Technological Uses of 76 ed.
CONversion of SERials Project: *see* CONSER
Cooke, Eileen, (photo) 290. *See also* Biographies 79 ed.
Cooney, Barbara: *see* Biographies 81 ed.
Cooper-Hewitt Museum, 56
Cooper, Kenneth R., 8, (photo) 8, 315
Cooper, Sandra M.: *see* Biographies 79 ed.
Cooper, Susan: *see* Biographies 77 ed.
Copyright, 109 (*also* 76-84 eds.)
　and academic libraries, 26
　in Britain, 313-314
　in Canada, 86, 311
　Chinese training program, 162
　and computer programs, 290-291
　and foreign markets, 168
　and new technologies, 180-181
　and OCLC, 206
　and phonograph records, 180-181
　and "pirates," 230
　and record rental, 180-181, 290
　and semiconductor chips, 109, 290
　and videotaping, 168, 281, 290
Copyright Clearance Center, 230
Cornich, L.M. (Bud), 192
Coronet-Perspective Films, 119
correctional institutions, library services for, 299
Corr, Graham, 164
costs
　analysis in public libraries, 223-224
　in antiquarian trade, 271
　books, 95, 99, 104-105
　database usage, 112
　legal publications (chart), 170
　mailing, 229, 290
　periodicals, 99, 104-105, 235, 260
　See also fees, library.
Coulombe, Dominique, 5, 165
Council, ALA: *see* ALA Report. *See also* 76-82 eds.
Council on Library Media Technical Assistants (COLT), 110 (*also* 79-84 eds.) *See* Council on Library Technical Assistants 77-78 eds.
Council on Library Resources (CLR) A & I project, 64

and bibliographic services, 64, 71, 99, 203-204
institute for research libraries, 115-116
Linked Systems Project, 71
and preservation, 217
research grants, 252-253
and research library internships, 115
Cowen, Ione, 5, 60
Cox, Carl Raymond: *see* Obituaries 77 ed.
Cox, Carl Thomas: *see* Obituaries 77 ed.
Craig, Florence: *see* Obituaries 82 ed.
Crampton, Patricia, 60, 98
(John) Crerar Library
　merger with U. of C., 67-68, 143
　new structure, (photo) 31, 32
Cretsos, James M.: *see* Biographies 80 ed.
Cronin, John, 16, (photo) 16
Culbertson, Don Steward: *see* Obituaries 81 ed.
Cummings, Martin M., 191, 202
Cummings, Pat, 3, 267, (photo) 268
Cunha, George M., 52
Cunningham, George, 7-8, 175, 315
Cunningham International Fellowship, 191
Currier, Lura Gibbons: *see* Obituaries 84 ed.
Curry, Peggy Simpson, 192
Custer, Arline (Kern): *see* Obituaries 76 ed.

(Elizabeth) Dafoe Scholarship (CLA), 87, 310
Dagnese, Joseph M., 287 *See also* Biographies 80 ed.
Dainton, Sir Frederick Sydney: *see* Biographies 78 ed.
Dalgleish, Alice: *see* Obituaries 80 ed.
(B.) Dalton Bookseller, 186, 187
Dalton, Jack: *see* Biographies 84 ed.
(John Cotton) Dana Public Relations Awards, 2, 54, 116, 173, 227-228, 277
Dansbury, Claudia, (photo) 45
Danton, J. Periam: *see* Biographies 84 ed.
Darling, Louise, 191
Dartmouth Medal, 2, 238, 240
Databases, Computer Readable, 110, 113 (*also* 77-84 eds.) *See* Machine-Readable Data Bases 76 ed.
　academic libraries and searching, 30
　Canada, 306
　and continuing education, 108
　directory of publicly available databases, 50
　ERIC system, 117
　full text online services, 112
　and hardware, (photo) 113, 148
　and I & R services, (photo) 113, 143-144
　information for disabled, 78
　international cooperation, 194
　LC software development, 181-182
　and medical libraries, 100, 202
　and NAL, 194, 195-196
　OCLC copyright issue, 109
　and personal computers, 25
　and pricing formulas, 26
　reference referral services, 144
　serials online, 233
　serials vendors, 261
　and software interfaces, 111-112
　See also individual database systems by acronym, eg: OCLC.
Data Base User Service, 50
Datalinx, 102, 105

Data Phase, 148
Dauphin Public Library (Harrisburg, Pennsylvania), 2, 227
David, Charles W., 17
Davidson, Mary Wallace: *see* Biographies 83 ed.
(Watson) Davis Awards, 5-6, 50-51
Davis, Charles Hargis: *see* Biographies 83 ed.
(Walter Royal) Davis Library (University of North Carolina, Chapel Hill), 28
Day, Melvin S.: *see* Biographies 77 ed.
deacidification, of library materials, 168, 179, 218 232
Deaf heritage Week, 137
deaf, library services for the, 137, 263, 265
　See also Association for Specialized and Cooperative Library Services; Blind and Physically Handicapped, Library Service for the; Health and Rehabilitative Library Services.
Dear Mr. Henshaw, 3, 7, 60, (photo) 97, 98
De Berry, Joseph: *see* Obituaries 80 ed.
Decade of the Disabled, 69, 138
De Coux, Elizabeth Ann, 54
DeGennaro, Richard, (photo) 27. *See also* Biographies 76 ed.
Delacorte Press Prize, 301, 302
Delaware, networking in, 207
Delaware report, 323-324
D'Elia, George, 3, 116, 185, 243
DePaola, Thomas Anthony: *see* Biographies 84 ed.
deposit collections, 265
depository libraries, 136
　See also Government Publications and Depository System.
DeProspo, Ernest R.: *see* Obituaries 84 ed.
deSola Pool, Ithiel, 252
de Sola Price, Derek, 252. *See also* Obituaries 84 ed.
Dewey Decimal system, computer classification, 88
(Melvil) Dewey Medal, 2, 9
DIALOG, 240
Dictionary of the British Book Illustrators, 6
Dillon, Leo and Diane: *see* Biographies 77 ed.
Disadvantaged, Library Service to the: *see* 76-78 eds. *See also* Social Responsibilities
disks
　compact, 236
　optical, 112
Distinguished Library Service Award for School Administrators (AASL), 3, 40, 258
Distinguished Service Award (AALL), 39
Distinguished Service Award (archives), 52
Distinguished Service Award for School Administrators (CSLA), 87, 309
Distinguished Services Award (CALA), 98
District of Columbia report, 324-325
Division of Library Programs (CLEI), 171
Division of National Dissemination Programs (CLEI), 171-172
Divison of Technology, Resource Assessment and Development (CLEI), 171-172
Dix, William Shepherd: *see* Biographies 76 ed.; Obituaries 79 ed.
Dixon, Rebecca Danforth: *see* Biographies 83 ed.

381

Doares, Juanita S., 287
DOBIS, 199
DOCLINE, 205
Documents to the People Award, 2, 134
Dodd, James B.: see Biographies 81 ed.
Dodson, Howard, 72
(Janet) Doe Lecturer, 191
Doerr, Harriet, 5, 232
Dolnick, Sandy, 128
Doms, Keith: see Biographies 83 ed.
donations: see Gifts, Bequests and Endowments
Donovan, Ann F., 70
Dorf, Maxine, 2, 70
The Double Life of Pocahontas, 5
Dougherty, Richard, 166
Douglas, William O.: see Biographies 76 ed.
downloading, 26, 109
(Robert B.) Downs Award, 6
Downs, Robert Bingham: see Biographies 77 ed.
Doyle, Robert P., 8
Drennan, Henry Thomas: see Biographies 79 ed.
Drexel University Library (Philadelphia), 31
Dreyfus, John, 269
Dryfout, John, 56
(Miriam) Dudley Award for Bibliographic Instruction, 2, 33, 61
Duggins, Lydia A., 1, 49, 188
Dun & Bradstreet v. Greenmoss, 146
Dunkin, Paul Shaner: see Obituaries 76 ed.
Dunlap, Connie: see Biographies 80 ed.
Duran Daniel Flores: see Biographies 79 ed.
Dwyer, Melva, 87
Dynix, 148–149

Ebsco Subscription Services, 166
Ebsconet, 102, 105, 261
Echelman, Shirley: see Biographies 78 ed., 82 eds.
Eckstein, Otto, 146
Edge, Sigrid: see Obituaries 82 ed.
Education Amendments of 1984, 292
education, and libraries: see *Alliance for Excellence: Librarians Respond to A Nation at Risk*
Education Consolidation and Improvement Act of 1981, 172, 255
Education Film Library Association, 119
Education for Economic Security Act (PL 98–377), 168
Education, Library, 114–117 (also 76–84 eds.)
and accreditation, 32–36, (chart) 34–35
admissions: see 78 ed., "Passing Through the Turnstile: A View of Library School Admissions"
ARL institute, 64
in Britain, 314
in Canada, 309–311
centennial activities, 176
and children's services, 59
grants for, 171
and preservation studies, 218
and rural librarianship, 223
and school library media specialists, 257–258
training for future, 213–214
and visiting scholars, 161
See also 77 ed., "Patterns of Education and Accreditation for Librarianship: Canada, Great Britain, and Australia"; 78 ed. "Passing Through the Turnstile:

A View of Library School Admissions"; 81 ed. "Ninety Years of Library Instruction at Iowa State"; 84 ed. "Education for Librarianship: The Way It Is."
Education Practice File project, 117
Egoff, Sheila, 311. See also Biographies 80 ed.
Eichenberg, Fritz, 8, (photo) 8, 60
Eighteenth Century Short-Title Catalog, 71
Einhorn, Nathan R.: see Obituaries 84 ed.
elderly, library service to: see older adults, library service to
electronic communications
mail, 29–30
ordering systems, 105
publishing, 111–112
See also 80 ed. "Libraries and the Information Age"
(Ida and George) Eliot Prize, 191
Ellenberger, Jack S.: see Biographies 77 ed.
Elliott, Carl Atwood: see Biographies 83 ed.
Elsmo, Nancy, (photo) 231
employment: see Personnel and Employment; Job Market
endowments: see Gifts, Bequests and Endowments
energy conservation, for libraries, (photo) 82
English as a Second Language program, 186, 266
(Marian) *English, et al. v. Evergreen School District, et al.*, 127
Epstein, Dena Julia (Polacheck): see Biographies 78 ed.
Equality Award (ALA), 2, 292
equipment
and automation of libraries, 147
for blind and handicapped, (photos) 75, 137, 138, 265
security, 259
See also Furniture and Equipment 76, 77 eds.
ERIC (Educational Resources Information Center), 117–118 (also 79–84 eds.)
Eshelman William R.: see Biographies 79 ed.
Esquire, 235
Ethics: see 76, 77 eds.
ethnic groups, library service to
local programs, 266
See also Ethnic Groups, Library Service to 77, 78 eds.; individual groups by name.
evaluation: see Measurement and Evaluation
Evans, Luther: see Obituaries 82 ed.
Evans, Max, 52
Everett Anderson's Goodbye, 3, 267
Exceptional Service Award (ASCLA), 1, 70, 138
Exemplary Outreach Programs, 188
exhibits
awards for, 3
and Black Americans, 73
British Library, 315
censorship, (photos) 152–153, 154, 226, 230
commercial: see 76 ed.
Dallas Cowboys, (photo) 221
folk artifacts, (photo) 194
historical, 273–274
informational, (photos) 136, 137
Orwell's *1984*, (photo) 36
recommended books, (photo) 255
special opening—NYPL hall, 84–85, (photos) 84
theatrical memorabilia, (photos) 283
"Women of Courage," 210
Exhibits Round Table: see 76–83 eds.

Exxon Education Foundation, 103, 217

Facente, Gary, (photo), 43. See also Biographies 83 ed.
Facts on File Award, 2, 238
Facts on File, Inc., 240A
Fadiman, Clifton, 131
Fair, Ethel Marion: see Obituaries 81 ed.
fair use, 109
Fang, Josephine R., 162
Fast, Elizabeth: see Obituaries 78 ed.
Faust, Clarence Henry: see Obituaries 76 ed.
(Frederich Winthrop) Faxon Scholarship, 4
federal funding for libraries
administration of, 171
appropriations, (chart) 291
and buildings, 79–80
and collection management, 100–101
and research, 253
See also specific agencies, laws by name.
Federal Librarians Round Table, 118 (also 76–84 eds.)
Federal Library and Information Center Committee (FLICC), 204
Federal Library and Information Network: see FEDLINK
Federal Library Committee: see Federal Library and Information Center Committee (FLICC)
FEDLINK (Federal Library and Information Network), 180, 204
fees, for services
database searching, 30
and medical libraries, 190–191, 202
NAL policies, 196
NCLIS study, 197
See also 78 ed. "The Dilemma of Fees for Service: Issues and Action for Librarians"
Fennell, D. Pauline, 87–309
Fenner, Phyllis: see Obituaries 83 ed.
Fernandez, Maggie, 4
fiber optics, and communications, 282
FID: see International Federation for Documentation
Film Library Information Council (FLIC), 119
Films, 118–121 (also 76–84 eds.)
stills of, (photos) 38, 119, 120
Films, Children's, 121–127 (also 76–84 eds.)
award winners, (photos) 121–125
stills of, (photos) 122–125
Films for Young Adults, 23–24
Filmstrips: see 76–82 eds.
financing, library: see funding, for libraries
fingerprinting, of children, (photo) 263, 264
fire, damage due to, 85, 149–150, (photos) 150, (photo) 151
First Amendment
aspects of, 127, 128, 258
and young adults, 127, 297
Fischer, Margaret T.: see Biographies 78 ed.
Fitzgerald, Francis, (photo) 44
Fitzpatrick, Kelly: see Biographies 82 ed.
Flannery, Melissa C., 89
Florida, networking in, 207
Florida report, 325–327
Fontaine, Everett O.: see Obituaries 77 ed.
Ford, William D., 8–9, (photo) 8
foreign language materials
braille and recordings, 77
Latin American, 259

LC program, 77
reviews of, 183
Spanish, 266
Fort Lauderdale Main Library (Florida), (photo) 81
Foundations, Private: see 80–84 eds.; see Foundations and Funding Agencies 76–79 eds. See also 80 ed., "Foundations Funding for Libraries."
Fox, Paula: see Biographies 79 ed.
Frank, Andrew, 193
Franklin, John Hope: see Biographies 76 ed.
Frantz, Ray W., Jr.: see Biographies 79 ed.
Frarey, Carlyle James: see Obituaries 77 ed.
fraud, in advertising, 240A
(George) Freedley Memorial Award, 283
Freedman, Barbara, 4, 60
freedom of information: see Intellectual Freedom
Freedom of Information Act (FOIA), 153. See also 76 ed.
Freedom to Read Award, 301
Freedom to Read Committee (AAP), 153–154
Freedom to Read Foundation, 127–128 (also 76–84 eds.)
and school personnel, 258
Freedom to Read Week, 86
Free Library of Philadelphia, 188
(W.H.) Freeman Company, 3
Fresno County Public Library (California), 188
Friendly Booth Award, 166
Friends of Libraries, 128–129 (also 76–84 eds.)
and library support, 284
and public relations, 228
special activities, (photos) 78, 129
Friends of the North Carolina Public Libraries, 129
Friends of the Salt Lake City Public Library, 129
Friends of the Thomas Branigan Memorial Library (Las Cruces, New Mexico), 129
Fritz, Jean, 5. See also Biographies 77 ed.
Fruge, August, 231
Fuller, Muriel L.: see Obituaries 79 ed.
funding, for libraries
and buildings, 83, 85
drives for, (photo) 221
federal: see federal funding, for libraries; specific agencies and laws by name
private, 102
and public libraries, 221, 223
and social responsibilities, 266–267
See also 77 ed. "Financing the Public Library."
fundraising
kit for, 107
special materials, (photo) 182
Furniture and Equipment: see 76, 77 eds. See also equipment.
Fussler, Herman Howe: see Biographies 77 ed.
Futuretrack 5, (photo) 302

Gagliardo, Ruth Garver: see Obituaries 81 ed.
Gale, Jay, (photo) 302
Gale Research Company Financial Development Award, 2
Gallagher, Marian G., 39
Galler, Anne, 87
Galvin, Thomas, (photo) 160, 166. See also Biographies 79, 82 eds.
Gamble, Olive, (photo) 37, (photo) 131

Gard, Betty, (photo) 238
Gary, James A., III, (photo) 285
Gasaway, Laura N., 6
Gates, Francis L.: see Biographies 81 ed.
Gaver, Mary Virginia: see Biographies 77 ed.
Geac Computers International, 148, 307
Geer, Helen, 17
Geisel, Theodore Seuss: see Biographies 81, 83 eds.
Gell, Marilyn: see Biographies 80 ed.
genealogy: see 78 ed., "Genealogy as it Relates to Library Service"
General Accounting Office (GAO), 152–153
General Electric Foundation, 68, 186, 242
General Information Program (PGI) (UNESCO), 159
General Services Administration (GSA), 53
Georgia report, 327–329
Germain, Claire, 39
German Book Trade Peace Prize, 231
(J. Paul) Getty Center for the History of Art and the Humanities, 57
(J. Paul) Getty Trust, 57
Getz, Malcolm, 253
Gifts, Bequests and Endowments, 130–134 (also 76–84 eds.)
for literacy programs, (photo) 187
NAL and floriculture, 196
personal papers, 131
soft sculpture, (photo) 94
Gilchrist, Ellen, 232
Giles, Louise (Jones): see Obituaries 77 ed.
(Louise) Giles Minority Scholarship, 4
Gill, Gregory, 52
Ginader, George Hall: see Biographies 82 ed.
Gleaves, Edwin S., (photo) 164
The Glorious Flight Across the Channel with Louis Bleriot, 2, 12–13, 60, 97, 98
Goble, Paul: see Biographies 80 ed.
Goff, Frederick: see Obituaries 83 ed.
Goldstein, Elliot, (photo) 156
Goldstein, Harold: see Biographies 82 ed.
Goodrum, Charles A.: see Biographies 78 ed.
Gorilla, 6, 98
Gorman, Michael: see Biographies 78 ed.
Gottesman Exhibition Hall (New York Public Library), (photo) 84
(Murray) Gottlieb Prize, 191
Gottschalk, Louis Moreau, (photo) 271
Gould, Donald, 4, 242
Gould, Martha, (photo) 44
Govan, James F.: see Biographies 83 ed.
Government Documents Round Table (GODORT), 134 (also 76–84 eds.)
Government Printing Office (GOP), 228
Government Publications and Depository System, 134–136 (also 76–84 eds.)
Graham, Mae L.: see Obituaries 84 ed.
Granheim, Else, 164
Grants
accreditation study, 114
ALA, description of, 4–5
automation, 130
cataloging and classification, 89
children's library services, 60
and Chinese library service, 162
and correctional institutions, 299
educational programs, 172

federal, 167–168, 171–172. See also specific agencies, laws by name.
foreign language materials, 77
foreign students, 163
HEA: see Higher Education Act
and historical collections, 274
historical records, 52
K.I.D.S., 301
librarianship in China, 162
library history, 176
literacy, 186
LSCA: see LSCA
medical libraries, 190
NEH: see National Endowment for the Humanities
NSF (charts), 244–252
preservation, 217
professional development, 165
research, 243, 252, 253 (charts) 244–252
research in library education, 59
See also federal funding for libraries; Foundations, Private; funding agencies by name; Research; Scholarships; state reports by name.
Grassroots Grants, 4
Greenaway, Everson: see Biographies 77 ed.
(Kate) Greenaway Medal, 6, 98
Greenwald, Evelyn, (photo) 144
Gregorian, Vartan, (photo) 84. See also Biographies 82 ed.
(John) Grierson Award, 120
Grolier Award for Research in School Librarianship in Canada, 87
Grolier Club, 269–270
Grolier Foundation Award, 2, 12, 60
Grolier National Library Week Grant, 4
Grosch, Audrey N.: see Biographies 79 ed.
Gross, Mason Welch: see Obituaries 78 ed.
Grove, Andrew S., 146
Guereña, Salvador, 5
A Guide to County Records in the Illinois Regional Archives, 52
Gwinn, Nancy E., 4, 104, 253

Haas, Eva, 54
Haas, Warren J., 2, 9, (photo) 9, 162. See also Biographies 79 ed.
Hackett, Linda, (photo) 138
(G.K.) Hall Company, 2, 138
(G.K.) Hall Large Print Community Service Award, 2, 138
Hall of Fame Award (IIA), 146
Hall of Fame Award (SLA), 6, 277
Halpenny, Frances, 310
(Philip M.) Hamer Award, 52
Hamilton, Virginia, (photo) 302. See also Biographies 76 ed.
Hammond, Jane Laura: see Biographies 76 ed.
handicapped: see Blind and Physically Handicapped, Library Service for the
Handles 5, 98
Haney, Chris, (photo) 305
Hannigan, Jane Anne, 1, 9, 70, 116
Harcourt, Ellen Knowles, 231
Hardesty, Vicki, 1, 40, 258
Harlan, Louis R., 233
Harrar, Joanne: see Biographies 84 ed.
Hart, Dorothy, 54
Hart, Thomas, (photo) 168
Harvin-Clarendon County Public Library, Manning, South Carolina, 2
Hashim, Elinor, (photo) 140, 196. See also Biographies 84 ed.
Hatfield, Senator Mark, 80
Haviland, Virginia: see Biographies 77, 83 eds.

383

Hawaii report, 329–330
Hawthorne-Longfellow Library (Bowdoin College, Brunswick, Maine), (photo) 29
Haycock, Kenneth R.: see Biographies 78 ed.
Haycraft, Howard: see Biographies 77 ed.
Health and Rehabilitative Library Services, 136–139 (also 76–84 eds.)
See also Association of Specialized and Cooperative Library Agencies; Blind and Physically Handicapped, Library Services for the.
Division (HRLSD): see 76–79 eds.
health information, and libraries, 139, 264
Hedlin, Edie, 52
Heim, Kathleen: see Biographies 83 ed.
Helminiak, Marion, 94
Henley, John C. III, 1, 49
Henne, Frances Elizabeth: see Biographies 77, 79 eds.
Hennen, Earl M., Jr., 52
Herring, Harold F., 9
Herzig, Alison Cragin, (photo) 97
Hewitt, A.R., 6
Hewitt, Vivian D., 6, 277. See also Biographies 79 ed.
Higham, Norman: see Biographies 84 ed.
Higher Education Act (HEA)
and Congressional revision, 26
Title II-A, (college library resources) 171
Title II-B, (library career training) 33, 114, 171, 185
Title II-C, (strengthening research library resources) 26, 99, 103, 171, 274
Hines, Theodore C.: see Obituaries 84 ed.
Hinton, Frances: see Biographies 81 ed.
Hirsch, Felix: see Obituaries 84 ed.
Hispanic Heritage Month, 241
Hispanics, library service to, 263, 264
Hoagland, Sister Mary Arthur, I.H.M.: see Biographies 78 ed.
Hofer, Philip, 275
Hogan, Kathleen, 87, 310
Holler, Suzanne E., (photo) 238
Holley, Edward G., see Biographies 76, 84 eds.
(Oliver Wendell) Holmes Award, 52
"Homework Centers," (photo) 297
Hood, Joan, 128
Hookway, Sir Harry, 315
Hoolihan, Christopher, 191
Horn, Andrew Harlis: see Obituaries 84 ed.
Horrocks, Norman, 310
Horton, Marion Louise, 17
hospitals, and libraries, 191, 192
Hotel du Lac, 233
House and Garden, 235
Houston (Texas) Public Library, 2, 227
(Bailey K.) Howard—ALA Goal Award, 4–5
(Amelia Frances) Howard-Gibbon Medal, 6, 87, 98
Howard, Joseph H., (photo) 195
Howell, Warren R., 276
Howells Journal, 192
HR 5938: see Record Rental Agreement
Hudson, Jan, 5, 87, 98
Humanities Projects in Libraries, 290
Humphry, John Ames: see Biographies 78 ed.
Hund, Carol, (photo) 138
Hunter, Mollie (Maureen McIlwraith): see Biographies 76 ed.
Hutton, Warwick, 5

Idaho report, 330–331
IFLA, 139–140 (also 77–84 eds.) See International Federation of Library Associations 76 ed.
conference and programs, 158
and continuing education, 108
Kenya conference, (photo) 140
UBC activities, 286
IFRT State Program Award, 155
ILLINET, 43, 207
Illinois Cooperative Conservation Program (ICCP), 217
Illinois networking in, 207
Illinois report, 331–332
Immroth, John Phillip: see Obituaries 77 ed.
(John Phillip) Immroth Memorial Award for Intellectual Freedom, 2, 156, 258, 303
independent learning: see "Independent Learning and the Future Role of Public Libraries" 76 ed.
Independent Libraries: see 76 ed.
Independent Research Libraries, 140, 143 (also 77–84 eds.)
Independent study in public libraries: see 76 ed. See also 76 ed., "Independent Learning and the Future Role of Public Libraries"
indexes: see Bibliography and Indexes
Indexing and Abstracting Services: see 76, 77 eds., see Abstracting and Indexing Services 78–84 eds.
Indian in the Cupboard, 211
Indiana, networking in, 207
Indiana report, 332–334
Indians, American: see American Indians
information age: see 80 ed., "Libraries and the Information Age"
Information and Referral Centers: see 76–78 eds.
Information and Referral Service, 143–145 (also 79–84 eds.) See Information and Referral Centers 76–78 eds.
use of databases, 144
Information Industry, 145–146 (also 77–84 eds.)
Information Industry Association, 145-146
information science: see 81 ed. "An Information Agenda for the 1980s"
Information Science and Automation Division: see 76, 77, 78 eds.;see Library and Information Technology Division 79–83 eds.
Information Science and Technology, Division of: see 79–81 eds.; see National Science Foundation, Divison of Information Science and Technology 82, 83, 84 eds.; see Science Information, Division of 76–78 eds.
Information Technology, 147–149
INFOSERV, 261
Innovacq, 101
In-Search, 240
Inskip, Robin, 310
Institute for International Information Programs, 25
Insurance for Libraries, 149–151 (also 76–84 eds.)
Integrated Academic Information Management Systems (IAIMS), 190, 202

integrated library systems (ILS), 203
Intellectual Freedom, 151–155 (also 76–84 eds.)
Canada, 308, 311
and children's services, 60
and court cases, 127
and movie rating codes, 126
NCLIS study on censorship, 197
and school personnel, 258
See also Freedom to Read Foundation; individual court cases by name; individual state reports by name.
Intellectual Freedom Award (AASL/SIRS), 1, 40, 258
Intellectual Freedom Committee, South Carolina Library Association, 3
Intellectual Freedom Round Table (IFRT), 155–156 (also 76–84 eds.)
Intellectual Freedom Round Table State Program Award, 3
INTELSAT, 282
interlibrary cooperation
and agricultural libraries, 194
in Britain, 313
and electronic mail, 29–30
funding for, 171
report on state cooperatives, 70
and resource sharing, 100
See also 76, 77 eds.; Networks; state reports by name.
International Board on Books for Young People (IBBY), 156–157 (also 76–83 eds.)
awards, 98, 157
international cooperation
and art librarians, 56–57
and Britain, 314
and copyright, 109
free exchange of information, 154
joint meetings of U.S.-U.K., 197
and music literature, 193
and NAL, 194
and standards, 279
U.S.—China exchanges of librarians, 161–163
International Federation for Documentation (FID): see 76–79 eds.
International Federation of Library Associations: see IFLA
International Legal Bibliography, 39
International Reading Association Award, 98
International Relations, 157–158, 163–164 (also 76–84 eds.)
International Relations Round Table (IRRT), 164–165 (also 76–84 eds.)
International School Librarianship: see 77 ed.
International Standard Bibliographic Description: see ISBD
In the Mouth of the Wolf, 6, 63
inventory, and automation, 148
Iowa report, 334–335
Ironweed, 233
Irving, Jan, 5, 60
ISBD (International Standard Bibliographic Description), 285–286
Islamic libraries: see 82 ed., "Islamic Libraries: Retrospective and Perspective"
Italian American Librarians Caucus, 165
Italian Americans and Libraries, 165 (also 76, 81–84 eds.) See Italian Americans 79–80 eds. See also Ethnic Groups, Library Service to 77, 78 eds.
Ives, Alan, 52

Jackson, Elmer M., Jr., 4, 49
Jackson-George Regional Library

System, Pascagoula, Mississippi, 2, 4, 138, 167, 238
Jackson, Sidney L.: see Obituaries 80 ed.
Jackson, W. Carl: see Obituaries 82 ed.
Jacobs, Leland Blair: see Biographies 84 ed.
Jacobs, Roger F.: see Biographies 82 ed.
Jacobson, Susan, (photo) 27
Jacobstein, J. Myron: see Biographies 79 ed.
Jamisen, Susan C., 240A
Janklow v. *The Viking Press, et al.*, 127
Jankowski, Mike, 5
Javits, Jacob Koppel: see Biographies 82 ed.
Jenkins, Jane, 175, 315
Jenkinson, David, 87
Jepson, William H.: see Biographies 83 ed.
Jerry, Sylvester, (photo) 169
Jewish Caucus: see 76 ed.
Jiping, Liu, 161
job information centers, 264
job market: see Personnel and Employment: Job Market
Johnson, Barbara Coe: see Biographies 76 ed.
Johnson, Mary Frances Kennon: see Obituaries 80 ed.
Johnson, Richard D., 1, 33, 61. See also Biographies 76 ed.
Joint Council on Educational Telecommunications: see 76 ed.
Jonah and the Great Fish, 5
Jonah, David Alonzo: see Obituaries 82 ed.
(J. Morris) Jones—ALA Goal Award, 5
Jones, Clara Stanton, (photo) 268. See also Biographies 76, 79, 84 eds.
Jones, Virginia Lacy, 17-18, (photo) 17, 72, 116, 268. See also Biographies 77, 81 eds.
Josephine, Helen B.: see Biographies 80 ed.
Josey, E.J., 72, (photo) 72, 158, 188, (photo) 268, 294. See also Biographies 81, 84 eds.
journals: see Publishing, Serials; Serials
Juergensmeyer, John E.: see Biographies 84 ed.
Junior Members Round Table (JMRT), 165-166 (*also* 76-84 eds.)
Jurkins, Jacquelyn J., 9-10

Kahn, Herman: see Obituaries 76 ed.
Kalp, Margaret Ellen: see Obituaries 79 ed.
Kaminstein, Abraham Louis: see Obituaries 78 ed.
Kansas, networking in, 207-208
Kansas report, 335-336
Kaye, Marilyn Janice: see Biographies 83 ed.
Kegan, Elizabeth Hamer: see Obituaries 80 ed.
Kehs, Constance N., 4, 60
(W.K.) Kellog Foundation, 100
Kennedy, Anna Clark, 18
Kennedy, Jane F., (photo) 180
Kennedy, Jessie, (photo) 221
Kennedy, William, 233
Kennickell, Ralph E., Jr., 135
Kentucky report, 336-337
Kerker, Ann Elizabeth: see Biographies 77 ed.
Kerney, Barbara, (photo) 129
Kilgour, Frederick, 162, 191. See also Biographies 76, 83 eds.
Kimmel, Margaret Mary, 10

(Coretta Scott) King Awards, 3, 267, 268
King, Coretta Scott, 43, 267, (photo) 268
King, Donald W.: see Biographies 84 ed.
(Martin Luther) King, Jr., Library (Dallas), (photo) 72
King Research, Inc., 211-212
Kirk, Thomas, 2, 33, 61
Kirkegaard, Preben: see Biographies 76 ed.
Kirkus, Virginia: see Obituaries 81 ed.
Kitchen, Paul Howard: see Biographies 76 ed.
Kleckner, Simone-Marie, 39
Knapp, Sara D., 3, 237-238, 240
(Helen) Knight Memorial Fund, 60
Knopf, Alfred A., 231
Knowledge Industry Publications, Inc. Award for Library Literature, 184
Knox, William T(yndall): see Obituaries 79 ed.
Kohlstedt Exhibit Awards, 3
Kozol, Jonathan, 49, 189
Kreimeyer, Vicki R., 210
Krug, Judith Fingeret: see Biographies 77 ed.
Krug, Richard E.: see Obituaries 84 ed.
Krummel, Donald W.: see Biographies 82 ed.
Krupp, Robert G., 6, 277
Kudej, Blanka, 39
Kuhlman, James R., (photo) 238
Kuhns, Pat (photo) 186
Kunze, Horst J.: see Biographies 81 ed.
Kurth, William H.: see Obituaries 78 ed.
Kurtz, Angelica, 87, 310
Kusche, Lawrence David: see Biographies 76 ed.

Labor Groups, Library Service to, 166-167 (*also* 76-84 eds.)
Labor Groups, Library Service to special award, 4, 167, 238
Lacy, Dan Mabry: see Biographies 76 ed.
Ladd, David, 109, 162, 231. See also Biographies 81 ed.
Ladenson, Alex: see Biographies 81 ed.
Laine, John, 306
Lamb, Gertrude: see Biographies 81 ed.
Lamb, William Kaye, 200
Lancour, Harold: see Obituaries 82 ed.
(Harold) Lancour Scholarship for Foreign Study, 70
Landau, Herbert B.: see Biographies 81 ed.
Land, (Reginald) Brian: see Biographies 76 ed
(Sister M. Claude) Lane Award, 52
Lang, Sister Franz: see Biographies 80 ed.
Lanier, Gene D., 2, 156, (photo) 156, 258, 303
large-print books, 138-139
Large Print Community Service Award, 2, 138
Lasky, Kathryn, (photo) 96
L'Association des directeurs de bibliothèques publiques de Québec, 305
Lathem, Edward Connery: see Biographies 78 ed.
Lathrop, Dorothy P.: see Obituaries 81 ed.
Latman, Alan, 109
Law and Legislation, 167-170 (*also* 76-84 eds.)

and ARL, 64
in Britain, 313
Canada, 304
and copyright, 109, 290, 292
and IIA activities, 145-146
and medical libraries, 190-191
serials v. consumer products, 234
See also specific laws and cases by name; individual state reports by name.
Law Libraries, 170 (*also* 76-84 eds.)
Law Library Publication Award, 39
Lawrey, Keith, 175, 315
Laws of Trinidad and Tobago, 6
(Samuel) Lazerow Fellowship, 242
Learning Corporation of America (LCA), 118
Leeds, Byron: see Biographies 84 ed.
Lee, Joel M.: see Biographies 79 ed.
Lee, Mollie Huston: see Obituaries 83 ed.
legislation: see Law and Legislation
Legislative Leadership Award (MPLA), 192
Leiby, Jack, (photo) 130
Leigh, Janet, (photo) 129
Leiter, Joseph, 191
(Joseph) Leiter NLM/MLA Lectureship, 191
(Waldo Gifford) Leland Prize, 52
L'Engle, Madeleine, 6, 10, 89, 98
Leone, Joe, (photo) 113
Le Regroupement québécois de l'information documentaire, 305-306
Lerner, Adele A., 10-11
Lerner, Louis Abraham, 18. See also Biographies 78 ed.
"Let's Talk About It" project, 38, 69
Levy, Evelyn: see Obituaries 78 ed.
Lewis, Jean R., 70
Lewis, Peter Ronald: see Biographies 78 ed.
Libraries and Education Improvement, Center for (CLEI), 171-172
Libraries and Learning Resources, Office of: see 76-80 eds.
Libraries and Learning Technologies, Office of (OLLT): see 81-83 eds.; see Libraries and Learning Resources, Office of 76-80 eds.
libraries, retrospect on: see 79 ed., "To Praise the Past—To Forge the Future"
Library Administration and Management Association (LAMA), 172-174 (*also* 79-84 eds.) see Library Administration Division 76-78 eds.
Library Administration and Management Association (LAMA)
 public relations activities, 226-227
 regional institutes, 215
Library Administration Division: see 76-78 eds.
Library and Information Services Council (LISC), 313
Library and Information Technology Association (LITA), 174-175 (*also* 79-84 eds.) See Information Science amd Automation Division 76-78 eds.
Library and Information Technology Association/Gaylord Award, 3, 174
Library Association (Britain), 175-176 (*also* 84 ed.)
and copyright, 314
See also 78 ed., "The Library Association Centenary."
Library associations: see 78 ed. "1977: The Library Association Centenary"; 79 ed. "The Fine Art of Associating"; 82 ed. "The

Characteristics of National Professional Associations in the Library/Information Fields"
Library Bill of Rights, 155
LIbrary Contribution Award (MPLA), 192
library directors
  characteristics of, 27
  male/female percentages, 294
Library Education Centennial, 116
Library Education Division: see 76-78 eds.
Library History, 176-177 (also 83, 84 eds.) See American Library History 76-82 eds.
  ALA history, (photo) 177
  institute for study, 177
Library History Round Table (LHRT), 177-178 (also 80-84 eds.) See American Library History Round Table 76-79 eds.
Library Instruction Round Table (LIRT), 178-179 (also 79-84 eds.)
Library Journal, 183
Library of Congress (LC), 179-182 (also 76-84 eds.)
  cooperation with NAL, 194
  Foreign Language Program, 77
  Linked Systems Project, 204
  Name Authority Cooperative, 71
  and preservation, 218
  service to blind and physically handicapped, 76-77
  study of books in future, 181
  subject cataloging manual, 88-89
Library of Parliament (Canada), 200
Library Periodical Award, 4, 184
Library Press, 182-184 (also 76-84 eds.)
Library Research Round Table (LRRT), 184-185 (also 76-84 eds.)
Library Research Round Table Research Award, 3, 116, 185, 243
Library Services and Construction Act: see LSCA
Library Staff Development Grant, 5, 215-216
library technicians, in Canada, 310
Liebaers, Herman: see Biographies 77 ed.
Lieberman, J. Ben, 276
Lilly Endowment Fund, 51, 63
Lindberg, Donald A.B., 11, (photo) 11, 202
Lindgren, Astrid, 1, 60, 97, 98
Lindquist, Jennie D.: see Obituaries 78 ed.
Linked Systems Project (LSP), 71, 181-182, 204, 205, 206
(Joseph W.) Lippincott Award, 3, 15
Lippincott, Joseph Wharton: see Obituaries 77 ed.
Lister Hill National Center for Biomedical Communication, 202
Literacy Award (ALTA), 1, 49, 188
Literacy Programs, Library, 185-189 (also 76-84 eds.)
  cooperative planning, (photo) 42
  LC recommendations for future, 181
  local programs, 37, 264, 265
  NCLIS pilot project, 196-197
  and public libraries, 219
  special activities, (photo) 186, 187
  worldwide programs, 160
  See also individual state reports by name.
A Little Fear, 5
A Little Love, 302
Livingston, Lawrence G.: see Obituaries 79 ed.
Lobel, Arnold: see Biographies 82 ed.
Lodwick, Ellen, (photo) 238

logos and symbols
  Canadian, 86
  U.S., (photo) 219
London Illustrated 1604-1851, 5
Longworth, Alan: see Biographies 82 ed.
Lorenz, John George: see Biographies 76 ed.
Lorenzi, Nancy M.: see Biographies 83 ed.
Lorimer, Myrtle, 87
Louisiana report, 337-339
Love, Erika: see Biographies 79 ed.
Lovejoy, Eunice, 1, 70, 138
(Edward R.) Loveland Memorial Award, 191
Low, Edmon: see Biographies 76 ed.; Obituaries 84 ed.
Lowrie, Jean: see Biographies 79 ed.
LSCA (Library Services and Construction Act)
  appropriations for, 167-168, 289 (chart) 291
  and correctional institutions, 299
  and handicapped, 77
  and preservation, 217
  revisions in, 167, 289-290
  Title I (Library Services), 167
  Title II (Public Construction), 79-80, 220-221
  Title III (Interlibrary Cooperation and Resource Sharing), 101, 171
  Title IV (Library Services for Indian Tribes), 40-41
  Title V (Foreign Language Material Acquisition), 77, 167
  Title VI (Library Literacy Programs), 167, 185, 219
  See also individual state reports by name.
Lucker, Jay K.: see Biographies 81 ed.
Lukasavich, William, (photo) 140
Luskay, Jack R.: see Biographies 80 ed.
Lustberg, Arch, 69
Lutheran Church Library Association Minneapolis, Minnesota, 2, 227
Lyman, Helen Huguenor: see Biographies 80 ed.
Lynch, Beverly P., 11, (photo) 11, 166
Lynch, Mary Jo, 223. See also Biographies 79 ed.
Lynch, Sister Mary Dennis: see Biographies 84 ed.
Lynchburg Public Library (Virginia), (photo) 81
Lyons, Dean, 5, 60

McAnanama, Judith, 11, (photo) 11, 85, (photo) 87
McCarthy, Mary, 6, 233
McColvin Medal, 6
McCormick, Kenneth D., 233
McCusker, Sister Lauretta, 89
McDermott, Gerald, 91. See also Biographies 76 ed.
MacDonald, Alan (Hugh): see Biographies 81 ed.
Macdonald, Sir John A., 200
McElderry, Margaret K(nox): see Biographies 76 ed.
McFadden, David Revere, 56
(John P.) McGovern Award Lecturer, 191
McGraw, Harold, 231
McGregor, Della Louise: see Obituaries 79 ed.
McGregor, Jane Ann: see Biographies 82 ed.
McGuire, Alice Brooks: see Obituaries 76 ed.
(Melvin) McKay Trust, 130
McKenna, F(rank) E(ugene): see Biographies 77 ed.; Obituaries 79 ed.

McKenzie, Dorothy C.: see Biographies 79 ed.
McLaughlin, Jim, 296
MacLeish, Archibald: see Obituaries 83 ed.
MacMillan Encyclopedia of Architects, 56
MacMillan Publishing Company, 56
McNally, Joe, (photo) 305
McNamara, Brooks: see Biographies 78 ed.
McNamara, Margaret Craig: see Biographies 76 ed.; Obituaries 82 ed.
Machine-Readable Data Bases: see 76 ed; see Databases, Computer Readable 77-83 eds.
Machlup, Fritz, 252
magazines: see Publishing, Serials; Serials
MAGERT Honor Award, 3
Mahar, Mary Helen: see Biographies 80 ed.
Maine, networking in, 208
Maine report, 339-340
Major Benefactors Honor Award (ALTA), 1, 49
Major Microforms Project (OCLC), 63-64
Mali, Jane Lawrence, (photo) 97
Malone, Violet, (photo) 42
Management, Library
  ARL studies, 68
  considerations for leadership, 27
  and continuing education, 108
  LAMA activities, 172-174
  and public relations, 226-227
  See also 76-82 eds.
(Margaret) Mann Citation, 3, 89, 253
Manuscript Society, 269
maps
  state, 240A
  tactile, 76
Mark, Jan, 5, 98
Martell, Charles R., 11-12, (photo) 11
(Allie Beth) Martin Award, 3, 224, 225
Martin, Lowell A.: see Biographies 80 ed.
Martin, Susan K., 287
Maryland, networking in, 208
Maryland report, 340-341
Massachusetts report, 341
Matheson, Nina W.: see Biographies 84 ed.
Mathews, Anne, (photo) 140
Mazzei, Philip, 165
M'Bow, Secretary General Amadou-Mahtar, 43, (photo) 159
Meadow, Charles, 310
Meadows, Sharon, 310-311
Mearns, David C.: see Obituaries 82 ed.
Measurement and Evaluation: see 76-84 eds.
Media Center for Children (MCC), 123-124
Mediation, Arbitration and Inquiry: see 76-81 eds.
Medical Americana in the Library of the Wellcome Institute for the History of Medicine, 259
Medical Libraries, 189-191 (also 76-84 eds.)
Medical Library Assistance Act (MLAA), 190, 192
Medical Library Association (MLA), 191-192 (also 76-84 eds.)
  and continuing education, 108
Medical Literature Analysis and Retrieval System: see MEDLARS
Medina, Sue O'Neal: see Biographies 84 ed.
MEDLARS (Medical Literature Analysis and Retrieval System),

190, 202
MEDLARS III project, 190, 202
Meisel, Martin, 283
Melcher, Daniel, 231. *See also* Biographies 77 ed.
(Frederic G.) Melcher Scholarships, 4, 60
(Andrew) Mellon Foundation, 64, 115
MELVYL, 28
mentally ill, library services for the, 138
mentally retarded, library service to, 138, 264
Meredith, Louise: *see* Obituaries 76 ed.
Meritorious Civilian Service Medal, 54
Meritorious Person's Award (Alberta Teacher's Association), 310
(LeRoy C.) Merritt Humanitarian Fund: *see* 76 ed.
Merwine, Glenda, 42, 170, 214
Merwine v. State of Mississippi, 42, 170, 214
Metcalfe, John Wallace: *see* Obituaries 83 ed.
Metcalf, Keyes Dewitt: *see* Biographies 77 ed.; Obituaries 84 ed.
Metzdorf, Robert Frederic: *see* Obituaries 76 ed.
(Fred) Meyer Charitable Trust Library Program, 99, 100
Meyer, Helen Honig: *see* Biographies 77 ed.
Micelthwaite, Lucy, 6
Michigan report, 341–342
Microcomputer Award (AASL/Follet Library Book Company), 40
microcomputers
  and cataloging, 88
  and children, (photo) 92, 93–94
  and disabled, 136–137
  increase in use of, 28
  and inventory, (photo) 100
  in library, 148
  and public libraries, 219
  serials on, 234
  uses of (photos), 130, 147, 149, 220, 234, 307
microfiche, microfilm, microforms: *see* Micrographics
Microform Project (ARL), 63, 71
Micrographics
  ARL microform project, 63, 71
  history of: *see* 76 ed., "Micrographics: An Eventful Forty Years—What Next?"
  and LC, 180
  OCLC microform project, 63–64
  and state documents, 195
  See also 77–84 eds.
microphotography: *see* Micrographics
Micropublishers International, 104
Midwest Cooperative Conservation Program, 217
(Carl) Milam lecturer, 164
Milczewski, Marion A.: *see* Obituaries 82 ed.
Miller, Laurence A., (photo) 156
Mills, Shirley C.: *see* Biographies 79 ed.
Minnesota Library Association, 5
Minnesota report, 342–343
minorities
  and job recruitment, 214
  scholarships for, 4, 171, 191, 277
Mirsky, Phyllis, (photo) 12, 191
Mish, John L.: *see* Obituaries 84 ed.
Mississippi, networking in, 208
Mississippi report, 343–344
Missouri report, 344–346
Mitchell, Eleanor, 18, 164–165
MLA Minority Scholarship, 191
Moeller-Peiffer, Kathleen, 5, 165

Moltz, R. Kathleen: *see* Biographies 76 ed.
Monnin, Catherine, 2, 238
Montana report, 346–347
Moon, Eric: *see* Biographies 77, 82 eds.
Moore, Bessie, 12. *See also* Biographies 81 ed.
Moore, Everett Thomson: *see* Biographies 76 ed.
Moore, Lilian, 91
Morgan, Jane Hale, (photo) 221
Morris, Effie Lee, 60, 72, (photo) 268, 296
Morton, Elizabeth Homer: *see* Obituaries 78 ed.
Mosby, John, 1, 49
Mosher, Paul H., 4, 104, 253
motion pictures, and lending, 155
Mount, Ellis, 6, 116, 277
Mountain Plains Library Association (MPLA), 192. *See under* Regional Library Associations 76–84 eds.
Mouw, James, 5, 165
(Isadore Gilbert) Mudge Citation, 3, 237–238, 240
(Gerd) Muehsam Award (ARLIS/NA), 55
Muir, Helen, 4, 49
Mulroney, Brian, 304
multimedia materials: *see* 76–78 eds. *See also* Films; Films, Children's; Recordings, Sound; School Libraries and Media Programs; Telecommunications.
Mumford, L(awrence) Quincy: *see* Biographies 76 ed.; Obituaries 83 ed.
Munn, Ralph: *see* Obituaries 76 ed.
Museum of Modern Art Library (New York), (photo) 56
museums
  and media, 123
  with libraries, (photo) 56, 200
Music Library Association (MLA), 192–193 (*also* 76–84 eds.)
Musisi, J.S., 158
MWR Meritorious Award, 54
My Mamma Needs Me, 3, 267
Myers. Margaret, 2, 292

NACO (Name Authority Cooperation) project, 71, 195, 205
Naftalin, Frances Healy: *see* Biographies 79 ed.
Name Authority Cooperation project: *see* NACO project
The Name Authority Cooperative/Name Authority File Service (NACO), 71
National Advertising Council, Inc., 186
National Advisory Board on Rural Information Needs (NABRIN), 222
National Agricultural Library (NAL), 194–196 (*also* 76–84 eds.)
National Agricultural Library networking activities, 204–205
National Archives and Records Administration (NARA), 52, 53, 290
National Book Critics Circle Award, 233
National Center for Education Statistics (NCES), 243
National Collections Inventory Project (NCIP), 99, 101, 105
National Commission on Libraries and Information Science (NCLIS), 196–197 (*also* 76–84 eds.)
National Commission on Libraries and Information Science

(NCLIS)
  and cataloging manual, 89
  and continuing education, 107
  and rural needs, 222
National Council on Quality Continuing Library and Information Science Education, 107
National Diffusion Network (NDN), 172
National Endowment for the Humanities (NEH), 197–199 (*also* 76–84 eds.)
  A & I project, 64
  and censorship exhibit, 154
  challenge grants to libraries, 99, 102
  historical projects, 274
  Humanities Projects in Libraries, 290
  and independent research libraries, 143
  "Let's Talk About It" project, 38, 69
  and library history, 176
  1985 appropriation, library projects, 168
  Preservation Planning Program studies, 64, 68, 99, 217
  and social responsibilities, 264
  southwest culture project, (photo) 198
  videodisk project in China, 162
  See also individual state reports by name.
National Federation of Abstracting and Information Services (NFAIS), 25
National Geographic, 235
National Historical Publications and Records Commission, 290
  and grants, 52, 274
National Information Standards Organization (NISO), 102, 278–279
National Librarians Association: *see* 78–83 eds.
National Libraries: *see* 76 ed. *See also* Principal Libraries of the World 77 ed.
National Library of Canada, 199–202
National Library of Medicine (NLM), 202 (*also* 76–84 eds.)
  and computerization, 100, 190
  and networking, 205
National Library Week, (photo) 36, 228, 230, 296. *See also* 76 ed.
National Magazine Awards, 235
National Medal for Literature, 6, 233
National Micrographics Association (NMA): *see* 76–83 eds.
National Rehabilitation Information Center (NARIC), 78
National Science Foundation, Division of Information Science and Technology: *see* 82–84 eds.; *see* Information Science and Technology, Division of 79–81 eds.; *see* Science Information Service, Division of 76–78 eds.
National Science Foundation Grants, (charts) 244–252
National Security Agency (NSA), 127
National Technical Information Service (NTIS), 203 (*also* 76–84 eds.)
  cooperation with China, 25
A Nation at Risk, 36, 42, 59, 60, 108, 181, 197, 219, 225, 254, 255, 292, 303
National Union Catalog: *see* 76 ed.
Navy Libraries, 54
Nebraska, networking in, 208
Nebraska report, 347–348
Nellis (Nevada) Air Force Base Library, 2, 227

Nelson, James, (photo) 156
Nelson, Milo: see Biographies 79 ed.
Nemeyer, Carol A.: see Biographies 76, 82 eds.
Nesbitt, Elizabeth: see Obituaries 78 ed.
Networks, 203–209 (also 76–84 eds.)
   in Canada, 199, 306
   and independent research libraries, 143
   See also specific networks by name; interlibrary cooperation 76–77 eds.; individual state reports by name.
Neufeld, M. Lynne: see Biographies 81 ed.
Nevada, networking in, 208
Nevada report, 348–349
Newbery Medal, 3, 7, 60, 97, 98
Newbery Medal Honor Books, (photos) 96, 98
New England Library Association (NELA), 209. See under Regional Library Associations 79–84 eds.
New Hampshire report, 349
New Jersey, networking in, 208
New Jersey report, 350
Newman, Jerald C.: see Biographies 84 ed.
Newman, Paul, 81
Newman, Ralph G.: see Biographies 76 ed.
New Mexico, networking in, 208
New Mexico report, 350
The New Republic, 235
New York Library Association, 5
New York Magazine, 235
New York, networking in, 208
New York Public Library, 84–85, (photo) 84, 143, 154
New York report, 351–353
New York University, 253
News Media Support Award (MPLA), 192
newspapers
   in Canada, 199, 201
   talking, 77
The New Yorker, 235
Nigh, Gov. George, (photo) 113
1984
   conference on, 270–271
   exhibit on, (photo) 36
(Richard M.) Nixon Presidential Library, 85
Nobel Prize for Literature, 233
Non-English-Speaking, Library Service to: see 76 ed.
nonprint materials: see audiovisual materials; Films, Films, Children's; Recordings, Sound; Telecommunications; viedo materials
Noonan, Eileen, 89
North American Collections Inventory Project (NCIP), 63
North Carolina Association of School Libraries, 4
North Carolina Foreign Language Center, 77
North Carolina report, 353
North Dakota report, 353–354
Northeast Document Conservation Center, 64, 217
Northwest Conservation Center, 217
Norwood, Frank W.: see Obituaries 84 ed.
Nostlinger, Christine, 98, 157
Notable Books of 1984, 21
Notable Children's Books, 21–22
Notable Children's Films, 23, 121, (photos) 121
Notable Children's Filmstrips, 23
Notable Children's Recordings, 22–23
Notables, 21–24 (also 79–83 eds.). see Notable Books 76–78 eds.

Notables
   ALSC lists, 60
(Marcia C.) Noyes Award, 191
Nutt, Ken, 6, 87, 98
Nyholm, Jens Peter: see Obituaries 84 ed.
Obituaries, 16–20 (also 76–84 eds.)
   See also individual state reports by name.
Oboler, Eli M., 155. See also Obituaries 84 ed.
O'Brien, Elmer John: see Biographies 79 ed.
O'Brien, Patrick M., (photos) 131, 187
Ochs, Jacki, 120
OCLC (Online Computer Library Center)
   activities and concerns, 206
   and copyright protection, 109
   direct orders to vendors, 101
   and FEDLINK, 204
   Major Microforms Project, 63–64
   overview of, 29
   revenue sources, 149
   and serials, 261
   and tax status, 170
(Scott) O'Dell Award for Historical Fiction, 96, 98
O'Dell, Scott: see Biographies 79 ed.
Ofek, Uriel: see Biographies 79 ed.
Office for Library Personnel Resources (OLPR), 116
Office for Research (OFR) (ALA), 242
Office of Management and Budget (OMB)
   and Circular A-76, 118
   and printing regulations, 135
Office of Management Studies (OMS)
   and continuing education, 107
   library management institutes, 216
   Preservation Planning Program, 64, 68, 99, 217
   support for NCIP, 63
Office of Personnel Management (OPM), 214
Ohio Conservation Committee, 217–218
Ohio report, 354–355
Oja, Carol J., 193
Oklahoma report, 355–356
older adults, library service to
   local programs, 38, 264
   NCLIS memorandum, 196
   see also 76, 77 eds.; Adult Library Services 79 ed.; Adults, Library Services to 78, 80–84 eds.
Oliver, Mary, 233
(Shirley) Olofson Memorial Awards, 5, 165
O'Neill, Rep. Thomas P., Jr., 27
(Thomas P.) O'Neill, Jr., Library (Boston College), (photo) 27, 31
Online Computer Library Center: see OCLC
Online Network of Continuing Education (ONCE), 108
Optical Disk Pilot Program (LC), 179–180, 218
optical laser disk, 112
oral history, and Black Americans, 72–73
Oral History Association, 210 (also 78–84 eds.)
Oregon report, 356–357
Organization of American States (OAS): see 76–84 eds.
Organizations and Associations: see 76–78 eds.
Orr, Leslye, (photo) 75
Oryx Press, 3
Outside, 235
Outstanding Information Science Teacher's Award (ASIS), 50, 116

Pacific Northwest Library Association (PNLA), 210–211.

See under Regional Library Associations 76–84 eds.
Palmer, Raymond A.: see Biographies 83 ed.
Panek, Dennis, 91
(Lucille Micheels) Pannell Award, 296
Pare, Richard, 56
Parent, Roger H., 12, (photo) 12. See also Biographies 80 ed.
Parks, Martha: see Obituaries 82 ed.
A Passion for Films: Henri Langlois and the Cinémathèque Française, 283
Paterson, Katherine Womeldorf: see Biographies 79, 82 eds.
Paul, Sandra K., 233
pay parity, 213, 214, 294–295, 309
Paz, Octavio, 231
Pell, Claiborne: see Biographies 84 ed.
Pellowski, Anne, 156. See also Biographies 80, 81 eds.
Penney, Pearce J.: see Biographies 83 ed.
Pennsylvania, networking in, 208
Pennsylvania report, 357–358
People for the American Way, 258
Peoples, Clinton T., (photo) 131
People's Republic of China, and librarianship, 161
Peppin, Brigid, 6
periodicals: see Serials
Perkins, Carl Dewey, 18–19, (photo) 18, 292. See also Biographies 76 ed.
(Carl D.) Perkins Vocational Education Act, 292
Perline, 101, 105, 261
Personal Bibliographic System, 70
Personnel and Employment: Affirmative Action: see 76–81 eds.
Personnel and Employment: Collective Bargaining: see 81 ed.
Personnel and Employment: Compensation, 211–213 (also 82–84 eds.)
   academic libraries, 32
   ARL statistics, (charts) 65–66
   Canada, 310
   entry-level librarians, (charts) 295
   LJ report, 115, (charts) 295
   males vs. females, 211–212, 292–293, (chart) 295
   See also 76 ed. Personnel and Employment: Salaries
Personnel and Employment: Job Market
   Canada, 307
   school libraries, 257
   See also 76–82 eds.
Personnel and Employment: Performance Appraisal: see 76–81 eds.
Personnel and Employment: Recruitment and Selection, 213–214 (also 82–84 eds.)
Personnel and Employment: Staff Development, 215–216 (also 76–84 eds.)
Peterson, Carolyn Sue, 2, 12, (photo) 12, 60
Peterson, Col. Donald H., 268
(Howard V.) Phalin—World Book Graduate Scholarship, 87, 310
Phillips, Warren H., 146
Phinazee, Annette L.: see Obituaries 84 ed.
Phinney, Eleanor: see Obituaries 83 ed.
photocopying, royalties for, 312
Photography and Architecture, 1839–1939, 56
(Esther J.) Piercy Award, 3, 89, 253
Pierpont Morgan Library, 143
Pike, Nancy M., 55–56

Pilpel, Harriet Fleischl: see
    Biographies 77 ed.
Piternick, Anne B.: see Biographies
    77 ed.
Pizer, Irwin, 191
Placzek, Adolf, 56
Plaza Junior High School Library,
    Virginia Beach, Virginia 2, 227
Polish Americans: see 79 ed.
Pomerantz, Barbara, 6, 63
Poole, Jay Martin: see Biographies 80
    ed.
pornography,
    Canadian response to, 85–86
    issues in, 127–128
Posner, Ernst: see Obituaries 81 ed.
Posner Prize, 52
Post, Jeremiah B., 3
postal rates, and books, 229
posters, (photos) 91, 227, 230, 263,
    276
Potter, William Gray: see
    Biographies 84 ed.
Powell, Benjamin E.: see Obituaries
    82 ed.
Powell, Lawrence Clark: see
    Biographies 82 ed.
Powers, Sister Mary Luella: see
    Obituaries 84 ed.
preschoolers, and libraries, 264
Preservation of Library Materials,
    216–218 (also 76–84 eds.)
    ARL activities, 64, 68
    in Britain, 314
    disaster preparedness, (photo) 217
    informational newsletter, (photo)
        218
    LC activities, 179–180
    microfilming of theological
        literature, 51
    NEH grants, 102
    SOLINET project, 99
    See also Binding 76, 78–80 eds.;
        78 ed., "Our Fragile Inheritance:
        The Challenge of Preserving
        Library Materials"
Preservation Planning Program
    (ARL), 64, 68, 99, 217
presidential libraries, 85
President's Award (AASL), 1, 40,
    258
President's Award (LVA), 188
Price, Kathleen M.: see Biographies
    84 ed.
Price, Robin M., 259
prices: see costs
Prince Georges County Memorial
    Library System, Hyattsville,
    Maryland, 5, 215–216
Principal Libraries of the World: see
    76, 77 eds.
printing, history of, 269, 270
Processing Centers: see 76, 77 eds.
Professional Development Grants, 5,
    165
Professional Education and Training
    for Research Librarianship
    (PETREL) program, 252
Program for Art on Film and Video,
    119–120
Project, LEER, 266
Project, 2000, 51
promotional materials: see
    bookmarks; posters; streamers
Proposition 13: see 79 ed.,
    "Proposition 13 Sends
    California Libraries Reeling"
Provensen, Alice and Martin, 2,
    12–13, (photo) 12, 60, 97, 98
Public Archives of Canada, 52
publications
    ACRL, 61
    ALA, 44, (chart) 47–48
    art librarianship, 56, 57
    blind and handicapped services,
        70, 136–137
    in Canada, 311

censorship, 235
children's services, 60
collection management, 103, 104
historical materials, 274–275
information industry, 146
information technology, 174
interlibrary cooperation, 70
library history, 177
library management, 174
literacy, 188
preservation, 218
public relations, 228
reference librarianship, 238
research, 253
resource sharing, 101
and rural issues, 222
school library media programs,
    258
security, 258–259
sound recordings, 236
special libraries, 276–277
women in librarianship, 294
public broadcasting: see
    Telecommunications
Public Information Office (ALA),
    225–226
Public Law 98-377: see Education
    for Economic Security Act
Public Law 98-450: see Record
    Rental Amendment
Public Law 98-480: see Library
    Services and Construction Act
Public Law 98-511: see Education
    Amendments of 1984
Public Law 98-524: see (Carl D.)
    Perkins Vocational Education
    Act
Public Law 98-573: see Tariff and
    Trade Act
Public Law 98-620: see
    Semiconductor Chip Protection
    Act
Public Libraries, 218–221, 223–224
    (also 76–84 eds.)
    and adult services, 37
    and buildings, 80–82
    in Canada, 305–307
    collection diversity study, 154
    and data collection, 243
    development program, 224,
        242–243
    and funding, 221, 223
    and salaries, 212
    and social responsibilities,
        264–266
    special activities, (photos) 220,
        221, 241, 263
    and state aid, 287, (chart) 289
    statistical study, 287, (chart) 288
    See also 76 ed. "Independent
        Learning and the Future Role of
        Public Libraries"; 77 ed.
        "Financing the Public Library";
        81 ed. "The Late Great Public
        Library—R.I.P."
Public Library Association (PLA),
    224–225 (also 76–84 eds.)
    and rural library services, 222
Public Library Development
    Program, 224, 242–243
Public Relations, 225–228 (also
    76–84 eds.)
    awards, 2, 54, 116, 173, 227–228,
        277
    and information industry, 146
    and posters, (photos) 227, 230
    special activities, (photos) 226,
        227
    and special libraries, 276
Public Relations Section (LAMA),
    226–227
Publishing, ALA: see 76–82 eds.
Publishing, Book, 228–233 (also
    76–84 eds.)
    LC publications, 180
publishing, electronic, 111–112,
    229–230

Publishing Hall of Fame, 231
Publishing, Serials, 233–235 (also
    78–84 eds.) See also Publishing,
    magazines; Publishing,
    Newspaper 76, 77 eds.
    music librarianship, 193
    new journals, 182
Pugh, Michelle, 5
Pulitzer Prize, 233
(Herbert W.) Putnam Honor Award,
    5
Putnam Publishing Group Awards,
    5, 60
Quinn, Patrick M., 52
Rachow, Louis A(ugust): see
    Biographies 79, 82 eds.
radio, and reading service, 78
Railey, Valerie Ann, 277
Rain of Fire, 98
Rambo, Marjorie, 1, 54, 55, 224, 225
Randall, David Anton: see Obituaries
    76 ed.
Ransom, Harry Huntt: see Obituaries
    77 ed.
rare books and manuscripts
    at auction, 271
    new donations, 131–132
    in special collections, 268
    summer studies in, 272
    See also Special Collections.
Rare Books and Manuscripts Section
    (ACRL), 268–269
Raskin, Ellen: see Biographies 80 ed.
Rath, Bernie, 79
Ratha's Creature, 98
Rayward, W. Boyd: see Biographies
    80 ed.
reading
    library programs, (photos) 37, 93,
        94
    survey on, 229
reaching machines, (photos) 75, 137,
    138
Reagan, President Ronald, 53, 69
(Ronald) Reagan Presidential
    Library, 85
Realia: see 76–78 eds.
*Realities: Educational Reform in a
    Learning Society*, 42, 108, 292
*Realizations: Narrative, Pictorial
    and Theatrical Arts in
    Nineteenth Century England*,
    283
Record Rental Amendment of 1984,
    109, 180, 290
Recordings, Sound, 235–237 (also
    76–84 eds.)
    and copyright, 109, 180–181
    encyclopedia on cassettes, 264
    and lending, (photo) 235
    and talking newspapers, 77
Reed, Sarah Rebecca: see Obituaries
    79 ed.
(Sarah Rebecca) Reed Scholarship,
    70
Reese, Ernest J.: see Obituaries 77 ed.
Reference: see 76 ed.: see Reference
    Services 77–84 eds.
**Reference and Adult Services
    Division (RASD)**, 237–239 (also
    76–84 eds.)
    Carnegie Fund Grant recipient, 4
Reference Services, 239–241 (also
    77–84 eds.) See also Reference
    76 ed.
REFORMA, 241–242 (also 76–84
    eds.)
Regina Medal, 6, 10, 89, 98
Regional Library Associations: see
    77–84 eds.; see individual
    associations by name this ed.
Regional Medical Libraries, 205
REHABDATA, 78
Remini, Robert V., 232
remodeling and additions: see
    Buildings

389

repair and restoration: see
  Preservation of Library Materials
Research, 242-253 (also 76-84 eds.)
  ALISE Awards, 59
  funding for, 171, (charts) 244-252
  health sciences information
    processing, 202
  literacy learning program, 189
  new ASIS Award, 50
  Research and Development Award
    (CLA), 87
  Research Development Grant
    (LRRT), 243
  Research Development Prize Paper
    (LRRT), 185
  Research Libraries Group (RLG)
    direct vendor order transmission,
      101
    general information, 205-206
    and RLIN, 29, 102, 205-206
  Research Libraries Information
    Network: see RLIN
  resource sharing
    in Canada, 199, 201
    publications on, 101
**Resources and Technical Services
  Division** (RTSD), 253-254 (also
  76-84 eds.)
  regional institutes, 215
Retired Teachers Association (RTA),
  239
Rhoads, (James) Berton: see
  Biographies 80 ed.
Rhode Island report, 358-360
Rhydwen, David, 6, 277
Richards, John Stewart: see
  Obituaries 80 ed.
Richardson, John V., Jr., 59, 243
Richardson, Roland, (photo) 37
Richmond (Virginia) Public School
  System, 3, 40
Ricking, Myrl: see Obituaries 78 ed.
Ringer, Barbara Alice: see
  Biographies 76 ed.
Risser, Meg, 296
Rittenhouse Award, 191
Riverside-Brookfield Township High
  School, Riverside, Illinois, 3, 40
RLIN (Research Libraries Information
  Network)
  and interlibrary loan, 29
  new records, 102
  types of records, 205-206
Robbins-Carter, Jane, 13, (photo) 13
Roberts, Edward Graham, 268
Robinson, Charles, 224
Rogers, Frank Bradway, 191
(Frank Bradway) Rogers Information
  Advancement Award, 191
Rogers, Joseph W., 19
Rogers, Mary Margaret, (photo) 168
Rogers, Mr. Fred, (photo) 94
Rogers, Rutherford D., 162. See also
  Biographies 78 ed.
Rohan, Joan, (photo) 168
Rolark, Calvin, (photo) 42
Rollins, Charlemae Hill: see
  Obituaries 80 ed.
Ronia, the Robber's Daughter, 1, 60,
  (photo) 97, 98
Roos, Jean Carolyn: see Obituaries 83
  ed.
Rossell, Beatrice Sawyer: see
  Obituaries 77 ed.
Rosswurm, K.M., (photo) 238
Roth, Harold Lee: see Obituaries 83
  ed.
Rothrock, Mary U. (Topey): see
  Obituaries 77 ed.
Roud, Richard, 283
royalties
  for lending of books, 233
  for lending of phonograph records,
    109, 180-181
  and photocopying, 312
RTSD/Blackwell North America
  Scholarship Award, 4, 104, 253

Ruffner, Frederick G., 13, (photo) 13
rural communities, library services
  to
  ASIS activities, 50
  NCLIS and USDA efforts, 196
  overview of, 222-223

Safley, Ellen D., (photo) 238
SAGE (Service to the Aging), 264
salaries, for librarians: see Personnel
  and Employment: Compensation
San Francisco Public Library, (photo)
  80
San Juan Capistrano Regional Branch
  Library (California), (photo) 82
Sargent, Charles W.: see Biographies
  82 ed.
satellite communications
  and academic libraries, 28
  and archives, 196
  document delivery in Britain, 314
  uses of, 281, 282-283
Sauls, Joyce, (photo) 72
Saunders, Wilfred, 313, 315. See
  also Biographies 81 ed.
Sawyer, Danford L., 135, 231
*Scandinavian Modern Design,
  1880-1980*, 56
Scarry, Patricia: see Biographies 81
  ed.
Scarry, Richard, 131
Schaefer, Mayor William Donald,
  (photo) 285
Schindel, Morton: see Biographies
  80 ed.
Schlafley, Phyllis, 258
Schmidt, Angela, 87, 311
Schmidt, C. James: see Biographies
  81 ed.
Scholarships
  ACRL, 4, 242
  ALA, description of, 4
  archives, 52
  Beta Phi Mu, 70
  Canadian Library Association, 87,
    310
  Catholic Library Association, 89
  children's services, 4, 60
  foreign study, 70
  medical librarianship, 191
  minority, 4, 171, 191, 277
  new LITA, 174
  resource development, 253
  SLA, 277
**School Libraries and Media
  Programs**, 254-258 (also 79-84
  eds.) See School Libraries and
  media Centers 76-78 eds.
  in Britain, 313
  Canada, 308-309
  NCLIS statement, 197
  problems and trends, 256-257
  and salaries, 212
  and statistics, 243
School Library Journal, 183
School Library Media Month, 255
School Library Media Program of the
  Year Award (AASL), 3, 40
Schrader, Alvin, 59, 243
Schram, Tex, (photo) 221
Schultz, Charles R., 52
Science Information, Division of: see
  77-78 eds., see Science
  Information Service, Office of 76
  ed.; see Information Science and
  Technology, Division of 79-81
  eds.; see National Science
  Foundation, Division of
  Information Science and
  Technology 82-84 eds.
(Margaret B.) Scott Award of Meritt,
  87, 309
Scott, Marianne, 13, (photo) 13, 201.
  See also Biographies 82 ed.
Scott, Marilyn, 3, 40, 258
(Margaret B.) Scott Memorial Award,
  87

Scupholm, Paul, (photo) 221
Seal, Bob, (photo) 113
Sealock, Richard B., 19, (photo) 19
secondary services: see Abstracting
  and Indexing Services
The Secret Agent, 120
Security Systems, 258-259 (also
  76-84 eds.)
  academic and research libraries, 31
  SPEC kit, 99, 103, 258
  survey on, 99
Segal, Jo An S., 14, 206
Seifert, Jaroslav, 233
Semi-conductor Chip Protection Act
  of 1984, 109, 290
semiconductor chips, and copyright,
  109, 290
**Seminar on the Acquistion of Latin
  American Library Materials**
  (SALALM), 259-260 (also 79-84
  eds.)
Sendak, Maurice, 4, 95. See also
  Biographies 84 ed.
senior citizens: see older adults,
  library service to
SERHOLD, 205
Serials, 260-262 (also 76-84 eds.)
  costs of, 99, 104-105, 235, 260
  indexing of religious literature, 51
Serials Industry Systems Advisory
  Committee (SISAC), 279
(John) Sessions Memorial Award, 4,
  167, 238
Seventeen, 235
Shactman, Bella Evelyn, 19
Shank, Russell: see Biographies 78
  ed.
Shared Resources System (SHARES)
  (AMIGOS), 206
(Ralph R.) Shaw Award for Library
  Literature: see Knowledge
  Industry Publications, Inc.
  Award for Library Literature
Shaw, Spencer G.: see Biographies
  83 ed.
Shaw, Thomas Shuler: see
  Obituaries 76 ed.
Sheehy, Eugene P.: see Biographies
  78 ed.
Sheehy, Gail, 276
Sheeran, Ruth Jellicoe, 87
Sheldon, Brooke E., 43, 106, 107,
  116, 164. See also Biographies
  83 ed.
Shepard, Marietta Daniels, 19-20,
  164-165
Shera, Jesse Hauk: see Biographies
  77 ed.; Obituaries 83 ed.
Shinn, James R., 31
Shipman, Joseph Collins: see
  Obituaries 78 ed.
Shores, Louis: see Obituaries 82 ed.
Sieburth, Jan, 209
The Sign of the Beaver, (photo) 96,
  98
Simmons, Mabel, (photo) 195
Simon and Schuster
  Communications, 119
(Fannie) Simon Award, 233
Simone, Debby L., (photo) 238
Simon, Seymour, 91
(Constance Lindsay) Skinner Award:
  see Women's National Book
  Association Award
Smith, Carleton Sprague, 193
Smith, Emille, (photo) 42
Smith, G. Roysce, 79
Smith, Heather, 5, 165
Smith, Lillian Helena: see Obituaries
  84 ed.
Social Responsibilities, 262-267
  (also 76-84 eds.)
  fingerprinting of children, (photo)
    263
  See also special groups by name,
    eg. blind and handicapped,
    correctional institutions.

390

Social Responsibilities Round table
(SRRT), 267–268 (also 76–84 eds.)
The Social Transformation of American Medicine, 233
Sociedad de Bibliotecarios de Puerto Rico, 227. See also 76–77, 80–82 eds.
Society of American Archivists, 294
solar heating, for libraries, (photo) 82
SOLINET (Southeastern Library network), 99, 206–207, 217
Sommer, June, (photo) 137
Sony Corp. of America v. Universal City Studios, Inc., 109, 290
SOUL (Serials Online Union Listers), 261
South Carolina Library Association Intellectual Freedom Committee, 155, 156
South Carolina, networking in, 208
South Carolina report, 360–362
South Dakota, networking in, 208–209
South Dakota report, 362–363
Southeastern Library Association (SELA), 268. See under Regional Library Associations 76–84 eds.
Southern California Answering Network (SCAN), (photo) 144
Southern University Library (Baton Rouge), 31
Southwestern Library Association (SWLA): see under Regional Library Associations 76–84 eds.
Sowby, Richard, (photo) 138
Spalding, C. Sumner: see Biographies 76 ed.
Speare, Elizabeth, (photo) 96, 98
SPEC: see Systems and Procedures Exchange Center
SPEC Flyers
 automation and staff training, 29
 copyright policies, 26–27
 electronic mail, 30
 microcomputers in libraries, 28
 new bibliographic databases, 30
 security in ARL libraries, 31
 strategic planning, 27
Special Collections, 268–276 (also 76, 78–82, 84 eds.)
 Arthur Conan Doyle Collection, (photo) 305
 and Black Americans, 73
 children's literature, 131
 cookbooks, 132
 foreign topics, 133
 illustrations, 131
 in independent research libraries, 143
 literature, 132
 music, 130
 natural history, 132–133
 personal papers, 132
 photos of, 270
 theater materials, 130–131
Special Librarianship in Canada Award (CASLIS), 87
Special Libraries, 276–277 (also 76–84 eds.)
 in Canada, 309
 and salaries, 212
Special Libraries Association (SLA)
 and anniversary conference, 276, (photo) 277
 and continuing education, 107–108
Special Libraries Association (John Cotton) Dana Award, 6, 116, 277
Special Libraries Association Hall of Fame, 6, 277
Special Libraries Association (H.W.) Wilson Company Award, 6
Spencer, Rita, 87, 309
Spicer, Erik J.: see Biographies 80 ed.
Spier, Peter: see Biographies 79 ed.

Spivacke, Harold: see Obituaries 78 ed.
Spring-Gifford, Christine, 87
staff development: see Personnel and Employment: Staff Development; Continuing Professional Education
Staff Organizations Round Table (SORT), 278 (also 76–84 eds.)
stamps, commemorative, (photos) 52, 180, 186, 228, 229
Standard Network Interconnection (LC), 204
Standards, 278–279 (also 76–84 eds.)
 art libraries, 55
 ASCLA projects, 68–69
 and buildings, 80, 173
 cataloging of microcomputer software, 88
 CIP, 286
 continuing education, 106
 for federal librarians, 118
 I & R services, 143
 library service, 67
 and LITA activities, 175
 and ordering of library materials, 102
 paper quality, 102
 and public libraries, 224
 and school library media programs, 40
 and serials, 261
 and services for blind, 75
Standing Committee on Library Education (SCOLE), 116
Standing Conference of National and University Libraries (SCONUL), 314
Stanford University, 253
Stark v. Osseo School district, 127
Stark v. School District No. 1, 127
Starr, Paul, 233
state aid
 ASCLA report, 69
 and public libraries, 168–169, 287, (chart) 289
state library agencies
 and rural issues, 222
 and social responsibilities, 262–264
State University of New York at Albany Library Friends, 129
statistics
 ARL members, (chart) 67
 book publishing, 228–229
 booksellers, 78–79
 independent research libraries, (charts) 141–142
 librarianship: salaries and placement, 211–213
 library education, 114–115, (charts) 116
 library overview, 243
 public libraries, 219–220
 research grants, 244–252
Status of Women in Libraries Committee, 4
Steinitz, Kate Trauman: see Obituaries 76 ed.
Steuermann, Clara: see Biographies 76 ed.
Stevens, Charles H.: see Obituaries 80 ed.
Stevenson, Grace Thomas: see Biographies 77 ed.
(Helen Gordon) Stewart Award, 310
Stillwell, Margaret Bingham, 276
Stockey, Bill, (photo) 94
Stockham, Ken: see Biographies 83 ed.
Stone, Elizabeth, 89, 106. See also Biographies 77, 81 eds.
Stones for Ibarra, 5, 232
storage, and disks, 112, 179–180, 218, 236
streamers, (photo) 91

Strip, A.C.: see Biographies 82 ed.
Stuart-Stubbs, Dean Basil, 311
Stueart, Robert D., 59, 163. See also Biographies 84 ed.
Sugaring Time, (photo) 96
Sullivan, Peggy: see Biographies 80 ed.
summer reading programs, (photos) 93
Summers, F. William: see Biographies 83 ed.
Summit, Roger, 3, 174
support staff, use of, 214
Surridge, Ronald, 14, (photo) 14, 315
Sutherland, Zena B.: see Biographies 84 ed.
Sweeney, Joyce, 301, 302
Sweetgrass, 5, 87, 98
Swerdlove, Dorothy L., 14
Sylvestre, Guy, 200, 201
Systems and Procedures Exchange Center (SPEC) Flyers: see SPEC Flyers
 general activities, 68
 inventory of automation resources, 68
 kit on collection security, 99, 103, 258

Talbot, Richard J., 14–15, (photo) 15
Talking Books program, 264, 265
Tannehill, Robert S., Jr., 6, 50–51
Tariff and Trade Act, 292
tariffs, and educational materials, 159–160
Tate, Elizabeth: see Biographies 80 ed.
Tate, Horace E.: see Biographies 79 ed.
Tauber, Maurice F.: see Obituaries 81 ed.
taxation
 and books in Britain, 176, 313–314
 and OCLC, 206
(Sydney) Taylor Body of Work Award, 63
Taylor, Charles F.: see Obituaries 81 ed.
Taylor, Franzine Kenneth, 277
Taylor, Mayor Starke, (photo) 221
Taylor, Mildred D.: see Biographies 78 ed.
Taylor, Nettie Bancroft, 3, (photo) 14, 15
technical information specialists, and exchange programs, 163
Ted Hughes: A Bibliography 1946-1980, 5
Tees, Miriam H(adley): see Biographies 76 ed.
Telecommunications, 279–283: see Telecommunications and Public Broadcasting 77–83 eds.
 and Fairness Doctrine, 155
 and medical libraries, 190
 public relations efforts, 225–226
 See also 77 ed. "Telecommunications"
Teletypewriter (TTY), 265
television
 closed captioned programs, 137
 cooperation with magazines, 234
 educational programs, 171–172
 and Fairness Doctrine, 155
 See also 76 ed. Television in Libraries
Tennessee report, 363–365
Terkel, Studs, 268
Texas, networking in, 209
Texas report, 365–366
Thaddeus, 97
Theatre Library Association, 283–284 (also 76–84 eds.)
theft, losses due to, 31
Thomas, F. Nell, 4
Thomas, Gerald, (photo) 140
Thompson, Deborah, 54

391

Thompson, (William) Godfrey: see Biographies 79 ed.
Thorpe, Frederick A.: see Biographies 77 ed.
(Frederick A.) Thorpe Traveling Fellowship, 224
Tiffany, Burton Chatterton: see Biographies 76 ed.
Tighe, Ruth Liepman: see Biographies 82 ed.
The Times Atlas of the Oceans, 2, 238, 240
Tobin, Carol, (photo) 238
Tocatlian, Jacques: see Biographies 80 ed.
Toe, Samuel Polkah, 52
To Live In Two Worlds: American Indian Youth Today, 302
Tomchyshyn, Terri, 165
Tom, Marilynn, (photo) 129
(José) Toribio Medina Award, 259
Tormey, John, (photo) 131
toys and games
  and disabled, 139
  See also 76-79 eds.
Trace, Timothy, 276
translation
  of agricultural materials, 195
  award for, 1, 60, 97,. 98
Trejo, Arnulfo D., 242
Trelease, Jim, 268
Trezza, Alphonse F.: see Biographies 76, 84 eds.
Trivial Pursuit, 305
Trotti, John Boone: see Biographies 78 ed.
Trustee Citations (ALTA), 4, 49
Trustees, 284-285 (also 76-84 eds.)
Tseng, Sally C., 98
Tsuneishi, Warren, (photo) 164
Turnbaugh, Roy, 52
tutoring, literacy, (photos) 187

UBC: see Universal Bibliographic Control
Ulveling, Ralph A.: see Obituaries 81 ed.
UNESCO
  Canadian support for, 85
  and IFLA contracts, 158, 163
  and U.S. withdrawal, 43, 109, 157-158, 159-160, 196
  See also 76-83 eds.
United Board for Christian Higher Education in Asia, 161, 162
United Kingdom Report, 312-315
  See London Correspondent's Report 76-84 eds.
United States National Commission for UNESCO, 159
Universal Bibliographic Control
  (UBC), 285-286 (also 76-79, 81-84 eds.)
Universal Serials and Book Exchange (USBE), 286-287 (also 76-84 eds.)
University of Texas Health Science Center, San Antonio, Texas, 2, 227
University Press of New England, 56
Urban Libraries Council, 287-289 (also 78-84 eds.)
Urban Professionals, Library Service to: see 76 ed.
U.S.—China Science and Technology Protocol, 161
U.S. Constitution, bicentennial celebration of, 154
U.S. Department of Education, and literacy grants, 186
  regional seminar on libraries, 197
use studies, 102
user surveys, 215
U.S. Information Agency, 162-163
U.S.—People's Republic of China Cultural Agreement, 161
U.S. Supreme Court

and serials, 234
and videotaping, 109, 168, 281, 290
Utah, networking in, 209
Utah report, 366-367
UTLAS, 149

Value Added Tax (VAT), 313
Van Allsburg, Chris: see Biographies 83 ed.
Vance Bibliographies, 71
van der Zee, John, (photo) 37, (photo) 131
Van House, Nancy, 59, 243
Vanity Fair, 235
Van Jackson, Wallace: see Biographies 77 ed.
Van Nostrand Reinhold Company, Inc., 238, 240
Vann, Sarah Katherine: see Biographies 83 ed.
vendors
  direct orders to, 105
  and library systems, 148-149
  and movie ratings, 155
  and shady practices, 104
Vermont report, 367-369
Vickery, Brian, 315
Victory Over Japan, 5, 232
video materials
  and lending, 155
  on literacy, 188
Viking Press, 1, 60, 97, 98
Virginia, networking in, 209
Virginia report, 369-370
Virgin Islands, networking in, 209
Virgo, Julie A. C.: see Biographies 78 ed.
visiting scholars, 161
Visualtek Reader, 265
Vitolo, Bill, (photo) 138
Vitz, Carl Peter Paul: see Obituaries 82 ed.
Vocational Education Act: see (Carl D.) Perkins Vocational Education Act
Voight, Cynthia: see Biographies 84 ed.
volunteers, library, (photo) 187, (photo) 265
Vosper, Robert Gordon: see Biographies 78 ed.
voter registration center, 265

Waddell, John Neal: see Obituaries 76 ed.
Walgren, Rep. Douglas, (photo) 160
Walker, Estellene Paxton, 20, (photo) 20
Wallace, Linda K., 15, (photo) 15, 226
Waller, Theodore: see Biographies 77 ed.
Walls, Esther J., (photo) 164
Walsh, Sandra, 3, 185, 243
Walter, Midlred P., 3
Walter, Roger, 175, 315
Wang, Chi, 161
Wang, Helen (photo) 138
Waples, Douglas: see Obituaries 79 ed.
Warner, Robert M., 52. See also Biographies 81 ed.
Warwick, James, (photo) 130
Washington Library for the Blind and Physically Handicapped (Seattle), (photo) 74
Washington Library network: see WLN
Washington, Mayor Harold, (photo) 263
Washington Report, 289-292 (also 76-84 eds.)
Washington state report, 371
Watanabe, Ruth T.: see Biographies 79 ed.
Watanabe, Shigeo: see Biographies

78 ed.
WEBNET, 28
Wedgeworth, Robert, 43, 128, (photo) 140, 159, 180
weeding, issues in, 102
Weeks, Ann Carlson: see Biographies 83 ed.
Welch, William, 164
(Leonard) Wertheimer Mutlilingual Award, 224
Westall, Robert, 302
West, Dorothy, (photo) 210
West Virginia, networking in, 209
West Virginia report, 371-372
Wezeman, Frederick: see Obituaries 82 ed.
Wheatley Medal, 6
White, Carl M.: see Obituaries 84 ed.
(E.H.) White Company, 171
White House Conference on Library and Information Services: see 76-77 eds.; feature article 80 ed.
White House Conference on Library and Information Services (WHCLIS) Taskforce, 185, 264
White, Karen, (photo) 138
White, Louise, 311
White, Lucien W.: see Obituaries 76 ed.
Whitenack, Carolyn I.: see Biographies 77 ed.
Whitney Fund Grants, 5
Whitney, Virginia P.: see Biographies 77 ed.
Wichers, Jean Elaine: see Obituaries 84 ed.
Wiegand, Wayne A., 59, 177, 243
Wiese, Bernice (Marion): see Obituaries 78 ed.
Wijnstroom, Margreet: see Biographies 77 ed.
Wilcox, Alice Erlander: see Biographies 76 ed.
(Laura Ingalls) Wilder Medal, 4
Wilkinson, Margaret Ann, 311
Willard, Nancy: see Biographies 83 ed.
Williams, Mabel: see Biographies 81 ed.
Williams, Martha E., 50
(Margaret) Williams Trust Fund, 311
Wilmeth, Don Burton: see Biographies 83 ed.
(H.W.) Wilson Company
  A & I project, 64
  and academic research librarianship, 115
  and accreditation conference, 58
  and awards, 4, 5, 6, 173, 184, 215-216, 227
  exhibit award winner, 3
  online indexes, 233
  and WILSONLINE, 71
(H.W.) Wilson Company Scholarship, 311
Wilson, David, 52
Wilson, Jane B(liss): see Biographies 76 ed.
Wilson Library Bulletin, 182-183
(H.W.) Wilson Library Periodical Award, 4, 184
(H.W.) Wilson Library Staff Development Grant, 5, 215-216
WILSONLINE, 71, 240
Wilson, Louis Round: see Obituaries 80 ed.
  See also 77 ed. "The Centenary of a Giant of Librarianship: Louis Round Wilson"
Wilson, Marjorie P., 191
(H.W.) Wilson Scholarship, 87
Winchell, Constance M.: see Obituaries 84 ed.
Winkler, Paul Walter: see Biographies 76 ed.
Winnie-the-Pooh: see Biographies 77 ed.

Winslow, Amy: *see* Obituaries 81 ed.
(Justin) Winsor Prize Essay Award, 4, 178
Wisconsin, networking in, 209
Wisconsin report, 372–374
(George) Wittenborn Awards, 55
WLN (Washington Library Network), 206
Wofford, Azile M.: *see* Obituaries 78 ed.
Wolfe, Deborah, (photo) 210
Woodward, Rupert C.: *see* Obituaries 82 ed.
Women in Librarianship, 292–296 (*also 80–82, 84 eds.*). See Women in Librarianship, Status of 76–79, 83 eds.
  AALL resolution on sexual harassment, 170
  Canada, 309
  discrimination case, 32
  pay parity issue, 213, 214, 294–295, 309
  and salaries, 211–212, 292–293, (chart) 295
  slide/tape program, (photo) 293
Women's National Book Association (WNBA), 296 (*also 78–84 eds.*)

Women's National Book Association Award, 60, 72, 296
The Words of Martin Luther King, Jr., 267
The Work of August Saint-Gaudens, 56
World Book Childcraft Grant, 89
World Book Encyclopedia, cassette form, 264
Wright, Benjamin H., (photo) 42
Wright, Keith C., 224
Wrightson, Patricia, 5
Wright Wyllis Eaton: *see* Obituaries 80 ed.
Wu, Julia Li: *see* Biographies 84 ed.
Wynne-Jones, Tim, 6, 87, 98
Wyoming report, 374–375

Xerox Foundation
  A & I project, 64

YASD/Baker & Taylor Conference Grants, 5
YASD/VOYA Research Grant, 5, 243
Yeatman, Joseph Lawrence, 4, 178
Yenawine, Wayne S.: *see* Obituaries 82 ed.
Yeo, Ronald: *see* Biographies 79 ed.

Young Adult Library Services, 297–300 (*also 76–84 eds.*)
  access to video materials, 155
  reference materials for, (photos) 297
Young Adult Literature, 300–302 (*also 76–84 eds.*)
  prominent authors and books, (photos) 301–302
  See also Children's Literature; International Board on Books for Young People.
Young Adult Services Division (YASD), 303 (*also 76–84 eds.*)
  Carnegie Fund Grant recipient, 4
Young, Christina Carr, (photo) 45
Young, James Bradford, 193
A Young Man's Guide to Sex, 302
Young, Marian C.: *see* Obituaries 80 ed.
Young Readers' Choice Award (PNLA), 211

Zar, Rose, 6, 63
Zelinsky, Paul O., 91
Zenger, John Peter, 154
Zoom at Sea, 6, 87, 98